T0180323

More information about this subseries at http://www.springer.com/series/7412

Hiroshi Ishikawa · Cheng-Lin Liu ·
Tomas Pajdla · Jianbo Shi (Eds.)

Computer Vision – ACCV 2020

15th Asian Conference on Computer Vision
Kyoto, Japan, November 30 – December 4, 2020
Revised Selected Papers, Part III

Springer

Editors
Hiroshi Ishikawa
Waseda University
Tokyo, Japan

Tomas Pajdla
Czech Technical University in Prague
Prague, Czech Republic

Cheng-Lin Liu
Institute of Automation of Chinese Academy
of Sciences
Beijing, China

Jianbo Shi
University of Pennsylvania
Philadelphia, PA, USA

ISSN 0302-9743 ISSN 1611-3349 (electronic)
Lecture Notes in Computer Science
ISBN 978-3-030-69534-7 ISBN 978-3-030-69535-4 (eBook)
https://doi.org/10.1007/978-3-030-69535-4

LNCS Sublibrary: SL6 – Image Processing, Computer Vision, Pattern Recognition, and Graphics

This Springer imprint is published by the registered company Springer Nature Switzerland AG
The registered company address is: Gewerbestrasse 11, 6330 Cham, Switzerland

Preface

The Asian Conference on Computer Vision (ACCV) 2020, originally planned to take place in Kyoto, Japan, was held online during November 30 – December 4, 2020. The conference featured novel research contributions from almost all sub-areas of computer vision.

We received 836 main-conference submissions. After removing the desk rejects, 768 valid, complete manuscripts were submitted for review. A pool of 48 area chairs and 738 reviewers was recruited to conduct paper reviews. As in previous editions of ACCV, we adopted a double-blind review process to determine which of these papers to accept. Identities of authors were not visible to reviewers and area chairs; nor were the identities of the assigned reviewers and area chairs known to authors. The program chairs did not submit papers to the conference.

Each paper was reviewed by at least three reviewers. Authors were permitted to respond to the initial reviews during a rebuttal period. After this, the area chairs led discussions among reviewers. Finally, an interactive area chair meeting was held, during which panels of three area chairs deliberated to decide on acceptance decisions for each paper, and then four larger panels were convened to make final decisions. At the end of this process, 254 papers were accepted for publication in the ACCV 2020 conference proceedings.

In addition to the main conference, ACCV 2020 featured four workshops and two tutorials. This is also the first ACCV for which the proceedings are open access at the Computer Vision Foundation website, by courtesy of Springer.

We would like to thank all the organizers, sponsors, area chairs, reviewers, and authors. We acknowledge the support of Microsoft's Conference Management Toolkit (CMT) team for providing the software used to manage the review process.

We greatly appreciate the efforts of all those who contributed to making the conference a success, despite the difficult and fluid situation.

December 2020

Hiroshi Ishikawa
Cheng-Lin Liu
Tomas Pajdla
Jianbo Shi

Organization

General Chairs

Ko Nishino   Kyoto University, Japan
Akihiro Sugimoto   National Institute of Informatics, Japan
Hiromi Tanaka   Ritsumeikan University, Japan

Program Chairs

Hiroshi Ishikawa   Waseda University, Japan
Cheng-Lin Liu   Institute of Automation of Chinese Academy
    of Sciences, China
Tomas Pajdla   Czech Technical University, Czech Republic
Jianbo Shi   University of Pennsylvania, USA

Publication Chairs

Ichiro Ide   Nagoya University, Japan
Wei-Ta Chu   National Chung Cheng University, Taiwan
Marc A. Kastner   National Institute of Informatics, Japan

Local Arrangements Chairs

Shohei Nobuhara   Kyoto University, Japan
Yasushi Makihara   Osaka University, Japan

Web Chairs

Ikuhisa Mitsugami   Hiroshima City University, Japan
Chika Inoshita   Canon Inc., Japan

AC Meeting Chair

Yusuke Sugano   University of Tokyo, Japan

Area Chairs

Mathieu Aubry   École des Ponts ParisTech, France
Xiang Bai   Huazhong University of Science and Technology,
    China
Alex Berg   Facebook, USA
Michael S. Brown   York University, Canada

Additional Reviewers

Sathyanarayanan
   N. Aakur
Mahmoud Afifi
Amit Aides
Noam Aigerman
Kenan Emir Ak
Mohammad
   Sadegh Aliakbarian
Keivan Alizadeh-Vahid
Dario Allegra
Alexander Andreopoulos
Nikita Araslanov
Anil Armagan
Alexey Artemov
Aditya Arun
Yuki M. Asano
Hossein Azizpour
Seung-Hwan Baek
Seungryul Baek
Max Bain
Abhishek Bajpayee
Sandipan Banerjee
Wenbo Bao
Daniel Barath
Chaim Baskin
Anil S. Baslamisli
Ardhendu Behera
Jens Behley
Florian Bernard
Bharat Lal Bhatnagar
Uttaran Bhattacharya
Binod Bhattarai
Ayan Kumar Bhunia
Jia-Wang Bian
Simion-Vlad Bogolin
Amine Bourki
Biagio Brattoli
Anders G. Buch
Evgeny Burnaev
Benjamin Busam
Holger Caesar
Jianrui Cai
Jinzheng Cai

Fanta Camara
Necati Cihan Camgöz
Shaun Canavan
Jiajiong Cao
Jiale Cao
Hakan Çevikalp
Ayan Chakrabarti
Tat-Jen Cham
Lyndon Chan
Hyung Jin Chang
Xiaobin Chang
Rama Chellappa
Chang Chen
Chen Chen
Ding-Jie Chen
Jianhui Chen
Jun-Cheng Chen
Long Chen
Songcan Chen
Tianshui Chen
Weifeng Chen
Weikai Chen
Xiaohan Chen
Xinlei Chen
Yanbei Chen
Yingcong Chen
Yiran Chen
Yi-Ting Chen
Yun Chen
Yun-Chun Chen
Yunlu Chen
Zhixiang Chen
Ziliang Chen
Guangliang Cheng
Li Cheng
Qiang Cheng
Zhongwei Cheng
Anoop Cherian
Ngai-Man Cheung
Wei-Chen Chiu
Shin-Fang Ch'ng
Nam Ik Cho
Junsuk Choe

Chiho Choi
Jaehoon Choi
Jinsoo Choi
Yukyung Choi
Anustup Choudhury
Hang Chu
Peng Chu
Wei-Ta Chu
Sanghyuk Chun
Ronald Clark
Maxwell D. Collins
Ciprian Corneanu
Luca Cosmo
Ioana Croitoru
Steve Cruz
Naresh Cuntoor
Zachary A. Daniels
Mohamed Daoudi
François Darmon
Adrian K. Davison
Rodrigo de Bem
Shalini De Mello
Lucas Deecke
Bailin Deng
Jiankang Deng
Zhongying Deng
Somdip Dey
Ferran Diego
Mingyu Ding
Dzung Anh Doan
Xingping Dong
Xuanyi Dong
Hazel Doughty
Dawei Du
Chi Nhan Duong
Aritra Dutta
Marc C. Eder
Ismail Elezi
Mohamed Elgharib
Sergio Escalera
Deng-Ping Fan
Shaojing Fan
Sean Fanello

Moshiur R. Farazi
Azade Farshad
István Fehérvári
Junyi Feng
Wei Feng
Yang Feng
Zeyu Feng
Robert B. Fisher
Alexander Fix
Corneliu O. Florea
Wolfgang Förstner
Jun Fu
Xueyang Fu
Yanwei Fu
Hiroshi Fukui
Antonino Furnari
Ryo Furukawa
Raghudeep Gadde
Vandit J. Gajjar
Chuang Gan
Bin-Bin Gao
Boyan Gao
Chen Gao
Junbin Gao
Junyu Gao
Lin Gao
Mingfei Gao
Peng Gao
Ruohan Gao
Nuno C. Garcia
Georgios Georgakis
Ke Gong
Jiayuan Gu
Jie Gui
Manuel Günther
Kaiwen Guo
Minghao Guo
Ping Guo
Sheng Guo
Yulan Guo
Saurabh Gupta
Jung-Woo Ha
Emanuela Haller
Cusuh Ham
Kai Han
Liang Han

Tengda Han
Ronny Hänsch
Josh Harguess
Atsushi Hashimoto
Monica Haurilet
Jamie Hayes
Fengxiang He
Pan He
Xiangyu He
Xinwei He
Yang He
Paul Henderson
Chih-Hui Ho
Tuan N.A. Hoang
Sascha A. Hornauer
Yedid Hoshen
Kuang-Jui Hsu
Di Hu
Ping Hu
Ronghang Hu
Tao Hu
Yang Hua
Bingyao Huang
Haibin Huang
Huaibo Huang
Rui Huang
Sheng Huang
Xiaohua Huang
Yifei Huang
Zeng Huang
Zilong Huang
Jing Huo
Junhwa Hur
Wonjun Hwang
José Pedro Iglesias
Atul N. Ingle
Yani A. Ioannou
Go Irie
Daisuke Iwai
Krishna Murthy
    Jatavallabhula
Seong-Gyun Jeong
Koteswar Rao Jerripothula
Jingwei Ji
Haiyang Jiang
Huajie Jiang

Wei Jiang
Xiaoyi Jiang
Jianbo Jiao
Licheng Jiao
Kyong Hwan Jin
Xin Jin
Shantanu Joshi
Frédéric Jurie
Abhishek Kadian
Olaf Kaehler
Meina Kan
Dimosthenis Karatzas
Isay Katsman
Muhammad Haris Khan
Vijeta Khare
Rawal Khirodkar
Hadi Kiapour
Changick Kim
Dong-Jin Kim
Gunhee Kim
Heewon Kim
Hyunwoo J. Kim
Junsik Kim
Junyeong Kim
Yonghyun Kim
Akisato Kimura
A. Sophia Koepke
Dimitrios Kollias
Nikos Kolotouros
Yoshinori Konishi
Adam Kortylewski
Dmitry Kravchenko
Sven Kreiss
Gurunandan Krishnan
Andrey Kuehlkamp
Jason Kuen
Arjan Kuijper
Shiro Kumano
Avinash Kumar
B. V. K. Vijaya Kumar
Ratnesh Kumar
Vijay Kumar
Yusuke Kurose
Alina Kuznetsova
Junseok Kwon
Loic Landrieu

Dong Lao
Viktor Larsson
Yasir Latif
Hei Law
Hieu Le
Hoang-An Le
Huu Minh Le
Gim Hee Lee
Hyungtae Lee
Jae-Han Lee
Jangho Lee
Jungbeom Lee
Kibok Lee
Kuan-Hui Lee
Seokju Lee
Sungho Lee
Sungmin Lee
Bin Li
Jie Li
Ruilong Li
Ruoteng Li
Site Li
Xianzhi Li
Xiaomeng Li
Xiaoming Li
Xin Li
Xiu Li
Xueting Li
Yawei Li
Yijun Li
Yimeng Li
Yin Li
Yong Li
Yu-Jhe Li
Zekun Li
Dongze Lian
Zhouhui Lian
Haoyi Liang
Yue Liao
Jun Hao Liew
Chia-Wen Lin
Guangfeng Lin
Kevin Lin
Xudong Lin
Xue Lin
Chang Liu

Feng Liu
Hao Liu
Hong Liu
Jing Liu
Jingtuo Liu
Jun Liu
Miaomiao Liu
Ming Liu
Ping Liu
Siqi Liu
Wentao Liu
Wu Liu
Xing Liu
Xingyu Liu
Yongcheng Liu
Yu Liu
Yu-Lun Liu
Yun Liu
Zhihua Liu
Zichuan Liu
Chengjiang Long
Manuel López Antequera
Hao Lu
Hongtao Lu
Le Lu
Shijian Lu
Weixin Lu
Yao Lu
Yongxi Lu
Chenxu Luo
Weixin Luo
Wenhan Luo
Diogo C. Luvizon
Jiancheng Lyu
Chao Ma
Long Ma
Shugao Ma
Xiaojian Ma
Yongrui Ma
Ludovic Magerand
Behrooz Mahasseni
Mohammed Mahmoud
Utkarsh Mall
Massimiliano Mancini
Xudong Mao
Alina E. Marcu

Niki Martinel
Jonathan Masci
Tetsu Matsukawa
Bruce A. Maxwell
Amir Mazaheri
Prakhar Mehrotra
Heydi Méndez-Vázquez
Zibo Meng
Kourosh Meshgi
Shun Miao
Zhongqi Miao
Micael Carvalho
Pedro Miraldo
Ashish Mishra
Ikuhisa Mitsugami
Daisuke Miyazaki
Kaichun Mo
Liliane Momeni
Gyeongsik Moon
Alexandre Morgand
Yasuhiro Mukaigawa
Anirban Mukhopadhyay
Erickson R. Nascimento
Lakshmanan Nataraj
K. L. Navaneet
Lukáš Neumann
Shohei Nobuhara
Nicoletta Noceti
Mehdi Noroozi
Michael Oechsle
Ferda Ofli
Seoung Wug Oh
Takeshi Oishi
Takahiro Okabe
Fumio Okura
Kyle B. Olszewski
José Oramas
Tribhuvanesh Orekondy
Martin R. Oswald
Mayu Otani
Umapada Pal
Yingwei Pan
Rameswar Panda
Rohit Pandey
Jiangmiao Pang
João P. Papa

Toufiq Parag
Jinsun Park
Min-Gyu Park
Despoina Paschalidou
Nikolaos Passalis
Yash Patel
Georgios Pavlakos
Baoyun Peng
Houwen Peng
Wen-Hsiao Peng
Roland Perko
Vitali Petsiuk
Quang-Hieu Pham
Yongri Piao
Marco Piccirilli
Matteo Poggi
Mantini Pranav
Dilip K. Prasad
Véronique Prinet
Victor Adrian Prisacariu
Thomas Probst
Jan Prokaj
Qi Qian
Xuelin Qian
Xiaotian Qiao
Yvain Queau
Mohammad Saeed Rad
Filip Radenovic
Petia Radeva
Bogdan Raducanu
François Rameau
Aakanksha Rana
Yongming Rao
Sathya Ravi
Edoardo Remelli
Dongwei Ren
Wenqi Ren
Md Alimoor Reza
Farzaneh Rezaianaran
Andrés Romero
Kaushik Roy
Soumava Kumar Roy
Nataniel Ruiz
Javier Ruiz-del-Solar
Jongbin Ryu
Mohammad Sabokrou

Ryusuke Sagawa
Pritish Sahu
Hideo Saito
Kuniaki Saito
Shunsuke Saito
Ken Sakurada
Joaquin Salas
Enrique Sánchez-Lozano
Aswin Sankaranarayanan
Hiroaki Santo
Soubhik Sanyal
Vishwanath Saragadam1
Yoichi Sato
William R. Schwartz
Jesse Scott
Siniša Šegvić
Lorenzo Seidenari
Keshav T. Seshadri
Francesco Setti
Meet Shah
Shital Shah
Ming Shao
Yash Sharma
Dongyu She
Falong Shen
Jie Shen
Xi Shen
Yuming Shen
Hailin Shi
Yichun Shi
Yifei Shi
Yujiao Shi
Zenglin Shi
Atsushi Shimada
Daeyun Shin
Young Min Shin
Kirill Sidorov
Krishna Kumar Singh
Maneesh K. Singh
Gregory Slabaugh
Chunfeng Song
Dongjin Song
Ran Song
Xibin Song
Ramprakash Srinivasan
Erik Stenborg

Stefan Stojanov
Yu-Chuan Su
Zhuo Su
Yusuke Sugano
Masanori Suganuma
Yumin Suh
Yao Sui
Jiaming Sun
Jin Sun
Xingyuan Sun
Zhun Sun
Minhyuk Sung
Keita Takahashi
Kosuke Takahashi
Jun Takamatsu
Robby T. Tan
Kenichiro Tanaka
Masayuki Tanaka
Chang Tang
Peng Tang
Wei Tang
Xu Tang
Makarand Tapaswi
Amara Tariq
Mohammad Tavakolian
Antonio Tejero-de-Pablos
Ilias Theodorakopoulos
Thomas E. Bishop
Diego Thomas
Kai Tian
Xinmei Tian
Yapeng Tian
Chetan J. Tonde
Lei Tong
Alessio Tonioni
Carlos Torres
Anh T. Tran
Subarna Tripathi
Emanuele Trucco
Hung-Yu Tseng
Tony Tung
Radim Tylecek
Seiichi Uchida
Md. Zasim Uddin
Norimichi Ukita
Ernest Valveny

Nanne van Noord
Subeesh Vasu
Javier Vazquez-Corral
Andreas Velten
Constantin Vertan
Rosaura G. VidalMata
Valentin Vielzeuf
Sirion Vittayakorn
Konstantinos Vougioukas
Fang Wan
Guowei Wan
Renjie Wan
Bo Wang
Chien-Yi Wang
Di Wang
Dong Wang
Guangrun Wang
Hao Wang
Hongxing Wang
Hua Wang
Jialiang Wang
Jiayun Wang
Jingbo Wang
Jinjun Wang
Lizhi Wang
Pichao Wang
Qian Wang
Qiaosong Wang
Qilong Wang
Qingzhong Wang
Shangfei Wang
Shengjin Wang
Tiancai Wang
Wenguan Wang
Wenhai Wang
Xiang Wang
Xiao Wang
Xiaoyang Wang
Xinchao Wang
Xinggang Wang
Yang Wang
Yaxing Wang
Yisen Wang
Yu-Chiang Frank Wang
Zheng Wang
Scott Wehrwein

Wei Wei
Xing Wei
Xiu-Shen Wei
Yi Wei
Martin Weinmann
Michael Weinmann
Jun Wen
Xinshuo Weng
Thomas Whelan
Kimberly Wilber
Williem Williem
Kwan-Yee K. Wong
Yongkang Wong
Sanghyun Woo
Michael Wray
Chenyun Wu
Chongruo Wu
Jialian Wu
Xiaohe Wu
Xiaoping Wu
Yihong Wu
Zhenyao Wu
Changqun Xia
Xide Xia
Yin Xia
Lei Xiang
Di Xie
Guo-Sen Xie
Jin Xie
Yifan Xing
Yuwen Xiong
Jingwei Xu
Jun Xu
Ke Xu
Mingze Xu
Yanyu Xu
Yi Xu
Yichao Xu
Yongchao Xu
Yuanlu Xu
Jia Xue
Nan Xue
Yasushi Yagi
Toshihiko Yamasaki
Zhaoyi Yan
Zike Yan

Keiji Yanai
Dong Yang
Fan Yang
Hao Yang
Jiancheng Yang
Linlin Yang
Mingkun Yang
Ren Yang
Sibei Yang
Wenhan Yang
Ze Yang
Zhaohui Yang
Zhengyuan Yang
Anbang Yao
Angela Yao
Rajeev Yasarla
Jinwei Ye
Qi Ye
Xinchen Ye
Zili Yi
Ming Yin
Zhichao Yin
Ryo Yonetani
Ju Hong Yoon
Haichao Yu
Jiahui Yu
Lequan Yu
Lu Yu
Qian Yu
Ruichi Yu
Li Yuan
Sangdoo Yun
Sergey Zakharov
Huayi Zeng
Jiabei Zeng
Yu Zeng
Fangneng Zhan
Kun Zhan
Bowen Zhang
Hongguang Zhang
Jason Y. Zhang
Jiawei Zhang
Jie Zhang
Jing Zhang
Kaihao Zhang
Kaipeng Zhang

Lei Zhang
Mingda Zhang
Pingping Zhang
Qian Zhang
Qilin Zhang
Qing Zhang
Runze Zhang
Shanshan Zhang
Shu Zhang
Wayne Zhang
Xiaolin Zhang
Xiaoyun Zhang
Xucong Zhang
Yan Zhang
Zhao Zhang
Zhishuai Zhang
Feng Zhao
Jian Zhao
Liang Zhao
Qian Zhao
Qibin Zhao

Ruiqi Zhao
Sicheng Zhao
Tianyi Zhao
Xiangyun Zhao
Xin Zhao
Yifan Zhao
Yinan Zhao
Shuai Zheng
Yalin Zheng
Bineng Zhong
Fangwei Zhong
Guangyu Zhong
Yaoyao Zhong
Yiran Zhong
Jun Zhou
Mo Zhou
Pan Zhou
Ruofan Zhou
S. Kevin Zhou
Yao Zhou
Yipin Zhou

Yu Zhou
Yuqian Zhou
Yuyin Zhou
Guangming Zhu
Ligeng Zhu
Linchao Zhu
Rui Zhu
Xinge Zhu
Yizhe Zhu
Zhe Zhu
Zhen Zhu
Zheng Zhu
Bingbing Zhuang
Jiacheng Zhuo
Mohammadreza
  Zolfaghari
Chuhang Zou
Yuliang Zou
Zhengxia Zou

Contents – Part III

Optimization, Statistical Methods, and Learning

Robot Vision

Recognition and Detection

End-to-End Model-Based Gait Recognition

Xiang Li[1,2]([✉]), Yasushi Makihara[2], Chi Xu[1,2], Yasushi Yagi[2], Shiqi Yu[3],
and Mingwu Ren[1]

[1] Nanjing University of Science and Technology, Nanjing, China
lixiangmzlx@gmail.com, xuchisherry@gmail.com, renmingwu@mail.njust.edu.cn
[2] Osaka University, Osaka, Japan
{makihara,yagi}@am.sanken.osaka-u.ac.jp
[3] Southern University of Science and Technology, Shenzhen, China
yusq@sustech.edu.cn

Abstract. Most existing gait recognition approaches adopt a two-step procedure: a preprocessing step to extract silhouettes or skeletons followed by recognition. In this paper, we propose an end-to-end model-based gait recognition method. Specifically, we employ a skinned multi-person linear (SMPL) model for human modeling, and estimate its parameters using a pre-trained human mesh recovery (HMR) network. As the pre-trained HMR is not recognition-oriented, we fine-tune it in an end-to-end gait recognition framework. To cope with differences between gait datasets and those used for pre-training the HMR, we introduce a reconstruction loss between the silhouette masks in the gait datasets and the rendered silhouettes from the estimated SMPL model produced by a differentiable renderer. This enables us to adapt the HMR to the gait dataset without supervision using the ground-truth joint locations. Experimental results with the OU-MVLP and CASIA-B datasets demonstrate the state-of-the-art performance of the proposed method for both gait identification and verification scenarios, a direct consequence of the explicitly disentangled pose and shape features produced by the proposed end-to-end model-based framework.

1 Introduction

A video of a walking person contains abundant information about his/her gait pose sequence (i.e., dynamic parameters) and his/her body shape (i.e., static parameters). Gait recognition aims to identify a walking person using such dynamic and static parameters, and has a number of merits: identification at a distance; identification without subject cooperation; and difficulty in spoofing. These merits make gait recognition one of the most important solutions for person identification from CCTV footage, which has a wide range of applications in surveillance systems, forensics, and criminal investigation [1–3].

Gait recognition approaches are generally either model-based [4–12] or appearance-based [13–31]. The former mainly relies on the parameters of an articulated human model (e.g., the size of a link and a joint angle sequence), which

© Springer Nature Switzerland AG 2021
H. Ishikawa et al. (Eds.): ACCV 2020, LNCS 12624, pp. 3–20, 2021.
https://doi.org/10.1007/978-3-030-69535-4_1

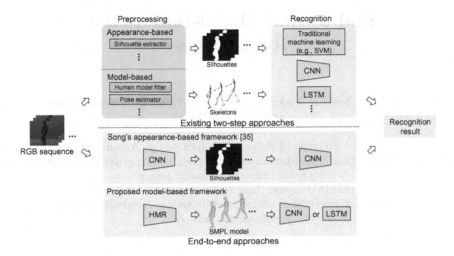

Fig. 1. While existing two-step approaches require a preprocessing step to first extract skeletons or silhouettes from RGB gait sequences before using a recognition network, the proposed method is an end-to-end model-based framework that estimates an SMPL model using a pre-trained HMR network, and subsequently uses the explicit parameterized pose and shape features of the SMPL model for recognition.

are less sensitive to apparent changes caused by covariates (e.g., view angles, carrying status, and clothing), but are generally hard to extract accurately, particularly from low-resolution images. The latter approach mainly relies on human silhouette-based representations (e.g., gait energy images (GEIs) [13], frequency-domain features [25], and chrono-gait images [32]), which are easy to extract, even from low-resolution images, but are relatively sensitive to the aforementioned covariates.

Both approaches typically apply a preprocessing step to extract the pose structure or silhouettes from raw RGB videos with some additional algorithms, as shown in Fig. 1. For example, human body pose estimation methods (e.g., OpenPose [33]) are used to extract the joint locations; traditional background subtraction or deep learning-based semantic segmentation methods (e.g., RefineNet [34]) are used to segment the silhouettes. The preprocessing step is, however, not optimally designed for the latter recognition step. Hence, two-step approaches are not necessarily optimal in terms of recognition.

Several studies have proposed end-to-end appearance-based gait recognition frameworks [35,36] that make the whole process optimal for recognition tasks, as they directly output the recognition results from the input RGB image sequences. For example, Song et al. [35] proposed a framework combining two convolutional neural networks (CNNs) that handle silhouette segmentation and gait recognition, respectively. Zhang et al. [36] proposed an end-to-end model that directly extracts latent pose and appearance features from masked RGB image sequences via disentangled representation learning (DRL), and obtains recognition results by subsequently feeding the latent pose feature sequence (i.e., motion information) to a long short-term memory (LSTM) framework. These methods [35,36] are appearance-based approaches, and hence still suffer from the aforementioned sensitivity to covariates (e.g., view).

By contrast, the bottleneck of model-based approaches (e.g., difficulty of human model fitting) is being resolved by recent advances in deep learning-based human model fitting [33,37,38]. For example, Kanazawa et al. [37] proposed a human mesh recovery (HMR) network that could directly estimate a parametric 3D human model (i.e., a skinned multi-person linear (SMPL) model [39]) to describe the 3D human body and shape from a single RGB image. In this paper, we therefore describe the integration of a human model estimation method [37] with gait recognition, and propose the first end-to-end model-based gait recognition approach.

The contributions of this study can be summarized as follows.

(1) **End-to-end model-based gait recognition**

We propose an end-to-end model-based gait recognition method for the first time. More specifically, given an RGB gait sequence, we first extract pose and shape features by fitting the SMPL model and subsequently feed the pose and shape features to a recognition network. The whole network is then trained in an end-to-end manner. Unlike the existing DRL method [36], which provides implicit (or not physically interpretable) pose and appearance features, our method produces explicit (or physically interpretable) pose and shape features as a direct consequence of the model-based approach, which can be regarded as a kind of explicit DRL method for gait recognition.

(2) **A human model fine-tuning scheme using a differentiable renderer without pose supervision**

We fine-tune a pre-trained HMR network [37] to make it optimal for gait recognition tasks as well as being adapted to different subject populations in a target gait dataset (i.e., transfer learning). Because gait datasets do not usually provide ground-truth poses (i.e., 2D joint locations), which are needed to train the HMR network [37], we instead use silhouette masks of the target dataset. More specifically, we fine-tune the HMR network using the reconstruction loss between the silhouette masks and rendered silhouettes from an estimated 3D human model with a differentiable renderer, in addition to other losses (e.g., recognition loss).

(3) **State-of-the-art performance using our model-based approach**

We achieve state-of-the-art performance on two gait datasets, namely OU-MVLP [20] and CASIA-B [40], demonstrating the robustness of the proposed method against various covariates (e.g., views, clothes, carried objects). Because appearance-based approaches are believed to be better than model-based approaches in the gait recognition research community (indeed, model-based approaches have not outperformed appearance-based approaches for the last decade, to the best of our knowledge), our work is sure to generate some excitement by demonstrating that a model-based approach can outperform state-of-the-art appearance-based approaches.

2 Related Work

2.1 Gait Recognition

Model-based approaches mainly rely on the recognition of the human pose structure and movement. Early traditional approaches [4–9] suffered from a high computational cost and inaccurate human model fitting to a low-resolution image, and hence achieved relatively poor recognition performance. Thanks to recent advances in human pose estimation methods (e.g., Flowing ConvNets [41] and OpenPose [33]), human model estimation is no longer the bottleneck, resulting in an increasing number of model-based approaches [10–12]. These usually perform two-step recognition, in which the pose information (e.g., joint heat maps or exact joint locations) is first estimated, and then LSTM or CNN is applied to further extract discriminant features for recognition. These techniques have enabled great improvements compared with traditional model-based approaches.

Appearance-based approaches mainly rely on the recognition of human silhouettes. Unfortunately, the silhouette-based representations are easily affected by many covariates (e.g., view angles, carrying status, and clothing), which cause larger intra-subject differences than the subtle inter-subject differences. The many attempts to mitigate these negative effects of covariates can generally be separated into discriminative and generative approaches. Discriminative approaches [13–23,42] mainly focus on extracting discriminative features or subspaces that are invariant to the covariates, whereas generative approaches [24–31] specialize in generating gait features under the same covariate conditions. In particular, the introduction of deep learning techniques has significantly improved the recognition accuracy. For example, some CNN-based discriminative approaches [19–23] apply a Siamese/triplet network to learn similarity metrics for a pair/triplet of input GEIs/silhouettes. Some generative adversarial network-based approaches [30,31] generate a gait template from other covariate conditions to produce a canonical condition with no covariates (e.g., no carried object) or a target covariate condition (e.g., side view).

Both families, however, require a preprocessing step to extract the joint locations or silhouette-based representations given RGB gait sequences. Although [35] proposed an end-to-end framework for silhouette segmentation and gait recognition, it relies on the extracted silhouettes (i.e., appearance-based representation), and hence still suffers from sensitivity to covariates (e.g., view).

2.2 Disentangled Representation Learning

DRL is generally designed to separate the input data into disjoint meaningful variables, and has been widely studied in many areas (e.g., pose-invariant face recognition [43], shape-guided human image generation [44]). With regard to gait, there have been relatively few studies. Zhang et al. [36] employed an autoencoder-based CNN to directly extract latent pose and appearance features from RGB imagery, and then applied LSTM-based pose features for recognition. Li et al. [45] proposed a disentanglement method for the identity and covariate features for GEIs. They first used an encoder to extract the latent identity and covariate features, and then used a two-stream decoder to reconstruct GEIs with and without covariates.

The latent features used in [36, 45] are not, however, physically interpretable because of the implicit disentanglement process. Moreover, the features may not be perfectly disentangled when certain assumptions (e.g., appearance consistency within a sequence) are violated. In contrast, our method realizes explicit disentanglement into the physically interpretable 3D joints and shape features of an SMPL model.

2.3   3D Human Pose and Shape Estimation

Most approaches formulate this problem as the estimation of parameters for a parametric 3D human model (i.e., SMPL [39]). For example, Pavlakos et al. [38] used a ConvNet to predict 2D pose heat maps and silhouettes from an RGB image, and then used these to infer the pose and shape parameters of the SMPL through two individual networks. Kanazawa et al. [37] designed an end-to-end HMR network that directly estimates the pose and shape parameters of human meshes from a single RGB image. The HMR network is trained in an adversarial manner to determine whether the estimated parameters are real or not using a large database of 3D human meshes.

As the estimated SMPL model accurately captures the statistics of human 3D pose and shape, it could be used for numerous tasks (e.g., motion imitation or appearance transfer in human image synthesis [46]). In this paper, we explore the usage of the SMPL model for gait recognition. We mainly rely on the existing HMR network [37] to estimate the pose and shape parameters.

3   End-to-End Model-Based Gait Recognition

3.1   Overview

An overview of the proposed network is shown in Fig. 2. Given a period of size-normalized and registered RGB gait sequence, the SMPL model containing the pose and shape features is first estimated using a pre-trained HMR network [37]. The estimated shape features are further aggregated by an average pooling layer to produce a common shape for all frames. Thereafter, we render 2D binary silhouettes with a differentiable renderer from the 3D human mesh generated by the common shape, frame-by-frame pose, and camera parameters. The HMR network is then fine-tuned without pose supervision, instead using the reconstruction loss between the silhouette masks in the gait datasets and the rendered silhouettes. In this way, the estimated SMPL model becomes more identity-preserving. Finally, the shape feature and the latent pose features filtered by LSTM/CNN are used for recognition. The whole network is trained in an end-to-end manner with multiple losses, which are responsible for the identity-preserving SMPL model estimation and gait recognition.

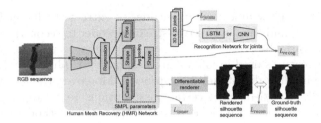

Fig. 2. Overview of the proposed network. For each input RGB sequence, an HMR [37] network first extracts the SMPL parameters, which are further rendered to 2D binary silhouettes for comparison with the silhouette masks in the gait datasets. The shape and pose features of the SMPL are then used for recognition.

3.2 HMR Network [37]

Given an input RGB gait sequence, the HMR network estimates a 3D human body mesh derived from the SMPL model [39], which factors the human body into shape β and pose θ components. The shape $\beta \in \mathbb{R}^{10}$ is defined in a low-dimensional principal component analysis shape space, which describes the height, weight, and body proportions of individuals. The pose $\theta \in \mathbb{R}^{72}$ is the combination of the relative 3D rotations of 23 joints in an axis–angle representation (23×3) with respect to its parent in the kinematic tree and the 3D root orientation, which describes the joint locations of individuals. The SMPL model outputs a triangulated mesh with 6,890 vertices, and is differentiable with respect to θ and β. Additionally, the weak-perspective camera parameter $k \in \mathbb{R}^3$ is also estimated. As a result, the HMR network first encodes the input image into a 2,048-dimensional feature using ResNet-50 [47], and then predicts the 85-dimensional vector $\Theta = [\beta^T, \theta^T, k^T]^T$ using an iterative 3D regression network.

The HMR network was trained using six datasets with different properties: four datasets [48–51] with 2D joint information (i.e., pose and body part length) from over 4,000 subjects and two datasets [52,53] with full 3D information, including body part thickness, but from a limited number of subjects (i.e., just five and eight subjects, respectively). Therefore, the subject diversity is good for the pose and the body part length, while it is limited for the body part thickness. Consequently, the estimation accuracy for the body part thickness is not as high as that for the pose and body part length (e.g., joint locations).

3.3 Shape Consistency and Pose/Camera Smoothness

Because the original HMR network is designed for a single image, it ignores the shape consistency and the pose and camera continuities within a sequence. We therefore modify the HMR network by introducing the inner loss L_{inner} of the estimated parameters Θ (i.e., combination of shape consistency and pose/camera smoothness) as additional constraints, as described below.

Suppose that N gait sequences $\{S_i\}(i = 1, \ldots, N)$ are given and the i-th sequence is composed of T_i frames. The HMR network first estimates the parameters $\boldsymbol{\Theta}_i^j = [\boldsymbol{\beta}_i^{j^T}, \boldsymbol{\theta}_i^{j^T}, \boldsymbol{k}_i^{j^T}]^T$ for the j-th frame of the i-th sequence frame-by-frame. To make the shape $\boldsymbol{\beta}_i^j$ consistent within the input sequence S_i, we aggregate each frame in an average pooling layer to produce a common shape $\bar{\boldsymbol{\beta}}_i = \frac{1}{T_i} \sum_{j=1}^{T_i} \boldsymbol{\beta}_i^j$. This common shape $\bar{\boldsymbol{\beta}}_i$ then replaces each frame's shape $\boldsymbol{\beta}_i^j$ in the final estimated SMPL model.

Furthermore, suppose that N gait sequences are composed of C subjects, and denote the set of sequence indices for the c-th subject as $\mathcal{S}_c$. We then introduce the shape-based inner loss L_{shape} to make the common shapes $\bar{\boldsymbol{\beta}}_i$ within the same subject closer to each other:

$$L_{\text{shape}} = \frac{1}{C} \sum_{c=1}^{C} \frac{1}{|\mathcal{S}_c|(|\mathcal{S}_c| - 1)} \sum_{i \in \mathcal{S}_c} \sum_{l \in \mathcal{S}_c - \{i\}} \|\bar{\boldsymbol{\beta}}_i - \bar{\boldsymbol{\beta}}_l\|_2^2. \tag{1}$$

As for the pose $\boldsymbol{\theta}_i^j$ and camera $\boldsymbol{k}_i^j$, they are considered to change smoothly within a gait sequence S_i. We therefore introduce the pose-based inner loss L_{pose} and camera-based inner loss L_{cam} as

$$L_{\text{pose}} = \frac{1}{N} \sum_{i=1}^{N} \left(\frac{1}{T_i - 1} \sum_{j=1}^{T_i - 1} \|\boldsymbol{\theta}_i^{j+1} - \boldsymbol{\theta}_i^j\|_2^2 + \frac{1}{T_i - 2} \sum_{j=2}^{T_i - 1} \|\boldsymbol{\theta}_i^{j+1} - 2\boldsymbol{\theta}_i^j + \boldsymbol{\theta}_i^{j-1}\|_2^2 \right),$$

$$L_{\text{cam}} = \frac{1}{N} \sum_{i=1}^{N} \left(\frac{1}{T_i - 1} \sum_{j=1}^{T_i - 1} \|\boldsymbol{k}_i^{j+1} - \boldsymbol{k}_i^j\|_2^2 + \frac{1}{T_i - 2} \sum_{j=2}^{T_i - 1} \|\boldsymbol{k}_i^{j+1} - 2\boldsymbol{k}_i^j + \boldsymbol{k}_i^{j-1}\|_2^2 \right),$$
$$\tag{2}$$

where the first and second terms of each expression are first- and second-order smoothness terms, respectively.

The final inner loss L_{inner} is a weighted summation of the above mentioned three losses, and can be written as

$$L_{\text{inner}} = \lambda_{\text{shape}} L_{\text{shape}} + \lambda_{\text{pose}} L_{\text{pose}} + \lambda_{\text{cam}} L_{\text{cam}}, \tag{3}$$

where λ_{shape}, λ_{pose}, and λ_{cam} are the weight parameters.

3.4   Transfer Learning Using a Differentiable Renderer

As the pre-trained HMR network is insufficient in terms of subject diversity, particularly for the body part thickness (see Subsect. 3.2), we fine-tune the HMR network to improve the coverage. Because publicly available gait datasets never provide the ground-truth SMPL parameters $\{\boldsymbol{\theta}, \boldsymbol{\beta}\}$, we instead exploit the silhouette masks provided by the gait datasets, which adequately reflect the body part thickness. More specifically, we render 2D binary silhouettes from the 3D human mesh obtained from the HMR network, and fine-tune the HMR network so that the rendered silhouettes match the silhouette masks in the gait datasets.

In this way, we can adapt the HMR network to the subject population in the gait datasets through transfer learning.

For the purpose of the 3D-to-2D projection, we introduce a neural renderer [54] as a differentiable renderer, which can be integrated with the whole framework through end-to-end training. Given the shape, pose, and camera parameters $\boldsymbol{\Theta}_i^j$ of the j-th frame of the i-th sequence, as estimated by the HMR network, we render the binary silhouette with the differential render as $\hat{\boldsymbol{b}}(\boldsymbol{\Theta}_i^j)$. We then compute the reconstruction loss between the silhouette masks $\{\boldsymbol{b}_i^j\}$ and the rendered silhouettes as

$$L_{\text{recont}} = \frac{1}{N} \sum_{i=1}^{N} \frac{1}{T_i} \sum_{j=1}^{T_i} \|\boldsymbol{b}_i^j - \hat{\boldsymbol{b}}(\boldsymbol{\Theta}_i^j)\|_2^2. \tag{4}$$

3.5   Constraints on Joint Locations

If we fine-tune the HMR network using only the silhouette masks, we may produce corrupted poses from overfitting to the silhouette masks because the poses (or joint locations) are ambiguous in a textureless silhouette mask. For example, the silhouette masks may have some extra parts with loose clothes or carried objects, which are never considered in SMPL models of real humans, and unlikely joint locations may be estimated by overfitting the rendered silhouettes to the silhouette masks with these extra parts. However, thanks to the good coverage of the subject diversity for the pose and body part length, the pre-trained HMR network can estimate the joint locations accurately, even for external datasets (i.e., the gait datasets considered in this paper).

Therefore, we introduce the joint loss L_{joints} to constrain the 3D and 2D joint locations. The parameters $\boldsymbol{\Theta}_i^j$ and $\tilde{\boldsymbol{\Theta}}_i^j$ at the j-th frame of the i-th sequence given by the fine-tuned and pre-trained HMR networks, respectively, are transformed to the 3D and 2D joint locations using the mapping functions $\boldsymbol{x}_{\text{3D}}(\boldsymbol{\Theta})$ and $\boldsymbol{x}_{\text{2D}}(\boldsymbol{\Theta})$, respectively. The joint loss L_{joints} is defined as

$$L_{\text{joints}} = \frac{1}{N} \sum_{i=1}^{N} \frac{1}{T_i} \sum_{j=1}^{T_i} \sum_{\text{dim}\in\{\text{2D},\text{3D}\}} \|\boldsymbol{x}_{\text{dim}}(\boldsymbol{\Theta}_i^j) - \boldsymbol{x}_{\text{dim}}(\tilde{\boldsymbol{\Theta}}_i^j)\|_2^2. \tag{5}$$

3.6   Disentangled Shape and Pose Features for Gait Recognition

The explicitly disentangled shape and pose features given by the HMR network are separately fed into recognition networks. For simplicity, let us drop the sequence index in this subsection.

Regarding the shape feature, we directly use the averaged shape feature $\boldsymbol{f}_{\text{shape}} = \bar{\boldsymbol{\beta}} \in \mathbb{R}^{10}$ of a given sequence for recognition.

For the pose feature, we first concatenate the 3D and 2D joint locations for a sequence with T frames as $P = \{\boldsymbol{p}^j | \boldsymbol{p}^j \in \mathbb{R}^{120}, j = 1, \ldots, T\}$,[1] and feed them

---

[1] Five dimensions of 23 joints + one root joint sum up to $5 \times (23 + 1) = 120$.

into an LSTM/CNN for spatiotemporal feature extraction. We use a three-layer LSTM with 256 hidden units in each cell following [36]. Once we obtain an LSTM output sequence $H = \{h^j | h^j \in \mathbb{R}^{256}, j = 1, \ldots, T\}$, we take the average $f_{\text{pose}}^{\text{LSTM}} = (1/T) \sum_{j=1}^{T} h^j \in \mathbb{R}^{256}$ as the pose feature for recognition.

We also use a CNN on the pose features, for which [12] mentioned that CNNs could outperform the LSTM. First, a 2D matrix is formed from the concatenated 3D and 2D joint locations of T frames as $[p^1, \ldots, p^T] \in \mathbb{R}^{120 \times T}$. We employ a relatively simple CNN architecture consisting of three convolutional layers and one fully connected layer. Each convolutional layer is followed by a batch normalization layer and ReLU activation function. We set the kernel size to 3×3, and use 64, 128, and 256 channels in the respective layers. The feature size is reduced in the row direction by setting the vertical stride to 2, as there is a limited frame number in the column direction. Finally, we use the 52-dimensional output from the last fully connected layer as the pose features for recognition, $f_{\text{pose}}^{\text{CNN}} \in \mathbb{R}^{52}$. Each feature $f \in \{f_{\text{shape}}, f_{\text{pose}}^{\text{LSTM}}, f_{\text{pose}}^{\text{CNN}}\}$ is taken separately for training and testing.

In the training stage, following [20,45], we use different loss functions ($L_{\text{recog}} \in \{L_{\text{trip}}, L_{\text{cont}}\}$) for different recognition tasks (gait identification and verification). For gait identification, we assume that a mini-batch of sequences contains N_{trip} triplets $\{f_Q^i, f_G^i, f_I^i\}(i = 1, \ldots, N_{\text{trip}})$, where a subject of f_G^i is the same as that of f_Q^i whereas a subject of f_I^i is different from that of f_Q^i. The triplet loss [55] is defined as

$$L_{\text{trip}} = \frac{1}{N_{\text{trip}}} \sum_{i=1}^{N_{\text{trip}}} \max(m - \|f_Q^i - f_I^i\|_2^2 + \|f_Q^i - f_G^i\|_2^2, 0), \qquad (6)$$

where m is the margin.

For gait verification, we assume that a mini-batch of sequences contains N_{pair} pairs $\{f_P^i, f_G^i\}(i = 1, \ldots, N_{\text{pair}})$, and the i-th pair has a binary label y_i (if $y_i = 1$, the pair is from the same subject sequence; if $y_i = 0$, the pair is from different subject sequences). The normalized contrastive loss [56] for the same and different subject pairs is defined as

$$L_{\text{cont}} = \frac{1}{N_s} \sum_{i=1}^{N_{\text{pair}}} y_i \|f_P^i - f_G^i\|_2^2 + \frac{1}{N_d} \sum_{i=1}^{N_{\text{pair}}} (1 - y_i) \max(m - \|f_P^i - f_G^i\|_2^2, 0), \quad (7)$$

where N_s, N_d are the number of same and different subject pairs in this batch.

3.7 Joint Loss Function

We train the whole network in an end-to-end manner with a joint loss function. This is a weighted summation of the aforementioned losses, and is defined as

$$L_{\text{total}} = \lambda_{\text{inner}} L_{\text{inner}} + \lambda_{\text{recont}} L_{\text{recont}} + \lambda_{\text{joints}} L_{\text{joints}} + \lambda_{\text{recog}} L_{\text{recog}}, \qquad (8)$$

where λ_{inner}, λ_{recont}, and λ_{joints} are the weight parameters.

In a test case, we use the trained model to extract the feature f for the input RGB sequences, then compute the L2 distance between f for two sequences as a dissimilarity score for matching.

4 Experiments

4.1 Datasets

We evaluated our method on two datasets: OU-MVLP [20] and CASIA-B [40].

OU-MVLP is currently the largest database with various view variations. There are 10,307 subjects with 14 view angles ($0°$, $15°$, ..., $90°$; $180°$, $195°$, ..., $270°$). Each subject has two sequences (#00, #01). Following the protocol of [20], 5,153 subjects were selected for the training set and the remaining 5,154 subjects were placed in the test set. Sequence #00 and sequence #01 were assigned as a probe and a gallery, respectively. Probes that did not have corresponding galleries (i.e., non-enrolled probes) were excluded from the test set.

CASIA-B is one of the most frequently used gait databases. There are 124 subjects with 11 view angles ($0°$, $18°$, ..., $180°$). Each subject has 10 sequences per view. Six are in the normal walking condition (NM), two are carrying a bag (BG), and the remaining two are wearing a coat (CL). We applied the protocol of using the first 74 subjects for training, with the remaining 50 subjects used for testing. In the test cases, NM #1–4 were assigned as galleries, and the other six were divided into three probes: NM #5–6, BG #1–2, and CL #1–2.

4.2 Implementation Details

We simply obtained the size-normalized and registered human silhouettes from the raw silhouettes provided by the datasets based on the region center and height, and cropped the raw RGB sequences using the corresponding locations. As for other real-scene videos, some state-of-the-art human detection and segmentation methods (e.g., Mask R-CNN [57] and RefineNet [34]) could be applied to obtain the required RGB sequences and silhouettes for training and testing.

The cropped RGB sequences were then scaled to 224×224 to fit the pre-trained HMR [37] model, and the corresponding silhouette masks were resized to a smaller 64×64 size to reduce the memory requirements. The frame number T in a period was set to 15. Thus, we generally selected 15 frames at equal intervals from a period in sequences, while omitting sequences with fewer than 15 frames.

For both datasets, other layers besides the HMR (which is initialized with a pre-trained model provided by [37]) used the default initialization. Adam [58] was chosen as the optimizer. The learning rate was initially set to 10^{-4}, and then decreased to 10^{-5} after a certain number of iterations M. For OU-MVLP, we set $M = 30K$ and the total number of iterations to 60K. For CASIA-B, we basically set $M = 10K$ and the total number of iterations to 15K; sometimes, we decreased the learning rate earlier or applied early stopping to prevent overfitting to the small training set. For each training iteration, we randomly selected eight

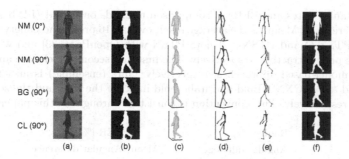

Fig. 3. Visualization of estimation results under different views and walking conditions on CASIA-B: (a) RGB inputs; (b) silhouette masks; (c) estimated SMPL models; (d) estimated 3D joint locations; (e) estimated 2D joint locations; (f) rendered silhouettes.

subjects and eight sequences per subject to generate all possible triplets or pairs in a mini-batch. The margin m in Eqs. (6) and (7) was set to 0.2. The hyperparameters of the inner loss and the joint loss functions in Eqs. (3) and (8) were experimentally set to $\lambda_{shape} = 1$, $\lambda_{pose} = 0.1$, $\lambda_{cam} = 0.00001$, $\lambda_{inner} = 1$, $\lambda_{recont} = 1$, $\lambda_{joints} = 100$, and $\lambda_{recog} = 1$.

We evaluated the recognition performance in terms of the Rank-1 identification rate (denoted as Rank-1) and the equal error rate (denoted as EER) for the identification and verification tasks, respectively.

4.3 Feature Visualization

Some of the estimation results given by the proposed method are visualized in Fig. 3. This figure shows that the proposed method can estimate reasonable SMPL models under view, clothing, and carrying status variations, i.e., it obtains a similar body thickness between frontal and side views, and successfully excludes carried bags or clothing in the estimated SMPL models to some extent (e.g., the third row of Fig. 3). This is beneficial for robust gait recognition against changes in view, clothing, and carried objects. In addition, the pose (or joint locations) is also reasonably estimated, although some of the joints are not realistic (i.e., both left and right arms stay forward); this will be examined in future research.

4.4 Comparison Using OU-MVLP

The benchmarks included both appearance-based approaches [18–20, 22, 25, 60, 61][2] and a model-based approach [11]. The deep models were trained using all 14 views. As mentioned in Subsect. 3.4, we trained and tested three features given by the proposed method (i.e., "pose_LSTM", "pose_CNN", and "shape") separately. Following [20], we selected four typical views (i.e., 0°, 30°, 60°, 90°) and present the test results averaged over each angular difference in Table 1. We also present more comprehensive results for some benchmarks in Table 2.

---

[2] While the original GaitSet paper [22] reported results including the non-enrolled probes, the results here exclude the non-enrolled probes to ensure a fair comparison.

Table 1. Rank-1 rates and EERs of comparison methods on OU-MVLP based on the angular differences. "Mean" is the average result over all 16 probe and gallery view combinations. PTSN-O and PTSN-α denote PTSN with OpenPose [33] and with Alpha-Pose [59] as pose extractors, respectively. The first and second blocks are appearance-based and model-based approaches, respectively. Ours (ensemble) is an ensemble of "shape" and "pose_CNN". Bold and italic bold indicate the best and the second-best accuracies, respectively. This convention is consistent throughout this paper.

Methods	Rank-1 [%]					EER [%]				
	Angular difference				Mean	Angular difference				Mean
	0°	30°	60°	90°		0°	30°	60°	90°	
Direct Match	77.4	2.4	0.2	0.0	20.3	6.5	25.2	41.4	46.2	27.2
LDA [60]	81.6	10.1	0.8	0.1	24.4	6.2	22.7	35.7	40.1	24.0
VTM [25]	77.4	2.7	0.6	0.2	20.5	6.5	26.8	34.2	38.5	25.0
GEINet [18]	85.7	40.3	13.8	5.4	40.7	2.4	5.9	12.7	17.2	8.1
LB [19]	89.9	42.2	15.2	4.5	42.6	1.0	3.3	6.7	9.3	4.3
Takemura's [20]	89.5	55.0	30.0	17.3	52.7	1.0	2.0	3.4	4.2	2.4
PSTN [61]	93.9	69.2	41.9	25.9	63.1	0.6	1.5	2.8	3.7	1.9
GaitSet [22]	99.1	96.4	86.9	79.8	92.6	0.25	0.42	0.68	0.92	0.51
PTSN-O [11]	48.1	18.4	6.6	2.1	18.8	8.8	11.9	15.4	20.5	13.1
PTSN-α [11]	59.7	31.0	13.2	4.7	30.4	6.6	8.7	12.3	17.8	10.2
Ours (shape)	**99.6**	*97.7*	*95.0*	**91.4**	*96.7*	**0.12**	**0.19**	*0.23*	*0.29*	*0.19*
Ours (pose_LSTM)	88.1	61.9	47.3	35.1	61.5	0.36	0.55	0.79	1.06	0.62
Ours (pose_CNN)	98.3	91.9	81.9	74.5	88.8	*0.19*	*0.30*	0.41	0.58	0.33
Ours (ensemble)	*99.5*	**98.2**	**95.2**	*91.3*	**96.9**	**0.12**	**0.19**	**0.14**	**0.28**	**0.17**

Table 2. Rank-1 rates and EERs averaged over the 14 gallery views, where the identical view is excluded. Ours is an ensemble. GaitPart [42] only provides the mean Rank-1 rate.

	Methods	Probe view														
		0°	15°	30°	45°	60°	75°	90°	180°	195°	210°	225°	240°	255°	270°	Mean
Rank -1 [%]	PTSN-O	6.4	11.0	15.4	18.8	17.6	15.1	8.8	5.2	10.6	10.5	17.3	14.6	11.6	7.7	12.2
	PTSN-α	11.8	19.0	23.9	26.5	24.9	20.6	14.7	6.1	11.6	14.2	22.1	21.3	17.9	14.3	17.8
	GaitSet	*84.7*	*93.6*	*96.7*	*96.7*	*93.6*	*95.3*	*94.2*	*86.9*	*92.8*	*96.0*	*96.1*	*93.0*	*94.5*	*92.8*	*93.3*
	GaitPart	–	–	–	–	–	–	–	–	–	–	–	–	–	–	*95.1*
	Ours	**92.8**	**96.2**	**96.8**	**96.3**	**94.7**	**96.6**	**96.6**	**93.5**	**95.4**	**96.3**	**96.7**	**96.5**	**96.5**	**96.2**	**95.8**
EER [%]	PTSN-O	16.0	13.3	13.0	11.2	11.6	12.8	17.1	17.6	14.9	18.9	12.3	13.2	14.9	18.2	14.6
	PTSN-α	15.1	12.5	11.9	11.1	11.2	12.5	14.8	22.2	17.8	21.3	11.8	11.9	13.0	14.7	14.4
	GaitSet	*1.45*	*0.93*	*0.76*	*0.75*	*0.99*	*0.79*	*0.86*	*2.80*	*1.61*	*1.53*	*2.20*	*1.83*	*1.15*	*1.00*	*1.33*
	Ours	**0.34**	**0.34**	**0.20**	**0.18**	**0.31**	**0.26**	**0.17**	**0.28**	**0.28**	**0.36**	**0.34**	**0.21**	**0.20**	**0.20**	**0.26**

The results indicate that the proposed method using the shape feature outperforms state-of-the-art appearance- and model-based approaches in terms of both identification and verification tasks. As the view variation increases from 0° to 90°, the accuracy of the existing methods decreases rapidly, whereas our

Table 3. Rank-1 rates [%] of comparison methods on CASIA-B using the first 74 subjects for training. The mean result over all 10 gallery views for each probe view is given, where the identical view is excluded.

Probe	Methods	Probe view											
		0°	18°	36°	54°	72°	90°	108°	126°	144°	162°	180°	Mean
NM #5–6	ViDP [62]	–	–	–	64.2	–	60.4	–	65.0	–	–	–	–
	CNN ensemble [19]	88.7	95.1	98.2	96.4	94.1	91.5	93.9	97.5	98.4	95.8	85.6	94.1
	Takemura's [20]	83.2	91.2	95.8	93.4	91.2	87.8	89.4	93.6	96.0	95.8	81.6	90.8
	PSTN [61]	87.0	93.8	96.2	94.4	92.2	91.8	92.0	95.0	96.0	96.4	84.8	92.7
	Song's GaitNet [35]	75.6	91.3	91.2	92.9	92.5	91.0	91.8	93.8	92.9	94.1	81.9	89.9
	Zhang's GaitNet [36]	91.2	92.0	90.5	95.6	86.9	92.6	93.5	96.0	90.9	88.8	89.0	91.6
	GaitSet [22]	90.8	*97.9*	**99.4**	96.9	93.6	91.7	95.0	*97.8*	*98.9*	96.8	85.8	95.0
	GaitPart [42]	94.1	**98.6**	*99.3*	**98.5**	94.0	92.3	95.9	**98.4**	**99.2**	*97.8*	90.4	96.2
	PoseGait [12]	55.3	69.6	73.9	75.0	68.0	68.2	71.1	72.9	76.1	70.4	55.4	68.7
	Ours (shape)	**97.1**	97.3	98.4	*98.4*	*97.4*	**98.3**	**97.7**	96.2	96.9	97.1	*97.5*	*97.5*
	Ours (pose_LSTM)	65.1	59.5	67.2	67.9	66.2	68.1	72.0	66.0	65.2	65.4	64.0	66.1
	Ours (pose_CNN)	87.1	88.3	93.8	95.4	92.1	92.8	90.5	90.7	88.5	92.4	91.7	91.2
	Ours (ensemble)	*96.9*	97.1	98.5	*98.4*	**97.7**	*98.2*	*97.6*	97.6	98.0	**98.4**	**98.6**	**97.9**
BG #1–2	LB [19]	64.2	80.6	82.7	76.9	64.8	63.1	68.0	76.9	82.2	75.4	61.3	72.4
	Zhang's GaitNet [36]	83.0	87.8	88.3	93.3	82.6	74.8	89.5	91.0	86.1	81.2	85.6	85.7
	GaitSet [22]	83.8	91.2	91.8	88.8	83.3	81.0	84.1	90.0	*92.2*	**94.4**	79.0	87.2
	GaitPart [42]	89.1	**94.8**	**96.7**	**95.1**	88.3	**94.9**	89.0	*93.5*	**96.1**	*93.8*	*85.8*	*91.5*
	PoseGait [12]	35.3	47.2	52.4	46.9	45.5	43.9	46.1	48.1	49.4	43.6	31.1	44.5
	Ours (shape)	*92.0*	91.7	92.2	93.0	*92.7*	91.6	*92.8*	92.3	88.4	86.5	83.4	90.6
	Ours (pose_LSTM)	53.9	50.5	52.4	51.9	49.1	50.6	47.1	49.4	47.0	44.2	45.7	49.3
	Ours (pose_CNN)	86.8	81.2	84.6	86.8	84.9	83.0	83.9	82.8	82.1	84.0	83.2	83.9
	Ours (ensemble)	**94.8**	*92.9*	*93.8*	*94.5*	**93.1**	*92.6*	**94.0**	**94.5**	89.7	93.6	**90.4**	**93.1**
CL #1–2	LB [19]	37.7	57.2	66.6	61.1	55.2	54.6	55.2	59.1	58.9	48.8	39.4	54.0
	Zhang's GaitNet [36]	42.1	58.2	65.1	70.7	68.0	70.6	65.3	69.4	51.5	50.1	36.6	58.9
	GaitSet [22]	61.4	75.4	80.7	77.3	72.1	70.1	71.5	73.5	*73.5*	68.4	50.0	70.4
	GaitPart [42]	70.7	**85.5**	**86.9**	**83.3**	77.1	72.5	**76.9**	**82.2**	**83.8**	**80.2**	66.5	**78.7**
	PoseGait [12]	24.3	29.7	41.3	38.8	38.2	38.5	41.6	44.9	42.2	33.4	22.5	36.0
	Ours (shape)	*72.1*	74.1	77.2	79.0	*77.3*	*76.7*	75.2	*76.0*	70.1	72.8	**74.8**	75.1
	Ours (pose_LSTM)	40.4	42.5	41.7	38.9	34.9	34.9	37.5	36.1	34.8	33.5	32.0	37.0
	Ours (pose_CNN)	63.0	62.4	66.3	65.2	61.9	58.2	58.3	59.1	56.8	55.4	55.6	60.2
	Ours (ensemble)	**78.2**	*81.0*	*82.1*	*82.8*	**80.3**	76.9	75.5	77.4	72.3	*73.5*	*74.2*	*77.6*

method mitigates the degradation. This demonstrates the robustness of our method against view variations.

However, our method performs worse with the pose feature than with the shape feature. This is partly because the extraction accuracy of the pose feature is sometimes degraded by self-occlusions when only a single-view sequence is used (e.g., both arms stay forward in Fig. 3). We also find that "pose_CNN" performs better than "pose_LSTM," which is consistent with the conclusions of the recent pose-based gait recognition study [12]. Despite the above mentioned difficulty, our method using the pose feature (CNN) outperforms most of the benchmarks and is even comparable to GaitSet [22], the state-of-the-art appearance-based method (i.e., slightly worse Rank-1 rate, but better EER).

Moreover, we constructed an ensemble of "shape" and "pose_CNN" by averaging their dissimilarity scores, and this produced a further improvement.

4.5 Comparison Using CASIA-B

Table 3 compares the results from our method with those given by other bench-marks. We only report the Rank-1 rates, because few previous studies evaluated the verification accuracy. For three different probe sets, we trained three separate models for our method. Our method (ensemble) is comparable with the latest state-of-the-art GaitPart [42], i.e., 1.7% and 1.6% better for "NM" and "BG," but 1.1% worse for "CL", and achieves the best or the second-best accuracy in most cases. Additionally, compared with the two-step model-based approach with pose information [12], our pose-based method (pose_CNN) exhibits significantly better performance. This is because our method trains the human model fitting along with recognition tasks in an end-to-end manner, whereas the method of [12] extracts poses with the pre-trained OpenPose [33], which is not optimized for recognition.

4.6 Ablation Study of Loss Functions

We conducted ablation studies using our method with the shape feature (i.e., the best individual feature), and analyze the effect of the proposed loss functions on the recognition performance in Table 4. The pre-trained HMR without recognition loss L_{recog} yields the worst accuracy (the first row), whereas introducing the recognition loss L_{recog} significantly improves the accuracy (the second to the fifth rows). When we separately turn off the inner loss L_{inner}, joint loss

Table 4. Ablation study of our method (shape) on CASIA-B under NM probe setting.

Pre-trained HMR	Fine-tuned HMR	Fine-tuned loss			L_{recog}	Rank-1 [%]
		L_{inner}	L_{joints}	L_{recon}		
√						4.1
	√		√	√	√	94.3
	√	√		√	√	*94.8*
	√	√	√		√	93.6
	√	√	√	√	√	**97.5**

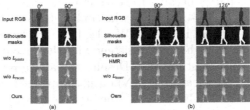

Fig. 4. Rendered semantic silhouettes comparison: (a) effect of L_{joints} and L_{recon}; (b) effect of L_{inner}.

L_{joints}, and reconstruction loss L_{recon} (see the second to the fourth rows), the accuracy decreases by 3–4%, indicating the contribution of each loss term. Moreover, we show a qualitative comparison of the rendered semantic silhouettes in Fig. 4. In line with our expectations, L_{joints} avoids the pose corruption problem and L_{recon} enables wider body shapes to be learned from the silhouette masks; L_{inner} helps learn continuous poses, which can fix the error estimations of the pre-trained HMR. All the results indicate that our method can accurately estimate the SMPL models from RGB sequences, which is beneficial for future gait recognition studies.

5   Conclusion

We have proposed an end-to-end model-based gait recognition approach that models the human gait via an SMPL model and provides explicitly disentangled shape and pose representations. We evaluated the recognition performance of shape and pose features for different recognition tasks. The experimental results on two datasets show that our method outperforms a number of state-of-the-art approaches. Because current recognition networks for pose features ignore the structure information between joints (e.g., limb length), more suitable networks will be investigated in the future.

Acknowledgement. This work was supported by JSPS KAKENHI Grant No. JP18H04115, JP19H05692, and JP20H00607, and the National Natural Science Foundation of China (Grant No. 61727802).

References

1. Bouchrika, I., Goffredo, M., Carter, J., Nixon, M.: On using gait in forensic biometrics. J. Forensic Sci. **56**, 882–889 (2011)
2. Iwama, H., Muramatsu, D., Makihara, Y., Yagi, Y.: Gait verification system for criminal investigation. IPSJ Trans. Comput. Vis. Appl. **5**, 163–175 (2013)
3. Lynnerup, N., Larsen, P.: Gait as evidence. IET Biometrics **3**, 47–54 (2014)
4. Wagg, D., Nixon, M.: On automated model-based extraction and analysis of gait. In: Proceedings of the 6th IEEE International Conference on Automatic Face and Gesture Recognition, pp. 11–16 (2004)
5. Yam, C., Nixon, M., Carter, J.: Automated person recognition by walking and running via model-based approaches. Pattern Recogn. **37**, 1057–1072 (2004)
6. Bobick, A., Johnson, A.: Gait recognition using static activity-specific parameters. In: CVPR, vol. 1, pp. 423–430 (2001)
7. Cunado, D., Nixon, M., Carter, J.: Automatic extraction and description of human gait models for recognition purposes. Comput. Vis. Image Underst. **90**, 1–41 (2003)
8. Yamauchi, K., Bhanu, B., Saito, H.: 3D human body modeling using range data. In: ICPR, pp. 3476–3479 (2010)
9. Ariyanto, G., Nixon, M.: Marionette mass-spring model for 3d gait biometrics. In: Proceedings of the 5th IAPR International Conference on Biometrics, pp. 354–359 (2012)

10. Feng, Y., Li, Y., Luo, J.: Learning effective gait features using LSTM. In: ICPR, pp. 325–330 (2016)
11. Liao, R., Cao, C., Garcia, E.B., Yu, S., Huang, Y.: Pose-based temporal-spatial network (PTSN) for gait recognition with carrying and clothing variations. In: Zhou, J., et al. (eds.) CCBR 2017. LNCS, vol. 10568, pp. 474–483. Springer, Cham (2017). https://doi.org/10.1007/978-3-319-69923-3_51
12. Liao, R., Yu, S., An, W., Huang, Y.: A model-based gait recognition method with body pose and human prior knowledge. Pattern Recogn. **98**, 107069 (2020)
13. Han, J., Bhanu, B.: Individual recognition using gait energy image. IEEE Trans. Pattern Anal. Mach. Intell. **28**, 316–322 (2006)
14. Xu, D., Yan, S., Tao, D., Zhang, L., Li, X., Zhang, H.: Human gait recognition with matrix representation. IEEE Trans. Circuits Syst. Video Technol. **16**, 896–903 (2006)
15. Lu, J., Tan, Y.P.: Uncorrelated discriminant simplex analysis for view-invariant gait signal computing. Pattern Recogn. Lett. **31**, 382–393 (2010)
16. Guan, Y., Li, C.T., Roli, F.: On reducing the effect of covariate factors in gait recognition: a classifier ensemble method. IEEE Trans. Pattern Anal. Mach. Intell. **37**, 1521–1528 (2015)
17. Makihara, Y., Suzuki, A., Muramatsu, D., Li, X., Yagi, Y.: Joint intensity and spatial metric learning for robust gait recognition. In: CVPR, pp. 5705–5715 (2017)
18. Shiraga, K., Makihara, Y., Muramatsu, D., Echigo, T., Yagi, Y.: Geinet: View-invariant gait recognition using a convolutional neural network. In: ICB (2016)
19. Wu, Z., Huang, Y., Wang, L., Wang, X., Tan, T.: A comprehensive study on cross-view gait based human identification with deep CNNs. IEEE Trans. Pattern Anal. Mach. Intell. **39**, 209–226 (2017)
20. Takemura, N., Makihara, Y., Muramatsu, D., Echigo, T., Yagi, Y.: On input/output architectures for convolutional neural network-based cross-view gait recognition. IEEE Trans. Circuits Syst. Video Technol. **29**, 2708–2719 (2019)
21. Zhang, K., Luo, W., Ma, L., Liu, W., Li, H.: Learning joint gait representation via quintuplet loss minimization. In: CVPR (2019)
22. Chao, H., He, Y., Zhang, J., Feng, J.: Gaitset: regarding gait as a set for cross-view gait recognition. In: AAAI (2019)
23. Li, X., Makihara, Y., Xu, C., Yagi, Y., Ren, M.: Joint intensity transformer network for gait recognition robust against clothing and carrying status. IEEE Trans. Inf. Forensics Secur. 1 (2019)
24. Kusakunniran, W., Wu, Q., Zhang, J., Li, H.: Support vector regression for multi-view gait recognition based on local motion feature selection. In: CVPR, San Francisco, CA, USA, pp. 1–8 (2010)
25. Makihara, Y., Sagawa, R., Mukaigawa, Y., Echigo, T., Yagi, Y.: Gait recognition using a view transformation model in the frequency domain. In: Leonardis, A., Bischof, H., Pinz, A. (eds.) ECCV 2006. LNCS, vol. 3953, pp. 151–163. Springer, Heidelberg (2006). https://doi.org/10.1007/11744078_12
26. Makihara, Y., Tsuji, A., Yagi, Y.: Silhouette transformation based on walking speed for gait identification. In: CVPR, San Francisco, CA, USA (2010)
27. Muramatsu, D., Shiraishi, A., Makihara, Y., Uddin, M., Yagi, Y.: Gait-based person recognition using arbitrary view transformation model. IEEE Trans. Image Process. **24**, 140–154 (2015)
28. Mansur, A., Makihara, Y., Aqmar, R., Yagi, Y.: Gait recognition under speed transition. In: CVPR, pp. 2521–2528 (2014)

29. Akae, N., Mansur, A., Makihara, Y., Yagi, Y.: Video from nearly still: an application to low frame-rate gait recognition. In: CVPR, Providence, RI, USA, pp. 1537–1543 (2012)
30. Yu, S., et al.: GaiTGANv 2: invariant gait feature extraction using generative adversarial networks. Pattern Recogn. **87**, 179–189 (2019)
31. He, Y., Zhang, J., Shan, H., Wang, L.: Multi-task GANs for view-specific feature learning in gait recognition. IEEE Trans. Inf. Forensics Secur. **14**, 102–113 (2019)
32. Wang, C., Zhang, J., Wang, L., Pu, J., Yuan, X.: Human identification using temporal information preserving gait template. IEEE Trans. Pattern Anal. Mach. Intell. **34**, 2164–2176 (2012)
33. Cao, Z., Hidalgo, G., Simon, T., Wei, S.E., Sheikh, Y.: OpenPose: realtime multi-person 2D pose estimation using Part Affinity Fields. arXiv preprint arXiv:1812.08008 (2018)
34. Lin, G., Milan, A., Shen, C., Reid, I.D.: RefineNet: multi-path refinement networks for high-resolution semantic segmentation. In: CVPR, pp. 5168–5177 (2017)
35. Song, C., Huang, Y., Huang, Y., Jia, N., Wang, L.: GaitNet: an end-to-end network for gait based human identification. Pattern Recogn. **96**, 106988 (2019)
36. Zhang, Z., et al.: Gait recognition via disentangled representation learning. In: CVPR, Long Beach, CA (2019)
37. Kanazawa, A., Black, M.J., Jacobs, D.W., Malik, J.: End-to-end recovery of human shape and pose. In: CVPR, pp. 7122–7131 (2018)
38. Pavlakos, G., Zhu, L., Zhou, X., Daniilidis, K.: Learning to estimate 3D human pose and shape from a single color image. In: CVPR (2018)
39. Loper, M., Mahmood, N., Romero, J., Pons-Moll, G., Black, M.J.: SMPL: a skinned multi-person linear model. ACM Trans. Graph. (Proc. SIGGRAPH Asia) **34**, 248:1–248:16 (2015)
40. Yu, S., Tan, D., Tan, T.: A framework for evaluating the effect of view angle, clothing and carrying condition on gait recognition. In: ICPR, Hong Kong, China, vol. 4, pp. 441–444 (2006)
41. Pfister, T., Charles, J., Zisserman, A.: Flowing convnets for human pose estimation in videos. In: ICCV (2015)
42. Fan, C., et al.: Gaitpart: temporal part-based model for gait recognition. In: CVPR (2020)
43. Tran, L., Yin, X., Liu, X.: Disentangled representation learning GAN for pose-invariant face recognition. In: CVPR (2017)
44. Esser, P., Sutter, E., Ommer, B.: A variational U-net for conditional appearance and shape generation. In: CVPR (2018)
45. Li, X., Makihara, Y., Xu, C., Yagi, Y., Ren, M.: Gait recognition via semi-supervised disentangled representation learning to identity and covariate features. In: CVPR (2020)
46. Liu, W., Piao, Z., Min, J., Luo, W., Ma, L., Gao, S.: Liquid warping GAN: a unified framework for human motion imitation, appearance transfer and novel view synthesis. In: ICCV (2019)
47. He, K., Zhang, X., Ren, S., Sun, J.: Identity mappings in deep residual networks. In: Leibe, B., Matas, J., Sebe, N., Welling, M. (eds.) ECCV 2016. LNCS, vol. 9908, pp. 630–645. Springer, Cham (2016). https://doi.org/10.1007/978-3-319-46493-0_38
48. Lin, T.-Y., et al.: Microsoft COCO: common objects in context. In: Fleet, D., Pajdla, T., Schiele, B., Tuytelaars, T. (eds.) ECCV 2014. LNCS, vol. 8693, pp. 740–755. Springer, Cham (2014). https://doi.org/10.1007/978-3-319-10602-1_48
49. Andriluka, M., Pishchulin, L., Gehler, P., Schiele, B.: 2D human pose estimation: New benchmark and state of the art analysis. In: CVPR (2014)

50. Johnson, S., Everingham, M.: Learning effective human pose estimation from inaccurate annotation. In: CVPR (2011)
51. Johnson, S., Everingham, M.: Clustered pose and nonlinear appearance models for human pose estimation. In: BMVC (2010)
52. Ionescu, C., Papava, D., Olaru, V., Sminchisescu, C.: Human3.6m: large scale datasets and predictive methods for 3D human sensing in natural environments. IEEE Trans. Pattern Anal. Mach. Intell. **36**, 1325–1339 (2014)
53. Mehta, D., et al.: Monocular 3D human pose estimation in the wild using improved CNN supervision. In: Fifth International Conference on 3D Vision (3DV) (2017)
54. Hiroharu Kato, Y.U., Harada, T.: Neural 3D mesh renderer. In: CVPR (2018)
55. Wang, J., et al.: Learning fine-grained image similarity with deep ranking. In: CVPR (2014)
56. Hadsell, R., Chopra, S., LeCun, Y.: Dimensionality reduction by learning an invariant mapping. In: CVPR, vol. 2, pp. 1735–1742 (2006)
57. He, K., Gkioxari, G., Dollár, P., Girshick, R.B.: Mask R-CNN. In: ICCV (2017)
58. Kingma, D.P., Ba, J.: Adam: a method for stochastic optimization. arXiv preprint (2014)
59. Fang, H.S., Xie, S., Tai, Y.W., Lu, C.: RMPE: regional multi-person pose estimation. In: The IEEE International Conference on Computer Vision (ICCV) (2017)
60. Otsu, N.: Optimal linear and nonlinear solutions for least-square discriminant feature extraction. In: ICPR, pp. 557–560 (1982)
61. Xu, C., Makihara, Y., Li, X., Yagi, Y., Lu, J.: Cross-view gait recognition using pairwise spatial transformer networks. IEEE Trans. Circuits Syst. Video Technol. 1 (2020)
62. Hu, M., Wang, Y., Zhang, Z., Little, J.J., Huang, D.: View-invariant discriminative projection for multi-view gait-based human identification. IEEE Trans. Inf. Forensics Secur. **8**, 2034–2045 (2013)

Horizontal Flipping Assisted Disentangled Feature Learning for Semi-supervised Person Re-identification

Gehan Hao[1], Yang Yang[2], Xue Zhou[1,3(✉)], Guanan Wang[2], and Zhen Lei[2]

[1] School of Automation Engineering, University of Electronic Science and Technology of China (UESTC), Chengdu 611731, China
zhouxue@uestc.edu.cn
[2] National Laboratory of Pattern Recognition (NLPR), Institute of Automation, Chinese Academy of Sciences, Beijing 100190, China
[3] Shenzhen Institute of Advanced Study, UESTC, Shenzhen, China

Abstract. In this paper, we propose to learn a powerful Re-ID model by using less labeled data together with lots of unlabeled data, *i.e.* semi-supervised Re-ID. Such kind of learning enables Re-ID model to be more generalizable and scalable to real-world scenes. Specifically, we design a two-stream encoder-decoder-based structure with shared modules and parameters. For the encoder module, we take the original person image with its horizontal mirror image as a pair of inputs and encode deep features with identity and structural information properly disentangled. Then different combinations of disentangling features are used to reconstruct images in the decoder module. In addition to the commonly used constraints from identity consistency and image reconstruction consistency for loss function definition, we design a novel loss function of enforcing consistent transformation constraints on disentangled features. It is free of labels, and can be applied to both supervised and unsupervised learning branches in our model. Extensive results on four Re-ID datasets demonstrate that by reducing 5/6 labeled data, Our method achieves the best performance on Market-1501 and CUHK03, and comparable accuracy on DukeMTMC-reID and MSMT17.

1 Introduction

Person Re-Identification (Re-ID) aims to automatically match the underlying identities of person images from non-overlapping camera views [1]. As an essential task in video surveillance of distributed multi-cameras, Re-ID is very important for individual-specific long-term behavior analysis. Due to variations of view angles, poses and illuminations in different cameras, it's very challenging to tackle this task.

In person Re-ID community, many models have been proposed, which mainly focus on three parts: hand-crafted descriptor design, metric learning and deep Re-ID models. Hand-crafted person descriptors [2–4] try to design features that are robust to different view angles, poses, and illuminations. Metric learning

© Springer Nature Switzerland AG 2021
H. Ishikawa et al. (Eds.): ACCV 2020, LNCS 12624, pp. 21–37, 2021.
https://doi.org/10.1007/978-3-030-69535-4_2

[5,6] aims to learn a feature projected space wherein the similarity of same person is higher than that of different person. With successful application of deep Convolution Neural Network (CNN), deep Re-ID [7–13], models are able to straightly learn robust and discriminative features in a compact end-to-end manner, which have gained more and more attention.

Based on whether identity labels are used, deep Re-ID models can be roughly divided into supervised and unsupervised ones. The former trains models with a supervised loss such as classification loss [10] and triplet loss [14]. The latter solves unsupervised Re-ID with cross-dataset domain-adaptation learning [15–17], tracklet information [18], or clustering-based pseudo-labels learning [19]. Although the above two kinds of Re-ID methods have achieved promising progress, they still suffer from their inherent weaknesses. Supervised Re-ID methods require massive cross-camera identity-labels to avoid over-fitting a training set. Obtaining such labels can be very time-consuming and expensive. In unsupervised Re-ID methods, domain-adaptation learning also needs source labeled data, tracklet-based methods rely on accurate tracking results, and pseudo-labels are sensitive to initial parameters. Besides, existing unsupervised Re-ID methods are still far from supervised ones in terms of accuracy.

In this paper, we formulate Re-ID problem in a semi-supervised way by leveraging a few labeled and lots of unlabeled data. Our semi-supervised Re-ID method enjoys the following two merits. 1) Compared with pure supervised Re-ID methods, our method requires less labeled data. Besides, auxiliary by mega unlabeled data, it avoids over-fitting on the training set. 2) Compared with pure unsupervised Re-ID methods, ours can achieve better accuracy by exhaustively exploring the limited labeled data.

In order to learn more robust and discriminative deep global features for Re-ID task, disentangled feature learning (DFL) is introduced in our work. Usually, DFL requires multi-inputs to disentangle features with different semantics. In our work, we found that a pair of horizontally flipped images changed the person structural information while maintaining the identity and attribute characteristics unchanged, and showed a symmetrical distribution. Then, we simply take the original person image with its horizontal mirror image as two inputs of DFL module, which does not need extra complicated operations and costs like other methods [11,20–23]. DFL module is designed in an encoder-decoder way to disentangle identity-aware features and structure-aware features, which has been applied on the original image and its horizontal mirror image respectively. With respect to the four disentangled features, two identity-aware features from the original image and its mirror image should be the same, meanwhile, two structure-aware features should satisfy mirror symmetry. However, the above invariance and equivariance constraints are often missing in the normal Re-ID training process, which only considers image-level identity labels. After that, four different combinations of disentangling features are used to reconstruct images in the decoder module.

Our main contributions can be summarised as below:

(1) We propose a novel semi-supervised Re-ID framework, which consists of two branches with shared feature disentanglement models, one for supervised task and the other for unsupervised task. It alleviates limitation of labeled data by exploiting lots of unlabeled data.
(2) We exploit unsupervised data by disentangling images and its horizontal flipping images into structure-aware and identity-aware features in a self-supervised way. A consistent transformation constrained loss function including identity invariance and structure equivariance is defined on disentangled features, which is free of labels.
(3) Extensive results on four Re-ID datasets demonstrate that by reducing 5/6 labeled data, Our method achieves the best performance on Market-1501 and CUHK03, and comparable accuracy on DukeMTMC-reID and MSMT17.

2 Related Work

2.1 Semi-supervised Person Re-identification

There are a few early semi-supervised work on person Re-ID. Figueira et al. [24] propose a method that combines multiple semi-supervised feature learning frameworks to deal jointly with the appearance-based and learning-based Re-ID problem. Liu et al. [25] propose a semi-supervised coupled dictionary learning method, which jointly learns two coupled dictionaries in the training phase from both labeled and unlabeled images. However, these non-deep-learning methods can only achieve good results on small-scale datasets.

In recent years, with the development of deep CNN, some deep semi-supervised person Re-ID methods have been presented. The first semi-supervised approach [26] that performs pseudo-labeling by considering complex relationships between unlabeled and labeled training samples in the feature space. They adopt a generative adversarial network to generate additional artificial sample data as unlabeled data. Huang et al. [27] introduce multi-pseudo regularized labels and distribute them to the generated data to supplement the real training data in a semi-supervised manner. Liu et al. [22] design a simple but effective learning mechanism that merely substitutes the last fully-connected layer with the proposed Transductive Centroid Projection (TCP) module. Fan et al. [28] propose a simple and progressive unsupervised deep learning framework, whose purpose is to use k-means clustering to estimate the labels of unlabeled training samples, and extend it to semi-supervised Re-ID. Xin et al. [29] propose a semi-supervised method that combines multi-view clustering and deep metric learning to repeatedly update the pseudo-labels of unlabeled training samples.

Different from the above methods, our method does not follow the idea of pseudo labelling and clustering, but construct an encoder-decoder feature disentanglement framework which can be learned not relying on the labels.

2.2 DFL-Based Person Re-identification

In recent years, disentangled feature learning (DFL)-based person Re-ID has gained more and more attention [11,20,22,23,30–34]. DFL is expected to provide gains by separating the underlying structure of data into uncorrelated meaningful variables, which helps determine what types of hidden features are actually learned [35]. Current DFL-based Re-ID methods usually adopt GAN or auto-encoder model to separate different attributes (i.e., appearance or pose, etc.) from multi-inputs of a person. Among them, posture is the most considered attribute. Ma et al. [22] use a complex multi-branch model to decompose the input person image into the foreground, background, and pose to generate a specific image, but the model cannot be trained end-to-end. Qian et al. [20] generate a normalized pose image for each person, but there are only 8 predefined poses. Ge et al. [11] also guide the network to learn pose-invariant features, but utilizing human key points to describe pose features, which is time-consuming. Based on previous work, Li et al. [23] not only extract pose features, but also use additional key features of human body.

Therefore, most of the current work can be summarized as follows: 1) Additional annotations are used, such as human keypoint features. They define characteristics of human posture information as constraints to guide the network to learn identity-invariant features. 2) Requiring person samples with different postures for learning identity-invariant features. However, both methods have their shortcomings. The first requires the introduction of additional annotations, which increases the complexity of the network. Samples that meet the conditions of second method are difficult to find. Either you need to select samples with different poses or using GAN to generate these multi-pose samples. Even if you find these kinds of samples, different posture images caused by different perspectives will bring confusion in attributes, resulting ambiguity in identity. For example, the chaos of carrying school bag due to changes in camera view, or the chaos of long hair because the person turns around.

In order to avoid the above disadvantages and make full use of existing data, we simply horizontally flip the original image without introducing extra annotations or complicated GAN model. The horizontal mirror image implicitly reflects structural information and enjoys several merits: identity and attributes invariance, and structural symmetrical equivariance.

3 Our Approach

In this section, we firstly describe the overall architecture of our network. Then, we introduce Disentangled Feature Learning for semi-supervised Re-ID task, followed by loss functions explanation.

3.1 Overall Framework

The overall architecture of the proposed framework is shown in Fig. 1. Our semi-supervised framework consists of two branches: a supervised branch and an unsupervised branch. For each branch, we design an Encoder-Decoder network to realize feature disentanglement and reconstruction. We take a pair of original image I_O and its horizontal mirror image I_T along with the label Y as

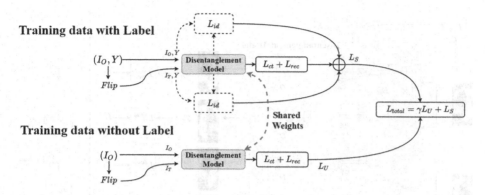

Fig. 1. Overview of our framework. Our Semi-supervised framework consists of two branches with shared feature disentanglement models, one for supervised task and the other for unsupervised task. The labeled and unlabeled data are simultaneously adopted to train the whole framework.

three inputs for supervised branch, and omit the label for unsupervised branch. The final loss L_{Total} equals to the weighted summation of supervised branch loss L_S and unsupervised branch loss L_U. Constraints on label consistency L_{id}, image reconstruction L_{rec}, and consistent transformations on disentangled features L_{ct} are considered for designing supervised loss L_S. While only L_{ct} and L_{rec} are considered in unsupervised loss L_U. The detailed description about feature disentanglement model and loss functions design are referred to next following subsections. Due to sharing parameters and training as a whole, under the strong label guidance learning in the supervised branch, the unsupervised branch can effectively make full use of a large amount of unlabeled data.

3.2 Disentangled Feature Learning

For person Re-ID tasks, it is very important to mine person identity information with different structural information under different views. We hope to guide the network to learn how to disentangle the mixed global features into independent structure-aware features and identity-aware features. Previously, some methods build pairs of images which have same identity but different structures, effectively disentangling features through Siam network. However, for unlabeled data, we cannot find samples that have same identity but different structures. Here we are inspired by data augmentation, and can obtain new mirror structural samples through flipping and horizontal displacement operations. Mirror samples meet our requirements for a pair of person samples: 1) the same identity 2) different structure.

Thus, we design an encoder-decoder-based feature disentanglement network which requires a pair of inputs, shown in Fig. 2(a). DenseNet-121 [36] pretrained on ImageNet [37] is chosen as our auto-encoder backbone by removing the final pooling and fully-connected layers. Please note that, although most existing Re-ID methods take ResNet-50 as CNN backbone, we choose a smaller DenseNet-121

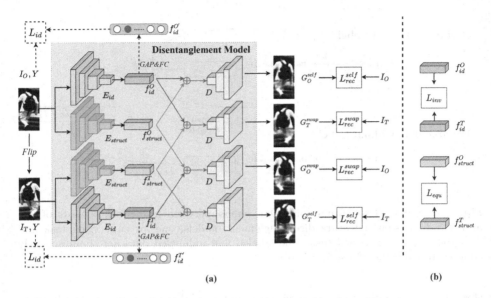

Fig. 2. Disentangled feature learning network for Re-ID task. (a) Encoder-decoder-based backbone to disentangle identity-aware features from structure-aware features. Both self-reconstruction and swap-reconstruction are considered in the reconstruction loss function. $G_{\{O,T\}}^{\{self,swap\}}$ denotes the generated reconstruction image after decoder module in each path, corresponding to operation $D(\cdot, \cdot)$ in Eq. (2) and Eq. (3). The dotted lines indicate that these parts only exist in supervised branch. (b) Illustration of consistent transformation constraints on disentangled features.

compared with ResNet-50 ($8M$ params *vs.* $25.5M$ params). Taking the original image input I_O as an example, two auto-encoders (E_{id} and E_{struct}) with the same structures but different parameters are respectively applied to encode identity-aware features f_{id}^O and structure-aware features f_{struct}^O. We define a Horizontal Flipping Transformation $T(\cdot)$, which is used to generate the horizontal flipped image $I_T = T(I_O)$. By analogy, f_{id}^T and f_{struct}^T can be also decomposed from the horizontal flipped image I_T. The superscript O and T denote the original image and its horizontal flipping image, respectively. Then, we concatenate two disentangled features with different semantics, resulting four different combinations followed by a decoder network D to reconstruct images. Decoder D consists of 5 transposed convolutional layers followed by batch normalization [38], leaky ReLU [39] and dropout [40].

In order to guarantee that the disentangled features encoding semantic information, the reconstructed images should satisfy the following criteria: 1) Self-reconstruction. If both identity-aware features and structure-aware features are decomposed from the same image, i.e., (f_{id}^O and f_{struct}^O) or (f_{id}^T and f_{struct}^T), the reconstructions are certainly similar with themselves corresponding input images, i.e., I_O or I_T; 2) Swap-reconstruction. If the decomposed identity-aware features and structure-aware features are from different input images, i.e., (f_{id}^O

and f_{struct}^T) or (f_{id}^T and f_{struct}^O), the reconstructions are consistent with the image from which the structure-aware features are disentangled, i.e., I_T or I_O.

Therefore, by obeying the above criteria, we define the final reconstruction loss function L_{rec} composed of two kinds of reconstructions:

$$L_{rec} = L_{rec}^{self} + L_{rec}^{swap} \tag{1}$$

The first item L_{rec}^{self} follows the first criteria, each reconstruction is similar to itself, i.e.,

$$L_{rec}^{self} = ||I_O - D(f_{id}^O, f_{struct}^O)||_2 + ||I_T - D(f_{id}^T, f_{struct}^T)||_2 \tag{2}$$

where $D(\cdot, \cdot)$ denotes the reconstructed image by concatenating two decomposed features, $||\cdot||_2$ is the pixel-wise L_2 loss. The second item L_{rec}^{swap} follows the second criteria. Disentangled identity-aware features and structure-aware features are expected to be independent of each other. Obviously, identity features do not change after flipping the image, and the reconstructed image is determined by the structure-aware features. Thus, the second reconstruction loss can be defined as follows:

$$L_{rec}^{swap} = ||I_O - D(f_{id}^T, f_{struct}^O)||_2 + ||I_T - D(f_{id}^O, f_{struct}^T)||_2 \tag{3}$$

3.3   Consistent Transformation Constraints

Traditional supervised Re-ID frameworks [21–23] are trained under the identity label guidance to encode the global person features. Different from them, in our work we adopt a disentangled feature learning framework to decompose semantic mixed features into independent features with different characteristic.

As described in Subsect. 3.2, with respect to a pair of image and its horizontal mirror inputs, four disentangled features are obtained. Among them, two are identity-aware features, the other two are structure-aware features. Because horizontal flipping will not change the person identity, these two disentangled identity-aware features should satisfy invariant properties. At the same time, the two structure-aware features accordingly presents equivariant transformation as two images, i.e., the output feature maps of flipped images are also flipped to ensure the consistency of structure features. Figure 3 is an illustration of these constraints. The left part in Fig. 3 displays identity invariance constraint, therein the generated two identity-aware features f_{id}^O and f_{id}^T should maintain invariant. The right part in Fig. 3 displays structure equivariance constraint, therein two structure-aware features f_{struct}^O and f_{struct}^T should maintain horizontal symmetry.

Therefore, following the above ideas we respectively design the identity invariance transformation loss function L_{inv} and structure equivariance transformation loss function L_{equ} as:

$$L_{inv} = D_{KL}(f_{id}^O || f_{id}^T) \tag{4}$$

$$L_{equ} = D_{KL}(f_{struct}^O || T(f_{struct}^T)) \tag{5}$$

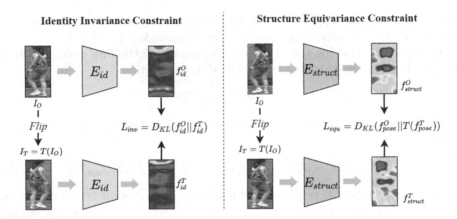

Fig. 3. Illustration of consistent transformation constraints on disentangled features. **Identity Invariance Constraint (left)** The identity information does not change as the image is horizontally flipped. **Structure Equivariance Constraint (right)** The structure information is flipped equivariantly as the image is horizontally flipped. Grad-CAM [41] is adopted for feature maps visualization.

where $D_{KL}(\cdot)$ is the Kullback–Leibler divergence distance. With respect to KL divergence applied on feature maps ($f_{id}^O, f_{id}^T, f_{struct}^O, f_{struct}^T$), we firstly apply Softmax operation along channel dimension to enforce a discrete distribution at each element location, then element-wise KL divergence loss is applied between pre-transform and after-transform feature maps.

The overall loss function under these two consistent transformation constraints could be defined as:

$$L_{ct} = L_{inv} + L_{equ} \tag{6}$$

These two constraints reflect the intrinsic correlation among disentangled features, which guarantees the disentangled feature learning well conducted. This loss function is free of labels, can be applied both supervised learning and unsupervised learning.

3.4   Semi-supervised Training and Testing

Annotating person Re-ID datasets is a very time-consuming task. We introduce a semi-supervised method to train Re-ID model using less labeled data by making full use of unlabeled data. Our model consists of a supervised branch and an unsupervised branch, where two branches share the same parameters.

For the unsupervised branch, the disentangled features get the consistent transformation constrained loss L_{ct}, and then different combinations of features are concatenated into the decoder to reconstruct images under the reconstruction loss L_{rec}. In this case, the unsupervised training loss L_U is defined as:

$$L_U = \alpha L_{ct} + \beta L_{rec} \tag{7}$$

where α and β control the relative importance of the corresponding objectives. We empirically set $\alpha = 5$, $\beta = 0.3$ in our experiments.

For the supervised branch, in addition to the unsupervised loss mentioned above, we use the identity label as a strong supervised signal to guide our model to disentangle identity-aware and structure-aware features more effectively. Here we use cross-entropy loss function L_{id} applied on the two identity feature vectors ($f_{id}^{O'}$ and $f_{id}^{T'}$), which are generated by GAP&FC operation based on the disentangled feature maps (f_{id}^O and f_{id}^T). As shown in Fig. 1 and Fig. 2, L_{id} denoted by dashed line is only valid for supervised branch. In this case, the supervised training loss L_S is defined as:

$$L_S = \alpha L_{ct} + \beta L_{rec} + L_{id} \tag{8}$$

In our training process, supervised branch and unsupervised branch are trained as a whole. We define the overall loss function L_{total} as follows:

$$L_{total} = \gamma L_U + L_S \tag{9}$$

where γ is the weighting parameter. The training loss L_{total} is used to optimize the whole network. The unsupervised branch is trained under the guidance of supervised branch to make the feature disentangling be more successful and effective.

During testing, we input each test image in conjunction with its horizontal flipping image into ID encoder model (E_{id} in Fig. 2) respectively, and take the mean of two disentangled id-aware feature vectors ($f_{id}^{O'}$ and $f_{id}^{T'}$) as the final global feature vector. Cosine similarity is used for matching with gallery images.

4   Experiments

4.1   Experimental Configurations

We evaluate our proposed method on 4 datasets (Market-1501 [3], DukeMTMC-reID [13], CUHK03 [42] and MSMT17 [43]) under both semi-supervised and fully-supervised settings. When using the semi-supervised setting, we split training set into the labeled and unlabeled data according to identities. Under the fully-supervised setting, we view all images in training set as labeled ones. Cumulative match curve (CMC) and mean average precision (mAP) are used as evaluation protocols. The detailed description about 4 datasets are given as follows. **Market-1501** [3] consists of 32,668 labeled images of 1,501 identities captured by 6 cameras; wherein 12,936 images are for training and 19,732 images are for testing. **DukeMTMC-reID** [13] collects from 8 cameras and is comprised of 36,411 labeled images of 1,404 identities. Especially, 702 identities are for training and the others are for testing. **CUHK03** [42] contains 14,096 images of 1,467 identities, captured by 6 camera views. Among these identities, 767 identities with a total of 7368 images are used for training and 700 identities with a total of 6728 images are for testing. **MSMT17** [43] has 126,441 images of

Table 1. Comparison with five state-of-the-art Re-ID methods when labeled data *ratio* is set to 1/6. Our method achieves the best performance on Market-1501 and CUHK03, and comparable accuracy on DukeMTMC-reID and MSMT17.

Methods	Market-1501		DukeMTMC-reID		CUHK03		MSMT17	
	Rank-1	mAP	Rank-1	mAP	Rank-1	mAP	Rank-1	mAP
IDE (arXiv) [10]	30.4	18.5	40.1	21.5	11.7	10.5	13.7	6.4
MGN (MM'2018) [45]	75.4	52.0	**69.1**	50.1	19.5	20.4	55.3	21.6
PCB (ECCV'2018) [7]	74.1	48.2	68.4	45.8	23.2	21.4	23.2	12.4
BoT (CVPRW'2019) [9]	65.6	42.3	60.5	41.0	16.5	16.4	34.6	14.5
ABD-Net (ICCV'2019) [8]	68.0	48.1	68.0	48.2	26.0	25.2	**45.4**	21.0
Ours	**77.8**	**54.5**	69.0	**50.5**	**32.9**	**29.8**	44.5	**29.3**

4,101 identities captured by a 15-camera network (12 outdoor, 3 indoor). This large dataset is closer to the real scene in terms of environment diversity and amount of identities. 1041 identities with 32621 samples are for training and 3060 identities with 93820 samples are for testing.

During training, the input images are resized to 256×128 augmented by random erasing operation [44]. The batch size is set 96. Considering that the encoders are pre-trained on ImageNet, its initial learning rate is 0.01, which is smaller than the two fully connected layers and decoder, whose learning rates are 0.1. The learning rates are decayed to its $0.1\times$ and $0.01\times$ at 70th and 80th epochs, and end at 90 epochs.

4.2 Comparison with State-of-the-Art Under Semi-supervised Setting

We denote the proportion of labeled data in the training set as *ratio* and the rest are used as unlabeled data. We evaluate the effectiveness of our approach with different settings of *ratio*. For example, in the Market-1501 dataset, there are 751 pedestrians in the training set. If we define *ratio* is 1/3, we only select 250 identities as the labeled data, and the remaining images of 501 identities as the unlabeled data.

We compare ours with 5 state-of-the-art Re-ID methods, including IDE [10], MGN [45], PCB [7], BoT [9] and ABD-Net [8]. Multiple experiments are conducted on different datasets by setting *ratio* to 1/3, 1/6 and 1/12. Quantitative comparison results are shown in Fig. 4. We found that the lower the percentage of labeled data, the better our method worked. When the proportion of labeled data is 1/12, our method has got Rank-1 scores increased by 51.9%, 16.7%, 6.0%, 3.7% and 1.8%, and has got mAP increased by 31.9%, 12.9%, 5.2%, 4.8% and 5.1%, compared with IDE, BoT, MGN, PCB and ABD-Net methods. Among them, MGN and PCB methods extract stripe-level features of the target, IDE and BoT directly use global features, and ABD-Net extracts features through attention mechanism based on channel dimension and spatial dimension.

We especially show the experimental results by setting *ratio* to 1/6 in Table 1. For example, on Market-1501, the global feature-based methods IDE and BoT

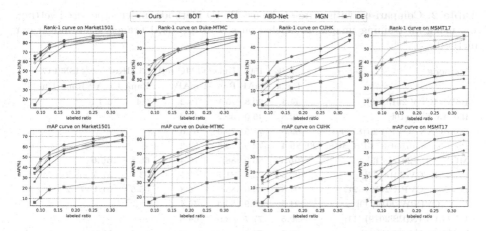

Fig. 4. Semi-supervised quantitative comparison results of six methods on Market-1501, DukeMTMC-reID, CUHK03, MSMT17 under different *ratio* values.

have poor results. Their Rank-1 are 30.4% and 65.6%, respectively. Global features learned in Re-ID task have limited capability of extracting effective and discriminative features. Stripe-based methods perform well on Market-1501 and DukeMTMC-reID. For example, MGN achieves 75.4%, 69.1% Rank-1 scores and 52.0%, 50.1% mAP on Market-1501 and DukeMTMC-reID datasets. This shows that on small datasets, local features help improve performance. Attention-based ABD-Net perform well in CUHK03, with 26.0% Rank-1 and 25.2% mAP scores, respectively. This also shows that the attention-based method can effectively mine deeper features. Through feature disentangling and consistent transformation constraints, our method only considering global features achieves the best accuracy on Market-1501 and CUHK03, and comparable accuracy on DukeMTMC-reID and MSMT17, which demonstrates that our proposed method is capable of effectively extracting more robust features.

4.3 Comparison with State-of-the-Art Under Supervised Setting

In this section, fully supervised setting is applied. The unsupervised branch is invalid in our method. We report the performance comparisons of ours and 11 state-of-the-art Re-ID models including hand-crafted methods [3], attention-based methods [8], stripe-based methods [7,45], global feature methods [9,10,47], and GAN-based methods [11,20,21,46]. The quantitative comparison results are shown in Table 2.

As we can see, the hand-crafted features has got the worst accuracy on all four datasets. For example, on Market-1501, its Rank-1 is 44.4%, much lower than deep Re-ID methods, which achieve around 90%. Among deep Re-ID methods, GAN-based methods [11,20,21,46] are not so satisfying. The reasons may be that GAN import some noise to the generated images, and attention mechanism is not so useful for well-cropped images. For example, Cam-GAN and Pose-Normalized

Table 2. Comparison with state-of-the art Re-ID methods under supervised setting, *i.e.* using all training images as labeled ones. Unsupervised branch is invalid in our method.

Methods	Market-1501		DukeMTMC-reID		CUHK03		MSMT17	
	Rank-1	mAP	Rank-1	mAP	Rank-1	mAP	Rank-1	mAP
BoW (ICCV'2015) [3]	44.4	20.8	25.1	12.2	6.4	6.4	–	–
IDE (arXiv) [10]	72.5	46.0	65.2	44.9	–	–	–	–
Cam-GAN (CVPR'2018) [46]	89.5	71.5	78.3	57.6	–	–	–	–
Pose-Normalized (CVPR'2018) [20]	89.4	72.6	73.6	53.2	–	–	–	–
MGN (MM'2018) [45]	**95.7**	86.9	88.7	78.4	66.8	**66.0**	–	–
PCB (ECCV'2018) [7]	92.3	73.3	81.7	66.1	63.7	57.5	68.2	40.4
DG-Net (CVPR'2019) [21]	94.8	86.0	86.6	74.8	65.6	61.1	77.2	52.3
BoT (CVPRW'2019) [9]	94.5	85.9	86.4	76.4	–	–	–	–
FD-GAN (NIPS'2019) [11]	90.5	77.7	80.0	64.5	–	–	–	–
VCFL (ICCV'2019) [47]	89.3	74.5	–	–	61.4	55.6	–	–
ABD-Net (ICCV'2019) [8]	95.6	**88.2**	**89.0**	**78.6**	–	–	–	–
Ours	95.0	86.7	88.9	78.0	**68.8**	64.9	**78.8**	**55.9**

perform less than 90% on Market-1501. Compared with the above two kinds of methods, global feature-based methods [9, 10, 47] achieve very good performance. For example, BoT achieves 94.5% and 86.4% Rank-1 scores, and 85.9% and 76.4% mAP scores on Market and DukeMTMC-reID, respectively. Unsurprisingly, stripe-based methods achieve better accuracy than the global feature-based methods. Take MGN as an example, it gets 95.7% and 88.7% Rank-1 scores, and 86.9% and 78.4% mAP scores on Market-1501 and DukeMTMC-reID, respectively. Finally, our method uses only global features and achieves comparable performance with stripe-based methods on Market-1501 and DukeMTMC-reID, even better accuracy on CUHK03 and MSMT17. The analysis above demonstrates the effectiveness of our proposed methods under supervised setting.

4.4   Ablation Analysis and Effect of Hyper-Parameters γ, α and β

Our method introduces two main parts, namely, disentangling feature learning (DFL) and the Consistent Transformation loss (CT loss), which are systematically analyzed through experiments. The performance of each component in fully-supervised task and semi-supervised task are shown in Fig. 5.

Baseline. If CT loss and DFL are disabled, our model degenerates into a classification model containing only one DenseNet-121 branch. Since our model only uses the cross entropy loss function, our baseline model also uses the cross entropy loss function.

Baseline+DFL. We simultaneously input a pair of structure mirror images and add a DFL module.

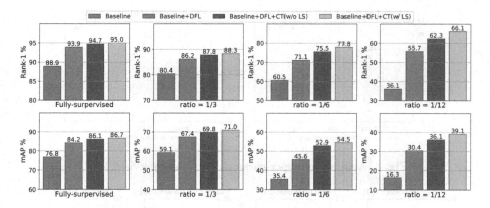

Fig. 5. Ablation analysis of three components on Market-1501. **DFL** refers to disentangled feature learning. **CT** means Consistent Transformation loss. **LS** represents label smooth adopted as a trick in our method. The first column is for fully-supervised case, and the last three columns are for semi-supervised cases with different labeled *ratio* values.

Baseline+DFL+CT Loss. Consistent transformation constraints are introduced for disentangled identity-aware features and structure-aware features.

As each component is applied one by one, we can observe significant performance improvements from Fig. 5. For the fully-supervised case (the first column in Fig. 5), Rank-1 is 88.9% when no strategies are used. When incrementally applying DFL, CT, SL, Rank-1 is increased to 93.9%, 94.7% and 95.0%, respectively. When reducing the proportion of labeled data in semi-supervised case, the effect of adding these strategies to the model is becoming more and more obvious. For example, when the *ratio* is 1/12, after adding DFL and CT, Rank-1 increases by 26.2%, and mAP increases by 19.8% compared with baseline. These three modules also have different impacts on model performance. As the results showing, DFL has the greatest impact on model performance. It also verifies that the combination of these components is complementary and conducive to achieve better performance.

The Effect of Hyper-Parameters γ, α *and* β ***in the Loss Function.*** In the total loss function, we set a parameter γ for unsupervised loss. The performance of our model is also related to this parameter. As can be seen from Fig. 6, when the parameter γ is 0.01, the performance of the model is the best. Particularly, when $\gamma = 0$ means only the supervised branch of the framework is valid. Therefore, it has verified that by utilizing the labeled data together with unlabeled data can bring performance improvement. Figure 7 shows the performance analysis on α and β. We choose $\alpha = 5$ and $\beta = 0.3$ because of their better performance.

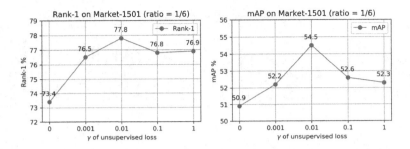

Fig. 6. Analysis on hyper-parameter γ of unsupervised loss

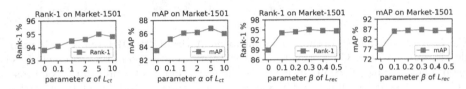

Fig. 7. Analysis on hyper-parameters α and β.

5   Conclusion

In this paper, we proposed a novel semi-supervised Re-ID framework, which consists of two branches with shared feature disentanglement models, one for supervised task and the other for unsupervised task. It alleviates limitation of labeled data by exploiting lots of unlabeled data. Furthermore, we design a free-of-label loss function to enforce consistent transformation constraints on disentangled features, which can be applied to both supervised and unsupervised learning branches. We have shown in ablation analysis experiments, the combination of above components play a very important role in performance improvement. A series of comparison results with stat-of-the-art methods have shown the good performance of ours in both semi-supervised and supervised tasks, and also demonstrated that our method can make full use of labeled data and unlabeled data. In the future, we plan to establish deeper connections between supervised and unsupervised branches and design a better training strategies.

Acknowledgment. This work was supported in part by the National Natural Science Foundation of China (No. 61972071), the National Key Research & Development Program (No. 2020YFC2003901), the 2019 Fundamental Research Funds for the Central Universities, the Research Program of Zhejiang lab (No. 2019KD0AB02), the Open Project Program of the National Laboratory of Pattern Recognition (NLPR No. 201900014) and Sichuan Science and Technology Program (No. 2020YJ0036).

References

1. Gong, S., Cristani, M., Yan, S., Loy, C.C.: Person Re-identification. Springer, London (2014). https://doi.org/10.1007/978-1-4471-6296-4

2. Satta, R.: Appearance descriptors for person re-identification: a comprehensive review. arXiv preprint arXiv:1307.5748 (2013)
3. Zheng, L., Shen, L., Tian, L., Wang, S., Wang, J., Tian, Q.: Scalable person re-identification: a benchmark. In: 2015 IEEE International Conference on Computer Vision (ICCV), pp. 1116–11244 (2015)
4. Yang, Y., Yang, J., Yan, J., Liao, S., Yi, D., Li, S.Z.: Salient color names for person re-identification. In: Fleet, D., Pajdla, T., Schiele, B., Tuytelaars, T. (eds.) ECCV 2014. LNCS, vol. 8689, pp. 536–551. Springer, Cham (2014). https://doi.org/10.1007/978-3-319-10590-1_35
5. Farenzena, M., Bazzani, L., Perina, A., Murino, V., Cristani, M.: Person re-identification by symmetry-driven accumulation of local features. In: 2010 IEEE Computer Society Conference on Computer Vision and Pattern Recognition, pp. 2360–2367 (2010)
6. Yang, Y., Liao, S., Lei, Z., Li, S.Z.: Large scale similarity learning using similar pairs for person verification. In: Proceedings of the Thirtieth AAAI Conference on Artificial Intelligence, pp. 3655–3661 (2016)
7. Sun, Y., Zheng, L., Yang, Y., Tian, Q., Wang, S.: Beyond part models: person retrieval with refined part pooling (and a strong convolutional baseline). In: Ferrari, V., Hebert, M., Sminchisescu, C., Weiss, Y. (eds.) ECCV 2018. LNCS, vol. 11208, pp. 501–518. Springer, Cham (2018). https://doi.org/10.1007/978-3-030-01225-0_30
8. Chen, T., et al.: ABD-Net: attentive but diverse person re-identification, pp. 8351–8361 (2019)
9. Luo, H., et al.: Bag of tricks and a strong baseline for deep person re-identification. In: The IEEE Conference on Computer Vision and Pattern Recognition (CVPR) Workshops (2019)
10. Zheng, L., Yang, Y., Hauptmann, A.G.: Person re-identification: past, present and future. arXiv preprint arXiv:1610.02984 (2016)
11. Ge, Y., et al.: FD-GAN: pose-guided feature distilling GAN for robust person re-identification, pp. 1222–1233 (2018)
12. Chen, W., Chen, X., Zhang, J., Huang, K.: Beyond triplet loss: a deep quadruplet network for person re-identification. In: Proceedings of the IEEE Conference on Computer Vision and Pattern Recognition, pp. 403–412 (2017)
13. Ristani, E., Solera, F., Zou, R., Cucchiara, R., Tomasi, C.: Performance measures and a data set for multi-target, multi-camera tracking. In: Hua, G., Jégou, H. (eds.) ECCV 2016. LNCS, vol. 9914, pp. 17–35. Springer, Cham (2016). https://doi.org/10.1007/978-3-319-48881-3_2
14. Hermans, A., Beyer, L., Leibe, B.: In defense of the triplet loss for person re-identification. arXiv preprint arXiv:1703.07737 (2017)
15. Liu, J., Zha, Z., Chen, D., Hong, R., Wang, M.: Adaptive transfer network for cross-domain person re-identification, pp. 7202–7211 (2019)
16. Zhong, Z., Zheng, L., Luo, Z., Li, S., Yang, Y.: Invariance matters: exemplar memory for domain adaptive person re-identification, pp. 598–607 (2019)
17. Tang, H., Zhao, Y., Lu, H.: Unsupervised person re-identification with iterative self-supervised domain adaptation. In: 2019 IEEE/CVF Conference on Computer Vision and Pattern Recognition Workshops (CVPRW), pp. 1536–1543. IEEE (2019)
18. Li, M., Zhu, X., Gong, S.: Unsupervised person re-identification by deep learning tracklet association. In: Ferrari, V., Hebert, M., Sminchisescu, C., Weiss, Y. (eds.) ECCV 2018. LNCS, vol. 11208, pp. 772–788. Springer, Cham (2018). https://doi.org/10.1007/978-3-030-01225-0_45

19. Yu, H., Zheng, W., Wu, A., Guo, X., Gong, S., Lai, J.: Unsupervised person re-identification by soft multilabel learning, pp. 2148–2157 (2019)
20. Qian, X., et al.: Pose-normalized image generation for person re-identification. In: Ferrari, V., Hebert, M., Sminchisescu, C., Weiss, Y. (eds.) ECCV 2018. LNCS, vol. 11213, pp. 661–678. Springer, Cham (2018). https://doi.org/10.1007/978-3-030-01240-3_40
21. Zheng, Z., Yang, X., Yu, Z., Zheng, L., Yang, Y., Kautz, J.: Joint discriminative and generative learning for person re-identification, pp. 2138–2147 (2019)
22. Liu, Y., Song, G., Shao, J., Jin, X., Wang, X.: Transductive centroid projection for semi-supervised large-scale recognition. In: Ferrari, V., Hebert, M., Sminchisescu, C., Weiss, Y. (eds.) ECCV 2018. LNCS, vol. 11209, pp. 72–89. Springer, Cham (2018). https://doi.org/10.1007/978-3-030-01228-1_5
23. Li, Y.J., Lin, C.S., Lin, Y.B., Wang, Y.C.F.: Cross-dataset person re-identification via unsupervised pose disentanglement and adaptation. In: Proceedings of the IEEE International Conference on Computer Vision, pp. 7919–7929 (2019)
24. Figueira, D., Bazzani, L., Minh, Q.H., Cristani, M., Bernardino, A., Murino, V.: Semi-supervised multi-feature learning for person re-identification. In: AVSS, pp. 111–116 (2013)
25. Liu, X., Song, M., Tao, D., Zhou, X., Chen, C., Bu, J.: Semi-supervised coupled dictionary learning for person re-identification, pp. 3550–3557 (2014)
26. Ding, G., Zhang, S., Khan, S., Tang, Z., Zhang, J., Porikli, F.: Feature affinity-based pseudo labeling for semi-supervised person re-identification. IEEE Trans. Multimed. **21**, 2891–2902 (2019)
27. Huang, Y., Xu, J., Wu, Q., Zheng, Z., Zhang, Z., Zhang, J.: Multi-pseudo regularized label for generated data in person re-identification. IEEE Trans. Image Process. **28**, 1391–1403 (2019)
28. Fan, H., Zheng, L., Yan, C., Yang, Y.: Unsupervised person re-identification: clustering and fine-tuning. ACM Trans. Multimed. Comput. Commun. Appl. (TOMM) **14**, 1–18 (2018)
29. Xin, X., Wang, J., Xie, R., Zhou, S., Huang, W., Zheng, N.: Semi-supervised person re-identification using multi-view clustering. Pattern Recogn. **88**, 285–297 (2019)
30. Wang, G., Zhang, T., Cheng, J., Liu, S., Yang, Y., Hou, Z.: RGB-infrared cross-modality person re-identification via joint pixel and feature alignment. In: 2019 IEEE/CVF International Conference on Computer Vision (ICCV), pp. 3622–3631 (2019)
31. Wang, G., Zhang, T., Yang, Y., Cheng, J., Chang, J., Hou, Z.: Cross-modality paired-images generation for RGB-infrared person re-identification. In: AAAI 2020: The Thirty-Fourth AAAI Conference on Artificial Intelligence (2020)
32. Wang, G., Yang, Y., Cheng, J., Wang, J., Hou, Z.: Color-sensitive person re-identification. In: Proceedings of the 28th International Joint Conference on Artificial Intelligence, IJCAI 2019, pp. 933–939 (2019)
33. Wang, G., et al.: High-order information matters: learning relation and topology for occluded person re-identification. In: 2020 IEEE Conference on Computer Vision and Pattern Recognition (CVPR) (2020)
34. Wang, G., Gong, S., Cheng, J., Hou, Z.: Faster person re-identification. In: Vedaldi, A., Bischof, H., Brox, T., Frahm, J.-M. (eds.) ECCV 2020. LNCS, vol. 12353, pp. 275–292. Springer, Cham (2020). https://doi.org/10.1007/978-3-030-58598-3_17
35. Li, X., Makihara, Y., Xu, C., Yagi, Y., Ren, M.: Gait recognition via semi-supervised disentangled representation learning to identity and covariate features. In: CVPR 2020: Computer Vision and Pattern Recognition, pp. 13309–13319 (2020)

36. Huang, G., Liu, Z., Der Maaten, L.V.: Weinberger, K.Q.: Densely connected convolutional networks, pp. 2261–2269 (2017)
37. Deng, J., Dong, W., Socher, R., Li, L.J., Li, K., Fei-Fei, L.: ImageNet: a large-scale hierarchical image database. In: IEEE Conference on Computer Vision and Pattern Recognition, CVPR 2009, pp. 248–255. IEEE (2009)
38. Ioffe, S., Szegedy, C.: Batch normalization: accelerating deep network training by reducing internal covariate shift. In: International Conference on Machine Learning, pp. 448–456 (2015)
39. Xu, B., Wang, N., Chen, T., Li, M.: Empirical evaluation of rectified activations in convolutional network. arXiv preprint arXiv:1505.00853 (2015)
40. Hinton, G.E., Srivastava, N., Krizhevsky, A., Sutskever, I., Salakhutdinov, R.R.: Improving neural networks by preventing co-adaptation of feature detectors. arXivpreprint arXiv:1207.0580 (2012)
41. Selvaraju, R.R., Das, A., Vedantam, R., Cogswell, M., Parikh, D., Batra, D.: Grad-CAM: why did you say that? arXiv preprint arXiv:1611.07450 (2016)
42. Li, W., Zhao, R., Xiao, T., Wang, X.: DeepReID: deep filter pairing neural network for person re-identification. In: Proceedings of the IEEE Conference on Computer Vision and Pattern Recognition, pp. 152–159 (2014)
43. Wei, L., Zhang, S., Gao, W., Tian, Q.: Person transfer GAN to bridge domain gap for person re-identification. In: 2018 IEEE/CVF Conference on Computer Vision and Pattern Recognition, pp. 79–88 (2018)
44. Zhong, Z., Zheng, L., Kang, G., Li, S., Yang, Y.: Random erasing data augmentation. arXiv preprint arXiv:1708.04896 (2017)
45. Wang, G., Yuan, Y., Chen, X., Li, J., Zhou, X.: Learning discriminative features with multiple granularities for person re-identification, pp. 274–282 (2018)
46. Zhong, Z., Zheng, L., Zheng, Z., Li, S., Yang, Y.: Camera style adaptation for person re-identification. In: Proceedings of the IEEE Conference on Computer Vision and Pattern Recognition, pp. 5157–5166 (2018)
47. Liu, F., Zhang, L.: View confusion feature learning for person re-identification, pp. 6639–6648 (2019)

MIX'EM: Unsupervised Image Classification Using a Mixture of Embeddings

Ali Varamesh$^{(\boxtimes)}$ and Tinne Tuytelaars

ESAT-PSI, KU Leuven, Leuven, Belgium
{ali.varamesh,tinne.tuytelaars}@esat.kuleuven.be

Abstract. We present MIX'EM, a novel solution for unsupervised image classification. MIX'EM generates representations that by themselves are sufficient to drive a general-purpose clustering algorithm to deliver high-quality classification. This is accomplished by building a mixture of embeddings module into a contrastive visual representation learning framework in order to disentangle representations at the category level. It first generates a set of embedding and mixing coefficients from a given visual representation, and then combines them into a single embedding. We introduce three techniques to successfully train MIX'EM and avoid degenerate solutions; (i) diversify mixture components by maximizing entropy, (ii) minimize instance conditioned component entropy to enforce a clustered embedding space, and (iii) use an associative embedding loss to enforce semantic separability. By applying (i) and (ii), semantic categories emerge through the mixture coefficients, making it possible to apply (iii). Subsequently, we run K-means on the representations to acquire semantic classification. We conduct extensive experiments and analyses on STL10, CIFAR10, and CIFAR100-20 datasets, achieving state-of-the-art classification accuracy of 78%, 82%, and 44%, respectively. To achieve robust and high accuracy, it is essential to use the mixture components to initialize K-means. Finally, we report competitive baselines (70% on STL10) obtained by applying K-means to the "normalized" representations learned using the contrastive loss.

1 Introduction

In the span of a few years, supervised image classification has made remarkable progress and even surpassed humans on specific recognition tasks [1]. Its success depends on few important factors, namely, stochastic gradient descent to optimize millions of parameters, GPUs to accelerate high-dimensional matrix computations, and access to vast amounts of manually annotated data [2]. Although a particular optimization method or high-performance hardware is not theoretically essential for supervised learning methods, labeled data is. In fact, access

Electronic supplementary material The online version of this chapter (https://doi.org/10.1007/978-3-030-69535-4_3) contains supplementary material, which is available to authorized users.

H. Ishikawa et al. (Eds.): ACCV 2020, LNCS 12624, pp. 38–55, 2021.
https://doi.org/10.1007/978-3-030-69535-4_3

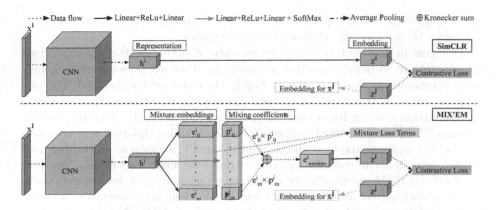

Fig. 1. Our proposed architecture with a mixture of embeddings module (bottom row), compared to the contrastive representation learning framework (top row). Components in green are devised in MIX'EM.

to large-scale labeled data is vital if we want to get the top performance [3,4]. Hence, one of the current major challenges in modern computer vision is being able to do unsupervised visual recognition. That means eliminating the costly and not always feasible process of manual labeling [5,6]. In this context, visual representation learning has recently demonstrated great success in discarding manual labels by relying on self-supervision [7–13]. We believe self-supervised representation learning has paved the way for unsupervised recognition.

In self-supervised visual representation learning, a pretext (auxiliary) task provides a supervision signal (without manual labels) for training a representation encoder. One particularly successful pretext task is to treat each image instance in a dataset as a unique class and use them as supervision labels for training a classifier using the cross-entropy objective [9]. However, it is computationally prohibitive to implement at a scale of millions of images. In practice, it is simplified such that given a mini-batch containing transformations of different images, transformations of a particular image should be classified as the same [11,12]. By training a linear classifier on representations generated by such an encoder, we can achieve high accuracy, close to that of an end-to-end trained fully supervised ImageNet classifier: 76.5% compared to 78.3% in terms of top-1 accuracy, respectively. [11]. They have even outperformed supervised representations on some variants of object detection and segmentation [12].

The fact that a linear layer, with very limited discriminative power [14], can deliver such high accuracy on the complex ImageNet classification task signals presence of powerful semantic clues in the representations. Hence, we hypothesize that by just knowing the expected number of classes, an off-the-shelf clustering method must be able to deliver high accuracy clustering similarly. However, our experiments show that K-means trained on "normalized" representations generated by the recent SimCLR method [11] achieves clustering accuracy of 70%

on STL10 compared to top-1 accuracy of 87% by a supervised linear classifier. Therefore there is significant room for improvement.

Our goal in this work is to impose semantic structure on the self-supervised representations to boost clustering accuracy. In other words, we want to generate representations that are already highly clustered or disentangled. For this purpose, we build a mixture of embeddings module into the contrastive visual representation learning framework [11], as illustrated in Fig. 1. The mixture components [15–17] are expected to specialise on embedding different semantic categories. For a given sample, each component should generate an embedding and predict how much it contributes to the combined final embedding. We have designed MIX'EM essentially by taking inspiration from a few recent works [18–24] showing that mixture models can divide their input-output space in a meaningful manner without being directly supervised. MIX'EM takes advantage of the contrastive visual learning framework for guiding training a mixture model without interfering with its mechanisms (see Table 3).

In addition to the contrastive representation learning loss, we introduce three key techniques to successfully train MIX'EM end-to-end. A naive attempt to train using only the contrastive loss would quickly converge to a degenerate solution that assigns all samples to a single component, bypassing all other paths. To avoid this issue and achieve high accuracy, we (i) maximize the entropy of coefficient distribution to diversify the mixture components; (ii) minimize the entropy of components conditioned on the input to enforce separation of the embedding space; and enabled by (i) and (ii), (iii) we use an associative embedding loss [25, 26] to directly enforce semantic coherency inter/intra mixture components. Figure 2 presents visualizations of the embeddings when gradually plugging in each of the loss terms. The resulting representations significantly boost K-means' performance up to 78% on the STL10 dataset, without interfering with the contrastive learning process. We summarise our contributions as follows:

- We propose MIX'EM, a solution for unsupervised image classification using a mixture of embedding module. MIX'EM disentangles visual representations semantically at the category level, such that an off-the-shelf clustering method can be applied to acquire robust image classification.
- We introduce three techniques to successfully train MIX'EM in an unsupervised manner and avoid degenerate solutions.
- We introduce a technique to initialize K-means algorithm using the mixture components in MIX'EM and achieve significantly higher accuracy. This eliminates the need to run K-means with multiple random initializations.

2   Related Work

Our work relates to a few different lines of research. It is the most related to the self-supervised representation learning, as our goal in the first place is to train a better representation encoder without using manually labeled data. However, beyond that, we want the representations to be highly structured such that

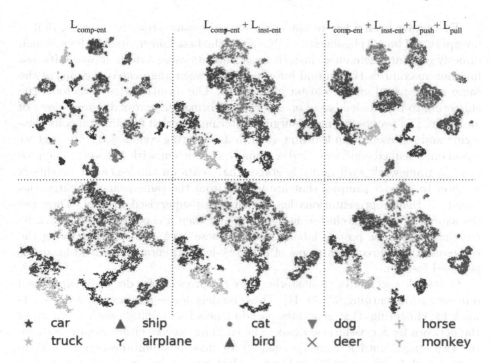

Fig. 2. tSNE visualization of embeddings learned by MIX'EM on STL10. Top row: embeddings from the dominant component ($e^i_{m'}$ s.t. $m' = \arg\max_{m'}(p^i_{m'})$); Bottom row: the final mixture embedding (z^i). By adding our loss terms (explained in Sect. 3.2), embedding space gets increasingly more disentangled at category level. Samples are marked and color coded based on their ground truth label.

reliable semantic clustering is possible using an off-the-shelf clustering method. We develop our idea on the recent research [11,27] which empirically proves using noise contrastive loss [28] and heavy augmentation for visual representation learning outperforms other popular approaches, including mutual information maximization [7,29], generative models [30,31], image rotation prediction [8], predicting patch position [32], clustering [33], solving jigsaw puzzles [34], and image colorization [35]. In this work, we also advocate using contrastive loss for self-supervised representation learning. However, we are particularly interested in enforcing category-level semantic disentanglement on the representation space.

To the best of our knowledge, this is the first work to set out to impose semantic structure on self-supervised visual representations learned using the contrastive loss. We show that the representations generated by MIX'EM result in high accuracy semantic clustering only by applying K-means to them. Existing works on unsupervised image classification using self-supervised representations [36–38] should benefit from adapting our proposed module, as it is an internal module that can be plugged-in without altering the output mechanism.

There have been a few recent works with the same objective as ours, that is unsupervised image classification. IIC [38] is the best known among them, which directly generates semantic clustering assignments using a deep network. Its loss function maximizes the mutual information between augmented versions of the same image based on the cluster assignment. The intuitive goal is to force the clustering to be decided based on invariant information across different views of an image. [37] proposes a max-margin clustering criterion for simultaneous clustering and representation learning, such that clustering confidence is the highest based on a defined confidence index. Finally, concurrent with our work, [36] proposes a framework with multiple stages that relies on the k-nearest neighbors method to extract samples that are ideally from the same semantic categories based on their representations learned in a self-supervised fashion. They use the samples to train a clustering network, and then a classification network by treating clusters as pseudo labels. None of these works concern improving the representations directly in terms of category-level disentanglement in an unsupervised fashion.

Our work also relates to clustering-based approaches for deep self-supervised representation learning [33,39–41]. These models devise a branch in a deep network for clustering; that generates pseudo labels for training another branch of the network for a classification task. The training process either iterate between the two stages until it converges [33,39] or does it simultaneously [42]. Generating high-level semantic labels using clustering, however, is not the goal in this line of work. Instead, they combine clustering and classification in order to build a pretext task for representation learning. Often the best representations are achieved with over-clustering. For example, [33] achieves the best mAP on the Pascal VOC 2007 object detection task when the representations are learned using a 10000-way clustering stage.

Finally, [43] is also related to our work, where representations are split into "shared" and "exclusive" parts. It maximizes mutual information for the shared and minimizes for the exclusive component across paired samples. However, they use supervision to pair images for training. Moreover, the work is not concerned with semantic clustering. Based on their problem formulation and results, the disentanglement focuses a foreground-background separation.

3 Method

In this section, first we review the contrastive learning framework as proposed in SimCLR [11] (the principles are similar to [9,12,13]). Next, we show how to integrate a mixture of embeddings module in this framework.

3.1 Contrastive Learning of Visual Representation

Contrastive learning of visual representations is built upon the intuition that different transformations of an image should have the same characteristics, which identifies them as bearing the same semantics. In practice, this means that given a dataset with images containing a single dominant object (like ImageNet or CIFAR10/100), an ideal encoder should map different augmentations of an image to a very compact neighborhood. This interpretation implies considering every image in a dataset as a distinct class and training a classification network using cross-entropy loss [9]. However, having as many classes as the number of samples in a large dataset is not scalable. A streamlined version of this idea, SimCLR [11], is based on doing instance classification within mini-batches of images.

In SimCLR, the goal is to train an encoder to generate visual representations. We denote the encoder function with f such that $h^i = f(x^i)$, where $x^i \in D$ is an RGB image from the unlabeled dataset D. Encoder f is implemented using a deep convolutional neural network. Training then will proceed by contrasting representations h^i in order to pull together similar images in the space. h^i is the representation intended to be used by downstream tasks. However, Chen et al. [11] show that, before computing the contrastive loss, applying a further non-linear g layer to h^i results in significant improvement. So in the following definitions, the contrastive loss will be computed on $z^i = g(h^i)$.

At training, given a mini-batch of N images, $\{x^i\}_{i=1}^{N}$, every image is augmented twice using a sequence of random transformations to generate 2N samples $\{\hat{x}^j\}_{j=1}^{2N}$. Then, the similarity between every pair u and v of the 2N samples is computed using function $sim(u,v) = z_u^T.z_v/\|z_u\|\|z_v\|$. Next, counteractive loss for a positive pair (i.e. two augmentations of the same image x_i) is implemented in form of cross-entropy loss for a 2N-1 way classification task, where the logits are set to the pairwise similarities of a given view with its positive counterpart, and 2N-2 views from the remaining augmented samples. The contrastive loss $l_c(\hat{x}^{j_1}, \hat{x}^{j_2})$ for a positive pair $\hat{x}^{j_1}$ and $\hat{x}^{j_2}$ (two views of the image x^j) is shown in the Eq. (1), where τ is a temperature parameter [11]. The contrastive loss is computed for both views of each of the N images. The total contrastive loss $L_{contrast}$ is shown in Eq. (2).

$$l_c(\hat{x}^{j_1}, \hat{x}^{j_2}) = -\log \frac{exp(sim(\hat{x}^{j_1}, \hat{x}^{j_2})/\tau)}{\sum_{k=1}^{2N} \mathbb{1}_{[k \neq j_1]} exp(sim(\hat{x}^{j_1}, \hat{x}^{k})/\tau)} \tag{1}$$

$$L_{contrast} = \frac{1}{2N} \sum_{k=1}^{N} l_c(\hat{x}^{k_1}, \hat{x}^{k_2}) + l_c(\hat{x}^{k_2}, \hat{x}^{k_1}) \tag{2}$$

3.2   Mixture Embedding

SimCLR computes the contrastive loss after embedding the target representations (h) into another space (z) via the non-linear layer, g. In MIX'EM, we replace this layer with multiple parallel non-linear layers, each generating an embedding and a coefficient to determine how much the embedding contributes to the final embedding, z^i. Figure 1 depicts the architecture of MIX'EM and how it differs from the regular contrastive representation learning pipeline. Given input x^i, and representation $h^i = f(x^i)$ generated by the encoder, our model replaces $z^i = g(h^i)$ with the function $z^i = g(\psi(h^i))$, where the function ψ is defined in Eq. (3). M in Eq. (3) indicates the number of mixture components. g_m is a non-linear layer similar to g and specializes in generating embedding for samples that component m is responsible for. Mixing coefficient p_m^i indicates the prior probability of sample x_i being generated by the component m. The coefficients p^i for x^i are computed from h^i using a non-linear layer g_p and softmax function.

$$\psi(h^i) = \sum_{m=1}^{M} p_m^i * g_m(h^i)) \quad s.t. \quad p^i = softmax(g_p(h^i)) \quad (3)$$

With the mixture module, we expect the network to distribute input samples across components, as this should make the task easier [15,21]. Each mixture component should generate embeddings for certain semantic categories and guide the backpropagation process conditioned on the input. However,if we train MIX'EM only using the contrastive loss, it will quickly lead to a degenerate solution that assigns all samples to a single component. Therefore, we devise three loss terms to avoid such degenerate solutions and adequately train MIX'EM to meet our goals.

Entropy Maximization Across Components. In a degenerate solution, the coefficients p^i provide the lowest information from an information theory point of view; always, a particular component is equal to one. However, we want the model to be more diverse in the assignment of the components. We expect it to be dependent on the input image, not to ignore it. Given that we do not have any means to directly supervise the mixture module, we can instead maximize the entropy of the marginal distribution of mixtures p, which would take the highest value when all components are equally probable. As we will show in the experiments, this term indeed avoids the degenerate solution. Moreover, it will result in semantically meaningful components; that is, components will focus on different categories. We believe this is due to the simultaneous backpropagation of the contrastive loss, imposing minimal semantic regularization. In fact, without the contrastive loss, training would fail. The entropy maximization loss term is shown in Eq. (4), and is equal to the negative of entropy $H(p)$.

$$L_{comp-ent} = -H(p) = \sum p_m \log p_m \quad s.t. \quad p_m = 1/N \sum_{i=0}^{N} p_m^i \quad (4)$$

Conditional Component Entropy Minimization. Maximizing entropy of marginal p diversifies the components. However, we would like to separate the representation space based on the most discriminative aspect of objects. For a given image, ideally, we want one of the mixture components to have close to full confidence so that it can be interpreted as an indicator of the true category. This, in turn, would mean reducing the entropy of the mixture components given an instance. We know that entropy would be minimized in practice if all probability mass is assigned to a single component. Therefore, given an image, we add a loss term that pushes the probability of the dominant (max) component to the highest value. Equation (5) shows the instance based entropy minimization loss term.

$$L_{inst-ent} = \sum_{i=0}^{N} 1 - max\{p_m^i\}_{m=1}^{M} \tag{5}$$

Associative Embedding Loss. Both entropy-based loss terms above are principled techniques to guide the training. However, they do not directly take into account the semantics. Intuitively, samples' ideal assignment to the components should pick up on visual clues that minimize the distance between samples with the same dominant mixture component. At the same time, it should maximize the distance of samples with different dominant components. In a supervised setting, it is straightforward to implement a loss function like this given the true semantic labels; however, here we do not have access to such labels. The good news, however, is that just training MIX'EM with $L_{comp-ent}$ and $L_{inst-ent}$ would result in each component specializing in one category. In quantitative words, evaluating MIX'EM by treating the dominant component index as cluster label, on STL10, we get an accuracy of 73% (row (3) of the fourth column in Table 1.)

Therefore, we introduce a third loss term to enforce semantic coherency by relying on the index of the dominant component as a pseudo-ground-truth label. This loss, called associative embedding, is inspired by the work of Newell et al. [25,26] on scene graph generation and human pose estimation. Using the dominant component index as the class label, we want to pull the embeddings assigned to a component as close as possible to each other. We implement this by minimizing the distance of all embeddings by a component m and the average embedding for the component on samples with m as their dominant component (pull loss). Simultaneously, we wish to push the average embedding of different components away from each other (push loss). We implement this by directly maximizing the pairwise distance of the average embedding of components. Equations (6)–(8) show formal specification of pull and push loss terms. Note that E_m is vital for the both losses, and we are able to compute it only by means of using the dominant components in MIX'EM.

$$\mu_m = \frac{1}{|E_m|} \sum_{i \in E_m} e_m^i \quad s.t. \quad E_m = \{i \mid \arg\min_{m'}(p_{m'}^i) = m\} \tag{6}$$

$$L_{pull} = \frac{1}{M} \sum_{m=1}^{M} \sum_{i \in E_m} ||e_m^i - \mu_m||_2 \tag{7}$$

$$L_{push} = -\frac{1}{M} \sum_{m=1}^{M} \sum_{m'=1}^{M} \mathbb{1}_{[m \neq m']} ||\mu_m - \mu_{m'}||_2 \tag{8}$$

Total Loss. Equation (9) shows the total loss we use to train MIX'EM.

$$L_{total} = L_{contrast} + \lambda_1 L_{comp-ent} + \lambda_2 L_{inst-ent} + \lambda_3 L_{push} + \lambda_4 L_{pull} \qquad (9)$$

3.3 Clustering to Acquire Classification

Once MIX'EM is trained, we apply the K-means algorithm to the representations or the embeddings to generate the final clusters. Our experiments show that K-means on representations delivers superior performance. We also tried using other off-the-shelf clustering methods including spectral clustering [44], and obtained similar results. Moreover, the dominant mixture component index also provides a highly accurate classification, as shown in the next section.

4 Experiments

We experiment with three standard datasets, STL10 [45], CIFAR10 [46], and CIFAR100–20 [46] (CIFAR100 with 20 super-classes). STL10 is a subset of ImageNet designed to benchmark self-supervised and unsupervised methods. It includes 100k unlabeled images and train/test labeled splits with 5k/8k images. The labeled splits have ten categories, and the unlabeled split includes a similar but broader set of categories. We use ResNet-18 [1] for all the experiments. Since CIFAR10 and CIFAR100-20 images are already in small resolution (32×32), we remove the down-sampling in the first convectional layer and the max-pooling layer for experiments on them.

We assume to know the number of categories in the datasets and use the same number of mixture components for the main results, but also provide results with larger number of components. As a potential application in the real world, consider labeling items from a set of already known classes in a supermarket [47] or in a warehouse. Nevertheless, if the number of classes is not known in advance, there are techniques to estimate it [48].

For each dataset, we first train the bare SimCLR for 600 epochs with embedding dimension 256 without the mixture embedding component. For this stage, on STL10 we use the train and unlabled splits, and on CIFAR10/100-20 we use the train split. We call this model "base SimCLR encoder." Next, we continue training with/without the mixture embedding module with a lower embedding dimension to investigate various aspects under equal conditions. We set embedding dimension to 32, as it gives slightly better results. In the rest of the paper, by "SimCLR", we mean the version trained further on the base SimCLR encoder.

For the evaluation of the semantic clustering, we use the three popular metrics: clustering accuracy (ACC), normalized mutual information (NMI), and adjusted rand index (ARI). For ACC, we use the Hungarian method to map cluster indices to the ground-truth labels. Following the standard practice for unsupervised settings [38,40], we train MIX'EM on the combination of all labeled data and evaluate on the test split. To gain a better understanding of the role of data in unsupervised learning, in ablation studies, we also provide separate evaluations for when test data is not used in the training of MIX'EM. Unless specified otherwise, the results are obtained by taking the average of five separate trainings and are accompanied by the standard deviation.

Training hyper-parameters, including learning rate, mini-batch size, learning schedule, the loss weight terms (λ_1, λ_2, λ_3, and λ_4), and augmentation configuration are determined by trying few different values for each dataset. Details for the training setup are provided in the supplementary material. Given enough computational resources, we believe that extending the experiments to a larger dataset like ImageNet would be straightforward.

Table 1. Effect of different MIX'EM loss terms when evaluated on STL10. Randomly initialized K-means is repeated 50 for times. "Max Comp" means doing clustering by using the dominant component indices as the final cluster labels.

Method	ACC		NMI		ARI	
	K-means	Max Comp	K-means	Max Comp	K-means	Max Comp
(1) SimCLR	65.01 ± 1.79	–	66.2 ± 0.66	–	43.94 ± 1.09	–
(2) + representation normalization	69.95 ± 0.78	–	67.05 ± 0.33	–	55.37 ± 0.78	–
MIX'EM						
(3) $+L_{comp-ent}$	69.88 ± 0.17	31.83 ± 0.29	66.52 ± 0.08	20.61 ± 0.15	54.43 ± 0.23	12.15 ± 0.17
(4) $+L_{inst-ent}$	76.21 ± 0.12	73.45 ± 0.03	67.27 ± 0.07	64.3 ± 0.04	60.16 ± 0.16	55.88 ± 0.05
(5) + MIX'EM initializes K-means	76.21 ± 0.09	73.45 ± 0.03	67.23 ± 0.08	64.3 ± 0.04	60.12 ± 0.11	55.88 ± 0.05
(6) $+L_{push} + L_{pull}$	$\mathbf{77.76 \pm 0.08}$	68.44 ± 0.44	$\mathbf{68.03 \pm 0.07}$	64.08 ± 0.1	$\mathbf{61.35 \pm 0.1}$	54.66 ± 0.09
(7) – MIX'EM initializes K-means	70.78 ± 0.19	68.44 ± 0.44	67.57 ± 0.42	64.08 ± 0.1	55.95 ± 0.16	54.66 ± 0.09

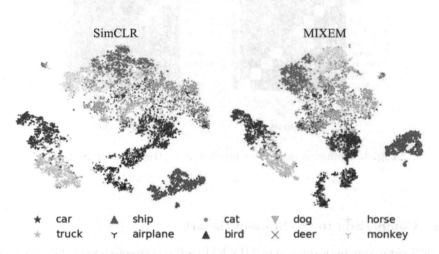

Fig. 3. tSNE visualization of representation on STL10 to illustrate the category-level disentanglement. Samples are marked and colored based on their true label.

4.1 Results

We begin by analyzing the effect of each loss term on STL10. Table 1 shows that, starting from contrastive loss alone (SimCLR) [11], gradually adding various MIX'EM loss terms consistently improves the performance. Row (2) illustrates the importance of normalizing the representations before applying K-means. Rows (4) vs. (5), and (6) vs. (7) show using MIX'EM to initialize the K-means results in significant improvement.

In Fig. 3 we present the tSNE [49] visualization of the representations for SimCLR and MIX'EM. In line with the quantitative evaluation, MIX'EM representations are more disentangled and constitute more compact clusters. Using contrastive loss alone does not adequately pull samples from similar categories to each other, resulting in a sparse space. The mixture module guides the training process via mixing coefficients, forcing the encoder to allocate more compact regions to different categories.

In Fig. 2, the top row displays the tSNE visualization of the embeddings for the dominant component of each image as we gradually add MIX'EM loss terms. The bottom row shows how, in turn, the mixture embeddings get more disentangled as we do so. For a category level analysis of MIX'EM, we show the accuracy confusion matrix in Fig. 4. The animal categories are clearly more difficult to discriminate and benefit the most from MIX'EM. In the supplementary material, we provide more visualizations that indicate how the correct category is very hard to recognize in some images.

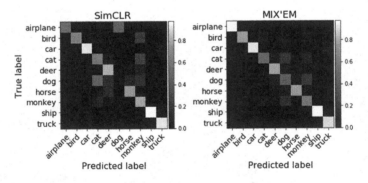

Fig. 4. Confusion matrix for prediction vs. true label on STL10.

4.2 Comparison to the State-of-the-art

Table 2 compares performance of MIX'EM to the state-of-the-art. On the more challenging dataset of STL10, our model outperforms all other works by a large margin. On CIFAR, our model outperforms other works, except SCAN [36] (concurrent work) when further trained with a classification objective. MIX'EM has

Table 2. Comparison to the state-of-the-art in unsupervised image classification.

Dataset	CIFAR10			CIFAR100-20			STL10		
Metric	ACC	NMI	ARI	ACC	NMI	ARI	ACC	NMI	ARI
Linear classifier on SimCLR (supervised)	89.6±0.2	79.91±0.3	79.15±0.35	79.69±0.15	64.38±0.15	61.54±0.26	87.22±0.09	77.1±0.13	74.88±0.15
DEC [50]	30.1	25.7	16.1	18.5	13.6	5.0	35.9	27.6	18.6
DAC [51]	52.2	40.0	30.1	23.8	18.5	8.8	47.0	36.6	25.6
DeepCluster [33]	37.4	-	-	18.9	-	-	65.6	-	-
ADC [52]	32.5	-	-	16.0	-	-	53	-	-
PICA [37]	0.561	0.645	0.467	-	-	-	0.592	0.693	0.504
IIC [38]	61.7	51.1	41.1	25.7	22.5	11.7	59.6	49.6	39.7
SCAN [36]	81.8±0.3	71.2±0.4	66.5±0.4	42.2±3.0	44.1±1.0	26.7±1.3	75.5±2.0	65.4±1.2	59.0±1.6
SCAN [36] w/classification	87.6±0.4	78.7±0.5	75.8±0.7	45.9±2.7	46.8±1.3	30.1±2.1	76.7±1.9	68.0±1.2	61.6±1.8
SimCLR + K-means	79.72±0.22	69.56±0.28	62.06±0.43	42.58±0.74	43.7±0.59	24.43±0.81	69.95±0.78	67.05±0.33	55.37±0.78
MIX'EM + K-means	81.87±0.23	70.85±0.26	66.59±0.37	43.77±0.51	46.41±0.11	27.12±0.33	77.76±0.08	68.03±0.07	61.35±0.1
MIX'EM max component	82.19±0.21	71.35±0.27	67.15±0.32	39.19±0.44	43.59±0.14	26.67±0.12	68.44±0.44	64.08±0.1	54.66±0.09

very low standard deviation, which would be of high importance in a real-world application. On STL10 and CIFAR100-20, standard deviation of SCAN is about an order of magnitude higher. Since MIX'EM improves representations in terms of separability, SCAN should benefit from using MIX'EM as the representation encoder. On CIFAR100-20 for all models, the results are generally worse compared to other datasets. This is mainly due to the some confusing mapping of classes to super-classes. For example, "bicycle" and "train" both are mapped to "vehicles 1" and most animals are divided based on size, rather than semantics.

4.3   Ablation Studies

Number of the Mixture Components. Although we set the number of mixture components to be the same as the number of categories, it is not necessary to do so. With 20 and 40 components on STL10, clustering accuracy is relatively stable: 76.22% and 75.53%, respectively, compared to 77.76% with 10 components. In these cases, where we have more mixture components than classes, we initialize K-Means using the most frequent components. As MIX'EM is a solution for clustering to a known number of categories, we believe it is optimal to use that information in the design.

Initializing K-Means Using MIX'EM. K-means lacks a robust initialization method and the standard procedure is to run K-means many times using random initialization and choose the best one in terms of inertia. We experimented with up to 100 runs and found 50 times to work the best on our models. However, this is neither reliable nor efficient on large scale datasets. With random initialization, K-means is not guaranteed to find the best clustering within practical limits (see large fluctuations in accuracy across different runs in Fig. 5). Running K-means for 50 times on representations of dimensionality 512 takes about 21 seconds on the relatively small STL10 test split (8k images and 10 classes). On 10k images of CIFAR100-20/CIFAR100 with 20/100 classes it takes 112/221 seconds on average. This will get worse on larger datasets with even more categories.

In MIX'EM, we use the mean of representations by each component, based on samples with the same dominant mixture component, to initialize K-means. This

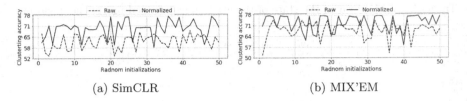

(a) SimCLR   (b) MIX'EM

Fig. 5. K-means with standard random initialization fluctuates heavily over different runs and does not guarantee converging to an optimal solution (on STL10).

eliminates need for multiple random initializations, while consistently delivering higher accuracy. Rows (4), (5), (6) and (7) in Table 1 show the performance with MIX'EM initialization. In particular, rows (6) and (7) illustrate how K-means with 50 random initialization can be far worse than using MIX'EM for initialization. A single run with MIX'EM initialization, on average, takes 0.27, 1.5, and 3 seconds on STL10, CIFAR100-20, and CIFAR100, in order.

Effect on Contrastive Representation Learning. In MIX'EM, the contrastive loss is vital for successful training. This raises the question of how the mixture module influences the performance of representations in terms of accuracy of a linear classifier trained on the frozen features generated by the encoder, which is the standard measure to evaluate self-supervised representations [10,11,35]. To answer this, we train a linear classifier on the frozen base SimCLR encoder, SimCLR, and various forms of MIX'EM. According to Table 3, the mixture module neither improves nor hurts the representation quality the linear classification task. This implies that the representation learned using Sim-CLR contain rich information enough to easily train a supervised linear classifier without further disentanglement of the representation. However, for the unsupervised setting, category-level disentanglement of the representation seems essential, as we observed a significant boost in clustering accuracy using MIX'EM.

Table 3. MIX'EM does not disrupt contrastive learning objective while imposing category-level disentanglement on representations. (evaluated on STL10)

	Model	Supervised linear classifier accuracy
(0)	base SimCLR encoder	86.1
(1)	SimCLR	87.21 ± 0.1
	MIX'EM	
(2)	+ entropy maximization	87.25 ± 0.05
(3)	+ component entropy minimization	87.15 ± 0.06
(4)	+ associative embedding loss	87.22 ± 0.09

Effect of Using Test Data in Training. We investigate three scenarios regarding data splits used for training of MIX'EM and SimCLR; (1) using both train and test splits for training. This is the standard setting as we do not use the available labels for training [38,40]. (2) only using the train split for training; (3) using the train and unlabeled splits (on STL10 only) for training. Note that we always evaluate on the test split. The results are presented in Table 4.

Table 4. The effect of data splits used for training MIX'EM and SimCLR on the K-Menas clustering performance. All evaluations are on test split.

Dataset	Training splits	Method	ACC	NMI	ARI
STL10	train+unlabled	SimCLR	67.44 ± 0.71	64.90 ± 0.1	51.26 ± 0.18
		MIX'EM	71.04 ± 1.13	62.56 ± 0.85	52.29 ± 1.41
	train	SimCLR	65.57 ± 0.4	63.72 ± 0.2	50.50 ± 0.38
		MIX'EM	74.20 ± 0.06	65.19 ± 0.06	55.89 ± 0.1
	train+test	SimCLR	69.95 ± 0.78	67.05 ± 0.33	55.37 ± 0.78
		MIX'EM	77.76 ± 0.08	68.03 ± 0.07	61.35 ± 0.1
CIFAR10	train	SimCLR	77.74 ± 0.08	67.21 ± 0.15	58.54 ± 0.16
		MIX'EM	79.51 ± 0.41	68.29 ± 0.28	63.29 ± 0.44
	train+test	SimCLR	79.72 ± 0.22	69.56 ± 0.28	62.06 ± 0.43
		MIX'EM	81.87 ± 0.23	70.85 ± 0.26	66.59 ± 0.37

Scenario (1) vs. (2). Using test split in training consistently improves performance, having a more significant impact on STL10. We argue that this is due to the size and visual difficulty of STL10. CIFAR10 has 50k training and 10k test images. But, on STL10 there is only 5k training and 8k test images. Hence, on STL10, using test split in training means 160% additional data, while on CIFAR10 it is just a 20% addition. In the future, a more controlled experiment by progressively removing fractions of training data should be helpful for making a more informed conclusion. Additionally, STL10 is a subset of ImageNet and is visually more complex. On CIFAR100-20 trend is quite similar to CIFAR10.

Scenario (2) vs. (3). Unlabeled split of STL10 contains 100k images; however, we do not know the distribution of the categories, and it contains unknown distractor categories. Therefore, despite increasing training data by a large factor, performance drops in this scenario. MIX'EM presumes access to the expected number of categories, which does not hold for the unlabeled set. We believe this is the reason why the accuracy of K-means on SimCLR does not drop as much in this case. Nevertheless, MIX'EM still is significantly more accurate.

5   Conclusion

We presented MIX'EM, a novel solution for unsupervised image classification. MIX'EM builds a mixture of embeddings module into SimCLR in order to impose semantic structure on the representations. To successfully train MIX'EM, we introduce various loss terms. MXI'EM sets a new stat-of-the-art unsupervised accuracy on STL10 and performs on par with current models on CIFAR. We also show that applying K-means itself on normalized representations from Sim-CLR results in impressively high accuracy. We believe this can be used as a new measure for evaluating the quality of self-supervised representation learning methods. The results we publish here could be further improved by using the latest findings in contrastive visual representation learning [53]. In the future, we would like to explore the impact of our model on image retrieval and instance segmentation tasks. Moreover, studying the theoretical aspects of MIX'EM could provide insight for further improvements.

Acknowledgments. This work was partially funded by the FWO SBO project HAPPY.

References

1. He, K., Zhang, X., Ren, S., Sun, J.: Deep residual learning for image recognition. In: Proceedings of the IEEE Conference on Computer Vision and Pattern Recognition, pp. 770–778 (2016)
2. Krizhevsky, A., Sutskever, I., Hinton, G.E.: ImageNet classification with deep convolutional neural networks. In: Advances in Neural Information Processing Systems, pp. 1097–1105 (2012)
3. Sun, C., Shrivastava, A., Singh, S., Gupta, A.: Revisiting unreasonable effectiveness of data in deep learning era. In: Proceedings of the IEEE International Conference on Computer Vision, pp. 843–852 (2017)
4. He, K., Girshick, R., Dollár, P.: Rethinking imagenet pre-training. In: Proceedings of the IEEE International Conference on Computer Vision, pp. 4918–4927 (2019)
5. Lin, T.-Y., et al.: Microsoft COCO: common objects in context. In: Fleet, D., Pajdla, T., Schiele, B., Tuytelaars, T. (eds.) ECCV 2014. LNCS, vol. 8693, pp. 740–755. Springer, Cham (2014). https://doi.org/10.1007/978-3-319-10602-1_48
6. Deng, J., Dong, W., Socher, R., Li, L.J., Li, K., Fei-Fei, L.: ImageNet: a large-scale hierarchical image database. In: 2019 IEEE Conference on Computer Vision and Pattern Recognition, pp. 248–255 (2009)
7. Bachman, P., Hjelm, R.D., Buchwalter, W.: Learning representations by maximizing mutual information across views. In: Advances in Neural Information Processing Systems, pp. 15535–15545 (2019)
8. Gidaris, S., Singh, P., Komodakis, N.: Unsupervised representation learning by predicting image rotations. arXiv preprint arXiv:1803.07728 (2018)
9. Wu, Z., Xiong, Y., Yu, S.X., Lin, D.: Unsupervised feature learning via nonparametric instance discrimination. In: Proceedings of the IEEE Conference on Computer Vision and Pattern Recognition, pp. 3733–3742 (2018)
10. van den Oord, A., Li, Y., Vinyals, O.: Representation learning with contrastive predictive coding. arXiv preprint arXiv:1807.03748 (2018)

11. Chen, T., Kornblith, S., Norouzi, M., Hinton, G.: A simple framework for contrastive learning of visual representations. arXiv preprint arXiv:2002.05709 (2020)
12. He, K., Fan, H., Wu, Y., Xie, S., Girshick, R.: Momentum contrast for unsupervised visual representation learning. In: Proceedings of the IEEE/CVF Conference on Computer Vision and Pattern Recognition, pp. 9729–9738 (2020)
13. Tian, Y., Krishnan, D., Isola, P.: Contrastive multiview coding. arXiv preprint arXiv:1906.05849 (2019)
14. Asano, Y.M., Rupprecht, C., Vedaldi, A.: A critical analysis of self-supervision, or what we can learn from a single image. arXiv preprint arXiv:1904.13132 (2019)
15. McLachlan, G.J., Basford, K.E.: Mixture models: inference and applications to clustering, vol. 84. M. Dekker New York (1988)
16. Jordan, M.I., Jacobs, R.A.: Hierarchical mixtures of experts and the EM algorithm. Neural Comput. 6, 181–214 (1994)
17. Bishop, C.M.: Mixture density networks (1994)
18. Greff, K., et al.: Multi-object representation learning with iterative variational inference. arXiv preprint arXiv:1903.00450 (2019)
19. Chen, M., Artières, T., Denoyer, L.: Unsupervised object segmentation by redrawing. In: Advances in Neural Information Processing Systems, pp. 12726–12737 (2019)
20. Li, C., Lee, G.H.: Generating multiple hypotheses for 3D human pose estimation with mixture density network. In: Proceedings of the IEEE Conference on Computer Vision and Pattern Recognition, pp. 9887–9895 (2019)
21. Lee, S., Purushwalkam, S., Cogswell, M., Crandall, D., Batra, D.: Why M heads are better than one: training a diverse ensemble of deep networks. arXiv preprint arXiv:1511.06314 (2015)
22. Ye, Q., Kim, T.K.: Occlusion-aware hand pose estimation using hierarchical mixture density network. In: Proceedings of the European Conference on Computer Vision (ECCV), pp. 801–817 (2018)
23. Makansi, O., Ilg, E., Cicek, O., Brox, T.: Overcoming limitations of mixture density networks: a sampling and fitting framework for multimodal future prediction. In: Proceedings of the IEEE Conference on Computer Vision and Pattern Recognition, pp. 7144–7153 (2019)
24. Varamesh, A., Tuytelaars, T.: Mixture dense regression for object detection and human pose estimation. In: Proceedings of the IEEE/CVF Conference on Computer Vision and Pattern Recognition, pp. 13086–13095 (2020)
25. Newell, A., Deng, J.: Pixels to graphs by associative embedding. In: Advances in Neural Information Processing Systems, pp. 2171–2180 (2017)
26. Newell, A., Huang, Z., Deng, J.: Associative embedding: end-to-end learning for joint detection and grouping. In: Advances in Neural Information Processing Systems, pp. 2277–2287 (2017)
27. Chen, X., Fan, H., Girshick, R., He, K.: Improved baselines with momentum contrastive learning. arXiv preprint arXiv:2003.04297 (2020)
28. Gutmann, M., Hyvärinen, A.: Noise-contrastive estimation: a new estimation principle for unnormalized statistical models. In: Proceedings of the Thirteenth International Conference on Artificial Intelligence and Statistics, pp. 297–304 (2010)
29. Hjelm, R.D., et al.: Learning deep representations by mutual information estimation and maximization. arXiv preprint arXiv:1808.06670 (2018)
30. Donahue, J., Krähenbühl, P., Darrell, T.: Adversarial feature learning. arXiv preprint arXiv:1605.09782 (2016)
31. Dumoulin, V., et al.: Adversarially learned inference. arXiv preprint arXiv:1606.00704 (2016)

32. Doersch, C., Gupta, A., Efros, A.A.: Unsupervised visual representation learning by context prediction. In: Proceedings of the IEEE International Conference on Computer Vision, pp. 1422–1430 (2015)
33. Caron, M., Bojanowski, P., Joulin, A., Douze, M.: Deep clustering for unsupervised learning of visual features. In: Proceedings of the European Conference on Computer Vision (ECCV), pp. 132–149 (2018)
34. Noroozi, M., Favaro, P.: Unsupervised learning of visual representations by solving jigsaw puzzles. In: Leibe, B., Matas, J., Sebe, N., Welling, M. (eds.) ECCV 2016. LNCS, vol. 9910, pp. 69–84. Springer, Cham (2016). https://doi.org/10.1007/978-3-319-46466-4_5
35. Zhang, R., Isola, P., Efros, A.A.: Colorful image colorization. In: Leibe, B., Matas, J., Sebe, N., Welling, M. (eds.) ECCV 2016. LNCS, vol. 9907, pp. 649–666. Springer, Cham (2016). https://doi.org/10.1007/978-3-319-46487-9_40
36. Van Gansbeke, W., Vandenhende, S., Georgoulis, S., Proesmans, M., Van Gool, L.: Learning to classify images without labels. arXiv preprint arXiv:2005.12320 (2020)
37. Huang, J., Gong, S., Zhu, X.: Deep semantic clustering by partition confidence maximisation. In: Proceedings of the IEEE/CVF Conference on Computer Vision and Pattern Recognition, pp. 8849–8858 (2020)
38. Ji, X., Henriques, J.F., Vedaldi, A.: Invariant information clustering for unsupervised image classification and segmentation. In: Proceedings of the IEEE International Conference on Computer Vision, pp. 9865–9874 (2019)
39. Asano, Y.M., Rupprecht, C., Vedaldi, A.: Self-labelling via simultaneous clustering and representation learning. arXiv preprint arXiv:1911.05371 (2019)
40. Yang, J., Parikh, D., Batra, D.: Joint unsupervised learning of deep representations and image clusters. In: Proceedings of the IEEE Conference on Computer Vision and Pattern Recognition, pp. 5147–5156 (2016)
41. Yan, X., Misra, I., Gupta, A., Ghadiyaram, D., Mahajan, D.: Clusterfit: improving generalization of visual representations. In: Proceedings of the IEEE/CVF Conference on Computer Vision and Pattern Recognition, pp. 6509–6518 (2020)
42. Zhan, X., Xie, J., Liu, Z., Ong, Y.S., Loy, C.C.: Online deep clustering for unsupervised representation learning. In: Proceedings of the IEEE/CVF Conference on Computer Vision and Pattern Recognition, pp. 6688–6697 (2020)
43. Sanchez, E.H., Serrurier, M., Ortner, M.: Learning disentangled representations via mutual information estimation. arXiv preprint arXiv:1912.03915 (2019)
44. Von Luxburg, U.: A tutorial on spectral clustering. Stat. Comput. **17**, 395–416 (2007)
45. Coates, A., Ng, A., Lee, H.: An analysis of single-layer networks in unsupervised feature learning. In: Proceedings of the Fourteenth International Conference on Artificial Intelligence And Statistics, pp. 215–223 (2011)
46. Krizhevsky, A., Hinton, G., et al.: Learning multiple layers of features from tiny images (2009)
47. Han, K., Rebuffi, S.A., Ehrhardt, S., Vedaldi, A., Zisserman, A.: Automatically discovering and learning new visual categories with ranking statistics. arXiv preprint arXiv:2002.05714 (2020)
48. Han, K., Vedaldi, A., Zisserman, A.: Learning to discover novel visual categories via deep transfer clustering. In: Proceedings of the IEEE International Conference on Computer Vision, pp. 8401–8409 (2019)
49. van der Maaten, L., Hinton, G.: Visualizing data using T-SNE. J. Mach. Learn. Res. **9**, 2579–2605 (2008)
50. Xie, J., Girshick, R., Farhadi, A.: Unsupervised deep embedding for clustering analysis. In: International Conference on Machine Learning, pp. 478–487 (2016)

51. Chang, J., Wang, L., Meng, G., Xiang, S., Pan, C.: Deep adaptive image clustering. In: Proceedings of the IEEE International Conference on Computer Vision, pp. 5879–5887 (2017)
52. Haeusser, P., Plapp, J., Golkov, V., Aljalbout, E., Cremers, D.: Associative deep clustering: training a classification network with no labels. In: Brox, T., Bruhn, A., Fritz, M. (eds.) GCPR 2018. LNCS, vol. 11269, pp. 18–32. Springer, Cham (2019). https://doi.org/10.1007/978-3-030-12939-2_2
53. Tian, Y., Sun, C., Poole, B., Krishnan, D., Schmid, C., Isola, P.: What makes for good views for contrastive learning. arXiv preprint arXiv:2005.10243 (2020)

Backbone Based Feature Enhancement for Object Detection

Haoqin Ji[1,2], Weizeng Lu[1,2], and Linlin Shen[1,2(✉)]

[1] Computer Vision Institute, School of Computer Science and Software Engineering,
Shenzhen University, Shenzhen, China
{jihaoqin2019,luweizeng2018}@email.szu.edu.cn, llshen@szu.edu.cn
[2] Shenzhen Institute of Artificial Intelligence and Robotics for Society,
Shenzhen, China

Abstract. FPN (Feature Pyramid Networks) and many of its variants have been widely used in state of the art object detectors and made remarkable progress in detection performance. However, almost all the architectures of feature pyramid are manually designed, which requires ad hoc design and prior knowledge. Meanwhile, existing methods focus on exploring more appropriate connections to generate features with strong semantics features from inherent pyramidal hierarchy of deep ConvNets (Convolutional Networks). In this paper, we propose a simple but effective approach, named BBFE (Backbone Based Feature Enhancement), to directly enhance the semantics of shallow features from backbone ConvNets. The proposed BBFE consists of two components: reusing backbone weight and personalized feature enhancement. We also proposed a fast version of BBFE, named Fast-BBFE, to achieve better trade-off between efficiency and accuracy. Without bells and whistles, our BBFE improves different baseline methods (both anchor-based and anchor-free) by a large margin (∼2.0 points higher AP) on COCO, surpassing common feature pyramid networks including FPN and PANet.

Keywords: Feature enhancement · Object detection

1 Introduction

As one of the most fundamental and challenging tasks in computer vision, object detection aims to accurately detect the objects of predefined categories in digital images. Benefited from the development of deep ConvNets (Convolutional Networks) [1] and GPUs computing power in recent years, modern object detectors (e.g., SSD [2], YOLO [3], RetinaNet [4], Faster R-CNN [5], Cascade R-CNN [6]) have achieved impressive progress. However, object detection still faces many challenges, e.g. there usually exists objects with various scales in the same picture. To solve this problem, a traditional idea is to use an image pyramid [7] to build a feature pyramid and then detect objects of different scales in different feature maps, which is effective but brings huge computing cost. As shown in

© Springer Nature Switzerland AG 2021
H. Ishikawa et al. (Eds.): ACCV 2020, LNCS 12624, pp. 56–70, 2021.
https://doi.org/10.1007/978-3-030-69535-4_4

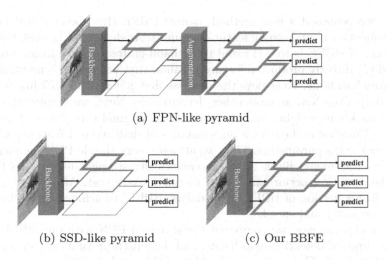

(a) FPN-like pyramid

(b) SSD-like pyramid   (c) Our BBFE

Fig. 1. (a) Designing additional augmentation to enhance detection capability of original features. (b) Using pyramidal feature hierarchy that have semantics from low to high levels. (c) Building a strong pyramid from backbone directly. In this figure, thicker outlines denote semantically stronger features.

Fig. 1(b), SSD (Single Shot Detector) [2] is one of the first attempts to combine the predictions from pyramidal feature hierarchy directly to handle objects of various sizes, but the performance is limited due to the limited semantics available in shallow level feature maps. After that, FPN (Feature Pyramid Network) [8] proposes to create a feature pyramid with strong semantics at all scales by developing an efficient top-down pathway with lateral connections after the bottom-up pathway, which shows significant improvements with small extra cost.

The success of FPN attracts wide attention from the community. After that, a series of subsequent works, such as FPR [9], PANet [10], and M2Det [11], propose to further improve the pyramid architectures like FPN from different aspects to obtain enriched features. As shown in Fig. 1(a), Most of the existing works related to pyramidal feature fusion can be summarized into two steps: (1) select one or more feature maps from multiple levels of deep ConvNets and denote them as $\{C_2, C_3, \ldots\}$; (2) carefully design the multi-scale features fusion module and augment $\{C_2, C_3, \ldots\}$ to $\{P_2, P_3, \ldots\}$ that contain richer semantic information. Finally, these high-level features are applied to the subsequent detection process. Although these works promote detection accuracy remarkably, designing a suitable feature fusion scheme is of great challenge, which requires rich experience and prior knowledge.

The feature hierarchy computed by backbone has an inherent multi-scale, pyramidal shape, which we call SSD-like pyramid. In SSD-like pyramid, while the deepest feature map has the strongest semantic features, the shallower feature maps have lower-level features. What if we continue to apply the subsequent layers of ConvNets to the shallow feature maps of the SSD-like pyramid? Inspired by that, we proposed a new method, named BBFE (Backbone Based Feature Enhancement), to build strong feature pyramids. As shown in Fig. 1(c), the basic motivation of BBFE is to: (1) avoid using hand-crafted feature fusion architecture and (2) directly produce a feature pyramid that has strong semantics at all scales from backbone. To achieve this goal, we first generate an SSD-like pyramid from a deep ConvNet, as most other detectors do. Next, we employ the RBW (reusing backbone weight) module to reuse the original convolutional layers of backbone ConvNet and enhance the semantics of shallow-layer features, without introducing extra parameters. Then we attach a very simple PFE (personalized feature enhancement) block on each semantically stronger feature, to further boost the detection performance with marginal extra cost. After that, we proposed a faster version of BBFE, named Fast-BBFE, to achieve better trade-off between accuracy and speed.

In our experiments, we compared the standard FPN with our BBFE using different types of detection algorithms, and demonstrate competitiveness of the proposed method. The main contributions of this work can be summarized as:

- Propose a RBW module to get semantically strong features directly from the standard backbone, without additional hand-crafted architectures;
- Propose a more powerful BBFE approach consisting of RBW and a lightweight detection neck PFE, which can be generalized to all detectors and replace FPN for better detection performance;
- Without using any tricks, our approach achieves a consistent improvement (~2.0 points higher AP) on both anchor-based and anchor-free detectors.

2   Related Work

Benefited from the success of deep ConvNets [1] and the great increase in computing power, the CNN-based object detectors have greatly advanced the performance of hand-crafted features [12,13]. In order to efficiently detect objects of various scales simultaneously in a single image and further push the upper bound of detection accuracy, deep object detectors usually adopt multiple feature layers. Using image pyramid [7] to construct feature pyramid is a reasonable solution, but it is time-consuming because of the large computation burden to independently generate features on each image scale. To better address this issue, lots of works have been proposed.

Applying Multi-layer Features. Reusing feature maps from different layers computed in the forward propagation of ConvNet is a useful way to deal with the problem of scales. SSD [2] directly utilizes several original feature maps of backbone layers to improve detection performance. SDP+CRC [14] uses features in multiple layers to detect objects of different scales by using the proposed scale-dependent pooling and cascaded rejection classifiers. MSCNN [15] applies deconvolutional layers on multiple feature maps of a CNN to increase their resolutions, and later these refined feature maps are used to make predictions. RFBNet [16] proposes a multi-branch convolution block similar to the Inception block, and combine them with the dilated convolution to further enhance the discriminability and robustness of features.

Fusing Multi-layer Features. Recent works exploit lateral or skip connections to fuse information between different layers to produce combined features. DSOD [17] follows the SSD framework and fuses multi-scale prediction responses with an elaborated dense structure. FPN [8] passes semantic information from deep layers to shallow layers by a concise top-down pathway, which further shows the power of feature fusion. Furthermore, a series of improved FPN are proposed. PANet [10] adds another bottom-up path with lateral connections on the basis of FPN to shorten the information path. FPR [9] adaptively concatenates multiple layers extracted from backbone network and then spread semantics to all scales through a more complex module. Libra R-CNN [18] proposes a BFP (Balanced Feature Pyramid) to aggregates multiple features and refine the integrated feature with the non-local module [19], then scatter it to all scales. NAS-FPN [20] adopts NAS (Neural Architecture Search) [21] to find a new feature pyramid architecture, which consists of free connections to fuse features of different scales. Other representative methods, such as DSSD (Deconvolutional Single Shot Detector) [22], TDM (Top Down Modulation) [23], STDN (Scale Transfer Detection Network) [24], RefineDet [25] and M2Det [11], also made impressive progress in multi-layers fusion.

Most of the existing studies, except NAS-FPN, manually design the connection between backbone features and pyramidal features. Considering that it might be ad hoc to manually design architectures for fusing features across scale, our work focuses on building a semantic feature pyramid directly from the backbone, which is a simple and near parameter-free method that only reuses the original convolutional layers.

3   Method

The overall pipeline of BBFE is shown in Fig. 2. Taking a single-scale image of an arbitrary size as input, our goal is to directly build a high-level semantic feature pyramid by reusing original layers. All the components and details will be introduced in this section.

3.1   Reusing Backbone Weight

As shown in Fig. 2, the dotted box represents the proposed RBW (reusing backbone weight) module, which is based on the backbone ConvNet's pyramidal feature hierarchy $\{C_2, C_3, C_4, C_5\}$. $\{C_2, C_3, C_4, C_5\}$ are the output of different convolutional blocks and have semantics from low to high levels. The deepest layer C_5 has the strongest semantics and can be used for subsequent detection without further improvement. For other layers, we continue to apply the later convolutional blocks to shallower features to enrich their semantics. For example, C_3 is the output of conv2, so we continue to apply conv3 and conv4 to C_3 to enrich its semantic information. When reusing a convolutional block, we

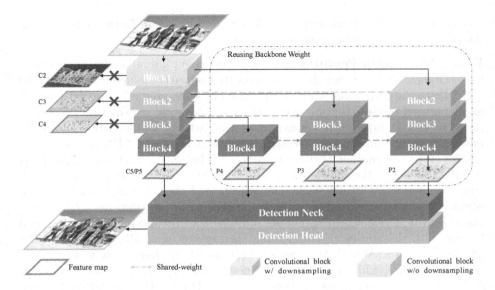

Fig. 2. Overview of the proposed BBFE. $\{C_2, C_3, C_4, C_5\}$ denotes the original pyramidal feature hierarchy of backbone ConvNets, C_5 and P_5 are identical. Feature maps with red crosses are not required and will not be generated in our approach. We firstly enhance the middle-level features $\{C_2, C_3, C_4\}$ into semantically strong features $\{P_2, P_3, P_4\}$ by reusing the backbone weight (no extra parameters) while maintaining their original resolutions. Then $\{P_2, P_3, P_4, P_5\}$ are further enriched by detection neck (e.g. the PFE block) before the subsequent detection.

need to change the down-sampling operation in order to keep the spatial size of output and input layer consistent. To be specific, if the down sampling operation is related to the stride of the convolution kernel, we will reset the stride and padding value. If the downsampling operation is associated with the pooling layer, we simply skip that layer.

We strengthen multi-scale feature presentations by reusing the original convolution blocks, with the removal of down-sampling operation. Compared to previous studies, our method can obtain semantic features without requirement of complex structures for feature fusion and feature enhancement. The proposed RBW does not require any additional parameters and can be easily generalized to other detectors. It's a parameter-free approach for feature pyramid enhancement.

3.2 Personalized Feature Enhancement

Object detectors leverage feature pyramid to detect small objects from high resolution images and detect large objects from low resolution images. Because many convolution kernels are shared for feature extraction, RBW module may generate similar semantic information for feature maps generated by different branches, which limit the representation ability cross scales. To alleviate the problem, we

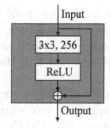

Fig. 3. The overview of the personalized feature enhancement block.

introduce the PFE (personalized feature enhancement) block shown in Fig. 3 and separately attach it on each layer to make features more discriminative. To avoid complex manual design, we simply adopt a residual block consisting of a 3×3 convolution and ReLU function. Inspired by ResNet [26], our hypothesis is that the shortcut enables input features to retain their original representation if extra convolution destroys the learned semantic information. Based on RBW, the PFE block can further improve the detection accuracy with marginal extra cost.

In addition, the detection neck (PFE block) can be replaced by other existing components (e.g. Non-Local [19]) for better accuracy, which may introduce too much calculations. In this paper, simplicity is central to our design.

3.3 Fast-BBFE

The combination of RBW module and PFE block forms a simple and effective approach named BBFE (backbone based feature enhancement) for enhancing

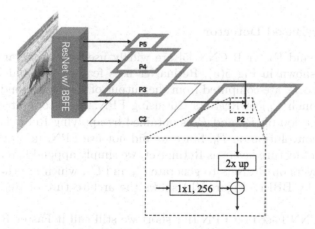

Fig. 4. The overview of the Fast-BBFE: Using BBFE to obtain semantic features except C_2. P_2 is generated by merging C_2 and P_3 after simple dimension transformation.

detection ability of each feature map. The speed of BBFE is inversely proportional to the scale of the feature map. Backbone ConvNet computes a feature hierarchy consisting of feature maps at several scales with a scaling step of 2, and the largest feature map will cost most of the time due to the removal of down-sampling.

To address this issue, we apply BBFE to the original features except the biggest one, which is built through FPN-way separately. We denote the output of each residual blocks of ResNets as $\{C_2, C_3, C_4, C_5\}$, and note that they have strides of $\{4, 8, 16, 32\}$ pixels with respect to the input image. We firstly utilize BBFE to enhance $\{C_3, C_4, C_5\}$ to $\{P_3, P_4, P_5\}$, and then generate P_2 by merging C_2 and P_3, as shown in Fig. 4. We up-sample the spatial resolution of P_3 by a factor of 2 using nearest neighbor up-sampling, and use a 1×1 convolutional layer to reduce the channel dimensions of C_2, then merge the up-sampled map with C_2 by element-wise addition to produce P_2. Unlike FPN, we use the PFE block to reduce the aliasing effect of up-sampling. We call BBFE with this module Fast-BBFE, which achieves better trade-off between accuracy and efficiency. As Table 2 shows, RetinaNet [4] using Fast-BBFE surpasses FPN based RetinaNet in both accuracy and speed.

4   Object Detection

State of the art object detectors available in literature can be mainly categorized into anchor-based and anchor-free approaches. Our method is a generic solution for building strong semantic feature pyramids based on backbone ConvNets. In this section, we generalize BBFE to different types of object detectors. To demonstrate the effectiveness and simplicity of BBFE and Fast-BBFE, we make minimal and reasonable modifications to these algorithms to adapt them to our methods.

4.1   Anchor-Based Detector

RetinaNet [4] and Faster R-CNN [5] are widely used one-stage and two-stage methods. As shown in Fig. 5(a), RetinaNet uses feature pyramid levels P_3 to P_7, where P_3 to P_5 are computed from the output of the corresponding residual stage (C_3 through C_5) of ResNets [26] using FPN. P_6 is computed via a 3×3 stride-2 convolution on P_5, and P_7 is obtained by applying ReLU followed by a 3×3 stride-2 convolution on P_6. Since we did not use FPN, in order to get the same number of feature layers as RetinaNet, we simply append two 3×3 stride-2 convolution layers on ResNets to generate C_6 and C_7, which are then enhanced to P_6 and P_7 by BBFE. Figure 5(b) shows the architecture of RetinaNet with BBFE.

Faster R-CNN based on FPN (for short we still call it Faster R-CNN) uses feature pyramid levels P_2 to P_6, where P_2 to P_5 are the output of ResNets corresponding to C_2 to C_5, and P_6 is generated by applying max-pooling on P_6.

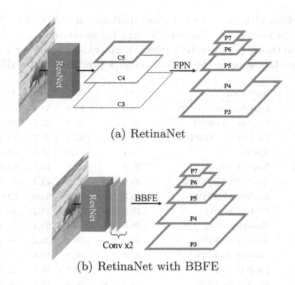

(a) RetinaNet

(b) RetinaNet with BBFE

Fig. 5. (a) Original RetinaNet that uses FPN by default. (b) Replacing FPN with BBFE and appending two extra 3 × 3 conv layers on backbone to generate the same number of feature maps as FPN.

Analogous to the RetinaNet combined with BBFE, we firstly add a 3 × 3 convolutional layer to Faster R-CNN backbone and generate the feature hierarchy $\{C_2, C_3, C_4, C_5, C_6\}$, where C_6 is the output of the extra conv layer, then use BBFE to directly obtain feature pyramid $\{P_2, P_3, P_4, P_5, P_6\}$.

4.2   Anchor-Free Detector

Anchor-free detectors can be divided into center-based and keypoint-based methods. For example, FCOS [27] proposes a novel centerness score and predicts object bounding box with four distances. RepPoints [28] represents objects as a set of sample points and learns to automatically arrange themselves in a particular manner. Although the algorithm details are different, both FCOS and RepPoints use common backbone networks and detection necks to extract and enhance features. Similar to RetinaNet, we replace FPN with BBFE in FCOS and RepPoints using the approach shown in Fig. 5.

5   Experiments

5.1   Datasets and Evaluation Metrics

We conduct all experiments on the challenging COCO dataset [29], which consists of 115k images for training (*train-2017*) and 5k images for validation (*val-2017*). We use the *train-2017* split for training and perform all ablation studies on the *val-2017* subset, then report our main results on the *test dev* split (20k

Table 1. Comparison with the state-of-the-art methods on COCO *test-dev*. The symbol "*" means our implementation. The number in [ ] denotes the relative improvement. We exclude all the training and testing tricks in our experiments for fair comparison. All the settings are the same as the default settings provided in the MMDetection.

Method	Backbone	AP	AP_{50}	AP_{75}	AP_S	AP_M	AP_L
YOLOv3 [33]	DarkNet-59	33.0	57.9	34.4	18.3	35.4	41.9
SSD513 [2]	ResNet-101-SSD	31.2	50.4	33.3	10.2	34.5	49.8
DSSD513 [22]	ResNet-101-DSSD	33.2	53.3	35.2	13.0	35.4	51.1
RefineDet512 [25]	ResNet-101	36.4	57.5	39.5	16.6	39.9	51.4
Mask R-CNN [34]	ResNet-101-FPN	38.2	60.3	41.7	20.1	41.1	50.2
Mask R-CNN [34]	ResNeXt-101-FPN	39.8	62.3	43.4	22.1	43.2	51.2
Libra R-CNN [18]	ResNet-101-FPN	40.3	61.3	43.9	22.9	43.1	51.0
ExtremeNet [35]	Hourglass-104	40.2	55.5	43.2	20.4	43.2	53.1
CornerNet [36]	Hourglass-104	40.5	56.5	43.1	19.4	42.7	53.9
Faster R-CNN*	ResNet-50-FPN	36.5	58.6	39.2	21.5	39.4	44.7
FCOS*	ResNet-50-FPN	37.1	56.5	39.6	20.5	39.8	46.7
RepPoints*	ResNet-50-FPN	38.6	59.7	41.5	22.7	41.8	47.2
RetinaNet*	ResNet-50-FPN	35.8	56.0	38.3	20.0	39.0	43.9
RetinaNet*	ResNet-101-FPN	38.0	58.7	40.8	21.3	41.6	47.5
RetinaNet*	ResNeXt-101-FPN	40.2	61.3	43.5	23.1	43.9	50.9
Faster R-CNN (ours)	ResNet-50-Fast-BBFE	38.1[+1.6]	59.9	41.5	23.2	40.9	47.4
FCOS (ours)	ResNet-50-Fast-BBFE	38.3[+1.2]	57.9	40.9	22.0	40.9	48.4
RepPoints (ours)	ResNet-50-Fast-BBFE	39.5[+0.9]	60.8	42.5	23.6	42.7	48.6
RetinaNet (ours)	ResNet-50- Fast-BBFE	36.9[+1.1]	57.5	39.7	21.4	40.2	45.5
RetinaNet (ours)	ResNet-101- Fast-BBFE	38.9[+0.9]	59.6	42.0	22.3	42.4	49.0
RetinaNet (ours)	ResNeXt-101- Fast-BBFE	41.1[+0.9]	62.4	44.5	23.9	44.8	51.7
Faster R-CNN (ours)	ResNet-50-BBFE	38.6[+2.1]	60.4	41.7	23.7	41.3	47.6
FCOS (ours)	ResNet-50-BBFE	39.4[+2.3]	58.9	42.2	24.1	41.7	48.9
RepPoints (ours)	ResNet-50-BBFE	40.3[+1.7]	61.4	43.5	25.2	43.2	48.8
RetinaNet (ours)	ResNet-50-BBFE	37.8[+2.0]	58.5	40.8	22.6	40.8	46.7
RetinaNet (ours)	ResNet-101-BBFE	40.0[+2.0]	60.7	43.3	24.0	43.1	49.9
RetinaNet (ours)	ResNeXt-101-BBFE	41.6[+1.4]	62.8	44.8	25.0	45.0	52.4

images with disclosed labels) by uploading our detection results to the evaluation server. All the experiment results are reported using standard COCO-style AP (Average Precision) metrics, including AP, AP_{50}, AP_{75}, AP_S, AP_M, AP_L.

5.2 Implementation Details

All the experiments are implemented based on PyTorch [30] and MMDetection [31] for fair comparisons. For the main results, we select four representative detectors as our baseline, and use ResNet backbone initialized with the weights pretrained on ImageNet [32]. The input images are resized to have their shorter side being 800 and their longer side less or equal to 1333. We use 4 GPUs (2 images per GPU) to train detectors with SGD (Stochastic Gradient Descent) for 12 epochs, which is commonly referred as 1x training schedule. According to the linear scaling rule, the initial learning rate was set to 0.005 and decreased by 0.1 after epoch 8 and 11. Weight decay and momentum are set as 0.0001 and 0.9, respectively. All other hyper-parameters follow the settings in MMDetection.

5.3   Main Results

Without loss of generality, we verify the effectiveness of BBFE and Fast-BBFE on different types of detectors and compare them with other state-of-the-art detectors on *test dev* split of COCO benchmark. The results are reported in Table 1. Many researches adopt longer training schedule and scale jitters as well as multi-scale/flip testing to make their detectors achieve better results. For a fair comparison, we exclude all the training and testing tricks in all experiments. We firstly reimplement the baseline methods equipped with FPN, which generally perform better than that reported in their papers. Then we make minimal changes to the original object detectors to fit our BBFE and Fast-BBFE introduced in Sect. 4.

As Table 1 shows, by replacing FPN with Fast-BBFE and BBFE, Faster R-CNN based on ResNet-50 achieves 38.1 AP and 38.6 AP, respectively, which is 1.6 points and 2.1 points higher than ResNet50-FPN based Faster R-CNN. As for one-stage detector, The AP of RetinaNet with BBFE using different backbones is improved by 1.4 ~ 2.0 points. As for anchor-free detectors, BBFE improves the AP of FCOS and RepPoints by 2.2 and 1.6 points, respectively, when using ResNet50 as backbone. The improvement of RepPoints is relatively small, because the original RepPoints uses Group Normalization [37] in standard FPN to boost performance. Without bells and whistles, The proposed BBFE bring significant improvements to various backbones and detectors, which demonstrates the robustness and generalization ability of our method.

5.4   Ablation Studies

Overall Ablation Studies. For a better understanding to our approach, we further conduct a series of ablation studies and report results in Table 2. We gradually add RBW (reusing backbone weight), PFE (personalized feature enhancement) and the fast version of the combination of the previous two modules on

Table 2. Ablation studies on COCO *test-dev*.

w/RBW?	w/PFE?	Fast-BBFE?	FPS	AP	AP_{50}	AP_{75}	AP_S	AP_M	AP_L
			13.3	34.4	54.0	36.7	17.8	38.3	47.0
✓			10.8	36.1	56.3	38.8	19.7	40.0	48.2
	✓		13.4	34.4	54.1	36.8	18.0	38.4	46.7
✓		✓	14.6	35.0	54.7	37.2	18.4	39.2	47.1
✓	✓		10.7	**36.4**	**56.4**	**39.1**	**20.4**	40.5	**48.5**
✓	✓	✓	**14.6**	35.4	55.4	38.0	18.6	39.6	47.7

ResNet-50-FPN RetinaNet600 baseline. The first row of Table 2 shows the result of the original RetinaNet600, which use FPN by default. We replace the FPN architecture in RetinaNet with our methods and show the corresponding results in rows 2 through 6.

Reusing Backbone Weight. Reusing backbone weight achieves 1.7 points higher box AP than the ResNet-50-FPN RetinaNet600 baseline, demonstrating the power of this simple approach, which does not introduce any additional parameters or utilize any FPN-like feature fusion methods.

Personalized Feature Enhancement. Personalized feature enhancement further improves the box AP from 36.1 to 36.4, where most of the improvements are from AP_S, i.e. 0.7 points increase. Row 5 of Table 2 indicates that the PFE block can boost performance with marginal extra cost (FPS reduced from 10.8 to 10.7).

Fast-BBFE. Based on BBFE, Fast-BBFE achieves a better trade-off in accuracy and efficiency. The last row in Table 2 shows that Fast-BBFE achieves better precision and increasing speed over the baseline, which can even compete with ResNet-50-FPN RetinaNet800 (35.5 AP and 12.6 FPS).

Table 3. Comparisons with other feature pyramidal architectures on COCO *test-dev.*

Architecture	AP	AP_{50}	AP_{75}	AP_S	AP_M	AP_L
FPN [8]	35.5	55.6	38.1	21.2	39.3	45.9
BFP [18]	35.7	56.2	38.0	20.8	40.2	46.2
PANet [10]	35.9	55.9	38.4	20.9	40.1	46.3
FPN + BFP	36.4	56.9	38.6	21.2	40.4	48.1
BBFE (ours)	**37.3**	**57.6**	**40.0**	**22.9**	**41.2**	**47.6**
BBFE + FPN	36.8[−0.5]	57.8	39.4	23.4	40.4	46.3
BBFE + PANet	38.2[+0.9]	58.5	**41.2**	23.7	**42.4**	**49.4**
BBFE + BFP	**38.3[+1.0]**	**59.3**	41.0	**24.7**	42.1	47.8

Comparisons with Other Feature Pyramid. To further demonstrate the effectiveness of our method, we compared in Table 3 with common hand-crafted feature pyramidal networks including FPN, BFP, and PANet. Our experiments are performed on ResNet-50 RetinaNet with the image scale of [1333, 800]. NAS-FPN is not involved because its experimental conditions in MMDetection are quite different from other algorithms. As Table 3 shows, our BBFE yields 0.9 ~ 1.8 points higher AP over other FPNs on the same baseline. In particular, compared with the method of FPN combined with BFP in row 4, BBFE has a more balanced increase in AP_S (+1.7 points), AP_M (+1.9 points) and AP_L (+1.7 points), which further demonstrates that our method consistently enhances the feature map of all scales.

Our BBFE is able to achieve 37.3 AP on COCO dataset, which is 1.8 points higher than ResNet-50-FPN RetinaNet. Furthermore, we tried to combine BBFE with other feature pyramid structures to achieve further improvements and the corresponding results are shown in the last three rows of Table 3. BBFE increases the AP of PANet and BFP by 0.9 and 1.0 points, respectively. However, using standard FPN after BBFE gets worse performance. As FPN focus on passing the semantic information down to the shallow layers one by one to enhance low-level features, it is not suitable for features already containing strong semantic information, which is the case of BBFE.

6   Discussion

Why can BBFE Improve Detection Performance? We take ResNet-50 Faster R-CNN (without FPN) for example. The feature activations output by all stages of ResNet-50 are denoted as $\{C_2, C_3, C_4, C_5\}$, which have semantics from shallow to deep layers. Inspired by CAM [38], we visualize the features to better understand their properties. As shown in Fig. 6, the redder area means richer semantic information. Intuitively, low-level features focus on the edge information, while high-level features focus on the semantic information of the object. The shallow layers are not suitable for detection due to the weak semantics. BBFE use the same convolutional layers on feature maps of different scales, which greatly alleviates this problem. The comparison of C_2 and P_2, C_3 and P_3 as well as C_4 and P_4 in Fig. 6 shows that BBFE can add semantic information into low level features and retain the original edge feature at the same time, so as to reasonably improve the detection capability.

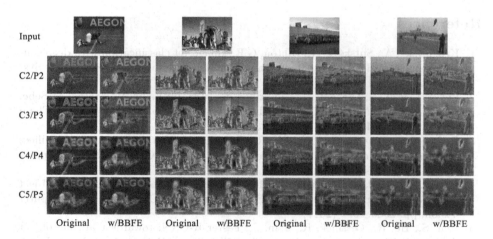

Fig. 6. Heatmap visualization. From top to bottom: the original image, feature maps from different depths of ConvNets. The odd columns represent the original features, and the even columns represent features enhanced by BBFE.

Runtime Analysis. ResNet-50-FPN can run at 12.6 FPS on 800×1333 input images, which outperforms ResNet-50-Fast-BBFE (11.7 FPS). However, as listed in Table 2, ResNet-50-Fast-BBFE runs at 14.6 FPS while ResNet-50-FPN only operates at 13.3 FPS on 600×1000 input images. Although the proposed BBFE obtains feature maps in parallel, the inference time of BBFE is limited on the slowest branch. Increasing the input resolution cause heavy computations, due to the size of largest feature maps. Conventional FPN runs slower than Fast-BBFE on smaller images as it needs to wait for the backbone to generate pyramidal feature hierarchy. However, it is less sensitive to the image resolutions, due to the down-sampling layers. All the runtimes are tested on a single Tesla V100 GPU.

7   Conclusion

In this paper, we propose a near parameter-free approach, named BBFE, to directly build a semantic feature pyramid from detection backbone without additional feature fusions. Compared with existing FPNs, our BBFE is simple and requires no hand-crafted effort by exploring the potential of backbone ConvNets. The experiments on COCO dataset demonstrate that our method can produce significant improvements upon mainstream detectors without any training or testing tricks. We also proposed Fast-BBFE to achieve better trade-off between accuracy and efficiency. Moreover, our approach can be combined with other FPNs to further improve the performance of object detection.

Acknowledgement. This work is supported by the National Natural Science Foundation of China (Grant No. 91959108 and U1713214).

References

1. Krizhevsky, A., Sutskever, I., Hinton, G.E.: ImageNet classification with deep convolutional neural networks. In: Advances in Neural Information Processing Systems, pp. 1097–1105 (2012)
2. Liu, W., et al.: SSD: single shot multibox detector. In: Leibe, B., Matas, J., Sebe, N., Welling, M. (eds.) ECCV 2016. LNCS, vol. 9905, pp. 21–37. Springer, Cham (2016). https://doi.org/10.1007/978-3-319-46448-0_2
3. Redmon, J., Divvala, S., Girshick, R., Farhadi, A.: You only look once: unified, real-time object detection. In: Proceedings of the IEEE Conference on Computer Vision and Pattern Recognition, pp. 779–788 (2016)
4. Lin, T.Y., Goyal, P., Girshick, R., He, K., Dollár, P.: Focal loss for dense object detection. In: Proceedings of the IEEE International Conference on Computer Vision, pp. 2980–2988 (2017)
5. Ren, S., He, K., Girshick, R., Jian, S.: Faster R-CNN: towards real-time object detection with region proposal networks. IEEE Trans. Pattern Anal. Mach. Intell. **39** (2015)
6. Cai, Z., Vasconcelos, N.: Cascade R-CNN: delving into high quality object detection. In: Proceedings of the IEEE Conference on Computer Vision and Pattern Recognition, pp. 6154–6162 (2018)

7. Adelson, E.H., Anderson, C.H., Bergen, J.R., Burt, P.J., Ogden, J.M.: Pyramid methods in image processing. RCA Eng. **29**, 33–41 (1984)
8. Lin, T.Y., Dollár, P., Girshick, R., He, K., Hariharan, B., Belongie, S.: Feature pyramid networks for object detection. In: Proceedings of the IEEE Conference on Computer Vision and Pattern Recognition, pp. 2117–2125 (2017)
9. Kong, T., Sun, F., Tan, C., Liu, H., Huang, W.: Deep feature pyramid reconfiguration for object detection. In: Proceedings of the European Conference on Computer Vision (ECCV), pp. 169–185 (2018)
10. Liu, S., Qi, L., Qin, H., Shi, J., Jia, J.: Path aggregation network for instance segmentation. In: Proceedings of the IEEE Conference on Computer Vision and Pattern Recognition, pp. 8759–8768 (2018)
11. Zhao, Q., et al.: M2Det: a single-shot object detector based on multi-level feature pyramid network. In: Proceedings of the AAAI Conference on Artificial Intelligence, vol. 33, pp. 9259–9266 (2019)
12. Dalal, N., Triggs, B.: Histograms of oriented gradients for human detection. In: 2005 IEEE Computer Society Conference on Computer Vision and Pattern Recognition (CVPR 2005), vol. 1, pp. 886–893. IEEE (2005)
13. Lowe, D.G.: Distinctive image features from scale-invariant keypoints. Int. J. Comput. Vis. **60**, 91–110 (2004)
14. Yang, F., Choi, W., Lin, Y.: Exploit all the layers: fast and accurate CNN object detector with scale dependent pooling and cascaded rejection classifiers. In: Proceedings of the IEEE Conference on Computer Vision and Pattern Recognition, pp. 2129–2137 (2016)
15. Cai, Z., Fan, Q., Feris, R.S., Vasconcelos, N.: A unified multi-scale deep convolutional neural network for fast object detection. In: Leibe, B., Matas, J., Sebe, N., Welling, M. (eds.) ECCV 2016. LNCS, vol. 9908, pp. 354–370. Springer, Cham (2016). https://doi.org/10.1007/978-3-319-46493-0_22
16. Liu, S., Huang, D., et al.: Receptive field block net for accurate and fast object detection. In: Proceedings of the European Conference on Computer Vision (ECCV), pp. 385–400 (2018)
17. Shen, Z., Liu, Z., Li, J., Jiang, Y.G., Chen, Y., Xue, X.: DSOD: learning deeply supervised object detectors from scratch. In: Proceedings of the IEEE International Conference on Computer Vision, pp. 1919–1927 (2017)
18. Pang, J., Chen, K., Shi, J., Feng, H., Ouyang, W., Lin, D.: Libra R-CNN: towards balanced learning for object detection. In: Proceedings of the IEEE Conference on Computer Vision and Pattern Recognition, pp. 821–830 (2019)
19. Wang, X., Girshick, R., Gupta, A., He, K.: Non-local neural networks. In: Proceedings of the IEEE Conference on Computer Vision and Pattern Recognition, pp. 7794–7803 (2018)
20. Ghiasi, G., Lin, T.Y., Le, Q.V.: NAS-FPN: learning scalable feature pyramid architecture for object detection. In: Proceedings of the IEEE Conference on Computer Vision and Pattern Recognition, pp. 7036–7045 (2019)
21. Zoph, B., Le, Q.V.: Neural architecture search with reinforcement learning. arXiv preprint arXiv:1611.01578 (2016)
22. Fu, C.Y., Liu, W., Ranga, A., Tyagi, A., Berg, A.C.: DSSD: deconvolutional single shot detector. arXiv preprint arXiv:1701.06659 (2017)
23. Shrivastava, A., Sukthankar, R., Malik, J., Gupta, A.: Beyond skip connections: top-down modulation for object detection. arXiv preprint arXiv:1612.06851 (2016)
24. Zhou, P., Ni, B., Geng, C., Hu, J., Xu, Y.: Scale-transferrable object detection. In: proceedings of the IEEE Conference on Computer Vision and Pattern Recognition, pp. 528–537 (2018)

25. Zhang, S., Wen, L., Bian, X., Lei, Z., Li, S.Z.: Single-shot refinement neural network for object detection. In: Proceedings of the IEEE Conference on Computer Vision and Pattern Recognition, pp. 4203–4212 (2018)
26. He, K., Zhang, X., Ren, S., Sun, J.: Deep residual learning for image recognition. In: Proceedings of the IEEE Conference on Computer Vision and Pattern Recognition, pp. 770–778 (2016)
27. Tian, Z., Shen, C., Chen, H., He, T.: FCOS: fully convolutional one-stage object detection. In: Proceedings of the IEEE International Conference on Computer Vision, pp. 9627–9636 (2019)
28. Yang, Z., Liu, S., Hu, H., Wang, L., Lin, S.: Reppoints: point set representation for object detection. In: Proceedings of the IEEE International Conference on Computer Vision, pp. 9657–9666 (2019)
29. Lin, T.-Y., et al.: Microsoft COCO: common objects in context. In: Fleet, D., Pajdla, T., Schiele, B., Tuytelaars, T. (eds.) ECCV 2014. LNCS, vol. 8693, pp. 740–755. Springer, Cham (2014). https://doi.org/10.1007/978-3-319-10602-1_48
30. Paszke, A., et al.: Pytorch: an imperative style, high-performance deep learning library. In: Advances in Neural Information Processing Systems, pp. 8026–8037 (2019)
31. Chen, K., et al.: MMDetection: open MMLab detection toolbox and benchmark. arXiv preprint arXiv:1906.07155 (2019)
32. Russakovsky, O., et al.: ImageNet large scale visual recognition challenge. Int. J. Comput. Vis. **115**, 211–252 (2015)
33. Redmon, J., Farhadi, A.: YOLOv3: an incremental improvement. arXiv preprint arXiv:1804.02767 (2018)
34. He, K., Gkioxari, G., Dollár, P., Girshick, R.: Mask R-CNN. In: Proceedings of the IEEE International Conference on Computer Vision, pp. 2961–2969 (2017)
35. Zhou, X., Zhuo, J., Krahenbuhl, P.: Bottom-up object detection by grouping extreme and center points. In: Proceedings of the IEEE Conference on Computer Vision and Pattern Recognition, pp. 850–859 (2019)
36. Law, H., Deng, J.: Cornernet: detecting objects as paired keypoints. In: Proceedings of the European Conference on Computer Vision (ECCV), pp. 734–750 (2018)
37. Wu, Y., He, K.: Group normalization. In: Proceedings of the European Conference on Computer Vision (ECCV), pp. 3–19 (2018)
38. Zhou, B., Khosla, A., Lapedriza, A., Oliva, A., Torralba, A.: Learning deep features for discriminative localization. In: Proceedings of the IEEE Conference on Computer Vision and Pattern Recognition, pp. 2921–2929 (2016)

Long-Term Cloth-Changing Person Re-identification

Xuelin Qian[1], Wenxuan Wang[1], Li Zhang[2], Fangrui Zhu[2], Yanwei Fu[2(✉)], Tao Xiang[3], Yu-Gang Jiang[1], and Xiangyang Xue[1,2]

[1] School of Computer Science, Shanghai Key Lab of Intelligent Information Processing, Fudan University, Shanghai, China
{xlqian15,wxwang19,ygj,xyxue}@fudan.edu.cn
[2] School of Data Science, and MOE Frontiers Center for Brain Science, Shanghai Key Lab of Intelligent Information Processing, Fudan University, Shanghai, China
{lizhangfd,18210980021,yanweifu}@fudan.edu.cn
[3] University of Surrey, Guildford, UK
t.xiang@surrey.ac.uk

Abstract. Person re-identification (Re-ID) aims to match a target person across camera views at different locations and times. Existing Re-ID studies focus on the short-term cloth-consistent setting, under which a person re-appears in different camera views with the same outfit. A discriminative feature representation learned by existing deep Re-ID models is thus dominated by the visual appearance of clothing. In this work, we focus on a much more difficult yet practical setting where person matching is conducted over long-duration, *e.g.*, over days and months and therefore inevitably under the new challenge of changing clothes. This problem, termed Long-Term Cloth-Changing (LTCC) Re-ID is much understudied due to the lack of large scale datasets. The first contribution of this work is a new LTCC dataset containing people captured over a long period of time with frequent clothing changes. As a second contribution, we propose a novel Re-ID method specifically designed to address the cloth-changing challenge. Specifically, we consider that under cloth-changes, soft-biometrics such as body shape would be more reliable. We, therefore, introduce a shape embedding module as well as a cloth-elimination shape-distillation module aiming to eliminate the now unreliable clothing appearance features and focus on the body shape information. Extensive experiments show that superior performance is achieved by the proposed model on the new LTCC dataset. The dataset is available on the project website: https://naiq.github.io/LTCC_Perosn_ReID.html.

Electronic supplementary material The online version of this chapter (https://doi.org/10.1007/978-3-030-69535-4_5) contains supplementary material, which is available to authorized users.

H. Ishikawa et al. (Eds.): ACCV 2020, LNCS 12624, pp. 71–88, 2021.
https://doi.org/10.1007/978-3-030-69535-4_5

1   Introduction

Person re-identification (Re-ID) aims at identifying and associating a person at different locations and times monitored by a distributed camera network. It underpins many crucial applications such as multi-camera tracking [1], crowd counting [2], and multi-camera activity analysis [3].

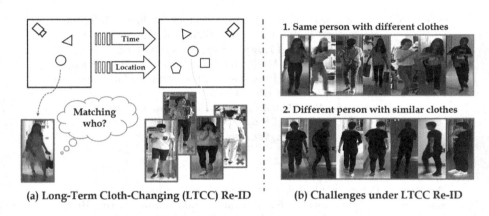

(a) Long-Term Cloth-Changing (LTCC) Re-ID   (b) Challenges under LTCC Re-ID

Fig. 1. Illustration of the long-term cloth-changing Re-ID task and dataset. The task is to match the same person under cloth-changes from different views, and the dataset contains same identities with diverse clothes.

Re-ID is inherently challenging as a person's appearance often undergoes dramatic changes across camera views. Such a challenge is captured in existing Re-ID datasets, including Market-1501 [4], DukeMTMC [5] and CUHK03 [6], where the appearance changes are caused by changes in body pose, illumination [7], occlusion [8–10] and camera view angle [11,12]. However, it is noted that in these popular datasets each person is captured across different camera views within a short period of time on the same day. As result, each wears the same outfit. We call the Re-ID under this setting as short-term cloth-consistent (STCC) Re-ID. This setting has a profound impact on the design of existing Re-ID models – most existing models are based on deep neural networks (DNNs) that extract feature representations invariant to these changes. Since faces are of too low resolutions to be useful, these representations are dominated by the clothing appearance.

In this paper, we focus on a more challenging yet practical new Long-Term Cloth-Changing (LTCC) setting (see Fig. 1 (a)). Under this setting, a person is matched over a much longer period of time, e.g., days or even months. As a result, clothing changes are commonplace, though different parts of the outfit undergo changes at different frequencies – the top is more often than the bottom and shoe changes are the least common. Such a setting is not only realistic but also crucial for certain applications. For instance, if the objective is to capture a criminal suspect after a crime is committed, he/she may change outfits even over short-term as a disguise. However, LTCC Re-ID is largely ignored so far. One primary reason is the lack of large-scale datasets featuring clothing changes.

The first contribution of this paper is thus to provide such a dataset to fill in the gap between research and real-world applications. The new Long-Term Cloth-Changing (LTCC) dataset (see Fig. 1 (b)) is collected over two months. It contains 17, 138 images of 152 identities with 478 different outfits captured from 12 camera views. This dataset was completed under pedestrian detection and careful manual labeling of both person identities and clothing outfit identities. Due to the long duration of data collection, it also features drastic illumination, viewing angle, and pose changes as in existing STCC datasets, but additionally clothing and carrying changes and occasionally hairstyle changes. Furthermore, it also includes many persons wearing similar clothing, as shown in Fig. 1 (b).

With cloth-changing now commonplace in LTCC Re-ID, existing Re-ID models are expected to struggle (see Table 1) because they assume that the clothing appearance is consistent and relies on clothing features to distinguish people from each other. Instead, it is now necessary to explore identity-relevant biological traits (*i.e.*, soft-biometrics) rather than cloth-sensitive appearance features. A number of naive approaches can be considered. First, can a DNN 'does the magic' again, *i.e.*, figures out automatically what information is cloth-change-invariant? The answer is no, because a) the soft-biometrics information is subtle and hard to compute without any network architectural change to assist in the extraction; and b) in a real-world, some people will wear the same outfit or at least keep part of the outfit unchanged (*e.g.*, shoes) even over a long duration. The network thus receives a mixed signal regarding what information is discriminative. Second, would adding a cloth-changing detector be a solution so that models can be switched accordingly? The answer is also negative since detecting changes for the same person needs person Re-ID to be solved in the first place.

To overcome these difficulties, we propose a novel DNN for LTCC Re-ID. The key idea is to remove the cloth-appearance related information completely and only focus on view/pose-change-insensitive body shape information. To this end, we introduce a Shape Embedding (SE) to help shape feature extraction and a Cloth-Elimination Shape-Distillation (CESD) module to eliminate cloth-related information. Concretely, the SE module aims to extract body pose features. This is achieved by encoding the position/semantic information of human body joints, and leveraging the relation network [13] to explore the implicit correlations between each pair of body joints. The CESD module, on the other hand, is designed to learn identity-relevant biological representation. Based on the features extracted from SE module, we adaptively distill the shape information by re-scaling the original image feature. To better disentangle the identity-relevant features from the residual (*i.e.*, the difference between the original information and the re-scaled shape information), we explicitly add the clothing identity constrain to ensure the identity-irrelevant clothing feature to be eliminated.

Contribution. Our contributions are as follows: (1) We introduce a new Long-Term Cloth-Changing (LTCC) dataset, designed to study the more challenging yet practical LTCC Re-ID problem. (2) We propose a novel model for LTCC Re-

ID. It contains a shape embedding module that efficiently extracts discriminative biological structural feature from keypoints, and a cloth-elimination shape-distillation module that learns to disentangle identity-relevant features from the cloth-appearance features. (3) Extensive experiments validate the efficacy of our Re-ID models in comparison with existing Re-ID models.

2   Related Work

Short-Term Cloth-Consistent Re-ID. With the popularization of surveillance system in the real-world, person re-identification task attracts more and more attention. As mentioned earlier, almost all existing Re-ID datasets [4,14,15] were captured during short-period of time. As a result, for the same person, the clothing appearances are more or less consistent. In the deep-learning era, more efforts have been made in developing approaches for automatic person re-identification by learning discriminative features [16,17] or robust distance metrics [18,19]. These models are robust against changes caused by pose, illumination and view angles as they are plenty in those datasets. However, they are vulnerable to clothing changes as the models are heavily reliant on the clothing appearance consistency.

Long-Term Cloth-Changing Re-ID Datasets. Barbosa et al. [20] proposed the first cloth-changing Re-ID dataset. However, the dataset is too small to be useful for deep learning based Re-ID. More recently iQIYI-VID [21] is introduced which is not purposefully built for LTCC but does contain some cloth-changing images. However, it is extracted from on-line videos, unrepresentative of real-world scenarios and lack of challenges caused illumination change and occlusion. Similarly, Huang et al. [22,23] collect Celebrities-ReID dataset containing clothing variations. Nevertheless, the celebrity images are captured in high quality by professional photographers, so unsuited for the main application of Re-ID, i.e. video surveillance using CCTV cameras. Another related work/dataset is Re-ID in photo albums [24,25]. It involves person detection and recognition with high-resolution images where face is the important clue to solve this task. However, this setting is not consistent with canonical Person Re-ID, where pedestrians are captured by non-overlapped surveillances with low resolution. Note that a concurrent work [26] also introduced an LTCC dataset, called PRCC which is still not released. Though featuring outfit changes, PRCC is a short-term cloth-changing dataset so it contains less drastic clothing changes and bare hairstyle changes. Further, with only 3 cameras instead of 12 in our LTCC dataset, it is limited in view-angle and illumination changes. In contrast, our LTCC Re-ID aims at matching persons over long time from more cameras, with more variations in visual appearance, e.g., holding different bags or cellphones, and wearing hats as shown in Fig. 1(b).

Long-Term Cloth-Changing Re-ID Models. Recently, Xue et al. [27] particularly address the cloth-change challenge by downplaying clothing information and emphasizing face. In our dataset, face resolution is too low to be useful and we take a more extreme approach to remove clothing information completely. Zheng *et al.* [17] propose to switch the appearance or structure codes and leverage the generated data to improve the learned Re-ID features. Yang *et al.* [26] introduce a method to capture the contour sketch representing the body features. These two works mainly focus on learning invariant and discriminative Re-ID features by taking clothing information into account. In contrast, our model focuses solely on extracting soft-biometries features and removes the model dependency on clothing information completely.

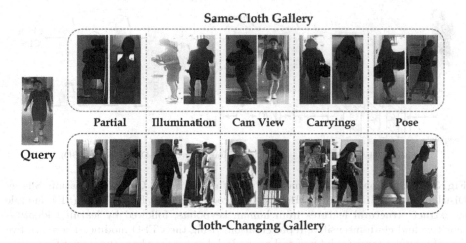

Fig. 2. Examples of one person wearing the same and different clothes in LTCC dataset. There exist various illumination, occlusion, camera view, carrying and pose changes.

3 Long-Term Cloth-Changing (LTCC) Dataset

Data Collection. To facilitate the study of LTCC Re-ID, we collect a new Long-Term Cloth-Changing (LTCC) person Re-ID dataset. Different from previous datasets [4–6,28], this dataset aims to support the research of long-term person re-identification with the added challenge of cloth changes. During dataset collection, an existing CCTV network is utilized which is composed of twelve cameras installed on three floors in an office building. A total of 24-h videos are captured over two months. Person images are then obtained by applying the Mask-RCNN [29] detector.

Statistics. We release the first version of LTCC dataset with this paper, which contains 17,138 person images of 152 identities, as shown in Fig. 2. Each identity is captured by at least two cameras. To further explore the cloth-changing Re-ID scenario, we assume that different people will not wear identical outfits (however visually similar they may be), and annotate each image with a cloth label as well.

Note that the changes of the hairstyle or carrying items, *e.g.*, hat, bag or laptop, do not affect the cloth label. Finally, dependent on whether there is a cloth-change, the dataset can be divided into two subsets: one cloth-change set where 91 persons appearing with 417 different sets of outfits in 14,756 images, and one cloth-consistent subset containing the remaining 61 identities with 2,382 images without outfit changes. On average, there are 5 different clothes for each cloth-changing person, with the numbers of outfit changes ranging from 2 to 14.

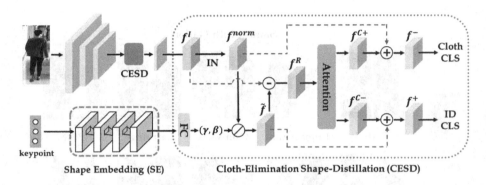

Fig. 3. Illustration of our framework and the details of Cloth-Elimination Shape-Distillation (CESD) module. Here, we introduce Shape Embedding (SE) module to extract structural features from human keypoints, followed by learning identity-sensitive and cloth-insensitive representations using the CESD module. There are two CESD modules (green solid box and green dash box). Both share the same SE module, but we only show the detail of CESD in the second one. '$\oslash$' denotes the operation of re-scale in the Eq. 4. (Color figure online)

Comparison with Previous Datasets. Comparing to the most widely-used cloth-consistent Re-ID datasets such [4–6], our dataset is gathered primarily to address the new LTCC Re-ID task, which challenges the Re-ID under a more realistic yet difficult setting. Comparing to few cloth-changing datasets [22,30], ours is collected in a natural and long-term way without any human intervention. Concretely, our dataset includes not only various cloth-changing (*e.g.*, top, bottom, shoe-wear), but also diverse human pose (*e.g.*, squat, run, jump, push, bow), large changes of illumination (*e.g.*, from day to night, indoor lighting) and large variations of occlusion (*e.g.*, self-occlusion, partial), as shown in Fig. 2. More details can be found in Supplementary Material.

4 Methodology

Under the LTCC Re-ID setting, the clothing appearance becomes unreliable and can be considered as a distraction for Re-ID. We thus aim to learn to extract biological traits related to soft biometrics, with a particular focus on body shape information in this work. Unfortunately, learning the identity-sensitive feature directly from body shape [31] is a challenging problem on its own. Considering the recent success in body parsing or human body pose estimation [32] from RGB images, we propose to extract identity-discriminative shape information whilst eliminating clothing information with the help of an off-the-shelf body pose estimation model. Specifically, given a generic DNN backbone, we first introduce a Shape Embedding (SE) module to encode shape information from human body keypoints. Then we propose a Cloth-Elimination Shape-Distillation (CESD) module, which is able to utilize shape embedding to adaptively distill the identity-relevant shape feature and explicitly disentangle the identity-irrelevant clothing information.

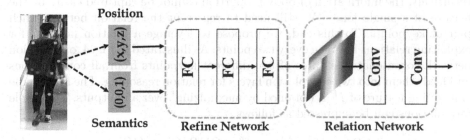

Fig. 4. The detailed structure of the Shape Embedding (SE) module.

4.1 Shape Embedding (SE)

Humans can easily recognize an old friend in an unseen outfit from the back (no face). We conjecture that this is because the body shape information is discriminative enough for person identification. Here, 'shape' is a general term referring to several *unique* biological traits, *e.g.*, stature and body-part proportion. One intuitive way to represent body shape is to employ joints of human body and model the relations between each pair of points. For example, the relation between points of left-shoulder and left-hip reflects the height of the upper body.

Representation. We employ an off-the-shelf pose detector [33,34], which is trained without using any re-id benchmark data, to detect and localize n human body joints as shown in Fig. 4. Each point n_i is represented by two attributes, position P_i and semantics S_i (*i.e.*, corresponding to which body joint). Concretely, $P_i = (\frac{x_i}{w}, \frac{y_i}{h}, \frac{w}{h})$ where (x_i, y_i) denotes the coordinates of joint i in the person image and (w, h) represents the original width and height of the image. S_i is a n-dimensional one-hot vector to index the keypoint i (*e.g.*, head and knee). If one of the points is undetectable, we set P_i as $(-1, -1, \frac{w}{h})$.

Embedding. The two keypoint representation parts are first encoded with learnable embedding weights W individually. Then, we employ a refinement network to integrate the two parts and improve the representation of each keypoint, which can be formulated as

$$f_i = \mathcal{F}\left(W_p P_i^{\mathsf{T}} + W_s S_i^{\mathsf{T}}\right) \in \mathbb{R}^{d_2}, \tag{1}$$

where $W_p \in \mathbb{R}^{d_1 \times 3}$ and $W_s \in \mathbb{R}^{d_1 \times 13}$ are two different embedding weights; $\mathcal{F}(\cdot)$ denotes the refinement network with several fully-connected layers to increase the dimension from d_1 to d_2. In this paper, we have two hidden layers and set $d_1 = 128$, $d_2 = 2048$.

After the embedding, we now obtain a set of keypoint features $f \in \mathbb{R}^{n \times d_2}$. Intuitively, the information of body proportion cannot be captured easily by the feature of a single joint. We still need to represent the relation between each pair of keypoints. To this end, we propose to leverage a relation network for exploiting relations between every two points. As illustrated in Fig. 4, our relation network concatenates features of two different keypoints from all combinations and feeds them into two convolution layers for relation reasoning. The final shape embedding feature of f^P is obtained by maximizing[1] over all outputs. The whole formulations can be expressed as follows,

$$H_{ij} = [f_i \; ; \; f_j], \qquad f^p = \mathrm{GMP}\left(Conv_\theta(H)\right) \tag{2}$$

where $f^P \in \mathbb{R}^{d_2}$ and $H \in \mathbb{R}^{n \times n \times d_2}$; GMP and θ denote global max pooling and parameters of convolution layers, respectively. $[*; *]$ denotes the operation of concatenation.

4.2   Cloth-Elimination Shape-Distillation (CESD)

Person images contain clothing and shape information. Disentangling the two and focusing on the latter is the main idea behind our model for LTCC Re-ID. Recently, many works on visual reasoning [35,36] or style transfer [37,38] are proposed to solve a related similar problem with adaptive normalization. Inspired by these works, we introduce a cloth-elimination shape-distillation module. It is designed to utilize the shape embedding to explicitly disentangle the clothing and discriminative shape information from person images[2]. The final extracted feature thus contains the information transferred from shape embedding and the ones from a task-driven attention mechanism. Specifically, we denote both the input image and shape features by $f^I \in \mathbb{R}^{h \times w \times c}$ and $f^P \in \mathbb{R}^{d_2}$, where h, w, c indicate the height, width and number of channel, respectively.

---

[1] Max pooling is found to be more effective than alternatives such as avg pooling; possible reason is that it is more robust against body pose undergoing dramatic changes.

[2] We found empirically that directly using shape embeddings as Re-ID features leads to worse performance. A likely reason is that the detected 2D keypoints may be unreliable due to occlusion. So, we treat them as intermediate ancillary features.

Shape Distillation. Inspired by adaptive instance normalization [37], we first try to reduce the original style information in the input by performing instance normalization [39]. Then, we distill the shape information by re-scaling the normalized feature with the parameters γ and β calculated from f^P. These two steps can be expressed as,

$$f^{norm} = \frac{f^I - \mathrm{E}\left[f^I\right]}{\sqrt{\mathrm{Var}\left[f^I\right] - \epsilon}}, \tag{3}$$

$$\begin{aligned} \widetilde{f} = (1 + \Delta\gamma)\, f^{norm} + \beta, \\ where\ \Delta\gamma = \mathcal{G}_s\left(f^P\right),\quad \beta = \mathcal{G}_b\left(f^P\right) \end{aligned} \tag{4}$$

where $\mathrm{E}\left[\cdot\right]$ and $\mathrm{Var}\left[\cdot\right]$ denote the mean and variance of image features calculated per-dimension separately for each sample; $\mathcal{G}_s\left(\cdot\right)$ and $\mathcal{G}_b\left(\cdot\right)$ are both one fully-connected layer to learn new parameters of scale and bias. Particularly, rather than directly predicting γ, we output the offset $\Delta\gamma$ in case of re-scaling factor value for the feature activation being too low.

Cloth Elimination. To further enhance the representation of identity-sensitive but cloth-insensitive feature, we propose to eliminate the identity-irrelevant clothing clue from the final image features. As shown in Fig. 3, given the image feature f^I and the transferred feature $\widetilde{f}$, we first obtain the residual feature $f^R \in \mathbb{R}^{h \times w \times c}$ by computing the difference between f^I and $\widetilde{f}$,

$$f^R = f^I - \widetilde{f} \tag{5}$$

For f^R, it inevitably includes some discriminative features (e.g., contour) and features that are sensitive to cloth changes. Since reducing intra-distance of the same identity with different clothing is the primary objective here, we propose to leverage the self-attention mechanism to explicitly disentangle the residual feature into two parts, the cloth-irrelevant feature $f^{C-} \in \mathbb{R}^{h \times w \times c}$ and the cloth-relevant feature $f^{C+} \in \mathbb{R}^{h \times w \times c}$, which can be formulated as follows,

$$\alpha = \phi\left(\mathcal{G}^2\left(\mathrm{GAP}\left(f^R\right)\right)\right), \tag{6}$$

$$f^{C+} = \alpha f^R,\quad f^{C-} = (1 - \alpha) f^R \tag{7}$$

where $\mathcal{G}^i$ denotes the i-th layer of a convolution neural network with ReLU activation function, GAP is the global average pooling operation, ϕ is a sigmoid activation function and $\alpha \in \mathbb{R}^{1 \times 1 \times c}$ is the learned attention weights.

By adding the cloth-irrelevant feature f^{C-} to the re-scaled shape feature $\widetilde{f}$, we add one more convolutional layer to refine it and obtain the identity-relevant feature of f^+. Analogously, we sum the cloth-relevant feature f^{C+} and the normalized feature f^{norm} followed by a different convolutional layer to get the final cloth-relevant feature f^-, that is,

$$f^+ = \mathrm{Conv}_\theta\left(\widetilde{f} + f^{C-}\right),\quad f^- = \mathrm{Conv}_\phi\left(f^{norm} + f^{C+}\right). \tag{8}$$

4.3   Architecture Details

Figure 3 gives an overview of our framework. Particularly, a widely-used network of ResNet-50 [40] is employed as our backbone for image feature embedding. We insert the proposed CESD module after *res3* and *res4* blocks. For each CESD module, we apply two classification losses (person ID and cloth ID) to support the learning of identity-relevant feature f^+ and cloth-relevant feature f^- respectively. Therefore, the overall loss of our framework is,

$$\mathcal{L} = \sum_{i=1}^{2} \lambda_i \mathcal{L}^i_{clothing} + \sum_{i=1}^{2} \mu_i \mathcal{L}^i_{id}, \tag{9}$$

where $\mathcal{L}^i_{clothing}$ and $\mathcal{L}^i_{id}$ denote the cross-entropy loss of clothing and identity classification from the i-th CESD module, respectively; λ_i and μ_i are both coefficients which control the contribution of each term. Intuitively, the feature at the deeper layer is more important and more relevant to the task, thus, we empirically set λ_1, λ_2 to $0.3, 0.6$ and μ_1, μ_2 to $0.5, 1.0$ in all experiments.

5   Experiment

5.1   Experimental Setup

Implementation Details. Our model is implemented on the Pytorch framework, and we utilize the weights of ResNet-50 pretrained on ImageNet [41] for initialization. For key points, we first employ the model from [33,34] for human joints detection to obtain 17 key points. Then, we average 5 points from face (*i.e.*, nose, ear, eye) as one point of 'face', given us the 13 human key joints and their corresponding coordinates. During training, the input images are resized to 384×192 and we only apply random erasing [42] for data augmentation. SGD is utilized as the optimizer to train networks with mini-batch 32, momentum 0.9, and the weight decay factor for L2 regularization is set to 0.0005. Our model is trained on one NVIDIA TITAN Xp GPU for total 120 epochs with an initial learning rate of 0.01 and a reduction factor of 0.1 every 40 epochs. During testing, we concatenate features f^+ from all CESD modules as the final feature.

Evaluation Settings. We randomly split the LTCC dataset into training and testing sets. The training set consists of 77 identities, where 46 people have cloth changes and the rest of 31 people wear the same outfits during recording. Similarly, the testing set contains 45 people with changing clothes and 30 people wearing the same outfits. Unless otherwise specified, we use all training samples for training. For better analyzing the results of long-term cloth-changing Re-ID in detail, we introduce two test settings, as follows, (1) *Standard Setting*: Following the evaluation in [4], the images in the test set with the same identity and the same camera view are discarded when computing evaluation scores, *i.e.*, Rank-k and mAP. In other words, the test set contains both cloth-consistent and cloth-changing examples. (2) *Cloth-changing Setting*: Different from [4], the images with same identity, camera view and clothes are discarded during testing. This setting examines specifically how well a Re-ID model copes with cloth changes.

Table 1. Results comparisons of our model and other competitors. 'Standard' and 'Cloth-changing' mean the standard setting and cloth-changing setting, respectively. '(Image)' or '(Parsing)' represents that the input data is person image or body parsing. '†' denotes that only identities with clothes changing are used for training. '§' indicates our simple implementation of the siamese network using face images detected by [43].

Methods	Standard		Cloth-changing		Standard[†]		Cloth-changing[†]	
	Rank-1	mAP	Rank-1	mAP	Rank-1	mAP	Rank-1	mAP
LOMO [44] + KISSME [45]	26.57	9.11	10.75	5.25	19.47	7.37	8.32	4.37
LOMO [44] + XQDA [44]	25.35	9.54	10.95	5.56	22.52	8.21	10.55	4.95
LOMO [44] + NullSpace [46]	34.83	11.92	16.45	6.29	27.59	9.43	13.37	5.34
ResNet-50 (Image) [40]	58.82	25.98	20.08	9.02	57.20	22.82	20.68	8.38
PCB (Image) [47]	65.11	30.60	23.52	10.03	59.22	26.61	21.93	8.81
HACNN [48]	60.24	26.71	21.59	9.25	57.12	23.48	20.81	8.27
MuDeep [49]	61.86	27.52	23.53	10.23	56.99	24.10	18.66	8.76
OSNet [47]	67.86	32.14	23.92	10.76	63.48	29.34	24.15	10.13
ResNet-50 (Parsing) [40]	19.87	6.64	7.51	3.75	18.86	6.16	6.28	3.46
PCB (Parsing) [47]	27.38	9.16	9.33	4.50	25.96	7.77	10.54	4.04
ResNet-50 + Face[§] [27]	60.44	25.42	22.10	9.44	55.37	22.23	20.68	8.99
Ours	**71.39**	**34.31**	**26.15**	**12.40**	**66.73**	**31.29**	**25.15**	**11.67**

5.2 Comparative Results

LTCC Dataset. We evaluate our proposed method on the LTCC dataset and compare it with several competitors, including hand-crafted features of LOMO [44] + KISSME [45], LOMO [44] + XQDA [44], LOMO [44] + NullSpace [46], deep learning baseline as ResNet-50 [40], PCB [47], and strong Re-ID methods MuDeep [49], OSNet [47] and HACNN[3] [48]. In addition, we try to leverage human parsing images, which are semantic maps containing body structure information [50]. Please find more quantitative and qualitative studies in Supplementary Material.

A number of observations can be made from results in Table 1. (1) Our method beats all competitors with a clear margin under both evaluation settings. As expected, the re-identification results under the cloth-changing setting are much lower than the standard setting, which verify the difficulty of LTCC Re-ID. Under cloth-changing setting, where the training and testing identities both with different clothes, our method surpass the general baseline 'ResNet-50 (Image)' with 4.47%/3.29% of Rank-1/mAP, and it also outperforms strong baseline 'PCB (Image)' by 3.22%/2.86%. (2) Meanwhile, our model also achieves better results than those advanced Re-ID methods, where some of them are designed with multi-scale or attention mechanism to extract more discriminative features under the general Re-ID problem. Such results indicate that our proposed method can better eliminate negative impact of cloth changes and explore more soft-biometrics identity-relevant features. (3) Following the idea of [27],

---

[3] OSNet is trained with the size of 384×192 and the cross-entropy loss as ours for a fair comparison. HACNN is trained with 160×64 as required by the official code.

we build a siamese network applying the information of face for LTCC Re-ID. Intuitively, more information, *i.e.*, face, leads to better performance. However, face feature is sensitive to factors of illumination, occlusion and resolution, so it is not the optimal way for the cloth-changing Re-ID. (4) Comparing the performance of 'ResNet-50 (Parsing)' and 'ResNet-50 (Image)', as well as 'PCB (Parsing)' and 'PCB (Image)', we can find that the models trained on person images have superior accuracy than those using parsing. This suggests that the identity-sensitive structural information is hard to capture directly from images. As a result, applying it alone for re-identification is unhelpful.

Table 2. Results of the multi-shot setting on BIWI dataset. '*' denotes the results are reported from original paper [26]. Note that, the same baselines (*i.e.*, ResNet-50 [40], PCB [47]) implemented by us yield better results than those reported in [26].

Methods	Still setting		Walking setting	
	Rank-1	Rank-5	Rank-1	Rank-5
ResNet-50 [40]	41.26	65.13	37.08	65.01
PCB [47]	46.36	72.37	37.89	**70.21**
SPT+ASE* [26]	21.31	66.10	18.66	63.88
HACNN [48]	42.71	64.89	37.32	64.27
MuDeep [49]	43.46	**73.80**	38.41	65.35
OSNet [51]	47.14	72.52	38.87	61.22
Ours	**49.51**	71.44	**39.80**	66.23

BIWI Dataset. Additional experimental results on BIWI [30] dataset are further presented and discussed. Please refer to Supplementary Material for more details about dataset introduction and implementation details. From the results shown in Table 2, we can make the following observations: (1) Our method achieves the highest performance on Rank-1 at both settings (Rank-1 of 49.51% and 39.80% compared to the closest competitor OSNet [51] which gives 47.14% and 38.87% at Still and Walking setting respectively). (2) Our method beats the state-of-the-art competitor SPT+ASE [26], which is designed for cloth-changing re-ID specifically, by over 28% and 21% on Rank-1 under the Still and Walking setting, respectively. Note that we adopt the same training/test split and pretrain strategy as SPT+ASE [26]. (3) We also notice that the performance of Still setting are generally higher than the Walking setting. This confirms the conclusion drawn in the main paper as 'Still' subset involve fewer variations of pose and occlusions.

5.3 Ablation Study

Effectiveness of Shape Embedding Module. Our shape embedding (SE) module is designed to exploit the shape information from human joints, so that

Table 3. Comparing the contributions of each component in our method on LTCC dataset. 'w/ Cloth label' means the model is also trained with clothes labels. 'RN' and 'Attn' refer to the relation network and the design of self-attention in CESD module, respectively. 'w/ single CESD' indicates that we only insert one CESD module after res4 block. Note that all models of variants are trained only with images of identities who have more than one outfit.

Methods	Standard setting			Cloth-changing setting		
	Rank-1	Rank-5	mAP	Rank-1	Rank-5	mAP
ResNet-50 [40]	57.20	71.19	22.82	20.68	31.84	8.38
ResNet-50 [40] w/ Cloth label	63.08	75.05	29.16	20.89	31.64	9.46
Ours w/o SE	65.92	76.29	29.84	22.10	31.86	10.28
Ours w/o RN	65.51	75.89	29.37	21.29	31.67	10.05
Ours w/o Attn	64.09	76.70	28.82	22.31	34.12	9.78
Ours w/ single CESD	64.21	**77.51**	29.46	23.73	34.30	10.19
Ours	**66.73**	77.48	**31.29**	**25.15**	**34.48**	**11.67**

it can facilitate the task of long-term cloth-changing Re-ID. Here, we compare several variants to evaluate its effectiveness. 'Ours w/o SE': a model without the SE module. 'Ours w/o RN': a model where the keypoint feature in SE module is encoded directly with several FC layers instead of the relation network.

We have three observations from the results in Table 3. (1) The variants of 'Ours w/o SE' and 'Ours w/o RN' achieve very similar results and both are clearly inferior to the full model. It clearly verifies that the shape information can be better encoded with the relations between two different points rather than the feature from an individual point. (2) With the information from human body shape, 'Ours' obtains a better performance than 'Ours w/o SE' (about 3% higher on Rank-1), which demonstrates the effectiveness of our shape embedding module. (3) Comparing the gap of our model with/without SE module between two different settings, we notice that the shape information contributes about 1% to the accuracy of Rank-1 under the standard setting, but 3 points under the cloth-changing setting, which shows that under the LTCC ReID task, the biological traits, e.g., body shape, is more important and helpful.

Effectiveness of Cloth-Elimination Shape-Distillation Module. Our proposed CESD module aims to distill the shape features and remove the cloth-relevant features from the input. We consider three variants in the analysis. Concretely, we first compare our full model with 'ResNet50 w/ Cloth label', whereby a vanilla ResNet-50 is trained with identity and clothes labels. The results under the two settings in Table 3 show that the clothes label helps the model a bit under the standard setting but not on the more challenging cloth-changing setting. Meanwhile, it is clear that it is our model rather than the clothes label that plays the main part. Secondly, we compare our full model with 'Ours w/o Attn', where a variant removes the self-attention block. It shows that 'Ours' gets about 2–3% higher accuracy on Rank-1/mAP under both settings,

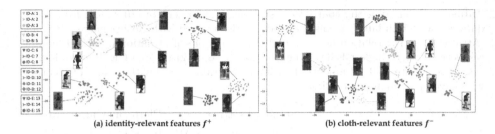

(a) identity-relevant features f^+ (b) cloth-relevant features f^-

Fig. 5. Visualization of the identity-relevant features and cloth-relevant features learned from CESD using t-SNE [52]. In (a) and (b), each color represents one identity which is randomly selected from the testing set, and each symbol (circle, rhombus, triangle, cross, *etc.*) with various color indicates different clothes. In the legend, the capital letters behind the 'ID' indicate the identity labels, and the numbers are used to represent the clothing category. Best viewed in color and zoomed in. (Color figure online)

which clearly suggests the benefit of the proposed CESD module on LTCC Re-ID by explicitly disentangling and eliminating the cloth-relevant features. Considering the features from the last two blocks of ResNet-50 are deep features, which are more relevant to the specific task, we then evaluate the effect of different number of CESD modules. From Table 3, we can conclude that inserting one CESD module after *res3* and *res4* blocks individually is better than 'Ours w/ single CESD', which achieves around 2 points higher on Rank-1 and mAP. It further demonstrates the effectiveness of our CESD module.

Visualization of Features Learned from CESD. As described in Sect. 4, our CESD module can disentangle the input feature into two spaces, the identity-relevant and the cloth-relevant. To verify our motivation and better understand its objective, we visualize the learned features from the last CESD module using t-SNE [52]. Specifically, we randomly select images of five identities in the testing set, and each of them appeared in more than one outfits. We can observe that (1) with the overview of Fig. 5, the samples with the same identity are clustered using identity-relevant feature f^+, and the distances between images which have similar appearances are closer than those with large clothing discrepancy based on the cloth-relevant feature f^-. (2) As for Fig. 5 (b), images with warm color appearances are clustered at the top of feature space, and those with cold color are centered at the lower right corner. For example, the girl wearing a khaki dress (blue circle) has more similar appearance feature f^- to the boy with pink shorts (pink circle), and images at the bottom of the space are clustered due to wearing similar dark clothes. (3) In the identity-relevant feature space of Fig. 5 (a), identities denoted by blue, yellow and purple have smaller intra-class distances comparing with the distances in the cloth-relevant space in (b). (4) Interestingly, there is a special case denoted by a yellow inverted triangle in both spaces. His body shape is similar to the pink one, so in (a) he is aggregated closer to the pink cluster. Meanwhile, he, wearing black pants and dark shorts (affected by illumination), is surrounded by the images having dark clothes in (b). In conclusion, our model can successfully disentangle the identity-relevant features with the cloth-relevant features.

6 Conclusion

In this paper, to study the Re-ID problem under more realistic conditions, we focus on Long-Term Cloth-Changing (LTCC) Re-ID, and introduce a new large-scale LTCC Dataset, which has no cloth-consistency constraint. LTCC has 152 identities with 478 different clothes of 17,128 images from 12 cameras, and among them, there are 91 persons showing clothing changes. To further solve the problem of dramatic appearance changes, we propose a task-driven method, which can learn identity-sensitive and cloth-insensitive representations. We utilize the relation between the human keypoints to extract biological structural features and apply attention mechanism to disentangle the identity-relevant features from clothing-related information. The effectiveness of proposed method is validated through extensive experiments.

Acknowledgment. This work was supported in part by Science and Technology Commission of Shanghai Municipality Projects (19511120700, 19ZR1471800), NSFC Projects (U62076067, U1611461).

References

1. Wang, X., Tieu, K., Grimson, W.: Correspondence-free multi-camera activity analysis and scene modeling. In: IEEE Conference on Computer Vision and Pattern Recognition (2008)
2. Chan, A., Vasconcelos, N.: Bayesian poisson regression for crowd counting. In: IEEE International Conference on Computer Vision (2009)
3. Berclaz, J., Fleuret, F., Fua, P.: Multi-camera tracking and atypical motion detection with behavioral maps. In: Forsyth, D., Torr, P., Zisserman, A. (eds.) ECCV 2008. LNCS, vol. 5304, pp. 112–125. Springer, Heidelberg (2008). https://doi.org/10.1007/978-3-540-88690-7_9
4. Zheng, L., Shen, L., Tian, L., Wang, S., Wang, J., Tian, Q.: Scalable person re-identification: a benchmark. In: IEEE International Conference on Computer Vision (2015)
5. Zheng, Z., Zheng, L., Yang, Y.: Unlabeled samples generated by GAN improve the person re-identification baseline in vitro. In: IEEE International Conference on Computer Vision (2017)
6. Li, W., Zhao, R., Xiao, T., Wang, X.: Deepreid: deep filter pairing neural network for person re-identification. In: IEEE Conference on Computer Vision and Pattern Recognition (2014)
7. Bąk, S., Carr, P., Lalonde, J.-F.: Domain adaptation through synthesis for unsupervised person re-identification. In: Ferrari, V., Hebert, M., Sminchisescu, C., Weiss, Y. (eds.) ECCV 2018. LNCS, vol. 11217, pp. 193–209. Springer, Cham (2018). https://doi.org/10.1007/978-3-030-01261-8_12

8. Zheng, W.S., Li, X., Xiang, T., Liao, S., Lai, J., Gong, S.: Partial person re-identification. In: IEEE International Conference on Computer Vision (2015)
9. Miao, J., Wu, Y., Liu, P., Ding, Y., Yang, Y.: Pose-guided feature alignment for occluded person re-identification. In: IEEE International Conference on Computer Vision (2019)
10. He, L., Wang, Y., Liu, W., Zhao, H., Sun, Z., Feng, J.: Foreground-aware pyramid reconstruction for alignment-free occluded person re-identification. In: IEEE International Conference on Computer Vision (2019)
11. Qian, X., et al.: Pose-normalized image generation for person re-identification. In: Ferrari, V., Hebert, M., Sminchisescu, C., Weiss, Y. (eds.) ECCV 2018. LNCS, vol. 11213, pp. 661–678. Springer, Cham (2018). https://doi.org/10.1007/978-3-030-01240-3_40
12. Sun, X., Zheng, L.: Dissecting person re-identification from the viewpoint of viewpoint. In: IEEE Conference on Computer Vision and Pattern Recognition (2019)
13. Santoro, A., et al.: A simple neural network module for relational reasoning. In: Neural Information Processing Systems (2017)
14. Wei, L., Zhang, S., Gao, W., Tian, Q.: Person transfer GAN to bridge domain gap for person re-identification. In: IEEE Conference on Computer Vision and Pattern Recognition (2018)
15. Ristani, E., Solera, F., Zou, R., Cucchiara, R., Tomasi, C.: Performance measures and a data set for multi-target, multi-camera tracking. In: Hua, G., Jégou, H. (eds.) ECCV 2016. LNCS, vol. 9914, pp. 17–35. Springer, Cham (2016). https://doi.org/10.1007/978-3-319-48881-3_2
16. Wang, G., Yang, Y., Cheng, J., Wang, J., Hou, Z.: Color-sensitive person re-identification. In: International Joint Conference on Artificial Intelligence (2019)
17. Zheng, Z., Yang, X., Yu, Z., Zheng, L., Yang, Y., Kautz, J.: Joint discriminative and generative learning for person re-identification. In: IEEE Conference on Computer Vision and Pattern Recognition (2019)
18. Paisitkriangkrai, S., Shen, C., van den Hengel, A.: Learning to rank in person re-identification with metric ensembles. In: IEEE Conference on Computer Vision and Pattern Recognition (2015)
19. Shen, Y., Xiao, T., Li, H., Yi, S., Wang, X.: End-to-end deep kronecker-product matching for person re-identification. In: IEEE Conference on Computer Vision and Pattern Recognition (2018)
20. Barbosa, I.B., Cristani, M., Del Bue, A., Bazzani, L., Murino, V.: Re-identification with RGB-D sensors. In: Fusiello, A., Murino, V., Cucchiara, R. (eds.) ECCV 2012. LNCS, vol. 7583, pp. 433–442. Springer, Heidelberg (2012). https://doi.org/10.1007/978-3-642-33863-2_43
21. Liu, Y., et al.: IQIYI-VID: a large dataset for multi-modal person identification. arXiv preprint arXiv:1811.07548 (2018)
22. Huang, Y., Wu, Q., Xu, J., Zhong, Y.: Celebrities-ReID: a benchmark for clothes variation in long-term person re-identification. In: International Joint Conference on Neural Networks (2019)
23. Huang, Y., Xu, J., Wu, Q., Zhong, Y., Zhang, P., Zhang, Z.: Beyond scalar neuron: adopting vector-neuron capsules for long-term person re-identification. IEEE Trans. Circuits Syst. Video Technol. **30**, 3459–3471 (2019)
24. Joon Oh, S., Benenson, R., Fritz, M., Schiele, B.: Person recognition in personal photo collections. In: IEEE International Conference on Computer Vision (2015)
25. Zhang, N., Paluri, M., Taigman, Y., Fergus, R., Bourdev, L.: Beyond frontal faces: improving person recognition using multiple cues. In: IEEE Conference on Computer Vision and Pattern Recognition (2015)

26. Yang, Q., Wu, A., Zheng, W.S.: Person re-identification by contour sketch under moderate clothing change. IEEE Trans. Pattern Anal. Mach. Intell. (2019)
27. Xue, J., Meng, Z., Katipally, K., Wang, H., van Zon, K.: Clothing change aware person identification. In: IEEE Conference on Computer Vision and Pattern Recognition Workshops (2018)
28. Li, W., Zhao, R., Wang, X.: Human reidentification with transferred metric learning. In: Lee, K.M., Matsushita, Y., Rehg, J.M., Hu, Z. (eds.) ACCV 2012. LNCS, vol. 7724, pp. 31–44. Springer, Heidelberg (2013). https://doi.org/10.1007/978-3-642-37331-2_3
29. He, K., Gkioxari, G., Dollár, P., Girshick, R.: Mask R-CNN. In: IEEE International Conference on Computer Vision (2017)
30. Munaro, M., Fossati, A., Basso, A., Menegatti, E., Van Gool, L.: One-shot person re-identification with a consumer depth camera. In: Gong, S., Cristani, M., Yan, S., Loy, C.C. (eds.) Person Re-Identification. ACVPR, pp. 161–181. Springer, London (2014). https://doi.org/10.1007/978-1-4471-6296-4_8
31. Chao, H., He, Y., Zhang, J., Feng, J.: Gaitset: regarding gait as a set for cross-view gait recognition. In: AAAI Conference on Artificial Intelligence (2019)
32. Liang, X., Gong, K., Shen, X., Lin, L.: Look into person: joint body parsing & pose estimation network and a new benchmark. IEEE Trans. Pattern Anal. Mach. Intell. **41**, 871–885 (2018)
33. Fang, H.S., Xie, S., Tai, Y.W., Lu, C.: RMPE: regional multi-person pose estimation. In: IEEE International Conference on Computer Vision (2017)
34. Xiu, Y., Li, J., Wang, H., Fang, Y., Lu, C.: Pose flow: efficient online pose tracking. In: British Machine Vision Conference (2018)
35. Perez, E., De Vries, H., Strub, F., Dumoulin, V., Courville, A.: Learning visual reasoning without strong priors. arXiv preprint arXiv:1707.03017 (2017)
36. Perez, E., Strub, F., De Vries, H., Dumoulin, V., Courville, A.: Film: visual reasoning with a general conditioning layer. In: AAAI Conference on Artificial Intelligence (2018)
37. Huang, X., Belongie, S.: Arbitrary style transfer in real-time with adaptive instance normalization. In: IEEE International Conference on Computer Vision (2017)
38. Ghiasi, G., Lee, H., Kudlur, M., Dumoulin, V., Shlens, J.: Exploring the structure of a real-time, arbitrary neural artistic stylization network. arXiv preprint arXiv:1705.06830 (2017)
39. Ulyanov, D., Vedaldi, A., Lempitsky, V.: Instance normalization: the missing ingredient for fast stylization. arXiv preprint arXiv:1607.08022 (2016)
40. He, K., Zhang, X., Ren, S., Sun, J.: Deep residual learning for image recognition. In: IEEE Conference on Computer Vision and Pattern Recognition (2015)
41. Deng, J., Dong, W., Socher, R., Li, L.J., Li, K., Fei-Fei, L.: ImageNet: a large-scale hierarchical image database. In: IEEE Conference on Computer Vision and Pattern Recognition (2009)
42. Zhong, Z., Zheng, L., Kang, G., Li, S., Yang, Y.: Random erasing data augmentation. arXiv preprint arXiv:1708.04896 (2017)
43. Tang, X., Du, D.K., He, Z., Liu, J.: PyramidBox: a context-assisted single shot face detector. In: Ferrari, V., Hebert, M., Sminchisescu, C., Weiss, Y. (eds.) ECCV 2018. LNCS, vol. 11213, pp. 812–828. Springer, Cham (2018). https://doi.org/10.1007/978-3-030-01240-3_49
44. Liao, S., Hu, Y., Zhu, X., Li., S.Z.: Person re-identification by local maximal occurrence representation and metric learning. In: IEEE Conference on Computer Vision and Pattern Recognition (2015)

45. Kittur, A., Chi, E.H., Suh, B.: Crowdsourcing user studies with mechanical Turk. In: ACM Computer-Human Interaction (CHI) Conference on Human Factors in Computing Systems (2008)
46. Zhang, L., Xiang, T., Gong, S.: Learning a discriminative null space for person re-identificatio. In: IEEE Conference on Computer Vision and Pattern Recognition (2016)
47. Sun, Y., Zheng, L., Yang, Y., Tian, Q., Wang, S.: Beyond part models: person retrieval with refined part pooling (and a strong convolutional baseline). In: Ferrari, V., Hebert, M., Sminchisescu, C., Weiss, Y. (eds.) ECCV 2018. LNCS, vol. 11208, pp. 501–518. Springer, Cham (2018). https://doi.org/10.1007/978-3-030-01225-0_30
48. Li, W., Zhu, X., Gong, S.: Harmonious attention network for person re-identification. In: IEEE Conference on Computer Vision and Pattern Recognition (2018)
49. Qian, X., Fu, Y., Xiang, T., Jiang, Y.G., Xue, X.: Leader-based multi-scale attention deep architecture for person re-identification. IEEE Trans. Pattern Anal. Mach. Intell. **42**, 371–385 (2019)
50. Gong, K., Liang, X., Zhang, D., Shen, X., Lin, L.: Look into person: self-supervised structure-sensitive learning and a new benchmark for human parsing. In: IEEE Conference on Computer Vision and Pattern Recognition (2017)
51. Zhou, K., Yang, Y., Cavallaro, A., Xiang, T.: Omni-scale feature learning for person re-identification. In: IEEE International Conference on Computer Vision (2019)
52. van der Maaten, L., Hinton, G.: Visualizing data using T-SNE. J. Mach. Learn. Res. (2008)

Any-Shot Object Detection

Shafin Rahman[1,2,3]([ID]), Salman Khan[2,4]([ID]), Nick Barnes[2]([ID]),
and Fahad Shahbaz Khan[4]([ID])

[1] North South University, Dhaka, Bangladesh
shafin.rahman@northsouth.edu
[2] Australian National University, Canberra, ACT 2601, Australia
nick.barnes@anu.edu.au
[3] Data61, CSIRO, Canberra, ACT 2601, Australia
[4] MBZ University of Artificial Intelligence, Abu Dhabi, UAE
{salman.khan,fahad.khan}@mbzuai.ac.ae

Abstract. Previous work on novel object detection considers zero or
few-shot settings where none or few examples of each category are available
for training. In real world scenarios, it is less practical to expect
that 'all' the novel classes are either unseen or have few-examples. Here,
we propose a more realistic setting termed 'Any-shot detection', where
totally unseen and few-shot categories can simultaneously co-occur during
inference. Any-shot detection offers unique challenges compared to
conventional novel object detection such as, a high imbalance between
unseen, few-shot and seen object classes, susceptibility to forget base-
training while learning novel classes and distinguishing novel classes from
the background. To address these challenges, we propose a unified any-
shot detection model, that can concurrently learn to detect both zero-
shot and few-shot object classes. Our core idea is to use class semantics
as prototypes for object detection, a formulation that naturally minimizes knowledge forgetting and mitigates the class-imbalance in the
label space. Besides, we propose a rebalanced loss function that emphasizes difficult few-shot cases but avoids overfitting on the novel classes
to allow detection of totally unseen classes. Without bells and whistles,
our framework can also be used solely for Zero-shot object detection
and Few-shot object detection tasks. We report extensive experiments
on Pascal VOC and MS-COCO datasets where our approach is shown
to provide significant improvements.

1 Introduction

Traditional object detectors are designed to detect the categories on which they
were originally trained. In several applications, such as self-driving cars, it is
important to extend the base object detector with novel categories that were
never seen before. The current 'novel' object detection models proposed in the

Electronic supplementary material The online version of this chapter (https://
doi.org/10.1007/978-3-030-69535-4_6) contains supplementary material, which is available to authorized users.

© Springer Nature Switzerland AG 2021
H. Ishikawa et al. (Eds.): ACCV 2020, LNCS 12624, pp. 89–106, 2021.
https://doi.org/10.1007/978-3-030-69535-4_6

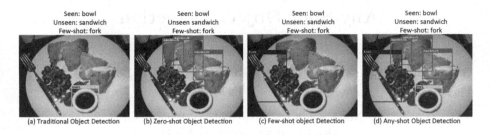

Fig. 1. (a) A traditional object detection method only detects seen objects. In the same vein, zero and few-shot object detection methods can detect (b) unseen or (c) few-shot objects. (d) Our proposed Any-shot detection method can *simultaneously* detect seen, unseen and few-shot objects.

literature target either of the two distinct settings, *Zero-shot detection* (ZSD) and *Few-shot detection* (FSD). In the former setting, it is assumed that totally unseen objects appear during inference and a model must learn to adapt for novel categories using only their class description (semantics). In the latter setting, a small and fixed-number of novel class samples are available for model adaptation. However, in a practical scenario, restricting the novel classes to be always unseen (with zero visual examples) or always with few-shot examples can limit the generality of the model.

In a real-world scenario, both unseen and few-shot classes can be simultaneously of interest. Moreover, we may encounter a few examples of a novel class that was previously supposed to be unseen. In such a case, an adaptive model must leverage from new information to improve its performance in an online fashion. To address these requirements, we introduce a new '*Any-shot Detection*' (ASD) protocol where a novel class can have zero or a few training examples. Since, the existing object detection models can either work for zero-shot or few-shot settings, we develop a unified framework to address the ASD problem (see Fig. 1). Remarkably, since the ASD task sits at the continuum between ZSD and FSD, our model can be directly applied to both these problems as well.

The ASD task poses new challenges for novel object detection. First, a high data imbalance between unseen, few-shot and seen classes can lead to a biased detection model. Additionally, the fine-tuning performed on few-shot examples can lead to forgetting previously acquired knowledge, thereby deteriorating model performance on seen and unseen classes. To overcome these challenges, we propose to learn a mapping from the visual space to the semantic space where class descriptors serve as fixed prototypes. The semantic prototypes in our approach encode inherent class relationships (thus enabling knowledge transfer from the seen to the unseen), helps us disentangle totally unseen concepts from the background and can be automatically updated to align well with the visual information. Besides, we introduce a novel rebalancing loss function for the fine-tuning stage that functions on few-shot examples. This loss serves two objectives, i.e., to focus on the errors made for few-shot classes and at the same time avoid overfitting them so that it remains generalizable to totally unseen categories.

Our main contributions are:

- A unified framework that can accommodate ZSD, FSD, ASD and their generalized settings.
- Learning with semantic class-prototypes that are well aligned with visual information and help minimize forgetting old concepts.
- An end-to-end solution with a novel loss function that rebalances errors to penalize difficult cases yet remains generalizable to unseen objects.
- Extensive experiments with new ASD setup, as well as comparisons with traditional FSD and ZSD frameworks demonstrating significant improvements.

2   Related Work

N-shot Recognition: There exist three types of methods for n-shot recognition. The *first* body of work targets only zero-shot recognition (ZSR) [1–3]. They perform training with seen data and test on unseen (or unseen+seen) data. To relate seen and unseen classes, they use semantic embeddings e.g., attributes [4] or word vectors [5,6]. The ZSR task has been investigated under popular themes such as transduction [7,8], domain adaptation [8,9], adversarial learning [10] and class-attribute association [11,12]. The *second* body of work targets only few-shot recognition (FSR) task [13]. This task leverages few labeled examples to classify novel classes. Most popular methods to solve FSR are based on meta-learning where approaches perform metric learning to measure the similarity between input and novel classes [14–16], adapt the meta-learner by calculating gradient updates for novel classes [16] or predict the classifier weights for novel classes [17]. The *third* body of work addresses both zero- and few-shot learning together [18–21]. These approaches are the extended version of ZSR or FSR methods that consider word vectors to accommodate both problems within a single framework. Our current work belongs to the third category, but instead of a recognition task, we focus on the detection problem, that is more challenging.

Zero-Shot Detection: Different from traditional object detection (where only seen objects are detected), ZSD aims to detect both seen and/or unseen objects. Pioneering works on ZSD attempt to extend established object detection methods to enable ZSD. For example, [22–24] and [25,26] employ pre-computed object proposals [27], YOLOv2 [28] and Faster-RCNN [29] based methods for ZSD, respectively. Recent methods for ZSD employ specialized polarity loss [30], explore transductive settings [31] and use raw textual description instead of only class-names [32]. All the above methods focus on only ZSD and Generalized ZSD tasks but cannot accommodate FSD scenario when new instances of unseen images become available. In this paper, we propose a method that can perform ZSD, FSD, and ASD tasks seamlessly, including their generalized cases.

Few-Shot Detection: FSD methods attempt to detect novel classes for which only a few instances (1–10) are available during the inference stage [33,34]. Among the early attempts of FSD, [35] proposed a regularizer that works on standard object detection models to detect novel classes. Later, [36] proposed

	Zero-shot	Few-shot	Any-shot
Recognition	Ziad et al. [CVPR'17] Xian et al. [CVPR'18] Song et al. [CVPR'18] Zhao et al. [NeurIPS'18]	Vinyals et al. [NeurIPS'16] Snell et al. [NeurIPS'17] Qi et al. [CVPR'18] Chen et al. [ICLR'19]	Tsai et al. [ICCV'17] Rahman et al. [TIP'18] Schonfeld et al. [CVPR'19] Xian et al. [CVPR'19]
Detection	Bansal et al. [ECCV'18] Demirel et al. [BMVC'18] Li et al. [AAAI'19] Rahman et al. [ICCV'19]	Chen et al. [AAAI'18] Dong et al. [TPAMI'19] Karlinsky et al. [CVPR'19] Kang et al. [ICCV'19]	**?**

Fig. 2. The any-shot object detection (ASD) problem has not been addressed in the literature before. Importantly, an ASD system can automatically perform both ZSD and FSD, which no prior approach can simultaneously offer.

a distant metric learning-based approach that learned representative vectors to facilitate FSD. The drawback of the above FSD methods is that they cannot handle seen/base classes during test time. Recently, [37] proposed to train a base network with seen data and then fine-tune it by meta-network learning that predicts scores for both seen and novel classes by re-weighing the base network features. This approach can perform generalized FSD but cannot accommodate ZSD or ASD scenario. In this paper, we address the mentioned gap in the literature (see Fig. 2).

3   Novel Object Detection

Novel object detection refers to enhancing the ability of a traditional object detector model to detect a new set of classes that were not present during training. We propose a unified Any-shot Detection (ASD) setting[1] where novel classes include both few-shot and unseen (zero-shot) classes. This is in contrast to the existing works on novel object detection that treat zero and few-shot detection in an isolated manner. In the absence of the unseen class and few-shot classes, our problem becomes identical to a conventional FSD and ZSD task, respectively. In this way, our proposed ASD settings unifies ZSD and FSD in a *single* framework.

3.1   Problem Formulation

Assume a total of C object classes are present in a given test set that need to be detected. Out of these, $S(>0)$ seen classes have many, $Q(\geq 0)$ few-shot classes have few and $U(\geq 0)$ unseen classes has no examples available in the training dataset and $C = S+Q+U$. Here, $T = Q+U$ represents the total number of novel classes that become available during the inference stage. For each class, a semantic description is available as a d-dimensional embedding vector. The semantic embeddings of all classes are denoted by $W = [W_s, W_f, W_u] \in \mathbb{R}^{d \times C}$,

---

[1] Our any-shot detection setting is different from [19], which considers zero and few-shot problems *separately* for a simpler *classification* task.

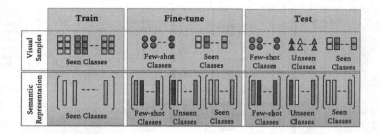

Fig. 3. An overview of Any-shot Detection setting.

where $\boldsymbol{W}_s \in \mathbb{R}^{d \times S}$, $\boldsymbol{W}_f \in \mathbb{R}^{d \times Q}$ and $\boldsymbol{W}_u \in \mathbb{R}^{d \times U}$ are semantic vectors for seen, few-shot and unseen classes, respectively.

The base training set $(\mathcal{D}_{tr})$ contains N_{tr} images with instances from S seen classes. Each training image $\boldsymbol{I}$ is provided with a set of bounding boxes, where each box $\mathbf{b}_{tr}$ is provided with a seen label $\mathbf{y}_{tr} \in \{0,1\}^S$. Similarly, when $Q>0$, we have a fine-tuning dataset $(\mathcal{D}_{ft})$ with N_{ft} images containing instances from both seen and few-shot classes for which bounding box $\mathbf{b}_{ft}$ and class label $\mathbf{y}_{ft} \in \{0,1\}^C$ annotations are present. During inference, we have a testing dataset $\mathcal{D}_{ts}$ with N_{ts} images where each image can contain any number of seen and novel class objects (see Fig. 3).

Our task is to perform any-shot detection, defined as:

Definition 1. Any-shot detection: *When $Q>0$ and $U>0$, predict object labels and associated bounding boxes for T novel classes, that include both zero and few-shot classes.*

In comparison, the traditional zero and few-shot problems can be defined as: (a) **Few-shot detection:** When $Q>0$ but $U = 0$, predict object labels and associated bounding boxes for all Q classes. (b) **Zero-shot detection:** When $Q = 0$ but $U>0$, predict object labels and associated boxes for all U classes. Note, if $Q = U = 0$ then the problem becomes equivalent to a traditional detection task.

We also study the generalized ASD problem defines as:

Definition 2. Generalized any-shot detection: *When $\{S, Q, U\} \subset \mathbb{Z}^+$, predict object labels and box locations for all C classes, that include seen, zero and few-shot classes.*

In the same vein, generalized zero and few-shot detection problems aim to detect seen classes in addition to novel ones. Next, we describe our approach for ASD and GASD.

3.2 Method

Our goal is to design a model that can *simultaneously* perform zero, few, and many-shot detection. This model is trained with seen classes, and is quickly

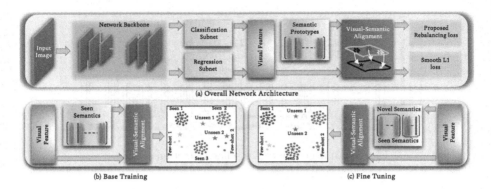

Fig. 4. (a) Network architecture. The visual-semantic alignment is performed using (b) seen semantics during base training and with (c) seen and novel semantics during fine-tuning. The visual features from the classification and regression units are separately used for visual-semantic alignment and subsequent loss calculation.

adapted during inference for zero-shot and few-shot classes. This problem set-up has the following major challenges: *(a) Adaptability:* A trained model must be flexible enough to incorporate new classes (with no or few examples) on the go, *(b) Learning without Forgetting:* While the model is adapted for new classes, it must not forget the previous knowledge acquired on seen classes, and *(c) Class Imbalance:* The classes representations are highly imbalanced: some with many instances, some with none and others with only a few. Therefore, the learning regime must be robust against the inherent imbalance in the ASD setting.

At a high-level, our proposed approach has two main components that address the above mentioned problems. First, we consider the semantic class prototypes to serve as anchors in the prediction space, thereby providing the flexibility to extend to any number of novel classes without the need to retrain network parameters. We show that such a representation also helps in avoiding catastrophic forgetting that is likely to occur otherwise. Furthermore, we propose a new loss formulation to address the class imbalance problem, that specifically focuses on difficult cases and minimizes model's bias against rare classes. We elaborate the novel aspects of our approach below.

Learning Without Forgetting. Traditional object detection models are static approaches that cannot dynamically adapt to novel classes. The flexibility to introduce novel object classes, after the base model training, requires special consideration, e.g., by posing it as an incremental learning problem [38–40]. In such cases, since classifier weights for novel categories are learned from scratch, the knowledge distillation concept [41] is applied to avoid forgetting the old learning. Such a strategy is not useful in our case because unlike previous approaches, we do not have access to many examples of the new task and a subset of novel classes has no training examples available.

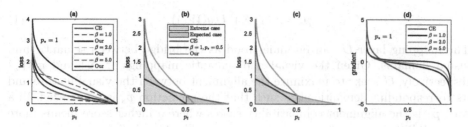

Fig. 5. Loss visualization. The colored dotted lines represent β-controlled penalty function, $h(.)$ and the solid lines represent loss functions. **(a)** The red line represents cross entropy (CE) which is compared to our loss with $\beta = 1, 2$ and 5 shown as black, green and blue lines, respectively. **(b)** Our loss (green line) with fixed $p_* = 0.5$. Here, our loss can be less than CE (red line) for the expected case. **(c)** Our loss curve (green line) with dynamic p_*. Here, our loss calculates the same value as CE (red line) for the expected case. The red shaded region represents extreme case since $p < p_*$ and blue shaded region represents expected or moderate case $p \geq p_*$. **(d)** Derivatives of CE and our loss for different β. See the supplementary material for the gradient analysis. (Color figure online)

To allow adding novel classes without forgetting old concepts, our approach seeks to disentangle the feature learning and classification stages. Precisely, we develop a training mechanism in which adding new classes does not require re-training base-network's parameters. This is achieved by defining the output decision space in the form of semantic class prototypes. These semantic class representatives are obtained in an unsupervised manner using a large text corpus, such as the Wikipedia, and encode class-specific attributes as well as the inter-class relationships [5,6].

During base-model training, the model learns to map visual features to semantic space. At the same time, the semantic space is well-aligned with the visual concepts using a learnable projection. Note that only seen class semantics are used during the training stage. Once the base-model is trained, novel classes (both zero and few-shot) can be accommodated at inference time taking advantage of the semantic class descriptions of the new classes. For novel classes whose new few-examples are available during inference, we fine-tune the model to adapt semantic space, but keeping the base-model's architecture unchanged. Essentially, this means that adding new classes does not demand any changes to the architecture of the base-network. Still, the model is capable of generating predictions for novel classes since it has learned to relate visual information with semantic space during training (see Fig. 4).

Formally, a training image X is fed to a deep network $f(\cdot)$, that produces a visual feature vector $f(X) \in \mathbb{R}^n$ corresponding to a particular box location. In a parallel stream, seen word vectors W_s, are passed through a light-weight subnet denoted by $g(\cdot)$, producing the transformed word vectors $g(W_s)$. Then, we connect the visual and semantic streams via a trainable layer, $U \in \mathbb{R}^{n \times d}$. Finally, a set of seen scores p_s is obtained by applying a sigmoid activation function (σ). The overall computation is given by,

$$p_s = \sigma\big(f(X)^T U g(W_s)\big). \tag{1}$$

The mapping layer U can be understood as the bridge between semantic and visual domains. Given the visual and semantic mappings, $f(X)$ and $g(W_s)$ respectively, U seeks to maximize the alignment between the visual feature and its corresponding semantic class such that the prediction p_s is maximized. In a way, p_s is the alignment compatibility scores where a higher score means more compatibility between feature and semantics. The function $f(\cdot)$ can be implemented with a convolutional network backbone (e.g. ResNet [42]) and $g(\cdot)$ can be implemented as a fixed or trainable layer. In the fixed case, fixed word vectors can be directly used for alignment i.e., $g(W_s) = W_s$. In the trainable case, W_s can be updated using a trainable metric $M \in \mathbb{R}^{d \times v}$ and a word vocabulary $D \in \mathbb{R}^{v \times d}$, resulting in $g(W_s) = \delta(W_s M D)$ where, v is the size of the word vocabulary and δ is a tanh activation. In our experiments, we find a trainable $g(W_s)$ achieves better performance.

We propose a two step training procedure. The first step involves training the base model, where Eq. 1 is trained with only images and semantics of seen classes. In the second step of fine-tuning, when novel class information becomes available, we replace W_s by W and train it with few-shot examples. Equation 1 then becomes $p = \sigma\big(f(X)^T U g(W)\big)$, where, p contains scores of both seen and novel classes. In this manner, model is quickly adapted for novel classes.

Notably, although our network can predict scores for all classes, no new tunable weights are added. In both steps, our network tries to align the feature with its corresponding semantics. From the network's perspective it does not matter how many classes are present. It only cares how compatible a feature is with the corresponding class semantics. This is why our network does not forget the seen classes as these semantic prototypes serve as an anchor to retain previous knowledge. Adding new classes is therefore not a new task for the network. During fine-tuning, the model still performs the same old task of aligning feature and semantics.

Learning with Imbalance Data. After base training on seen classes, novel classes become available during inference stage i.e., few-shot images and the word vectors of both zero and few-shot classes. Here, the few-shot image may contain seen instances as well. In this way, the fine-tuning stage contains an imbalanced data distribution and the model must minimize bias towards the already seen classes. To this end, we propose a rebalancing loss for the fine-tuning stage.

Suppose, $p \in p$ is the alignment score for a visual feature and the corresponding class semantics. As the fine-tuning is done on rare data, we need to penalize the cross-entropy (CE) loss based on the quality of alignment. If the network makes a mistake, we increase the penalty and if the network is already performing well, we employ a low or negative penalty. Suppose, the penalty $h(\cdot)$ is a function of p and p_* where p_* determines the penalization level, then,

$$L(p) = -\log p + \beta\, h(p, p_*), \tag{2}$$

where, β is a hyper-parameter. Here, $h(p, p_*)$ is given by,

$$h(p, p_*) = \log(1 + p_* - p), \tag{3}$$

where $(p_* - p)$ represents the violation of the expected alignment that controls the margin of the penalty function. We explore two alternatives for selecting p_*, a fixed value in range $0 < p_* \le 1$ and a dynamically adjusted value based on $p_* = \max_{i \in C} p_i$. We can get the following scenarios based on the choice of p_* and positive alignment quality p:

- *Expected case, $p > p_*$:* Negative penalty to calculate lower loss compared to CE (lower bounded by 0).
- *Moderate case, $p = p_*$:* Zero penalty and the calculated loss is equal to regular CE.
- *Extreme case, $p < p_*$:* High penalty in comparison to regular CE loss.

Plugging the penalty definition from Eq. 3 to Eq. 2 and enforcing positive loss values $L(p) \in \mathbb{R}^+$, we obtain,

$$L(p) = \max\left[0, -\log \frac{p}{(1 + p_* - p)^\beta}\right]. \tag{4}$$

After adding an α-balanced modulating factor from focal loss [43], we have,

$$L(p) = \max\left[0, -\alpha_t(1 - p_t)^\gamma \log p_t\right], \text{where, } p_t = \begin{cases} \frac{p}{(1+p_*-p)^\beta}, & \text{if } y = 1 \\ 1 - p, & \text{otherwise.} \end{cases}$$

Here, β is a parameter that focuses on hard cases and y is the corresponding value from the one-hot encoded ground-truth vector. With $\beta = 0$, Eq. 5 becomes equivalent to focal loss and with $\beta = 0$, $\gamma = 0$, $\alpha = 1$, Eq. 5 becomes CE loss.

Since several objects can co-occur in the same scene, the fine-tuning data can have seen instances. To emphasise rare classes more than the seen ones, we apply our rebalancing loss only on the novel class examples. For a seen anchor, only the focal loss is calculated. Thus, the final loss is,

$$L = \lambda L(s) + (1 - \lambda)L(n). \tag{5}$$

For the case of $L(s)$ and $L(n)$, $\beta = 0$ and $\beta > 0$ respectively. $L(s)$ and $L(n)$ represent the compatibility scores of seen and novel (few-shot and unseen) classes i.e., $s \in \{1, 2, .., S\}$ and $n \in \{1, 2, .., T\}$.

During inference when a test image is presented, a simple forward pass provides compatibility scores of seen, few-shot and unseen classes for each bounding box. If the score is higher than a threshold, we consider it a correct detection.

Analysis: Based on the quality of alignment, our proposed loss penalizes positive anchors. This scenario helps in the class imbalance problem. Especially, in the extreme case, when the network fails to detect a positive few-shot anchor, we highly penalize our network predictions. It gives extra supervision to the

Table 1. ASD results on MSCOCO.

#-Shot	Method	ASD			GASD			
		unseen	FS	HM	seen	unseen	FS	HM
1	Baseline-I	3.74	1.60	2.25	**54.11**	2.04	0.73	1.60
	Baseline-II	8.57	21.39	12.23	51.89	3.79	9.62	7.74
	Ours	**16.57**	**23.50**	**19.44**	51.70	**10.75**	**11.83**	**15.23**
5	Baseline-I	4.16	2.69	3.27	**54.15**	2.35	1.20	2.35
	Baseline-II	8.69	26.19	13.05	51.67	4.85	18.20	10.70
	Ours	**18.22**	**26.31**	**21.53**	51.18	**12.70**	**18.34**	**19.63**
10	Baseline-I	3.45	2.95	3.18	**54.25**	1.89	1.56	2.53
	Baseline-II	7.26	31.14	11.78	51.00	4.12	25.00	9.91
	Ours	**13.21**	**33.52**	**18.95**	51.18	**9.71**	**26.96**	**18.79**

Table 2. Ablation study with 5-shot case.

Method	ASD			GASD			
	unseen	FS	HM	seen	unseen	FS	HM
Baseline-I	4.16	2.69	3.27	**54.15**	2.35	1.20	2.35
Baseline-II	8.69	26.19	13.05	51.67	4.85	18.20	10.70
Ours with FL	13.69	23.81	16.61	51.20	9.21	16.34	15.85
Ours with AL	7.03	24.17	10.89	50.74	5.94	17.46	12.23
Ours ($p_* = 0.3$)	17.20	26.85	20.97	51.48	11.84	19.21	19.24
Ours ($p_* = 0.5$)	15.24	24.02	18.65	50.65	10.38	17.06	17.17
Ours ($p_* = 1.0$)	16.17	27.17	20.27	50.58	11.29	19.83	18.90
Ours*	16.60	24.05	19.64	51.32	11.09	16.71	17.70
Ours	**18.22**	**26.31**	**21.53**	51.18	**12.70**	**18.34**	**19.63**

network that it must not make errors on the few-shot classes. In contrast, for the expected and moderate cases, we reduce the loss which avoids the network becoming too confident on few-shot examples. Since, unseen objects are more related to the seen objects as compared to background, a low penalty on confident cases implicitly promotes discovering unseen classes. In effect, this leads to low overfitting on the few-shot classes that helps in achieving good performance on totally unseen classes.

Loss Shape Analysis: In Fig. 5, we visualize the loss. Figure 5 (a) shows how the shape of binary cross entropy (CE) changes with different values of β. β controls the penalty $h(.)$ which modifies CE loss. For a fixed $p_* = 1$, increasing β calculates a higher penalty for a wrong prediction. For a fixed margin penalty $p_* = 0.5$ in Fig. 5 (b), a network can predict a lower, equal and higher score than p_*. Correspondingly, it enables the network to calculate a less, equal and higher penalty for expected, moderate and extreme cases, respectively. In contrast, for the dynamic margin penalty case Fig. 5 (c), the predicted score can be at best $p_* = \max_{i \in C} p_i$. Therefore, the extreme case works similarly to the fixed p_* scenario but for the other cases, the network calculates a loss equal to CE/Focal loss. The dynamic p_* estimates the quality of predicted scores based on the current anchor specific situation. E.g., for a given anchor, a small predicted score (e.g., 0.1) for the ground-truth class can be considered as good prediction if all other predictions are <0.1. It helps to make a good balance between seen, few-shot and unseen predictions because the loss does not unnecessarily tries to maximize the ground-truth class score and thus avoids over-fitting.

3.3   Implementation Details

We implement our framework with a modified version of the RetinaNet architecture proposed in [30] (see Fig. 4(a)). It incorporates the word vectors at the penultimate layers of classification and regression subnets. While performing the base training with focal loss at the first step, we follow the recommended process in [30], where only seen word vectors are used in word processing network, $g(.)$ (see Fig. 4(b)). During the fine-tuning step, we update the base model with newly available data and our proposed loss function. As shown in Fig. 4(c), fine-tuning uses both seen and novel word vectors inside $g(.)$. Note that, in addition to novel class data, the small dataset used for fine-tuning includes some seen instances as well. We train our model for 10 epochs during the fine-tuning stage. After the fine-tuning is finished, our framework can detect seen, few-shot, and unseen classes simultaneously. We use the Adam optimizer for each training stage.

4 Experiments

Datasets: We evaluate our work on the MSCOCO-2014 [44] and PASCAL VOC 2007/12 datasets. For the MSCOCO experiment, we adopt the 65/15 seen/unseen split setting used in [30,31]. In both ZSD and FSD experiments, we consider unseen classes as the novel ones. However, in ASD experiments, we further split 15 novel classes into 8 few-shot and 7 unseen classes. We use the same 62,300 images during training where no single instance of novel classes is present. For testing ASD, we use 10,098 images where each image contains at least one novel object. However for GASD testing, we use the entire validation set of 40,504 images. We randomly choose additional images with a few (1/5/10) annotated bounding boxes for each novel category while performing FSD/ASD on MSCOCO. These images may contain some seen objects as well. For the PAS-CAL VOC 2007/12 experiment, we adopt three 15/5 seen/novel split settings from [37]. As recommended, we use train+val sets from PASCAL VOC 2007 and 2012 as training data and test-set from PASCAL VOC 2007 for evaluation. For fine-tuning, we use the images provided by Kang *et al.* [37] as few-shot data. For both MSCOCO and PASCAL VOC classes and vocabulary texts, we use 300-dimensional and ℓ_2 normalized word2vec vectors [5]. We have used same set of 4717 vocabulary atoms as used in [30] which are originally taken from [45].

Evaluation Criteria: For FSD and ASD, we evaluate our method with mean average precision (mAP). To report GFSD and GASD, we calculate the harmonic mean of the individual seen and novel class mAP. For ZSD, we report also recall@100 (RE) results as recommended in [22].

Validation Experiment: α, β, γ and λ are the hyper-parameter of our model. Among them, α and γ are specific to focal loss. Thus, we fix the recommend

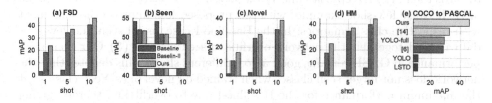

Fig. 6. FSD performance. (a) 1-, 5- and 10-shot detection mAP, (b), (c) and (d) seen, unseen and harmonic mean (HM) of GFSD. (e) 10-shot detection mAP for MSCOCO to PASCAL experiment.

Table 3. Base class (of Novel set 1) mAP on Pascal VOC 2007 test set.

Method	aero	bike	boat	bottle	car	cat	chair	table	dog	horse	person	plant	sheep	train	tv	mean
LSTD [46]	74.8	68.7	**57.1**	44.1	**78.0**	83.4	46.9	64.0	**78.7**	**79.1**	70.1	39.2	58.1	**79.8**	71.9	66.3
Kang *et al.* [37]	73.6	**73.1**	56.7	41.6	76.1	78.7	42.6	**66.8**	72.0	77.7	68.5	42.0	57.1	74.7	70.7	64.8
Ours	**80.4**	52.8	50.2	**55.9**	76.9	**85.1**	**49.8**	54.0	76.8	72.7	**81.1**	**44.8**	**61.7**	79.0	**76.8**	**66.5**

value $\alpha = 0.25$ and $\gamma = 2$ following [43]. We validate β and λ by creating a validation dataset based on splitting 65 seen classes into 55 seen and 10 novel classes. From the validation experiment, we select $\beta = 5$ and $\lambda = 0.1$. Detailed validation results are presented in the supplementary material.

Baseline Methods: Here, we introduce our baseline methods.

- *Baseline-I:* A RetinaNet architecture where fixed semantics are used in semantic processing pipeline i.e. $g(\boldsymbol{W}_s) = \boldsymbol{W}_s$ and the training is done with the basic focal loss. The fine-tuning step uses all seen and novel class data together.
- *Baseline-II:* The second baseline approach is identical to Baseline-I, except that the fine-tuning step uses novel class data and a few examples of seen. Finally, *Ours* denote the complete approach where the RetinaNet architecture is trained with adaptive prototypes in the semantic processing pipeline i.e. $g(\boldsymbol{W}_s) = \delta(\boldsymbol{W}_s \boldsymbol{M} \boldsymbol{D})$ and the training is done with our proposed loss.

4.1 ASD Performance

Here, we discuss the ASD and GASD performance with the 65/8/7 split of MSCOCO. For ASD, we show the performance of novel classes (i.e. unseen and few-shot classes) and the harmonic mean of individual performances. For GASD, we report separate seen, few-shot, unseen mAP and their harmonic mean mAP to show the overall performance.

Main Results: In Table 1, we report the our main results and comparisons with the baselines. Our observations are as follows: **(1)** Using more few-shot examples generally helps. However the effect of higher shots on the unseen performance is not always positive since more instances of few-shot classes can bias the model towards them. **(2)** Except Baseline-1, few-shot mAP is always better than unseen mAP because few-shot examples with our proposed loss improve the alignment with respective class semantics. In the Baseline-I case, as all seen and few-shot data is used together, the network overfits to seen classes. **(3)** Our seen class performance in GASD remains good across different shots. This denotes that the network does not forget seen classes when trained on novel ones. Seen classes get the maximum performance for the Baseline-I due to overfitting, thereby giving poor performance on novel classes. **(4)** Across different shots, Baseline-II beats the Baseline-I method as it is less prone to overfitting. With the proposed adaptive semantic prototypes and our loss function, we beat Baseline-II. **(5)** The improvement for unseen mAP is greater than few-shot or seen mAP irrespective

Table 4. FSD mAP of novel classes on Pascal VOC 2007 test set.

Method	Novel Set 1						Novel Set 2						Novel Set 3					
	bird	bus	cow	mbike	sofa	mean	aero	bottle	cow	horse	sofa	mean	boat	cat	mbike	sheep	sofa	mean
LSTD [46]	23.1	22.6	15.9	0.4	0.0	12.4	12.6	0.7	11.3	0.4	0.0	5.0	0.0	36.6	21.4	16.9	0.0	15.0
Kang et al. [37]	26.1	19.1	**40.7**	20.4	**27.1**	26.7	29.4	**4.6**	34.9	6.8	**37.9**	22.7	**11.7**	48.2	17.4	34.7	**30.1**	28.4
Ours	**37.4**	**23.0**	23.7	**37.0**	25.0	**29.2**	**32.0**	1.1	**39.2**	**55.5**	25.1	**30.6**	4.4	**66.9**	**43.7**	**49.0**	25.5	**37.9**

of the number of shots, ASD, or GASD tasks. It tells us that our loss formulation not only tackles the class imbalance of few-shot classes but also promotes detection of unseen classes. In Fig. 7 and Fig. 1 of the supplementary material, we show qualitative results for GASD.

Ablation Studies: In Table 2, we report ablation experiments on MSCOCO dataset with with alternate versions of our approach. Baseline-I and Baseline-II operate with fixed semantics. For the rest of the cases, we use our adaptive semantic-prototype approach (Sect. 3.2) to update the word vectors. Here, we first use a basic focal loss [43] (FL) to train the network. This approach outperforms both baselines because of the adaptable semantic prototypes. Then, we try two variants of FL: Anchor Loss [47] (AL) and a modified anchor loss with our loss penalty definition for few-shot classes. We notice that these variations do not work well in both ASD and GASD cases because AL penalizes negative anchors that network confuses with positive ones. This idea is beneficial for traditional recognition cases, but unsuitable for ZSD/FSD/ASD scenarios. This is because a negative anchor may contain an unseen object which is closely related to seen or few-shot semantics, and we do not want to suppress the anchor even though it predicts similar scores as the positive ones. Next, we apply our loss by fixing p_* to a constant value e.g., 0.3, 0.5, and 1. These trials outperform both baselines and FL based methods since the network emphasizes few-shot examples based on the quality of the visual-semantic alignment. Finally, alongside the adaptive semantics, we apply our final loss formulation which dynamically selects p_*. Our loss beats all previously described settings because it brings better emphasis on novel classes. Notably, we also experiment with the Our* case that applies our loss to all predictions (instead of just the novel scores) i.e., $\beta > 0$ for all classes. However, it does not perform as well as Ours potentially because the representations suitable for seen classes are already learnt well.

4.2   FSD Performance

If $U = 0$, our ASD framework becomes a few-shot detection problem. In this paper, we experiment on FSD with the following three different dataset setups.

MSCOCO: Here we consider all 15 novel classes of the MSCOCO split [30] as few-shot classes. We report mAP results of 1, 5 and 10-shot detection tasks of Baseline-I, Baseline-II, and Ours model in Fig. 6 (a–d). Besides, we report generalized FSD results. Overall, FSD performance improves with more examples.

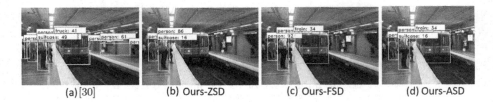

| (a) [30] | (b) Ours-ZSD | (c) Ours-FSD | (d) Ours-ASD |

Fig. 7. Qualitative comparison with [30] and Our method. Object bounding boxes: Yellow (seen), blue (few-shot) and pink (unseen). *(best viewed with zoom)* (Color figure online)

Table 5. ZSD results on MS-COCO dataset. Our rebalancing loss used in the fine-tuning stage (applied on seen data) leads to improved results.

Method		GZSD		
Split in [22] (↓)	ZSD (mAP/RE)	Seen (mAP/RE)	Unseen (mAP/RE)	HM (mAP/RE)
SB [22]	0.70/24.39	–	–	–
DSES [22]	0.54/27.19	–/15.02	–/15.32	–/15.17
Baseline	5.91/18.67	36.57/42.21	2.64/17.60	4.93/24.84
Ours	**7.78/32.83**	34.50/41.66	**3.06/27.34**	**5.63/33.01**

When trained with the adaptive semantic prototypes and rebalancing loss, our model successfully outperforms both baselines.

MSCOCO to PASCAL: It is a cross-dataset experiment. Following [37], we use 20 PASCAL VOC classes (overlapped with MSCOCO) as the few-shot classes and the remaining 60 MSCOCO classes as seen. This setting performs base training on MSCOCO seen classes and fine-tunes the base model using the 10-shot examples of the PASCAL VOC dataset. Finally, the PASCAL VOC 2007 test set is used to evaluate FSD. In Fig. 6(e), our method outperforms others including a recent approach [37].

PASCAL VOC 2007/12: Using three 15/5 novel-splits proposed in [37], we compare FSD performance of our work with Kang *et al.* [37] and LSTD [46] in Tables 3 and 4. We achieve better performance than them in both novel and base class detection with 3-shot detection settings.

4.3 ZSD Performance

For ZSD case, after the base training, we do not have any more data to fine-tune. Thus, we perform the second step of fine-tuning with the same data used in the first step but apply our loss instead of the focal loss. As $Q = 0$, we consider each seen class as a few-shot class during the second step. It emphasizes all seen classes in the same way. But, based on the dynamic choice of p_*, the network penalizes a bad prediction by calculating high loss and compensates a good prediction with no penalty. We notice that it helps to improve ZSD performance. We apply this process with the 48/17 split setting of [22] on MSCOCO. We report the mAP and Recall (RE) scores of this experiment in Table 5. With the recommended setting of [22], our work outperforms other methods in both ZSD and GZSD.

5   Conclusion

In this paper, we propose a unified any-shot detection approach where novel classes include both unseen and few-shot objects. Traditional approaches consider solving zero and few-shot tasks separately, whereas our approach encapsulates both tasks into a common framework. This approach does not forget the base training while learning novel classes, which helps to perform generalized ASD. Moreover, we propose a new loss function to learn new tasks. This loss penalizes the wrong prediction of a novel class more than the seen classes. We evaluate the proposed ASD tasks on the challenging MSCOCO and PASCAL VOC datasets. Besides, we compare ZSD and FSD performance of our approach with established state-of-the-art methods. Our first ASD framework delivers strong performance on ZSD, FSD, and ASD tasks.

References

1. Xian, Y., Lampert, C.H., Schiele, B., Akata, Z.: Zero-shot learning-a comprehensive evaluation of the good, the bad and the ugly. IEEE Trans. Pattern Anal. Mach. Intell. **41**, 2251–2265 (2019)
2. Chen, H., et al.: Generalized zero-shot vehicle detection in remote sensing imagery via coarse-to-fine framework. In: Proceedings of the Twenty-Eighth International Joint Conference on Artificial Intelligence, IJCAI-19, International Joint Conferences on Artificial Intelligence Organization, pp. 687–693 (2019)
3. Chao, W.-L., Changpinyo, S., Gong, B., Sha, F.: An empirical study and analysis of generalized zero-shot learning for object recognition in the wild. In: Leibe, B., Matas, J., Sebe, N., Welling, M. (eds.) ECCV 2016. LNCS, vol. 9906, pp. 52–68. Springer, Cham (2016). https://doi.org/10.1007/978-3-319-46475-6_4
4. Farhadi, A., Endres, I., Hoiem, D., Forsyth, D.: Describing objects by their attributes. In: CVPR, pp. 1778–1785. IEEE (2009)
5. Mikolov, T., Sutskever, I., Chen, K., Corrado, G., Dean, J.: Distributed representations of words and phrases and their compositionality. In: Proceedings of the 26th International Conference on Neural Information Processing Systems, NIPS 2013, vol. 2, pp. 3111–3119. Curran Associates Inc., USA (2013)
6. Pennington, J., Socher, R., Manning, C.D.: Glove: global vectors for word representation. In: EMNLP, pp. 1532–1543 (2014)
7. Song, J., Shen, C., Yang, Y., Liu, Y., Song, M.: Transductive unbiased embedding for zero-shot learning. In: The IEEE Conference on Computer Vision and Pattern Recognition (CVPR) (2018)
8. Zhao, A., Ding, M., Guan, J., Lu, Z., Xiang, T., Wen, J.R.: Domain-invariant projection learning for zero-shot recognition. In: Bengio, S., Wallach, H., Larochelle, H., Grauman, K., Cesa-Bianchi, N., Garnett, R. (eds.) Advances in Neural Information Processing Systems 31, pp. 1019–1030. Curran Associates, Inc. (2018)

9. Kodirov, E., Xiang, T., Fu, Z., Gong, S.: Unsupervised domain adaptation for zero-shot learning. In: The IEEE International Conference on Computer Vision (ICCV) (2015)

10. Xian, Y., Lorenz, T., Schiele, B., Akata, Z.: Feature generating networks for zero-shot learning. In: The IEEE Conference on Computer Vision and Pattern Recognition (CVPR) (2018)

11. Al-Halah, Z., Tapaswi, M., Stiefelhagen, R.: Recovering the missing link: predicting class-attribute associations for unsupervised zero-shot learning. In: The IEEE Conference on Computer Vision and Pattern Recognition (CVPR) (2016)

12. Al-Halah, Z., Stiefelhagen, R.: Automatic discovery, association estimation and learning of semantic attributes for a thousand categories. In: The IEEE Conference on Computer Vision and Pattern Recognition (CVPR) (2017)

13. Chen, W.Y., Liu, Y.C., Kira, Z., Wang, Y.C., Huang, J.B.: A closer look at few-shot classification. In: International Conference on Learning Representations (2019)

14. Vinyals, O., Blundell, C., Lillicrap, T., Kavukcuoglu, K., Wierstra, D.: Matching networks for one shot learning. In: Proceedings of the 30th International Conference on Neural Information Processing Systems, NIPS'16, pp. 3637–3645. Curran Associates Inc., USA (2016)

15. Snell, J., Swersky, K., Zemel, R.: Prototypical networks for few-shot learning. In: Advances in Neural Information Processing Systems, pp. 4077–4087 (2017)

16. Ravi, S., Larochelle, H.: Optimization as a model for few-shot learning. In: International Conference on Learning Representations (ICLR) (2017)

17. Qi, H., Brown, M., Lowe, D.G.: Low-shot learning with imprinted weights. In: The IEEE Conference on Computer Vision and Pattern Recognition (CVPR) (2018)

18. Schonfeld, E., Ebrahimi, S., Sinha, S., Darrell, T., Akata, Z.: Generalized zero- and few-shot learning via aligned variational autoencoders. In: The IEEE Conference on Computer Vision and Pattern Recognition (CVPR) (2019)

19. Xian, Y., Sharma, S., Schiele, B., Akata, Z.: f-VAEGAN-D2: a feature generating framework for any-shot learning. In: The IEEE Conference on Computer Vision and Pattern Recognition (CVPR) (2019)

20. Rahman, S., Khan, S., Porikli, F.: A unified approach for conventional zero-shot, generalized zero-shot, and few-shot learning. IEEE Trans. Image Process. **27**, 5652–5667 (2018)

21. Tsai, Y.H., Huang, L., Salakhutdinov, R.: Learning robust visual-semantic embeddings. In: The IEEE International Conference on Computer Vision (ICCV) (2017)

22. Bansal, A., Sikka, K., Sharma, G., Chellappa, R., Divakaran, A.: Zero-shot object detection. In: Ferrari, V., Hebert, M., Sminchisescu, C., Weiss, Y. (eds.) ECCV 2018. LNCS, vol. 11205, pp. 397–414. Springer, Cham (2018). https://doi.org/10.1007/978-3-030-01246-5_24

23. Demirel, B., Cinbis, R.G., Ikizler-Cinbis, N.: Zero-shot object detection by hybrid region embedding. In: British Machine Vision Conference (BMVC) (2018)

24. Zhu, P., Wang, H., Saligrama, V.: Zero shot detection. IEEE Trans. Circuits Syst. Video Technol 1 (2019)

25. Rahman, S., Khan, S., Porikli, F.: Zero-shot object detection: learning to simultaneously recognize and localize novel concepts. In: Jawahar, C.V., Li, H., Mori, G., Schindler, K. (eds.) ACCV 2018. LNCS, vol. 11361, pp. 547–563. Springer, Cham (2019). https://doi.org/10.1007/978-3-030-20887-5_34

26. Rahman, S., Khan, S.H., Porikli, F.: Zero-shot object detection: joint recognition and localization of novel concepts. Int. J. Comput. Vis. **128**, 2979–2999 (2020)

27. Zitnick, C.L., Dollár, P.: Edge boxes: locating object proposals from edges. In: Fleet, D., Pajdla, T., Schiele, B., Tuytelaars, T. (eds.) ECCV 2014. LNCS, vol. 8693, pp. 391–405. Springer, Cham (2014). https://doi.org/10.1007/978-3-319-10602-1_26

28. Redmon, J., Farhadi, A.: Yolo9000: better, faster, stronger. In: The IEEE Conference on Computer Vision and Pattern Recognition (CVPR) (2017)

29. Ren, S., He, K., Girshick, R., Sun, J.: Faster R-CNN: towards real-time object detection with region proposal networks. IEEE Trans. Pattern Anal. Mach. Intell. **39**, 1137–1149 (2017)

30. Rahman, S., Khan, S., Barnes, N.: Polarity loss for zero-shot object detection. arXiv preprint arXiv:1811.08982 (2018)

31. Rahman, S., Khan, S., Barnes, N.: Transductive learning for zero-shot object detection. In: The IEEE International Conference on Computer Vision (ICCV) (2019)

32. Li, Z., Yao, L., Zhang, X., Wang, X., Kanhere, S., Zhang, H.: Zero-shot object detection with textual descriptions. In: Proceedings of the AAAI Conference on Artificial Intelligence, vol. 33, pp. 8690–8697 (2019)

33. Dong, X., Zheng, L., Ma, F., Yang, Y., Meng, D.: Few-example object detection with model communication. IEEE Trans. Pattern Anal. Mach. Intell. **41**, 1641–1654 (2019)

34. Wang, Y.X., Hebert, M.: Model recommendation: generating object detectors from few samples. In: The IEEE Conference on Computer Vision and Pattern Recognition (CVPR) (2015)

35. Chen, H., Wang, Y., Wang, G., Qiao, Y.: LSTD: a low-shot transfer detector for object detection. In: McIlraith, S.A., Weinberger, K.Q., (eds.) Proceedings of the Thirty-Second AAAI Conference on Artificial Intelligence, (AAAI 2018), New Orleans, Louisiana, USA, 2–7 February 2018, pp. 2836–2843. AAAI Press (2018)

36. Karlinsky, L., et al.: RepMet: representative-based metric learning for classification and few-shot object detection. In: The IEEE Conference on Computer Vision and Pattern Recognition (CVPR) (2019)

37. Kang, B., Liu, Z., Wang, X., Yu, F., Feng, J., Darrell, T.: Few-shot object detection via feature reweighting. In: The IEEE International Conference on Computer Vision (ICCV) (2019)

38. Li, Z., Hoiem, D.: Learning without forgetting. IEEE Trans. Pattern Anal. Mach. Intell. **40**, 2935–2947 (2018)

39. Chen, G., Choi, W., Yu, X., Han, T., Chandraker, M.: Learning efficient object detection models with knowledge distillation. In: Proceedings of the 31st International Conference on Neural Information Processing Systems, NIPS 2017, pp. 742–751. Curran Associates Inc., USA (2017)

40. Shmelkov, K., Schmid, C., Alahari, K.: Incremental learning of object detectors without catastrophic forgetting. In: Proceedings of the IEEE International Conference on Computer Vision, pp. 3400–3409 (2017)

41. Hinton, G., Vinyals, O., Dean, J.: Distilling the knowledge in a neural network. arXiv preprint arXiv:1503.02531 (2015)

42. He, K., Zhang, X., Ren, S., Sun, J.: Deep residual learning for image recognition. In: The IEEE Conference on Computer Vision and Pattern Recognition (CVPR) (2016)

43. Lin, T.Y., Goyal, P., Girshick, R., He, K., Dollar, P.: Focal loss for dense object detection. IEEE Trans. Pattern Anal. Mach. Intell. (2018)

44. Lin, T.-Y., et al.: Microsoft COCO: common objects in context. In: Fleet, D., Pajdla, T., Schiele, B., Tuytelaars, T. (eds.) ECCV 2014. LNCS, vol. 8693, pp. 740–755. Springer, Cham (2014). https://doi.org/10.1007/978-3-319-10602-1_48

45. Chua, T.S., Tang, J., Hong, R., Li, H., Luo, Z., Zheng, Y.T.: NUS-WIDE: a real-world web image database from National University of Singapore. In: CIVR, Santorini, Greece, 8–10 July 2009
46. Chen, H., Wang, Y., Wang, G., Qiao, Y.: LSTD: a low-shot transfer detector for object detection. In: Thirty-Second AAAI Conference on Artificial Intelligence (2018)
47. Ryou, S., Jeong, S.G., Perona, P.: Anchor loss: modulating loss scale based on prediction difficulty. In: The IEEE International Conference on Computer Vision (ICCV) (2019)

Background Learnable Cascade
for Zero-Shot Object Detection

Ye Zheng[1,2], Ruoran Huang[1,2], Chuanqi Han[1,2], Xi Huang[1], and Li Cui[1(✉)]

[1] Institute of Computing Technology, Chinese Academy of Sciences,
Beijing 100190, China
zhengye@ict.ac.cn, lcui@ict.ac.cn
[2] University of Chinese Academy of Sciences, Beijing 100190, China

Abstract. Zero-shot detection (ZSD) is crucial to large-scale object detection with the aim of simultaneously localizing and recognizing unseen objects. There remain several challenges for ZSD, including reducing the ambiguity between background and unseen objects as well as improving the alignment between visual and semantic concept. In this work, we propose a novel framework named Background Learnable Cascade (BLC) to improve ZSD performance. The major contributions for BLC are as follows: (i) we propose a multi-stage cascade structure named Cascade Semantic R-CNN to progressively refine the alignment between visual and semantic of ZSD; (ii) we develop the semantic information flow structure and directly add it between each stage in Cascade Semantic R-CNN to further improve the semantic feature learning; (iii) we propose the background learnable region proposal network (BLRPN) to learn an appropriate word vector for background class and use this learned vector in Cascade Semantic R-CNN, this design makes "Background Learnable" and reduces the confusion between background and unseen classes. Our extensive experiments show BLC obtains significantly performance improvements for MS-COCO over state-of-the-art methods (Code has been made available at https://github.com/zhengye1995/BLC).

Keywords: Zero-shot object detection · Multi-stage structure · Background learnable · Semantic information flow

1 Introduction

Zero-shot learning (ZSL) is widely used to reason about objects belonging to unseen classes that have never been observed during training. Traditional ZSL researches focus on the classification problem of unseen objects and achieve high classification accuracy [1]. However, there still exists a large gap between ZSL settings and real-world scenarios. ZSL just focuses on recognizing unseen objects, not detecting them. For example, most of datasets used as ZSL benchmark only have one dominant object in each sample [2–4], while in real-world, various objects may appear in a single image without being precisely localized.

© Springer Nature Switzerland AG 2021
H. Ishikawa et al. (Eds.): ACCV 2020, LNCS 12624, pp. 107–123, 2021.
https://doi.org/10.1007/978-3-030-69535-4_7

To simultaneously localize and recognize unseen objects, some preliminary attempts [5–8] for zero-shot object detection (ZSD) have been reported. ZSD introduces a more practical setting to detect novel objects that are not observed during training. On this foundation, Rahman et al. [9], Li et al. [10], Zhao et al. [11] and Zhu et al. [12] make improvements to boost ZSD performance. These achievements combine the visual-semantic mapping relationship in ZSL with the deep learning based detection model in traditional object detection methods to detect unseen objects. However, these works still have their limitations: (i) can not gradually optimize the visual-semantic alignment to properly map visual features to semantic information; (ii) lack of a handy pipeline to learn a discriminative background class semantic embedding representation, while this representation is important for reducing the confusion between background and unseen classes; (iii) rely on pre-trained weights that were learned from seen or unseen datasets.

We therefore propose a novel framework named Background Learnable Cascade (BLC) for ZSD, including three components: Cascade semantic R-CNN, semantic information flow and BLRPN. BLC is motivated on the cognitive science about how humans reason objects through semantic information. Humans can use semantic information such as words to describe the characteristics of objects, and conversely, humans can also reason the categories for objects from the semantic description. Based on the past life experience, humans have established an abstract visual-semantic mapping relationship for seen objects and transfer it to recognize unseen objects. For example, humans can recognize the zebra with the language description "a horse with black and white stripes" and the visual memory of horse even if they had never seen a zebra before. Inspirited by this, BLC develops a visual-semantic alignment substructure named semantic branch to learn the visual-semantic relationship between seen objects' images and word vectors. Then transfers this alignment from seen classes to unseen classes to detect unseen objects. In order to progressively refine the visual-semantic alignment, BLC develops Cascade Semantic R-CNN by integrating the semantic branch in a multi-stage architecture based on Cascade R-CNN [13]. This combination can take advantage of the cascade structure and multi-stage refinement policy. In Cascade Semantic R-CNN, the semantic branches in later stages only benefit from better localized bounding boxes without direct semantic information connections. To remedy this problem, BLC further designs semantic information flow structure to improve the semantic information flow by directly connecting semantic branches in each cascade stage. The semantic feature in the current stage will be modulated through fully connected layers and fed to the next stage. This design promotes the circulation of semantic information between each stage and is beneficial to learn a proper visual-semantic relationship. Due to the coarse word vector for background class used in semantic branch is inability to exactly represent the complex background, BLC develops a novel framework denoted as background learnable region proposal network (BLRPN) to learn an appropriate word vector for background class. Our study shows that replacing the coarse background word vector in semantic branch with the new one learned from BLRPN can effectively increases the recall rate for unseen classes.

Our main contributions of Background Learnable Cascade (BLC) are: (i) we develop Cascade Semantic R-CNN, which effectively integrates multi-stage structure and cascade strategy into zero-shot object detection by first integrating cascade with the semantic branch; (ii) we develop semantic information flow structure among each cascade stage to improve the semantic feature learning; (iii) we develop a background learnable region proposal network (BLRPN) to learn a more appropriate background class semantic word vector reducing the confusion between background and unseen classes; (iv) extensive experiments on two different MS-COCO splits show significant performance improvement in terms of mAP and recall.

2   Related Work

Zero-Shot Recognition. In the past few years, several works have been proposed [1,2,14–26] for zero-shot image recognition. Most approaches of ZSL [21,27–36] have employed the relationship between seen and unseen classes to optimize recognition of unseen objects. The most classic way is to learn the alignment between the visual and semantic information by using extra source data. This alignment can classify unseen image categories by using labeled image data and semantic representations trained with unsupervised fashion from unannotated text data. In our work, we follow this methodology to detect objects for unseen classes.

Object Detection. Deep learning based object detection methods have made great progress in the past several years, e.g., YOLO [37], SSD [38], RetinaNet [39], Faster R-CNN [40], R-FCN [41], MASK R-CNN [42], DCN [43], CornerNet [44], CenterNet [45] and FCOS [46]. The recent multi-stage structures have further boosted performance for object detection, e.g., Cascade R-CNN [13] and Cascade RPN [13]. The multi-stage cascade strategy progressively refine the results and we also adopt this strategy to refine visual-semantic alignment in our BLC.

Recent Achievements for ZSD. In recent years, some ZSD approaches have been proposed. Rahman et al. [7] combine ConSE [22] and Faster R-CNN [40] with a max-margin loss and a meta-class clustering loss to tackle the problem of ZSD. Bansal et al. [5] employ a background-aware model to solve the confusion for background class in ZSD, and they use additional data to densely sample training classes. They also propose a generalization version of ZSD called generalized zero-shot object detection (GZSD) which aims to detect seen and unseen objects together. Demirel et al. [6] adopt the hybrid region embedding to improve performance. Zhu et al. [8] introduce ZS-YOLO, which is built on a one-step YOLOv2 [47] detector. Rahman et al. [9] propose polarity loss to cluster semantic and develop an end-to-end network based RetinaNet [39]. Li et al. [10] address ZSD with textual descriptions by jointly learning visual units, visual-unit attention and word-level attention.

There are some key differences between our work and previous works: (i) to the choice of evaluation datasets, Rahman et al. [7] and Zhu et al. [8] use the ILSVRC-2017 detection dataset [3]. This dataset is restrictive for evaluate ZSD, in comparison with our choice — MS-COCO [48]. Because each image in ILSVRC-2017 detection dataset only has one dominant object, which exists a big gap with the real scene. We follow the choices and splits for dataset introduced by Bansal et al. [5] and Rahman et al. [9] in MS-COCO). These dataset splits are more challenging and closer to the real scene settings. (ii) for the representation of background class, most of them just use a trivial representation for background class, e.g., the semantic vectors for 'background' word [5] and the mean vectors for all seen classes [7]. These representations are not the optimal solution to address the confusion between background and unseen classes. Bansal et al. [5] propose a background-aware approach based on an iterative EM-like training procedure, but it is complex and inefficient for datasets with a small number of categories like MS-COCO. In contrast, our BLRPN, as an end-to-end framework, can learn a reasonable representation for background class through only one training process without iterations while not be affected by the sparsity of category; (iii) in the aspect of the optimization strategy, all of these previous works just refine the visual-semantic alignment once, which may not enough to optimize this alignment. In BLC, we adopt multi-stage architecture to progressively refine this alignment to improve the performance of ZSD. (iv) for the training process, most of them need fine tune their model based on additional pre-trained weights, which are learned from seen or unseen-class data, while our work, as stated above, just needs a simple and straightforward training process without any additional pre-trained weights on seen or unseen data.

3   Background Learnable Cascade

In this section, we elaborate Background Learnable Cascade (BLC). We first introduce our semantic branch about learning the alignment between the visual and semantic information. Then we introduce Cascade Semantic R-CNN which integrates our semantic branch with a multi-stage cascade structure. Since Cascade Semantic R-CNN does not use the semantic information between each stage, we develop semantic information flow structure via incorporating a direct path to reinforce the information flow among semantic branches. Moreover, in consideration of further reducing the confusion between background and unseen classes, we develop BLRPN to learn a discriminative word-embedding representation for background objects. Finally, we describe the details of training process, loss function and inference settings.

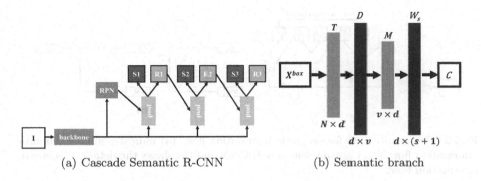

(a) Cascade Semantic R-CNN   (b) Semantic branch

Fig. 1. The architecture for Cascade Semantic R-CNN. (a) is the overview architecture and (b) indicates the details for semantic branch. In figure (b), T, M are trainable FC layers and D, W_s are fixed FC layers. For an input image I, a backbone network (ResNet) is used to obtain the features. Then these features will be forwarded to the Region Proposal Network (RPN) to generate a set of object proposals. After we use a RoI pooling layer to map the proposals' features to a set of fix size objective features, we forward them through the semantic branches (purple $S1,S2$ and $S3$) and the regression branch (green $R1,R2$ and $R3$) in 3 cascade stages to get category scores and bounding boxes for objects. (Color figure online)

3.1   Model Architecture

Semantic Branch. We propose semantic branch to learn the alignment between the visual and semantic information. The details about our semantic branch denoted as S are illustrated in Fig. 1(b). The basic idea is derived from [9] which uses the relationship between the visual features and the semantic embedding as the bridge to detect unseen objects. There are four main components in semantic branch. $W_s \in \mathbb{R}^{d \times (s+1)}$ is a fixed FC layer, whose parameters are the stacked semantic word vectors of background and seen classes. More specifically, d is the dimension of word vector for each class, s denotes the number of seen classes and 1 denotes the background class. As shown in Fig. 4, each class has a corresponding word vector v_c ($1 \times d$ dimension) in W_s. For background class, we use the mean word vector $v_b = \frac{1}{s}\sum_{c=1}^{s} v_c$ in our baseline and this v_b will be improved in our BLRPN. Since the word vector quantity for W_s is limited and causes the serious sparsity of semantic representation, we add an external vocabulary $D \in \mathbb{R}^{d \times v}$ to enhance the richness of semantic information, where v is the number of words in this external vocabulary. D is also implemented by a fixed FC layer like W_s. To overcome the limitation of fixed semantic representation of W_s and D, we make an updatable representation by introducing an adjustable FC layer M to semantic branch which can be regarded as an attention mechanism in visual-semantic alignment. With this adaptive M whose dimension is $v \times d$, semantic branch can update the semantic word embedding space to learn a more flexible and reliable alignment. $T \in \mathbb{R}^{N \times d}$ is an FC layer which is used to adjust the dimension of input objective feature $\mathbf{x}^{box}$ to fit the subsequent model. In detail, it transforms $\mathbf{x}^{box}$ from N dimension to d dimension. With these above

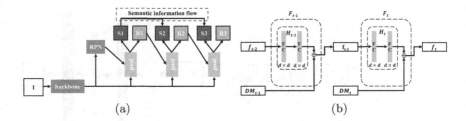

Fig. 2. The architecture for semantic information flow. (a) indicates adding semantic information flow into Cascade Semantic R-CNN and (b) shows the details of semantic information flow.

components, our semantic branch projects the input visual feature tensors to the semantic space and then gets the category score **c**. The calculation process is summarized as follows:

$$S = \delta(W_s MDT),$$
$$\mathbf{c} = \sigma(S(\mathbf{x}^{box})), \tag{1}$$
$$= \sigma(\delta(W_s MDT)\mathbf{x}^{box}).$$

Where, $\delta(\cdot)$ denotes a tanh activation function, $\sigma(\cdot)$ is the softmax activation function and **c** represents the category score.

Cascade Semantic R-CNN. In order to gradually refine the visual-semantic alignment, we integrate above semantic branch into Cascade R-CNN to develop Cascade Semantic R-CNN. We replace the classification branch of each stage for Cascade R-CNN with our semantic branch, as shown in Fig. 1. In particular, the semantic branches for each stage do not share parameter weights. This framework progressively refines predictions through the semantic branches and bounding box regression branches. The whole pipeline is summarized as follows:

$$\mathbf{x}_t^{box} = \mathcal{P}(\mathbf{x}, \mathbf{r}_{t-1}), \qquad \mathbf{r}_t = \mathcal{R}_t(\mathbf{x}_t^{box}), \tag{2}$$
$$\mathbf{c}_t = \sigma(\mathbf{S}_t(\mathbf{x}_t^{box})) = \sigma(\delta(W_s M_t DT_t)\mathbf{x}_t^{box}).$$

Here, **x** represents the visual feature from backbone network which is based on ResNet-50 [49] and the Feature Pyramid Networks (FPN) [50]. $\mathbf{r}_{t-1}$ is the RoIs for $(t-1)$-th stage and $\mathbf{x}_t^{box}$ represents the objective feature derived from **x** and the input RoIs $\mathbf{r}_{t-1}$. $\mathcal{P}(\cdot)$ is a pooling operator and we use RoI Align [42] here. $\mathcal{R}_t$ and $\mathcal{S}_t$ indicate the bounding box regression branch and the semantic branch at the t-th stage, respectively. $\mathbf{c}_t$ represents category score predictions for t-th stage. This process will be iterated in each stage.

Semantic Information Flow. In Cascade Semantic R-CNN, the visual-semantic alignment in semantic branches of each stage is purely based on the visual objective features $\mathbf{x}_t^{box}$. This design does not have direct information flow between semantic branches for each stage, failing to make full use of the relevance of semantic information in different stages and progressively refine semantic representing. With the aim of making up this issue, we develop a semantic information flow structure between semantic branches among each cascade stage by forwarding the modulated semantic information from previous stages to current stage, as illustrated in Fig. 2. We show the calculation process for semantic information flow as follows:

$$\mathbf{f}_1 = DM_1$$
$$\mathbf{f}_2 = \mathcal{F}_2(\mathbf{f}_1, DM_2)$$
$$\vdots \tag{3}$$
$$\mathbf{f}_t = \mathcal{F}_t(\mathbf{f}_{t-1}, DM_t)).$$

Where, $\mathbf{f}_t$ represents the semantic information for t-th stage derived from $\mathcal{F}_t$ which combines the semantic information of current stage and the preceding one. DM_t indicates the local semantic information for t-th stage. $\mathcal{F}$ is a function which fuses the semantic information for last stage and current stage with two steps. First, modulating the input semantic information for preceding stage $\mathbf{f}_{t-1}$ with two FC layers $\mathcal{H}_t$. Then, adding this modulated feature with the semantic information of current stage DM_t in an element-wise manner. The calculation details for $\mathcal{F}$ in t-th stage are:

$$\mathcal{F}_t(\mathbf{f}_{t-1}, DM_t)) = \mathcal{H}_t(\mathbf{f}_{t-1}) + DM_t \tag{4}$$

After adding the semantic information flow into Cascade Semantic R-CNN, the calculation process for $\mathbf{c}_t$ in Eq. 2 will be changed with replacing original DM_t with new $\mathbf{f}_t$:

$$\mathbf{c}_t = \sigma(\mathbf{S}_t(\mathbf{x}_t^{box})) = \sigma(\delta(W_s \mathbf{f}_t T_t) \mathbf{x}_t^{box}). \tag{5}$$

The semantic features will benefit from this approach and can help to learn a robust visual-semantic alignment and improve zero shot detection performance.

Background Learnable RPN (BLRPN). In Cascade Semantic R-CNN, the W_s in semantic branch adopts a coarse mean word vector v_b for background class, which may not reasonably represent the background class and further reduce the confusion between background and unseen classes. We need a new background semantic vector to replace the old one because this "replace" strategy can avoid modifying Cascade Semantic R-CNN structure and introducing extra computation. Since the background visual concept is very complex, the better idea is to learn background semantic vector from various background visual data. In order to ensure that the learned background class word vector can directly replace the original one, the learning process needs to be consistent with the

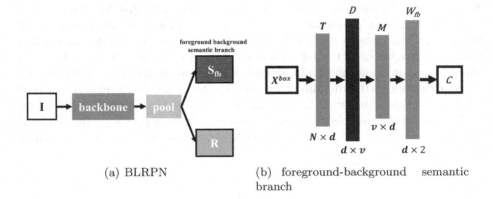

(a) BLRPN

(b) foreground-background semantic branch

Fig. 3. The architecture for BLRPN. (a) is the overview architecture and (b) indicates the details about foreground-background semantic branch S_{fb}. In S_{fb}, D is fixed while T, M and W_{fb} are trainable FC layers. c is the foreground background binary classification score.

process it Cascade Semantic R-CNN. Based on above analysis, we develop Background Learnable RPN to learn this new background semantic vector and use it to replace the coarse one in W_s. In Fig. 3, we develop a foreground-background semantic branch S_{fb} and integrate it into the original RPN. S_{fb} is modified from our semantic branch for consistency, and the details are illustrated in Fig. 3(b). The only difference between S_{fb} and semantic branch S is that the W_s in S is replaced by the W_{fb} in S_{fb}. We implement W_{fb} with an FC layer without bias and make it trainable. The parameters of $W_{fb} \in \mathbb{R}^{d \times 2}$ contain two word vectors, one is v_b for background class and the other is v_f for foreground class, so v_b as the new background word vector will be updated during training. v_f is initialized with a uniform random distribution and the v_b is initialized with the mean word vectors for all seen classes, which is the same as W_s. During training, we feed the visual features derived from the backbone network to the foreground-background branch and get the foreground-background classification score. The details are:

$$S_{fb} = \delta(W_{fb}MDT),$$
$$\mathbf{c} = \sigma(S_{fb}(\mathbf{x}^{box})), \tag{6}$$
$$= \sigma(\delta(W_{fb}MDT)\mathbf{x}^{box}).$$

After calculating the loss, we back propagate all gradients to update trainable parameters includes W_{fb}. W_{fb} will be updated means that we can learn the target background class semantic vector v_b in the course of training BLRPN. As shown in Fig. 4, we use this new v_b to replace the old one for background class in W_s. Finally, we retrain our Cascade Semantic R-CNN model with this new W_s and effectively improve the performance for unseen objects. Overall, BLRPN learns the new v_b by establishing the alignment between visual concepts and semantic representation of background classes.

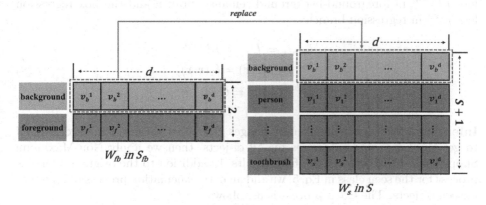

Fig. 4. W_s is the word vectors for background and other seen classes, it includes 1 background class and s seen classes, each class has a $1 \times d$ dimensional word vector. W_{fb} is the word vectors for background and foreground classes, it includes 1 background class and 1 foreground class, each class has a $1 \times d$ word vector. Here, we replace the v_b in W_s with that in W_{fb} learned from BLRPN.

3.2 Learning

Training Process. Compared with previous achievements [5–8] needing multi-step training and pre-trained weights on seen or unseen data, the training process of our model is very simple and convenient with a two step manner. First we train BLRPN to get v_b and use it to obtain a new W_s. Then we train our Cascade Semantic R-CNN equipped with semantic information flow with this new W_s. It needs to be emphasized that we only adopt the ImageNet pre-trained weights in the above training processes without any pre-trained weights of seen-class data.

Loss Function. First, we introduce the loss function of Cascade Semantic R-CNN. In each stage t for Cascade Semantic R-CNN, the box regression branch predicts the RoIs r_t and the semantic branch predicts category score c_t. The loss function L_{cs} is:

$$L_{cs} = \sum_{t=1}^{3} \alpha_t (L_t^{reg} + L_t^{sem}),$$
$$L_t^{reg}(\mathbf{r}_t, \widehat{\mathbf{r}}_t) = \ell_1(\mathbf{r}_t, \widehat{\mathbf{r}}_t), \tag{7}$$
$$L_t^{sem}(c_t, \widehat{c}_t) = CE(c_t, \widehat{c}_t).$$

Here, L_t^{sem} represents classification loss for semantic branch which adopts cross-entropy (CE) loss function. L_t^{reg} is the loss of the boxes predictions at stage t, which uses smooth $\ell 1$ loss. The coefficient α_t is the loss weight for each stage, we follow the settings in Cascade R-CNN [13] and set α_t to [1,0.5,0.25] for 3 stages.

The loss function of BLRPN denoted as L_{blrpn} is consists of the classification loss L^{fbsem} in foreground-background semantic branch and the box regression loss L^{reg} in regression branch:

$$L_{blrpn} = L^{reg} + L^{fbsem},$$
$$L^{reg}(\mathbf{r}, \hat{\mathbf{r}}) = \ell_1(\mathbf{r}, \hat{\mathbf{r}}),$$
$$L^{fbsem}(c, \hat{c}) = CE(c, \hat{c}). \tag{8}$$

Inference. We forward the input images through Cascade Semantic R-CNN to get the boxes and categories for all objects, then we apply Non-Maximum Suppression (NMS) to get the final results. In addition to the original inference process for the seen class in Eq. 5, we add an extra calculation process to inference unseen objects. The extra process is as follows:

$$\mathbf{c}_{unseen} = W_u W_s^{\mathsf{T}} \sigma(\delta(W_s f T) \mathbf{x}^{box}). \tag{9}$$

Where, $W_u \in \mathbb{R}^{d \times (u+1)}$ denotes the stacking word vectors for background and unseen classes, u indicates the number of unseen classes. The other components are same as Eq. 5. For an input object feature $\mathbf{x}^{box}$, we first map this visual feature to the category probability of seen classes. Then we use the transpose of W_s to transform this probability back to semantic space, finally we get unseen category score from the semantic space through W_u. For GZSD task, we simultaneously execute the above two reasoning process, so as to achieve the simultaneous reasoning of seen and unseen objects.

4   Experiments

4.1   Datasets

We perform experiments on MS-COCO dataset [48]. MS-COCO (2014) includes 82783 training images and 40504 validation images with 80 classes. We follow the datasets settings in [5] and [9] for MS-COCO. We divide the dataset with two different splits: (i) 48 seen classes an 17 unseen classes; (ii) 65 seen classes and 15 unseen classes. The seen classes are training set and unseen classes are test set. Both splits remove all images from the training set which contain any object from seen classes. Specially, the images for unseen classes in test set still have objects for seen classes in order to maintain the number of samples in the test set. Following [9], we use extra vocabulary from NUS-WIDE [51] and remove MS-COCO classes names and all tags with no word-vectors. We use a 300 dimensional word2vec [52] with a ℓ_2 normalization for MS-COCO classes and extra vocabulary.

Table 1. Comparison of the proposed BLC with the previous state-of-the-art zsd work on two splits of COCO. Seen/Unseen refers to the split of datasets. The proposed BLC can achieve 10.6 mAP and 48.87 Recall@100 for 48/17 split, 14.7 mAP and 54.68 Recall@100 for 65/15 split, significantly surpasses all other work. "ms" indicates multi-scale training and test.

Method	Seen/Unseen	Recall@100			mAP
		0.4	0.5	0.6	0.5
SB [5]	48/17	34.46	22.14	11.31	0.32
DSES [5]	48/17	40.23	27.19	13.63	0.54
TD [10]	48/17	45.50	34.30	18.10	–
PL [9]	48/17	–	43.59	–	10.10
BLC	48/17	**49.63**	**46.39**	**41.86**	9.90
BLC (ms)	48/17	**51.33**	**48.87**	**45.03**	10.60
PL [9]	65/15	–	37.72	–	12.40
BLC	65/15	**54.18**	**51.65**	**47.86**	13.10
BLC (ms)	65/15	**57.23**	**54.68**	**51.22**	14.70

4.2 Evaluation Protocol

We report the evaluation results on ZSD and GZSD task like previous work [5,9] over two splits for MS-COCO. We use recall and mAP as metrics, these metrics for boxes are all evaluated across IoU thresholds in 0.4, 0.5 and 0.6. In particular, the evaluation for recall is based on Recall@K [5], which means the recall when only the top K detections are selected from an image, we set K to 100 by following the settings in [5].

4.3 Implementation Details

In all experiments, we adopt ResNet-50 [49] as the backbone network with FPN [50]. We train all models with 4 GPUs (two images per GPU) for 12 epochs with a SGD optimizer which momentum is 0.9 and weight-decay is 0.0001. The initial learning rate for the optimizer is set to 0.01, and decreased by 0.1 after 8 and 11 epochs. The long edge and short edge of images are resized to 1333 and 800 without changing the aspect ratio. We use horizontal flip during training and the multi-scale for training is set to [400,1400]. We implement our model in PyTorch [53] and the pre-trained model is from PyTorch official model zoo.

4.4 Quantitative Results

Results in Benchmarks. We compare Background Learnable Cascade with the state-of-the-art zero-shot detection approaches on two splits of MS-COCO in Table 1. We can observe that: (i) for 48/17 split, we compare our approaches with SB [5], DSES [5], TD [10] and PL [9]. Our BLC surpasses all of them in

Table 2. Effects of each component in our work. Results are reported on 48/17 split and 65/15 split of MS-COCO, respectively.

	Cascade Semantic	Semantic Info	BLRPN	Recall@100			mAP
				0.4	0.5	0.6	0.5
48/17	✓			40.96	38.75	35.25	9.3
	✓	✓		43.84	41.73	38.11	9.5
	✓		✓	48.52	45.41	41.04	9.6
	✓	✓	✓	**49.63**	**46.39**	**41.86**	**9.9**
65/15	✓			49.75	47.28	43.87	12.4
	✓	✓		51.49	49.05	45.07	12.7
	✓		✓	53.38	51.03	47.39	12.9
	✓	✓	✓	**54.18**	**51.65**	**47.86**	**13.1**

Recall@100 and mAP, brings up to 33.72% (4×) and 10.28% (33×) gain in terms of Recall@100 and mAP; (ii) for 65/15 split, compared with PL [9], our BLC brings 16.96% gain for Recall@100 and 2.3% improvement for mAP. Moreover, in other previous works, Recall@100 drops severely as IoU threshold increasing while our BLC can still maintain a high Recall@100 indicating our approach is more robust for stringent IoU threshold.

Component-Wise Analysis. We investigate the contributions of the main components for BLC. "Cascade Semantic" means the baseline Cascade Semantic R-CNN, "Semantic Flow" denotes the semantic information flow, "BLRPN" represents the new background class word vector learned from our background learnable region proposal network. The results for 48/17 and 65/15 splits are shown in Table 2, respectively.

Class-Wise Performance. We report the Recall@100 on two splits of MS-COCO for each unseen classes in Table 3. Our BLC makes significant improvement on both splits: (i) for the split of 48/17, BLC substantially boosts baseline in the most of classes. For the classes which are hard to detect, BLC achieves 2.1×, 1.6×, 3.7×, 1.4×, 2.1×, 1.5× and 2.5× improvement on Recall@100 for "skateboard", "cup", "knife", "cake", "keyboard", "sink" and "scissors" classes, respectively; (ii) for the split of 65/15, BLC also obtains further improvement compared with baseline. We also note that BLC is unable to detect any true positive for the class "umbrella" and "tie", the Recall@100 rate for the class "hair drier" is also unsatisfying. The main reason is that there are fewer classes are semantically similar with these poor classes in training dataset, which makes them difficult to detect.

Table 3. Class-wise Recall@100 for 48/17 and 65/15 splits of MS-COCO with the IoU threshold is 0.5. Our BLC achieves significant improvement in most of unseen classes compared with Cascade Semantic R-CNN baseline.

48/17 split of MS-COCO

Method	Overall	bus	dog	cow	elephant	umbrella	tie	skateboard	cup	knife	cake	couch	keyboard	sink	scissors	airplane	cat	snowboard
baseline	38.73	72.9	**94.6**	67.3	68.1	0.0	0.0	19.9	24.0	12.4	24.0	63.7	11.6	9.2	8.3	48.3	70.7	**63.4**
BLC	**46.39**	**77.4**	88.4	**71.9**	**77.2**	0.0	0.0	**41.7**	**38.0**	**45.6**	**34.3**	**65.2**	**23.8**	**14.1**	**20.8**	48.3	**79.9**	61.8

65/15 split of MS-COCO

Method	Overall	airplane	train	parking meter	cat	bear	suitcase	frisbee	snowboard	fork	sandwich	hot dog	toilet	mouse	toaster	hair drier
baseline	47.28	53.9	70.6	5.9	90.2	85.1	40.7	25.9	59.9	33.7	76.9	64.4	33.2	3.3	**64.1**	1.4
BLC	**51.28**	**58.7**	**72.0**	**10.2**	**96.1**	**91.6**	**46.9**	**44.1**	**65.4**	**37.9**	**82.5**	**73.6**	**43.8**	**7.9**	35.9	**2.7**

Table 4. This table shows Recall@100 and mAP (IoU threshold = 0.5) for our BLC and other stat of the art over GZSD task. HM denotes the harmonic average for seen and unseen classes.

Method	Seen/Unseen	Seen		Unseen		HM	
		mAP	Recall	mAP	Recall	mAP	Recall
DSES [5]	48/17	-	15.02	-	15.32	-	15.17
PL [9]	48/17	35.92	38.24	4.12	26.32	7.39	31.18
BLC	48/17	**42.10**	**57.56**	**4.50**	**46.39**	**8.20**	**51.37**
PL [9]	65/15	34.07	36.38	12.40	37.16	18.18	36.76
BLC	65/15	**36.00**	**56.39**	**13.10**	**51.65**	**19.20**	**53.92**

Generalized Zero-Shot Detection (GZSD) Results. The generalized zero-shot detection task is more realistic that both seen and unseen classes are presented during evaluation. We report the performance for GZSD in Table 4 under on both splits over MS-COCO. The score threshold is 0.2 for seen classes and 0.05 for unseen classes, respectively. The IoU threshold for mAP is 0.5. Our BLC exceeds other stat-of-the-art methods in terms of mAP and recall@100.

4.5   Qualitative Results

For intuitively evaluating the qualitative results, we give some detection results in Fig. 5 for BLC on two splits of MS-COCO. We find that BLC can precisely detect unseen classes under different situations. For example, BLC detects objects under densely packed scenes, e.g., "airplanes", "elephants" and "hot dogs", as well as successfully captures small objects like the tiny "airplane". It is noteworthy that multiple objects are also detected by BLC from messy background like "cat"

Fig. 5. Examples for detection results of BLC on 48/17 and 65/15 splits of MS-COCO. All these objects are belong unseen classes.

and "couch". The main issue in BLC is the misclassification for unseen objects which belong to the same meta class due to lacking of enough information to distinguish them, and we can see it as cases of "elephant" and "cat".

5   Conclusions

In this paper, we propose a novel framework for ZSD named Background Learnable Cascade (BLC), which includes Cascade Semantic R-CNN, semantic information flow and BLRPN. Cascade Semantic R-CNN progressively refines the visual-semantic alignment, semantic information flow improves the semantic feature learning and BLRPN learns a appropriate word vector for background class to reduce the confusion between background and unseen classes. Experiments in two splits of MS-COCO show that BLC outperforms several state of the art under both ZSD and GZSD tasks.

Acknowledgement. The paper is supported by the National Natural Science Foundation of China (NSFC) under Grant No. 61672498 and the National Key Research and Development Program of China under Grant No. 2016YFC0302300.

References

1. Zhang, Z., Saligrama, V.: Zero-shot learning via joint latent similarity embedding. In: Proceedings of the IEEE Conference on Computer Vision and Pattern Recognition, pp. 6034–6042 (2016)
2. Nilsback, M.E., Zisserman, A.: Automated flower classification over a large number of classes. In: 2008 Sixth Indian Conference on Computer Vision, Graphics & Image Processing, pp. 722–729. IEEE (2008)
3. Russakovsky, O., et al.: ImageNet large scale visual recognition challenge. Int. J. Comput. Vis. **115**, 211–252 (2015)
4. Welinder, P., et al.: Caltech-UCSD birds 200 (2010)
5. Bansal, A., Sikka, K., Sharma, G., Chellappa, R., Divakaran, A.: Zero-shot object detection. In: Proceedings of the European Conference on Computer Vision (ECCV), pp. 384–400 (2018)
6. Demirel, B., Cinbis, R.G., Ikizler-Cinbis, N.: Zero-shot object detection by hybrid region embedding. arXiv preprint arXiv:1805.06157 (2018)
7. Rahman, S., Khan, S., Porikli, F.: Zero-shot object detection: learning to simultaneously recognize and localize novel concepts. In: Jawahar, C.V., Li, H., Mori, G., Schindler, K. (eds.) ACCV 2018. LNCS, vol. 11361, pp. 547–563. Springer, Cham (2019). https://doi.org/10.1007/978-3-030-20887-5_34
8. Zhu, P., Wang, H., Saligrama, V.: Zero shot detection. IEEE Trans. Circuits Syst. Video Technol. (2019)
9. Rahman, S., Khan, S., Barnes, N.: Improved visual-semantic alignment for zero-shot object detection. In: 34th AAAI Conference on Artificial Intelligence (2020)
10. Li, Z., Yao, L., Zhang, X., Wang, X., Kanhere, S., Zhang, H.: Zero-shot object detection with textual descriptions. In: Proceedings of the AAAI Conference on Artificial Intelligence, vol. 33, pp. 8690–8697 (2019)
11. Zhao, S., et al.: GTNet: generative transfer network for zero-shot object detection. arXiv preprint arXiv:2001.06812 (2020)
12. Zhu, P., Wang, H., Saligrama, V.: Don't even look once: synthesizing features for zero-shot detection. In: Proceedings of the IEEE/CVF Conference on Computer Vision and Pattern Recognition, pp. 11693–11702 (2020)
13. Cai, Z., Vasconcelos, N.: Cascade R-CNN: delving into high quality object detection. In: Proceedings of the IEEE Conference on Computer Vision and Pattern Recognition, pp. 6154–6162 (2018)
14. Bendale, A., Boult, T.E.: Towards open set deep networks. In: Proceedings of the IEEE Conference on Computer Vision and Pattern Recognition, pp. 1563–1572 (2016)
15. Changpinyo, S., Chao, W.L., Gong, B., Sha, F.: Synthesized classifiers for zero-shot learning. In: Proceedings of the IEEE Conference on Computer Vision and Pattern Recognition, pp. 5327–5336 (2016)
16. Elhoseiny, M., Saleh, B., Elgammal, A.: Write a classifier: zero-shot learning using purely textual descriptions. In: Proceedings of the IEEE International Conference on Computer Vision, pp. 2584–2591 (2013)
17. Frome, A., et al.: Devise: a deep visual-semantic embedding model. In: Advances in Neural Information Processing Systems, pp. 2121–2129 (2013)
18. Jain, L.P., Scheirer, W.J., Boult, T.E.: Multi-class open set recognition using probability of inclusion. In: Fleet, D., Pajdla, T., Schiele, B., Tuytelaars, T. (eds.) ECCV 2014. LNCS, vol. 8691, pp. 393–409. Springer, Cham (2014). https://doi.org/10.1007/978-3-319-10578-9_26

19. Kodirov, E., Xiang, T., Gong, S.: Semantic autoencoder for zero-shot learning. In: Proceedings of the IEEE Conference on Computer Vision and Pattern Recognition, pp. 3174–3183 (2017)
20. Lampert, C.H., Nickisch, H., Harmeling, S.: Learning to detect unseen object classes by between-class attribute transfer. In: 2009 IEEE Conference on Computer Vision and Pattern Recognition, pp. 951–958. IEEE (2009)
21. Lampert, C.H., Nickisch, H., Harmeling, S.: Attribute-based classification for zero-shot visual object categorization. IEEE Trans. Pattern Anal. Mach. Intell. **36**, 453–465 (2013)
22. Norouzi, M., et al.: Zero-shot learning by convex combination of semantic embeddings. arXiv preprint arXiv:1312.5650 (2013)
23. Rahman, S., Khan, S., Porikli, F.: A unified approach for conventional zero-shot, generalized zero-shot, and few-shot learning. IEEE Trans. Image Process. **27**, 5652–5667 (2018)
24. Xian, Y., Schiele, B., Akata, Z.: Zero-shot learning-the good, the bad and the ugly. In: Proceedings of the IEEE Conference on Computer Vision and Pattern Recognition, pp. 4582–4591 (2017)
25. Zhang, Z., Saligrama, V.: Zero-shot learning via semantic similarity embedding. In: Proceedings of the IEEE International Conference on Computer Vision, pp. 4166–4174 (2015)
26. Zhang, Z., Saligrama, V.: Zero-shot recognition via structured prediction. In: Leibe, B., Matas, J., Sebe, N., Welling, M. (eds.) ECCV 2016. LNCS, vol. 9911, pp. 533–548. Springer, Cham (2016). https://doi.org/10.1007/978-3-319-46478-7_33
27. Al-Halah, Z., Stiefelhagen, R.: Automatic discovery, association estimation and learning of semantic attributes for a thousand categories. In: Proceedings of the IEEE Conference on Computer Vision and Pattern Recognition, pp. 614–623 (2017)
28. Al-Halah, Z., Tapaswi, M., Stiefelhagen, R.: Recovering the missing link: predicting class-attribute associations for unsupervised zero-shot learning. In: Proceedings of the IEEE Conference on Computer Vision and Pattern Recognition, pp. 5975–5984 (2016)
29. Xian, Y., Lampert, C.H., Schiele, B., Akata, Z.: Zero-shot learning-a comprehensive evaluation of the good, the bad and the ugly. IEEE Trans. Pattern Anal. Mach. Intell. **41**, 2251–2265 (2018)
30. Zablocki, E., Bordes, P., Soulier, L., Piwowarski, B., Gallinari, P.: Context-aware zero-shot learning for object recognition. In: International Conference on Machine Learning, PMLR, pp. 7292–7303 (2019)
31. Luo, R., Zhang, N., Han, B., Yang, L.: Context-aware zero-shot recognition. arXiv preprint arXiv:1904.09320 (2019)
32. Krishna, R., et al.: Visual genome: connecting language and vision using crowdsourced dense image annotations. Int. J. Comput. Vis. **123**, 32–73 (2017)
33. Mishra, A., Krishna Reddy, S., Mittal, A., Murthy, H.A.: A generative model for zero shot learning using conditional variational autoencoders. In: Proceedings of the IEEE Conference on Computer Vision and Pattern Recognition Workshops, pp. 2188–2196 (2018)
34. Kumar Verma, V., Arora, G., Mishra, A., Rai, P.: Generalized zero-shot learning via synthesized examples. In: Proceedings of the IEEE Conference on Computer Vision and Pattern Recognition, pp. 4281–4289 (2018)
35. Verma, V.K., Rai, P.: A simple exponential family framework for zero-shot learning. In: Ceci, M., Hollmén, J., Todorovski, L., Vens, C., Džeroski, S. (eds.) ECML PKDD 2017. LNCS (LNAI), vol. 10535, pp. 792–808. Springer, Cham (2017). https://doi.org/10.1007/978-3-319-71246-8_48

36. Verma, V.K., Brahma, D., Rai, P.: Meta-learning for generalized zero-shot learning. In: AAAI, pp. 6062–6069 (2020)
37. Redmon, J., Divvala, S., Girshick, R., Farhadi, A.: You only look once: unified, real-time object detection. In: Proceedings of the IEEE Conference on Computer Vision and Pattern Recognition, pp. 779–788 (2016)
38. Liu, W., et al.: SSD: single shot multibox detector. In: Leibe, B., Matas, J., Sebe, N., Welling, M. (eds.) ECCV 2016. LNCS, vol. 9905, pp. 21–37. Springer, Cham (2016). https://doi.org/10.1007/978-3-319-46448-0_2
39. Lin, T.Y., Goyal, P., Girshick, R., He, K., Dollár, P.: Focal loss for dense object detection. In: Proceedings of the IEEE International Conference on Computer Vision, pp. 2980–2988 (2017)
40. Ren, S., He, K., Girshick, R., Sun, J.: Faster R-CNN: towards real-time object detection with region proposal networks. In: Advances in Neural Information Processing Systems, pp. 91–99 (2015)
41. Dai, J., Li, Y., He, K., Sun, J.: R-FCN: object detection via region-based fully convolutional networks. In: Advances in Neural Information Processing Systems, pp. 379–387 (2016)
42. He, K., Gkioxari, G., Dollár, P., Girshick, R.: Mask R-CNN. In: Proceedings of the IEEE International Conference on Computer Vision, pp. 2961–2969 (2017)
43. Dai, J., et al.: Deformable convolutional networks. In: Proceedings of the IEEE International Conference on Computer Vision, pp. 764–773 (2017)
44. Law, H., Deng, J.: Cornernet: detecting objects as paired keypoints. In: Proceedings of the European Conference on Computer Vision (ECCV), pp. 734–750 (2018)
45. Duan, K., Bai, S., Xie, L., Qi, H., Huang, Q., Tian, Q.: Centernet: keypoint triplets for object detection. In: Proceedings of the IEEE International Conference on Computer Vision, pp. 6569–6578 (2019)
46. Tian, Z., Shen, C., Chen, H., He, T.: FCOS: fully convolutional one-stage object detection. In: Proceedings of the IEEE International Conference on Computer Vision, pp. 9627–9636 (2019)
47. Redmon, J., Farhadi, A.: YOLO9000: better, faster, stronger. In: Proceedings of the IEEE Conference on Computer Vision and Pattern Recognition, pp. 7263–7271 (2017)
48. Lin, T.-Y., et al.: Microsoft COCO: common objects in context. In: Fleet, D., Pajdla, T., Schiele, B., Tuytelaars, T. (eds.) ECCV 2014. LNCS, vol. 8693, pp. 740–755. Springer, Cham (2014). https://doi.org/10.1007/978-3-319-10602-1_48
49. He, K., Zhang, X., Ren, S., Sun, J.: Deep residual learning for image recognition. In: Proceedings of the IEEE Conference on Computer Vision and Pattern Recognition, pp. 770–778 (2016)
50. Lin, T.Y., Dollár, P., Girshick, R., He, K., Hariharan, B., Belongie, S.: Feature pyramid networks for object detection. In: Proceedings of the IEEE Conference on Computer Vision and Pattern Recognition, pp. 2117–2125 (2017)
51. Chua, T.S., Tang, J., Hong, R., Li, H., Luo, Z., Zheng, Y.: NUS-WIDE: a real-world web image database from National University of Singapore. In: Proceedings of the ACM International Conference on Image and Video Retrieval, pp. 1–9 (2009)
52. Mikolov, T., Sutskever, I., Chen, K., Corrado, G.S., Dean, J.: Distributed representations of words and phrases and their compositionality. In: Advances in Neural Information Processing Systems, pp. 3111–3119 (2013)
53. Paszke, A., et al.: Automatic differentiation in pytorch (2017)

Unsupervised Domain Adaptive Object Detection Using Forward-Backward Cyclic Adaptation

Siqi Yang[1(✉)], Lin Wu[2], Arnold Wiliem[1], and Brian C. Lovell[1]

[1] The University of Queensland, Brisbane, Australia
siqi.yang@uq.net.au, arnold.wiliem@ieee.org, lovell@itee.uq.edu.au
[2] Hefei University of Technology, Hefei, China
xiaoxian.wu9188@gmail.com

Abstract. We present a novel approach to perform the unsupervised domain adaptation for object detection through forward-backward cyclic (FBC) training. Recent adversarial training based domain adaptation methods have shown their effectiveness on minimizing domain discrepancy via marginal feature distributions alignment. However, aligning the marginal feature distributions does not guarantee the alignment of class conditional distributions. This limitation is more evident when adapting object detectors as the domain discrepancy is larger compared to the image classification task, *e.g.*, various number of objects exist in one image and the majority of content in an image is the background. This motivates us to learn domain-invariance for category-level semantics via gradient alignment for instance-level adaptation. Intuitively, if the gradients of two domains point in similar directions, then the learning of one domain can improve that of another domain. We propose Forward-Backward Cyclic Adaptation to achieve gradient alignment, which iteratively computes adaptation from source to target via backward hopping and from target to source via forward passing. In addition, we align low-level features for adapting image-level color/texture via adversarial training. However, the detector that performs well on both domains is not ideal for the target domain. As such, in each cycle, domain diversity is enforced by two regularizations: 1) maximum entropy regularization on the source domain to penalize confident source-specific learning and 2) minimum entropy regularization on target domain to intrigue target-specific learning. Theoretical analysis of the training process is provided, and extensive experiments on challenging cross-domain object detection datasets have shown our approach's superiority over the state-of-the-art.

1 Introduction

Object detection is a fundamental problem in computer vision [1–5], which can be applied to many scenarios such as face and pedestrian detection [6] and self-

Electronic supplementary material The online version of this chapter (https://doi.org/10.1007/978-3-030-69535-4_8) contains supplementary material, which is available to authorized users.

© Springer Nature Switzerland AG 2021
H. Ishikawa et al. (Eds.): ACCV 2020, LNCS 12624, pp. 124–142, 2021.
https://doi.org/10.1007/978-3-030-69535-4_8

Fig. 1. (a) Due to domain discrepancy, the detector trained on the source domain does not perform well on the target. Green boxes indicate false positives and red indicate missing objects. (b) Feature visualization of the detection results on target images generated by source-only model. It is difficult to align feature at instance-level without category information due to the existence of false detections on the background. (Color figure online)

driving cars [7]. However, due to the variations in shape and appearance, lighting conditions and backgrounds, a model trained on the source data might not perform well on the target—a problem known as *domain discrepancy*. A common approach to maximizing the performance on the target domain is via fine-tuning a pre-trained model with a large amount of target data. However, annotating bounding boxes for target objects is time-consuming and expensive. Hence, unsupervised domain adaptation methods for object detection are highly desirable.

Unsupervised domain adaptation for image classification has been extensively studied [8–13]. Most methods are developed to learn domain-invariant features by simultaneously minimizing the source error and the domain discrepancy through feature distribution alignment. Standard optimization criteria include maximum mean discrepancy [8,9] and distribution moment matching [14,15]. Recent adversarial training based methods have shown their effectiveness in learning domain-invariance by matching the marginal distributions of both source and target features [10,11,16]. However, this does not guarantee the alignment of class conditional distributions [17–20]. For example, aligning the target cat class to the source dog class can easily meet the objective of reducing the cost of source/target domain distinction, but the semantic categories are wrong. The limitation of adversarial learning is more evident when the domain discrepancy between two domains is larger, such as in object detection.

In object detection, performing domain alignment is more challenging compared to alignment in the image classification task in the following two aspects: (1) the input image may contain multiple objects, while there is only one centered object in the classification task; (2) the images in object detection are dominated by background and non-objects. Therefore, performing global adversarial learning (*i.e.,* marginal feature distributions) at the image-level is not sufficient for such challenging tasks due to the limitations discussed above. Chen *et al.* [21] made the first attempt to apply adversarial domain alignment to object detection, where the marginal feature distributions were aligned at both image-level and instance-level. However, due to the domain shift, the detector may not

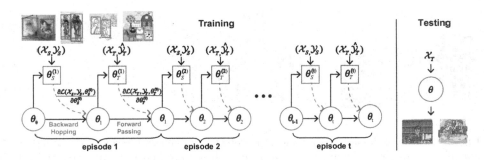

Fig. 2. The diagram of the proposed forward-backward cyclic adaptation for unsupervised domain adaptive object detection. In each episode, the training proceeds to achieve two goals: 1) gradient alignment across the source $\mathcal{X}_s$ and target $\mathcal{X}_t$ to achieve domain invariant detectors; and 2) encouraging domain-diversity to boost the target detector performance.

be accurate and many non-object proposals from the backgrounds are used for domain alignment (Fig. 1). This amplifies the limitation of adversarial domain training and hence limited gains can be achieved.

To tackle the limitation, efforts have been made to improve the image-level adaptation [22] and instance-level adaptation [23, 24] respectively. Saito *et al.* [22] proposed to weakly align the image-level features from the high-level layer, where the globally similar images have higher priorities to be aligned. In instance-level adaptation, Zhu *et al.* [23] proposed to filter the non-objects via grouping and then select source-like target instances according to the scores of the domain classifier. Zhuang *et al.* [24] proposed category-aware domain discriminators for instance-level alignment, where each category has its own domain discriminator.

We argue that explicit feature distribution alignment is not a necessary condition to learn domain-invariance. Instead, we remark that *domain-invariance* of category-level semantics can be learned by gradient alignment, where the inner product between the gradients of category-level classification loss from different domains is maximized. Intuitively, if the inner product is positive, taking a gradient step at the examples from one domain can decrease the loss at the examples from another domain. In other words, the learning of one domain can improve the learning of another domain and therefore lead to domain-invariance. More importantly, the gradients of category-level classification loss can encode class conditional information. Therefore, gradient alignment shows its advantages on the challenging instance-level adaptation for object detection.

In this work, we propose a Forward-Backward Cyclic Adaptation (FBC) approach to learn adaptive object detectors. In each cycle, the games of *Forward Passing*, an adaptation from source to target, and *Backward Hopping*, an adaptation from target to source, are played sequentially. Each adaptation is a domain transfer, where the training is first initialized with the model trained on the previous domain and then finetuned with the images in the current domain. We provide a theoretical analysis to show that by computing the forward and backward adaptation sequentially via Stochastic Gradient Descent (SGD), gradient alignment can be achieved. Our proposed approach is also related to the cycle consistency utilized in both machine translation [25] and image-to-image translation [26,27] with a similar intuition that the mappings of an example transferred from source to target and then back to the source domain should have the same results. In addition to instance-level adaptation via gradient alignment, we leverage adversarial domain training for image-level adaptation. Low-level features are aligned to learn the domain-invariance of holistic color and textures.

However, a detector with good generalization on both domains may not be the optimal solution for the target domain. To address this, we introduce *domain-diversity* into the training objective to avoid overfitting on the source domain and encourage target-specific learning on the target domain. We adopt two regularizers: (1) a maximum entropy regularizer on source domain and (2) a minimum entropy regularizer on the target domain.

We conduct experiments on four domain-shift scenarios and experimental results show the effectiveness of our proposed approach. **Contributions:** (1) We propose a forward-backward cyclic adaptation approach to learn unsupervised domain adaptive object detectors through image-level adaptation via adversarial domain alignment and instance-level adaptation via gradient alignment; (2) The proposed gradient alignment effectively aligns category-level semantics at the instance-level; (3) To achieve good performance on the target domain, we explicitly enforce domain-diversity via entropy regularization to further approximate the domain-invariant detectors closer to the optimal solution to target space; (4) The proposed method is simple yet effective and can be applied to various architectures.

2 Related Work

Object Detection. Deep object detection methods [1–3,5,28,29] can be roughly grouped into two-stage detectors, *e.g.,* Faster R-CNN [1] and single-stage detectors, *e.g.,* SSD [2] and YOLO [3]. Faster R-CNN consists of two networks: a region proposal network and an R-CNN that classifies the proposals. Other methods like FPN [5] and RetinaNet [29] proposed to leverage a combination of features from different levels to improve the feature representations.

Unsupervised Domain Adaptation for Image Classification. A vast number of deep learning based unsupervised domain adaptation methods are presented for image classification. Many adaptation methods [8–11,14,16,30] are proposed to reduce the domain divergence based on the following theory:

Theorem 1 (Ben-David et al. [31]). *Let* $h : \mathcal{X} \rightarrow \mathcal{Y}$ *be a hypothesis in the hypothesis space* $\mathcal{H}$*. The expected error on target domain* $\epsilon_T(h)$ *is bounded by*

$$\epsilon_T(h) \leq \epsilon_S(h) + \frac{1}{2}d_{\mathcal{H}\Delta\mathcal{H}}(\mathcal{D}_S, \mathcal{D}_T) + \lambda, \forall h \in \mathcal{H}, \tag{1}$$

where $\epsilon_S(h)$ is the expected error on the source domain,

$$d_{\mathcal{H}\Delta\mathcal{H}}(\mathcal{D}_S, \mathcal{D}_T) = 2 \sup_{h,h'\in\mathcal{H}} \left| \Pr_{x\sim\mathcal{D}_S}[h(x) \neq h'(x)] - \Pr_{x\sim\mathcal{D}_T}[h(x) \neq h'(x)] \right| \text{ measures domain diver-}$$

gence, and λ is the expected error of ideal joint hypothesis, $\lambda = \min_{h\in\mathcal{H}}[\epsilon_S(h) + \epsilon_T(h)]$.

To minimize the divergence, various methods have been proposed to align the distributions of features from source and target domains, *e.g.*, maximum mean discrepancy [8,9], correlation alignment [14], joint distribution discrepancy loss [30] and adversarial training [10,11,16]. Adversarial training based methods [10,11,16] align the marginal distributions of source and target features, where the feature generator is trained to confuse the domain classifier. Although these methods have demonstrated impressive results, recent works [17,18,22,32,33] have shown that aligning marginal distributions without considering class conditional distributions does not guarantee small $d_{\mathcal{H}\Delta\mathcal{H}}(\mathcal{D}_S, \mathcal{D}_T)$. To address this, Luo *et al.* [19] proposed a semantic-aware discriminator and Xie *et al.* [17] proposed to align the semantic prototypes for each class. Some works [17,32,33] proposed to minimize the joint hypothesis error λ with pseudo labels in addition to the marginal distribution alignment. Some other methods proposed to use the predictions of a classifier as pseudo labels for unlabeled target samples [12,34,35]. Lee *et al.* [36] argued that training with pseudo labels is equivalent to entropy regularization, which favors a low-density separation between classes.

Unsupervised Domain Adaptation for Object Detection. Domain adaptive object detection has received much attention in the past two years [21–24,37–40]. The DA-Faster [21] was proposed to align domains at both image-level and instance-level by adding two domain classifiers to the Faster R-CNN. However, due to the limitation of domain adversarial training and inaccurate instance predictions, the improvement is limited. To improve the efficiency of image-level adaptation, multi-feature alignment [22,24,37,39] has been proposed. In strong-weak domain alignment (SWDA) [22], Saito *et al.* proposed to strongly align low-level image features and weakly align high-level image features. Through weak alignment, the target images that are globally similar to source images have higher priorities to be aligned. Focal loss [29] is used in the domain classifier to achieve it. To address the inaccurate instance problem in instance-level adaptation, Zhu *et al.* [23] proposed to first filter non-object instances via grouping and then emphasize the target instances that are similar to the source for adversarial domain alignment. However, the category-level semantics are not studied in the traditional adversarial alignment. Zhuang *et al.* [24] proposed image-instance full alignment (iFAN) for category-aware instance-level adaptation, where each category owns a domain discriminator. Unlike using adversarial training, our proposed method aligns category-level semantics via gradient alignment.

Gradient-Based Meta Learning and Continual Learning. Our method is also related to recent gradient-based meta-learning methods: MAML [41] and Reptile [42], which are designed to learn a good initialization for few-shot learning and have demonstrated good within-task generalization. Reptile [42] suggested that SGD automatically maximizes the inner products between the gra-

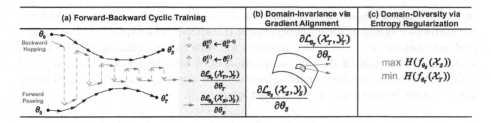

Fig. 3. (a) Illustration of the model updates in our proposed forward-backward cyclic adaptation method. The θ_0 is the initial model and the θ_S^* and θ_T^* are the optimal solutions for source and target domain, respectively. (b) We propose that domain-invariance occurs when the gradients of source and target samples are pointing in similar directions. (c) The domain diversity is implemented by maximum entropy regularization on the source domain and minimum entropy regularization on the target domain.

dients computed on different minibatches of the same task, and results in within-task generalization. Riemer *et al.* [43] integrated the Reptile with an experience replay module for the task of continual learning, where the transfer between examples is maximized via gradient alignment. Inspired by these methods, we leverage the generalization ability of Reptile [42] to improve the generalization across domains for unsupervised domain adaptation via gradient alignment.

Entropy Regularization. The maximum entropy principle proposed by Jaynes [44] has been applied to reinforcement learning [45, 46] to prevent early convergence and supervised learning to improve generalization [47–50]. On the contrary, the entropy minimization has been used for unsupervised clustering [51], semi-supervised learning [52] and unsupervised domain adaptation [9,53] to encourages low density separation between clusters or classes (Fig. 3).

3 Forward-Backward Domain Adaptation for Object Detection

3.1 Overview

In unsupervised domain adaptation, N_S labeled images $\{\mathcal{X}_S, \mathcal{Y}_S\} = \{x_S^i, y_S^i\}_{i=1}^{N_S}$ from the source domain with a distribution $\mathcal{D}_S$ are given. We have N_T unlabeled images $\mathcal{X}_T = \{x_T^j\}_{j=1}^{N_T}$ from the target domain with a different distribution $\mathcal{D}_T$, but the ground truth labels $\mathcal{Y}_T = \{y_T^j\}_{j=1}^{N_T}$ are not accessible during training. Note that in object detection, each label in $\mathcal{Y}_S$ or $\mathcal{Y}_T$ is composed of a set of bounding boxes with their corresponding class labels. Our goal is to learn a neural network (parameterized by θ) $f_\theta : \mathcal{X}_T \to \mathcal{Y}_T$ that can make accurate predictions on the target samples without the need for labeled training data.

In this work, we argue that aligning the feature distributions is not a necessary condition to reduce the $d_{\mathcal{H}\Delta\mathcal{H}}(\mathcal{D}_S, \mathcal{D}_T)$ in Theorem 1. Unlike the above-mentioned distribution alignment based methods, we cast the domain adaptation into an optimization problem to learn the domain-invariance. We propose to utilize gradient alignment for category-aware instance-level adaptation. For image-level adaptation, local feature alignment via adversarial training is performed. As the ultimate goal of domain adaptation is to achieve good performance on the target domain, we further introduce *domain-diversity* into training to boost the detection performance in the target space.

3.2   Gradient Alignment via Forward-Backward Cyclic Training

Recent gradient-based meta-learning methods [41,42,54], designed for few-shot learning, have demonstrated their success in approximating learning algorithms and shown their ability to generalize well to new data from unseen distributions. Inspired by these methods, we propose to learn the *domain-invariance* via gradient alignment to achieve generalization across domains.

Gradient Alignment for Domain-Invariance. Suppose that we have neural networks that learn the predictions for source and target samples as f_{θ_S} : $\mathcal{X}_S \to \mathcal{Y}_S$ and $f_{\theta_T} : \mathcal{X}_T \to \mathcal{Y}_T$. The network parameters θ_S and θ_T are updated via minimizing the empirical risks, $\mathcal{L}_{\theta_S}(\mathcal{X}_S, \mathcal{Y}_S) = \frac{1}{N_S} \sum_{i=1}^{N_S} \ell(f_{\theta_S}(x_S^i), y_S^i)$ and $\mathcal{L}_{\theta_T}(\mathcal{X}_T, \mathcal{Y}_T) = \frac{1}{N_T} \sum_{j=1}^{N_T} \ell(f_{\theta_T}(x_T^j), y_T^j)$, where $\ell(\cdot)$ is the cross-entropy loss. Inspired by methods for continual learning [43,55], when the parameters θ_S and θ_T are shared and the gradient updates are in small steps, we could assume the function $\mathcal{L}_\theta$ is linear. If the following condition is satisfied, the gradient updates at source samples could decrease the loss at target samples and vice verse:

$$\frac{\partial \mathcal{L}_{\theta_S}(\mathcal{X}_S, \mathcal{Y}_S)}{\partial \theta_S} \cdot \frac{\partial \mathcal{L}_{\theta_T}(\mathcal{X}_T, \mathcal{Y}_T)}{\partial \theta_T} > 0, \tag{2}$$

where the $\cdot$ is the inner-product operator. This indicates that the learning of one domain could improve the learning of another domain. Therefore, we propose that domain-invariance could be learned by maximizing the inner products of gradients from different domains. Moreover, this gradient alignment can encode category-level semantics as the gradients are generated from the classification losses $\mathcal{L}_{\theta_S}(\mathcal{X}_S, \mathcal{Y}_S)$ and $\mathcal{L}_{\theta_T}(\mathcal{X}_T, \mathcal{Y}_T)$. It is different from the feature alignment by a domain classifier in adversarial training based methods [10,11,16,21,22], where class information is not explicitly considered. Thus, we use gradient alignment for instance-level adaptation.

Recall Theorem 1, once $d_{\mathcal{H}\Delta\mathcal{H}}(\mathcal{D}_S, \mathcal{D}_T)$ is minimized, the generalization error on target domain $\epsilon_T(h)$ is bounded by the shared error of ideal joint hypothesis, $\lambda = \min_{h \in \mathcal{H}}[\epsilon_S(h) + \epsilon_T(h)]$. As suggested in [31], it is important to have a classifier performing well on both domains. Therefore, similar to the previous works [17,33,36], we resort to using pseudo labels $\hat{\mathcal{Y}}_T = \{\hat{y}_T^j\}_{j=1}^{N_T}$ to optimize the upper bound for the λ. These pseudo labels are the detections on the target images produced by the source detector f_{θ_S} and are updated with the updates

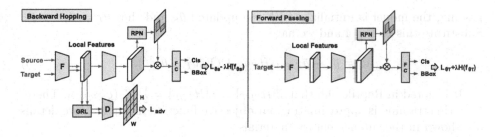

Fig. 4. Network architecture.

of f_{θ_S}. Our objective function of gradient alignment is to minimize the $\mathcal{L}_g$:

$$\mathcal{L}_{\theta_S}(\mathcal{X}_S, \mathcal{Y}_S) + \mathcal{L}_{\theta_T}(\mathcal{X}_T, \hat{\mathcal{Y}}_T) - \alpha \frac{\partial \mathcal{L}_{\theta_S}(\mathcal{X}_S, \mathcal{Y}_S)}{\partial \theta_S} \cdot \frac{\partial \mathcal{L}_{\theta_T}(\mathcal{X}_T, \hat{\mathcal{Y}}_T)}{\partial \theta_T}. \tag{3}$$

Forward-Backward Cyclic Training. To achieve the above objective, we propose an algorithm that sequentially plays the game of *Backward Hopping* on the source domain and *Foward Passing* on the target domain, and a shared network parameterized by θ is updated iteratively. We initialize the shared network θ with ImageNet [56] pre-trained model. Let us denote a cycle of performing forward passing and backward hopping as an episode. In the backward hopping phase of episode t, the network parameterized by $\theta_S^{(t)}$ is first initialized with the model $\theta_T^{(t-1)}$ from the previous episode $t-1$. And the model $\theta_S^{(t)}$ is then optimized with one image per time via stochastic gradient descent (SGD) on N_S labeled source images $\{\mathcal{X}_S, \mathcal{Y}_S\}$. In forward passing, the model $\theta_T^{(t)}$ is initialized with $\theta_S^{(t)}$ and trained with pseudo labeled target samples $\{\mathcal{X}_T, \hat{\mathcal{Y}}_T\}$. The training procedure is shown in Fig. 2 (Fig. 4).

Theoretical Analysis. We provide a theoretical analysis to show how our proposed forward and backward training strategy can achieve the objective of gradient alignment in Eq. 3. For simplicity, we only analyze the gradient computations in one episode and denote the gradient obtained in one episode as g_e. We then have $g_e = g_S + g_T$, where g_S is obtained in backward hopping $g_S = \frac{\partial \mathcal{L}_{\theta_S}(\mathcal{X}_S, \mathcal{Y}_S)}{\partial \theta_S}$ and g_T is the gradient obtained in forward passing $g_T = \frac{\partial \mathcal{L}_{\theta_T}(\mathcal{X}_T, \hat{\mathcal{Y}}_T)}{\partial \theta_T}$.

According to Taylor's theorem, the gradient of forward passing can be expanded as $g_T = \bar{g}_T + \bar{H}_T(\theta_T - \theta_0) + O(\|\theta_T - \theta_0\|^2)$, where $\bar{g}_T$ and $\bar{H}_T$ are the gradient and Hessian matrix at initial point θ_0. Then the overall gradient g_e can be rewritten as:

$$g_e = g_S + g_T = \bar{g}_S + \bar{g}_T + \bar{H}_T(\theta_T - \theta_0) + O(\|\theta_T - \theta_0\|^2). \tag{4}$$

Let us denote the initial parameters in one episode as θ_0. In our proposed forward and backward training strategy, the model parameters of backward hopping are first initialized with $\theta_S = \theta_0$ and are updated by $\theta_0 - \alpha g_S$. In forward passing, the model is initialized with the updated θ_S and thus $\theta_T = \theta_0 - \alpha g_S$. Substitute this to Eq. 4 and we have

$$g_e = \bar{g}_S + \bar{g}_T - \alpha \bar{H}_T \bar{g}_S + O(\|\theta_T - \theta_0\|^2). \qquad (5)$$

It is noted in Reptile [42] that $\mathbb{E}[\bar{H}_S \bar{g}_T] = \mathbb{E}[\bar{H}_T \bar{g}_S] = \frac{1}{2}[\frac{\partial}{\partial \theta_0}(\bar{g}_S \cdot \bar{g}_T)]$. Therefore, this training is approximating our objective function in Eq. 3. More details are shown in the supplementary materials.

3.3 Local Feature Alignment via Adversarial Training

Domain adversarial training has demonstrated its effectiveness in reducing domain discrepancy of low-level features, *e.g.,* local texture and color, regardless of class conditional information [21,22]. Therefore, we align the low-level features at the image-level in combination with gradient alignment on the source domain. We utilize the gradient reversal layer (GRL) proposed by Ganin and Lempitsky [10] for adversarial domain training, where the gradients of the domain classifier are reversed for domain confusion. Following SWDA [22], we extract local features F from a low-level layer as the input of the domain classifier D and the least-squares loss [26,57] is used to optimize the domain classifier. The loss of adversarial training is as follows:

$$\mathcal{L}_{adv} = \frac{1}{2} \frac{1}{N_S WH} \sum_{i,w,h} D(F(x_S^i))_{wh}^2 + \frac{1}{2} \frac{1}{N_S WH} \sum_{j,w,h} (1 - D(F(x_T^j))_{wh})^2, \quad (6)$$

where H and W are the height and width of the output feature map of the domain classifier.

3.4 Domain Diversity via Entropy Regularization

The ultimate goal of domain adaptation is to achieve good performance on the target domain. However, a model that only learns the domain-invariance is not an optimal solution for the target domain, as

$$\epsilon_T(h) \leq \epsilon_T(h^a) + \epsilon_T(h, h^a), \qquad (7)$$

where $h^a = \arg\min_{h \in \mathcal{H}}[\epsilon_S(h) + \epsilon_T(h)]$. Moreover, in the absence of ground truth labels for target samples, the learning of domain-invariance largely relies on the source samples, which might lead to overfitting on the source domain and limiting its ability to generalize well on target domain. Therefore, it is crucial to introduce the domain-diversity into the training to encourage more emphasis on target-specific information.

We define the domain diversity as a combination of two regularizations: (1) maximum entropy regularization on the source domain to avoid overfitting and (2) minimum entropy regularization on unlabeled target domain to leverage target-specific information. Low entropy corresponds to high confidence. To avoid the overfitting when training with source data, we utilize the maximum entropy regularizer [47] to penalize the confident predictions with low entropy:

$$\max_{\theta_S} H(f_{\theta_S}(\mathcal{X}_S)) = -\sum_{i=1}^{N_S} f_{\theta_S}(x_S^i) \log(f_{\theta_S}(x_S^i)). \tag{8}$$

On the contrary, to leverage unlabeled target domain data, we exploit the minimum entropy regularizer. The entropy minimization has been used for unsupervised clustering [51], semi-supervised learning [52] and unsupervised domain adaptation [9,53] to encourages low density separation between clusters or classes. Here, we minimize the entropy of class conditional distribution:

$$\min_{\theta_T} H(f_{\theta_T}(\mathcal{X}_T)) = -\sum_{j=1}^{N_T} f_{\theta_T}(x_T^j) \log(f_{\theta_T}(x_T^j)). \tag{9}$$

We define the objective of domain diversity is to minimize the following function:

$$\mathcal{L}_{div}(\mathcal{X}_S, \mathcal{X}_T) = -H(f_{\theta_S}(\mathcal{X}_S)) + H(f_{\theta_T}(\mathcal{X}_T)). \tag{10}$$

3.5 Overall Objective

To learn domain-invariance for adapting object detectors, we perform gradient alignment for high-level semantics and domain adversarial training on local features for low-level information. The loss function of domain-invariance is:

$$\mathcal{L}_{inv}(\mathcal{X}_S, \mathcal{Y}_S, \mathcal{X}_T) = \mathcal{L}_g(\mathcal{X}_S, \mathcal{Y}_S, \mathcal{X}_T) + \lambda\mathcal{L}_{adv}(\mathcal{X}_S, \mathcal{X}_T), \tag{11}$$

where λ balances the trade-off between gradient alignment loss and adversarial training loss.

Maximizing the domain-diversity contradicts the intention of learning domain-invariance. However, without access to the ground truth labels of target samples, the accuracy of the target samples relies on the domain-invariance information learned from the source domain. Consequently, it is important to accomplish the trade-off between learning domain-invariance and domain-diversity. We use a hyperparameter γ to balance the trade-off. Our overall objective function is

$$\min_{\theta} \mathcal{L}_{inv}(\mathcal{X}_S, \mathcal{Y}_S, \mathcal{X}_T) + \gamma\mathcal{L}_{div}(\mathcal{X}_S, \mathcal{X}_T). \tag{12}$$

The full algorithm is outlined in Algorithm 1.

Algorithm 1. Forward-Backward Cyclic Domain Adaptation for Object Detection

---

Input: Source samples $\{x_S^i, y_S^i\}_{i=1}^{N_S}$, target samples $\{x_T^j\}_{j=1}^{N_T}$, ImageNet pre-trained model θ_0, hyperparameters α, β, γ, λ, number of iterations N_{itr}

Output: A shared model θ

1: Initialize θ with θ_0
2: **for** t in N_{itr} **do**
3:     //*Backward Hopping:*
4:     $\theta_S^{(t)} \leftarrow \theta$
5:     **for** i, j in N_S, N_T **do**
6:         $\theta_S^{(t)} \leftarrow \theta_S^{(t)} - \alpha \nabla_{\theta_S^{(t)}} (\mathcal{L}_{\theta_S^{(t)}}(x_S^i, y_S^i) + \lambda \mathcal{L}_{adv}(x_S^i, x_T^j) - \gamma \mathrm{H}(f_{\theta_S^{(t)}}(x_S^i)))$
7:     **end for**
8:     $\theta \leftarrow \theta - \beta \theta_S^{(t)}$
9:     Generate pseudo labels $\hat{y}_T = f_{\theta_S^{(t)}}(x_T^j), j = 1, ..., N_T$
10:     //*Forward Passing:*
11:     $\theta_T^{(t)} \leftarrow \theta$
12:     **for** j in N_T **do**
13:         $\theta_T^{(t)} \leftarrow \theta_T^{(t)} - \alpha \nabla_{\theta_T^{(t)}} (\mathcal{L}_{\theta_T^{(t)}}(x_T^j, \hat{y}_T^j) + \gamma \mathrm{H}(f_{\theta_T^{(t)}}(x_T^j)))$
14:     **end for**
15:     $\theta \leftarrow \theta - \beta \theta_T^{(t)}$
16: **end for**

---

4   Experiments

In this section, we evaluate the proposed forward-backward cycling adaptation approach (FBC) on four cross-domain detection datasets.

4.1   Implementation Details

Following DA-Faster [21] and SWDA [22], we use the Faster-RCNN [1] as our detection framework. All training and test images are resized with the shorter side of 600 pixels and the training batch size is 1. Our method is implemented using Pytorch. The source only model is fine-tuned on the pre-trained ImageNet [56] model with labeled source samples without adaptation For the evaluation, we measure the mean average precision (mAP) with a threshold of 0.5 across all classes. More details are shown in supplementary materials.

Table 1. Results (%) on the adaptation from PASCAL [58] to Clipart Dataset [59]. The DA-Faster†is the reported result in SWDA [22].

Method	aero	bike	bird	boat	bottle	bus	car	cat	chair	cow	table	dog	horse	motor	prsn	plnt	sheep	sofa	train	tv	mAP
Source only	24.2	47.1	24.9	17.7	26.6	47.3	30.4	11.9	36.8	26.4	10.1	11.8	25.9	74.6	42.1	24.0	3.8	27.2	37.9	29.9	29.5
DA-Faster†[21]	15.0	34.6	12.4	11.9	19.8	21.1	23.2	3.1	22.1	26.3	10.6	10.0	19.6	39.4	34.6	29.3	1.0	17.1	19.7	24.8	19.8
SWDA [22]	26.2	48.5	32.6	33.7	38.5	54.3	37.1	18.6	34.8	58.3	17.0	12.5	33.8	65.5	61.6	52.0	9.3	24.9	54.1	49.1	38.1
FBC (ours)	43.9	64.4	28.9	26.3	39.4	58.9	36.7	14.8	46.2	39.2	11.0	11.0	31.1	77.1	48.1	36.1	17.8	35.2	52.6	50.5	**38.5**

4.2 Adaptation Between Dissimilar Domains

We evaluate the adaptation performance on two pairs of dissimilar domains: PASCAL [58] to Clipart [59], and PASCAL [58] to Watercolor [59]. For the two domain shifts, we use the same source-only model trained on PASCAL. Following SWDA [22], we use ResNet101 [60] as the backbone network for Faster R-CNN detector and the settings of training and test sets are the same.

Datasets. PASCAL VOC dataset [58] is used as the source domain in these two domain shift scenarios. This dataset consists of real images with 20 object classes. The training set contains 15K images. The two dissimilar target domains are Clipart dataset [59] with comic images and Watercolor dataset [59] with artistic images. Clipart dataset has the same 20 object classes as the PASCAL, while Watercolor only has six. Clipart dataset 1K comic images, which are used for both training (without labels) and testing. There 2K images in the Watercolor dataset: 1K for training (without labels) 1K for testing.

Results on the Clipart Dataset [59]. In the original paper of DA-Faster [21], they do not evaluate the Clipart and Watercolor datasets. Thus, we follow with the results of DA-Faster [21] reported in SWDA [22]. As shown in Table 1, in comparison to the source only model, DA-Faster [21] degrades the detection performance significantly, with a drop of 8 percentage points in mAP. DA-Faster [21] adopts two domain classifiers on both image-level and instance-level features. However, the source/target domain confusion without considering the semantic information will lead to the wrong alignment of semantic classes across domains. The problem is more challenging when domain shift in object detection is large, i.e., PASCAL [58] to Clipart [59]. In Clipart, the comic images contain objects that are far different from those in PASCAL w.r.t. the shapes and appearance, such as sketches. To address this, the SWDA [22] conducts a weak alignment on the image-level features by training the domain classifier with a focal loss. With the additional help of a domain classifier on lower level features and context regularization, the SWDA [22] can boost the mAP of detection from 27.8% to 38.1% with an increase of 10.3 points. Our proposed FBC can achieve the highest mAP of 38.5%. In the ablation studies (Table 2), we can see that using gradient alignment only could also obtain good performance in this challenging adaptation scenario.

Results on the Watercolor Dataset [59]. The adaptation results are summarized in Table 3. In Watercolor, most of the images contain only one or two

Table 2. Ablation studies of the proposed method on the adaptation from PAS-CAL [58] to Clipart Dataset [59]. G: gradient alignment, L: local feature alignment and D: domain diversity.

G	L	D	aero	bike	bird	boat	bottle	bus	car	cat	chair	cow	table	dog	horse	motor	prsn	plnt	sheep	sofa	train	tv	mAP
✓			28.8	64	21.1	19.1	39.7	60.7	29.5	14.2	46.4	29.3	21.8	8.9	28.8	72.7	51.3	32.9	12.8	28.1	52.7	49.5	35.6
✓	✓		32.1	57.6	24.4	23.7	34.1	59.3	32.2	9.1	40.3	41.3	27.8	11.9	30.2	72.9	48.8	38.3	6.1	33.1	46.5	48	35.9
		✓	31.8	53.0	21.3	25.0	36.1	55.9	30.4	11.6	39.3	21.0	9.4	14.5	32.4	79.0	44.9	37.8	6.2	35.6	43.0	53.5	34.1
✓	✓	✓	43.9	64.4	28.9	26.3	39.4	58.9	36.7	14.8	46.2	39.2	11.0	11.0	31.1	77.1	48.1	36.1	17.8	35.2	52.6	50.5	**38.5**

Table 3. Results (%) on the adaptation from PASCAL [58] to Watercolor [59]. The DA-Faster†is the reproduced result in SWDA [21]. G: gradient alignment, L: local feature alignment and D: domain diversity.

Method	G	L	D	bike	bird	car	cat	dog	prsn	mAP
Source only (ours)				66.7	43.5	41.0	26.0	22.9	58.9	43.2
DA-Faster† [21]				75.2	40.6	48.0	31.5	20.6	60.0	46.0
SWDA [22]				82.3	55.9	46.5	32.7	35.5	66.7	53.3
FBC (ours)	✓			90.0	46.5	51.3	33.2	29.5	65.9	52.9
	✓		✓	88.7	48.2	46.6	38.7	35.6	64.1	53.6
		✓		89.0	47.2	46.1	39.9	27.7	65.0	52.5
	✓	✓	✓	90.1	49.7	44.1	41.1	34.6	70.3	**55.0**

objects with less variations of shape and appearance than those in the Clipart. As reported in SWDA [22], the source only model can achieve quite good results with an mAP of 44.6% and DA-Faster [21] can improve it slightly by only 1.4 points. SWDA [22] performs much better than DA-Faster [21] and obtain a high mAP of 53.3%. The gain from adaptation is 8.7 points. The mAP of our proposed FBC is 55.0%, which is 1.5% higher than that of SWDA. Even without the local feature alignment via adversarial training, our proposed forward-backward cyclic adaptation method (53.6%) can achieve state-of-the-art performance.

Feature Visualization. To visualize the adaptability of our method, we use the Grad-cam [61] to show the evidence (heatmap) for the last fully connected layer in the object detectors. The high value in the heatmap indicates the evidence why the classifiers make the classification. Figure 5 shows the differences of classification evidence before and after adaptation. As we can see, the adapted detector is able to classify the objects (*e.g.*, persons) based on more semantics (*e.g.*, faces, necks, joints). It demonstrates that the adapted detector has addressed the discrepancy on the appearance of real and cartoon objects.

4.3 Adaptation from Synthetic to Real Images

As the adaptation from the synthetic images to the real images can potentially reduce the efforts of collecting the real data and labels, we evaluate the adaptation performance in the scenario of Sim10k [62] to Cityscapes [63].

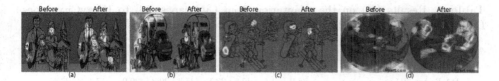

Fig. 5. Feature visualization for showing the evidence for classifiers before and after domain adaptation using Grad-cam [61].

Table 4. Results (%) on the adaptation from Sim10k [62] to Cityscapes [63]. The DA-Faster†is the reproduced result in SWDA [21]. G: gradient alignment, L: local feature alignment and D: domain diversity.

Method	G	L	D	AP on Car
Source only (ours)				31.2
DA-Faster [21]				39.0
DA-Faster† [21]				34.2
MAF [37]				41.1
SWDA [22]				42.3
Zhu *et al.* [23]				43.0
iFAN [24]				**46.2**
FBC (ours)	✓			38.2
	✓		✓	39.2
		✓		41.4
	✓	✓	✓	42.7

Datasets. The source domain, Sim10k [62], contains synthetic images that are rendered by the computer game Grand Theft Auto (GTA). It provides 58,701 bounding box annotations for cars 10 K images. The target domain, Cityscapes [63], consists of real images captured by car-mounted video cameras for driving scenarios. It comprises 2,975 images for training and 500 images for validation. We use its training set for adaptation without labels and validation set for evaluation. The adaptation is only evaluated on class *car* as Sim10k only provides annotations for car.

Results. Results are shown in Table 4. The reported mAP gain of DA-Faster [21] in its original report (7.8 points) is significantly different from its reproduced gain (−0.4 points) in SWDA [22]. It implies that a lot of efforts are needed to reproduce the reported results of DA-Faster [21]. Our proposed FBC has a competitive result of mAP, 42.7%, which is 0.4% higher than that of SWDA and on par with that of Zhu *et al.* (43 %). iFAN *et al.* [24] achieve the best performance with an mAP of 46.2%. We note that for image-level adaptation, iFAN adopts four domain classifiers for aligning multi-level features, whereas we only align the features from a single layer. Despite this, our proposed method

Table 5. Results (%) on the adaptation from Cityscapes [63] to FoggyCityscapes Dataset [64]. G: gradient alignment, L: local feature alignment and D: domain diversity.

Method	G	L	D	prsn	rider	car	truck	bus	train	motor	bcycle	mAP
Source only (ours)				22.4	34.2	27.2	12.1	28.4	9.5	20.0	27.1	22.9
DA-Faster [21]				25.0	31.0	40.5	22.1	35.3	20.2	20.0	27.1	27.6
Zhu *et al.* [23]				33.5	38.0	48.5	26.5	39.0	23.3	28.0	33.6	33.8
MAF [37]				28.2	39.5	43.9	23.8	39.9	33.3	29.2	33.9	34.0
SWDA [22]				29.9	42.3	43.5	24.5	36.2	32.6	30.0	35.3	34.3
Diversify& Match [38]				30.8	40.5	44.3	27.2	38.4	34.5	28.4	32.2	34.6
iFAN [24]				32.6	48.5	22.8	40.0	33.0	45.5	31.7	27.9	35.3
Xie *et al.* [39]				33.2	44.2	44.8	28.2	41.8	28.7	30.5	36.5	36.0
FBC (ours)	✓			25.8	35.6	35.5	18.4	29.6	10.0	24.5	30.3	26.2
	✓	✓		29.0	37.0	35.6	18.9	32.1	10.7	25.0	31.3	27.5
			✓	31.6	45.1	42.6	26.4	37.8	22.1	29.4	34.6	33.7
	✓	✓	✓	31.5	46.0	44.3	25.9	40.6	39.7	29.0	36.4	**36.7**

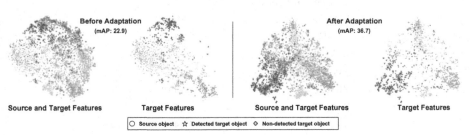

Fig. 6. t-SNE visualization of features before and after domain adaptation from Cityscape to FoggyCityScape. Different colors represent different classes. Target features are displayed alone on the right for better visualization. (Color figure online)

could obtain better results than iFAN in the adaptation from Cityscapes to FoggyCityscapes.

4.4 Adaptation Between Similar Domains

Datasets. The target dataset, FoggyCityscapes [64], is a synthetic foggy dataset where images are rendered from the Cityscapes [63]. The annotations and data splits are the same as the Cityscapes. The adaptation performance is evaluated on the validation set of FoggyCityscapes.

Results. It can be seen in Table 5 that our proposed FBC method outperforms the baseline methods, which boosts the mAP to 36.7%. It is noteworthy that MAF (34.0%), iFAN (35.5 %) and Xie *et al.* (36.0 %) utilize multiple domain classifiers for multi-layer image-level feature alignment, whereas we only use single-layer features. If without the local feature alignment, our proposed method can only obtain limited gain. It is because, in this scenario, the main difference between these two domains is the local texture. But with the combination of gradient alignment and domain diversity, our full model could achieve state-of-the-art performance.

t-SNE Visualization. We visualize the differences of features before and after adaptation via t-SNE visualization [65] in Fig. 6. The features are output from the ROI pooling layer and 100 images are randomly selected. After adaptation, the distributions of source and target features are well aligned with regard to the object classes. More importantly, as shown in Fig. 6, different classes are better distinguished and more target objects are detected for each class after adaptation. This demonstrates the effectiveness of our proposed adaptation method for object detection.

5 Conclusions

We address unsupervised domain adaptation for object detection task where the target domain does not have labels. A forward-backward cyclic adaptation method is proposed. This method was based on the intuition that domain invariance of category-level semantics could be learned when the gradient directions of source and target were aligned. Theoretical analysis was presented to show that the proposed method achieved the gradient alignment goal. Local feature alignment via adversarial training was performed for learning domain-invariance of holistic color/textures. Furthermore, we proposed a domain diversity constraint to penalize confident source-specific learning and intrigue target-specific learning via entropy regularization.

Acknowledgements. This research was funded by the Australian Government through the Australian Research Council and Sullivan Nicolaides Pathology under Linkage Project LP160101797. Lin Wu was supported by NSFC U19A2073, the Fundamental Research Funds for the Central Universities under Grant No.JZ2020HGTB0050.

References

1. Ren, S., He, K., Girshick, R., Sun, J.: Faster R-CNN: towards real-time object detection with region proposal networks. In: NeurIPS (2015)
2. Liu, W., et al.: SSD: single shot multibox detector. In: Leibe, B., Matas, J., Sebe, N., Welling, M. (eds.) ECCV 2016. LNCS, vol. 9905, pp. 21–37. Springer, Cham (2016). https://doi.org/10.1007/978-3-319-46448-0_2
3. Redmon, J., Divvala, S., Girshick, R., Farhadi, A.: You only look once: unified, real-time object detection. In: CVPR (2016)
4. Long, J., Shelhamer, E., Darrell, T.: Fully convolutional networks for semantic segmentation. In: CVPR (2015)
5. Lin, T.Y., Dollár, P., Girshick, R., He, K., Hariharan, B., Belongie, S.: Feature pyramid networks for object detection. In: CVPR (2017)
6. Hu, P., Ramanan, D.: Finding tiny faces. In: CVPR (2017)
7. Chen, X., Ma, H., Wan, J., Li, B., Xia, T.: Multi-view 3D object detection network for autonomous driving. In: CVPR (2017)
8. Long, M., Cao, Y., Wang, J., Jordan, M.I.: Learning transferable features with deep adaptation networks. In: ICML (2015)
9. Long, M., Zhu, H., Wang, J., Jordan, M.I.: Unsupervised domain adaptation with residual transfer networks. In: NeurIPS (2016)

10. Ganin, Y., Lempitsky, V.: Unsupervised domain adaptation by backpropagation. In: ICML (2015)
11. Tzeng, E., Hoffman, J., Saenko, K., Darrell, T.: Adversarial discriminative domain adaptation. In: CVPR (2017)
12. Saito, K., Ushiku, Y., Harada, T.: Asymmetric tri-training for unsupervised domain adaptation. In: ICML (2017)
13. Saito, K., Watanabe, K., Ushiku, Y., Harada, T.: Maximum classifier discrepancy for unsupervised domain adaptation. In: CVPR (2018)
14. Sun, B., Saenko, K.: Deep CORAL: correlation alignment for deep domain adaptation. In: Hua, G., Jégou, H. (eds.) ECCV 2016. LNCS, vol. 9915, pp. 443–450. Springer, Cham (2016). https://doi.org/10.1007/978-3-319-49409-8_35
15. Tzeng, E., Hoffman, J., Darrell, T., Saenko, K.: Simultaneous deep transfer across domains and tasks. In: ICCV (2015)
16. Tzeng, E., Hoffman, J., Zhang, N., Saenko, K., Darrell, T.: Deep domain confusion: maximizing for domain invariance. arXiv preprint arXiv:1412.3474 (2014)
17. Xie, S., Zheng, Z., Chen, L., Chen, C.: Learning semantic representations for unsupervised domain adaptation. In: ICML (2018)
18. Shu, R., Bui, H.H., Narui, H., Ermon, S.: A DIRT-T approach to unsupervised domain adaptation. In: ICLR (2018)
19. Luo, Y., Zheng, L., Guan, T., Yu, J., Yang, Y.: Taking a closer look at domain shift: category-level adversaries for semantics consistent domain adaptation. arXiv preprint arXiv:1809.09478 (2018)
20. Kumar, A., et al.: Co-regularized alignment for unsupervised domain adaptation. In: NeurIPS (2018)
21. Chen, Y., Li, W., Sakaridis, C., Dai, D., Van Gool, L.: Domain adaptive faster R-CNN for object detection in the wild. In: CVPR (2018)
22. Saito, K., Ushiku, Y., Harada, T., Saenko, K.: Strong-weak distribution alignment for adaptive object detection. In: CVPR (2019)
23. Zhu, X., Pang, J., Yang, C., Shi, J., Lin, D.: Adapting object detectors via selective cross-domain alignment. In: CVPR (2019)
24. Zhuang, C., Han, X., Huang, W., Scott, M.R.: iFAN: image-instance full alignment networks for adaptive object detection. In: AAAI (2020)
25. He, D., et al.: Dual learning for machine translation. In: NeurIPS (2016)
26. Zhu, J.Y., Park, T., Isola, P., Efros, A.A.: Unpaired image-to-image translation using cycle-consistent adversarial networks. In: ICCV (2017)
27. Yi, Z., Zhang, H., Tan, P., Gong, M.: DualGAN: unsupervised dual learning for image-to-image translation. In: ICCV (2017)
28. Girshick, R.: Fast R-CNN. In: ICCV (2015)
29. Lin, T.Y., Goyal, P., Girshick, R., He, K., Dollár, P.: Focal loss for dense object detection. In: CVPR (2017)
30. Long, M., Zhu, H., Wang, J., Jordan, M.I.: Deep transfer learning with joint adaptation networks. In: ICML (2017)
31. Ben-David, S., Blitzer, J., Crammer, K., Kulesza, A., Pereira, F., Vaughan, J.W.: A theory of learning from different domains. Mach. Learn. 79, 151–175 (2010)
32. Kang, G., Jiang, L., Yang, Y., Hauptmann, A.G.: Contrastive adaptation network for unsupervised domain adaptation. In: CVPR (2019)
33. Chen, C., et al.: Progressive feature alignment for unsupervised domain adaptation. In: CVPR (2019)
34. Sener, O., Song, H.O., Saxena, A., Savarese, S.: Learning transferrable representations for unsupervised domain adaptation. In: NeurIPS (2016)

35. Chen, M., Weinberger, K.Q., Blitzer, J.: Co-training for domain adaptation. In: NeurIPS (2011)
36. Lee, D.H.: Pseudo-label: the simple and efficient semi-supervised learning method for deep neural networks. In: Workshop on Challenges in Representation Learning, ICML, vol. 3, no. 2 (2013)
37. He, Z., Zhang, L.: Multi-adversarial faster-RCNN for unrestricted object detection. In: ICCV (2019)
38. Kim, T., Jeong, M., Kim, S., Choi, S., Kim, C.: Diversify and match: a domain adaptive representation learning paradigm for object detection. In: CVPR (2019)
39. Xie, R., Yu, F., Wang, J., Wang, Y., Zhang, L.: Multi-level domain adaptive learning for cross-domain detection. In: ICCV Workshops (2019)
40. Hsu, H.K., et al.: Progressive domain adaptation for object detection. In: The IEEE Winter Conference on Applications of Computer Vision (2020)
41. Finn, C., Abbeel, P., Levine, S.: Model-agnostic meta-learning for fast adaptation of deep networks. In: ICML (2017)
42. Nichol, A., Schulman, J.: Reptile: a scalable metalearning algorithm. arXiv preprint arXiv:1803.02999, vol. 2 (2018)
43. Riemer, M., et al.: Learning to learn without forgetting by maximizing transfer and minimizing interference. In: ICLR (2019)
44. Jaynes, E.T.: Information theory and statistical mechanics. Phys. Rev. **106**, 620 (1957)
45. Williams, R.J., Peng, J.: Function optimization using connectionist reinforcement learning algorithms. Conn. Sci. **3**, 241–268 (1991)
46. Mnih, V., et al.: Asynchronous methods for deep reinforcement learning. In: ICML, pp. 1928–1937 (2016)
47. Pereyra, G., Tucker, G., Chorowski, J., Kaiser, L., Hinton, G.: Regularizing neural networks by penalizing confident output distributions. arXiv preprint arXiv:1701.06548 (2017)
48. Liu, H., Jin, S., Zhang, C.: Connectionist temporal classification with maximum entropy regularization. In: NeurIPS (2018)
49. Dubey, A., Gupta, O., Raskar, R., Naik, N.: Maximum-entropy fine grained classification. In: NeurIPS (2018)
50. Zhu, X., Zhou, H., Yang, C., Shi, J., Lin, D.: Penalizing top performers: conservative loss for semantic segmentation adaptation. In: Ferrari, V., Hebert, M., Sminchisescu, C., Weiss, Y. (eds.) ECCV 2018. LNCS, vol. 11211, pp. 587–603. Springer, Cham (2018). https://doi.org/10.1007/978-3-030-01234-2_35
51. Palubinskas, G., Descombes, X., Kruggel, F.: An unsupervised clustering method using the entropy minimization. In: ICPR (1998)
52. Grandvalet, Y., Bengio, Y.: Semi-supervised learning by entropy minimization. In: NeurIPS (2005)
53. Luo, Z., Zou, Y., Hoffman, J., Fei-Fei, L.F.: Label efficient learning of transferable representations acrosss domains and tasks. In: NeurIPS (2017)
54. Ravi, S., Larochelle, H.: Optimization as a model for few-shot learning. In: ICLR (2016)
55. Lopez-Paz, D., et al.: Gradient episodic memory for continual learning. In: NeurIPS, pp. 6467–6476 (2017)
56. Deng, J., Dong, W., Socher, R., Li, L.J., Li, K., Fei-Fei, L.: ImageNet: a large-scale hierarchical image database. In: CVPR (2009)
57. Mao, X., Li, Q., Xie, H., Lau, R.Y., Wang, Z., Paul Smolley, S.: Least squares generative adversarial networks. In: ICCV (2017)

58. Everingham, M., Van Gool, L., Williams, C.K., Winn, J., Zisserman, A.: The pascal visual object classes (VOC) challenge. IJCV **88**, 303–338 (2010)
59. Inoue, N., Furuta, R., Yamasaki, T., Aizawa, K.: Cross-domain weakly-supervised object detection through progressive domain adaptation. In: CVPR (2018)
60. He, K., Zhang, X., Ren, S., Sun, J.: Deep residual learning for image recognition. In: CVPR (2016)
61. Selvaraju, R.R., Cogswell, M., Das, A., Vedantam, R., Parikh, D., Batra, D.: Grad-CAM: visual explanations from deep networks via gradient-based localization. In: ICCV (2017)
62. Johnson-Roberson, M., Barto, C., Mehta, R., Sridhar, S.N., Rosaen, K., Vasudevan, R.: Driving in the matrix: can virtual worlds replace human-generated annotations for real world tasks? arXiv preprint arXiv:1610.01983 (2016)
63. Cordts, M., et al.: The cityscapes dataset for semantic urban scene understanding. In: CVPR (2016)
64. Sakaridis, C., Dai, D., Van Gool, L.: Semantic foggy scene understanding with synthetic data. IJCV **126**, 1–20 (2018)
65. Maaten, L.V.D., Hinton, G.: Visualizing data using t-SNE. J. Mach. Learn. Res. **9**, 2579–2605 (2008)

COG: COnsistent Data AuGmentation for Object Perception

Zewen He[1,2](✉) , Rui Wu[3], and Dingqian Zhang[2]

[1] Institute of Automation, Chinese Academy of Sciences, Beijing, China
hezewen2014@ia.ac.cn
[2] School of Computer and Control Engineering, University of Chinese Academy of Science, Beijing, China
[3] Horizon Robotics, Beijing, China

Abstract. Recently, data augmentation techniques for training convnets emerge one after another, especially focusing on image classification. They're always applied to object detection without further careful design. In this paper we propose COG, a general domain migration scheme for augmentation. Specifically, based on a particular augmentation, we first analyze its inherent inconsistency, and then adopt an adaptive strategy to rectify ground-truths of the augmented input images. Next, deep detection networks are trained on the rectified data to achieve better performance. Our extensive experiments show that our method COG's performance is superior to its competitor on detection and instance segmentation tasks. In addition, the results manifest the robustness of COG when faced with hyper-parameter variations, etc.

1 Introduction

Over the past two decades, the vision community has made considerable progress on object perception, including image classification [1], object detection [2] and instance segmentation [3]. This is mainly due to the emergence of deep convolutional neural networks (CNNs) and massive annotated data. Along with the increase of CNNs' capacity (including depth, width etc.), accuracies of theses tasks continue to increase. However, this growth may bring catastrophic overfitting phenomenon. In order to improve CNN's generalization and robustness, data augmentation strategies are often used to generate data with more diverse input distribution.

Existing augmentation techniques mainly stem from the image classification community. They usually contain three categories: 1). spatial transformation, such as random scale, flip, rotation; 2). color distortion, such as randomly changing pixel value in color space like RGB or HSV; 3). information dropping or stitching, such as randomly dropping regions; These methods try to change different properties of original images to obtain more training data, and then achieve considerable accuracy improvement.

Nevertheless, most augmentation methods are first proposed for the image classification task. They are always transferred to other tasks with little change.

H. Ishikawa et al. (Eds.): ACCV 2020, LNCS 12624, pp. 143–154, 2021.
https://doi.org/10.1007/978-3-030-69535-4_9

This direct migration is not quite reasonable. Because image classification just inputs one image and outputs a single label. The robustness requires that even if randomly changing input, the output label should be the same. But this requirement is not appropriate for other tasks, such as object detection and instance segmentation, which needs precise localization. For example in the detection task, if the augmentation randomly removes the half body of one annotated person from the image (please see Fig. 2d), we need to figure out which bounding-box(bbox) matches the augmented input most consistently. The possible choices contain 1). original person box; 2). the person with half body; 3). the person disappears. The **first choice** will force the model trying to detect objects under severe occlusion, but this may be difficult if the whole person is occluded; The **second choice** wants to force the model obtaining accurate boundaries of objects, but this may fetch ambiguity of person category (the whole body and the half body both belong to the person category); The **third choice** just goes over to the opposite side of the first choice, namely deleting the ground-truth of objects (as ignored when training) which are under severe occlusion. In practice, the annotator also needs to make choices when meeting crowd scenes with occlusion. As far as we observe, most annotation in COCO [4] and CrowdHuman [5], characterize the whole outline of each object, namely the 1st choice. It's because the occlusion here is mainly from other foreground objects like horses or cars that can provide context information for predicting occluded targets. However, this is not the optimal choice for data augmentation. For example, GridMask [6] also makes the 1st choice as shown in Fig. 2e, but this will bring inconsistency if 90% of the object is occluded by the gray areas. The gray areas don't bring extra context information. Therefore, more intelligent choices are needed here.

We believe that the key factor of making optimal choices is making the pair, namely (input image, output box, and label), consistent. If the occlusion is a little, the original gt-bbox can be reserved; If the occlusion is not severed but cannot be ignored, gt-bbox can be rectified; If the occlusion is very severe, the original gt-bbox can be removed. In this way, the best strategy is making the choice adaptively based on the degree of occlusion. Figure 1a shows different choices under different occlusion levels. To validate our hypothesis, we start from one augmentation method (GridMask) originated from the classification domain, and then point out the inconsistency when migrating to the detection domain directly. Next, we propose the COG method to rectify the inconsistency adaptively. The general difference are shown in Fig. 2. Finally, COG can obtain higher performance in detection and instance segmentation tasks, which means that better choices are made in COG when facing region removal. The performance shown in Fig. 1b validates the superiority of COG.

In short, our main contribution can be summarized as follows:

- we analyze the inconsistency between input images and corresponding labels when encountering data augmentation in the detection task.
- we propose COG to rectify this inconsistency adaptively.

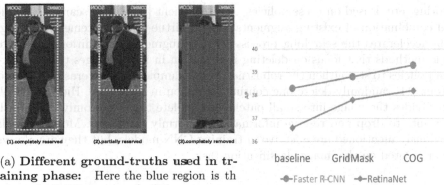

(a) **Different ground-truths used in tr-aining phase:** Here the blue region is th gt-mask of this person. And the gray region means that **GridMask** method occludes some part. The green and solid line is the gt-bbox of this person used in **GridMask**. The yellow and dash line is the gt-bbox of this person used in **COG**.According to the occlusion level, **COG** provides gt-bbox adaptively.

(b) **mAP on test-dev:** For both Faster R-CNN and RetinaNet, **COG** is superior to **GridMask**.

Fig. 1. COG v.s. GridMask: The left side shows the different target boxes used by the two methods, and the right side shows the results of the two methods.

– we conduct extensive experiments and validate that our method benefits different detectors under various settings. Besides, comparable improvements have been achieved in other perception tasks.

The rest of this paper is organized as follows. Section 2 presents some related works about object detection and corresponding data augmentation. Section 3 analyzes the inconsistency and proposes COG. Experiment studies, including a comparison of the results and corresponding analysis, are presented in Sect. 4. Finally, we conclude in Sect. 5.

2   Related Work

We will introduce general data augmentation paradigms used in training CNN models. Next object detection and specially designed augmentation methods are also described.

2.1   Data Augmentation

Regularization is an effective technique to prevent CNN from over-fitting. Data augmentation is a special regularization which only operates on the data. It aims to increase the diversity of input distribution and is also easy to deploy. The basic augmentation policy consists of random flipping, random cropping, and random coloring, etc. Based on these policies, AutoAugment [7] tries to search the optimal combination of existing augmentations in virtue of reinforcement learning. [8,9] accelerates the searching process of AutoAugment. In addition, there are some methods that focus on deleting information in input images through certain policies to strengthen the robustness. For example, random erasing [10] and cutout [11] randomly delete one continuous region in the image. Hide-and-Seek [12] divides the image into small patches and delete them randomly. GridMask [6] wants to drop and reserve information uniformly in images. Most methods previously mentioned are effective in training CNN models, but they are always experimented on the image classification task.

2.2   Object Detection

The object detection task attempts to locate and classify possible targets in the image at the same time. Benefit from the representation capacity of deep conv-feature, CNN-based detectors [2,13–16] have become a dominant paradigm in the object detection community. The R-CNN series and its variants [2,3,17] gradually increase the upper bound of the performance on two-stage detectors. In particular, Faster R-CNN [2] is the principal architecture in these methods. It adopts a shared backbone network to extract features for subsequent proposal generation and RoI classification, resulting in real-time detection and rising accuracy. Besides, one-stage methods like RetinaNet [18] also work well.

Together with these efficient detectors, particular augmentation strategies are also designed for detection applications. Mosaic [19] tries to mix 4 training images with different contexts. This strategy significantly reduces the need for a larger mini-batch size. GridMask [6] can be extended to detection without special modification. Deep reinforcement learning is also used in [20] to find a set of best strategies for object detection automatically. InstaBoost [21] boosts the performance on instance segmentation by probability map guided copy-pasting techniques.

3   Method

We will formally introduce our COG, namely COnsistent auGmentation, in this section. To facilitate understanding, Sect. 3.1 analyzes the inconsistency in original GridMask. Then, Sect. 3.2 details the COG paradigm and its implementation.

3.1   Inconsistency in GridMask

Original GridMask. Original GridMask [6] is a simple, general, and efficient strategy for data augmentation. Given an input image, GridMask randomly removes some regions which are distributed across the image uniformly. In other words, the removed regions are neither a continuous region [11] nor random pixels in dropout. They are disconnected pixel sets which are aligned to grids, as illustrated in Fig. 2d. These gray regions with grid shape guarantee that both information deletion and reserve co-exist in augmentation.

In detail, the operation of GridMask can be summarized by Eq. 1.

$$\hat{\mathbf{x}} = \mathbf{x} \times \mathbf{M} \tag{1}$$

Concretely, $\mathbf{x} \in R^{H \times W \times C}$ denotes the original input image, $\mathbf{M} \in \{0,1\}^{H \times W}$ denotes the corresponding binary mask matrix, and $\hat{\mathbf{x}} \in R^{H \times W \times C}$ is the augmentation result generated by GridMask. For the binary mask $\mathbf{M}$, if $\mathbf{M}_{i,j} = 1$, we keep the original pixel (i,j) in $\mathbf{x}$; otherwise the pixel value at position (i,j) will be set to the mean RGB value, namely 0 value after image normalization.

Figure 2c displays the $\mathbf{M}$ with grid-shape and corresponding control parameters. It should be noted that the dark gray areas denote the regions where $\mathbf{M}_{i,j} = 0$; while the light white areas denote the regions where $\mathbf{M}_{i,j} = 1$. The parameters here contains $(r, d, \delta_x, \delta_y)$, which control the exact appearance of $\mathbf{M}$. Among them, d means the length of one grid unit; $1 - r$ means the proportion of the removed gray square in one grid unit; δ_x, δ_y means the start pixel of the first grid unit in an image.

In order to increase the diversity of $\mathbf{M}$, these hyper-parameters will be generated randomly for each image. Unless otherwise specified, the d is sampled from $[d_l, d_h] = [32, 512]$, δ_x, δ_y is sampled from $[0, d-1]$, and the r is set to 0.5 like original GridMask [6].

Inconsistency Details. Although the original GridMask can increase the robustness of the detection model and improve the performance by nearly 1.0 points on COCO [4], there also exists inconsistency. The main inconsistency originates from mismatching between $\hat{\mathbf{x}}$, namely input image after GridMask, and the adopted ground-truth $gt(\mathbf{x})$ (including category labels and geometry bboxes in this image). If there is no augmentation, the input image $\mathbf{x}$ and corresponding ground-truth $gt(\mathbf{x})$ match perfectly. Because the $gt(\mathbf{x})$ is from the official annotation. But when GridMask is employed on some $\mathbf{x}$ to get $\hat{\mathbf{x}}$, some region in $\mathbf{x}$ is removed. At this moment, parts of some objects may be covered by the gray regions. Then, the original annotations of these objects don't match to $\hat{\mathbf{x}}$ well, as shown in Fig. 2e. In other words, the original GridMask uses the changed image $\hat{\mathbf{x}}$ and the original but fixed annotation $gt(\mathbf{x})$ to train the CNN model. This strategy can be explained as increasing the robustness for occlusion, as the **first choice** mentioned in Sect. 1. The CNN model will be trained to infer the whole object's category and geometry bbox when given a part of this object.

We argue that this approach may be challenged when the occlusion is severe in GridMask in both qualitative and quantitive perspectives. Qualitatively, the occlusion is inevitable as shown in Fig. 2e. Even as an annotation worker, such as MTurk, he/she may feel difficult to give precise bounding-box. Quantitively, our statistical result shows that about 25.1% area of the foreground gt-masks are occluded when using default GridMask settings. This occlusion level cannot be ignored. Because we think that both the object itself and context features are important for object localization and recognition. If the occlusion is severe,

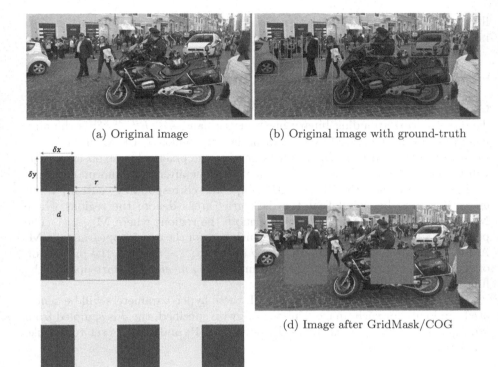

(a) Original image   (b) Original image with ground-truth

(d) Image after GridMask/COG

(c) Mask used in GridMask/COG

(e) GridMask image with ground-truth: all (f) COG image with ground-truth: changed
bboxes are marked by green rectangles.   bboxes are marked by yellow rectangles.

Fig. 2. Original v.s. GridMask v.s. COG Blue regions represent the gt-mask.
Green rectangles represent the gt-bbox. (Color figure online)

the available information only stems from context. This may lead to ambiguity
because the same context may contain different objects.

Intuitively, Fig. 1a illustrates the same gt-bboxes used in GridMask under
different occlusion levels. Even if the whole person is almost completely occluded,
GridMask still gives it a bounding-box annotation for training. This is unreasonable and inconsistent.

3.2   Rectifying Ground-Truth

As previously mentioned, there exists inconsistency between changed input
image $\hat{\mathbf{x}}$ and the unchanged ground-truth $gt(\mathbf{x})$. We should rectify original

ground-truth $gt(\mathbf{x})$ to $gt(\hat{\mathbf{x}})$ and try to make the matching degree between $\hat{\mathbf{x}}$ and $gt(\hat{\mathbf{x}})$ as high as possible. In other words, we should find better choice from the three candidates adaptively, as Sect. 1 mentioned.

The rectifying procedure in our method is displayed in Algorithm 1. In detail, for original input image $\mathbf{x}$, whose corresponding gt is $gt(\mathbf{x})$. There're N annotated objects in $gt(\mathbf{x})$. For each annotated object obj_k, there exists one category label c_k, one bounding box b_k, and one mask annotation $\mathbf{GM}_k$. Here, $\mathbf{GM}$ means the ground-truth mask for the object. As shown in Fig. 2b, the b_k and $\mathbf{GM}_k$ are the green bbox and blue region respectively. Specifically in COCO dataset, the c_k is $0 - 1$ vector with 80 dimension; the b_k is (x_k, y_k, w_k, h_k), which represents the (x, y) coordinate of the top-left corner, width and height of b_k; the $\mathbf{GM}_k$ is also a binary mask matrix which shape is $H \times W$. If the pixel at (i, j) in x is in fore-ground region of b_k, then $\mathbf{GM}_k(i, j)$ is 1, otherwise 0. When GridMask operation is adopted, the binary mask $\mathbf{M}$ is shown in Fig. 2c.

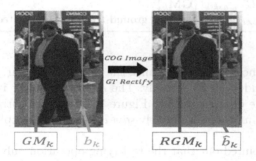

Fig. 3. Rectifying Procedure: Left fig represents original image and corresponding ground-truth: gtbbox b_k and gtmask $\mathbf{GM}_k$; Right fig represents image after GridMask operation and corresponding ground-truth after rectifying (when $thres_l < saveRatio_k < thres_h$): new gt-bbox $\hat{b}_k$ and gt-mask $\mathbf{RGM}_k$.

The core idea of Algorithm 1 is making a perfect tradeoff between object and context when rectifying. Concretely, COG calculates the reserved region $\mathbf{RGM}$ of each b_k under $\mathbf{M}$, and then provide a revised $\hat{b}_k$. As shown in Fig. 3, the blue region at left is original $\mathbf{GM}$, and the blue region at right is $\mathbf{RGM}$. All $\hat{b}_k$ constitute the new ground-truth for $\hat{\mathbf{x}}$. In detail, according to the $saveRatio$, namely the ratio between $area(\mathbf{RGM})$ and $area(\mathbf{GM})$, different strategies will be used.

First, if $saveRatio_k$ is higher than $thres_h$, the $\hat{b}_k$ is the same as b_k. We consider this object as unbroken but just occluded, the object information doesn't disappear. Second, if $saveRatio_k$ is lower than $thres_h$ but higher than $thres_l$, the $\hat{b}_k$ is the minimum enclosing rectangle of $\mathbf{RGM}_k$. We consider this object as broken but still existent, the image has dropped part of the object information. The remanent object information and context information can be used to predict the object category but no precise localization for the original object. So we acknowledge that the object still exists but the corresponding gt-bbox should be

---

Algorithm 1. Rectifying Ground-Truth

Input: $\mathbf{M}, GT = \{(b_k, \mathbf{GM}_k), where \quad k \in [1, ..., N]\}$

Output: $\hat{GT}_{bbox}, \hat{GT}_{mask}$

0: $\hat{GT}_{bbox} \leftarrow \varnothing, \hat{GT}_{mask} \leftarrow \varnothing,$

1: **For** $k \in [1, ..., N]$ **do**

2:     $\mathbf{RGM}_k = \mathbf{M} \times \mathbf{GM}_k$

3:     $saveRatio_k = area(\mathbf{RGM}_k)/area(\mathbf{GM}_k)$

4:     **if** $saveRatio_k > thres_h$

5:         $\hat{b}_k = b_k$

6:         $\hat{\mathbf{GM}}_k = \mathbf{GM}_k$

7:     **elseif** $saveRatio_k > thres_l$

8:         $\hat{b}_k = minEncloseRectangle(\mathbf{RGM}_k)$

9:         $\hat{\mathbf{GM}}_k = \mathbf{RGM}_k$

10:    **else**

11:        continue

12:    $\hat{GT}_{bbox} \leftarrow \hat{GT}_{bbox} \cup \{\hat{b}_k\}$

13:    $\hat{GT}_{mask} \leftarrow \hat{GT}_{mask} \cup \{\hat{\mathbf{GM}}_k\}$

14:Output $\{\hat{GT}_{bbox}, \hat{GT}_{mask}\}$ as new ground-truth for augmented image

---

changed to the truncated version. Third, the $\hat{b}_k$ will disappear. We consider that this object is occluded by $\mathbf{M}$ severely. The remanent object information is too little to predict the object category. Figure 1a illustrates corresponding results under different occlusion levels, namely $saveRatio_k$. It also explains COG's superiority intuitively.

It should be pointed out that the rectifying operation only changes ground-truth in accordance with the occlusion situation in the current image. So if $thres_h$ and $thres_l$ are set to 0.0, then the generated $\hat{GT}$ is the same as GT, namely the original GridMask. Besides, although it now uses $\mathbf{GM}_k$ to calculate $saveRatio_k$, it can also only use b_k to get a course rectification. More details about this will be described in Sect. 4.3.

4 Experiments

Extensive experiments are conducted on object detection and instance segmentation to verify the effectiveness of COG. As described below, we firstly depict common settings in detail for a fair comparison. Then, the main results and ablation study are provided to validate COG's advantage over other competitors and robustness to hyper-parameter variation.

4.1 Common Settings

Dataset Description. Experiments are performed on COCO [4] following the official dataset split. In other words, all models are trained on train2017(118k images) and evaluated on val2017(5k images). The results on test-dev(20k+ images) are submitted to the official server for evaluation.

Common Implementation and Hyper-parameters. Two-stage Faster R-CNN [2] is employed for detection, and Mask R-CNN [3] is employed for instance segmentation. We implements our method and competitors based on MMDetection [22] framework. The details will be described from input images to outputs. In our experiments, first, input images are always resized to a single scale $(800, 1333)$ in both training and testing phases. Second, backbones in detection models generally include vanilla ResNet [1] (abbr. R50 for ResNet-50). After that, FPN is adopted to extract features of multiple resolutions. For post-processing, Non-Maximum Suppression (NMS) is substitute by Soft-NMS [23] to remove possible duplicate bboxes.

Besides, all models are trained on 8 GPUs for 24 epochs. The learning rate is initialized with 0.00125*batch-size with a gradual warmup strategy, then divided by 10 at 16-th and 22-th epoch successively.

Hyper-parameters in COG. Without specification, the upper bound and lower bound are set to $[0.25, 0.9]$ in COG. The probability of augmentation operation is set to a constant value, namely 0.7, for both GridMask and COG. We also set $drange = [32, 512]$ and $r = 0.5$ for both COG and GridMask, as Sect. 3.1 mentioned.

Competitor Methods. Except for self-comparison, our proposed COG is compared with GridMask [6] which belongs to current SOTA methods.

Evaluation Metrics. Standard COCO metrics [4], including AP (mean AP over multiple IoU thresholds) for object detection, AP^{mask} for instance segmentation are reported. Note that the best results in each table are in **boldface**.

4.2 Main Results

To verify the effectiveness of COG, we compare COG with GridMask in different detectors (such as Faster RCNN and RetinaNet), when integrated with FPN. Table 1 shows the results on COCO val dataset. For baseline Faster RCNN with R50 backbone, our re-implemented baseline AP is 38.0, which surpasses that in [22] because all models are equipped with Soft-NMS. Compared with the baseline, while GridMask improves the AP by 0.6 points, COG boosts additional 0.5 points further. Also for RetinaNet, while GridMask improves the AP by 0.9 points, COG boosts additional 0.4 points further. The same performance improvement can be observed in the COCO test-dev dataset, as shown in Table 2. We can conclude that COG is superior to GridMask in the detection task.

Among them, the accuracy improvement is higher in AP_M and AP_L, compared with AP_S. First, we argue that because the object with a smaller scale will be occluded by the gray region with higher probability. So more small objects are removed in the training phase and relatively more medium or large objects participate in the training process. Second, when more medium or large objects are reserved, the rectified gt-bbox also diminishes the inconsistency in the original GridMask.

Table 1. Detection results on COCO val

Method	Backbone	AP	AP_S	AP_M	AP_L
FPN (baseline)	R50	38.0	22.0	41.7	49.3
GridMask+FPN	R50	38.6(+0.6)	22.7	42.4	49.2
COG+FPN	R50	**39.1(+1.1)**	**23.0**	**43.1**	**49.7**
RetinaNet (baseline)	R50	36.3	19.5	39.7	47.6
GridMask+RetinaNet	R50	37.2(+0.9)	21.3	41.2	48.5
COG+RetinaNet	R50	**37.6(+1.3)**	**21.5**	**41.7**	**48.9**

Table 2. Detection results on COCO test-dev

AP	AP_S	AP_M	AP_L
38.3	21.9	41.3	47.6
38.8(+0.5)	22.5	42.0	47.6
39.3(+1.0)	**22.9**	**42.6**	**48.1**
36.6	19.6	39.4	46.1
37.8(+1.2)	21.3	41.1	47.2
38.2(+1.6)	**21.5**	**41.7**	**47.9**

4.3 Ablation Study

Hyperparameter Settings. In this section, results of Faster R-CNN with COG under different hyper-parameters are displayed in Table 3.

Firstly, we experiment with the upper and lower bound of *saveRatio*, namely $thres_h$ and $thres_l$, on COG+FPN. We need to reserve the original annotation when occlusion is not severe to get robustness, We also need to reserve the visible section or delete it when occlusion is severe. So the upper bound cannot be very high or very low. Similarly, the lower bound cannot be very low. According to the result, the upper bound $thres_h = 0.9$ and lower bound $thres_l = 0.25$ performs best. Secondly, we experiment with different *drange*, namely $[d_l, d_h]$ mentioned in Subsect. 3.1, on COG and original GridMask. It seems that the expanded range for d is not good for GridMask but okay for COG.

These variations show the robustness of the COG paradigm.

Table 3. Detection results of COG under different hyper-parameters. This demonstrates that COG is robust to different settings. Details are explained in Subsect. 4.3.

Method	drange	maskratio	AP
COG+FPN	[32, 512]	[0.25, 0.5]	38.7
COG+FPN	[32, 512]	[0.25, 0.75]	38.8
COG+FPN	[32, 512]	[0.25, 0.9]	**39.1**
COG+FPN	[32, 512]	[0.25, 1.0]	38.8
COG+FPN	[32, 512]	[0.3, 0.9]	39.0
COG+FPN	[32, 512]	[0.4, 0.9]	38.7
COG+FPN	[2, 800]	[0.25, 0.9]	38.9
GridMask+FPN	[2, 800]	[0.25, 0.9]	38.5

Table 4. Detection Results of COG with other variations. This demonstrates that COG is robust to different training settings. Details are explained in Subsect. 4.3.

Method	step_list	prob_list	AP
COG+FPN	[,24]	[,0.7]	**39.1**
COG+FPN	[2,24]	[0.0,0.7]	39.0
COG+FPN	[1,2,4]	[0.0,0.7,0.9]	39.0
COG+FPN	[23,24]	[0.7,0.3]	38.9
Changing loss weight	RPN	RCNN	
COG+FPN	True	True	38.8
GridMask+FPN	True	True	38.5
Using bbox ratio	drange	bboxratio	
COG+FPN	[32, 512]	[0.3, 0.8]	39.0
COG+FPN	[32, 512]	[0.3, 0.9]	38.8

Variations of COG. We also experiment with more variations on COG to validate its robustness.

The first variation is changing the probability of augmentation. For example in Table 4, step_list = $[2, 24]$ and prob_list = $[0.0, 0.7]$ means setting COG's probability to 0.0 before the 2-th epoch and setting this probability to 0.7 between

2-th and 24-th epoch. We can see that the performance of COG is consistent regardless of the variation of COG's probability. The second variation is changing the loss weight of k_{th} gt-bbox by the $saveRatio_k$ adaptively but adopting the original ground-truth in training. If the $saveRatio_k$ is low, then the corresponding loss weight also decreases. It can be regarded as a soft version of ground-truth rectification. From the results in Table 4, we can see that adaptively changing loss weight doesn't make a difference for COG and GridMask. The third variation is using bbox save ratio but not mask save ratio. In detail, the save ratio is $saveRatio_k = \mathrm{Area}(bb_k^{res})/\mathrm{Area}(bb_k)$. Here, bb_k means the k_{th} gt-bbox, bb_k^{res} means the maximum rectangle that hasn't been occluded by GridMask in bb_k. From the results in Table 4, we can see that only using bbox annotation for calculating save ratio in COG can also achieve similar performance.

COG on Instance Segmentation. We also experiment with COG on the instance segmentation task to validate its effectiveness on rectifying gt-mask annotations. As shown in Table 5, COG surpasses GridMask 0.4 points on AP and 0.2 points on Mask AP.

Table 5. Mask RCNN's results on COCO val

Method	Backbone	AP	AP_S	AP_M	AP_L	AP^{mask}	AP_S^{mask}	AP_M^{mask}	AP_L^{mask}
FPN (baseline)	R50	39.1	22.3	42.5	51.0	34.8	18.5	37.9	47.8
GridMask+FPN	R50	39.2	23.3	43.1	50.2	35.2	18.8	38.7	47.4
COG+FPN	R50	**39.6**	23.3	**43.6**	**50.6**	**35.4**	**18.9**	**38.9**	**48.0**

5   Conclusion

In this paper, we propose COG, an adaptive rectification strategy for data augmentation, which eliminates the inherent inconsistency. The experimental studies validate that COG can improve data augmentation's performance on different perception tasks. It's also robust to various settings for hyper-parameters and training configurations. COG provides a new perspective to migrate data augmentation from label-based domain(classification) to location-based domain (detection). Further, we can extend COG to considering both image and current network's state simultaneously.

References

1. He, K., Zhang, X., Ren, S., Sun, J.: Deep residual learning for image recognition. In: Proceedings of CVPR, pp. 770–778 (2016)
2. Ren, S., He, K., Girshick, R., Sun, J.: Faster R-CNN: towards real-time object detection with region proposal networks. In: Proceedings of NIPS, pp. 91–99 (2015)
3. He, K., Gkioxari, G., Dollár, P., Girshick, R.: Mask R-CNN. In: Proceedings of IEEE ICCV, pp. 2980–2988 (2017)

4. Lin, T.-Y., et al.: Microsoft COCO: common objects in context. In: Fleet, D., Pajdla, T., Schiele, B., Tuytelaars, T. (eds.) ECCV 2014. LNCS, vol. 8693, pp. 740–755. Springer, Cham (2014). https://doi.org/10.1007/978-3-319-10602-1_48
5. Shao, S., et al.: CrowdHuman: a benchmark for detecting human in a crowd. arXiv preprint arXiv:1805.00123 (2018)
6. Chen, P., Liu, s., Hengshuang, Z., Jiaya, J.: Gridmask data augmentation. arXiv preprint arXiv:2001.04086 (2020)
7. Cubuk, E.D., Zoph, B., Mané, D., Vasudevan, V., Le, Q.V.: AutoAugment: learning augmentation strategies from data. In: Proceedings of IEEE CVPR, pp. 113–123 (2019)
8. Lim, S., Kim, I., Kim, T., Kim, C., Kim, S.: Fast AutoAugment. arXiv preprint arXiv:1905.00397 (2019)
9. Hataya, R., Zdenek, J., Yoshizoe, K., Nakayama, H.: Faster AutoAugment: learning augmentation strategies using backpropagation. arXiv preprint arXiv:1911.06987 (2019)
10. Zhong, Z., Zheng, L., Kang, G., Li, S., Yang, Y.: Random erasing data augmentation. In: AAAI (2020)
11. DeVries, T., Taylor, G.W.: Improved regularization of convolutional neural networks with cutout. arXiv preprint arXiv:1708.04552 (2017)
12. Singh, K.K., Hao, Y., Sarmasi, A., Pradeep, G., Yongjae, L.: Hide-and-Seek: a data augmentation technique for weakly-supervised localization and beyond (2018)
13. Girshick, R., Donahue, J., Darrell, T., Malik, J.: Rich feature hierarchies for accurate object detection and semantic segmentation. In: Proceedings of IEEE CVPR, pp. 580–587 (2014)
14. Liu, W., et al.: SSD: single shot multibox detector. In: Leibe, B., Matas, J., Sebe, N., Welling, M. (eds.) ECCV 2016. LNCS, vol. 9905, pp. 21–37. Springer, Cham (2016). https://doi.org/10.1007/978-3-319-46448-0_2
15. Redmon, J., Farhadi, A.: YOLOv3: an incremental improvement. arXiv preprint arXiv:1804.02767 (2018)
16. Li, Y., Chen, Y., Wang, N., Zhang, Z.: Scale-aware trident networks for object detection. arXiv preprint arXiv:1901.01892 (2019)
17. Cai, Z., Vasconcelos, N.: Cascade R-CNN: delving into high quality object detection. In: Proceedings of CVPR, pp. 6154–6162 (2018)
18. Lin, T.Y., Goyal, P., Girshick, R., He, K., Dollár, P.: Focal loss for dense object detection. In: Proceedings of IEEE ICCV, pp. 2999–3007 (2017)
19. Bochkovskiy, A., Wang, C.Y., Liao, H.Y.M.: YOLOv4: optimal speed and accuracy of object detection. arXiv preprint arXiv:2004.10934 (2020)
20. Zoph, B., Cubuk, E.D., Ghiasi, G., Lin, T.Y., Shlens, J., Le, Q.V.: Learning data augmentation strategies for object detection. arXiv preprint arXiv:1906.11172 (2019)
21. Fang, H.s., Sun, J., Wang, R., Gou, M., Li, Y., Lu, C.: InstaBoost: boosting instance segmentation via probability map guided copy-pasting. In: Proceedings of IEEE ICCV, pp. 682–691 (2019)
22. Chen, K., et al.: MMDetection: open MMLab detection toolbox and benchmark. arXiv preprint arXiv:1906.07155 (2019)
23. Bodla, N., Singh, B., Chellappa, R., Davis, L.S.: Soft-NMS – improving object detection with one line of code. In: Proceedings of IEEE ICCV, pp. 5562–5570 (2017)

Synthesizing the Unseen for Zero-Shot Object Detection

Nasir Hayat[1(✉)], Munawar Hayat[1,2], Shafin Rahman[3], Salman Khan[1,2], Syed Waqas Zamir[1], and Fahad Shahbaz Khan[1,2]

[1] Inception Institute of Artificial Intelligence, Abu Dhabi, UAE
nh2218@nyu.edu
[2] MBZ University of AI, Abu Dhabi, UAE
{munawar.hayat,salman.khan,fahad.khan}@mbzuai.ac.ae
[3] North South University, Dhaka, Bangladesh

Abstract. The existing zero-shot detection approaches project visual features to the semantic domain for seen objects, hoping to map unseen objects to their corresponding semantics during inference. However, since the unseen objects are never visualized during training, the detection model is skewed towards seen content, thereby labeling unseen as background or a seen class. In this work, we propose to *synthesize* visual features for unseen classes, so that the model learns both seen and unseen objects in the visual domain. Consequently, the major challenge becomes, *how to accurately synthesize unseen objects merely using their class semantics?* Towards this ambitious goal, we propose a novel generative model that uses class-semantics to not only generate the features but also to discriminatively separate them. Further, using a unified model, we ensure the synthesized features have high diversity that represents the intra-class differences and variable localization precision in the detected bounding boxes. We test our approach on three object detection benchmarks, PASCAL VOC, MSCOCO, and ILSVRC detection, under both conventional and generalized settings, showing impressive gains over the state-of-the-art methods. Our codes are available at https://github.com/nasir6/zero_shot_detection.

Keywords: Zero-shot object detection · Generative adversarial learning · Visual-semantic relationships

1 Introduction

Object detection is a challenging problem that seeks to simultaneously localize and classify object instances in an image [1]. Traditional object detection methods work in a supervised setting where a large amount of annotated data is used to train models. Annotating object bounding boxes for training such models is a labor-intensive and expensive process. Further, for many rare occurring objects, we might not have any training examples. Humans, on the other hand, can easily identify unseen objects solely based upon the objects' attributes

© Springer Nature Switzerland AG 2021
H. Ishikawa et al. (Eds.): ACCV 2020, LNCS 12624, pp. 155–170, 2021.
https://doi.org/10.1007/978-3-030-69535-4_10

or their natural language description. Zero Shot Detection (ZSD) is a recently introduced paradigm which enables simultaneous localization and classification of previously *unseen* objects. It is arguably the most extreme case of learning with minimal supervision [2,3].

ZSD is commonly accomplished by learning to project visual representations of different objects to a pre-defined semantic embedding space, and then performing nearest neighbor search in the semantic space at inference [2–5]. Since the unseen examples are never visualized during training, the model gets significantly biased towards the seen objects [6,7], leading to problems such as confusion with background and mode collapse resulting in high scores for only some unseen classes. In this work, we are motivated by the idea that if an object detector can visualize the unseen data distribution, the above-mentioned problems can be alleviated. To this end, we propose a conditional feature generation module to synthesize visual features for unseen objects, that are in turn used to directly adapt the classifier head of Faster-RCNN [1]. While such feature synthesis approaches have been previously explored in the context of zero-shot classification, they cannot be directly applied to ZSD due to the unique challenges in detection setting such as localizing multiple objects per image and modeling diverse backgrounds.

The core of our approach is a novel feature synthesis module, guided by semantic space representations, which is capable of generating diverse and discriminative visual features for unseen classes. We generate exemplars in the feature space and use them to modify the projection vectors corresponding to unseen classes in the Faster-RCNN classification head. The major contributions of the paper are: **(i)** it proposes a novel approach to visual feature synthesis conditioned upon class-semantics and regularized to enhance feature diversity, **(ii)** feature generation process is jointly driven by classification loss in the semantic space for both seen and unseen classes, to ensure that generated features are discriminant and compatible with the object-classifier, **(iii)** extensive experiments on Pascal VOC, MSCOCO and ILSVRC detection datasets to demonstrate the effectiveness of the proposed method. For instance, we achieve a relative mAP gain of 53% on MS-COCO dataset over existing state-of-the-art on ZSD task. Our approach is also demonstrated to work favorably well for Generalized ZSD (GZSD) task that aims to detect both *seen* and *unseen* objects.

2   Related Work

Zero-Shot Recognition: The goal of Zero shot learning (ZSL) is to classify images of unseen classes given their textual semantics in the form of wordvecs [8], text-descriptions [5,9] or human annotated attributes [10]. This is commonly done by learning a joint embedding space where semantics and visual features can interact. The embeddings can be learnt to project from visual-to-semantic [11], or semantic-to-visual space [8]. Some methods also project both visual and semantic features into a common space [12]. The existing methods which learn a projection or embedding space have multiple inherent limitations such as the hubness problem [13] caused by shrinked low dimensional semantic space with limited or no diversity to encompass variations in the visual image space. These methods are therefore prone to mis-classify unseen samples into seen due to non-existence of training samples for the unseen. Recently, generative approaches deploying variational auto-encoders (VAEs) or generative adverserial networks (GANs) have shown promises for ZSL [14–17]. These approaches model the underlying data distribution of visual feature space by training a generator and a discriminator network that compete in a minimax game, thereby synthesizing features for unseen classes conditioned on their semantic representations.

Zero-Shot Detection: The existing literature on zero shot learning is dominated by zero shot classification (ZSC). Zero Shot Detection (ZSD), first introduced in [2,3], is significantly more challenging compared with ZSC, since it aims to simultaneously localize and classify an unseen object. [2] maps visual features to a semantic space and enforces max-margin constraints along-with meta-class clustering to enhance inter-class discrimination. The authors in [3] incorporate an improved semantic mapping for the background in an iterative manner by first projecting the seen class visual features to their corresponding semantics and then the background bounding boxes to a set of diverse unseen semantic vectors. [4] learns an embedding space as a convex combination of training class wordvecs. [5] uses a Recurrent Neural Network to model natural language description of objects in the image.

Unlike ZSC, synthetic feature generation for unseen classes is less investigated for ZSD and only [18] augments features. Ours is a novel feature synthesis approach that has the following major differences from [18] **(i)** For feature generation, we only train a single GAN model, in comparison to [18] which trains three isolated models. Our unified GAN model is capable of generating diverse and distinct features for unseen classes. **(ii)** We propose to incorporate a semantics guided loss function, which improves feature generation capability of the generator module for unseen categories. **(iii)** To enhance diversification amongst the generated features, we incorporate a mode seeking regularization term. We further compare our method directly with [18] and show that it outperforms [18] by a significant margin, while using a single unified generation module.

3   Method

Motivation: Most of the existing approaches for ZSD address this problem in the semantic embedding space. This means that the visual features are mapped to semantic domain where unseen semantics are related with potential unseen object features to predict decision scores. We identify three problems with this line of investigation. **(i)** *Unseen background confusion:* Due to the low objectness scores for unseen objects, they frequently get confused as background during inference. To counter this, [3,19] use external data in the form of object annotations or vocabulary that are neither seen nor unseen. **(ii)** *Biasness problem:* Since, unseen objects are never experienced during training, the model becomes heavily biased towards seen classes. For this, approaches usually design specialized loss functions to regularize learning [2,19]. **(iii)** *Hubness problem:* Only a few unseen classes get the highest scores in most cases. Addressing the problem in semantic space intensifies the hubness issue [20]. Very recently, GTNet [18] attempted to address these issues in the visual domain instead of the semantic space. Similar to [15], they generate synthesized features to train unseen classes in a supervised manner. We identify two important drawbacks in this approach. **(i)** They train multiple GAN models to incorporate variance due to intra-class differences and varying overlaps with ground-truth (IoU). These generative models are trained in a sequential manner, without an end-to-end learning mechanism, making it difficult to fix errors in early stages. **(ii)** In addition to synthesized unseen object features, they need to generate synthesized background features. As the background semantic is not easy to define, synthesized background features become too noisy than that of object features, thereby significantly hindering the learning process. In this paper, we attempt to solve this problem by training one unified GAN model to generate synthesized unseen object features that can be used to train with real background features without the help of synthesized background features. Further, without requiring multiple sequential generative models to inject feature diversity [18], we propose a simple regularization term to promote diversity in the synthesized features.

3.1   Overview

Problem Formulation: Consider the train set $\mathcal{X}^s$ contains image of seen objects and the test set $\mathcal{X}^u$ contains images of seen+unseen objects. Each image can have multiple objects. Let's denote $\mathcal{Y}_s = \{1, \cdots S\}$ and $\mathcal{Y}_u = \{S+1, \cdots S+U\}$ respectively as the label sets for seen and unseen classes. Note that S and U denote total number of seen and unseen classes respectively, and $\mathcal{Y}_S \cap \mathcal{Y}_u = \emptyset$. At training, we are given annotations in terms of class labels $y \in \mathcal{Y}_s$ and bounding-box coordinates $b \in \mathbb{R}^4$ for all seen objects in $\mathcal{X}^s$. We are also given semantic embeddings $\mathbf{W}_s \in \mathbb{R}^{d \times S}$ and $\mathbf{W}_u \in \mathbb{R}^{d \times U}$ for seen and unseen classes respectively (e.g., Glove [21] and fastText [22]). At inference, we are required to correctly predict the class-labels and bounding-box coordinates for the objects in images of $\mathcal{X}^u$. For ZSD settings, only unseen predictions are required, while for generalized ZSD, both seen and unseen predictions must be made.

We outline different steps used for our generative ZSD pipeline in Algorithm 1 and Fig. 1 illustrates our method. The proposed ZSD framework is designed to work with any two-stage object detector. For this paper, we implement Faster-RCNN model with ResNet-101 backbone. We first train the Faster-RCNN model $\phi_{\texttt{faster-rcnn}}$ on the training images $\mathcal{X}^s$ comprising of only seen objects and their corresponding ground-truth annotations. Given an input image $\mathbf{x} \in \mathcal{X}^s$, it is first represented in terms of activations of a pre-trained ResNet-101. Note that the backbone ResNet-101 was trained on ImageNet data by *excluding* images belonging to the overlapping unseen classes of the evaluated ZSD datasets. The extracted features are feed-forwarded to the region proposal network (RPN) of Faster-RCNN, which generates a set of candidate object bounding box proposals at different sizes and aspect ratios. These feature maps and the proposals are then mapped through an RoI pooling layer, to achieve a fixed-size representation

---

Algorithm 1. The proposed feature synthesis base ZSD method

Input: $\mathcal{X}^s, \mathcal{X}^u, y \in \mathcal{Y}_s, b, \mathbf{W}_s, \mathbf{W}_u$

1: $\phi_{\text{faster-rcnn}} \leftarrow$ Train Faster-RCNN using seen data $\mathcal{X}^s$ and annotations
2: $\mathbf{F}_s, \mathbf{Y}_s \leftarrow$ Extract features for b-boxes of $\mathcal{X}^s$ using RPN of $\phi_{\text{faster-rcnn}}$
3: $\phi_{\text{Ws-cls}} \leftarrow$ Train $\phi_{\text{Ws-cls}}$ using $\mathbf{F}_s, \mathbf{Y}_s$
4: $\phi_{\text{Wu-cls}} \leftarrow$ Define $\phi_{\text{Wu-cls}}$ using $\phi_{\text{Ws-cls}}$ by replacing $\mathbf{W}_s$ with $\mathbf{W}_u$
5: $\mathbf{G} \leftarrow$ Train GAN by optimizing loss in Eq. 1
6: $\tilde{\mathbf{F}}_u, \mathbf{Y}_u \leftarrow$ Syntesize features for unseen classes using $\mathbf{G}$ and $\mathbf{W}_u$
7: $\phi'_{\text{cls}} \leftarrow$ Train ϕ_{cls} using $\tilde{\mathbf{F}}_u, \mathbf{Y}_u$
8: $\phi_{\text{faster-rcnn}} \leftarrow$ Update $\phi_{\text{faster-rcnn}}$ with ϕ'_{cls}
9: Evaluate $\phi_{\text{faster-rcnn}}$ on $\mathcal{X}^u$

Output: Class labels and bbox-coordinates for $\mathcal{X}^u$

---

for each proposal. Let's denote the feature maps corresponding to K bounding box proposals of an image with $\mathbf{f}_i \in \mathbb{R}^{1024}, i = 1, \cdots K$. The features $\mathbf{f}_i$ are then passed through two modules: bounding-box-regressor, and object-classifier. Once $\phi_{\text{faster-rcnn}}$ is trained on the seen data $\mathcal{X}^s$, we use it to extract features for seen object anchor boxes. All candidate proposals with an intersection-over-union (IoU) ≥ 0.7 are considered as foreground, whereas the ones with IoU ≤ 0.3 are considered backgrounds. For N_{tr} training images in $\mathcal{X}^s$, we therefore get bounding-box features $\mathbf{F}_s \in \mathbb{R}^{1024 \times K.N_{tr}}$ and their class-labels $\mathbf{Y}_s \in \mathbb{R}^{K.N_{tr}}$. Next, we learn a unified generative model to learn the relationship between visual and semantic domains.

3.2 Unified Generative Model

Given object features $\mathbf{F}_s$, their class-labels $\mathbf{Y}_s$, and semantic vectors $\mathbf{W}_s$ for seen training data $\mathcal{X}^s$, our goal is to learn a conditional generator $\mathbf{G} : \mathcal{W} \times \mathcal{Z} \mapsto \mathcal{F}$, which takes a class embedding $\mathbf{w} \in \mathcal{W}$ and a random noise vector $\mathbf{z} \sim \mathcal{N}(0, 1) \in \mathbb{R}^d$ sampled from a Gaussian distribution and outputs the features $\tilde{\mathbf{f}} \in \mathcal{F}$. The generator $\mathbf{G}$ learns the underlying distribution of the visual features $\mathbf{F}_s$ and their relationship with the semantics $\mathbf{W}_s$. Once trained, the generator $\mathbf{G}$ is used to generate unseen class visual features. Specifically, our feature generation module optimizes the following objective function,

$$\min_{\mathbf{G}} \max_{\mathbf{D}} \alpha_1 \mathcal{L}_{\text{WGAN}} + \alpha_2 \mathcal{L}_{C_s} + \alpha_3 \mathcal{L}_{C_u} + \alpha_4 \mathcal{L}_{\text{div}}, \tag{1}$$

where $\mathcal{L}_{\text{WGAN}}$ minimizes the Wasserstein distance, conditioned upon class semantics, $\mathcal{L}_{C_s}$ ensures the seen class features generated by $\mathbf{G}$ are suitable and aligned with a pre-trained classifier ϕ_{cls}, and $\mathcal{L}_{C_u}$ ensures the synthesized features for unseen classes are aligned with their semantic representations $\mathbf{W}_u$. $\alpha_1, \alpha_2, \alpha_3, \alpha_4$ are the weighting hyper-parameters optimized on a held-out validation set. The proposed approach is able to generate sufficiently discriminative visual features to train the softmax classifier. Each term in Eq. 1 is discussed next.

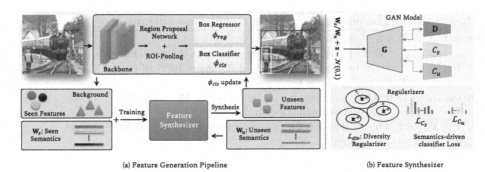

(a) Feature Generation Pipeline   (b) Feature Synthesizer

Fig. 1. Overview of proposed generative ZSD approach.

3.3   Conditional Wasserstein GAN

We build upon improved WGAN [23] and extend it to conditional WGAN
(cWGAN), by integrating the class embedding vectors. The loss $\mathcal{L}_{\texttt{WGAN}}$ is given
by,

$$\mathcal{L}_{\texttt{WGAN}} = \mathbb{E}[\mathbf{D}(\mathbf{f}, y)] - \mathbb{E}[\mathbf{D}(\tilde{\mathbf{f}}, y)] + \lambda\mathbb{E}[(||\nabla_{\hat{\mathbf{f}}}\mathbf{D}(\hat{\mathbf{f}}, y)||_2 - 1)^2], \qquad (2)$$

where $\mathbf{f}$ are the real visual features, $\tilde{\mathbf{f}} = \mathbf{G}(\mathbf{w}, \mathbf{z})$ denotes the synthesized visual
features conditioned upon class semantic vector $\mathbf{w} \in \mathbf{W}_s$, $\hat{\mathbf{f}} = \alpha\mathbf{f} + (1 - \alpha)\tilde{\mathbf{f}}$,
$\alpha \sim \mathcal{N}(0, 1)$ and λ is the penalty coefficient. The first two terms provide an
approximation of the Wasserstein distance, while the third term enforces gradi-
ents to a unit norm along the line connecting pairs of real and generated features.

3.4   Semantically Guided Feature Generation

Our end goal is to augment visual features using the proposed generative module such that they enhance discrimination capabilities of the classifier $\phi_{\texttt{cls}}$. In
order to encourage the synthesized features $\tilde{\mathbf{f}} = \mathbf{G}(\mathbf{w}, \mathbf{z})$ to be meaningful and
discriminative, we optimize the logliklihood of predictions for synthesized seen-
class features,

$$\mathcal{L}_{C_s} = -\mathbb{E}[\log p(y|\mathbf{G}(\mathbf{w}, \mathbf{z}); \phi_{\texttt{cls}})], \quad s.t., \mathbf{w} \in \mathbf{W}_s, \qquad (3)$$

where, $y \in \mathcal{Y}_s$ denotes the ground-truth seen class labels, and $p(y|\mathbf{G})$ is the class
prediction probability computed by the linear softmax classifier $\phi_{\texttt{cls}}$. Note that
$\phi_{\texttt{cls}}$ was originally trained on the seen data $\mathcal{X}^s$ and is kept frozen for the purpose
of computing $\mathcal{L}_{C_s}$. While the conditional Wasserstein GAN captures underlying
data distribution of visual features, the $\mathcal{L}_{C_s}$ term enforces additional constraint
and acts as a regularizer to enforce the generated features to be discriminative.

    The $\mathcal{L}_{C_s}$ term in Eq. 3 can act as a regularizer for seen classes only. This is
because $\mathcal{L}_{C_s}$ employs pre-trained $\phi_{\texttt{cls}}$ which was learnt for seen data. In order to
enhance the generalization capability of our generator $\mathbf{G}$ towards unseen classes,
we propose to incorporate another loss term $\mathcal{L}_{C_u}$. For this purpose, we redefine

the classifier head in terms of class semantics, as $\phi_{\text{Ws-cls}} : \mathbf{f} \to \text{fc} \to \mathbf{W}_s \to$ softmax $\to y_{pr}$, where $\mathbf{f} \in \mathbb{R}^{1024}$ are the input features, fc is the learnable fully-connected layer with weight matrix $\mathbf{W}_{\text{fc}} \in \mathbb{R}^{1024 \times d}$ and bias $\mathbf{b}_{\text{fc}} \in \mathbb{R}^d$, $\mathbf{W}_s \in \mathbb{R}^{d \times S}$ are the fixed non-trainable seen class semantics. The outputs of fc layer are matrix multiplied with $\mathbf{W}_s$ followed by softmax operation to compute class predictions y_{pr}. The classifier $\phi_{\text{Ws-cls}}$ is trained on the features $\mathbf{F}_s$ and ground-truth labels $\mathbf{Y}_s$ of seen class bounding boxes. We can then easily define an unseen classifier $\phi_{\text{Wu-cls}}$ by replacing the semantics matrix $\mathbf{W}_s$ in $\phi_{\text{Ws-cls}}$ with $\mathbf{W}_u$. The semantics guided regularizer loss term $\mathcal{L}_{C_u}$ for synthesized unseen samples is then given by,

$$\mathcal{L}_{C_u} = -\mathbb{E}[\log p(y|\mathbf{G}(\mathbf{w}, \mathbf{z}); \phi_{\text{Wu-cls}})], \quad s.t., \mathbf{w} \in \mathbf{W}_u. \tag{4}$$

The $\mathcal{L}_{C_u}$ term therefore incorporates the unseen class-semantics information into feature synthesis, by ensuring that unseen features, after being projected onto fc layer are aligned with their respective semantics vectors.

3.5 Enhancing Synthesis Diversity

Variations in synthesized features are important for learning a robust classifier. Our cWGAN based approach maps a single class semantic vector to multiple visual features. We observed that the conditional generation approach can suffer from mode collapse [24] and generate similar output features conditioned upon prior semantics only, where the noise vectors (responsible for variations in the generated features) get ignored. In order to enhance the diversity of synthesized features, we adapt the mode seeking regularization which maximizes the distance between generations with respect to their corresponding input noise vectors [25]. For this purpose, we define the diversity regularization loss $\mathcal{L}_{\text{div}}$ as,

$$\mathcal{L}_{\text{div}} = \mathbb{E}[\|\mathbf{G}(\mathbf{w}, \mathbf{z_1}) - \mathbf{G}(\mathbf{w}, \mathbf{z_2})\|_1 / \|\mathbf{z_1} - \mathbf{z_2}\|_1]. \tag{5}$$

$\mathcal{L}_{\text{div}}$ encourages the $\mathbf{G}$ to diversify the synthesized feature space and enhance chances of generating features from minor modes.

3.6 Unseen Synthesis and Detection

Optimizing the loss defined in Eq. 1 results in conditional visual feature generator $\mathbf{G}$. We can synthesize an arbitrarily large number of features $\tilde{\mathbf{f}}_u = \mathbf{G}(\mathbf{z}, \mathbf{w})$ for each unseen class by using its corresponding class semantics vector $\mathbf{w} \in \mathbf{W}_u$ and a random noise vector $\mathbf{z} \sim \mathcal{N}(\mathbf{0}, \mathbf{1})$. Repeating the process for all unseen classes, we get synthesized features $\tilde{\mathbf{F}}_u$ and their corresponding class-labels $\mathbf{Y}_u$, which can then be used to update softmax classifier ϕ_{cls} of $\phi_{\text{faster-rcnn}}$ for unseen classes. At inference, a simple forward pass through $\phi_{\text{faster-rcnn}}$ predicts both class-wise confidence scores and offsets for the bounding-box coordinates. We consider a fixed number of proposals from the RPN (100 in our case) and apply non-maximal suppression (NMS) with a threshold of 0.5 to obtain final detections. The classification confidence for the proposals are directly given by ϕ_{cls}, whereas the bounding-box offset coordinates of an unseen class are estimated by the predictions for the seen class with maximum classification response. We observe that this is a reasonable assumption since visual features for the unseen class and its associated confusing seen class are similar. For the case of Generalized zero-shot-detection (GZSD), we simply consider all detections from seen and unseen objects together, whereas for ZSD, detections corresponding to seen objects are only considered.

4   Results

Datasets: We extensively evaluate our proposed ZSD method on three popular object detection datasets: MSCOCO 2014 [26], ILSVRC Detection 2017 [27] and PASCAL VOC 2007/2012 [28]. For MSCOCO, we use 65/15 seen/unseen split proposed in [19]. As argued in [19], this split exhibits rarity and diverseness of the unseen classes in comparison to another 48/17 split proposed in [3]. We use 62,300 images for training set and 10,098 images from the validation set for testing ZSD and GZSD. For ILSVRC Detection 2017, we follow the 177/23 seen/unseen split proposed in [2] that provides 315,731 training images and 19,008 images for testing. For PASCAL VOC 2007/2012, we follow the 16/4 seen/unseen split proposed in [4] that uses a total of 5,981 images from the train set of 2007 and 2012 and 1,402 images for testing from val+test set of PASCAL VOC 2007. To test the seen detection results, it uses 4,836 images from the test+val set of 2007. For all these datasets, the testing set for ZSD contains at least one unseen object per image.

Implementation Details: We rescale each image to have the smaller side of 600, 800 and 600 pixels respectively for PASCAL VOC, MSCOCO and ILSVRC Detection datasets. For training our generative module, we consider different anchor bounding boxes with an IoU ≥ 0.7 as foregrounds, whereas IoU ≤ 0.3 boxes are considered as background. We ignore other bounding-boxes with an IoU between 0.3 and 0.7, since a more accurate bounding box helps GAN in learning discriminative features. We first train our Faster-RCNN model on seen data for 12 epochs using standard procedure as in [29]. Our category classifier ϕ_{cls}, and bounding-box regressor ϕ_{reg} both have a single fully-connected layer. The trained model is then used to extract visual features corresponding to bounding-boxes of ground-truth seen objects. We then train our generative model to learn the underlying data distribution of the extracted seen visual features.

The generator **G** and discriminator **D** of our GAN model are simple single-layered neural networks with 4096 hidden units. Through out our experiments, the loss re-weighting hyper-parameters in Eq. 1 are set as, $\alpha_1 = 1.0, \alpha_2 = 0.1, \alpha_3 = 0.1, \alpha_4 = 1.0$, using a small held-out validation set. The noise vector **z** has the same dimensions as the class-semantics vector $\mathbf{w} \in \mathbb{R}^d$ and is drawn from a unit Gaussian distribution with zero mean. We use $\lambda = 10$ as in [23]. For training of our cWGAN model, we use Adam optimizer with learning rate 10^{-4}, $\beta_1 = 0.5, \beta_2 = 0.999$. The loss term $\mathcal{L}_{C_u}$ is included after first 5 epochs, when the generator **G** has started to synthesize meaningful features. Once the generative module is trained, we synthesize 300 features for each unseen class, conditioned upon their class-semantics, and use them to train ϕ_{cls} for 30 epochs using Adam optimizer. To encode class-labels, unless mentioned otherwise, we use the FastText [30] embedding vectors learnt on large corpus of non-annotated text. The implementation of the proposed method in Pytorch is available at https://github.com/nasir6/zero_shot_detection.

Evaluation Metrics: Following previous works [3,19], we report recall@100 (RE) and mean average precision (mAP) with IoU = 0.5. We also report per-class average prevision (AP) to study category-wise performance. For GZSD, we report Harmonic Mean (HM) of performances for seen and unseen classes.

4.1   Comparisons with the State-of-the-Art

Comparison Methods: We compare our method against a number of recently proposed state-of-the-art ZSD and GZSD methods. These include: **(a) SB, LAB** [3], which is a background-aware approach that considers external annotations from object instances belonging to neither seen or unseen. This extra information helps SB, LAB [3] to address the confusion between unseen and background. **(b) DSES** [3] is a version of above approach that does not use background-aware representations but employs external data sources for background. **(c) HRE** [4]: A YOLO based end-to-end ZSD approach based on the convex combination of region embeddings. **(d) SAN** [2]: A Faster-RCNN based ZSD approach that takes advantage of super-class information and a max-margin loss to understand unseen objects better. **(e) PL-48, PL-65** [19]: A RetinaNet based ZSD approach that uses polarity loss for better alignment of visual features and semantics. **(f) ZSDTD** [5]: This approach uses textual description instead of a single-word class-label to define semantic representation. The additional textual description enriches the semantic space and helps to better relate semantics with the visual features. **(g) GTNet** [18]: uses multiple GAN models along with textual descriptions similar to [5], to generate unseen features to train a Faster-RCNN based ZSD model in a supervised manner. **(h) Baseline:** The baseline method trains a standard Faster-RCNN model for seen data $\mathcal{X}^s$. To extend it to unseen classes for ZSD, it first gets seen predictions $\mathbf{p}_s$, and then project them onto class semantics to get unseen predictions $\mathbf{p}_u = \mathbf{W}_u \mathbf{W}_s^T \mathbf{p}_s$ as in [19]. **(i) Ours:** This is our proposed ZSD approach.

MSCOCO Results: Our results and comparisons with different state-of-the-art methods for ZSD and GZSD on MSCOCO dataset are presented in Table 1. *(a) ZSD results:* The results demonstrate that our proposed method achieves a significant gain on both metrics (mAP and RE) over the existing methods on ZSD setting. The gain is specifically pronounced for the mAP metric, which is more challenging and meaningful to evaluate object detection algorithms. This is because mAP penalizes false positives while the RE measure does not impose any penalty on such errors. Despite the challenging nature of mAP metric, our method achieves a relative mAP gain of 53% over the second-best method

Table 1. ZSD and GZSD performance of different methods on MSCOCO in terms of mAP and recall (RE). Note that our proposed feature synthesis based approach achieves a significant gain over the existing state-of-the-art. For the mAP metric, compared with the second best method PL-65 [19], our method shows a relative gain of 53% on ZSD and 38% on harmonic mean of seen and unseen for GZSD.

Metric	Method	Seen/Unseen split	ZSD	GZSD		
				seen	unseen	HM
mAP	SB [3]	48/17	0.70	–	–	–
	DSES [3]	48/17	0.54	–	–	–
	PL-48 [19]	48/17	10.01	35.92	4.12	7.39
	PL-65 [19]	65/15	12.40	34.07	12.40	18.18
	Baseline	65/15	8.80	36.60	8.80	14.19
	Ours	65/15	**19.0**	**36.90**	**19.0**	**25.08**
RE	SB [3]	48/17	24.39	–	–	–
	DSES [3]	48/17	27.19	15.02	15.32	15.17
	PL-48 [19]	48/17	43.56	38.24	26.32	31.18
	PL-65 [19]	65/15	37.72	36.38	37.16	36.76
	Baseline	65/15	44.40	56.40	44.40	49.69
	Ours	65/15	**54.0**	**57.70**	**53.90**	**55.74**

Table 2. Class-wise AP comparison of different methods on unseen classes of MSCOCO for ZSD. The proposed method shows significant gains for a number of individual classes. Compared with the second best method PL [19], our method shows an absolute mAP gain of 6.6%.

Method	Overall	aeroplane	train	parking meter	cat	bear	suitcase	frisbee	snow-board	fork	sand-wich	hot dog	toilet	mouse	toaster	hair drier
PL-Base [19]	8.48	4.0	28.7	.29	18.0	0.0	13.1	11.3	24.3	13.8	9.6	2.0	1.1	.24	.73	0.0
PL [19]	12.40	20.0	48.2	.63	28.3	13.8	12.4	21.8	15.1	8.9	8.5	.87	5.7	.04	1.7	.03
Ours-Baseline	8.80	1.9	31.8	0.0	59.3	3.8	0.6	0.1	19.6	10.7	2.8	0.0	0.8	0.0	0.0	0.0
Ours	**19.0**	10.1	**48.7**	**1.2**	**64.0**	**64.1**	12.2	0.7	**28.0**	**16.4**	**19.4**	0.1	**18.7**	**1.2**	0.5	**0.2**

(PL [19]). We attribute such remarkable improvement to the fact that our approach addresses the zero shot learning problem by augmenting the visual features. In contrast, previous approaches such as SB [3], DSES [3], PL [19] map visual features to the semantic space that limits their flexibility to learn strong representations mainly due to the noise in semantic domain. In comparison, our approach helps in reducing the biases towards the seen classes during training, avoids unseen-background confusion, and minimizes the hubness problem.

In Fig. 2, we further show comparisons for ZSD recall@100 rates by varying the IoU. Note that the compared methods in Fig. 2 use additional information in the form of textual description of concepts instead of a single-word class name. Even though, our proposed method uses much simpler semantic information

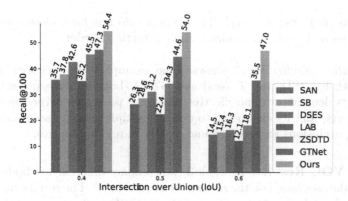

Fig. 2. Comparison of SAN [2], SB/DES/LAB [3], ZSDTD [5], GTNet [18] in terms of Recall@100 rates for different IoU settings on MSCOCO dataset. The proposed method consistently shows improved performance over existing state-of-the-art methods.

(only semantic vectors for class labels), the results in Fig. 2 indicate that our method consistently outperforms several established methods by a large margin for a variety of IoU settings. This comparison includes a recent generative ZSD approach, GTNet [18], that employs an ensemble of GANs to synthesize features.

(b) GZSD results: Our GZSD results in Table 1 also achieve a significant boost in performance. The generated synthesized features allow training of the detection model in a supervised manner. In this way, unseen instances get equal emphases as seen class objects during training. We note that the GZSD setting is more challenging and realistic since both seen and unseen classes are present at inference. An absolute HM mAP gain of 6.9% for GZSD is therefore quite significant for our proposed method.

Compared with the baseline, which projects visual features to semantic space, our results demonstrate the effectiveness of augmenting the visual space, and learning a discriminative classifier for more accurate classification. These baseline results further indicate the limitations of mapping multiple visual features to a single class-semantic vector. One interesting trend is that the baseline still performs reasonably well according to the RE measure (in some cases even above the previous best methods), however the considerably low mAP scores tell us that the inflated performance from the baseline is prone to many false positives, that are not counted in the RE measure. For this reason, we believe the mAP scores are a more faithful depiction of ZSD methods.

(c) Class-wise performances: Our class-wise AP results on MSCOCO in Table 2 show that the performance gain for the proposed method is more pronounced for *'train'*, *'bear'* and *'toilet'* classes. Since our feature generation is conditioned upon class-semantics, we observe that the feature synthesis module generates more meaningful features for unseen classes which have similar semantics in the seen data. The method shows worst performance for classes *'parking-meter'*,

'*frisbee*', '*hot dog*' and '*toaster*'. These classes do not have close counterparts among the seen classes, which makes their detection harder.

(d) Qualitative results: Fig. 3 shows some examples of detections from our method both for ZSD (top 2 rows) and GZSD (bottom 2 rows) settings. The visual results demonstrate the effectiveness of the proposed method in localizing unseen objects, and its capability to detect multiple seen+unseen objects with challenging occlusions and background clutter in real-life images.

PASCAL VOC Results: In Table 3, we compare different methods on PAS-CAL VOC dataset based on the setting mentioned in [4]. The results suggest that the proposed method achieves state-of-the-art ZSD performance. A few examples images on PASCAL VOC shown in Fig. 5 demonstrate the capability of our method to detect multiple unseen objects in real-life scenarios. The results in Table 3 further indicate that in addition to the unseen detection case, our method performs very well in the traditional seen detection task. We outperform the current best model PL [19] by a significant margin, i.e., 73.6% vs. 63.5% for seen detection and 64.9% vs. 62.1% for unseen detection. A t-SNE visualization of our synthesized features for unseen classes is shown in Fig. 4. We observe that our generator can effectively capture the underlying data distribution of visual

Zero Shot Detection (ZSD)

Generalized Zero Shot Detection (GZSD)

Fig. 3. Qualitative results on MSCOCO for ZSD (top 2 rows) and GZSD (bottom 2 rows). Seen classes are shown with green and unseen with red. *(best seen when zoomed)* (Color figure online)

features. The similar classes occur in close proximity of each other. We further observe that the synthesized features form class-wise clusters that are distinctive, thus aiding in learning a discriminative classifier on unseen classes. Synthesized features for similar classes (*bus* and *train*) are however sometimes confused with each other due to high similarity in their semantic space representation.

Table 3. mAP scores on PASCAL VOC'07. *Italic* classes are unseen.

Method	Seen	Unseen	aeroplane	bicycle	bird	boat	bottle	bus	cat	chair	cow	d.table	horse	motrobike	person	p.plant	sheep	tvmonitor	*car*	*dog*	*sofa*	*train*
HRE [4]	57.9	54.5	68.0	72.0	74.0	48.0	41.0	61.0	48.0	25.0	48.0	73.0	75.0	71.0	73.0	33.0	59.0	57.0	55.0	82.0	55.0	26.0
PL [19]	63.5	62.1	74.4	71.2	67.0	50.1	50.8	67.6	84.7	44.8	68.6	39.6	74.9	76.0	79.5	39.6	61.6	66.1	63.7	87.2	53.2	44.1
Ours	**73.6**	**64.9**	**83.0**	**82.8**	**75.1**	**68.9**	**63.8**	**69.5**	**88.7**	**65.1**	**71.9**	**56.0**	**82.6**	**84.5**	**82.9**	**53.3**	**74.2**	**75.1**	59.6	**92.7**	**62.3**	**45.2**

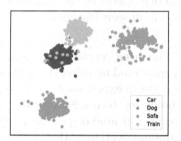
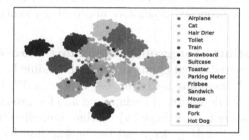

Fig. 4. A t-SNE visualization of synthesized features by our approach for unseen classes on PASCAL VOC dataset (left) and MSCOCO dataset (right). The generated features form well-separated and distinctive clusters for different classes.

Fig. 5. Example unseen detections on PASCAL VOC. *(best seen when zoomed).* (Color figure online)

ILSVRC DET 2017 Results: In Table 4, we report ZSD results on ILSVRC Detection dataset based on the settings mentioned in [2]. We can notice from the results that, in most of the object categories, we outperform our closed competitor SAN [2] by a large margin. Note that for a fair comparison, we

Table 4. ZSD class-wise AP for unseen classes of ILSVRC DET 2017 dataset.

	mean	p.box	syringe	harmonica	maraca	burrito	pineapple	electric-fan	iPod	dishwasher	canopener	plate-rack	bench	bowtie	s.trunk	scorpion	small	hamster	tiger	ray	train	unicycle	golfball	h.bar
Baseline	12.7	0.0	3.9	0.5	0.0	36.3	2.7	1.8	1.7	12.2	2.7	7.0	1.0	0.6	22.0	19.0	1.9	40.9	75.3	0.3	28.4	17.9	12.0	4.0
SAN (L_{mm})	15.0	0.0	8.0	0.2	0.2	39.2	2.3	1.9	3.2	11.7	4.8	0.0	0.0	7.1	23.3	25.7	5.0	50.5	75.3	0.0	44.8	7.8	28.9	4.5
SAN [2]	16.4	5.6	1.0	0.1	0.0	27.8	1.7	1.5	1.6	7.2	2.2	0.0	4.1	5.3	26.7	65.6	4.0	47.3	71.5	21.5	51.1	3.7	26.2	1.2
Ours	**24.3**	**6.2**	**18.6**	**0.7**	**5.9**	**50.9**	**8.2**	**2.1**	**55.3**	11.5	**14.3**	3.0	**15.4**	2.7	11.4	41.9	**16.4**	**79.6**	67.6	14.5	**69.5**	**31.8**	**30.7**	0.1

do not compare our method with reported results in [5,18], since both these methods use additional information in the form of textual description of class-labels. It has been previously shown in [5] that the additional textual description information boosts performance across the board. For example, in their paper, SAN [2] reports an mAP of 16.4 using single-word description for class-labels, whereas, [5] reports an mAP of 20.3 for SAN using multi-word textual description of class-labels. Our improvements over SAN again demonstrates the significance of the proposed generative approach for synthesizing unseen features.

Distinct Foreground Bounding Boxes: The seen visual features are extracted based upon the anchor bounding boxes generated by using the ground-truth bounding boxes for seen classes in $\mathcal{X}^s$. We perform experiments by changing the definition of background and foreground bounding-boxes. Specifically, we consider two settings: **(a)** Distinct bounding-boxes: foreground object has a high overlap (IoU ≥ 0.7), and the background has minimal overlap with the object (IoU ≤ 0.3), and **(b)** Overlapping bounding-boxes: foreground has a medium overlap with the object of interest (IoU > 0.5), and some background boxes have medium overlap with the object (IoU < 0.5). We achieve an mAP of 19.0 vs 11.7 for distinct and overlapping boundig boxes respectively on MSCOCO 65/15 split. This suggests that the generative module synthesizes the most discriminant features when the bounding-boxes corresponding to the real visual features have a high overlap with the respective object and minimal background.

5   Conclusion

The paper proposed a feature synthesis approach for simultaneous localization and categorization of objects in the framework of ZSD and GZSD. The proposed method can effectively learn the underlying visual-feature data distribution, by training a generative adversarial network model conditioned upon class-semantics. The GAN training is driven by a semantic-space unseen classifier, a seen classifier and a diversity enhancing regularizer. The method can therefore synthesize high quality unseen features which are distinct and discriminant for the subsequent classification stage. The proposed framework generalizes well to both seen and unseen objects and achieves impressive performance gains on a number of evaluated benchmarks including MSCOCO, PASCAL VOC and ILSVRC detection datasets.

References

1. Ren, S., He, K., Girshick, R., Sun, J.: Faster R-CNN: towards real-time object detection with region proposal networks. In: Advances in Neural Information Processing Systems, pp. 91–99 (2015)
2. Rahman, S., Khan, S., Porikli, F.: Zero-shot object detection: learning to simultaneously recognize and localize novel concepts. In: Jawahar, C.V., Li, H., Mori, G., Schindler, K. (eds.) ACCV 2018. LNCS, vol. 11361, pp. 547–563. Springer, Cham (2019). https://doi.org/10.1007/978-3-030-20887-5_34
3. Bansal, A., Sikka, K., Sharma, G., Chellappa, R., Divakaran, A.: Zero-shot object detection. In: Proceedings of the European Conference on Computer Vision (ECCV), pp. 384–400 (2018)
4. Demirel, B., Cinbis, R.G., Ikizler-Cinbis, N.: Zero-shot object detection by hybrid region embedding. arXiv preprint arXiv:1805.06157 (2018)
5. Li, Z., Yao, L., Zhang, X., Wang, X., Kanhere, S., Zhang, H.: Zero-shot object detection with textual descriptions. In: Proceedings of the AAAI Conference on Artificial Intelligence, vol. 33, pp. 8690–8697 (2019)
6. Hayat, M., Khan, S., Zamir, S.W., Shen, J., Shao, L.: Gaussian affinity for max-margin class imbalanced learning. In: Proceedings of the IEEE International Conference on Computer Vision (ICCV) (2019)
7. Khan, S., Hayat, M., Zamir, S.W., Shen, J., Shao, L.: Striking the right balance with uncertainty. In: Proceedings of the IEEE Conference on Computer Vision and Pattern Recognition (CVPR) (2019)
8. Zhang, L., Xiang, T., Gong, S.: Learning a deep embedding model for zero-shot learning. In: Proceedings of the IEEE Conference on Computer Vision and Pattern Recognition, pp. 2021–2030 (2017)
9. Lei Ba, J., Swersky, K., Fidler, S., et al.: Predicting deep zero-shot convolutional neural networks using textual descriptions. In: Proceedings of the IEEE International Conference on Computer Vision, pp. 4247–4255 (2015)
10. Annadani, Y., Biswas, S.: Preserving semantic relations for zero-shot learning. In: Proceedings of the IEEE Conference on Computer Vision and Pattern Recognition, pp. 7603–7612 (2018)
11. Lampert, C.H., Nickisch, H., Harmeling, S.: Attribute-based classification for zero-shot visual object categorization. IEEE Trans. Pattern Anal. Mach. Intell. 36, 453–465 (2013)
12. Akata, Z., Reed, S., Walter, D., Lee, H., Schiele, B.: Evaluation of output embeddings for fine-grained image classification. In: Proceedings of the IEEE Conference on Computer Vision and Pattern Recognition, pp. 2927–2936 (2015)
13. Dinu, G., Lazaridou, A., Baroni, M.: Improving zero-shot learning by mitigating the hubness problem. arXiv preprint arXiv:1412.6568 (2014)
14. Chen, L., Zhang, H., Xiao, J., Liu, W., Chang, S.F.: Zero-shot visual recognition using semantics-preserving adversarial embedding networks. In: Proceedings of the IEEE Conference on Computer Vision and Pattern Recognition, pp. 1043–1052 (2018)
15. Xian, Y., Lorenz, T., Schiele, B., Akata, Z.: Feature generating networks for zero-shot learning. In: Proceedings of the IEEE Conference on Computer Vision and Pattern Recognition, pp. 5542–5551 (2018)
16. Zhu, Y., Elhoseiny, M., Liu, B., Peng, X., Elgammal, A.: A generative adversarial approach for zero-shot learning from noisy texts. In: Proceedings of the IEEE Conference on Computer Vision and Pattern Recognition, pp. 1004–1013 (2018)

17. Khan, S.H., Hayat, M., Barnes, N.: Adversarial training of variational auto-encoders for high fidelity image generation. In: Proceedings of the IEEE Winter Conference on Applications of Computer Vision (2018)
18. Zhao, S., Gao, C., Shao, Y., Li, L., Yu, C., Ji, Z., Sang, N.: GTNet: generative transfer network for zero-shot object detection. arXiv arXiv:2001 (2020)
19. Rahman, S., Khan, S., Barnes, N.: Polarity loss for zero-shot object detection. arXiv preprint arXiv:1811.08982 (2018)
20. Zhang, L., Xiang, T., Gong, S.: Learning a deep embedding model for zero-shot learning. In: CVPR (2017)
21. Pennington, J., Socher, R., Manning, C.D.: GloVe: global vectors for word representation. In: Proceedings of the 2014 Conference on Empirical Methods in Natural Language Processing (EMNLP), pp. 1532–1543 (2014)
22. Joulin, A., Grave, É., Bojanowski, P., Mikolov, T.: Bag of tricks for efficient text classification. In: Proceedings of the 15th Conference of the European Chapter of the Association for Computational Linguistics: Volume 2, Short Papers, pp. 427–431 (2017)
23. Gulrajani, I., Ahmed, F., Arjovsky, M., Dumoulin, V., Courville, A.C.: Improved training of Wasserstein GANs. In: Advances in Neural Information Processing Systems, pp. 5767–5777 (2017)
24. Salimans, T., Goodfellow, I., Zaremba, W., Cheung, V., Radford, A., Chen, X.: Improved techniques for training GANs. In: Advances in Neural Information Processing Systems, pp. 2234–2242 (2016)
25. Mao, Q., Lee, H.Y., Tseng, H.Y., Ma, S., Yang, M.H.: Mode seeking generative adversarial networks for diverse image synthesis. In: Proceedings of the IEEE Conference on Computer Vision and Pattern Recognition, pp. 1429–1437 (2019)
26. Lin, T.-Y., et al.: Microsoft COCO: common objects in context. In: Fleet, D., Pajdla, T., Schiele, B., Tuytelaars, T. (eds.) ECCV 2014. LNCS, vol. 8693, pp. 740–755. Springer, Cham (2014). https://doi.org/10.1007/978-3-319-10602-1_48
27. Russakovsky, O., et al.: ImageNet large scale visual recognition challenge. Int. J. Comp. Vis. 115(3), 211–252 (2015). https://doi.org/10.1007/s11263-015-0816-y
28. Everingham, M., Van Gool, L., Williams, C.K., Winn, J., Zisserman, A.: The pascal visual object classes (VOC) challenge. Int. J. Comput. Vis. 88, 303–338 (2010)
29. Chen, K., et al.: MMDetection: open MMLab detection toolbox and benchmark. arXiv preprint arXiv:1906.07155 (2019)
30. Mikolov, T., Grave, E., Bojanowski, P., Puhrsch, C., Joulin, A.: Advances in pre-training distributed word representations. In: Proceedings of the International Conference on Language Resources and Evaluation (LREC 2018) (2018)

Fully Supervised and Guided Distillation
for One-Stage Detectors

Deyu Wang[1], Dongchao Wen[1]($\boxtimes$) (iD), Junjie Liu[1], Wei Tao[1], Tse-Wei Chen[2],
Kinya Osa[2], and Masami Kato[2]

[1] Canon Information Technology (Beijing) Co., LTD., Beijing, China
{wangdeyu,wendongchao,liujunjie,taowei}@canon-ib.com.cn
[2] Device Technology Development Headquarters, Canon Inc., Ota City, Japan
twchen@ieee.org

Abstract. Model distillation has been extended from image classification to object detection. However, existing approaches are difficult to focus on both object regions and false detection regions of student networks to effectively distill the feature representation from teacher networks. To address it, we propose a fully supervised and guided distillation algorithm for one-stage detectors, where an excitation and suppression loss is designed to make a student network mimic the feature representation of a teacher network in the object regions and its own high-response regions in the background, so as to excite the feature expression of object regions and adaptively suppress the feature expression of high-response regions that may cause false detections. Besides, a process-guided learning strategy is proposed to train the teacher along with the student and transfer knowledge throughout the training process. Extensive experiments on Pascal VOC and COCO benchmarks demonstrate the following advantages of our algorithm, including the effectiveness for improving recall and reducing false detections, the robustness on common one-stage detector heads and the superiority compared with state-of-the-art methods.

1 Introduction

With the rapid development of deep learning, there are an increasing number of practical applications with deep neural networks applied to intelligent devices, such as face recognition in mobile phones, human body detection in smart cameras, and pathogenic cell analysis in medical microscopes, etc. Since these applications are extremely demanding in terms of accuracy, speed and memory, some efficient network architectures are proposed, such as MobileNet [1], MobileNetV2 [2], ShuffleNet [3], ShuffleNetV2 [4] and IGCV2 [5]. In addition, some existing methods [6–8] mainly focus on physically pruning networks to reduce redundant weights of larger models and obtain thinner and shallower

Electronic supplementary material The online version of this chapter (https:// doi.org/10.1007/978-3-030-69535-4_11) contains supplementary material, which is available to authorized users.

© Springer Nature Switzerland AG 2021
H. Ishikawa et al. (Eds.): ACCV 2020, LNCS 12624, pp. 171–188, 2021.
https://doi.org/10.1007/978-3-030-69535-4_11

models. However, these methods only consider the effectiveness and compactness of network structures, but ignore to simulate the network potential on the premise of keeping structure unchanged. So, in order to achieve this, our intuition is to make compact student networks learn from larger teacher networks, because the teacher has more robust feature representation and can mine deeper information, which are valuable knowledge for guiding student networks.

An effective algorithm to induce the training of a student network by transferring experience from a teacher network is knowledge distillation [9]. Nowadays, there have been many well-designed distillation works, including the works for classification [10–13] and the works for detection [14–17]. However, existing methods decide what knowledge should be transferred mostly based on human experience or teacher's attention, but neglect to consider what knowledge the student wants to receive. As in the detection distillation methods, feature representation mimicry is generally based on full features or teacher's attention, which will undoubtedly bring two problems: (1) The former will introduce unnecessary computation and a large amount of noise from unimportant area. (2) The latter will ignore valuable knowledge in the background, because the teacher's attention tends to the foreground. Besides, most of works heavily rely on trained teacher models, which ignore the knowledge in the teacher's training process.

To tackle the mentioned limitations, we propose a fully supervised and guided distillation algorithm for one-stage detectors, which consists of three parts: (a) Inter-layer representation supervision. (b) Training process supervision. (c) Network output supervision. For the inter-layer supervision, we find that the regions where objects are detected show higher response in the feature maps and the high-response feature regions in the background are more likely to cause false detections. Therefore, in addition to mimicking the feature representation in the object regions, we also consider the importance of student's high-response feature regions and merge them into the mimicry regions to distill representation more effectively. For the training process supervision, the teacher and the student are initialized with ImageNet pre-trained models and trained together for detection task. The knowledge in the teacher's training process is continuously transferred to help the student find a better local minimum. For the output supervision, we use a multi-task loss to jointly perform the network training and mimicry learning. The contributions in this paper are summarized as follows:

- We present a novel fully supervised and guided distillation algorithm for one-stage detectors which achieves comprehensive coverage of distillation in the inter-layer representation, training process and network output.
- We design an excitation and suppression loss which innovatively considers from the perspective of the student about the importance of its high-response feature regions, so that it makes the student focus on mimicking the feature representation not only in the object regions but also in such high-response regions to improve recall and reduce false detections.
- We propose a process-guided learning strategy, where the teacher is trained along with the student and continuously transfers knowledge throughout the training process to help the student find a better local minimum.

– We verify our algorithm on the representative network structures by using public benchmarks and achieve compelling results.

The rest of paper is organized as follows. The related work is first given in Sect. 2. And then we elaborate and analyze our algorithm in Sect. 3. Next experiments are shown in Sect. 4. Lastly we conclude the paper in Sect. 5.

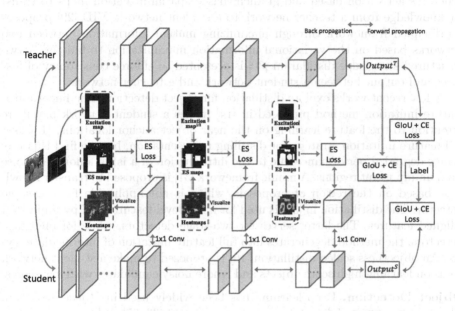

Fig. 1. Overall architecture of our fully supervised and guided distillation algorithm. The proposed architecture consists of three parts: inter-layer representation supervision, training process supervision and network output supervision. The ES loss is proposed for inter-layer representation supervision, which combines the object regions (excitation map) with the high-response feature regions (suppression map) of student network to generate ES maps, and using such maps as masks to make student network focus on mimicking the representation of teacher network in these regions. As for training process supervision, the teacher network receives labels to train along with the student network and transfer knowledge throughout the training phase. We employ a multi-task loss for network training and output distillation.

2   Related Work

Knowledge Distillation. Inspired by pioneering works [9,18], there are various related approaches proposed [17,19–23]. For the distillation approaches focused on the task of classification, FitNets [24] devises a hint-based training approach to transfer representation of intermediate layers from a teacher network to a student network. Deep mutual learning proposed in [25] allows two networks to learn the output distribution from each other so as to improve performance together. Similarity-preserving knowledge distillation [26] uses the pairwise activation similarities within each input mini-batch to supervise the training of a student network with a trained teacher network. Flow-based method [27] generates distilled knowledge by determining the knowledge as the flow of the solving procedure calculated with the proposed FSP matrix. Attention transfer [28] generates activation-based and gradient-based spatial attention maps to transfer knowledge from a teacher network to a student network. VID [29] proposes a principled framework through maximizing mutual information between two networks based on the variational information maximization technique. A two structured knowledge distillation [30] is presented to enforce consistency of features and output between a student network and a teacher network.

A few recent works explore distillation for object detection. The fine-grained feature imitation method proposed in [14] makes a student network pay more attention to the feature learning on the near object anchor locations. [15] uses full feature imitation strategy for distilling representation, but we find this way brings degraded performance due to the introduction of a large amount of noise from unimportant regions. A mimic framework [31] is proposed to transfer knowledge based on the region of proposals, which is not applicable for one-stage detector. The distillation in [32] is used for multi-level features and pyramid ROI Aligned features. The latter serves for two-stage detectors, while for one-stage detectors, the method degenerates into full feature imitation of intermediate layers. An objectness scaled distillation [16] is proposed to make a student network focus on learning high score objects and ignore noisy candidates with low scores.

Object Detection. Deep learning has been widely used in object detection. There are two types of detectors: one-stage detectors [33–37] and two-stage detectors [38–42]. One-stage detectors are designed to be satisfied with the requirement of real-time detection and can be easily deployed into applications. With the development of one-stage detectors, many compact one-stage detectors are proposed such as ThunderNet [43] and PeleeNet [44], which are faster and require fewer resources. Two-stage detectors care more about the detection accuracy. Following the R-CNN [42,45,46] series, there are many efficient two-stage detectors proposed such as light-Head R-CNN [47] and Libra R-CNN [48], which further improve detection accuracy as well as speed up network inference.

3   Method

Figure 1 illustrates the overall framework of fully supervised and guided distillation algorithm (FSGD) which has three parts: (a) Inter-layer representation supervision. (b) Training process supervision. (c) Network output supervision. As for inter-layer representation supervision, we comprehensively consider the importance of feature expression in the object regions and the high-response regions of student network to propose an excitation and suppression loss function. In the training process supervision, a process-guided learning strategy is

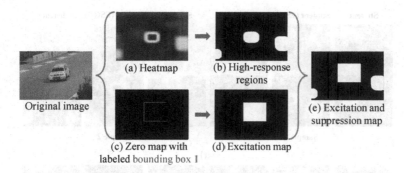

Fig. 2. Generation steps of an excitation and suppression map. (a) Visualization of the feature map from a student network. (b) High-response regions are generated based on (a) with its values greater than a threshold (Defined in Sect. 3.1 ES Loss). (c) The bounding box 1 obtained from ground truth is drawn in a zero map. (d) Generating an excitation map based on the bounding box region of (c). (e) Combining (b) and (d) by union operation to obtain an excitation and suppression map.

proposed to make a teacher network train along with a student network and continuously transfer knowledge. For network output supervision, we use a multi-task loss to optimize networks as well as transfer knowledge. In what follows, we elaborate these parts one by one.

3.1   Inter-layer Representation Supervision

As mentioned in [28], not all the information in the feature maps of a teacher network is important for guiding a student network, and the knowledge transferred from valuable regions is more beneficial than from the overall feature maps. Inspired by it, we propose a novel excitation and suppression loss function to make a student focus on mimicking the feature representation in the object regions and its own high-response regions from a teacher so as to improve recall and reduce false detections.

Generation of Excitation and Suppression Map (ES Map). By visualizing the feature maps of detectors, there are usually many high-response regions at the location of objects. Thus, the features in the object regions are quite important for object detection. In order to help the student network mimic the feature representation in the object regions, we directly regard the bounding box regions of ground truth as object regions and add them into a zero map (an image whose all pixel values are zero) to get an excitation map as shown in Fig. 2(c) and Fig. 2(d). Then, this map is used as a mask to make the student network learn the feature representation in the object regions so as to excite feature expression in such regions. As shown in sample 1 and sample 2 of Fig. 3(a), this way helps the student network reduce missed detections to improve recall, and promotes the precision of detected objects.

Additionally, although small networks often have the same representation capacity as large networks according to the observation [18,49], it is hard to

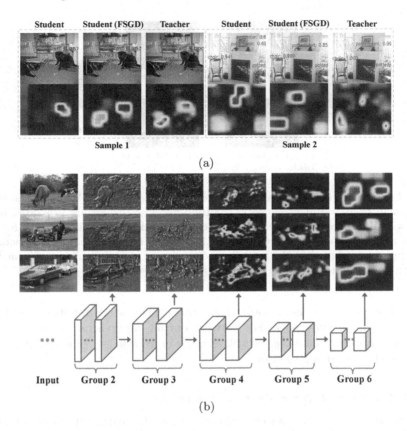

Fig. 3. (a) Qualitative demonstration on the gain from our inter-layer representation supervision. The top row shows the detection results of two samples and the bottom row visualizes the corresponding feature maps at the end of the student backbone. (b) Visualization of feature maps at the end of each supervised groups for some samples. We can see that group 2 and group 3 still express some low-level features, but there are more semantic information in the feature maps of group 4, group 5 and group 6.

achieve the same representation level as large networks due to difficulty of optimization [49], so that the student may have more false detections in the complex background. Interestingly, like object regions, there are also many high-response feature regions at the location of false detections. That is, in these regions, the student's feature values are large, but for the teacher, since it has less false detection, most of feature values are small. Therefore, we can use the teacher's features as targets to guide the student to suppress its large feature values, so as to alleviate false detection. Specifically, for each supervised channel, we further merge the high-response feature regions of the student into the excitation map to generate an excitation and suppression map as illustrated in Fig. 2(e). Then, the ES maps generated from all channels are used as masks to make the student focus on exciting feature expression in the object regions to improve recall and suppressing feature expression in the high-response regions to reduce false detections as shown in sample 2 of Fig. 3(a).

Excitation and Suppression Loss (ES Loss). To ensure the same size of feature maps, the supervised layers of the student and teacher networks should be from the groups with the same scale. Besides, 1×1 convolution layers are introduced into the student network for addressing inconsistent number of channels. Then, we define s as the aligned feature maps of the student network and t as the corresponding feature maps of the teacher network, the ES loss function is defined as:

$$L_{ES} = \frac{1}{N_E + N_S} \sum_{i=1}^{W} \sum_{j=1}^{H} \sum_{c=1}^{C} (I_E \cup I_S^c)(s_{ijc} - t_{ijc})^2, \quad (1)$$

where I_E is the excitation mask generated based on ground truth, and I_S^c is the suppression mask of the cth channel in the feature maps, which is generated by using:

$$I_S^c = \cup_{x=1}^{W} \cup_{y=1}^{H} I(s_c, \alpha, x, y)(\neg I_E) \quad (2)$$

with an indicator function $I(s_c, \alpha, x, y) = \begin{cases} 1 & s_{xyc} > \alpha \times \max(s_c) \\ 0 & s_{xyc} \leq \alpha \times \max(s_c) \end{cases}$. Here W, H and C denote the width, height and channel of feature maps respectively. N_E is the number of excitation points in the excitation mask and N_S is the number of suppression points in the suppression mask. It is noted that α is a filter factor to control the generation of suppression regions. When $\alpha = 1$, only object regions are kept while all background regions are also included when $\alpha = 0$, and more details about the impact of α can be found in Sect. 4.3.

3.2   Training Process Supervision

Existing distillation methods for object detection are almost result-guided, which means that the knowledge is transferred from trained teacher models. However, we find that, for detection task, training a teacher network along with a student network and continuously transferring knowledge can help the student network converge better as shown in Fig. 4. So, we use this training strategy in our algorithm and refer to it as process-guided learning.

Compared with the distillation methods based on trained teacher models, the process-guided learning is more effective for following reasons: (1) Compared with large networks, small networks are hard to train and find the right parameters that realize the desired function due to difficulty of optimization [49]. However, the process-guided learning can continuously transfer knowledge in the optimization process of teacher network, which can be regard as a constraint to guide the training of student network and make it converge better. (2) Because of the difficulty of optimization, the student network may fall into a suboptimal solution if directly regarding the features and output of a trained teacher model

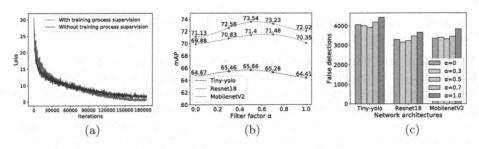

Fig. 4. (a) Loss analysis with/without training process supervision for Tiny-YOLO [36] with the guidance of Darknet53 [37] on Pascal VOC07 dataset. (b) and (c) demonstrate the impact of filter factor α: (b) Accuracy comparison for different α. (c) Comparison of total number of false detections by using different α when $P_{class} > 0.5$.

as the targets. Furthermore, compared with training the teacher model firstly and then distilling the student, this synchronous training strategy is time-saving.

Note that, as shown in Fig. 4(a), in the early stage of training, the loss value with training process supervision is higher and more unstable, but the opposite result is obtained in the late stage. Our analysis is that the knowledge obtained from the teacher is continuously changing for each iteration, and the degree of the change is relatively large at the early stage to lead the higher and unstable loss value. With the improvement of the teacher, the student receives more accurate targets so that the loss will be lower and more stable. Besides, we try to initialize models by random normal initializer in addition to ImageNet pre-training, and it presents the similar training situation as above. However, whichever initialization is used, the early instability is not too severe to cause divergence. Also, we find these ways are different in convergence speed (150 epochs by pre-training and 360 epochs by random initializer). Namely, initializing with ImageNet pre-training can speed up the convergence of our models.

3.3 Network Output Supervision

Since object detection requires localization in addition to classification, for these two types of tasks, we utilize following objective functions for training.

Probabilistic Objective Function. In the detectors, foreground judgment and classification belong to probabilistic tasks. So for this type of task, we both use cross entropy loss function. Given N samples $X = \{x_i\}_{i=1}^{N}$ from M classes, the objective function is defined as follows:

$$L_{CE} = -\sum_{i=1}^{N}\sum_{m=1}^{M} I(y_i, m)log(p^m(x_i)), \tag{3}$$

where $p^m(x_i)$ is the probability output of mth category of ith sample, and y_i is the label of sample i and I is an indicator function defined as

$$I(y_i, m) = \begin{cases} 1 & y_i = m \\ 0 & y_i \neq m \end{cases}.$$ For transferring knowledge from a teacher network to a student network, the objective function is modified as:

$$L(p_t \| p_s) = - \sum_{i=1}^{N} \sum_{m=1}^{M} p_t^m(x_i) log(p_s^m(x_i)), \tag{4}$$

where $p_t^m(x_i)$ and $p_s^m(x_i)$ are probability outputs of the teacher network and student network respectively.

As for probabilistic task, the advantages of using the same loss function are that gradient balance can be guaranteed without biasing towards one or some tasks, and no additional balancing factors are required to adjust different probabilistic loss functions.

Regression Objective Function. For object localization, we use GIoU loss [50] as our objective function which is defined as:

$$GIoU = \frac{A \cap B}{A \cup B} - \frac{C - (A \cup B)}{C}, \tag{5}$$

where A and B represent the regions of two bounding boxes, and C is the smallest rectangle region enclosing both A and B. The GIoU loss is defined as:

$$L_{GIoU} = 1 - GIoU. \tag{6}$$

Compared with traditional L2 loss function, the reason we use GIoU loss function is that, in the early stage of training, due to the large gap between the result of the teacher network and ground truth, the training of the student network will be unstable and often lead to divergence by using L2 loss function in the experiments. However, according to the property of GIoU loss function, the student network tries to regress a bounding box to cover the bounding boxes obtained from the teacher network and ground truth for each object, and gradually narrows the regressed box with the improvement of the teacher network. Finally, the student network can locate objects accurately. Therefore, GIoU loss function is more suitable for our algorithm and experiments also confirm this. In a nutshell, the optimization process of the student network with GIoU loss function is from coarse to fine.

3.4   Overall Objective Function

For the teacher network, it only uses ground truth for training, the overall loss function L_t is defined as:

$$L_t = L_{CE_1} + L_{GIoU_1}. \tag{7}$$

For the student network, the overall loss function L_s is defined as:

$$L_s = L_{ES} + L_{CE_2} + L(p_t \| p_s) + L_{GIoU_2} + L_{GIoU_t}, \tag{8}$$

In L_{GIoU_1} and L_{GIoU_2}, the bounding box A is from ground truth and the bounding box B is from network prediction, but in L_{GIoU_t}, the bounding box A is from the prediction of teacher network and the bounding box B is from student network. The targets of L_{CE_1} and L_{CE_2} both are from ground truth, and the target of $L(p_t\|p_s)$ is from the output of teacher network.

In this way, the student network learns to correctly predict the label of training samples as well as to match the output and specified features of the teacher network. At the same time, the teacher network also learns to correctly predict the label of training samples.

4   Experiments

In this section, we will evaluate our algorithm on Pascal VOC [51] and MS COCO [52] benchmarks. Firstly, we describe the experimental settings. Then, we compare the performance by introducing inter-layer representation supervision into different layers and discuss the impact of filter factor α with different values. After that, ablation experiments will be presented to explain the effects of different supervision. Lastly, we compare our algorithm with state-of-the-art methods and further verify it on some common one-stage detector heads.

4.1   Implementation Details

Backbone Networks. In our experiments, Tiny-YOLO [36], Resnet18 [53] and MobileNetV2 [2] are used as backbones of student networks for the following reasons: (1) Tiny-YOLO consists of continuous convolution and pooling operation, which is a typical network structure like VGG [54]. (2) Resnet18 can be used to represent the networks with Residual blocks [53] to verify our algorithm. (3) MobileNetV2 is composed of Depthwise Separable Convolution [1] which is a common building block used in many efficient networks. Therefore, these three networks contain the common structures used in most existing networks, which can be utilized to reflect the generality of our algorithm.

For another, Darknet53 [37] and Resnet50 [53] are used as backbones of teacher networks, and the reasons are that: (1) Since the teacher network and the student network are trained together in our algorithm, the time of each iteration depends on the teacher network and it will be longer when using a giant backbone such as Resnet101 [53]. So the use of mentioned backbones can save training time. (2) Based on the teacher networks with these backbones, the training of our algorithm can be easily set up and perform well in the single GPU (TITAN Xp), which is resource-saving. (3) The experiments verify that the teacher networks with above backbones can still significantly improve student networks and make them achieve competitive performance. Therefore, we use the aforementioned backbones into teacher networks.

Training Setup. We implement all networks and training procedures in TensorFlow and use the standard AdamOptimizer with default setting for training. The cosine schedule is used to adjust learning rate from 10^{-4} to 10^{-6} and the initial moving average decay is set to 0.9995. We only use single GPU (TITAN Xp) for each experiment and we use 4×8 batch size (4 sub-batch size and 8 subdivisions, the same strategy as mentioned in [37]) to train networks for 150 epochs. All teacher and student models in experiments are initialized with ImageNet pre-trained models. A single scale detection layer [37] is used as our main detector head and we also evaluate our algorithm by using other common detector heads such as SSD [35], DSSD [55] and RetinaNet [56]. Normal data augmentation methods are applied during training, such as random horizontal flipping, random cropping and random translating.

4.2 Multi-layer Supervision

The inter-layer representation supervision can be used to guide the feature representation of any layer in the student network. However, by considering the feature similarity in the adjacent layers or the same groups, we only introduce inter-layer supervision at the end of each group to avoid redundant mimicry. To verify which groups should be supervised for optimal performance, we conduct comparison experiments by using Tiny-YOLO [36] with the guidance of Darknet53 [37] on Pascal VOC dataset and the results are reported in Table 1.

Table 1. Comparison for different supervised groups on Pascal VOC07 dataset by using Tiny-YOLO with the guidance of Darknet53.

Group (Backbone)	mAP (%)
Last five groups	64.49
Last four groups	64.32
Last three groups	**65.66**
Last two groups	65.36
Last group	64.89

Generally, the first group of network is mainly responsible for low-level feature extraction and the features in deep layers are rich in semantic information, so we introduce the supervision into the end of each group from deep to shallow except the first group. As reported in Table 1, we can observe that the optimal result is obtained when introducing the supervision into the end of last three groups. To better understand why this case is the best, we visualize the feature maps of some samples in Fig. 3(b) and we find that group 2 and group 3 still express some low-level features. If we generate suppression regions for these groups by using the method mentioned in Sect. 3, the student network will learn a lot of low-level information in the useless regions of background. In contrast, as shown in Fig. 3(b), there are more semantic information in the feature maps of group 4, group 5 and group 6, and high-response regions are basically concentrated in the object regions, so the features in these regions are exactly what we want the student network to mimic. In the following experiments, we introduce inter-layer representation supervision to the last three groups of backbone networks.

4.3 Filter Factor α for ES Map

In Sect. 3, we use a filter factor α to control the generation of suppression regions. To better determine the value of α, we conduct a set of experiments on Pascal VOC dataset [51] with $\alpha = 0$, $\alpha = 0.3$, $\alpha = 0.5$, $\alpha = 0.7$ and $\alpha = 1$ respectively and the results are shown in Fig. 4(b) and Fig. 4(c).

When $\alpha = 0$, the student network focuses on mimicking the feature representation from overall features of the teacher network, but the accuracy has dropped as shown in Fig. 4(b). By observing the average pixel loss in the feature maps, the result with $\alpha = 0$ has a bigger loss value than others. Through analysis, we find that the full feature mimicry introduces a great deal of information from unimportant regions, which leads to performance degradation. In addition, when $\alpha = 1$, the student only focuses on the feature mimicry in the object regions. That is, the feature expression of false detections in the background cannot be suppressed. To verify this point, we simply count the total number of false detections with a classification score (P_{class}) greater than 0.5 for different α values and the results are shown in Fig. 4(c). The number of false detections with $\alpha = 1$ is more than others, which verifies the above point. More detection analysis can be found in supplementary material. From the results, $\alpha = 0.5$ offers the best performance, so a constant $\alpha = 0.5$ is used in all experiments.

4.4 Ablation Study

To further verify the effect of each component in our algorithm, we conduct ablation experiments by using Tiny-YOLO distilled with Darknet53 on VOC dataset. The results of different supervision combinations are shown in Table 2.

Table 2. Ablation experimental results for evaluating the effect of different combinations of the three supervisions on Pascal VOC07 dataset.

Network	Network output supervision	Training process supervision	Inter-layer supervision	mAP (%)
Darknet53 (teacher)	–	–	–	76.96
Tiny-YOLO (student)	–	–	–	57.10
	√	–	–	58.01
	√	√	–	59.72
	–	–	√	62.08
	√	–	√	63.37
	–	√	√	63.84
	√	√	√	**65.66**

Table 3. Experimental comparison of different distillation algorithms on Pascal VOC07 dataset (mAP, %).

Teacher	Darknet53	Darknet53	Darknet53	Resnet50	Resnet50	Resnet50
Student	Tiny-YOLO	Resnet18	MobileNetV2	Tiny-YOLO	Resnet18	MobileNetV2
Teacher	76.96	76.96	76.96	74.87	74.87	74.87
Student	57.10	69.19	68.59	57.10	69.19	68.59
Hints [24]	61.68	71.12	69.76	59.43	69.88	69.31
FSP [27]	61.23	71.32	69.44	59.17	69.23	68.79
OSD [16]	60.60	69.32	68.11	58.63	68.76	67.67
SP [26]	62.14	72.25	69.81	59.30	70.05	69.06
FFI [14]	62.26	71.83	70.34	59.21	70.25	69.15
FSGD (ours)	**65.66**	**73.54**	**71.40**	**61.28**	**71.01**	**70.11**

From Table 2, there is 0.91% improvement by using output supervision, which shows that conventional output distillation is not very effective for object detection. When we only use the inter-layer representation supervision, there is a significant improvement in performance, which indicates the feature representation distillation is more important for detection and also verifies the effectiveness of proposed ES loss. Besides, the training process supervision gives a further improvement for both output supervision and inter-layer supervision, and the reason we analyzed is that the dynamically evolved features and output from the teacher carry with the experience of step-by-step learning so as to promote the training process of the student. After introducing all supervision, our algorithm significantly boosts 8.56% mAP compared to the non-distilled student.

4.5 Experiment Results

As reported in Table 3, we compare our algorithm with Hints [24], FSP [27], objectness scaled distillation (OSD) [16], similarity-preserving distillation method (SP) [26] and distillation with fine-grained feature imitation (FFI) [14] on Pascal VOC benchmark. Overall, FSGD consistently outperforms the state-of-the-art methods. Especially for Tiny-YOLO, it achieves compelling 3.4% absolute improvement over the best competitor FFI. Note that Resnet18 is further boosted up to 73.54% by using FSGD, which has compelling 4.35% gains compared with original model. Besides, we find OSD method that only distills network output rarely promote the student networks, which also denotes that the distillation of intermediate representation is more important for object detection as mentioned in Sect. 4.4. Detailed analysis of class-wise performance for student networks can be found in the supplementary file.

To further verify the effectiveness of proposed algorithm, we present experimental results on the challenging COCO benchmark. As shown in Table 4, our algorithm significantly improves original student networks. Tiny-YOLO, MobileNetV2 and Resnet18 get respectively 3.36%, 2.43% and 4.83% boost of AP_{50} compared with non-distilled counterpart. And there are still obviously 1.57%, 1.87% and 3.49% absolute gains in AP. Noted that FSGD improves AR

Table 4. Performance verification of proposed FSGD algorithm on COCO dataset by using different teacher networks to distill different student networks.

Student	Teacher53	AP_{50} (%)	AP (%)	AR (%)
Tiny-YOLO	–	23.72	10.46	11.97
	Resnet50	26.02 (+2.30)	11.47 (+1.01)	12.81 (+0.84)
	Darknet53	27.08 (+3.36)	12.03 (+1.57)	13.38 (+1.41)
MobileNetV2	–	29.31	13.46	14.23
	Resnet50	30.46 (+1.15)	14.44 (+0.98)	15.01 (+0.78)
	Darknet53	31.74 (+2.43)	15.33 (+1.87)	15.50 (+1.27)
Resnet18	–	30.55	14.42	15.08
	Resnet50	33.77 (+3.22)	16.84 (+2.42)	17.11 (+2.03)
	Darknet53	35.38 (+4.83)	17.91 (+3.49)	17.63 (+2.55)

for each student model, which demonstrates that our algorithm can help improve recall as discussed in Sect. 3.1.

Besides, we use some common one-stage detector heads (SSD [35], DSSD [55], RetinaNet [56]) to verify the robustness of FSGD. Shown in Table 5, lightweight version of detector head are used into student networks. Similar to SSDLite [2], all the regular convolutions are replaced with separable convolutions (depthwise followed by 1 × 1 projection) in the prediction layers of DSSD and RetinaNet. We call them DSSDLite and RetinaLite. RetinaNet uses a 600 pixel train and test image scale. Experiments show that FSGD still can help to improve the performance of student networks with such detector heads.

Table 5. Robustness verification of FSGD algorithm on Pascal VOC07 by using SSD, DSSD and RetinaNet detector heads (mAP, %).

Teacher	Student	Non-distilled Student	FSGD
Resnet50 + SSD300 [35]	Resnet18 + SSDLite	73.62	76.83 (+3.21)
	MobileNetV2 + SSDLite	73.24	75.67 (+2.43)
Resnet50 + DSSD321 [55]	Resnet18 + DSSDLite	74.53	77.28 (+2.75)
	MobileNetV2 + DSSDLite	73.85	75.76 (+1.91)
Resnet50 + RetinaNet [56]	Resnet18 + RetinaLite	75.88	78.69 (+2.81)
	MobileNetV2 + RetinaLite	75.56	77.24 (+1.68)

5   Conclusions

In this work, a novel fully supervised and guided distillation algorithm is proposed to comprehensively transfer knowledge from inter-layer feature representation, training process and network output. Besides, we design an excitation and suppression loss to make the student network focus on mimicking valuable feature representation to improve recall and reduce false detections. Then, a process-guided learning strategy is proposed for transferring the knowledge in the training process of teacher network to help the student network find a better local minimum. Extensive experiments demonstrate the effectiveness and robustness of our algorithm on the representative network architectures.

References

1. Howard, A.G., et al.: MobileNets: efficient convolutional neural networks for mobile vision applications. arXiv preprint arXiv:1704.04861 (2017)
2. Sandler, M., Howard, A., Zhu, M., Zhmoginov, A., Chen, L.: MobileNetV 2: inverted residuals and linear bottlenecks. arXiv preprint arXiv:1801.04381 (2018)
3. Zhang, X., Zhou, X., Lin, M., Sun, J.: ShuffleNet: an extremely efficient convolutional neural network for mobile devices. In: The IEEE Conference on Computer Vision and Pattern Recognition (CVPR), pp. 6848–6856 (2018)
4. Ma, N., Zhang, X., Zheng, H.-T., Sun, J.: ShuffleNet V2: practical guidelines for efficient CNN architecture design. In: Ferrari, V., Hebert, M., Sminchisescu, C., Weiss, Y. (eds.) Computer Vision – ECCV 2018. LNCS, vol. 11218, pp. 122–138. Springer, Cham (2018). https://doi.org/10.1007/978-3-030-01264-9_8
5. Xie, G., Wang, J., Zhang, T., Lai, J., Hong, R., Qi, G.: IGCV2: interleaved structured sparse convolutional neural networks. In: The IEEE Conference on Computer Vision and Pattern Recognition (CVPR) (2018)
6. He, Y., Liu, P., Wang, Z., Yang, Y.: Pruning filter via geometric median for deep convolutional neural networks acceleration. In: The IEEE Conference on Computer Vision and Pattern Recognition (CVPR) (2019)
7. Lin, S., et al.: Towards optimal structured CNN pruning via generative adversarial learning. In: The IEEE Conference on Computer Vision and Pattern Recognition (CVPR) (2019)
8. Frankle, J., Carbin, M.: The lottery ticket hypothesis: finding sparse, trainable neural networks. In: International Conference on Learning Representations (ICLR) (2019)
9. Geoffrey, H., Oriol, V., Jeff, D.: Distilling the knowledge in a neural network. In: Neural Information Processing Systems (NIPS) (2015)
10. Mirzadeh, S., Farajtabar, M., Li, A., Ghasemzadeh, H.: Improved knowledge distillation via teacher assistant. In: The AAAI Conference on Artificial Intelligence (AAAI) (2020)
11. Liu, Y., Sheng, L., Shao, J., Yan, J., Xiang, S., Pan, C.: Multi-label image classification via knowledge distillation from weakly-supervised detection. In: ACM Multimedia, pp. 700–708 (2018)
12. Park, W., Kim, D., Lu, Y., Cho, M.: Relational knowledge distillation. In: The IEEE Conference on Computer Vision and Pattern Recognition (CVPR) (2019)
13. Byeongho, H., Minsik, L., Sangdoo, Y., Jin, Young, C.: Knowledge distillation with adversarial samples supporting decision boundary. In: The AAAI Conference on Artificial Intelligence (AAAI) (2019)
14. Wang, T., Yuan, L., Zhang, X., Feng, J.: Distilling object detectors with fine-grained feature imitation. In: The IEEE Conference on Computer Vision and Pattern Recognition (CVPR), pp. 4933–4942 (2019)

15. Chen, G., Choi, W., Yu, X., Han, T., Chandraker, M.: Learning efficient object detection models with knowledge distillation. In: Advances in Neural Information Processing Systems, vol. 30, pp. 742–751 (2017)
16. Mehta, R., Ozturk, C.: Object detection at 200 frames per second. In: Leal-Taixé, L., Roth, S. (eds.) ECCV 2018. LNCS, vol. 11133, pp. 659–675. Springer, Cham (2019). https://doi.org/10.1007/978-3-030-11021-5_41
17. Wei, Y., Pan, X., Qin, H., Ouyang, W., Yan, J.: Quantization mimic: towards very tiny CNN for object detection. In: Ferrari, V., Hebert, M., Sminchisescu, C., Weiss, Y. (eds.) ECCV 2018. LNCS, vol. 11212, pp. 274–290. Springer, Cham (2018). https://doi.org/10.1007/978-3-030-01237-3_17
18. Cristian, B., Rich, C., Alexandru, N.M.: Model compression. In: KDD (2006)
19. Junjie, L., et al.: Knowledge representing: efficient, sparse representation of prior knowledge for knowledge distillation. In: The IEEE Conference on Computer Vision and Pattern Recognition Workshops (2019)
20. Yu, L., Yazici, V.O., Liu, X., Weijer, J.V.D., Cheng, Y., Ramisa, A.: Learning metrics from teachers: compact networks for image embedding. In: The IEEE Conference on Computer Vision and Pattern Recognition (CVPR) (2019)
21. He, T., Shen, C., Tian, Z., Gong, D., Sun, C., Yan, Y.: Knowledge adaptation for efficient semantic segmentation. In: The IEEE Conference on Computer Vision and Pattern Recognition (CVPR) (2019)
22. Chen, L., Chunyan, Y., Lvcai, C.: A new knowledge distillation for incremental object detection. In: International Joint Conference on Neural Networks (IJCNN) (2019)
23. Yousong, Z., Chaoyang, Z., Chenxia, H.: Mask guided knowledge distillation for single shot detector. In: International Conference on Multimedia and Expo (ICME) (2019)
24. Romero, A., Ballas, N., Kahou, S.E., Chassang: FitNets: hints for thin deep nets. In: In Proceedings of International Conference on Learning Representations (2015)
25. Zhang, Y., Xiang, T., Hospedales, T.M., Lu, H.: Deep mutual learning. In: The IEEE Conference on Computer Vision and Pattern Recognition (CVPR) (2018)
26. Tung, F., Mori, G.: Similarity-preserving knowledge distillation. In: International Conference on Computer Vision (ICCV) (2019)
27. Yim, J., Joo, D., Bae, J., Kim, J.: A gift from knowledge distillation: fast optimization, network minimization and transfer learning. In: The IEEE Conference on Computer Vision and Pattern Recognition (CVPR), pp. 7130–7138 (2017)
28. Zagoruyko, S., Komodakis, N.: Paying more attention to attention: improving the performance of convolutional neural networks via attention transfer. In: International Conference on Learning Representations (ICLR) (2017)
29. Ahn, S., Hu, S.X., Damianou, A., Lawrence, N.D., Dai, Z.: Variational information distillation for knowledge transfer. In: The IEEE Conference on Computer Vision and Pattern Recognition (CVPR) (2019)
30. Liu, Y., Chen, K., Liu, C., Qin, Z., Luo, Z., Wang, J.: Structured knowledge distillation for semantic segmentation. In: The IEEE Conference on Computer Vision and Pattern Recognition (CVPR) (2019)
31. Li, Q., Jin, S., Yan, J.: Mimicking very efficient network for object detection. In: The IEEE Conference on Computer Vision and Pattern Recognition (CVPR) (2017)
32. Rui, C., Haizhou, A., Chong, S.: Learning lightweight pedestrian detector with hierarchical knowledge distillation. In: 2019 IEEE International Conference on Image Processing (ICIP) (2019)

33. Zhao, Q., et al.: M2Det: a single-shot object detector based on multi-level feature pyramid network. In: The AAAI Conference on Artificial Intelligence (AAAI) (2019)
34. Law, H., Deng, J.: CornerNet: detecting objects as paired keypoints. In: The European Conference on Computer Vision (ECCV) (2018)
35. Liu, W., Anguelov, D., Erhan, D., Szegedy, C., Reed, S., Fu, C.-Y., Berg, A.C.: SSD: single shot multibox detector. In: Leibe, B., Matas, J., Sebe, N., Welling, M. (eds.) ECCV 2016. LNCS, vol. 9905, pp. 21–37. Springer, Cham (2016). https://doi.org/10.1007/978-3-319-46448-0_2
36. Redmon, J., Farhadi, A.: YOLO9000: better, faster, stronger. In: The IEEE Conference on Computer Vision and Pattern Recognition (CVPR) (2017)
37. Redmon, J., Farhadi, A.: YOLOV3: an incremental improvement. arXiv preprint arXiv:1804.02767 (2018)
38. Cai, Z., Vasconcelos, N.: Cascade R-CNN: delving into high quality object detection. In: The IEEE Conference on Computer Vision and Pattern Recognition (CVPR) (2018)
39. He, K., Gkioxari, G., Dollar, P., Girshick, R.: Mask R-CNN. In: The IEEE Conference on Computer Vision and Pattern Recognition (CVPR) (2017)
40. Deng, J., Pan, Y., Yao, T., Zhou, W., Li, H., Mei, T.: Relation distillation networks for video object detection. In: The IEEE International Conference on Computer Vision (ICCV) (2019)
41. Jifeng, D., Yi, L., Kaiming, H., Jian, S.: R-FCN: object detection via region-based fully convolutional networks. In: Advances in Neural Information Processing Systems (NIPS) (2016)
42. Ren, S., He, K., Girshick, R., Sun, J.: Faster R-CNN: towards real-time object detection with region proposal networks. In: Advances in Neural Information Processing Systems (NIPS) (2015)
43. Qin, Z., Li, Z., Zhang, Z., Bao, Y., Yu, G., Peng, Y., Sun, J.: ThunderNet: towards real-time generic object detection on mobile devices. In: The IEEE International Conference on Computer Vision (ICCV) (2019)
44. Wang, R.J., Li, X., Ling, C.X.: Pelee: a real-time object detection system on mobile devices. In: Advances in Neural Information Processing Systems (NIPS), pp. 1967–1976 (2018)
45. Girshick, R., Donahue, J., Darrell, T., Malik, J.: Rich feature hierarchies for accurate object detection and semantic segmentation. In: The IEEE Conference on Computer Vision and Pattern Recognition (CVPR) (2014)
46. Girshick, R.: Fast R-CNN. In: International Conference on Computer Vision (ICCV) (2015)
47. Li, Z., Peng, C., Yu, G., Zhang, X., Deng, Y., Sun, J.: Light-head R-CNN: in defense of two-stage object detector. arXiv preprint arXiv:1711.07264 (2017)
48. Pang, J., Chen, K., Shi, J., Feng, H., Ouyang, W., Lin, D.: Libra R-CNN: towards balanced learning for object detection. In: The IEEE Conference on Computer Vision and Pattern Recognition (CVPR) (2019)
49. Ba, L.J., Caruana, R.: Do deep nets really need to be deep. In: Advances in Neural Information Processing Systems (NIPS) (2013)
50. Rezatofighi, H., Tsoi, N., Gwak, J., Sadeghian, A., Reid, I., Savarese, S.: Generalized intersection over union: a metric and a loss for bounding box regression. In: The IEEE Conference on Computer Vision and Pattern Recognition (CVPR) (2019)

51. Everingham, M., Van Gool, L., Williams, C.K.I., Winn, J., Zisserman, A.: The pascal visual object classes (VOC) challenge. Int. J. Comput. Vis. **88**, 303–338 (2010)
52. Lin, T.-Y., et al.: Microsoft COCO: common objects in context. In: Fleet, D., Pajdla, T., Schiele, B., Tuytelaars, T. (eds.) ECCV 2014. LNCS, vol. 8693, pp. 740–755. Springer, Cham (2014). https://doi.org/10.1007/978-3-319-10602-1_48
53. He, K., Zhang, X., Ren, S., Sun, J.: Deep residual learning for image recognition. In: The IEEE Conference on Computer Vision and Pattern Recognition (CVPR) (2016)
54. Simonyan, K., Zisserman, A.: Very deep convolutional networks for large-scale image recognition. In: ICLR (2015)
55. Fu, C.Y., Liu, W., Ranga, A., Tyagi, A., Berg, A.C.: DSSD: deconvolutional single shot detector. In: arXiv preprint arXiv:1701.06659 (2017)
56. Lin, T.Y., Goyal, P., Girshick, R., He, K., Dollar, P.: Focal loss for dense object detection. In: The IEEE International Conference on Computer Vision (ICCV) (2017)

Visualizing Color-Wise Saliency
of Black-Box Image Classification Models

Yuhki Hatakeyama[1]([✉]), Hiroki Sakuma[1], Yoshinori Konishi[1],
and Kohei Suenaga[2]

[1] SenseTime Japan, 4F, Oike Koto Building, 324 Oikeno-cho, Nakagyo-ku,
Kyoto, Japan
{hatakeyama,sakuma,konish}@sensetime.jp
[2] Graduate School of Informatics, Kyoto University, 36-1 Yoshida-Honmachi,
Sakyo-ku, Kyoto, Japan
ksuenaga@gmail.com

Abstract. Image classification based on machine learning is being commonly used. However, a classification result given by an advanced method, including deep learning, is often hard to interpret. This problem of interpretability is one of the major obstacles in deploying a trained model in safety-critical systems. Several techniques have been proposed to address this problem; one of which is RISE, which explains a classification result by a heatmap, called a *saliency map*, that explains the significance of each pixel. We propose *MC-RISE* (Multi-Color RISE), which is an enhancement of RISE to take color information into account in an explanation. Our method not only shows the saliency of each pixel in a given image as the original RISE does, but the significance of *color components* of each pixel; a saliency map with color information is useful especially in the domain where the color information matters (e.g., traffic-sign recognition). We implemented MC-RISE and evaluate them using two datasets (GTSRB and ImageNet) to demonstrate the effectiveness of our methods in comparison with existing techniques for interpreting image classification results.

1 Introduction

As machine learning is widely applied to image classification, there is a surging demand for the methods to explain classification results and visualize it. One can use such an explanation to check whether a trained model classifies images based on a rational and acceptable criterion, by which he or she can convince various stakeholders that the model is readily deployed.

One of the most popular ways of the visualization is by a *saliency map*—a heatmap overlaid on the original image that indicates which part of the image contributes to the classification result [1–14]. Figure 1 shows an example of a

Electronic supplementary material The online version of this chapter (https://doi.org/10.1007/978-3-030-69535-4_12) contains supplementary material, which is available to authorized users.

H. Ishikawa et al. (Eds.): ACCV 2020, LNCS 12624, pp. 189–205, 2021.
https://doi.org/10.1007/978-3-030-69535-4_12

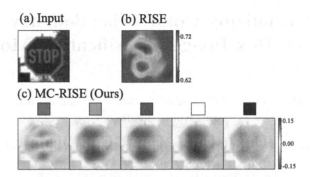

Fig. 1. Visual comparison between the saliency map of RISE [4] and the color sensitivity maps generated by our proposed method (MC-RISE). Best viewed in color. (Color figure online)

saliency map generated by a method called RISE [4]. Given the image (a) of a road sign "STOP" and a model that indeed classifies this image as a stop sign, RISE generates the saliency map (b), which indicates the part of (a) that contributes to the classification result by a heatmap. From this saliency map, we can figure out that the part of the sign surrounding the text "STOP" contributes positively to the classification result.

Among the explanation methods proposed so far, *model-agnostic* techniques such as LIME [1], SHAP [2], and RISE [4] generate a saliency map without accessing the internal information of a model, treating it as a black box. Although these procedures differ in their detail, they all share the following central idea: They compute a saliency map for a classification result by perturbing the given image and observing how the output of the perturbed image changes from the original. Concretely, given an image I, a model M, and its classification result, they compute a saliency map by (1) generating perturbed image $I_1, \ldots, I_N$ from I by masking a part of it, (2) computing the classification result $M(I_1), \ldots, M(I_N)$ for each perturbed image, and (3) comparing $M(I)$ with each $M(I_i)$. If the output of a perturbed image with a specific part unmasked tends to be the same as $M(I)$, then this part is considered to be important.

Although these model-agnostic explanation techniques give valuable insights about a classification result of an image, there is important information that has been overlooked by these methods: *colors*. They compute a saliency map indicating each pixel's existence, but they do not take the color information of a pixel into account. A *color-aware* explanation is effective especially in the application domains in which the colors in an image convey important information (e.g., traffic-sign recognition).

This paper proposes an extension of RISE [4] so that it generates a color-aware saliency map. We extend the original RISE so that it can compute a saliency map for each color of a given color set; we call our extended method *MC-RISE (Multi-Color RISE)*. Figure 1(c) shows the saliency maps generated by MC-RISE. It consists of five heatmaps, each of which corresponds to the significance of a certain color of each pixel; the associated color is shown above each heatmap. We can figure out that the red color at the peripheral part of the stop sign contributes much to the classification result, whereas the other colors do not contribute as much as red.

We also propose an enhancement to *debias* the original RISE. In our extension, the saliency of the pixels in an input image is close to 0 if it is irrelevant for the classification result. Notice that the heatmaps in Fig. 1(c) have value close to 0 for the irreverent pixels, whereas the heatmap generated by the original RISE in Fig. 1(b) does not contain a pixel of value 0; it is hard to figure out which part of the image is irreverent to the classification result from the latter saliency map.

The contributions of the paper are summarized as follows. (i) We propose a new model-agnostic explanation method for an image classifier, *MC-RISE*, which generates *color-aware* saliency maps for the classifier's decision. (ii) To improve the interpretability of the saliency map, we propose a method to debias the saliency map of RISE and incorporate it into MC-RISE. (iii) We qualitatively and quantitatively compare our method to existing model-agnostic explanation methods (LIME [1] and RISE [4]) in GTSRB [15] dataset and ImageNet [16] dataset, and showed that our method can extract additional information which can not be obtained by the existing methods, such as color-sensitivity.

Due to the space limitation, the proofs of theorems and several experimental results are in a separate supplementary material.

2 Related Work

Explanation-generating methods for an image classifier proposed so far can be categorized into the following two groups: (1) ones that treat a model as a *black box* and (2) ones that treat a model as a *white box*. The former observes the input–output relation in generating an explanation without using the internal information of a model; whereas the methods in the latter group assume that the internal information is accessible. As far as we know, our method is the first explanation-generating method for black-box models that considers color information in generating an explanation.

Many white-box methods compute a saliency map utilizing the classifier's gradient information. Grad-CAM [5] and its extension Grad-CAM++ [6] use the gradient with respect to an intermediate feature map to obtain class-specific weights for the feature map. Integrated gradient [7] and SmoothGrad [8] accumulate the gradients with respect to modified input images in order to get a more interpretable sensitivity map than a single gradient map. In [9–13], the relevance map for an intermediate layer is back-propagated layer-by-layer from the output layer to the input layer with a modified back-propagation rule.

However, it is pointed out that the explanation generated by gradient-based methods are not necessarily faithful to the classifier's decision process. Adebayo et al. [17] shows that some gradient-based methods are nearly independent of the classifier's weight, and act like a model-ignorant edge detector rather than an explanation of the classifier. [18–20] adversarially attack gradient-based methods and can manipulate a saliency map without regard to the classifier's output. From these results, we expect that the methods based on the input–output relation are more faithful to the classifier's actual behavior than gradient-based methods.

Other white-box methods include optimization-based methods and attention-based methods. In Meaningful perturbation [21], Extremal Perturbations [22], and FGVis [23], the image region to add perturbation (e.g. blurring, masking) are optimized by gradient descent with respect to an input image, and saliency information is extracted from the perturbed region. In [24], a visual question answering model with the attention mechanism is proposed and the attention maps can be interpreted as the relevant parts in an image.

LIME (Local Interpretable Model-agnostic Explanation) [1] and SHAP [2] are popular explanation-generating methods for a black-box image-classifier. Both perturb the given image preprocessed into a set of superpixels, observe how the output to the perturbed image, and generate an explanation based on the change in the output. Although their merits are widely appreciated, it is known that a generated explanation is not robust to how an image is decomposed into superpixels [25]. Our extension proposed in this paper is based on RISE [4] instead, which does not require a prior preprocessing of an input image. We will explain RISE in detail in Sect. 3.

Some black-box methods are based on these black-box techniques. IASSA [14] is an extension of RISE, which refines a saliency map by iteratively adapting the mask sampling process based on the previous saliency map and attention map. As extensions of the LIME framework, LORE [26] generates sample data with a genetic algorithm and fits decision trees instead of the linear regression model in LIME, and [27] incorporates the effect of higher-order interactions between input features.

Other black-box methods include Anchors [28], which searches for the minimal feature set which is sufficient for a correct prediction, and CXPlain [29], which trains the causal explanation model for the classifier's behavior when some input feature is removed.

3   RISE

This section explains an explanation-generating method RISE [4], which is the basis of our method. For a detailed exposition, see Petsiuk et al. [4].

We first designate several definitions to define RISE. An *image* is a mapping from a finite set Λ of *pixels* to $\mathbb{R}^3$. For an image i and a pixel λ, the tuple $i(\lambda) \in \mathbb{R}^3$ is the RGB value of λ in i. We write $\mathcal{I} = \{ i \mid i : \Lambda \to \mathbb{R}^3 \}$ for the set of images. We also designate the finite set of labels $\mathcal{L}$. We fix an image-classification model $M : \mathcal{I} \times \mathcal{L} \to [0, 1]$ throughout this paper; $M(i, l) \in [0, 1]$ is the model confidence in classifying i as l. For any i, we assume that $\sum_{l \in \mathcal{L}} M(i, l) = 1$.

A *mask* is an element of $\Lambda \to \{0, 1\}$. A mask m represents an image transformation that sets the RGB value of a pixel λ to $(0, 0, 0)$ if $m(\lambda) = 0$; the transformation keeps the original value of λ if $m(\lambda) = 1$ Therefore, the image $i \odot m$ that is obtained by applying the image transformation m to an image i is defined by $\lambda \mapsto i(\lambda) \times m(\lambda)$.

Given an image $i \in \mathcal{I}$ and a label $l \in \mathcal{L}$, we define the *saliency map* $S_{i,l}$ as $\lambda \mapsto \mathbb{E}_m[M(i \odot m, l) \mid m(\lambda) = 1]$, where the expectation is taken over all the possible masks. The intuition behind this definition is that λ can be considered to positively contribute to the classification of i to l if the model confidence of classifying the image to l remains high when λ *is not masked*.

Let X be a random variable whose value is a mask. Then, the definition of $S_{i,l}(\lambda)$ is equal to

$$\frac{1}{P[X(\lambda) = 1]} \sum_m M(i \odot m, l) \times m(\lambda) \times P[X = m] . \tag{1}$$

This expression shows that we can compute $S_{i,l}(\lambda)$ by computing the model confidence $M(i \odot m, l)$ for every mask m that does not mask λ and taking the weighted sum of these values.

Remark 1. In the actual implementation of RISE, the following optimizations are often applied.

– It is prohibitively expensive to precisely computing the value of the expression (1). Therefore, $S_{i,l}$ is approximated by the Monte-Carlo method. We randomly sample sufficiently many masks $m_1, \ldots, m_N$ and compute

$$S_{i,l}(\lambda) \approx \frac{1}{N} \sum_n \frac{m_n(\lambda)}{p} M(i \odot m_n, l) . \tag{2}$$

Here, p is $P[X(\lambda) = 1]$, m_n is the n-th mask, and N is the number of samples.
– RISE preprocesses a mask by bilinear interpolation before it applies the mask to an image. This is based on the intuition that (1) the saliency of a pixel is not binary and (2) a pixel that is close to an important pixel is often important. After this optimization, a mask is an element of $\Lambda \to [0, 1]$ instead of $\Lambda \to \{0, 1\}$.

Our extensions proposed in this paper also uses these optimizations.

4   Debiased RISE and MC-RISE

This section describes our extension to RISE. As we mentioned in Sect. 1, our extension consists of two enhancements of RISE: (1) MC-RISE, which generates *color-aware* saliency maps, and (2) *debiasing* saliency maps, which is a tweak to the RISE procedure so that the value of an irrelevant pixel in a saliency map is close to 0. We first present (2) in Sect. 4.1 and then (1) in Sect. 4.2.

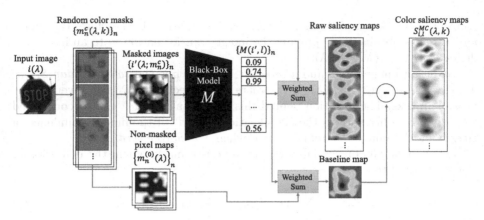

Fig. 2. Overview of our proposed method MC-RISE. An input image $i(\lambda)$ is randomly masked by given colors and the masked images $i'(\lambda; m_n^c)$ are fed to the black-box model M. Raw saliency maps are obtained by the weighted sum of the color masks $m_n^c(\lambda, k)$, where the weights are the output probabilities $M(i', l)$. Then a baseline map obtained from non-masked pixel maps $m_n^{(0)}(\lambda)$ is subtracted from them so that the saliency value in image parts irrelevant to classification is aligned to zero. (Color figure online)

4.1   Removing Bias from Saliency Maps

The range of the saliency values of a heatmap generated by RISE is highly variable depending on an input image. For example, the values in the saliency map at the first row in Fig. 4(c) ranges from 0.016 to 0.023, whereas the one at the third row ranges from 0.375 to 0.550. This variability of saliency values degrades interpretability because it makes *thresholding* saliency value difficult: There is no clear threshold to decide which pixel is positively important, which is negatively important, and which is irrelevant.

To address this problem, we tweak the definition of RISE so that the saliency value of an irrelevant pixel to be close to 0, a positively-important pixel to be positive, and a negatively-important pixel to be negative; in other words, our method generates a *debiased* saliency map. Concretely, we generate a saliency map using the following definition instead of Eq. (1):

$$S_{i,l}^{\mathrm{PN}}(\lambda) := \mathbb{E}_m[M(i \odot m, l)|m(\lambda) = 1] - \mathbb{E}_m[M(i \odot m, l)|m(\lambda) = 0] . \quad (3)$$

Intuition behind Eq. (3) is that we also need to use *negative* saliency $\mathbb{E}_m[M(i \odot m, l)|m(\lambda) = 0]$ of a pixel λ for the classification result l in computing a saliency map, not only using the positive saliency $\mathbb{E}_m[M(i \odot m, l)|m(\lambda) = 1]$ as RISE does. The expression $\mathbb{E}_m[M(i \odot m, l)|m(\lambda) = 0]$ indeed expresses the negative saliency of λ because its value becomes high if *masking out* the pixel λ increases the model confidence on average over the masks. To give the saliency as a single number, we calculate the difference of the positive saliency and the negative saliency. As a result, the sign of $S_{i,l}^{\mathrm{PN}}(\lambda)$ indicates whether positive or negative saliency is dominant at a given pixel λ.

Calculating the difference of the positive saliency and the negative saliency also makes the saliency value of an irrelevant pixel to be 0. We can prove that a saliency map generated from Eq. (3) is equipped with the following property (for the proof, see Section C in the supplementary material):

Proposition 1 (Irrelevant pixels). *If, for all binary mask samples, the output probability of class l from a black-box classifier M does not vary no matter whether a pixel λ in the mask m is retained or masked (i.e. $M(i \odot m, l)_{m(\lambda)=1} = M(i \odot m, l)_{m(\lambda)=0}$), then $S_{i,l}^{\mathrm{PN}}(\lambda) = 0$.*

This property justifies the following interpretation of $S_{i,l}^{\mathrm{PN}}$: A pixel whose value of $S_{i,l}^{\mathrm{PN}}$ is close to 0 has almost no effect on the classification result. It is worth noting that (1) the sign of the value of $S_{i,l}^{\mathrm{PN}}(\lambda)$ carries information on whether the pixel λ positively/negatively significant for the classification of i to l and (2) its absolute value expresses how significant λ is for the classification. In the original RISE, we can observe only that λ is more/less positively significant than another pixel λ' in the image i if the value of $S_{i,l}(\lambda)$ is larger/smaller than $S_{i,l}(\lambda')$. In Sect. 5.2, we empirically justify the above interpretation and argue that these properties render the interpretation of our saliency map easier than the one of the original RISE.

Equation (3) can be rewritten to the following equation that computes $S_{i,l}^{\mathrm{PN}}$ by a weighted sum over all masks m (see Section A in the supplementary material for the detailed derivation):

$$S_{i,l}^{\mathrm{PN}}(\lambda) = \sum_m \frac{m(\lambda) - p}{p(1 - p)} M(i \odot m, l) P[X = m] , \qquad (4)$$

where $p = P[X(\lambda) = 1]$. We approximate $S_{i,l}^{\mathrm{PN}}$ by Monte Carlo sampling and express it by the following equation:

$$S_{i,l}^{\mathrm{PN}}(\lambda) \approx \frac{1}{N} \sum_n \frac{m_n(\lambda) - p}{p(1 - p)} M(i \odot m_n, l) , \qquad (5)$$

where N is the number of mask samples and $\{m_n\}_{n=1}^N$ are randomly-sampled masks. We remark that Eq. (5) is obtained from Eq. (2) simply by replacing $\frac{m_n(\lambda)}{p}$ with $\frac{m_n(\lambda)-p}{p(1-p)}$; therefore, we can easily implement our debiasing method by modifying the implementation of RISE.

4.2   Multi-Colored RISE (MC-RISE)

We next present MC-RISE, our extension to RISE that explains the color-wise saliency of each pixel. The main idea of MC-RISE is to use a colored mask instead of a binary mask that RISE uses. Then, we can compute the positive/negative saliency of the given color component of a pixel from the response of the model to the masked image. The pseudocode for MC-RISE is presented in Section F in the supplementary material.

Color Masks. We explain the method to generate color masks and color-masked images in MC-RISE. We fix a set of colors $c_1, \ldots, c_K \in \mathbb{R}^3$ where each c_i is a 3-tuple of color values in the RGB colorspace. We are to generate a saliency map for each c_i. To this end, MC-RISE generates *colored masks* instead of the binary masks that RISE uses. The saliency map is computed from the change in the average model confidence for the color-masked image in a similar way to RISE. We will explain the details of the saliency-map computation later.

To generate a colored mask, MC-RISE first generates a low-resolution color mask $m_{\text{low}}(\lambda, k)$ of the size $h \times w$ (which is smaller than the input image's size), where λ is the position of a pixel and k is the index for masking color in the color set $\{c_k\}_k$. The low-resolution color mask $m_{\text{low}}(\lambda, k)$ is generated as follows:

1. For each pixel, MC-RISE randomly decides whether it is masked or not with a masking probability p_{mask}.
2. For each pixel that is decided to be masked, MC-RISE chooses the color used to mask it from the color set $\{c_k\}_k$ with the uniform probabilities.
3. Then, the color mask $m_{\text{low}}(\lambda, k)$ is defined as follows:

$$m_{\text{low}}(\lambda, k) = \begin{cases} 1 \text{ if } \lambda \text{ is masked with color } k. \\ 0 \text{ otherwise.} \end{cases} \tag{6}$$

Then, $m_{\text{low}}(\lambda, k)$ is converted to a high-resolution color mask $m^c(\lambda, k)$ by (1) resizing $m_{\text{low}}(\lambda, k)$ to the size $H \times W$ of input images using bilinear interpolation and (2) shifting the resized mask by a random number of pixels from $(0, 0)$ up to $(\lfloor H/h \rfloor, \lfloor W/w \rfloor)$ (i.e., the size of a low-resolution pixel). We remark that the computation of $m^c(\lambda, k)$ corresponds to the preprocessing of a mask in RISE mentioned in Remark 1.

We also compute a non-masked pixel map $m^{(0)}(\lambda)$ by

$$m^{(0)}(\lambda; m^c) = 1 - \sum_{k=1}^{K} m^c(\lambda, k) . \tag{7}$$

$m^{(0)}(\lambda; m^c)$ is 1 for non-masked pixels and 0 for masked pixels.

From a color mask m^c and an input image i, the color-masked image $i'(\lambda; m^c)$ is computed by $i'(\lambda; m^c) = i(\lambda)m^{(0)}(\lambda; m^c) + \sum_{k=1}^{K} c_k m^c(\lambda, k)$. Because of Eqs. (6) and (7), this expression can be seen as the alpha blending of an input image and the images uniformly filled with the masking colors $\{c_k\}_k$.

In Fig. 2, an example of a color mask $m^c(\lambda, k)$, a non-masked pixel map $m^{(0)}(\lambda)$, and a color-masked image $i'(\lambda; m^c)$ are presented.

Color-Aware Saliency Map. The saliency map of MC-RISE is defined by

$$S_{i,l}^{\text{MC}}(\lambda, k) := \mathbb{E}_{m^c \sim \mathcal{M}_c}[M(i'(\lambda; m^c))|m^c(\lambda, k) = 1]$$
$$-\mathbb{E}_{m^c \sim \mathcal{M}_c}[M(i'(\lambda; m^c))|m^{(0)}(\lambda) = 1] , \tag{8}$$

where $\mathcal{M}_c$ denotes the probability distribution of color masks induced by the above mask-generation procedure. $S_{i,l}^{\mathrm{MC}}(\lambda, k)$ represents how sensitively the model's confidence in classifying an image i to class l responds when the pixel λ in an input image is masked by the color c_k.

The debiasing method of a saliency map discussed in Sect. 4.1 is incorporated also into the definition of color saliency maps (Eq. (8)), where the baseline saliency map for non-masked pixels $(\mathbb{E}_{m^c \sim \mathcal{M}_c}[M(i'(\lambda; m^c))|m^{(0)}(\lambda) = 1]$, corresponding to the effect of retaining the pixel λ) is subtracted from the raw saliency maps $(\mathbb{E}_{m^c \sim \mathcal{M}_c}[M(i'(\lambda; m^c))|m^c(\lambda, k) = 1]$, corresponding to the effect of masking the pixel λ).

The formula to estimate a color saliency map with Monte Carlo sampling can be derived in a similar way to Sect. 4.1 (see Section B in the supplementary material for the detailed derivation);

$$S_{i,l}^{\mathrm{MC}}(\lambda, k) = \mathbb{E}_{m^c \sim \mathcal{M}_c}\left[\left(\frac{m^c(\lambda, k)}{p_{\mathrm{mask}}/K} - \frac{m^{(0)}(\lambda)}{1 - p_{\mathrm{mask}}}\right) M(i'(\lambda; m^c))\right]$$

$$\approx \frac{1}{N}\sum_n \left(\frac{K m_n^c(\lambda, k)}{p_{\mathrm{mask}}} - \frac{m_n^{(0)}(\lambda)}{1 - p_{\mathrm{mask}}}\right) M(i'(\lambda; m_n^c)), \qquad (9)$$

where N is the number of mask sampling and $\{m_n^c\}_{n=1}^N$ are color masks sampled from the distribution $\mathcal{M}_c$. In our implementation, $\frac{K m_n^c(\lambda, k)}{p_{\mathrm{mask}}}$ and $\frac{m_n^{(0)}(\lambda)}{1 - p_{\mathrm{mask}}}$ in Eq. (9) are separately accumulated using the same samples of color masks $\{m_n^c\}_n$; $S_{i,l}^{\mathrm{MC}}(\lambda, k)$ is computed by subtracting the weighted-sum of the second term (baseline map) from that of the first term (raw saliency maps), as illustrated in Fig. 2.

Interpretation of Color Saliency Maps. Since the debiasing method of Sect. 4.1 is incorporated into the definition of color saliency maps (Eq. (8)), we can interpret the sign of a color saliency map as a positive/negative effect on the decision given by the model as we discussed in Sect. 4.1. However, because the sign of a color saliency map represents the expected change in the model confidence by *color-masking* a pixel λ, the interpretation of the sign of a saliency value is different from the debiased RISE in Sect. 4.1, in which a saliency value represents the effect of *retaining* original pixels. Therefore, we can interpret the color saliency map $S_{i,l}^{\mathrm{MC}}(\lambda, k)$ as follows:

- If $S_{i,l}^{\mathrm{MC}}(\lambda, k)$ has a positive or negative value *for all* k, the model's output probability of class l should increase or decrease by any kind of color mask at a pixel λ, respectively. This suggests that the original *texture* at pixel λ is an obstacle or an important feature to the model, respectively, and its overall color is not relevant to the model's decision.
- If $S_{i,l}^{\mathrm{MC}}(\lambda, k) \sim 0$ *for all* k, any kind of masking at the pixel λ should not affect the model's output. It means that the pixel λ is irrelevant to the model's decision.

- If $S_{i,l}^{\mathrm{MC}}(\lambda, k) > 0$ *for some* k, the model's output probability of class l should increase by masking the pixel λ with the color c_k. This indicates that the presence of the color c_k at the pixel λ is an important feature for the model to classify an image as class l, but the original image lacks this feature.
- If $S_{i,l}^{\mathrm{MC}}(\lambda, k) < 0$ *for some* k, the model's output probability of class l should decrease by masking the pixel λ with the color c_k. This suggests that the pixel λ's original color is an influential feature for the model to classify an image as class l and masking it with the color c_k degrade the model's confidence for class l.
- If $S_{i,l}^{\mathrm{MC}}(\lambda, k) \sim 0$ *for some* k, color-masking the pixel λ with the color c_k should not affect the model's output. It suggests that the color c_k is similar to the original color of the pixel λ from the viewpoint of the model, therefore masking λ with other colors would affect the model's output.

5 Experiments

5.1 Experimental Settings

We use LIME [1] and RISE [4] as the baseline for the evaluation of our methods. We designated two kinds of models trained with different datasets for the evaluation.

- Models trained with GTSRB [15] dataset: We trained (1) VGG-16 [30] model with batch normalization and (2) ResNet-50 [31] model. We trained the models for 90 epochs with momentum SGD using cross-entropy loss. We set the learning rate to 10^{-1}, the momentum to 0.9, and the weight decay to 5×10^{-4}; we decayed the learning rate by a factor of 0.1 in every 30 epochs. We resized images to $H \times W = 96 \times 96$ pixels for training and evaluation.
- Models trained with ImageNet [16] dataset: We used the pretrained ResNet-50 model provided by PyTorch [32] for the evaluation. We cropped and resized images to $H \times W = 224 \times 224$ pixels for the evaluation.

For MC-RISE and RISE, the number of samples N was set to 8000 and the masking probability was set to 0.5. For MC-RISE, we used the following five colors: red ($c_k = (255, 0, 0)$ in the RGB colorspace), green ($c_k = (0, 255, 0)$), blue ($c_k = (0, 0, 255)$), white ($c_k = (255, 255, 255)$), and black ($c_k = (0, 0, 0)$). For LIME, the parameters that we used were the same as the original paper [1].

We also applied MC-RISE to a person re-identification model with metric learning. See Section D in the supplementary material for details.

5.2 Results

Qualitative Evaluation of the Debiasing Method. We qualitatively evaluated the debiasing method presented in Sect. 4.1. Figure 3 compares the saliency maps of RISE and our debiased saliency map; we used ImageNet dataset to generate these maps. In the saliency map generated by the original RISE (Fig. 3(b)),

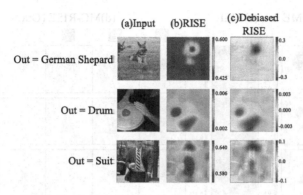

Fig. 3. Visual comparison between (b) raw saliency maps of RISE [4] and (c) debiased saliency maps calculated by our method. The parts of the image contributing positively/negatively to the output class have positive/negative intensity in (c), respectively. The background regions irrelevant to the model's output have near-zero intensity in (c). Best viewed in color. (Color figure online)

the saliency values of the background regions—which should be irrelevant to the decision of the model—largely differs depending on the input images both in their absolute values and in their relative magnitude (i.e., pseudo-color in the plots). In our debiased maps (Fig. 3(c)), the background regions of all the images have the saliency values that are close to zero. These results demonstrate that the debiased RISE computes a saliency map in which the saliency values of the irrelevant regions are close to zero as we intend.

The saliency maps on the second and third rows in Fig. 3(c) shows that the saliency values near the objects of the output class (i.e., Drum and Suit) are positive and that the saliency values near the "noisy" objects (i.e., heart-shaped weight and necktie) are negative. These behaviors are also in accordance with the interpretation we presented in Sect. 4.1.

Qualitative Evaluation of MC-RISE. Figure 4 compares saliency maps generated by LIME [1], RISE [4], and our method MC-RISE; we used GTSRB dataset to generate these saliency maps. The saliency values of MC-RISE on the third row are not sensitive to the colors (i.e. the sign and the values of $S_{i,l}^{\mathrm{MC}}(\lambda, k)$ is similar for all k). As we mentioned in Sect. 4.2, this suggests that the texture information is important for the model than the color information.

The saliency map of the image on the first row in Fig. 6 is sensitive to colors. In this image, the saliency near the white arrow is negative for all the colors; this suggests that the texture of this region (i.e., the arrow shape) is important for the model. In contrast, the values near the peripheral region of the sign in the green and the blue saliency maps are positive; this suggests that the blue-like color of this region is important for the model's decision. Notice that LIME nor RISE can detect the sensitivity to colors; in fact, these parts identified as salient

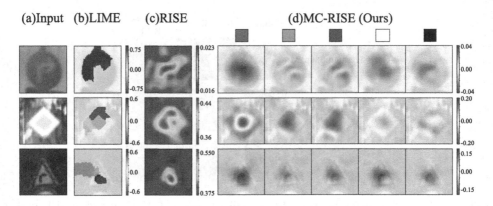

Fig. 4. Visual comparison among the saliency maps of (b) LIME [1], (c) RISE [4], and (d) the color saliency maps of MC-RISE in the GTSRB dataset. The boxes in the top row in (d) present the masking color used to obtain the maps in the same column. All samples are correctly classified by the model. Best viewed in color. (Color figure online)

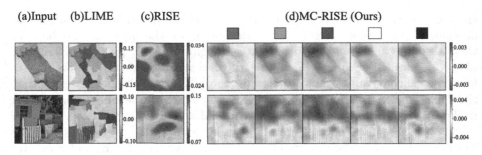

Fig. 5. Visual comparison among the saliency maps of (b) LIME [1], (c) RISE [4], and (d)the color saliency maps of MC-RISE in the ImageNet dataset. All samples are correctly classified by the model. Best viewed in color. (Color figure online)

in the green and the blue saliency maps are not necessarily identifiable in the saliency maps generated by LIME and RISE.

Figure 5 shows the comparison of the saliency maps in ImageNet dataset. Compared to maps in the GTSRB dataset, many of the maps in the ImageNet dataset have low color-dependency among the color saliency maps. This suggests that the model's decision is more dependent on the detailed texture of objects than on the color of image regions. In such cases, we can extract information about positive or negative saliency from the color saliency maps. For example, in the third-row samples in Fig. 5, color saliency maps are interpreted to mean that the upper part of the image is important for the classification output ("Mobile home" class), but the fences in the lower part of the image are reducing the model's confidence for the output class. From these observations, it is expected that MC-RISE can extract more useful information in domains where the color in

Table 1. Evaluations of CA-deletion metric (lower is better) in LIME [1], RISE [4], and MC-RISE (ours).

Dataset	Model	LIME	RISE	MC-RISE
GTSRB	VGG-16	0.1324	0.0664	**0.0270**
	ResNet50	0.1294	0.0627	**0.0204**
ImageNet	ResNet50	0.1146	0.1046	**0.0980**

image regions is highly important for classification, such as the GTSRB dataset, than domains where detailed texture is important such as the ImageNet dataset.

Quantitative Evaluation of MC-RISE. For the quantitative evaluation of MC-RISE, we first would like to establish the evaluation metrics we use. We adapt the *deletion* metric proposed by Petsiuk et al. [4]—which measures how well a saliency-map–based explanation of an image classification result localizes the important pixels—to our color-aware setting.

To explain the deletion metric, let i be an image and M be a model. The deletion metric is the AUC value of the plot of f where $f(j)$ is the model confidence of the image in which the 1st to the j-th important pixels are removed. The lower the deletion metric is, the better the saliency map localizes the important region; a lower metric value means that the model confidence drops rapidly because the saliency map successfully points out the important pixels.

Our metric, called *CA-deletion (color-aware deletion)* is derived from the deletion metric as follows. In the CA-deletion metric, pixels in an input image are removed by masking them with *the most sensitive color* obtained from the color saliency maps. Concretely, pixel λ is removed in the ascending order of $\min_k[S_{i,l}^{\mathrm{MC}}(\lambda, k)]$ and the removed pixel is filled by the color c_k where $k = \mathrm{argmin}_k[S_{i,l}^{\mathrm{MC}}(\lambda, k)]$. The model confidence for the pixel-removed images are plotted against the pixel-removal fractions; the CA-deletion value is the area-under-curve (AUC) of the plot. If a color saliency map correctly captures the model's sensitivity to color masking, this removal method must be effective to reduce the model confidence, resulting in a low value of the CA-deletion metric.[1]

Table 1 shows the evaluation result of MC-RISE in comparison with LIME and RISE. MC-RISE consistently outperforms RISE and LIME especially by a large margin in the GTSRB dataset. This indicates that MC-RISE can correctly capture the color-dependent sensitivity of the model, and effectively localize important pixels in an input image by using this information. The large margin in the GTSRB dataset is in accordance with our expectation that MC-RISE is especially effective in a domain, such as traffic sign classification, where color information conveys important information.

---

[1] Notice that other common metrics (e.g., pointing game) are not appropriate for evaluating MC-RISE because these metrics focus on the *positional* saliency; they do not consider the color saliency.

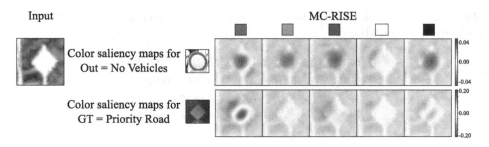

Fig. 6. Error analysis example in the GTSRB classification model with MC-RISE. Sensitivities for a red color mask at the center of the sign are opposite for the output class (No Vehicle) and the GT class (Priority road). It suggests that the absence of red color at the sign center is the cause of the error. Best viewed in color. (Color figure online)

Use Case: Error Analysis Using MC-RISE. We demonstrate a use case of MC-RISE for analyzing misclassified samples. Figure 6 shows the color saliency maps generated by MC-RISE for a sample in GTSRB dataset that is misclassified by our model. The input is an image of a "Priority road" sign, whereas our model misclassified it as a "No vehicles" sign.

The saliency maps for the output "No vehicles" class show that the colors other than white at the center part of the sign have a negative effect in classifying this image as "No vehicles". This suggests that, if the color of the center part were not white, then this image would not be classified as "No vehicles" class.

In contrast, in the saliency maps of the GT class (i.e., "Priority road" sign), the saliency map for red color has a strong positive value at the center of the sign, suggesting that the confidence of "Priority Road" class would largely increase if the color of the central part were red. From the above observations, we can hypothesize that the cause of the error is the absence of red color at the center of the sign (possibly due to overexposure). As one can observe, the information obtained by MC-RISE in addition to that obtained by the other methods, such as color-sensitivity or negative saliency, is indeed useful to explore the cause of the misclassification, especially when there is no objects which clearly hinder the correct decision of the model in an input image.

6   Conclusion

We proposed two extensions of a model-agnostic interpretation method RISE [4]. One is debiased RISE; it computes a saliency map in which the saliency of an unimportant pixel is close to 0; this makes the interpretation of a saliency map easier than RISE. Another is MC-RISE, which computes color-wise saliency; a saliency map for a color c computed by MC-RISE explains the saliency of the color c in each pixel. Such color-wise saliency is useful in application domains such as road sign recognition, in which colors convey significant information. We empirically demonstrated the effectiveness of our extensions.

We plan to extend our idea to use other features than colors; for example, by using masks that blur a part of an image, we expect that we can generate a saliency map that explains the significance of the clarity of the region.

Acknowledgment. We thank the reviewers for their fruitful comments.

References

1. Ribeiro, M.T., Singh, S., Guestrin, C.: "Why should I trust you?": Explaining the predictions of any classifier. In: SIGKDD 2016 (2016)
2. Lundberg, S.M., Lee, S.I.: A unified approach to interpreting model predictions. In: NIPS 2017 (2017)
3. Selvaraju, R.R., Cogswell, M., Das, A., Vedantam, R., Parikh, D., Batra, D.: Grad-CAM: visual explanations from deep networks via gradient-based localization. In: ICCV 2017 (2017)
4. Petsiuk, V., Das, A., Saenko, K.: RISE: randomized input sampling for explanation of black-box models. In: BMVC 2018 (2018)
5. Selvaraju, R.R., Cogswell, M., Das, A., Vedantam, R., Parikh, D., Batra, D.: Grad-CAM: visual explanations from deep networks via gradient-based localization. In: 2017 IEEE International Conference on Computer Vision (ICCV), pp. 618–626 (2017). ISSN 2380-7504
6. Chattopadhay, A., Sarkar, A., Howlader, P., Balasubramanian, V.N.: Grad-CAM++: generalized gradient-based visual explanations for deep convolutional networks. In: 2018 IEEE Winter Conference on Applications of Computer Vision (WACV), pp. 839–847 (2018)
7. Sundararajan, M., Taly, A., Yan, Q.: Axiomatic attribution for deep networks. In: Proceedings of the 34th International Conference on Machine Learning, ICML 2017, Sydney, NSW, Australia, vol. 70, pp. 3319–3328 (2017). JMLR.org
8. Smilkov, D., Thorat, N., Kim, B., Viégas, F., Wattenberg, M.: SmoothGrad: removing noise by adding noise. arXiv preprint (2017). arXiv:1706.03825
9. Zeiler, M.D., Fergus, R.: Visualizing and understanding convolutional networks. In: Fleet, D., Pajdla, T., Schiele, B., Tuytelaars, T. (eds.) ECCV 2014. LNCS, vol. 8689, pp. 818–833. Springer, Cham (2014). https://doi.org/10.1007/978-3-319-10590-1_53
10. Springenberg, J., Dosovitskiy, A., Brox, T., Riedmiller, M.: Striving for simplicity: the all convolutional net. In: International Conference on Learning Representations (2015)
11. Bach, S., Binder, A., Montavon, G., Klauschen, F., Müller, K.R., Samek, W.: On pixel-wise explanations for non-linear classifier decisions by layer-wise relevance propagation. PLoS ONE 10, e0130140 (2015)
12. Shrikumar, A., Greenside, P., Kundaje, A.: Learning important features through propagating activation differences. In: Precup, D., Teh, Y.W. (eds.) Proceedings of the 34th International Conference on Machine Learning. Proceedings of Machine Learning Research, International Convention Centre, Sydney, Australia, PMLR, vol. 70, pp. 3145–3153 (2017)
13. Zhang, J., Bargal, S.A., Lin, Z., Brandt, J., Shen, X., Sclaroff, S.: Top-down neural attention by excitation backprop. Int. J. Comput. Vision **126**(10), 1084–1102 (2017). https://doi.org/10.1007/s11263-017-1059-x

14. Vasu, B., Long, C.: Iterative and adaptive sampling with spatial attention for black-box model explanations. In: The IEEE Winter Conference on Applications of Computer Vision, pp. 2960–2969 (2020)
15. Stallkamp, J., Schlipsing, M., Salmen, J., Igel, C.: Man vs. computer: benchmarking machine learning algorithms for traffic sign recognition. Neural Netw. **32**, 323–332 (2012)
16. Russakovsky, O., et al.: ImageNet large scale visual recognition challenge. Int. J. Comput. Vision **115**(3), 211–252 (2015). https://doi.org/10.1007/s11263-015-0816-y
17. Adebayo, J., Gilmer, J., Muelly, M., Goodfellow, I., Hardt, M., Kim, B.: Sanity checks for saliency maps. In: Bengio, S., et al. (eds.) Advances in Neural Information Processing Systems, vol. 31, pp. 9505–9515. Curran Associates, Inc. (2018)
18. Heo, J., Joo, S., Moon, T.: fooling neural network interpretations via adversarial model manipulation. In Wallach, H., Larochelle, H., Beygelzimer, A., Alché-Buc, F.d., Fox, E., Garnett, R. (eds.) Advances in Neural Information Processing Systems, vol. 32, pp. 2925–2936. Curran Associates, Inc. (2019)
19. Dombrowski, A.K., Alber, M., Anders, C., Ackermann, M., Müller, K.R., Kessel, P.: Explanations can be manipulated and geometry is to blame. In: Wallach, H., et al. (eds.) Advances in Neural Information Processing Systems, vol. 32, pp. 13589–13600. Curran Associates, Inc. (2019)
20. Subramanya, A., Pillai, V., Pirsiavash, H.: Fooling network interpretation in image classification. In: Proceedings of the IEEE International Conference on Computer Vision, pp. 2020–2029 (2019)
21. Fong, R.C., Vedaldi, A.: Interpretable explanations of black boxes by meaningful perturbation. In: Proceedings of the IEEE International Conference on Computer Vision, pp. 3429–3437 (2017)
22. Fong, R., Patrick, M., Vedaldi, A.: Understanding deep networks via extremal perturbations and smooth masks. In: ICCV 2019 (2019)
23. Wagner, J., Kohler, J.M., Gindele, T., Hetzel, L., Wiedemer, J.T., Behnke, S.: Interpretable and fine-grained visual explanations for convolutional neural networks. In: Proceedings of the IEEE Conference on Computer Vision and Pattern Recognition, pp. 9097–9107 (2019)
24. Xu, K., et al.: Show, attend and tell: neural image caption generation with visual attention. In: International Conference on Machine Learning, pp. 2048–2057 (2015). ISSN 1938-7228. Section: Machine Learning
25. Schallner, L., Rabold, J., Scholz, O., Schmid, U.: Effect of superpixel aggregation on explanations in LIME – a case study with biological data. CoRR abs/1910.07856 (2019)
26. Guidotti, R., Monreale, A., Ruggieri, S., Pedreschi, D., Turini, F., Giannotti, F.: Local rule-based explanations of black box decision systems. arXiv preprint (2018). arXiv:1805.10820
27. Tsang, M., Cheng, D., Liu, H., Feng, X., Zhou, E., Liu, Y.: Feature interaction interpretability: a case for explaining ad-recommendation systems via neural interaction detection. In: International Conference on Learning Representations (2019)
28. Ribeiro, M.T., Singh, S., Guestrin, C.: Anchors: high-precision model-agnostic explanations. In: Thirty-Second AAAI Conference on Artificial Intelligence (2018)
29. Schwab, P., Karlen, W.: CXPlain: causal explanations for model interpretation under uncertainty. In: Wallach, H., Larochelle, H., Beygelzimer, A., Alché-Buc, F.d., Fox, E., Garnett, R. (eds.) Advances in Neural Information Processing Systems, vol. 32, pp. 10220–10230. Curran Associates, Inc. (2019)

30. Simonyan, K., Zisserman, A.: Very deep convolutional networks for large-scale image recognition. arXiv preprint arXiv:1409.1556 (2014)
31. He, K., Zhang, X., Ren, S., Sun, J.: Deep residual learning for image recognition. In: CVPR 2016 (2016)
32. Paszke, A., et al.: PyTorch: an imperative style, high-performance deep learning library. In: Wallach, H., Larochelle, H., Beygelzimer, A., Alché-Buc, F.d., Fox, E., Garnett, R. (eds.:) Advances in Neural Information Processing Systems, vol. 32, pp. 8026–8037. Curran Associates, Inc. (2019)

ERIC: Extracting Relations Inferred from Convolutions

Joe Townsend$^{(\boxtimes)}$ (ID), Theodoros Kasioumis (ID), and Hiroya Inakoshi (ID)

Fujitsu Laboratories of Europe LTD., 4th Floor, Building 3, Hyde Park Hayes,
11 Millington Road, Hayes, Middlesex UB3 4AZ, UK
{joseph.townsend,theodoros.kasioumis,hiroya.inakoshi}@uk.fujitsu.com

Abstract. Our main contribution is to show that the behaviour of kernels across multiple layers of a convolutional neural network can be approximated using a logic program. The extracted logic programs yield accuracies that correlate with those of the original model, though with some information loss in particular as approximations of multiple layers are chained together or as lower layers are quantised. We also show that an extracted program can be used as a framework for further understanding the behaviour of CNNs. Specifically, it can be used to identify key kernels worthy of deeper inspection and also identify relationships with other kernels in the form of the logical rules. Finally, we make a preliminary, qualitative assessment of rules we extract from the last convolutional layer and show that kernels identified are symbolic in that they react strongly to sets of similar images that effectively divide output classes into sub-classes with distinct characteristics.

1 Introduction

As public concern regarding the extent to which artificial intelligence can be trusted increases, so does the demand for so-called *explainable* AI. While accountability is a key motivator in recent years, other motivations include understanding how models may be improved, knowledge discovery through the extraction of concepts learned by the models but previously unknown to domain experts, means by which to test models of human cognition, and perhaps others.

This has led to extensive research into explaining how models trained through machine learning make their decisions [1–3], and the field of *Neural-Symbolic Integration* covers this work with respect to neural networks [4–8]. The latter began by largely focussing on modelling the behaviour of multi-layer perceptrons or recurrent neural networks as symbolic rules that describe strongly-weighted relationships between neurons in adjacent layers [4,5]. More recent work strives to explain deeper networks, including convolutional neural networks (CNNs) [5–8]. Most of these methods identify important input or hidden features with respect to a given class or convolutional kernel [9–15], but methods that extract rule or graph-based relationships between key features are also emerging [16–21]. Moreover it has been shown that a CNN's kernels may correspond to semantically meaningful concepts to which we can ascribe symbols or words [22].

© Springer Nature Switzerland AG 2021
H. Ishikawa et al. (Eds.): ACCV 2020, LNCS 12624, pp. 206–222, 2021.
https://doi.org/10.1007/978-3-030-69535-4_13

We show how the behaviour of a CNN can be approximated by a set of logical rules in which each rule's conditions map to convolutional kernels and therefore the semantic concepts they represent. We introduce *ERIC (Extracting Relations Inferred from Convolutions)*, which assumes each kernel maps to an individual concept, quantises the output of each kernel as a binary value, extracts rules that relate the binarised kernels to each other and visualises the concepts they represent. We also argue that the extracted rules simplify the task of identifying key kernels for inspection (using for example importance methods described above), as the number of kernels in a layer is often in the order of hundreds.

Although related work which extracts graph-based approximations has also made significant strides in this direction [19,20], so far nodes in the graph only correspond to positive instances of symbols, e.g. "If feature X is observed...", and not negative, e.g. "If X is not observed...". Propositional logic is able to express both (X and $\neg X$). Furthermore our method is entirely post-hoc and does not assume a convolutional architecture has been designed [17,18] or trained [23] to learn semantically meaningful kernels. However ERIC is not necessarily incompatible with such architectures either, allowing for flexible usage.

We begin with a literature survey in Sect. 2, and Sect. 3 outlines ERIC's architecture. In Sect. 4 we extract logic programs from multiple convolutional layers and show that these programs can approximate the behaviour of the original CNN to varying degrees of accuracy depending on which and how many layers are quantised. Section 4 ends with an analysis of extracted rules and argues that the kernels they represent correspond to semantically meaningful concepts. The discussion in Sect. 5 argues that the extracted rules faithfully represent how the CNN 'thinks', compares ERIC to other methods from the literature and also proposes future work. Section 6 presents our conclusion that kernels can be mapped to symbols that, regardless of their labels, can be manipulated by a logic program able to approximate the behaviour of the original CNN.

2   Background

2.1   Rule Extraction from Neural Networks

Since at least the 1990s efforts have been made to extract interpretable knowledge from neural networks, and during this period Andrews et al. defined three classes of extraction method [4]. *Pedagogical* methods treat a network as a black box and construct rules that explain the outputs in terms of the inputs. *Decompositional* methods extract separate rule sets for individual network parts (such as individual neurons) so that collectively all rules explain the behaviour of the whole model. *Eclectic* methods exhibit elements of both of the other classes.

Another important distinction between different classes of extraction method is the *locality* of an explanation [1,24]. Some extraction methods provide *local* explanations that describe individual classifications, wheras others are more *global* in that they provide explanations for the model as a whole.

Two important components for extracting rules from a network are *quantisation* and *rule construction* [5,6]. *Quantisation* maps input, hidden and output states of neural networks from the domain of real numbers to binary or categorical values, for example by thresholding. *Rule construction* forms the rules which describe the conditions under which these quantised variables take different values (e.g.. true or false) based on the values of other quantised variables.

In addition to measuring classification accuracy of an explainable approximation of a model, it is also common to record *fidelity* to the behaviour of the original model. In other words, *fidelity* is the accuracy of the approximation with respect to the outputs of the original model. Also, if a model is to be regarded as 'explainable', then there must be some means by which to quantify this quality. Explainability is a subjective quality and at the time of writing there does not appear to be a consensus on how to quantify it. Examples of the various approaches include counting extracted rules [4] or some assessment of how humans respond to or interact with extracted rules presented to them [24,25].

However explainability is quantified, it is often observed that there is a trade-off between an extraction method's explainability and its fidelity due to information loss that results from quantifying continuous variables. The preference of fidelity and accuracy over explainability or vice-versa may depend on the nature of the task or a user's preference [24]. If the model is advising a human decision-maker such as a doctor who has to justify their decisions to others, then explainability is key. For a task that is entirely automated but not safety-critical to the extent that such accountability is required, then explainability can be sacrificed for accuracy. That said, in the latter case, *some* explainability is still useful as humans may discover new knowledge by analysing what the automated system has learned. In situations where accountability is a priority, one may prefer network architectures that are themselves designed or trained with explainability in mind. Solutions like these are often described as *explainable-by-design* and for brevity we abbreviate these to *XBD-methods*. However in XBD methods it may be more difficult to discover new knowledge as they explore a more constrained search space during training.

Early work largely focussed on multi-layer perceptrons (MLPs) with one or very few hidden layers and also on recurrent neural networks. Research has since grown into explaining 'deeper' neural networks of several to many layers, be these MLPs that are deep in this particular sense [26–28] or more advanced architectures such as LSTMs [29], Deep Belief Networks [30] or CNNs [16–21]. Remaining subsections only cover methods that extract explanations from CNNs. The reader is referred to surveys in the literature regarding other network types [5–8]. We also acknowledge generic methods that treat arbitrary models as black boxes but do not cover them as they are *pedagogical* and by nature cannot decompose neural networks. These are also surveyed in the literature [2,3].

2.2   Feature Importance

A lot of existing research presents ways to visualise what CNNs 'see' [9–15]. These methods generally identify the responsibility of input pixels (or neurons in a hidden layer) with respect to activating the output neuron corresponding to a given class. This usually involves tracing the signal back from that output neuron, backwards through the network along stronger network weights until arriving at the input image. This signal may be the output activation [10,31], a gradient [9,32,33] or some other metric derived from the output [13,14]. These ideas can be used to analyse what a specific kernel responds to [10]. Furthermore, Zhou et al. show that semantic concepts can be observed from an analysis of a kernel's receptive field in CNNs trained to recognise scenes, and that kernels tend to have more semantic meaning at deeper network layers [22]. In related work Simon et al. provide a means of localising semantic parts of images [34].

2.3   Rule Extraction from CNNs

Compared with methods for visualising important features as in Sect. 2.2, methods that model the relationships between these features are relatively few.

Chen et al. introduce an XBD-model that includes a *prototype* layer that is trained to recognise a set of prototype components so that images can be classified by reference to these component parts. In other words, the CNN is trained to classify images in a human-like manner. For example, one kernel learns the concept of wing, another learns the concept of beak, and when an input image is classified the explanation can be given as $wing \wedge beak \rightarrow bird$.

The prototype method, and currently our own, assumes a one-to-one relationship between kernels and symbols. However it has been observed that this may not be the case [35]. It may be that the relationship between kernels and semantic concepts is in fact many-to-many. Zhang et al. disentangle concepts represented in this way and represent disentangled concepts and their relationship to each other in a hierarchical graph in which each layer of the hierarchy corresponds to a layer of the CNN [19,20]. However, the disentangled graphs in their current form show limited expressivity in that explanations are only composed of positive instances of parts. We extract rules in which conditions may be positive or negative. The work was extended to an XBD approach in which a CNN is trained with a loss function that encourages kernels to learn disentangled relations [23], and this was then used to generate a decision tree based on disentangled parts learned in the top convolutional layer [21].

Bologna and Fossati extract propositional rules from CNNs [18]. First they extract rules that approximate the dense layers, with antecedents corresponding to the outputs of individual neurons in the last convolutional layer, and then extract rules that summarise the convolutional layers, with antecedents mapped to input neurons. This work is to some extent XBD as it assumes that some layers of the original model are discretised. Only the dense layer rules are actually used for inference, with convolutional rules only used to provide explanations. The complexity of working with invdidual neurons as antecedents is cited as the reason for this decision. Other work described above (and ours) overcomes this by mapping symbols to *groups* of neurons (e.g.. prototype kernels or disentangled parts). One advantage over the disentanglement method is that extracted rules may include negated antecedents.

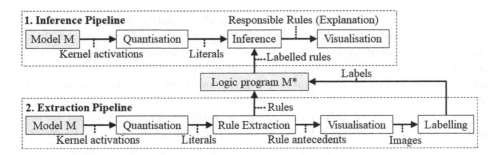

Fig. 1. ERIC Pipelines for *inference* and *rule extraction*.

3 ERIC Architecture

ERIC is a global explanation method that extracts rules conditioned on positive and negative instances of quantised kernel activations and is able to extract these rules from multiple convolutional layers. ERIC assumes CNNs have standard convolution, pooling and dense layers, and is indifferent with respect to whether the CNN has been trained with explainability in mind. ERIC is mostly decompositional in that rules explain kernel activations but partly pedagogical in that we only decompose a subset of convolutional layers and the output dense layer, and treat remaining layers as black boxes. Figure 1 presents an overview of the architecture as two pipelines sharing most modules. We explain the inference module first in Sect. 3.2 in order to formalise the target behaviour of extracted programs. All modules of the extraction pipeline are explained in Sect. 3.3.

3.1 Preliminaries

Let us consider a set of input images x indexed by i and a CNN M whose layers are indexed by $l = 1, \ldots, l^o$. Every layer has kernels indexed by $k = 1, \ldots, K_l$. $A_{i,l,k} \in \mathbb{R}^{h \times w}$ denotes an activation matrix output for a kernel, where h, w are natural numbers. Note that we treat the term *kernel* as synonymous with *filter* and we do not need to consider a kernel's input weights for our purposes in this paper. Let o refer to the softmax layer at the output of M, with index l^o. Let l^{LEP} denote the index of a special layer we call the *Logical Entry Point*, the layer after which and including we approximate kernel activations.

Let $b_{i,l,k} \in \{1, -1\}$ denote a binary truth value associated with $A_{i,l,k}$ as in Eq. 1 and 2. $b_{i,l,k}$ may be expressed as positive and negative literals $\mathcal{L}_{i,l,k} \equiv (b_{i,l,k} = 1)$ and $\neg \mathcal{L}_{i,l,k} \equiv (b_{i,l,k} = -1)$ respectively. A set of rules indexed by r at layer l is denoted $R_l = \{R_{l,r} = (D_{l,r}, C_{l,r})\}_r$, where $D_{l,r}$ and $C_{l,r}$ are sets of conjoined literals in the *antecedents* (conditions for satisfying the rule) and *consequents* (outcomes) of $R_{l,r}$ respectively. For example, $D_{l,r} = \mathcal{L}_{i,l-1,3} \wedge \neg \mathcal{L}_{i,l-1,6} \wedge \mathcal{L}_{i,l-1,7}$ and $C_{l,r} = \mathcal{L}_{i,l,2} \wedge \mathcal{L}_{i,l,3} \wedge \mathcal{L}_{i,l,5}$. $C_{l,r}$ may only contain positive literals as we assume *default negation*, i.e. by default all $b_{i,l,k} = -1$ ($\neg \mathcal{L}_{i,l,k}$) unless some $C_{l,r}$ determines otherwise.

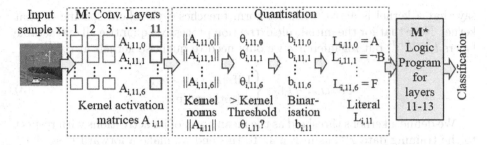

Fig. 2. Inference: kernel outputs at a designated layer are *quantised* and input to a *logic program* that approximates remaining layers. *Input sample* from Places365 [36].

3.2   Inference

Inference is summarised in Fig. 2. Equation 1 and 2 formalise the process by which we infer a binary approximation $b_{i,l,k}$ for activation tensor $A_{i,l,k}$ for any kernel. An extracted program approximates convolutional layers after and including layer l^{LEP}, at which point kernel activations are mapped to binary values via a quantisation function $Q(A_{i,l,k}, \theta_{l,k})$ so that these activations may be treated as the input to logic program M^* (Eq. 1). $Q(A_{i,l,k}, \theta_{l,k})$ is explained in detail later in Subsect. 3.3. The truths of all kernels in all following layers ($b_{i,l,k}$ for $l > l^{LEP}$) are derived through logical inference on the truths of binarised kernels from the previous layer $b_{i,l-1}$ according to a set of layer-specific rules R_l (Eq. 2).

$$b_{i,l^{LEP},k} = Q(A_{i,l^{LEP},k}, \theta_{l^{LEP},k}) \tag{1}$$

$$b_{i,l,k} = \begin{cases} 1 \text{ depending on } C_{l,r} \text{ for all } k \text{ if } \exists r(D_{l,r} = True) \\ -1 \text{ otherwise (default negation)} \end{cases} \tag{2}$$

3.3   Rule Extraction

Rule extraction is implemented as a pipeline of 5 modules (Fig. 1). First is the original **model** M for which we want to extract an approximation M^*. We do not need to say much about this except that ERIC assumes M has already been trained. Next in the **quantisation** stage we obtain binarisations for all kernels after and including layer l^{LEP} based on activations obtained for training data. We then **extract rules** which describe the relationship between kernels by reference to their binarisations. Then to interpret the meanings of individual kernels we first **visualise** each kernel as one or more images that represent what inputs the kernels strongly react to, before each kernel is assigned a **label** based on manual inspection, a process we plan to automate in future work.

Quantisation. Our quantisation function Q is defined in Eq. 3, where $\theta_{l,k}$ is a kernel-specific threshold and norm function $\|\cdot\|$ is the $l1$ norm[1]. Intuitively, we

---
[1] Preliminary experiments found that $l1$ norm yielded higher fidelity than $l2$ norm.

say that a kernel is active when its norm breaches a threshold specific to that kernel. Note that for the initial rule extraction process we quantise all extractable layers $l \geq l^{LEP}$ but for inference we only need to quantise kernels at l^{LEP}.

$$Q(A_{i,l,k}, \theta_{l,k}) = \begin{cases} 1 \text{ if } \|A_{i,l,k}\| > \theta_{l,k} \\ -1 \text{ otherwise} \end{cases} \tag{3}$$

We define a kernel's threshold as the mean norm of its activations with respect to the training data x^{tr}, as in Eq. 4. To this end we make a forward pass of x^{tr} in order to obtain $\{A_{i,l,k}^{tr}\}_{i,l,k}$, activations for each kernel $1 \leq k \leq K_l$ at each layer $l^{LEP} \leq l < l^o$ for each input training sample $1 \leq i \leq n$.

$$\theta_{l,k} = \frac{\sum_{i=1}^{n} \|A_{i,l,k}^{tr}\|}{n} \tag{4}$$

We can now use the quantisation function (Eq. 3) to obtain binarisations of all kernel activations according to Eq. 5. Where a convolutional layer outputs to a pooling layer, we take $A_{i,l,k}$ from the pooled output. As also shown in Eq. 5, we also need to treat output neurons as kernels of dimension 1×1 so that $b_{i,l^o}^{tr} = M(x_i^{tr})$. This enables us to extract rules that map kernel activations at layer $l^o - 1$ to the output classifications as inferred by M.

$$b_{i,l,k} = \begin{cases} o_{i,k}^{tr} \text{ if } l = l^o \\ Q(A_{i,l,k}^{tr}) \text{ otherwise} \end{cases} \tag{5}$$

Rule Extraction. We now extract rules that describe the activation at each kernel at every layer l given activations at layer $l - 1$. Thus, the following is applied layer-wise from l^o to l^{LEP}. We use a tree-based extraction algorithm similar to the C4.5 algorithm [37] to extract rules which describe conditions for which each kernel evaluates as true. As we assume default negation, we do not need to extract rules that describe when a kernel is false. Let us denote the training data $Z_l = \{(z_i, t_i) \mid i = 1, ..., n\}$ where $z_i \in \{True, False\}^{2K_{l-1}}$ and $t_i \in \{True, False\}$. Note that the length of z_l is twice the number of kernels at layer $l - 1$ because each kernel has positive and negative literals. $z_{l-1,k'} = True$ if it corresponds to a positive literal and its binary value is 1 or if it represents a negative literal and its binary value is -1. It is False otherwise. C4.5 generates a decision tree up to maximum depth d. Each path from the root of the tree to a leaf node represents a separate rule and nodes branch on rule conditions (i.e. antecedents). The maximum number of antecedents per rule is equal to $d+1$. C4.5 uses entropy as a branch selection criterion but based on a marginal improvement in fidelity observed in preliminary tests we chose to use gini index. Extraction can become intractable as more layers and therefore kernels are introduced due to combinatorial explosion. This can be moderated by reducing d or increasing another parameter α that we introduce for this purpose. Let P, Q represent sets of training instances that satisfy the path of conditions leading to a parent node and child node, respectively. We stop branching if $|Q|/|P| < \alpha$. If a leaf node represents multiple outcomes, we set the consequence to the modal value of Q. Finally, we simplify extracted programs by merging rules with complementary literals ($A \wedge B \to C$ and $A \wedge \neg B \to C$ become $A \to C$) and rules with identical antecedents but different consequents ($A \to B$ and $A \to C$ become $A \to B \wedge C$).

Kernel Visualisation and Labelling. To visualise what a kernel sees, we select the m images from x^{tr} which activate that kernel most strongly with respect to $\|A_{i,l,k}^{tr}\|$. We denote this visualisation as $\hat{x}_{l,k}^{m}$. A label is assigned to a kernel based on $\hat{x}_{l,k}^{m}$, which for the time being we do manually based on visual inspection but in future work plan to automate. For the time being, to defend the arguments of the paper, it is not so much the labels that are important as the distinction between the subsets of image that each kernel responds most strongly to.

4   Experiments

In Sects. 4.1 and 4.2 we outline the classification task and CNN configuration we use for our experiments. We then extract rules from a single convolutional layer in Sect. 4.3 and then multiple convolutional layers in Sect. 4.4. In Sect. 4.5 we visualise and label kernels and in Sect. 4.6 analyse some of the rules with these labels assigned to the antecedents.

4.1   Task

We chose to classify road scenes from the places365 dataset [36] for a number of reasons. First, we felt that a scene dataset was appropriate as scenes can easily be described by reference to symbolic entities within them which themselves could be described by a separate classifer (i.e. the kernel classifier) with a large vocabulary of labels. We selected a handful of 5 scenes to simplify the task given the complexity of rule extraction, and opted for roads in order to create a scenario where the distinction between scenes is particularly important (due to regulations, potential hazards, etc.). We wanted to demonstrate ERIC on a multi-class task and on multiple combinations of class. 3 is the minimum required for multi-class case and gives us $\binom{5}{3} = 10$ combinations of scenes (Table 1).

4.2   Network Model

For each combination of classes we train VGG16 (as defined for Tensorflow using Keras [38]) from scratch over 100 epochs using Stochastic Gradient Descent, a learning rate of 10^{-5}, categorical crossentropy and a batch size of 32.

4.3   Extraction from a Single Layer

We set $\alpha = 0.01$ so that branching stops if a branch represents less than 1% of the samples represented by its parent node. We iterate the logical entry point

Table 1. *Accuracies of the original model M and extracted program M*, with the number of unique variables (positive or negative literals) and rules for each M*, and the size of M* measured as the total number of antecedents across all rules. Results are shown for all sets of 3/5 classes:* **Desert road**, **Driveway**, **Forest**, **Highway** *and* **Street**.

Classes	Original M			Program M*			M − M*			M* stats		
	Train	Val.	Test.	Tr.	Val.	Te.	Tr.	Val.	Te.	Vars	Rules	Size
De, Dr, F	98.5	88.5	90.2	83.5	79.7	81.6	15.0	8.8	8.6	50	31	171
De, Dr, H	97.5	82.7	83.6	77.2	73.5	75.0	20.3	9.2	8.6	44	32	176
De, Dr, S	99.6	92.9	93.3	78.7	74.9	76.1	20.9	18.0	17.2	44	34	183
De, F, H	95.0	80.8	81.5	85.0	80.7	81.4	10.0	0.1	0.1	48	36	196
De, F, S	99.0	94.8	94.7	91.0	**89.4**	90.3	8.0	5.4	4.4	33	25	127
De, H, S	97.7	84.9	86.2	80.6	78.0	78.7	17.1	6.9	7.5	42	36	194
Dr, F, H	96.9	82.5	83.0	83.3	80.0	81.0	13.6	2.5	2.0	47	31	167
Dr, F, S	97.9	89.7	90.9	73.4	68.9	69.6	24.5	20.8	21.3	47	33	181
Dr, H, S	99.0	88.0	88.1	79.8	76.7	78.0	19.2	11.3	10.1	47	36	197
F, H, S	97.7	86.9	87.1	73.8	71.2	71.6	23.9	15.7	15.5	56	34	185

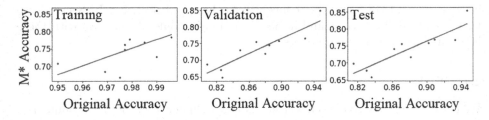

Fig. 3. *Original CNN accuracy compared to accuracy of extracted model M**

$l^{LEP} \in [Conv8 \ldots Conv13]$ and tree depth $d \in [1 \ldots 5]$ and observe the effects on accuracy, fidelity and the size of the extracted program. Size is measured as the sum length (number of entecedents) of all rules and is our metric for interpretability on the basis that larger programs take longer to read and understand. In all figures we average over all results except the variable we iterate over.

Figure 3 compares the average accuracy across all depths and layers for each class combination with the accuracy of the original model. The line of best fit shows that the accuracy of the extracted model is consistent with respect to that of the original model. In the validation set, accuracy drops by about 15% in each case. However average validation accuracy drops by an average of 10% for the optimal selection of depth and layer (Table 1). In summary, the loss in accuracy can be moderated by adjusting extraction parameters.

Figure 4 shows how accuracy, fidelity and program size are affected as we adjust the extraction layer and tree depth. Accuracy and fidelity both improve as tree depth (and therefore rule length) is increased, demonstrating that extraction benefits from quantising more kernels. However, the cost of this is a larger

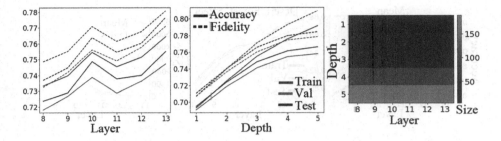

Fig. 4. *Accuracies, fidelities* and *program sizes* obtained from single-layer extraction.

logic program. Accuracy and fidelity both show a general increase as rules are extracted from higher layers. This is to be expected since 1) deeper layers are known to represent more abstract and discriminative concepts, and 2) by discretising one layer we also discard all the information encoded in any following layers. However, there is a spike at layer 10. Layers 10 and 13 of VGG16 pass through max-pooling filters, suggesting that pooling before quantisation may also be beneficial to accuracy. The choice of extraction layer has small but negligible effect on program size. However in our case all extraction layers have 512 kernels and results may differ when extracting from smaller or larger layers.

Optimal validation accuracies were found for *conv*13 and a tree depth of 5. Table 1 presents accuracies for all class combinations based on this configuration. The best validation accuracy was found for *Desert Road, Forest Road and Street* and Table 2 shows example rules extracted for this case. Note that literals are composed of two letters because an alphabet of A-Z is insufficient for all 512 kernels, and they can be renamed in the kernel labelling stage anyway. We carry the optimal parameters and scenario forward for all further tests.

4.4 Extraction from Multiple Layers

Given the higher complexity of extracting knowledge from multiple layers at once, we do not iterate different values for tree depth but fix it at 5. We also increase the value of α to 0.1 to enforce stricter stopping conditions and prevent

Table 2. 6/25 Extracted rules for classes = {desert road, forest road, street}.

1	$LW \land \neg SG \rightarrow street$
7	$CX \land \neg LW \land NI \land PO \land \neg SG \rightarrow street$
10	$\neg CK \land DO \land \neg HV \land JB \land NI \rightarrow forest$
13	$\neg AC \land CK \land \neg DO \land NI \land \neg SG \rightarrow forest$
17	$\neg AC \land \neg DO \land \neg JJ \land SG \rightarrow desert$
25	$AC \land \neg DO \land ID \land SG \rightarrow desert$

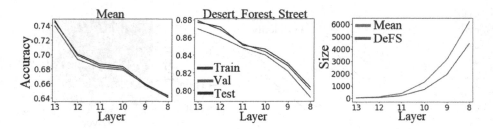

Fig. 5. *Accuracies, fidelities* and program *sizes* yielded from multi-layer extraction.

combinatorial explosion caused by observing relations between kernels at adjacent layers. Figure 5 shows the effect of incrementally adding layers starting from layer 13 only, then adding layer 12, and so on up to layer 8. Accuracy drops as more layers are added, presumably due to an increase in information loss as more and more kernels are quantised. Nonetheless accuracies are reasonable. However, the size of the logic program increases exponentially as more layers are added, emphasising the importance of adjusting d and α to moderate this.

4.5   Visualisation and Labelling

It can be difficult to know which kernels to examine when inspecting large CNNs such as VGG16 which has 512 in one layer. We have shown that using rule extraction this number can be reduced (the best case is 33 in Table 1). For now we assign labels manually with the intention of automating this process in future work. We label kernels represented by rules extracted for layer 13, with $m = 10$. That is, we choose a kernel's label based on the 10 images that activate it most strongly with respect to $l1$ norm values obtained from a forward pass of the training set. Fig. 6 presents 7/10 images[2] from $\hat{x}_{13,k}^{10}$ selected for 11 kernels.

The kernels clearly partition classes into further sub-classes with noticable similarities within them, supporting the findings of Zhou et al. [22]. Images for kernels 101, 184 and 334 are all taken from the street class but focus on different things: 101 seems to focus on *walls* mostly free from occlusion, 184 mostly on *cars* and 334 on *crowds* of people. Kernels 229, 369 and 500 mostly respond to the desert class but again distinguish between different features: 229 responds strongly to *cliffs* or mountains, 369 to *bends* in roads and 500 to desert with *grass* patches. The remaining kernels respond mostly to forest images but differences were less clear. Kernel 28 responds when *tree trunks* are more visible and 118 when the *tree tops* are visible. 88 was more difficult to choose a label for but we chose *grey* due to significant grey regions in some images. 269 was also difficult to choose for. A common feature appears to be something in the centre of the image such as cars on two occasions, a lake on another and planks of wood in another. It may be that the kernel has picked up on a regularity not immediatly

---

[2] Limited space made it difficult to show all 10 without compromising clarity.

Fig. 6. Kernel visualisations. All images from *Places365* dataset [36]

Fig. 7. Misclassifications: a *forest road* misclassified as a desert road, a *street* misclassified as a forest, and a *forest* misclassified as a street. Images from Places365 [36].

clear to human observers; an example of the need for a symbol for a possibly new concept to which we assign *TreesMisc* as a surrogate.

However we label the kernels, the initial 3-class dataset does not have the labels necessary to distinguish between these sub-classes even though the CNN is capable of doing so to the extent that, as we show in Sects. 4.3 and 4.4, they can be quantised and included in rules that approximate the CNN's behaviour.

4.6   Test Images

We now inspect some of the explanations given for classifications made on the test set, assigning the labels in Fig. 6 to the rules in Table 2. Rule 1 translates as $Crowd \wedge \neg Grass \rightarrow street$, i.e. "if you encounter people and no grass then you are in a street". Of course, in reality there are other situations where people may be found without grass, and some empty streets may have grass patches, so we as humans would not conclude we are in a street with this information alone. However, in this particular "Desert, Forest or Street" case on which the CNN was trained, one is significantly less likely to encounter people in the former two categories. Thus, this is enough information for the CNN to identify the location. Rule 7 translates as $Grey \wedge TreeTops \wedge Animal \rightarrow forest$. Animals may appear in streets, as would a grey surface, but when they appear together with trees it is more likely to be a forest. Rule 17 translates as $\neg TreeTrunk \wedge \neg TreeTops \wedge \neg TreesMisc \wedge Grass \rightarrow desert$, i.e. "if there is grass but no trees then it must be a desert". Again, there are many places with grass but no trees (e.g. a field) but in this particular task the CNN has no other concept of grass without trees.

Figure 7 shows three images for which both the original and approximated models made identical misclassifications. In the first example rule 17 misclassifies a forest road as a desert road. Although trees are present they are perhaps too few to activate the tree-related kernels, satisfying the negated tree-based antecedents. Grass by the road satisfies the other antecedent. In the second case rule 10 ($TreeTrunk \wedge \neg Wall \wedge TreeTops \wedge \neg Crowd \wedge \neg Animal \rightarrow forest$) confuses a street for a forest road as there are no animals in the street and many trees occlude the walls of the houses. The image from the forest set is misclassified as a street according to rule 1 as there are people and no grass.

5 Discussion and Future Work

ERIC quantises the outputs of kernels in a CNN and relates these kernels to each
other as logical rules that yield lower but reasonable accuracy. Our inspection of
these kernels supported existing findings that most exhibit a strong response to
sets of similar images with common semantic features [22]. We hope to automate
the process of labelling these symbols in future work, likely integrating existing
methods for mapping kernels or receptive fields to semantic concepts [19,20,
22,34]. However these methods have finite sets of labels originally provided by
humans with finite vocabularies. It may be that knowledge extraction methods
will find new and important symbols for which we need to invent new words.
ERIC provides a framework for discovering symbols that are important enough
to distinguish between classes but for which no labels yet exist.

Although the rules in Sect. 4.6 are not paths of reasoning humans are likely
to take, they nonetheless suffice to approximate the behaviour of the original
CNN. It would be unreasonable for a human to assume they are in a street just
because they see people and no grass, but for a CNN that has only seen streets,
forests and desert roads, it is a reasonable assumption. Being able to explain
how a machine 'thinks' does not necessarily mean that it thinks like a human.

An empirical comparison of performance of methods listed in the background
also remains to be addressed in future work, but for now we comment on how
they differ in terms of features. ERIC is a global explanation model that extracts
rules in which antecedents are composed of positive and negative instances of
quantised kernel activations, and is able to extract these rules from multiple
convolutional layers. ERIC lacks some features that may be of benefit such as
the ability to disentangle features and thus overcome assumptions regarding one-
to-one relationships between kernels and concepts. However relationships defined
using the disentanglement method do not include negated symbols as ERIC does.
Both methods have potentially mutually beneficial features and adapting ERIC
to disentangle representations would be an interesting future step.

Finally, although ERIC is not yet compatible with *architectures* designed for
explainability, we expect it would be compatible with weight matrices that have
been *trained* for explainability. We would like to test this hypothesis and use
ERIC as a framework for assessing how this affects fidelity and explainability.

6 Conclusions

We have shown that the behaviour of kernels across multiple convolutional layers
can be approximated using a logic program, and the extracted program can be
used as a framework in which we can begin to understand the behaviour of
CNNs and how they think. More specifically, it can be used to identify kernels
worthy of deeper inspection and their relationships with other kernels in the
form of logical rules. Our own inspections show that the kernels in the last
convolutional layer may be associated with concepts that are symbolic in the
sense that they are visually distinct from those represented by other kernels.

Some of these symbols were more interpretable from a human perspective than others. However regardless of what labels we assign, we have shown that these kernels can be used to construct symbolic rules that approximate the behaviour of the CNN to an accuracy that can be improved by adjusting rule length and the choice of layer or layers to extract from, at the cost of a larger and therefore less interpretable but nonetheless symbolic logic program. In the best case, we saw an average 10% drop in accuracy compared with the original model.

References

1. Ribeiro, M.T., Singh, S., Guestrin, C.: Why should I trust you?: explaining the predictions of any classifier. In: Proceedings of the 22nd ACM SIGKDD International Conference on Knowledge Discovery and Data Mining, pp. 1135–1144. ACM (2016)
2. Gilpin, L.H., Bau, D., Yuan, B.Z., Bajwa, A., Specter, M., Kagal, L.: Explaining explanations: an overview of interpretability of machine learning. In: 2018 IEEE 5th International Conference on Data Science and Advanced Analytics (DSAA), pp. 80–89. IEEE (2018)
3. Guidotti, R., Monreale, A., Ruggieri, S., Turini, F., Giannotti, F., Pedreschi, D.: A survey of methods for explaining black box models. ACM Comput. Surv. (CSUR) **51**, 93 (2018)
4. Andrews, R., Diederich, J., Tickle, A.B.: Survey and critique of techniques for extracting rules from trained artificial neural networks. Knowl.-Based Syst. **8**, 373–389 (1995)
5. Jacobsson, H.: Rule extraction from recurrent neural networks: a taxonomy and review. Neural Comput. **17**, 1223–1263 (2005)
6. Townsend, J., Chaton, T., Monteiro, J.M.: Extracting relational explanations from deep neural networks: a survey from a neural-symbolic perspective. IEEE Trans. Neural Networks Learn. Syst. **31**, 3456 (2019)
7. Zhang, Q., Zhu, S.: Visual interpretability for deep learning: a survey. Front. Inf. Technol. Electron. Eng. **19**, 27–39 (2018)
8. Lamb, L., Garcez, A., Gori, M., Prates, M., Avelar, P., Vardi, M.: Graph neural networks meet neural-symbolic computing: a survey and perspective. arXiv preprint arXiv:2003.00330 (2020)
9. Simonyan, K., Vedaldi, A., Zisserman, A.: Deep inside convolutional networks: visualising image classification models and saliency maps. arXiv preprint arXiv:1312.6034 (2013)
10. Zeiler, M.D., Fergus, R.: Visualizing and understanding convolutional networks. In: Fleet, D., Pajdla, T., Schiele, B., Tuytelaars, T. (eds.) ECCV 2014. LNCS, vol. 8689, pp. 818–833. Springer, Cham (2014). https://doi.org/10.1007/978-3-319-10590-1_53
11. Springenberg, J.T., Dosovitskiy, A., Brox, T., Riedmiller, M.: Striving for simplicity: the all convolutional net. arXiv preprint arXiv:1412.6806 (2014)
12. Bojarski, M., et al.: Visualbackprop: efficient visualization of CNNs. arXiv preprint arXiv:1611.05418 (2016)
13. Bach, S., Binder, A., Montavon, G., Klauschen, F., Müller, K., Samek, W.: On pixel-wise explanations for non-linear classifier decisions by layer-wise relevance propagation. PloS One **10**, e0130140 (2015)

14. Samek, W., Binder, A., Montavon, G., Lapuschkin, S., Müller, K.: Evaluating the visualization of what a deep neural network has learned. IEEE Trans. Neural Networks Learn. Syst. **28**, 2660–2673 (2017)
15. Shrikumar, A., Greenside, P., Kundaje, A.: Learning important features through propagating activation differences. arXiv preprint arXiv:1704.02685 (2017)
16. Frosst, N., Hinton, G.: Distilling a neural network into a soft decision tree. arXiv preprint arXiv:1711.09784 (2017)
17. Chen, C., Li, O., Tao, D., Barnett, A., Rudin, C., Su, J.K.: This looks like that: deep learning for interpretable image recognition. In: Advances in Neural Information Processing Systems, pp. 8930–8941 (2019)
18. Bologna, G., Fossati, S.: A two-step rule-extraction technique for a CNN. Electronics **9**, 990 (2020)
19. Zhang, Q., Cao, R., Wu, Y.N., Zhu, S.: Growing interpretable part graphs on convnets via multi-shot learning. In: Thirty-First AAAI Conference on Artificial Intelligence (2017)
20. Zhang, Q., Cao, R., Shi, F., Wu, Y.N., Zhu, S.: Interpreting CNN knowledge via an explanatory graph. In: Thirty-Second AAAI Conference on Artificial Intelligence (2018)
21. Zhang, Q., Yang, Y., Ma, H., Wu, Y.N.: Interpreting CNNs via decision trees. In: Proceedings of the IEEE Conference on Computer Vision and Pattern Recognition, pp. 6261–6270 (2019)
22. Zhou, B., Khosla, A., Lapedriza, A., Oliva, A., Torralba, A.: Object detectors emerge in deep scene CNNs. arXiv preprint arXiv:1412.6856 (2014)
23. Zhang, Q., Nian Wu, Y., Zhu, S.: Interpretable convolutional neural networks. In: Proceedings of the IEEE Conference on Computer Vision and Pattern Recognition, pp. 8827–8836 (2018)
24. Percy, C., d'Avila Garcez, A.S., Dragicevic, S., França, M.V., Slabaugh, G.G., Weyde, T.: The need for knowledge extraction: understanding harmful gambling behavior with neural networks. Front. Artif. Intell. Appl. **285**, 974–981 (2016)
25. Ribeiro, M.T., Singh, S., Guestrin, C.: Anchors: High-precision model-agnostic explanations. In: AAAI Conference on Artificial Intelligence (2018)
26. Zilke, J.R., Loza Mencía, E., Janssen, F.: DeepRED – rule extraction from deep neural networks. In: Calders, T., Ceci, M., Malerba, D. (eds.) DS 2016. LNCS (LNAI), vol. 9956, pp. 457–473. Springer, Cham (2016). https://doi.org/10.1007/978-3-319-46307-0_29
27. Schaaf, N., Huber, M.F.: Enhancing decision tree based interpretation of deep neural networks through l1-orthogonal regularization. arXiv preprint arXiv:1904.05394 (2019)
28. Nguyen, T.D., Kasmarik, K.E., Abbass, H.A.: Towards interpretable deep neural networks: an exact transformation to multi-class multivariate decision trees. arXiv preprint arXiv:2003.04675 (2020)
29. Murdoch, W.J., Szlam, A.: Automatic rule extraction from long short term memory networks. arXiv preprint arXiv:1702.02540 (2017)
30. Tran, S.N., d'Avila Garcez, A.S.: Deep logic networks: inserting and extracting knowledge from deep belief networks. IEEE Trans. Neural Networks Learn. Syst. **29**, 246 (2016)
31. Zhou, B., Khosla, A., Lapedriza, A., Oliva, A., Torralba, A.: Learning deep features for discriminative localization. In: 2016 IEEE Conference on Computer Vision and Pattern Recognition (CVPR), pp. 2921–2929. IEEE (2016)
32. Denil, M., Demiraj, A., De Freitas, N.: Extraction of salient sentences from labelled documents. arXiv preprint arXiv:1412.6815 (2014)

33. Selvaraju, R.R., Cogswell, M., Das, A., Vedantam, R., Parikh, D., Batra, D.: Grad-cam: visual explanations from deep networks via gradient-based localization. In: Proceedings of the IEEE international conference on computer vision, pp. 618–626 (2017)
34. Simon, M., Rodner, E., Denzler, J.: Part detector discovery in deep convolutional neural networks. In: Cremers, D., Reid, I., Saito, H., Yang, M.-H. (eds.) ACCV 2014. LNCS, vol. 9004, pp. 162–177. Springer, Cham (2015). https://doi.org/10.1007/978-3-319-16808-1_12
35. Xie, N., Sarker, M.K., Doran, D., Hitzler, P., Raymer, M.: Relating input concepts to convolutional neural network decisions. arXiv preprint arXiv:1711.08006 (2017)
36. Zhou, B., Lapedriza, A., Khosla, A., Oliva, A., Torralba, A.: Places: a 10 million image database for scene recognition. IEEE Trans. Pattern Anal. Mach. Intell. **40**, 1452 (2017)
37. Quinlan, J.R.: C4.5: programming for machine learning. The Morgan Kaufmann Series in Machine Learning, pp. 38–48. Morgan Kaufmann, San Mateo, CA (1993)
38. Chollet, F., et al.: Keras (2015). https://github.com/fchollet/keras

D2D: Keypoint Extraction with Describe to Detect Approach

Yurun Tian[1(✉)], Vassileios Balntas[2], Tony Ng[1], Axel Barroso-Laguna[1], Yiannis Demiris[1], and Krystian Mikolajczyk[1]

[1] Imperial College London, London, UK
{y.tian,tony.ng14,axel.barroso17,y.demiris,k.mikolajczyk}@imperial.ac.uk
[2] Scape Technologies, London, UK
vassileios@scape.io

Abstract. In this paper, we present a novel approach that exploits the information within the descriptor space to propose keypoint locations. Detect then describe, or jointly detect and describe are two typical strategies for extracting local features. In contrast, we propose an approach that inverts this process by first describing and then detecting the keypoint locations. Describe-to-Detect (D2D) leverages successful descriptor models without the need for any additional training. Our method selects keypoints as salient locations with high information content which are defined by the descriptors rather than some independent operators. We perform experiments on multiple benchmarks including image matching, camera localisation, and 3D reconstruction. The results indicate that our method improves the matching performance of various descriptors and that it generalises across methods and tasks.

1 Introduction

One of the main problems in computer vision is concerned with the extraction of 'meaningful' descriptions from images and sequences. These descriptions are then used for the correspondence problem which is critical for applications such as SLAM [1,2], structure from motion [3], retrieval [4], camera localisation [5–10], tracking [11], etc. The key issue is how to measure the 'meaningfulness' from the data and which descriptors are the most suitable for matching. Extensive survey of salient region detectors [12] attempts to identify the main properties expected from 'good' features including repeatability, informativeness, locality, quantity, accuracy, and efficiency. It has also been noted that the detector should be adapted to the needs of the application, *i.e.*, the data.

In contrast to the significant progress on local descriptors achieved with neural networks, keypoint detectors enjoyed little success from using learning methods, with few notable exceptions [13–15]. As a consequence, keypoint detectors

---

Electronic supplementary material The online version of this chapter (https://doi.org/10.1007/978-3-030-69535-4_14) contains supplementary material, which is available to authorized users.

© Springer Nature Switzerland AG 2021
H. Ishikawa et al. (Eds.): ACCV 2020, LNCS 12624, pp. 223–240, 2021.
https://doi.org/10.1007/978-3-030-69535-4_14

based on handcrafted filters such as Difference-of-Gaussians, Harris, Hessian [12], which all originate from research in 1980-ties are still used in many applications.

In the era of deep learning, there are three main research directions towards improving image matching, namely descriptor-only learning [16–20], detector-only learning [15,21], as well as jointly learnt detection-description [14,22–26]. What underlines the concept of disjoint frameworks is their sub-optimal compatibility between the detection and description. In contrast to the CNN based descriptors [16–18,20,27,28], the performance of jointly learnt detection-description [14,22,23,25] does not seem to generalise well across datasets and tasks [29]. CNN descriptors perform significantly better if trained and

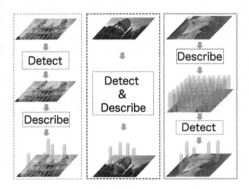

Fig. 1. Comparison of our proposed Describe-to-Detect framework (right) to the existing Detect-then-Describe and Detect-and-Describe frameworks.

applied in the same data domain. Similarly, different keypoint detectors are suitable for different tasks. With all available options, finding optimal pair of detector-descriptor for a dataset or a task requires extensive experiments. Therefore, an approach that adapts keypoint detector to a descriptor without training and evaluation is highly valuable for various applications (Fig. 1).

Our approach is inspired by detectors based on saliency measures [30,31], where the saliency was defined in terms of local signal complexity or unpredictability; more specifically the Shannon entropy of local descriptor was suggested. Despite the appealing idea, such methods failed to be widely adopted due to the complexity of the required dense local measurements. However, currently available CNN dense descriptors allow revisiting the idea of using saliency measured on descriptor maps to define keypoint locations. Top performing learnt descriptors [16–18,20] all share the same fully convolutional network (FCN) that adapts to varying image resolution and output dense descriptors. Furthermore, joint methods like SuperPoint [13], D2-Net [14] and R2D2 [25] also provide dense features. The proposed approach can be seen as a combination of the classical saliency-based methods [30,31] and the modern deep attention mechanisms [4,14,32].

In summary, our main contributions are:

– We propose a novel Describe-to-Detect (D2D) framework for keypoint detection that requires no training and adapts to any existing CNN based descriptor.
– We propose a relative and an absolute saliency measure of local deep feature maps along the spatial and depth dimensions to define keypoints.

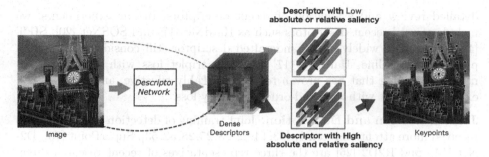

Fig. 2. The Describe-to-Detect pipeline. Locations with high variation across channels (high absolute saliency) as well as high saliency w.r.t spatial neighbours (relative saliency) are detected as keypoints.

– We demonstrate on several benchmarks and different tasks that matching performance of various descriptors can be consistently improved by our approach (Fig. 2).

2 Related Works

In this section, we briefly introduce some of the most recent learning-based methods for local feature detection and description. There are several survey articles that provide comprehensive reviews of this field [12, 33–35].

Local Feature Detection. Most of the existing learned [15, 21, 36–40] or hand-crafted [41–44] detectors are not descriptor-specific. The main property required from keypoints is their repeatability such that their descriptors can be correctly matched. TILDE [21] trains a piece-wise linear regression model as the detector that is robust to weather and illumination changes. CNN models are trained with feature covariant constraints in [36, 37]. Unsupervised trained QuadNet [38] assumes that the ranking of the keypoint scores should be invariant to image transformations. A similar idea is also explored in [39] to detect keypoint in textured images. AffNet [40] learns to predict the affine parameters of a local feature via the hard negative-constant loss based on the descriptors. Key.Net [15] combines hand-crafted filters with learnt ones to extract keypoints at different scale levels. Recently, it has been shown that pre-trained CNNs on standard tasks such as classification can be adapted to keypoint detection [45]. However, the local feature matching pipeline is by nature different from classification. In contrast, our method directly leverage CNNs pre-trained for description to achieve detection.

Local Feature Description. The emergence of several large scale local patch datasets [46–48] stimulated the development of deep local descriptors [16–18, 20, 49–51] that are independent of the detectors. However, this paper is concerned with keypoint detection. Therefore, we refer the reader to [47] for a detailed review and evaluation of recent descriptors. In our experiments, we include several recent descriptors such as HardNet [17] and SOSNet [20]. SIFT [41] is the most widely used handcrafted descriptor still considered as a well-performing baseline. HardNet [17] combines triplet loss with in-batch hard-negatives mining that has proven to be remarkably effective, and SOSNet [20] extends HardNet with a second-order similarity loss.

Joint Detection and Description. Joint training of detection-description has received more attention recently [13, 14, 22, 23, 25, 28, 52, 53]. SuperPoint [13], D2-Net [14], and R2D2 [25] are the three representatives of recent research direction, where patch cropping is replaced by fully convolutional dense descriptors. SuperPoint [13] leverages two separate decoders for detection and description on a shared encoder. Synthetic shapes and image pairs generated from random homographies are used to train the two parts. In D2-Net [14], local-maxima within and across channels of deep feature maps are defined as keypoints, with the same maps used for descriptors. R2D2 [25] aims at learning keypoints that are not only repeatable but also reliable together with robust descriptors. However, the computational cost for current joint frameworks is still high. Besides, the generation of training data is typically laborious and method-specific.

Therefore, a keypoint detection method that is based on a trained descriptor model, thus adapted to the data without requiring any training, can be considered a novel and significant contribution.

3   Describe-to-Detect

In this section, we first define keypoints in terms of the descriptor saliency, then we present our approach to integrate D2D with existing state-of-the-art methods.

3.1   What Is a Keypoint?

Despite the absence of a unified definition, it is widely accepted that keypoints should be image points that have the potential of being repeatably detected under different imaging conditions. As mentioned, according to [12], such points should satisfy several requirements such as repeatability, informativeness, locality, quantity, accuracy and efficiency.

In this work, we argue that the informativeness, which we refer to as saliency, is the property that can lead to satisfying most of the other requirements. We define the saliency in relative terms w.r.t the other descriptors in the neighbourhood, as well as in absolute terms as the information content of the descriptor. Our argument stems from the following assumptions:

Assumption 1. *A point in an image has a high absolute saliency if its corresponding descriptor is highly informative.*

The idea of exploiting salient regions in an image has been adopted by many classical [30, 31] methods as well as recent attention-based models [4, 14, 32]. In tasks such as image retrieval, saliency/attention is defined on image regions with rich semantic information [4,32]. In feature matching, local image structures that exhibit significant variations in shape and texture can be considered salient. However, absolute saliency alone is not sufficient for identifying keypoints. For instance, highly informative but spatially non-discriminative structures should be avoided as they cannot be uniquely and accurately localised. Therefore a relative saliency should also be considered.

Assumption 2. *A point in an image has a high relative saliency if its corresponding descriptor is highly discriminative in its spatial neighbourhood.*

The success of handcrafted detectors that define keypoints according to this criteria [15,41–44,54] validates this assumption. Descriptors on repeated textures can lead to geometrically noisy correspondences, therefore their spatial uniqueness is essential. Similarly to the absolute saliency, the relative saliency alone is not sufficient for detection. For example, corner points of uniform regions can exhibit high relative saliency, whereas their descriptors information content is not high.

Based on Assumptions 1 and 2, our definition for keypoints based on their corresponding descriptors is:

Definition 1. *A point in an image is a keypoint, if its corresponding descriptor's absolute and relative saliencies are both high.*

Definition 1 is a generalization of the keypoints defined for low-level pixel intensities, either by simple operators such as autocorrelation [54] or by early saliency based methods [30,31], to high-level descriptors. In contrast to existing Detect-then/and-Describe frameworks, in Definition 1, we define the detector by the properties of the descriptor. Thus, the key idea of Describe-to-Detect (D2D) is a description-guided detection. Moreover, we claim that descriptors that are specifically trained to be robust to the changes of imaging conditions can provide data driven discriminativeness and thus, more reliable detections. It is worth noting that our D2D differs from other works that utilize the deep feature map response, but do not exploit the full representation potential of a descriptor. For example, the detection step of D2-Net [14] is performed by considering each feature activation separately, as a score map for keypoint detection, whereas D2D detects keypoints via descriptor similarity in the metric space and therefore makes use of the rich information content across entire depth.

In summary, to identify the keypoints, Definition 1 is concerned with two properties: Firstly, when evaluating itself, the descriptor should be informative. Secondly, when comparing to others, the descriptor should be discriminative.

3.2 How to Detect a Keypoint?

Measuring the absolute saliency of a point can be achieved by computing the entropy of a descriptor. It has been shown in the design of binary descriptors [55,56], that selecting binary tests with high entropy will encourage compact and robust representation. Therefore, we propose to measure the informativeness of a descriptor by its entropy, interpreted as a N-dimensional random variable. Unlike in binary descriptors where discrete entropy can be computed directly, for real-valued descriptors differential entropy is needed. However, computing an accurate differential entropy requires probability density estimation, which is computationally expensive. Thus, similarly to the binary case [55,56], we employ the standard deviation as a proxy for the entropy:

$$S_{AS}(x,y) = \sqrt{\mathbb{E}[\boldsymbol{F}^2(x,y)] - \bar{F}(x,y)^2}, \tag{1}$$

where $\bar{F}(x,y)$ is the mean value of descriptor $\boldsymbol{F}(x,y)$ across its dimensions.

Measuring the relative saliency of a point is based on Assumption 2. A function that measures the relationship between a variable's current value and its neighbouring values is the autocorrelation. It has been successfully used by the classic Moravec corner detector [54] as well as the well known Harris detector [57]. However, their simple operators rely directly on pixel intensities which suffer from poor robustness to varying imaging conditions. The autocorrelation was implemented as a sum of squared differences (SSD) between the corresponding pixels of two overlapping patches:

$$S_{SSD}(x,y) = \sum_u \sum_v \boldsymbol{W}(u,v)(\boldsymbol{I}(x,y) - \boldsymbol{I}(x+u, y+v))^2, \tag{2}$$

where $I(x,y)$ indicate pixel intensity at (x,y), (u,v) are window indexes centered at (x,y), and $\boldsymbol{W}(u,v)$ are weights. A high value of $S_{SSD}(x,y)$ means low similarity. As a natural generalization of SSD for measuring the relative saliency, we replace pixel intensities with dense descriptors :

$$S_{RS}(x,y) = \sum_u \sum_v \boldsymbol{W}(u,v)||\boldsymbol{F}(x,y) - \boldsymbol{F}(x+u, y+v)||_2, \tag{3}$$

where $\boldsymbol{F}(x,y)$ indicates the descriptor centered at location (x,y), and $||\cdot||_2$ is the L2 distance. A high value of $S_{RS}(x,y)$ defines points with high relative saliency, i.e., this point stands out from its neighbours according to the description provided by the pre-trained descriptor model. Also note that even though relative saliency can be measured by different similarity metrics, we pick L2 distance as it is used in the matching stage.

Using Eqs. (1) and (3), we assign a score to each point by:

$$S_{D2D}(x,y) = S_{AS}(x,y)S_{RS}(x,y). \tag{4}$$

3.3   Dense Descriptors

All existing description methods can extract dense descriptors for a given image. For example, patch-based methods can be used to generate dense descriptors by extracting patches with a sliding window. However, such strategy is infeasible in large scale tasks such as 3D reconstruction, due to its computational cost. Fortunately, most recent state-of-the-art methods adopt the fully convolutional network architecture without fully-connected layers [13,14,16–18,20]. Thus, dense descriptor maps can be extracted with a single forward pass for images with various resolutions. To guarantee the efficiency, we apply the proposed D2D to fully convolutional network descriptors only. Specifically, in Sect. 4, we evaluate D2D with two state-of-the-art descriptors, *i.e.*, HardNet [17] and SOSNet [20]. We further validate D2D on joint detection-description methods SuperPoint [13] and D2-Net [14].

3.4   Implementation Details

Computation of $S_{AS}(x,y)$ is done on descriptors before L2 normalization, since it has an effect of reducing the standard deviation magnitude across the dimensions. It has been shown that the descriptor norm, that also reflects the magnitude of variance, is not helpful in the matching stage [47], however, we use the variance during the detection to identify informative points.

Computation of $S_{RS}(x,y)$. We define the size of the window $W(u,v)$ in Eq. (3) as r_{RS}. Considering that the receptive fields of neighbouring descriptors overlap and that the descriptor map resolution is typically lower than the input image, we sample the neighbouring descriptors with a step size of 2 and calculate the relative saliency with respect to the center descriptor. Please refer to the supplementary material for the detailed defination of $W(u,v)$. Note that the operation in Eq. (3) can be implemented efficiently with a convolution, therefore, when the window size r_{RS} is small and the sampling step is 2, the computational cost is negligible.

Combining D2D With Descriptors. To evaluate D2D we employ two current state-of-the-art patch-based descriptors, namely HardNet [17] and SOSNet [20]. Given the network architecture [16] and an input image of size $H \times W (H \geq 32, W \geq 32)$, the output feature map size is $(\lfloor H/4 \rfloor - 7) \times (\lfloor W/4 \rfloor - 7)$. The receptive field's size is 51×51. Therefore, each descriptor $F(x,y)$ describes a 51×51 region centered at $(4x + 14, 4y + 14)$. There are two stride-2 convolutional layers in the network, meaning that F describes each 51×51 patch with stride of 4. In other words, keypoints are at least 4 pixels away from each other. Such sparse sampling has also been validated in other works [25,58]. Finally, given S_{D2D} we directly take the top K ranked points as keypoints.

In D2-Net [14], the effect of downsampling layers is mitigated by upsampling the dense descriptors. However, with a large receptive overlap, dense F is redundant. For example, $F(x,y)$ and $F(x+1,y)$ describe two 51×51 patch with a 47×51 overlap. For networks such as HardNet [17] and SOSNet [20] that are trained to be insensitive to such small changes, additional interpolation of feature maps is unnecessary.

Also, note that the amount of content the network can see in a 51×51 region is defined by the resolution of the image. High resolution and dense sampling can make the neighbouring descriptors indistinguishable. An interesting question is

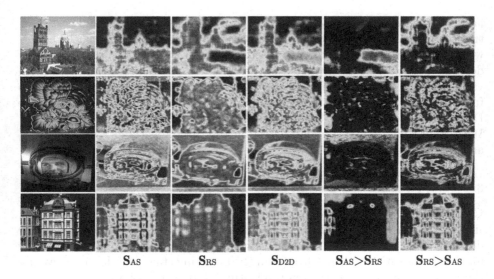

S_{AS} S_{RS} S_{D2D} $S_{AS}>S_{RS}$ $S_{RS}>S_{AS}$

Fig. 3. Visualization of the heat maps generated by D2D applied to HardNet [17]. From left to right the columns show images, heat maps of S_{AS}, S_{RS}, S_{D2D}, $\max(0, S_{AS}-S_{RS})$ and $\max(0, S_{RS}-S_{AS})$, respectively. S_{AS} and S_{RS} are normalized so that their values are in $[0, 1]$.

whether a multi-scale strategy to tackle the scale changes is needed. We show in Sect. 4 that single scale HardNet [17] and SOSNet [20] perform well in different tasks, which is in accordance with the observations from joint methods [14,25, 59]. We claim that there are two reasons for this: First, dramatic scale changes are rare in typical images of the same scenes. Second, scale changes are often global and the ranking of the detected keypoints is not affected by such changes [38].

Furthermore, we visualise some examples in Fig. 3 to show different components of the final keypoint score map and how S_{AS} and S_{RS} contribute to S_{D2D}. As shown, S_{AS} highlights all regions that have high intensity variations, while S_{RS} has high scores in structured areas. Finally, S_{D2D} combines the two parts, resulting in a low score for repetitive/non-textured areas and edges. Points with S_{RS} greater than S_{AS} are informative but not locally discriminative. This includes repetitive textures like tree leaves and tiles on building roof, as well as intensity noise in visually homogeneous regions. On the contrary, line structures are less informative but can be discriminative from the adjacent regions, which results in S_{AS} greater than S_{RS}.

4   Experiments

In this section, we present the results for various tasks on different datasets, and next, we conduct ablation studies and discussions.

4.1   Comparison with the state-of-the-art

We evaluate D2D on three different tasks, *i.e.*, image matching, visual localisation, and 3D reconstruction on three standard benchmarks, *i.e.*, Hpatches [47], Aachen Day-Night [60,61], and ETH SfM [62], respectively. Each of the tasks tests the compatibility of the detector and the descriptor from a different perspective. We employ HardNet and SOSNet trained on Liberty from UBC dataset [46]. For all experiments in this section, we set the window size r_{RS} to be 5.

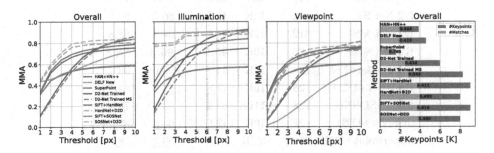

Fig. 4. Experimental results for the HPatches [47] dataset. The results are reported with Mean Matching Accuracy. We observe that the proposed D2D method significantly outperforms other approaches, especially in the crucial high-accuracy area of $< 5px$.

Image Matching. Hpatches [47] dataset contains 116 image sequences with ground truth homographies under different viewpoint or illumination changes. Following the evaluation protocol of [14,33], we report the mean matching accuracy (MMA). In Fig. 4, we plot the MMA curve for thresholds 1 to 10 pixels averaged over all image pairs. Also, we give the mean number of keypoints, mean number of mutual nearest neighbour matches per image pair, and the ratio between the two numbers.

As shown, combining D2D approach with HardNet and SOSNet can achieve superior or comparable results to other state-of-the-art methods. By comparing the curves of HardNet/SOSNet+D2D with SIFT+HardNet/SOSNet, we can observe that D2D finds more compatible keypoints for HardNet/SOSNet than SIFT. Also note that when using the SIFT detector, the MMA curves of HardNet and SOSNet almost overlap, however, D2D helps to further reveal their performance difference. This also demonstrates that the detector is a very crucial component of matching, and that optimising descriptor independently from the detector is insufficient. Moreover, we also see that D2D can detect more keypoints thus leading to a higher number of mutual nearest neighbour matches, which beneficial for various applications. Besides, HardNet+D2D also surpass AffNet+HardNet++, where AffNet is specifically trained with a descriptor loss. This shows that leveraging the absolute and relative saliency of descriptors is an effective approach to detect keypoints. Plead refer to the supplementary materials for more comparisons against different detection methods.

Table 1. Comparison to the state of the art on the Aachen Day-Night dataset. We report the percentages of successfully localized images within 3 error thresholds as in [14,25].

Method	#Dim	#Kp	0.5m, 2°	1m, 5°	5m, 10°
SIFT	128	11K	33.7	52.0	65.3
DELF(New)	1024	11K	39.8	61.2	85.7
HAN+HN++	128	11K	39.8	61.2	77.6
SuperPoint	128	3.7K	42.8	57.1	75.5
D2-Net SS	512	12K	44.9	66.3	88.8
D2-Net MS	512	12K	44.9	64.3	88.8
R2D2 (N=8)	128	10K	**45.9**	**66.3**	**88.8**
SIFT+HardNet	128	11K	34.7	52.0	69.4
HardNet+D2D	128	16K	_41.8_	_61.2_	_84.7_
SIFT+SOSNet	128	11ßK	36.7	53.1	70.4
SOSNet+D2D	128	16K	_42.9_	_64.3_	_85.7_
SuperPoint+D2D	256	3.7K	41.8	_59.2_	_78.6_
D2-Net SS+D2D	512	_8.3K_	_44.9_	_66.3_	_88.8_

Day-Night Visual Localisation. In this section, we further evaluate our method on the task of long-term visual localization using the Aachen Day-Night dataset [60,61]. This task evaluates the performance of local features under challenging conditions including day-night and viewpoint changes. Our evaluation is performed via a localisation pipeline[1] based on COLMAP [3] and The Visual Localization Benchmark[2].

In Table 1, we report the percentages of successfully localized images within three error thresholds. As can be seen, D2D significantly boost the performance of HardNet and SOSNet. Even though D2-Net and R2D2 are still the best performers on this dataset, their advantage may come from the training data or network architecture, i.e., D2-Net uses VGG16 network [63] pre-trained on ImageNet and then trained on MegaDepth [64] while R2D2 is also trained on Aachen Day-Night dataset. However, HardNet and SOSNet are only trained on 450K 32×32 patches from Liberty dataset [46]. We leave the training of D2D on larger datasets for better visual localisation performance as a further work. We will show in the next experiments that, these two models trained on patches labeled by an SfM pipeline are especially effective for 3D reconstruction tasks.

3D Reconstruction. We test our method on the ETH SfM benchmark [62] in the task of 3D reconstruction. We compare the reconstruction quality by comparing the number of registered images, reconstructed sparse and dense points,

---

[1] https://github.com/tsattler/visuallocalizationbenchmark/tree/master/local_feature_evaluation.

[2] https://www.visuallocalization.net/.

Table 2. Evaluation results on ETH dataset [62] for SfM. We can observe that with our proposed D2D, the shallow networks trained on local patches can significantly surpass deeper ones trained on larger datasets with full resolution images.

		#Reg. Images	#Sparse Points	#Dense Points	Track Length	Reproj. Error
Fountain 11 images	SIFT	11	14K	292K	4.79	**0.39px**
	SuperPoint	11	7K	304K	4.93	0.81px
	D2-Net	11	19K	301K	3.03	1.40px
	SIFT+HardNet	11	16K	303K	4.91	0.47px
	SIFT+SOSNet	11	16K	**306K**	4.92	0.46px
	HardNet+D2D	11	**20K**	304K	6.27	1.34px
	SOSNet+D2D	11	**20K**	305K	**6.41**	1.36px
Herzjesu 8 images	SIFT	8	7.5K	241K	4.22	**0.43px**
	SuperPoint	8	5K	**244K**	4.47	0.79px
	D2-Net	8	13K	221K	2.87	1.37px
	SIFT+HardNet	8	8K	239K	4.30	0.50px
	SIFT+SOSNet	8	8K	239K	4.31	0.50px
	HardNet+D2D	8	**13K**	242K	5.73	1.29px
	SOSNet+D2D	8	**13K**	237K	**6.06**	1.34px
South Building 128 images	SIFT	128	108K	**2.14M**	6.04	**0.54px**
	SuperPoint	128	125k	2.13M	7.10	0.83px
	D2-Net	128	178K	2.06M	3.11	1.36px
	SIFT+HardNet	128	159K	2.12M	5.18	0.62px
	SIFT+SOSNet	128	160K	2.12M	5.17	0.63px
	HardNet+D2D	128	**193K**	2.02M	8.71	1.33px
	SOSNet+D2D	128	184K	1.94M	**8.99**	1.36px
Madrid Metropolis 1344 images	SIFT	500	116K	**1.82M**	6.32	**0.60px**
	SuperPoint	702	125K	1.14M	4.43	1.05px
	D2-Net	787	229K	0.96M	5.50	1.27px
	SIFT+HardNet	793	306K	1.23M	3.84	0.93px
	SIFT+SOSNet	675	240K	1.27M	4.40	0.94px
	HardNet+D2D	**899**	**710K**	1.13M	5.31	1.08px
	SOSNet+D2D	865	626K	1.15M	6.00	1.14px
Gendar- menmarkt 1463 images	SIFT	1035	338K	**4.22M**	5.52	**0.69px**
	SuperPoint	1112	236K	2.49M	4.74	1.10px
	D2-Net	1225	541K	2.60M	5.21	1.30px
	SIFT+HardNet	1018	827K	2.06M	2.56	1.09px
	SIFT+SOSNet	1129	729K	3.05M	3.85	0.95px
	HardNet+D2D	1250	**1716K**	2.64M	5.32	1.16px
	SOSNet+D2D	**1255**	1562K	2.71M	**5.95**	1.20px

mean track length, and the reprojection error. Following [62], no nearest neighbour ratio test is conducted to better expose the matching performance of the descriptors.

The reconstruction results are listed in Table 2. With D2D, HardNet and SOSNet show consistent performance increase in terms of the number of registered images, the number of sparse points, and the track length, which are

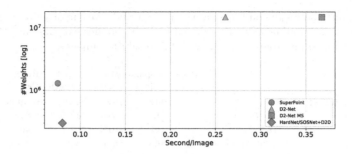

Fig. 5. Comparison of efficiency.

important indicators of the reconstruction quality. This observation is expected as in this experiment, both HardNet and SOSNet are trained on local patches that are extracted and labeled via the SfM pipeline, and therefore are more suitable for this task.

Moreover, an interesting observation which has also been observed by previous works [20,27], is that when the number of spare points increases, track length drops and reprojection error increases, especially with large scenes. A possible explanation for this phenomenon is that more robust descriptors manage to match harder keypoint pairs, which are characteristic for showing lower repeatability and localisation accuracy. The lack of repeatability and accuracy, in turn, aggravates the reprojection error on the detections. However, we observer this phenomenon can be alleviated by D2D which provides more accurate and repeatable keypoints that are compatible with the descriptors.

Efficiency. In this experiment, we compare the feature extraction speed of several methods. Specifically, we record the extraction time over 108 image sequences in Hpatches [47], where there are 648 images with various resolutions (the average resolution is 775×978). All methods are tested on a RTX 2080 GPU, and the results are shown in Fig. 5. SuperPoint and D2-Net has 1.3M and 15M parameters, respectively, whereas HardNet/SOSNet+D2D only relies 0.3M. HardNet/SOSNet+D2D is slightly slower than SuperPoint, due to the extra time that is mostly spend on ranking the $\mathbf{S}_{D2D}$ score of keypoints, whereas SuperPoint takes a thresholding operation.

In summary, from the results on three different tasks with three different datasets we observe that with D2D, patch-based descriptors HardNet and SOS-Net can achieve competitive performance compared to joint detection-description methods such as D2-Net and SuperPoint. With significantly less parameters and faster speed, HardNet and SOSNet can achieve comparable/superior results to/than the state-of-the-art methods. These results validate our hypothesis that the networks trained for descriptors can be also used for detection.

4.2 Ablation Study

Combining D2D with Joint Methods. In order to further validate the effectiveness of the proposed D2D, we test it in combination with detect-and-describe methods namely D2-Net[14] and SuperPoint [13]. Each of the two methods has its unique detection strategy: SuperPoint detects via thresholding of deep score maps while D2-Net selects local maxima. We adapt D2D in the following way: For SuperPoint, we generate a new threshhold α^* by:

$$\alpha^* = \frac{\mathbb{E}[S_{\text{D2D}}S_O]}{\mathbb{E}[S_O]}\alpha, \tag{5}$$

where α and S_O are the original threshold and score map, respectively. For D2-Net, we choose local maxima that also have high $\mathbf{S}_{\text{D2D}}$. Specifically, if (x, y) is a keypoint than it should be detected by the non-maxima-suppression as well as have:

$$S_{\text{D2D}}(x, y) > \mathbb{E}[S_{\text{D2D}}] \tag{6}$$

Table 3. Ablative study in terms of Absolute Saliency(AS) and Relative Saliency(RS). Numbers are in terms of the average MMA on Hpatches [47] across pixel error threshold 1 to 10.

AS	RS	SuperPoint	D2-Net	HardNet	SOSNet
$\checkmark$		67.51	61.20	71.38	72.66
	$\checkmark$	67.58	60.07	69.32	72.77
$\checkmark$	$\checkmark$	**67.64**	**61.42**	**72.40**	**75.40**

In Fig. 6(a), D2D helps to eliminate a large number of unmatchable keypoints, *i.e.*, improves the ratio of mutual nearest neighbour matches, while guaranteeing on par or superior performance. We suspect the slight performance drop of SuperPoint+D2D at lower thresholds is the side effect of reducing keypoints density, whereas D2Net with better keypoints localisation accuracy does not suffer from this problem. Moreover, in Table 1, SuperPoint+D2D achieves remarkably better localisation accuracy. D2-Net+D2D can maintain the same accuracy with much fewer detections indicating that keypoints not contributing to the localisation are filtered out by D2D. These results demonstrate that D2D can also improve the jointly trained detection-description methods.

Impact of Absolute and Relative Descriptor Saliency. In Table 3, we show how S_{AS} and S_{RS} impact the matching performance. We observe that each of the two terms enables the detection, and the performance is further boosted when they are combined. This indicates that the absolute and relative saliency, *i.e.*, informativeness and distinctiveness of a point are two effective and complementary factors.

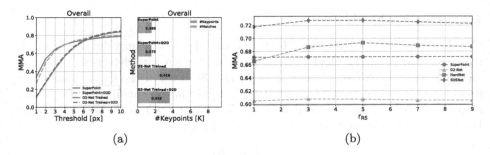

(a)   (b)

Fig. 6. (a) Performance of combining D2D with SuperPoint [13] and D2-Net [14] on Hpatches [47]. (b) Performance in terms of MMA with different choice of r_{RS}.

Table 4. Keypoint repeatability on Hpatches [47] with different detectors. Column: detector used on source image. Row: detector used on destination image. Numbers are the percentage of repeatability change in terms of the original repeatability (diagonal).

	SuperPoint	D2-Net	HardNet	SOSNet
SuperPoint	1	1.0154	0.745	0.765
D2-Net	1.136	1	0.675	0.690
HardNet	0.849	0.729	1	0.952
SOSNet	0.868	0.738	0.950	1

Impact of r_{RS}. Matching performance in terms of different window size r_{RS} for computing relative saliency is shown in Fig. 6(b), where the experiment is done using only S_{RS} as the keypoint score. For HardNet and SOSNet, the best r_{RS} is 5, which means that it is better to compare patches that are 20 pixels (stride 4 times 5) away from the center, which is approximately half of the receptive field size. Descriptors that are too close are indistinguishable.

Keypoint Complementarity. Table 4 shows the results of a repeatability test across different descriptors combined with D2D. This is to demonstrate the complementarity of keypoints detected with different methods. The off diagonal scores are normalised with the diagonal scores for example, keypoints from Hard-Net+D2D are compared to those detected by SOSNet+D2D. Low normalised repeatability score indicates that the keypoints are mostly different, i.e., different locations, thus the methods are complementary. Similarly HardNet and SOSNet give high score. This may be expected as both share the same architecture and similar training process. However, high score between SuperPoint and D2-Net which indicates that the two descriptors are not complementary, measure the same type of information that D2D uses for detecting keypoints.

5   Conclusion

We proposed a new Describe-to-Detect (D2D) framework for the task of keypoint detection given dense descriptors. We have demonstrated that CNN models trained to describe can also be used to detect. D2D is simple, does not require training, is efficient, and can be combined with any existing descriptor. We defined the descriptor saliency as the most important property and proposed an absolute and relative saliency measure to select keypoints that are highly informative in descriptor space and discriminative in their local spacial neighbourhood.

Our experimental evaluation on three different tasks and different datasets show that D2D offers a significant boost to the matching performance of various descriptors. It also improves results for camera localisation and 3D reconstruction.

Acknowledgements. This research was supported by UKEPSRC IPALM project EP/S032398/1.

References

1. Davison, A.J., Reid, I.D., Molton, N.D., Stasse, O.: MonoSLAM: real-time single camera slam. IEEE Trans. Pattern Anal. Mach. Intell. **29**, 1052–1067 (2007)
2. Mur-Artal, R., Montiel, J.M.M., Tardos, J.D.: ORB-SLAM: a versatile and accurate monocular SLAM system. IEEE Trans. Rob. **31**, 1147–1163 (2015)
3. Schonberger, J.L., Frahm, J.M.: Structure-from-motion revisited. In: Proceedings of the IEEE Conference on Computer Vision and Pattern Recognition (CVPR), pp. 4104–4113 (2016)
4. Radenović, F., Tolias, G., Chum, O.: Fine-tuning CNN image retrieval with no human annotation. IEEE Trans. Pattern Anal. Mach. Intell. **41**, 1655–1668 (2018)
5. Sattler, T., et al.: Benchmarking 6DoF urban visual localization in changing conditions. CoRR abs/1707.09092 (2017)
6. Yu, X., Zhuang, Z., Koniusz, P., Li, H.: 6DoF object pose estimation via differentiable proxy voting loss. In: British Machine Vision Conference (BMVC) (2020)
7. Shi, Y., Yu, X., Campbell, D., Li, H.: Where am i looking at? Joint location and orientation estimation by cross-view matching. In: Proceedings of the IEEE Conference on Computer Vision and Pattern Recognition (CVPR), pp. 4064–4072 (2020)
8. Shi, Y., Yu, X., Liu, L., Zhang, T., Li, H.: Optimal feature transport for cross-view image geo-localization, pp. 11990–11997 (2020)
9. Shi, Y., Liu, L., Yu, X., Li, H.: Spatial-aware feature aggregation for image based cross-view geo-localization. In: Advances in Neural Information Processing Systems (NeurIPS) (2019)
10. Du, H., Yu, X., Zheng, L.: Learning object relation graph and tentative policy for visual navigation. In: Vedaldi, A., Bischof, H., Brox, T., Frahm, J.-M. (eds.) ECCV 2020. LNCS, vol. 12352, pp. 19–34. Springer, Cham (2020). https://doi.org/10.1007/978-3-030-58571-6_2
11. Smeulders, A.W., Chu, D.M., Cucchiara, R., Calderara, S., Dehghan, A., Shah, M.: Visual tracking: an experimental survey. IEEE Trans. Pattern Anal. Mach. Intell. **36**, 1442–1468 (2013)
12. Tuytelaars, T., Mikolajczyk, K., et al.: Local invariant feature detectors: a survey. Found. Trends® Comput. Graph. Vis. **3**, 177–280 (2008)

13. DeTone, D., Malisiewicz, T., Rabinovich, A.: Superpoint: self-supervised interest point detection and description. In: Proceedings of the IEEE Conference on Computer Vision and Pattern Recognition Workshops, pp. 224–236 (2018)
14. Dusmanu, M., et al.: D2-Net: a trainable CNN for joint detection and description of local features. In: Proceedings of the IEEE Conference on Computer Vision and Pattern Recognition (CVPR) (2019)
15. Barroso-Laguna, A., Riba, E., Ponsa, D., Mikolajczyk, K.: Key.net: keypoint detection by handcrafted and learned CNN filters. Proceedings of the IEEE International Conference on Computer Vision (ICCV) (2019)
16. Tian, Y., Fan, B., Wu, F.: L2-net: deep learning of discriminative patch descriptor in Euclidean space. In: Proceedings of the IEEE Conference on Computer Vision and Pattern Recognition (CVPR), vol. 1, p. 6 (2017)
17. Mishchuk, A., Mishkin, D., Radenovic, F., Matas, J.: Working hard to know your neighbor's margins: local descriptor learning loss. In: Advances in Neural Information Processing Systems (NeurIPS), pp. 4826–4837 (2017)
18. He, K., Lu, Y., Sclaroff, S.: Local descriptors optimized for average precision. In: Proceedings of the IEEE Conference on Computer Vision and Pattern Recognition (CVPR), pp. 596–605 (2018)
19. Yu, X., et al.: Unsupervised extraction of local image descriptors via relative distance ranking loss. In: Proceedings of the IEEE International Conference on Computer Vision Workshops, pp. 1–8 (2019)
20. Tian, Y., Yu, X., Fan, B., Wu, F., Heijnen, H., Balntas, V.: SOSNet: second order similarity regularization for local descriptor learning. In: Proceedings of the IEEE Conference on Computer Vision and Pattern Recognition (CVPR), pp. 11016–11025 (2019)
21. Verdie, Y., Yi, K., Fua, P., Lepetit, V.: Tilde: a temporally invariant learned detector. In: Proceedings of the IEEE Conference on Computer Vision and Pattern Recognition (CVPR), pp. 5279–5288 (2015)
22. Yi, K.M., Trulls, E., Lepetit, V., Fua, P.: LIFT: Learned Invariant Feature Transform. In: Leibe, B., Matas, J., Sebe, N., Welling, M. (eds.) ECCV 2016. LNCS, vol. 9910, pp. 467–483. Springer, Cham (2016). https://doi.org/10.1007/978-3-319-46466-4_28
23. Ono, Y., Trulls, E., Fua, P., Yi, K.M.: LF-Net: learning local features from images. In: Advances in Neural Information Processing Systems (NeurIPS), pp. 6234–6244 (2018)
24. Shen, X., et al.: RF-Net: an end-to-end image matching network based on receptive field. In: Proceedings of the IEEE Conference on Computer Vision and Pattern Recognition (CVPR), pp. 8132–8140 (2019)
25. Revaud, J., et al.: R2D2: repeatable and reliable detector and descriptor. arXiv preprint arXiv:1906.06195 (2019)
26. Yang, T.Y., Nguyen, D.K., Heijnen, H., Balntas, V.: UR2KiD: unifying retrieval, keypoint detection, and keypoint description without local correspondence supervision. arXiv preprint arXiv:2001.07252 (2020)
27. Luo, Z., Shen, T., Zhou, L., Zhu, S., Zhang, R., Yao, Y., Fang, T., Quan, L.: Geodesc: Learning local descriptors by integrating geometry constraints. In: European Conference on Computer Vision (ECCV), Springer (2018) 170–185
28. Luo, Z., et al.: ContextDesc: Local descriptor augmentation with cross-modality context. In: Proceedings of the IEEE Conference on Computer Vision and Pattern Recognition (CVPR), pp. 2527–2536 (2019)
29. Jin, Y., et al.: Image matching across wide baselines: from paper to practice. arXiv preprint arXiv:2003.01587 (2020)

30. Kadir, T., Brady, M.: Saliency, scale and image description. Int. J. Comput. Vis. **45**, 83–105 (2001). https://doi.org/10.1023/A:1012460413855
31. Schiele, B., Crowley, J.L.: Recognition without correspondence using multidimensional receptive field histograms. Int. J. Comput. Vis. **36**, 31–50 (2000). https://doi.org/10.1023/A:1008120406972
32. Noh, H., Araujo, A., Sim, J., Weyand, T., Han, B.: Large-scale image retrieval with attentive deep local features. In: Proceedings of the IEEE International Conference on Computer Vision, pp. 3456–3465 (2017)
33. Mikolajczyk, K., Schmid, C.: A performance evaluation of local descriptors. IEEE PAMI **27**, 1615–1630 (2005)
34. Mikolajczyk, K., et al.: A comparison of affine region detectors. Int. J. Comput. Vis. **65**, 43–72 (2005)
35. Lenc, K., Vedaldi, A.: Large scale evaluation of local image feature detectors on homography datasets. arXiv preprint arXiv:1807.07939 (2018)
36. Lenc, K., Vedaldi, A.: Learning covariant feature detectors. In: Hua, G., Jégou, H. (eds.) ECCV 2016. LNCS, vol. 9915, pp. 100–117. Springer, Cham (2016). https://doi.org/10.1007/978-3-319-49409-8_11
37. Zhang, X., Yu, F.X., Karaman, S., Chang, S.F.: Learning discriminative and transformation covariant local feature detectors. In: Proceedings of the IEEE Conference on Computer Vision and Pattern Recognition (CVPR), pp. 6818–6826 (2017)
38. Savinov, N., Seki, A., Ladicky, L., Sattler, T., Pollefeys, M.: Quad-networks: unsupervised learning to rank for interest point detection. In: Proceedings of the IEEE Conference on Computer Vision and Pattern Recognition (CVPR), pp. 1822–1830 (2017)
39. Zhang, L., Rusinkiewicz, S.: Learning to detect features in texture images. In: Proceedings of the IEEE Conference on Computer Vision and Pattern Recognition (CVPR) (2018)
40. Mishkin, D., Radenović, F., Matas, J.: Repeatability is not enough: learning affine regions via discriminability. In: Ferrari, V., Hebert, M., Sminchisescu, C., Weiss, Y. (eds.) ECCV 2018. LNCS, vol. 11213, pp. 287–304. Springer, Cham (2018). https://doi.org/10.1007/978-3-030-01240-3_18
41. Lowe, D.G.: Distinctive image features from scale-invariant keypoints. In: Proceedings of the IEEE International Conference on Computer Vision (ICCV), vol. 60, pp. 91–110 (2004)
42. Leutenegger, S., Chli, M., Siegwart, R.: Brisk: Binary robust invariant scalable keypoints. In: Proceedings of the IEEE International Conference on Computer Vision (ICCV), pp. 2548–2555. IEEE (2011)
43. Alcantarilla, P.F., Bartoli, A., Davison, A.J.: KAZE features. In: Fitzgibbon, A., Lazebnik, S., Perona, P., Sato, Y., Schmid, C. (eds.) ECCV 2012. LNCS, vol. 7577, pp. 214–227. Springer, Heidelberg (2012). https://doi.org/10.1007/978-3-642-33783-3_16
44. Aldana-Iuit, J., Mishkin, D., Chum, O., Matas, J.: In the saddle: chasing fast and repeatable features. In: 2016 23rd International Conference on Pattern Recognition (ICPR), pp. 675–680. IEEE (2016)
45. Benbihi, A., Geist, M., Pradalier, C.: ELF: embedded localisation of features in pretrained CNN. In: Proceedings of the IEEE International Conference on Computer Vision (ICCV), pp. 7940–7949 (2019)
46. Brown, M., Hua, G., Winder, S.: Discriminative learning of local image descriptors. IEEE Trans. Pattern Anal. Mach. Intell. **33**, 43–57 (2011)

47. Balntas, V., Lenc, K., Vedaldi, A., Mikolajczyk, K.: HPatches: a benchmark and evaluation of handcrafted and learned local descriptors. In: Proceedings of the IEEE Conference on Computer Vision and Pattern Recognition (CVPR), vol. 4, p. 6 (2017)
48. Mitra, R., et al.: A large dataset for improving patch matching. arXiv preprint arXiv:1801.01466 (2018)
49. Simo-Serra, E., Trulls, E., Ferraz, L., Kokkinos, I., Fua, P., Moreno-Noguer, F.: Discriminative learning of deep convolutional feature point descriptors. In: Proceedings of the IEEE International Conference on Computer Vision (ICCV), pp. 118–126 (2015)
50. Balntas, V., Riba, E., Ponsa, D., Mikolajczyk, K.: Learning local feature descriptors with triplets and shallow convolutional neural networks. In: British Machine Vision Conference (BMVC), vol. 1, p. 3 (2016)
51. Keller, M., Chen, Z., Maffra, F., Schmuck, P., Chli, M.: Learning deep descriptors with scale-aware triplet networks. In: Proceedings of the IEEE Conference on Computer Vision and Pattern Recognition (CVPR). IEEE (2018)
52. Luo, Z., et al.: ASLFeat: learning local features of accurate shape and localization. arXiv preprint arXiv:2003.10071 (2020)
53. Germain, H., Bourmaud, G., Lepetit, V.: S2DNet: learning accurate correspondences for sparse-to-dense feature matching. arXiv preprint arXiv:2004.01673 (2020)
54. Moravec, H.P.: Obstacle avoidance and navigation in the real world by a seeing robot rover. Technical report, Stanford Univ CA Dept of Computer Science (1980)
55. Rublee, E., Rabaud, V., Konolige, K., Bradski, G.: ORB: an efficient alternative to sift or surf. In: Proceedings of the IEEE International Conference on Computer Vision (ICCV), pp. 2564–2571. IEEE (2011)
56. Balntas, V., Tang, L., Mikolajczyk, K.: Bold-binary online learned descriptor for efficient image matching. In: Proceedings of the IEEE Conference on Computer Vision and Pattern Recognition (CVPR), pp. 2367–2375 (2015)
57. Harris, C.G., Stephens, M., et al.: A combined corner and edge detector. In: Alvey Vision Conference. vol. 15, pp. 10–5244. Citeseer (1988)
58. Christiansen, P.H., Kragh, M.F., Brodskiy, Y., Karstoft, H.: Unsuperpoint: end-to-end unsupervised interest point detector and descriptor. arXiv preprint arXiv:1907.04011 (2019)
59. Sarlin, P.E., DeTone, D., Malisiewicz, T., Rabinovich, A.: Superglue: learning feature matching with graph neural networks. arXiv preprint arXiv:1911.11763 (2019)
60. Sattler, T., Weyand, T., Leibe, B., Kobbelt, L.: Image retrieval for image-based localization revisited. In: British Machine Vision Conference (BMVC), vol. 1, p. 4 (2012)
61. Sattler, T., et al.: Benchmarking 6DoF outdoor visual localization in changing conditions. In: Proceedings of the IEEE Conference on Computer Vision and Pattern Recognition (CVPR), pp. 8601–8610 (2018)
62. Schönberger, J.L., Hardmeier, H., Sattler, T., Pollefeys, M.: Comparative evaluation of hand-crafted and learned local features. In: Proceedings of the IEEE Conference on Computer Vision and Pattern Recognition (CVPR) (2017)
63. Simonyan, K., Zisserman, A.: Very deep convolutional networks for large-scale image recognition. arXiv preprint arXiv:1409.1556 (2014)
64. Li, Z., Snavely, N.: MegaDepth: learning single-view depth prediction from internet photos. In: Proceedings of the IEEE Conference on Computer Vision and Pattern Recognition, pp. 2041–2050 (2018)

Accurate Arbitrary-Shaped Scene Text Detection via Iterative Polynomial Parameter Regression

Jiahao Shi, Long Chen, and Feng Su$^{(\boxtimes)}$ (iD)

State Key Laboratory for Novel Software Technology, Nanjing University,
Nanjing 210023, China
suf@nju.edu.cn

Abstract. A number of scene text in natural images have irregular shapes which often cause significant difficulties for a text detector. In this paper, we propose a robust scene text detection method based on a parameterized shape modeling and regression scheme for text with arbitrary shapes. The shape model geometrically depicts a text region with a polynomial centerline and a series of width cues to capture global shape characteristics (e.g.. smoothness) and local shapes of the text respectively for accurate text localization, which differs from previous text region modeling schemes based on discrete boundary points or pixels. We further propose a text detection network PolyPRNet equipped with an iterative regression module for text's shape parameters, which effectively enhances the detection accuracy of arbitrary-shaped text. Our method achieves state-of-the-art text detection results on several standard benchmarks.

1 Introduction

Scene text carries useful semantic information for various content-based image applications such as image parsing, classification, and retrieval. Due to the complexity and wide variation of scene text's appearance and various contextual interferences such as complicated background and low contrast, to reliably detect scene text in natural images remains a challenging task.

Traditional scene text detection methods [1–3] usually work in a bottom-up manner which first localizes candidate character regions in the image with manually designed features and some classifiers and then combines them into text. The multi-stage detection pipeline often keeps these methods from achieving overall optimized performance.

More recent scene text detection methods [4–8] often employ deep neural networks such as convolutional neural network (CNN) and recurrent neural network (RNN) to automatically learn effective representations of text and predict text candidates in an end-to-end manner, which significantly enhance the detection performance compared to traditional methods.

© Springer Nature Switzerland AG 2021
H. Ishikawa et al. (Eds.): ACCV 2020, LNCS 12624, pp. 241–256, 2021.
https://doi.org/10.1007/978-3-030-69535-4_15

Compared to the detection performance on regular scene text which has been continuously improved to a rather high level, there is still large improvement space in the detection of arbitrarily shaped scene text such as multi-oriented and curved ones due to their largely varied irregular appearances. Accordingly, the focus of increasing researches [5–9] has turned to it and a number of promising results have been attained. On the other hand, most existing methods employ discrete boundary points or a pixel mask to depict a text region, and few efforts have been made on devising more effective shape models of text to capture its distinctive geometric characteristics beyond a general connected object, which limits potential performance improvements of existing text detection methods.

In this paper, we propose a robust scene text detection method based on a novel parameterized geometric shape modeling and iterative regression scheme for arbitrary-shaped text. The key contributions of our work are summarized as follows:

- We propose a geometric, parameterized shape model for text with arbitrary shapes. The model depicts one text region with a polynomial centerline that captures global shape characteristics such as smoothness of the text as an artificial object and a series of width cues capturing local text shape, which provides effective shape constraints and sufficient flexibility for accurate localization of the text region. The model essentially differs from the pixels- or boundary points-based representations of text region employed by most previous text detection methods.
- Based on the parameterized text shape model, we take the text detection task as a conditional shape parameter regression problem. Accordingly, we propose an end-to-end trainable detection network PolyPRNet that introduces an iterative shape parameter regression module on the basis of backbone networks, which iteratively refines the shape parameters of a potential text candidate for enhanced detection accuracy. We also devise an effective labeling scheme and corresponding loss functions for training the text detection network on the basis of the boundary points based annotations of text provided in most datasets.
- The proposed text detection method is evaluated on several challenging benchmark datasets and achieves state-of-the-art text detection results.

2   Related Work

Generally, existing scene text detection methods can be divided into two main categories: traditional methods employing multi-stage detection pipelines, and recent methods based on end-to-end deep neural networks.

Most traditional scene text detection methods [1–3, 10, 11] first employed connected component analysis or sliding windows to extract character candidates from the image, and then classified them to either text or non-text using some classifiers and finally grouped characters into text. Due to the bottom-up stepwise detection pipelines employed, however, these methods are usually difficult to be optimized holistically to attain state-of-the-art detection performance.

Recently, with deep learning techniques being extensively employed in diverse computer vision problems, a number of scene text detectors based on various deep neural network models such as CNN and RNN have emerged, which can be roughly classified into two categories: segmentation-based and regression-based.

Segmentation-based methods localize text regions in an image by inferring the text/non-text label of every pixel using some fully convolutional networks (FCN) [12]. For example, in [13], a multiresolution FCN was proposed for text detection, which classified pixels into three categories—non-text, text border, and text to help separate adjacent text. TextSnake [5] depicted one text instance by a sequence of overlapping disks centered at symmetric axes with variable radiuses and orientations, and then an FCN-based network was used to predict score maps of text center line, text region, and geometry attributes. PSENet [6] depicted text instances with kernels of different scales and, starting from the minimal scale, gradually expanded the kernel to separate and detect adjacent text instances utilizing multi-scale segmentation maps. LOMO [7] iteratively refined detected text proposals to handle long text and introduced a shape expression module to generate more accurate representation of text for detection. CRAFT [8] first localized individual character regions by inferring both character region probability and affinity probability between adjacent characters and then linked the detected characters belonging to one word as final detection results.

Regression-based methods first employ some object detection frameworks such as Faster R-CNN [14] and SSD [15] to generate a set of region proposals, and then predict text candidates by regressing text region parameters based on the proposals. For example, TextBoxes [16] extended SSD with text-box layers, in which the anchor scales and convolution kernel shapes were modified to better adapt to the text detection task. EAST [4] and Direct Regression [17] exploited fully convolutional networks to regress candidate text boxes based on the predicted offsets from each pixel to the box boundaries. In [9], RNN was exploited to predict a pair of boundary points of one potential text region at each time step until the stop label, which allowed the method to handle text regions with arbitrary shapes and adaptive number of boundary points.

Different from most state-of-the-art segmentation-based detection models for arbitrary-shaped text [5–8,18,19], we geometrically depict and regress one text region with a parametric shape model which effectively enhances the detection performance for text with arbitrary shapes.

3   Approach

In this work, we propose a novel polynomial-based parameterized shape modeling and iterative regression scheme for arbitrary-shaped text and, on the basis of it, a robust end-to-end scene text detection network PolyPRNet.

3.1   Polynomial-Based Parameterized Shape Model of Text Region

Existing scene text detection methods usually employ one of two different schemes to model a text region—a quadrangular or polygonal boundary depicted

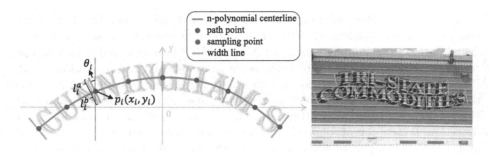

Fig. 1. Illustration of the proposed polynomial-based shape model of text region (left) and an example of text region (right) depicted by the shape model.

by discrete vertices, or a set of pixels constituting the text region in a segmentation manner. Both schemes encode only local or general (e.g.., connectedness) constraints between vertices or pixels and do not precisely capture distinctive holistic shape characteristics of text as one specific class of man-made objects.

In this work, we propose a parameterized text region modeling scheme that geometrically depicts the shape of one text with a polynomial centerline curve and a series of width cues along the centerline as shown in Fig. 1. Specifically, the n-polynomial centerline of a text region (n denoting the degree of the polynomial), which depicts the global layout and smoothness of the text, is formulated as:

$$y = a_n \times x^n + a_{n-1} \times x^{n-1} + \cdots + a_0 \tag{1}$$

where $a_n, a_{n-1}, \ldots, a_0$ are coefficients of respective polynomial terms, and x and y denote the coordinates of a point on the centerline.

Different from [20] that similarly employs a polynomial text centerline (for generating control points used to rectify text shape), as shown in Fig. 1, we further introduce a series of k *path points* located on the medial axis of the text region as the explicit constraints for the polynomial centerline—it should fit the path points as precisely as possible (as described in Sect. 3.2 and 3.5), which help attain more accurate prediction of centerline parameters.

Besides the centerline capturing the global shape characteristics of the text, we further depict the width and orientation of each local part of the text along the centerline with a series of m *width lines* as shown in Fig. 1. A width line is depicted by its intersection point p_i with the centerline, which is termed a *sampling point* with coordinates (x_i, y_i), and a pair of parameters l_i^a and l_i^b indicating its length above and below the centerline respectively and a parameter θ_i indicating its angle relative to y-axis. Unlike [20] employing a single width parameter, the two separate width parameters (l_i^a and l_i^b) allows the shape model to depict text with different-sized parts on the two sides of the centerline such as those comprising mixed upper and lower case characters and helps keep the smoothness of centerline. Moreover, the explicit depiction of the sampling points saves the computation of intersection points between the polynomial centerline and width lines to facilitate constructing a differentiable network with easier

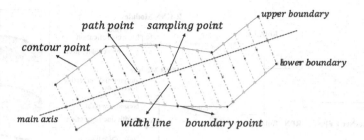

Fig. 2. Illustration of label generation for the text shape representation model.

gradient computation. The polynomial parameters $\{a_n, a_{n-1}, \ldots, a_0\}$ of the centerline and the parameters $\{x_i, y_i, l_i^a, l_i^b, \theta_i\}$ of the set of width lines together depict the geometric model of the text region.

Note the above parameterization scheme of text region applies to mainly horizontal text, for vertical ones, we exchange the roles of y and x in the scheme for effective representation of the text region. Accordingly, we employ two separate sets of shape model parameters for horizontal and vertical text respectively, which more accurately capture distinct characteristics of text in two different orientations for enhanced detection accuracy.

3.2   Label Generation

To derive training labels for the parameters of the proposed polynomial-based text shape model from the common polygonal annotations of text regions provided by most text datasets, we propose an effective labeling scheme for arbitrary snake-shaped text instances, i.e., text not forking into multiple branches.

Specifically, as shown in Fig. 2, given the polygon boundary of one text region provided by the dataset, we first divide it into four connected boundary segments: two line segments marking the head and tail positions of the text, and two polylines marking the upper and lower boundaries of the text. Next, we evenly sample a series of k *contour points* on the upper and lower boundaries of the text region respectively, which cover the total length of each boundary with equal spacing. Then, we connect every pair of two corresponding contour points on the upper and lower boundaries with a line segment denoted by $s_{i=1..k}$, and take its midpoint as one path point which is supposed to be located on the centerline of the text region. We further sample a set of m width lines from the line sequence $\{s_1, \cdots, s_k\}$, taking s_1 and s_k as the first and the last width lines respectively. We then take the midpoint (also a path point) of each width line as one sampling point and label its two endpoints as *boundary points*.

Moreover, we assign each text region a direction label represented as a 2-dim one-hot vector $\boldsymbol{d}$, which is set to horizontal ($d_0 = 1$) if the angle between the text's main axis (i.e., the line connecting the first and the last path points) and x-axis is less than $50°$, otherwise it is set to vertical ($d_1 = 1$). To accommodate text regions of varied sizes, we normalize the coordinates of all points to the

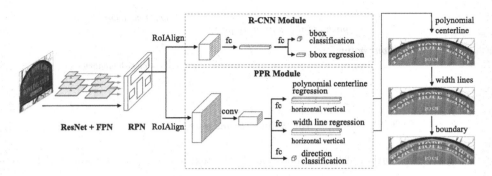

Fig. 3. Illustration of the architecture of the proposed text detection network.

range $[-0.5, 0.5]$ after generating the labels. Note that no information other than standard annotations provided by the dataset is exploited in the label generation process.

3.3   Network Architecture

We propose an end-to-end text detection network PolyPRNet on the basis of the polynomial-based text shape model, which adopts a two-stage R-CNN based framework as illustrated in Fig. 3.

In the first stage, the ResNet50 [21] and a Feature Pyramid Network (FPN) [22] with a four-level feature pyramid are employed to extract multi-level feature maps from the input image, which are then used as the shared input to subsequent network modules. Next, we employ the RPN network [14] to generate a set of text region proposals, and an RoIAlign operation [23], which evenly splits input RoI feature maps into 16×16 blocks, is applied on each proposal to generate feature maps of fixed size which preserve the proposal's exact spatial location information.

In the second stage, we employ an R-CNN module with a bounding box regression branch and a classification branch to refine the bounding box of a text region proposal generated by RPN with more accurate location information and assign it a text/non-text score. Specifically, in this work, we employ a Cascade R-CNN [24] as the R-CNN module, which comprises three stages with IoU thresholds $\{0.5, 0.55, 0.6\}$ and loss weights $\{1, 0.5, 0.25\}$ for each stage respectively.

Given the text region proposals generated by RPN, we introduce a *polynomial-based shape parameter regression (PPR)* module to infer the shape parameters and direction of a potential text candidate based on the proposed parameterized text shape model. Specifically, the feature maps of one text region proposal first undergo a 3×3 convolutional layer followed by two groups of 3×3 convolutional layers and 2×2 max-pooling layers. Finally, two full-connected layers are employed to predict the shape parameters of the candidate text region.

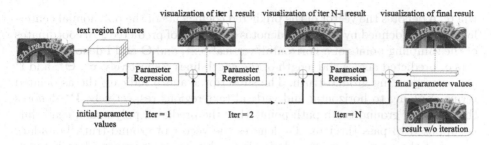

Fig. 4. Illustration of the iterative shape parameter regression pipeline. The 'Parameter Regression' block is composed of the last two full-connected layers of the PPR module for text shape parameter prediction. ⊕ denotes the addition operation. The black input to ⊕ is the shape parameter values obtained in the previous iteration, and the grey input is the predicted refinements to the parameter values. The output of ⊕ is the updated parameter values of the current iteration.

3.4 Iterative Shape Parameter Regression

To help attain optimal regression of shape parameters of a text region, we employ an iterative parameter regression pipeline as shown in Fig. 4. Specifically, with the values of shape parameters being initialized to zero, in each iteration, the parameter regression block takes the concatenation of the flattened feature maps of a text region and the vector of current shape parameter values as input, and predicts a refinement to be added to each current parameter value to generate its updated value for the next iteration. This iterative shape parameter regression process repeats until a predefined number (3 in this work) of refinement iterations is reached, which yields the final shape parameter values of the text candidate. Comparing the detection results shown in Fig. 4 with and without the iterative refinement process, the iteration mechanism effectively improves the accuracy of shape parameter regression.

3.5 Loss Functions

We define a multitask loss on each text region proposal as the sum of the loss L_{rpn} for the RPN subnetwork [14], the loss L_{rcnn} for the Cascade R-CNN subnetwork [24], and the loss L_{ppr} for the PPR module in the proposed PolyPRNet:

$$L = \lambda_1 L_{rpn} + \lambda_2 L_{rcnn} + \lambda_3 L_{ppr} \qquad (2)$$

where the weights λ_1, λ_2, and λ_3 are set to 1.0 in this work.

Specifically, the loss L_{ppr} is composed of the text region approximation loss L_{reg} and the text direction classification loss L_{dir}:

$$\begin{aligned}
L_{ppr} = &\lambda_4 I_{\mathbf{d}_0^* = 1} L_{reg}(\mathbf{a}_x, \mathbf{c}_x, \mathbf{\Theta}_x, \mathbf{l}_x, \mathbf{P}^*, \mathbf{c}_x^*, \mathbf{\Theta}_x^*, \mathbf{l}_x^*, \mathbf{T}^*) \\
&+\lambda_4 I_{\mathbf{d}_1^* = 1} L_{reg}(\mathbf{a}_y, \mathbf{c}_y, \mathbf{\Theta}_y, \mathbf{l}_y, \mathbf{P}^*, \mathbf{c}_y^*, \mathbf{\Theta}_y^*, \mathbf{l}_y^*, \mathbf{T}^*) \\
&+\lambda_5 L_{dir}(\mathbf{d}, \mathbf{d}^*)
\end{aligned} \qquad (3)$$

where, $\mathbf{a}$ denotes the vector of the predicted coefficients of the polynomial center-line function defined by Eq. (1). $\mathbf{c}$ denotes the vector of predicted x/y coordinates of the sampling points of a horizontal/vertical text, and Θ and $\mathbf{l}$ denote the vectors of predicted angles and length of the width lines respectively. $\mathbf{c}^*$, Θ^*, and $\mathbf{l}^*$ are corresponding ground-truth. The subscript x and y indicate the associated terms applying to horizontal and vertical text regions respectively. $\mathbf{P}^*$ denotes the vector of ground-truth path points that the predicted polynomial centerline is supposed to pass through. $\mathbf{T}^*$ denotes the vector of ground-truth boundary points of the text region. $L_{dir}(\mathbf{d}, \mathbf{d}^*)$ is the binary cross-entropy loss between the predicted text direction probability vector $\mathbf{d}$ and the ground-truth one-hot direction vector $\mathbf{d}^*$. I denotes the indicator function for the text direction. The balancing weights λ_4 and λ_5 are set to 5.0 and 0.5 respectively.

The text region approximation loss L_{reg} measures the approximation accuracy of the predicted text region relative to the ground-truth annotation, which is formulated as a combination of the approximation loss L_{reg}^{line} on the polynomial centerline and the approximation loss L_{reg}^{width} on the width lines:

$$L_{reg}(\mathbf{a}, \mathbf{c}, \Theta, \mathbf{l}, \mathbf{P}^*, \mathbf{c}^*, \Theta^*, \mathbf{l}^*, \mathbf{T}^*) = L_{reg}^{line}(\mathbf{a}, \mathbf{P}^*) + L_{reg}^{width}(\mathbf{a}, \mathbf{c}, \Theta, \mathbf{l}, \mathbf{c}^*, \Theta^*, \mathbf{l}^*, \mathbf{T}^*)$$
(4)

The centerline approximation loss L_{reg}^{line} measures the fitting accuracy of the predicted polynomial centerline (parameterized by $\mathbf{a}$) against the ground-truth path points $\mathbf{P}^*$, which is formulated as:

$$L_{reg}^{line}(\mathbf{a}, \mathbf{P}^*) = smooth_{L1}(sum(|f(\mathbf{a}, \mathbf{P}^*)|))$$
(5)

$$f(\mathbf{a}, \mathbf{P}^*) = \begin{bmatrix} a_n & a_{n-1} & .. & a_0 & -1 \end{bmatrix} \begin{bmatrix} u_1^n & .. & u_k^n \\ u_1^{n-1} & .. & u_k^{n-1} \\ .. & .. & .. \\ u_1^0 & .. & u_k^0 \\ v_1 & .. & v_k \end{bmatrix}$$
(6)

$$smooth_{L1}(x) = \begin{cases} 0.5x^2 & if\ |x| < 1 \\ |x| - 0.5 & otherwise \end{cases}$$
(7)

where u_i and v_i correspond to the coordinates x_i and y_i of the ith path point in $\mathbf{P}^*$ respectively if $\mathbf{d}_0^* \geq \mathbf{d}_1^*$, otherwise they correspond to y_i and x_i.

The width line approximation loss L_{reg}^{width} is formulated as:

$$L_{reg}^{width}(\mathbf{a}, \mathbf{c}, \Theta, \mathbf{l}, \mathbf{c}^*, \Theta^*, \mathbf{l}^*, \mathbf{T}^*) = smooth_{L1}(sum(|\mathbf{c} - \mathbf{c}^*|))$$
$$+ smooth_{L1}(sum(|\Theta - \Theta^*|)) + smooth_{L1}(sum(|\mathbf{l} - \mathbf{l}^*|))$$
$$+ smooth_{L1}(sum(|\mathbf{T} - \mathbf{T}^*|))$$
(8)

where $\mathbf{T}$ denotes the vector of predicted boundary points, whose coordinates are computed based on the predicted width line parameters Θ and $\mathbf{l}$ and the predicted sampling point coordinates computed based on $\mathbf{a}$ and $\mathbf{c}$.

3.6   Inference

Given an input text image, each text region proposal generated by the RPN network is first fed to the R-CNN module to obtain its accurate bounding box and classification score. Then, proposals whose scores fall below 0.7 (0.65 in multi-scale testing—see Sect. 4.4) are discarded, and non-maximum suppression [25] with IoU threshold 0.4 is applied on the proposals to obtain a set of at most 200 detection boxes with highest scores, which are fed to the PPR module for text region parameter prediction.

With the shape parameters predicted by the PPR module, we first determine the direction of the text to be the one corresponding to the greater probability in the predicted 2-dim direction vector. We then calculate the y coordinate of each sampling point on the polynomial centerline of a horizontal text region according to Eq. (1) given its predicted x coordinate—for a vertical text region, the roles of y and x are exchanged. Finally, given the predicted parameters θ_i, l_i^a, and l_i^b of a width line crossing the sampling point (x_i, y_i), we calculate the coordinates of its two endpoints and further obtain the polygonal boundary of the text region by sequentially connecting the endpoints of all width lines. Note that, for datasets adopting quadrangular annotations of text, we calculate the minimal area bounding rectangle of the predicted polygonal boundary of the text as the final detection result.

4   Experiments

4.1   Dataset

We evaluate our scene text detection method on four challenging benchmark datasets: TotalText, CTW1500, ICDAR2015, and ICDAR2017-MLT.

TotalText dataset [26] consists of 1255 and 300 images for training and testing respectively, which contain multi-oriented and curved text instances, each with a polygonal annotation comprising 10 vertices. **CTW1500** dataset [27] comprises 1000 training images and 500 testing images with a large number of challenging long curved text. Each text is annotated by a polygon with 14 vertices. **ICDAR2015** dataset [28] is composed of 1000 training images and 500 testing images, which contain accidental scene text instances with quadrangular annotations. **ICDAR2017-MLT** dataset [29] consists of 7200, 1800, and 9000 images for training, validation, and testing respectively, which contain multi-oriented, multi-scripting, and multi-lingual scene text instances with quadrangular annotations.

We adopt the standard evaluation protocol for text detection, which measures the detection performance by precision P, recall R, and f-measure F (i.e., the harmonic mean $\frac{2*P*R}{P+R}$ of P and R).

4.2   Implementation Details

We implement the proposed PolyPRNet on the basis of the PyTorch framework and conduct the experiments on one NVIDIA Tesla V100 GPU.

With the ResNet [21] backbone pre-trained on ImageNet dataset [30], we train the whole detection network end-to-end using stochastic gradient descent (SGD) with 0.0001 weight decay and 0.9 momentum and mini-batch of 10.

The training process comprises two stages: pre-training on a combined dataset and fine-tuning on each dataset. The pre-training dataset is the same as that employed in [6], which is composed of 10K images from ICDAR2015 dataset's training set and the training and validation sets of ICDAR2017-MLT dataset. We train the detection model on the pre-training dataset for 60K iterations with the learning rate starting from 0.01 and reduced to 0.001 for the last 20K iterations. In the fine-tuning stage, we train separate detection models for different test datasets using their own training sets on the basis of the pre-trained model. For curved text datasets TotalText and CTW1500, the learning rate is initialized to 0.01 for first 40K training iterations and is reduced to 0.001 for further 20K iterations. For ICDAR2015 and ICDAR2017-MLT datasets, the learning rate is set to 0.001 during 40K training iterations of the model.

We use a polynomial centerline of degree 3 and 5 width lines as default for depicting a text region, and the number of path points is set to 13 in the experiments.

4.3   Ablation Study

Effectiveness of Polynomial-Based Text Shape Modeling and Regression. We validate the effectiveness of the proposed polynomial-based text shape modeling and regression mechanism for scene text detection by comparing the performance of some variants of PolyPRNet in Table 1. Specifically, the model 'Cas. R-CNN' removes the PPR module from PolyPRNet and uses the Cascade R-CNN for text detection, which employs rectangular bounding boxes to depict text regions. The model 'Cas. R-CNN + QuadPR' employs a quadrangle to depict the text region and replaces the PPR module in PolyPRNet with a regression branch to predict the parameters of quadrangles. The model 'Cas. R-CNN + Mask' replaces the PPR module with the mask branch proposed in Mask R-CNN [23] for text candidate prediction. The model 'Cas. R-CNN + PPR' denotes the proposed PolyPRNet with the iterative shape parameter regression mechanism being removed for fair comparison with other variants in which this mechanism cannot be similarly employed.

As shown in Table 1, compared to the Cascade R-CNN backbone, introducing the PPR module significantly enhances the detection f-measure by 9–19%, which clearly demonstrates the effectiveness of the proposed text shape modeling and regression mechanism. Moreover, the proposed PPR module is more effective than the mask mechanism [23] as it effectively captures and exploits distinctive shape characteristics of text rather than low-level segmentation information. Figure 5 shows some examples of detection results by variant models in Table 1. The PPR-based detection model yields more accurate text region boundaries than other models.

To further evaluate the effectiveness of the PPR module, we combine it with the more general Faster R-CNN backbone. Compared to the detection

Table 1. Effectiveness of the proposed PPR module for enhancing text detection performance (%)

Model	TotalText			CTW1500			ICDAR2015		
	P	R	F	P	R	F	P	R	F
Cas. R-CNN	64.6	65.0	64.8	69.0	67.1	68.0	78.1	78.7	78.4
Cas. R-CNN + QuadPR	73.3	72.7	73.0	69.2	68.4	68.8	79.5	74.8	77.1
Cas. R-CNN + Mask	**86.5**	82.0	84.1	82.2	81.0	81.6	**89.4**	81.0	85.0
Cas. R-CNN + PPR	84.5	**84.7**	**84.6**	**84.2**	**82.7**	**83.4**	89.1	**86.0**	**87.5**

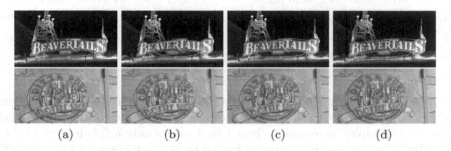

(a)   (b)   (c)   (d)

Fig. 5. Examples of detection results by variant text detection models in Table 1: (a) Cas. R-CNN, (b) Cas. R-CNN + QuadPR, (c) Cas. R-CNN + Mask, and (d) Cas. R-CNN + PPR.

f-measure 62.2%, 65.3%, and 76.7% attained by Faster R-CNN on TotalText, CTW1500, and ICDAR2015 datasets respectively, introducing the PPR module achieves again the significantly enhanced f-measure 83.5%, 82.7%, and 87.1% which reveal its effectiveness.

Influence of Degree of Polynomial. We investigate the influence of the degree of the polynomial text centerline on the detection performance in Table 2. It can be seen that, for curved text in TotalText dataset, the degree of the polynomial needs to be large enough to accommodate complex shapes of text, and the detection performance increases with the polynomial degree and reaches the peak around a degree of 5. On the other hand, for mostly straight text in ICDAR2015 dataset, as expected, different polynomial degrees do not change the detection performance much.

Influence of Number of Width Lines. We further inspect the influence of the number of width lines in the proposed text region shape model on the detection performance in Table 3. It can be seen that using more width lines to depict the text region usually yields better detection results due to the more accurate text boundary. For text instances in the experiment datasets, 5 to 9 width lines are generally sufficient for the detection task.

Table 2. Comparison of text detection performance (%) using different degrees (n) of polynomial for text region modeling

n	TotalText			ICDAR2015		
	P	R	F	P	R	F
1	82.0	82.2	82.1	89.2	85.8	87.5
2	84.1	83.5	83.8	88.4	86.0	87.1
3	84.5	84.7	84.6	89.1	86.0	87.5
4	84.6	84.7	84.7	**89.7**	85.8	**87.7**
5	84.8	**84.9**	**84.9**	88.6	**86.9**	**87.7**
6	**84.9**	84.7	84.8	89.4	85.7	87.5

Table 3. Comparison of text detection performance (%) using different numbers (m) of width lines for text region modeling

m	TotalText			ICDAR2015		
	P	R	F	P	R	F
3	83.9	83.4	83.6	88.3	86.0	87.1
5	84.5	**84.7**	84.6	89.1	86.0	87.5
7	85.1	84.1	84.6	89.1	**86.1**	87.6
9	**85.6**	84.5	**85.0**	89.9	86.0	**87.9**
11	83.9	83.6	83.8	89.4	85.7	87.5

Note that increasing the number (m) of width lines and the polynomial degree (n) has limited impact on the network's efficiency as the network size is enlarged little. For example, increasing n from 1 to 6 causes only a 0.4 drop in FPS on TotalText dataset, and increasing m from 3 to 11 results in a 0.2 drop in FPS.

Effectiveness of Iterative Shape Parameter Regression (IPR). We verify the effectiveness of the iterative shape parameter regression mechanism by comparing the detection performance with and without it in Table 4. It can be seen that, owing to the more accurate text boundaries predicted, iterative shape parameter regression effectively improves the detection results without introducing much computational overhead (e.g.. 0.2 drop in FPS on TotalText dataset compared to no IPR).

Table 4. Comparison of text detection performance (%) with and without IPR

Model	TotalText			CTW1500			ICDAR2015		
	P	R	F	P	R	F	P	R	F
w/o IPR	84.5	84.7	84.6	84.2	82.7	83.4	**89.1**	86.0	87.5
w. IPR	**86.3**	**85.0**	**85.6**	**84.3**	**83.4**	**83.8**	89.0	**86.6**	**87.8**

4.4 Comparison with State-of-the-Art Text Detection Methods

Curved Text Detection. To demonstrate the effectiveness of PolyPRNet for detecting curved text, in Table 6 and 5, we compare both the single-scale and the multi-scale (MS) performance of PolyPRNet with other state-of-the-art text detection methods on CTW1500 and TotalText datasets respectively, using the same evaluation scheme as [26]. In the single-scale testing, the shorter sides of a test image are scaled to 720, while in the multi-scale testing, they are scaled to

Table 5. Comparison of text detection performance (%) on TotalText dataset

Method	P	R	F	FPS
SegLink [31]	30.3	23.8	26.7	–
DeconvNet [26]	33.0	40.0	36.0	–
EAST [4]	50.0	36.2	42.0	–
TextSnake [5]	82.7	74.5	78.4	–
Wang et al. [9]	80.9	76.2	78.5	–
TextDragon [32]	84.5	74.2	79.0	–
PSENet-1s [6]	84.0	78.0	80.9	3.9
SPCNet [18]	83.0	82.8	82.9	–
CRAFT [8]	87.6	79.9	83.6	–
PAN [19]	89.3	81.0	85.0	39.6
PolyPRNet	86.3	**85.0**	**85.6**	13.5
LOMO MS [7]	87.6	79.3	83.3	–
PolyPRNet MS	**88.1**	**85.3**	**86.7**	3.7

Table 6. Comparison of text detection performance (%) on CTW1500 dataset

Method	P	R	F	FPS
SegLink [31]	42.3	40.0	40.8	10.7
EAST [4]	78.7	49.1	60.4	21.2
CTD+TLOC [27]	77.4	69.8	73.4	13.3
TextSnake [5]	67.9	**85.3**	75.6	1.1
Wang et al. [9]	80.1	80.2	80.1	–
TextDragon [32]	79.5	81.0	80.2	–
PSENet-1s [6]	84.8	79.7	82.2	3.9
CRAFT [8]	86.0	81.1	83.5	–
PAN [19]	**86.4**	81.2	83.7	39.8
PolyPRNet	84.3	83.7	**84.0**	14.1
LOMO MS [7]	**85.7**	76.5	80.8	–
PolyPRNet MS	85.4	**83.9**	**84.7**	3.8

$\{640, 720, 800\}$ respectively. For CTW1500 dataset, the number of width lines in the text shape model is set to 7 to correspond to the 14-vertices annotations in the dataset, and it is set to 5 for TotalText and other datasets.

On both TotalText and CTW1500 datasets, PolyPRNet surpasses all other methods on f-measure in both single-scale and multi-scale testings, which reveal the superiority of our method in detecting various curved scene text with the polynomial-based text shape model and iterative regression mechanism.

Multi-oriented Text Detection. We validate the effectiveness of PolyPRNet for detecting multi-oriented text in ICDAR2015 dataset. The shorter sides of a test image are scaled to 1320 in the single-scale testing and $\{720, 1320, 1920\}$ respectively in the multi-scale (MS) testing. As shown in Table 7, PolyPRNet achieves the highest f-measure in both single-scale and multi-scale testings in the comparison, demonstrating PolyPRNet's well capability to localize text with arbitrary orientations.

Multilingual Text Detection. We also evaluate PolyPRNet's performance on multilingual text in ICDAR2017-MLT dataset. The test images are scaled in the same way as for ICDAR2015 dataset in single-scale and multi-scale testings. As shown in Table 8, PolyPRNet yields the highest f-measure in the comparison, showing that the proposed polynomial-based text shape model effectively captures the largely varied shape characteristics of text in different languages.

Table 7. Comparison of text detection performance (%) on ICDAR2015 dataset

Method	P	R	F	FPS
MCN [33]	72.0	80.0	76.0	–
Lyu *et al.* [34]	**94.1**	70.7	80.7	3.6
TextSnake [5]	84.9	80.4	82.6	1.1
PAN [19]	84.0	81.9	82.9	26.1
TextDragon [32]	84.8	81.8	83.1	–
PixelLink [35]	85.5	82.0	83.7	7.3
PSENet-1s [6]	86.9	84.5	85.7	1.6
IncepText [36]	89.4	84.3	86.8	–
SPCNet [18]	88.7	85.8	87.2	–
Wang *et al.* [9]	89.2	86.0	87.6	–
PolyPRNet	89.0	**86.6**	**87.8**	7.4
RRD MS [37]	88.0	80.0	83.8	–
Lyu *et al.* MS [34]	89.5	79.7	84.3	–
LOMO MS [7]	87.6	**87.8**	87.7	–
PolyPRNet MS	**91.5**	86.1	**88.7**	1.5

Table 8. Comparison of text detection performance (%) on ICDAR2017-MLT dataset

Method	P	R	F	FPS
E2E-MLT [38]	64.6	53.8	58.7	–
He *et al.* [17]	76.7	57.9	66.0	–
Lyu *et al.* [34]	**83.8**	56.6	66.8	–
AF-RPN [39]	75.0	66.0	70.0	–
SPCNet [18]	73.4	66.9	70.0	–
PSENet [6]	73.8	**68.2**	70.9	–
PolyPRNet	81.2	66.8	**73.3**	7.4
Lyu *et al.* MS [34]	74.3	**70.6**	72.4	–
LOMO MS [7]	80.2	67.2	73.1	–
SPCNet MS [18]	80.6	68.6	74.1	–
PolyPRNet MS	**82.9**	69.3	**75.5**	1.5

Fig. 6. Examples of text detection results of our method.

4.5 Qualitative Results

Figure 6 shows some text detection results of our method. Notice the curved text in the images, regardless of their variant styles and tight spacing, are accurately localized. The results demonstrate our method's capability of robustly detecting text with varied shapes, orientations, sizes, and languages.

5 Conclusions

We present a robust scene text detection method with a polynomial-based parameterized shape modeling and regression scheme for arbitrary-shaped text, which effectively captures the shape characteristics of text and significantly enhances the performance of the R-CNN based detection backbone. The state-of-the-art text detection results our method obtains on standard benchmarks demonstrate its effectiveness.

Acknowledgments. The research was supported by the Natural Science Foundation of Jiangsu Province of China under Grant No. BK20171345 and the National Natural Science Foundation of China under Grant Nos. 61003113, 61321491, and 61672273.

References

1. Epshtein, B., Ofek, E., Wexler, Y.: Detecting text in natural scenes with stroke width transform. In: CVPR, pp. 2963–2970 (2010)
2. Yin, X., Yin, X., Huang, K., Hao, H.: Robust text detection in natural scene images. IEEE Trans. Pattern Anal. Mach. Intell. **36**, 970–983 (2014)
3. Tian, S., Pan, Y., Huang, C., Lu, S., Yu, K., Tan, C.L.: Text flow: a unified text detection system in natural scene images. In: ICCV, pp. 4651–4659 (2015)
4. Zhou, X., et al.: EAST: an efficient and accurate scene text detector. In: CVPR, pp. 2642–2651 (2017)
5. Long, S., Ruan, J., Zhang, W., He, X., Wu, W., Yao, C.: TextSnake: a flexible representation for detecting text of arbitrary shapes. In: Ferrari, V., Hebert, M., Sminchisescu, C., Weiss, Y. (eds.) ECCV 2018. LNCS, vol. 11206, pp. 19–35. Springer, Cham (2018). https://doi.org/10.1007/978-3-030-01216-8_2
6. Wang, W., et al.: Shape robust text detection with progressive scale expansion network. In: CVPR, pp. 9336–9345 (2019)
7. Zhang, C., et al.: Look more than once: an accurate detector for text of arbitrary shapes. In: CVPR, pp. 10544–10553 (2019)
8. Baek, Y., Lee, B., Han, D., Yun, S., Lee, H.: Character region awareness for text detection. In: CVPR, pp. 9365–9374 (2019)
9. Wang, X., Jiang, Y., Luo, Z., Liu, C., Choi, H., Kim, S.: Arbitrary shape scene text detection with adaptive text region representation. In: CVPR, pp. 6449–6458 (2019)
10. Sun, L., Huo, Q., Jia, W., Chen, K.: A robust approach for text detection from natural scene images. Pattern Recogn. **48**, 2906–2920 (2015)
11. Zhang, Z., Shen, W., Yao, C., Bai, X.: Symmetry-based text line detection in natural scenes. In: CVPR, pp. 2558–2567 (2015)
12. Long, J., Shelhamer, E., Darrell, T.: Fully convolutional networks for semantic segmentation. In: CVPR, pp. 3431–3440 (2015)
13. Wu, Y., Natarajan, P.: Self-organized text detection with minimal post-processing via border learning. In: ICCV, pp. 5010–5019 (2017)
14. Ren, S., He, K., Girshick, R.B., Sun, J.: Faster R-CNN: towards real-time object detection with region proposal networks. In: NIPS, pp. 91–99 (2015)
15. Liu, W., et al.: SSD: single shot multibox detector. In: Leibe, B., Matas, J., Sebe, N., Welling, M. (eds.) ECCV 2016. LNCS, vol. 9905, pp. 21–37. Springer, Cham (2016). https://doi.org/10.1007/978-3-319-46448-0_2
16. Liao, M., Shi, B., Bai, X., Wang, X., Liu, W.: TextBoxes: a fast text detector with a single deep neural network. In: AAAI, pp. 4161–4167 (2017)
17. He, W., Zhang, X., Yin, F., Liu, C.: Multi-oriented and multi-lingual scene text detection with direct regression. IEEE Trans. Image Process. **27**, 5406–5419 (2018)

18. Xie, E., Zang, Y., Shao, S., Yu, G., Yao, C., Li, G.: Scene text detection with supervised pyramid context network. In: AAAI, pp. 9038–9045 (2019)
19. Wang, W., et al.: Efficient and accurate arbitrary-shaped text detection with pixel aggregation network. In: ICCV, pp. 8439–8448 (2019)
20. Zhan, F., Lu, S.: ESIR: end-to-end scene text recognition via iterative image rectification. In: CVPR, pp. 2054–2063 (2019)
21. He, K., Zhang, X., Ren, S., Sun, J.: Deep residual learning for image recognition. In: CVPR, pp. 770–778 (2016)
22. Lin, T., Dollár, P., Girshick, R.B., He, K., Hariharan, B., Belongie, S.J.: Feature pyramid networks for object detection. In: CVPR, pp. 936–944 (2017)
23. He, K., Gkioxari, G., Dollár, P., Girshick, R.B.: Mask R-CNN. In: ICCV, pp. 2980–2988 (2017)
24. Cai, Z., Vasconcelos, N.: Cascade R-CNN: delving into high quality object detection. In: CVPR, pp. 6154–6162 (2018)
25. Girshick, R.B., Iandola, F.N., Darrell, T., Malik, J.: Deformable part models are convolutional neural networks. In: CVPR, pp. 437–446 (2015)
26. Chng, C.K., Chan, C.S.: Total-text: a comprehensive dataset for scene text detection and recognition. In: ICDAR, pp. 935–942 (2017)
27. Liu, Y., Jin, L., Zhang, S., Zhang, S.: Detecting curve text in the wild: new dataset and new solution. CoRR abs/1712.02170 (2017)
28. Karatzas, D., et al.: ICDAR 2015 competition on robust reading. In: ICDAR, pp. 1156–1160 (2015)
29. Nayef, N., et al.: ICDAR2017 robust reading challenge on multi-lingual scene text detection and script identification - RRC-MLT. In: ICDAR, pp. 1454–1459 (2017)
30. Krizhevsky, A., Sutskever, I., Hinton, G.E.: ImageNet classification with deep convolutional neural networks. In: NeurIPS, pp. 1106–1114 (2012)
31. Shi, B., Bai, X., Belongie, S.J.: Detecting oriented text in natural images by linking segments. In: CVPR, pp. 3482–3490 (2017)
32. Feng, W., He, W., Yin, F., Zhang, X., Liu, C.: TextDragon: an end-to-end framework for arbitrary shaped text spotting. In: ICCV, pp. 9075–9084 (2019)
33. Liu, Z., Lin, G., Yang, S., Feng, J., Lin, W., Goh, W.L.: Learning Markov clustering networks for scene text detection. In: CVPR, pp. 6936–6944 (2018)
34. Lyu, P., Yao, C., Wu, W., Yan, S., Bai, X.: Multi-oriented scene text detection via corner localization and region segmentation. In: CVPR, pp. 7553–7563 (2018)
35. Deng, D., Liu, H., Li, X., Cai, D.: PixelLink: detecting scene text via instance segmentation. In: AAAI, pp. 6773–6780 (2018)
36. Yang, Q., Cheng, M., Zhou, W., Chen, Y., Qiu, M., Lin, W.: IncepText: a new inception-text module with deformable PSROI pooling for multi-oriented scene text detection. In: IJCAI, pp. 1071–1077 (2018)
37. Liao, M., Zhu, Z., Shi, B., Xia, G.s., Bai, X.: Rotation-sensitive regression for oriented scene text detection. In: CVPR, pp. 5909–5918 (2018)
38. Bušta, M., Patel, Y., Matas, J.: E2E-MLT - an unconstrained end-to-end method for multi-language scene text. In: Carneiro, G., You, S. (eds.) ACCV 2018. LNCS, vol. 11367, pp. 127–143. Springer, Cham (2019). https://doi.org/10.1007/978-3-030-21074-8_11
39. Zhong, Z., Sun, L., Huo, Q.: An anchor-free region proposal network for Faster R-CNN-based text detection approaches. Int. J. Doc. Anal. Recogn. (IJDAR) **22**(3), 315–327 (2019). https://doi.org/10.1007/s10032-019-00335-y

Adaptive Spotting: Deep Reinforcement Object Search in 3D Point Clouds

Onkar Krishna$^{(\boxtimes)}$, Go Irie, Xiaomeng Wu, Takahito Kawanishi,
and Kunio Kashino

NTT Communication Science Laboratories, NTT Corporation, Atsugi City, Japan
{krishna.onkar.ru,xiaomeng.wu.px}@hco.ntt.co.jp, goirie@ieee.org

Abstract. In this paper, we study the task of searching for a query object of unknown position and pose in a scene, both given in the form of 3D point cloud data. A straightforward approach that exhaustively scans the scene is often prohibitive due to computational inefficiencies. High-quality feature representation also needs to be learned to achieve accurate recognition and localization. Aiming to address these two fundamental problems in a unified framework, we propose Adaptive Spotting, a deep reinforcement learning approach that jointly learns both the features and the efficient search path. Our network is designed to directly take raw point cloud data of the query object and the search bounding box and to sequentially determine the next pose to be searched. This network is successfully trained in an end-to-end manner by integrating a contrastive loss and a reinforcement localization reward. Evaluations on ModelNet40 and Stanford 2D-3D-S datasets demonstrate the superiority of the proposed approach over several state-of-the-art baselines.

1 Introduction

Objects in the real world are three-dimensional (3D). Understanding their appearances and semantics naturally requires 3D information processing. The external surfaces of 3D objects can be captured as point clouds, which have become easily acquirable with the proliferation of modern range sensors such as LiDAR and RGBD cameras, and with the improvement of SLAM and SfM accuracy. While such data have been used mainly for environment modeling towards robot control or autonomous driving purposes, the recent development of deep neural networks such as PointNet [1], which can directly handle 3D point cloud data, has opened new research avenues including point cloud-based classification/segmentation [1–3], detection [4–8], and retrieval [9,10].

In this paper, we consider the problem of point cloud-based object search. The task is to find a query object from a scene (reference map), both given in the form of 3D point cloud data; for example, we may want to find a chair specified by a user from an office room. It is different from the popular point cloud-based object recognition tasks mentioned earlier. In object classification, detection, and segmentation, the object classes to be classified/detected are known in advance,

© Springer Nature Switzerland AG 2021
H. Ishikawa et al. (Eds.): ACCV 2020, LNCS 12624, pp. 257–272, 2021.
https://doi.org/10.1007/978-3-030-69535-4_16

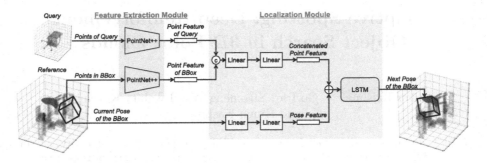

Fig. 1. Overview of our proposed network. Our model has two major modules: a feature extraction module and a localization module. Taking a query object and a current search bounding box in the reference map, the network sequentially determines the pose of the next bounding box. ⓒ and ⊕ indicate concatenation and element-wise addition, respectively.

while in our task the object to search is specified online as a query. The task most relevant to ours is object retrieval, where the common idea is to follow the successful approaches in 2D image retrieval. For example, the previous works [1, 9–11] use deep neural networks to represent each point cloud as a global feature, with which a query object is compared with multiple database objects. While the goal of object retrieval is to search a database, our task aims at finding a point cloud (query) that exists in a much larger point cloud (reference map) with unknown position and pose. One straightforward solution is to adapt existing object retrieval methods to our problem in a "sliding-window" manner, i.e., scanning the whole reference map using a small 3D bounding box with varying scale and orientation. However, this solution has to deal with a huge search space for accurate localization of the target object, making the overall search process fairly inefficient.

In this paper, we propose Adaptive Spotting, a point cloud search approach that significantly reduces the search space with greater matching accuracy. The idea is to learn efficient search path from data, i.e., using machine learning to pick and compare only highly prospective regions in the 3D reference map with a given query. Specifically, a recurrent neural network is employed to predict a sequence of 3D poses, each spotting a candidate 3D bounding box in the reference map and being expected to match with the query. The network is trained through reinforcement learning in an exploratory manner. No explicit supervision such as the 3D location of the target object or its class label is needed. In addition to the search path, our approach jointly learns point cloud feature representation in a unified framework, which provides a sharp insight into the similarity between the predicted target object and the query. To this end, we propose a novel loss configuration that integrates the feature contrastive loss with the reinforcement localization rewards. This configuration enables our model to learn more discriminative feature representation than traditional retrieval methods. We evaluate our approach on ModelNet40 and Stanford 2D-3D-S and show that it produces remarkable accuracy improvement with a greatly reduced number of matching processes and a much shorter run time.

2   Related Work

We briefly review two relevant areas to this paper: deep feature representation techniques for point cloud data and point cloud-based object retrieval and search.

Deep Feature Representation for Point Cloud Data. While the feature representation of point clouds has long relied on handcrafted features, the recent success of CNNs in 2D image representation has led to researches on deep point cloud representation.

Unlike 2D images, regular convolution kernels cannot be applied to unstructured 3D point cloud data. Hence, early attempts rasterized the point cloud into dense and regular voxel grids to make use of 3D volumetric convolutions. Two pioneers are VoxNet [12] and 3D ShapeNet [13], which integrate volumetric occupancy grid representations with supervised 3D CNNs for point cloud representation learning. Following these two studies, many methods have been proposed to handle the sparsity problem of raw point clouds [14–17]. Another direction of deep point cloud representation is to project the set of 3D points onto 2D planes so that standard 2D CNNs can be applied directly [18–20]. For example, MultiView CNN [18,19] tried to learn features using CNN in an end-to-end trainable fashion through multiple 2D projections of a 3D point cloud. This line of studies has achieved dominating performance on shape classification and retrieval tasks as reported in the competitions of the large scale 3D SHape REtrieval Contest (SHREC) [21]. However, it is nontrivial to extend them to our object search task or other 3D tasks such as point classification and shape completion.

More recently, a special type of neural network has been proposed that can be directly applied to raw point cloud data [1,2,22]. PointNet [1] is the pioneering network that directly processes point sets and uses a symmetric function to make the feature representation invariant to the order permutation of the input points. PointNet++ [2] is the extended version of PointNet and introduces a hierarchical architecture to exploit the local structures of the point set at multiple scales. Several other extensions have also been made to more effectively capture local to global shape characteristics of the input point cloud data [23–25]. In addition to these, several studies have been proposed that leverage the graph convolutional networks (GCNs) [26–28] for the point cloud convolution, given that the point cloud data can be readily modeled as a graph. Some studies such as [29] also introduced customized layers to capture the distribution of 3D points in a latent space.

In this study, we integrate PointNet++ [2] into our deep recurrent framework as a feature extraction module. The network is effectively trained in a fully end-to-end manner through our exploratory reinforcement learning and contrastive feature learning process.

Point Cloud-Based Object Retrieval and Search. The common approach to point cloud-based object retrieval is the same as in the case of 2D images: it represents each point cloud by a feature vector and searches by feature matching. Traditional studies rely on handcrafted features to describe the shape of the point cloud data (often in the normal direction). A typical example is to use local 3D descriptors such as [30–32] to identify objects that match the query. Such methods often require dense and accurate point cloud data, and the signal-to-noise ratio of the target object needs to be small.

In response to the recent growth of deep point cloud representation, several studies have worked on point cloud object retrieval based on deep features. An early attempt [9] used a PointNet pre-trained for object recognition [1] to extract deep features for 3D shape retrieval. PointNetVLAD [10] adapted the NetVLAD architecture [33], which was originally designed for 2D image retrieval, by replacing the conventional 2D CNN with PointNet. Its performance was evaluated in a point cloud-based place recognition task that aims to identify the urban block corresponding to a given query from a database of pre-segmented urban blocks. PCAN [11] is an extension of PointNetVLAD that involves 3D attention map to exploit higher-level contextual information, and is also proposed for the same place recognition task.

Unfortunately, these techniques cannot be directly applied to the problem we are considering in this work. Our object search task is to accurately localize an object in a reference map with unknown position and pose, whereas the techniques described above do not take into account this localization requirement. Of course, it is possible to leverage these techniques for feature extraction and search for the object based on a sliding window (i.e., a 3D bounding box in the reference map). However, such an exhaustive strategy is often prohibitively time-consuming. By association, it is not easy to find an optimal quantization level for the position and size (scale) of the bounding box, such that sufficient accuracy and small search space can be guaranteed simultaneously. Another potentially related field is robotics, where object search has long been explored [34,35]. However, most of the approaches are based on handcrafted features and heuristics.

Unlike the previous studies described above, our approach can predict the position and pose of the target object directly from the raw point cloud of the query and reference map. The conceptual idea of this study is somewhat similar to [36] and [37], where, however, only 2D images are taken into consideration. To the best of our knowledge, this is the first work that proposes an end-to-end reinforcement learning approach to object search on raw 3D point cloud data.

3   Adaptive Spotting

Given a pair of a query (target) object Q and a reference map R both represented as point clouds, our task is to find the correct pose of the target object in R that matches Q.

Following previous studies for 3D object detection [4,38], we represent the pose of the target object by a set of seven parameters, which are three for the translation, three for the scaling, and one for the rotation (yaw) relative to Q. This parameter set (or pose) is denoted by A_g. Given A_g, a 4×4 affine transformation matrix can be constructed, which represents the 3D mapping from Q to the target object in $\mathcal{R}$. We can bridge the geometric variation between the query and the target by applying the inverse of the above affine transformation to $\mathcal{R}$. Consequently, the points in the 3D bounding box, whose center is the origin and whose size is equal to the query, becomes the rectified target object and should match Q without viewpoint variation.

Given an arbitrary pose A, we use $\mathcal{R}(A)$ to denote the point cloud rectified from $\mathcal{R}$ according to A. For example, $\mathcal{R}(A_g)$ indicates the rectified target object. Our task is thus to find an affine matrix A such that $\mathcal{R}(A)$ matches Q.

3.1   Overview

Different from the naïve solution that exhaustively scans $\mathcal{R}$, we approach to this problem by sequential search. Specifically, we aim at determining a sequence of poses $\{A_t\}_{t=0}^{T}$ such that the search process can correctly reach A_g within T steps. Here, t is the time step and T is the length of the sequence.

We propose a deep reinforcement learning approach with a neural network that embraces PointNet++ [2] and LSTM in a unified framework. The schematic overview of our network is illustrated in Fig. 1. Our network consists of two major modules called *feature extraction module* and *localization module*, respectively. In the test stage, the behaviors of our network at each time step t can be summarized as follows.

1. The feature extraction module extracts point features from Q and $\mathcal{R}(A_t)$, which are denoted by $f(Q)$ and $f(\mathcal{R}(A_t))$, respectively. Here, $\mathcal{R}(A_t)$ indicates the predicted target object that has been rectified according to A_t.
2. The localization module receives the two sets of point features $f(Q)$ and $f(\mathcal{R}(A_t))$ as well as the current pose A_t to determine the next pose A_{t+1}.

These two sub-processes are repeated sequentially until the maximum number of time steps T is reached. The detail of the two modules is given in Sect. 3.2.

Consider a realistic training scenario, where a trainer asks an autonomous agent to find an object in an unknown place, i.e., the ground truth pose A_g is unavailable. In this case, the only thing the trainer can do for training is to tell the agent whether the object localized by the agent is the target or not. Since the localization is achieved in a sequential manner, the decision made at the current time step relies on all the past decisions, and the quality of the current decision cannot be evaluated independently from the past ones. Therefore, typical supervised learning methods that assume i.i.d. samples cannot be applied to our scenario. Fortunately, the problem can be modeled as a Partially Observable Markov Decision Process (POMDP), which can be handled by reinforcement learning. We thus propose using a reinforcement learning algorithm that requires neither the explicit supervision nor the i.i.d. assumption. We give the detail of our training algorithm in Sect. 3.3.

Our idea is inspired by the Recurrent Attention Models (RAMs) primarily designed for image recognition [39–41]. In this study, we introduce this mechanism into point cloud-based object search by incorporating it with feature embedding of unstructured 3D data, leading to the simultaneous end-to-end learning of point features and efficient search paths.

3.2   Details of Modules

This section gives the details of the feature extraction module and the localization module one by one. Hereafter, we simply use the term "BBox" to indicate the 3D bounding box that covers the predicted target object in the space of $\mathcal{R}$ but has not been rectified according to A_t.

Feature Extraction Module. This module extracts point features $f(\mathcal{Q})$ and $f(\mathcal{R}(A_t))$ from $\mathcal{Q}$ and $\mathcal{R}(A_t)$. Given a BBox that touches the true target object but does not fully overlap, the network is expected to move the BBox closer to the target at succeeding time steps. To make it possible, the network must know, e.g.., in which direction/angle the BBox is offset from the target, and such information must be acquirable from $f(\mathcal{Q})$ and $f(\mathcal{R}(A_t))$. Therefore, the point feature needs to be affine-variant: $f(\mathcal{R}(A_t))$ must change as the pose of $\mathcal{R}(A_t)$ changes.

In this study, we adopt PointNet++ [2] for this purpose but any deep, affine-variant feature extractor can be used here. Our feature extraction module consists of two identical PointNet++ networks with shared parameters; one for the query $\mathcal{Q}$ and the other for $\mathcal{R}(A_t)$. PointNet++ has a hierarchical architecture and alternately clusters and aggregates local points to extract a global feature vector that captures both global and local structures of the point cloud. This approach draws an analogy to convolution and pooling layers in standard CNNs. Specifically, we employ a three-level hierarchical architecture with 1024, 256, and 128 clusters, respectively. The final embedding is obtained by applying two fully connected (FC) layers with output dimensions of 512 and 64, respectively. The extracted features $f(\mathcal{Q})$ and $f(\mathcal{R}(A_t))$ are both fed to the subsequent localization module to determine the pose of the next BBox.

Localization Module. The main component of the localization module is an LSTM that sequentially predicts the pose A_{t+1} of the next BBox from three external inputs, namely $f(\mathcal{Q})$, $f(\mathcal{R}(A_t))$, and the current pose A_t.

We first concatenate $f(\mathcal{Q})$ and $f(\mathcal{R}(A_t))$ and employ two FC layers to generate a single 128D point feature vector. This feature reflects the appearance of $\mathcal{Q}$ and $\mathcal{R}(A_t)$ as well as the *relative* spatial relationship between the two point clouds. Meanwhile, A_t is encoded, by two FC layers of output dimensions 64 and 128, into a 128D pose feature vector. This feature represents the *absolute* spatial pose of the current BBox. The point and pose features are summed and then fed to the LSTM, as shown in Fig. 1.

The LSTM outputs the next 128D hidden state h_{t+1} to which a linear projection is applied to obtain the expected value $\hat{A}_{t+1}$ of the seven pose parameters.

That is, we assume that A_{t+1} is a stochastic variable and follows a Gaussian distribution whose mean is given by $\hat{A}_{t+1}$. Once $\hat{A}_{t+1}$ is predicted, A_{t+1} is obtained as a sample drawn from the distribution $\mathcal{N}(\hat{A}_{t+1}, \lambda I)$, where I is the identity matrix and λ is a hyperparmeter controlling the standard deviation.

For initialization, the first pose A_0 is determined randomly. If at any time $\mathcal{R}(A_t)$ contains no points, we take the center point, i.e., $(0,0,0)$, as $\mathcal{R}(A_t)$ and feed it to PointNet++ to inform the network about the lack of objectness.

3.3 Model Training

Let $\Theta = \{\theta_f, \theta_l\}$ be the parameters of the whole network, where θ_f and θ_l correspond to feature extraction and localization modules, respectively. Reinforcement learning is used to tune Θ. For simplicity, we use $s_{t-1} = \{\{P_\tau\}_{\tau=1}^{t-1}, \mathcal{Q}, \mathcal{R}\}$ to denote the set containing all the past predicted poses as well as the query and the reference. The policy of the reinforcement learning can then be represented as a conditional distribution $\pi(A_t|s_{t-1}; \Theta)$. Our goal is to maximize the total reward $R = \sum_{t=1}^{T} r_t$ w.r.t. Θ, where r_t is the reward value, typically one or zero, at time t (The definition of r_t is given in Sect. 4.2). The expected value of the total reward is then

$$J(\Theta) = \mathbb{E}_{p(s_T;\Theta)}[R], \tag{1}$$

where $p(s_T; \Theta)$ is the probabilistic distribution of s_T, which depends on the policy. Although the gradient w.r.t. Θ is non-trivial, it can be approximately computed by sampling the sequence $\{A_t, s_{t-1}\}_{t=1}^{T}$ from the policy in a similar way to Monte-Carlo approximation, which gives

$$\nabla_\Theta J(\Theta) \approx \frac{1}{M} \sum_{i=1}^{M} \sum_{t=1}^{T} \nabla_\Theta \log \pi(A_t^i|s_{t-1}^i; \Theta) R^i. \tag{2}$$

Here, M is the number of sampled sequences. With this equation, Θ can be iteratively updated through gradient ascent.

Training our model only with reinforcement learning often makes the learning process unstable. Hence, we involve another loss function suitable for the object search task to improve the stability. Specifically, we require the two point cloud features extracted by the feature extraction module to correctly reflect the similarity between $\mathcal{Q}$ and $\mathcal{R}(A_t)$, i.e., the distance between the two features should be small for matching pairs and large for non-matching pairs. To this end, we impose a loss function, which resembles contrastive loss, on the feature extraction module.

$$L(\theta_f) = \sum_{t=1}^{T} r_t d^2 + (1 - r_t) \max\{0, m - d\}^2, \tag{3}$$

where $d = \|f(\mathcal{Q}) - f(\mathcal{R}(A_t))\|$ and m is the margin of the hinge loss. Unlike the standard contrastive loss, Eq. 3 exploits the reward r_t to determine the loss value. It is piecewise differentiable, and so can be easily optimized with gradient descent.

4 Experiments

4.1 Datasets

We used two benchmark datasets, ModelNet40[1] [13] and Stanford 2D-3D-S[2] [42], to evaluate the performance of our approach. Examples of the query/reference pairs are shown in Fig. 2.

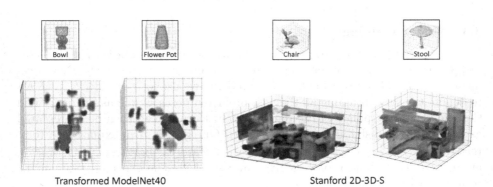

Fig. 2. Examples of our datasets. Pairs of query (top) and reference (bottom) are visualized. The examples of Stanford-2D-3D-S are textured for visualization purpose only. In our experiments, we use texture-less 3D points.

Transformed ModelNet40. ModelNet40 consists of 40 object classes with varying numbers (from 64 to 889) of clean CAD instances per class, each having the size $2 \times 2 \times 2$ and $1,024$ points. The total number of objects is $12,311$. We used this dataset to analyze the performance of our approach under the controlled setup. The dataset was originally created for object recognition and shape completion [13] and cannot be directly used for object search evaluation. Hence, we conducted the following processing to generate query/reference pairs from the original dataset.

Given an object of size $2 \times 2 \times 2$, we randomly sample a set A_g of seven pose parameters from the ranges of $[-1, 1]$ for 3D translation, $[0.8, 1.0]$ for 3D scaling, and $[0, 360)$ for 1D rotation, and transform the object to a new reference space (reference map). The reference map is no larger than $4 \times 4 \times 4$. 10 patches, each having 128 points, are randomly extracted from objects of other categories and added to the reference map as distractors. The reference map thus has $2,304$ points. The object described above is then regarded as the query and combined with the reference to form a query/reference pair.

This processing was applied to all the objects in the dataset, leading to $12,311$ query/reference pairs. We followed the practice of [43] for obtaining the training and testing sets, each consisting of $9,843$ and $2,468$ pairs, respectively.

---

[1] https://modelnet.cs.princeton.edu/.

[2] http://buildingparser.stanford.edu/dataset.html.

Stanford 2D-3D-S. To evaluate our approach in more realistic scenes, we made use of the Stanford 2D-3D-S dataset to create query/reference pairs. The Stanford 2D-3D-S dataset consists of 247 different halls originating from 6 large-scale indoor areas that cover $6,000$ m^2 in total. Instance-level annotations are provided for 13 object classes including structural elements (ceiling, floor, wall, beam, column, window, and door) and movable elements (table, chair, sofa, bookcase, board and clutter).

To generate query/reference pairs, we split each giant hall into $7^3 = 343$ regular partitions. Each partition is regarded as a reference map if it contains at least one object for which 70% of its points are inside the partition. All the movable elements, whose volumes are no less than $1/10$ of the reference map, are taken as queries.

We selected one out of the six indoor areas and used all the query/reference pairs derived from it for testing. All the other pairs were used for training. The resulting training set consists of $2,919$ queries and $1,504$ references, while the test set consists of 312 queries and 285 references. For this dataset, a search is determined to be successful if the approach finds an object that has the same class as the query.

4.2   Experimental Setup

Performance Metrics. We evaluated our approach in terms of success rate and search time. Given a query/reference pair, our approach predicts a sequence of T poses over the reference map, which are used to evaluate the success rate. With each pose, we can easily identify the corners of the predicted BBox. A point cloud search is considered as being successful if the 3D IoU [38] between the ground truth BBox and the predicted BBox is greater than a certain threshold. The success rate is defined as the ratio of the number of the query/reference pairs, where the search is successful, over the total number of tested pairs. The search time (in seconds) is the time required for predicting the T poses for each query/reference pair.

Baselines. To the best of our knowledge, there is no existing techniques that predict a sequence of 3D poses over a reference map to search for a 3D point cloud object. In this study, we compared our approach with state-of-the-art models developed for 3D object retrieval and classification, namely PointNet [1], PointNet++ [2], and PointNetVlad [10], which were adapted to out task in a "sliding window" manner. For each baseline, we slide a 3D BBox of three different scales over all three dimensions of the reference map with a certain sampling rate. For example, we have $2^3 \times 3 = 24$ BBoxes if the sampling rate is two and $7^3 \times 3 = 1,029$ BBoxes if the rate is seven. We then use baseline models to extract point features from the sampled BBoxes, and compare them with the query to find the best match. All the baselines were trained using ModelNet40 and Stanford 2D-3D-S datasets, separately. Their network configurations are the same as those reported in the original papers.

Learning Configurations. We trained the proposed network from scratch. We used Adam with a batch size of five for Transformed Modelnet40 and one for Stanford 2D-3D-S. The learning rate was kept in the range $[10^{-4}, 10^{-3}]$ with exponential decay. The hyperparameter λ in Sect. 3.2 (Localization Module), which is used for sampling out the next pose with the predicted expected value, is fixed to 0.22. We evaluate our approach by varying the maximum number of time steps T, which is sometimes referred to as "No. of BBoxes". The reward r_t in our implementation is determined based on the success (one) or failure (zero) of the search at time t. The search is considered as being successful if the 3D IoU [38] between the ground truth BBox and the predicted BBoxes at time t is greater than a threshold. Note that this simulator is the same as the scheme used to calculate the success rate during evaluation.

In the following sections, we first report the quantitative performance of our approach evaluated in terms of success rate and search time (in seconds). We performed extensive evaluation of our network by varying different parameters to understand their impact over search performance. These parameters include number of BBoxes, IoU threshold, and output dimensionality of the feature extraction module (PointNet++). Finally, we show qualitative results to demonstrate the effectiveness of our network in learning the search path.

Table 1. Results on Transformed ModelNet40. Values in the table are success rates along with the parenthesized average time (in seconds) required to process one query-reference pair. Results were obtained with the IoU threshold being 0.5 when a 64D PointNet++ feature vector was used.

No. of BBoxes	24	81	192	375	648	1029
PointNet++	0.12 (0.54)	0.16 (1.88)	0.16 (4.50)	0.26 (8.82)	0.28 (15.25)	− (36.70)
PointNet	0.13 (0.19)	0.24 (0.62)	0.31 (1.44)	0.29 (2.83)	0.30 (4.84)	0.32 (7.57)
PointNetVLAD	0.13 (1.05)	0.33 (3.55)	0.47 (8.35)	0.50 (16.69)	0.50 (28.94)	0.53 (45.67)
No. of BBoxes	4	6	8	10	12	24
Ours	0.44 (0.13)	0.52 (0.18)	0.57 (0.24)	0.65 (0.39)	0.68 (0.45)	0.74 (0.49)

4.3   Accuracy vs Number of BBoxes

Results on Transformed ModelNet40. Table 1 shows the performance of our network obtained by varying the number of BBoxes from 4 to 24 on the Transformed ModelNet40 dataset. Because the baselines could not achieve satisfactory success rates with such a small number of BBoxes, we show their performance obtained when varying the parameter in the range of 24 to 1,029. The procedure of BBox sampling for baseline methods has been described in Sect. 4.2.

Table 1 shows that the success rate increases as the number of search BBoxes increases for both our approach and the baselines. Our approach clearly outperformed all the baselines with a huge margin by processing only a very small number of BBoxes. For instance, with 24 BBoxes the success rate of our approach reached 0.74, while those of the baselines were less than 0.15. The baseline methods could not achieve the same level of accuracy as ours, even with over 1,000 search BBoxes. Moreover, our approach required much shorter search time than PointNet++ and PointNetVLAD. PointNet was the fastest among all the compared approaches because of its much simpler network architecture. Using the same network architecture, our approach achieved a huge gain in success rate (approximately six times) compared to PointNet++ without increasing the run time.

Table 2. Results on Stanford 2D-3D-S. Values in the table are success rates along with the parenthesized average time (in seconds) required to process one query-reference pair. Results were obtained with the IoU threshold being 0.4 when a 64D PointNet++ feature vector was used.

No. of BBoxes	81	192	375	648	1029
PointNet++	0.20 (1.38)	0.16 (3.30)	0.22 (6.55)	0.26 (11.40)	0.32 (18.15)
PointNet	0.14 (0.52)	0.14 (1.20)	0.12 (2.39)	0.12 (4.07)	0.18 (6.44)
PointNetVLAD	0.12 (3.16)	0.16 (7.53)	0.26 (14.67)	0.26 (25.47)	0.34 (40.95)
No. of BBoxes	55	65	75	85	95
Ours	0.29 (1.17)	0.33 (1.37)	0.35 (1.59)	0.35 (1.80)	0.42 (2.01)

Results on Stanford 2D-3D-S. Results on Stanford 2D-3D-S dataset are shown in Table 2. This dataset is more challenging than ModelNet40, because it contains meaningful and much larger scale of distractors (i.e., realistic objects whose classes are different from the query), as shown in Fig. 2. Our approach is more likely to be "trapped" by the distractors.

The performances for varying the number of BBoxes are shown in Table 2. Due to the larger size of the reference map and realistic distractive noises, we use the larger number of BBoxes in the range of 55 to 95 for this dataset than Transformed ModelNet40. Our approach achieved a much better balance between success rate and search time than the baseline methods. For example, our approach achieved a success rate of 0.42 with 2.01 seconds in average, while the success rates of the baselines were no higher than 0.16 at comparable search times. Results on Stanford 2D-3D-S dataset confirms that our network is easily scalable for object search in 3D real-world indoor scenes by efficiently exploring only prospective regions in a sequential manner.

4.4 Accuracy vs Feature Dimensionality

We studied the relationship between the discriminative power of our network and the dimensionality of the point feature extracted from the feature extraction module (PointNet++). As shown in Table 3, our approach attained the highest success rates when the feature dimension was set at 64 or 128. The success rate decreased as we further increased the number of feature dimensions. The reason may be overfitting due to an excessive number of feature dimensions. In particular, as shown in Fig. 1, our network uses the pose feature obtained from the 7D pose parameters by projecting them to the same number of dimensions as the point feature. Using too large dimension of the pose feature, say 512D, may readily raise the risk of overfitting. Also, it might become less informative for pose estimation after combined with the point feature.

Table 3. Success rate and search time (in seconds) obtained with varying feature dimensions of PointNet++ on both datasets. Results were obtained with 24 and 85 BBoxes, and the IoU threshold was set at 0.50 and 0.40 for Transformed ModelNet40 and Stanford 2D-3D-S datasets, respectively.

Feature length	32	64	128	256	512
Transformed ModelNet40					
Ours		0.62	0.74	0.68	0.63	0.48
Stanford 2D-3D-S					
Ours		0.34	0.38	0.38	0.35	0.33

Table 4. Success rates obtained with different IoU thresholds on Transformed Model-Net40. The IoU threshold is used to judge whether a search is successful or not. Based on this judgment, the reinforcement localization reward is determined during training, while the same threshold is used for calculating the success rate during testing.

IoU	0.35	0.40	0.45	0.50	0.55
No. of BBoxes = 648					
PointNet++	0.64	0.52	0.40	0.28	0.20
PointNet	0.69	0.56	0.42	0.30	0.20
PointNetVLAD	0.84	0.76	0.66	0.50	0.36
No. of BBoxes = 24					
Ours	1.0	0.97	0.86	0.74	0.44

4.5   Accuracy vs IoU Threshold

As mentioned in Sect. 4.2, while training our network we provided the reward r_t based on the search outcome, i.e., the success (one) or failure (zero) of the search at each time step t. We consider a search is successful if the 3D IoU between the predicted and ground truth BBoxes is greater than a certain threshold. Here, we aim to analyze the sensitivity of the performance to this threshold. To this end,

Table 5. Success rates obtained with different IoU thresholds on Stanford 2D-3D-S. The IoU threshold is used to judge whether a search is successful or not. Based on this judgment, the reinforcement localization reward is determined during training, while the same threshold is used for calculating the success rate during testing.

IoU	0.25	0.30	0.35	0.40	0.45	0.50
No. of BBoxes = 1029						
PointNet++	0.62	0.52	0.44	0.32	0.12	0.04
PointNet	0.56	0.42	0.30	0.18	0.14	0.06
PointNetVLAD	0.62	0.58	0.48	0.34	0.20	0.10
No. of BBoxes = 85						
Ours		0.61	0.56	0.52	0.35	0.26	0.17

we first trained our network with different IoU thresholds, ranging from 0.35 to 0.55 on Transformed ModelNet40 and 0.25 to 0.50 on Stanford 2D-3D-S. Then we evaluated the trained network and calculated the success rate with the same IoU threshold as used during training.

The results on Transformed ModelNet40 are shown in Table 4. The success rate is as high as 1.0 for IoU threshold 0.35 even if only 24 BBoxes are compared with the query. The performance then decreases as we raises the threshold. All the baseline methods also followed the same trend, but in all cases, they could not achieve the same level of accuracy as ours, even if a much larger number of BBoxes were processed. Results on Stanford 2D-3D-S are given in Table 5, which shows the same trend as the case of Transformed ModelNet40.

4.6 Qualitative Analysis

Figure 3 shows some examples of the search behavior of our approach on Stanford 2D-3D-S for given queries. In all the examples, our network is able to approach the target object within a small number of search steps. Some interesting behaviors can be observed. First, in all the examples, starting from a random initial position, our approach moves the BBox significantly at first, and then takes a finer step size for precise localization as soon as it touches the target object. This shows that our approach is able to learn a natural and efficient search strategy. Second, our approach prioritizes the areas where the query object is likely to be present. For example, in the case of (a), our approach moves the BBox quickly from a high initial position to the floor and then stays on the floor to look for the chair. In the example in (b), starting from a low initial position, our approach continues to search near the floor surface and successfully captures the target without searching unnecessarily high areas. These examples show that our approach can leverage the advantage of the inherent contextual information between the target object and the search space for lean object search.

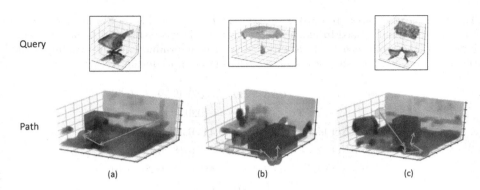

Fig. 3. Qualitative results on Stanford 2D-3D-S. For each query (top) and reference (bottom) pair, the target object and the final localization result by our approach are indicated by the red and green 3D BBoxes, respectively. Search paths are indicated by a sequence of orange arrows. The examples are textured for visualization purpose only. In our experiments, we use texture-less 3D points. (Color figure online)

5   Conclusions

In this study, we proposed Adaptive Spotting, a deep reinforcement learning approach to point cloud-based object search. This model takes the point clouds of a query and a reference map as input and leverages the internal state of the network to predict the next prospective position and pose to focus on. Using this model, the target object that corresponds to the query but is hidden in the reference can be efficiently localized in an exploratory way without being confused with clutter present in the reference. Our model significantly outperformed state-of-the-art deep point cloud networks and greatly reduced the number of matching processes and execution times, thereby making a noticeable improvement in the trade-off between accuracy and efficiency.

As one of the few examples of research dealing with point cloud-based object search based on end-to-end deep reinforcement learning, we believe this work revitalizes problems at the intersection of computer vision and other related fields including robotics, sensing, and machine learning. Exploring how to terminate the search process at any time step is an interesting direction for further research. We shall also investigate the impact of different exploration/reward strategies on the learning performance of our model to further optimize the accuracy-efficiency trade-off.

References

1. Qi, C.R., Su, H., Mo, K., Guibas, L.J.: PointNet: deep learning on point sets for 3D classification and segmentation. In: Proceedeings of CVPR, pp. 77–85 (2017)
2. Qi, C.R., Yi, L., Su, H., Guibas, L.J.: PointNet++: deep hierarchical feature learning on point sets in a metric space. In: Proceedings of NeurIPS, pp. 5099–5108 (2017)

3. Li, Y., Bu, R., Sun, M., Wu, W., Di, X., Chen, B.: PointCNN: convolution on X-transformed points. In: Proceedings of NeurIPS, pp. 828–838 (2018)
4. Qi, C.R., Liu, W., Wu, C., Su, H., Guibas, L.J.: Frustum PointNets for 3D object detection from RGB-D data. In: Proceedings of CVPR, pp. 918–927 (2018)
5. Xu, D., Anguelov, D., Jain, A.: PointFusion: deep sensor fusion for 3D bounding box estimation. In: Proceedings of CVPR, pp. 244–253 (2018)
6. Shi, S., Wang, X., Li, H.: PointRCNN: 3D object proposal generation and detection from point cloud. In: Proceedings of CVPR, pp. 770–779 (2019)
7. Qi, C.R., Litany, O., He, K., Guibas, L.J.: Deep hough voting for 3D object detection in point clouds. In: Proceedings of ICCV, pp. 9276–9285 (2019)
8. Du, L., et al.: Associate-3Ddet: perceptual-to-conceptual association for 3D point cloud object detection. In: Proceedings of CVPR (2020)
9. Pham, Q.H., et al.: RGB-D object-to-CAD retrieval. In: Proceedings of Eurographics Workshop on 3D Object Retrieval, pp. 45–52 (2018)
10. Uy, M.A., Lee, G.H.: PointNetVLAD: deep point cloud based retrieval for large-scale place recognition. In: Proceedings of CVPR, pp. 4470–4479 (2018)
11. Zhang, W., Xiao, C.: PCAN: 3D attention map learning using contextual information for point cloud based retrieval. In: Proceedings of CVPR, pp. 12436–12445 (2019)
12. Maturana, D., Scherer, S.A.: VoxNet: a 3D convolutional neural network for real-time object recognition. In: Proceedings of IROS, pp. 922–928 (2015)
13. Wu, Z., et al.: 3D ShapeNets: a deep representation for volumetric shapes. In: Proceedings of CVPR, pp. 1912–1920 (2015)
14. Wang, D.Z., Posner, I.: Voting for voting in online point cloud object detection. In: Proceedings of Robotics: Science and Systems (2015)
15. Riegler, G., Ulusoy, A.O., Geiger, A.: OctNet: learning deep 3D representations at high resolutions. In: Proceedings of CVPR, pp. 6620–6629 (2017)
16. Engelcke, M., Rao, D., Wang, D.Z., Tong, C.H., Posner, I.: Vote3Deep: fast object detection in 3D point clouds using efficient convolutional neural networks. In: Proceedings of ICRA, pp. 1355–1361 (2017)
17. Le, T., Duan, Y.: PointGrid: a deep network for 3D shape understanding. In: Proceedings of CVPR, pp. 9204–9214 (2018)
18. Su, H., Maji, S., Kalogerakis, E., Learned-Miller, E.: Multi-view convolutional neural networks for 3D shape recognition. In: Proc. ICCV. (2015) 945–953
19. Qi, C.R., Su, H., Nießner, M., Dai, A., Yan, M., Guibas, L.J.: Volumetric and multi-view CNNs for object classification on 3D data. In: Proceedings of CVPR, pp. 5648–5656 (2016)
20. Bai, S., Bai, X., Zhou, Z., Zhang, Z., Jan Latecki, L.: GIFT: a real-time and scalable 3D shape search engine. In: Proceedings of CVPR, pp. 5023–5032 (2016)
21. Savva, M., et al.: Large-scale 3D shape retrieval from ShapeNet Core55. In: Proceedings of Eurographics Workshop on 3D Object Retrieval (2016)
22. Li, J., Chen, B.M., Lee, G.H.: SO-net: self-organizing network for point cloud analysis. In: Proceedings of CVPR, pp. 9397–9406 (2018)
23. Hua, B.S., Tran, M.K., Yeung, S.K.: Pointwise convolutional neural networks. In: Proceedings of CVPR, pp. 984–993 (2018)
24. Tatarchenko, M., Park, J., Koltun, V., Zhou, Q.Y.: Tangent convolutions for dense prediction in 3D. In: Proceedings of CVPR, pp. 3887–3896 (2018)
25. Wu, W., Qi, Z., Li, F.: PointConv: deep convolutional networks on 3D point clouds. In: Proceedings of CVPR, pp. 9621–9630 (2019)
26. Qi, X., Liao, R., Jia, J., Fidler, S., Urtasun, R.: 3D graph neural networks for RGBD semantic segmentation. In: Proceedings of ICCV, pp. 5209–5218 (2017)

27. Yang, Y., Feng, C., Shen, Y., Tian, D.: FoldingNet: point cloud auto-encoder via deep grid deformation. In: Proceedings of CVPR, pp. 206–215 (2018)
28. Wang, Y., Sun, Y., Liu, Z., Sarma, S.E., Bronstein, M.M., Solomon, J.M.: Dynamic graph CNN for learning on point clouds. ACM Trans. Graph. (TOG) **38**, 146:1–146:12 (2019)
29. Su, H., et al.: SPLATNet: sparse lattice networks for point cloud processing. In: Proceedings of CVPR, pp. 2530–2539 (2018)
30. Rusu, R.B., Blodow, N., Marton, Z.C., Beetz, M.: Aligning point cloud views using persistent feature histograms. In: Proceedings of IROS, pp. 3384–3391 (2008)
31. Drost, B., Ulrich, M., Navab, N., Ilic, S.: Model globally, match locally: efficient and robust 3D object recognition. In: Proceedings of CVPR, pp. 998–1005 (2010)
32. Salti, S., Tombari, F., Di Stefano, L.: SHOT: unique signatures of histograms for surface and texture description. Comput. Vis. Image Underst. **125**, 251–264 (2014)
33. Arandjelovič, R., Gronat, P., Torii, A., Pajdla, T., Sivic, J.: NetVLAD: CNN architecture for weakly supervised place recognition. In: Proceedings of CVPR, pp. 5297–5307 (2016)
34. Saidi, F., Stasse, O., Yokoi, K., Kanehiro, F.: Online object search with a humanoid robot. In: Proceedings of IROS, pp. 1677–1682 (2007)
35. Aydemir, A., Pronobis, A., Gobelbecker, M., Jensfelt, P.: Active visual object search in unknown environments using uncertain semantics. IEEE Trans. Robot. **29**, 986–1002 (2013)
36. Nagaraja, V.K., Morariu, V.I., Davis, L.S.: Searching for objects using structure in indoor scenes. In: Proceedings of BMVC, pp. 53.1–53.11 (2015)
37. Krishna, O., Irie, G., Wu, X., Kawanishi, T., Kashino, K.: Learning search path for region-level image matching. In: Proceedings of ICASSP, pp. 1967–1971 (2019)
38. Zhou, D., Fang, J., Song, X., Guan, C., Yin, J., Dai, Y., Yang, R.: IoU loss for 2D/3D object detection. In: Proceedings of 3DV, pp. 85–94 (2019)
39. Mnih, V., Heess, N., Graves, A., Kavukcuoglu, K.: Recurrent models of visual attention. In: Proceedings of NeurIPS, pp. 2204–2212 (2014)
40. Ba, J., Mnih, V., Kavukcuoglu, K.: Multiple object recognition with visual attention. In: Proceedings of ICLR (2015)
41. Ablavatski, A., Lu, S., Cai, J.: Enriched deep recurrent visual attention model for multiple object recognition. In: Proceedings of WACV, pp. 971–978 (2017)
42. Armeni, I., Sax, A., Zamir, A.R., Savarese, S.: Joint 2D–3D-semantic data for indoor scene understanding. arXiv:1702.01105 (2017)
43. Notchenko, A., Kapushev, Y., Burnaev, E.: Large-scale shape retrieval with sparse 3d convolutional neural networks. In: van der Aalst, W.M.P., et al. (eds.) AIST 2017. LNCS, vol. 10716, pp. 245–254. Springer, Cham (2018). https://doi.org/10.1007/978-3-319-73013-4_23

Efficient Large-Scale Semantic Visual Localization in 2D Maps

Tomas Vojir[1,2]([envelope]) [ID], Ignas Budvytis[1] [ID], and Roberto Cipolla[1] [ID]

[1] University of Cambridge, Cambridge, UK
{ib255,rc10001}@cam.ac.uk
[2] Czech Technical University in Prague, Prague, Czech Republic
vojirtom@cmp.felk.cvut.cz

Abstract. With the emergence of autonomous navigation systems, image-based localization is one of the essential tasks to be tackled. However, most of the current algorithms struggle to scale to city-size environments mainly because of the need to collect large (semi-)annotated datasets for CNN training and create databases for test environment of images, key-point level features or image embeddings. This data acquisition is not only expensive and time-consuming but also may cause privacy concerns. In this work, we propose a novel framework for semantic visual localization in city-scale environments which alleviates the aforementioned problem by using freely available 2D maps such as OpenStreetMap. Our method does not require any images or image-map pairs for training or test environment database collection. Instead, a robust embedding is learned from a depth and building instance label information of a particular location in the 2D map. At test time, this embedding is extracted from a panoramic building instance label and depth images. It is then used to retrieve the closest match in the database.

We evaluate our localization framework on two large-scale datasets consisting of Cambridge and San Francisco cities with a total length of drivable roads spanning 500 km and including approximately 110k unique locations. To the best of our knowledge, this is the first large-scale semantic localization method which works on par with approaches that require the availability of images at train time or for test environment database creation.

1 Introduction

In this work, we propose a novel framework for semantic visual localization in 2D maps. Our work is motivated by the need for easy-to-use, scalable localization methods. One of the biggest challenges in achieving this goal includes the need of collecting large semi-annotated datasets of images [1–5], point clouds [6,7] or key-point level features [8] which is not only computationally expensive but

Electronic supplementary material The online version of this chapter (https://doi.org/10.1007/978-3-030-69535-4_17) contains supplementary material, which is available to authorized users.

also causes additional privacy concerns. In localization task, image datasets are collected for two reasons: (i) to learn image or key-point level features and embeddings [3–5,9], and (ii) to collect a database of images, image-level embeddings or 2D features of the test environment [3–5,7,9–11]. In most deep network approaches [7,10,11] or in conventional feature-based approaches [12,13], images from the same or sometimes similar [3] environments are used. In contrast, our method does not require any images in order to train our embedding network or to build a database of test environments. Instead, it leverages the freely available 2D maps (e.g. OpenStreetMap [14]). Hence, our approach allows us to train a framework for localization on large cities in less than 24 h effortlessly following the steps explained below.

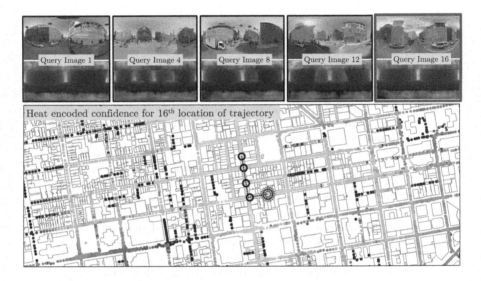

Fig. 1. This figure illustrates the typical results of our large scale semantic localization method. The top two rows show input query images with overlayed estimated building instances and estimated depth images for five locations of the query trajectory (marked by black circles). The bottom image shows the map locations similarity score for the last trajectory location encoded as a heat map (blue - low, red - high). The red circle marks the estimated most confident location for the 16th query image and the ground truth location is marked in purple. (Color figure online)

Our method consists of four key steps. Firstly, a 2D map of a city of interest is downloaded from OpenStreetMap [14]. Secondly, a set of 2D map locations are sampled from the map. For each location, a semantic descriptor which encodes surrounding building presence as well depth profile is extracted. Thirdly, an embedding network is trained to learn the mapping of semantic descriptors to a low dimension space. The mapping ensures that descriptors of spatially close locations in the 2D map are similar in the embedding space and vice-versa. Finally, at test time, embeddings are calculated on semantic descriptors extracted from the building instance label [15,16] and depth images [17] of the query image. They are then compared to the database of embeddings of the test environment locations to retrieve the most similar location.

The contributions of our work are as follows: (i) a novel semantic descriptor which encodes building instances and depth which can be efficiently extracted from both 2D map as well as from an RGB image, and (ii) a novel efficient localization framework which can be trained fully from 2D map data without any annotated images for training or for building a database for the test environment.

We evaluate our method on 110k Google StreetView images from Cambridge and San Francisco cities. Our dataset covers more 500 km of the total driving length, of which query trajectories cover 200 km. We significantly outperform binary semantic descriptor (BSD [18,19]) on both single location retrieval and trajectory retrieval. A typical trajectory localization result obtained by our network is shown in Fig. 1. We also outperform the most recent large scale localization approach [3], which requires the collection of images for training of their method, at the task of trajectory retrieval and demonstrate less sensitivity to the miss-match between training and test datasets. To the best of our knowledge, this is the first large scale semantic localization method which does not require images to train embedding network nor to build a representation of the test environment and works on par with localization techniques [3] which require the availability of images for training.

The rest of this work is divided as follows. Section 2 discusses relevant work in localization. Section 3 provides details of our proposed localization method. Sections 4 and 5 describe the experiment setup and corresponding results.

2 Related Work

In this section, we provide a description of related work for retrieval-based, end-to-end trained, and very large-scale localization methods.

Localization by Image Retrieval. Image retrieval localization methods [1,2, 4,5,8,9,20,21] work by finding the visually most similar image in a database of previously collected set of images and reporting the associated image pose of the best match. Images in the database are commonly represented by a collection of local features (e.g. SIFT [22]) which are often aggregated to a single feature vector per image (e.g. bag-of-visual-worlds [12], Fisher Vector [13]). To reduce the storage of the database, the compression of aggregated features is proposed [23] for efficient storage and fast matching of query images. To improve the localization pipeline, feature extraction, aggregation and compression stages can be replaced by end-to-end learned image representations [4,5,9] which yield better performance than the methods using hand-crafted features. The accuracy of the localization, assuming that correct closest database images can be retrieved, depends significantly on how densely the environment is sampled in order to build comprehensive database of the images. To refine the localization accuracy, several approaches have been proposed [6,24,25] that extend the retrieval-based localization by 3D information enabling precise 6-DoF camera pose estimation.

These methods use either (i) global 3D reconstruction [26–29] from all database images [6,24] and then establish 2D-3D matches to estimate the query image camera pose by PnP [30,31] algorithms or (ii) local 3D reconstruction from retrieved images [25] followed by a resection of the query image into the local reconstruction. There are two common issues which are encountered when performing large-scale localization: (i) the requirement of large storage space for the database, which is usually tackled by trying to compress the database without the loss in localization accuracy [25,32] and (ii) the high self-similarity of feature descriptors and local geometry [33] of unrelated images in large-scale datasets, which hinders the accuracy of successful retrieval of closest images.

End-to-End Localization. There are two general approaches in end-to-end deep learning based localization. The first set of approaches can be described as direct pose regression [10,34–36] methods. These methods train an end-to-end network to regress camera pose for a given input image. The training data consist of pairs of images and corresponding camera poses, where the camera pose is usually represented by GPS coordinates (coarse localization [36]) or camera position and orientation (6-DoF accurate localization [10,34,35]). It was shown recently by [7,37], that these direct pose regression approaches are more similar to image-based retrieval methods. The results for unseen test images are internally computed by interpolating poses of training images rather than by estimating accurate camera pose via the 3D structure of the scene. The training data size and the distribution of the training poses in the test environment are crucial for these methods. The second set of approaches attempt to regress 3D scene coordinates [7,11] for each image pixel followed by absolute pose estimation algorithm (whether differentiable [38] or not [30,31]) for accurate 6-DoF camera pose estimation. These methods generalize better for unseen test images than direct pose regression methods, but require structured training data (e.g. 3D mesh or point cloud) and are hard to scale to large scenes [38] because of training convergence difficulty or lack of training data. The scaling problem was partially addressed by [7] where the task of global scene coordinate regression was separated into two tasks of object recognition and local coordinate regression. This approach granted increased convergence speed and test accuracy. However, long training times and storage requirements of the 3D scene coordinates still prevent the scene coordinate regression works from being easily applied for city-size level environments.

Very Large Scale Localization. There are very few approaches which tackle very large-scale localization problems on maps of size larger than 5 km × 5 km. Examples of such works include [39], who proposed a method for localization by matching a query trajectory estimated by visual odometry [40] to a GPS map of road segments. This method is complementary to ours rather than a direct competitor. Also, note, they use trajectory shapes to localize and need "unique" road topology to be successful, where our method can work in urban environment with Manhattan-like road topology, as demonstrated in San Francisco city (see Sect. 5). Methods proposed in [18,19] use a very small and efficient-to-compute hand-crafted 4-bit binary semantic descriptor (BSD), which encodes the presence of junctions and building gaps in panoramic images. While Abonce et al. [3] proposed utilising a twin CNN-based embedding architecture for image and map-tile respectively for fast and efficient retrieval. The main disadvantage of [3] compared to our method is that it requires GPS annotated images for training, whereas we need only the map data. The method [3] also relies on the network to learn geometric and semantic information from images and map-tiles in a way suitable for this cross-modality matching, which is prone to overfitting. On the other hand, we explicitly provide structured semantic information during training (depth and building labels), which improves generalization (see Sect. 5). Moreover, our method is easily adaptable to a new city (downloading a 2D map and training) where [3] needs to collect a new set of training images. Our work is most similar to BSD [18,19] as we do not use images at train time, which enables us to very quickly deploy our localization method in new large-scale environments. However, unlike [18,19], our method outperforms image-based approache [3], which use images at train time, on several trajectory retrieval metrics.

3   Method

Our proposed semantic localization method consists of four key steps: (i) collecting the 2D map dataset, (ii) obtaining semantic descriptors for road locations in the 2D map, (iii) training of an embedding network for the aforementioned descriptors, and (iv) retrieving most similar individual locations and trajectories in the database for a given semantic descriptor extracted from the query image. These steps are explained in more detail below and in Figs. 2 and 3.

Obtaining 2D Map Data. The first step of our localization framework involves obtaining the 2D map data for the training of the embedding network and for the creation of the embeddings database of the test environment. Open-StreetMaps [14] service is used to download a 2D map, which contains a set of 2D polygons or 2D lines representing objects such as buildings or road centerlines. In this work, only building outlines are used for localization, however, other objects such as trees, road signs or road markings could be used. A partial illustration of a downloaded 2D map of the Cambridge (UK) city is shown at the top of Fig. 2. Note that the full map used in our experiments reported in Sect. 5 cover approximately a $5 \times 5\,\mathrm{km}^2$ area, which contains approximately 22000 buildings.

Obtaining Semantic Descriptors. The second step of our method involves extracting a semantic descriptor of an arbitrary location. This descriptor encodes two types of information about the location: the instance boundaries between buildings and corresponding distances between the query location and the buildings surrounding it. It is designed in such a way that it could be extracted both from a 2D map and from depth and building instance label images. In more detail, the following procedure is used to extract the semantic descriptor from a 2D map. For a given location $\mathbf{x}_i$ on a 2D map M, a quantised set of viewing directions $\Theta = \{\frac{i2\pi}{B}; \forall i \in N, s.t.\ 0 \leq i \leq B - 1\}$ are considered. For every

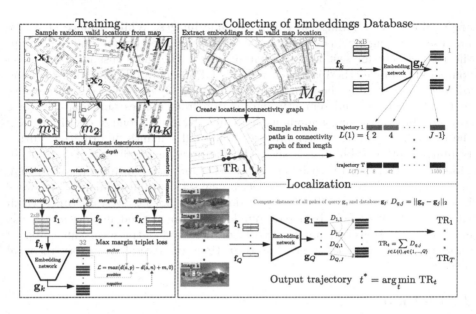

Fig. 2. This figure illustrates the key steps of our approach. During training, we randomly sample locations $\mathbf{x}_k$ from the 2D map M and extract the corresponding semantic descriptors $\mathbf{f}_k$ from visible local map m_k. Note that the extracted descriptors are semantically and geometrically augmented. The embedding network is then trained using max margin triplet loss, where positive samples come from augmentations and negative from different locations. To build a database for the test environment, semantic descriptors and their embeddings are extracted for J road locations (visualized as black dots in the map) of the 2D map M_d and possible drivable trajectories, $L(t), t \in \{1, ..., T\}$, are generated given the map locations connectivity graph. At localization time, the predicted labels and depth for each query image are used to extract a semantic descriptor $\mathbf{f}_q$ which is then passed through the learned embedding network. The individual embeddings $\mathbf{g}_q$ for query locations are compared with all database map embeddings $\mathbf{g}_j$ using Euclidean distance and the most similar trajectory, computed as the minimum sum location-wise distance $D_{q,j}$, is reported as the output.

viewing direction $\theta \in \Theta$, a ray is cast from the location of interest. For each ray the distance d_θ and corresponding building identity b_θ of the closest intersection is recorded. The vector $\mathbf{b} = [b_0, b_1, ...b_{B-1}]$ is transformed to vector $\mathbf{e} = [e_0, e_1, ...e_{B-1}]$ where $e_i = \exp\left(\frac{-0.5}{\sigma^2}\left[\min_{j \in \{l|b_l \neq b_{l+1}\}}(i - j \mod B)\right]^2\right)$, i.e. each element encodes the distance to the closest building edge. This representation removes building identities and allows for a robust matching with noisy building labels extracted from query images during the localization procedure. An example of such descriptor is illustrated in Fig. 3. The combined descriptor is obtained by simply concatenating $\mathbf{d} = [d_0, d_1, ...d_{B-1}]$ and $\mathbf{e}$ resulting in tensor $\mathbf{f}$ of shape $B \times 2$. At test time, building instance label and depth images are extracted using an off-the-shelf detection [15], semantic segmentation [16] as well as depth estimation [17] networks. Building instances with low Mask-

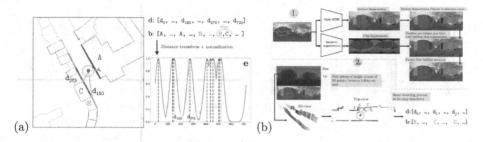

Fig. 3. The figure (a) illustrates the process of obtaining a semantic descriptor by casting rays uniformly around a given location in the map obtained from Open-StreetMap [14], and recording the distance of the first intersection d_θ and building label b_θ for each ray. The building labels are then converted to building edges and transformed to **e**. The final descriptor is obtained by simply concatenating **d** and **e**. The right figure (b) illustrates the process of extracting the semantic descriptor from the query image. In the first phase, the Mask-RCNN [15] is used to detect building instances. For each discretized column of the building instance segmentation image the most common building label is computed and used to label the corresponding columns of high resolution building class segmentation [16]. The second phase combines estimated depth in the height range of 1 m–20 m with the high-resolution instance segmentation to create a local map for which the same ray-casting procedure as for figure (a) is used to obtain **d** and **e** components of the final descriptor **f**.

RCNN [15] detection score (<0.9) are filtered out. For each discretized angle θ, the most common building for that angle is obtained and transferred to the high resolution building segmentation[1] to obtain the final building instance segmentation masks. For each pixel with a valid building label its' corresponding 3D point is computed from the depth image [17], resulting in the same type of semantic descriptor as extracted from the 2D map. The 3D points outside of the height range of 1m–20m (assuming ground plane corresponds to the x-y plane of the equirectangular image) are filtered out as this helps to remove most false detections in the sky, sidewalks and street areas. The remaining 3D points are orthographically projected onto the ground plane by ignoring the z-axis. The same procedure as for obtaining a semantic descriptor from the 2D map is then used. The whole descriptor extraction process is illustrated in Fig. 3. Note that by explicitly using semantic and geometric information, we can utilize heavy semantically and geometrically meaningful augmentation during the embedding network training, hence, making the descriptor embeddings more robust to changes captured by the augmentations. More implementation details are provided in Sect. 4.

Descriptor Embedding. The semantic descriptors **f** are embedded into 32 dimension vectors **g** using a 1D convolutional neural network. The architecture is inspired by the VGG network [41], where the context for features is pro-

---

[1] Note, we found that semantic segmentation networks obtain higher quality segmentations of building class labels.

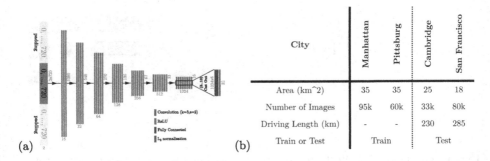

Fig. 4. The left figure shows the architecture of the embedding network. The table provides information about the datasets used in our experiments.

gressively enlarged to accommodate relations between faraway buildings. The exact architecture is described in Sect. 4. The CNN is trained using max-margin triplet loss [42,43], which encourages the similarity and dissimilarity of semantic descriptors from the same and different locations respectively. All triplets mining strategy [44] is used to generate triplets for batch training. As a result of requiring only 2D maps for training the embedding network, there is a virtually unlimited amount of training data available. More details for network training and data augmentations are described in Sect. 4.

Location Retrieval. To retrieve the set of most similar locations from the database, the semantic descriptor $\mathbf{f}_q$ is extracted for all query images I_q, where $q \in \{1, ..., Q\}$, and corresponding embeddings $\mathbf{g}_q$ are obtained using the aforementioned embedding network. The Euclidean distance: $D_{q,j} = \|\mathbf{g}_q - \mathbf{g}_j\|_2$ is measured between all query embeddings $\mathbf{g}_q$ and database embeddings $\mathbf{g}_j$. This procedure is illustrated on the right side of Fig. 2. In order to perform retrieval of trajectories, the trajectory is represented as an ordered set $L(t)$ of database indexes for all locations in the trajectory t in the order of trajectory traversal. The trajectory score TR_t for a trajectory t is calculated as a sum of the location-wise scores: $TR_t = \sum_{j \in L(t), q \in \{1,...,Q\}} D_{q,j}$. The most similar trajectory (i.e. the minimum score) is returned as an output. We follow the protocol of [3] for candidate trajectory generation as explained in Sect. 4.

4   Experimental Setup

In this section, we describe the details of the datasets, training procedure and evaluation protocol employed.

Datasets. Since public large scale datasets covering cities larger than $5km \times 5km$ with dense equirectangular images were not available at the time of publication we have collected our own dataset consisting of four cities: Pittsburgh, Manhattan, Cambridge (UK) and San Francisco. For each city, we obtained a detailed 2D building outline map from OpenStreetMap and a sample of Google StreetView images. For example, in case of Manhattan, a total area of 35 km^2 was covered

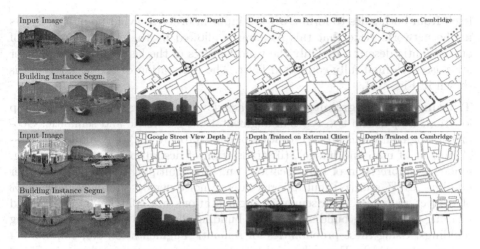

Fig. 5. This figure illustrates the qualitative performance of a single location retrieval of our method trained with Pittsburgh and Manhattan datasets. Three different columns on the right side correspond to different depths used at test time: (i) depth provided by Google StreetView (column 1), (ii) monocular depth estimation networks trained on external city images (column 2) and a similar network trained on Cambridge images (column 3). The quality of matches is encoded using a jet color scheme where best matches are encoded in red and worst matches in blue. Ground truth location is marked with a black circle. In the first row, due to the wrong depth of Google StreetView, the ground truth location produces a relatively weaker match than for depths obtained from monocular depth estimation networks. On the other hand, the second-row showcase where the images and map do not correspond and the depth estimated by the mono-depth approach hinders the localization. The results demonstrate the importance of depth quality for the localization. (Color figure online)

containing 55k buildings and 95k Google StreetView images. The corresponding details for other cities are provided in Fig. 4(b). In our experiments, we use OpenStreetMap data and images from Pittsburgh and Manhattan for training purposes (for competitors) and Cambridge as well as San Francisco for testing. When reporting accuracy results on Cambridge city we use San Francisco as validation data and similarly use Cambridge city as validation data for obtaining results on San Francisco. Note, however, since we do not require any images for training our embedding network it is also fair to use the 2D maps of the test environment for training.

Network Architecture. The CNN architecture used for semantic descriptor embedding consists of seven sequentially stacked convolutional layers and a final dense layer with 32 output units with L_2 normalization of the 32 dimensional vector. For the convolutional part of the architecture the number of channels is doubled for every layer. The first convolutional block contains 16 channels and the final one contains 1024. All convolutional layers have ReLU non-linearities, zero padding, kernel size 3 and stride 2. The input descriptor is padded with itself from both sides to form a $3B \times 2$ input in order to avoid boundary effects in the network. Note that this padding is allowed by the circular property of our semantic descriptors. Only the valid features of the last convolutional layer are passed to final fully connected layer. The illustration of the architecture is shown in Fig. 4(a).

Training Data Augmentation. For each descriptor of a given OpenStreetMap location, we perform two types of augmentation: geometric and semantic. Geometric augmentations are: (i) rotation of descriptor by $\pm 5°$ (e.g. modeling miss-alignment of map and image), (ii) translation of descriptor location $\pm 5m$ (e.g. modeling imprecision of map location) and (iii) multiplicative depth noise per building $\pm 10\%$ and (iv) multiplicative depth noise per descriptor element $\pm 5\%$ of correct distances. The semantic augmentations are splitting buildings and merging neighboring buildings, making building shorter or larger, and removing buildings. Using these probabilities for semantic augmentation 0.5, 0.3, 0.3, 0.4 and 0.2 respectively. Examples of descriptor augmentations are shown in Fig. 2 (left part).

Training Details. Adam optimizer with a learning rate of 0.0001 was used for training. For the building identity removal from descriptors a Gaussian with 0 mean and variance set to 5 was used. The variance was set empirically with slightly different values having a minimal effect. All the experiments reported on our method were trained in less 24 h on a single Titan X GPU.

Evaluation Protocol. Our localization framework is evaluated with respect to both single point and trajectory retrieval experiments. The quality of single point retrieval is examined by calculating the percentage of the successful retrieval of the query point for closest top 1%, 10% and 50% as shown in Fig. 7(b). The accuracy of the trajectory retrieval is evaluated by the percentage of successfully retrieved trajectories. The retrieval is considered successful if the locations of final points of the query and retrieved trajectory are within 10 m (a relaxed version of methodology used in [3]). For Cambridge and San Francisco cities we use 200 and 400 query trajectories correspondingly. They are matched 200K and 500K alternative trajectories. Testing locations are taken to match GPS coordinates of StreetView images for compatibility with the evaluation protocol of [3,18]. The alternative trajectories are generated by randomly traversing a graph made of testing locations as nodes and location connectivity as edges (see the illustration on the right side of Fig. 2 and the supplementary material for implementation details). The generating traversal algorithm prevents trajectories from visiting the same location twice. Query trajectories are selected at random with a constraint that a medium number of buildings within trajectory should be larger than 3. See the visualization of query and database trajectories in the material.

5   Experiments

We evaluate our proposed localization method on two tasks: single point retrieval and trajectory retrieval, on different city combinations, and compare with com-

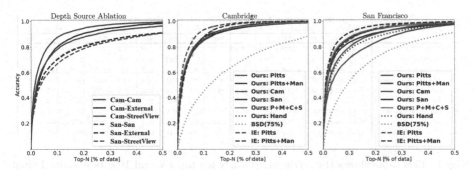

Fig. 6. The graph on the left shows the single point retrieval accuracy in top N% of locations. Our localization method is trained on Manhattan and Pittsburgh cities and tested using various depth predictions: (i) depth trained on the same city as tested on (blue), (ii) depth trained on external cities (orange) and (iii) depth accompanying the Google StreetView images (green). The depth trained on the same city achieves the highest accuracy highlighting the effect of good depth estimation on the retrieval performance. The middle and the right graphs show the same accuracy for various methods tested on Cambridge and San Francisco cities respectively. Our method trained on all four cities (P+M+C+S) achieved similar performance on both cities as best versions of IE for top-1% accuracy. However, unlike IE, our method performs consistently on both cities (note that the performance of IE versions differs significantly for Cambridge and San Francisco). For the full quantitative results please see Fig. 7. (Color figure online)

peting methods [3,18,19]. For the first competing method, we simulated binary semantic descriptor BSD [18] estimation from images by replacing the learned classifiers of junctions and building gaps with a classification accuracy of 75% as in [3]. For the second comparison, we directly employed our descriptors (denoted as Hand-Crafted). Finally, we re-implemented the localization method of [3], denoted as Image Embedding (IE), following the guidelines provided in the publication and evaluated it in two settings - trained on Pittsburgh and jointly on Pittsburgh and Manhattan. We evaluated our method trained on five different sets of cities: (i) Cambridge, (ii) San Francisco, (iii) Pittsburgh, (iv) Pittsburgh and Manhattan as well as (v) all four cities. It can be seen in the Figs. 8 and 7 that our network performs best when all four cities are used. Also, respectively a network trained on Cambridge data performs better on Cambridge query images than the one trained on the San Francisco city and the opposite. Since we do not use any images for training the embedding network, it is easy to leverage training data from 2D maps for test environments to boost performance, as demonstrated in these experiments.

5.1   Single Location Retrieval

In this experiment, we inspect the sensitivity of our method to errors in depth estimation and we compare our work to several state-of-the-art methods [3,18,19] in single query localization task.

Method	Single Query Localization [Top x%]						Trajectory Localization [Top 1]								
	Cambridge		San Francisco		Average		Cambridge			San Francisco			Average		
	1%	10%	1%	10%	1%	10%	80m	160m	320m	80m	160m	320m	80m	160m	320m
BSD (75%)	9.6	45.1	13.1	52.9	11.4	49.0	6.9	27.2	70.0	1.3	6.2	21.3	4.1	16.7	45.7
Ours: Hand-Crafted	37.4	86.3	38.6	78.1	38.0	82.2	15.2	31.8	62.2	13.8	24.3	55.3	14.5	28.1	58.8
Ours: Pittsburgh	41.2	86.2	34.2	71.3	37.7	78.8	30.4	53.5	88.0	18.7	35.3	70.3	24.6	44.4	79.2
Ours: Pittsburgh + Manhattan	44.2	87.8	47.7	83.6	46.0	85.7	29.0	58.5	86.6	35.3	58.9	86.2	32.2	58.7	86.4
Ours: Cambridge	43.5	85.1	39.3	79.9	41.4	82.5	28.6	59.0	85.7	21.5	43.9	77.8	25.1	51.5	81.8
Ours: San Francisco	41.4	85.9	49.4	86.6	45.4	86.3	26.7	53.0	84.8	37.0	61.3	90.8	31.9	57.2	87.8
Ours: All (P+M+C+SF)	45.1	86.4	51.4	87.6	48.3	87.0	30.9	62.7	90.8	42.8	72.7	93.8	36.9	67.7	92.3
IE: Pittsburgh	49.3	93.4	46.5	85.6	47.9	89.5	40.1	65.9	85.7	34.4	65.8	90.3	37.3	65.9	88.0
IE: Pittsburgh + Manhattan	35.9	87.8	53.9	91.1	44.9	89.5	16.1	35.9	63.6	42.6	71.4	92.0	29.4	53.7	77.8

Fig. 7. This table shows the retrieval accuracy for top 1% and 10% best ranked single locations and the accuracy of the correct trajectory retrieval at different lengths of 80 m, 160 m 320 m for various methods. The "average" column shows a combined score over Cambridge and San Francisco cities. The IE stands for the Image Embedding method [3]. The best and second best results are in bold green and blue respectively. Our method performs favorably against IE variations and, in total, outperforms IE in average performance for trajectory retrieval. Note that our single method trained on all cities (highlighted in bold) achieves consistently high performance. In contrast, the performance of variations of IE method fluctuates significantly depending on the combination of train and test data. (Color figure online)

Sensitivity to Incorrect Depth. We trained a semantic descriptor embedding network on a dataset consisting of the building outlines of Manhattan and Pittsburgh cities. At test time, depth images were obtained: (i) directly provided by the Google StreetView (Cam-StreetView and San-StreetView), (ii) from monocular depth estimation network trained on external cities (Cam-External and San-External) and (ii) from monocular depth estimation network trained directly on the images of Cambridge and San Francisco (Cam-Cam and San-San). The depth provided with the Google StreetView images was filtered and used to train the monocular depth networks as described above. Quantitative results are shown in Fig. 6 and Fig. 7. The best performance is obtained using a monocular depth network trained on the respective cities achieving 44.2% retrieval accuracy for top 1% predictions. Note that when testing using depth from a network trained on external cities the results have equally high accuracy on San Francisco city (48.1% at top-1%). As Google StreetView depth is provided using a planar approximation, some of the depth planes are missing or incorrectly placed, which significantly reduces the performance. Similarly, monocular depth estimation networks struggle to generalize in some cases and provide incorrect depth predictions. Figure 5 illustrates the qualitative results. For the rest of the experiments, we use the depth predictions obtained using the third method[2].

Comparison with Alternative Methods. Our network trained on all four cities achieved only a 4.2% and 2.5% lower top 1% accuracy on Cambridge and San Francisco respectively than IE [3]. On average, our method outperforms IE in the top 1% criterion, which shows that our model is more robust to the different test environments and less prone to overfitting. It is interesting to point out that

---

[2] Note that if LIDAR, stereo or other depth sensor data were available, they could be used instead.

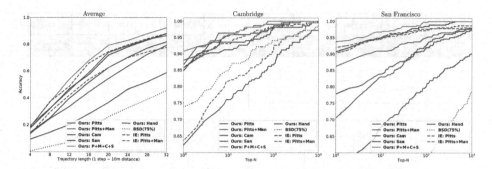

Fig. 8. The left graph shows the combined trajectory retrieval accuracy for Cambridge and San Francisco cities for varying trajectory length. Our method outperforms IE [3] in combined scores for almost all trajectory lengths. The middle and right graphs show the trajectory retrieval accuracy 320 m length trajectories on Cambridge and San Francisco, respectively, when considering top-N trajectories. Our method trained on all cities (P+M+C+S) is the top-performing with consistently high performance on both cities and converges to 100% retrieval accuracy when considering the top 100 most similar trajectories. Other methods need to consider ten times more trajectories.

single query localization performance correlates with the trajectory localization, but it is not the only factor. Our method performs better on average by 4.3% when longer driving scenario (>200m) is considered as shown in Fig. 7.

5.2   Trajectory Prediction

For the final set of experiments, we evaluated the same networks as in Sect. 5.1 for the trajectory retrieval task. Figures 7 and 8 illustrate quantitative results. In particular, the left-most graph in Fig. 8 shows that our network trained on all four cities achieves the highest combined (Cambridge + San Francisco) accuracy at all trajectory lengths larger than eight samples ($\approx$80m). The right side of the Fig. 8 show the trajectory retrieval accuracy for the trajectories of length 32 for Cambridge and San Francisco cities. It is important to note that the performance of the variants of Image Embedding [3] networks differ significantly when applied on Cambridge and San Francisco. The accuracy of the image embedding network trained on Pittsburgh and Manhattan cities decreases from 92.0% on San Francisco to 63.6% on Cambridge. This may be explained by the networks over-fitting to a particular dataset or type of city. All our networks, except for the one trained on Pittsburgh, show the biggest difference of 7.9% when evaluated on different cities. Two qualitative results demonstrating the strength and weaknesses of our and [3] methods are shown in Fig. 9. In the left example (Cambridge), our method fails mainly because of severe occlusion by trees in most query images. Note that at the beginning of the trajectory, our method was more confident because of the cross-road and later it become less clear because of the occlusions. In contrast, the IE does not suffer from occlusions by trees and is able to localize correctly. However, note that the second best trajectory for IE is in the same location but the wrong direction and it does not fully exploit cross-road

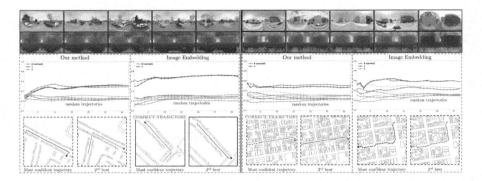

Fig. 9. This figure shows two examples of trajectory retrieval for Cambridge (left) and San Francisco (right). We show successful localization of our method (right) and a typical failure (left) and also compare it to IE [3]. The first two rows show input query images of the trajectory of length 32 with overlayed estimated building instances and depths. The plots in the middle show mean confidence of trajectories w.r.t. the number of query images. Each plot visualises scores for two most similar trajectories, the correct trajectory (red) and few random trajectories in order to illustrate confidence margins. (Color figure online)

structures (visible on the trajectory confidence graph). The second example on San Francisco (right part of the Figure) supports the previously mentioned IE issue that it does not learn the proper geometric structure and cannot take into account the width of the road.

6   Conclusions

We proposed a novel framework for semantic visual localization in 2D maps. Our work was motivated by the need for easy-to-use, scalable localization methods. Unlike most state-of-the-art large scale localization methods [3,6,7], our approach does not require any images at train time (either for training embedding or building database of the test environment). Hence, it enables us to train networks for localization on large cities in less than 24 h effortlessly. We achieved this by making use of the following procedure. We first obtain a freely available 2D building outline maps from OpenStreetMap [14] and use them for training a semantic embedding network for a descriptor containing depth and building instances visible from particular locations on such a map. At test time, we extract a similar descriptor from the building instance segmentation and depth predictions of the actual query images and use it to find the closest match to various locations of the map in the embedding space. We evaluated our method on two cities of Cambridge and San Francisco. Our method significantly outperformed binary semantic descriptor (BSD [18,19]) on both single location retrieval and trajectory retrieval. It also obtained higher combined retrieval accuracy than image-based localization method [3]. To the best of our knowledge, this is the first large scale semantic visualization method which works on par with localization techniques [3], which require images at train time.

References

1. Torii, A., Arandjelović, R., Sivic, J., Okutomi, M., Pajdla, T.: 24/7 place recognition by view synthesis. In: CVPR (2015)
2. Budvytis, I., Sauer, P., Cipolla, R.: Semantic localisation via globally unique instance segmentation. In: BMVC (2018)
3. Abonce, O.S., Zhou, M., Calway, A.: You are here: geolocation by embedding maps and images. arXiv:1911.08797 (2019)
4. Arandjelović, R., Gronat, P., Torii, A., Pajdla, T., Sivic, J.: NetVLAD: CNN architecture for weakly supervised place recognition. IEEE TPAMI **40**, 1437–1451 (2018)
5. Schönberger, J., Pollefeys, M., Geiger, A., Sattler, T.: Semantic visual localization. In: CVPR (2018)
6. Sattler, T., Havlena, M., Radenovic, F., Schindler, K., Pollefeys, M.: Hyperpoints and fine vocabularies for large-scale location recognition. In: ICCV (2015)
7. Budvytis, I., Teichmann, M., Vojir, T., Cipolla, R.: Large scale joint semantic re-localisation and scene understanding via globally unique instance coordinate regression. In: BMVC (2019)
8. Arandjelović, R., Zisserman, A.: DisLocation: scalable descriptor distinctiveness for location recognition. In: Cremers, D., Reid, I., Saito, H., Yang, M.-H. (eds.) ACCV 2014. LNCS, vol. 9006, pp. 188–204. Springer, Cham (2015). https://doi.org/10.1007/978-3-319-16817-3_13
9. Stenborg, E., Toft, C., Hammarstrand, L.: Long-term visual localization using semantically segmented images. In: ICRA (2018)
10. Kendall, A., Cipolla, R.: Geometric loss functions for camera pose regression with deep learning. In: CVPR (2017)
11. Brachmann, E., Rother, C.: Learning less is more - 6D camera localization via 3D surface regression. In: CVPR (2017)
12. Philbin, J., Chum, O., Isard, M., Sivic, J., Zisserman, A.: Object retrieval with large vocabularies and fast spatial matching. In: CVPR (2007)
13. Perronnin, F., Liu, Y., Sánchez, J., Poirier, H.: Large-scale image retrieval with compressed Fisher vectors. In: CVPR (2010)
14. Coast, S.: OpenStreetMap (2004)
15. Massa, F., Girshick, R.: MaskRCNN-benchmark: fast, modular reference implementation of Instance Segmentation and Object Detection algorithms in PyTorch (2018). https://github.com/facebookresearch/maskrcnn-benchmark
16. Zhu, Y., et al.: Improving semantic segmentation via video propagation and label relaxation. In: IEEE Conference on Computer Vision and Pattern Recognition (CVPR) (2019)
17. Yakubovskiy, P.: Segmentation models (2019). https://github.com/qubvel/segmentation_models
18. Panphattarasap, P., Calway, A.: Automated map reading: image based localisation in 2-D maps using binary semantic descriptors. In: IROS (2018)
19. Yan, F., Vysotska, O., Stachniss, C.: Global localization on OpenStreetMap using 4-bit semantic descriptors. In: ECMR (2019)
20. Chen, D.M., et al.: City-scale landmark identification on mobile devices. In: CVPR (2011)
21. Schindler, G., Brown, M., Szeliski, R.: City-scale location recognition. In: CVPR (2007)

22. Lowe, D.G.: Distinctive image features from scale-invariant keypoints. IJCV **60**, 91–110 (2004). https://doi.org/10.1023/B:VISI.0000029664.99615.94
23. Jegou, H., Douze, M., Schmid, C.: Product quantization for nearest neighbor search. IEEE TPAMI **33**, 117–128 (2011)
24. Sattler, T., Leibe, B., Kobbelt, L.: Fast image-based localization using direct 2D-to-3D matching. In: ICCV (2011)
25. Sattler, T., et al.: Are large-scale 3D models really necessary for accurate visual localization? In: CVPR (2017)
26. Agarwal, S., et al.: Building Rome in a day. In: ICCV (2009)
27. Crandall, D., Owens, A., Snavely, N., Huttenlocher, D.: Discrete-continuous optimization for large-scale structure from motion. In: CVPR (2011)
28. Schönberger, J.L., Radenović, F., Chum, O., Frahm, J.: From single image query to detailed 3D reconstruction. In: CVPR (2015)
29. Schönberger, J.L., Frahm, J.: Structure-from-motion revisited. In: CVPR (2016)
30. Kneip, L., Li, H., Seo, Y.: UPnP: an optimal O(n) solution to the absolute pose problem with universal applicability. In: Fleet, D., Pajdla, T., Schiele, B., Tuytelaars, T. (eds.) ECCV 2014. LNCS, vol. 8689, pp. 127–142. Springer, Cham (2014). https://doi.org/10.1007/978-3-319-10590-1_9
31. Lepetit, V., Moreno-Noguer, F., Fua, P.: EPnP: an accurate O(N) solution to the PnP problem. IJCV **81**, 155 (2009)
32. Camposeco, F., Cohen, A., Pollefeys, M., Sattler, T.: Hybrid scene compression for visual localization. In: CVPR (2019)
33. Sattler, T., Havlena, M., Schindler, K., Pollefeys, M.: Large-scale location recognition and the geometric burstiness problem. In: CVPR (2016)
34. Kendall, A., Grimes, M., Cipolla, R.: PoseNet: a convolutional network for real-time 6-DOF camera relocalization. In: ICCV (2015)
35. Walch, F., Hazirbas, C., Leal-Taixé, L., Sattler, T., Hilsenbeck, S., Cremers, D.: Image-based localization using LSTMs for structured feature correlation. In: ICCV (2016)
36. Weyand, T., Kostrikov, I., Philbin, J.: PlaNet - photo geolocation with convolutional neural networks. In: Leibe, B., Matas, J., Sebe, N., Welling, M. (eds.) ECCV 2016. LNCS, vol. 9912, pp. 37–55. Springer, Cham (2016). https://doi.org/10.1007/978-3-319-46484-8_3
37. Sattler, T., Zhou, Q., Pollefeys, M., Leal-Taixé, L.: Understanding the limitations of CNN-based absolute camera pose regression. In: CVPR (2019)
38. Brachmann, E., et al.: DSAC - differentiable RANSAC for camera localization. In: CVPR (2017)
39. Brubaker, M.A., Geiger, A., Urtasun, R.: Map-based probabilistic visual self-localization. IEEE TPAMI **38**, 652–665 (2016)
40. Nister, D., Naroditsky, O., Bergen, J.: Visual odometry. In: CVPR (2004)
41. Simonyan, K., Zisserman, A.: Very deep convolutional networks for large-scale image recognition. In: International Conference on Learning Representations (2015)
42. Hermans, A., Beyer, L., Leibe, B.. In defense of the triplet loss for person re-identification. arXiv preprint arXiv:1703.07737 (2017)
43. Vo, N.N., Hays, J.: Localizing and orienting street views using overhead imagery. In: Leibe, B., Matas, J., Sebe, N., Welling, M. (eds.) ECCV 2016. LNCS, vol. 9905, pp. 494–509. Springer, Cham (2016). https://doi.org/10.1007/978-3-319-46448-0_30
44. Ding, S., Lin, L., Wang, G., Chao, H.: Deep feature learning with relative distance comparison for person re-identification. Pattern Recogn. **48**, 2993–3003 (2015)

Synthetic-to-Real Unsupervised Domain Adaptation for Scene Text Detection in the Wild

Weijia Wu[1], Ning Lu[2], Enze Xie[3], Yuxing Wang[1], Wenwen Yu[4], Cheng Yang[1], and Hong Zhou[1(✉)]

[1] Key Laboratory for Biomedical Engineering of Ministry, Zhejiang University, HangZhou, China
zhouhong_zju@126.com
[2] Tencent Cloud Product Department, Shenzhen, China
[3] The University of Hong Kong, Pok Fu Lam, Hong Kong
[4] Xuzhou Medical University, Xuzhou, China

Abstract. Deep learning-based scene text detection can achieve preferable performance, powered with sufficient labeled training data. However, manual labeling is time consuming and laborious. At the extreme, the corresponding annotated data are unavailable. Exploiting synthetic data is a very promising solution except for domain distribution mismatches between synthetic datasets and real datasets. To address the severe domain distribution mismatch, we propose a synthetic-to-real domain adaptation method for scene text detection, which transfers knowledge from synthetic data (source domain) to real data (target domain). In this paper, a text self-training (TST) method and adversarial text instance alignment (ATA) for domain adaptive scene text detection are introduced. ATA helps the network learn domain-invariant features by training a domain classifier in an adversarial manner. TST diminishes the adverse effects of false positives (FPs) and false negatives (FNs) from inaccurate pseudo-labels. Two components have positive effects on improving the performance of scene text detectors when adapting from synthetic-to-real scenes. We evaluate the proposed method by transferring from SynthText, VISD to ICDAR2015, ICDAR2013. The results demonstrate the effectiveness of the proposed method with up to 10% improvement, which has important exploration significance for domain adaptive scene text detection. Code is available at https://github.com/weijiawu/SyntoReal_STD.

1 Introduction

Scene text detection and recognition [1–3] has received increasing attention due to its numerous applications in computer vision. Additionally, scene text detection [4–8] has achieved great success in the last few decades. However, these detection methods require manually labeling large quantities of training data, which is very expensive and time consuming. Whereas several public benchmarks [9–13] have already existed, they only covered a very limited range of

© Springer Nature Switzerland AG 2021
H. Ishikawa et al. (Eds.): ACCV 2020, LNCS 12624, pp. 289–303, 2021.
https://doi.org/10.1007/978-3-030-69535-4_18

Fig. 1. Examples of different datasets. The first row are from real ICDAR2013 [9], ICDAR2015 [10], and ICDAR2017 MLT [11], respectively. The second row is from Virtual SynthText [14], VISD [15], and UnrealText [16]. There remains a considerable domain gap between synthetic data and real data.

scenarios. In the real world, a specific application task usually requires the collection and annotation of a new training dataset, and it is difficult, even impossible, to collect enough labeled data. Therefore, the expensive cost of labeling has become a major problem for text detection applications based on deep learning methods.

With the great development of computer graphics, an alternative way is to utilize synthetic data, which is largely available from the virtual world, and the ground truth can be freely and automatically generated. SynthText [14] first provides a virtual scene text dataset and automatically generates synthetic images with word-level and character-level annotations. Zhan *et al.* [15] equipped text synthesis with selective semantic segmentation to produce more realistic samples. UnrealText [16] provides realistic virtual scene text images via a 3D graphics engine, which provides realistic appearance by rendering scene and text as a whole. Although synthetic data offer the possibility of substituting for real images in training scene text detectors, many previous works have also shown that training with only synthetic data degrades the performance on real data due to a phenomenon known as "domain shift". As shown in Fig. 1, unlike common objects, text has more diversity of shapes, colours, fonts, sizes, and orientations in real-world scenarios, which causes a large domain gap between synthetic data and real data. Therefore, the performance of the model degrades significantly when applying model learning only from synthetic data to real data.

To tackle the domain shift, we propose a synthetic-to-real domain adaptation approach for scene text detection, which aims to efficiently improve the model performance on real data by using synthetic data and unlabeled real data. Inspired by [17] and [18], a text self-training(TST) method and an adversarial text instance alignment(ATA) are proposed in our paper to reduce the domain shift. Self-training has achieved excellent results for domain adaptive object detection [19,20] and semantic segmentation [21]. However, scene text detection tasks with more diverse situations and complex backgrounds have not been explored in this direction to the best of our knowledge. To better apply self-training to scene text detection, TST is used to suppress the adverse impact of both false positives and false negatives that occur in pseudo-labels. In addition, we first utilize adversarial learning [18] help the model to learn discriminative features of text. The contributions of our paper are as follows:

- We introduce text self-training (TST) to improve the performance of domain adaptive scene text detection by minimizing the adverse effects of inaccurate pseudo-labels.
- We propose adversarial text instance alignment (ATA) to help the model learn domain-invariant features, which enhance the generalization ability of the model.
- We first introduce a synthetic-to-real domain adaptation method for scene text detection, which transfers knowledge from the synthetic data (source domain) to real data (target domain).

The proposed method is evaluated by extensive experiments for the scene text detection transfer task (*e.g., SynthText* [14]→*ICDAR2015* [10]). The experimental results demonstrate the effectiveness of the proposed approach for addressing the domain shift of scene text detection, which has important exploration significance for domain adaptive scene text detection.

2   Related Work

2.1   Scene Text Detection

Before the era of deep learning, SWT [22] and MSER [23] were two representative algorithms for conventional text detection methods. SWT obtains information about the text stroke efficiently, and MSER draws intensity stable regions as text candidates. Based on convolutional neural network knowledge, scene text detection [24,25] has made great progress. EAST [8] performs very dense predictions that are processed using locality-aware NMS. PixelLink [26] detects text instances by linking neighbouring pixels. PSENet [27] proposed a progressive scale algorithm to gradually expand the predefined kernels for scene text detection. In addition to the above methods based on strongly supervised learning, some weakly/semi-supervised methods are proposed to reduce the expansive cost of annotation. WeText [28] trains a text detection model on a small amount of character-level annotated text images, followed by boosting the performance with a much larger amount of weakly annotated images at word line level. WordSup [29] trains a character detector by exploiting word annotations in rich, large-scale real scene text datasets. [30] utilizes the network pretrained on synthetic data with full masks to enhance the coarse masks in a real image.

2.2 Domain Adaptation

Domain adaptation reduces the domain gap between training and testing data. Prior works [31] estimated the domain gap and minimized it. Recent methods use more effective methods to reduce the domain gap, such as incorporating a domain classifier with gradient reversal [18]. [32] addressed the domain shift by training domain discriminators on the image level and instance level. [17] introduced a weak self-training to diminish the adverse effects of inaccurate pseudo-labels, and designed adversarial background score regularization to extract discriminative features. For scene text, the domain adaptation method [33] converts a source-domain image into multiple images of different spatial views as in the target domain. Handwriting recognition [34] proposes AFDM to elastically warp extracted features in a scalable manner.

2.3 Self-training

Prior works used self-training [35,36] to compensate for the lack of categorical information. [37] bridged the gap between the source and target domains by adding both the target features and instances in which the current algorithm is the most confident. [38] used three networks asymmetrically, where two networks were used to label unlabeled target samples and one network was trained to obtain discriminative representations. Other works [21,39,40] also showed the effectiveness of self-training for domain adaptation. However, text detection still requires further exploration in the self-training method due to a lack of previous work.

3 Proposed Method

In this section, the problems caused by domain shifts are analysed. Furthermore, we introduce the principle of TST and ATA, and how to use them for domain adaptation. To evaluate our method, EAST [8] is adopted as the baseline.

3.1 Problem and Analysis

Although synthetic scene text data can be automatically generated with diversified appearance and accurate ground truth annotations, the model trained with only synthetic data cannot be directly applied to real scenes since there exists a significant domain shift between synthetic datasets and real datasets.

Viewing the problem from a probabilistic perspective is clearer. We refer to the synthetic data domain as the source domain and the real data domain as the target domain. The scene text detection problem can be viewed as learning the posterior $P(B|I)$, where I refers to the image features and B is the predicted bounding-box of text instances. Using the Bayes formula, the posterior $P(B|I)$ can be decomposed as:

$$P(B|I) = \frac{P(I|B) * P(B)}{P(I)} = \frac{P(I|B)}{P(I)} * P(B). \tag{1}$$

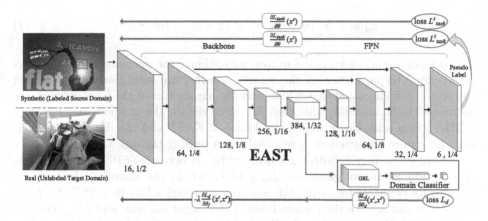

Fig. 2. The network architecture with the corresponding optimization object. θ represents the parameters of EAST. A domain classifier (green) is added after the feature extractor via a gradient reversal layer that multiplies the gradient by a certain negative constant during the backpropagation-based training. L_{task} refers to the original detection loss of EAST, and L_d is the loss of domain classifier. (Color figure online)

We make the covariate shift assumption in this task that the priori probability $P(B)$ is the same for the two domains. $P(I|B)$ refers to the conditional probability of I, which means that the likelihood of learning true features given that the predicted result is true. We also consider that $P(I|B)$ is the same for both domains. Therefore, the difference in posterior probability is caused by the priori probability $P(I)$. In other words, to detect text instances, the difference in detection results is caused by domain change features. To improve the generalization ability, the model should learn more domain-invariant features, keeping the same $P(I)$ regardless of which domain the input image belongs.

In the EAST [8] model, the image feature $P(I)$ refers to the features output from the backbone. Therefore, the feature map should be aligned between the source domain and the target domain (i.e., $P_s(I) = P_t(I)$). To achieve this goal, ATA is proposed to align the features, with more details in the next subsection.

3.2 Adversarial Text Instance Alignment

Motivated by [18], ATA is adopted to help the network learn domain-invariant features. In the EAST model, the image features $P(I)$ refer to the feature map outputs of the backbone (i.e., 384, 1/32 features in Fig. 2). To align the features $P(I)$ between the source domain and target domain, a domain classifier is used to confuse the feature domain.

In particular, the domain classifier is trained for each input image and predicts the domain label to which the image belongs. We assume that the model works with input samples $x \in X$, where X is the some input space. y_i denotes the domain label of the i-th training image, with $y_i = 0$ for the source domain and $y_i = 1$ for the target domain. $p_i(x)$ is the output of the domain classifier, and we use cross entropy as the loss function:

$$L_d = -\sum_i (y_i \times ln^{p_i(x)} + (1 - y_i) \times ln^{1-p_i(x)}). \qquad (2)$$

To learn domain-invariant features, we optimize the parameters in an adversarial way. The parameters of the domain classifier are optimized by minimizing the above domain classification loss, and the parameters of the base network are optimized by maximizing this loss. For more detail, the gradient reverse layer (GRL) [18] is added between the backbone of EAST and the domain classifier, and the sign of the gradient is reversed when passing through the GRL layer.

As shown in Fig. 2, both the feature pyramid network (FPN) and the backbone minimize the original loss L_{task} of EAST at the training phase. L_{task} specifically denotes the score map loss and geometries loss in EAST [8]. L_{task}^t refers to training with the pseudo-label in the target domain, and L_{task}^s denotes training with the source domain. Thus, different training objectives for various parameter spaces:

$$\begin{cases} L_f = min(L_{task}^t(\theta_f|x^t) + L_{task}^s(\theta_f|x^s) - \lambda L_d(\theta|(x^s, x^t))) & \theta_f \in F, \\ L_d = min(L_d(\theta_d|(x^s, x^t))) & \theta_d \in C, \qquad (3) \\ L_h = min(L_{task}^t(\theta_h|x^t) + L_{task}^s(\theta_h|x^s)) & \theta_h \in D, \end{cases}$$

where F, C, D are the parameter spaces of the backbone, the domain classifier and the FPN. The overall training objective is as follows:

$$L = L_f + L_h + \lambda L_d, \qquad (4)$$

where λ is the tradeoff parameter, we set it to 0.2 in all experiments. Through optimizing the loss, the network can learn more text domain-invariant features, transforming better from synthetic data to real data.

3.3   Text Self-training

Previous works [21,41] have shown the effectiveness of self-training. However, two major problems for self-training still need to be explored further: false positives (FP) and false negatives (FN) occurred in pseudo-label. Incorrect pseudo-labels will cause very serious negative effects to our networks. To overcome such problems, TST is designed to minimize the adverse effects of FP and FN.

Reducing False Negatives. Inspired by [17], a weak supervision way is utilized to minimize the effects of false negatives. The original score map loss in the EAST [8] is

$$L_s = -\sum_{i \in Pos} \beta Y^* log\widehat{Y} - \sum_{i \in Neg} (1 - \beta)(1 - Y^*)(1 - \widehat{Y}), \qquad (5)$$

where $\widehat{Y} = F_s$ is the prediction of the score map, and Y^* is the ground truth. While the network is optimized by backpropagation learning the loss of background (i.e., negative examples), FP occurring in pseudo-labels misleads the network. We assume that FPs are mainly selected by hard negative mining,

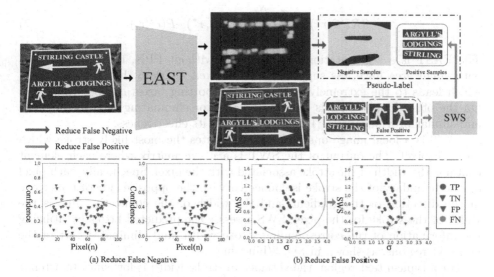

Fig. 3. Up: The framework of proposed text self-training. We utilize SWS to filter the positive samples in pseudo-label for minimizing false positives, and select a third of negative samples with low confidence as the final negative samples to minimize false negatives. Down: We present sample space representation for pseudo-label. (a): False negatives are effectively filtered out by weak training. (b): False positives are filtered out by the standard deviation (σ) of the stroke width and SWS. (Color figure online)

such as blurred text and unusual fonts similar to the background. To reduce the adverse effects of FP, we ignore some background examples that have the potential to be foregrounds with a confidence score.

Negative examples for EAST are a pixel map, a pixel is more likely to be considered a negative pixel while the corresponding confidence score higher. Thus, we choose a part of the negative sample pixels (*e.g.*, $Neg/3$) that have the lowest confidence score as the final negative examples, which is denoted as $\widehat{Neg}$ in Fig. 3(red line). The corresponding mathematical expression is $\widehat{Neg} = \eta Neg$, where η is set to 1/3 in all experiments. For those pixels that have a high confidence score, the network does not optimize this part loss. Finally, the modified loss function is defined as

$$L_{sw} = - \sum_{i \in Pos} \beta Y_i^* log\widehat{Y} - \sum_{i \in \widehat{Neg}} (1 - \beta)(1 - Y_i^*)(1 - \widehat{Y}). \tag{6}$$

Reducing False Positives. Corresponding to false negatives, false positives also cause serious interference to the network. Some patterns and designs in natural scenes are extremely easy to identify as text, which leads to inaccurate pseudo-labels. Replacing Supporting Region-based Reliable Score (SRRS) in [17], we propose a more reasonable Stroke Width Score (SWS) that utilizes the Stroke Width Transform (SWT) [22] to evaluate the predicted boxes of text instances. On the one hand, SRRS is not applicable to EAST based on segmentation. SRRS in [17] is define as:

$$SRRS(r^*) = \frac{1}{N_s} \sum_{i=1}^{N_s} IoU(r_i, r^*) \cdot P(c^*|r_i) \tag{7}$$

The EAST is a segmentation-based method without FPN, the text instances with small area have less supporting boxes (*i.e.,* r_i) than that with big area, which leads to the extremely unbalanced supporting boxes number (*i.e.,* N_s). On the other hand, SWT is more reasonable for eliminating non-text regions, and similar previous works [13,42] have shown its effectiveness.

SWT is a local image operator that computes the most likely stroke width for each pixel. The output of the SWT is a $n * m$ matrix where each element contains the width of the stroke associated with the pixel. Specifically, each pixel on the boundary of the stroke is connected with the opposite side of the stroke in the direction of the gradient, and the width of the connecting line is the width of the stroke for the pixel. SWS assesses the predicted boxes by utilizing the information of the corresponding stroke width, and eliminates part of the non-text regions, as shown in Fig. 3(blue line).

For a typical text region, the variance in stroke width is low since text tends to maintain a fixed stroke width. We denote the set of stroke widths in the v_{th} predicted box as W_n^v and the stroke width of the u_{th} pixel as $w_u^v \in W_n^v$. The standard deviation is as follows:

$$\sigma_v = \sqrt{\frac{1}{N} \sum_{u=1}^{N} (w_u^v - \mu^v)^2}, \tag{8}$$

where μ^v is the mean stroke width in the v_{th} predicted box. Therefore, each box has a standard deviation (σ) about the stroke width, and we choose reliable boxes with an upper threshold (ϵ_1). In addition, we further filter boxes by SWS:

$$SWS_v = \frac{w_v}{\sigma_v^2}, \tag{9}$$

w_v is the most common stroke width value for the v_{th} predicted box. By thresholding the score with a lower threshold ϵ_2, the boxes are further selected. Figure 3(b) shows that part of the FP is filtered out by SWS and σ.

4   Experiments

The proposed method is evaluated by transferring a scene text detector from synthetic datasets to real datasets. We adopt several pure synthetic data and real scene data (*i.e.,* SynthText [14] and ICDAR2015 [10]).

4.1   Dataset and Experimental Settings

Pure Synthetic Datasets. *SynthText* [14] is a large-scale dataset that contains 800 K synthetic images. These images are created by blending natural images with text rendered with random fonts, sizes, colours, and orientations, thus these images are quite realistic. *Verisimilar Image Synthesis Dataset(VISD)* [15] contains 10 k images synthesized with 10 k background images. Thus, there are no repeated background images for this dataset.

Table 1. The performance of different models on Syn2Real scene text detection dataset for SynthText/VISD→ICDAR2015 transfers. UL refers to the unlabeled data. * denotes the performance reported in UnrealText [16]. † refers to our testing performance.

Method	Source → Target (UL)	Annotation	Detection evaluation/%		
			Precision	Recall	F-score
PAN [43]	SynthText→ICDAR2015	Word	0.659	0.469	0.548
EAST [8]*	SynthText→ICDAR2015	Word	–	–	0.580
EAST [8]†	SynthText→ICDAR2015	Word	0.721	0.521	0.605
CCN [44]	SynthText→ICDAR2015	Character	–	–	0.651
EAST+Ours	SynthText→ICDAR2015	Word	0.690	0.670	0.680
EAST [8]*	VISD→ICDAR2015	Word	–	–	0.643
EAST [8]†	VISD→ICDAR2015	Word	0.640	0.652	0.645
EAST+Ours	VISD→ICDAR2015	Word	**0.748**	**0.727**	**0.738**

Real Datasets. *ICDAR2015* [10] is a multi-oriented text detection dataset for English text that includes 1,000 training images and 500 testing images. Scene text images in this dataset were taken by Google Glasses without taking care of positioning, image quality, and viewpoint. *ICDAR2013* [9] was released during the ICDAR 2013 Robust Reading Competition for focused scene text detection, consisting of high-resolution images, 229 for training and 233 for testing, containing texts in English.

Implementation Details. In all experiments, we used EAST [8] as a base network. Following the original paper, inputs were resized to 512×512, and we applied all augmentations used in the original paper. The network was trained with a batch input composed of 12 images, 6 images from the source domain, and the other 6 images from the target domain. The Adam optimizer was adopted as our learning rate scheme. All of the experiments used the same training strategy: (1) pretraining the network for 80 k iterations with ATA to learn domain-invariant features and (2) the pretrained model is used to generate corresponding pseudo-label (*i.e.,* pseudo-bounding box label and negative sample map) for each image in the target domain, then fine-tuning the pretrained model with generated pseudo-labels. In the process of generating pseudo-labels, we set ϵ_1 and ϵ_2 to 3.0 and 0.30 for stroke width elimination parameters. All of the experiments were conducted on a regular workstation (CPU: Intel(R) Core(TM) i7-7800X CPU @ 3.50 GHz; GPU: GTX 2080Ti).

4.2   Performance Comparison and Analysis

Synthetic→ICDAR2015 Transfer. Table 1 summarizes the performance comparisons for synthetic→ICDAR2015 transfer task. The EAST model as the baseline training with source-only had an unsatisfactory F-score (60.5% using SynthText and 64.5% using VISD), which can be regarded as a lower bound without adaptation. By combining with the proposed method, the F-score achieved

Table 2. The performance of different models on Syn2Real scene text detection dataset for SynthText/VISD→ICDAR2013 transfers. UL refers to the unlabeled data. * denotes the performance reported in UnrealText [16]. † refers to our testing performance.

Method	Source → Target(UL)	Annotation	Detection evaluation/%		
			Precision	Recall	F-score
EAST [8]*	SynthText→ICDAR2013	Word	–	–	0.677
EAST [8]†	SynthText→ICDAR2013	Word	0.669	0.674	0.671
EAST+Ours	SynthText→ICDAR2013	Word	0.805	0.765	0.784
EAST [8]*	VISD→ICDAR2013	Word	–	–	0.748
EAST [8]†	VISD→ICDAR2013	Word	0.783	0.705	0.742
EAST+Ours	VISD→ICDAR2013	Word	**0.830**	**0.781**	**0.805**

a 68.0% and 73.8% respectively, making 7.5% and 9.3% absolute improvements over the baseline. GCN [44] based on character annotation led to a performance improvement over that based on word annotation. However, the performances of GCN were still lower than our method, which utilizes self-training and adversarial learning. The experiment indicates the efficient performance of the proposed method in alleviating the domain discrepancy over the source and target data.

Synthetic→ICDAR2013 Transfer. To further verify the effectiveness of our proposed method, we conducted experiments by using ICDAR2013 as the target domain for the synthetic→real scene text detection transfer task. The experimental results are reported in Table 2. Specifically, for the SynthText→ICDAR2013 transfer task, compared with the baseline EAST training with source-only, we achieved an 11.3% performance improvement. Similar to synthetic→ICDAR2015 transfer experiment, VISD was also used as the source domain in the comparison experiment. After using ATA and TST, the proposed method achieved a 6.3% performance improvement over the baseline EAST, which exhibits the effectiveness of the method for reducing the domain shift. Note that for fair comparison, except for adding ATA and TST, the base network and experimental settings of the proposed method were the same as the baseline EAST.

ICDAR2013→ICDAR2015 Transfer. Table 3 shows the performance for ICDAR2013→ICDAR2015 Transfer task. The annotations of ICDAR2013 are rectangular boxes while that of ICDAR2015 are rotated boxes, which limits the transfer performance. However, comparing with the baseline EAST training with source-only, we achieved an 7.6% performance improvement.

4.3   Ablation Study

Component Analysis. To verify the effectiveness of the proposed method, we conducted ablation experiments for Syn2Real transfer task on four datasets: SynthText, VISD, ICDAR2015, and ICDAR2013. Table 3 shows the experimental results. For the SynthText→ICDAR2015 transfer task, the F-scores increased by 4.1% and 3.5% respectively, after using the TST and ATA. In addition, our

Table 3. Ablation study for the proposed Syn2Real scene text detection transfer. 'Baseline' denotes training only with labeled data in the source domain. ▲ denotes the increase in the F-score compared with the baseline training with source-only. UL refers to the unlabeled data. 'F-target' denotes pretrain in source domain and fine-tuning with original pseudo-bounding box in target domain.

Method	TST	ATA	Source→Target(UL)	Detection evaluation/%			Improv.
				Precision	Recall	F-score	
Baseline			SynthText→ICDAR2015	0.721	0.521	0.605	–
F-target				0.666	0.535	0.594	–
Ours	✓			0.693	0.605	0.646	▲ 4.1%
		✓		0.682	0.610	0.640	▲ 3.5%
	✓	✓		0.690	0.670	0.680	▲ 7.5%
Baseline			VISD→ICDAR2015	0.640	0.652	0.645	–
Ours	✓			0.702	0.658	0.695	▲ 5.0%
		✓		0.713	0.670	0.691	▲ 4.6%
	✓	✓		**0.748**	**0.727**	**0.738**	▲ 9.3%
Baseline			SynthText→ICDAR2013	0.669	0.674	0.671	–
Ours	✓			0.715	0.707	0.711	▲ 4.0%
		✓		0.736	0.721	0.729	▲ 5.8%
	✓	✓		0.805	0.765	0.784	▲ 11.3%
Baseline			VISD→ICDAR2013	0.783	0.705	0.742	–
Ours	✓			0.794	0.720	0.755	▲ 1.3%
		✓		0.802	0.751	0.776	▲ 3.4%
	✓	✓		**0.830**	**0.781**	**0.805**	▲ 6.3%
Baseline			ICDAR13→ICDAR2015	0.513	0.398	0.448	–
Ours	✓			0.546	0.459	0.505	▲ 5.7%
		✓		0.560	0.441	0.493	▲ 4.5%
	✓	✓		**0.563**	**0.490**	**0.524**	▲ 7.6%

method produced a higher recall rate of up to eight percent than the baseline, which shows the effectiveness of this approach on improving the robustness of the model. By combining both components, the F-score of the proposed method achieved a 68.0%, a 7.5% absolute improvement over the baseline. The VISD→ICDAR2015 transfer task exhibited better performance since VISD has a more realistic synthesis effect. In particular, the F-score using our method reached 73.8%, making the absolute improvement over the corresponding baseline 9.3%. For SynthText/VISD→ICDAR2015 transfers, the improved performances are also significant. We achieved a 11.3% performance improvement using SynthText and 6.3% performance improvement using VISD.

Parameter Sensitivity on TST. To explore the influence of threshold parameters (*i.e.*, ϵ_1 and ϵ_2) on SWS, we conducted several sets of comparative experiments, and the results shown are in Table 4. Threshold parameter ϵ_1 was utilized to filter the predicted box since we considered the standard deviation of the stroke width in the text region close to zero in an ideal situation. The network trained with $\epsilon_1 = 3$ showed better performance than the others, and the

Table 4. Model results for different values of ϵ_1 and ϵ_2 in Text Self-training (TST).

ϵ_2	ϵ_1	Detection evaluation/%			ϵ_1	ϵ_2	Detection evaluation/%		
		Precision	Recall	F-score			Precision	Recall	F-score
–	–	0.597	0.561	0.580	–	–	0.597	0.561	0.580
	2	0.636	0.543	0.581		0.20	0.621	0.556	0.586
	3	0.634	0.563	0.596		0.30	0.623	0.554	0.586
	4	0.612	0.565	0.588		0.40	0.645	0.550	0.594

(a) SynthText-to-ICDAR2013 Transfer   (b) SynthText-to-ICDAR2015 Transfer

Fig. 4. Examples of detection results for different models. The first row is the results of the baseline training with only source domain. The second row is the results of using the proposed method.

results were not sensitive to the parameters. Similar to ϵ_1, three different values $0.2, 0.3, 0.4$ were adopted to verify the parameter sensitivity of ϵ_2, and the result shows that the value(0.3) of ϵ_2 was reasonable.

Qualitative Analysis. Figure 4 shows four examples of detection results for synthetic-to-real transfer tasks. The exemplars show that the proposed method improves the robustness of the model.

5   Conclusions

In this paper, we first introduced a synthetic-to-real domain adaptation method for scene text detection, which transfers knowledge from synthetic data to real data. The proposed TST effectively minimizes the adverse effects of FNs and FPs for pseudo-labels, and the ATA helps the network to learn domain-invariant features in an adversarial way. We evaluated the proposed method on several common synthetic and real datasets. The experiments showed that our approach makes a great improvement for synthetic-to-real transfer text detection task.

Acknowledgments. This work is supported by the National Key Research and Development Project (2019YFC0118202), the National Natural Science Foundation of China Grant No. 61803332 and No. LQ18E050001.

References

1. He, W., Zhang, X.Y., Yin, F., Liu, C.L.: Deep direct regression for multi-oriented scene text detection. In: ICCV, pp. 745–753 (2017)
2. Wang, W., et al.: AE TextSpotter: learning visual and linguistic representation for ambiguous text spotting. arXiv preprint arXiv:2008.00714 (2020)
3. Wang, W., Xie, E., Sun, P., Wang, W., Tian, L., Shen, C.: TextSR: content-aware text super-resolution guided by recognition. arXiv preprint arXiv:1909.07113 (2019)
4. Liu, Z., Lin, G., Yang, S., Liu, F., Lin, W., Goh, W.L.: Towards robust curve text detection with conditional spatial expansion. In: CVPR, pp. 7269–7278 (2019)
5. Long, S., Ruan, J., Zhang, W., He, X., Wu, W., Yao, C.: TextSnake: a flexible representation for detecting text of arbitrary shapes. In: Ferrari, V., Hebert, M., Sminchisescu, C., Weiss, Y. (eds.) ECCV 2018. LNCS, vol. 11206, pp. 19–35. Springer, Cham (2018). https://doi.org/10.1007/978-3-030-01216-8_2
6. Xie, E., Zang, Y., Shao, S., Yu, G., Yao, C., Li, G.: Scene text detection with supervised pyramid context network. In: AAAI (2019)
7. Wang, W., et al.: Shape robust text detection with progressive scale expansion network. In: CVPR, pp. 9336–9345 (2019)
8. Zhou, X., et al.: EAST: an efficient and accurate scene text detector. In: CVPR, pp. 5551–5560 (2017)
9. Karatzas, D., et al.: ICDAR 2013 robust reading competition. In: 2013 12th ICDAR, pp. 1484–1493. IEEE (2013)
10. Karatzas, D., et al.: ICDAR 2015 competition on robust reading. In: 2015 13th ICDAR, pp. 1156–1160. IEEE (2015)
11. Nayef, N., et al.: ICDAR 2017 robust reading challenge on multi-lingual scene text detection and script identification-RRC-MLT. In: 2017 14th ICDAR, vol. 1, pp. 1454–1459. IEEE (2017)
12. Yuan, T.L., Zhu, Z., Xu, K., Li, C.J., Hu, S.M.: Chinese text in the wild. arXiv preprint arXiv:1803.00085 (2018)
13. Yao, C., Bai, X., Liu, W., Ma, Y., Tu, Z.: Detecting texts of arbitrary orientations in natural images. In: CVPR. IEEE (2012)
14. Gupta, A., Vedaldi, A., Zisserman, A.: Synthetic data for text localisation in natural images. In: CVPR, pp. 2315–2324 (2016)
15. Zhan, F., Lu, S., Xue, C.: Verisimilar image synthesis for accurate detection and recognition of texts in scenes. In: Ferrari, V., Hebert, M., Sminchisescu, C., Weiss, Y. (eds.) ECCV 2018. LNCS, vol. 11212, pp. 257–273. Springer, Cham (2018). https://doi.org/10.1007/978-3-030-01237-3_16
16. Long, S., Yao, C.: UnrealText: synthesizing realistic scene text images from the unreal world. arXiv preprint arXiv:2003.10608 (2020)
17. Kim, S., Choi, J., Kim, T., Kim, C.: Self-training and adversarial background regularization for unsupervised domain adaptive one-stage object detection. In: ICCV, pp. 6092–6101 (2019)
18. Ganin, Y., Lempitsky, V.: Unsupervised domain adaptation by backpropagation. arXiv preprint arXiv:1409.7495 (2014)

19. Rosenberg, C., Hebert, M., Schneiderman, H.:Semi-supervised self-training of object detection models. WACV/MOTION **2** (2005)
20. RoyChowdhury, A., et al.: Automatic adaptation of object detectors to new domains using self-training. In: CVPR, pp. 780–790 (2019)
21. Zou, Y., Yu, Z., Vijaya Kumar, B.V.K., Wang, J.: Unsupervised domain adaptation for semantic segmentation via class-balanced self-training. In: Ferrari, V., Hebert, M., Sminchisescu, C., Weiss, Y. (eds.) ECCV 2018. LNCS, vol. 11207, pp. 297–313. Springer, Cham (2018). https://doi.org/10.1007/978-3-030-01219-9_18
22. Epshtein, B., Ofek, E., Wexler, Y.: Detecting text in natural scenes with stroke width transform. In: CVPR, pp. 2963–2970. IEEE (2010)
23. Neumann, L., Matas, J.: A method for text localization and recognition in real-world images. In: Kimmel, R., Klette, R., Sugimoto, A. (eds.) ACCV 2010. LNCS, vol. 6494, pp. 770–783. Springer, Heidelberg (2011). https://doi.org/10.1007/978-3-642-19318-7_60
24. Xu, Y., Wang, Y., Zhou, W., Wang, Y., Yang, Z., Bai, X.: TextField: learning a deep direction field for irregular scene text detection. IEEE Trans. Image Process. **28**, 5566–5579 (2019)
25. Liao, M., Shi, B., Bai, X.: TextBoxes++: a single-shot oriented scene text detector. IEEE Trans. Image Process. **27**, 3676–3690 (2018)
26. Deng, D., Liu, H., Li, X., Cai, D.: PixelLink: detecting scene text via instance segmentation. In: AAAI (2018)
27. Li, X., Wang, W., Hou, W., Liu, R.Z., Lu, T., Yang, J.: Shape robust text detection with progressive scale expansion network. arXiv preprint arXiv:1806.02559 (2018)
28. Tian, S., Lu, S., Li, C.: WeText: scene text detection under weak supervision. In: ICCV (2017) 1492–1500
29. Hu, H., Zhang, C., Luo, Y., Wang, Y., Han, J., Ding, E.: WordSup: exploiting word annotations for character based text detection. In: ICCV, pp. 4940–4949 (2017)
30. Wu, W., Xing, J., Yang, C., Wang, Y., Zhou, H.: Texts as lines: text detection with weak supervision. Math. Probl. Eng. **2020** (2020)
31. Gong, B., Shi, Y., Sha, F., Grauman, K.: Geodesic flow kernel for unsupervised domain adaptation. In: CVPR, pp. 2066–2073. IEEE (2012)
32. Chen, Y., Li, W., Sakaridis, C., Dai, D., Van Gool, L.: Domain adaptive faster R-CNN for object detection in the wild. In: CVPR, pp. 3339–3348 (2018)
33. Zhan, F., Xue, C., Lu, S.: GA-DAN: geometry-aware domain adaptation network for scene text detection and recognition. In: ICCV, pp. 9105–9115 (2019)
34. Bhunia, A.K., Das, A., Bhunia, A.K., Kishore, P.S.R., Roy, P.P.: Handwriting recognition in low-resource scripts using adversarial learning. In: CVPR (2019)
35. Lee, D.H.: Pseudo-label: the simple and efficient semi-supervised learning method for deep neural networks. In: Workshop, ICML, vol. 3 (2013)
36. Choi, J., Jeong, M., Kim, T., Kim, C.: Pseudo-labeling curriculum for unsupervised domain adaptation. arXiv preprint arXiv:1908.00262 (2019)
37. Chen, M., Weinberger, K.Q., Blitzer, J.: Co-training for domain adaptation. In: Advances in neural information processing systems, pp. 2456–2464 (2011)
38. Saito, K., Ushiku, Y., Harada, T.: Asymmetric tri-training for unsupervised domain adaptation. arXiv preprint arXiv:1702.08400 (2017)
39. Shu, R., Bui, H.H., Narui, H., Ermon, S.: A DIRT-T approach to unsupervised domain adaptation. arXiv preprint arXiv:1802.08735 (2018)
40. Zhang, W., Ouyang, W., Li, W., Xu, D.: Collaborative and adversarial network for unsupervised domain adaptation. In: CVPR, pp. 3801–3809 (2018)
41. Inoue, N., Furuta, R., Yamasaki, T., Aizawa, K.: Cross-domain weakly-supervised object detection through progressive domain adaptation. In: CVPR (2018)

42. Özgen, A.C., Fasounaki, M., Ekenel, H.K.: Text detection in natural and computer-generated images. In: 2018 26th Signal Processing and Communications Applications Conference (SIU), pp. 1–4. IEEE (2018)

43. Wang, W., et al.: Efficient and accurate arbitrary-shaped text detection with pixel aggregation network. In: ICCV, pp. 8440–8449 (2019)

44. Xing, L., Tian, Z., Huang, W., Scott, M.R.: Convolutional character networks. In: ICCV, pp. 9126–9136 (2019)

Scale-Aware Polar Representation for Arbitrarily-Shaped Text Detection

Yanguang Bi and Zhiqiang Hu[✉]

SenseTime Research, Beijing, China
{biyanguang,huzhiqiang}@sensetime.com

Abstract. Arbitrarily-shaped text detection faces two major challenges: 1) various scales and 2) irregular angles. Previous works regress the text boundary in Cartesian coordinates as ordinary object detection. However, such grid space interleaves the unique scale and angle attributes of text, which seriously affects detection performance. The implicit disregard of text scale also impairs multi-scale detection ability. To better learn the arbitrary text boundary and handle the text scale variation, we propose a novel Scale-Aware Polar Representation (SAPR) framework. The text boundary is represented in Polar coordinates, where scale and angle of text could be both clearly expressed for targeted learning. This simple but effective transformation brings significant performance improvement. The explicit learning on separated text scale also promotes the multi-scale detection ability. Based on the Polar representation, we design line IoU loss and symmetry sine loss to better optimize the scale and angle of text with a multi-path decoder architecture. Furthermore, an accurate center line calculation is proposed to guide text boundary restoration under various scales. Overall, the proposed SAPR framework is able to effectively detect arbitrarily-shaped texts and tackle the scale variation simultaneously. The state-of-the-art results on multiple benchmarks solidly demonstrate the effectiveness and superiority of SAPR.

1 Introduction

Scene text detection plays an important role in numerous applications, such as real-time text translation, product identification, image retrieve and autonomous driving. In recent years, deep learning based methods exhibit promising detection performance [1–4]. The promotion mainly benefits from the development of Convolutional Neural Networks (CNN) [5] and research on detection [6–8] and segmentation [9,10]. However, many existing methods with quadrilateral bounding-box outputs may suffer from texts with arbitrary shapes. Consequently, more and more recent works [11–18] begin to focus on arbitrarily-shaped text detection.

The two basic and independent attributes of arbitrarily-shaped text are: 1) various scales and 2) irregular angles, which also become the major challenges in detection task. As shown in Fig. 1, the text prototypes could form arbitrary shapes based on scale and angle transformations. Since text is usually composed of multiple individual characters, the formulation of arbitrary boundary in Fig. 1

H. Ishikawa et al. (Eds.): ACCV 2020, LNCS 12624, pp. 304–321, 2021.
https://doi.org/10.1007/978-3-030-69535-4_19

Fig. 1. Scale and angle attributes are the two basic and independent attributes of text boundary, which could form arbitrary shapes. From a decomposition perspective, the shape formulation is actually the scaling and rotation of small local areas.

is actually the simple scaling and rotation of small local areas, which could be naturally expressed in Polar coordinates. Therefore, we are motivated to detect arbitrarily-shaped text using Polar representation.

Figure 2 presents the comparison of existing regular Cartesian representation and our novel Polar representation. For the scene text in Fig. 2(a), many methods [15,19–21] regress the text boundary in Cartesian coordinates, as shown in Fig. 2(b)–(c). Compared with Fig. 2(b), Fig. 2(c) is more reasonable and stable which only focuses on the nearest boundary. While this is common in ordinary object detection, the unique scale and angle attributes of text are interleaved in such grid space. The force learning of unrelated attributes seriously affects detection performance, as shown in following experiments. The scale attribute of text is also implicitly disregarded, which impairs multi-scale detection ability. The overall detection performance in Cartesian space is thus largely suppressed. Conversely, Fig. 2(d) shows our Polar representation for arbitrarily-shaped texts. The independent scale and angle attributes are both clearly expressed, which is beneficial to boundary learning. Furthermore, the scale attribute is explicitly extracted and allows more effective end-to-end optimization. The multi-scale detection ability is thus promoted. On the whole, the transformation from Cartesian space to Polar space is simple but effective, which breaks the grid bottlenecks and brings significant performance improvement.

Based on the novel Polar representation, a unified Scale-Aware Polar Representation (SAPR) framework is proposed to better detect arbitrarily-shaped text and handle scale variation simultaneously. We dedicatedly design line IoU loss and symmetry sine loss to optimize the scale and angle attributes of text, respectively. Compared with L_1 loss and monotonous cosine loss, the tailored losses bring more performance improvement. A novel network architecture with multi-path decoder is also developed to better extract features from different scales. Besides, we propose a more accurate calculation of text center line which is frequently used in text detection task to complete entire boundary. Instead of complicated network prediction, we simply encode the symmetry distances of scale attribute. The produced center line could automatically fit various scales. Integrating above work, the unified SAPR framework is able to effectively detect

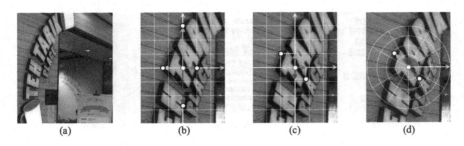

Fig. 2. (a) Arbitrarily-shaped texts. (b)–(c) Cartesian representations on global and local text. (d) The proposed Polar representation, which clearly depicts angle and scale attributes of text. Specifically, the scale attribute in (d) is decomposed into top distance (green arrow) and bottom distance (purple arrow). (Color figure online)

texts with arbitrary shapes and handle the scale variation. The state-of-the-art empirical results on different benchmarks, especially the large improvement on arbitrarily-shaped datasets, demonstrate the effectiveness of SAPR.

The contributions of this work are summarized as follows: (1) We propose a novel Polar representation to better model arbitrary text boundary and learn the scale attribute simultaneously; (2) Based on the Polar representation, we develop line IoU loss and symmetry sine loss with multi-path decoder architecture as a unified Scale-Aware Polar Representation (SAPR) framework; (3) Instead of learning segmentation or attractive links, we proposed a more accurate and simple text center line extraction based on the symmetry distances of scale attribute; (4) SAPR achieves state-of-the-art performances on challenging Total-Text, CTW1500 and MSRA-TD500 benchmarks, which contain curved, multi-oriented and long texts.

2   Related Work

In recent years, most of the scene text detection methods are based on deep learning. They can be roughly divided into two categories: regression based methods and segmentation based methods.

Regression based methods benefit from the development of general object detection. Inspired by the Faster RCNN [7], CTPN [1] detects horizontal texts by grouping adjacent and compact text components. TextBoxes [22] and RRD [23] adopt the architecture of SSD [8] to detect texts with different aspect ratios. As the anchor-free methods, EAST [2] and DeepReg [24] predict the text boundary directly, which is similar to DenseBox [6]. RRPN [3] generates proposals with different rotations to detect multi-oriented texts. PMTD [4] is built on Mask RCNN [25] and produces quadrilateral boundary from pyramid mask. [26] detects texts by localizing corner points of bounding boxes. Most of the regression-based methods only predict quadrilateral bounding boxes with fixed number of vertexes. Therefore, such methods are difficult to detect texts with arbitrary shapes. Besides, the limited receptive field of CNN also affects the detection performance on long texts.

Segmentation based methods benefit from the development of semantic segmentation. The Fully Convolutional Network (FCN) [9] and U-Net [10] are widely used structures. These methods aim to segment the text instances from backgrounds. For example, PixelLink [27] predicts the pixel classification and its neighborhood connections to obtain instances. With the rise of arbitrarily-shaped text detection trend, segmentation based methods become the main-stream because pixel-level classification is friendly to irregular shapes. However, the segmentation may cause adhesion when two text instances are close. There-fore, most of the segmentation based methods struggle to split adjacent texts. TextSnake [11], MSR [20] and LOMO [15] segment the center region and restore the boundary based on their regression results. TextField [17] predicts directional field to aggravate different instances. PSENet [28] predicts multiple kernels with different sizes and gradually merge them to produce final result. TextMoun-tain [18] segment the center region of texts which are unconnected, then assign boundary pixels to corresponding center.

It is worth noting that compared with heuristic TextSnake, our method learns the text boundary end-to-end using polar representation. TextSnake and LOMO limit the shape regression to center region, while our method adaptively repre-sents arbitrary texts anywhere. Moreover, our center line is calculated automat-ically with the symmetry scale distances in polar representation, which avoids extra complicated center learning.

3   Method

In this section, we first introduce the entire pipeline of SAPR framework. Next, the structure of network with multi-path decoder and the loss functions tailored for Polar representation are introduced. Then, the reconstruction of complete text boundary is presented in details. Finally, the label generation is described.

3.1   Scale-Aware Polar Representation Framework

The entire pipeline of SAPR framework is presented in Fig. 3. Overall, SAPR employs classification branch as mask to roughly locate texts and employs regres-sion branch to precisely refine the boundary in Polar space. Specially, the scale attribute is decomposed into top distance and bottom distance, as shown by the green and purple arrows in Fig. 2(d). The angle is defined as the counterclockwise rotation along the positive half axis. For an input image, the network produces text confidence from classification branch and angle, top distance, bottom dis-tance from regression branch. The text confidence map is segmented to obtain text mask, which is used to cover valid text regions in regression maps. Based on top distance and bottom distance, we calculate the center line and extract the skeleton. Each individual center line skeleton is used to integrate local boundary restored by regression results and form a complete text boundary.

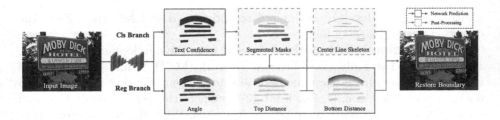

Fig. 3. The overview of SAPR framework. The center line skeleton is obtained automatically based on top distance and bottom distance, which guides the entire boundary restoration. The blue boxes with solid lines denote the outputs of network. The green boxes with dash lines denote post-processing. (Color figure online)

Based on the suitable representation in Polar space, SAPR could better learn arbitrary text boundary and handle the scale problem compared with Cartesian methods [15, 19–21]. Different from heuristic approach [11], SAPR directly learns the text boundary with more effective and end-to-end manner which also simplifies the boundary restoration. In addition, the center text line is calculated easily and accurately with symmetry distances of scale attribute, which avoids complicated network learning of segmentation [11, 15] or attractive links [29, 30]. It is worth noting that the instance segmentation [31] also employ the polar representation with single center and fixed angle prior. However, the above simple representation is not suitable to curved texts with complex ribbon shapes. In contrast, our polar representation with various local centers and flexible angles could precisely describe irregular boundary and obtain promising performance.

On the whole, the Polar representation artfully express the scale and angle attributes of arbitrarily-shaped texts. Many bottlenecks in ordinary Cartesian space are solved gracefully. Therefore, SAPR achieves significant improvement of detection performance.

3.2   Network

The network of SAPR follows the typical encoder-decoder structure shown in Fig. 4. As a powerful feature extractor, the encoder produces rich feature maps with multiple levels. Generally, single path structure like U-Net is employed as the decoder. However, simple decoder may be too weak to process the rich and abstract information passed from encoder under complex multi-task learning. Besides, the high-level semantic information from the deep layers would also be diluted gradually during fusion.

Inspired by DLA [32] and GridNet [33], we develop a new decoder with multiple paths to better utilize information under different scales. During decoding, each path creates new aggregated features which are passed to next path via residual connections. We concatenate outputs from different paths for two parallel branches: text/non-text classification and shape regression. The multi-path decoder has more powerful representation ability to extract and analyze information from encoder for abstract and complex regression. At the same time, residual connections allow network to automatically learn the utilization degree of features in different scales. Thus the aggregation produces more effective features for multi-scale text detection.

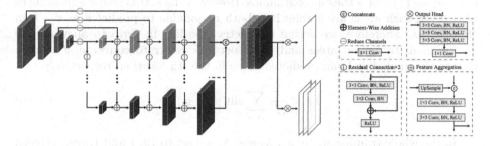

Fig. 4. The detailed structure of network with multi-path decoder. "Conv", "BN", "ReLU" and "UpSample" denote convolution, batch normalization, rectified linear unit and 2× bilinear up-sampling, respectively.

3.3 Loss Function

The loss for multi-task learning is formulated as

$$L = \lambda_1 L_{cls} + \lambda_2 L_{dis} + \lambda_3 L_\theta \tag{1}$$

where L_{cls}, L_{dis} and L_θ represent the losses of text/non-text classification, distance regression and angle regression, respectively.

Binary cross-entropy loss shown in Eq. 2 is employed as the classification loss for fair comparison. $\mathcal{M}$ is the training mask to ignore invalid regions. $\widehat{y}_i$ and y_i denote ground truth and predicted label in the ith location, respectively.

$$L_{cls} = \frac{1}{|\mathcal{M}|} \sum_{i \in \mathcal{M}} \left(-\widehat{y}_i \log y_i - (1 - \widehat{y}_i) \log (1 - y_i) \right) \tag{2}$$

Instead of using norm losses like L_2, L_1 and *Smooth* L_1, we design line IoU loss, i.e., the one-dimensional (1D) version of original IoU loss [34] for top and bottom distances regression. In Eq. 5, the $\widehat{d}_i^{top}$, $\widehat{d}_i^{bot}$, d_i^{top} and d_i^{bot} denote top distance label, bottom distance label, predicted top distance and predicted bottom distance in the ith location, respectively. $\mathcal{T}$ denotes valid text regions. The proposed line IoU loss could better handle texts with various heights and thus contributes to the multi-scale detection.

$$d_i^{inter} = \min \left(\widehat{d}_i^{top}, d_i^{top} \right) + \min \left(\widehat{d}_i^{bot}, d_i^{bot} \right) \tag{3}$$

$$\widehat{d}_i = \widehat{d}_i^{top} + \widehat{d}_i^{bot}, d_i = d_i^{top} + d_i^{bot} \tag{4}$$

$$L_{dis} = -\frac{1}{|\mathcal{T}|} \sum_{i \in \mathcal{T}} \log\left(\frac{d_i^{inter}}{\widehat{d_i} + d_i - d_i^{inter}}\right) \tag{5}$$

In horizontal text areas, the angle may change dramatically between 180° and 0°. The angle label is thus discontinuous. However, the actual shape appearances of texts in such areas are stable. It is both reasonable to predict θ or $\pi - \theta$ in these areas. Therefore, we design symmetry sine loss in Eq. 6 to alleviate the confusion in transition areas and make network easier to converge. $\widehat{\theta}_i$ and θ_i denote the angle label and predicted angle in the ith location, respectively.

$$L_\theta = \frac{1}{|\mathcal{T}|} \sum_{i \in \mathcal{T}} \sin(|\widehat{\theta}_i - \theta_i|) \tag{6}$$

In the whole training stage, λ_1, λ_2 and λ_3 are set to 10, 1 and 1, respectively.

3.4   Label Generation

The labels includes: (1) text confidence, (2) top distance, (3) bottom distance and (4) angle. Figure 5 shows the detailed label generation from polygon annotation.

Assuming that the annotations only include ordered vertexes. The preparation of label generation is finding the 4 key vertexes denoted by the green numbers 1–4 in Fig. 5. For convenience, each text instance annotation is formulated as $\mathcal{V} = \{v_1, ..., v_i, ..., v_n\}$ and $n \geq 4$, where n denotes the number of polygon vertexes. Each vertex v_i can be viewed as the intersection point of two adjacent sides denoted by $\vec{v_l}$ and $\vec{v_r}$. We define θ_i in Eq. 7 to measure degree of direction change of these two adjacent sides. The v_i is more likely to being a key vertex when θ_i is smaller, i.e., the adjacent sides construct a 90° angle.

$$\theta_i = |90° - \arccos(\vec{v_l} \cdot \vec{v_r} / (\|\vec{v_l}\| \|\vec{v_r}\|))| \tag{7}$$

The entire label generation requires the nearest two side points p_t and p_b on polygon annotation in the normal direction, which are the white points in Fig. 5. Firstly, we construct the two paths between key vertexes 1–2 and key vertexes 3–4, denoted by l_t and l_b. Then, these two paths are sampled densely as $l_t = \{p_{t1}, ..., p_{ti}...p_{tm}\}$ and $l_b = \{p_{b1}, ..., p_{bi}...p_{bm}\}$ where m is the number of sampled points. For any location p in text region, we can calculate the distance d_i between p and the each line determined by (p_{ti}, p_{bi}). In this way, the nearest two side points p_t and p_b assigned for current location p could be obtained as:

$$p_t = p_{\widehat{ti}}, p_b = p_{\widehat{bi}}, \tag{8}$$

$$\widehat{i} = \arg\min_i d_i. \tag{9}$$

The text confidence label is the height-shrunk version of complete text mask, while the length on reading direction remains unchanged. For the height-shrunk mask, a appropriate ratio helps avoiding adhesion and ambiguous regression in the edge area compared with the original ratio = 0 mask. A big ratio would

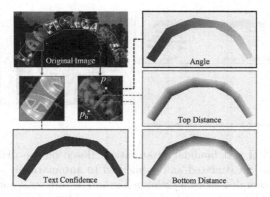

Fig. 5. The label generation based on original polygon annotation. The text confidence label is the height-shrunk version of complete text mask. The top distance and bottom distance labels are the lengths between current location p with the higher side point p_t and the lower side point p_b, respectively. The angle label is the angle between the local normal vector $\langle p_b, p_t \rangle$ with horizontal direction.

cause confusion to classify the surrounding text as background. The ratio is not sensitive and works well in [0.15, 0.4], so we chose 0.3. The top distance label (green arrow) and bottom distance label (purple arrow) are the lengths between current location p with the higher side point p_t and the lower side point p_b, respectively. The angle label (red sector) is the angle between the local normal vector $\langle p_b, p_t \rangle$ and horizontal direction which ranges from $0°$ to $180°$.

3.5   Text Boundary Restoration

Figure 6 presents the detailed text boundary restoration. Firstly, the centerness is calculated based on top distance and bottom distance:

$$c_i = \frac{2 * \min\left(d_i^{top}, d_i^{bot}\right)}{d_i^{top} + d_i^{bot}} \tag{10}$$

where d_i^{top}, d_i^{bot} and c_i denote predicted top distance, predicted bottom distance and centerness in the ith location, respectively. The centerness ranges in [0, 1] with mountain appearance where the regions closer to center have larger values. Then, the center line could be easily segmented and skeletonized from centerness map. Each center line skeleton is considered as a individual instance to avoid adhesion. For example, the two small texts in the bottom right corner of Fig. 6 are dense and stick together. The skeleton successfully separate the adhesive texts. Next, the anchor points are sampled on each center line skeleton evenly. Based on the Polar coordinates regression in its surrounding region, each anchor point could directly produce corresponding local boundary.

Specifically, the transformation from predicted Polar coordinates to Cartesian coordinates contains two steps: 1) scale restoration and 2) angle restoration.

Fig. 6. The details of text boundary restoration. Based on top distance and bottom distance, centerness is calculated and segmented to automatically obtain center line. Anchor points are sampled on each skeleton line and restore scale and angle attributes. The complete boundary is formed by integrating local boundaries.

Assuming that (x_i, y_i) denotes ith location in original image, where the regressed Polar coordinates are top distance d_i^{top}, bottom distance d_i^{bot} and angle θ_i. It is noteworthy that θ_i is the counterclockwise rotation along the positive half axis. The Cartesian coordinates of two local boundary points (x_i^t, y_i^t) and (x_i^b, y_i^b) are:

$$\begin{bmatrix} x_i^t & x_i^b \\ y_i^t & y_i^b \end{bmatrix} = \begin{bmatrix} \cos\Delta\theta & -\sin\Delta\theta \\ \sin\Delta\theta & \cos\Delta\theta \end{bmatrix} \begin{bmatrix} 0 & 0 \\ d_i^{top} & -d_i^{bot} \end{bmatrix} + \begin{bmatrix} x_i \\ y_i \end{bmatrix} \tag{11}$$

where $\Delta\theta = \theta - \dfrac{\pi}{2}$. The complete detection boundary is obtained by integrating the local boundary points.

Overall, the encoded centerness automatically produces accurate center line under different scales. The extracted skeletons naturally solve the adhesion problem. Besides, it avoids complicated network prediction of segmentation [11,15] or attractive links [29,30] to integrate local boundaries. The entire text boundary restoration is thus simplified and more robust.

4   Experiments

4.1   Datasets

SynthText [35] is a synthetic dataset which contains 800K synthetic images. The texts are artificially rendered with random attributes. Like other methods, SynthText is used to pre-train our network.

Total-Text [36] is a recently released word-level dataset. It consists 1255 training images and 300 testing images with horizontal, multi-oriented, and curved texts. The annotations are polygons with variable vertexes.

CTW1500 [37] is a text-line based text dataset with 1000 training images and 500 testing images. Similar to Total-Text, the texts are also horizontal, multi-oriented, and curved. The annotations are polygons with fixed 14 vertexes.

MSRA-TD500 [38] is a line-level dataset with 300 training images and 200 test images of multi-oriented and long texts. The annotations are rotated rectangles. The training set is relatively small, so we also include 400 images from HUST-TR400 [39] according to previous works [2,11,26].

Fig. 7. Qualitative results of SAPR on different benchmarks. From top to bottom in rows: Total-Text, CTW1500, MSRA-TD500.

4.2   Implementation Details

We use ResNet50 [5] pre-trained on ImageNet [40] as the backbone of network, which produces 4 levels feature maps denoted by C_2, C_3, C_4 and C_5. Their channels are reduced to 32, 64, 128 and 256, respectively. The decoder is equipped with 3 paths. The output channel of aggregation module is the same as the minimum channel number of two input features. The final outputs have strides of 4 pixels with respect to the input image.

The training contains two phase: pre-train and fine-tune. The model is optimized using ADAM with batch-size 32 and the learning rate decreases under cosine schedule. We use SynthText [35] to pre-train the model for 1 epoch. The learning rate is from 1×10^{-3} to 1×10^{-4}. Then, we fine-tune the model on different benchmarks for 100 epochs, respectively. The learning rate is from 3×10^{-4} to 1×10^{-5}. The blurred texts labeled as DO NOT CARE are ignored in training.

During the data augmentation, we set the short sides of training images in [640, 1280] randomly. The heights of images are set in ratio [0.7, 1.3] randomly while widths keep unchanged. The images are rotated in $[-15°, 15°]$ randomly. 640×640 random patches are cropped as the final training data.

During the evaluation on three benchmarks, the short sides of images are all fixed to 960 to report the single scale results. The evaluation on MSRA-TD500 requires box with fixed 4 vertexes, so we extract rotated rectangle with the minimum area around original detected polygon as the final result.

Table 1. Quantitative results of different methods on Total-Text, CTW1500 and MSRA-TD500 benchmarks. The best score is highlighted in bold.

Datasets	Total-text			CTW1500			MSRA-TD500		
Method	Precision	Recall	F-score	Precision	Recall	F-score	Precision	Recall	F-score
SegLink [29]	30.3	23.8	26.7	-	-	-	86.0	70.0	77.0
EAST [2]	50.0	36.2	42.0	-	-	-	87.3	67.4	76.1
CENet [41]	59.9	54.4	57.0	-	-	-	85.9	75.3	80.2
CTD [37]	74.0	71.0	73.0	74.3	65.2	69.5	84.5	77.1	80.6
SLPR [19]	-	-	-	80.1	70.1	74.8	-	-	-
TextSnake [11]	82.7	74.5	78.4	67.9	**85.3**	75.6	83.2	73.9	78.3
SAE [13]	-	-	-	82.7	77.8	80.1	84.2	**81.7**	82.9
MSR [20]	85.2	73.0	78.6	84.1	79.0	81.5	87.4	76.7	81.7
AGBL [42]	84.9	73.5	78.8	83.9	76.6	80.1	86.6	72.0	78.6
TextField [17]	81.2	79.9	80.6	83.0	79.8	81.4	87.4	75.9	81.3
PSENet [28]	84.0	78.0	80.9	84.8	79.7	82.2	-	-	-
FTSN [43]	84.7	78.0	81.3	-	-	-	87.6	77.1	82.0
SWSL [44]	80.6	82.3	81.4	77.0	79.9	78.5	-	-	-
SegLink++ [30]	82.1	80.9	81.5	82.8	79.8	81.3	-	-	-
IncepText [45]	-	-	-	-	-	-	87.5	79.0	83.0
MCN [46]	-	-	-	-	-	-	88.0	79.0	83.0
Relation [47]	86.0	80.5	83.1	85.8	80.9	83.3	87.2	79.4	83.1
LOMO [15]	87.6	79.3	83.3	85.7	76.5	80.8	-	-	-
CRAFT [16]	87.6	79.9	83.6	86.0	81.1	83.5	88.2	78.2	82.9
ContourNet [48]	86.9	**83.9**	85.4	83.7	84.1	83.9	-	-	-
SAPR (ours)	**89.5**	82.6	**85.9**	**89.8**	83.2	**86.4**	**92.5**	75.7	**83.3**

4.3   Comparisons with State-of-the-Art Methods

Arbitrarily-Shaped Text. Total-Text and CTW1500 are recently introduced datasets with arbitrarily-shaped texts. They are specially curated as the two most important benchmarks to evaluate the arbitrarily-shaped text detection performance. The quantitative comparisons on Total-Text and CTW1500 are shown in Table 1. SAPR achieves the new state-of-the-art performances on both challenging datasets with significant improvements. SAPR designs better polar representation thus output boundaries are more accurate with high confidence. Therefore, we use higher threshold to show precision superiority while suppress recall. Some detection results are presented in the first and second rows of Fig. 7, where arbitrarily-shaped texts under different scales are all precisely located. It solidly demonstrates the effectiveness of Polar representation and tailored framework on arbitrarily-shaped text detection.

Regular Text. We also evaluate SAPR on regular quadrilateral texts to prove the generalization ability. Among the different regular datasets, MSRA-TD500 is more challenging with a large amount of multi-oriented and extreme long texts. The quantitative comparison result is shown in Table 1 and SAPR still achieves the state-of-the-art performance. Some detection results are presented in the third row of Fig. 7, where the texts with multiple orientations and extreme long lengths are all accurately detected under various scales. This comparison indicates that SAPR could also seamlessly adapt to other types of text detection.

Fig. 8. The qualitative comparison between Cartesian baseline and SAPR under different scales. The red arrow, green arrow and yellow arrow denote false alarm, miss and inaccurate boundary, respectively. (Color figure online)

Table 2. Comparison of Cartesian baseline and SAPR framework. "F", "F-small", "F-medium" and "F-large" denote the overall F-score, F-scores of small, medium and large texts, respectively.

Method	Polar space	Multi-path decoder	Line IoU loss	Symmetry sine loss	F	F-small	F-medium	F-large
Cartesian baseline	-		-	-	77.3	66.1	74.1	78.4
	-	✓	-	-	78.4	68.5	75.4	79.6
SAPR (ours)	✓				81.6	70.4	81.1	84.0
	✓	✓			82.7	72.7	82.4	84.1
	✓	✓	✓		85.3	77.3	**85.3**	87.1
	✓	✓	✓	✓	**85.9**	**77.9**	84.5	**87.5**

4.4 Ablation Study

Scale-Aware Polar Representation. To exhibit the effectiveness of SAPR, we train a similar model using the Cartesian representation [15,20] in Fig. 2(c) as baseline while other configurations remain the same. Meanwhile, we divide texts into small, medium and large inspired by COCO dataset [49] to clearly demonstrate the scale-aware ability. For Total-Text, the texts with height in (0,

27), (27, 50) and (50, ∞) are defined as small, medium and large, which occupy 42%, 31% and 27% of entire dataset, respectively.

Table 2 presents the detailed ablation results. During the evaluation, we use single path decoder, L_1 loss and monotonous cosine loss [2] as substitutes. The Cartesian baseline obtains 77.3% F-score. When our Polar representation is adopted, the F-score obviously increases to 81.6%. The F-scores of all three scale ranges also obtain promising improvement. It solidly demonstrates that the proposed Polar representation clearly decouple the independent scale and angle attributes of text, which is more suitable for learning distinguish features and improves detection performance. At the same time, the explicit learning of scale attribute also contributes to multi-scale detection ability.

Furthermore, the multi-path decoder promotes both the performances of Cartesian baseline and SAPR. It indicates the effectiveness of proposed multi-path structure to extract features from multiple scales. With the line IoU loss, the overall F-score increases obviously to 85.3% where the F-small obtains around 5% absolute improvement. Moreover, symmetry sine loss brings 0.6% absolute improvement. It proves that the tailored losses could effectively describe and optimize the scale and angle attributes of text. On the whole, the F-scores of overall and different scale ranges are gradually improved with proposed components. It demonstrates the effectiveness of SAPR framework to detect arbitrarily-shaped texts and handle the scale variation problem. In particular, the evaluation tool DetEval [50] allows many-to-one and one-to-many matches which may slightly affect the detection results in current scale range [51].

Figure 8 shows qualitative comparison between Cartesian baseline and SAPR under different scales. The decoupling learning of independent angle and scale attributes is beneficial for network to explore more essential features of texts, which effectively reduces the false alarms (red arrow). Meanwhile, the miss of vague and indistinguishable text (green arrow) which are easy to mix with background are also improved. In addition, the Cartesian baseline may produce inaccurate boundaries with low quality (yellow arrow). By contrast, SAPR precisely locates texts with arbitrary shapes and various scales, which solidly demonstrates the superior performance of SAPR.

Table 3. The comparison of mean and variance of F-scores over dataset with multiple scale-fluctuations.

Method	F-score mean	F-score variance
Cartesian baseline	75.1	3.17
SAPR (ours)	**83.7**	**2.51**

Although SAPR exhibits promising performances on different benchmarks, there are two types of fail cases: (1) The texts with blurry appearance are difficult to distinguish by the classification branch; (2) The boundary of too small/short texts produced by the regression branch may be not accurate and unstable.

Scale Robustness. To further confirm the scale-aware ability, the short sides of input images in Total-Text dataset are set in [640, 1280] with step 40 to obtain the F-score fluctuation as metric. Table 3 presents the mean and variance of F-scores with multiple scale-fluctuations. SAPR achieves 8.6% absolute F-score improvement compared with Cartesian baseline. Meanwhile, the variance also decreases obviously. It solidly demonstrates that the Polar representation clearly separates scale attribute of text, which allows more focused and effective learning on scale problem. With tailored line IoU loss, SAPR is able to be robust to complex scale variation.

Table 4. Comparison of decoder with paths of different numbers.

#Path	1	2	3	4
Params (M)	35.44	34.43	32.53	33.59
Flops (G)	11.04	7.95	7.43	8.14
F-score	83.5	84.4	**85.9**	83.7

Table 5. Comparison of center line generation between common direct segmentation and our distance encoding.

Center line	Precision	Recall	F-score
Direct segmentation	83.9	77.3	80.5
Distance encode	**89.5**	**82.6**	**85.9**

Center Line Generation. We propose to use local top and bottom distance to encode the center line of text. For comparison, the classification branch is added a new channel to predict center line as baseline. During inference, the center line is directly segmented from the output of corresponding channel. As shown in Table 5, encoding the distance to produce center line achieves 5.4% absolute improvement compared with direct segmentation. Actually, it is hard for network to learn the accurate center line, which is imagined artificially and prone to confused by the similar texts in surrounding sides. From the perspective of symmetry distance, encoding the top and bottom could naturally and easily produce reasonable center line with better quality.

Number of Decoder Path. The number of paths in decoder would affect final performance. We design decoders with paths of different numbers to find the best configuration. The parameters and flops (224×224 input) are tried to set similar by adjusting channels for fair comparison. Table 4 shows the comparison on Total-Text dataset. Compared with single-path decoder, multi-path decoders usually have better performance. However, more paths may be too complex to be trained efficiently with limited data. The decoder with 3 paths achieves the highest F-score, which is selected as our default configuration.

5   Conclusion

In this paper, we reveal the basic independent attributes of arbitrarily-shaped text boundary: 1) various scales and 2) irregular angles. Cartesian based methods interleave the independent angle and scale attributes, which affects detection performance and suppresses multi-scale detection ability. We propose a novel Scale-Aware Polar Representation (SAPR) framework to better learn arbitrary shapes and handle the scale variation of text. The decoupling learning of scale and angle attributes in Polar coordinates produces promising improvement. We then propose line IoU loss and symmetry sine loss to effectively optimize the scale and angle, respectively. The base network is equipped with multi-path decoder to better utilize the multi-scale features. A more accurate and simple center line calculation is also developed to automatically fit various scales. Extensive experiments on benchmarks and ablation study solidly demonstrate the scala-aware ability and excellent performance of SAPR.

References

1. Tian, Z., Huang, W., He, T., He, P., Qiao, Yu.: Detecting text in natural image with connectionist text proposal network. In: Leibe, B., Matas, J., Sebe, N., Welling, M. (eds.) ECCV 2016. LNCS, vol. 9912, pp. 56–72. Springer, Cham (2016). https://doi.org/10.1007/978-3-319-46484-8_4
2. Zhou, X., et al.: East: an efficient and accurate scene text detector. In: Proceedings of the IEEE Conference on Computer Vision and Pattern Recognition, pp. 5551–5560 (2017)
3. Ma, J., et al.: Arbitrary-oriented scene text detection via rotation proposals. IEEE Trans. Multimed. **20**, 3111–3122 (2018)
4. Liu, J., Liu, X., Sheng, J., Liang, D., Li, X., Liu, Q.: Pyramid mask text detector. arXiv preprint arXiv:1903.11800 (2019)
5. He, K., Zhang, X., Ren, S., Sun, J.: Deep residual learning for image recognition. In: Proceedings of the IEEE Conference on Computer Vision and Pattern Recognition, pp. 770–778 (2016)
6. Huang, L., Yang, Y., Deng, Y., Yu, Y.: DenseBox: unifying landmark localization with end to end object detection. arXiv preprint arXiv:1509.04874 (2015)
7. Ren, S., He, K., Girshick, R., Sun, J.: Faster R-CNN: towards real-time object detection with region proposal networks. In: Advances in Neural Information Processing Systems, pp. 91–99 (2015)
8. Liu, W., et al.: SSD: single shot MultiBox detector. In: Leibe, B., Matas, J., Sebe, N., Welling, M. (eds.) ECCV 2016. LNCS, vol. 9905, pp. 21–37. Springer, Cham (2016). https://doi.org/10.1007/978-3-319-46448-0_2
9. Long, J., Shelhamer, E., Darrell, T.: Fully convolutional networks for semantic segmentation. In: Proceedings of the IEEE Conference on Computer Vision and Pattern Recognition, pp. 3431–3440 (2015)

10. Ronneberger, O., Fischer, P., Brox, T.: U-Net: convolutional networks for biomedical image segmentation. In: Navab, N., Hornegger, J., Wells, W.M., Frangi, A.F. (eds.) MICCAI 2015. LNCS, vol. 9351, pp. 234–241. Springer, Cham (2015). https://doi.org/10.1007/978-3-319-24574-4_28

11. Long, S., Ruan, J., Zhang, W., He, X., Wu, W., Yao, C.: TextSnake: a flexible representation for detecting text of arbitrary shapes. In: Proceedings of the European Conference on Computer Vision (ECCV), pp. 20–36 (2018)

12. Wang, X., Jiang, Y., Luo, Z., Liu, C.L., Choi, H., Kim, S.: Arbitrary shape scene text detection with adaptive text region representation. In: Proceedings of the IEEE Conference on Computer Vision and Pattern Recognition, pp. 6449–6458 (2019)

13. Tian, Z., et al.: Learning shape-aware embedding for scene text detection. In: Proceedings of the IEEE Conference on Computer Vision and Pattern Recognition, pp. 4234–4243 (2019)

14. Liu, Z., Lin, G., Yang, S., Liu, F., Lin, W., Goh, W.L.: Towards robust curve text detection with conditional spatial expansion. In: Proceedings of the IEEE Conference on Computer Vision and Pattern Recognition, pp. 7269–7278 (2019)

15. Zhang, C., et al.: Look more than once: an accurate detector for text of arbitrary shapes. arXiv preprint arXiv:1904.06535 (2019)

16. Baek, Y., Lee, B., Han, D., Yun, S., Lee, H.: Character region awareness for text detection. In: Proceedings of the IEEE Conference on Computer Vision and Pattern Recognition, pp. 9365–9374 (2019)

17. Xu, Y., Wang, Y., Zhou, W., Wang, Y., Yang, Z., Bai, X.: TextField: learning a deep direction field for irregular scene text detection. IEEE Trans. Image Process. 28(11), 5566–5579 (2019)

18. Zhu, Y., Du, J.: TextMountain: accurate scene text detection via instance segmentation. arXiv preprint arXiv:1811.12786 (2018)

19. Zhu, Y., Du, J.: Sliding line point regression for shape robust scene text detection. In: 2018 24th International Conference on Pattern Recognition (ICPR), pp. 3735–3740. IEEE (2018)

20. Xue, C., Lu, S., Zhang, W.: MSR: multi-scale shape regression for scene text detection. arXiv preprint arXiv:1901.02596 (2019)

21. Qiao, L., et al.: Text perceptron: towards end-to-end arbitrary-shaped text spotting. arXiv preprint arXiv:2002.06820 (2020)

22. Liao, M., Shi, B., Bai, X., Wang, X., Liu, W.: TextBoxes: a fast text detector with a single deep neural network. In: Thirty-First AAAI Conference on Artificial Intelligence (2017)

23. Liao, M., Zhu, Z., Shi, B., Xia, G.S., Bai, X.: Rotation-sensitive regression for oriented scene text detection. In: Proceedings of the IEEE Conference on Computer Vision and Pattern Recognition, pp. 5909–5918 (2018)

24. He, W., Zhang, X.Y., Yin, F., Liu, C.L.: Deep direct regression for multi-oriented scene text detection. In: Proceedings of the IEEE International Conference on Computer Vision, pp. 745–753 (2017)

25. He, K., Gkioxari, G., Dollár, P., Girshick, R.: Mask R-CNN. In: Proceedings of the IEEE International Conference on Computer Vision, pp. 2961–2969 (2017)

26. Lyu, P., Yao, C., Wu, W., Yan, S., Bai, X.: Multi-oriented scene text detection via corner localization and region segmentation. In: Proceedings of the IEEE Conference on Computer Vision and Pattern Recognition, pp. 7553–7563 (2018)

27. Deng, D., Liu, H., Li, X., Cai, D.: PixelLink: detecting scene text via instance segmentation. In: Thirty-Second AAAI Conference on Artificial Intelligence (2018)

28. Wang, W., et al.: Shape robust text detection with progressive scale expansion network. arXiv preprint arXiv:1903.12473 (2019)
29. Shi, B., Bai, X., Belongie, S.: Detecting oriented text in natural images by linking segments. In: Proceedings of the IEEE Conference on Computer Vision and Pattern Recognition, pp. 2550–2558 (2017)
30. Tang, J., Yang, Z., Wang, Y., Zheng, Q., Xu, Y., Bai, X.: SegLink++: detecting dense and arbitrary-shaped scene text by instance-aware component grouping. Pattern Recogn. **96**, 106954 (2019)
31. Xie, E., et al.: PolarMask: single shot instance segmentation with polar representation. In: Proceedings of the IEEE/CVF Conference on Computer Vision and Pattern Recognition, pp. 12193–12202 (2020)
32. Yu, F., Wang, D., Shelhamer, E., Darrell, T.: Deep layer aggregation. In: Proceedings of the IEEE Conference on Computer Vision and Pattern Recognition, pp. 2403–2412 (2018)
33. Fourure, D., Emonet, R., Fromont, E., Muselet, D., Tremeau, A., Wolf, C.: Residual conv-deconv grid network for semantic segmentation. arXiv preprint arXiv:1707.07958 (2017)
34. Yu, J., Jiang, Y., Wang, Z., Cao, Z., Huang, T.: UnitBox: an advanced object detection network. In: Proceedings of the 24th ACM International Conference on Multimedia, pp. 516–520. ACM (2016)
35. Gupta, A., Vedaldi, A., Zisserman, A.: Synthetic data for text localisation in natural images. In: Proceedings of the IEEE Conference on Computer Vision and Pattern Recognition, pp. 2315–2324 (2016)
36. Ch'ng, C.K., Chan, C.S.: Total-Text: a comprehensive dataset for scene text detection and recognition. In: 2017 14th IAPR International Conference on Document Analysis and Recognition (ICDAR), vol. 1, pp. 935–942. IEEE (2017)
37. Liu, Y., Jin, L., Zhang, S., Luo, C., Zhang, S.: Curved scene text detection via transverse and longitudinal sequence connection. Pattern Recogn. **90**, 337–345 (2019)
38. Yao, C., Bai, X., Liu, W., Ma, Y., Tu, Z.: Detecting texts of arbitrary orientations in natural images. In: 2012 IEEE Conference on Computer Vision and Pattern Recognition, pp. 1083–1090. IEEE (2012)
39. Yao, C., Bai, X., Liu, W.: A unified framework for multioriented text detection and recognition. IEEE Trans. Image Process. **23**, 4737–4749 (2014)
40. Deng, J., Dong, W., Socher, R., Li, L.J., Li, K., Fei-Fei, L.: ImageNet: a large-scale hierarchical image database. In: 2009 IEEE Conference on Computer Vision and Pattern Recognition, pp. 248–255. IEEE (2009)
41. Li, J., Zhang, C., Sun, Y., Han, J., Ding, E.: Detecting text in the wild with deep character embedding network. In: Jawahar, C.V., Li, H., Mori, G., Schindler, K. (eds.) ACCV 2018. LNCS, vol. 11364, pp. 501–517. Springer, Cham (2019). https://doi.org/10.1007/978-3-030-20870-7_31
42. Chen, J., Lian, Z., Wang, Y., Tang, Y., Xiao, J.: Irregular scene text detection via attention guided border labeling. Sci. China Inf. Sci. **62** (2019). Article number: 220103. https://doi.org/10.1007/s11432-019-2673-8
43. Dai, Y., et al.: Fused text segmentation networks for multi-oriented scene text detection. In: 2018 24th International Conference on Pattern Recognition (ICPR), pp. 3604–3609. IEEE (2018)
44. Qin, X., Zhou, Y., Yang, D., Wang, W.: Curved text detection in natural scene images with semi-and weakly-supervised learning. arXiv preprint arXiv:1908.09990 (2019)

45. Yang, Q., et al.: IncepText: a new inception-text module with deformable PSROI pooling for multi-oriented scene text detection. arXiv preprint arXiv:1805.01167 (2018)
46. Liu, Z., Lin, G., Yang, S., Feng, J., Lin, W., Goh, W.L.: Learning Markov clustering networks for scene text detection. arXiv preprint arXiv:1805.08365 (2018)
47. Ma, C., Zhong, Z., Sun, L., Huo, Q.: A relation network based approach to curved text detection. In: 2019 International Conference on Document Analysis and Recognition (ICDAR), pp. 707–713. IEEE (2019)
48. Wang, Y., Xie, H., Zha, Z.J., Xing, M., Fu, Z., Zhang, Y.: ContourNet: taking a further step toward accurate arbitrary-shaped scene text detection. In: Proceedings of the IEEE/CVF Conference on Computer Vision and Pattern Recognition, pp. 11753–11762 (2020)
49. Lin, T.-Y., et al.: Microsoft COCO: common objects in context. In: Fleet, D., Pajdla, T., Schiele, B., Tuytelaars, T. (eds.) ECCV 2014. LNCS, vol. 8693, pp. 740–755. Springer, Cham (2014). https://doi.org/10.1007/978-3-319-10602-1_48
50. Wolf, C., Jolion, J.M.: Object count/area graphs for the evaluation of object detection and segmentation algorithms. IJDAR 8, 280–296 (2006). https://doi.org/10.1007/s10032-006-0014-0
51. Xue, C., Lu, S., Zhan, F.: Accurate scene text detection through border semantics awareness and bootstrapping. In: Proceedings of the European Conference on Computer Vision (ECCV), pp. 355–372 (2018)

Branch Interaction Network for Person Re-identification

Zengming Tang(iD) and Jun Huang[(✉)](iD)

Shanghai Advanced Research Institute, Chinese Academy of Sciences,
Shanghai, China
{tangzengming2019,huangj}@sari.ac.cn

Abstract. Most existing Person Re-identification (Re-ID) models aim
to learn global and multi-granularity local features by designing a multi-
branch structure and performing a uniform partition with the various
number of divisions in different branches. However, the uniform partition
is likely to separate meaningful regions in a single branch, and interaction between various branches disappeared after the split. In this paper,
we propose the Branch Interaction Network (BIN), a multi-branch network architecture with three branches for learning coarse-to-fine features.
Instead of traditional uniform partition, a horizontal overlapped division
is employed to make sure essential local areas between adjacent parts
are covered. Additionally, a novel attention module called Inter-Branch
Attention Module (IBAM) is introduced to model contextual dependencies in the spatial domain across branches and learn better shared and
specific representations for each branch. Extensive experiments are conducted on three mainstream datasets, i.e., DukeMTMC-reID, Market-
1501 and CUHK03, showing the effectiveness of our approach, which
outperforms the state-of-the-art methods. For instance, we achieve a top
result of 90.50% mAP and 92.06% rank-1 accuracy on DukeMTMC-reID
with re-ranking.

1 Introduction

Person re-identification (Re-ID) aims to retrieve a person of interest across non-
overlapping camera views in a large image gallery with a given probe. Recently,
deep learning methods dominate this community, which obtain state-of-the-art
results. Deeply-learned features provide discriminative representation ability but
still are not robust for many challenges like variations in view angle, pose, and
illumination.

To relieve these issues, many part-based methods [1–3] are proposed to learn
part features and achieve promising results. They can be categorized into two
groups by the number of branches. The first group applies single branch methods,
which split the deep feature maps into several pre-defined patches and promote
the network to focus on fine-grained features in each local region. The second
group, using multiple branch methods, combines local and global information in
different granularities and learns coarse-to-fine representations. Although they

© Springer Nature Switzerland AG 2021
H. Ishikawa et al. (Eds.): ACCV 2020, LNCS 12624, pp. 322–337, 2021.
https://doi.org/10.1007/978-3-030-69535-4_20

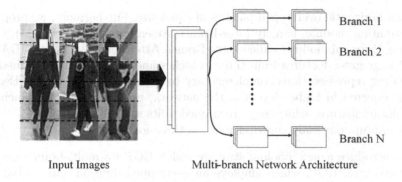

Input Images   Multi-branch Network Architecture

Fig. 1. Overview of problems in the single branch and multiply branch interaction. Left: uniform partition on input images. Heads are divided into two parts, which diminish the representational capability in head regions. Right: multi-branch network architecture. Strong relations between branches vanished after the split.

push the performance of Re-ID to a new level, they still suffer from the problems of learning in the single branch and ignore the correlation between different branches.

Feature Learning in the Single Branch. By the uniform partition, local information is preserved, which is robust for occlusion and partial pedestrian retrieval. For example, Part-based Convolutional Baseline (PCB) [1] is implemented by partitioning feature maps into 6 horizontal stripes. Nevertheless, in PCB, as the number of stripes increases, retrieval accuracy improves at first, but drop dramatically in the end. Over-increased numbers break the balance between learning fine-grained features and extracting meaningful body region information. In other words, the division will separate important semantic parts, as illustrated in Fig. 1.

Correlation Between Different Branches. Multi-branch networks have gained state-of-the-art performance by sharing lower layers of network and extracting different granularity features at the higher layers in different branches, as shown in Fig. 1. Since lower layers capture the same low-level features for different branches with the same input image, branch relatedness in lower layers is built. Besides, sharing lower layers keeps the model parameters in a low level. However, during testing, features of all branches are concatenated, but context information between them vanish after the split during training. As a result, interaction among branches is neglected in higher layers of the network.

In this paper, we propose a novel Branch Interaction Network (BIN) to address the above problems. The network learns coarse-to-fine representations for Re-ID in a multi-branch structure. It has three branches. One is for capturing coarsest information i.e., global information, while others are for learning multi-level fine-grained information with the various number of partitions. In order to preserve the consistency of meaningful regions across equally-sliced parts, Horizontal Overlapped Pooling (HOP) is adopted to extract local features on horizontal overlapped patches of equal size. Furthermore, we propose a new attention module, namely Inter-Branch Attention Module (IBAM), which contains three submodules called Inter-Branch Attention Submodule (IBASM). IBAM aggregates features from three branches and produces three refined corresponding representations complementary to the other two branches. Besides, IBAM, injected in higher layers of the network, promotes all the branches to learn shared features while they are trained in its specific granularity.

To sum up, our main contributions are three-fold:

- We introduce a new pooling strategy called HOP on multi-branch network architecture. HOP, which employs an overlapped division and Global Max Pooling (GMP) to obtain a vector representation, is shown superior to the combination of original uniform partition and GMP.
- We incorporate a novel attention module into BIN to model spatial contextual, multi-level dependencies across branches. It is found that complementary information efficiently promotes the performance of Re-ID. To the best of our knowledge, this is the first work which builds strong relations between different branches for Re-ID.
- We conduct extensive experiments on three datasets and show that BIN achieves competitive results in comparison with state-of-the-art methods. HOP and IBAM are also verified that each enhances accuracy.

2   Related Works

This section mainly discusses part-based and attention-based Re-ID, which are strongly related to our method.

2.1   Part-Based Re-ID

Part-based methods focus on learning local parts information for region-level embeddings of person. It can be divided into two groups, as mentioned in Sect. 1. In the single branch methods, considering that methods slicing the last feature map horizontally into a small fixed number may not be robust for challenges like low resolution, viewpoint variation, HPM [4] explore a coarse-to-fine pyramid model to discover sufficient part descriptors of a given person. OSNet [5] achieves multi-scale feature learning by designing a omni-scale residual block. Multiple branch methods are proposed to model multiple information such as fine-grained features, pose information in different branches. It is proved that integrating the local and global features can promote the results. In CA^3Net [6], appearance network consisting of three branches is designed to extract global, horizontal human parts and vertical human parts features. In order to overcome the misaligned problem, pose information is utilized in FEN [7] to match the feature from global and local body parts.

Different from previous part-based methods, we crop the feature maps into overlapped patches to learn local features as well as preserve essential information.

2.2 Attention-Based Re-ID

The attention mechanism can enhance features, which helps to locate meaningful regions. Mancs [8] emphasize discriminative features by the proposed fully attention block (FAB). HA-CNN [9] extracts features by jointly learning hard region-level and soft pixel-level attention. Person attributes like gender, handbag can guide attention mechanisms to find meaningful information. In AANet [10], latent attribute regions are located by combining class sensitive activation regions from each attribute in attribute detection task. A^3M [11] proposes an attribute-category reciprocal attention module to leverage attribute information, and it is helpful to select key features for Re-ID.

Previous methods strengthen representational capability by utilizing information from single branch. However, we propose the IBAM to help BIN generate more discriminative features by combining information from different branches.

3 Branch Interaction Network (BIN)

In this section, we first describe the overall architecture of Branch Interaction Network (BIN). Then the proposed Horizontal Overlapped Pooling (HOP) is discussed, followed by a novel attention module named Inter-Branch Attention Module (IBAM). Finally, we discuss the relations between the proposed modules and some existed methods.

3.1 Overview

As is shown in Fig. 2, the BIN is a multi-branch network, including a base network and three independent branches. ResNet-50 [12] is applied for our feature extraction backbone. The base network consists of previous layers before conv4_2, which is capable of generating shared low-level visual features. Specifically, three branches are directly borrowed from subsequent layers after conv4_1, namely Stripe 1 Branch (S1B), Stripe 2 Branch (S2B), Stripe 3 Branch (S3B) based on the number of stripes. S1B performs the global-level person re-identification task, while S2B and S3B perform part-level and global-level feature learning. In S2B and S3B, we remove the last spatial down-sampling operation to enrich the granularity. As a result, feature tensors T_1, T_2, T_3, the output of conv5 from S1B, S2B and S3B have different spatial sizes. In order to integrate multi-branch features, we inject IBAM on the outputs of conv4 to exploit complementary information across branches. Refined feature maps are fed into the following layers.

With the Global Max Pooling (GMP), BIN generates global feature representations $g_i (i = 1, 2, 3)$ for each branch. A parameter shared 1×1 convolution layer, followed with a batch normalization layer and ReLU layer, is applied to

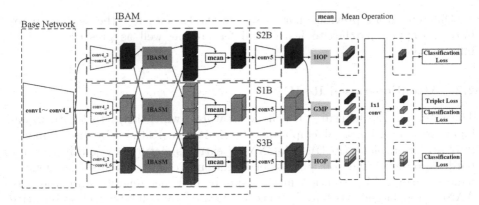

Fig. 2. The overall architecture of the proposed BIN. BIN contains a base network and three independent branches, i.e., S1B, S2B, S3B. IBAM is added after conv4 to capture complementary information among branches. BIN extracts global features by employing GMP on three branches and learns local features by applying HOP on S2B and S3B. The whole network is trained with triplet loss and classification loss.

reduce the dimension from 2048-dim $g_i(i = 1, 2, 3)$ to 256-dim $u_i(i = 1, 2, 3)$. Finally, each $u_i(i = 1, 2, 3)$ is trained with triplet loss [13] and classification loss. Specifically, triplet loss on global features can be formulated as :

$$L_{tri}^g = \sum_{i=1}^{N_g} \left(\frac{1}{N_t} \sum_{j=1}^{N_t} \left[m + \left\| u_i^{(j)} - u_i^{(j+)} \right\|_2 - \left\| u_i^{(j)} - u_i^{(j-)} \right\|_2 \right]_+ \right) \quad (1)$$

where N_g and N_t are the numbers of global features and sampled triplets, $u_i^{(j)}$, $u_i^{(j+)}$, $u_i^{(j-)}$ are the feature u_i extracted from anchor, positive and negative samples in j-th triplet respectively, m is the margin parameter, and $[\cdot]_+$ denotes $max(\cdot, 0)$. Classification loss on global features can be formulated as :

$$L_{cls}^g = \sum_{i=1}^{N_g} \left(-\frac{1}{N} \sum_{j=1}^{N} log \frac{\exp(((W^i)_{y_j})^T u_i)}{\sum_{k=1}^C \exp(((W^i)_k)^T u_i)} \right) \quad (2)$$

where N, C are the number of input images and identities, y_j is the ground truth of j-th input image. $(W^i)_k$ denotes the weight matrix for k-th identity in the fully connected layer whose input is u_i.

With our proposed HOP, BIN partitions $T_i(i = 2, 3)$ into 2 and 3 horizontal stripes in S2B and S3B, and pools these stripes to generate column feature vectors i.e., p_m^n, where m, n refer to the m-th stripe in Stripe n Branch. The dimension of p_m^n is also reduced to 256 by the 1×1 convolution layer. Finally, dimension-reduced features v_m^n are only trained with classification loss. Classification loss on local features are formulated as :

$$L_{cls}^l = \sum_{n=2}^{N_b} \sum_{m=1}^{n} \left(-\frac{1}{N} \sum_{j=1}^{N} log \frac{\exp(((W_m^n)_{y_j})^T v_m^n)}{\sum_{k=1}^{C} \exp(((W_m^n)_k)^T v_m^n)} \right) \qquad (3)$$

where N_b is the number of branches, $(W_m^n)_k$ is the weight matrix for k-th identity in the fully connected layer whose input is v_m^n. And the final loss is defined as following:

$$L = \frac{1}{N_{tri}} L_{tri}^g + \lambda \frac{1}{N_{cls}} \left(L_{cls}^g + L_{cls}^l \right) \qquad (4)$$

where N_{tri} and N_{cls} are the numbers of features trained with triplet loss and classification loss, λ is a trade-off parameter. Specifically, we set λ to 2 in the following experiments.

3.2   Horizontal Overlapped Pooling (HOP)

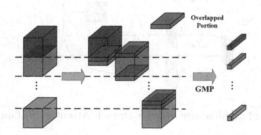

Fig. 3. Illustration of HOP. Firstly, uniform partition is performed on the feature map. Then, each stripe is padded with two overlapped portions. Finally, we pool them by GMP.

Given an input feature map $F \in \mathbb{R}^{C \times H \times W}$, locating meaningful parts by original uniform partition may cause within-part inconsistency, and introduce many outliers near division lines. HOP is proposed to solve this problem by making meaningful regions covered in adjacent parts. It has two parameters, which are l and k. l is the total height of overlapped areas in one stripe. k is the number of partitions. When $k = 1$, we remain the global information. In BIN, we keep the $k = 2$ in S2B and $k = 3$ in S3B.

The HOP is illuminated in Fig. 3. Firstly, we perform a uniform partition on the feature map horizontally. With the aim of devoting equal attention to each stripe, parts on the top or bottom are extended in one direction while others are extended in two directions to keep the same spatial size. An overlapped portion is a smaller 3D tensor whose size is $C \times h \times W$, where h refers to its height. As a result, $l = 2h$. However, it is obvious that l can be an odd number when $k = 2$. To make HOP universal, we require that l must be an even number. Finally, each horizontal stripe is pooled by GMP to generate a part-level vector.

3.3   Inter-Branch Attention Module (IBAM)

Features extracted from different branches help together to boost the feature representative capability. In order to model spatial contextual dependencies between branches, an IBAM is applied, as shown in Fig. 2. Features from paired branches are fed into an Inter-Branch Attention Submodule (IBASM), and output paired refined features. BIN has three branches, and form $C_3^2 = 3$ combinations when we choose paired branches. As a result, each branch is selected twice and has two refined outputs which build contextual dependencies between features from various branches. A mean operation on these two outputs is performed to update the original features.

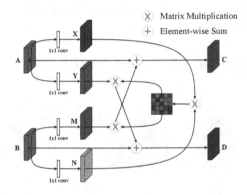

Fig. 4. The detail architecture of Inter-Branch Attention Submodule (IBASM).

Specifically, IBASM captures the similarity between input paired feature maps and aggregate together to produce more discriminative features. Figure 4 depicts the detail structure of IBASM. Given two feature maps $A \in \mathbb{R}^{C \times H \times W}$, $B \in \mathbb{R}^{C \times H \times W}$ from different branches, a 1×1 convolution layer is employed to generate four new feature maps X, Y, M, and N, where $X, Y, M, N \in \mathbb{R}^{\frac{C}{8} \times H \times W}$. These four feature maps are reshaped to $\mathbb{R}^{\frac{C}{8} \times L}$, where $L = H \times W$ is the number of feature locations. Pixel-wise similarity is calculated by matrix multiplication between transposed X and N, and then normalized to obtain the spatial attention map $S \in \mathbb{R}^{L \times L}$, as shown below:

$$S_{i,j} = \frac{\exp(m_{i,j})}{\sum_{i=1}^{L} \exp(m_{i,j})}, m_{ij} = X_i^T N_j \tag{5}$$

where X_i, N_j denote the ith and j^{th} spatial features of X and N respectively.

To calculate the output C, BIN first predicts A by exploiting the information from input B based on spatial attention map S. The prediction is reshaped to $\mathbb{R}^{C \times H \times W}$, then BIN performs an element-wise sum between weighted prediction and original A. The output C denotes refined A guided by B, which is defined as :

$$C_j = \gamma_1 \sum_{i=1}^{L} S^T{}_{i,j} M_i + A_j \tag{6}$$

where γ_1 is a learnable weight which is initialized as 0. The output D denotes refined B guided by A, which is defined as :

$$D_j = \gamma_2 \sum_{i=1}^{L} S_{i,j} Y_i + B_j \tag{7}$$

As a result, IBASM keeps the size unchanged. With this property, IBAM and IBASM can be incorporated into any existing multi-branch architecture.

Armed with our proposed IBASM, spatial contextual, multi-level dependencies across branches are well established, and the shared information in multi-granularity features are utilized in higher layers.

3.4 Discussion

To highlight the difference between our proposed modules and other related methods, we provide a brief discussion on the relations between them.

Relations Between HOP and OBM. OBM [14] propose a multiple overlapping blocks structure to pool features from overlapping regions. OBM requires pyramid-like horizontal partitions. However, HOP performs on a single scale, which is a lightweight method in the training procedure for its relatively fewer fully connected layers.

Relations Between HOP and RPP. RPP [1] is proposed to relocate outliers incurred by uniform partition to the parts they are closest to. In other words, RPP aims to address problems brought by "hard" partition. However, HOP focuses on keeping the balance between learning fine-grained features and extracting meaningful region information. HOP is a new kind of "hard" partition, and uniform partition can be seen a special case of HOP when $l = 0$.

Relations Between IBASM and Non-local Block. In some ways, IBASM can be regarded as a variation of the non-local block [15]. IBASM differs from non-local block in: (1) IBASM takes two input features while non-local block takes one input feature. IBASM performs non-local operation on two features. This modification helps model refine one input feature with the consideration of the other input feature. (2) IBASM produces two output features correspond to two refined input features by the guidance from each other. "Encoder-decoder attention" layers from [16] and pairwise non-local operation from [17] both take two input features to compute non-local operation and produce one output feature corresponds to one refined input feature guided by the other input feature.

Relations Between IBAM and Dual Attention Block. We make the comparison with IBAM and dual attention block [18] on image input. Given an image input, feature sequence is formed by rearranging feature vectors by locations. Dual attention block contains inter-sequence attention and intra-sequence attention. They have similarities because they both seek to find relations between branches or sequences. IBAM and dual attention block differ in: For the same image, intra-sequence attention refined itself by focusing on context-aware information in the single scale, and inter-sequence attention generates aligned counterpart by focusing on consistent regions from the opposite image. However, IBAM is designed to model spatial contextual dependencies from features with multiple granularity from the same image. IBAM has the capability to aggregate complementary information in multiple granularity.

Relations Between IBAM and PS-MCNN. IBAM has some similarities with PS-MCNN [19], because both are designed to interact with different branches. However, our IBAM is different from PS-MCNN in three aspects. (1) IBAM aims to build relations between different branches with various granularities while PS-MCNN focuses on building relations between different branches with various attribute groups. (2) IBAM builds interactions between all branches by modeling the relations of paired branches while PS-MCNN introduces a new Shared Network (SNet) to learn shared information for all branches. Besides, IBAM considers the spatial information in the process of interaction, which is ignored by PS-MCNN. (3) IBAM is a module that can be easily embedded into any multi-branch network architecture, while PS-MCNN is a network designed for building interactions among different branches with various attribute groups specifically. Our IBAM is more general than PS-MCNN.

4 Experiments

We conduct experiments on three Re-ID datasets: DukeMTMC-reID [20], Market-1501 [21] and CUHK03 [22]. First, we compare the retrieval accuracy of BIN with state-of-the-art methods on these three datasets. Then, we carry out ablation studies on DukeMTMC-reID dataset to verify the effectiveness of each component.

4.1 Datasets and Evaluation Protocol

DukeMTMC-reID. This dataset is a subset of the DukeMTMC for Re-ID. It contains 36,411 images of 1,812 persons from 8 cameras. There are 1,404 identities appear in more than two cameras, and the other 408 identities appear in only one camera, which are regarded as distractors. There are 16,522 images of 702 persons in the training set, and the rest 702 persons are included in the testing set, which consists of 2,228 query images and 17,661 gallery images.

Market-1501. This dataset includes 32,668 images of 1,501 identities detected by the Deformable Part Model (DPM) detector from 6 cameras. Specifically, the training set contains 12,936 images of 751 persons, and the testing set includes 3,368 query images and 19,732 gallery images of 750 persons.

CUHK03. This dataset consists of 14,097 images of 1,467 identifies captured by 6 cameras. It provides two types of annotations, which are manually labeled pedestrian bounding boxes and DPM-detected bounding boxes. We perform experiments on both of them.

Evaluation Protocol. In our experiments, we adopt standard Re-ID metrics: Cumulative Matching Characteristic (CMC) at rank-1, and the mean Average Precision (mAP) on all candidate datasets. All the experiments are conducted under the single query model.

4.2 Implementation Details

The implementation of our proposed BIN is based on the Pytorch framework. We initialize parameters of the BIN with the weights of ResNet-50 [12] pretrained on ImageNet.

During training, the input images are resized to 384×128 to keep more detailed information. We deploy random horizontal flip, normalization and random erasing [23] for data augmentation. A mini-batch is randomly sampled with 4 identities, and each identity contains 4 images. The margin in the triplet loss is 1.2 in all our experiments. The model is trained for 500 epochs. Adam optimizer is utilized to update the weight parameters with weight decay 5^{-4}. The initial learning rate is 2^{-4}, then decayed to 2^{-5}, 2^{-6} after 320, 380 epochs.

During testing, images are resized to 384×128 and normalized before fed into the network. Global features from all branches and local features from horizontally sliced parts are concatenated as the final pedestrian representation.

4.3 Comparison with State-of-the-Art Methods

BIN is compared with 14 existing state-of-the-art methods on three datasets: DukeMTMC-reID, Market-1501 and CUHK03 in Table 1. The compared methods are categorized into single branch methods (S), multi-branch methods (M) and attention-based methods regardless of the number of branches (A). Results in detail are discussed as follows.

DukeMTMC-reID. The proposed BIN achieves 89.36% Rank-1 accuracy and 79.60% mAP, which outperforms all published methods by a large margin. Note that : (1) The gaps between our method and single branch methods indicate that multi-branch structure is necessary: about 0.76% and 6.10% improvement in Rank-1 accuracy and mAP respectively. These methods focus on global information, local details or both of them in the single branch, which is insufficient for Re-ID. In contrast with single branch methods, our method can capture robust features in multiple granularities from various branches. (2) Although multi-branch methods integrate complementary information into final pedestrian representations, e.g., AANet [10] integrates key attribute information in a unified framework. BIN surpasses them, exceeding the MGN [2], which achieves the best results in this category, by 0.66% in Rank-1 accuracy and 1.20% in mAP. We argue that these methods neglect the interaction among branches.

Table 1. Comparison with state-of-the-art methods on three mainstream datasets. Red and Blue indicate our results and the best results of previous methods respectively. Best results of all methods are marked in bold. "−" denotes not available, "RK" denotes re-ranking operation.

Methods		DukeMTMC-reID		Market-1501		CUHK03			
						Labeled		Detected	
		Rank-1	mAP	Rank-1	mAP	Rank-1	mAP	Rank-1	mAP
S	MLFN [24] (CVPR2018)	81.00	62.80	90.00	74.30	54.70	49.20	52.80	47.80
	PCB+RPP [1] (ECCV2018)	83.30	69.20	93.80	81.60	−	−	63.70	57.50
	HPM [4] (AAAI2019)	86.60	74.30	94.20	82.70	−	−	63.90	57.50
	OSNet [5] (ICCV2019)	88.60	73.50	94.80	84.90	−	−	72.30	67.80
M	PSE [25] (CVPR2018)	79.80	62.00	87.70	69.00	−	−	−	−
	HA-CNN [9] (CVPR2018)	80.50	63.80	91.20	75.70	44.40	41.00	41.70	38.60
	CA^{3}Net [6] (ACM MM2018)	84.60	70.20	93.20	80.00	−	−	−	−
	CAMA [26] (CVPR2019)	85.80	72.90	94.70	84.50	70.10	66.50	66.60	64.20
	MGN [2] (ACM MM2018)	88.70	78.40	**95.70**	86.90	68.00	67.40	66.80	66.00
A	MGCAM [27] (CVPR2018)	−	−	83.79	74.33	50.14	50.21	46.71	46.87
	DuATM [18] (CVPR2018)	81.82	64.58	91.42	76.62	−	−	−	−
	Mancs [8] (ECCV2018)	84.90	71.80	93.10	82.30	69.00	63.90	65.50	60.50
	AANet-50 [10] (CVPR2019)	86.42	72.56	93.89	82.45	−	−	−	−
	CASN [28] (CVPR2019)	87.70	73.70	94.40	82.80	73.70	68.00	71.50	64.40
BIN		89.36	79.60	94.80	87.27	74.29	72.43	72.57	69.83
BIN (RK)		92.06	90.50	95.69	94.07	83.66	81.71	79.43	81.66

On the contrary, our method remains the strong relations between different branches, which is proved efficient. (3) Compared to attention-based methods, our methods boost CASN [28] by 1.66% in Rank-1 accuracy and 5.90% in mAP. Most attention-based methods build intra-branch contextual dependencies in the spatial or channel dimension. However, we model inter-branch non-local dependencies, which is more competent. With the help of re-ranking [29], we achieve a top result of 92.06% rank-1 accuracy and 90.50% mAP, which is a giant breakthrough.

Some visual examples of BIN on DukeMTMC-reID dataset are illustrated in Fig. 5. Given a query pedestrian image, BIN can retrieve the same person images in low-resolution, view angle variation and occlusion, which shows its robustness for most exiting challenges.

Market-1501. We report the 94.80% Rank-1 accuracy and 87.27% mAP, which significantly surpass most of the recent start-of-the-art methods. Although the Rank-1 accuracy of BIN is slightly lower than MGN(95.7%), BIN achieves the top mAP, outperforms the MGN by a large margin of 0.37%.

CUHK03. As is illustrated in Table 1, we compare the BIN against other methods on the CUHK03 dataset in two types of annotation settings, i.e., labeled and detected. BIN still achieves the best result of Rank-1 accuracy 74.29%, mAP 72.43% on the labeled setting, and Rank-1 accuracy 72.57%, mAP 69.83% on the detected setting, which surpasses the 1st best-compared method by Rank-1/mAP = 0.59%/4.43% and 1.07%/5.43% respectively.

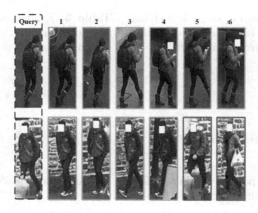

Fig. 5. Top-6 ranking list for given query images on DukeMTMC-reID dataset from BIN. Correct and false matches are highlighted by green and red borders respectively. (Color figure online)

4.4   Ablation Study

To investigate the effectiveness of each component in our proposed BIN, we conduct a series of ablation experiments on DukeMTMC-reID dataset.

Multi-branch Structure. Table 2 compares single branch and multi-branch models. For single branch models, with the increase of horizontal stripes, we extract more detail-rich representations, and the accuracy is increased as well. S1B+S2B($l = 0$) means multi-branch network architecture with two branches of S1B and S2B, and so as S1B+S3B($l = 0$), S1B+S2B($l = 0$) + S3B($l = 0$). The multi-branch structure is superior to each composed single branch and gains further improvements, e.g., S1B+S2B outperform S1B and S2B in Rank-1/mAP by 8.39%/12.90% and 1.89%/2.66%. However, with the increase of k in single branch, the improvement seems to be marginal but enlarge the model parameters, e.g., S2B($l = 0$) outperforms S1B in mAP by 10.24% but S3B($l = 0$) outperforms S2B($l = 0$) in mAP by 0.9%. With the increase of the number of branches, the performance shows the same trend, e.g., S1B+S3B($l = 0$) outperforms S1B in mAP by 13.20% but S1B+S2B($l = 0$)+S3B($l = 0$) outperforms S1B+S2B($l = 0$) in mAP by 2.61%. As a result, we adopt S1B+S2B($l = 0$)+S3B($l = 0$) as the multi-branch model for the following experiments.

Effectiveness of Triplet Loss. Our proposed BIN is trained with triplet loss and classification loss. Triplet loss plays a vital role for surpervising the whole network. Table 3 shows the effectiveness of triplet loss.

Effectiveness of HOP. We define l of HOP in S2B as l_2 and l of HOP in S3B as l_3. Figure 6 compares the HOP operations with different l. As is shown in Fig. 6a, when l_3 is set to 0, there is an improvement in accuracy when l_2 is increased, indicating the effectiveness of HOP. However, the retrieval accuracy drop dramatically when l_2 is further increased. We also increase l_3 when l_2 is set

Table 2. Comparison of single branch and multi-branch models. l means the parameter l of HOP in corresponding branch.

Model	Rank-1	mAP
S1B	78.64	61.62
S2B($l=0$)	85.14	71.86
S3B($l=0$)	86.09	72.76
S1B+S2B($l=0$)	87.03	74.52
S1B+S3B($l=0$)	87.15	74.82
S1B+S2B($l=0$)+S3B($l=0$)	**88.15**	**77.13**

Table 3. Evaluation of the effectiveness of triplet loss. "Triplet" refers to the triplet loss.

Model	Rank-1	mAP
S1B+S2B($l=0$)+S3B($l=0$)	**88.15**	**77.13**
S1B+S2B($l=0$)+S3B($l=0$) w/o Triplet	85.01	71.45

Table 4. Comparison of different l in different branches.

Model	Rank-1	mAP
S1B+S2B($l=0$)+S3B($l=0$)	88.15	77.13
S1B+S2B($l=2$)+S3B($l=2$)	**88.87**	**77.77**
S1B+S2B($l=2$)+S3B($l=4$)	88.69	77.28
S1B+S2B($l=4$)+S3B($l=2$)	88.73	77.57
S1B+S2B($l=4$)+S3B($l=4$)	88.46	77.19

Table 5. Comparison on adding IBAM in different positions.

Model	Rank-1	mAP
S1B+S2B($l=2$)+S3B($l=2$)	88.87	77.77
S1B+S2B($l=2$)+S3B($l=2$))+IBAM(conv4) (Our proposed BIN)	**89.36**	**79.60**
S1B+S2B($l=2$)+S3B($l=2$)+IBAM(conv5)	89.09	79.20

to 0 in Fig. 6b. They keep the same trend in performance, i.e., rise first, then decrease. With the increase of l in single branch, HOP helps to cover meaningful regions between adjacent parts, but will damage representational capability in local information slightly. As a result, a proper l is needed. We find that l_2 and l_3 both equal 2 can achieve the best results, as shown in Table 4.

Effectiveness of IBAM. Table 5 reports the effectiveness of IBAM. We add the IBAM on the output of conv4 and conv5 to compare the performance. Specifically, since the inputs of IBAM need to have the same size, we remove the last spatial down-sample operation in the conv5 layer of S1B when adding the IBAM following ResNet conv5. Multi-branch models with IBAM in various positions lead a significant performance improvement. The growth of the IBAM after conv4 is greater than after conv5. Although PCB finds that removing the last spatial down-sample operation in ResNet increases person retrieval accuracy, we argue that the remaining down-sample operation in S1B will produce complementary features. To better understand the IBAM used in our BIN, we visualize the activation maps extracted from the output of each branch in Fig. 7. First, BIN w/o IBAM is not sufficient to capture robust information about input image, e.g., shins in the first input image are ignored. Comparing the activation maps, we see that BIN can extract more discriminative features in each branch with the help of IBAM. Second, the activation maps from S1B in BIN w/o IBAM mainly cover the main body of pedestrians but ignore some detailed regions, e.g., arms in the second image. With the help of IBAM, S1B from BIN focus on the main body and local parts because S1B interacts with S2B and S3B. Third, the distribution of the activation maps from S2B and S3B in BIN w/o IBAM is too scattered, which means BIN w/o IBAM fails in modeling consecutive local areas

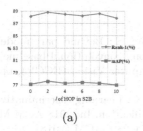 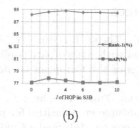

(a)   (b)

Fig. 6. Parameter analysis for l in S2B and S3B. (a) Rank-1 and mAP changes with l_2 while l_3 is set to 0. (b) Rank-1 and mAP changes with l_3 while l_2 is set to 0.

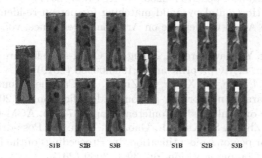

Fig. 7. Visualizaion of activation maps extracted from each branch. For each spatial position, the maximum of all channels is assigned for this part in activation maps. For each input image, the activation maps in first row are generated from our proposed BIN while the activation maps in second row are produced from BIN w/o IBAM.

in S2B and S3B. With the help of IBAM, S2B and S3B can concentrate more on meaningful local regions because of complementary information from S1B.

5 Conclusions

This paper proposes the BIN, a multi-branch network for Re-ID. The multi-branch structure is necessary to capture coarse-to-fine information. HOP is an improvement on the traditional uniform partition and GMP, while IBAM is an extension of attention mechanism. Each component is verified in boosting the robustness of BIN. Extensive experiments on three datasets demonstrate that BIN achieves the state-of-the-art performance. In the future, we will explore the correlation between inter-branch attention mechanism and intra-branch attention mechanism.

Acknowledgments. This paper was supported by National Key R&D Program of China (2019YFC1521204).

References

1. Sun, Y., Zheng, L., Yang, Y., Tian, Q., Wang, S.: Beyond part models: person retrieval with refined part pooling (and a strong convolutional baseline). In: Proceedings of the European Conference on Computer Vision (ECCV), pp. 480–496 (2018)
2. Wang, G., Yuan, Y., Chen, X., Li, J., Zhou, X.: Learning discriminative features with multiple granularities for person re-identification. In: 2018 ACM Multimedia Conference on Multimedia Conference, pp. 274–282. ACM (2018)
3. Li, W., Zhu, X., Gong, S.: Person re-identification by deep joint learning of multiloss classification. In: Proceedings of the 26th International Joint Conference on Artificial Intelligence, pp. 2194–2200. AAAI Press (2017)
4. Fu, Y., et al.: Horizontal pyramid matching for person re-identification. In: Proceedings of the AAAI Conference on Artificial Intelligence, vol. 33, pp. 8295–8302 (2019)
5. Zhou, K., Yang, Y., Cavallaro, A., Xiang, T.: Omni-scale feature learning for person re-identification. arXiv preprint arXiv:1905.00953 (2019)
6. Liu, J., Zha, Z.J., Xie, H., Xiong, Z., Zhang, Y.: Ca 3 net: Contextual-attentional attribute-appearance network for person re-identification. In: 2018 ACM Multimedia Conference on Multimedia Conference, pp. 737–745. ACM (2018)
7. Su, C., Li, J., Zhang, S., Xing, J., Gao, W., Tian, Q.: Pose-driven deep convolutional model for person re-identification. In: Proceedings of the IEEE International Conference on Computer Vision, pp. 3960–3969 (2017)
8. Wang, C., Zhang, Q., Huang, C., Liu, W., Wang, X.: Mancs: A multi-task attentional network with curriculum sampling for person re-identification. In: Proceedings of the European Conference on Computer Vision (ECCV), pp. 365–381 (2018)
9. Li, W., Zhu, X., Gong, S.: Harmonious attention network for person re-identification. In: Proceedings of the IEEE Conference on Computer Vision and Pattern Recognition, pp. 2285–2294 (2018)
10. Tay, C.P., Roy, S., Yap, K.H.: Aanet: ttribute attention network for person re-identifications. In: Proceedings of the IEEE Conference on Computer Vision and Pattern Recognition, pp. 7134–7143 (2019)
11. Han, K., Guo, J., Zhang, C., Zhu, M.: Attribute-aware attention model for fine-grained representation learning. In: 2018 ACM Multimedia Conference on Multimedia Conference, pp. 2040–2048. ACM (2018)
12. He, K., Zhang, X., Ren, S., Sun, J.: Deep residual learning for image recognition. In: Proceedings of the IEEE Conference on Computer Vision and Pattern Recognition, pp. 770–778 (2016)
13. Hermans, A., Beyer, L., Leibe, B.: In defense of the triplet loss for person re-identification. arXiv preprint arXiv:1703.07737 (2017)
14. Chen, Y., Zhao, C., Sun, T.: Single image based metric learning via overlapping blocks model for person re-identification. In: Proceedings of the IEEE Conference on Computer Vision and Pattern Recognition Workshops (2019)
15. Wang, X., Girshick, R., Gupta, A., He, K.: Non-local neural networks. In: Proceedings of the IEEE Conference on Computer Vision and Pattern Recognition, pp. 7794–7803 (2018)
16. Vaswani, A., et al.: Attention is all you need. In: Advances in Neural Information Processing Systems, pp. 5998–6008 (2017)
17. Fu, Z., Chen, Y., Yong, H., Jiang, R., Zhang, L., Hua, X.S.: Foreground gating and background refining network for surveillance object detection. IEEE Trans. Image Process. **28**, 6077–6090 (2019)

18. Si, J., et al.: Dual attention matching network for context-aware feature sequence based person re-identification. In: Proceedings of the IEEE Conference on Computer Vision and Pattern Recognition, pp. 5363–5372 (2018)
19. Cao, J., Li, Y., Zhang, Z.: Partially shared multi-task convolutional neural network with local constraint for face attribute learning. In: Proceedings of the IEEE Conference on Computer Vision and Pattern Recognition, pp. 4290–4299 (2018)
20. Ristani, E., Solera, F., Zou, R., Cucchiara, R., Tomasi, C.: Performance measures and a data set for multi-target, multi-camera tracking. In: Hua, G., Jégou, H. (eds.) ECCV 2016. LNCS, vol. 9914, pp. 17–35. Springer, Cham (2016). https://doi.org/10.1007/978-3-319-48881-3_2
21. Zheng, L., Shen, L., Tian, L., Wang, S., Wang, J., Tian, Q.: Scalable person re-identification: a benchmark. In: Proceedings of the IEEE International Conference on Computer Vision, pp. 1116–1124 (2015)
22. Li, W., Zhao, R., Xiao, T., Wang, X.: Deepreid: deep filter pairing neural network for person re-identification. In: Proceedings of the IEEE Conference on Computer Vision and Pattern Recognition, pp. 152–159 (2014)
23. Zhong, Z., Zheng, L., Kang, G., Li, S., Yang, Y.: Random erasing data augmentation. In: AAA, vol. I, pp. 13001–13008 (2020)
24. Chang, X., Hospedales, T.M., Xiang, T.: Multi-level factorisation net for person re-identification. In: Proceedings of the IEEE Conference on Computer Vision and Pattern Recognition, pp. 2109–2118 (2018)
25. Saquib Sarfraz, M., Schumann, A., Eberle, A., Stiefelhagen, R.: A pose-sensitive embedding for person re-identification with expanded cross neighborhood re-ranking. In: Proceedings of the IEEE Conference on Computer Vision and Pattern Recognition, pp. 420–429 (2018)
26. Yang, W., Huang, H., Zhang, Z., Chen, X., Huang, K., Zhang, S.: Towards rich feature discovery with class activation maps augmentation for person re-identification. In: Proceedings of the IEEE Conference on Computer Vision and Pattern Recognition, pp. 1389–1398 (2019)
27. Song, C., Huang, Y., Ouyang, W., Wang, L.: Mask-guided contrastive attention model for person re-identification. In: Proceedings of the IEEE Conference on Computer Vision and Pattern Recognition, pp. 1179–1188 (2018)
28. Zheng, M., Karanam, S., Wu, Z., Radke, R.J.: Re-identification with consistent attentive siamese networks. In: Proceedings of the IEEE Conference on Computer Vision and Pattern Recognition, pp. 5735–5744 (2019)
29. Zhong, Z., Zheng, L., Cao, D., Li, S.: Re-ranking person re-identification with k-reciprocal encoding. In: Proceedings of the IEEE Conference on Computer Vision and Pattern Recognition, pp. 1318–1327 (2017)

BLT: Balancing Long-Tailed Datasets with Adversarially-Perturbed Images

Jedrzej Kozerawski[1]([⊠]), Victor Fragoso[2]([⊠]), Nikolaos Karianakis[2]([⊠]), Gaurav Mittal[2]([⊠]), Matthew Turk[1,3]([⊠]), and Mei Chen[2]([⊠])

[1] UC Santa Barbara, Santa Barbara, USA
jkozerawski@ucsb.edu
[2] Microsoft, Bengaluru, India
{victor.fragoso,nikolaos.karianakis,
gaurav.mittal,mei.chen}@microsoft.com
[3] Toyota Technological Institute at Chicago, Chicago, USA
mturk@ttic.edu

Abstract. Real visual-world datasets tend to have few classes with large numbers of samples (*i.e.*, head classes) and many others with smaller numbers of samples (*i.e.*, tail classes). Unfortunately, this imbalance enables a visual recognition system to perform well on head classes but poorly on tail classes. To alleviate this imbalance, we present BLT, a novel data augmentation technique that generates extra training samples for tail classes to improve the generalization performance of a classifier. Unlike prior long-tail approaches that rely on generative models (*e.g.*, GANs or VQ-VAEs) to augment a dataset, BLT uses a gradient-ascent-based image generation algorithm that requires significantly less training time and computational resources. BLT avoids the use of dedicated generative networks, which adds significant computational overhead and require elaborate training procedures. Our experiments on natural and synthetic long-tailed datasets and across different network architectures demonstrate that BLT consistently improves the average classification performance of tail classes by 11% w.r.t. the common approach that balances the dataset by oversampling tail-class images. BLT maintains the accuracy on head classes while improving the performance on tail classes.

1 Introduction

Visual recognition systems deliver impressive performance thanks to the vast publicly available amount of data and convolutional neural networks (CNN) [1–6]. Despite these advancements, the majority of the state-of-the-art visual recognition systems learn from artificially balanced large-scale datasets. These

Code available at: http://www.github.com/JKozerawski/BLT.

Electronic supplementary material The online version of this chapter (https://doi.org/10.1007/978-3-030-69535-4_21) contains supplementary material, which is available to authorized users.

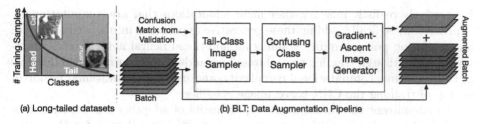

(a) Long-tailed datasets   (b) BLT: Data Augmentation Pipeline

Fig. 1. (a) Real-world datasets are often naturally imbalanced as they present a long-tail distribution over classes. Some classes (*e.g.*, cats) have an abundant number of training instances (head classes) while others (*e.g.*, lemurs) have fewer training examples (tail classes). (b) BLT augments a training batch by generating images from existing tail class images to compensate for the imbalance in a long-tailed dataset. Unlike existing methods that rely on generative networks such as GANs or VAEs, BLT uses an efficient gradient ascent-based algorithm to generate hard examples that are tailored for tail classes. We show that BLT is flexible across different architectures and improves the performance of tail classes without sacrificing that of the head classes.

datasets are not representative of the data distribution in most real-world applications [7–12]. The statistics of the real visual world follow a long-tailed distribution [13–17]. These distributions have a handful of classes with a large number of training instances (head classes) and many classes with only a few training samples (tail classes); Fig. 1(a) illustrates a long-tailed dataset.

The main motivation for visual recognition is to understand and learn from the real visual world [14]. While the state of the art can challenge human performance on academic datasets, it is missing an efficient mechanism for learning tail classes. As Van Horn and Perona found [14], training models using long-tailed datasets often leads to unsatisfying tail performance. This is because the imbalance in real-world datasets imposes a bias that enables a visual recognition system to perform well on head classes but often poorly on tail classes.

To alleviate the bias imposed from a long-tailed dataset, learned classifiers need to generalize for tail classes while simultaneously maintaining a good performance on head classes. Recent efforts that aim to learn from long-tailed datasets modify the training loss functions [18–22], over- or under-sample a dataset to balance it [23,24], or hallucinate or generate additional training instances (*e.g.*, images or features) [25]. Despite the progress of these efforts, the performance of visual recognition systems still falls short when trained using long-tailed datasets. There are two reasons that make these systems struggle on these long-tailed datasets. First, the information from the gradients of tail-class samples gets diminished given the prevalence of the head-class instances in the mini-batch. Second, more frequent sampling of instances from the tail classes reduces their training error but does not help the classifier to generalize.

Recent advances on generative approaches (*e.g.*, GANs [26,27] and autoencoders [28]) enable the development of data augmentation techniques that make the generation of additional training samples for tail classes on the fly useful to address dataset imbalance. Although these generative approaches can hallucinate impressively realistic imagery, they incur adaptations that are computationally expensive. Specifically, adding these generative approaches into a per-batch data augmentation policy requires training an additional neural network and adapting its sophisticated training procedures. This adds significant overhead in terms of training time, computational complexity, and use of computational resources on top of training the CNN-based image classifier.

To circumvent the cumbersome requirements of adopting a generative approach in long-tail recognition, we propose an efficient solution for Balancing Long-Tailed datasets (BLT) which, at its core, embraces gradient ascent-based adversarial image hallucination [29–31]. This approach removes the requirement of using an additional network to generate images for tail classes (e.g., GANs or autoencoders). As a result, BLT waives the need for extensive training procedures for the generator, thus keeping the computational complexity and resources low. Instead of perturbing images to purely confuse a CNN-based image classifier, as it is done for increasing robustness of a CNN [32–34], BLT perturbs tail-class images in a batch to make them hard examples, adds them to the batch, and proceeds with the regular training procedure. BLT generates hard examples by computing image perturbations that make the classifier confuse an image from a tail class with a confusing class based on the confusion matrix. Figure 1(b) shows an overview of our proposed data augmentation technique.

Our experiments on publicly available real and synthetic long-tail image-classification datasets show that BLT consistently increases the average classification accuracy of tail classes across different network architectures while maintaining the performance on head classes. Our experiments show that BLT increases the classification performance on tail classes by 11% w.r.t. the common approach of oversampling tail-class images to balance a long-tailed dataset.

The contributions of this work are the following:

1. BLT, a data augmentation technique that uses gradient ascent-based adversarial image generation to compensate the imbalance in a long-tailed dataset;
2. A quantitative analysis to demonstrate that BLT improves the generalization of a classifier on tail classes while maintaining its overall performance; and
3. An extensive evaluation on synthetically and organically long-tailed datasets to validate the flexibility of BLT on different network architectures.

2   Related Work

The main challenge of learning models from long-tailed datasets involves learning parameters that generalize well from few training instances while maintaining the accuracy of head classes. Many of the existing methods that address the problem of learning from a long-tailed dataset modify the training loss, balance the dataset via sampling techniques, or hallucinate data. Since BLT uses techniques designed to address classification robustness, this section also covers adversarial image perturbations, and image and feature hallucinations.

2.1   Learning from Long-Tailed Datasets

The simplest techniques that deal with long-tailed datasets use random sampling to artificially create a more balanced training set [23]. The two most common techniques are oversampling and undersampling. Oversampling picks training instances from tail classes more often. On the other hand, undersampling selects instances from head classes less frequently. In practice, oversampling tail classes tends to alleviate the bias from long-tailed datasets. Liu et al. [24] proposed an approach that exploits data balancing and a modular architecture to solve learning from an long-tailed dataset but also in an open-set scenario [35].

A different set of approaches adapt the training loss function to learn from long-tailed datasets. Lin et al. [20] proposed an object detection loss designed to penalize more the misclassified ones. Song et al. [21] presented a loss that forces a network to learn a feature embedding that is useful for few-shot learning. Cui et al. [18] presented a loss designed to better re-weight by means of the effective number of samples. Dong et al. [19] presented class rectification loss which formulates a scheme for batch incremental hard sample mining of minority attribute classes. Zhang et al. [22] developed a loss with the goal to reduce overall intra-class variations while enlarging inter-class differences. Zhong et al. [36] used different loss functions for head and tail class data while simultaneously introducing a noise resistant loss. Huang et al. [37] presented a quintuplet loss that forces a network to have both inter-cluster and inter-class margins.

The closest group of approaches to BLT hallucinate new data for tail classes to compensate for the imbalance in the dataset. Yin et al. [25] presented a face-recognition approach that generates new instances in feature space for tail classes. Their approach used an encoder-decoder architecture to produced novel features. Wang et al. [16] introduced MetaModelNet, a network that can hallucinate parameters given some knowledge from head classes. While these approaches alleviate the imbalance in a long-tailed dataset, they require training additional networks besides the CNN-based classifier.

2.2   Generating Novel Data for Few-Shot Learning

The methods that leverage image generation techniques the most are those that tackle the one- and few-shot learning problems [38–41]. Peng et al. [42] created a method that used a generator-discriminator network that adversarially learned to generate data augmentations. Their method aimed to generate hard examples in an on-line fashion. Hoffman et al. [43] presented an approach that hallucinates features obtained by a depth prediction network for improving object detection. Zhang et al. [44] introduced a one-shot learning approach that hallucinated foreground objects on different backgrounds by leveraging saliency maps. Hariharan and Girshick [45] presented a method that used visual analogies to generate new samples in a feature space for few-shot categories. Gidiaris and Komodakis [46] generated weights for novel classes based on attention. Pahde et al. [47] used StackGAN to generate images based on textual image descriptions for few-shot learning. Wang et al. [48] hallucinated temporal features for action recognition from few images. Wang *et al.* [49] hallucinated examples using GANs trained in an end-to-end fashion combined with a classifier for few-shot classification. Chen *et al.* [50] presented a network that learns how to deform training images for more effective one-shot learning. Although these networks did not generate realistic images, Chen and colleagues demonstrated that they were still beneficial for one-shot learning. While many of these approaches can generate realistic imagery, they unfortunately lack adoption because they require a significant amount of effort to make them work as desired. Nevertheless, inspired by Chen *et al.* [50], we argue that images do not need to look realistic in order to compensate the lack of data of tail classes. Given this argument, we focus on efficient image generation via adversarial perturbations.

2.3   Adversarially-Perturbed Images

The goal of adversarial images is to fool CNNs [30,32,33,51] or increase the robustness of a CNN-based classifier [52–56]. While some techniques use GANs [51] for generating adversarial images, there exist others that construct adversarial images by means of gradient ascent [30] or by solving simple optimization problems [32,33]. The benefit of using adversarially-perturbed images as hard examples was shown by Rozsa *et al.* [57]. Because we are interested in generating images in an efficient manner, we focus on the gradient ascent-based method of Nguyen *et al.* [30]. This method computes the gradient of the posterior probability for a specific class with respect to an input image using back propagation [58]. Then, the method uses these gradients to compute an additive perturbation yielding a new image. While these methods have been useful to show weaknesses and increase robustness of many visual recognition systems, there has not been any approach exploiting these adversarial examples to learn from a long-tailed dataset.

Unlike many methods described in Sect. 2.2, BLT does not require dedicated architectures for image generations (*e.g.*, GANs or VAEs) and complex training procedures which can take days to train [59]. Instead, BLT uses the underlying trained CNN-based model combined with a gradient ascent method [30] to generate adversarial examples from tail-class images that are added to a batch.

3   BLT: An Efficient Data Augmentation Technique for Balancing Long-Tailed Datasets

The main goal of BLT is to augment a batch by generating new images from existing ones in order to compensate for the lack of training data in tail classes. With the constraint of not increasing the computational overhead considerably, we investigate the use of adversarial image perturbations [29–31] to generate novel images. Although these techniques create noise-induced imagery, we show that they are effective in compensating the imbalance in a long-tailed dataset and efficient to generate. We first review how to generate new images by perturbing existing ones via the gradient ascent technique [29–31].

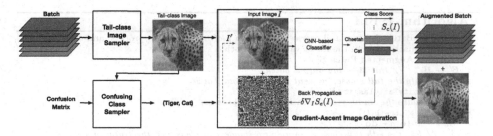

Fig. 2. BLT samples a tail-class image I from the batch and its confusion matrix from the latest validation epoch. Then, our algorithm passes I through the CNN and evaluates its class scores $S_c(I)$. Via back-propagation, our method computes the image perturbation that increases the class score of a selected confusing class (*e.g.*, cat) and adds the perturbation to the original image to produce I'. The perturbed image becomes the new input, *i.e.*, $I \leftarrow I'$. The technique iterates until the class score of a target non-true class reaches certain threshold or an iteration limit. Finally, BLT augments the input batch with the generated image to resume the regular training procedure.

3.1 Generating Images with Gradient Ascent-Based Techniques

Generating an image via gradient ascent [29–31] requires evolving an image by applying a sequence of additive image perturbations. We review this technique assuming that we aim to confuse a classifier. Confusing a classifier requires maximizing the posterior probability or logit of a non-true class given an input image I. Mathematically, this confusion can be posed as follows: $I^* = \arg\max_I S_c(I)$, where $S_c(I)$ is the score (*e.g.*, logit) of class c given I.

To confuse a classifier, the goal is to maximize the score $S_c(I)$ for a non-true class c. To generate image I^*, the technique first computes the gradient of the scoring function $\nabla_I S_c(I)$ corresponding to a non-true class c w.r.t. to an input image I using backpropagation. Then, the technique adds a scaled gradient to the input image I, *i.e.*, $I \leftarrow I + \delta\nabla_I S_c(I)$, to produce a new image I. This technique repeats this process until the score $S_c(I)$ for a non-true class is large enough to confuse a classifier. Unlike generative approaches (*e.g.*, GANs or VQ-VAEs) that require an additional architecture to generate images (*e.g.*, encoder-decoder networks), specialized losses, and sophisticated training procedures, this technique evolves the image I using the underlying neural network and keeps its parameters frozen. Thus, BLT saves memory because it avoids the parameters of a generative model and uses efficient implementations of backpropagation from deep learning libraries to compute the image perturbations. Further, BLT is about 7 times more efficient than GANs as generating images for ImageNet-LT adds 3 h and 53 min to the regular 3 h 10 min training time for a vanilla CNN (compared to additional 48 h to just train a GAN [59]).

3.2 Augmenting a Batch with Generated Tail-Class Hard Examples

The goal of BLT is to generate images from tail classes using gradient ascent techniques to compensate for the imbalance in a long-tailed dataset. As a data aug-

---

Algorithm 1: BLT

Input : Batch $\mathcal{B}$, list of tail classes $\mathcal{T}$, fraction p of tail classes to process, and confusion matrix $\mathcal{C}$ from the latest validation epoch

Output: Augmented Batch $\mathcal{B}'$

1   $\mathcal{B}' \leftarrow \mathcal{B}$ // Initialize the output batch.
2   // Identify the tail classes present in the original batch.
3   $l \leftarrow$ IdentifyTailClasses $(\mathcal{B}, \mathcal{T})$
4   // Calculate the number of the tail classes to process.
5   $n_\mathcal{T} \leftarrow \lceil p \times$ Length$(l) \rceil$
6   **for** $i \leftarrow 0$ **to** $n_\mathcal{T}$ **do**
7   // For the i-th tail class c, sample an image I of class c in the training set.
8     $(I, c) \leftarrow l\,[i]$
9   // Select a confusing class c' for the i-th tail class c.
10     $c' \leftarrow$ SelectConfusingClass $(\mathcal{C}, c)$.
11   // Sample a class score for $S_{c'}(\cdot)$.
12     $s_{c'} \leftarrow$ SampleClassScore ()
13   // Generate an adversarial image via iterative gradient ascent; see Sec. 3.1.
14     $I' \leftarrow$ HallucinateImage $(I, c', s_{c'})$
15   // Augment batch with the generated hard example.
16     $\mathcal{B}' += (I', c)$
17   **end**
18   **return** $\mathcal{B}'$

---

mentation technique, BLT generates new images from existing tail-class images in a batch. These additional images are generated in such a way that they become hard examples (*i.e.*, confusing examples for tail classes). To this end, BLT uses the results of a validation process to detect the most confusing classes for tail classes. Then, it perturbs the images in the batch belonging to tail classes in such a way that the resultant images get a higher confusing class score. Subsequently, BLT appends the hard examples to the batch preserving their original tail-class labels and resumes the normal training procedure.

Algorithm 1 summarizes BLT. Given a batch $\mathcal{B}$, a list of tail classes $\mathcal{T}$, the fraction p of tail-class samples to process, and the confusion matrix from the latest validation epoch $\mathcal{C}$, BLT first initializes the augmented batch $\mathcal{B}'$ by copying the original input batch $\mathcal{B}$. Then, it iterates the training samples in the batch $\mathcal{B}$ and creates a list l which contains the identified tail-class samples (step 3). Next, BLT computes the number $n_\mathcal{T}$ of tail samples to process using the fraction p where $0 \leq p \leq 1$ in step 5. Then in steps 6–17, for each tail-class sample $(I, c) \in l$, BLT selects a confusing class c' for the tail class c from the confusion matrix $\mathcal{C}$ (step 10). Then, in step 12 BLT computes a minimum class score $s_{c'}$. Next, in step 14, BLT triggers the generation of a new image via the gradient ascent technique with a starting image I, target class c', and class score threshold $s_{c'} \geq S_{c'}(I')$. Lastly, BLT appends the new hard example (I', c) to the augmented batch $\mathcal{B}'$ (step 16) and returns it in step 18. When the input batch $\mathcal{B}$ does not contain any tail classes, then we return the input batch, *i.e.*, $\mathcal{B}' = \mathcal{B}$.

Our implementation of BLT selects a confusing class in step 4 by using information from the confusion matrix $\mathcal{C}$ for a given tail class c. Specifically, BLT computes a probability distribution over all classes using the confusion matrix scores for a tail class c. Then, it uses the computed distribution to sample for a confusing class c'. This strategy will select the most confusing classes more often.

Subsequently, BLT computes the minimum class score $s_{c'}$ by randomly choosing a confidence value from within 0.15 and 0.25. Our implementation runs the gradient ascent image generation procedure with a learning rate $\delta = 0.7$. It stops running when $S_{c'}(I') \geq s_{c'}$ or when it reaches 15 iterations. BLT freezes the weights of the underlying network, since the goal is to generate new images. Figure 2 illustrates how BLT operates.

BLT is independent of model architecture. However, there is an important aspect of using BLT and a class balancer (e.g., oversampling [23]). Since BLT operates on a batch $\mathcal{B}$, it is possible that the batch contains many tail-class samples triggering BLT more often. When this happens, our experiments show that the performance of the head classes decreases. To mitigate this issue, the balancer needs to reduce the sampling frequency for tail classes. We introduce a procedure to achieve this for the widely adopted balancer: oversampling via class weights.

The simplest balancer uses class weights $w_i \geq 0$ to define its sampling policy using the inverse frequency, i.e., $w_i = n_i^{-1} \cdot \sum_i^N n_i$, where n_i is the number of training samples for the i-th class. This balancer then normalizes the weights to compute a probability distribution over the N classes, and uses this distribution as a sampling policy. This balancer samples tail classes more frequently because their corresponding weights w_i tend to be higher. To reduce these weights of tail-classes, we introduce the following adaptation,

$$w_i = \frac{\sum_i^N n_i}{n_i^\gamma}, \tag{1}$$

where γ is the exponent that inflates or deflates the weights w_i. When $0 < \gamma < 1$, the proposed balancer samples head-class instances more frequently than the inverse-frequency balancer. On the other hand, when $\gamma > 1$, the balancer favors tail classes more frequently than the inverse-frequency balancer. This simple adaptation is effective in maintaining the performance of head-classes while significantly increasing the performance of tail classes (see Sect. 4.1).

3.3   Squashing-Cosine Classifier

We use an adapted cosine classifier combined with the Large-Margin Softmax Loss [60]. This is because it is a strict loss and forces a classifier to find a decision boundary with a desired margin. We generalize the squashing cosine classifier implemented by Liu et al. [24] by adding two parameters that allow us to balance the accuracy drop of head classes and the accuracy gain of tail classes. The adapted squashing-cosine classifier computes the following class scores or logits for class c as follows:

$$\mathrm{logit}_c(\mathbf{x}) = \left(\frac{\alpha \cdot \|\mathbf{x}\|}{\beta + \|\mathbf{x}\|}\right) \frac{\mathbf{w}_c^{\mathsf{T}} \mathbf{x}}{\|\mathbf{w}_c\| \|\mathbf{x}\|}, \tag{2}$$

where $\mathbf{x} \in \mathbb{R}^d$ is the feature vector of an image I, $\mathbf{w}_c \in \mathbb{R}^d$ is the weight vector for class c, α is a scale parameter, and β controls the squashing factor. We obtain the cosine classifier used by Liu et al. [24] when $\alpha = 16$ and $\beta = 1$.

3.4   BLT as a Bi-level Optimization and Regularization per Batch

BLT can be seen as a learning process that uses bi-level optimization and regularization terms for tail classes at every batch. This is because the added images to the batch come from a gradient ascent procedure. Since the images in a batch go through the training loss and procedure, they consequently contribute gradients for the learning process. BLT can be seen as the following per-batch problem:

$$
\underset{\theta}{\text{minimize}} \quad \frac{1}{|\mathcal{B}|} \sum_{(I_i, c_i) \in \mathcal{B}} \mathcal{H}\left(f_\theta\left(I_i\right), c_i\right) + \lambda [\![c_i \in \mathcal{T}]\!] \mathcal{H}\left(f_\theta\left(I'_{c_i}\right), c_i\right)
$$

$$
\text{subject to} \quad I'_{c_i} = \arg\max_I f_\theta\left(I_i\right), s_{c'_i} \geq f_\theta\left(I_i\right); \forall c_i \in \mathcal{T},
$$

(3)

where $f_\theta\left(\cdot\right)$ is the CNN-based classifier with parameters θ; $\mathcal{H}\left(\cdot\right)$ is a classification loss (*e.g.*, the Large-Margin Softmax loss or binary cross entropy loss); $[\![\cdot]\!]$ is the Iverson bracket; c_i is the class of I_i; c'_i is the class to confuse the classifier using gradient ascent techniques; and λ is the penalizing factor for mistakes on the generated images. Our implementation uses $\lambda = 1$.

BLT adapts its learning process at every batch. This is because in a stochastic gradient descent learning process, the parameters θ of the CNN-based classifier change at every batch. Thanks to this bi-level optimization and regularization, BLT generates images for tail classes that compensate the long-tailed dataset and forces the CNN-based classifier to generalize well on few-shot classes.

4   Experiments

This section presents a series of experiments designed to validate the benefits of BLT on long-tailed datasets. The experiments comprise an ablation study that reveals the performance effect of the BLT parameters and image classification experiments on synthetic and naturally long-tailed datasets that measure the accuracy of BLT applied on different architectures. We implemented BLT on PyTorch, and trained and ran CNN-based classifiers; see the supplementary material for all implementation details (*e.g.*, learning rate policies, optimizer, etc.). Our code is available at: http://www.github.com/JKozerawski/BLT.

Datasets. We use two synthetic long-tailed datasets, ImageNet-LT [24] (1k classes, 5–1280 images/class) and Places-LT [24] (365 classes, 5–4980 images/class), and a naturally long-tailed dataset, iNaturalist 2018 [61]. We create a validation set from the training set for iNaturalist because BLT selects confusing classes at each validation epoch; the iNaturalist dataset does not contain a test set. To do so, we selected 5 training samples for every class and discarded the classes with less than 5 samples in the training set. We used the iNaturalist validation set modulo the removed classes. The modified iNaturalist dataset contains $8,122$ classes and preserves its natural imbalance with minimum of 2 and maximum of 995 imgs/class. Unless otherwise specified, we assume that the many-shot classes have more than 100 training images, the medium-shot classes have more than 20 and less or equal to 100 images, and the few-shot classes have less or equal to 20 training images. Every experiment reports the overall accuracy which is calculated as the average of per-class accuracies.

4.1 Ablation Study

We study the performance effect of the parameters in the adapted cosine classifier (see Sect. 3.3), the adapted balancer detailed in Sect. 3.2, the fraction p of tail-class images in a batch to process (see Sect. 3.2), the compensation of imbalance with common image augmentations versus those of BLT, and the effect of batch size on the accuracy achieved by BLT. We use ImageNet-LT dataset and ResNet-10 backbone for this study, and use a batch size of 256 for most experiments.

Squashing-Cosine Classifier. We study the effect on performance of the parameters of the adapted cosine classifier. For this experiment, we set $p = 0.5$ and $\gamma = 1.0$ and keep them fixed while varying the parameters α (scaling factor) and β (squashing factor) of the classifier. In Fig. 3(a) we see that the performance of few-shot classes decreases by about 3% and the accuracy of many-shot or head classes improves by about 4% when α increases. We see in Fig. 3(b) that the accuracy of few-shot or tail classes improves by about 2% and the performance of many-shot or head classes drops on average by 1% when β increases. Thus, setting these parameters properly can help a recognition system control gains or losses in the performance on head and tail classes.

Balancer. We analyze the effect of the parameter γ in the adapted weight-based balancer described in Sect. 3.2. For this experiment, we set $p = 0.5$, $\alpha = 20$, and $\beta = 0.5$ and keep them fixed while varying the γ parameter. In Fig. 3(c), we observe that the accuracy of many-shot or head classes decreases by about 11% while the performance of medium-shot and few-shot or tail classes improves by about 2% when γ increases. Thus, this parameter helps BLT control the decrease in the performance on head classes.

Fraction of Tail-class Images to Adversarially Perturb. We examine the classification accuracy as a function of the fraction of tail-class images in a batch to process (*i.e.*, p) by BLT. For this experiment we set $\alpha = 20$, $\beta = 0.5$, $\gamma = 1.0$ and vary p between 0 and 0.5. We observe in Fig. 3(d) that the accuracy of few-shot improves by about 6% while the performance of many- and medium-shot classes fall by about 2% when p increases.

Hallucinations vs Augmentations. BLT changes the statistics of the batch by supplementing it with hallucinated tail-class images. While this technique is effective in improving the accuracy of tail classes (see Sect. 4.2), it prompts the question whether one can improve the accuracy of tail classes by augmenting the batch with images computed with an alternative approach, such as common image-augmentation techniques. To answer this question, we augment a batch with the same number of tail-class images using common augmentation techniques (*i.e.*, rotations, crops, mirror flips and color jitter) instead of hallucinated samples from BLT. For this experiment, we set $\alpha = 20$, $\beta = 0.5$, $\gamma = 1.0$, $p = 0.5$ and let the gradient ascent technique iterate in BLT for no more than 15 iterations; and included BLT without appending images to the batch and dubbed

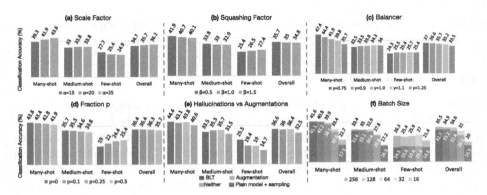

Fig. 3. Top-1 classification accuracy as a function of parameters (**a–d**); comparison between BLT, common image augmentation, and sample balancing baselines (**e**); and the effect of batch size (**f**). (**a**) The performance of few-shot or tail classes deteriorates and the accuracy of many-shot or head classes improves when α increases. (**b**) The accuracy of tail classes improves and the accuracy of head classes decreases when β increases. (**c**) The many-shot accuracy decreases while the medium-shot and few-shot accuracy improves when γ increases. (**d**) The few-shot accuracy improves while the medium-shot and many-shot accuracy decreases as p increases. (**e**) Adding tail-class images in the batch (via sample balancing or image augmentations) improves the accuracy of few-shot classes. However, BLT further improves the accuracy of tail classes compared to common augmentations and BLT without appending images to the batch (Neither) while preserving the medium-shot and many-shot accuracy. (**f**) BLT (lightly colored bars) maintains the accuracy improvement on few-shot classes over plain balanced models (solidly colored bars) as the batch size decreases.

it "Neither". Figure 3(e) shows that the performance of tail classes increases by augmenting the batch with tail-class images regardless of the image generation techniques (*i.e.*, image augmentations or gradient ascent techniques). However, the hard examples generated by BLT increase the accuracy of few-shot or tail classes compared to common image augmentation techniques by about 6% at a cost of an increase in confusion between medium- and few-shot classes.

Batch Size. Given that BLT operates on a batch, its size can affect the performance of BLT. We train a Resnet-10 model combined with BLT and a balancer with batch sizes varying from 16 to 256 and measure their accuracies. Figure 3(f) shows the accuracies of the model combined with BLT (lightly colored bars) and sampling or balancer (solidly colored bars). We can observe that the accuracies of many- and medium-shot from BLT remain similar to those of the balancer and decrease when the batch size decreases. On the other hand, accuracies of few-shot classes remain stable when the batch size decreases and the accuracies of BLT are higher than those of the balancer.

4.2   Image Classification on Long-Tailed Datasets

The goal of this experiment is to measure the accuracy gain on tail classes that BLT brings. Similar to the experiments presented by Liu *et al.* [24], we used

Table 1. Top-1 classification accuracy on ImageNet-LT. BLT maintains high many-shot accuracy, improves the accuracy of few-shot classes, and keeps the overall accuracy high. We show the highest accuracy in **bold** and the second highest in *italic*.

Methods	Many	Medium	Few	Overall
Plain model	**52.4**	23.1	4.5	31.6
Plain model + sampling	40.6	31.5	14.7	32.5
Lifted Loss [21]	35.8	30.4	17.9	30.8
Range Loss [22]	35.8	30.3	17.6	30.7
FSLwF [46]	40.9	22.1	15.0	28.4
OLTR [24]	43.2	**35.1**	*18.5*	*35.6*
OLTR [24] (Repr.)	39.5	32.5	18.4	33.1
Focal Loss [20]	37.8	31.2	15.0	31.4
CB [18]	29.7	24.7	17.4	25.6
CB Focal Loss [18]	28.0	23.6	17.4	24.4
BLT (Ours)	*44.4*	*33.5*	**25.5**	**36.6**

ResNet-10 and two-stage training approach. The first stage trains the underlying model without special long-tail techniques. On the other hand, the second stage starts from the weights learned in the first stage and applies all the techniques that reduce the bias from long-tailed datasets.

BLT Maintains the Accuracy of Head Classes While Increasing the Accuracy of Tail Classes on ImageNet-LT and Places-LT. Table 1 and Table 2 show the results of image classification on ImageNet-LT and Places-LT datasets [24], respectively. These Tables report results of methods that were only trained from scratch. Every row in both Tables present the results of different state-of-the-art approaches or baselines that deal with long-tailed datasets. The results in Table 1 of Lifted Loss [21], Range Loss [22], FSLwF [46], and OLTR [24] come from those reported by Liu *et al.* [24]. We reproduce the results with publicly available code for the remaining baselines. The columns in both Tables show the top-1 accuracy for many-shot, medium-shot and few-shot classes. The right-most column shows the overall top-1 accuracy. We can observe that the results of the baseline model trained without any technique to address the bias in long-tailed datasets shows that the head-classes (Many column) achieve higher accuracy than classes with fewer training examples; compare with Medium and Few columns. When adding a sampling balancer method in order to select few-shot examples more often, the performance of tail classes (see Few column) improves. We can observe that our proposed solution increases the accuracy of the few-shot categories while maintaining a competitive accuracy compared to the baselines on the many-shot and medium-shot classes. Please see supplemental material for additional results that include variants of BLT.

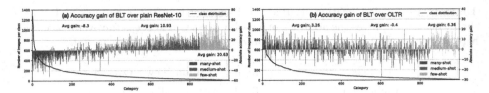

Fig. 4. Accuracy gains for every class on the ImageNet-LT dataset of BLT w.r.t. the plain ResNet-10 model and OLTR [24]. We see in **(a)** that BLT has average gains on medium- and few-shot classes of 10.93% and 20.63%, respectively. We can observe in **(b)** that BLT achieved 3.26% and 6.36% average classification gains on many- and few-shot classes, respectively.

Table 2. Top-1 classification accuracy on Places-LT and iNaturalist 2018. BLT maintains high many-shot accuracy, while it improves the few-shot and overall accuracy. We show in **bold** and *italic* the highest and the second highest accuracy, respectively.

Methods	Places-LT				iNaturalist 2018			
	Many	Medium	Few	Overall	Many	Medium	Few	Overall
Plain model	**37.8**	13.0	0.8	19.3	**70.6**	53.0	40.4	46.8
Plain model + sampling	27.8	25.3	7.0	22.4	48.8	*53.4*	47.1	49.0
OLTR [24] (Repr.)	29.1	*26.0*	8.3	*23.4*	44.8	**53.7**	**52.1**	**51.8**
Focal Loss [20]	27.6	25.5	7.0	22.3	28.6	39.0	36.9	36.6
CB [18]	20.5	19.0	12.6	18.2	16.6	25.4	29.1	26.8
CB Focal Loss [18]	18.6	17.7	*12.8*	17.0	14.0	22.1	27.2	24.5
BLT (Ours)	*31.0*	**27.4**	**14.1**	**25.9**	*53.7*	52.5	*49.9*	*51.0*

BLT Maintains the Accuracy of Head Classes High While Lifting the Accuracy of Tail Classes on iNaturalist 2018. Table 2 shows the classification results on the naturally long-tailed dataset iNaturalist [61]. All methods use ResNet-34 as the backbone. Although many few-shot classes only have two images, our solution increased the accuracy of tail classes (see Few column). In particular, BLT increases the overall accuracy and keeps the performance of many- and medium-shot classes high. The difference in behavior of all methods between ImageNet-LT, Places-LT, and iNaturalist can be attributed to the "longer tail" of iNaturalist. The number of few-shot classes in iNaturalist is about 63% of all classes, compared to 21% for Places-LT, and 15% for ImageNet-LT. Moreover, many few-shot classes only have two images for training in iNaturalist dataset while ImageNet-LT and Places-LT have at least five. Thus, iNaturalist presents a more challenging scenario for the baselines because few-shot classes dominate.

Accuracy gains on ImageNet-LT. Figs. 4(a, b) show the accuracy boost for many-shot (head classes), medium-shot and few-shot (tail) classes w.r.t. to the plain ResNet-10 model and OLTR [24]. We can see that BLT achieved average gains in accuracy for medium- and few-shot classes by 10.93% and 20.63%, respectively. The performance drop of head (many-shot) classes occurs because the baseline model has a strong bias due to the imbalance in the dataset. In Fig. 4(b) we observe that BLT achieves 3.26% and 6.36% average gains

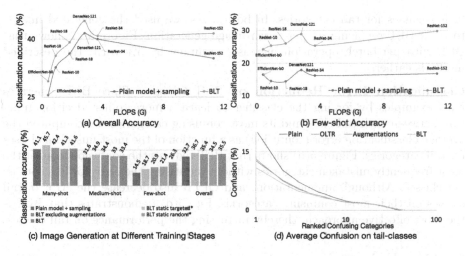

Fig. 5. Top-1 classification accuracy vs FLOPS for BLT and plain model with sample balancing across different architectures (**a–b**). BLT preserves high overall accuracy for all backbones (**a**) while significantly increasing the performance for few-shot classes (**b**). Influence of generating images at different training stages (**c**). Two approaches of generating images statically (*) cannot increase the few-shot accuracy above the level of BLT excluding augmentations, while dynamic image generation (BLT) increases the performance by 5.4%. Overall, we see a favorable trade-off as a 7.6% increase in few-shot accuracy leads to a modest 1.2% drop in overall accuracy. Average classification error (confusion) on tail classes as a function of the ranked misclassified categories (**d**). Because BLT uses hard examples to force the CNN-based classifier learn a more robust decision function for tail classes, it reduces the errors on the most confusing classes.

respectively on many- and few-shot classes w.r.t. OLTR. The accuracy gains on tail classes of BLT over OLTR are consistent; only a few tail classes declined (see yellow bars).

Performance as a Function of Network Depth on ImageNet-LT. Fig. 5(a–b) demonstrates that BLT increases the overall top-1 accuracy compared to the plain model with a balancer oversampling tail-classes for all tested backbones (see Fig. 5(a)). It also improves the accuracy on few-shot classes by a significant margin (see Fig. 5(b)). We used architectures with different depths and complexity (in FLOPS) such as EfficientNet-b0 [62], ResNet-28, and ResNet-152 [1].

Influence of Dynamic Image Generation. Because a network changes the topology of its feature space every batch, we study the effect of generating new tail-class images at different training stages (*e.g.*, at every batch or one time) and using them for training. To do so, we trained BLT excluding augmentations from scratch on ImageNet-LT and computed its confusion matrix $\mathcal{C}'$. We tested two augmentation strategies. The first is BLT static targeted: we generated images using BLT strategy using $\mathcal{C}'$. The second is BLT static random: we generated images using gradient ascent techniques and randomly selected confusing classes for tail categories. In both cases, we used the generated images to train BLT replacing its per-batch image generation. Figure 5(c) shows that BLT with per-batch operation increases accuracy by 5% w.r.t. the described methods earlier.

Classification Error Reduction on Tail Classes. Since BLT generates hard examples by forcing the classifier to learn a more robust decision function between each tail class and its most confusing categories, we computed the average classification error (confusion) as a function of the most mistaken classes for tail categories. Figure 5(d) shows that BLT reduces the confusion against the most frequently mistaken categories without increasing the error for less confusing classes. Although augmentations and OLTR also decrease the error of tail classes on their most confusing categories, Fig. 5(d) demonstrates that BLT is the most effective approach, thereby increasing the performance on tail classes.

5   Conclusion

We presented BLT, a data augmentation technique that compensates the imbalance of long-tailed classes by generating hard examples via gradient ascent techniques [29–31] from existing training tail-class examples. It generates hard examples for tail classes via gradient ascent at every batch using information from the latest confusion matrix. BLT circumvents the use of dedicated generative models (*e.g.*, GANs [26,27] or VAEs [28]), which increase computational overhead and require sophisticated training procedures. These hard examples force the CNN-based classifier to produce a more robust decision function yielding an accuracy increase for tail classes while maintaining the performance on head classes. BLT is a novel, efficient, and effective approach. The experiments on synthetically and organic long-tailed datasets as well as across different architectures show that BLT improves learning from long-tailed datasets.

References

1. He, K., Zhang, X., Ren, S., Sun, J.: Deep residual learning for image recognition. In: Proceedings of the IEEE Conference on Computer Vision and Pattern Recognition (2016)
2. Huang, G., Liu, Z., Van Der Maaten, L., Weinberger, K.Q.: Densely connected convolutional networks. In: Proceedings of the IEEE Conference on Computer Vision and Pattern Recognition (2017)
3. Krizhevsky, A., Sutskever, I., Hinton, G.E.: ImageNet classification with deep convolutional neural networks. In: Advances in Neural Information Processing Systems (2012)
4. Mnih, V., et al.: Human-level control through deep reinforcement learning. Nature **518**, 529 (2015)
5. Simonyan, K., Zisserman, A.: Very deep convolutional networks for large-scale image recognition. In: International Conference on Learning Representations (2015)
6. Szegedy, C., et al.: Going deeper with convolutions. In: Proceedings of the IEEE Conference on Computer Vision and Pattern Recognition (2015)

7. Deng, J., Dong, W., Socher, R., Li, L.J., Li, K., Fei-Fei, L.: ImageNet: a large-scale hierarchical image database. In: Proceedings of the IEEE Conference on Computer Vision and Pattern Recognition (2009)
8. Griffin, G., Holub, A., Perona, P.: Caltech-256 object category dataset (2007)
9. Lin, T.Y., et al.: Microsoft COCO: common objects in context. In: Fleet, D., Pajdla, T., Schiele, B., Tuytelaars, T. (eds.) ECCV 2014. LNCS, vol. 8693, pp. 740–755. Springer, Cham (2014). https://doi.org/10.1007/978-3-319-10602-1_48
10. Nene, S.A., Nayar, S.K., Murase, H., et al.: Columbia object image library (1996)
11. Quattoni, A., Torralba, A.: Recognizing indoor scenes. In: Proceedings of the IEEE Conference on Computer Vision and Pattern Recognition (2009)
12. Russakovsky, O., et al.: ImageNet large scale visual recognition challenge. Int. J. Comput. Vis. 115, 211–252 (2015)
13. Salakhutdinov, R., Torralba, A., Tenenbaum, J.: Learning to share visual appearance for multiclass object detection. In: Proceedings of the IEEE Conference on Computer Vision and Pattern Recognition (2011)
14. Van Horn, G., Perona, P.: The devil is in the tails: fine-grained classification in the wild. arXiv preprint arXiv:1709.01450 (2017)
15. Wang, Y.X., Hebert, M.: Learning from small sample sets by combining unsupervised meta-training with CNNs. In: Proceedings of the Advances in Neural Information Processing Systems (2016)
16. Wang, Y.X., Ramanan, D., Hebert, M.: Learning to model the tail. In: Proceedings of the Advances in Neural Information Processing Systems (2017)
17. Zhu, X., Anguelov, D., Ramanan, D.: Capturing long-tail distributions of object subcategories. In: Proceedings of the IEEE Conference on Computer Vision and Pattern Recognition (2014)
18. Cui, Y., Jia, M., Lin, T.Y., Song, Y., Belongie, S.: Class-balanced loss based on effective number of samples. In: Proceedings of the IEEE Conference on Computer Vision and Pattern Recognition (2019)
19. Dong, Q., Gong, S., Zhu, X.: Class rectification hard mining for imbalanced deep learning. In: Proceedings of the IEEE International Conference on Computer Vision (2017)
20. Lin, T.Y., Goyal, P., Girshick, R., He, K., Dollár, P.: Focal loss for dense object detection. In: Proceedings of the IEEE International Conference on Computer Vision (2017)
21. Oh Song, H., Xiang, Y., Jegelka, S., Savarese, S.: Deep metric learning via lifted structured feature embedding. In: Proceedings of the IEEE Conference on Computer Vision and Pattern Recognition (2016)
22. Zhang, X., Fang, Z., Wen, Y., Li, Z., Qiao, Y.: Range loss for deep face recognition with long-tailed training data. In: Proceedings of the IEEE International Conference on Computer Vision (2017)
23. He, H., Garcia, E.A.: Learning from imbalanced data. IEEE Trans. Knowl. Data Eng. 21, 1263–1284 (2009)
24. Liu, Z., Miao, Z., Zhan, X., Wang, J., Gong, B., Yu, S.X.: Large-scale long-tailed recognition in an open world. In: Proceedings of the IEEE Conference on Computer Vision and Pattern Recognition (2019)
25. Yin, X., Yu, X., Sohn, K., Liu, X., Chandraker, M.: Feature transfer learning for face recognition with under-represented data. In: Proceedings of the IEEE Conference on Computer Vision and Pattern Recognition (2019)
26. Arjovsky, M., Chintala, S., Bottou, L.: Wasserstein generative adversarial networks. In: Proceedings of the International Conference on Machine Learning (2017)

27. Goodfellow, I., et al.: Generative adversarial nets. In: Proceedings of the Advances in Neural Information Processing Systems (2014)
28. van den Oord, A., Vinyals, O., et al.: Neural discrete representation learning. In: Proceedings of the Advances in Neural Information Processing Systems (2017)
29. Erhan, D., Bengio, Y., Courville, A., Vincent, P.: Visualizing higher-layer features of a deep network. University of Montreal, vol. 1341, p. 1 (2009)
30. Nguyen, A., Yosinski, J., Clune, J.: Deep neural networks are easily fooled: high confidence predictions for unrecognizable images. In: Proceedings of the IEEE Conference on Computer Vision and Pattern Recognition (2015)
31. Simonyan, K., Vedaldi, A., Zisserman, A.: Deep inside convolutional networks: Visualising image classification models and saliency maps. In: Workshop at International Conference on Learning Representations (2014)
32. Moosavi-Dezfooli, S.M., Fawzi, A., Frossard, P.: DeepFool: a simple and accurate method to fool deep neural networks. In: Proceedings of the IEEE Conference on Computer Vision and Pattern Recognition (2016)
33. Moosavi-Dezfooli, S.M., Fawzi, A., Fawzi, O., Frossard, P.: Universal adversarial perturbations. In: Proceedings of the IEEE Conference on Computer Vision and Pattern Recognition (2017)
34. Salman, H., et al.: Provably robust deep learning via adversarially trained smoothed classifiers. In: Proceedings of the Advances in Neural Information Processing Systems (2019)
35. Scheirer, W.J., de Rezende Rocha, A., Sapkota, A., Boult, T.E.: Toward open set recognition. IEEE Trans. Pattern Anal. Mach. Intell. **35**, 1757–1772 (2012)
36. Zhong, Y., et al.: Unequal-training for deep face recognition with long-tailed noisy data. In: Proceedings of the IEEE Conference on Computer Vision and Pattern Recognition (2019)
37. Huang, C., Li, Y., Change Loy, C., Tang, X.: Learning deep representation for imbalanced classification. In: Proceedings of the IEEE Conference on Computer Vision and Pattern Recognition (2016)
38. Zhang, R., Che, T., Ghahramani, Z., Bengio, Y., Song, Y.: MetaGAN: an adversarial approach to few-shot learning. In: Proceedings of the Advances in Neural Information Processing Systems (2018)
39. Jang, Y., Zhao, T., Hong, S., Lee, H.: Adversarial defense via learning to generate diverse attacks. In: Proceedings of the IEEE International Conference on Computer Vision (2019)
40. Zhang, J., Zhao, C., Ni, B., Xu, M., Yang, X.: Variational few-shot learning. In: Proceedings of the IEEE International Conference on Computer Vision, pp. 1685–1694 (2019)
41. Mullick, S.S., Datta, S., Das, S.: Generative adversarial minority oversampling. In: The IEEE International Conference on Computer Vision (ICCV) (2019)
42. Peng, X., Tang, Z., Yang, F., Feris, R.S., Metaxas, D.: Jointly optimize data augmentation and network training: adversarial data augmentation in human pose estimation. In: Proceedings of the IEEE Conference on Computer Vision and Pattern Recognition (2018)
43. Hoffman, J., Gupta, S., Darrell, T.: Learning with side information through modality hallucination. In: Proceedings of the IEEE Conference on Computer Vision and Pattern Recognition (2016)
44. Zhang, H., Zhang, J., Koniusz, P.: Few-shot learning via saliency-guided hallucination of samples. In: Proceedings of the IEEE Conference on Computer Vision and Pattern Recognition (2019)

45. Hariharan, B., Girshick, R.: Low-shot visual recognition by shrinking and halluci-nating features. In: Proceedings of the IEEE International Conference on Computer Vision (2017)
46. Gidaris, S., Komodakis, N.: Dynamic few-shot visual learning without forgetting. In: Proceedings of the IEEE Conference on Computer Vision and Pattern Recog-nition (2018)
47. Pahde, F., Nabi, M., Klein, T., Jahnichen, P.: Discriminative hallucination for multi-modal few-shot learning. In: Proceedings of the IEEE International Confer-ence on Image Processing (2018)
48. Wang, Y., Zhou, L., Qiao, Y.: Temporal hallucinating for action recognition with few still images. In: Proceedings of the IEEE Conference on Computer Vision and Pattern Recognition (2018)
49. Wang, Y.X., Girshick, R., Hebert, M., Hariharan, B.: Low-shot learning from imag-inary data. In: Proceedings of the IEEE Conference on Computer Vision and Pat-tern Recognition (2018)
50. Chen, Z., Fu, Y., Wang, Y.X., Ma, L., Liu, W., Hebert, M.: Image deformation meta-networks for one-shot learning. In: Proceedings of the IEEE Conference on Computer Vision and Pattern Recognition (2019)
51. Goodfellow, I., Shlens, J., Szegedy, C.: Explaining and harnessing adversarial exam-ples. In: Proceedings of the International Conference on Learning Representations (2015)
52. Chen, H., Zhang, H., Boning, D., Hsieh, C.J.: Robust decision trees against adver-sarial examples. arXiv preprint arXiv:1902.10660 (2019)
53. Ilyas, A., Santurkar, S., Tsipras, D., Engstrom, L., Tran, B., Madry, A.: Adversarial examples are not bugs, they are features. In: Proceedings of the Advances in Neural Information Processing Systems (2019)
54. Liu, A., Liu, X., Zhang, C., Yu, H., Liu, Q., He, J.: Training robust deep neural networks via adversarial noise propagation. arXiv preprint arXiv:1909.09034 (2019)
55. Lopes, R.G., Yin, D., Poole, B., Gilmer, J., Cubuk, E.D.: Improving robustness without sacrificing accuracy with patch gaussian augmentation. arXiv preprint arXiv:1906.02611 (2019)
56. Madry, A., Makelov, A., Schmidt, L., Tsipras, D., Vladu, A.: Towards deep learning models resistant to adversarial attacks. arXiv preprint arXiv:1706.06083 (2017)
57. Rozsa, A., Rudd, E.M., Boult, T.E.: Adversarial diversity and hard positive gen-eration. In: Proceedings of the IEEE Conference on Computer Vision and Pattern Recognition Workshops (2016)
58. Rumelhart, D.E., Hinton, G.E., Williams, R.J., et al.: Learning representations by back-propagating errors. Cogn. Model. 5, 1 (1988)
59. Brock, A., Donahue, J., Simonyan, K.: Large scale GAN training for high fidelity natural image synthesis. arXiv preprint arXiv:1809.11096 (2018)
60. Liu, W., Wen, Y., Yu, Z., Yang, M.: Large-margin softmax loss for convolu-tional neural networks. In: Proceedings of the International Conference on Machine Learning (2016)
61. Van Horn, G., et al.: The inaturalist species classification and detection dataset. In: Proceedings of the IEEE Conference on Computer Vision and Pattern Recognition (2018)
62. Tan, M., Le, Q.V.: EfficientNet: rethinking model scaling for convolutional neural networks. arXiv preprint arXiv:1905.11946 (2019)

Jointly Discriminating and Frequent Visual Representation Mining

Qiannan Wang, Ying Zhou, Zhaoyan Zhu, Xuefeng Liang$^{(\boxtimes)}$ ⓘ, and Yu Gu

School of Artificial Intelligence, Xidian University, Xi'an, China
xliang@xidian.edu.cn

Abstract. Discovering visual representation in an image category is a challenging issue, because the visual representation should not only be discriminating but also frequently appears in these images. Previous studies have proposed many solutions, but they all separately optimized the discrimination and frequency, which makes the solutions sub-optimal. To address this issue, we propose a method to discover the jointly discriminating and frequent visual representation, named as JDFR. To ensure discrimination, JDFR employs a classification task with cross-entropy loss. To achieve frequency, JDFR uses triplet loss to optimize within-class and between-class distance, then mines frequent visual representations in feature space. Moreover, we propose an attention module to locate the representative region in the image. Extensive experiments on four benchmark datasets (*i.e.* CIFAR10, CIFAR100-20, VOC2012-10 and Travel) show that the discovered visual representations have better discrimination and frequency than ones mined from five state-of-the-art methods with average improvements of 7.51% on accuracy and 1.88% on frequency.

1 Introduction

Visual patterns are basic visual elements that commonly appear in images and tend to convey higher-level semantics than raw pixels. Thus, mining visual patterns is a fundamental issue in computer vision, and have been applied to many vision tasks, such as object recognition [1,2], object detection [3], and scene classification [1], to name a few. The visual representation of a category is a type of visual pattern that represents the discernible regularity in the visual world and captures the essential nature of visual objects or scenes. Unlike visual pattern, visual representation does not have to appear in every image of a category. Recently, it has been utilized in the tourism industry. By mining visual representations from travel photos, users can discover useful information about tourism destinations for travel recommendation [4–6]. Visual representation has

---

Electronic supplementary material The online version of this chapter (https://doi.org/10.1007/978-3-030-69535-4_22) contains supplementary material, which is available to authorized users.

two properties [1,7]: 1) *discrimination*, which means it represents only a particular image category rather than the other categories; 2) *frequency*, which means it frequently appears in images of the category.

To tackle this issue, handcrafted features, *i.e.* SIFT [8] and HOG [9], were firstly used for visual pattern mining. Due to the scale invariability and tolerating a certain distortion in a local space, they are regarded as low-level visual patterns. However, the local feature is limited in its capability of expressing the semantics of images. Recently, convolutional neural network (CNN) has been often utilized as a feature extractor [1,2,10,11], as it is able to learn the high-level semantic representation of images. The CNN features were associated with association rules [1], clustering algorithm [10], and unsupervised max-margin analysis [3] to discover visual patterns. The discrimination or frequency of these patterns was separately guaranteed through varied optimizations. In addition, other studies [12,13] applied image co-saliency detection to find the visual patterns that appear in all images.

Aforementioned methods still face two issues regarding visual representation mining. Firstly, the separation of discrimination and frequency will make the solution sub-optimal. Secondly, image co-saliency requires the representation to appear in all images.

To address the above issues, we propose a jointly discriminating and frequent visual representation mining method (JDFR) to discover the visual representations that are simultaneously discriminating and frequent. In JDFR, the end-to-end network is jointly optimized by cross-entropy loss and triplet loss. The cross-entropy loss ensures the discrimination of visual representation using a classification task. The triplet loss ensures the frequency by exploring the highly dense visual representations in the feature space, which have a close within-class distance and a sufficient between-class distance. Since the visual representation often is only a region in the image, we design an attention module to locate the most discriminating regions in the images.

Therefore, our main contributions are as follows:

- We propose an end-to-end framework jointly optimized by cross-entropy loss and triplet loss to discover the discriminating and frequent visual representations.
- We designed a channel and spatial attention module to locate the visual representations in images.
- Experiments show that our JDFR outperforms five state-of-the-arts on four benchmark datasets.

2   Related Work

2.1   Visual Pattern Mining

Since understanding visual pattern is a fundamental issue in visual cognition, many studies have been conducted on this issue. Handcrafted features [8,9,14,15] were first applied for visual pattern mining. Doersch C et al. [9] used the HOG descriptor to represent visual patterns, which were iteratively optimized by SVM. However, such local features can not well represent the semantic information of images well, and thus are usually regarded as low-level visual patterns.

Recently, CNN demonstrated a remarkable performance on many vision tasks [1,2,10,11], because its high-level features can represent better semantic information. Li et al. [1] extracted features from image patches using a CNN model, and retrieved semantic patches from these features based on association rules. Since the frequency and discrimination of these patches were optimized separately, the method did not achieve a desirable performance on the classification task. Zhang et al. [10] mined visual patterns using the mean shift in a binary feature space, and thus was able to ensure the frequency. Moreover, they enhanced the discrimination by leveraging contrast images. However, their outputs were images instead of visual patterns, meanwhile, the frequency and the discrimination were optimized independently as well. Yang et al. [3] exploited the hierarchical abstraction of CNN and utilized unsupervised max-margin analysis to locate visual patterns in images. This method is effective for discrimination but cannot guarantee the frequency. An emerging study [7] is able to mine visual patterns simply by analyzing filter activations in CNN. Due to the empirical design of the methodology, there is no solid theory that supports the two aforementioned properties of visual representation, especially the frequency. Furthermore, other studies [16–18] have shown that the frequently occurring images could be found by clustering methods.

One can see that none of aforementioned methods is able to jointly optimize the discrimination and the frequency. By contrast, we propose a new framework (JDFR) that is able to mine the best discriminating and frequent representations using the joint optimization.

2.2   Image Co-saliency Detection

Some studies [19–29] consider the visual pattern mining as an image co-saliency problem, which refers to detecting the common salient objects or regions in a set of relevant images. Image co-saliency detection methods can be grouped into three categories: bottom-up, fusion-based and learning-based methods. Bottom-up methods score image regions based on feature priors to simulate visual attention. Fu et al. [23] proposed three visual attention cues including contrast, spatial and corresponding ones. Later, they proposed a two-stage propagation framework using background and foreground cues [19]. Fusion-based methods ensembled the detection results of existing saliency or co-saliency methods. For example, Cao et al. [24] obtained the self-adaptive weight via a rank constraint to combine the co-saliency maps. Huang et al. [25] used multiscale superpixels to jointly detect salient object via low-rank analysis. Studies [26,27] have discovered inter-image correspondence through the high-level semantic features extracted from CNNs. Learning based methods have developed significantly in recent years because of the breakthrough of deep learning models [20,21,28]. Wei et al. [22] proposed an end-to-end framework based on the FCN to discover co-salient objects. Ge et al. [28] proposed an unsupervised CNN to jointly optimize the co-saliency maps.

However, there is a significant difference between image co-saliency detection and visual representation mining. Image co-saliency requires the same pattern appearing in all images. Instead, visual representation is a pattern that represents the major characteristic of the category, not necessarily to appear in each image.

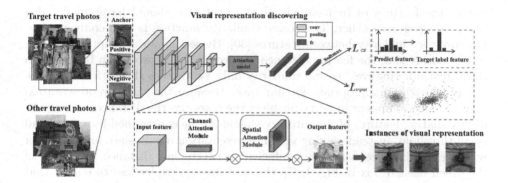

Fig. 1. The schematic diagram of our JDFR. Best viewed in color.

3 The Proposed Method

Since visual representations should be the most discriminating and frequent image regions in an image category, we firstly employ a classification task to discover the discriminating images. For frequency, we then apply the triplet loss to make features of the visual representation of one category close, but features belonging to different categories far in the feature space. Finally, we utilize an attention module to locate the representative region in each image. The schematic diagram of our method is illustrated in Fig. 1.

3.1 The Classification Task for Discriminating Images

The images are discriminating for a category when they represent the characteristics of the data in the category well. Therefore, discovering discriminating images can be considered as a classification task. The more discriminating the images are, the higher classification accuracy they achieve. We define a classification network with parameters as $f(\cdot)$. Given an image x and its label y, the network predicts its label $\hat{y} = f(x)$ that indicates which category x belongs to. Please refer to the yellow dashed box in Fig. 1. To optimize the network, we employ the cross-entropy loss $L_{CE}(y, \hat{y})$ that is

$$L_{CE} = \sum_{j=1}^{m} \sum_{i=1}^{n} -y_{ji} log(\hat{y}_{ji}) - (1 - y_{ji}) log(1 - \hat{y}_{ji}), \tag{1}$$

where m is the number of categories, n is the number of images in a category, y_{ji} denotes the ground truth, and $\hat{y}_{ji}$ denotes the output of the network.

3.2 The Triplet Loss for Frequent Visual Representation

The frequent visual representation of a category should represent the majority of the data and its features should have a highly dense distribution. In other words, the features of frequent visual representation should have smaller distance between each other. The cosine similarity function is commonly used to measure the similarity between features [30]. By setting an appropriate threshold for cosine loss, the feature distance learned by the network can be less than the threshold. However, cosine similarity only guarantees the within-class distance, which is inappropriate for our task. Because the visual representation may not always appear in every image of the category, the distances among the discriminating features of the category should not be constrained by a fixed and small threshold. Instead, mining visual representation requires not only a proper within-class distance, but also a sufficient between-class distance, as shown in the green dashed box in Fig. 1. To this end, we use triplet loss to ensure that an image x_i^a(anchor) in the i-th category is closer to other samples x_i^p (positive) than the image x_j^n (negative) in the j-th category [31], as shown in the blue dashed box in Fig. 1. This can be formulated as:

$$\|g(x_i^a) - g(x_i^p)\|_2^2 + \alpha < \|g(x_i^a) - g(x_j^n)\|_2^2 \qquad i \neq j, \tag{2}$$

where $g(x)$ denotes the feature vector of the sample x, and α is the margin (between-class distance) between positive and negative pairs. In this work, $g(x)$ is the high-level feature in the network because it involves the semantic information. We use Euclidean distance to measure the similarity between the features. The network is optimized by

$$L_{triplet} = \sum_{i=1}^{t} [\|g(x_i^a) - g(x_i^p)\|_2^2 - \|g(x_i^a) - g(x_j^n)\|_2^2 + \alpha]_+, \tag{3}$$

where, t denotes the number of triples. By using triplet loss, the mined visual representations can be frequent.

3.3 Attention Modules for Locating Visual Representation

The visual representation, is often a region in the image rather than the whole image, especially for the image that contains multiple objects. Meanwhile, it is expected to be discriminating for the category. To locate the most discriminating region in an image, we must address two problems: 1) How to find the discriminating object in each image? 2) How to locate the most discriminating region?

For the first problem, since different channels in the feature map F focuses on different objects in the image, we design a channel attention module that explores the inter-channel relationship of features to find the most discriminating object in each image. Average-pooling, $AvgPool_s$, is applied on the intermediate feature map, F, to aggregate spatial information. Max-pooling, $MaxPool_s$, is applied on F to aggregate distinctive object features. In order to obtain a finer channel-wise attention, we put them into a multi-layer perceptron (MLP) with one hidden layer to produce a channel attention map $M_c \in \mathbb{R}^{(c \times 1 \times 1)}$, which shows the weight of each channel. It can be formulated as:

$$M_c(F) = \sigma(MLP(AvgPool_s(F)) + MLP(MaxPool_s(F)))$$
$$= \sigma(W_1(W_0(F_c^{avg})) + W_1(W_0(F_c^{max}))), \qquad (4)$$

$$F' = M_c(F) \otimes F, \qquad (5)$$

where σ is the sigmoid function, $W_0 \in \mathbb{R}^{(c/r \times c)}$ and $W_1 \in \mathbb{R}^{(c \times c/r)}$ are the MLP weights, r is the reduction ratio, $F_c^{avg} \in \mathbb{R}^{(c \times 1 \times 1)}$ and $F_c^{max} \in \mathbb{R}^{(c \times 1 \times 1)}$ denote the average-pooled features and the max-pooled features, respectively, $\otimes$ denotes the element-wise multiplication, and F' is the channel feature map.

For the second problem, we design a spatial attention module that explores the inter-spatial relationship of the features. Due to the effectiveness of pooling operations along the channel axis in highlighting informative regions [32], we apply average pooling, $AvgPool_c$, and max-pooling, $MaxPool_c$, along the channel axis to locate the most discriminating region on F'. They are then concatenated and convolved by a standard convolution filter. Please refer to the red dashed box in Fig. 1. It can be formulated as:

$$M_s(F') = \sigma(f^{7 \times 7}([AvgPool_c(F'); MaxPool_c(F')])), \qquad (6)$$

$$F'' = M_s(F') \otimes F', \qquad (7)$$

where $f^{7 \times 7}$ is a convolution operation with the size of 7×7, and F'' is the feature map with attention.

To form the attention module, the channel attention and spatial attention are combined in a sequential manner with channel first order. We place it following the last convolution layer in the network. After training, the optimized attention module can locate the most discriminating region in each image, as shown in Fig. 2.

3.4 The Unified Model and Optimization

To ensure both discrimination and frequency of visual representations, we jointly optimize the network using the cross-entropy loss and triplet loss. The overall objective function is

$$\min_\theta L = \beta L_{triplet} + \gamma L_{CE}, \qquad (8)$$

where β and γ are constants to balance the contributions of the two losses.

4 Experiments

In this section, we firstly describe the experiment set-up, including datasets, implementation details, and evaluation metrics. Then, we examine the effectiveness of our method by comparing it with five state-of-the-arts on four benchmark datasets. Finally, we conduct ablation studies by controlling major influence factors.

4.1 Experiment Set-up

Datasets. Four datasets are selected in our experiment. First, we choose three benchmark datasets that are commonly used for visual pattern mining evaluation, there are CIFAR-10 [33], CIFAR-100-20 [33], and VOC2012-10 [34]. Since many categories in CIFAR100 are very challenging for visual representation mining, we select 20 categories from it, named as CIFAR100-20. VOC2012 is originally designed for object detection, so all images contain multiple objects. In many cases, the shared objects are too small to be representative. Therefore, we select 10 categories with representative objects from VOC2012, named as VOC2012-10. The travel photo dataset is collected from the popular travel website, TripAdvisor[1]. Photos from one travel destination belong to a category. Details of datasets are shown in Table 1. The Test sets are used for discovering the visual representation, and the Train and Validation sets with category labels are used for training our model.

Table 1. Details of four datasets.

Dataset	CIFAR10	CIFAR100-20	VOC2012-10	Travel
Category	10	20	10	20
Train	40000	8000	4905	64904
Validation	10000	2000	786	16227
Test	10000	2000	948	20000

Implementation Details. In this work, all the experiments were implemented by PyTorch on an NVIDIA 2080Ti with 11 GB of on-board memory. We fine-tuned the pre-trained VGG-19 on each training set. The VGG-19 was jointly trained by cross-entropy loss and triplet loss, and was optimized using Stochastic Gradient Descent (SGD) with an initial learning rate of 0.1. To balance the two loss functions, the hyperparameters β and γ were set to 0.3 and 0.7 respectively. The training stopped when no significant reduction of the validation error occurred, about 50 epochs. To find the most frequent representations, we applied a density-based clustering algorithm for mining task, and the number of features

---

[1] https://www.tripadvisor.com.

with the highest density was set as $N_u = 20$. Thus, 20 visual instances would be discovered for the visual representation from each category.

Competing Methods. The recent study [1] reported that the CNN-based visual patterns mining methods had largely outperformed the traditional hand-crafted based methods. Therefore, we compared JDFR with five state-of-the-arts for performance evaluation, which are all CNN-based methods. They are (1) Mid-level Deep Pattern Mining (MDPM) [1], (2)Contrastive Binary Mean Shift (CBMS) [10], (3) Part-level Convolutional Neural Network model (P-CNN) [3], (4) PatternNet [7] and (5) Masked-guided FCN (MFCN) [35]. Since only the code of MDPM was available from authors, we strictly implemented other methods according to their papers. The CNNs in P-CNN, PatternNet and MFCN were fine-tuned on the training set as well. P-CNN was trained with cross-entropy loss and SGD with momentum technique and the initial learning rate of 1e−3 that was the best rate in our tests. Since the detailed setting of experimental parameters were not given in the PatternNet, we trained it with MSE loss and Adam with the best initial learning rate of 1e−4, while the experimental parameters of MFCN used were consistent with the original paper.

4.2   Evaluation Metrics

The following two metrics were employed to evaluate the effectiveness of our model:

Discrimination Evaluation. Previous works for visual pattern mining used the image classification task as a proxy to evaluate their performances. Thus, we followed their protocol and trained a ResNet50 for classifying images to the corresponding categories, which is for evaluating the discrimination of the discovered visual representations. The results were an average accuracy and F1-score of those 20 instances of visual representation retrieved by the clustering step. Since MDPM divided the input image to a set of patches for subsequent processing, it was evaluated on the retrieved visual patches.

Frequency Evaluation. Intuitively, the discrimination cannot evaluate the frequency of discovered visual representation directly. Few previous studies explicitly measured it either. In this paper, we proposed a new metric (Frequency rate, FR) to compute the percentage of the images that are similar to the discovered visual representations in the high-level feature space. This is defined as:

$$\mathrm{FR} = \frac{1}{N_w \times N_u \times N} \sum_{w=1}^{N_w} \sum_{u=1}^{N_u} \sum_{v=1}^{N} \left\| S_{u,v}^w \geq T_f \right\|_0, \tag{9}$$

where, $S_{u,v}^w = cos(p_u^w, p_v^w)$ is a cosine similarity, p_u^w and p_v^w are the feature maps coming from the last convolution layer of aforementioned ResNet50. p_u^w is the

Table 2. Comparison among six approaches on discrimination of discovered visual representations.

Method	CIFAR10		CIRAR100-20		VOC2012-10		Travel	
	mAcc	F1	mAcc	F1	mAcc	F1	mAcc	F1
MDPM [1]	0.7820	0.7800	0.7800	0.7750	0.8000	0.8100	0.7800	0.8530
CBMS [10]	0.8800	0.8790	0.8630	0.8640	0.8650	0.8663	0.8630	0.9550
P-CNN[3]	0.8850	0.8880	0.8800	0.8750	0.8720	0.8715	0.8800	0.9725
PatternNet [7]	0.8300	0.8330	0.8200	0.8250	0.7950	0.7963	0.8200	0.9374
MFCN [35]	0.8450	0.8440	0.8434	0.8452	0.8312	0.8416	0.8434	0.9057
JDFR (Ours)	**0.9650**	**0.9650**	**0.9450**	**0.9440**	**0.9100**	**0.9100**	**0.9975**	**0.9975**

feature map of one image from w-th category, and p_v^w is the feature map of an instance of discovered visual representation from w-th category. N_w, N_u, and N are the number of categories, the number of images in each category, and the number of retrieved instances of visual representation(s), respectively. T_f denotes the similarity threshold. In this work, it was set three levels: 0.866, 0.906, and 0.940, which are corresponding to 30°, 25°, and 20° between two feature vectors, respectively.

4.3 Result and Analysis

Quantitative Results and Comparison. For the discrimination of visual representation, classification accuracy and F1-score are used for evaluation. The results of JDFR and five state-of-the-arts on four datasets are listed in Table 2. It shows that JDFR outperforms other five competing methods. MDPM performs the worst because it divides the image into patches, which could lose some semantic information. Surprisingly, PatternNet concentrates on mining discriminating patterns, but achieves the second worse performance, the reason might be that the discriminating information of their result is only provided by one max-pooling layer (last convolution), which lacks of adequate high-level semantic features. MFCN reaches the third worse since it is designed for co-saliency detection, which requires the visual pattern must appear in all images. P-CNN achieves the second best because P-CNN is more robust than other methods by using multi-scale information of images. JDFR performs the best on all datasets due to optimizing both discrimination and frequency of the visual representations. Compared with P-CNN, JDFR only improves 3.8% accuracy and 3.85% F1-score on VOC2012-10, but improves 8.0% accuracy and 7.7% F1-score on CIFAR10. Moreover, one can see that most methods perform better on VOC2012-10 and Travel than CIFAR10 and CIFAR100-20. The possible explanation is that our network has a fixed architecture of Conv module, and the feature map in the high-level layer becomes rather small when the input is small. Thus, the resolution of images in CIFAR10 and CIFAR100-20 is much smaller than the one in VOC2012-10 and Travel, which makes high-level features of images in CIFAR contain less semantics. In addition, all methods perform better on CIFAR10 than CIFAR100-20. We can observe that the number of training images in CIFAR100-20 is smaller than CIFAR10, which can make the trained network sub-optimal.

Table 3. Comparison of six approaches on frequency of discovered representations at three thresholds T_f.

Datasets	T_f	MDPM [1]	CBMS [10]	P-CNN [3]	PatternNet [7]	MFCN [35]	JDFR (Ours)
CIFAR10	0.940 (20°)	0.1025	0.1565	0.1533	0.1473	0.1516	**0.1733**
	0.906 (25°)	0.3289	0.5169	0.5224	0.4856	0.5003	**0.5429**
	0.866 (30°)	0.5673	0.8689	0.8792	0.8386	0.8515	**0.9122**
CIFAR100-20	0.940 (20°)	0.0322	0.0425	0.0489	0.0406	0.0372	**0.0523**
	0.906 (25°)	0.1540	0.2039	0.2153	0.2002	0.2037	**0.2346**
	0.866 (30°)	0.3370	0.5511	0.5314	0.5468	0.5531	**0.5880**
VOC2012-10	0.940 (20°)	0.0425	0.0665	0.0725	0.0627	0.0780	**0.0923**
	0.906 (25°)	0.1489	0.2410	0.2312	0.2245	**0.2468**	0.2415
	0.866 (30°)	0.3556	0.4789	0.4456	0.4289	0.4774	**0.4876**
Travel	0.940 (20°)	0.0752	0.1277	0.1000	0.1163	0.1325	**0.1668**
	0.906 (25°)	0.1428	0.2603	0.3002	0.2375	0.2470	**0.3348**
	0.866 (30°)	0.2555	0.4109	0.4355	0.3926	0.4058	**0.5076**

Fig. 2. Instances of discovered visual representations by JDFR from VOC2012-10. The first row lists the original images, the second row shows the attention maps after joint optimization, and the last row demonstrates the discovered instances of visual representation. Best viewed in color.

Fig. 3. Instances of discovered visual representations by JDFR from Travel. Best viewed in color.

Secondly, we compare the frequency of discovered visual representations at a varied threshold T_f on four datasets. The result is similar to the classification evaluation, as shown in Table 3. The visual representations discovered by JDFR are more frequent than ones from other methods at almost all thresholds. MFCN discovers the most frequent representation on VOC2012-10 when $T_f = 25°$. But it is just slightly higher than ours. Although MDPM uses a frequent pattern mining algorithm, it still performs the worst. PatternNet and P-CNN focus on mining the discriminating patterns, while their results also have high frequencies. All the above results demonstrate that our JDFR can discover better discriminating and frequent visual representations.

Qualitative Results and Comparison. To subjectively evaluate the performance of our method, we illustrate the attention maps and discovered visual representations of ten categories in VOC2012-10 in Fig. 2 and ten tourism destinations in Travel Fig. 3, respectively. One can see that they contain the symbolic content and represent these categories well.

Fig. 4. Instances of visual representation of aeroplane category in VOC2012-10 discovered by (a) MDPM [1], (b) CBMS [10], (c) P-CNN [3], (d) PatternNet [7], (e) MFCN [35] and (f) JDFR (ours), respectively. Best viewed in color.

For the qualitative comparison, we list ten instances of visual representation discovered by six approaches from aeroplane category in VOC2012-10, as shown in Fig. 4, and Manneken Pis in Travel, as shown in Fig. 5, respectively. One can observe that MDPM produces the worst result marked with the blue box, because it utilizes image patches that may merely have a part of the symbolic object. CBMS finds the frequent images in the yellow box instead of the visual representation in the images. P-CNN and PatternNet are able to discover the

Fig. 5. Instances of visual representation of Manneken Pis in Travel photo dataset discovered by (a) MDPM [1], (b) CBMS [10], (c) P-CNN [3], (d) PatternNet [7], (e) MFCN [35] and (f) JDFR (ours), respectively. Best viewed in color.

visual representations but include a few off-target errors only marked with the red boxes. MFCN is designed to mine the co-existing objects across all images. Thus, it finds the same object in dataset highlighted in green box, but does not work on images which include other objects only. By contrast, our method can retrieve consistent instances of visual representations.

4.4 Ablative Study

Variants of Model. To further verify our main contributions, we firstly compare JDFR with the model only with cross-entropy loss and only with triplet loss, respectively. Here, we set $\alpha = 1.5$ and $T_f = 20°$ because 20° is the strictest threshold of similarity measure. Results are listed in Table 4.

Table 4. Ablation study of JDFR on four datasets.

	mAcc			F1			FR 0.940 (20°)		
	CE	Triplet	CE + Triplet	CE	Triplet	CE + Triplet	CE	Triplet	CE+Triplet
CIFAR10	0.9100	0.8850	**0.9650**	0.9100	0.8850	**0.9650**	0.1667	0.1731	**0.1893**
CIFAR100-20	0.9050	0.8500	**0.9450**	0.9050	0.8490	**0.9440**	0.0405	0.0365	**0.0482**
VOC2012-10	**0.9100**	0.8350	**0.9100**	**0.9100**	0.8270	**0.9100**	0.0650	0.0634	**0.0715**
Travel	0.9800	0.9650	**0.9975**	0.9800	0.9640	**0.9975**	0.1464	0.1569	**0.1668**

One can observe JDFR achieves the best frequent and discriminating performance on four datasets. Specifically, JDFR improves 1.6% frequency on

CIFAR10 compared with the Triplet model. The average improvement on all datasets is 1.15%. Analogously, JDFR improves 5.5% accuracy and 5.5% F1-score on CIFAR10 compared with the CE model. On average, JDFR raises the accuracy 2.8% and F1-score 2.8%. These results demonstrate that joint optimization does improve the both frequency and discrimination of visual representations.

| (a) car | (b) bicycle | (c) bus | (d) dog |

Fig. 6. Four images from VOC2012-10 with labels of car, bicycle, bus and dog, respectively. The labels are indicated by yellow box. The shared object is shown in red box. (Color figure online)

Moreover, we find the frequency on VOC2012-10 increases the least among four datasets, and the accuracy is not improved. This might be caused by the characteristics of VOC2012-10. Each image in VOC2012-10 has multiple objects which may be shared with images belonging to other categories. For instance, Fig. 6(a) and Fig. 6(b) are labeled by car and bicycle, respectively. But they both include car and bicycle. Figure 6(c) and Fig. 6(d) are other examples that contain both bus and dog but have different labels. This suggests that many images, which are in different categories, may have very similar semantic features. In this case, triplet loss can not contribute much for the classification task. Thus, the discrimination performance of JDFR on VOC2012-10 is identical to the one of CE model. Since it does enlarge the between-class distance, the performance of frequency is still improved.

Table 5. Comparison of JDFR performance with different α.

	mAcc			F1			FR 0.940 (20°)		
	$\alpha = 1$	$\alpha = 1.5$	$\alpha = 2$	$\alpha = 1$	$\alpha = 1.5$	$\alpha = 2$	$\alpha = 1$	$\alpha = 1.5$	$\alpha = 2$
CIFAR10	0.9600	**0.9650**	0.9600	0.9600	**0.9650**	0.9590	0.1934	0.1899	**0.2042**
CIFAR100-20	0.9280	**0.9450**	0.9400	0.9270	**0.9440**	0.9380	**0.0556**	0.0482	0.0508
VOC2012-10	0.8950	0.9100	**0.9200**	0.8960	0.9100	**0.9150**	0.0691	0.0715	**0.0742**
Travel	**0.9975**	**0.9975**	0.9925	**0.9975**	**0.9975**	0.9925	**0.1843**	0.1668	0.1657

Varied Margin α. The margin α can adjust the between-class distance. We test varied α and show the results in Table 5. Due to the characteristics of VOC2012-10, the larger value of α can improve both frequency and discrimination of visual representations. However, an overlarge α is not appropriate to other data. One can observe that the best overall performance on all datasets can be reached when $\alpha = 1.5$. Therefore, We choose this setting for all experiments in this paper.

5 Conclusion

In this work, we propose a jointly discriminating and frequent visual representation mining method (JDFR) to address the problem of discovering visual representations. Unlike previous studies focusing on either the discriminating patterns or frequent patterns, JDFR can optimize both the discrimination and frequency of discovered visual representations simultaneously. Moreover, our channel and spatial attention modules help to locate the representations in images. To evaluate the effectiveness of JDFR, we conduct experiments on four diverse datasets. The results of classification accuracy and frequency demonstrate that JDFR is able to discover the best visual representation in comparing with five state-of-the-art methods.

Acknowledgments. This work is supported by the Science and Technology Plan of Xi'an (20191122015KYPT011JC013), the Fundamental Research Funds of the Central Universities of China (No. JX18001) and the Science Basis Research Program in Shaanxi Province of China (No. 2020JQ-321, 2019JQ-663).

References

1. Li, Y., Liu, L., Shen, C., Van Den Hengel, A.: Mining mid-level visual patterns with deep CNN activations. IJCV **121**, 344–364 (2017)
2. Chen, Z., Maffra, F., Sa, I., Chli, M.: Only look once, mining distinctive landmarks from convnet for visual place recognition. In: IROS, pp. 9–16 (2017)
3. Yang, L., Xie, X., Lai, J.: Learning discriminative visual elements using part-based convolutional neural network. Neurocomputing **316**, 135–143 (2018)
4. Memon, I., Chen, L., Majid, A., Lv, M., Hussain, I., Chen, G.: Travel recommendation using geo-tagged photos in social media for tourist. Wirel. Pers. Commun. **80**, 1347–1362 (2015)
5. Vu, H.Q., Li, G., Law, R., Ye, B.H.: Exploring the travel behaviors of inbound tourists to Hong Kong using geotagged photos. Tour. Manage. **46**, 222–232 (2015)
6. Bronner, F., De Hoog, R.: Vacationers and eWOM : who posts, and why, where, and what? J. Travel Res. **50**, 15–26 (2011)
7. Li, H., Ellis, J.G., Zhang, L., Chang, S.F.: Automatic visual pattern mining from categorical image dataset. Int. J. Multimedia Inf. Retrieval **8**, 35–45 (2019)
8. Lowe, D.G.: Object recognition from local scale-invariant features. In: ICCV, vol. 2, pp. 1150–1157 (1999)
9. Doersch, C., Singh, S., Gupta, A., Sivic, J., Efros, A.A.: What makes Paris look like Paris? Commun. ACM **58**, 103–110 (2015)
10. Zhang, W., Cao, X., Wang, R., Guo, Y., Chen, Z.: Binarized mode seeking for scalable visual pattern discovery. In: CVPR, pp. 3864–3872 (2017)
11. Simonyan, K., Zisserman, A.: Very deep convolutional networks for large-scale image recognition. arXiv:1409.1556 (2014)

12. Tan, Z., Liang, W., Wei, F., Pun, C.M.: Image co-saliency detection by propagating superpixel affinities. In: ICASSP (2013)
13. Chang, K.Y., Liu, T.L., Lai, S.H.: From co-saliency to co-segmentation: an efficient and fully unsupervised energy minimization model. In: CVPR, pp. 2129–2136 (2011)
14. Zhang, B., Gao, Y., Zhao, S., Liu, J.: Local derivative pattern versus local binary pattern: face recognition with high-order local pattern descriptor. IEEE TIP **19**, 533–544 (2009)
15. Kim, S., Jin, X., Han, J.: Disiclass: discriminative frequent pattern-based image classification. In: KDD Workshop on Multimedia Data Mining (2010)
16. Lapuschkin, S., Binder, A., Montavon, G., Muller, K.R., Samek, W.: Analyzing classifiers: Fisher vectors and deep neural networks. In: CVPR, pp. 2912–2920 (2016)
17. Gong, Y., Pawlowski, M., Yang, F., Brandy, L., Bourdev, L., Fergus, R.: Web scale photo hash clustering on a single machine. In: CVPR, pp. 19–27 (2015)
18. Chum, O., Matas, J.: Large-scale discovery of spatially related images. IEEE TPAMI **32**, 371–377 (2009)
19. Fu, H., Xu, D., Lin, S., Liu, J.: Object-based RGBD image co-segmentation with mutex constraint. In: CVPR, pp. 4428–4436 (2015)
20. Fu, H., Xu, D., Zhang, B., Lin, S.: Object-based multiple foreground video co-segmentation. In: CVPR, pp. 3166–3173 (2014)
21. Tang, K., Joulin, A., Li, L.J., Fei-Fei, L.: Co-localization in real-world images. In: CVPR, 1464–1471 (2014)
22. Wei, L., Zhao, S., Bourahla, O.E.F., Li, X., Wu, F.: Group-wise deep co-saliency detection. arXiv:1707.07381 (2017)
23. Fu, H., Cao, X., Tu, Z.: Cluster-based co-saliency detection. IEEE TIP **22**, 3766–3778 (2013)
24. Cao, X., Tao, Z., Zhang, B., Fu, H., Feng, W.: Self-adaptively weighted co-saliency detection via rank constraint. IEEE TIP **23**, 4175–4186 (2014)
25. Huang, R., Feng, W., Sun, J.: Saliency and co-saliency detection by low-rank multiscale fusion. In: ICME (2015)
26. Luo, Y., Jiang, M., Wong, Y., Zhao, Q.: Multi-camera saliency. IEEE TPAMI **37**, 2057–2070 (2015)
27. Bors, A.G., Papushoy, A.: Image retrieval based on query by saliency content. In: Benois-Pineau, J., Le Callet, P. (eds.) Visual Content Indexing and Retrieval with Psycho-Visual Models. MSA, pp. 171–209. Springer, Cham (2017). https://doi.org/10.1007/978-3-319-57687-9_8
28. Ge, C., Fu, K., Liu, F., Bai, L., Yang, J.: Co-saliency detection via inter and intra saliency propagation. Signal Process. Image Commun. **44**, 69–83 (2016)
29. Li, H., Ngan, K.N.: A co-saliency model of image pairs. IEEE TIP **20**, 3365–3375 (2011)
30. Nguyen, H.V., Bai, L.: Cosine similarity metric learning for face verification. In: Kimmel, R., Klette, R., Sugimoto, A. (eds.) ACCV 2010. LNCS, vol. 6493, pp. 709–720. Springer, Heidelberg (2011). https://doi.org/10.1007/978-3-642-19309-5_55
31. Schroff, F., Kalenichenko, D., Philbin, J.: FaceNet: a unified embedding for face recognition and clustering. In: CVPR, pp. 815–823 (2015)
32. Zagoruyko, S., Komodakis, N.: Paying more attention to attention: Improving the performance of convolutional neural networks via attention transfer. arXiv:1612.03928 (2016)

33. Krizhevsky, A., Hinton, G.: Learning multiple layers of features from tiny images (2009)
34. Shetty, S.: Application of convolutional neural network for image classification on pascal VOC challenge 2012 dataset. arXiv:1607.03785 (2016)
35. Zhang, K., Li, T., Liu, B., Liu, Q.: Co-saliency detection via mask-guided fully convolutional networks with multi-scale label smoothing. In: CVPR, pp. 3095–3104 (2019)

Discrete Spatial Importance-Based Deep Weighted Hashing

Yang Shi[1], Xiushan Nie[2(✉)], Quan Zhou[1], Xiaoming Xi[2], and Yilong Yin[1(✉)]

[1] Shandong University, 1500 Shunhua Road, Jinan, Shandong Province, China
shiyang@mail.sdu.edu.cn, woodschou@outlook.com, ylyin@sdu.edu.cn
[2] Shandong Jianzhu University,
1000 Fengming Road, Jinan, Shandong Province, China
niexiushan@163.com, fyzq10@126.com

Abstract. Hashing is a widely used technique for large-scale approximate nearest neighbor searching in multimedia retrieval. Recent works have proved that using deep neural networks is a promising solution for learning both feature representation and hash codes. However, most existing deep hashing methods directly learn hash codes from a convolutional neural network, ignoring the spatial importance distribution of images. The loss of spatial importance negatively affects the performance of hash learning and thus reduces its accuracy. To address this issue, we propose a new deep hashing method with weighted spatial information, which generates hash codes by using discrete spatial importance distribution. In particular, to extract the discrete spatial importance information of images effectively, we propose a method to learn the spatial attention map and hash code simultaneously, which makes the spatial attention map more conductive to hash-based retrieval. The experimental results of three widely used datasets show that the proposed deep weighted hashing method is superior to the state-of-the-art hashing method.

Keywords: Hashing · Neural networks · Spatial importance

1 Introduction

With the rapid developments in science and technology, people can use the sensors around them more conveniently, which greatly increases the amount of data uploaded through the sensors, including a large number of images and videos. Therefore, the ability to deal with this data has become an urgent problem, and the approximate nearest search is a method to solve it. As one of the approximate nearest search methods, hashing maps the high-dimensional data into a compact binary code in the Hamming space. Hashing greatly reduces the required storage

Y. Yin—This work was supported in part by the National Natural Science Foundation of China (61671274, 61876098), National Key R & D Program of China (2018YFC0830100, 2018YFC0830102) and special funds for distinguished professors of Shandong Jianzhu University.

H. Ishikawa et al. (Eds.): ACCV 2020, LNCS 12624, pp. 372–387, 2021.
https://doi.org/10.1007/978-3-030-69535-4_23

space and the calculation of the hamming distance of XOR binary codes is much faster than that of the Euclidean distances of the original data. Because of its excellent storage capacity and efficient computing power, hashing has attracted wide attention from researchers.

At the same time, with the rapid development of deep learning research, deep model has achieved remarkable improvements in computer vision performance including image classification [1], image retrieval [2], video classification [3] and other directions [4–7]. Therefore, many deep hashing methods have been developed, which can learn both deep features and hash codes. At present, the key concept of deep hashing methods is to obtain the hash codes of images by putting the images directly into convolutional neural networks (CNNs). Unfortunately, this simple operation does not distinguish the importance of the region of the image, every pixel in the image has the same impact on the hash code learning, which may lead to suboptimal performance [8]. Recently, the research on fully convolutional networks (FCN) [9] in image positioning shows that the feature map of a convolution layer can retain a great deal of spatial information. Therefore, the ability to optimize hash codes with this spatial information has become an important new research topic.

To fully use the spatial importance information, in this study, we propose a deep hashing method with weighted discrete spatial importance (SIWH). To explore spatial importance information, we designed an effective hash-based spatial attention model to adaptively learn the spatial importance closely related to the target. Meanwhile, we also used a CNN to extract semantic information, which is much richer in detail than the handcrafted features of images [10].

In summary, we emphasize the following three contributions:

(1) We propose a unified framework to learn weighted hash codes using discrete spatial importance distributions, which can assign different hash code lengths to images according to their spatial importance. After reviewing available research, we believe that this is the first attempt to learn weighted hashing according to the importance of spatial position.
(2) We develop an effective hash-guide spatial attention model. In this model, the spatial attention network and hash learning network are trained simultaneously, which makes the spatial information conducive to hash code generation.
(3) We make an extensive evaluation of three widely used image retrieval benchmarks. The experimental results show that our method significantly outperforms the state-of-the-art methods' results, which demonstrates the superiority and effectiveness of our method.

The rest of this paper is organized as follows. In Sect. 2, we briefly review related works. The proposed method is introduced in Sect. 3. The extensive experiments and discussions of the experimental results are provided in Sect. 4, and we present conclusions in Sect. 5.

2   Related Works

In this section, we will briefly review the related hashing methods, including shallow-based and deep-based models.

In general, hashing methods can be divided into two categories data-independent and data-dependent [11]. In the early years of these methods' development, researchers focused on data-independent hashing methods, such as LSH [12] and its variants (SKLSH) [13]. The LSH method generates hash codes through random projection. However, to achieve satisfactory performance, these data-independent methods often need a long hash code.

To obtain more compact binary codes, data-dependent hash methods have been proposed in more recent years. These methods attempt to learn hash functions from a training set, and they can be divided into unsupervised methods and supervised methods [14]. Unsupervised methods only use unmarked training data to learn hash functions. For example, spectral hashing (SH) [15] minimizes the weighted hamming distance of image pairs, where the weight is defined as the similarity measure of the image pairs. Iterative quantization (ITQ) [16] attempts to minimize quantization errors on projected image descriptors to reduce the information loss caused by the difference between the real value feature space and the binary hamming space.

Compared to unsupervised methods, supervised methods provide better accuracy due to the usage of label information. Predictable discriminative binaries (DBC) [17] look for hyperplanes as hash functions that separate categories with large margins. Minimal loss hashing (MLH) [18] optimizes the upper bound of hinged losses to learn the hash function.

Meanwhile, semi-supervised hashing (SSH) [19], uses rich unmarked data to standardize hash functions. Although the above methods use linear projections as hash functions, they have difficulty in handling linearly indivisible data. To overcome this limitation, supervised hashing with kernels (KSH) [20] and binary reconstructive embedding (BRE) [21] are proposed to study the similarity–preserving hash function in kernel space.

With the wide application of deep learning in recent years, deep hashing frameworks have attracted more and more attention in hashing methods. Deep hashing (DH) [22] uses nonlinear deep networks to generate improved hash codes. Fang et al. [23] and Lai et al. [24] were the first to attempt to combine learning feature representations and hash functions. Lu et al. [25] used a deep network with a stacked fully connected layer to construct multiple hierarchical nonlinear transforms to learn binary hash codes. Deep supervised hashing (DSH) [2] tries to maintain similarity and minimize binary loss. A supervised semantics preserving hash (SSDH) [26] constructs the underlying hashing layer to generate hash code by directly minimizing classification errors on the hashing layer output. Li et al. [27] proposed deep pairwise labels supervised hashing (DPSH), which uses pairwise labels to perform both feature learning and hash code learning. Deep supervised discrete hashing (DSDH) [28] develops DPSH based on the ideal assumption that hash codes should be classified. Cao et al. [29] proposed deep Cauchy hashing (DCH), which designed loss functions based on the

Cauchy distribution to generate highly concentrated hash codes. Jiang et al. [30] proposed the Deep discrete supervised hashing (DDSH), which uses pairwise supervised information to directly guide the discrete coding program and the deep characteristic learning program. Jiang et al. [31] proposed asymmetric deep supervised hashing (ADSH), which processes query points and database points in an asymmetric path. Deep ordinal hashing (DOH [32]) learns a group of ranking-based hash functions by jointly exploiting the local spatial information and the global semantic information. In general, deep supervised hashing can significantly improve performance.

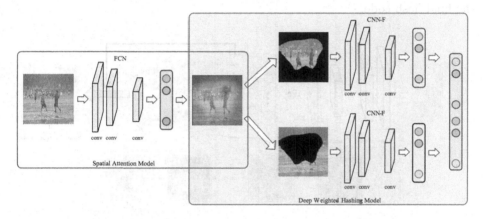

Fig. 1. Framework of the proposed SIWH method, which consists of two components: Spatial Attention Model and Deep Weighted Hashing Model

However, the aforementioned deep-learning-based hashing methods use the deep model to generate semantics of whole images, which ignore the spatial importance distribution of the images. To fully use this information, in this work, we propose a spatial attention module to learn a weighted hash. In the proposed method, we first use the spatial attention model to obtain the importance of each position, and then learn the weighted hash function with the allocation of the hash code length appropriately according to the different importance information.

At the same time, attention models have been extensively studied in image/video subtitling [33] and object detection [8]. [34] proposed that attention model can selectively learn significant areas of images in specific visual tasks. And [4] proposed attention model to learn the attention position of image subtitle. Although attention model has been successfully used in various visual tasks, it is still not fully utilized in image retrieval.

3   Discrete Spatial Importance-Based Deep Weighted Hashing

In this section, we describe the proposed deep hashing framework in detail. The entire framework is shown in Fig. 1. Firstly, the spatial attention model is used to generate the spatial attention map for the input image by FCN network. Then, the attention mask is generated according to the spatial attention map, and the attention and non-attention parts of the input image are divided by the mask. After that, the attention and the non-attention parts are put into CNN network learning hash function. Finally, the learned hash codes are combined to generate the final hash code.

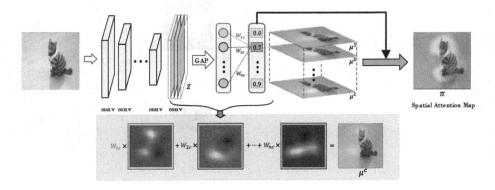

Fig. 2. An imaginary illustration of the Spatial Attention Model.

3.1   Notation and Definition

Suppose $\mathbf{X} = \{x_n\}_{n=1}^N$ be a set of N images, $\mathbf{Y} = \{\mathbf{y}_n\}_{n=1}^N$ is the set of their corresponding binary label vectors, where $\{\mathbf{y}_n\} \in \{0,1\}^C$, and C defines the total number of the categories. The non-zero entry in $\mathbf{y}_n$ indicates that the nth image belongs to the corresponding class. Let $\mathbf{S} = \{s_{ij}\} \in \{0,1\}^{N \times N}$ be the similarity matrix, where $s_{ij} = 1$ if the image pair (x_i, x_j) shares at least one common class, otherwise $s_{ij} = 0$. Hash coding learns a collection of K-bit binary codes $\mathbf{B} \in \{0,1\}^{K \times N}$, where the nth column $\mathbf{b}_n \in \{0,1\}^K$ denotes the binary codes for the nth sample x_n. Our goal is to learn a set of mappings $H : x \to \mathbf{b}$, which maps the image x into a hash code $\mathbf{b}$.

3.2   Network Architecture

The proposed method uses two networks, in which the FCN model aims to capture spatial principal distribution information using the spatial attention model, and the CNN model explores semantic information. For CNN networks, we utilize CNN-F [35] as the backbone, where the first five convolutional layers and the first two fully connected layers of CNN-F are denoted as $conv1$, $conv2$, $conv3$, $conv4$, $conv5$, $fc6$ and $fc7$, respectively. Based on these layers, we design a task-specific fully connected layer fck. For FCN networks, we use a FCN network with VGG [36] as its backbone to extract the attention position. The FCN network adopts the first 5 convolutional layers of the VGG network, containing $conv1$, $conv2$, $conv3$, $conv4$, and $conv5$. In the proposed network, we use a convolutional layer $conv6$ to replace the first fully connected layer $fc6$ of the VGG network. Behind the above layers, there is a fully connected fcc layer for classification prediction. In particular, we perform global average pooling on the $conv5$ layer and provide the output to the fully connected classification layer (i.e. fcc). The average of these feature maps will be used to generate the probability output of the fcc layer. Furthermore, we introduce an intuitive method for extracting image spatial importance by utilizing the weight matrix of the fcc layer and the feature map of the $conv5$ layer. Like the CNN network, the $conv6$ layer is designed to learn visual descriptors by encoding spatial information.

3.3   Spatial Attention Model

Intuitively, when searching for relevant images in the database, we always pay more attention on the regions that are highly related to the main objects or peoples in the image. Consequently, we introduce a hash-guide spatial attention model, which aims to generate object-specific spatial attention map for hash learning. Figure 2 illustrates the generation of the spatial attention map.

As is shown in Fig. 2, we use the Full Convolution Network with the global average pooling to generate the attention locations of the image. Specifically, we perform the global average pooling on $conv5$ layer and provide the output to the fully-connected classification layer (fcc). The outputs of the global average pooling can be regarded as the spatial average of feature maps of the $conv5$ layer. Those spatial average values are used to generate the probabilistic outputs of the fcc layer.

In this section, we introduce an intuitive way to produce the spatial attention map by projecting the weight matrix of the fcc layer on the feature maps of the $conv5$ layer.

Let $\mathbf{Z}_{uv}$ define the channel-wise representation at the spatial location (u, v) of the $conv5$ layer of the FCN network, which can be computed as

$$\mathbf{Z}_{uv} = \Psi_F(x; \mathbf{\Omega}_F), \tag{1}$$

where $\mathbf{Z}_{uv} \in \mathbb{R}^{M_F}$ with M_F being the number of feature maps. The notations $u \in \{1, \cdots, U\}$ and $v \in \{1, \cdots, V\}$, where U and V are the width and height of feature maps. The notation x represents the input image, and Ψ_F defines the non-linear projection function for the FCN network. The notation $\mathbf{\Omega}_F = \{\mathbf{W}_F^d, \mathbf{c}_F^d\}_{d=1}^{D_F}$ defines a set of non-linear projection parameters with D_F being the depth of the FCN network.

Considering the weight matrix, $\mathbf{W} \in \mathbb{R}^{M_F \times C}$ performs a mapping of the spatial average values to the semantic class labels. We define the object-specific local response at the spatial location (u, v) as μ_{uv}^c, which can be obtained by

$$\mu_{uv}^c = max(\mathbf{w}_c^T \mathbf{z}_{uv}, 0), \; for \; c = 1, \cdots, C, \tag{2}$$

where $\mathbf{w}_c$ is the cth column of $\mathbf{W}$. μ_{uv}^c indicates the importance at the spatial location (u, v) in the input image x which is classified to the cth class. As each spatial location (u, v) corresponds to a different local patch in the original image, the local response μ_{uv}^c indicates the relative similarity of the local image patch to the cth class.

Essentially, we can obtain local discriminative information at different spatial locations for a particular class. The larger value of μ_{uv}^c indicates that the image patch at the spatial location (u, v) is more related to the cth class. Inversely, the smaller value of μ_{uv}^c indicates it is less related to the cth class. Therefore, μ^c is the attention map for class c. By integrating μ^c together, we can define the spatial attention map π to identify all the object-specific image patches. Specifically, the local response at (u, v), denoted as π_{uv}, is defined as follows

$$\pi_{uv} = \sum_{c=1}^{C} p_c \mu_{uv}^c / \sum_{c=1}^{C} p_c \tag{3}$$

where p_c is the cth probabilistic output of the classification (i.e., fcc) layer of FCN network.

3.4   Deep Weighted Hashing Model

Given a query image, users typically pay more attention to the attention area of the query image. Therefore, differently weighted hash codes should be assigned between attention and non-attention areas during hash learning. To achieve this purpose, in the proposed SIWH, we first generate an attention mask using the spatial attention map, and then learn weighted hash codes for different attention areas.

Using the attention map obtained before, we assign 1 to the location whose response value is equal or greater than the threshold value t, and assign a 0 to the rest, generating the attention mask $\mathbf{A}$. We can also swap the 0 and the 1 in $\mathbf{A}$ to generate $\bar{\mathbf{A}}$. Then, we expand the attention mask $\mathbf{A}$ to the size of the image x, which is $\mathbf{A}'$. We then multiply $\mathbf{A}'$ with the image x to get the attention image of x, which is denoted as x^1. Similarly, we use $\bar{\mathbf{A}}$ and the image x to generate x^2.

Next, we put the attention image x^1 and non-attention image x^2 into two CNN networks to learn hash codes. First, we define the feature representation extracted from the $fc8$ layer of the CNN network as $\mathbf{g}^1$ and $\mathbf{g}^2$, computed by

$$\mathbf{g}^1 = \Psi_{C^1}(x^1; \mathbf{\Omega}_{C^1}), \; \mathbf{g}^2 = \Psi_{C^2}(x^2; \mathbf{\Omega}_{C^2}), \tag{4}$$

where $\mathbf{g}^1 \in \mathbb{R}^{M_{C^1}}$ and $\mathbf{g}^2 \in \mathbb{R}^{M_{C^2}}$. The notation Ψ_{C^1} and Ψ_{C^2} define the non-linear projection function for the two CNN networks, respectively. $\Omega_{C^1} = \{\mathbf{W}_{C^1}^d, \mathbf{c}_{C^1}^d\}_{d=1}^{D_{C^1}}$ and $\Omega_{C^2} = \{\mathbf{W}_{C^2}^d, \mathbf{c}_{C^2}^d\}_{d=1}^{D_{C^2}}$ define two sets of non-linear projection parameters with D_{C^1} and D_{C^2} being the depths of the CNN networks, respectively.

We can use a symbolic function to get the hash code $\mathbf{b}^1$ and $\mathbf{b}^2$, which are computed by

$$\mathbf{b}^1 = sgn(\mathbf{g}^1), \ \mathbf{b}^2 = sgn(\mathbf{g}^2). \tag{5}$$

Then, we can define $\mathbf{b}$ as the whole hash code, which can be calculated as $\mathbf{b} = \mathbf{b}^1 \oplus \mathbf{b}^2$, where $\oplus$ denotes the connect operation. We define K as the code length of $\mathbf{b}$, K^1 and K^2 are the code lengths of $\mathbf{b}^1$ and $\mathbf{b}^2$ respectively, and $K = K^1 + K^2$.

3.5 Objective Function

As mentioned earlier, given the binary codes $\mathbf{B} = \{\mathbf{b}_i\}_{i=1}^N$ and the pairwise labels $\mathbf{S} = \{s_{ij}\}$ for all the images, we can define the likelihood of the pairwise labels [37]:

$$p(s_{ij} \mid \mathbf{B}) = \begin{cases} \sigma(\theta_{ij}), & s_{ij} = 1 \\ 1 - \sigma(\theta_{ij}), & s_{ij} = 0 \end{cases} \tag{6}$$

where $\theta_{ij} = \frac{1}{2}\mathbf{b}_i^T\mathbf{b}_j$, and $\sigma(\theta_{ij}) = \frac{1}{1+e^{-\theta_{ij}}}$. Please note that $\mathbf{b}_i \in \{-1, 1\}^K$.

By taking the negative log-likelihood of the observed pairwise labels in S, we can obtain the following optimization equation:

$$\begin{aligned} \min_{\mathbf{B}} L_s &= -\log p(\mathbf{S} \mid \mathbf{B}) = -\sum_{s_{ij} \in \mathbf{S}} \log p(s_{ij} \mid \mathbf{B}) \\ &= -\sum_{s_{ij} \in \mathbf{S}} (s_{ij}\theta_{ij} - \log(1 + e^{\theta_{ij}})). \end{aligned} \tag{7}$$

It is easy to find that the above optimization problem can make the hamming distance between two similar points as small as possible and the hamming distance between two different similar points as large as possible. This fits perfectly with the goal of supervised hash of paired tags.

The problem in (7) is a discrete optimization problem, which is difficult to solve. However, we can solve this problem by directly transferring $\mathbf{b}_i$ from discrete value to a continuous relaxation $\mathbf{d}_i$. Therefore, a quantization loss term is included as follows:

$$\min_{\mathbf{B}} L_q = \sum_{i=1}^{N} \| \mathbf{b}_i - \mathbf{d}_i \|_2^2, \tag{8}$$

where $\mathbf{d}_i$ is the real value output of the network.

In the FCN, the classification loss term is defined as the cross entropy loss, which is expressed as follows:

$$\min_{\mathbf{B}} L_c = -\sum_{i=1}^{N}(y_i \log \bar{y}_i + (1 - y_i) \log(1 - \bar{y}_i)), \tag{9}$$

where $\bar{y}_i$ is the prediction value output of the network.

Thus, the final objective function is as follows:

$$\begin{aligned}
\min_{\mathbf{B}} L &= L_s + \eta L_q + \beta L_c \\
&= -\sum_{s_{ij} \in \mathbf{S}}(s_{ij}\theta_{ij} - \log(1 + e^{\theta_{ij}})) \\
&\quad + \eta \sum_{i=1}^{N} \| \mathbf{b}_i - \mathbf{d}_i \|_2^2 \\
&\quad - \beta \sum_{i=1}^{N}(y_i \log \bar{y}_i + (1 - y_i) \log(1 - \bar{y}_i)),
\end{aligned} \tag{10}$$

where η and β are the hyper-parameters.

Among these terms, we need to optimize parameters for $\boldsymbol{\Omega}_F = \{\mathbf{W}_F^d, \mathbf{c}_F^d\}_{d=1}^{D_F}$ and $\boldsymbol{\Omega}_{C^*} = \{\mathbf{W}_{C^*}^d, \mathbf{c}_{C^*}^d\}_{d=1}^{D_{C^*}}$. The parameters $\mathbf{W}_*^d$ and $\mathbf{c}_*^d$ can be automatically updated by applying SGD with BP algorithm in pytorch.

4   Experiment

In this section, we report the results of our extensive experiments to verify the efficiency of the proposed method (SIWH) on three widely used image retrieval datasets, including CIFAR-10 [38], NUS-WIDE [39], and MS-COCO [40]. The CIFAR-10 dataset is a single-label dataset, while the NUS-WIDE and MS-COCO dataset are multi-label datasets.

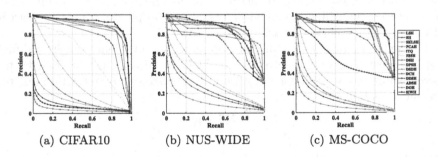

(a) CIFAR10   (b) NUS-WIDE   (c) MS-COCO

Fig. 3. The results of Precision-recall curves with respect to 64-bit hash code on three datasets.

Table 1. The results of mAP with respect to different code lengths on the three datasets.

Method	CIFAR10				NUS-WIDE				MS-COCO			
	24 bits	48 bits	64 bits	128 bits	24 bits	48 bits	64 bits	128 bits	24 bits	48 bits	64 bits	128 bits
LSH	0.2722	0.3586	0.4490	0.4887	0.0654	0.1882	0.2993	0.3900	0.0868	0.1462	0.1774	0.3007
SH	0.2346	0.2959	0.3187	0.5168	0.1238	0.1729	0.2358	0.3448	0.0837	0.1048	0.1289	0.2373
SKLSH	0.2378	0.2983	0.3872	0.5517	0.0922	0.1387	0.2596	0.4354	0.0551	0.1369	0.1893	0.3966
PCAH	0.1430	0.1720	0.1863	0.2018	0.0924	0.0809	0.0890	0.1131	0.0662	0.0633	0.0702	0.0918
ITQ	0.3648	0.4245	0.4283	0.4502	0.3109	0.3884	0.4139	0.4571	0.2289	0.2862	0.3085	0.3515
FSSH	0.6853	0.7124	0.6919	0.7204	0.3959	0.3716	0.4462	0.5411	0.3105	0.3415	0.4063	0.4316
DSH	0.7864	0.7830	0.7834	0.7835	0.6598	0.6653	0.6587	0.6598	0.5153	0.5069	0.5147	0.5072
DPSH	0.8821	0.8853	0.8858	0.8876	0.8390	0.8429	0.8423	0.8468	0.6623	0.6871	0.6965	0.7073
DSDH	0.8985	0.9004	0.9002	0.8970	0.8225	0.8328	0.8347	0.8415	0.6988	0.7191	0.7220	0.7227
DCH	0.8753	0.8752	0.8749	0.8273	0.7552	0.7632	0.7647	0.7602	0.5858	0.5954	0.5948	0.5953
DDSH	0.8452	0.8861	0.8916	0.8993	0.7352	0.8102	0.8083	0.7957	0.5821	0.6032	0.6142	0.6162
ADSH	0.8957	0.9040	0.9060	0.9059	0.8582	0.8893	0.8890	0.8873	0.6351	0.6376	0.6508	0.6617
DOH	0.8651	0.8616	0.8697	0.8739	0.7830	0.7846	0.7808	0.7935	0.7336	0.7487	0.7537	0.7521
SIWH	**0.9231**	**0.9304**	**0.9294**	**0.9316**	**0.8673**	**0.8948**	**0.9023**	**0.9109**	**0.7522**	**0.7986**	**0.8007**	**0.8153**

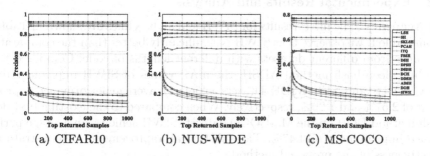

| (a) CIFAR10 | (b) NUS-WIDE | (c) MS-COCO |

Fig. 4. The results of P@N curves with respect to 64-bit hash code on three datasets.

4.1 Baselines and Evaluation Metrics

We compare the proposed SIWH method with thirteen state-of-the-art image hashing methods, including six non-deep hashing methods (LSH [12], SH [15], SKLSH [13], PCAH [41], ITQ [16], and FSSH [42]) and seven deep hashing methods (ADSH [31], DPSH [27], DSH [2], DDSH [30], DSDH [28], DCH [29], and DOH [32]). We have briefly reviewed these hashing methods in Sect. 2 above. Among them, LSH, SH, and SHLSH are unsupervised hash methods, and the rest are supervised hash methods.

For the non-deep methods, we use the CNN-F network to extract the 4096-dimensional features of the $fc7$ layer. For all deep methods, we use the same network (CNN-F) for equivalent comparison. The parameters of all comparison methods were selected as their default values.

In addition, we use three widely used indicators to evaluate search performance: mean average accuracy (mAP), top N precision (P@N), and Precision-Recall curves (PR).

4.2 Experimental Settings

We implemented the proposed SIWH method using the open source pytorch framework on the NVIDIA TITAN XP GPU server. In addition to the layers from VGG, $conv1$ to $conv5$, and $fc6$ to $fc7$, we use "kaiming" initialization to initialize the network. Our network is trained by using a small batch random gradient descent with learning speed set to 10^{-5}. In all experiments, we fixed the minimum batch size to be 16. The hyperparameters η and β of the two loss functions are set to 1e−2 and 3e−2 respectively.

SIWH involves two hyperparameters, namely the threshold value of the attention mask t and the proportion of the attention hash code K^1/K. For t, we use a linear search to select t in 0.5, 0.625, 0.75, 0, 875. Specifically, for the CIFAR-10 data set, we set t to 0.875 and for the NUS-WIDE and MS-COCO data sets, we set t to 0.75. For K^1/K, we conducted a comparative experiment of the parameters.

4.3 Experimental Results and Analysis

(1) **Accuracy.** The mAP results for SIWH and all baselines are shown in Table 1. From Table 1, we observe that SIWH is significantly better than the comparative baselines from different datasets with different lengths of code. Compared with the best deep hash method ADSH, the mAP values of SIWH implemented on the CIFAR10 and NUS-WIDE datasets achieve an average performance improvement of 2.57% and 1.29%, respectively. When compared to the existing best deep hash method DOH on the MS-COCO dateset, SIWH achieves an average performance improvement of 4.47%. The substantial improvements demonstrate the effectiveness of the proposed method.

In Fig. 3, we plot the PR curves for a 64-bit code length on the three datasets. Specifically, the PR curve represents overall performance, and the PR curve near the upper right indicates superior performance. As shown in Fig. 3, SIWH achieves superior performance compared to the benchmarks of the other methods on all datasets. Additionally, SIWH can achieve higher accuracy at lower recall points, which is preferred for an actual image retrieval system.

In Fig. 4, we report the performance of P@N in terms of a 64-bit code length, and dependent on the number of top samples returned. We observe that SIWH performs better than any of the comparison methods on different datasets.

Overall, it was observed from the experimental results that in terms of mAP, P@N, and PR curves, SIWH was significantly better than the baseline for all comparisons on the different datasets. Such a major improvement shows the superiority of the proposed hashing method.

Table 2. The mAP results of Our method and its variants.

Method	CIFAR10				NUS-WIDE				MS-COCO			
	24 bits	48 bits	64 bits	128 bits	24 bits	48 bits	64 bits	128 bits	24 bits	48 bits	64 bits	128 bits
SIWH-wa	0.7853	0.7809	0.7951	0.8095	0.5947	0.6698	0.7084	0.7260	0.5570	0.5727	0.5922	0.6043
SIWH-oa	0.8343	0.8444	0.8400	0.8566	0.6337	0.6421	0.6445	0.6526	0.5370	0.5509	0.5821	0.5891
SIWH-ona	0.4601	0.4794	0.4466	0.4558	0.2163	0.2352	0.2553	0.2131	0.2327	0.2326	0.2461	0.2434
SIWH	**0.9231**	**0.9304**	**0.9294**	**0.9316**	**0.8673**	**0.8948**	**0.9023**	**0.9109**	**0.7522**	**0.7986**	**0.8007**	**0.8153**

Table 3. The mAP results of Our method with different K^1/K.

K^1/K (%)	CIFAR10				NUS-WIDE				MS-COCO			
	24 bits	48 bits	64 bits	128 bits	24 bits	48 bits	64 bits	128 bits	24 bits	48 bits	64 bits	128 bits
87.5	0.8941	0.8944	0.8996	0.8936	0.8479	0.8295	0.8363	0.8452	0.7281	0.7653	0.7979	0.7959
75	**0.9231**	**0.9304**	**0.9294**	**0.9316**	**0.8673**	**0.8948**	**0.9023**	**0.9109**	**0.7522**	**0.7986**	**0.8007**	**0.8153**
62.5	0.8927	0.8843	0.8816	0.8922	0.8451	0.8370	0.8453	0.8476	0.7058	0.7556	0.7936	0.7904
50	0.8713	0.8790	0.8821	0.8857	0.8238	0.8272	8247	0.8215	0.7066	0.7646	0.7807	0.7907

Table 4. The mAP results of Our method With Different Attention.

Method	CIFAR10				NUS-WIDE				MS-COCO			
	24 bits	48 bits	64 bits	128 bits	24 bits	48 bits	64 bits	128 bits	24 bits	48 bits	64 bits	128 bits
Classification	0.8921	0.8990	0.9055	0.8964	0.8097	0.8018	0.8192	0.8016	0.6566	0.6655	0.6606	0.6737
Hashing	**0.9231**	**0.9304**	**0.9294**	**0.9316**	**0.8673**	**0.8948**	**0.9023**	**0.9109**	**0.7522**	**0.7986**	**0.8007**	**0.8153**

(2) **Comparison with Variants.** In the proposed deep network, we construct a spatial attention model to learn spatial importance distribution information and combine it with a CNN network to learn hash codes uniformly. To prove the influence of spatial attention models, we studied three variations of SIWH: 1) SIWH-wa: the proposed SIWH learns hash codes without an attention model; 2) SIWH-oa: the proposed SIWH learns hash codes only using the attention region; and 3) SIWH-ona: the proposed SIWH learns hash codes only using the non-attention region.

Table 2 presents the mAP results for SIWH and the three variations described above. As we can see, the proposed method is superior to SIWH using no attention method. Therefore, the spatial attention model utilized by the proposed hashing method can be used to generate an identifiable hash code and will produce higher retrieval performance. Additionally, our method is significantly better than using either the attention or non-attention area alone. This result demonstrates that our integration is effective.

(3) **Effect Of Parameter.** One of the parameters involved in the proposed SIWH is the threshold value of attention mask t. To verify sensitivity, we performed experiments to analyze the effects on different datasets by using a linear search in 0.5, 0.625, 0.75, 0.875. The retrieval performance expressed by mAP is shown in Fig. 5. For the CIFAR10 data set, the performance impact under different settings is very small. However, on NUS-WIDE and MS-COCO, when t is set to 0.5, the performance is slightly reduced. As shown in Fig. 5, for CIFAR-10, we can set t to 0.875. For NUS-WIDE and MS-COCO, we can set t to 0.75.

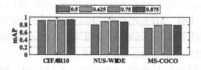

Fig. 5. The mAP with respect to different t for 64-bits hash code on three datasets.

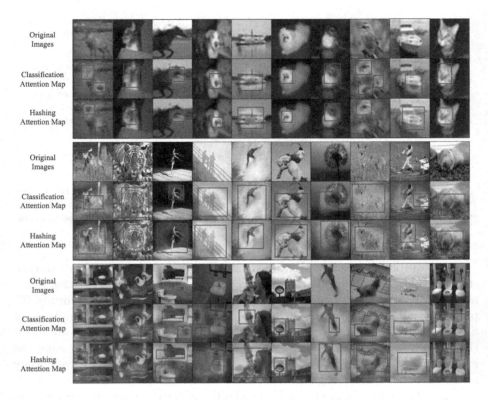

Fig. 6. Some visual examples of spatial attention maps for CIFAR-10, NUS-WIDE and MS-COCO datasets, respectively. The first line shows the original images. The second line represents the classification attention maps. The third line displays the DWSH-D hashing attention maps. The bottom line indicates the DWSH-C hashing attention maps. (Color figure online)

The proposed SIWH also involves another parameter, the proportion of the attention hash code K^1/K. We set different values for it, and the retrieval performance represented by mAP is shown in Table 3. We found that on all three datasets, when K1/K was set to 0.75, the performance was superior to the rest.

(4) **Comparison With Classification Attention.** Generally, most attention models are used for classification. However, in the proposed method SIWH, the attention model is guided by the hash learning process. In fact, there exists many differences between classification-guided and hash-guided attention map generation. Some visual examples of spatial attention maps are shown in Fig. 6, including classification-guided and hash-guided attention maps. It can be seen that both attention models can learn to distinguish the attention regions, which are indicated by the red border areas, and we can also see that there are some differences in the attention regions selected.

In the proposed method, the generation of the attention map is guided by hash learning. Therefore, we explored the performance difference between the hash-guided attention model and classification-guided attention model, and the mAP performance is shown in Table 4, where the mAP of hash-guide model is superior to that of the classification-guided model. It is indicated that the proposed attention model is beneficial to hash-based retrieval tasks.

5 Conclusions

In this study, we propose a novel deep weighted hashing method that learns hash codes by discrete spatial importance. Specifically, two network branches are designed to generate hash codes while simultaneously learning the spatial importance distribution. The proposed method can generate distinguishable hash codes with high quality, thus achieving excellent performance in image retrieval. Many experimental results on three datasets verify the superiority of the proposed method in learning hash codes for image retrieval. In future work, we will investigate how to learn the weights automatically for the weighted hash codes.

References

1. Krizhevsky, A., Sutskever, I., Hinton, G.E.: ImageNet classification with deep convolutional neural networks. In: Neural Information Processing Systems, pp. 1097–1105 (2012)
2. Liu, H., Wang, R., Shan, S., Chen, X.: Deep supervised hashing for fast image retrieval. In: Computer Vision and Pattern Recognition, pp. 2064–2072 (2016)
3. Liong, V.E., Lu, J., Tan, Y.P., Zhou, J.: Deep video hashing. IEEE Trans. Multimed. **19**, 1209–1219 (2017)
4. Long, C., Zhang, H., Xiao, J., Nie, L., Chua, T.S.: SCA-CNN: spatial and channel-wise attention in convolutional networks for image captioning. In: Computer Vision and Pattern Recognition, pp. 6298–6306 (2017)
5. Nie, X., Li, X., Chai, Y., Cui, C., Xi, X., Yin, Y.: Robust image fingerprinting based on feature point relationship mining. IEEE Trans. Inf. Forensics Secur. **13**, 1509–1523 (2018)
6. Nie, X., Jing, W., Cui, C., Zhang, J., Zhu, L., Yin, Y.: Joint multi-view hashing for large-scale near-duplicate video retrieval. IEEE Trans. Knowl. Data Eng. **32**, 1951–1965 (2019)
7. Nie, X., Yin, Y., Sun, J., Liu, J., Cui, C.: Comprehensive feature-based robust video fingerprinting using tensor model. IEEE Trans. Multimed. **19**, 785–796 (2016)
8. Zhou, B., Khosla, A., Lapedriza, A., Oliva, A., Torralba, A.: Learning deep features for discriminative localization. In: Computer Vision and Pattern Recognition, pp. 2921–2929 (2015)
9. Shelhamer, E., Long, J., Darrell, T.: Fully convolutional networks for semantic segmentation. IEEE Trans. Pattern Anal. Mach. Intell. **39**, 640–651 (2017)
10. Oquab, M., Bottou, L., Laptev, I., Sivic, J.: Learning and transferring mid-level image representations using convolutional neural networks. In: Computer Vision and Pattern Recognition, pp. 1717–1724 (2014)
11. Wang, J., Zhang, T., Song, J., Sebe, N., Shen, H.T.: A survey on learning to hash. IEEE Trans. Pattern Anal. Mach. Intell. **40**, 769–790 (2018)

12. Andoni, A., Indyk, P.: Near-optimal hashing algorithms for approximate nearest neighbor in high dimensions. Commun. ACM **51**, 117–122 (2008)
13. Liuz, Y., Cuiz, J., Huang, Z., Liz, H., Shenx, H.T.: SK-LSH: an efficient index structure for approximate nearest neighbor search. Proc. VLDB Endow. **7**, 745–756 (2014)
14. Wang, J., Liu, W., Kumar, S., Chang, S.F.: Learning to hash for indexing big data - a survey. Proc. IEEE **104**, 34–57 (2016)
15. Weiss, Y., Torralba, A., Fergus, R.: Spectral hashing. In: International Conference on Neural Information Processing Systems, pp. 1753–1760 (2008)
16. Yunchao, G., Svetlana, L., Albert, G., Florent, P.: Iterative quantization: a procrustean approach to learning binary codes for large-scale image retrieval. IEEE Trans. Pattern Anal. Mach. Intell. **35**, 2916–2929 (2013)
17. Rastegari, M., Farhadi, A., Forsyth, D.: Attribute discovery via predictable discriminative binary codes. In: Fitzgibbon, A., Lazebnik, S., Perona, P., Sato, Y., Schmid, C. (eds.) ECCV 2012. LNCS, vol. 7577, pp. 876–889. Springer, Heidelberg (2012). https://doi.org/10.1007/978-3-642-33783-3_63
18. Norouzi, M., Blei, D.M.: Minimal loss hashing for compact binary codes. In: Proceedings of the 28th International Conference on Machine Learning (ICML-11), pp. 353–360. Citeseer (2011)
19. Wang, J., Kumar, S., Chang, S.: Semi-supervised hashing for large-scale search. IEEE Trans. Pattern Anal. Mach. Intell. **34**, 2393–2406 (2012)
20. Liu, W., Wang, J., Ji, R., Jiang, Y.G., Chang, S.F.: Supervised hashing with kernels. In: Computer Vision and Pattern Recognition, pp. 2074–2081. IEEE (2012)
21. Kulis, B., Darrell, T.: Learning to hash with binary reconstructive embeddings. In: Advances in Neural Information Processing Systems, pp. 1042–1050 (2009)
22. Liong, V.E., Lu, J., Gang, W., Moulin, P., Jie, Z.: Deep hashing for compact binary codes learning. In: Computer Vision and Pattern Recognition, pp. 2475–2483 (2015)
23. Fang, Z., Huang, Y., Liang, W., Tan, T.: Deep semantic ranking based hashing for multi-label image retrieval. In: Computer Vision and Pattern Recognition, pp. 1556–1564 (2015)
24. Lai, H., Pan, Y., Liu, Y., Yan, S.: Simultaneous feature learning and hash coding with deep neural networks. In: Computer Vision and Pattern Recognition, pp. 3270–3278 (2015)
25. Lu, J., Liong, V.E., Zhou, J.: Deep hashing for scalable image search. IEEE Trans. Image Process. **26**, 2352–2367 (2017)
26. Yang, H., Lin, K., Chen, C.: Supervised learning of semantics-preserving hash via deep convolutional neural networks. IEEE Trans. Pattern Anal. Mach. Intell. **40**, 437–451 (2018)
27. Li, W.J., Wang, S., Kang, W.C.: Feature learning based deep supervised hashing with pairwise labels. In: International Joint Conference on Artificial Intelligence, pp. 1711–1717 (2016)
28. Li, Q., Sun, Z., He, R., Tan, T.: Deep supervised discrete hashing. In: Advances in Neural Information Processing Systems, pp. 2479–2488 (2017)
29. Cao, Y., Long, M., Liu, B., Wang, J.: Deep Cauchy hashing for hamming space retrieval. In: Proceedings of the IEEE Conference on Computer Vision and Pattern Recognition, pp. 1229–1237 (2018)
30. Jiang, Q.Y., Cui, X., Li, W.J.: Deep discrete supervised hashing. IEEE Trans. Image Process. **27**, 5996–6009 (2018)
31. Jiang, Q.Y., Li, W.J.: Asymmetric deep supervised hashing. In: Thirty-Second AAAI Conference on Artificial Intelligence, pp. 3342–3349 (2018)

32. Jin, L., Shu, X., Li, K., Li, Z., Qi, G., Tang, J.: Deep ordinal hashing with spatial attention. IEEE Trans. Image Process. **28**, 2173–2186 (2019)
33. You, Q., Jin, H., Wang, Z., Chen, F., Luo, J.: Image captioning with semantic attention. In: Computer Vision and Pattern Recognition, pp. 4651–4659 (2016)
34. Xu, K., et al.: Show, attend and tell: neural image caption generation with visual attention. Comput. Sci. 2048–2057 (2015)
35. Chatfield, K., Simonyan, K., Vedaldi, A., Zisserman, A.: Return of the devil in the details: delving deep into convolutional nets. arXiv preprint arXiv:1405.3531 (2014)
36. Simonyan, K., Zisserman, A.: Very deep convolutional networks for large-scale image recognition. Comput. Sci. (2014)
37. Zhang, P., Zhang, W., Li, W.J., Guo, M.: Supervised hashing with latent factor models. In: International ACM SIGIR Conference on Research and Development in Information Retrieval, pp. 173–182 (2014)
38. Krizhevsky, A., Hinton, G.: Learning multiple layers of features from tiny images. Technical report, Citeseer (2009)
39. Chua, T.S., Tang, J., Hong, R., Li, H., Luo, Z., Zheng, Y.: NUS-WIDE: a real-world web image database from National University of Singapore. In: Proceedings of the ACM International Conference on Image and Video Retrieval, p. 48. ACM (2009)
40. Lin, T.-Y., et al.: Microsoft COCO: common objects in context. In: Fleet, D., Pajdla, T., Schiele, B., Tuytelaars, T. (eds.) ECCV 2014. LNCS, vol. 8693, pp. 740–755. Springer, Cham (2014). https://doi.org/10.1007/978-3-319-10602-1_48
41. Wang, X.J., Zhang, L., Jing, F., Ma, W.Y.: AnnoSearch: image auto-annotation by search. Comput. Vis. Pattern Recogn. **2**, 1483–1490 (2006)
42. Luo, X., Nie, L., He, X., Wu, Y., Chen, Z.D., Xu, X.S.: Fast scalable supervised hashing. In: International ACM SIGIR Conference on Research and Development in Information Retrieval, pp. 735–744. ACM (2018)

Low-Level Sensor Fusion for 3D Vehicle Detection Using Radar Range-Azimuth Heatmap and Monocular Image

Jinhyeong Kim, Youngseok Kim, and Dongsuk Kum[⊠]

Korea Advanced Institute of Science and Technology, Daejeon, Republic of Korea
{1994kjhg,youngseok.kim,dskum}@kaist.ac.kr

Abstract. Robust and accurate object detection on roads with various objects is essential for automated driving. The radar has been employed in commercial advanced driver assistance systems (ADAS) for a decade due to its low-cost and high-reliability advantages. However, the radar has been used only in limited driving conditions such as highways to detect a few forwarding vehicles because of the limited performance of radar due to low resolution or poor classification. We propose a learning-based detection network using radar range-azimuth heatmap and monocular image in order to fully exploit the radar in complex road environments. We show that radar-image fusion can overcome the inherent weakness of the radar by leveraging camera information. Our proposed network has a two-stage architecture that combines radar and image feature representations rather than fusing each sensor's prediction results to improve detection performance over a single sensor. To demonstrate the effectiveness of the proposed method, we collected radar, camera, and LiDAR data in various driving environments in terms of vehicle speed, lighting conditions, and traffic volume. Experimental results show that the proposed fusion method outperforms the radar-only and the image-only method.

1 Introduction

A frequency-modulated continuous-wave (FMCW) radar and RGB camera have been widely used in advanced driver assistant systems (ADAS) thanks to their many advantages for mass production. Commercial radars and cameras have advantages of low-maintenance, high-reliability, and low-cost due to their stable design and mature market. Despite the many advantages of radar, the radar used in ADAS is limited to detecting a few forwarding vehicles as the radar data is processed using traditional signal processing algorithms. Learning-based methods are expected to show better performance when replacing existing rule-based algorithms. However, 3D object detection utilizing low-level radar data in deep learning frameworks has not yet been thoroughly investigated.

J. Kim and Y. Kim—Contributed equally to this work.
This work was done when Jinhyeong Kim was at KAIST, prior to joining SOCAR.

© Springer Nature Switzerland AG 2021
H. Ishikawa et al. (Eds.): ACCV 2020, LNCS 12624, pp. 388–402, 2021.
https://doi.org/10.1007/978-3-030-69535-4_24

The automotive FMCW radar can measure distances to distant objects and can operate robustly even in harsh weather conditions due to the nature of fundamental design and long wavelength. However, the long wavelength of radar also restricts its performance. The radar suffers from a low angular resolution and accuracy that makes it challenging to separate adjacent vehicles. Contrarily, the camera has a high angular resolution due to the dense pixels and dense RGB pixels can provide visual cues to classify the category of objects. As shown in Table 1, the camera and radar have very complementary properties. Therefore, the camera-radar sensor fusion is promising to complement the shortcomings of each sensor and improve the detection performance.

This paper aims to detect 3D vehicles by sensor fusion network using the radar range-azimuth heatmap and image data, as illustrated in Fig. 1. To demonstrate the effectiveness of the proposed fusion method on the various driving environment, we constructed a dataset because none of the public datasets contains the low-level radar with 3D annotations.

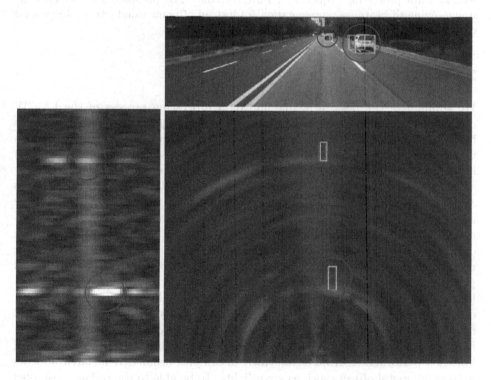

Fig. 1. Detection results of the proposed fusion method on the camera image (top), radar range-azimuth heatmap in the polar coordinate system (left), and radar in the Cartesian coordinate system (right). White and green boxes refer to ground truths and prediction results. (Color figure online)

Table 1. Characteristics of sensors widely used in vehicle intelligence.

	Classification	Radial accuracy	Angular accuracy	Weather condition	Lighting condition	Measuring range	Cost	Maintenance	Reliability
Camera	○	△	○	×	×	×	○	○	○
Radar	△	○	△	○	○	○	○	○	○
LiDAR	△	○	○	△	△	△	×	×	×

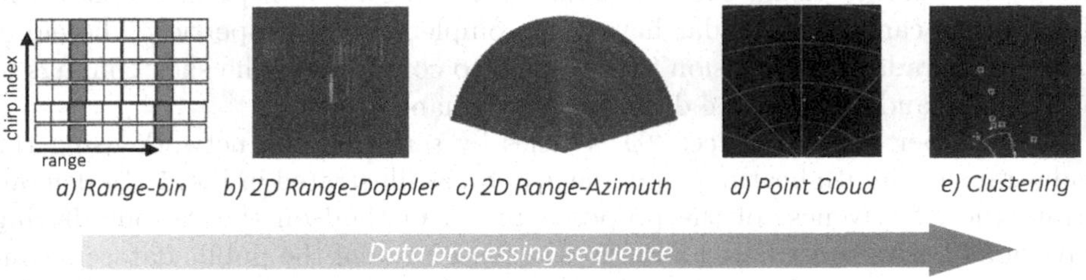

a) Range-bin   b) 2D Range-Doppler   c) 2D Range-Azimuth   d) Point Cloud   e) Clustering

Data processing sequence

Fig. 2. Data processing sequence of FMCW radar. The proposed method uses 2D Range-Azimuth heatmap representation (c) instead of point cloud (d) or object-level representation (e).

2   Background

We summarize the basic principle and data processing process of the FMCW radar in Fig. 2. The FMCW radar transmits a chirp signal that linearly increases frequency and receives the reflected signal. The frequency difference between transmitted and received signal obtained by Analog-to-Digital Converter (ADC) is calculated by Fast Fourier Transform (FFT) to calculate the distance (Fig. 2-a). The velocity and angle are estimated by measuring the phase difference across signals. The velocity can be calculated by two chirps measured at a successive time (Fig. 2-b), and the angle is calculated by the same chirp measured from multiple RX antennas. As a result, a 3D radar tensor with a range-azimuth-Doppler dimension is obtained as a result of FFTs (Fig. 2-c). In this paper, this radar representation is referred to as a radar heatmap. After that, conventional signal processing techniques such as Constant False-Alarm Rate (CFAR) [1] process low-level data to identify valid point targets among clutters (Fig. 2-d). Finally, objects are detected by a clustering algorithm and verified using filtering and tracking algorithms (Fig. 2-e). Conventional signal processing algorithms using hand-coded features (e.g., CFAR, MUSIC) works robustly in simple scenarios, but their performance drops significantly in complex urban driving environments with many metal objects such as streetlights. To be able to use radar in complex environments, we design a learning-based method to fully exploit information on image-like radar range-azimuth heatmap representation (Fig. 2-c) rather than object-level representation (Fig. 2-e).

3   Related Work

Dataset for Autonomous Driving. A number of public datasets for autonomous driving have recently been published. KITTI [2] provides a monocular and stereo camera, 3D LiDAR for many computer vision tasks such as 3D object detection, tracking, and depth prediction. However, it is pointed out that the diversity of the dataset may not be sufficient because data is only collected during the daytime and on sunny days. Apolloscape [3] collected a total of 143,969 frames, which contains the largest labels among public datasets and it claims to have a higher diversity compared to KITTI. However, KITTI and Apolloscape do not provide radar data. NuScenes [4] is a multimodal dataset for 3D object detection and tracking tasks and contains radar data, but radar data is processed as a point cloud representation. We argue that a lot of valuable information can be lost during the signal processing. Oxford RobotCar [5] provides camera, 3D LiDAR, and radar data as range-azimuth heatmap representation, which is the same representation used in this paper. However, RobotCar [5] does not provide 3D object labels because the dataset is aimed at the odometry task. The synthetic datasets such as Virtual KITTI [6] are used as alternatives to address the data limitation issue. However, it is known to be challenging to generate synthetic radar data since the radar beam is difficult to simulate due to the nature of electromagnetic waves.

Learning-Based Object Detection Using Low-Level Radar Data. Only a few studies have been conducted using low-level radar data for object detection. We assume this is because of the absence of the public dataset containing low-level radar data and the ground truth label. He et al. [7] and Kwon et al. [8] use a time-serial micro-Doppler map to classify human activities using a convolutional neural network (CNN) and multi-layer perceptron (MLP), but their works do not consider detecting the position of the object. Brodeski et al. [9] and Zhang et al. [10] utilize U-Net [11] like architecture to detect objects on the range-Doppler map. These studies, however, are demonstrated in restricted environments such as a chamber and a vacant lot. Major et al. [12] collect radar range-azimuth-Doppler data on highway driving scenario and detect vehicles on a bird's eye view (BEV). They employ a one-stage detection network SSD [13] and it provides good detection performance in highway environment, but it is not be guaranteed to work well in complex urban situation.

Sensor Fusion-Based Object Detection. The number 3D object detection studies have been conducted using multiple sensors, mainly LiDAR and camera. MV3D [14] generates 3D proposals from BEV LiDAR feature map and projects proposals into a front view LiDAR and image feature map to fuse a projected region of interest (RoI). Similarly, AVOD [15] projects 3D anchors to LiDAR and image feature maps, respectively. RoIs from different feature maps are fused on region proposal network (RPN) stage and generate high-recall object proposals. Few methods exploit radar and camera sensors but not fully investigated on detecting 3D objects. Chadwick et al. [16] focus on detecting distant vehicles by using object-level radar data. It projects radar data into the image plane and detects a 2D bounding box using SSD [13] in the image pixel coordinate system rather than vehicle coordinate system. Meyer and Kuschk [17] exploit radar point cloud and camera to detect 3D vehicle using AVOD [15] architecture. Lim et al. [18] utilize low-level radar and camera. Images are projected into the BEV plane using Inverse Perspective Mapping (IPM) to match the coordinate system with radar, on the dataset collected in [12]. However, their experiments are conducted in the highway driving scenario and assume a planar road scene to use IPM, but IPM approach is difficult to be adopted to the road with slope.

4   Dataset

4.1   Sensor Configuration

We use the Hyundai Ioniq vehicle platform equipped with a camera, radar, and LiDAR to collect data. Sensor specifications and placements are described in Table 2 and Fig. 3. We mount radar and LiDAR on the front bumper parallel to the ground, while the camera is mounted on the top of the vehicle.

Table 2. Sensor specification.

Sensor	Specification
Camera	**1 × FLIR Blackfly**, 10 Hz capture frequency, RGB, 1/1.8" CMOS, 1920 × 704 resolution, auto exposure, JPEG compressed
Radar	**1 × TI AWR1642**, 10 Hz capture frequency, 77 to 81-GHz FMCW, 4Rx and 2Tx antennas, 120° horizontal FoV, ≤55 m range
LiDAR	**3 × IBEO LUX**, 25 Hz capture frequency, 4 beams, 85° horizontal FoV, ≤80m range

We carefully calibrated intrinsic parameters and extrinsic parameters to obtain a reliable ground truth and to transform the coordinate system between sensors. First, we calibrated the camera to be undistorted and rectified by intrinsic parameters, then calibrated extrinsic parameters between camera and LiDAR using the approach proposed in [19]. After that, 6-DOF rigid transformation parameters between LiDAR and radar are obtained using a laser scanner while keeping the two sensors are mounted in parallel.

For the radar, built-in subsystems such as analog-to-digital converter (ADC), digital signal processing (DSP), and ARM-based processer are integrated with the radar sensor and process the signal as Fig. 2. In this paper, we use low-level range-azimuth data instead of a point cloud or object-level data to fully exploit the potential of radar. We modify the C++ implemented radar firmware of chip to access 2D range-azimuth data from the radar.

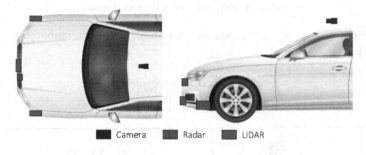

Fig. 3. Sensor placements of vehicle platform.

In order to reduce the data misalignment between multiple sensors, we synchronize data using CPU time. As a result, radar and LiDAR data captured closest to the camera are used, and data is sampled at 2Hz.

4.2 Data Acquisition and Annotation

Driving data has been recorded while driving around campus, urban areas, and motorways in Daejeon, Korea. After recording raw data, we select interesting scenes considering the diversity of data with respect to the speed of ego vehicle, the volume of traffic, and lighting conditions. 'Stop' means that the ego vehicle slows down and stopped while surrounding vehicles are moving (e.g., stopping at intersection or red traffic light), 'Low' means that the ego vehicle drives below 40kph (e.g., campus), and 'Normal' is a general road driving environment that drives above 40kph. The scenes according to the light condition consist of 'Sunny,' 'Cloudy,' and 'Night.'

This paper focuses on demonstrating the effectiveness of the proposed method on detecting car class. We carefully annotated the 3D position, size, and orientation of the car. The ground truths label are annotated using LiDAR point clouds and transformed into the radar coordinate system. Note that we annotated vehicles with more than half of the vehicle is inside the image frame, and vehicles located within 50 meters.

4.3 Dataset Analysis

We carefully split collected data into a train set and test set while making sure that training and testing data does not come from the same scene. We analyze the distribution of the dataset in terms of the ego vehicle speed, lighting conditions, distance to annotation, and the number of annotation in frame in Table 3 and Fig. 4. The distribution analysis shows that our dataset can represent the complex urban driving scenarios.

Table 3. Statistics of collected dataset.

Split	Size (Hr)	Number of frames	Number of annotations
Training set	0.78	5512	9115
Test set	0.32	2232	5853
Total	1.10	7744	14968

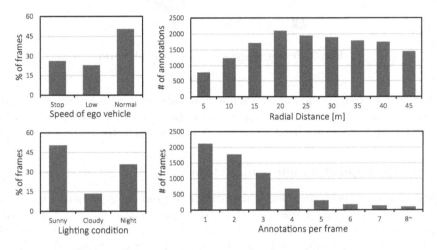

Fig. 4. Distributions of collected dataset consists of ratio of driving conditions, distance of annotation from the ego vehicle, and the number of annotations in each frame.

5   Methodology

The performance of the sensor fusion-based object detection network can vary depending on the stage in which the two modalities are combined. Sensor fusion methods can be broadly categorized into early, middle, and late fusion, and each method has its strengths and weaknesses. The conventional sensor fusion method for ADAS is the late fusion method that combines object-level outputs processed by each modality, which has advantages of high flexibility and modularity. However, it discards the benefit of rich information of intermediate features. While, the early fusion method combines the two raw sensor data and feeds it into the network. It can utilize the information of the raw data, however, two modalities have to be on the same coordinate system so that two modalities can be aligned. Meanwhile, middle fusion is a compromise between early and late fusion because it combines feature representations from two modalities at intermediate layers. It can fully exploit both input data by using appropriate feature extractor for each modality, and network design is advantageous because the coordinate systems of the two sensors do not have to be the same.

As illustrated in Fig. 5, our proposed method has a middle fusion method that combines the region of interest (RoI) features from two modalities based on a two-stage object detection architecture with region proposal network (RPN) and detection head following AVOD [15] architecture.

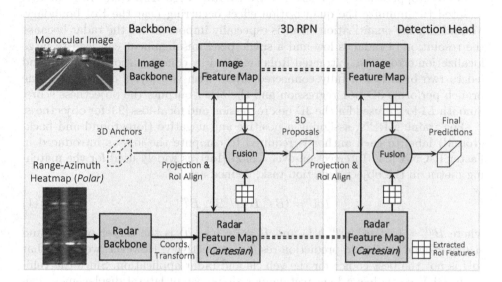

Fig. 5. Overall architecture of the proposed radar-image fusion method.

5.1 Radar Representation and Backbone

The 2D range-azimuth heatmap is naturally obtained in range-azimuth (polar) coordinate system, but the polar coordinate system has several shortcomings to detect objects on 3D space. In the polar coordinate system, the physical distance between two adjacent data in the polar space increases as the radial distance increases. As also claimed in [12], detecting objects in polar feature map has inferior performance than detecting objects in Cartesian space. Following [12], we extract features in polar space then explicitly transforms the extracted feature map into Cartesian space using bilinear interpolation.

The radar and image backbone has a modified VGG16 [20] model and a feature pyramid network (FPN) [21]. The width and height of input decrease by half using max pooling, while the number of feature increases from 32 to 256 every 2, 2, 3, and 3 layers. The network takes the image with a size of 1920×704 and range-azimuth radar in polar space with a size of 128×64. The radar input has a resolution of 0.4392 m and 1.9 degree. The last radar feature map is transformed to Cartesian space with a size of 560×610 with 0.1 m resolution.

5.2 3D Region Proposal Network

In the 3D region proposal network (RPN) stage, a 3D anchor is used to generate proposals. Similar to 2D RPN, 3D RPN generates anchors in 3D space within a range of radar Cartesian space. Two Region of Interests (RoIs) are obtained by projecting given 3D anchor into two feature maps of each modality, and RoIs are cropped into 7×7 size feature by RoI Align [22]. Here, RoI Align is adopted to minimize the quantization effect occurring near the RoI boundary. Minimizing the quantization effect is especially important for the radar because the resolution of radar is low and a single pixel misalignment can lead to large localization error. Two extracted RoIs are fused by concatenation operation and fed to two branches of fully connected layers with two layers of size 256. One branch performs 3D box regression and the other outputs the objectness score. Smooth $L1$ loss is used for the 3D box regression and focal-loss [23] for objectness.

For training RPN, assigning a positive and negative (foreground and background) label to each anchor is required to compute the loss as introduced in Faster R-CNN [24]. Intersection-over-Union (IoU) is widely used for the matching metric in the object detection task, defined as:

$$IoU = |B \cap B^{gt}|/|B \cup B^{gt}| \tag{1}$$

where $B^{gt} = (x^{gt}, y^{gt}, w^{gt}, h^{gt})$ and $B = (x, y, w, h)$ is the center position and size of ground truth and prediction results, respectively. However, we claim that IoU is not the best choice for the vehicle and radar application. Since the vehicle in BEV space has a long rectangular shape, small lateral displacement can greatly reduce the IoU, as an example shown in Fig. 6. The IoU can be especially fatal to the radar because the radar has low lateral accuracy. We claim that the IoU threshold is inconsistent and it can inhibit the network generalization. Therefore, we proposed the distance matching metric using L2 norm between center positions of ground truth and prediction as follows:

$$Distance\ matching = \|(x^{gt}, y^{gt}) - (x, y)\|_2 \tag{2}$$

In the RPN stage, anchor closer than $2\,\mathrm{m}$ are regarded as positive, and farther than $2.5\,\mathrm{m}$ are regarded as a background during training schemes. Predicted proposals are filtered by 2D non-maximum suppression (NMS) at an IoU threshold of 0.8 in BEV space.

5.3   Detection Head

In the detection head stage, the top 100 proposals from the RPN are projected onto each coordinate system again, and the RoI fusion proceeds as same in the RPN. The extracted features are cropped and resized to 7×7 and fused through a concatenation operation used as an input to fully connected layers. The final detection head consists of one branch of a fully connected layer, which consists of three layers of size 2048 to output object probability, box regression, and orientation. Similar to RPN, proposals closer than $1\,\mathrm{m}$ are considered as positive, and farther than $1.25\,\mathrm{m}$ are negative. NMS threshold of 0.001 IoU is used to remove prediction results that are overlapped with each other.

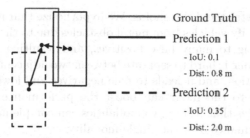

Fig. 6. Example of the IoU matching metric and the distance matching metric. The prediction 1 is closer to the ground truth than prediction 2 but it has a lower score when using IoU due to the shape of the vehicle.

5.4 Implementation Details

We apply multi-task loss for position and size regression, orientation, and classification in an end-to-end fashion same as [15].

$$L_{total} = \lambda_{cls}L_{cls} + \lambda_{reg}L_{reg} + \lambda_{dir}L_{dir} \qquad (3)$$

In (3), the regression and orientation terms use smooth $L1$ loss and weights are experimentally set to $\lambda_{cls} = 5$, $\lambda_{reg} = 3$, and $\lambda_{dir} = 5$. The classification loss for RPN has the focal loss [17] following:

$$FL(p_t) = -\alpha_t(1 - p_t)^\gamma \log(p_t) \qquad (4)$$

We use $\alpha = 0.3$ and $\gamma = 2.25$ to enforce positive and negative samples to have a 1:3 ratio. The proposed network was trained using Adam optimizer, with an initial learning rate of 0.0001 with a decay of 0.8 for every 33k iterations until 220k iterations.

6 Experiments

We evaluate the performance of the proposed method using three different metrics and compare with a radar-only and an image-only method. The radar baseline method has the same architecture as the proposed two-stage method without the image branch. For the image baseline, the state-of-the-art image-based 3D detection method M3D-RPN [25] is trained and evaluated on our dataset.

We use the average precision (AP) metric using bird's-eye-view (BEV) IoU threshold of 0.5 and 0.7 used in KITTI [2] and center distance threshold of 0.5, 1.0, and 2.0 meters used in NuScenes [4]. We also evaluate the localization performance using root-mean-square error (RMSE).

6.1 Quantitative Evaluation

Table 4 and 5 analyze AP performances using IoU and distance metrics. Results show that the image method has a better performance than the radar baseline method in most metrics and thresholds. We hypothesize that it is difficult for the radar alone to classify vehicles from metal obstacles due to the lack of contextual information, leading to many false positives, and resulting in poor precision. Moreover, radar alone is hard to separate between two adjacent objects due to the low angular resolution, and it leads to true negatives and lower recall. However, adding the image to the radar can boost the performance on all evaluation metrics. This verifies that fusing two modalities can complement each other and yield higher performance over the single modality.

Table 4. Average Precision (AP) using IoU matching.

Method	Modality	$AP_{BEV,IoU}$	
		IoU = 0.5	IoU = 0.7
M3D-RPN	Image	39.46	11.71
Radar baseline	Radar	26.88	12.91
Proposed	Radar+Img	**46.16**	**16.30**

Table 5. Average Precision (AP) using distance matching.

Method	Modality	$AP_{BEV,dist}$		
		0.5 m	1.0 m	2.0 m
M3D-RPN	Image	16.31	39.37	64.71
Radar baseline	Radar	15.36	32.98	44.34
Proposed	Radar+Img	**26.92**	**51.06**	**66.26**

The RMSE in a longitudinal and lateral direction is shown in Table 6. Note that only results detected in all three methods using 2.0 m distance threshold are used to calculate the RMSE for the fair comparison. The radar baseline method has a low longitudinal error, and the image method has a low lateral error, which is reasonable given the characteristics of each sensor. As can be seen, fusing camera and radar sensors together contributes to reduce the localization errors in longitudinal and lateral directions, thus improve overall performance.

6.2 Qualitative Results

We visualize qualitative results of radar, image, and fusion method in Fig. 7. Note that all figures are best viewed in color with zoom in. We observe that the radar baseline method often suffers from false positives and separating adjacent vehicles, and the image method typically fails to detect distant vehicles. The proposed method is able to detect and classify vehicles accurately.

Table 6. Root-mean-square error (RMSE) on prediction results using 2 m distance threshold.

Method	Modality	RMSE [m]	
		Longitudinal	Lateral
M3D-RPN	Image	0.2486	**0.1529**
Radar baseline	Radar	0.2219	0.2080
Proposed	Radar+Img	**0.2210**	0.1828

Figure 8 shows the advantage of fusion method compared to the radar baseline. As highlighted, radar alone suffers from detecting clutter signals as object (blue circle, false positive) and fails to separate adjacent vehicles (red circle, true negative). The proposed fusion method overcomes weaknesses of radar alone method by utilizing visual cues.

6.3 Ablation Study

As we hypothesized in Sect. 5.2, the IoU matching is not suitable for the vehicle and radar application due to the shape of the vehicle and the characteristic of radar. To verify the benefit of the distance matching, we compare the proposed network with the network trained using the IoU metric. For the RPN stage, anchors with IoU less than 0.25 are considered as negative, while IoU greater than 0.3 are considered as positive. For the detection head stage, proposals with IoU less and greater than 0.35 and 0.4 are considered as negative and positive. For better understanding, we note that 0.4 IoU and 1.0 m distance thresholds are similar. Both networks are trained in the same manner as explained in Sect. 5.4.

Fig. 7. Qualitative comparison on test set using radar-only (top), image-only (middle), and proposed fusion method (bottom). The 3D bounding box is projected into the image space and BEV space for the visualization. White and red box denotes the ground truth and green and blue box denotes the prediction results. (Color figure online)

Fig. 8. Qualitative results in challenging scenarios. Predictions results using proposed fusion method (top), radar-only (bottom), and radar range-azimuth heatmap input (right).

As shown in Table 7 and Fig. 9, the number of positive samples on the RPN stage using distance matching is larger than the IoU matching even two networks use a similar matching threshold. More positive samples during training can help to converge faster and lead to better performance. As a result, the distance matching shows better performance on both IoU and the distance evaluation metric by 4.44% and 4.53%.

Table 7. Comparison between IoU and distance matching method.

Training metric	# of positive anchors on RPN	Evaluation metric	AP [%]
IoU	4.3	IoU (0.5)	41.72
		Dist. (1.0 m)	46.53
Distance	20.4	IoU (0.5)	**46.16**
		Dist. (1.0 m)	**51.06**

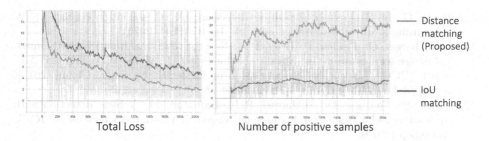

Fig. 9. Visualization of total loss and the number of samples by iteration.

7   Conclusion

In this paper, we introduced the sensor fusion-based 3D object detection method using radar range-azimuth heatmap and monocular image. We demonstrated the proposed low-level sensor fusion network on the collected dataset and showed the benefit of the proposed fusion method over radar alone method. In addition, we showed that the proposed distance matching method helps the network train stable and yields better performance compared to the IoU method in radar application. The proposed method has shown the potential to achieve high performance even with inexpensive radar and camera sensors.

Acknowledgement. This research was supported by the Technology Innovation Program (No. 10083646) funded By the Ministry of Trade, Industry & Energy, Korea and the KAIST-KU Joint Research Center, KAIST, Korea.

References

1. Rohling, H.: Radar CFAR thresholding in clutter and multiple target situations. IEEE Trans. Aerosp. Electron. Syst. (1983)
2. Geiger, A., Lenz, P., Urtasun, R.: Are we ready for autonomous driving? The KITTI vision benchmark suite. In: CVPR (2012)
3. Huang, X., et al.: The apolloscape dataset for autonomous driving. In: CVPR Workshop (2018)
4. Caesar, H., et al.: nuScenes: a multimodal dataset for autonomous driving. In: CVPR (2020)
5. Barnes, D., Gadd, M., Murcutt, P., Newman, P., Posner, I.: The Oxford radar robotcar dataset: a radar extension to the Oxford robotcar dataset. In: ICRA (2020)
6. Gaidon, A., Wang, Q., Cabon, Y., Vig, E.: Virtualworlds as proxy for multi-object tracking analysis. In: CVPR (2016)
7. He, Y., Yang, Y., Lang, Y., Huang, D., Jing, X., Hou, C.: Deep learning based human activity classification in radar micro-doppler image. In: EuRAD (2018)
8. Jihoon, K., Seungeui, L., Nojun, K.: Human detection by deep neural networks recognizing micro-doppler signals of radar. In: EuRAD (2018)
9. Brodeski, D., Bilik, I., Giryes, R.: Deep radar detector. In: RadarConf (2019)

10. Zhang, G., Li, H., Wenger, F.: Object detection and 3D estimation via an FMCW radar using a fully convolutional network. In: ICASSP (2020)
11. Ronneberger, O., Fischer, P., Brox, T.: U-Net: convolutional networks for biomedical image segmentation. In: Navab, N., Hornegger, J., Wells, W.M., Frangi, A.F. (eds.) MICCAI 2015. LNCS, vol. 9351, pp. 234–241. Springer, Cham (2015). https://doi.org/10.1007/978-3-319-24574-4_28
12. Major, B., Fontijne, D., Sukhavasi, R.T., Hamilton, M.: Vehicle detection with automotive radar using deep learning on range-azimuth-doppler tensors. In: ICCV Workshop (2019)
13. Liu, W., et al.: SSD: single shot multibox detector. In: Leibe, B., Matas, J., Sebe, N., Welling, M. (eds.) ECCV 2016. LNCS, vol. 9905, pp. 21–37. Springer, Cham (2016). https://doi.org/10.1007/978-3-319-46448-0_2
14. Chen, X., Ma, H., Wan, J., Li, B., Xia, T.: Multi-view 3D object detection network for autonomous driving. In: CVPR (2017)
15. Ku, J., Mozifian, M., Lee, J., Harakeh, A., Waslander, S.: Joint 3D proposal generation and object detection from view aggregation. In: IROS (2018)
16. Chadwick, S., Maddern, W., Newman, P.: Distant vehicle detection using radar and vision. In: ICRA (2019)
17. Meyer, M., Kuschk, G.: Deep learning based 3D object detection for automotive radar and camera. In: EuRAD (2019)
18. Lim, T., Major, B., Fontijne, D., Hamilton, M.: Radar and camera early fusion for vehicle detection in advanced driver assistance systems. In: NeurIPS Workshop (2019)
19. Huang, J.K., Grizzle, J.W.: Improvements to target-based 3D lidar to camera calibration. IEEE Access (2020)
20. Simonyan, K., Zisserman, A.: Very deep convolutional networks for large-scale image recognition. In: ICLR (2015)
21. Lin, T.Y., Dollar, P., Girshick, R., He, K., Hariharan, B., Belongie, S.: Feature pyramid networks for object detection. In: CVPR (2017)
22. He, K., Gkioxari, G., Dollar, P., Girshick, R.: Mask R-CNN. In: ICCV (2017)
23. Lin, T., Girshick, R., Doll, P., He, K., Dollar, P.: Focal loss for dense object detection. In: ICCV (2017)
24. Ren, S., He, K., Girshick, R., Sun, J.: Faster R-CNN: towards real-time object detection with region proposal networks. In: NeurIPS (2015)
25. Brazil, G., Liu, X.: M3D-RPN: Monocular 3D region proposal network for object detection. In: ICCV (2019)

MLIFeat: Multi-level Information Fusion Based Deep Local Features

Yuyang Zhang[1,2], Jinge Wang[3], Shibiao Xu[1,2(✉)], Xiao Liu[3],
and Xiaopeng Zhang[1,2]

[1] National Laboratory of Pattern Recognition, Institute of Automation,
Chinese Academy of Sciences, Beijing, China
{yuyang.zhang,shibiao.xu,xiaopeng.zhang}@nlpr.ia.ac.cn
[2] School of Artificial Intelligence, University of Chinese Academy of Sciences,
Beijing, China
[3] Megvii Technology, Beijing, China
wjg172184@163.com,liuxiao@foxmail.com

Abstract. Accurate image keypoints detection and description are of central importance in a wide range of applications. Although there are various studies proposed to address these challenging tasks, they are far from optimal. In this paper, we devise a model named MLIFeat with two novel light-weight modules for multi-level information fusion based deep local features learning, to cope with both the image keypoints detection and description. On the one hand, the image keypoints are robustly detected by our Feature Shuffle Module (FSM), which can efficiently utilize the multi-level convolutional feature maps with marginal computing cost. On the other hand, the corresponding feature descriptors are generated by our well-designed Feature Blend Module (FBM), which can collect and extract the most useful information from the multi-level convolutional feature vectors. To study in-depth about our MLIFeat and other state-of-the-art methods, we have conducted thorough experiments, including image matching on HPatches and FM-Bench, and visual localization on Aachen-Day-Night, which verifies the robustness and effectiveness of our proposed model.

1 Introduction

For a long time, image keypoints detection and their local feature description have been active and open research problems in computer vision. It is an essential processing step for various visual-based applications such as SfM [1], SLAM [2–6], Visual Localization [7,8], and Image Retrieval [9]. With the industry's

Y. Zhang—Part of the contribution was made by Y. Zhang when he was an intern at Megvii Research Beijing, Megvii Technology, China.

Electronic supplementary material The online version of this chapter (https://doi.org/10.1007/978-3-030-69535-4_25) contains supplementary material, which is available to authorized users.

H. Ishikawa et al. (Eds.): ACCV 2020, LNCS 12624, pp. 403–419, 2021.
https://doi.org/10.1007/978-3-030-69535-4_25

Fig. 1. Visualization samples of detecting and matching on FM-Bench [20], Aachen-Day-Night [21] and HPatches [22]. The proposed method can successfully find image correspondences even under large illumination or viewpoint changes.

rapid development, these applications is required to deal with more complex and challenging scenarios (various conditions such as day, night, and seasons). As the image keypoints detection and description are the critical components of these high-level algorithms, there is an urgent need to improve their precision, which is of great significance (Fig. 1).

Over the past two decades, there are many excellent algorithms proposed to solve the above problem. Both the traditional hand-crafted methods [10–14] and the deep-learning-based methods [15–17] have made a breakthrough. Especially the deep-learning-based algorithms, such as SuperPoint [15], D2-net [16], and R2D2 [18], have greatly improved the accuracy of both the keypoints detection and the local feature description. However, most previous methods [15,16,18,19] deploy the top-layer feature map to detect keypoints and extract descriptors, which is problematic. Firstly, detecting keypoints on the top-layer feature map with reduced spatial size will inevitably enlarge the detection error. More importantly, it is hard for the descriptors extracted from the top-layer feature to distinguish keypoints with the same high-level semantics but the different local structures, as they lack the low-level structural information. Motivated by such observation, we propose two novel lightweight modules to mitigate each limitation separately. Specifically, to reduce the systematic detection error, we design a Feature Shuffle Module (FSM), which can efficiently reorganize the feature maps from low-resolution to high-resolution with marginal computing cost and detect the keypoints with high precision from these shuffled feature maps. To encode necessary structural information to each descriptor, we further devise a Feature Blend Module (FBM), capable of collecting rich information from the multi-level convolutional features and constructing the most discriminative descriptor.

In brief, there are three main contributions in this paper: 1) we design a novel Feature Shuffle Module (FSM) to detect the keypoints accurately; 2) we devise a novel Feature Blend Module (FBM) to generate robust descriptors; 3) with the power of the two lightweight modules, we present a novel model named MLIFeat to detect keypoints and extract descriptors jointly. To analyze the proposed method's strengths, we have conducted comprehensive experiments on HPatches [22], FM-Bench [20], and Aachen-Day-Night [21], which show that our proposed MLIFeat reaches state-of-the-art performance.

2 Related Work

For a long time, the hand-crafted methods are the preference of most high-level algorithms. Among them, SIFT [10] plays a vital role in computer vision [1], which utilizes Difference-of-Gaussian to detect the keypoints and then constructs the corresponding descriptors through gradients of their surrounding pixels. Besides, ORB [11] is a commonly used algorithm due to its fast and robust features. More comprehensive evaluation results can be found in [14,23,24].

With the development of deep learning technology, many learned local features [17,25,26] emerge, which detect keypoints based on the hand-crafted methods and extract the descriptors via neural network. Among them, L2-Net [17] proposed a network architecture stacking by several convolution layers to extract the descriptor of an image patch and deployed an n-pair loss to train the model end-to-end. Hardnet [25] proposed a hard-mining strategy to train the network more efficiently, which improved the model performance significantly. SOS-Net [26] used the second-order similarity to regularize the descriptors' potential distribution. Since these methods take an image patch as input, the performance of their descriptors is still limited in some challenge scenarios [14,15].

In contrast to the above hybrid methods, many unified architectures have proposed to detect the keypoints and describe [15,16,27,28] the local feature jointly in recent years. Among them, LIFT [27] and LF-Net [28] both proposed a two-stage algorithm to first detect the keypoints via a score map predicted by one sub-network and then input the corresponding image patches to another sub-network to generate the descriptors. Different from the above two-stage methods, SuperPoint [15] raised a more unified architecture constructed by a common encoder followed by two separate branches to detect the keypoints and extract the descriptors. DELF [29] and D2-Net [16] proposed a describe-and-detect approach that utilizes the dense feature descriptors to detect the keypoints. R2D2 [18] raised an algorithm that trains the model to detect and describe the keypoints only in the discriminate image region. UnsuperPoint [30] deployed an unsupervised pipeline to learn both the keypoints detector and the local feature descriptor. Recently, ASLFeat [19] utilized the powerful DCN to extract the descriptors, which can correctly match under challenging scenarios. However,

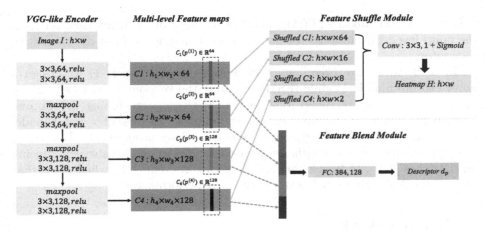

Fig. 2. The network architecture of our **MLIFeat**, which is designed by integrating the common used VGG-like encoder with the Feature Shuffle Module(FSM) and the Feature Blend Module(FBM). Specifically, the backbone encoder takes a single-scale image I as input and output the feature maps at scales. The FSM further utilizes these feature maps to predict the heatmap H. Besides, given a point $p \in I$ and its down-sampled location $p^{(m)}$ in each feature map C_m, the corresponding feature vector $C_m(p^{(m)})$ is looked up from C_m with bi-linear interpolation. Then the FBM blends all feature vectors to generate the descriptor d_p.

most of these methods ignore the importance of low-level structural information (e.g., shape, scales) to the keypoints detection and descriptors extraction, resulting in sub-optimal performance. To mitigate this limitation, in this paper, we carefully devise two novel and intuitive light-weight modules to take the advantages of multi-level feature maps to largely promote the precision of keypoints and the robustness of descriptors.

3   Proposed Method

3.1   Network Architecture

Our model consists of three core components: the backbone feature encoder, the Feature Shuffle Module (FSM), and the Feature Blend Module (FBM). The backbone feature encoder takes a single-scale image as input and generates a series of convolutional feature maps with semantic information from low to high. The well-designed Feature Shuffle Module and Feature Blend Module further take these feature maps as input and output the detected keypoints and their corresponding descriptors. Since the detection and description are relatively independent of the feature extracting, we take the commonly used VGG-like [15, 16, 31] encoder as our backbone network due to its efficiency and accuracy. The whole network architecture can be seen in Fig. 2.

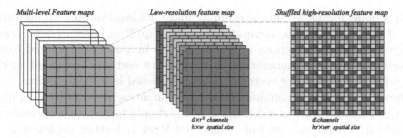

Fig. 3. The visualization of the pixel shuffle operation. Each depth channel's features are scattered into the corresponding spatial region according to a scale ratio r, resulting in a high-resolution feature map with reduced depth channel. The whole process is fast and casts no extra memory resources, which is very suitable for real-time keypoints detection.

Backbone Feature Encoder. The process of the encoder is a feed-forward computation of the backbone network, which produces the feature maps at several scales with a scaling step of 2. Considering the original image as $I \in \mathbb{R}^{h \times w}$, the corresponding feature maps at scales can be denoted as $C_m \in \mathbb{R}^{h_m \times w_m \times d_m}$, where $m \in \{1, 2, 3, 4\}$ and $d \in \{64, 64, 128, 128\}$. The size of C_m and the size of I satisfies $h = h_m \times 2^{m-1}, w = w_m \times 2^{m-1}$. This feature extraction process can be formulated as:

$$C_1, C_2, C_3, C_4 = Encoder(I). \tag{1}$$

Keypoint Detection with Feature Shuffle Module. Inspired by the pixel shuffle operation raised in [32], we propose a novel Feature Shuffle Module (FSM) that takes the multi-level feature maps as input and predicts the keypoint heatmap with the same resolution as the input image.

Specifically, our Feature Shuffle Module first reorganizes each low-resolution feature map $C_m \in \mathbb{R}^{h_m \times w_m \times d_m}$ to a high-resolution one $C_m^s \in \mathbb{R}^{h \times w \times d_m/4^{m-1}}$ via the pixel shuffle operation, which is shown in Fig. 3. Since the shuffled feature maps have the same spatial size, they can be processed by a unified $Conv$ layer to generate the final heatmap, which implicitly fuses multi-level semantics and naturally leads to a prediction with high precision. And the whole process can be abstracted as:

$$H = FSM(C_1, C_2, C_3, C_4). \tag{2}$$

During the model inference, the Non-Maximum-Suppression (NMS) is first applied to the predicted heatmap. A point is then marked as a keypoint while its response value in H exceeds a fixed detection threshold α.

Local Feature Description with Feature Blend Module. To further make full use of the multi-level semantics, we design a novel Feature Blend Module (FBM) that can extract the most discriminative information from the multi-level feature vectors to construct the descriptor.

For a point $p = [x, y]^T$ in the original image, its location in each feature map $C_m \in \mathbb{R}^{h_m \times w_m \times d_m}$ can be computed by $p^{(m)} = p/2^i = [x/2^m, y/2^m]^T$ and the corresponding feature vector $C_m(p^{(m)}) \in \mathbb{R}^{d_m}$ is bi-linear interpolated from the feature map C_m. After generating all the feature vectors corresponding to the same point, a long feature vector C_{cat} is constructed by concatenation.

Though C_{cat} already contains multi-level semantics from low to high, directly using this feature vector as a descriptor will certainly introduce noise and useless information. Therefore, one fully-connected layer is further deployed to filter noise and compress the valid semantics to produce a compact descriptor $d_p \in \mathbb{R}^{dim}$, where $dim = 128$. The FBM is illustrated in Fig. 2 and the whole process can be generalized as:

$$D = FBM(C_1, C_2, C_3, C_4, P), \tag{3}$$

where $P = \{p_1, p_2, ..., p_n\}$ denotes a bunch of keypoints and their corresponding descriptors are denoted as $D = \{d_1, d_2, ..., d_n\}$.

3.2   Data Preparation for Joint Training

To train our MLIFeat with FSM and FBM jointly, we use the COCO [33] and MegaDepth [34] as our training dataset. The former are collected from plenty of diverse scenes, which ensures the robustness of the whole model. And the latter contains image pairs with known poses and depth, which can further enhance the local features' distinguishability.

Image Keypoints Supervising. As the original COCO and MegaDepth do not have ground truth labels for the keypoint detection, we deploy the Iterative Homographic Adaptation [15] to generate the keypoints pseudo-ground truth label $Y \in \mathbb{R}^{h \times w}$ for each image in both datasets: 1) Construct a synthetic dataset as source dataset; 2) Use the source dataset to train a detector; 3) Label the target dataset (COCO and MegaDepth); 4) Change the source to the newly labeled target datasets and back to the step two until converged. More details can be found in our supplementary material.

Correspondences Generation. For the descriptor training, the correspondences between the image pair are required. Different from the MegaDepth, the images in COCO are relatively independent. Thus, for an image I in COCO, a random homography is sampled and an image I' is synthesized based on the homography, resulting in the pairwise image. Then, for both dataset, n randomly sampled correspondences are constructed based either on the homography in COCO or on the pose in MegaDepth, which can be formulated as:

$$P = RandomSample(\cdot) \quad P', V = Transform(P), \tag{4}$$

where P, P' are the corresponding points between the image pair and $V \in \mathbb{B}^n$ is a valid mask denoting the validity of each projected point, as not all the transformed points are located in the image boundaries.

3.3   Definition of Loss Function

Detector Loss. Given a heatmap $H \in \mathbb{R}^{h \times w}$ predicted from Eq. (2) and its corresponding keypoints pseudo-ground truth label Y, the weighted binary cross entropy loss can be formulated as:

$$L_{bce}(H, Y) = \frac{1}{hw} \sum_{u,v}^{h,w} (-\lambda Y_{u,v} log(H_{u,v}) - (1 - Y_{u,v}) log(1 - H_{u,v})), \qquad (5)$$

where λ is used for balancing the ratio between positive and negative samples because the number of positive samples is much smaller than the number of negative samples. And in our paper, we empirically set $\lambda = 200$.

Descriptor Loss. Given the points set P in I and their corresponding points set P' in I' generated from Eq. (4), the descriptors D, D' of these points can be extracted from FBM respectively. Then, for a descriptor $d_{p_i} \in D$, its *positive pair distance* is defined as:

$$p(d_{p_i}) = ||d_{p_i} - d_{p'_i}||_2, \qquad (6)$$

where $d_{p'_i} \in D'$ is the corresponding descriptor of d_{p_i}. And its *hardest negative pair distance* is formulated as:

$$n(d_{p_i}) = ||d_{p_i} - d_{p'_{k*}}||_2, \qquad (7)$$

where

$$k^* = \underset{k \neq i}{\arg\min} ||d_{p_i} - d_{p'_k}||_2 \ \& \ ||p'_k - p'_i||_2 > \theta \ \& \ p'_k \text{ within the boundaries.} \quad (8)$$

The empirical threshold $\theta = 16$ is used to ensure that the spatial distance between p'_{k*} and p'_i is beyond a certain value, as the two descriptors are too similar to distinguish from each other when they are very close in the image, which is harmful to the training. Besides, the selected negative sample $d_{p'_{k*}}$ is also required to locate within the image boundaries, or it is invalid. Given $p(d_{p_i})$ and $n(d_{p_i})$, we define our hardest triplet descriptor loss as:

$$l_{triplet}(d_{p_i}) = \max(0, p(d_{p_i}) - n(d_{p_i}) + 1). \qquad (9)$$

And the whole loss constructed for the descriptors D, D' is summed as:

$$L_{triplet}(D, D', V) = \sum_{i=1}^{n} \frac{l_{triplet}(d_{p_i}) v_i}{\sum_{j=1}^{n} v_j}, \qquad (10)$$

where $v_i \in V$ indicating the validity of the correspondence between d_{p_i} and $d_{p'_i}$.

Total Loss. Based on above definition, the total loss is formulated as:

$$L_{total}(H, H', D, D'; Y, Y', V) = L_{bce}(H, Y) + L_{bce}(H', Y') + L_{triplet}(D, D', V). \tag{11}$$

The sampling of both the transformation and correspondences is processed with the training procedure in parallel, which prevents the network from overfitting.

3.4 Parameters Setting

For model training, we use Adam optimizer [35] with $\beta_1 = 0.9$, $\beta_2 = 0.999$, $lr = 0.001$ and $weight\,decay = 10^{-4}$. The training image size is set to 240×320 with the training batch size setting to 16. The whole training process typically converges in about 30 epochs. Besides, during the model evaluation, the NMS radius is set to 4 pixels. And the detection threshold α is set to 0.9 to balance the number and reliability of the keypoints.

4 Experiments

4.1 Image Matching on HPatches

Dataset. We use the popular HPatches [22], which includes 116 scenes with 580 image pairs exhibiting a large change in either illumination or viewpoints. The ground truth homography between each image pair is provided for the evaluation. Following D2net [16], we exclude eight high-resolution sequences, leaving 108 scenes for a fair comparison.

Evaluation Protocols. For a comprehensive evaluation, three standard metrics are used: 1) Homography accuracy ($\%HA$), a.k.a the ratio of correct estimated homography. 2) Matching score ($\%M.S.$), a.k.a the ratio of correct matches and the minimum number of keypoints in the shared view. 3) Mean matching accuracy ($\%MMA$), a.k.a the ratio of correct matches and possible matches. Here, the matches are found by the mutual nearest search for all methods, and a match is defined to be correct if the point distance is below some error threshold after projecting from one image to another. Besides, the homography is estimated based on the matches, and it is defined to be correct when its warping error is below some error thresholds [15].

Comparative Methods. We compare our methods with 1) hand-craft method ROOT-SIFT [36] and DSP-SIFT [13]. 2) learned shape estimator HesAffNet [37] plus learned patch descriptors HardNet++ [25]. 3) Joint local feature learning state-of-the-art approaches including SuperPoint [15], D2net [16], R2D2 [18], and recent ASLFeat [19]. To ensure the fairness and reproducibility of results, we report all the results based on the public implementations with default parameters. Except for speed evaluation, all evaluations are conducted based on the original resolution images in HPatches.

Table 1. Ablation experiments of proposed modules. *orig* means the SuperPoint publicly released model, and *impl* is the reimplemented baseline under our training protocol. SuperPoint + FSM replaces the SuperPoint detection head with our Feature Shuffle Module. SuperPoint + FBM replaces the SuperPoint description head with our Feature Blend Module. And MLIFeat is the backbone of SuperPoint plus two proposed modules that significantly improves the baseline model's performance.

HPatches dataset (error threshold @3px)									
Configs	Total			Illumination			Viewpoint		
	M.S.	MMA	HA	M.S.	MMA	HA	M.S.	MMA	HA
SuperPoint *orig*	0.424	0.645	0.726	0.456	0.694	0.892	0.394	0.599	0.571
SuperPoint *impl*	0.456	0.683	0.713	**0.502**	0.734	0.889	0.413	0.637	0.557
SuperPoint + FSM	0.464	0.710	0.730	0.489	0.742	0.896	0.439	0.679	0.575
SuperPoint + FBM	0.460	0.698	0.734	0.496	0.748	**0.915**	0.427	0.651	0.575
MLIFeat	**0.475**	**0.728**	**0.756**	0.500	**0.763**	0.892	**0.453**	**0.696**	**0.629**

Baseline. In this paper, we use the same backbone as SuperPoint and present our reimplementation of SuperPoint(*our impl*) as our baseline. Specifically, *our impl* is differs from the original SuperPoint(*orig*) in mainly two aspects: 1) Different training dataset (COCO and MegaDepth vs. only COCO). 2) Different loss formulation (hardest-triplet [25] vs. pairwise-contrastive [15]). Under the same training protocol, it is fair to compare our MLIFeat with the new baseline.

Ablation on Training Protocol. Due to the newly added dataset and more powerful loss function, as shown in Table 1, *our impl* outperforms *orig* in %MMA and %M.S.. However, it's interesting to find that the %HA of *our impl* is slightly worse than the *orig*. It lies in that the %HA is not a direct metric to assess and is affected by both the homography estimation algorithm's accuracy and the quality of the matched points. Generally speaking, only when the matching is sufficiently good can the corresponding estimated homography be improved.

Ablation on FSM. When replacing the original detection head in SuperPoint with our proposed Feature Shuffle Module, it is evident in Table 1 that this variant outperforms the baseline in almost metrics. Such improvement is reasonable that FSM detects keypoints from the high-resolution multi-level information fused feature map. Especially when viewpoint changes, points detected from low-resolution prone to large errors. However, applying FSM, the accuracy of the keypoints improves obviously, e.g., %MMA from 0.637 to 0.679, which indicates that FSM will reduce the systematic errors caused by low-resolution feature map.

Ablation on FBM. Similarly, utilizing the Feature Blend Module yields better results, for it promotes the discriminability of the descriptors by the multi-level

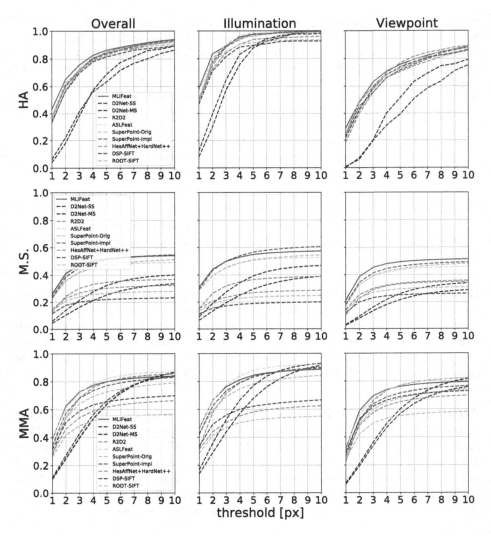

Fig. 4. Comparisons on HPatches Dataset [22] with Homography Accuracy (%HA), Matching Scores (%M.S.), and Mean Matching Accuracy (%MMA). Our method achieves either the best or the comparable performances within a threshold of 3px.

feature vectors. The lower-level feature vector contains more structural information about the neighbor of the keypoints. Meanwhile, the high-level feature vector encodes more semantics information from a wider spatial region. Such a combination is simple but effective. And it is convenient to take our FBM in most current methods to further improve their descriptors' performances.

Comparisons with Other Methods. The comprehensive comparisons results with other methods are illustrated in Fig. 4. Within a small threshold (3px), MLIFeat outperforms other methods on almost all error metrics. Even within a relaxed error bound, our method is still at the top three ranks in all models. Furthermore, when comparing with the most recent ASLFeat who utilizes the complex Deformable Convolutional network to generate descriptors with high precision, our MLIFeat still generates comparable results, which strongly verifies the effectiveness of the proposed two modules.

In addition, experiments are conducted to compare the size and speed of the proposed model and other joint learning methods, which is shown in Table 2. Specifically, the speed is average on HPatches with the same image size(480×640) under TitanV, and the size is the sum of all the parameters contained in each model. With the light-weight FSM and FBM, our MLIFeat reaches the fastest speed. Though R2D2 has the smallest model size, it cast too much time to detect keypoints and extract descriptors, making the whole algorithm very slow.

Table 2. Size and speed comparisons of the joint learning methods. The speed is averaged on HPatches(480×640) with TitanV. We can see that our MLIFeat reaches the fastest speed under the same experimental protocol.

	MLIFeat	SuperPoint	ASLFeat	R2D2	D2Net
Size	2.6 Mb	5.0 Mb	5.2 Mb	**1.9 Mb**	29 Mb
Speed	**32 fps**	28 fps	21 fps	8 fps	6 fps

4.2   Image Matching on FM-Bench

The widely used HPatches dataset may not comprehensively reflect the algorithm's performance in real applications [19], since it exhibits only homography. Therefore, the same as ASLFeat, we resort to the newly proposed FM-Bench [20] to further evaluate each method's matching performance.

Dataset. FM-Bench comprises four datasets captured in practical scenarios: the TUM dataset [38] in indoor SLAM settings, the KITTI dataset [39] in driving scenes, the Tanks and Temples dataset(T&T) [40] for wide-baseline reconstruction and the Community Photo Collection(CPC) [41] for wild reconstruction from web images. For each dataset, 1000 overlapping image pairs are chosen for evaluation, with ground-truth fundamental matrix pre-computed.

Evaluation Protocols. A full matching pipeline including outlier rejection (ratio test) and geometric verification (RANSAC) is performed, and the final estimated pose accuracy is evaluated. FM-Bench utilizes ground-truth pose to generate a set of virtual correspondences, then use the estimated pose to measure the average of normalized symmetric epipolar distance, and finally computes the ratio of correct estimates as *%Recall*. A pose is defined as correct for its distance error is below a certain threshold (0.05 as default). Besides, FM-Bench also reports intermediate results such as the inlier ratio (*%Inlier/%Inlier-m*) and correspondence number (*%Corr/%Corr-m*) after/before RANSAC.

Table 3. Evaluation results on FM-Bench [20] for pair-wise image matching, where *Recall* denotes the percentage of accurate pose estimation(within the error threshold 0.05), *Inlier* and *Inlier-m*, *Corrs* and *Corrs-m* denote the inlier ratio and correspondence number after/before RANSAC. The results of other methods come from the paper [19] except ASLFeat, ROOT-SIFT, and DSP-SIFT, which the are evaluated using their publicly released models with the default setting. The best and the second best are marked red and blue, respectively.

FM-Bench Dataset(error threshold @0.05)								
Methods	**TUM** [38] (indoor SLAM settings)				**KITTI** [39] (driving SLAM settings)			
	Recall	Inlier	Inlier-m	Corrs(-m)	Recall	Inlier	Inlier-m	Corrs(-m)
ROOT-SIFT [36]	58.40	75.33	62.46	68 (308)	92.20	98.34	91.11	158 (520)
DSP-SIFT [13]	55.60	74.54	56.44	66 (380)	92.40	98.22	87.60	154 (573)
HesAffNet+HardNet++ [37]	51.70	75.70	62.06	101 (657)	90.40	98.09	90.64	233 (1182)
D2Net-MS [16]	34.50	67.61	49.01	74 (1279)	71.40	94.26	73.25	103 (1832)
R2D2 [18]	57.70	73.70	61.53	260 (1912)	78.80	97.53	86.49	278 (1804)
ASLFeat [19]	59.10	76.17	69.13	149 (742)	92.00	98.64	96.27	446 (1459)
SuperPoint *orig* [15]	45.80	72.79	64.06	39 (200)	86.10	98.11	91.52	73 (392)
SuperPoint *impl*	49.80	73.95	68.32	43 (193)	87.70	98.28	93.95	76 (367)
MLIFeat	52.90	74.10	67.29	65 (358)	89.10	98.25	95.07	140 (772)
	T&T [40] (wide-baseline reconstruction)				**CPC** [39] (wild reconstruction)			
ROOT-SIFT [36]	78.00	81.38	63.38	93 (756)	41.20	78.31	62.27	65 (369)
DSP-SIFT [13]	74.50	79.80	60.07	90(846)	34.00	75.83	56.29	58(367)
HesAffNet+HardNet++ [37]	82.50	84.71	70.29	97 (920)	47.40	82.58	72.22	65 (405)
D2Net-MS [16]	68.40	71.79	55.51	78 (2603)	31.30	56.57	49.85	84 (1435)
R2D2 [18]	73.00	80.81	65.31	84 (1462)	43.00	82.40	67.28	91 (954)
ASLFeat [19]	88.60	85.56	79.08	297 (2070)	52.90	87.88	82.29	177 (1062)
SuperPoint *orig* [15]	81.80	83.87	70.89	52 (535)	40.50	75.28	64.68	31 (225)
SuperPoint *impl*	85.00	85.95	78.00	57 (491)	44.60	86.16	79.98	40 (273)
MLIFeat	88.80	86.21	78.63	103 (1006)	53.50	86.52	80.78	72 (535)

Comparisons with Other Methods. As we can observe in Table 3, for the *Recall* metric, MLIFeat is superior to other methods in T&T and CPC dataset, which are scenes with wide baseline, and it is slightly inferior to ASLFeat in TUM and KITTI dataset, which are scenes with short baseline. Since the baseline of image pair in TUM and KITTI dataset is short [20], image from one to another does not vary too much. The transformation between the image pair can be approximated to an affine transformation, which is precisely the advantage of ASLFeat whose descriptors are generated by the affine-constraint *DCN*[19].

In contrast, the image pair in T&T and CPC dataset exhibits large viewpoint and illumination changes. To correctly match the keypoints, it is required that the descriptors contain not only the local structural information but high-level semantics as well. Though FBM is not as powerful as *DCN* to extract the affine-invariant descriptors, the multi-level semantics fused descriptors are much more robust in these challenging wide-baseline dataset.

4.3 Visual Localization

In this section, we evaluate our MLIFeat and other methods under the task of visual localization [18,42], where the goal is to retrieve the pose of an image within a given environment. In this benchmark, methods will face challenges such as day-night transitions and significant viewpoint changes between scene modeling and image localization. It is particularly meaningful to evaluate each method's performance under this real-world application because it further reflects the local feature's robustness.

Dataset. The evaluation is conducted on the Aachen-Day-Night dataset [21]: For each of the 98 night-time images in the dataset, up to 20 relevant day-time images with known camera poses are given. After exhaustive feature matching between the day-time images in each set, their known poses are used to triangulate the scenes' 3D structure. Finally, these resulting 3D models are used to localize the night-time query images [16].

Evaluation Protocols. We follow the public evaluation pipeline proposed in *The Visual Localization Benchmark* , which takes the custom features as input, then relies on COLMAP [43] for image registration, and finally generates the percentages of successfully localized images within three tolerances $(0.25\,\text{m}, 2°)$ / $(0.5\,\text{m}, 5°)$ / $(5\,\text{m}, 10°)$. It is noting that the evaluation rule and tolerances are changed after recent updating in the website, and all of our results are based on the new rule.

Comparisons with Other Methods. The comparison results are illustrated in Table 4. Consistent with the above evaluation, our MLIFeat outperforms other methods in the most strict tolerance. However, it is interesting to find that D2Net recovers all the query images' poses for the most relaxed tolerance$(5\,\text{m}, 10°)$. On the one hand, D2Net is fine-tuned from the VGG pre-trained on ImageNet, making its descriptors implicitly contain much more semantics than others. On the other hand, the dataset MegaDepth used for fine-tuning D2Net is close to the scenes contained in Aachen. Therefore, despite having large keypoints localization error, the matched keypoints still belong to the same place, which ensures the recovery of poses within the most relaxed tolerance.

Analogously, when contrast SuperPoint *impl* and SuperPoint *orig* in Table 4, there is an evident improvement from *orig* to *impl* (79.6 to 86.7 and 88.8 to 94.9). With the above analysis of D2Net, it is easy to find that such an improvement is mainly due to the extra MegaDepth training dataset. Since the scenes

Table 4. Evaluation results on the Aachen-Day-Night dataset. We report the average feature number of each method, the descriptor's dimension, and the percentages of successfully localized images within three error thresholds. The best and second best are marked in red and blue, respectively. It can be observed that our MLIFeat achieves the best results within the most strict threshold.

Aachen-Day-Night Dataset					
Methods	#Features	Dim	Correctly localized queries(%)		
			0.25 m, 2°	0.5 m, 5°	5 m, 10°
ROOT-SIFT [36]	11K	128	49.0	53.1	61.2
DSP-SIFT [13]	11K	128	41.8	48.0	52.0
HesAffNet+HardNet++ [37]	11K	128	52.0	65.3	73.5
D2Net-SS [16]	19K	512	72.4	88.8	100
D2Net-MS [16]	14K	512	75.5	88.8	100
R2D2 [18]	10K	128	74.5	85.7	**99.0**
ASLFeat [19]	10K	128	**77.6**	**87.8**	98.0
SuperPoint [15] *Orig*	7K	256	73.5	79.6	88.8
SuperPoint *Impl*	7K	256	76.5	86.7	94.9
MLIFeat	7K	128	78.6	88.8	96.9

in MegaDepth are close to Aachen, the descriptors trained from MegaDepth perform much better in Aachen than that in other test datasets (HPathces and FM-Bench). Furthermore, it is interesting to find the DSP-SIFT, ROOT-SIFT and HardNet++ performs much worse in this task. It might due to the descriptors from these methods are extracted from the image patch, which lacks enough global semantics to handle large illumination changes(day v.s night). Thus, for the challenge localization task, to learn descriptors with rich semantics or add auxiliary semantic learning, e.g., classification, will both increase the accuracy of such a problem.

5 Conclusion

In this paper, we propose a novel deep model for multi-level information fusion based deep local features learning (MLIFeat), to cope with the image keypoints detection and description simultaneously. Two novel feature fusion modules, Feature Shuffle Module (FSM) and the Feature Blend Module (FBM), are cascaded to the commonly used encoder (SuperPoint backbone used in our paper). The Feature Shuffle Module can efficiently utilize the multi-level feature maps to detect the keypoints with high precision via the pixel shuffle operation. And the Feature Blend Module can make the full use of the multi-level feature vectors to generate the discriminative descriptors. To evaluate our model and other state-of-the-art methods, we have conducted extensive experiments, including image matching on HPatches and FM-Bench, and visual localization on Aachen-Day-Night. These evaluation results not only validate the effectiveness of our MLIFeat but also give insight into the performances of current methods under different tasks, which is beneficial to the development of the related algorithm.

Future Work. To further improve the deep local feature's precision, better keypoints supervisory signals should be developed, as the current pseudo-ground label still contains noise. Besides, as analyzed above, additional semantic information should be embedded in the descriptors, enabling the model to handle more challenging scenarios.

Acknowledgement. This work was supported in part by the National Natural Science Foundation of China (Nos. 91646207, 61620106003, 61971418, 61771026, 62071157 and 61671451).

References

1. Schönberger, J.L., Frahm, J.M.: Structure-from-motion revisited. In: Conference on Computer Vision and Pattern Recognition (CVPR) (2016)
2. Mur-Artal, R., Montiel, J.M.M., Tardos, J.D.: Orb-slam: a versatile and accurate monocular slam system. IEEE Trans. Rob. **31**, 1147–1163 (2015)
3. Mur-Artal, R., Tardós, J.D.: Orb-slam2: an open-source slam system for monocular, stereo, and rgb-d cameras. IEEE Trans. Rob. **33**, 1255–1262 (2017)
4. Engel, J., Schöps, T., Cremers, D.: LSD-SLAM: large-scale direct monocular SLAM. In: Fleet, D., Pajdla, T., Schiele, B., Tuytelaars, T. (eds.) ECCV 2014. LNCS, vol. 8690, pp. 834–849. Springer, Cham (2014). https://doi.org/10.1007/978-3-319-10605-2_54
5. Forster, C., Pizzoli, M., Scaramuzza, D.: Svo: fast semi-direct monocular visual odometry. In: IEEE International Conference on Robotics and Automation (ICRA), vol. 2014, pp. 15–22. IEEE (2014)
6. Engel, J., Koltun, V., Cremers, D.: Direct sparse odometry. IEEE Trans. Pattern Anal. Mach. Intell. **40**, 611–625 (2017)
7. Sattler, T., et al.: Benchmarking 6dof outdoor visual localization in changing conditions. In: Proceedings of the IEEE Conference on Computer Vision and Pattern Recognition, pp. 8601–8610 (2018)
8. Taira, H., et al.: Inloc: indoor visual localization with dense matching and view synthesis. In: Proceedings of the IEEE Conference on Computer Vision and Pattern Recognition, pp. 7199–7209 (2018)
9. Wang, X., Hua, Y., Kodirov, E., Hu, G., Garnier, R., Robertson, N.M.: Ranked list loss for deep metric learning. In: Proceedings of the IEEE Conference on Computer Vision and Pattern Recognition, pp. 5207–5216 (2019)
10. Lowe, D.G.: Distinctive image features from scale-invariant keypoints. Int. J. Comput. Vision **60**, 91–110 (2004)
11. Rublee, E., Rabaud, V., Konolige, K., Bradski, G.: Orb: An efficient alternative to sift or surf. In: International Conference on Computer Vision, vol. 2011, pp. 2564–2571. IEEE (2011)
12. Alcantarilla, P.F., Bartoli, A., Davison, A.J.: Kaze features. In: European Conference on Computer Vision, Springer (2012) 214–227
13. Dong, J., Soatto, S.: Domain-size pooling in local descriptors: Dsp-sift. In: Proceedings of the IEEE Conference on Computer Vision and Pattern Recognition, pp. 5097–5106 (2015)

14. Schonberger, J.L., Hardmeier, H., Sattler, T., Pollefeys, M.: Comparative evaluation of hand-crafted and learned local features. In: Proceedings of the IEEE Conference on Computer Vision and Pattern Recognition, pp. 1482–1491 (2017)
15. DeTone, D., Malisiewicz, T., Rabinovich, A.: Superpoint: self-supervised interest point detection and description. In: Proceedings of the IEEE Conference on Computer Vision and Pattern Recognition Workshops, pp. 224–236 (2018)
16. Dusmanu, M., Rocco, I., Pajdla, T., Pollefeys, M., Sivic, J., Torii, A., Sattler, T.: D2-net: a trainable CNN for joint detection and description of local features. In: CVPR 2019 (2019)
17. Tian, Y., Fan, B., Wu, F.: L2-net: deep learning of discriminative patch descriptor in euclidean space. In: Proceedings of the IEEE Conference on Computer Vision and Pattern Recognition, pp. 661–669 (2017)
18. Revaud, J., Weinzaepfel, P., De Souza, C., Pion, N., Csurka, G., Cabon, Y., Humenberger, M.: R2d2: Repeatable and reliable detector and descriptor. arXiv preprint arXiv:1906.06195 (2019)
19. Luo, Z., et al.: Aslfeat: learning local features of accurate shape and localization. In: Proceedings of the IEEE/CVF Conference on Computer Vision and Pattern Recognition, pp. 6589–6598 (2020)
20. Bian, J.W., et al.: An evaluation of feature matchers for fundamental matrix estimation. arXiv preprint arXiv:1908.09474 (2019)
21. Sattler, T., Weyand, T., Leibe, B., Kobbelt, L.: Image retrieval for image-based localization revisited. In: BMVC (2012)
22. Balntas, V., Lenc, K., Vedaldi, A., Mikolajczyk, K.: Hpatches: a benchmark and evaluation of handcrafted and learned local descriptors. In: Proceedings of the IEEE Conference on Computer Vision and Pattern Recognition, pp. 5173–5182 (2017)
23. Schmid, C., Mohr, R., Bauckhage, C.: Evaluation of interest point detectors. Int. J. Comput. Vision 37, 151–172 (2000)
24. Mikolajczyk, K., Schmid, C.: A performance evaluation of local descriptors. IEEE Trans. Pattern Anal. Mach. Intell. 27, 1615–1630 (2005)
25. Mishchuk, A., Mishkin, D., Radenovic, F., Matas, J.: Working hard to know your neighbor's margins: local descriptor learning loss. In: Advances in Neural Information Processing Systems, pp. 4826–4837 (2017)
26. Tian, Y., Yu, X., Fan, B., Wu, F., Heijnen, H., Balntas, V.: Sosnet: second order similarity regularization for local descriptor learning. In: Proceedings of the IEEE Conference on Computer Vision and Pattern Recognition, pp. 11016–11025 (2019)
27. Yi, K.M., Trulls, E., Lepetit, V., Fua, P.: LIFT: learned invariant feature transform. In: Leibe, B., Matas, J., Sebe, N., Welling, M. (eds.) ECCV 2016. LNCS, vol. 9910, pp. 467–483. Springer, Cham (2016). https://doi.org/10.1007/978-3-319-46466-4_28
28. Ono, Y., Trulls, E., Fua, P., Yi, K.M.: Lf-net: learning local features from images. In: Advances in Neural Information Processing Systems, pp. 6234–6244 (2018)
29. Noh, H., Araujo, A., Sim, J., Weyand, T., Han, B.: Large-scale image retrieval with attentive deep local features. In: Proceedings of the IEEE International Conference on Computer Vision, pp. 3456–3465 (2017)
30. Christiansen, P.H., Kragh, M.F., Brodskiy, Y., Karstoft, H.: Unsuperpoint: End-to-end unsupervised interest point detector and descriptor. arXiv preprint arXiv:1907.04011 (2019)
31. Simonyan, K., Zisserman, A.: Very deep convolutional networks for large-scale image recognition. arXiv preprint arXiv:1409.1556 (2014)

32. Shi, W., et al.: Real-time single image and video super-resolution using an efficient sub-pixel convolutional neural network. In: Proceedings of the IEEE Conference on Computer Vision and Pattern Recognition, pp. 1874–1883 (2016)
33. Lin, T.Y., et al.: Microsoft COCO: common objects in context. In: Fleet, D., Pajdla, T., Schiele, B., Tuytelaars, T. (eds.) ECCV 2014. LNCS, vol. 8693, pp. 740–755. Springer, Cham (2014). https://doi.org/10.1007/978-3-319-10602-1_48
34. Li, Z., Snavely, N.: Megadepth: learning single-view depth prediction from internet photos. In: Proceedings of the IEEE Conference on Computer Vision and Pattern Recognition, pp. 2041–2050 (2018)
35. Kingma, D.P., Ba, J.: Adam: A method for stochastic optimization. arXiv preprint arXiv:1412.6980 (2014)
36. Arandjelović, R., Zisserman, A.: Three things everyone should know to improve object retrieval. In: 2012 IEEE Conference on Computer Vision and Pattern Recognition, pp. 2911–2918. IEEE (2012)
37. Mishkin, D., Radenovic, F., Matas, J.: Repeatability is not enough: learning affine regions via discriminability. In: Proceedings of the European Conference on Computer Vision (ECCV), pp. 284–300 (2018)
38. Sturm, J., Engelhard, N., Endres, F., Burgard, W., Cremers, D.: A benchmark for the evaluation of rgb-d slam systems. In: 2012 IEEE/RSJ International Conference on Intelligent Robots and Systems, pp. 573–580. IEEE (2012)
39. Geiger, A., Lenz, P., Urtasun, R.: Are we ready for autonomous driving? the kitti vision benchmark suite. In: Conference on Computer Vision and Pattern Recognition (CVPR) (2012)
40. Knapitsch, A., Park, J., Zhou, Q.Y., Koltun, V.: Tanks and temples: Benchmarking large-scale scene reconstruction. ACM Trans. Graph. (ToG) 36, 1–13 (2017)
41. Wilson, K., Snavely, N.: Robust global translations with 1DSfM. In: Fleet, D., Pajdla, T., Schiele, B., Tuytelaars, T. (eds.) ECCV 2014. LNCS, vol. 8691, pp. 61–75. Springer, Cham (2014). https://doi.org/10.1007/978-3-319-10578-9_5
42. Svärm, L., Enqvist, O., Kahl, F., Oskarsson, M.: City-scale localization for cameras with known vertical direction. IEEE Trans. Pattern Anal. Mach. Intell. 39, 1455–1461 (2016)
43. Schonberger, J.L., Frahm, J.M.: Structure-from-motion revisited. In: Proceedings of the IEEE Conference on Computer Vision and Pattern Recognition, pp. 4104–4113 (2016)

CLASS: Cross-Level Attention and Supervision for Salient Objects Detection

Lv Tang[1] and Bo Li[2(✉)]

[1] State Key Laboratory for Novel Software Technology, Nanjing University,
Nanjing, China
luckybird1994@gmail.com
[2] Youtu Lab, Tencent, Shanghai, China
libraboli@tencent.com

Abstract. Salient object detection (SOD) is a fundamental computer vision task. Recently, with the revival of deep neural networks, SOD has made great progresses. However, there still exist two thorny issues that cannot be well addressed by existing methods, indistinguishable regions and complex structures. To address these two issues, in this paper we propose a novel deep network for accurate SOD, named CLASS. First, in order to leverage the different advantages of low-level and high-level features, we propose a novel non-local cross-level attention (CLA), which can capture the long-range feature dependencies to enhance the distinction of complete salient object. Second, a novel cross-level supervision (CLS) is designed to learn complementary context for complex structures through pixel-level, region-level and object-level. Then the fine structures and boundaries of salient objects can be well restored. In experiments, with the proposed CLA and CLS, our CLASS net consistently outperforms 13 state-of-the-art methods on five datasets.

1 Introduction

Salient object detection (SOD) is a fundamental task in computer vision, which is derived with the goal of detecting and segmenting the most distinctive objects from visual scenes. As a preliminary step, SOD plays an essential role in various visual systems, such as object recognition [1,2], semantic segmentation [3], visual tracking [4] and image-sentence matching [5].

Recently, with the application of deep convolutional neural networks (CNNs), salient object detection has achieved impressive improvements over conventional hand-crafted feature based approaches. Owing to their efficiency and powerful capability in visual feature representation, the CNN-based methods have pushed the performance of SOD to a new level, especially after the emergence of fully convolutional neural networks (FCNs). However, there still exist two thorny issues that cannot be well addressed by existing SOD methods. First, it is difficult to keep the uniformity and wholeness of the salient objects in some complex

Electronic supplementary material The online version of this chapter (https://doi.org/10.1007/978-3-030-69535-4_26) contains supplementary material, which is available to authorized users.

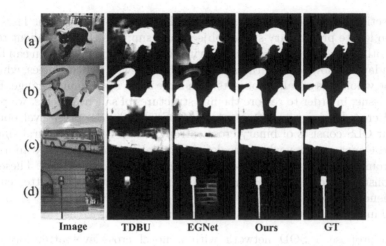

Fig. 1. Issues that cannot be well addressed by existing SOD methods. In (a)(b), some "salient-like" regions and large appearance change between salient object parts usually confuse the models to cause wrong predictions. In (c)(d), it is hard to maintain the fine structures and boundaries of salient objects. Images and ground-truth masks (GT) are from [6,7]. Results are generated by TDBU [8], EGNet [9] and our approach.

detecting scenes. As shown in Fig. 1(a)(b), some "salient-like" regions and large appearance change between salient object parts usually confuse the models to cause wrong predictions. Second, it is hard to maintain the fine structures and boundaries of salient objects (see Fig. 1(c)(d)). These two issues hinder the further development of SOD, and make it still a challenging task.

To alleviate the first problem, some methods [8,10–16] attempt to enhance the feature by aggregating multi-level and multi-scale features or adopting attention mechanisms to guide the models to focus on salient regions. However, these mechanisms ignore the relationships between the object parts and the complete salient object, leading to wrong prediction in complex real-world scenarios. For the second problem, methods [9,17–20] try to maintain the fine structures by introducing some special boundary branch or adding extra boundary supervision. These branches can provide boundary details to restore the salient contour, but they inevitably contain some noise edges might influence the final prediction (like the bricks in Fig. 1(d)). Meanwhile, these pixel-level boundary supervisions not only cannot capture enough context of complex structures but need extra cost to get boundary labels.

In this paper, to address the aforementioned two issues, we propose a novel convolutional neural network, named CLASS, which achieves remarkable performance in detecting accurate salient objects. For the first issue, inspired by non-local mechanism [21,22], we develop a novel attention module to capture the relationships between regions and the complete salient object. Unlike the conventional self-attention mechanism, we want to capture features dependencies through different levels, which is called cross-level attention module (CLA). On one hand, low-level features which contain the fine spatial details can guide the selection of high-level through non-local position dependencies. Thus it can assist to locate preliminary salient objects and suppress the non-salient regions. On the other hand, high-level features with rich semantic information can be used as a guidance of low-level features through channel-wise dependencies, which can keep the wholeness of salient objects with large inner appearance change. For the second issue, in order to restore the fine structures of salient objects, we propose a novel cross-level supervision strategy (CLS). Unlike the pixel-level boundary loss, our CLS consists of binary cross entropy loss, a novel structural similarity loss and F-measure loss, which are designed to learn complementary information from ground truth through pixel-level, region-level and object-level. These cross-level constraints can provide context of complex structures to better calibrate the saliency values.

The main contributions of this paper can be summarize as:

(1) We propose a SOD network with a novel cross-level attention mechanism, which can keep the uniformity and wholeness of the detected salient objects by modeling the channel-wise and position-wise features dependencies through different levels.
(2) We introduce a novel cross-level supervision to train our network across three different levels: pixel-level, region-level and object-level. The complementarity between these losses can help restoring the fine structures and boundaries of salient objects.
(3) We conduct comprehensive experiments on five public SOD benchmark datasets. The results demonstrate that with the above two components the proposed CLASS net consistently outperforms state-of-the-art algorithms, which proves the effectiveness and superiority of our method.

2   Related Work

Over the past decades, a large amount of SOD algorithms have been developed. Traditional models [23–27] detect salient objects by utilizing various heuristic saliency priors with hand-crafted features. More details about the traditional methods can be found in the survey [28]. Here we mainly focus on deep learning based saliency detection models, especially the latest FCN-based methods in recent three years.

Lots of FCN-based models are devoted to exploring various feature enhancement strategies to improve the ability of localization and awareness of salient objects. Hou et al. [10] introduced short connections to the skip-layer structures within the HED [29] architecture, which provided rich multi-scale feature maps at each layer. Zhang et al. [12] aggregated multi-level feature maps into multiple resolutions, which were then fused to predict saliency maps in a recursive manner. Liu et al. [13] proposed a pixel-wise contextual attention to guide the network learning to attend global and local contexts. Chen et al. [15] propose a reverse attention network, which restore the missing object parts and details by erasing the current predicted salient regions from side-output features. Feng et al. [16] designed the attentive feedback modules to control the message passing between encoder and decoder blocks. Wu et al. [11] introduced skip connection between multi-level features and a holistic attention module to refine the detection results by enlarging the coverage area of the initial saliency map. Wang et al. [8] proposed to integrate both top-down and bottom-up saliency inference by using multi-level features in an iterative and cooperative manner. However, these above mechanisms lack consideration of the relationships between the object parts and the complete salient object, leading to wrong prediction in complex real-world scenarios. Unlike these methods, we propose the cross-level attention module: the non-local position-wise and channel-wise features dependencies through different levels. The cross-level position attention can guide the network to suppress the non-salient regions, while the cross-level channel attention can keep the wholeness of salient objects with large inner appearance change.

Recently, some methods consider leveraging boundary information to restore the fine structures of salient objects. These methods usually utilize some special boundary branch or adding extra boundary supervision to get the boundary information. Li et al. [17] transferred salient knowledge from an existing contour detection model as useful priors to facilitate feature learning in SOD. In [9,14,18,20], edge features from some sophisticated edge detection branches or modules were fused with salient features as complementary information to enhance the structural details for accurate saliency detection. However, these branches inevitably contain some noise edges that might influence the final prediction (like the bricks in Fig. 1(d)). Liu et al. [19] proposed to utilize extra edge supervision to jointly train an edge detection branch and a SOD branch, which can assist the deep neural network to refine the details of salient objects. Feng et al. [16] presented a boundary-enhanced loss as a supplement to the cross-entropy loss for learning fine boundaries. These pixel-level boundary supervisions cannot capture enough context of complex structures and also increase labeling cost. Different form the above methods, our novel cross-level supervision strategy (CLS), which consists of binary cross entropy loss, a novel structural similarity loss and F-measure loss, are designed to train our network across three different levels: pixel-level, region-level and object-level. With the learned complementary context of complex structures, it is much easier for our network to maintain the fine structures and boundaries of salient objects. For more information about the DNN-based methods, please refer to survey [30,31].

3 Proposed Method

In this section, we first describe the overall architecture of the proposed deep salient object detection network, and then elaborate our main contributions, which are corresponding to cross-level attention module and cross-level supervision respectively.

3.1 Architecture

As illustrated in Fig. 2, the proposed CLASS net has a simple U-Net-like Encoder-Decoder architecture [32]. The ResNet-50 [33] is used as backbone

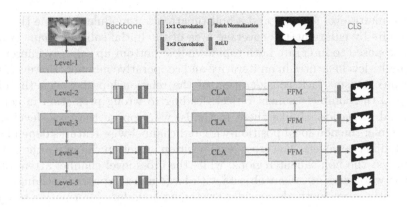

Fig. 2. An overview of proposed CLASS net. ResNet-50 is used as the backbone encoder. Cross-level attention module (CLA) is used to capture the long-range features dependencies between the high-level features and the low-level features. Feature fusion module (FFM) is a basic module to fuse features for decoder. Cross-level supervision (CLS) in each stages help to ease the optimization of CLASS net.

feature encoder, which has five residual modules for encoding, named as level-1 to level-5 respectively. Because level-1 feature brings too much computational cost but little performance improvement, we don't use it for following process as suggested in work [11]. Between the encoder and decoder, we add two convolution blocks as the bridge. The 1×1 convolutional layer compresses the channels of high-level features for subsequent processing and the 3×3 convolutional layer transfers features for SOD task. Each of these convolution layers is followed by a batch normalization [34] and a ReLU activation [35]. The high-level feature in level-5 is denoted as $\{F_h | h = 5\}$, while the other three levels features are denoted as $\{F_l | l = 2, 3, 4\}$. Then cross-level attention modules are used to capture the long-range features dependencies between the high-level features (F_h) and the low-level features (F_l). For the decoder, we use a feature fusion module (FFM) to delicately aggregate the output features of CLA module in each stage and the upsampled features from the previous stage in a bottom-up manner. The output of each decoder stage is defined as $\{D_i | i = 2, 3, 4\}$. Cross-level supervision (CLS) is applied in each stage to train our CLASS net jointly. The output of the last stage is taken as the final saliency prediction.

3.2 Cross-Level Attention Module

Discriminant feature representations are essential for accurate SOD, while most existing methods cannot well keep the uniformity and wholeness of the salient objects in some complex scenes because of lacking consideration of the relationships between the indistinguishable regions and the salient object. To address this problem, inspired by non-local mechanism [21,22], we develop a novel attention module to capture the long-range features dependencies. However, features

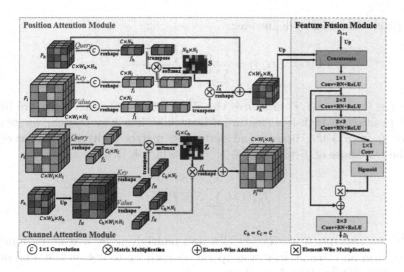

Fig. 3. An overview of the proposed Cross-Level Attention Module and Feature Fusion Module. Cross-Level Attention Module contains Position Attention and Channel Attention.

in different levels usually have different recognition information. Common non-local models [22], which rely on a single layer feature, exhibit limited ability in capturing sufficient long range dependencies. Unlike them, we want to leverage the advantages of features in different levels and propose the cross-level attention module. As illustrated in Fig. 3, we design two parts in CLA to model the channel-wise and position-wise features dependencies across the high-level feature and the low-levels features.

Position Attention Module. In some complex detecting scenes, there exist some non-salient regions which have "salient-like" appearance. These regions usually share some similar attributes with real salient regions like the high visual contrast. Thus, the saliency-like regions may also have high saliency semantics at the high-level layer. So the high-level feature which lacks low-level cues is difficult to distinguish saliency-like regions. We want to use the rich spatial details of low-level features as a guidance to make the high-level layer concentrate on real salient positions and then learn more discriminative features to suppress the non-salient regions. Specifically, as illustrated in Fig. 3, the input of Position Attention Module is a high-level feature map $F_h \in \mathcal{R}^{C \times H_h \times W_h}$ and a low-level feature map $F_l \in \mathcal{R}^{C \times H_l \times W_l}$. To be specific, for *Query* branch, we first add a 1×1 convolution layer on F_h and reshape the feature to $f_h \in \mathcal{R}^{C \times N_h}$, where $N_h = H_h \times W_h$. Meanwhile, for *Key* branch, we also use a 1×1 convolution layer on F_l and reshape the feature to $f_l \in \mathcal{R}^{C \times N_l}$, where $N_l = H_l \times W_l$. After that, we perform a matrix multiplication between the transpose of f_h and f_l, then apply a *softmax* function to calculate the spatial attention map $\mathbf{S} \in \mathcal{R}^{N_h \times N_l}$.

Each pixel value in **S** is defined as:

$$S(i,j) = \frac{exp(f_h^i \cdot f_l^j)}{\sum_{j=1}^{N_l} exp(f_h^i \cdot f_l^j)}, \tag{1}$$

where $i \in [1, N_h]$, $S(i,j)$ measures the jth position in low-level feature impact on i^{th} position in high-level feature. Meanwhile, like *Key* branch, we generate feature $\hat{f}_l$ from *Value* branch and perform a matrix multiplication between S and the transpose of $\hat{f}_l$ to get $f_h' \in \mathcal{R}^{C \times N_h}$, which is defined as:

$$f_h'(i) = \sum_{j=1}^{N_l} S(i,j)\hat{f}_l(j), \tag{2}$$

Finally, we reshape f_h' to $\mathcal{R}^{C \times H_h \times W_h}$ and multiply it by a scale parameter α and perform an element-wise sum operation with F_h to obtain the final output $F_h^{out} \in \mathcal{R}^{C \times H_h \times W_h}$. It is defined as:

$$F_h^{out} = \alpha \cdot f_h' + F_h, \tag{3}$$

where α is initialized as 0 and gradually learns to assign more weight [36].

Channel Attention Module. In some complicated scenarios, salient objects may have large inner appearance change. These appearance variations are mainly reflected in the difference in the channels of low-level features. Since the channel of the low-level features contains almost no semantic information but low-level visual appearance cues, it is hard to maintain the semantic consistency of the object parts. To address this issue, we want to use the rich semantics of channels in high-level features to guide the selection of low-level features, which equips our network with the power of assigning saliency label to different-looking regions to keep the wholeness of salient objects. Specifically, as illustrated in Fig. 3, for channel attention module, we first use bilinear to upsample F_h to the spatial size of F_l, denoted as $f_H \in \mathcal{R}^{C_h \times H_l \times W_l}$, where $C_h = C$. For *Query* branch, we reshape F_l to $f_L \in \mathcal{R}^{C_l \times N_l}$, where $C_l = C$. For *Key* branch, we reshape f_H to $\mathcal{R}^{C_h \times N_l}$. Next, we perform a matrix multiplication between f_L and the transpose of f_H and apply a softmax function to get the channel attention map $\mathbf{Z} \in \mathcal{R}^{C_l \times C_h}$. Each pixel value in **Z** can be calculated as:

$$Z(i,j) = \frac{exp(f_L^i \cdot f_H^j)}{\sum_{j=1}^{C_h} exp(f_L^i \cdot f_H^j)}, \tag{4}$$

where $i \in [1, C_l]$, $Z(i,j)$ measures the jth channel of high-level feature impact on i^{th} channel of low-level feature. At the same time, for *Value* branch, we reshape f_H to $\mathcal{R}^{C_h \times N_l}$ and perform a matrix multiplication with **Z** to get $f_L' \in \mathcal{R}^{C_l \times N_l}$, which is defined as:

$$f_L'(i) = \sum_{j=1}^{C_h} Z(i,j) f_H(j), \tag{5}$$

Finally, we reshape f'_L to $\mathcal{R}^{C_l \times H_l \times W_l}$ and multiply it by a scale parameter β and perform an element-wise sum operation with F_l to obtain the final output $F_l^{out} \in \mathcal{R}^{C \times H_l \times W_l}$. It is defined as:

$$F_l^{out} = \beta \cdot f'_L + F_l, \tag{6}$$

where β is initialized as 0 and gradually learns to assign more weight.

3.3 Feature Fusion Module

As illustrated in Fig. 3, Each decoder network stage contains feature F_l^{out}, F_h^{out} from cross-level attention module, $D_{i+1} \in \mathcal{R}^{C \times \frac{H_l}{2} \times \frac{W_l}{2}}$ from previous decoder network stage. As these features contain different level information, we can not simply sum up these features for decoding. Inspired by SENet [37], we use an attention based feature fusion module to aggregate and refine these features effectively. Specifically, we first concatenate the three features then apply a 1×1 and two 3×3 convolutional layer with batch normalization and ReLU activation function to balance the scales of the features. Then we use a 1×1 convolutional layer and *sigmoid* function to compute a weight map, which amounts to feature selection and combination. Finally, guided by this weight map, we can archive an effective feature representation D_i for following process. Figure 3 shows the details of this design.

3.4 Cross-Level Supervision

Through the cross-level attention, features are enhanced for better keeping the uniformity and wholeness of the salient objects. Then we focus on restoring the fine structures and boundaries of salient objects. Toward this end, we propose a novel cross-level supervision strategy (CLS) to learn complementary context information from ground truth through pixel-level, region-level and object-level.

Let $\mathcal{I} = \{I_n\}_{n=1}^N$ and their groundtruth $\mathcal{G} = \{G_n\}_{n=1}^N$ denote a collection of training samples where N is the number of training images. After saliency detection, saliency maps are $\mathcal{S} = \{S_n\}_{n=1}^N$. In SOD, binary cross entropy (BCE) is the most widely used loss function, and it is a pixel-wise loss which is defined as:

$$L_{Pixel} = -\big(G_n log(S_n) + (1 - G_n)log(1 - S_n)\big). \tag{7}$$

From the formula of BCE loss, we find that it only considers the independent relationship between each pixel, which cannot capture enough context of complex structures, leading to blurry boundaries.

To address this problem, we propose to model region-level similarity as a supplement to the pixel-level constraint. Following the setting of [38,39], we use the sliding window fashion to generate two corresponding regions from saliency map S_n and groundtruth G_n, denoted as $S_n^{region} = \{S_n^i : i = 1, ...M\}$ and $G_n^{region} = \{G_n^i : i = 1, ...M\}$, where M is the total number of region. Then, we adopt the simplified 2-Wasserstein distance [40,41] to evaluate the distributional similarity between S_n^i and G_n^i. Thus the proposed network can be trained by minimizing the similarity distance SSD_i between the corresponding regions, which is defined as:

$$SSD_i = ||\mu_{S_n^i} - \mu_{G_n^i}||_2^2 + ||\sigma_{S_n^i} - \sigma_{G_n^i}||_2^2, \tag{8}$$

where local statistics $\mu_{S_n^i}$, $\sigma_{S_n^i}$ is mean and std vector of S_n^i, $\mu_{G_n^i}$, $\sigma_{G_n^i}$ is mean and std vector of G_n^i. Finally, the overall loss function is defined as:

$$L_{Region} = \frac{1}{M} \sum_{i=1}^{M} SSD_i, \tag{9}$$

Pixel-level and region-level constraints can only capture local context for salient objects, a global constraint is still needed for accurate SOD. F-measure is often used to measure the overall similarity between the saliency map of the detected object and its groundtruth [42–44]. Hence we want to directly optimize the F-measure to learn the global information, called object-level supervision. For easy remembering, we denote F-measure as F_β in the following. The predicted saliency map S_n is a non-binary map, so we calculate F_β value via two steps. First, multiple thresholds are applied to the predicted saliency map to obtain multiple binary maps. Then, these binary maps are compared to the groundtruth. Hence, the whole process of calculating F_β is nondifferentiable. However, we can modify it to be differentiable. Considering pixel value $G_n(x,y)$ and $S_n(x,y)$, if $G_n(x,y) = 1$ and $S_n(x,y) = p$, it means this pixel has p probability to be true positive and $(1-p)$ probability to be false negative; if $G_n(x,y) = 0$ and $S_n(x,y) = p$, it means this pixel has p probability to be true negative and $1 - p$ to be false positive. So, we can calculate precision and recall by following Formulation:

$$precision = \frac{TP}{TP + FP} = \frac{S_n \cdot G_n}{S_n \cdot G_n + S_n \cdot (1 - G_n)} = \frac{S_n \cdot G_n}{S_n + \epsilon}, \tag{10}$$

$$recall = \frac{TP}{TP + FN} = \frac{S_n \cdot G_n}{S_n \cdot G_n + (1 - S_n) \cdot G_n} = \frac{S_n \cdot G_n}{G_n + \epsilon}, \tag{11}$$

$$F_\beta = \frac{(1 + \beta^2) \cdot precision \cdot recall}{\beta^2 \cdot precision + recall}, \tag{12}$$

where $\cdot$ means pixel-wise multiplication, $\epsilon = 1e^{-7}$ is a regularization constant to avoid division of zeros. L_{Object} loss function is defined as:

$$L_{Object} = 1 - F_\beta. \tag{13}$$

Note that all parts of our network are trained jointly, and the over all loss function is given as:

$$L = L_{Object} + L_{Region} + L_{Pixel}. \tag{14}$$

In addition, as show in Fig. 2, we use multi-level supervision as an as an auxiliary loss to facilitate sufficient training. The network has K levels and the whole loss is defined as:

$$L_{Final} = \sum_{i=1}^{K=4} \frac{1}{2^{i-1}} L_i. \tag{15}$$

In this loss function, high level loss has smaller weight because of its larger error. Finally, these cross-level constraints can provide context of complex structures to better calibrate the saliency values.

4   Experiments

4.1   Implementation Details

Following the works [9,11,18,20], we train our proposed network on DUTS-TR. ResNet-50 [33] is used as the backbone network. For a more comprehensive demonstration, we also trained our network with VGG-16 [45] backbone. The whole network is trained end-to-end by stochastic gradient descent(SGD). Maximum learning rate is set to 0.005 for ResNet-50 or VGG-16 backbone and 0.05 for other parts. Warm-up and linear decay strategies are used to adjust the learning rate. Momentum and weight decay are set to 0.9 and 0.0005. Batchsize is set to 32 and maximum epoch is set to 100. We use Pytorch[1] to implement our model. Only horizontal flip and multi-scale input images are utilized for data augmentation as done in [15,16,18,20]. A RTX 2080Ti GPU is used for acceleration. During testing, the proposed method runs at about 40 fps with about 352×352 resolution without any post-processing. Our code has been released.[2]

We comprehensively evaluated our method on five representative datasets, including HKU-IS [46], ECSSD [47], PASCAL-S [6], DUT-OMRON [7] and DUTS [48], which contain 4447, 1000, 850, 5168 and 5019 images respectively. All datasets are human-labeled with pixel-wise ground-truth. Among them, more recent datasets PASCAL-S and DUT-TE are more challenging with salient objects that have large appearance change and complex background.

4.2   Evaluation Metrics

To evaluate the performance of the proposed method, four widely-used metrics are adopted: (1) Precision-Recall (PR) curve, which shows the tradeoff between precision and recall for different threshold (ranging from 0 to 255). (2) F-measure, (F_β), a weighted mean of average precision and average recall, calculated by $F_\beta = \frac{(1+\beta^2) \times Precision \times Recall}{\beta^2 \times Precision + Recall}$. We set β^2 to be 0.3 as suggested in [43]. (3) Mean Absolute Error (MAE), which characterize the average 1-norm distance between ground truth maps and predictions. (4) Structure Measure (S_m), a metric to evaluate the spatial structure similarities of saliency maps based on both region-aware structural similarity S_r and object-aware structural similarity S_o, defined as $S_\alpha = \alpha * S_r + (1 - \alpha) * S_o$, where $\alpha = 0.5$ [39].

---

[1] https://pytorch.org/.

[2] https://github.com/luckybird1994/classnet.

Table 1. Performance of 13 sotas and the proposed method on five benchmark datasets. Smaller MAE, larger F_β and S_m correspond to better performance. The best results of different backbones are in blue and red fonts. "†" means the results are post-processed by dense conditional random field(CRF) [49]. MK: MSRA10K [24], DUTS: DUTS-TR [48], MB: MSRA-B [50].

Models	Training dataset	ECSSD			DUTS-TE			DUT-OMRON			PASCAL-S			HKU-IS		
		F_β	S_m	MAE	F_β	S_m	MAE	F_β	S_m	MAE	F_β	S_m	MAE	F_β	S_m	MAE
VGG-16 backbone																
Amulet (ICCV2017) [12]	MK	0.868	0.894	0.059	0.678	0.804	0.085	0.647	0.781	0.098	0.757	0.814	0.097	0.841	0.886	0.051
C2SNet (ECCV2018) [17]	MK	0.853	0.882	0.059	0.710	0.817	0.066	0.664	0.780	0.079	0.754	0.821	0.085	0.839	0.873	0.051
RAS (ECCV2018) [15]	MB	0.889	0.893	0.056	0.751	0.839	0.059	0.713	0.814	0.062	0.777	0.792	0.101	0.871	0.887	0.045
PiCA-V (CVPR2018) [13]	DUTS	0.885	0.914	0.046	0.749	0.861	0.054	0.710	0.826	0.068	0.789	0.842	0.077	0.870	0.906	0.042
DSS† (TPAMI2019) [10]	MB	0.904	0.882	0.052	0.808	0.820	0.057	0.740	0.790	0.063	0.801	0.792	0.093	0.902	0.878	0.040
PAGE (CVPR2019) [14]	MK	0.906	0.912	0.042	0.777	0.854	0.052	0.736	0.824	0.062	0.806	0.835	0.075	0.882	0.903	0.037
AFNet (CVPR2019) [16]	DUTS	0.908	0.913	0.042	0.792	0.867	0.046	0.738	0.826	0.057	0.820	0.848	0.070	0.888	0.905	0.036
CPD-V (CVPR2019) [11]	DUTS	0.915	0.910	0.040	0.813	0.867	0.043	0.745	0.818	0.057	0.820	0.838	0.072	0.896	0.904	0.033
TSPOA (ICCV2019) [51]	DUTS	0.900	0.907	0.046	0.776	0.860	0.049	0.716	0.818	0.061	0.803	0.836	0.076	0.882	0.902	0.038
BANet-V (ICCV2019) [18]	DUTS	0.910	0.913	0.041	0.789	0.861	0.046	0.731	0.819	0.061	0.812	0.834	0.078	0.887	0.902	0.037
EGNet-V (ICCV2019) [9]	DUTS	0.913	0.913	0.041	0.800	0.878	0.044	0.744	0.813	0.057	0.809	0.837	0.076	0.893	0.910	0.035
Ours	DUTS	0.917	0.915	0.038	0.833	0.880	0.039	0.749	0.820	0.057	0.838	0.853	0.062	0.909	0.915	0.031
ResNet50 backbone																
PiCA-R (CVPR2018) [13]	DUTS	0.886	0.917	0.046	0.759	0.869	0.051	0.717	0.832	0.065	0.792	0.848	0.074	0.870	0.904	0.043
TDBU (CVPR2019) [8]	MK	0.880	0.918	0.041	0.767	0.865	0.048	0.739	0.837	0.061	0.775	0.844	0.070	0.878	0.907	0.038
CPD-R (CVPR2019) [11]	DUTS	0.917	0.918	0.037	0.805	0.869	0.043	0.747	0.825	0.056	0.820	0.842	0.070	0.891	0.905	0.034
SCRN (ICCV2019) [20]	DUTS	0.918	0.927	0.037	0.808	0.885	0.040	0.746	0.837	0.056	0.827	0.848	0.062	0.896	0.916	0.034
BANet (ICCV2019) [18]	DUTS	0.923	0.924	0.035	0.815	0.879	0.040	0.746	0.832	0.059	0.823	0.845	0.069	0.900	0.913	0.032
EGNet (ICCV2019) [9]	DUTS	0.920	0.925	0.037	0.815	0.887	0.039	0.755	0.837	0.053	0.817	0.846	0.073	0.901	0.918	0.031
Ours	DUTS	0.933	0.928	0.033	0.856	0.894	0.034	0.774	0.838	0.052	0.849	0.863	0.059	0.921	0.923	0.028

4.3   Comparisons with the State-of-the-Arts

We compare our approach CLASS net with 13 state-of-the-art methods, including Amulet [12], C2SNet [17], RAS [15], PiCAnet [13], DSS [10], PAGE [14], AFNet [16], CPD [11], TSPOANet [51], TDBU [8], SCRN [20], BANet [18] and EGNet [9]. For fair comparison, we obtain the saliency maps of these methods from authors or the deployment codes provided by authors.

Quantitative Evaluation. The proposed approach is compared with 13 state-of-the-art SOD methods on five datasets, and the results are reported in Table 1 and Fig. 4. From Table 1, we can see that our method consistently outperforms other methods across all the five benchmark datasets. It is noteworthy that our method improves the F-measure and S-measure achieved by the best-performing existing algorithms by a large margin on two challenging datasets PASCAL-S (F_β: 0.849 against 0.827, S_m: 0.863 against 0.848) and DUTS-TE (F_β: 0.856 against 0.815, S_m: 0.894 against 0.887). As for MAE, our method obviously exceed other state-of-the-art algorithms on all five datasets. When using VGG-16 as backbone, our method still consistently outperfrom other methods, which verifies that our proposed CLA and CLS can achieve great performance with different backbone. For overall comparisons, PR curves of different methods are displayed in Fig. 4. One can observe that our approach noticeably higher than all the other methods. These observations present the efficiency and robustness of our CLASS net across various challenging datasets, which indicates that the perspective of CLA for the problem of SOD is useful.

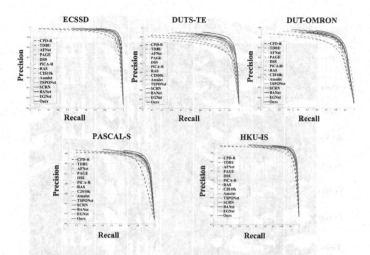

Fig. 4. Comparison of the PR curves across five benchmark datasets.

Qualitative Evaluation. To exhibit the superiority of the proposed approach, Fig. 5 show representative examples of saliency maps generated by our approach and other state-of-the-art algorithms. As can be seen, the proposed method can keep the uniformity and wholeness of the salient objects meanwhile maintain the fine structures and boundaries in various challenging scenes. From the column of 1 and 2 in Fig. 5, we can observe that with the influence of "salient-like" regions (mountain and water reflection), existing methods usually give wrong predictions. While, in our method, by the guidance of position-wise cross-level attention, the salient objects are accurately located and the non-salient regions are well suppressed. Example in third column with large inner appearance change can cause incomplete detection problem in existing methods. With the help of channel-wise cross-level attention, our method can better keep the wholeness of the salient object. Moreover, for the case of multiple and small objects in the of 4 to 6, our method can detect all the salient objects with the relationship information captured by cross-level attention, whereas the other methods mostly miss objects or introduce some background noise. From the column of 7 and 8, we can find that most existing methods cannot maintain the fine structures and boundaries of objects in the case of low contrast between salient object and background as well as the complicated scene. Note that some methods with special edge branches (EGNet, BANet and SCRN) can keep some structural details of example in column 8 and 9. However, These branches inevitably contain some noise edges can introduce background noise in the final prediction. It can be clearly observed that our method achieves impressive performance in all these cases, which indicates the effectiveness of cross-level supervision in maintaining the fine structures and boundaries of salient objects.

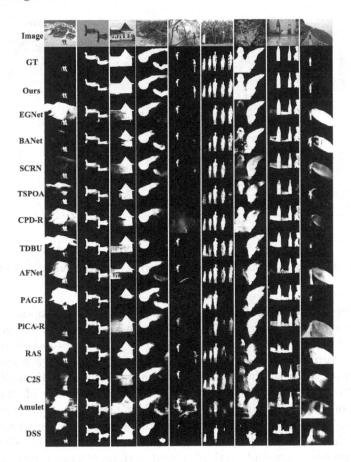

Fig. 5. Qualitative comparisons of the state-of-the-art algorithms and our approach.

4.4   Ablation Studies

To validate the effectiveness of the proposed components of our method, we conduct a series of experiments on three datasets with different settings.

Supervision Ablation. To investigate the effectiveness of our proposed cross-level supervision, we conduct a set of experiments over different losses based on a baseline U-Net architecture. As listed in Table 2, we can observe a remarkable and consistent improvement brought by different level supervisions. Compared with only using pixel-level supervision, adding region-level structural similarity supervision can significantly improve the performance on all three metrics, especially the S-measure, which shows its ability of maintaining fine structures and boundaries of salient objects. Object-level supervision further improve the performance on F-measure. When these supervision are combined and applied at each stage (MS), we can get the best SOD results. In addition, by comparing setting No.9 and No.10, we can find that CLS is still useful even when the results is advanced.

Table 2. Ablation study on different settings of supervision and architecture.

Ablation		Configurations							ECSSD			PASCAL-S			DUT-TE		
		Pixel level	Region level	Object level	MS	CLA-C	CLA-P	FFM	F_β	S_m	MAE	F_β	S_m	MAE	F_β	S_m	MAE
Loss	1	✓							0.900	0.910	0.043	0.808	0.838	0.072	0.782	0.873	0.044
	2	✓	✓						0.915	0.918	0.040	0.825	0.846	0.068	0.820	0.882	0.039
	3	✓	✓	✓					0.918	0.919	0.089	0.832	0.850	0.067	0.837	0.885	0.038
	4	✓	✓	✓	✓				0.920	0.920	0.088	0.838	0.853	0.064	0.841	0.887	0.037
Architecture	5	✓	✓	✓	✓			✓	0.923	0.922	0.087	0.842	0.855	0.062	0.845	0.888	0.036
	6	✓	✓	✓	✓	✓	✓		0.930	0.926	0.034	0.847	0.860	0.060	0.852	0.892	0.035
	7	✓	✓	✓	✓	✓		✓	0.927	0.924	0.036	0.845	0.859	0.062	0.850	0.889	0.036
	8	✓	✓	✓	✓		✓	✓	0.926	0.925	0.036	0.844	0.858	0.061	0.851	0.891	0.035
	9	✓			✓	✓	✓	✓	0.919	0.925	0.087	0.830	0.861	0.063	0.813	0.891	0.039
	10	✓	✓	✓	✓	✓	✓	✓	0.933	0.928	0.083	0.849	0.863	0.059	0.856	0.894	0.034

Architecture Ablation. To prove the effectiveness of our CLASS net, we report the quantitative comparison results of our model with different architectures. As shown in Table 2, Comparing No.5 and No.4, only using FFM can slightly improve the performance. Comparing No.6 and No.4, More significant improvements can be observed when we add channel-wise cross-level attention (CLA-C) and position-wise cross-level attention (CLA-P). Comparing No.7 with No.5, or No.8 with No.5, independently using CLA-C or CLA-P can also improve the performance. Finally, a best performance can be achieved through the combination of the CLA and FFM compared with baseline architecture (No.4), which verifies the compatibility of the two attentions and effectiveness of the features fusion module. For more comprehensive analyses of our proposed method, please refer to the supplementary materials.[3]

5 Conclusions

In this paper, we revisit the two thorny issues that hinder the development of salient object detection. The issues consist of indistinguishable regions and complex structures. To address these two issues, in this paper we propose a novel deep network for accurate SOD, named CLASS. For the first issue, we propose a novel non-local cross-level attention (CLA), which can leverage the advantages of features in different levels to capture the long-range feature dependencies. With the guidance of the relationships between low-level and high-level features, our model can better keep the uniformity and wholeness of the salient objects in some complex scenes. For the second issue, a novel cross-level supervision (CLS) is designed to learn complementary context for complex structures through pixel-level, region-level and object-level. Then the fine structures and boundaries of salient objects can be well restored. Extensive experiments on five benchmark datasets have validated the effectiveness of the proposed approach.

References

1. Rutishauser, U., Walther, D., Koch, C., Perona, P.: Is bottom-up attention useful for object recognition? In: CVPR (2), pp. 37–44 (2004)

---

[3] https://arxiv.org/abs/2009.10916.

2. Ren, Z., Gao, S., Chia, L., Tsang, I.W.: Region-based saliency detection and its application in object recognition. IEEE Trans. Circ. Syst. Video Technol. **24**, 769–779 (2014)
3. Wei, Y., et al.: STC: a simple to complex framework for weakly-supervised semantic segmentation. IEEE Trans. Pattern Anal. Mach. Intell. **39**, 2314–2320 (2017)
4. Hong, S., You, T., Kwak, S., Han, B.: Online tracking by learning discriminative saliency map with convolutional neural network. In: ICML, Proceedings of JMLR Workshop and Conference, JMLR.org (2015), vol. 37, pp. 597–606 (2015)
5. Ji, Z., Wang, H., Han, J., Pang, Y.: Saliency-guided attention network for image-sentence matching. In: ICCV (2019)
6. Li, Y., Hou, X., Koch, C., Rehg, J.M., Yuille, A.L.: The secrets of salient object segmentation. In: CVPR, pp. 280–287 (2014)
7. Yang, C., Zhang, L., Lu, H., Ruan, X., Yang, M.: Saliency detection via graph-based manifold ranking. In: CVPR, pp. 3166–3173 (2013)
8. Wang, W., Shen, J., Cheng, M., Shao, L.: An iterative and cooperative top-down and bottom-up inference network for salient object detection. In: CVPR, Computer Vision Foundation/IEEE, pp. 5968–5977 (2019)
9. Zhao, J.X., Liu, J.J., Fan, D.P., Cao, Y., Yang, J., Cheng, M.M.: EGNet: Edge guidance network for salient object detection. In: ICCV (2019)
10. Hou, Q., Cheng, M., Hu, X., Borji, A., Tu, Z., Torr, P.H.S.: Deeply supervised salient object detection with short connections. IEEE Trans. Pattern Anal. Mach. Intell. **41**, 815–828 (2019)
11. Wu, Z., Su, L., Huang, Q.: Cascaded partial decoder for fast and accurate salient object detection. In: CVPR, pp. 3907–3916 (2019)
12. Zhang, P., Wang, D., Lu, H., Wang, H., Ruan, X.: Amulet: aggregating multi-level convolutional features for salient object detection. In: ICCV, pp. 202–211 (2017)
13. Liu, N., Han, J., Yang, M.: PiCANet: learning pixel-wise contextual attention for saliency detection. In: CVPR, pp. 3089–3098 (2018)
14. Wang, W., Zhao, S., Shen, J., Hoi, S.C.H., Borji, A.: Salient object detection with pyramid attention and salient edges. In: CVPR, pp. 1448–1457 (2019)
15. Chen, S., Tan, X., Wang, B., Hu, X.: Reverse attention for salient object detection. In: Ferrari, V., Hebert, M., Sminchisescu, C., Weiss, Y. (eds.) ECCV 2018. LNCS, vol. 11213, pp. 236–252. Springer, Cham (2018). https://doi.org/10.1007/978-3-030-01240-3_15
16. Feng, M., Lu, H., Ding, E.: Attentive feedback network for boundary-aware salient object detection. In: CVPR, pp. 1623–1632 (2019)
17. Li, X., Yang, F., Cheng, H., Liu, W., Shen, D.: Contour knowledge transfer for salient object detection. In: Ferrari, V., Hebert, M., Sminchisescu, C., Weiss, Y. (eds.) ECCV 2018. LNCS, vol. 11219, pp. 370–385. Springer, Cham (2018). https://doi.org/10.1007/978-3-030-01267-0_22
18. Su, J., Li, J., Zhang, Y., Xia, C., Tian, Y.: Selectivity or invariance: boundary-aware salient object detection. In: ICCV (2019)
19. Liu, J., Hou, Q., Cheng, M., Feng, J., Jiang, J.: A simple pooling-based design for real-time salient object detection. In: CVPR, pp. 3917–3926 (2019)
20. Wu, Z., Su, L., Huang, Q.: Stacked cross refinement network for edge-aware salient object detection. In: ICCV (2019)
21. Buades, A., Coll, B., Morel, J.: A non-local algorithm for image denoising. In: CVPR, pp. 60–65 (2005)
22. Wang, X., Girshick, R.B., Gupta, A., He, K.: Non-local neural networks. In: CVPR, pp. 7794–7803 (2018)

23. Itti, L., Koch, C., Niebur, E.: A model of saliency-based visual attention for rapid scene analysis. IEEE Trans. Pattern Anal. Mach. Intell. **20**, 1254–1259 (1998)
24. Cheng, M., Mitra, N.J., Huang, X., Torr, P.H.S., Hu, S.: Global contrast based salient region detection. IEEE Trans. Pattern Anal. Mach. Intell. **37**, 569–582 (2015)
25. Wang, J., Jiang, H., Yuan, Z., Cheng, M., Hu, X., Zheng, N.: Salient object detection: a discriminative regional feature integration approach. Int. J. Comput. Vis. **123**, 251–268 (2017)
26. Wang, T., Zhang, L., Lu, H., Sun, C., Qi, J.: Kernelized subspace ranking for saliency detection. In: ECCV, vol. 9912, pp. 450–466 (2016)
27. Klein, D.A., Frintrop, S.: Center-surround divergence of feature statistics for salient object detection. In: ICCV, pp. 2214–2219 (2011)
28. Borji, A., Cheng, M., Hou, Q., Jiang, H., Li, J.: Salient object detection: a survey. Comput. Vis. Media **5**, 117–150 (2019)
29. Xie, S., Tu, Z.: Holistically-nested edge detection. Int. J. Comput. Vis. **125**, 3–18 (2017)
30. Wang, W., Lai, Q., Fu, H., Shen, J., Ling, H.: Salient object detection in the deep learning era: an in-depth survey. CoRR abs/1904.09146 (2019)
31. Han, J., Zhang, D., Cheng, G., Liu, N., Xu, D.: Advanced deep-learning techniques for salient and category-specific object detection: a survey. IEEE Signal Process. Mag. **35**, 84–100 (2018)
32. Ronneberger, O., Fischer, P., Brox, T.: U-Net: convolutional networks for biomedical image segmentation. In: MICCAI, vol. 9351, pp. 234–241 (2015)
33. He, K., Zhang, X., Ren, S., Sun, J.: Deep residual learning for image recognition. In: CVPR, pp. 770–778 (2016)
34. Ioffe, S., Szegedy, C.: Batch normalization: accelerating deep network training by reducing internal covariate shift. In: ICML, JMLR.org, vol. 37, pp. 448–456 (2015)
35. Hahnloser, R.H.R., Seung, H.S.: Permitted and forbidden sets in symmetric threshold-linear networks. In: NIPS, pp. 217–223. MIT Press (2000)
36. Zhang, H., Goodfellow, I.J., Metaxas, D.N., Odena, A.: Self-attention generative adversarial networks. In: ICML, vol. 97, pp. 7354–7363 (2019)
37. Hu, J., Shen, L., Sun, G.: Squeeze-and-excitation networks. In: CVPR, 7132–7141 (2018)
38. Wang, Z., Bovik, A.C., Sheikh, H.R., Simoncelli, E.P.: Image quality assessment: from error visibility to structural similarity. IEEE Trans. Image Process. **13**, 600–612 (2004)
39. Fan, D., Cheng, M., Liu, Y., Li, T., Borji, A.: Structure-measure: a new way to evaluate foreground maps. In: ICCV, pp. 4558–4567 (2017)
40. Berthelot, D., Schumm, T., Metz, L.: BEGAN: boundary equilibrium generative adversarial networks. CoRR abs/1703.10717 (2017)
41. He, R., Wu, X., Sun, Z., Tan, T.: Wasserstein CNN: learning invariant features for NIR-VIS face recognition. IEEE Trans. Pattern Anal. Mach. Intell. **41**, 1761–1773 (2019)
42. Margolin, R., Zelnik-Manor, L., Tal, A.: How to evaluate foreground maps. In: CVPR, pp. 248–255 (2014)
43. Borji, A., Cheng, M., Jiang, H., Li, J.: Salient object detection: a benchmark. IEEE Trans. Image Process. **24**, 5706–5722 (2015)
44. Wang, W., Shen, J., Dong, X., Borji, A.: Salient object detection driven by fixation prediction. In: CVPR, IEEE Computer Society, pp. 1711–1720 (2018)
45. Simonyan, K., Zisserman, A.: Very deep convolutional networks for large-scale image recognition. In: ICLR (2015)

46. Li, G., Yu, Y.: Visual saliency based on multiscale deep features. In: CVPR, pp. 5455–5463 (2015)
47. Shi, J., Yan, Q., Xu, L., Jia, J.: Hierarchical image saliency detection on extended CSSD. Trans. Pattern Anal. Mach. Intell. **38**, 717–729 (2016)
48. Wang, L., et al.: Learning to detect salient objects with image-level supervision. In: CVPR, 3796–3805 (2017)
49. Krähenbühl, P., Koltun, V.: Efficient inference in fully connected CRFs with Gaussian edge potentials. In: NIPS, pp. 109–117 (2011)
50. Liu, T., et al.: Learning to detect a salient object. IEEE Trans. Pattern Anal. Mach. Intell. **33**, 353–367 (2011)
51. Liu, Y., Zhang, Q., Zhang, D., Han, J.: Employing deep part-object relationships for salient object detection. In: ICCV (2019)

Cascaded Transposed Long-Range Convolutions for Monocular Depth Estimation

Go Irie[✉], Daiki Ikami, Takahito Kawanishi, and Kunio Kashino

NTT Corporation, Kanagawa 243-0124, Japan
goirie@ieee.org,go.irie.nv@hco.ntt.co.jp

Abstract. We study the shape of the convolution kernels in the upsampling block for deep monocular depth estimation. First, our empirical analysis shows that the depth estimation accuracy can be improved consistently by only changing the shape of the two consecutive convolution layers with square kernels, e.g., $(5 \times 5) \rightarrow (5 \times 5)$, to two "long-range" kernels, one having the transposed shape of the other, e.g., $(1 \times 25) \rightarrow (25 \times 1)$. Second, based on this observation, we propose a new upsampling block called Cascaded Transposed Long-range Convolutions (CTLC) that uses parallel sequences of two long-range convolutions with different kernel shapes. Experiments with NYU Depth V2 and KITTI show that our CTLC offers higher accuracy with fewer parameters and FLOPs than state-of-the-art methods.

1 Introduction

Depth information often provides useful clues for recognizing the 3D structure of a scene, which is essential for many practical applications such as 3D scene reconstruction, navigation, and autonomous driving. While the performance of depth sensors has improved, obtaining dense and accurate depth information still requires high-end sensors. Unfortunately, such sensors cannot always be available due to limitations of device size or cost constraints. To overcome this issue, depth estimation from a single RGB image has received much attention in recent years.

Monocular depth estimation is an ill-posed problem; it is impossible to recover the depth of a scene from only a single RGB image without any assumptions or knowledge about the scene. Modern approaches rely on deep convolutional neural networks (CNNs) to learn a direct mapping from an RGB image to a corresponding depth map [1–3]. The majority of existing methods can be grouped into supervised [2–4] and self-supervised approaches [5]. The former uses ground truth depth maps measured by a depth sensor to train the prediction network, and the latter instead trains the network using a stereo pair or a

Electronic supplementary material The online version of this chapter (https://doi.org/10.1007/978-3-030-69535-4_27) contains supplementary material, which is available to authorized users.

© Springer Nature Switzerland AG 2021
H. Ishikawa et al. (Eds.): ACCV 2020, LNCS 12624, pp. 437–453, 2021.
https://doi.org/10.1007/978-3-030-69535-4_27

sequence of moving frames that can be used to estimate depth. Although the self-supervised approach has a significant advantage of being trainable without explicit ground truth information, the supervised approach still tends to accurate. In this paper, we consider the supervised approach for monocular depth estimation.

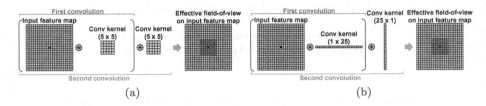

Fig. 1. Kernel shape and effective field-of-view. (a) Two convolution layers whose kernel shapes are (5×5) are applied to the input feature map. The size of the effective field of view, i.e., the number of the pixels on the input feature map used to compute the value of the output feature map at the position of the black pixel, is 9×9 (green pixels). (b) The shape of the two convolution kernels is changed to (1×25) and (25×1), respectively. Although the number of parameters and FLOPs are exactly the same as the case of (a), the area of the effective field-of-view (green) is dramatically increased to 25×25. (Color figure online)

A common approach is to use an encoder-decoder type CNN. The encoder part is typically built by using a Fully Convolutional Network (FCN) to extract a low-resolution feature map, and the decoder part upsamples the feature map to recover the target depth map by applying several upsampling blocks. Previous studies have explored diverse aspects of this common strategy to improve the final prediction performance, including network architectures [1–3,6], loss functions [1,3,4,7], and usage of additional cues such as sparse depth [4,8] or relative depth information [9], just to name a few.

We focus on the shape of the convolution kernels in the upsampling blocks. To the best of our knowledge, the only existing method that has focused on the shape of the kernels in the upsampling blocks is Whole Strip Masking (WSM) [10]. WSM uses a "long-range" convolution whose kernel is designed so that either of its vertical or horizontal length is equal to that of the input feature map. By stacking several WSM blocks, the receptive field spanned by the network as a whole effectively covers a wide area of the input RGB image. However, a single WSM layer only looks at pixels on approximately the same vertical or horizontal line to compute each output pixel value. This may overlook potential dependencies between vertical and horizontal directions on each intermediate feature map, which should be a powerful clue for accurate depth estimation. Another disadvantage would be that, because the kernel size depends on the size of the input feature map, it can only be applied to images of the same size (similar to a CNN that has fully connected layers), which may not always be desirable in practice.

We propose a modified upsampling block called Cascaded Transposed Long-range Convolutions (CTLC) free from these problems. Unlike WSM that applies a single long-range convolution separately to the input feature map, the core idea of our CTLC is to sequentially apply two long-range convolutions, one having the spatially transposed shape of the other. More specifically, suppose there are two consecutive convolution layers with normal square kernels, $(5 \times 5) \rightarrow (5 \times 5)$, as shown in Fig. 1a. Our CTLC changes their shapes to $(1 \times 25) \rightarrow (25 \times 1)$ as in Fig. 1b. A notable advantage of our CTLC block is that the resulting area of the effective field-of-view is dramatically increased, without changing the number of parameters and FLOPs. Moreover, unlike WSM, the kernel size of CTLC does not depend on the size of the input image, so it can be applied to images of any size. Our final CTLC block is configured to apply multiple convolutional sequences with different kernel shapes in parallel to capture different levels of contextual information of the input feature map by a single upsampling block. Experiments on two standard benchmark datasets for monocular depth estimation, namely NYU Depth V2 [11] and KITTI [12], demonstrate that our CTLC block yields consistently better accuracies than existing upsampling blocks and can outperform several state-of-the-art methods.

2   Related Work

We briefly review previous studies on supervised monocular depth estimation and upsampling block that are relevant to this work.

2.1   Supervised Monocular Depth Estimation

Supervised methods assume that ground truth depth maps, usually measured by a range imaging system such as an infrared camera or LiDAR, are available during the training and train a model so that the error between the model's output and the ground truth depth map is minimized. Early attempts addressed the problem using probabilistic structured prediction models, such as Markov Random Fields (MRFs) and Conditional Random Fields (CRFs) [13–15], or an external database to obtain a depth map with RGB content similar to the target scene [16]. These methods generally used hand-crafted features, but designing useful features has often been a difficult problem. Modern approaches use deep learning. The ability to learn features directly from the data has been shown to improve performance significantly, and since then, a variety of researches have been conducted on network architecture design, loss function, and so on.

Network Architectures. One of the key requirements for the network architecture is to effectively model the multiscale nature of the depth estimation task, which has been a mainstream of the architecture study. Eigen et al. proposed using multiple FCNs, where each FCN aims to infer different scale levels of the depth map [1,2]. Liu et al. [17] proposed a model that incorporates a CRF into the FCN to obtain a smoother depth map [17]. Xu et al. [6] also used a variant of CRFs to fuse multiscale outputs extracted from the intermediate layers.

Lee et al. [18] fused multiple depth predictions at different cropping rates with the weights obtained by Fourier domain analysis. Fu et al. [7] proposed to use Atrous Spatial Pyramid Pooling (ASPP) that is originally proposed for semantic segmentation tasks [19] to capture the different levels of contextual information of the feature map. Lee et al. [20] also used an extended version of ASPP called Dense ASPP [21].

Loss Functions. [4] investigated several standard loss functions, such as the mean absolute error (MAE) and the mean square error (MSE). Robust and "anti-robust" loss functions have also been explored in several studies [3,22]. [1] introduced a scale-invariant loss to mitigate a harmful effect that the average scale of the scene dominates the overall prediction error. [23] proposed an attention-driven loss to take into account the long-tail distribution of depth values. Fu et al. proposed to solve the problem as an ordinal regression problem by quantizing depth values [7].

Other Attempts. Several studies have focused on densifying sparse depth maps with the help of RGB images [4,24]. Given the strong correlation between structured visual prediction tasks, such as depth estimation, semantic segmentation, and normal map estimation, some studies explored multi-task learning approaches of these tasks [2,25]. [26] showed that the result could be improved by explicitly modeling the uncertainties of the depth information.

The focus of this work is on the network architecture, more specifically the upsampling block, which will be described in detail in the next subsection.

2.2   Upsampling Block

The majority of the existing architectures for monocular depth estimation have a feature extraction backbone to extract a low-resolution feature map and upsampling blocks to recover the target depth size. Hence, the performance of the upsampling block greatly affects the final depth estimation accuracy. Given a general architecture that has a feature extraction backbone (e.g., ResNet-50 [27]) and an upsampling network consisting of a sequence of four upsampling blocks, Laina et al. [3] explored several types of upsampling blocks including unpooling (UnPool), upconvolution (UpConv), deconvolution (DeConv) and upprojection (UpProj), and showed that UpProj outperforms the others. The most relevant research to our work would be WSM [10]. As discussed in the introduction, a major drawback of WSM is that it cannot capture dependencies between vertical and horizontal directions on each intermediate feature map, and our CTLC overcomes this weakness. Vertical pooling [28] that pools the input feature map along the vertical direction and RowColCNN [29] that uses long-range kernels for image distortion correction have also the same weakness as WSM. Our experimental results in Sect. 4 will demonstrate that our CTLC can achieve significantly better performance than Vertical Pooling and WSM.

Several upsampling networks have also been explored in some neighboring fields, such as image classification and semantic segmentation. Atrous convolution [19] was originally proposed for semantic segmentation, performing convolutions at "wider intervals" to ensure larger receptive fields. DUpsampling [30] is a trainable upsampling layer that has been proposed to generate finer segmentation results from low-resolution images. More recently, several methods [31,32] proposed using self-attention for CNNs [33] to integrate information over the entire image. Inception V3, which is a well-known architecture proposed by Szegedy et al. for image classification, uses an idea of decomposing a square convolution kernel into two vertical and horizontal kernels [34]. Unlike their method that reduces the number of parameters for efficient convolution operations, our CTLC changes only the shape of the kernel without changing the number of parameters, which has not been considered in [34].

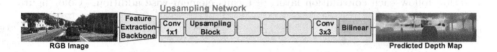

Fig. 2. Our architecture of entire depth estimation network. The entire structure follows [3] and consists of two major parts. One is a feature extraction backbone (encoder) that is typically constructed by using an image classification network such as ResNet-50 and DenseNet-161. The other is an upsampling network (decoder) which has one (1×1) convolution layer to reduce the number of channels by half, four upsampling blocks, one (3×3) convolution layer, and one bilinear upsampling layer to predict the target depth map.

3   Method

We describe the details of our CTLC upsampling block in this section. We first present the entire architecture of our depth estimation network used in this paper. We next explain the core idea of our CTLC upsampling block and prove its effectiveness by showing empirical results of how the shape of the convolution kernel affects the final depth estimation performance. Finally, we introduce the final architecture of our CTLC upsampling block.

3.1   Entire Architecture of Depth Estimation Network

The entire architecture of our depth estimation network is illustrated in Fig. 2. Overall, this has the same structure proposed in some previous work [3,4] and consists of a feature extraction backbone and an upsampling network. The feature extraction backbone takes an RGB scene image and outputs a low-resolution feature map. Following [3,4], we use popular CNN architectures for image classification (e.g., ResNet-50) pre-trained on ImageNet and adapt them to our depth estimation task by discarding a few top layers. We will detail this adaptation process later in Sect. 4. The upsampling network is built by stacking several upsampling blocks in which each doubles the spatial resolution of the input feature map while reducing the number of channels into a half [3]. Typically, four blocks are involved, resulting in a 16 times larger feature map than that generated by the feature extraction backbone.

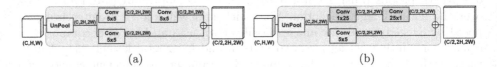

Fig. 3. Architecture of upsampling block. (a) UpProj and (b) our CTLC blocks with $(1 \times 25) \rightarrow (25 \times 1)$ convolutions. (C, H, W) means the number of channels, height, and width of the input feature map. A batch normalization layer and a ReLU activation function follow each convolution layer. $\oplus$ means element-wise addition. (Color figure online)

3.2   Core Concept of CTLC

We start from UpProj that is a simple and effective upsampling block proposed in [3] and introduce the core concept of our CTLC.

The architecture of the UpProj block is given in Fig. 3a. After the input feature map is doubled in size by the UnPool layer, it passes through two separate branches and then fused into a single feature map with an element-wise addition. While the bottom branch in Fig. 3a simply applies a single (5×5) convolution to the input feature map, the upper branch uses a sequence of two convolutions which we denote by $(5 \times 5) \rightarrow (5 \times 5)$ for brevity[1].

The goal of our CTLC is to achieve a larger effective field of view both vertically and horizontally than the square convolutions while keeping the computational costs the same. The key idea is to modify the kernel shape of the two consecutive convolutions in the upper branch, such that (1) each is longer in either direction and (2) one is to be the transpose of the other. Such a modification can be done systematically as follows. Suppose we have two consecutive convolutions with size k, i.e., $(k \times k) \rightarrow (k \times k)$. We can obtain the CTLC versions of them as $(\lceil k/c \rceil \times \lceil ck \rceil) \rightarrow (\lceil ck \rceil \times \lceil k/c \rceil)$, where $0 < c \leq k$ is a parameter to control the aspect ratio. For instance, when we set $c = 5$ for the case of $k = 5$, we have $(1 \times 25) \times (25 \times 1)$. We consider only the case where both sides of each kernel are odd, in order to keep the size of the input and output feature maps exactly the same, and thus the possible combinations we have for $k = 5$ are the following four patterns: $(9 \times 3) \rightarrow (3 \times 9)$, $(3 \times 9) \rightarrow (9 \times 3)$, $(25 \times 1) \rightarrow (1 \times 25)$ and $(1 \times 25) \rightarrow (25 \times 1)$. The example of the resulting CTLC block with $(1 \times 25) \rightarrow (25 \times 1)$ kernels can be illustrated in Fig. 3b.

---

[1] Although [3] uses $(5 \times 5) \rightarrow (3 \times 3)$, we in this work restrict it to be $(5 \times 5) \rightarrow (5 \times 5)$ for systematic discussion.

Table 1. Impact of kernel shapes in upsampling block on depth estimation performance. The scores are evaluated on NYU Depth V2 dataset. All the kernels have almost the same number of parameters (5×5). The best score for each metric and each feature extraction backbone (DenseNet-161 or ResNet-50) is shown in bold.

Backbone	Kernel shape	Higher is better			Lower is better			
		δ_1	δ_2	δ_3	AbsRel	SqRel	RMSE	$RMSE_{log}$
DenseNet-161	$(5 \times 5) \to (5 \times 5)$	0.850	0.975	0.995	0.126	0.075	0.431	0.156
	$(9 \times 3) \to (3 \times 9)$	0.857	0.977	0.995	0.122	0.072	0.426	0.154
	$(3 \times 9) \to (9 \times 3)$	0.857	0.978	**0.996**	0.121	0.071	0.425	0.153
	$(25 \times 1) \to (1 \times 25)$	0.867	0.978	0.995	0.119	0.070	0.412	0.148
	$(1 \times 25) \to (25 \times 1)$	**0.871**	**0.979**	0.995	**0.116**	**0.068**	**0.409**	**0.147**
	$(H \times 1) \to (1 \times W)$	0.873	0.978	0.996	0.118	0.070	0.407	0.147
	$(1 \times W) \to (H \times 1)$	0.871	0.979	0.996	0.115	0.068	0.413	0.147
ResNet-50	$(5 \times 5) \to (5 \times 5)$	0.812	0.965	0.992	0.143	0.094	0.478	0.177
	$(9 \times 3) \to (3 \times 9)$	0.829	0.968	0.993	0.137	0.087	0.459	0.169
	$(3 \times 9) \to (9 \times 3)$	0.828	0.968	0.993	0.137	0.087	0.461	0.170
	$(25 \times 1) \to (1 \times 25)$	0.863	0.977	0.994	0.120	0.073	0.418	0.150
	$(1 \times 25) \to (25 \times 1)$	**0.867**	**0.980**	**0.995**	**0.117**	**0.069**	**0.413**	**0.148**
	$(H \times 1) \to (1 \times W)$	0.864	0.976	0.994	0.120	0.073	0.413	0.150
	$(1 \times W) \to (H \times 1)$	0.866	0.979	0.996	0.117	0.070	0.413	0.149

To examine the impact of the kernel shapes on the final depth estimation accuracy, we evaluate the accuracy when we change only the kernel shapes while keeping the rest (further details of the protocol will be given later in Sect. 4). We tested two feature extraction backbone networks, DenseNet-161 and ResNet-50. Table 1 shows the results for the five different combinations of the kernel shapes. The results show that the shape of the convolution kernels significantly affects the final depth prediction performance. Interestingly, the performance of the square kernel is the worst for both feature extraction backbone networks, and the longer the kernel shapes, the better the performance. We also evaluated cases that use kernels having the same lengths as the input feature map as adopted in WSM [10], e.g., $(1 \times W) \to (H \times 1)$, but they did not give a consistent performance improvement over our CTLC counterparts such as $(1 \times 25) \to (25 \times 1)$, despite their non-negligible increases in the number of parameters[2]. These results suggest the effectiveness of the core concept of our CTLC.

There are several possible reasons. First, the sequence of a long-range convolution and its transposition allows the upsampling block to have a far larger field of view than a sequence of two square kernels, as shown in Fig. 1. The importance of the size of the field of view in deep monocular depth estimation has been pointed out in several studies, e.g., [3]. However, to the best of our knowledge, there has been no attempt to increase its size by changing only the shape of the convolution kernels in monocular depth estimation. Another reason may be that information obtained from pixels in the horizontal and vertical lines is often vital in depth estimation. An RGB image and a depth map captured

---

[2] For example, $(1 \times W) \to (H \times 1)$ has 1.46 times the number of parameters than $(1 \times 25) \to (25 \times 1)$ for the DenseNet-161 backbone.

in a natural setting are often taken almost parallel to the ground. In this case, in which case, if no object is present in the scene, pixels in the same horizontal line are considered to be almost equidistant from the camera. Furthermore, a recent study on deep monocular depth estimation [35] suggests that the network pays attention to the vertical position of the object to estimate the depth. From these observations, the pixels on the same horizontal and vertical lines provide important clues, which can be effectively captured by our CTLC.

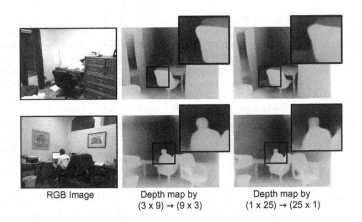

RGB Image   Depth map by   Depth map by
$(3 \times 9) \rightarrow (9 \times 3)$ $(1 \times 25) \rightarrow (25 \times 1)$

Fig. 4. Examples of estimated depth map. Each row shows an RGB image (left) and corresponding depth maps estimated by $(3 \times 9) \rightarrow (9 \times 3)$ (center) and $(1 \times 25) \rightarrow (25 \times 1)$ (right), respectively. The area inside the black frame is enlarged and displayed at the top right of each image.

3.3   Final CTLC Block

We propose our final CTLC block by introducing two modifications to the architecture shown in Fig. 3b. One is the parallelization of CTLCs to improve the accuracy, and the other is leveraging the idea of sub-pixel convolution [36] to reduce the number of parameters and FLOPs.

Parallel CTLC. Figure 4 shows some examples of the depth maps estimated by the upsampling block with $(3 \times 9) \rightarrow (9 \times 3)$ and $(1 \times 25) \rightarrow (25 \times 1)$. The results shown in Table 1 show that $(1 \times 25) \rightarrow (25 \times 1)$ tends to perform better than $(3 \times 9) \rightarrow (9 \times 3)$ in average. However, looking at the examples in the figure, we can see that $(3 \times 9) \rightarrow (9 \times 3)$ better recovers corners and roundish objects (such as a human) than $(1 \times 25) \rightarrow (25 \times 1)$. This may be because $(3 \times 9) \rightarrow (9 \times 3)$ is closer to square than $(1 \times 25) \rightarrow (25 \times 1)$, and thus is useful for restoring local shapes that would otherwise be difficult to recover without looking vertical and horizontal directions at the same time. Furthermore, since the second convolution sees only the features aggregated by the first convolution, the order of the kernels to be applied determines the priority of the directions. According to the suggestion above by [35], this should be determined based on the presence or absence of objects. These discussions suggest that a single sequence of CTLC may not be sufficient to capture the full spectrum of depth information.

We, therefore, propose a CTLC block that uses multiple sequences of different kernel shapes in parallel. The architecture of the proposed parallel CTLC block is indicated by the red dotted box in Fig. 5. The input feature map passes through parallel branches of four CTLCs with different shape patterns and then concatenated into a single feature map. Compared to the original CTLC block having only a single branch, the number of channels in each branch is reduced to $1/4$. The concatenated feature map is linearly projected by (1×1) convolution. This parallel architecture allows the upsampling block to effectively capture different context information, which leads to better estimation accuracy.

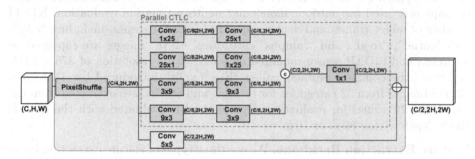

Fig. 5. Full CTLC block. (C, H, W) means the number of channels, height, and width of the input feature map. A batch normalization layer and ReLU follow each convolution layer. ⓒ and ⊕ mean concatenation and element-wise addition, respectively.

Sub-pixel Convolution. UnPool is not efficient because it doubles the spatial resolution of the input feature map without reducing the number of channels. Only a quarter of the pixels in the resulting feature map have non-zero values. This increases the number of parameters of the subsequent convolution layers and requires more FLOPs. We resolve this issue based on the idea of sub-pixel convolution [36] and replace UnPool with the pixel shuffle operation (PixelShuffle) that relocates the pixels of the tensor of shape $C \times H \times W$ to that of $C/4 \times 2H \times 2W$. The number of channels can be reduced to $1/4$ while retaining the same information. This makes it possible to suppress both the number of parameters and FLOPs to $1/3$ or less without losing depth estimation accuracy. Figure 5 shows the architecture of our final CTLC block. Unless otherwise specified, the proposed method uses this architecture for the upsampling block.

4   Experiments

We evaluate the performance of our CTLC upsampling block for monocular depth estimation.

4.1   Protocol

We follow the common protocol adopted in most of the previous papers (e.g., [2–4]) as detailed below.

Dataset. We use two datasets that are commonly used to evaluate monocular depth estimation. The first one is **NYU Depth V2** [11] which is the most widely-used benchmark dataset for indoor depth estimation tasks. It consists of RGB and depth images of 464 indoor scenes with a resolution of 480×640. Following the official split, we sampled 48k RGB-depth pairs from the raw RGB/depth sequences of the official training set (249 scenes) for training and used all the 654 images from the official test set (215 scenes) for evaluation. Each depth map is spatiotemporally aligned with the corresponding RGB image and hole-filled by applying a cross-bilateral filter. The second one is **KITTI** [12] which is frequently used for outdoor monocular depth estimation evaluation. KITTI consists of image frames and depth maps of 61 outdoor scenes, including "city", "residential", "road", and "campus" categories. All the images are captured by a camera and LiDAR sensor mounted on a car with a resolution of 375×1241. Following the common protocol called "Eigen split" introduced by [1], we use $23,488$ images from 32 categories for training and 697 images extracted from the remaining 29 scenes for evaluation. Our method is evaluated with the ground truth depth within 80 m or 50 m.

Feature Extraction Backbone. We use three types of feature extraction backbone networks including DenseNet-161 [37], ResNet-50 [27], and MobileNetV2 [38]. The original architecture of DenseNet-161/ResNet-50 consists of four dense/residual blocks for feature extraction and one classification block (a fully-connected layer after a global average pooling layer) at the top to output the final classification results. Following [3,4], we adapted these architectures to the monocular depth estimation task by replacing their classification block with the upsampling network shown in Fig. 2. For MobileNetV2, we also replaced the top convolution and average pooling layers for classification with the upsampling network. The parameters are initialized with those pre-trained on ImageNet and fine-tuned with the training set of the corresponding dataset.

Training Details. We use PyTorch for implementing all the models and running the experiments. The training is performed using Adam optimizer for 50 epochs. The learning rate is initially set to 10^{-4} and polynomially decayed during training to 10^{-5}. Other parameters we use are $\beta_1 = 0.9$, $\beta_2 = 0.999$, a weight decay of 10^{-4}, and a mini-batch size of 6. For all the experiments, we use the scale-invariant loss [1] to train our networks.

$$\ell(e) = \frac{1}{n} \sum_i^n e_i^2 - \frac{1}{n^2} \left(\sum_i^n e_i \right)^2 \tag{1}$$

where e_i and n are the pixel-level difference at i-th pixel between the estimated and ground truth depth maps and the number of pixels, respectively. We also use several standard data augmentation techniques commonly used in monocular depth estimation [1,4,7]. The RGB and depth images are randomly rotated in $[-5,+5]$ (deg), horizontally flipped with a 50% chance, and each of the RGB values is scaled by $[0.5, 1.5]$. We train our model on a random crop of size 416×544 for NYU Depth V2 and 385×513 for KITTI.

Table 2. Comparison of upsampling blocks on NYU Depth V2 with three backbone networks. #Params and GFLOPs are the number of trainable parameters and gigaFLOPs of each upsampling network, respectively. "Ours (UP)" and "Ours (PS)" use UnPool and PixelShuffle for upsampling, respectively. The best and the second-best are in bold and underlined, respectively.

Backbone	Upsampling Block	Higher is better			Lower is better				#Params (million)	GFLOPs
		δ_1	δ_2	δ_3	AbsRel	SqRel	RMSE	RMSE$_{log}$		
ResNet-50	UpConv [3]	0.773	0.955	0.990	0.157	0.111	0.520	0.194	25.2	117.2
	UpProj [3]	0.812	0.965	0.992	0.143	0.094	0.478	0.177	58.2	293.0
	Sub-pixel Conv [36]	0.802	0.962	0.992	0.147	0.099	0.485	0.181	18.1	117.2
	Atrous Conv [19]	0.855	0.975	<u>0.994</u>	0.125	0.075	0.427	0.156	58.2	293.0
	Self-attention [33]	0.830	0.970	<u>0.994</u>	0.136	0.086	0.452	0.167	25.7	120.6
	DUpsampling [30]	0.840	0.972	**0.995**	0.129	0.079	0.442	0.162	123.9	<u>53.3</u>
	DASPP [21]	0.857	**0.978**	**0.995**	0.121	0.074	0.433	0.154	97.5	332.6
	WSM [10]	0.812	0.969	0.993	0.158	0.102	0.474	0.176	**17.4**	38.0
	Ours (UP)	**0.866**	<u>0.976</u>	<u>0.994</u>	<u>0.119</u>	<u>0.073</u>	**0.412**	0.149	41.4	256.3
	Ours (PS)	<u>0.865</u>	**0.978**	**0.995**	**0.117**	**0.071**	<u>0.415</u>	0.150	<u>17.7</u>	77.4
DenseNet-161	UpConv [3]	0.843	0.975	<u>0.995</u>	0.128	0.077	0.436	0.160	24.4	136.2
	UpProj [3]	0.850	0.975	<u>0.995</u>	0.126	0.075	0.431	0.156	57.5	340.6
	Sub-pixel Conv [36]	0.846	0.975	**0.996**	0.127	0.075	0.430	0.158	<u>17.4</u>	136.3
	Atrous Conv [19]	0.866	0.977	<u>0.995</u>	0.118	0.070	0.419	0.150	57.5	340.6
	Self-attention [33]	0.861	<u>0.978</u>	<u>0.995</u>	0.121	0.071	0.417	0.151	24.9	140.0
	DUpsampling [30]	0.856	0.977	**0.996**	0.122	0.072	0.426	0.153	123.2	<u>66.7</u>
	DASPP [21]	<u>0.874</u>	0.979	<u>0.995</u>	<u>0.115</u>	<u>0.068</u>	0.410	<u>0.146</u>	96.8	385.3
	WSM [10]	0.830	0.975	<u>0.995</u>	0.150	0.091	0.456	0.167	21.8	**44.2**
	Ours (UP)	**0.877**	0.979	<u>0.995</u>	0.114	0.067	**0.404**	**0.145**	50.6	297.1
	Ours (PS)	<u>0.874</u>	0.979	<u>0.995</u>	<u>0.115</u>	<u>0.068</u>	<u>0.406</u>	<u>0.146</u>	16.9	89.4
MobileNetV2	UpConv [3]	0.773	0.955	0.990	0.157	0.111	0.520	0.194	7.6	45.8
	UpProj [3]	0.778	0.952	0.989	0.157	0.115	0.526	0.196	17.8	114.5
	Sub-pixel Conv [36]	0.762	0.949	0.988	0.162	0.120	0.541	0.201	<u>5.4</u>	45.8
	Atrous Conv [19]	0.820	0.967	<u>0.992</u>	0.138	0.092	0.478	0.174	17.8	114.5
	Self-attention [33]	0.801	0.960	0.990	0.150	0.103	0.498	0.183	7.7	47.5
	DUpsampling [30]	0.805	<u>0.964</u>	**0.993**	0.143	0.095	0.489	0.178	106.8	<u>20.8</u>
	DASPP [21]	0.827	0.967	<u>0.992</u>	**0.133**	0.089	0.474	<u>0.170</u>	29.9	133.5
	WSM [10]	0.788	0.959	0.991	0.163	0.115	0.515	0.188	6.8	**14.8**
	Ours (UP)	**0.833**	0.967	0.991	<u>0.134</u>	<u>0.090</u>	<u>0.466</u>	0.169	15.7	100.3
	Ours (PS)	<u>0.829</u>	0.967	<u>0.992</u>	0.135	**0.089**	**0.465**	0.169	5.3	30.2

Evaluation Metrics. We employ the following metrics for evaluation. The predicted and ground truth depth values at i-th pixel ($1 \leq i \leq n$) are denoted by $\hat{z}_i$ and z_i^*.

- δ_α: ratio of pixels whose relative error is within 1.25^α. We use $\alpha \in \{1, 2, 3\}$. Higher is better.

- AbsRel: mean absolute relative error, i.e., $\frac{1}{n}\sum_i^n |z_i^* - \hat{z}_i|/z_i^*$. Lower is better.
- SqRel: squared version of absolute relative error, i.e., $\frac{1}{n}\sum_i^n (z_i^* - \hat{z}_i)^2/z_i^*$. Lower is better.
- RMSE: root mean square error, i.e., $\sqrt{\frac{1}{n}\sum_i^n (z_i^* - \hat{z}_i)^2}$. Lower is better.
- RMSE$_{\log}$: logarithmic root mean square error, i.e., $\sqrt{\frac{1}{n}\sum_i^n (\log z_i^* - \log \hat{z}_i)^2}$. Lower is better.

Table 3. Comparison with state-of-the-art methods on NYU Depth V2. The best and the second-best scores for each metric and backbone network are shown in bold and are underlined, respectively.

Method	Backbone	Higher is better			Lower is better	
		δ_1	δ_2	δ_3	AbsRel	RMSE
Saxena et al. [14]	-	0.447	0.745	0.897	0.349	1.214
Eigen et al. [2]	VGG	0.769	0.950	0.988	0.158	0.641
Liu et al. [17]	AlexNet (Custom)	0.650	0.906	0.976	0.213	0.759
Laina et al. [3]	ResNet-50	0.811	0.953	0.988	0.127	0.573
Kendall et al. [26]	DenseNet (Custom [39])	0.817	0.959	0.989	**0.110**	0.506
Xu et al. [6]	ResNet-50	0.811	0.954	0.987	0.121	0.586
Ma et al. [4]	ResNet-50	0.810	0.959	0.989	0.143	0.514
Lee et al. [18]	ResNet-152	0.815	0.963	0.991	0.139	0.572
Fu et al. [7]	ResNet-101	0.828	0.965	0.992	<u>0.115</u>	0.509
Qi et al. [25]	ResNet-50	0.834	0.960	0.990	0.128	0.569
Heo et al. [10]	ResNet-50	0.816	0.964	0.992	0.135	0.571
Lee et al. [40]	DenseNet-161	0.837	0.971	<u>0.994</u>	0.131	0.538
Ours	ResNet-50	<u>0.865</u>	<u>0.978</u>	**0.995**	0.117	<u>0.415</u>
Ours	DenseNet-161	**0.874**	**0.979**	**0.995**	<u>0.115</u>	**0.406**

4.2   Comparison with Existing Upsampling Blocks

We first compare our CTLC with the following eight existing upsampling blocks. For all the upsampling blocks, we use the same base network architecture given in Fig. 2 and the training protocol.

- **UpConv** [3] uses only the bottom branch of UpProj. Other parts of the entire network is the same as that shown in Fig. 2.
- **UpProj** [3] which is exactly Fig. 3a.
- **Sub-pixel Conv** [36] is the same as UpProj except that it uses PixelShuffle instead of UnPool.
- **Atrous Conv** [19] changes the dilation rate of all convolution layers in the upper branch of UpProj to 2.
- **Self-attention** [33] uses UpConv as the base architecture, but a self-attention block (see Fig. 2 in [33]) is placed on top of the first two upsampling blocks.

- **DUpsampling** [30] uses three (5×5) convolutions and one DUpsampling layers, following [30].
- **DASPP** [21] is the same as the UpProj but has one DASPP block before the first upsampling block right after the feature extraction backbone network.
- **WSM** [10] uses the WSM block (see Fig. 5 in [10]) for each upsampling block in Fig. 2.

We use NYU Depth V2 for this experiment.

Table 4. Comparison with state-of-the-art methods on KITTI. "cap" gives the maximum depth used for evaluation. "Ours (raw)" and "Ours (GT)" are trained with raw depth maps and post-processed ground truth depth maps, both available on the official page. The best scores for each metric are shown in bold.

Method	Backbone	Cap	Higher is better			Lower is better			
			δ_1	δ_2	δ_3	AbsRel	SqRel	RMSE	RMSE$_{log}$
Saxena et al. [14]	-	80 m	0.601	0.820	0.926	0.280	3.012	8.734	0.361
Eigen et al. [1]	AlexNet	80 m	0.692	0.899	0.967	0.190	1.515	7.156	0.270
Liu et al. [17]	AlexNet (Custom)	80 m	0.647	0.882	0.961	0.217	1.841	6.986	0.289
Godard et al. [5]	ResNet-50	80 m	0.861	0.949	0.976	0.114	0.898	4.935	0.206
Kuznietsov et al. [41]	ResNet-50	80 m	0.862	0.960	0.986	0.113	0.741	4.621	0.189
Gan et al. [28]	ResNet-50	80 m	0.890	0.964	0.985	0.098	0.666	3.933	0.173
Fu et al. [7]	ResNet-101	80 m	0.932	0.984	0.994	0.072	0.307	**2.727**	0.120
Ours (raw)	DenseNet-161	80 m	0.896	0.972	0.990	0.093	0.519	3.856	0.155
Ours (GT)	DenseNet-161	80 m	**0.951**	**0.992**	**0.998**	**0.064**	**0.271**	2.945	**0.101**
Garg et al. [42]	Alexnet (Custom)	50 m	0.740	0.904	0.962	0.169	1.080	5.104	0.273
Godard et al. [5]	ResNet-50	50 m	0.873	0.954	0.979	0.108	0.657	3.729	0.194
Kuznietsov et al. [41]	ResNet-50	50 m	0.875	0.964	0.988	0.108	0.595	3.518	0.179
Gan et al. [28]	ResNet-50	50 m	0.898	0.967	0.986	0.094	0.552	3.133	0.165
Fu et al. [7]	ResNet-101	50 m	0.936	0.985	0.995	0.071	0.268	2.271	0.116
Ours (raw)	DenseNet-161	50 m	0.911	0.975	0.991	0.086	0.399	2.933	0.145
Ours (GT)	DenseNet-161	50 m	**0.956**	**0.994**	**0.999**	**0.065**	**0.199**	**2.141**	**0.098**

The results are presented in Table 2. Overall, we observe that our CTLC outperforms all the other upsampling blocks for all the feature extraction backbone networks. This clearly shows the effectiveness of our CTLC block. The results provide several interesting observations. First, when compared to UpProj which is used as the basic model of CTLC, we can see that CTLC consistently improves performance and significantly reduces the number of parameters and FLOPs. This proves the validity of the idea of changing the shape of two consecutive convolutions into spatially transposed long-range convolutions. Second, replacing UnPool (Ours (UP)) with PixelShuffle (Ours (PS)) greatly reduces the number of CTLC parameters and FLOPs while maintaining accuracy. Note that depending on the architecture of the upsampling block, accuracy may not always be maintained. More specifically, there is no significant difference in accuracy between UpProj and Sub-pixel Conv when DenseNet-161 is selected as the feature extraction backbone. However, using ResNet-50 or MobileNetV2 gives a performance gap between them. This may be because our CTLC has a much longer field-of-view than the range of the pixels shuffled by PixelShuffle, which also illustrates its advantage. Third, our CTLC is significantly more accurate than WSM that also uses long-range convolutions. Unlike CTLC, WSM compresses the input feature map vertically or horizontally using a convolutional layer of the same length as the input feature map. This reduces FLOPs, but can result in significant loss of spatial information. In contrast, our CTLC mitigates this by using the cascades of two long-range convolutions to capture spatial information in both directions efficiently. This may allow CTLC to achieve high accuracy with fewer parameters than other methods, including WSM.

Table 5. Ablation study. Performance on NYU Depth V2 with DenseNet-161 feature extraction backbone is reported. #Params and GFLOPs are the number of trainable parameters and gigaFLOPs of each upsampling network, respectively. The best scores for each metric are shown in bold.

Method	Higher is better			Lower is better		#Params (million)	GFLOPs
	δ_1	δ_2	δ_3	AbsRel	RMSE		
UpProj	0.850	0.975	0.995	0.126	0.431	57.5	340.6
+ Long-range	0.871	0.979	0.995	0.119	0.412	57.5	340.6
+ Parallel CTLC	**0.877**	**0.979**	**0.995**	**0.114**	**0.404**	50.6	297.1
+ PixelShuffle	0.874	**0.979**	**0.995**	0.115	0.406	**16.9**	**89.4**

Comparison with State-of-the-Art Methods. We compare the performance of our CTLC with several state-of-the-art monocular depth estimation methods. The results with NYU Depth V2 and KITTI are given in Table 3 and Table 4, respectively. Overall, our method outperforms all the other methods in most cases, which proves the remarkable superiority of our CTLC. The diversity of some detailed configurations over the different methods (e.g., differences of feature extraction backbone networks) makes it not easy to perform entirely fair comparisons for all the methods. However, ours achieves better performance even with ResNet-50 backbone than several methods that adopt much stronger backbone networks such as DenseNet with 100 layers [26] or ResNet-101 [7].

Ablation Study. We conduct an ablation study to analyze the effectiveness of each idea of our method. The results on NYU Depth V2 are shown in Table 5. From the normal UpProj block, the depth estimation accuracy is improved by changing the two convolution kernels in the upper branch to a pair of transposed long-range convolutions $(1 \times 25) \rightarrow (25 \times 1)$ (+ Long-range) without changing the number of parameters and FLOPs. Introducing a parallel CTLC block (+ Parallel CTLC) further improves accuracy. Finally, by replacing UnPool with PixelShuffle, both the number of parameters and FLOPs are significantly reduced while preserving accuracy. These results confirm the validity of each idea.

5   Conclusions

We introduced an upsampling block called Cascaded Transposed Long-range Convolutions (CTLC) for monocular depth estimation. Despite its simplicity of changing the kernel shape of two successive convolutions to spatially transposed long-range convolutions, it yields significantly better performance at reasonably smaller computational costs compared with existing upsampling blocks. We also demonstrated that the depth estimation network involving our final CTLC block outperforms the state-of-the-art depth estimation methods. One interesting suggestion is that changing the shape of the convolution kernels can boost the depth estimation performance, which will bring a new possibility for improving the performance of depth estimation in a way that can be easily applied to many types of network architectures. Applying the idea to other structured prediction tasks such as image segmentation would be an interesting future direction.

References

1. Eigen, D., Puhrsch, C., Fergus, R.: Depth map prediction from a single image using a multi-scale deep network. In: Proceedings of NeurIPS (2014)
2. Eigen, D., Fergus, R.: Predicting depth, surface normals and semantic labels with a common multi-scale convolutional architecture. In: Proceedings of ICCV (2015)
3. Laina, I., Rupprecht, C., Belagiannis, V.: Deeper depth prediction with fully convolutional residual networks. In: Proceedings of 3DV (2016)
4. Ma, F., Karaman, S.: Sparse-to-dense: depth prediction from sparse depth samples and a single image. In: Proceedings of ICRA (2018)
5. Godard, C., Aodha, O.M., Brostow, G.J.: Unsupervised monocular depth estimation with left-right consistency. In: Proceedings of CVPR (2017)
6. Xu, D., Ricci, E., Ouyang, W., Wang, X., Sebe, N.: Multi-scale continuous CRFs as sequential deep networks for monocular depth estimation. In: Proceedings of CVPR (2017)
7. Fu, H., Gong, M., Wang, C., Batmanghelich, K., Tao, D.: Deep ordinal regression network for monocular depth estimation. In: Proceedings of CVPR (2018)
8. Chen, Z., Badrinarayanan, V., Drozdov, G., Rabinovich, A.: Estimating depth from RGB and sparse sensing. In: Ferrari, V., Hebert, M., Sminchisescu, C., Weiss, Y. (eds.) ECCV 2018. LNCS, vol. 11208, pp. 176–192. Springer, Cham (2018). https://doi.org/10.1007/978-3-030-01225-0_11
9. Ron, D., Duan, K., Ma, C., Xu, N., Wang, S., Hanumante, S., Sagar, D.: Monocular depth estimation via deep structured models with ordinal constraints. In: Proceedings of 3DV (2018)
10. Heo, M., Lee, J., Kim, K.-R., Kim, H.-U., Kim, C.-S.: Monocular depth estimation using whole strip masking and reliability-based refinement. In: Ferrari, V., Hebert, M., Sminchisescu, C., Weiss, Y. (eds.) ECCV 2018. LNCS, vol. 11208, pp. 39–55. Springer, Cham (2018). https://doi.org/10.1007/978-3-030-01225-0_3
11. Silberman, N., Hoiem, D., Kohli, P., Fergus, R.: Indoor segmentation and support inference from RGBD images. In: Fitzgibbon, A., Lazebnik, S., Perona, P., Sato, Y., Schmid, C. (eds.) ECCV 2012. LNCS, vol. 7576, pp. 746–760. Springer, Heidelberg (2012). https://doi.org/10.1007/978-3-642-33715-4_54

12. Geiger, A., Lenz, P., Stiller, C., Urtasun, R.: Vision meets robotics: the KITTI dataset. IJRR **32**, 1231–1237 (2013)
13. Saxena, A., Chung, S.H., Ng, A.Y.: Learning depth from single monocular images. In: Proceedings of NeurIPS (2006)
14. Saxena, A., Sun, M., Ng, A.Y.: Make3D: learning 3D scene structure from a single still image. IEEE TPAMI **31**, 824–840 (2009)
15. Liu, B., Gould, S., Koller, D.: Single image depth estimation from predicted semantic labels. In: Proceedings of CVPR (2010)
16. Karsch, K., Liu, C., Kang, S.B.: Depth transfer: Depth extraction from video using non-parametric sampling. IEEE TPAMI **36**, 2144–2158 (2014)
17. Liu, F., Shen, C., Lin, G., Reid, I.: Learning depth from single monocular images using deep convolutional neural fields. IEEE TPAMI **38**, 2024–2039 (2016)
18. Lee, J.H., Heo, M., Kim, K.R., Kim, C.S.: Single-image depth estimation based on Fourier domain analysis. In: Proceedings of CVPR (2018)
19. Chen, L.C., Papandreou, G., Kokkinos, I., Murphy, K., Yuille, A.L.: DeepLab: semantic image segmentation with deep convolutional nets, atrous convolution, and fully connected CRFs. IEEE TPAMI **40**, 834–848 (2017)
20. Lee, J.H., Han, M.K., Ko, D.W., Suh, I.H.: From big to small: Multi-scale local planar guidance for monocular depth estimation. In: arXiv preprint arXiv:1907.10326. (2019)
21. Yang, M., Yu, K., Zhang, C., Li, Z., Yang, K.: DenseASPP for semantic segmentation in street scenes. In: Proceedings of CVPR (2018)
22. Irie, G., Kawanishi, T., Kashino, K.: Robust learning for deep monocular depth estimation. In: Proceedings of ICIP (2019)
23. Jiao, J., Cao, Y., Song, Y., Lau, R.: Look deeper into depth: monocular depth estimation with semantic booster and attention-driven loss. In: Ferrari, V., Hebert, M., Sminchisescu, C., Weiss, Y. (eds.) ECCV 2018. LNCS, vol. 11219, pp. 55–71. Springer, Cham (2018). https://doi.org/10.1007/978-3-030-01267-0_4
24. Cheng, X., Wang, P., Yang, R.: Depth estimation via affinity learned with convolutional spatial propagation network. In: Ferrari, V., Hebert, M., Sminchisescu, C., Weiss, Y. (eds.) ECCV 2018. LNCS, vol. 11220, pp. 108–125. Springer, Cham (2018). https://doi.org/10.1007/978-3-030-01270-0_7
25. Qi, X., Liao, R., Liu, Z., Urtasun, R., Jia, J.: GeoNet: geometric neural network for joint depth and surface normal estimation. In: Proceedings of CVPR (2018)
26. Kendall, A., Gal, Y.: What uncertainties do we need in Bayesian deep learning for computer vision? In: Proceedings of NeurIPS (2017)
27. He, K., Zhang, X., Ren, S., Sun, J.: Deep residual learning for image recognition. In: Proceedings of CVPR (2015)
28. Gan, Y., Xu, X., Sun, W., Lin, L.: Monocular depth estimation with affinity, vertical pooling, and label enhancement. In: Ferrari, V., Hebert, M., Sminchisescu, C., Weiss, Y. (eds.) ECCV 2018. LNCS, vol. 11207, pp. 232–247. Springer, Cham (2018). https://doi.org/10.1007/978-3-030-01219-9_14
29. Rengarajan, V., Balaji, Y., Rajagopalan, A.N.: Unrolling the shutter: CNN to correct motion distortions. In: Proceedings of CVPR (2017)
30. Tian, Z., He, T., Shen, C., Yan, Y.: Decoders matter for semantic segmentation: data-dependent decoding enables flexible feature aggregation. In: Proceedings of CVPR (2019)
31. Wang, X., Girshick, R., Gupta, A., He, K.: Non-local neural networks. In: Proceedings of CVPR (2018)
32. Huang, Z., Wang, X., Huang, L., Huang, C., Wei, Y., Liu, W.: CCNet: criss-cross attention for semantic segmentation. In: Proceedings of ICCV (2019)

33. Zhang, H., Goodfellow, I., Metaxas, D., Odena, A.: Self-attention generative adversarial networks. In: Proceedings of ICML (2019)
34. Szegedy, C., Vanhoucke, V., Ioffe, S., Shlens, J., Wojna, Z.: Rethinking the inception architecture for computer vision. In: Proceedings of CVPR (2016)
35. van Dijk, T., de Croon, G.: How do neural networks see depth in single images? In: Proceedings of ICCV (2019)
36. Shi, W., et al.: Real-time single image and video super-resolution using an efficient sub-pixel convolutional neural network. In: arXiv preprint arXiv:1609.05158. (2016)
37. Huang, G., Liu, Z., van der Maaten, L., Weinberger, K.Q.: Densely connected convolutional networks. In: Proceedings of CVPR (2017)
38. Sandler, M., Howard, A., Zhu, M., Zhmoginov, A., Chen, L.C.: MobileNetV2: Inverted residuals and linear bottlenecks. In: Proceedings of CVPR (2018)
39. Jégou, S., Drozdzal, M., Vázquez, D., Romero, A., Bengio, Y.: The one hundred layers tiramisu: fully convolutional densenets for semantic segmentation. In: Proceedings of CVPR Workshops (2017)
40. Lee, J.H., Kim, C.S.: Monocular depth estimation using relative depth maps. In: Proceedings of CVPR (2019)
41. Kuznietsov, Y., Stückler, J., Leibe, B.: Semi-supervised deep learning for monocular depth map prediction. In: Proceedings of CVPR (2017)
42. Garg, R., B.G., V.K., Carneiro, G., Reid, I.: Unsupervised CNN for single view depth estimation: geometry to the rescue. In: Leibe, B., Matas, J., Sebe, N., Welling, M. (eds.) ECCV 2016. LNCS, vol. 9912, pp. 740–756. Springer, Cham (2016). https://doi.org/10.1007/978-3-319-46484-8_45

Optimization, Statistical Methods, and Learning

Bridging Adversarial and Statistical Domain Transfer via Spectral Adaptation Networks

Christoph Raab(✉) ⓘ, Philipp Väth, Peter Meier, and Frank-Michael Schleif ⓘ

University of Applied Sciences Würzburg-Schweinfurt, Würzburg, Germany
{christoph.raab,frank-michael.schleif}@fhws.de

Abstract. Statistical and adversarial adaptation are currently two extensive categories of neural network architectures in unsupervised deep domain adaptation. The latter has become the new standard due to its good theoretical foundation and empirical performance. However, there are two shortcomings. First, recent studies show that these approaches focus too much on easily transferable features and thus neglect important discriminative information. Second, adversarial networks are challenging to train. We addressed the first issue by the alignment of transferable spectral properties within an adversarial model to balance the focus between the easily transferable features and the necessary discriminatory features, while at the same time limiting the learning of domain-specific semantics by relevance considerations. Second, we stabilized the discriminator networks training procedure by Spectral Normalization employing the Lipschitz continuous gradients. We provide a theoretical and empirical evaluation of our improved approach and show its effectiveness in a performance study on standard benchmark data sets against various other state of the art methods.

1 Introduction

The ability to learn sophisticated functions and non-trivial data distributions are some of the main advantages of deep learning networks. In recent years, this capability has led to a drastic increase in classification accuracy in computer vision [1] and natural language processing [2], making them state of the art models in these fields. These flexible network architectures tend to overfit on the given training distribution while showing poor generalization on related distributions. Especially in real application scenarios, the training and test domains are different, and the networks cannot generalize well to the test distribution [3].

Unsupervised deep domain adaptation is a commonly utilized technique where fine-tuning of networks [4] is insufficient, due to missing test labels or significant differences between related domains [5]. During the training process,

Electronic supplementary material The online version of this chapter (https://doi.org/10.1007/978-3-030-69535-4_28) contains supplementary material, which is available to authorized users.

© Springer Nature Switzerland AG 2021
H. Ishikawa et al. (Eds.): ACCV 2020, LNCS 12624, pp. 457–473, 2021.
https://doi.org/10.1007/978-3-030-69535-4_28

the networks learn discriminative features for the classification task and simultaneously learn an invariant representation by minimizing a statistical discrepancy between two or more domains [3,5,6]. Statistical adaptation [7] is usually integrated as a regularization term into the network. To some extent, these methods can be interpreted as minimizing the discrepancy between one or more (higher) central moments of the domains [6]. The obtained representation should neglect source-specific domain characteristics such as light and camera settings in an image classification task.

However, statistical adaptation networks are naturally restricted in creating invariant features concerning the chosen discrepancy measure. In contrast, domain adversarial neural networks (DANN) [8] consist of a classifier network and a domain classifier on top of the feature extractor (bottleneck output). The learning process is a min-max game related to GANs [9]. The network feature extractor tries to fool the domain classifier (discriminator) by learning an adversarial representation expected to be invariant to the source and target domain. Supported by the domain adaptation theory [10], minimizing the domain classifier loss and reverse propagating the resulting gradient to the feature extractor facilitates learning a transferable representation.

Recent work [7] revealed that DANN type networks focus too much on easily transferable features associated with large singular values, neglecting discriminative features assigned to mid-size singular values. We derive the spectral alignment of both domains during learning, reducing the influence of large singular values while balancing the relevance of source and target domain. Therefore, we consider transferable and discriminative features of the source and target domain as sufficiently similar after learning. Hence, it is not necessary to reduce the influence of high singular values. Additionally, when striving for domain invariant representations, a minimization of domain-specific influences [11] of the primary learning domain, i.e., small source singular values, should take place.

To bridge the gap between statistical adaptation and adversarial enhancement in a single loss function, we propose the *Relevance Spectral Loss* (RSL) within our *Adversarial Spectral Adaptation Network* (ASAN). It aligns the spectrum of the source and target domain in the learning and adaptation process and simultaneously minimizes the influence of domain-specific features relative to the overall spectrum. The proposed RSL is related to moment-matching networks [3,5,6], due to the relationship of (squared) singular values to the variance and the second central momentum. Hence, minimizing RSL aligns not only discrepancies between spectral properties [7], i.e., transferability and discriminability, of the adversarial features, but also the statistical properties, i.e., second-order momentum. To obtain better control of the gradients from the domain classifier and to lower training difficulties of adversarial networks, we utilize the process by Spectral Normalization [12] of the discriminator weights. The ASAN model shows superior classification performance compared to state of the art methods.

The contributions of this paper are summarized in the following:

- Proposing the *Relevance Spectral Loss* (RSL), underlying reasoning of RSL and integration of Spectral Normalization [12] into our *ASAN* (Sect. 3–3.4).

- Theoretical evaluation of the gradient and the learning properties of the proposed *Adversarial Spectral Adaptation Network* (Sect. 3.5–3.6).
- Empirical evaluation on benchmark datasets against competitive networks and an analysis of its properties showing the efficiency of ASAN (Sect. 4).

2 Background and Related Work

In unsupervised deep domain adaptation [3,6,8,13], we consider a labeled source dataset $D_s = \{\mathbf{X}_s, Y_s\} = \{\mathbf{x}_i, y_i\}_{i=1}^n \overset{i.i.d.}{\sim} p(\mathcal{S})$ in the source domain $\mathcal{S}$ and an unlabeled target dataset $D_t = \{\mathbf{X}_t\} = \{\mathbf{x}_j\}_{j=1}^m \overset{i.i.d.}{\sim} p(\mathcal{T})$ in the target domain $\mathcal{T}$ with same label space $\forall i, j : y_i, y_j \in \mathcal{Y}$ but different distributions $p(\mathcal{S}) \neq p(\mathcal{T})$. The overall goal is (still) to learn a classifier model, but additionally, it should generalize to a related target domain. The input feature space $\mathcal{X}$ is the initial representation of the source and target, i.e., $\mathbf{X}_s, \mathbf{X}_t \in \mathcal{X}$.

Initially, we consider a neural network $g : \mathcal{X} \to \mathcal{Y}$ with the parameters θ and given D_s, minimizing a classification loss - most often the cross-entropy $\mathcal{L}(g(\mathbf{x}; \theta), y) = -\sum_{i \in \mathcal{Y}} y_i log(g(\mathbf{x}_s; \theta)_i)$. The expected loss or risk of the network is $\mathcal{R}[\mathcal{L}(g(x; \theta), y)]$ and during learning the empirical risk approximates the risk by

$$\min_{\theta} \mathbb{E}[\mathcal{L}(g(\mathbf{X}_s; \theta), Y_s)]. \tag{1}$$

The network architecture is composed of multiple hidden layers followed by an output or classification layer. Consider $g(\mathbf{X}_s; \theta)_l = a(f(\mathbf{X}_s; \theta)_l)_l$ as the layer l with an activation function $a(\cdot)_l$ and parameter layer $f(\cdot)_l$ for the given source data and $g(\mathbf{X}_t; \theta)_l$ for the target data analogously. Recent network architectures roughly distinguish between the categories of statistical adaptation [3,5,6,13] and adversarial adaptation [7,14–17].

In *statistical* adaptation, approaches use one or more higher layers, i.e., the fully connected layers of the network, to adapt the output distributions of the (hidden) layers $g(\mathbf{X}_s; \theta)_l$ and $g(\mathbf{X}_t; \theta)_l$ [6]. This leads to very individualized approaches. To measure the difference between the output distributions of the network, a divergence measure $dist : g(\mathbf{X}_s; \theta)_l \times g(\mathbf{X}_t; \theta)_l \to \mathbb{R}_0^+$ is employed and added to the objective function:

$$\min_{\theta} \mathbb{E}[\mathcal{L}(g(\mathbf{X}_s; \theta), Y_s)] + \eta \cdot dist(g(\mathbf{X}_s; \theta)_l, g(\mathbf{X}_t; \theta)_l). \tag{2}$$

The dissimilarity measure is used as a regularization. The parameter $\eta \in [0, \infty)$ controls the trade-off between aligning the statistical divergence and minimizing the classification objective. A commonly used dissimilarity measure is the Maximum Mean Discrepancy (MMD) [18], which is the difference in mean of the domain data matrices in a reproducing kernel Hilbert space (RKHS). The minimization of MMD in the proposed networks can be seen as an alignment of statistical moments given a particular kernel, e.g., RBF-Kernel, of the two domains [19].

The authors of [6] proposed the Central Moment Discrepancy for domain adaptation, which explicitly minimizes higher central moments. The CORAL loss [3], minimizing the difference of the full covariance matrices between two domains. Our proposal is a particular case of CORAL. By aligning *only* the singular spectra of the domains, we align the covariances as a side effect. However, our ASAN minimizes a diagonal matrix, which is easier to learn, making it favorable over CORAL. An interpretation of our loss is the minimization of the second central moment between domains. Further, we do not rely on a particular kernel matrix nor kernel function, but any positive semi-definite (psd) kernel can be used. Due to this flexibility, it is also relatively easy to extend, e.g., relevance weighting as proposed in Sect. 3.3.

Since our ASAN combines statistical and *adversarial* adaptation, we now introduce adversarial learning: let the b_{th} layer of the network be the bottleneck layer and consider the network from the first to the b_{th} layer as the feature extractor $f : \mathcal{X} \to \mathcal{F}$ with parameters θ_f. From the $b + 1_{th}$ layer to the output, let $g : \mathcal{F} \to \mathcal{Y}$ be the classifier network with parameters θ_g, where $\mathcal{F}$ is a latent feature space and $\mathcal{Y}$ is the label space. Usually $b \leq l$ for the domain regularization layer. Additionally, let $d : \mathcal{F} \to \mathcal{C} = \{-1, 1\}$ be a domain classifier with parameters θ_d, predicting the domain of samples. Adversarial domain adaptation yields to minimize the loss of $d(\cdot)$, by propagating the reversed gradients from $d(\cdot)$ to $f(\cdot)$ and trying to confuse $d(\cdot)$ [8]. The Gradient-Reversal-Layer is defined as $R(x) = x$ and $\frac{\partial R}{\partial x} = -\lambda \mathbf{I}$, where $\mathbf{I}$ is the identity matrix. The invariant representation is achieved at the saddle point of

$$\min_{\theta_f, \theta_g, \theta_d} \mathbb{E}[\mathcal{L}(g(f(\mathbf{X}_s; \theta_f); \theta_g), Y_s))] + \lambda \mathbb{E}[\mathcal{L}_d(d(R[f(\mathbf{X}; \theta_f)]; \theta_d), Y_d)] \quad (3)$$

where $Y_d = [1n, -1m]$ are the domain labels of source size n and target size m and $\mathbf{X} = [\mathbf{X}_s, \mathbf{X}_t]$. The vanilla DANN [8] implements the cross-entropy for $\mathcal{L}_d$. Other authors [15] used the Wasserstein distance in $\mathcal{L}_d$ because of the intuitive expression of distribution differences [20]. DANN-type networks have also been extended to *normalized* Wasserstein distances [21].

The Conditional Domain Adaptation Network (CDAN) [16] enriches bottleneck features with class conditional confidences via multi-linear mapping $T : \mathcal{F} \times \mathcal{Y} \to \mathcal{F}_c$, which is fed into the discriminator, i.e., $d(T(\cdot))$. CDAN is the baseline in related networks and is extended in this work due to its good performance. The SDAN [22] integrates the Spectral Normalization (SN) [12] to obtain 1-Lipschitz continuous gradients. SN is also a building block in our network, but SDAN does no statistical alignment during learning.

None of the adversarial networks above explicitly define $dist(\cdot)$ in Eq. (3) in the same way as statistical deep learning does in Eq. (2). In this sense, the Batch-Spectral-Penalization (BSP) network is related to us in terms of shrinking the first k singular values, given features from $f(\cdot)$, to lower the influence of easily transferable features. However, our ASAN network explicitly defines $dist(\cdot)$ to align the spectra, which is crucial to be less dependent on the source feature spectrum. In [23], an element-wise comparison of distributions in the label space is implemented and [14] where $l < b$, aligning distributions in low-level filters.

Our proposed loss directly modifies adversarial and statistical characteristics in one loss, making it superior to discussed approaches.

3   Model

This section presents the main contribution: The reasoning behind the Relevance Spectral Loss (RSL) in Sect. 3.1 and 3.2. Afterward, the loss itself in Sect. 3.3 and the combination with SN in Sect. 3.4. Further, we analyze the learning and theoretical properties in Sect. 3.5 and 3.6, respectively. We present the architecture of the network in Fig. 1.

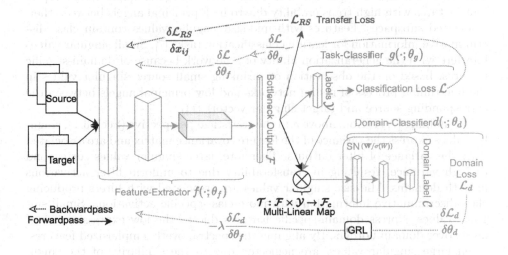

Fig. 1. Architectural overview of our proposed ASAN model, extending the CDAN [16] network by our $\mathcal{L}_{RS}$ and Spectral Normalization [12] (SN). GRL is the Gradient-Reversal-Layer [8].

3.1   Statistical Properties of Singular Values

Given the background in Sect. 2, let $\mathbf{X}_s^l$ and $\mathbf{X}_t^l$ be the output of the source and target from layer b or more precise the output of $f(\cdot)$ called bottleneck features. The Singular Value Decomposition (SVD) of these outputs is given with $\mathbf{X}_s^l = \mathbf{U}\mathbf{\Sigma}\mathbf{V}^T$ and $\mathbf{X}_t^l = \mathbf{L}\mathbf{T}\mathbf{R}^T$. Here $\mathbf{R}, \mathbf{V} \in \mathbb{R}^{d \times d}$, $\mathbf{U} \in \mathbb{R}^{n \times n}$ and $\mathbf{L} \in \mathbb{R}^{m \times m}$ are matrices. Further, $\mathbf{U}, \mathbf{L}, \mathbf{V}$ and $\mathbf{R}$ are column-orthogonal. $\mathbf{\Sigma}$ is a $n \times d$ matrix wherein all entries $\sigma_{ij} = 0$ iff $i \neq j$ and $\mathbf{T}$ is a $m \times d$ matrix wherein all entries $t_{ij} = 0$ iff $i \neq j$. Furthermore, by σ_k we denote the singular value in the k-th column of $\mathbf{\Sigma}$. For a linear covariance function, we can decompose the respective kernel with the eigenvalue decomposition and the SVD into

$$\mathbf{K} = \mathbf{C}\mathbf{D}\mathbf{C}^{-1} = \mathbf{X}^T\mathbf{X} = (\mathbf{V}\mathbf{\Sigma}\mathbf{U}^T)(\mathbf{U}\mathbf{\Sigma}\mathbf{V}^T) = \mathbf{C}\mathbf{\Sigma}^2\mathbf{C}^{-1}, \qquad (4)$$

where $\mathbf{C}$ are the eigenvectors (right singular vectors of $\mathbf{X}$) and $\mathbf{D}$ are the eigenvalues of $\mathbf{K}$. The singular values $\boldsymbol{\Sigma}$ of $\mathbf{X}$ are the square root eigenvalues of $\mathbf{K}$. Accordingly, the entries of the diagonal of $\mathbf{D}, \boldsymbol{\Sigma}^2$ give the variance of the columns of $\mathbf{K}$. Assuming that the expected values $\mathbb{E}_s(\mathbf{X}_s^l) = 0, \mathbb{E}_t(\mathbf{X}_t^l) = 0$, we got $tr(\boldsymbol{\Sigma}^2) = tr(\mathbf{X}^t \mathbf{X})$. Hence, minimizing the difference between $\boldsymbol{\Sigma}$ and $\mathbf{T}$ is the same as minimizing covariance matrices differences on the diagonal. Subsequently, we assume the same batch sizes for both domains during training.

3.2 Relationship of Feature Characteristics and Singular Values

Given $\boldsymbol{\Sigma}$ and $\mathbf{T}$ produced by a DANN [8] network, each spectrum associated with their features is separable into three areas. Large singular values represent features with high transferability due to high principal angels between their associated subspaces. Features with mid-size singular values contain class discriminative information for learning classification tasks [7]. Small singular values interfere with the generalization ability of a network because of domain-specific features, based on the observation of shrinking small source singular values in the fine-tuning process of neural networks and low principal angels between the corresponding source and target singular vectors [11].

Combining [7,11] from above and the statistical perspective (Sect. 3.1), singular values express the variance of the feature covariance matrix and are associated with the variance of filter outputs. Therefore, large singular values correspond to high variance, resulting in transferability due to uniform filter activations in both domains. Mid-size singular values are associated with filters producing class-discriminative information with more class-specific activations. Small singular values express domain-specific features due to the low expressiveness of filters over domain borders. By aligning the spectra, overly emphasized features, given large singular values, are neglected due to the similarity of the singular values, while the discriminative features are aligned. Aligning the statistics (Sect. 3.1) and shrink domain-specific signals [11] enables rich adaptation without the need for devastating transferable features [7], which is counter-intuitive in adaptation tasks.

3.3 Relevance Spectral Alignment

The approach [7] of shrinking the k highest or smallest k singular values from both domains for domain adaptation comes with the drawback that they are still related to the source spectrum. In some sense, it is counter-intuitive to shrink the influence of highly transferable features in the adaptation task. However, by aligning the most significant singular values, the network does not rely on one spectrum. The expressed variances of the features are the result of two domains. Following the same reasoning, the classification task is enhanced by not relying on the description of one but the alignment of two spectra. Only the domain-specific contents should be shrunk due to low expressiveness over domain borders [11], which we consider as relevance weighing of domain-specific features. Finally, we define our proposed Relevance Spectral loss as

$$\mathcal{L}_{RS} = ||(\boldsymbol{\Sigma}_n - \mathbf{T}_n) + (\boldsymbol{\Sigma}_k^2 - \mathbf{T}_k)||_F^2 \tag{5}$$

where $\boldsymbol{\Sigma}_n$ and $\mathbf{T}_n$ are the largest $n - k$ singular values and $\boldsymbol{\Sigma}_k$ and $\mathbf{T}_k$ are the smallest k singular values respectively. Further, $|| \cdot ||_F^2$ is the squared Frobenius norm. We follow the fine-tuning perspective of [11] and actively shrink only the k smallest source singular values. However, we show in Sect. 3.5 that the respective target singular values are also minimized during learning. The loss can be integrated into any layer as a regularization term or simultaneously used in multiple layers, as suggested by [13]. Here we use our proposed approach in the bottleneck layer.

$\mathcal{L}_{RS}$ has three main benefits. The network aligns the source and target spectrum during learning and depends not only on the source spectrum in $\mathcal{F}$. Assuming the properties as in Sect. 3.1, the network minimizes the difference of the diagonal entries of covariance matrices, making it related to [3,6], which adapts the second central moment. Domain-specific information [11] in the last k source singular values is minimized during the adversarial adaptation process. Simultaneously, discriminative and transferable features [7] in the largest $n - k$ are encouraged to be large and similar over domain borders. Summarizing, $\mathcal{L}_{RS}$ bridges statistical and enhances adversarial adaptation formulated in one loss, making ASAN favorable in simplicity and theoretical understanding.

3.4 Stabilize Discriminator Gradients

The domain classifier $d(\cdot)$ is related to the discriminator in GANs [22]. The GAN discriminator suffers from unstable gradients and saturation of training due to perfect predictions [24]. The occurrence of these problems is also possible in training the domain classifier. We integrate Spectral Normalization [12] in the domain classifier network to tackle this problem by regularizing the gradients to be 1-Lipschitz [12] and avoid the situation where the gradients coming from $d(\cdot)$ are devastating gradients from $\mathcal{L}_{RS}$. Let $\mathbf{W}$ be parameters in an arbitrary layer of $d(\cdot)$, then SN [12] has the form

$$\mathbf{W}_{sn} = \frac{\mathbf{W}}{\sigma(\mathbf{W})}, \tag{6}$$

where $\sigma(\mathbf{W})$ is the largest singular value of the parameters $\mathbf{W}$ and $||\mathbf{W}_{sn}||_{lip} \leq 1$. We implement SN [12] into every layer of the domain classifier, and SN takes place after the forward pass and before gradient propagation. In the following, we call the combination of $\mathcal{L}_{RS}$, SN and CDAN-baseline the *Adversarial Spectral Adaptation Network*. See Fig. 1 for an architectural overview.

3.5 Learning Procedure

From the perspective of statistical adaptation, data-driven gradients are common [3,6,13]. Therefore, we follow the suggestions and learn the RSL given the source

$\frac{\partial \mathcal{L}_{RS}}{\partial \mathbf{x}_s}$ and target data $\frac{\partial \mathcal{L}_{RS}}{\partial \mathbf{x}_t}$. Given the definition of the covariance-matrix in Eq. (4) and following [25,26], the derivative of a singular value σ and a squared singular value σ^2 w.r.t a sample point is

$$\frac{\partial \sigma_e}{\partial x_{ij}} = u_{ie} v_{je}, \qquad \frac{\partial \sigma_e^2}{\partial x_{ij}} = v_{ie} v_{je}. \qquad (7)$$

where u_{ie} and v_{je} are the components of the left and right singular vectors of $\mathbf{X}$. The derivative of the e_{th} singular value is given by the j_{th} feature of the i_{th} data-sample and is defined for any $\sigma_i \neq \sigma_j$. For a detailed description of the derivative of singular and eigen-values, see [25,26].

Looking once more at Eq. (5), the loss needs a derivative for each domain. The source-based derivative of $\mathcal{L}_{RS}$ is given by the derivative of σ_k w.r.t. the source data x_{ij}^s, therefore

$$\frac{\partial \mathcal{L}_{RSL}}{\partial x_{ij}^s} = \frac{\partial \sigma_e}{\partial x_{ij}^s} \sqrt{\Sigma_{e=1}^{n-k}(\sigma_e - t_e)^2 + \Sigma_{i=k+1}^{n}(\sigma_e^2 - t_e)^2}^2 \qquad (8)$$

$$= 2\Sigma_{e=1}^{n-k}(\sigma_e - t_e)\frac{\partial \sigma_e}{\partial x_{ij}^s} + 2\Sigma_{e=k+1}^{n}(\sigma_e^2 - t_e)\frac{\partial \sigma_e^2}{\partial x_{ij}^s} \qquad (9)$$

$$= 2\left(\Sigma_{e=1}^{n-k}(\sigma_e - t_e) \cdot |u_{ie} v_{je}| + \Sigma_{e=k+1}^{n}(\sigma_e^2 - t_e) \cdot |v_{ie} v_{je}|\right). \qquad (10)$$

Let l_{ie} and r_{je} be the singular vector components of the target data. The target-based derivative of $\mathcal{L}_{RS}$ is analogously given by t_k w.r.t target data x_{ij}^t as

$$\frac{\partial \mathcal{L}_{RSL}}{\partial x_{ij}^t} = -2\left(\Sigma_{e=1}^{n-k}(\sigma_e - t_e) \cdot |l_{ie} r_{je}| + \Sigma_{e=k+1}^{n}(\sigma_e^2 - t_e) \cdot |l_{ie} r_{je}|\right). \qquad (11)$$

The derivatives give some interesting insights to discuss. The absolute value of the singular-vector components is not a derivative product but was added afterward to avoid sign flipping of singular-vectors [27]. Sign flipping leads to wrongly directed gradients. Both derivations point in opposite directions leading to equilibrium at $\mathcal{L}_{RS} = 0$ because every iteration makes a step towards the respective other domain.

The difference between the $n - k$ largest singular values from the source and target is regularized by the component-wise correlation of the row and column spaces given a source or target data point. This prevents a too drastic focus on one of the spaces. The smallest k source singular values are regularized by the component-wise correlation of right singular vectors given feature x_{ij}. Consequently, the smallest k target singular values are mitigated while the target spectrum adapts to the source spectrum.

3.6   Theoretical Properties

The analysis of ASAN relies on the work of Zhao et al. [28], which extends the domain adaptation theory of Ben-David et al. [10]. To improve the readability, we adapt the former notation as follows: let $\varepsilon(s)$ and $\varepsilon(t)$ be the risk of classifier $g(\cdot)$

on the source and target domain. $\varepsilon(d)$ is the risk of the trained domain classifier $d(\cdot)$. Further, let $min\{\mathbb{E}_{p(S)}[|f_s - f_t|], \mathbb{E}_{p(T)}[|f_s - f_t|]\}$ be the expected divergence between the optimal labeling function of source f_s and target f_t w.r.t the source and target marginal distributions. Define $d_{\tilde{\mathcal{H}}}(p(S), p(T)) = \sup_{\tilde{h} \in \tilde{\mathcal{H}}} |Pr_{p(S)}(\tilde{h} = 1) - Pr_{p(T)}(\tilde{h} = 1)|$ as the disagreement of hypothesis $\tilde{h}$ on the source and target distribution given $\tilde{\mathcal{H}} = \{sgn(|h(\mathbf{x}) - h'(\mathbf{x})| - z) \mid h, h' \in \mathcal{H}, 0 \leq z \leq 1\}$, where $\mathcal{H}$ is a hypothesis class with finite VC dimension. Conveniently, this is referred to as the difference in marginal distribution [28]. The domain adaptation theory by [28] states that

$$\varepsilon(t) \leq \varepsilon(s) + d_{\tilde{\mathcal{H}}}(p(S), p(T)) + min\{\mathbb{E}_{p(S)}[|f_s - f_t|], \mathbb{E}_{p(T)}[|f_s - f_t|]\}. \quad (12)$$

Assuming a fixed representation obtained from $f(\cdot)$, it is shown for CDAN that learning $d(\cdot)$ yields an upper bound, i.e., $d_{\tilde{\mathcal{H}}}(p(S), p(T)) \leq \sup |\varepsilon(d)|$ where $z = 0$ [16]. This is done under the assumption that the hypothesis class $\mathcal{H}_d$ of $d(\cdot)$ is rich enough to contain $d_{\tilde{\mathcal{H}}}$, i.e., $d_{\tilde{\mathcal{H}}} \subset \mathcal{H}_d$ for $z = 0$. This is not an unrealistic scenario, since we are able to choose $d(\cdot)$ as a multi-layer perceptron approximating any function [8,16]. Following this reasoning, we assume that $\mathcal{H}_d$ is also rich enough that $d_{\tilde{\mathcal{H}}} \subset \mathcal{H}_d$ for $0 \leq z \leq 1$ and bound Eq. (12) by

$$\varepsilon(t) \leq \varepsilon(s) + \sup |\varepsilon(d)| + min\{\mathbb{E}_{p(S)}[|f_s - f_t|], \mathbb{E}_{p(T)}[|f_s - f_t|]\}. \quad (13)$$

See [8,16,28] for technical details about the proof. Hence, minimizing $\sup |\varepsilon(d)|$ by learning $d(\cdot; \theta_d)$, influenced by learning $\mathcal{L}_{RS}$, yields an upper bound for the risk of $g(\cdot)$ on the target domain, i.e., $f(\cdot)$ learns an invariant representation. In particular, the last term of Eq. 13, i.e., $min\{\cdot\}$, is the limitation of ASAN, since it does not approximate the labeling functions. Therefore, the performance of DANN-type networks is limited to differences in ground truth labeling of source and target, see Fig. 1 in [28].

Time Complexity. The SVD required for $\mathcal{L}_{RS}$ is $\mathcal{O}(min(p, d_f)^2)$ where p is the batch size and d_f is the dimension of the bottleneck space $\mathcal{F}$. The input space is usually high dimensional due to RGB image data, e.g., $d_x = 3 \times 224 \times 224 = 150.528$ in Resnet50 [1]. Given the computational complexity of convolution [29] and $d_f = 256 \ll d_x$ in ASAN, the computation of SVD at the bottleneck layer does not increase the complexity class of the network. Further, SN uses a *modified* power iteration converging in one iteration [12]. In practice, the time requirements of our extensions are neglectable in comparison to the Resnet50 training time.

4   Experiments

We provide the experimental validation of the ASAN architecture against state-of-the-art domain adaptation networks on standard benchmark datasets. The PyTorch code is published at https://github.com/ChristophRaab/ASAN.

4.1   Datasets

Office-31 [30] is an image data set with 4652 photographs, each assigned to one of the 31 classes. The dataset is divided into the three domains Amazon (**A**), **D**igital **S**ingle-**L**ens **R**eflex camera (**D**) and Webcam (**W**). The domain adaptation task is to learn on one domain and test on another. The shift between the domains results from differences in surroundings and camera characteristics. The tasks are **A→W, D→W, W→D, A→D, D→A** and **W→A**.

Image-Clef is another image dataset and was released in 2014 as part of the ImageClef domain adaptation challenge. It contains 12 common classes from domains Caltech-256 (**C**), ImageNet ILSVRC2012 (**I**), and PAS-CALVOC2012 (**P**) with an total of 1.800 photos. The test setting, again similar to Office-31, is **I→P, P→I, I→C, C→I, C→P** and **P→C**.

Office-Home [31] is more comprehensive and more difficult than Office-31 with 65 classes and 15.500 images in total. The dataset domains are Art (**A**), containing painting and sketches, Clipart (**C**), Product (**P**), containing product images without background, and real-world (**R**), containing objects from regular cameras. The test setting for domain adaptation is **A→C, A→P, A→R, C→A, C→P, C→R, P→A, P→C, P→R, R→A, R→C** and **R→P**.

4.2   Implementation Details

Architecture. Following the architectural style of CDAN+E (+E : Entropy reweighting)[16], the Resnet50 bottleneck network [1] pre-trained on Imagnet represents the feature extractor $f(\cdot)$. The classifier $g(\cdot)$ on top of $f(\cdot)$ is a fully connected network matching $\mathcal{F}$ to the task depended label space $\mathcal{Y}$, e.g., with 31 dimensions for Office-31. The classifier loss is cross-entropy. The domain classifier $d(\cdot)$ has three fully connected layers, while the first two have RELU activations and dropout, and the last has sigmoid activation. The input of the discriminator $d(\cdot)$ is the result of the multi-linear map $T(f, g) = f(\mathbf{X}) \otimes g(\mathbf{X})$ [16]. The loss of $d(\cdot)$ is binary-cross-entropy. In the adaptation process, the whole network is fine-tuned on the domain adaptation task. Beyond that, we extend the following: all discriminator layers are regularized with SN [12]. The proposed RSL is computed from the source and target bottleneck features and propagated to the feature extractor.

Competitive Methods. We compare our network against the following recent adversarial networks: Domain Adversarial Neural Network (**DANN**) [8], Conditional Domain Adversarial Network (**CDAN**) [16], Batch Spectral Penalization (**BSP**) [7], Spectral Normalized CDAN (**SDAN**) [22], Joint Adaptation Network (**JAN**) [13], Stepwise Adaptive Feature Norm (**SAFN**) [32] and Enhanced Transport Distance (**ETN**) [33]. Note that the authors of ETN have not provided the standard deviation in their results. But we still want to show the performance against very recent works.

Experimental Setup. We follow the standard study protocol [13] for unsupervised deep domain adaptation and use all available labeled source and unlabeled target data. The results are the mean and standard deviation given three random runs using the best-reported target accuracy per training process. All approaches use the same feature extractor. Reported results of former work are directly copied in the result Tables 1, 2, and 3 if the experimental designs are the same. The classifier and discriminator are trained from scratch with a learning rate ten times the feature extractors learning rate.

Parameters. The ASAN hyper-parameters are optimized as in [34] on the Office-31 dataset and set to $k = 11$ and $\eta = 10e^{-3}$ for all datasets. The supplementary gives more details about the tuning and behavior of k. All parameters are trained via mini-batch SGD with a momentum of 0.9. The initial learning rate $\zeta_0 = 0.001$ is modified by a progress based adjustment of $\zeta_p = \zeta_0(1 + \alpha \cdot p)^{-\beta}$, where $\alpha = 10$, $\beta = 0.75$, and $0 \leq p \leq 1$ depending on the training process as suggested by [8]. The λ parameter for the discriminator contribution to the overall loss is progressively increased from 0 to 1 based on $(1 - exp(-\delta \cdot x))/(1 + exp(-\delta \cdot x))$, with $\delta = 10$ as suggested for adversarial architectures [16].

4.3   Performance Results

We report the experiments for Office-31 in Table 1, for Image-Clef in Table 2, and Office-Home in Table 3 as accuracy (0–100%). Overall, **the ASAN architecture** outperforms the compared algorithms in two out of three datasets, while having the **overall best mean performance**. The results are obtained by optimizing the parameters only on the Office-31 dataset. This shows the robustness of the performance of our ASAN in terms of parameter sensitivity across changing tasks, making it a stable approach and easily applicable to related real-world scenarios. At Office-31, ASAN reports the best performance at four out of six comparisons, while showing the best mean performance. The second-best performing algorithm is SDAN, which also relies on CDAN and SN. However, due to no additional alignment, our ASAN is superior to SDAN by learning a bottleneck space, aligning both domain spectra. Further, the BSP approach seems to not create an invariant representation by shrinking the first k singular values competitive with ASANs spectral alignment (RSL). At Image-Clef, ASAN is only second-best in performance. However, better than related CDAN and SDAN. This suggests that learning our proposed RSL within ASAN improves CDAN, leading to better performance than related methods. At Office-Home, ASAN demonstrates outstanding performance by outperforming in ten out of twelve tasks. The results are comparable with the results of Office-31. The ASAN is best, ETN is second, and SDAN is third in mean performance. Again, RSL, combined with SN, is superior to related approaches such as BSP, SDAN, or CDAN and, further, outperforms very recent benchmark performances of ETN. Office-31 and Office-Home experiments demonstrate the ASANs parameter robustness:

the parameters optimized on Office-31 are used in different but related tasks and show robust generalization capacities. Robust parametrization and excellent performance make our ASAN favorable.

Table 1. Mean prediction **accuracy** with standard deviation on the **Office-31** dataset over three random runs.

Dataset	A→W	D→W	W→D	A→D	D→A	W→A	Avg.
Resnet [1]	68.4±0.2	96.7±0.1	99.3±0.1	68.9±0.2	62.5±0.3	60.7±0.3	76.1
DANN (2015) [8]	82.0±0.4	96.9±0.2	99.1±0.1	79.7±0.4	68.2±0.4	67.4±0.5	82.2
JAN (2017) [13]	85.4±0.3	97.4±0.2	99.8±0.2	84.7±0.3	68.6±0.3	70.0±0.4	84.3
CDAN (2018) [16]	93.1±0.2	98.2±0.2	**100±0**	89.8±0.3	70.1±0.4	68.0±0.4	86.6
BSP (2019) [7]	93.3±0.2	98.2±0.2	**100±0**	93.0±0.2	73.6±0.3	72.6±0.3	88.5
SDAN (2020) [22]	95.3±0.2	98.9±0.1	**100±0**	**94.7±0.3**	72.6±0.2	71.7±0.2	88.9
ETN (2020) [33]	92.1	**100.0**	**100.0**	88.0	71.0	67.8	86.2
ASAN (ours)	**95.6±0.4**	98.8±0.2	**100±0**	94.4±0.9	**74.7±0.3**	**74.0±0.9**	**90.0**

Table 2. Mean prediction **accuracy** with standard deviation on the **Image-clef** dataset over three random runs.

Dataset	I→P	P→I	I→C	C→I	C→P	P→C	Avg.
Resnet [1]	74.8±0.3	83.9±0.1	91.5±0.3	78.0±0.2	65.5±0.3	91.2±0.3	80.7
DANN (2015) [8]	75.0±0.6	86.0±0.3	96.2±0.4	87.0±0.5	74.3±0.5	91.5±0.6	85.0
JAN (2017) [13]	76.8±0.4	88.0±0.2	94.7±0.2	89.5±0.3	74.2±0.3	91.7±0.3	85.8
CDAN (2018) [16]	77.7±0.3	90.7±0.2	97.7±0.3	91.3±0.3	74.2±0.2	94.3±0.3	87.7
SAFN (2019) [32]	78.0±0.4	91.7±0.4	96.2±0.1	91.1±0.6	77.0±0.2	94.7±0.1	88.1
SDAN (2020) [22]	78.1±0.2	91.5±0.2	97.5±0.2	92.1±0.3	76.6±0.3	95.0±0.1	88.4
ETN (2020) [33]	**81.0**	91.7	**97.9**	**93.3**	**79.5**	**95.0**	**89.7**
ASAN (ours)	78.9±0.4	**92.3±0.5**	97.4±0.5	92.1±0.3	76.4±0.7	94.4±0.2	88.6

Table 3. Mean prediction **accuracy** on the **Office-Home** dataset over three random runs.

Dataset	A→C	A→P	A→R	C→A	C→P	C→R	P→A	P→C	P→R	R→A	R→C	R→P	Avg
Resnet [1]	34.9	50.0	58.0	37.4	41.9	46.2	38.5	31.2	60.4	53.9	41.2	59.9	46.1
DANN [8]	45.6	59.3	70.1	47.0	58.5	60.9	46.1	43.7	68.5	63.2	51.8	76.8	57.6
JAN [13]	45.9	61.2	68.9	50.4	59.7	61.0	45.8	43.4	70.3	63.9	52.4	76.8	58.3
CDAN [16]	49.0	69.3	74.5	54.4	66.0	68.4	55.6	48.3	75.9	68.4	55.4	80.5	63.8
BSP [7]	52.0	68.6	76.1	58.0	70.3	70.2	58.6	50.2	77.6	72.2	59.3	81.9	66.3
SDAN [22]	52.0	72.0	76.3	59.4	71.7	72.6	58.6	52.0	79.2	71.6	58.1	82.8	67.1
ETN [33]	51.3	71.9	**85.7**	57.6	69.2	**73.7**	57.8	51.2	79.3	70.2	57.5	82.1	67.3
ASAN	**53.6**	**73.0**	77.0	**62.1**	**73.9**	72.6	**61.6**	**52.8**	79.8	**73.3**	60.2	**83.6**	**68.6**

4.4   Convergence and Spectral Analysis

We report the convergence behavior of our RSL within the ASAN architecture compared to related networks in Fig. 2. The data is obtained by training on $\mathbf{A} \rightarrow \mathbf{W}$ from Office-31 dataset. The $\mathcal{A}$-Distance [35] is defined as $\mathcal{A} = 2(2 - 1\varepsilon)$, where ε is the error of the trained domain classifier. The $\mathcal{A}$-Distance is related to the $d_{\tilde{\mathcal{H}}}(\mathcal{S}, \mathcal{T})$ in Sect. 3.6 and measures the domain classifiers inability to distinguish the source and target domain. In contrast, a low $\mathcal{A}$-Distance is an indicator for an invariant representation [35]. The proposed RSL and the $\mathcal{A}$-Distance of our ASAN and BSP are shown in Fig. 2a, which we compare due to the commonality of manipulating the feature spectra. The interpolated lines (red, purple, brown) show the overall learning trend while the colored areas (blue, orange, green) show the fluctuation during learning. We observe that our network learns a better invariant representation via an almost all-time lower $\mathcal{A}$-Distance by not relying on only one spectrum. The plot shows that spectral differences represented by RSL are effectively reduced. Interestingly, the trend curves of the $\mathcal{A}$-Distance of ASAN and the RSL are similar in shape, allowing the presumption that learning RSL is related to learning an invariant representation, i. e., minimizing the $\mathcal{A}$-Distance. Figure 2b represents the target accuracy during learning. It is observable that the ASAN network converges very fast in a higher target accuracy than related approaches. Further, the saturation is very stable and practically does not change once reached. This behavior of ASAN is related to the Spectral Normalization by giving well-defined gradients back to the feature extractor. This assumption is verified in Fig. 2c, where the learning and evaluation process of ASAN itself and ASAN without Spectral Normalization (ASAN w/o SN) is plotted. The target accuracy of ASAN (red) remains stable while the accuracy of ASAN w/o SN (green), after reaching the best performance similar to ASAN, has a decline in target accuracy. In contrast, ASAN remains stable at high accuracy. The trends of train loss (brown for ASAN and purple for ASAN w/o SN) show an almost all-time lower learning loss of ASAN. The fluctuation of the train losses shows that ASAN (blue) is more stable than ASAN w/o SN

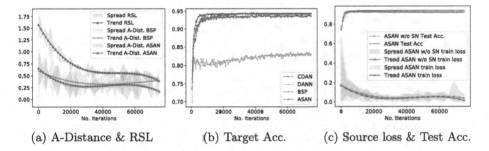

(a) A-Distance & RSL   (b) Target Acc.   (c) Source loss & Test Acc.

Fig. 2. Learning process of ASAN compared to related networks over time given $\mathbf{A} \rightarrow \mathbf{W}$ images from Office-31 dataset. Best viewed on computer display. (Color figure online)

(orange) and, most of the time, lower in value. Additional results on hyperparameter behavior and an ablation study are presented in the supplementary.

4.5   Feature Analysis

We evaluate the empirical feature representation of the bottleneck features given $A \rightarrow W$ images from the Office-31 dataset. The result is reported in Fig. 3 based on T-SNE [36]. The plot is split into two parts: the top row (Fig. 3a–3c) is a scatter plot of the bottleneck features of trained DANN, CDAN, and ASAN colored with ground truth domain labels. Blue shows the source, and red shows the target domain. ASAN shows the superiority of creating a domain invariant representation by almost perfectly assigning all red points to a blue cluster compared to CDAN and DANN. The bottom row (Fig. 3d–3f) shows the same representation but with classification labels. The class-label plots show that ASAN representations are easily classifiable by a neural network. However, some points are still located in the wrong cluster, representing the limitation of ASAN described in Sect. 3.6. The ASAN, DANN, and CDAN do not approximate the label distribution of target during learning. Therefore, the target accuracy of ASAN is bounded by the distribution differences of label distributions [28]. As a result, the label distribution difference is directly related to the remaining missclassified samples. However, as shown in the performance evaluation (Sect. 4.3), ASAN performs considerably better than remaining networks and is, therefore,

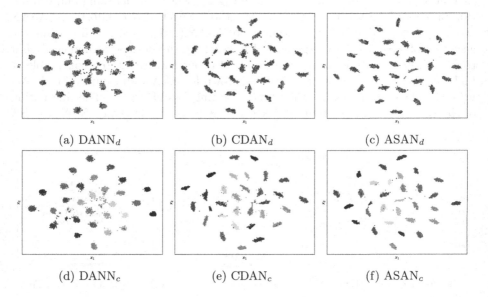

(a) DANN$_d$ (b) CDAN$_d$ (c) ASAN$_d$

(d) DANN$_c$ (e) CDAN$_c$ (f) ASAN$_c$

Fig. 3. T-SNE [36] of bottleneck features of selected networks given $A \rightarrow W$ images from Office-31 dataset. <Name>$_d$ and <Name>$_c$ show the outputs with ground truth domain and classification labels respectively. For the first row, blue shows the source, and red shows the target domain Best viewed in color. (Color figure online)

the preferable choice. Additional results to feature, convergence, and spectral analysis are offered in the supplementary material of the contribution.

5   Conclusion

We proposed the ASAN architecture, integrating Relevance Spectral Alignment and Spectral Normalization into the existing CDAN method. ASAN learns a bottleneck space, aligning both domain spectra while minimizing domain-specific information. The theoretical inspection of the gradients of RSL suggests that ASAN learns an invariant representation, empirically confirmed on three standard domain adaptation datasets. Further, ASAN has robust parametrization, making it easy to apply to other tasks. Compared to related approaches, ASAN is more stable and converges faster to a better solution. Prior theoretical evaluations of CDAN show that the performance of the domain classifier bounds the label-classifier of ASAN. Future research should target class conditional or cluster-based spectral alignment.

References

1. He, K., Zhang, X., Ren, S., Sun, J.: Deep residual learning for image recognition. In: Proceedings of the IEEE Computer Society Conference on Computer Vision and Pattern Recognition, Volume 2016-December, pp. 770–778 (2016)
2. Young, T., Hazarika, D., Poria, S., Cambria, E.: Recent trends in deep learning based natural language processing [review article]. IEEE Comput. Intell. Mag. **13**, 55–75 (2018)
3. Sun, B., Saenko, K.: Deep CORAL: correlation alignment for deep domain adaptation. In: Hua, G., Jégou, H. (eds.) ECCV 2016. LNCS, vol. 9915, pp. 443–450. Springer, Cham (2016). https://doi.org/10.1007/978-3-319-49409-8_35
4. Yosinski, J., Clune, J., Bengio, Y., Lipson, H.: How transferable are features in deep neural networks? In: Ghahramani, Z., Welling, M., Cortes, C., Lawrence, N.D., Weinberger, K.Q. (eds.) Advances in Neural Information Processing Systems 27, pp. 3320–3328. Curran Associates, Inc. (2014)
5. Long, M., Cao, Y., Wang, J., Jordan, M.I.: Learning transferable features with deep adaptation networks. In: Bach, F., Blei, D. (eds.) Proceedings of the 32nd International Conference on Machine Learning. Volume 37 of Proceedings of Machine Learning Research, Lille, France, pp. 97–105. PMLR (2015)
6. Zellinger, W., Grubinger, T., Lughofer, E., Natschläger, T., Saminger-Platz, S.: Central moment discrepancy (CMD) for domain-invariant representation learning. In: 5th International Conference on Learning Representations, ICLR 2017, Toulon, France, 24–26 April 2017, Conference Track Proceedings (2017)
7. Chen, X., Wang, S., Long, M., Wang, J.: Transferability vs. discriminability: batch spectral penalization for adversarial domain adaptation. In: Chaudhuri, K., Salakhutdinov, R. (eds.) Proceedings of the 36th International Conference on Machine Learning. Volume 97 of Proceedings of Machine Learning Research, Long Beach, California, USA, pp. 1081–1090. PMLR (2019)
8. Ganin, Y., Lempitsky, V.S.: Unsupervised domain adaptation by backpropagation. In: Proceedings of the 32nd International Conference on Machine Learning, ICLR 2015, Lille, France, 6–11 July 2015, pp. 1180–1189 (2015)

9. Goodfellow, I., et al.: Generative adversarial nets. In: Ghahramani, Z., Welling, M., Cortes, C., Lawrence, N.D., Weinberger, K.Q. (eds.) Advances in Neural Information Processing Systems 27, pp. 2672–2680. Curran Associates, Inc. (2014)
10. Ben-David, S., Blitzer, J., Crammer, K., Kulesza, A., Pereira, F., Vaughan, J.W.: A theory of learning from different domains. Mach. Learn. **79**, 151–175 (2010). https://doi.org/10.1007/s10994-009-5152-4
11. Chen, X., Wang, S., Fu, B., Long, M., Wang, J.: Catastrophic forgetting meets negative transfer: batch spectral shrinkage for safe transfer learning. In: Wallach, H., et al. (eds.) Advances in Neural Information Processing Systems 32, pp. 1908–1918. Curran Associates, Inc. (2019)
12. Miyato, T., Kataoka, T., Koyama, M., Yoshida, Y.: Spectral normalization for generative adversarial networks. In: International Conference on Learning Representations (2018)
13. Long, M., Zhu, H., Wang, J., Jordan, M.I.: Deep transfer learning with joint adaptation networks. In: Proceedings of the 34th International Conference on Machine Learning - Volume 70. ICML 2017, pp. 2208–2217. JMLR.org (2017)
14. Hoffman, J., et al.: CyCADA: cycle-consistent adversarial domain adaptation. In: Dy, J., Krause, A. (eds.) Proceedings of the 35th International Conference on Machine Learning. Volume 80 of Proceedings of Machine Learning Research, Stockholmsmässan, Stockholm, Sweden, pp. 1989–1998. PMLR (2018)
15. Shen, J., Qu, Y., Zhang, W., Yu, Y.: Wasserstein distance guided representation learning for domain adaptation. In: McIlraith, S.A., Weinberger, K.Q. (eds.) Proceedings of the Thirty-Second AAAI Conference on Artificial Intelligence, (AAAI-18), New Orleans, Louisiana, USA, 2–7 February 2018, pp. 4058–4065. AAAI Press (2018)
16. Long, M., Cao, Z., Wang, J., Jordan, M.I.: Conditional adversarial domain adaptation. In: Advances in Neural Information Processing Systems 31: Annual Conference on Neural Information Processing Systems 2018, NeurIPS 2018, 3–8 December 2018, Montréal, Canada, pp. 1647–1657 (2018)
17. Li, S., Liu, C.H., Xie, B., Su, L., Ding, Z., Huang, G.: Joint adversarial domain adaptation. In: Proceedings of the 27th ACM International Conference on Multimedia, New York, NY, USA, pp. 729–737. ACM (2019)
18. Gretton, A., Borgwardt, K.M., Rasch, M.J., Schölkopf, B., Smola, A.: A kernel two-sample test. J. Mach. Learn. Res. **13**, 723–773 (2012)
19. Li, Y., Swersky, K., Zemel, R.: Generative moment matching networks. In: Bach, F., Blei, D. (eds.) Proceedings of the 32nd International Conference on Machine Learning. Volume 37 of Proceedings of Machine Learning Research, Lille, France, pp. 1718–1727. PMLR (2015)
20. Arjovsky, M., Chintala, S., Bottou, L.: Wasserstein generative adversarial networks. In: Precup, D., Teh, Y.W. (eds.) Proceedings of the 34th International Conference on Machine Learning. Volume 70 of Proceedings of Machine Learning Research., International Convention Centre, Sydney, Australia, pp. 214–223 PMLR (2017)
21. Balaji, Y., Chellappa, R., Feizi, S.: Normalized Wasserstein for mixture distributions with applications in adversarial learning and domain adaptation. In: 2019 IEEE/CVF International Conference on Computer Vision (ICCV), pp. 6499–6507. IEEE (2019)
22. Zhao, L., Liu, Y.: Spectral normalization for domain adaptation. Information **11**, 68 (2020)

23. Rakshit, S., Chaudhuri, U., Banerjee, B., Chaudhuri, S.: Class consistency driven unsupervised deep adversarial domain adaptation. In: 2019 IEEE/CVF Conference on Computer Vision and Pattern Recognition Workshops (CVPRW), pp. 657–666. IEEE (2019)

24. Arjovsky, M., Bottou, L.: Towards principled methods for training generative adversarial networks. In: 5th International Conference on Learning Representations, ICLR 2017, Toulon, France, 24–26 April 2017, Conference Track Proceedings. OpenReview.net (2017)

25. Papadopoulo, T., Lourakis, M.I.A.: Estimating the Jacobian of the singular value decomposition: theory and applications. In: Vernon, D. (ed.) ECCV 2000. LNCS, vol. 1842, pp. 554–570. Springer, Heidelberg (2000). https://doi.org/10.1007/3-540-45054-8_36

26. Petersen, K.B., Pedersen, M.S.: The Matrix Cookbook (2008)

27. Bro, R., Acar, E., Kolda, T.G.: Resolving the sign ambiguity in the singular value decomposition. J. Chemometr. **22**, 135–140 (2008)

28. Zhao, H., Combes, R.T.D., Zhang, K., Gordon, G.: On learning invariant representations for domain adaptation. In: Chaudhuri, K., Salakhutdinov, R. (eds.) Proceedings of the 36th International Conference on Machine Learning. Volume 97 of Proceedings of Machine Learning Research, Long Beach, California, USA, pp. 7523–7532. PMLR (2019)

29. He, K., Sun, J.: Convolutional neural networks at constrained time cost. In: 2015 IEEE Conference on Computer Vision and Pattern Recognition (CVPR), vol. 15, pp. 5353–5360. IEEE (2015)

30. Saenko, K., Kulis, B., Fritz, M., Darrell, T.: Adapting visual category models to new domains. In: Daniilidis, K., Maragos, P., Paragios, N. (eds.) ECCV 2010. LNCS, vol. 6314, pp. 213–226. Springer, Heidelberg (2010). https://doi.org/10.1007/978-3-642-15561-1_16

31. Venkateswara, H., Eusebio, J., Chakraborty, S., Panchanathan, S.: Deep hashing network for unsupervised domain adaptation. In: 2017 IEEE Conference on Computer Vision and Pattern Recognition (CVPR), Volume 2017-January, pp. 5385–5394. IEEE (2017)

32. Xu, R., Li, G., Yang, J., Lin, L.: Larger norm more transferable: an adaptive feature norm approach for unsupervised domain adaptation. In: 2019 IEEE/CVF International Conference on Computer Vision (ICCV), Volume 2019-October, pp. 1426–1435. IEEE (2019)

33. Li, M., Zhai, Y.M., Luo, Y.W., Ge, P.F., Ren, C.X.: Enhanced transport distance for unsupervised domain adaptation. In: IEEE/CVF Conference on Computer Vision and Pattern Recognition (CVPR), pp. 13936–13944 (2020)

34. Zhong, E., Fan, W., Yang, Q., Verscheure, O., Ren, J.: Cross validation framework to choose amongst models and datasets for transfer learning. In: Balcázar, J.L., Bonchi, F., Gionis, A., Sebag, M. (eds.) ECML PKDD 2010. LNCS (LNAI), vol. 6323, pp. 547–562. Springer, Heidelberg (2010). https://doi.org/10.1007/978-3-642-15939-8_35

35. Ben-David, S., Blitzer, J., Crammer, K., Pereira, F.: Analysis of representations for domain adaptation. In: Schölkopf, B., Platt, J.C., Hoffman, T. (eds.) Advances in Neural Information Processing Systems 19, pp. 137–144. MIT Press (2007)

36. van der Maaten, L., Hinton, G.: Visualizing data using t-SNE. J. Mach. Learn. Res. **164**, 10 (2008)

Large-Scale Cross-Domain Few-Shot Learning

Jiechao Guan[1], Manli Zhang[1], and Zhiwu Lu[2(✉)]

[1] School of Information, Renmin University of China, Beijing, China
[2] Beijing Key Laboratory of Big Data Management and Analysis Methods,
Gaoling School of Artificial Intelligence, Renmin University of China, Beijing, China
luzhiwu@ruc.edu.cn

Abstract. Learning classifiers for novel classes with a few training examples (shots) in a new domain is a practical problem setting. However, the two problems involved in this setting, few-shot learning (FSL) and domain adaption (DA), have only been studied separately so far. In this paper, for the first time, the problem of large-scale cross-domain few-shot learning is tackled. To overcome the dual challenges of few-shot and domain gap, we propose a novel Triplet Autoencoder (TriAE) model. The model aims to learn a latent subspace where not only transfer learning from the source classes to the novel classes occurs, but also domain alignment takes place. An efficient model optimization algorithm is formulated, followed by rigorous theoretical analysis. Extensive experiments on two large-scale cross-domain datasets show that our TriAE model outperforms the state-of-the-art FSL and domain adaptation models, as well as their naive combinations. Interestingly, under the conventional large-scale FSL setting, our TriAE model also outperforms existing FSL methods by significantly margins, indicating that domain gaps are universally present.

1 Introduction

Large-scale visual recognition has been the central focus of the computer vision research recently. It faces two major challenges: lack of sufficient training samples for each class and the significant domain gap between the training and test data. Both problems have long been identified, which leads to two extensively studied areas: few-shot learning (FSL) [1–3] and domain adaption (DA) [4,5].

A FSL model is provided with a set of source classes and a set of target ones with no overlap in the label space between the two. Each source class has sufficient labeled samples, whereas each target class has only a few labeled samples. The goal of FSL is thus to learn transferable knowledge from the source classes, and develop a robust recognition model for recognizing novel/target

---

Electronic supplementary material The online version of this chapter (https://doi.org/10.1007/978-3-030-69535-4_29) contains supplementary material, which is available to authorized users.

H. Ishikawa et al. (Eds.): ACCV 2020, LNCS 12624, pp. 474–491, 2021.
https://doi.org/10.1007/978-3-030-69535-4_29

object classes. Meta-learning based FSL methods [6–14] have shown state-of-the-art performance on several medium-scale benchmarks (e.g. miniImageNet [15]). Recently, large-scale FSL [16–18], which focuses on more challenging datasets such as the ImageNet 1K classes, starts to attract increasing attentions.

Different from FSL, domain adaptation (DA) [4,5] aims to generalize a learned model to different domains but assumes that the class labels are shared between the training and test domains. Recent DA methods focus on the unsupervised domain adaptation (UDA) setting, under which the target domain training data are unlabeled [19–24]. It is thus clear that both FSL and DA problems need to be solved by knowledge transfer. However, due to the different problem settings, they are largely treated as two separate problems.

In this paper, we argue that the two problems are actually closely intertwined, and thus should be solved jointly. In particular, existing large-scale FSL methods [16–18,25–27] assume that both source and target classes come from the same domain. However, in real-world scenarios, the target novel classes are not only represented by a handful of examples, but also need to be recognized from a

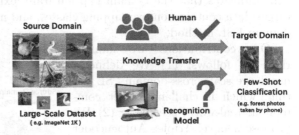

Fig. 1. Illustration of our proposed large-scale cross-domain few-shot learning setting.

domain different from the domain of the source classes (see Fig. 1). For example, it is assumed that an object recognizer is trained with the ImageNet 1K dataset and installed on a user's mobile phone. When the user comes across some new object categories during exploring a forest, he/she resorts to a FSL model to recognize the new classes. The domain gap between the images in ImageNet and the photos taken by her/his phone in the forest are clearly very different in style. Conventional FSL methods thus become inadequate because such domain changes between the source and target classes are not considered. We therefore define a new large-scale cross-domain FSL problem (see Fig. 1). It is clearly more challenging than the FSL and DA problems on their own. Moreover, it is also noted that a naive combination of existing FSL and domain adaptation methods does not offer a valid solution (see Fig. 4).

To solve this challenging problem, we propose a novel Triplet Autoencoder (TriAE) model. As illustrated in Fig. 2, it addresses both FSL and domain adaptation problems simultaneously by learning a joint latent subspace [22,28,29]. Intuitively, since class name semantic embedding is domain invariant, we utilize a semantic space (e.g., a word embedding space [30]) to learn the latent space. There are now three spaces: the visual feature space of the source domain, the visual feature space of the target domain, and the semantic space of both source and target classes. To construct the relationship among these three spaces, we choose to learn a shared latent subspace. Specifically, we leverage an encoder-decoder paradigm [31–34] between the semantic space and latent subspace for knowledge transfer (essential for FSL), and also learn encoder-decoder projections between the latent subspace and visual feature space. Domain alignment then takes place in the same latent subspace. The resultant model (see Fig. 3) can be decomposed into a pair of dual autoencoders (one for modeling source classes, and the other for target novel classes). We provide an efficient model optimization algorithm, followed by rigorous theoretical analysis. Extensive experiments on two large-scale cross-domain datasets show that our TriAE outperforms the state-of-the-art FSL and domain adaptation models. Importantly, it is noted that under the conventional large-scale FSL setting (i.e., without explicit domain gap), the proposed model also beats existing FSL models by significant margins. This indicates that the domain gap naturally exists in FSL as the source and target data contain non-overlapping classes, and needs to be bridged by a cross-domain FSL method.

Our contributions are summarized as follows: (1) We define a new large-scale cross-domain FSL setting, which is challenging yet common in real-world scenarios. (2) We propose a novel Triplet Autoencoder model, which seamlessly unifies FSL and domain adaptation into the same framework. (3) We provide an efficient model optimization algorithm for training the proposed TriAE model, followed by rigorous theoretical analysis. (4) The proposed TriAE model is shown to achieve the state-of-the-art performance on both new and conventional large-scale FSL problems. The code and dataset will be released soon.

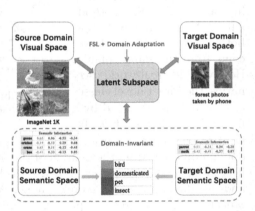

Fig. 2. Schematic of the proposed TriAE model for large-scale cross-domain FSL.

2   Related Work

Large-Scale FSL. Meta-learning based approaches [6–14, 35–37] have achieved great success on small- or medium-scale FSL datasets. More recently, large-scale FSL [16–18, 25–27, 38] becomes topical. Squared Gradient Magnitude (SGM) [16] proposes a Feature Hallucination strategy to augment target classes' samples based on target class centroids. Covariance-Preserving Adversarial Augmentation Network (CP-AAN) [27] resorts to adversarial learning for covariance-preserving target feature hallucination. Instead of feature synthesis, Parameter Prediction from Activations (PPA) [17] aims to explore the relationship between the logistic regression parameters and activations in a deep neural network, and

Large-Scale Diffusion (LSD) [26] constructs a large-scale semi-supervised graph over external data for label propagation. Knowledge Transfer with Class Hierarchy (KTCH) [18] constructs a tree-structured class hierarchy to formulate hierarchical classification loss functions for representation learning. However, existing large-scale FSL methods assume that both source and target classes come from the same domain. When they are deployed under the new cross-domain FSL setting, they are clearly beaten by our TriAE model (see Tables 1 and 2). Note that although cross-domain dataset (i.e. miniImageNet → CUB [39]) is used for FSL in [40], it is just used to evaluate the cross-dataset performance of conventional FSL methods. In contrast, we consider a dataset where the domain gap is much bigger (e.g. natural images vs. cartoon-like ones) and develop a model to specifically tackle the problem.

Domain Adaptation. Domain adaptation [4,5] aims to generalize the learned model to different domains. To alleviate the domain shift, some domain adaptation methods find a shared latent space that both source and target domains can be mapped into [22,28,41–45], to ensure that in the shared space the learned model cannot distinguish whether a sample is from the source or target domain [20–22,46,47]. Recently, adversarial learning [19–24] has also shown promising results on domain adaptation. Among these domain adaptation models, Few-shot Adversarial Domain Adaptation (FADA) [22] takes on board the few-shot domain adaptation setting, which is most similar to our proposed large-scale cross-domain FSL setting. But there is a clear difference: FADA assumes that the source and target domains share the same set of object classes, whereas in our proposed setting, the source and target domains consist of two non-overlapped sets of object classes (i.e. source and target classes). Moreover, FADA focuses on few-shot domain adaptation over medium-scale datasets (e.g. Office [48]), while we construct two new large-scale datasets from ImageNet2012/2010 and ImageNet2012/DomainNet (for cross-domain FSL), which are both more challenging yet more realistic for performance evaluation.

Domain-Invariant Semantic Space. The semantic space has been regarded as domain-invariant to handle numerous machine learning problems where the source and target classes are non-overlapped or from different domains (e.g., zero-shot learning [49–52] in computer vision, and machine translation [53,54] in natural language processing). However, few previous works have adopted the semantic space for solving the large-scale FSL problem. One exception is [18], but cross-domain FSL is not considered. Note that, after obtaining the class names in real-world application scenarios, it is trivial to project these class names into the semantic space [30,55]. Therefore, we take advantage of this easily-accessible semantic information into our large-scale FSL optimization framework, for knowledge transfer from the source classes to the target ones.

3   Methodology

3.1   Problem Definition

We formally define the large-scale cross-domain FSL problem as follows. Let C_s denote the set of source classes and C_t denote the set of target classes ($C_s \bigcap C_t = \emptyset$). We are given a large-scale sample set $\mathcal{D}_s$ from source classes, a few-shot sample set $\mathcal{D}_t$ from target classes, and a test set $\mathcal{T}$ from target classes. For the large-scale sample set $\mathcal{D}_s$, we collect the visual features of all samples as $\mathbf{X}^s \in R^{d \times n_s}$, where d is the dimension of visual feature vectors and n_s is the number of samples. We further collect the semantic representations of all samples in $\mathcal{D}_s$ as $\mathbf{Y}^s \in R^{k \times n_s}$, where $\mathbf{y}_i^s$ (i.e. the i-th column vector of $\mathbf{Y}^s$) is set as a k-dimensional class semantic embedding according to the source class label of the i-th sample ($i = 1, ..., n_s$). Similarly, the few-shot sample set $\mathcal{D}_t$ can be represented as $\mathbf{X}^t \in R^{d \times n_t}$ and $\mathbf{Y}^t \in R^{k \times n_t}$, where $n_t = K \times |C_t|$ ($n_t \ll n_s$) is the number of samples under the K-shot learning setting. In this paper, the class semantic embeddings of both source and target classes are extracted using the same word2vec model. Note that the source and target classes are assumed to come from different domains under our new FSL setting. For simplicity, we utilize the same source data pre-trained ResNet50 [56] to extract visual features for both source and target classes. The goal of large-scale cross-domain FSL is to obtain good classification results on the test set $\mathcal{T}$.

3.2   Latent Representation Learning over Source Classes

As shown in Fig. 3, a Triplet Autoencoder is proposed to model the triple relationship among $\mathbf{X}^s$, $\mathbf{X}^t$, and $\mathbf{Y}^s/\mathbf{Y}^t$. Following the idea of training the well-known triplet network [57], this triplet relationship can be resolved by first modeling the relationship between $\mathbf{X}^s$ and $\mathbf{Y}^s$, and then modeling the relationship between $\mathbf{X}^t$ and $\mathbf{Y}^t$. In other words, we choose to decompose the proposed TriAE into a pair of dual autoencoders: one is designed for latent representation learning over source classes (see Eq. (1)), and the other is designed for the subsequent domain adaptation and FSL over target classes (see Eq. (6)).

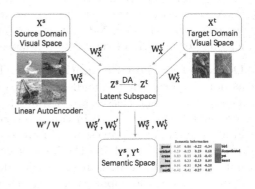

Fig. 3. Architecture of Triplet Autoencoder (TriAE). Note that only linear autoencoder is employed as the backbone model.

Concretely, for latent representation learning over source classes, we utilize a linear matrix projection and its transpose to mimic the encoder-decoder paradigm between the latent subspace and visual feature space/semantic embedding space. This results in a dual autoencoder model, which is optimized by minimizing the objective function:

$$
\begin{aligned}
F^{(s)} = {}& \|\mathbf{W}_X^{s\prime}\mathbf{X}^s - \mathbf{Z}^s\|_F^2 + \|\mathbf{X}^s - \mathbf{W}_X^s\mathbf{Z}^s\|_F^2 + \eta\|\mathbf{W}_X^s\|_F^2 \\
&+ \gamma(\|\mathbf{W}_Y^{s\prime}\mathbf{Y}^s - \mathbf{Z}^s\|_F^2 + \|\mathbf{Y}^s - \mathbf{W}_Y^s\mathbf{Z}^s\|_F^2 + \eta\|\mathbf{W}_Y^s\|_F^2)
\end{aligned}
\tag{1}
$$

where $\mathbf{Z}^s \in R^{r\times n_s}$ is the latent representation of training samples from source classes, r is the dimensionality of the latent subspace, $\mathbf{W}_X^s(\in R^{d\times r})/\mathbf{W}_Y^s(\in R^{k\times r})$ is the projection matrix from the latent subspace to the visual feature space/semantic embedding space, η is a positive regularization parameter, and γ is a positive weighting coefficient that controls the importance of the two autoencoders (i.e. the first three terms and the last three terms). In this work, we empirically set $\eta = 0.001$.

The optimization problem min $F^{(s)}$ can be solved by two alternating steps: 1) $\hat{\mathbf{W}}_X^s, \hat{\mathbf{W}}_Y^s = \arg\min_{\mathbf{W}_X^s,\mathbf{W}_Y^s} F^{(s)}(\mathbf{W}_X^s, \mathbf{W}_Y^s, \hat{\mathbf{Z}}^s)$; 2) $\hat{\mathbf{Z}}^s = \arg\min_{\mathbf{Z}^s} F^{(s)}(\hat{\mathbf{W}}_X^s, \hat{\mathbf{W}}_Y^s, \mathbf{Z}^s)$. In this work, $\hat{\mathbf{Z}}^s$ is initialized with the partial least squares (PLS) regression model [58]. Firstly, by setting $\frac{\partial F^{(s)}(\mathbf{W}_X^s,\mathbf{W}_Y^s,\hat{\mathbf{Z}}^s)}{\partial \mathbf{W}_X^s} = 0$ and $\frac{\partial F^{(s)}(\mathbf{W}_X^s,\mathbf{W}_Y^s,\hat{\mathbf{Z}}^s)}{\partial \mathbf{W}_Y^s} = 0$, we have the following two equations:

$$
(\mathbf{X}^s\mathbf{X}^{s\prime} + \eta\mathbf{I})\mathbf{W}_X^s + \mathbf{W}_X^s(\hat{\mathbf{Z}}^s\hat{\mathbf{Z}}^{s\prime}) = 2\mathbf{X}^s\hat{\mathbf{Z}}^{s\prime}
\tag{2}
$$

$$
(\mathbf{Y}^s\mathbf{Y}^{s\prime} + \eta\mathbf{I})\mathbf{W}_Y^s + \mathbf{W}_Y^s(\hat{\mathbf{Z}}^s\hat{\mathbf{Z}}^{s\prime}) = 2\mathbf{Y}^s\hat{\mathbf{Z}}^{s\prime}
\tag{3}
$$

Equation (2)–(3) can both be solved efficiently by the Matlab built-in function 'Sylvester' with the Bartels-Stewart algorithm [59]. Secondly, by setting $\frac{\partial F^{(s)}(\hat{\mathbf{W}}_X^s,\hat{\mathbf{W}}_Y^s,\mathbf{Z}^s)}{\partial \mathbf{Z}^s} = 0$, we can obtain a linear equation:

$$
(\hat{\mathbf{W}}_X^{s\prime}\hat{\mathbf{W}}_X^s + \gamma\hat{\mathbf{W}}_Y^{s\prime}\hat{\mathbf{W}}_Y^s + (1+\gamma)\mathbf{I})\mathbf{Z}^s = 2(\hat{\mathbf{W}}_X^{s\prime}\mathbf{X}^s + \gamma\hat{\mathbf{W}}_Y^{s\prime}\mathbf{Y}^s)
\tag{4}
$$

Since $\hat{\mathbf{W}}_X^{s\prime}\hat{\mathbf{W}}_X^s + \gamma\hat{\mathbf{W}}_Y^{s\prime}\hat{\mathbf{W}}_Y^s + (1+\gamma)\mathbf{I}$ is a positive definite matrix, Eq. (4) has one explicit unique solution.

3.3 Domain Adaptation and Few-Shot Learning over Target Classes

Once the optimal latent representation $\hat{\mathbf{Z}}^s$ is learned over the sufficient training samples from source classes, we further exploit it for the subsequent domain adaptation and FSL over target classes. Similar to most domain adaptation methods based on shared subspace learning [22,28,43–45], we choose to learn a latent subspace in which the learner is unable to distinguish whether a sample is from the source or target domain. The domain adaptation loss function is defined as:

$$
F^{(a)} = \sum_{i=1}^{n_s}\sum_{j=1}^{n_t}[(\boldsymbol{\omega}'(\hat{\mathbf{z}}_i^s - \mathbf{z}_j^t))^2 + \lambda\|\hat{\mathbf{z}}_i^s - \mathbf{z}_j^t\|_2^2]
\tag{5}
$$

Algorithm 1: Triplet Autoencoder (TriAE)

Input: Visual features $\mathbf{X}^s, \mathbf{X}^t$; semantic representations $\mathbf{Y}^s, \mathbf{Y}^t$; parameters
$\quad \beta, \gamma, \lambda$
Output: $\hat{\mathbf{W}}^t_X, \hat{\mathbf{W}}^t_Y$
1. Initialize $\hat{\mathbf{Z}}^s$ with the PLS regression model [58];
while *a stopping criterion is not met* **do**
$\quad$ 2. With the learned representation $\hat{\mathbf{Z}}^s$, find $\hat{\mathbf{W}}^s_X$ and $\hat{\mathbf{W}}^s_Y$ by solving
$\quad$ Eqs. (2)-(3);
$\quad$ 3. With the learned projections $\hat{\mathbf{W}}^s_X$ and $\hat{\mathbf{W}}^s_Y$, update $\hat{\mathbf{Z}}^s$ by solving Eq. (4);
end
4. Initialize $\hat{\mathbf{Z}}^t$ with the PLS regression model [58];
while *a stopping criterion is not met* **do**
$\quad$ 5. With the learned representations $\hat{\mathbf{Z}}^s$ and $\hat{\mathbf{Z}}^t$, find $\hat{\omega}$ in Eq. (8) according
$\quad$ to Prop. 1;
$\quad$ 6. With the learned representations $\hat{\mathbf{Z}}^t$, find $\hat{\mathbf{W}}^t_X$ and $\hat{\mathbf{W}}^t_Y$ by solving
$\quad$ Eqs. (9)-(10);
$\quad$ 7. With the learnt projections $\hat{\mathbf{W}}^t_X, \hat{\mathbf{W}}^t_Y$, and $\hat{\omega}$, update $\hat{\mathbf{Z}}^t$ by solving
$\quad$ Eq. (11);
end
8. Return $\hat{\mathbf{W}}^t_X$ and $\hat{\mathbf{W}}^t_Y$.

---

where $\hat{\mathbf{z}}^s_i$ is the optimal latent representation of i-th sample from the source domain (i.e. $\hat{\mathbf{Z}}^s = [\hat{\mathbf{z}}^s_1, ..., \hat{\mathbf{z}}^s_{n_s}]$), $\mathbf{z}^t_j$ is the latent representation of j-th sample from the target domain, ω is a normalized linear projection/column vector (i.e. $\|\omega\|_2 = 1$) to map the latent representations ($\hat{\mathbf{z}}^s_i$ & $\mathbf{z}^t_j$) into the real field R^1, and λ is a positive regularization parameter. In the above loss function, the first term aims to maximize the confusion between $\hat{\mathbf{z}}^s_i$ and $\mathbf{z}^t_j$ in the projected space R^1, and the second term aims to maximize the confusion in the original latent space.

For FSL over target classes, we propose another dual autoencoder model, similar to that used in Eq. (1). Let $\mathbf{Z}^t = [\mathbf{z}^t_1, ..., \mathbf{z}^t_{n_t}]$. The objective function is defined as:

$$
\begin{aligned}
F^{(t)} = &\|\mathbf{W}^{t'}_X \mathbf{X}^t - \mathbf{Z}^t\|^2_F + \|\mathbf{X}^t - \mathbf{W}^t_X \mathbf{Z}^t\|^2_F + \eta\|\mathbf{W}^t_X\|^2_F \\
&+ \gamma(\|\mathbf{W}^{t'}_Y \mathbf{Y}^t - \mathbf{Z}^t\|^2_F + \|\mathbf{Y}^t - \mathbf{W}^t_Y \mathbf{Z}^t\|^2_F + \eta\|\mathbf{W}^t_Y\|^2_F)
\end{aligned}
\tag{6}
$$

where η and γ are exactly the same as in Eq. (1). By combining Eq. (5) and Eq. (6) with a weighting coefficient β, we have the final loss function L:

$$
L = F^{(t)} + \beta F^{(a)}
\tag{7}
$$

The optimization problem $\min L$ can be solved by three alternate steps: 1) $\hat{\omega} = \arg_\omega \min F^{(a)}(\omega, \hat{\mathbf{Z}}^t)$; 2) $\hat{\mathbf{W}}^t_X, \hat{\mathbf{W}}^t_Y = \arg\min_{\mathbf{W}^t_X, \mathbf{W}^t_Y} F^{(t)}(\mathbf{W}^t_X, \mathbf{W}^t_Y, \hat{\mathbf{Z}}^t)$; 3) $\hat{\mathbf{Z}}^t = \arg\min_{\mathbf{Z}^t} L(\hat{\omega}, \hat{\mathbf{W}}^t_X, \hat{\mathbf{W}}^t_Y, \mathbf{Z}^t)$. In this work, $\hat{\mathbf{Z}}^t$ is initialized with the PLS regression model [58]. Firstly, we find the best $\hat{\omega}$ by solving the following optimization problem according to Proposition 1:

$$\hat{\boldsymbol{\omega}} = \arg_{\boldsymbol{\omega}} \min F^{(a)}(\boldsymbol{\omega}, \hat{\mathbf{Z}}^t) = \arg_{\boldsymbol{\omega}} \min \sum_{i=1}^{n_s} \sum_{j=1}^{n_t} (\boldsymbol{\omega}'(\hat{\mathbf{z}}_i^s - \hat{\mathbf{z}}_j^t))^2 \qquad (8)$$

Secondly, by setting $\frac{\partial F^{(t)}(\mathbf{W}_X^t, \mathbf{W}_Y^t, \hat{\mathbf{Z}}^t)}{\partial \mathbf{W}_X^t} = 0$ and $\frac{\partial F^{(t)}(\mathbf{W}_X^t, \mathbf{W}_Y^t, \hat{\mathbf{Z}}^t)}{\partial \mathbf{W}_Y^t} = 0$, we can obtain two equations:

$$(\mathbf{X}^t \mathbf{X}^{t'} + \eta \mathbf{I})\mathbf{W}_X^t + \mathbf{W}_X^t(\hat{\mathbf{Z}}^t \hat{\mathbf{Z}}^{t'}) = 2\mathbf{X}^t \hat{\mathbf{Z}}^{t'} \qquad (9)$$

$$(\mathbf{Y}^t \mathbf{Y}^{t'} + \eta \mathbf{I})\mathbf{W}_Y^t + \mathbf{W}_Y^t(\hat{\mathbf{Z}}^t \hat{\mathbf{Z}}^{t'}) = 2\mathbf{Y}^t \hat{\mathbf{Z}}^{t'} \qquad (10)$$

Thirdly, by setting $\frac{\partial L(\hat{\boldsymbol{\omega}}, \hat{\mathbf{W}}_X^t, \hat{\mathbf{W}}_Y^t, \mathbf{Z}^t)}{\partial \mathbf{Z}^t} = 0$, we have the following equation:

$$\begin{aligned}[\hat{\mathbf{W}}_X^{t'}\hat{\mathbf{W}}_X^t + \gamma \hat{\mathbf{W}}_Y^{t'}\hat{\mathbf{W}}_Y^t + (1+\gamma)\mathbf{I}]\mathbf{Z}^t + \beta(\hat{\boldsymbol{\omega}}\hat{\boldsymbol{\omega}}' + \lambda \mathbf{I})\mathbf{Z}^t(\mathbf{B}\mathbf{B}') \\ = 2\hat{\mathbf{W}}_X^{t'}\mathbf{X}^t + 2\gamma\hat{\mathbf{W}}_Y^{t'}\mathbf{Y}^t + \beta(\hat{\boldsymbol{\omega}}\hat{\boldsymbol{\omega}}' + \lambda \mathbf{I})\hat{\mathbf{Z}}^s\mathbf{A}\mathbf{B}'\end{aligned} \qquad (11)$$

where the formal definitions of $\mathbf{A}, \mathbf{B}$ are given in Proposition 1. Notably, according to Proposition 4, we can find the unique solution $\hat{\mathbf{Z}}^t$ of Eq. (11).

The complete algorithm for training our triplet autoencoder model is outlined in Algorithm 1. Once the optimal projections $\hat{\mathbf{W}}_X^t$ and $\hat{\mathbf{W}}_Y^t$ are learned, the class label of a test sample $\mathbf{x}^*$ is predicted as $l_{\mathbf{x}^*} = \arg\min_j \|\hat{\mathbf{W}}_X^{t'}\mathbf{x}^* - \hat{\mathbf{W}}_Y^{t'}\bar{\mathbf{y}}_j^t\|_2$, where $\bar{\mathbf{y}}_j^t$ is the semantic embedding of j-th target class using the word2vec model ($j = 1, ..., |C_t|$).

3.4   Theoretical Analysis

We finally give theoretical analysis for Algorithm 1. Specifically, Proposition 1 and Proposition 2 provide an efficient approach to finding the solution $\hat{\boldsymbol{\omega}}$ of Eq. (8), and Proposition 3 and Proposition 4 guarantee the solution uniqueness of Eqs. (9)–(11). Their proofs can be found in the suppl. material.

Proposition 1. $\sum_{i=1}^{n_s} \sum_{j=1}^{n_t} (\boldsymbol{\omega}'(\hat{\mathbf{z}}_i^s - \hat{\mathbf{z}}_j^t))^2 = \boldsymbol{\omega}'(\hat{\mathbf{Z}}^s\mathbf{A} - \hat{\mathbf{Z}}^t\mathbf{B})(\hat{\mathbf{Z}}^s\mathbf{A} - \hat{\mathbf{Z}}^t\mathbf{B})'\boldsymbol{\omega}$,

where $\mathbf{A} = \begin{pmatrix} \mathbf{1}_{n_t}' & 0 & ... & 0 \\ 0 & \mathbf{1}_{n_t}' & ... & 0 \\ ... & ... & ... & ... \\ 0 & 0 & ... & \mathbf{1}_{n_t}' \end{pmatrix} \in R^{n_s \times (n_t \times n_s)}, \mathbf{B} = (\mathbf{I}_{n_t}, \mathbf{I}_{n_t}, ..., \mathbf{I}_{n_t}) \in$

$R^{n_t \times (n_t \times n_s)}$, $\mathbf{1}_{n_t}$ is n_t-dimensional vector with all elements 1, and $\mathbf{I}_{n_t} \in R^{n_t \times n_t}$ is an identity matrix. Therefore, the solution $\hat{\boldsymbol{\omega}}$ of Eq. (8) is exactly the smallest eigenvector of $(\hat{\mathbf{Z}}^s\mathbf{A} - \hat{\mathbf{Z}}^t\mathbf{B})(\hat{\mathbf{Z}}^s\mathbf{A} - \hat{\mathbf{Z}}^t\mathbf{B})'$.

Proposition 2. $(\hat{\mathbf{Z}}^s\mathbf{A} - \hat{\mathbf{Z}}^t\mathbf{B})(\hat{\mathbf{Z}}^s\mathbf{A} - \hat{\mathbf{Z}}^t\mathbf{B})' = \hat{\mathbf{Z}}^s\mathbf{A}\mathbf{A}'\hat{\mathbf{Z}}^{s'} - \hat{\mathbf{Z}}^s\mathbf{A}\mathbf{B}'\hat{\mathbf{Z}}^{t'} - \hat{\mathbf{Z}}^t\mathbf{B}\mathbf{A}'\hat{\mathbf{Z}}^{s'} + \hat{\mathbf{Z}}^t\mathbf{B}\mathbf{B}'\hat{\mathbf{Z}}^{t'}$. Since $\mathbf{A}\mathbf{A}' = n_t\mathbf{I}_{n_s}, \mathbf{B}\mathbf{B}' = n_s\mathbf{I}_{n_t}, \mathbf{B}\mathbf{A}' = (\mathbf{1}_{n_t}, \mathbf{1}_{n_t}, ..., \mathbf{1}_{n_t}) \in R^{n_t \times n_s}$, and $\mathbf{A}\mathbf{B}' = (\mathbf{B}\mathbf{A}')'$, the computation of $(\hat{\mathbf{Z}}^s\mathbf{A} - \hat{\mathbf{Z}}^t\mathbf{B})(\hat{\mathbf{Z}}^s\mathbf{A} - \hat{\mathbf{Z}}^t\mathbf{B})'$ has a linear time cost $\mathcal{O}(r^2(n_t + n_s))$ ($r \ll n_t + n_s$).

Remark 1. Let $\mathbf{G} = \hat{\mathbf{Z}}^s\mathbf{A} - \hat{\mathbf{Z}}^t\mathbf{B}$. If we directly calculate $\mathbf{G}$ and then $\mathbf{GG}'$, the total flops cost is $2rn_tn_s(n_t + n_s + r + 1)$ and the computation cost is $\mathcal{O}(rn_tn_s(n_t + n_s))$, which is much higher than that given by **Proposition 2**.

Proposition 3. *According to the eigenvalue decomposition of positive semi-definite matrices, we have* $\mathbf{X}^t\mathbf{X}^{t'} = \mathbf{U}_1\mathbf{\Sigma}_1\mathbf{U}_1'$, $\hat{\mathbf{Z}}^t\hat{\mathbf{Z}}^{t'} = \mathbf{U}_2\mathbf{\Sigma}_2\mathbf{U}_2'$, *as well as* $\mathbf{Y}^t\mathbf{Y}^{t'} = \mathbf{U}_3\mathbf{\Sigma}_3\mathbf{U}_3'$, *where* $\mathbf{\Sigma}_1 = diag(\lambda_1^{(1)}, ..., \lambda_d^{(1)})$, $\mathbf{\Sigma}_2 = diag(\lambda_1^{(2)}, ..., \lambda_r^{(2)})$, *and* $\mathbf{\Sigma}_3 = diag(\lambda_1^{(3)}, ..., \lambda_k^{(3)})$. *Let* $\mathbf{C} = (\frac{2}{\lambda_i^{(1)}+\eta+\lambda_j^{(2)}})_{d\times r}$ *and* $\mathbf{D} = (\frac{2}{\lambda_i^{(3)}+\eta+\lambda_j^{(2)}})_{k\times r}$. *Both Eq. (9) and Eq. (10) have and only have one solution:*

$$\hat{\mathbf{W}}_X^t = \mathbf{U}_1[(\mathbf{U}_1'\mathbf{X}^t\hat{\mathbf{Z}}^{t'}\mathbf{U}_2)\odot\mathbf{C}]\mathbf{U}_2' \quad \hat{\mathbf{W}}_Y^t = \mathbf{U}_3[(\mathbf{U}_3'\mathbf{Y}^t\hat{\mathbf{Z}}^{t'}\mathbf{U}_2)\odot\mathbf{D}]\mathbf{U}_2'$$

where $\odot$ *means Hardamard product of two matrices (i.e. element-wise product).*

Proposition 4. *Let* $\mathbf{H} = (1 + \gamma + n_s\beta\lambda)\mathbf{I} + \hat{\mathbf{W}}_X^{t'}\hat{\mathbf{W}}_X^t + \gamma\hat{\mathbf{W}}_Y^{t'}\hat{\mathbf{W}}_Y^t + n_s\beta\hat{\omega}\hat{\omega}'$. *Since* $\mathbf{BB}' = n_s\mathbf{I}_{n_t}$ *and* $\mathbf{H}$ *is positive definite, Eq. (11) has and only has one solution:*

$$\hat{\mathbf{Z}}^t = \mathbf{H}^{-1}[2\hat{\mathbf{W}}_X^{t'}\mathbf{X}^t + 2\gamma\hat{\mathbf{W}}_Y^{t'}\mathbf{Y}^t + \beta(\hat{\omega}\hat{\omega}' + \lambda\mathbf{I})\hat{\mathbf{Z}}^s\mathbf{AB}']$$

According to Proposition 2, the computation of $(\hat{\mathbf{Z}}^s\mathbf{A} - \hat{\mathbf{Z}}^t\mathbf{B})(\hat{\mathbf{Z}}^s\mathbf{A} - \hat{\mathbf{Z}}^t\mathbf{B})'$ has a linear time cost. Given that $(\hat{\mathbf{Z}}^s\mathbf{A} - \hat{\mathbf{Z}}^t\mathbf{B})(\hat{\mathbf{Z}}^s\mathbf{A} - \hat{\mathbf{Z}}^t\mathbf{B})' \in R^{r\times r}$, its smallest eigenvector can be found very efficiently. According to Proposition 1, finding the solution $\hat{\omega}$ of Eq. (8) thus has a linear time cost. Moreover, Proposition 3 and Proposition 4 give explicit solutions for Eqs. (9)–(11) (and also guarantee the solution uniqueness). Note that Proposition 3 similarly holds for Eqs. (2)–(3).

4   Experiments

4.1   Experiment Setup

Datasets and Settings. We take the 1,000 classes from ILSVRC2012 (ImageNet) as the source classes as in [18,34], with 200 samples per class. Based on ILSVRC2012, we construct two large-scale datasets for evaluation. (1) **ImageNet 2012-2010**: The 360 classes from ILSVRC2010 (not included in ILSVRC 2012) are used as the target classes, with 150 samples per class. To construct a cross-domain dataset, we adopt pre-trained MSG-Net [60] for style transfer over all samples from ILSVRC2010 360 classes, and take the style-transferred samples from these 360 classes as the final target data. (2) **ImageNet2012-DomainNet**: We choose the Infograph dataset (all infographic images) in DomainNet [61], remove the overlapped ILSVRC2012 1K classes from the original 345 Infograph classes, and leave the non-overlapped 144 classes as the target domain (see more details in the suppl. material). With each target Domain-Net category containing samples from dozens to hundreds, the target domain includes 20,661 images in total. As in [18], each dataset is split into three parts: a large-scale sample set of sufficient labeled samples from source classes, a K-shot sample set of few labeled samples from target classes, and a test set of the rest samples from target classes. Note that this dataset is more challenging than ImageNet2012-2010 since the target domain is real and the domain gap is bigger.

Visual, Semantic, and Latent Spaces. As in [18], we utilize the ResNet50 [56] model pre-trained by us on the source ILSVRC2012 1K classes to extract 2,048-dimensional visual feature vectors. To obtain the semantic representations, we use the same 1,000-dimensional word vectors as in [18,34], which are obtained by training a skip-gram text model on a corpus of 4.6M Wikipedia documents. In this work, the shared latent subspace is initialized by running PLS regression [58] with visual feature vectors and semantic word vectors as two groups of inputs. The dimension of the latent shared subspace is a hyperparameter, and we empirically set it as $r = 300$ in all experiments.

Evaluation Metric and Hyperparameter. Unlike the n-way K-shot evaluation protocol widely used in the conventional FSL setting [9,14], we choose to evaluate the performance over all target classes (but not over a subset of target classes for one trial), similar to that in other large-scale FSL works [16,18]. Top-1 accuracy over the test set is used for each trial, and average Top-1 accuracy is computed. Note that we *reproduce the results of all baseline methods* under our new FSL setting, and thus it is still fair to make comparison between the proposed TriAE and other FSL/domain adaptation methods.

Algorithm 1 for training our TriAE model has three hyperparameters to tune: β (see Eq. (11)), γ (see Eqs. (4) and (11)), and λ (see Eq. (11)). Note that the K-shot sample set is not used to directly compute the classification loss for training our TriAE model. Instead, we select the hyperparameters using the Top-1 classification accuracy computed over the K-shot sample set. Additional experiments in the suppl. material show that the influence of the hyperparameters on our model's performance is small.

Compared Methods. We select representative/latest FSL and domain adaptation baselines. (1) **FSL Baselines**: We first select the latest large-scale FSL methods including SGM [16], PPA [17], LSD [26], and KTCH [18]. Moreover, the latest meta-learning-based FSL models (e.g., Prototypical Network (PN) [13], Matching Network (MN) [11], MetaOptNet [62], and Baseline++ [40]) are also selected as baselines. Note that PN, MN, and MetaOptNet are designed and evaluated under the n-way K-shot setting. When extending them to our proposed setting, we replace their backbone with ResNet50 for fair comparison: the n-way K-shot setting is still used for model training over the source classes, but when adapting to the target classes, the learned model is only used to extract the visual features of the few-shot sample set and thus a logistic regression (LR) classifier has to be trained for finally recognizing the target classes (as in [26]). In addition, another baseline is obtained by conducting the naive Nearest Neighbor (NN) search based on the pretrained ResNet50. (2) **Domain Adaptation Baselines**: We further compare with the latest unsupervised domain adaptation

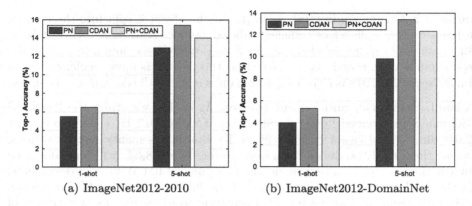

(a) ImageNet2012-2010   (b) ImageNet2012-DomainNet

Fig. 4. Comparative results among PN, CDAN, and PN+CDAN on two large-scale cross-domain datasets. For each method, an extra LR classifier is trained for large-scale classification.

Table 1. Comparative accuracies (%, top-1) for large-scale cross-domain FSL on ImageNet2012-2010. 'LR' means that an extra LR classifier is trained for large-scale classification. 'K' denotes the number of shots per target class. ‡ highlights that the extra LR is *even stronger* than recent FSL-based classifiers (see Fig. 4).

Model	LR?	K = 1	K = 2	K = 5	K = 10	K = 20
NN	w/o	3.5	5.3	8.3	11.3	13.7
MN [11]	w	3.4	5.2	8.7	12.6	14.8
PN [13]	w	5.5	7.6	12.9	13.8	15.0
MetaOptNet [62]	w	5.7	7.7	12.8	13.9	15.2
Baseline++ [40]	w/o	4.9	7.4	11.7	16.0	19.0
PPA [17]	w/o	4.1	6.4	11.8	15.1	17.6
SGM [16]	w/o	3.9	6.3	12.1	16.2	19.1
LSD [26]	w/o	5.7	8.0	12.4	15.6	19.0
KTCH [18]	w/o	5.9	8.7	13.5	17.0	19.4
CoGAN [20]	w	5.5	8.1	12.2	16.9	19.3
ADDA [21]	w	5.4	7.3	11.8	14.5	15.7
CDAN‡ [24]	w	6.5	9.8	15.4	20.6	24.2
AFN‡ [63]	w	7.0	9.9	15.7	20.5	24.2
TriAE (ours)	w/o	**7.9**	**11.6**	**17.3**	**22.4**	**26.3**

methods such as Coupled Generative Adversarial Network (CoGAN) [20], Adversarial Discriminative Domain Adaptation (ADDA) [21], Conditional Adversarial Domain Adaptation (CDAN) [24], and Adaptive Feature Norm (AFN) [63]. We first evaluate these domain adaptation methods with ResNet50 as backbone for visual feature learning and then conduct LR classification for FSL.

Table 2. Comparative accuracies (%, top-1) for large-scale cross-domain FSL on ImageNet2012-DomainNet. ‡ highlights that the extra LR is *even stronger* than recent FSL-based classifiers.

Model	LR?	K = 1	K = 2	K = 5	K = 10	K = 20
NN	w/o	2.5	4.0	7.4	10.3	13.0
MN [11]	w	3.1	4.3	8.0	11.9	14.1
PN [13]	w	3.7	4.8	9.5	12.7	14.4
MetaOptNet [62]	w	3.1	4.8	9.6	12.8	14.9
Baseline++ [40]	w/o	3.2	4.6	9.5	13.2	16.2
PPA [17]	w/o	3.8	5.8	11.2	14.9	17.4
SGM [16]	w/o	3.6	5.9	11.5	15.5	20.8
LSD [26]	w/o	3.2	4.4	9.0	12.5	15.5
KTCH [18]	w/o	3.7	5.1	10.7	15.1	18.6
CoGAN [20]	w	5.2	7.4	12.4	15.2	18.9
ADDA [21]	w	3.3	4.6	8.2	11.2	14.4
CDAN‡ [24]	w	5.3	7.5	13.4	17.7	22.1
AFN‡ [63]	w	3.9	6.1	10.8	15.3	20.5
TriAE (ours)	w/o	**6.4**	**9.3**	**16.0**	**20.2**	**24.8**

We assume that *naively combining FSL and domain adaptation* for large-scale cross-domain FSL is not effective and this is the place where our major technical novelty lies. To validate this, we conduct experiments by directly combining a representative FSL method (i.e. PN [13]) and a representative domain adaptation method (i.e. CDAN [24]). Concretely, we utilize CDAN to train a feature extractor and then apply the feature extractor to PN (denoted as PN+CDAN). Under the large-scale FSL evaluation protocol, we have to train an extra LR classifier for final recognition. The comparative results in Fig. 4 show that adding FSL to domain adaptation even causes performance degradation (see PN+CDAN vs. CDAN). Moreover, it is also observed that under the large-scale FSL evaluation protocol, a basic classifier like LR even yields better classification performance than FSL-based classifiers. In the following experiments, we thus ignore the naive combination of FSL and domain adaptation as a baseline.

4.2 Comparative Results

The comparative results of large-scale cross-domain FSL on the two datasets are presented in Tables 1 and 2. We can make the following observations: (1) Our TriAE model significantly outperforms the state-of-the-art large-scale FSL methods [16–18,26], because of explicitly solving the domain adaptation problem under the new cross-domain FSL setting. (2) Our TriAE model also clearly outperforms the latest unsupervised domain adaptation (UDA) methods [20,21,24,63]. In particular, the improvements achieved by our TriAE model over these UDA methods on the more challenging ImageNet2012-DomainNet dataset are larger. This suggests that our model can better cope with the large domain gap in the dataset. (3) The latest UDA methods (i.e. CDAN and AFN) clearly yield better results than existing large-scale FSL methods. This is interesting because they were originally designed for a shared class label space across the source and target domains. This result seems to suggest that solving the domain gap problem is more critical under the new cross-domain FSL setting. (4) The latest meta-learning-based FSL methods (i.e. MetaOptNet and Baseline++) generally perform worse than existing large-scale FSL methods, indicating that these approaches are not suitable for the proposed more challenging FSL setting.

4.3   Further Evaluation

Ablation Study. Our full TriAE model can be simplified as follows: (1) When only the large-scale sample set from source classes is used for projection learning, we can obtain $\hat{\mathbf{W}}_X^s, \hat{\mathbf{W}}_Y^s$ and then utilize these two projections directly for image classification over target classes. That is, our TriAE degrades to the model proposed in Sect. 3.2, denoted as AE_s. (2) When only the few-shot sample set from target classes is used to learn $\mathbf{W}_X^t, \mathbf{W}_Y^t$ but without updating $\hat{\mathbf{Z}}^t$, our TriAE degrades to one ablative model AE_t0. (3) We can further introduce the alternate optimization steps from Eqs. (9)–(11) into AE_t0, resulting in another ablative model AE_t1 (i.e. TriAE with $\beta = 0$). Note that the semantic information is used in AE_s, AE_t0, and AE_t1. (4) We take on board the fourth ablative model AE_pca (i.e. TriAE with $\gamma = 0$), which utilizes PCA [64] to reduce the dimension of $\mathbf{X}^s$ ($\mathbf{X}^t$) and obtain the latent representation $\mathbf{Z}^s$ ($\mathbf{Z}^t$), without exploiting the semantic embedding. After mapping the visual features of few-shot target-class images into the latent subspace for generating target class representations, AE_pca projects a test image into the latent subspace for NN search. We conduct the ablation study under the large-scale cross-domain FSL setting. The ablative results in Fig. 5(a) show that: (i) The unsatisfactory performance of AE_s indicates that there does exist a large gap between the source and target domains; (ii) The marginal improvements achieved by AE_t1 over AE_t0 validate the effectiveness of the alternate optimization steps used for training our TriAE; (iii) The dominance of our TriAE over AE_pca demonstrates the advantage of introducing the semantic embedding into FSL; (iv) The performance gains obtained by our TriAE over AE_t1 validate the effectiveness of our linear domain adaptation strategy.

Convergence Analysis. To provide convergence analysis for our TriAE model, we define three baseline projection matrices: (1) $\mathbf{W}_X^*, \mathbf{W}_Y^*$ – learned by AE_t0 with the whole labeled data from target classes (i.e. both few-shot sample set and test set); (2) $\mathbf{W}_X^s, \mathbf{W}_Y^s$ – learned by AE_s only with the large-scale sample set from source classes; (3) $\mathbf{W}_X^t, \mathbf{W}_Y^t$ – learned by AE_t0 only with the few-shot sample set from target classes. As we have mentioned, $\hat{\mathbf{W}}_X^t, \hat{\mathbf{W}}_Y^t$ are learned by our TriAE model using the large-scale sample set and few-shot sample set. We can directly compare $\mathbf{W}_X^s/\mathbf{W}_Y^s$, $\mathbf{W}_X^t/\mathbf{W}_Y^t$, and $\hat{\mathbf{W}}_X^t/\hat{\mathbf{W}}_Y^t$ to $\mathbf{W}_X^*/\mathbf{W}_Y^*$ by

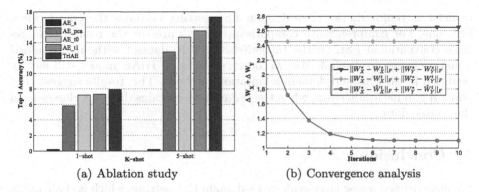

(a) Ablation study   (b) Convergence analysis

Fig. 5. (a) Ablative results under the large-scale cross-domain 1-shot and 5-shot settings. (b) Convergence analysis of our TriAE model under the large-scale cross-domain 5-shot setting.

Table 3. Comparative accuracies (%, top-1) for large-scale conventional FSL on ImageNet2012-2010. As in [18], the original ImageNet2012-2010 is used, without style transfer.

Model	LR?	$K=1$	$K=2$	$K=5$	$K=10$	$K=20$
NN	w/o	8.2	11.4	16.6	20.6	23.4
MN [11]	w	7.0	10.1	18.5	24.9	26.2
PN [13]	w	9.9	15.2	21.8	25.2	28.5
MetaOptNet [62]	w	10.2	16.4	22.3	26.8	30.3
Baseline++ [40]	w/o	10.5	16.4	25.2	32.1	38.0
PPA [17]	w/o	15.1	21.4	25.6	28.0	30.7
SGM [16]	w/o	14.8	21.4	33.0	39.1	43.4
LSD [26]	w/o	17.8	22.2	29.0	33.7	38.3
KTCH [18]	w/o	20.2	27.3	36.6	41.8	45.0
CoGAN [20]	w	10.1	16.3	25.0	32.5	38.2
ADDA [21]	w	10.0	15.4	22.2	25.5	27.2
CDAN [24]	w	14.7	21.1	31.5	38.9	43.4
AFN [63]	w	16.4	23.7	34.1	41.0	44.7
TriAE (ours)	w/o	**20.5**	**27.8**	**37.6**	**43.7**	**48.7**

computing the matrix distances among them. Note that $\mathbf{W}_X^*, \mathbf{W}_Y^*$ are considered to be the best projection matrices for recognizing the target classes. The results in Fig. 5(b) show that: (i) Our TriAE algorithm converges very quickly; (ii) $\hat{\mathbf{W}}_X^t, \hat{\mathbf{W}}_Y^t$ get closer to $\mathbf{W}_X^*, \mathbf{W}_Y^*$ with more iterations and finally become the closest to $\mathbf{W}_X^*, \mathbf{W}_Y^*$.

Conventional FSL. In this paper, style transfer is performed on ImageNet2012-2010 to construct a large-scale cross-domain dataset. When style transfer is removed, the cross-domain FSL setting becomes the conventional FSL one. For comprehensive comparison, we also present the results of large-scale conventional FSL on the ImageNet2012-2010 dataset without the added domain change in Table 3. We can observe that our TriAE model still clearly beats all latest FSL and domain adaptation methods. This results suggest that domain gap naturally exists when the target data contains different classes from the source data.

5   Conclusion

We have defined a new large-scale cross-domain FSL setting, which is challenging yet common in real-world scenarios. To overcome the large-scale cross-domain FSL challenge, we propose a Triplet Autoencoder model, which can address both FSL and domain adaptation problems by learning a joint latent subspace. We further provide an efficient model optimization algorithm, followed by rigorous theoretical algorithm analysis. The proposed model is shown to achieve state-of-the-art performance on both new and conventional large-scale FSL problems.

Acknowledgements. This work was supported in part by National Natural Science Foundation of China (61976220 and 61832017), and Beijing Outstanding Young Scientist Program (BJJWZYJH012019100020098).

References

1. Li, F., Fergus, R., Perona, P.: One-shot learning of object categories. TPAMI **28**, 594–611 (2006)
2. Gidaris, S., Komodakis, N.: Dynamic few-shot visual learning without forgetting. In: CVPR, pp. 4367–4375 (2018)
3. Oreshkin, B., López, P.R., Lacoste, A.: Tadam: task dependent adaptive metric for improved few-shot learning. In: Advances in Neural Information Processing Systems, pp. 721–731 (2018)
4. Pan, S.J., Yang, Q.: A survey on transfer learning. TKDE **22**, 1345–1359 (2010)
5. Pan, S.J., Tsang, I.W., Kwok, J.T., Yang, Q.: Domain adaptation via transfer component analysis. IEEE Trans. Neural Netw. **22**, 199–210 (2011)
6. Santoro, A., Bartunov, S., Botvinick, M., Wierstra, D., Lillicrap, T.: Meta-learning with memory-augmented neural networks. In: ICML, pp. 1842–1850 (2016)
7. Andrychowicz, M., et al.: Learning to learn by gradient descent by gradient descent. In: Advances in Neural Information Processing Systems, pp. 3981–3989 (2016)
8. Ravi, S., Larochelle, H.: Optimization as a model for few-shot learning. In: ICLR (2017)
9. Finn, C., Abbeel, P., Levine, S.: Model-agnostic meta-learning for fast adaptation of deep networks. In: ICML, pp. 1126–1135 (2017)
10. Munkhdalai, T., Yu, H.: Meta networks. In: ICML, pp. 2554–2563 (2017)
11. Vinyals, O., Blundell, C., Lillicrap, T., Kavukcuoglu, K., Wierstra, D.: Matching networks for one shot learning. In: Advances in Neural Information Processing Systems, pp. 3630–3638 (2016)

12. Bertinetto, L., Henriques, J.F., Valmadre, J., Torr, P.H.S., Vedaldi, A.: Learning feed-forward one-shot learners. In: Advances in Neural Information Processing Systems, pp. 523–531 (2016)
13. Snell, J., Swersky, K., Zemel, R.: Prototypical networks for few-shot learning. In: Advances in Neural Information Processing Systems, pp. 4077–4087 (2017)
14. Sung, F., Yang, Y., Zhang, L., Xiang, T., Torr, P.H.S., Hospedales, T.M.: Learning to compare: relation network for few-shot learning. In: CVPR, pp. 1199–1208 (2018)
15. Russakovsky, O., et al.: ImageNet large scale visual recognition challenge. IJCV 115, 211–252 (2015). https://doi.org/10.1007/s11263-015-0816-y
16. Hariharan, B., Girshick, R.B.: Low-shot visual recognition by shrinking and hallucinating features. In: ICCV, pp. 3037–3046 (2017)
17. Qiao, S., Liu, C., Shen, W., Yuille, A.L.: Few-shot image recognition by predicting parameters from activations. In: CVPR, pp. 7229–7238 (2018)
18. Li, A., Luo, T., Lu, Z., Xiang, T., Wang, L., Wen, J.: Large-scale few-shot learning: knowledge transfer with class hierarchy. In: CVPR, pp. 7212–7220 (2019)
19. Goodfellow, I.J., et al.: Generative adversarial nets. In: Advances in Neural Information Processing Systems, pp. 2672–2680 (2014)
20. Liu, M., Tuzel, O.: Coupled generative adversarial networks. In: Advances in Neural Information Processing Systems, pp. 469–477 (2016)
21. Tzeng, E., Hoffman, J., Saenko, K., Darrell, T.: Adversarial discriminative domain adaptation. In: CVPR, pp. 2962–2971 (2017)
22. Motiian, S., Jones, Q., Iranmanesh, S.M., Doretto, G.: Few-shot adversarial domain adaptation. In: Advances in Neural Information Processing Systems, pp. 6673–6683 (2017)
23. Hong, W., Wang, Z., Yang, M., Yuan, J.: Conditional generative adversarial network for structured domain adaptation. In: CVPR, pp. 1335–1344 (2018)
24. Long, M., Cao, Z., Wang, J., Jordan, M.I.: Conditional adversarial domain adaptation. In: Advances in Neural Information Processing Systems, pp. 1647–1657 (2018)
25. Qi, H., Brown, M., Lowe, D.G.: Low-shot learning with imprinted weights. In: CVPR, pp. 5822–5830 (2018)
26. Douze, M., Szlam, A., Hariharan, B., Jégou, H.: Low-shot learning with large-scale diffusion. In: CVPR, pp. 3349–3358 (2018)
27. Gao, H., Shou, Z., Zareian, A., Zhang, H., Chang, S.: Low-shot learning via covariance-preserving adversarial augmentation networks. In: Advances in Neural Information Processing Systems, pp. 983–993 (2018)
28. Motiian, S., Piccirilli, M., Adjeroh, D.A., Doretto, G.: Unified deep supervised domain adaptation and generalization. In: ICCV, pp. 5716–5726 (2017)
29. Klys, J., Snell, J., Zemel, R.: Learning latent subspaces in variational autoencoders. In: Advances in Neural Information Processing Systems, pp. 6444–6454 (2018)
30. Mikolov, T., Sutskever, I., Chen, K., Corrado, G.S., Dean, J.: Distributed representations of words and phrases and their compositionality. In: Advances in Neural Information Processing Systems, pp. 3111–3119 (2013)
31. Ranzato, M., Boureau, Y., Chopra, S., LeCun, Y.: A unified energy-based framework for unsupervised learning. In: AISTATS, pp. 371–379 (2007)
32. Rifai, S., Vincent, P., Muller, X., Glorot, X., Bengio, Y.: Contractive auto-encoders: explicit invariance during feature extraction. In: ICML, pp. 833–840 (2011)
33. Reed, S.E., Akata, Z., Yan, X., Logeswaran, L., Schiele, B., Lee, H.: Generative adversarial text to image synthesis. In: ICML, pp. 1060–1069 (2016)

34. Kodirov, E., Xiang, T., Gong, S.: Semantic autoencoder for zero-shot learning. In: CVPR, pp. 4447–4456 (2017)
35. Sun, Q., Liu, Y., Chua, T.S., Schiele, B.: Meta-transfer learning for few-shot learning. In: CVPR, pp. 403–412 (2019)
36. Jamal, M.A., Qi, G.J.: Task agnostic meta-learning for few-shot learning. In: CVPR, pp. 11719–11727 (2019)
37. Zhang, J., Zhang, M., Lu, Z., Xiang, T., Wen, J.: AdarGCN: adaptive aggregation GCN for few-shot learning. arXiv preprint arXiv:2002.12641 (2020)
38. Guan, J., Lu, Z., Xiang, T., Li, A., Zhao, A., Wen, J.R.: Zero and few shot learning with semantic feature synthesis and competitive learning. TPAM I, 1–14 (2020)
39. Wah, C., Branson, S., Welinder, P., Perona, P., Belongie, S.: The caltech-UCSD birds-200-2011 dataset. Technical Report CNS-TR-2011-001, California Institute of Technology (2011)
40. Chen, W., Liu, Y., Kira, Z., Wang, Y.F., Huang, J.: A closer look at few-shot classification. In: ICLR (2019)
41. Long, M., Ding, G., Wang, J., Sun, J., Guo, Y., Yu, P.S.: Transfer sparse coding for robust image representation. In: CVPR, pp. 407–414 (2013)
42. Muandet, K., Balduzzi, D., Schölkopf, B.: Domain generalization via invariant feature representation. In: ICML, pp. 10–18 (2013)
43. Long, M., Cao, Y., Wang, J., Jordan, M.I.: Learning transferable features with deep adaptation networks. In: ICML, pp. 97–105 (2015)
44. Ganin, Y., et al.: Domain-adversarial training of neural networks. JMLR 17, 59:1–59:35 (2016)
45. Motiian, S., Piccirilli, M., Adjeroh, D.A., Doretto, G.: Information bottleneck learning using privileged information for visual recognition. In: CVPR, pp. 1496–1505 (2016)
46. Tzeng, E., Hoffman, J., Darrell, T., Saenko, K.: Simultaneous deep transfer across domains and tasks. In: ICCV, pp. 4068–4076 (2015)
47. Ganin, Y., Lempitsky, V.S.: Unsupervised domain adaptation by backpropagation. In: ICML, pp. 1180–1189 (2015)
48. Saenko, K., Kulis, B., Fritz, M., Darrell, T.: Adapting visual category models to new domains. In: Daniilidis, K., Maragos, P., Paragios, N. (eds.) ECCV 2010. LNCS, vol. 6314, pp. 213–226. Springer, Heidelberg (2010). https://doi.org/10.1007/978-3-642-15561-1_16
49. Zhao, A., Ding, M., Guan, J., Lu, Z., Xiang, T., Wen, J.R.: Domain-invariant projection learning for zero-shot recognition. In: Advances in Neural Information Processing Systems, pp. 1019–1030 (2018)
50. Huo, Y., Guan, J., Zhang, J., Zhang, M., Wen, J.R., Lu, Z.: Zero-shot learning with few seen class samples. In: ICME, pp. 1336–1341 (2019)
51. Liu, G., Guan, J., Zhang, M., Zhang, J., Wang, Z., Lu, Z.: Joint projection and subspace learning for zero-shot recognition. In: ICME, pp. 1228–1233 (2019)
52. Li, A., Lu, Z., Guan, J., Xiang, T., Wang, L., Wen, J.-R.: Transferrable feature and projection learning with class hierarchy for zero-shot learning. Int. J. Comput. Vis. 128(12), 2810–2827 (2020). https://doi.org/10.1007/s11263-020-01342-x
53. Garcia, E.M., Tiedemann, J., España-Bonet, C., Màrquez, L.: Word's vector representations meet machine translation. In: EMNLP 2014 Workshop on Syntax, Semantics and Structure in Statistical Translation, pp. 132–134 (2014)
54. McCann, B., Bradbury, J., Xiong, C., Socher, R.: Learned in translation: contextualized word vectors. In: Advances in Neural Information Processing Systems, pp. 6297–6308 (2017)

55. Mikolov, T., Chen, K., Corrado, G., Dean, J.: Efficient estimation of word representations in vector space. In: ICLR 2013 Workshop (2013)
56. He, K., Zhang, X., Ren, S., Sun, J.: Deep residual learning for image recognition. In: CVPR, pp. 770–778 (2016)
57. Hoffer, E., Ailon, N.: Deep metric learning using triplet network. In: Feragen, A., Pelillo, M., Loog, M. (eds.) SIMBAD 2015. LNCS, vol. 9370, pp. 84–92. Springer, Cham (2015). https://doi.org/10.1007/978-3-319-24261-3_7
58. Rosipal, R., Krämer, N.: Overview and recent advances in partial least squares. In: Saunders, C., Grobelnik, M., Gunn, S., Shawe-Taylor, J. (eds.) SLSFS 2005. LNCS, vol. 3940, pp. 34–51. Springer, Heidelberg (2006). https://doi.org/10.1007/11752790_2
59. Bartels, R.H., Stewart, G.W.: Solution of the matrix equation ax+xb=c [F4] (algorithm 432). Commun. ACM 15, 820–826 (1972)
60. Zhang, H., Dana, K.: Multi-style generative network for real-time transfer. arXiv preprint arXiv:1703.06953 (2017)
61. Peng, X., Bai, Q., Xia, X., Huang, Z., Saenko, K., Wang, B.: Moment matching for multi-source domain adaptation. In: ICCV, pp. 1406–1415 (2019)
62. Lee, K., Maji, S., Ravichandran, A., Soatto, S.: Meta-learning with differentiable convex optimization. In: CVPR, pp. 10657–10665 (2019)
63. Xu, R., Li, G., Yang, J., Lin, L.: Unsupervised domain adaptation: an adaptive feature norm approach. CoRR abs/1811.07456 (2018)
64. Maćkiewicz, A., Ratajczak, W.: Principal components analysis (PCA). Comput. Geosci. 19, 303–342 (1993)

Channel Pruning for Accelerating Convolutional Neural Networks via Wasserstein Metric

Haoran Duan and Hui Li[✉]

Key Laboratory of Wireless-Optical Communications, Chinese Academy of Sciences,
School of Information Science and Technology,
University of Science and Technology of China, Hefei, China
hrduan@mail.ustc.edu.cn, mythlee@ustc.edu.cn

Abstract. Channel pruning is an effective way to accelerate deep convolutional neural networks. However, it is still a challenge to reduce the computational complexity while preserving the performance of deep models. In this paper, we propose a novel channel pruning method via the Wasserstein metric. First, the output features of a channel are aggregated through the Wasserstein barycenter, which is called the basic response of the channel. Then the *channel discrepancy* based on the Wasserstein distance is introduced to measure channel importance, by considering both the channel's feature representation ability and the substitutability of the basic responses. Finally, channels with the least discrepancies are removed directly, and the loss in accuracy of the pruned model is regained by fine-tuning. Extensive experiments on popular benchmarks and various network architectures demonstrate that the proposed approach outperforms the existing methods.

Keywords: Channel pruning · Wasserstein metric · CNNs

1 Introduction

In recent years, convolutional neural networks (CNNs) have made great achievements in various computer vision tasks [1–4]. However, the superior performance of CNNs relies on its huge computation and memory cost, which makes these CNNs very difficult to deploy on the devices with limited resources, such as mobile phones or embedded gadgets, etc. To expand the application scope of the CNNs, the research on model compression has attracted great interest.

Recent developments in model compression can be divided into three categories, namely, quantization, low-rank approximation, and network pruning. Network quantization compresses the original network by using few bits to represent each weight. However, the quantization error leads to low training efficiency of the network. Low-rank approximation aims to compress and accelerate the network through tensor decomposition, but these methods often suffer from

© Springer Nature Switzerland AG 2021
H. Ishikawa et al. (Eds.): ACCV 2020, LNCS 12624, pp. 492–505, 2021.
https://doi.org/10.1007/978-3-030-69535-4_30

expensive fine-tuning processes and performance degradation. Network pruning has two branches, *i.e.*, weight pruning and filter/channel pruning. Weight pruning simply removes weights parameters in filters, which may lead to non-structured sparsity. Thus the specific hardware structure is required for efficient inference. In contrast, channel pruning can significantly reduce memory footprint and boost the inference speeds by directly discarding redundant channels. Moreover, channel pruning is hardware-friendly and it can be easily integrated with other model compression techniques.

In recent work [5], the greedy algorithm is used to remove redundant channels by minimizing the reconstruction error before and after pruning. Regularization-based methods [6–9] introduce the sparsity penalty to the training objective. For these methods, more training epochs and extra optimization are required to achieve an optimal pruning result, which leads to low efficiency for large networks and datasets. In [10] channel pruning is implemented based on feature reconstruction, which leads to the problem of redundant feature maps due to the absence of the analysis on the relationship among the channels. Wang *et al.* [11] explore the linear relationship among the channels through clustering feature maps. However, the clustering results are only obtained by specific inputs, which do not apply to various input categories. LFC *et al.* [12] prunes one filter of the filter pairs with the largest correlation. LFC only considers the linear relationship of filters while ignoring the nonlinear relationships of filters. Moreover, the extra optimization is needed to increase correlations. To address the above issues, we propose a novel pruning method via the Wasserstein metric.

The concept of the Wasserstein metric or distance derives from optimal transport theory [13], which provides many powerful tools for probability measures and distributions. The Wasserstein distance measures the similarity or discrepancy between distributions by computing the minimal cost of transporting all the mass contained in one distribution to another. The Wasserstein distance satisfies all metric axioms and has many favorable properties, and the details are referred to [13].

In this paper, we aim to identify the most replaceable channels by summarizing the output features of channels, which can reflect the channels' contributions to the layer. Specifically, to prune the most redundant channels in a pre-trained model, the Wasserstein barycenter [14,15] is first utilized to aggregate the output features of a channel. The Wasserstein barycenter is defined as the basic response of the channel, which represents the unique output characteristics of the channel and is independent of the specific input category. This property allows us to identify redundant channels by analyzing the discrepancy between the basic responses. After obtaining the basic response of channels, we further propose *channel discrepancy* to measure the differences between channels and the channel's feature representation ability. Channels with minimal *channel discrepancy* can be substituted by other channels. By directly identifying and removing the channels that contribute the least to each layer, the proposed method avoids the tedious feature reconstruction process. After pruning all redundant channels, the pruned model is fine-tuned to recover performance. Given a pre-trained model, the proposed method can construct a compact model with comparable or even higher performance.

The main contributions of this work can be summarized as follows:

- A novel channel pruning approach via the Wasserstein metric is proposed. The *channel discrepancy* is introduced to measure the contribution of the channel, which provides a new perspective for understanding channel redundancy. And the non-iterative pruning manner makes the proposed method more efficient than previous methods.
- To our knowledge, this is the first work to introduce the Wasserstein metric for pruning deep convolutional neural networks. The Wasserstein metric can be regarded as a new indicator of channel importance, which expands the current evaluation criteria.
- Extensive experiments on popular datasets and various network architectures demonstrate that the proposed pruning approach outperforms the previous methods. On CIFAR-10 [1], the proposed approach achieves about 60% FLOPs reduction of ResNet-56 and ResNet-110 with an accuracy gain of 0.02% and 0.27% respectively. On ImageNet [16], the pruned ResNet-101 achieves a 58.8% FLOPs reduction with a loss of 0.64% in the top-1 accuracy.

2   Related Work

Low-Rank Approximation. Denton *et al.* [17] introduce tensor decompositions based on SVD to approximate the weight matrix in CNNs. Jaderberg *et al.* [18] achieve a 4.5× speedup with little performance loss by approximating filter banks via low-rank filters. Lebedev *et al.* [19] utilize the Canonical Polyadic decomposition on the kernel tensors, which can be efficiently computed by existing algorithms.

Network Quantization. Chen *et al.* [20] propose to hash the network weights into different groups and the weight value is shared in each group. In [21], networks are quantized with binary weights which significantly reduces memory usage. Rastegari *et al.* [22] propose XNOR-Net to approximate convolutions with bitwise operations. Compared to standard networks, the proposed XNOR-Net can achieve a similar performance but more efficient. Zhao *et al.* [23] introduce outlier channel splitting to improve network quantization without retraining. To enhance the representational capability, Liu *et al.* [24] use a identity mapping to propagate the real-valued information before binarization.

Network Pruning. Recent work on network pruning can be categorized into two sub-families: weight pruning and channel pruning. In early weight pruning work, LeCun *et al.* [25] and Hassibi *et al.* [26] propose to remove redundant weights based on second-order derivatives of the loss function. Han *et al.* [27]

evaluate the importance of weights based on the magnitude and remove unimportant weights with small absolute values. Guo *et al.* [28] integrate pruning and splicing operations, by which incorrect pruned connections could be recovered if they are found to be important. However, weight pruning can cause irregular connections, which requires specialized hardware to accelerate. Thus channel pruning is more preferred than weight pruning. Channel pruning directly discards unimportant channels without affecting network structure. Li *et al.* [29] utilize ℓ_1-norm to measure the importance of each filter. Based on Lasso regression, He *et al.* [10] and Luo *et al.* [5] prune networks in a layer-by-layer manner by selecting the filters that minimizing the reconstruction error. He *et al.* [30] propose a soft manner pruning approach to preserve the model capacity. In [9], the saliency of each filter is globally evaluated and dynamically updated. Ye *et al.* [8] apply scaling factors to each channel and add the sparse penalty to the training objective. He *et al.* [31] introduce the Geometric Median to prune the fewer contribution filters in the network.

3   Preliminaries

In this section, we give a review of the key concepts used in our proposed method.

3.1   Wasserstein Distance

The p-Wasserstein distance [13], or the Monge-Kantorovich distance of order p, quantifying the discrepancy between two distributions μ_0 and μ_1 is defined as

$$\mathbf{W}_p\left(\mu_0, \mu_1\right) = \left(\inf_{\pi \in \Pi(\mu_0, \mu_1)} \int_{M \times M} d\left(x, y\right)^p \mathrm{d}\pi\left(x, y\right)\right)^{\frac{1}{p}}, \qquad (1)$$

where M denotes the compact embedding space and $d : M \times M \to \mathbb{R}_+$ denotes the geodesic distance function. $\Pi(\mu_0, \mu_1)$ is the set of joint distributions of (μ_0, μ_1) having μ_0 and μ_1 as marginals.

The Wasserstein distance satisfies all metric axioms. It seeks a transport plan $\pi \in \Pi(\mu_0, \mu_1)$ with the optimal cost of transporting distribution μ_0 to μ_1, where the cost of moving a unit of mass from x to y is

$$d\left(x, y\right)^p = \|x - y\|_p^p \qquad (2)$$

the cost $d\left(x, y\right)$ equals ℓ_1-norm, and $d\left(x, y\right)^2$ is calculated by the squared Euclidean distance.

3.2   Wasserstein Barycenter

Given a set of distributions $\{\mu_1, \mu_2, \ldots, \mu_k\}$, the Wasserstein barycenter μ with respect to the Wasserstein metric, is defined as the following minimization problem:

$$\mu = arg \min_{\mu} \sum_{i=1}^{k} \alpha_i \mathbf{W}_2^2\left(\mu, \mu_i\right), \qquad (3)$$

where $(\alpha_1, \alpha_2, \ldots, \alpha_k)$ are non-negative weights summing to 1, and $\mathbf{W}_2^2$ denotes the squared 2-Wasserstein distance.

The Wasserstein barycenter tries to summarize the collection of distributions, which can describe the geometry characteristics better than the Euclidean average.

3.3   Smoothed Wasserstein Distance

The computation of the normal version of the Wasserstein distance has high time complexity, which scaling super-cubically in the size of the domain. Adding an entropic regularization term to the original distance makes the problem strictly convex. Specifically, the squared 2-Wasserstein distance with an entropic regularization term is defined as

$$\mathbf{W}_{2,\gamma}^2 (\mu_0, \mu_1) = \inf_{\pi \in \Pi(\mu_0, \mu_1)} \left[\int_{M \times M} d(x, y)^2 \, \pi(x, y) \, \mathrm{d}x\mathrm{d}y - \gamma \mathbf{H}(\pi) \right], \qquad (4)$$

where $\mathbf{H}(\pi)$ denotes the differential entropy of π on $M \times M$ and $\gamma > 0$ is the regularization parameter.

The smoothed version of the Wasserstein distance can be solved iteratively by Sinkhorn-Knopp algorithm [32], with a linear convergence rate. Another good feature of the smoothed Wasserstein distance is that the computation can be carried out simultaneously using elementary linear algebra operations, which could take advantage of parallel GPGPU architectures to get further acceleration.

According to (3) and (4) , the original barycenter problem can be modified as follows

$$\mu = arg \min_{\mu} \sum_{i=1}^{k} \alpha_i \mathbf{W}_{2,\gamma}^2 (\mu, \mu_i). \qquad (5)$$

There has been a lot of excellent work aiming to solve (5). Our proposed method employs the fast convolution [15], which enhances Sinkhorn's efficiency by avoiding explicit pairwise distance computation and via the pre-factored diffusion operator.

4   Method

4.1   Notions

Let N denote a part of the samples of the training set. Considering the l-th layer of an L-layer CNN model, let n^l $(l \in [1, 2, \ldots, L])$ denote the number of input channels, k denote the spatial size of filters and h^l/w^l denote the height/weight of the input feature maps. Given the input feature maps $\mathbf{X}^l \in \mathbb{R}^{N \times n^l \times h^l \times w^l}$, the output feature maps $\mathbf{Y}^l (i.e., \mathbf{X}^{l+1} \in \mathbb{R}^{N \times n^{l+1} \times h^{l+1} \times w^{l+1}})$ can be computed by applying weights $\boldsymbol{\theta}^l \in \mathbb{R}^{n^{l+1} \times n^l \times k \times k}$.

For the i-th sample and the j-th channel of the l-th layer, the output feature map can be formulated as

$$\mathbf{Y}_{i,j}^l = \sigma\left(\boldsymbol{\theta}_j^l \otimes \mathbf{X}_i^l + \mathbf{b}^l\right), \tag{6}$$

where $\sigma\left(\cdot\right)$ denotes nonlinear activation functions and $\otimes$ denotes the convolutional operation. In the following, the bias term $\mathbf{b}^l$ and the layer index l are omitted for simplicity.

4.2   The Basic Response of Channel

In the previous works [5,10], all feature maps are reconstructed to preserve the ability of the channel but ignore that the output features corresponding to the redundant channel and the important channel have different contributions to the layer output. Thus the less important feature maps are also recovered by mistake.

In this paper, without reconstructing the feature maps directly, we aim to summarize the output features by the Wasserstein barycenter, which is defined as the basic response of the channel. By aggregating the output feature maps, the basic response could represent the unique output characteristics of the channel, which is independent of the specific input category. Therefore, by analyzing the discrepancy between the basic responses, it is possible to identify channels that need to discard.

The j-th channel's output $\mathbf{Y}_{:,j} = \{\mathbf{Y}_{1,j}, \mathbf{Y}_{2,j}, \ldots, \mathbf{Y}_{N,j}\}$ is a collection of output features learned from N training samples. According to (5), the basic response, or the barycenter of the j-th channel is

$$\boldsymbol{\Lambda}_j = \arg\min_{\boldsymbol{\Lambda}} \sum_{i=1}^{N} \frac{1}{N} \mathbf{W}_2^2\left(\boldsymbol{\Lambda}, \mathbf{Y}_{i,j}\right), \tag{7}$$

where the basic response $\boldsymbol{\Lambda}_j$ summarizes the set of output distributions, and remain the same shape of output feature map. Then the basic responses of the l-th layer are $\{\boldsymbol{\Lambda}_j\}_{j=1}^{n^{l+1}}$. According to (7), the calculation of the basic responses does not require any training or reconstruction process.

4.3   Channel Discrepancy

We introduce the Wasserstein distance as a new indicator of channel importance, due to its superior ability to measure the discrepancy of distributions. Once obtained the basic responses of each channel, the discrepancy $d_{j,k}$ of the j-th and the k-th channel is defined as

$$d_{j,k} = \mathbf{W}_2^2\left(\boldsymbol{\Lambda}_j, \boldsymbol{\Lambda}_k\right). \tag{8}$$

$d_{j,k}$ measures the difference between the basic responses of the two channels. The larger the value of discrepancy, the greater the difference between the output of

Algorithm 1. Algorithm of channel pruning

Input: Training data $\mathcal{D}$, pre-trained model $\mathcal{M}$ with weights $\left\{\boldsymbol{\theta}^l\right\}_{l=1}^L$, pruning rate P_l,
number of training samples N to compute the basic response.
Output: The pruned model with selected channels.
1: Forward model and get the output feature maps $\left\{\mathbf{Y}^l\right\}_{l=1}^L$.
2: **for** layer l in model $\mathcal{M}$ **do**
3:     **for** channel in layer l **do**
4:         Compute basic response of channel via (7).
5:     **end for**
6:     Compute *channel discrepancy* via (11).
7:     Remove P_l-rate channels with smallest *channel discrepancy*.
8: **end for**
9: Fine-Tune the pruned model.

---

the two channels. The *layer-discrepancy* LD_j of the j-th channel is the average
of the discrepancy between one channel and other channels, *i.e.*,

$$LD_j = \frac{1}{n^{l+1} - 1} \sum_{k=1, j \neq k}^{n^{l+1}} d_{j,k} \tag{9}$$

where n^{l+1} is the number of channels in the l-th layer. The channel with high
layer-discrepancy means that its output feature is unique and irreplaceable,
therefore is important to the layer.

The redundancy of a channel depend on not only the *layer-discrepancy* but
also its feature representation ability. An important channel is very active for
different inputs. The more active the channel is, the richer the output feature
maps. Such ability is called the *output-discrepancy*. According to (7) the *output-
discrepancy* OD_j can be computed by

$$OD_j = \sum_{i=1}^N \frac{1}{N} \mathbf{W}_2^2 \left(\boldsymbol{\Lambda}_j, \mathbf{Y}_{i,j}\right), \tag{10}$$

where $\boldsymbol{\Lambda}_j$ represents the basic response and $\mathbf{Y}_{i,j}$ denotes the output feature maps
of the j-th channel. The *output-discrepancy* measures the feature representation
ability of the channel. The less redundant channel has large *output-discrepancy*.

For the j-th channel in the l-th layer, by combining both *layer-discrepancy*
and *output-discrepancy*, we have a joint discrepancy formula as follows

$$D_j = LD_j + \beta OD_j = \frac{1}{n^{l+1} - 1} \sum_{k=1, j \neq k}^{n^{l+1}} d_{j,k} + \beta \sum_{i=1}^N \frac{1}{N} \mathbf{W}_2^2 \left(\boldsymbol{\Lambda}_j, \mathbf{Y}_{i,j}\right), \tag{11}$$

where the two terms are balanced by β. D_j measures the channel's contribution
to the entire layer and is called the *channel discrepancy*.

The *channel discrepancy* not only considers the mutual relationship between
channels but also considers the channel's feature representation ability, therefore

Table 1. Comparison of pruning results for VGG-16 on CIFAR-10. "B. Top-k" and "P. Top-k" denote the top-k accuracy of the baseline and pruned model respectively. "Top-k↓ (%)" means the top-k accuracy loss of pruned model compared to its baseline (smaller is better). "FLOPs↓ (%)" denotes the reduction of FLOPs.

Model	Method	B. Top-1 (%)	P. Top-1 (%)	Top-1↓ (%)	FLOPs↓ (%)
VGG-16	L1	93.25	93.40	−0.15	34.2
	CP	**93.99**	93.67	0.32	50.0
	ThinNet	**93.99**	93.85	0.14	50.0
	Ours	93.73 ± 0.16	**93.99 ± 0.28**	−0.26	**50.4**

channels with the smallest *channel discrepancy* can be directly identified and safely pruned.

4.4 Pruning Algorithm

The proposed pruning algorithm can be described in the following steps to prune the redundant channels at a pruning rate P_l:

1. For each channel's output feature maps $Y_{:,j}$ in Y, calculate its corresponding basic response Λ_j through (7).
2. Obtain the *channel discrepancy* by using (11).
3. Remove P_l-rate channels in l-th layer with the minimal *channel discrepancy*, and the related channels in the next layer are removed in the meanwhile.

All the channels with less discrepancies will be directly identified and then pruned together. The performance of the pruned model can be quickly restored after fine-tuning. This non-iterative pruning manner makes our method more effective than the previous methods. Algorithm 1 details the procedures of our pruning technique.

5 Experiments

5.1 Experimental Settings

The proposed pruning algorithm is evaluated on CIFAR-10 [1] and ImageNet [16] with popular CNN networks, including VGGNet [2] and ResNet [3]. The CIFAR-10 dataset 50K training images 10K validation images of 10 classes, and the ImageNet dataset consists of 1.28M training images and 50k validation images in 1000 classes. The CIFAR-10 experiments follow the same hyper-parameters setting in [3], training schedule and data argumentation in [33], and the "mean ± std" of accuracy is reported by running the experiment three times. For the ImageNet experiments, we follow the default settings in [3]. The training schedule is same as FPGM [31]. To balance the performance and efficiency, the number of the training samples, N is set to 256. The computations (elementwise arithmetic) of the Wasserstein distance and barycenter are accelerated by four NVIDIA GTX 1080 Ti GPUs.

Table 2. Pruning performance of Resnet-56 and Resnet-110 on CIFAR-10. For ResNet-56, our method achieves the highest performance with similar FLOPs reduction compared to previous methods. For ResNet-110, with 70% of the FLOPs reduced, the pruned model could still maintain almost the same performance as the baseline.

Model	Method	B. Top-1(%)	P. Top-1(%)	Top-1↓ (%)	FLOPs↓ (%)
ResNet-56	L1	93.04	93.06	−0.02	27.6
	CP	92.80	91.80	1.00	50.0
	ThinNet	**93.80**	92.98	0.82	49.8
	SFP	93.59	93.35	0.24	52.6
	AMC	92.80	91.90	0.90	50.0
	LFC	93.57	93.32	0.25	61.5
	FPGM	93.59	93.26	0.33	52.6
	Ours (40%)	93.28 ± 0.26	93.69 ± 0.24	−0.41	39.4
	Ours (50%)	93.28 ± 0.26	**93.71 ± 0.14**	**−0.43**	49.4
	Ours (60%)	93.28 ± 0.26	93.30 ± 0.34	−0.02	**59.4**
ResNet-110	L1	93.53	93.55	−0.02	15.9
	SFP	**93.68**	93.86	−0.18	40.8
	FPGM	**93.68**	93.74	−0.16	52.3
	Ours (40%)	93.59 ± 0.31	**94.22 ± 0.28**	**−0.63**	39.4
	Ours (50%)	93.59 ± 0.31	94.11 ± 0.43	−0.52	49.5
	Ours (60%)	93.59 ± 0.31	93.86 ± 0.37	−0.27	59.5
	Ours (70%)	93.59 ± 0.31	93.83 ± 0.42	−0.24	**69.9**

5.2   VGG-16 on CIFAR-10

VGGNet is widely used for vision tasks, which has a plain and straight forward network architecture. We select VGG-16 as a representative model. Following PFEC [29], the VGG-16 with Batch Normalization layer is used in the experiment, which is trained from scratch with 93.73% accuracy. When pruning, 30% convolution channels of each convolution layer in VGG-16 has been removed.

Table 1 shows the results compared with PFEC, CP [10] and ThinNet [5]. With 50.4% of FLOPs reduction, our pruning method could even gain a 0.26% improvement on accuracy.

5.3   ResNet on CIFAR-10

We also make experiments for Resnet-56 and ResNet-110 on CIFAR-10 dataset with different pruning rates. Table 2 shows the results.

For ResNet-56, we achieves similar FLOPs reduction (59.4% *vs.* 61.5%) compared to LFC [12], and maintains almost the same accuracy with respect to baseline model (−0.02%), while LFC drops 0.25%. Moreover, By setting the pruning rate to 50%, the proposed method achieves the best accuracy. With similar FLOPs reduction, our method preserves the highest performance by comparison with CP, ThinNet, SFP [30], AMC [34], and FPGM.

Table 3. Pruning results for Resnet-50 and Resnet-101 on ImageNet. Our proposed method achieves the best top-1 accuracy and top-5 accuracy compared with the existing methods.

Model	Method	B. Top-1 (%)	P. Top-1 (%)	Top-1↓ (%)	Top-5↓ (%)	FLOPs↓ (%)
ResNet-50	ThinNet	72.88	71.01	1.87	1.12	**55.8**
	GAL	76.15	71.95	4.20	1.93	43.0
	SN	76.10	74.90	1.20	–	43.0
	SFP	76.15	62.14	14.01	8.27	41.8
	GDP	75.13	71.89	3.24	1.59	51.3
	LFC	75.30	73.40	1.90	0.80	50.4
	Taylor	**76.18**	74.50	1.68	–	44.9
	FPGM	76.15	74.83	1.32	0.55	53.5
	Ours(45%)	76.15	**75.27**	**0.88**	**0.37**	50.4
ResNet-101	BN-ISTA	76.40	74.56	1.84	–	52.7
	Taylor	**77.37**	75.95	1.42	–	**63.5**
	Ours(50%)	**77.37**	**76.73**	**0.64**	**0.39**	58.8

Table 4. Pruning results by different measures. "A" with "B": compute barycenter by "A" and discrepancy by "B".

ResNet-56 (50%)	Our method	WB with JS	EB with WD	EB with JS
	93.71	93.51	93.34	93.30

For ResNet-110, by setting the pruning rate to 40%, our method achieves 94.22% accuracy, which is 0.63% higher than the baseline. As more FLOPs are reduced, the improved performance starts to decrease, but still performs better than previous methods. Under a FLOPs reduction of 69.9%, the pruned model can still exceed the baseline by 0.24%.

It is worth noting that for pruning the pre-trained model of ResNet-56 or ResNet-110, our method outperforms the baseline under various pruning ratios. However, previous methods suffer performance loss under high FLOPs reduction. These results verify the ability of our algorithm to compress the model while maintaining or even achieving better performance.

5.4   ResNet on ImageNet

To further verify the effectiveness of the proposed pruning method, we test ResNet-50 and ResNet-101 as two variants of ResNet on ImageNet, specifically the ILSVRC2012 version. Following [5,30], the shortcut connections are maintained for simplicity. We report our results in Table 3.

Methods like GAL [35], SFP, and GDP [9] suffer a lot from FLOPs reduction of ResNet-50, while our method achieves the best results with the only 0.88% top-1 and 0.37% top-5 accuracy loss, which outperforms the previous channel pruning methods (ThinNet, SN [36], SFP, LFC, FPGM, Taylor [37]). The reason is that our method removes channels with the least contribution to the networks

Table 5. Resnet-56 pruning results on CIFAR-10 using different orders $(p = 1, 2)$ of Wasserstein distance.

Pruning ratio	FLOPs↓ (%)	Top-1 accuracy (%)	
		$p = 1$	$p = 2$
40%	39.4	93.57	**93.64**
50%	49.4	93.47	**93.71**
60%	59.4	93.09	**93.30**

according to the *channel discrepancy*, thus the model could keep high performance after pruning. The pruned model of ResNet-101 maintains high top-1 accuracy (76.73%), and the top-5 accuracy only decreases by 0.39%, while the accuracy drops of BN-ISTA [8] and Taylor are much larger than our method.

6 Discussions

6.1 Comparing Wasserstein Metric with Other Measures

The Kullback-Leibler (KL) divergence and Jensen-Shannon (JS) divergence are commonly used to quantify the divergence between two distributions. The JS divergence is symmetric while the KL divergence is not. As bin-by-bin dissimilarity measures, these divergences only consider the relationships of bins belonging to the same index but ignore the information across bins [38]. Moreover, they require distributions to have joint supports [39]. However, Wasserstein distance (WD) can handle these problems well and be aware of the spatial information, thus captures perfectly the underlying probability space of the distributions [13].

Meanwhile, as a probability measure, Wasserstein barycenter (WB) captures important characteristics and preserves the basic structure of distributions better than the Euclidean barycenter (EB) [14].

To demonstrate the discussions above, we experiment with the EB/WB to compute barycenters, and JS/WD to compute the discrepancies. Results for ResNet-56 on CIFAR-10 are reported in Table 4, which show the effectiveness of our method.

6.2 Influence of the Order of the Wasserstein Distance

The discrepancies of channels can be computed using different orders of the Wasserstein distance. According to (2), the transport cost is ℓ_1-norm corresponding to the 1-Wasserstein distance for $p = 1$, and is squared Euclidean distance corresponding to the squared 2-Wasserstein distance for $p = 2$.

We explore the influence of the above two Wasserstein distances by pruning ResNet-56 on CIFAR-10. Top-1 accuracy drops of the pruned model are reported in Table 5. Obviously, the squared 2-Wasserstein distance achieves better results

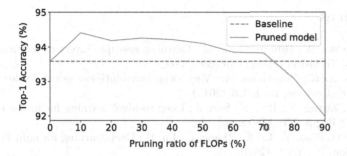

Fig. 1. Accuracy of ResNet-110 on CIFAR-10 regarding different pruning ratio of FLOPs. The dashed line and solid curve denote the baseline and pruned model respectively.

compared to the 1-Wasserstein distance, which means that 2-Wasserstein distance can find redundant channels more effectively. In addition, the proposed method is completely using the squared 2-Wasserstein distance to maintain consistency.

6.3 Varying Pruning Ratio of FLOPs

We conducted further experiments for ResNet-110 on CIFAR-10 with varying pruning ratios of FLOPs. Results are shown in Fig. 1. According to Fig. 1, when the pruning ratio increases to 10%, the performance rises sharply. It means that after pruning, the redundancy of ResNet is reduced, thereby alleviating the overfitting of the model. When the pruning ratio of FLOPs changes from 20% to 70%, the accuracy is slowly decreasing. As the pruning ratio larger than 70%, the accuracy of the pruned model drops dramatically, because the performance is limited by the high pruning ratio. It is worth noting that the pruned model always maintains a higher performance than the baseline when the pruning ratio is less than 70%. Overall, the high performance of the pruned model illustrates the powerful ability of the proposed method in compressing redundant models.

7 Conclusions

In this paper, a novel channel pruning method is proposed via the Wasserstein metric to accelerate CNN models. The Wasserstein barycenter is utilized to generate the basic response, which integrates the output features and summarizes the basic characteristics of each channel. Then the *channel discrepancy* of each channel measures the channel contribution, by considering both the channel's feature representation ability and channel relationships based on the Wasserstein distance. Finally, channels with the smallest discrepancies are selected and pruned. The comprehensive experiments on various popular network architectures verify the superior performance of the proposed method compared with the existing methods.

References

1. Krizhevsky, A., Hinton, G., et al.: Learning multiple layers of features from tiny images. Technical report, Citeseer (2009)
2. Simonyan, K., Zisserman, A.: Very deep convolutional networks for large-scale image recognition. In: ICLR (2015)
3. He, K., Zhang, X., Ren, S., Sun, J.: Deep residual learning for image recognition. In: CVPR, pp. 770–778 (2016)
4. Wang, T., Piao, Y., Li, X., Zhang, L., Lu, H.: Deep learning for light field saliency detection. In: ICCV (2019)
5. Luo, J.H., Wu, J., Lin, W.: ThiNet: a filter level pruning method for deep neural network compression. In: ICCV, pp. 5058–5066 (2017)
6. Wen, W., Wu, C., Wang, Y., Chen, Y., Li, H.: Learning structured sparsity in deep neural networks. In: NIPS, pp. 2074–2082 (2016)
7. Liu, Z., Li, J., Shen, Z., Huang, G., Yan, S., Zhang, C.: Learning efficient convolutional networks through network slimming. In: ICCV, pp. 2736–2744 (2017)
8. Ye, J., Lu, X., Lin, Z., Wang, J.Z.: Rethinking the smaller-norm-less-informative assumption in channel pruning of convolution layers. In: ICLR (2018)
9. Lin, S., Ji, R., Li, Y., Wu, Y., Huang, F., Zhang, B.: Accelerating convolutional networks via global & dynamic filter pruning. In: IJCAI, pp. 2425–2432 (2018)
10. He, Y., Zhang, X., Sun, J.: Channel pruning for accelerating very deep neural networks. In: ICCV, pp. 1389–1397 (2017)
11. Wang, D., Zhou, L., Zhang, X., Bai, X., Zhou, J.: Exploring linear relationship in feature map subspace for convnets compression. arXiv preprint arXiv:1803.05729 (2018)
12. Singh, P., Verma, V.K., Rai, P., Namboodiri, V.P.: Leveraging filter correlations for deep model compression. arXiv preprint arXiv:1811.10559 (2018)
13. Villani, C.: Optimal Transport: Old And New, vol. 338. Springer, Heidelberg (2008). https://doi.org/10.1007/978-3-540-71050-9
14. Cuturi, M., Doucet, A.: Fast computation of Wasserstein barycenters. In: ICML (2014)
15. Solomon, J., et al.: Convolutional Wasserstein distances: efficient optimal transportation on geometric domains. ACM Trans. Graph. **34**, 66 (2015)
16. Russakovsky, O., et al.: ImageNet large scale visual recognition challenge. In: IJCV, pp. 211–252 (2015)
17. Denton, E.L., Zaremba, W., Bruna, J., LeCun, Y., Fergus, R.: Exploiting linear structure within convolutional networks for efficient evaluation. In: NIPS, pp. 1269–1277 (2014)
18. Jaderberg, M., Vedaldi, A., Zisserman, A.: Speeding up convolutional neural networks with low rank expansions. In: BMVC (2014)
19. Lebedev, V., Ganin, Y., Rakhuba, M., Oseledets, I.V., Lempitsky, V.S.: Speeding-up convolutional neural networks using fine-tuned CP-decomposition. In: ICLR (2015)
20. Chen, W., Wilson, J., Tyree, S., Weinberger, K., Chen, Y.: Compressing neural networks with the hashing trick. In: ICML, pp. 2285–2294 (2015)
21. Courbariaux, M., Hubara, I., Soudry, D., El-Yaniv, R., Bengio, Y.: Binarized neural networks: training deep neural networks with weights and activations constrained to+ 1 or −1. arXiv preprint arXiv:1602.02830 (2016)

22. Rastegari, M., Ordonez, V., Redmon, J., Farhadi, A.: XNOR-Net: ImageNet classification using binary convolutional neural networks. In: Leibe, B., Matas, J., Sebe, N., Welling, M. (eds.) ECCV 2016. LNCS, vol. 9908, pp. 525–542. Springer, Cham (2016). https://doi.org/10.1007/978-3-319-46493-0_32

23. Zhao, R., Hu, Y., Dotzel, J., De Sa, C., Zhang, Z.: Improving neural network quantization without retraining using outlier channel splitting. In: ICML, pp. 7543–7552 (2019)

24. Liu, Z., Luo, W., Wu, B., Yang, X., Liu, W., Cheng, K.T.: Bi-real net: binarizing deep network towards real-network performance. IJCV **128**, 202–219 (2020)

25. LeCun, Y., Denker, J.S., Solla, S.A.: Optimal brain damage. In: NIPS, pp. 598–605 (1990)

26. Hassibi, B., Stork, D.G.: Second order derivatives for network pruning: optimal brain surgeon. In: NIPS, pp. 164–171 (1993)

27. Han, S., Mao, H., Dally, W.J.: Deep compression: compressing deep neural networks with pruning, trained quantization and Huffman coding. In: ICLR (2016)

28. Guo, Y., Yao, A., Chen, Y.: Dynamic network surgery for efficient DNNs. In: NIPS, pp. 1379–1387 (2016)

29. Li, H., Kadav, A., Durdanovic, I., Samet, H., Graf, H.P.: Pruning filters for efficient convnets. In: ICLR (2017)

30. He, Y., Kang, G., Dong, X., Fu, Y., Yang, Y.: Soft filter pruning for accelerating deep convolutional neural networks. In: IJCAI (2018)

31. He, Y., Liu, P., Wang, Z., Hu, Z., Yang, Y.: Filter pruning via geometric median for deep convolutional neural networks acceleration. In: CVPR, pp. 4340–4349 (2019)

32. Cuturi, M.: Sinkhorn distances: lightspeed computation of optimal transport. In: NIPS (2013)

33. Zagoruyko, S., Komodakis, N.: Wide residual networks. In: BMVC (2016)

34. He, Y., Lin, J., Liu, Z., Wang, H., Li, L.-J., Han, S.: AMC: AutoML for model compression and acceleration on mobile devices. In: Ferrari, V., Hebert, M., Sminchisescu, C., Weiss, Y. (eds.) ECCV 2018. LNCS, vol. 11211, pp. 815–832. Springer, Cham (2018). https://doi.org/10.1007/978-3-030-01234-2_48

35. Lin, S., et al.: Towards optimal structured CNN pruning via generative adversarial learning. In: CVPR, pp. 2790–2799 (2019)

36. Yu, J., Yang, L., Xu, N., Yang, J., Huang, T.S.: Slimmable neural networks. In: ICLR (2019)

37. Molchanov, P., Mallya, A., Tyree, S., Frosio, I., Kautz, J.: Importance estimation for neural network pruning. In: CVPR (2019)

38. Rubner, Y., Tomasi, C., Guibas, L.J.: The earth mover's distance as a metric for image retrieval. IJCV **40**, 99–121 (2000)

39. Arjovsky, M., Chintala, S., Bottou, L.: Wasserstein GAN. In: ICML, pp. 214–223 (2017)

Progressive Batching for Efficient Non-linear Least Squares

Huu Le[1]($\boxtimes$)(iD), Christopher Zach[1](iD), Edward Rosten[2,3](iD),
and Oliver J. Woodford[2,3](iD)

[1] Chalmers University, Gothenburg, Sweden
`huul@chalmers.se`
[2] Snap, Inc., London, UK
[3] Snap, Inc., Santa Monica, USA

Abstract. Non-linear least squares solvers are used across a broad range of offline and real-time model fitting problems. Most improvements of the basic Gauss-Newton algorithm tackle convergence guarantees or leverage the sparsity of the underlying problem structure for computational speedup. With the success of deep learning methods leveraging large datasets, stochastic optimization methods received recently a lot of attention. Our work borrows ideas from both stochastic machine learning and statistics, and we present an approach for non-linear least-squares that guarantees convergence while at the same time significantly reduces the required amount of computation. Empirical results show that our proposed method achieves competitive convergence rates compared to traditional second-order approaches on common computer vision problems, such as image alignment and essential matrix estimation, with very large numbers of residuals.

1 Introduction

Non-linear least squares (NLLS) solvers [1] are the optimizers of choice for many computer vision model estimation and fitting tasks [2], including photometric image alignment [3], essential matrix estimation [2] and bundle adjustment [4]. Fast convergence due to the second-order gradient model, and a simple, efficient implementation due to Gauss' approximation of the Hessian, make it a highly effective tool for these tasks. Nevertheless, the (non-asymptotic) computational efficiency of these methods can significantly impact the overall performance of a vision system, and the need to run such tasks in real-time, at video frame-rate, for applications such as Augmented Reality, leads to ongoing research to improve NNLS solvers.

This work was partially supported by the Wallenberg AI, Autonomous Systems and Software Program (WASP) funded by the Knut and Alice Wallenberg Foundation.

Electronic supplementary material The online version of this chapter (https://doi.org/10.1007/978-3-030-69535-4_31) contains supplementary material, which is available to authorized users.

© Springer Nature Switzerland AG 2021
H. Ishikawa et al. (Eds.): ACCV 2020, LNCS 12624, pp. 506–522, 2021.
https://doi.org/10.1007/978-3-030-69535-4_31

Standard NLLS solvers such as the Gauss-Newton (GN) [5] or Levenberg-Marquardt (LM) method [6,7] evaluate all residuals and their Jacobians (first derivatives of the residual function) at every iteration. Analogous to large-scale machine learning, utilizing all the data available to a problem can therefore substantially and unnecessarily slow down the optimization process. No improvements in solver efficiency have seen widespread adoption for model fitting, to address this problem. In practice, systems are engineered to pre-select a sparse set of data to avoid it, requiring some tuning on the part of the implementer to ensure that enough data is included for robustness and accuracy, while not too much is included, to keep computation time within budget. These design decisions, made at "compile time", do not then adapt to the unknown and variable circumstances encountered at run time.

Inspired by the stochastic methods used to accelerate large-scale optimization problems in machine learning, we introduce a stochastic NLLS optimizer that significantly reduces both computation time and the previously linear relationship between number of residuals and computation time, at no cost to accuracy. Our method has the following novel features:

- A stochastic, variable batch size approach for non-linear least squares that can be easily integrated into existing NLLS solvers for model fitting applications.
- A statistical test to determine the acceptance of an update step computed from a batch, without evaluating all residuals, that also progressively increases the batch size.
- Guaranteed convergence to a local minimum of the original problem, since all residuals are automatically included in the final iterations.

By adjusting the batch size at run time, according to a reasoned, statistical test, our algorithm is able to invest more computational resources when required, and less when not. This avoids the need to tightly tune the number of residuals at compile time, and can therefore lead to more accurate performance as a result.

We evaluate our method on a number of two-view geometry problems involving geometric and photometric residuals, such as essential matrix estimation and homography fitting, with promising results[1]. In particular, we empirically show that our new approach has much faster convergence rates compared to conventional approaches.

2   Related Work

2.1   Non-linear Least Squares

Fully second-order optimizers, such as NLLS methods, benefit from both the automatic choice of the step size and from modelling the dependency between variables, which results in faster convergence (rates) than first order and even quasi-Newton methods. Gauss replaced the Hessian of Newton's method with an approximation for least squares costs in 1809, creating the original NLLS

---

[1] Our source code is available at https://github.com/intellhave/ProBLM.

solver, the Gauss-Newton method [5]. Since the Gauss-Newton method does not guarantee convergence, the Levenberg-Marquardt algorithm [6,7] extends Gauss-Newton with back-tracking (i.e. conditional acceptance of new iterates) and diagonal damping of the (approximate) Hessian. More recently, a further modification of the Gauss-Newton method, variable projection (VarPro [8–10]), has been proposed for a particular class of separable problems, resulting in wider convergence basins to reach a global solution.

Since many model fitting tasks are solved using NLLS, several acceleration techniques have been developed to address problems of scale and real-time operation. However, these techniques are not generic, but instead exploit task specific properties. For example, certain image alignment tasks have been accelerated by the inverse compositional algorithm [3], which computes Jacobians once only, in the reference frame, or by learning a hyperplane approximation to the pseudo-inverse [11]. Truncated and inexact Newton methods [5] typically use iterative solvers such as conjugate gradients (CG) to approximately solve the linear system. These can converge in less time on larger scale problems, such as bundle adjustment (BA), especially when efficient, BA specific preconditioners are used [12]. In a framework such as RANSAC [13], convergence for each subproblem is not required so significant speedups are available by allowing a reduced probability of convergence [14].

Huge gains in efficiency are available if the problem exhibits a conditional independence structure. Bundle adjustment and related bipartite problem instances use techniques such as the Schur complement [4] (or more generally column reordering [15]) to reduce the size of the linear system to be solved in each iteration. Other linear systems have linear time solvers: Kalman smoothing [16] is a special case of using belief propagation [17] to solve linear least squares and such techniques can be applied to non-linear, robust least squares over tree structures [18].

2.2 Stochastic Methods

Stochastic first order methods [19,20], which are now common for large-scale optimization in machine learning, compute approximate (first order) gradients using subsets of the total cost, called batches, thereby significantly accelerating optimization. The randomness of the method (and the intermediate solutions) requires certain provisions in order to obtain guarantees on convergence. Due to their stochastic nature these methods empirically return solutions located in "wide" valleys [21,22].

In addition to first-order methods stochastic second-order one have also been investigated (e.g. [23–26]). One main motivation to research stochastic second-order methods is to overcome some shortcomings of stochastic first-order methods such as step size selection by introducing curvature (2nd-order) information of the objective. Due to the scale of problems tackled, many of these proposed algorithms are based on the L-BFGS method [27,28], which combines line search with low-rank approximations for the Hessian. The main technical difference between stochastic first-order and second-order methods is that the update direction in stochastic gradient methods is an unbiased estimate of the true descent direction, which is generally not the case for stochastic second-order updates. Convergence of stochastic methods relies on controlling the variance of the iterates, and consequently requires e.g. diminishing step sizes in stochastic first order methods [19, 29] or e.g. shrinking trust region radii [26] for a second order method. Without diminishing variances of the iterates, it is only possible to return approximate solutions [30]. Hence, using a proper stochastic method to minimize an NNLS instance over a finite number of residuals will never fully benefit from the fast convergence rates of 2nd order methods.

A number of recent proposals for stochastic methods use batches with an adaptive (or dynamically adjusted) batch size. This is in particular of interest in the second-order setting, since increasing the batch is one option to control the variance of the iterates (another option being reducing the step size). [31] and [32] propose schemes to adjust the batch size dynamically, which mostly address the first-order setup. Bollapragada et al. [24] propose a randomized qausi-Newton method, that is designed to have similar benefits as the stochastic gradient method. The method uses progressively larger sets of residuals, and the determination of the sample size is strongly linked with the underlying L-BFGS algorithm. A trust region method with adaptive batch size is described in [33], where the decision to accept a new iterate is based on the full objective (over all residuals), rather than the batch subset, limiting the benefits of this method. Similarly, [34] and [35] propose stochastic second-order methods that build on stochastic approximations of the Hessian but require computation of the full gradient (which was later relaxed in [36]).

The stochastic approaches above target optimizations with a large number of model parameters, which each depend on a large number of residuals. The scale of such problems does usually not permit the direct application of standard NLLS solvers. In many model fitting problems in computer vision, the number of variables appearing in the (Schur-complement reduced) linear system is small, making NLLS a feasible option. L-BFGS [37] (and any quasi-Newton method) has a disadvantage compared to Gauss-Newton derivatives for NNLS problem instances, since the NNLS objective is near quadratic when close to a local minimum. Thus, L-BFGS is not favoured in these applications, due to its slower convergence rate than NLLS (which is also empirically verified in Sect. 5). We note that the progressive batching of residuals introduced in this work can in principle also be applied to any local optimization method that utilizes backtracking to conditionally accept new iterates.

3   Background

3.1   Problem Formulation

Our work tackles the following NLLS problem:

$$\min_{\boldsymbol{\theta}} \sum_{i=1}^{N} f_i(\boldsymbol{\theta}), \quad \text{where} \quad f_i(\boldsymbol{\theta}) = \|\mathbf{r}_i(\boldsymbol{\theta})\|_2^2 \tag{1}$$

where $\boldsymbol{\theta} \in \mathbb{R}^d$ is the vector containing the desired parameters, N specifies the number of available measurements (residuals), and $\mathbf{r}_i : \mathbb{R}^d \mapsto \mathbb{R}^p$ is the function that computes the residual vector (of length p) of the i-th measurement.

It is worth noting that, while we start by introducing the standard NLLS formulation as per (1), our proposed method is directly applicable to robust parameter estimation problems through the use of methods such as Iteratively Reweighted Least Squares (IRLS) [38], since each step of IRLS can be reformulated as a special instance of (1). More specifically, with the use of a robust kernel ψ to penalize outlying residuals, the robust parameter estimation is defined as,

$$\min_{\boldsymbol{\theta}} \sum\nolimits_{i=1}^{N} g_i(\boldsymbol{\theta}), \quad \text{where} \quad g_i(\boldsymbol{\theta}) = \psi(\|\mathbf{r}_i(\boldsymbol{\theta})\|). \tag{2}$$

3.2   Levenberg-Marquardt Method

While our progressive batching approach is applicable to any second-order algorithm, here we employ Levenberg-Marquardt (LM) as the reference solver, as it is the most widely used method in a number of computer vision problems. In this section we briefly review LM and introduce some notations which are also later used throughout the paper.

At the t-th iteration, denote the current solution as $\boldsymbol{\theta}^{(t)}$ and $\{\mathbf{r}_i(\boldsymbol{\theta}^{(t)})\}_{i=1}^{N}$ as the set of residual vectors for all measurements. The LM algorithm involves computing the set of Jacobians matrices $\{\mathbf{J}_i^{(t)} \in \mathbb{R}^{p \times d}\}$, where, using $\mathbf{r}_i^{(t)}$ as shorthand for $\mathbf{r}_i(\boldsymbol{\theta}^{(t)})$,

$$\mathbf{J}_i^{(t)} = \left[\frac{\partial \mathbf{r}_i^{(t)}}{\partial \boldsymbol{\theta}_1^{(t)}} \frac{\partial \mathbf{r}_i^{(t)}}{\partial \boldsymbol{\theta}_2^{(t)}} \cdots \frac{\partial \mathbf{r}_i^{(t)}}{\partial \boldsymbol{\theta}_d^{(t)}} \right]. \tag{3}$$

Based on the computed Jacobian matrices and the residual vectors, the gradient vector $\mathbf{g}^{(t)}$ and approximate Hessian matrix $\mathbf{H}^{(t)}$ are defined as follows:

$$\mathbf{g}^{(t)} := \sum\nolimits_{i=1}^{N} (\mathbf{J}_i^{(t)})^T \mathbf{r}_i^{(t)}, \qquad \mathbf{H}^{(t)} := \sum\nolimits_{i=1}^{N} (\mathbf{J}_i^{(t)})^T \mathbf{J}_i^{(t)}, \tag{4}$$

where $(.)^T$ denotes the matrix transpose operation. Given $\mathbf{g}^{(t)}$ and $\mathbf{H}^{(t)}$, LM computes the step $\Delta\boldsymbol{\theta}$ by solving

$$\Delta\boldsymbol{\theta}^{(t)} \leftarrow -(\mathbf{H}^{(t)} + \lambda\mathbf{I})^{-1}\mathbf{g}^{(t)}, \tag{5}$$

where λ is the damping parameter that is modified after each iteration depending on the outcome of the iteration. In particular, if the computed step leads to a reduction in the objective function, i.e., $f(\boldsymbol{\theta}^{(t)} + \Delta\boldsymbol{\theta}^{(t)}) < f(\boldsymbol{\theta}^{(t)})$, the step is accepted and $\boldsymbol{\theta}$ is updated by setting $\boldsymbol{\theta}^{t+1} \leftarrow \boldsymbol{\theta}^t + \Delta\boldsymbol{\theta}$, while the damping λ is decreased by some factor. On the other hand, if $f(\boldsymbol{\theta}^{(t)} + \Delta\boldsymbol{\theta}^{(t)}) \geq f(\boldsymbol{\theta}^{(t)})$, $\Delta\boldsymbol{\theta}^{(t)}$ is rejected, λ is increased accordingly and (5) is recomputed; this is repeated until the cost is reduced.

4   Proposed Algorithm

In this section, we describe our proposed algorithm that is computationally cheaper than conventional second-order approaches. The main idea behind our algorithm is that, instead of computing the Jacobians of all residuals (as described in Sect. 3.2), we utilize only a small fraction of measurements to approximate the gradient and Hessian, from which the update step is computed.

Let $\mathcal{S}^{(t)} \subseteq \{1 \ldots N\}$ denote the subset of residual indices that are used at the t-th iteration (note that the set of subsampled indices can remain the same throughout many iterations, i.e., $\mathcal{S}^{t_0} = \cdots = \mathcal{S}^t (t_0 \leq t)$). For the ease of notation, we use $\mathcal{S}$ to specify the subset being used at the current iteration. Given a subset $\mathcal{S}$, analogous to (4), we use the notation $\mathbf{g}_{\mathcal{S}}$ and $\mathbf{H}_{\mathcal{S}}$ to denote the approximate gradient and Hessian obtained by only using residuals in the subset $\mathcal{S}^{(t)}$, i.e.

$$\mathbf{g}_{\mathcal{S}}^{(t)} := \sum_{i \in \mathcal{S}^{(t)}} \mathbf{J}_i^{(t)} \mathbf{r}_i^{(t)} \qquad \mathbf{H}_{\mathcal{S}}^{(t)} := \sum_{i \in \mathcal{S}^{(t)}} (\mathbf{J}_i^{(t)})^T \mathbf{J}_i^{(t)}. \qquad (6)$$

We also define the subset cost $f_{\mathcal{S}}^{(t)}$ as $f_{\mathcal{S}}^{(t)} := \sum_{i \in \mathcal{S}} f_i(\boldsymbol{\theta})$. Similar to (5), the approximate update step is denoted by $\Delta \hat{\boldsymbol{\theta}}_{\mathcal{S}^{(t)}}$, and is computed by

$$\Delta \boldsymbol{\theta}_{\mathcal{S}}^{(t)} \leftarrow -(\mathbf{H}_{\mathcal{S}}^{(t)} + \lambda \mathbf{I})^{-1} \mathbf{g}_{\mathcal{S}}^{(t)}. \qquad (7)$$

Note that depending on the characteristic of $\mathcal{S}^{(t)}$, $\mathbf{g}_{\mathcal{S}}^{(t)}$ and $\mathbf{H}_{\mathcal{S}}^{(t)}$ can be very far from the true $\mathbf{g}^{(t)}$ and $\mathbf{H}^{(t)}$, respectively. As a consequence, the update step $\Delta \boldsymbol{\theta}_{\mathcal{S}}^{(t)}$ computed from (7), despite resulting in a reduction in $f_{\mathcal{S}}^{(t)}$, may lead to an increase in the original cost $f^{(t)}$. However, as the number of measurements can be very large, computing the whole set of residuals at each iteration to determine the acceptance of $\Delta \boldsymbol{\theta}_{\mathcal{S}^{(t)}}$ is still very costly. Hence, we employ statistical approaches. Specifically, we only accept $\Delta \boldsymbol{\theta}_{\mathcal{S}}^{(t)}$ if, with a probability not less than $1 - \delta$ ($0 < \delta < 1$), a reduction in $f_{\mathcal{S}}^{(t)}$ also leads to a reduction in the true cost $f^{(t)}$. More details are discussed in the following sections.

4.1   A Probabilistic Test of Sufficient Reduction

We now introduce a method to quickly determine if an update step $\Delta \boldsymbol{\theta}_{\mathcal{S}}^{(t)}$ obtained from (7) also leads to a sufficient reduction in the original cost with a high probability. To begin, let us define $\boldsymbol{\theta}^{(t+1)} := \boldsymbol{\theta}^{(t)} + \Delta \boldsymbol{\theta}_{\mathcal{S}}^{(t)}$, and denote by

$$X_i = f_i(\boldsymbol{\theta}^{(t+1)}) - f_i(\boldsymbol{\theta}^{(t)}) \qquad (8)$$

the change of the i-th residual. We convert X_i to a random variable by drawing the index i from a uniform distribution over $\{1, \ldots, N\}$. Taking K random indices (which form the subset $\mathcal{S}$) yields the random variables $(Y_1, \ldots, Y_K)$, where

$$Y_k = X_{i_k} \qquad i_k \sim U\{1, \ldots, N\}. \qquad (9)$$

We can observe that the expectation

$$\mathbb{E}[Y_k] = f(\boldsymbol{\theta}^{(t+1)}) - f(\boldsymbol{\theta}^{(t)}) = \sum_i \left(f_i(\boldsymbol{\theta}^{(t+1)}) - f_i(\boldsymbol{\theta}^{(t)}) \right), \qquad (10)$$

represents the total change of the true objective, and at each iteration we are interested in finding $\boldsymbol{\theta}^{(t+1)}$ such that $\mathbb{E}[Y_k] < 0$. To obtain a lower bound for the random variables (which will be useful for the test introduced later), we can clamp Y_k to a one-sided range $[a, \infty)$ by introducing $Z_k := \max(a, Y_k)$. It can be noted that $\mathbb{E}[Y_k] \le \mathbb{E}[Z_k]$ and therefore $P(\mathbb{E}[Y_k] \ge 0) \le P(\mathbb{E}[Z_k] \ge 0)$, hence we can safely use $\mathbb{E}[Z_k]$ as a proxy to evaluate $\mathbb{E}[Y_k]$.

We introduce $S_K := \sum_{k=1}^{K} Z_k$, representing (an upper bound to) the observed reduction, i.e. $S_K \ge f_S(\boldsymbol{\theta}^{(t+1)}) - f_S(\boldsymbol{\theta}^{(t)})$. Recall that, during optimization, S_K is the only information available to the algorithm, while our real information of interest is the expectation $\mathbb{E}[Z_k]$. Therefore, it is necessary to establish the relation between $\mathbb{E}[Z_k]$ and S_K. Assume that $S_K < 0$ (i.e., the update step leads to a reduction in the observed cost), given a probability $0 < \delta < 1$, and a scalar $0 \le \alpha < 1$, we are interested in the following criterion,

$$P\left(\mathbb{E}[S_K] \le \alpha S_K\right) \ge 1 - \delta, \qquad (11)$$

indicating whether the true cost is also reduced by at least a fraction α of the observed reduction S_K with probability $1 - \delta$. Using Hoeffding's inequality [39][2], we obtain

$$P(\mathbb{E}[S_K] \ge \alpha S_K) = P\left(S_K - \mathbb{E}[S_K] \le (1 - \alpha)S_K\right) \le \exp\left(-\frac{2(1-\alpha)^2 S_K^2}{K(b-a)^2}\right), \quad (12)$$

where $b \in \mathbb{R}$ is the upper bound of the random variables Z_k ($Z_k \le b \ \forall k$). While the lower bound a can be freely chosen, computing b is often more involved in practice (we will discuss several options to choose b in the following section).[3]

In order for (11) to hold, we require the r.h.s. of (12) to be upper-bounded by a user-specified confidence level $\delta \in (0, 1)$, i.e., $\exp\left(-\frac{2(1-\alpha)^2 S_K^2}{K(b-a)^2}\right) \le \delta$, which leads to the condition

$$S_K \le -\frac{b-a}{1-\alpha} \cdot \sqrt{\frac{-K \log \delta}{2}} \qquad (\le 0). \qquad (13)$$

Thus, if the condition (13) is satisfied, we can confidently accept the step computed from the subset S. More specifically, based on S_K, the following steps are applied for the LM iterations on the subset:

1. $S_K \ge 0$: increase λ (e.g. $\lambda \leftarrow 10\lambda$), since the LM step was not successful for even the optimized function (the subsample version of the true objective).

---

[2] Hoeffding's inequality is one of the main tools in statistical learning theory, but has seem limited use in computer vision so far (e.g. [40]).

[3] Note that these bounds may depend on the current iteration, hence a and b should be understood as $a^{(t)}$ and $b^{(t)}$.

2. $S_K \leq 0$ but Eq. (13) is not satisfied: increase the sample set to K^+, λ remains unchanged.
3. $S_K \leq 0$ but Eq. (13) is satisfied: decrease λ (e.g. $\lambda \leftarrow \lambda/10$)

Note that Hoeffding's inequality also holds for sample sets without replacement. This means that indices i_k can be unique and obtained by random shuffling the residuals at the beginning of the algorithm. Let π be a random permutation of $\{1, \ldots, N\}$. Then S_K is given by $S_K = \{\pi(k) : k = 1, \ldots, K\}$. Thus, it is not necessary to draw batches at every iteration, which drastically reduces the variance of the iterates $\theta^{(t)}$. Further, using slightly more general versions of Hoeffding's inequality allows residual specific upper and lower bounds $[a_i, b_i]$, which can be useful especially when residuals can be grouped (e.g. into groups for the data terms and for a regularizer).

4.2   Bounding the Change of Residuals

Lower Bound a. Observe that, both the l.h.s. and r.h.s. of the criterion (13) depend on the lower bound a. Due to the fact that $\mathbb{E}[Y_k] \leq \mathbb{E}[Z_k]$, the condition (13) is valid for any choices of $a < 0$. One fast option to search for a is to successively select the observed reductions Y_k as values for a, and test whether the condition (13) is satisfied for any of them.

Upper Bound b. While choosing the upper bound b used in (13) is generally hard, in practice it can be approximated using several options:

1. Each f_i has range $[0, \bar{f}]$. This is the case e.g. when all $\mathbf{r}_i$ are continuous and the domain for θ is compact. It is also the case when f_i are robustified, i.e. $f_i(\theta) = \psi(\|\mathbf{r}_i(\theta)\|)$, where $\psi : \mathbb{R}_{\geq 0} \to [0, 1]$ is a robust kernel (such as the Geman-McClure or the Welsch kernels). If the upper bound $\bar{f}$ for each f_i is known, then b in Eq. (13) is given by $b = \bar{y}$ (since the worst case increase of a term f_i is from 0 to $\bar{y}$).
2. Each f_i is Lipschitz continuous with constant L_f. In this case we have $|f_i(\theta) - f_i(\theta')| \leq L_f \|\theta - \theta'\|$, in particular for $\theta = \theta^{(t)}$ and $\theta = \theta^{(t+1)}$. This implies that $|f_i(\theta^{(t+1)}) - f_i(\theta^{(t)})| \leq L_f \|\theta^{(t+1)} - \theta^{(t)}\|$ for all i, and b in Eq. (13) is therefore given by $b = L_f \|\theta^{(t+1)} - \theta^{(t)}\|$. This computation of b can be extended straightforwardly if all f_i are Hölder continuous.

In our experiments, we test our algorithm on both robustified and non-robustified problems. In order to approximate L_f for non-robustified cases, we propose to use the maximum change in sampled residuals, i.e.,

$$L_f = \max_{i \in S} \frac{|f_i(\theta^{(t+1)}) - f_i(\theta^{(t)})|}{\|\theta^{(t+1)} - \theta^{(t)}\|}. \tag{14}$$

4.3   Determining New Sample Sizes

At any iteration, when the condition (13) fails, the sample size K is increased to $K^+ > K$, and the algorithm continues with an extended subset $\mathcal{S}^+$ with $|\mathcal{S}^+| = K^+$. In this work, we approximate K^+ as follows: we use the estimate $\hat{S}_{K+} = K^+ S_K / K$ for S_{K+} and choose K^+ such that the condition Eq. (13) is satisfied for our estimate $\hat{S}_{K+}$. After simplification we obtain

$$K^+ = -\frac{K^2(b-a)^2 \log \delta}{2S_K^2(1-\alpha)^2}. \tag{15}$$

If we introduce $\tilde{\delta} := \exp(2S_K^2/(K(b-a)^2))$ as the confidence level such that $P(\mathbb{E}[S_K] \geq 0) \leq \tilde{\delta}$ under the observed value S_K, then K^+ can be stated as $K^+ = K \frac{\log \delta}{\log \tilde{\delta}}$. If $K^+ > N$, then the new batch size is at most N. In summary, K^+ is given by

$$K^+ = \min\left\{ N, \left\lceil -\frac{K^2(b-a)^2 \log \delta}{2S_K^2(1-\alpha)^2} \right\rceil \right\}. \tag{16}$$

4.4   Relaxing the Condition (13)

If T_S iterations of LM steps on subsampled residuals are applied, then the probability that *all* of these iterations led to a decrease of the full objective is given by $(1-\delta)^{T_S}$. Asking for all steps to be true descent steps can be very restrictive, and makes the condition (13) unnecessarily strict.[4] In practice one is interested that (i) most iterations (but not necessarily all) lead to a descent of the true objective, and that (ii) the true objective is reduced at the end of the algorithm (or for a number of iterations) with very high probability. Let t_0 and t be two iterations counters $t_0 < t$ such that the sample sets are constant, $\mathcal{S}^{(t_0)} = \ldots = \mathcal{S}^{(t)}$. Let $T_S = t - t_0 + 1$ be the number of successful LM iterations, that use the current sample set $\mathcal{S}^{(t)}$, and introduce the total observed reduction of the sampled cost after T (successful) iterations,

$$U_K^{(t_0,t)} := \sum_{r=t_0}^{t} S_K^{(r)}, \tag{17}$$

and recall that $S_K = U_K^{(t_0,t_0)}$. Let the current iteration be a successful step (leading to a reduction of the sampled objective $f_{\mathcal{S}_K^{(t)}}$). With the introduction of U_k, following the same reasoning as introduced in Sect. 4.1, our relaxed criterion reads:

$$U_K^{(t_0,t)} \leq -\frac{1-\alpha}{b-a}\sqrt{\frac{-K \log \delta}{2}} \tag{18}$$

---

[4] If we allow a "failure" probability η_0 for only increasing steps, then δ is given by $\delta = 1 - \sqrt[T_S]{(1-\eta_0)}$. E.g., setting $T_S = 100$ and $\eta_0 = 10^{-4}$ yields $\delta \approx 10^{-6}$.

If the above criterion (with $\alpha \in (0,1)$) is not satisfied, then with probability $\eta \in [0,1)$ the step is temporarily accepted (and λ reduced). With probability $1 - \eta$ the step is rejected and the sample size is increased. The rationale is that allowing further iterations with the current sample set may significantly reduce the objective value. If the condition (18) is never satisfied for the current sample set $\mathcal{S}^{(t_0)}$, then the expected number of "wasted" iterations is $1/(1 - \eta)$ (using the properties of the geometric series).

Algorithm 1. Stochastic Levenberg-Marquardt

Require: Initial solution $\boldsymbol{\theta}^{(0)}$, initial batch size K_0, maximum iterations `max_iter`
Require: Confidence level $\delta \in (0,1)$, margin parameter $\alpha \in [0,1)$
 1: Randomly shuffle the residuals $\{f_i\}$ and initialize $t \leftarrow 0$, $K \leftarrow K_0$
 2: **while** $t <$ `max_iter` and a convergence criterion is not met **do**
 3: $\quad \mathcal{S}^{(t)} \leftarrow \{1, \dots, K\}$
 4: $\quad$ Compute $\mathbf{g}_{\mathcal{S}^{(t)}}$ and $\mathbf{H}_{\mathcal{S}^{(t)}}$

$$\mathbf{g}_{\mathcal{S}^{(t)}} := \sum\nolimits_{i \in \mathcal{S}^{(t)}} \mathbf{J}_i^{(t)} \mathbf{r}_i^{(t)} \qquad \mathbf{H}_{\mathcal{S}^{(t)}} := \sum\nolimits_{i \in \mathcal{S}^{(t)}} (\mathbf{J}_i^{(t)})^T \mathbf{J}_i^{(t)}. \qquad (19)$$

$\quad$ and solve

$$\Delta\boldsymbol{\theta}^{(t)} \leftarrow (\mathbf{H}_{\mathcal{S}^{(t)}} + \lambda\mathbf{I})^{-1} \mathbf{g}_{\mathcal{S}^{(t)}} \qquad \boldsymbol{\theta}^{(t+1)} \leftarrow \boldsymbol{\theta}^{(t)} + \Delta\boldsymbol{\theta}^{(t)} \qquad (20)$$

 5: $\quad$ Determine current lower and upper bounds a and b, and set

$$S_K \leftarrow \sum\nolimits_{i \in \mathcal{S}^{(t)}} \max\left\{ a, \left(f_i(\boldsymbol{\theta}^{(t+1)}) - f_i(\boldsymbol{\theta}^{(t)}) \right) \right\}. \qquad (21)$$

 6: $\quad$ **if** $S_K \geq 0$ **then**
 7: $\quad\quad \boldsymbol{\theta}^{(t+1)} \leftarrow \boldsymbol{\theta}^{(t)}$ and $\lambda \leftarrow 10\,\lambda$ $\qquad\qquad\qquad\qquad\qquad$ ▷ Failure step
 8: $\quad$ **else if** S_K satisfies Eq. (13) **then**
 9: $\quad\quad \lambda \leftarrow \lambda/10$ $\qquad\qquad\qquad\qquad\qquad\qquad\qquad\qquad\qquad$ ▷ Success step
10: $\quad$ **else**
11: $\quad\quad \boldsymbol{\theta}^{(t+1)} \leftarrow \boldsymbol{\theta}^{(t)}$ and increase K using Eq. (16)
12: $\quad$ **end if**
13: $\quad t \leftarrow t + 1$
14: **end while**
15: **return** $\boldsymbol{\theta}^{(t)}$

4.5 The Complete Algorithm

We illustrate the complete method in Algorithm 1, which essentially follows a standard implementation of the Levenberg-Marquardt method. One noteworthy difference is that the implementation distinguishes between three scenarios depending on the reduction gain S_K (failure step, success step and insufficient step). For clarity we describe the basic (non-relaxed) variant of the method, and refer to the supplementary material for the implementation based on the relaxed test (Eq. (18) and the details of estimating the lower bound a. In the experiments we refer to our algorithm using the acronym *ProBLM* (**Pro**gressive **Ba**tching **LM**).

4.6   Convergence

When `max_iter`$\to \infty$, then the convergence properties of the algorithm are the same as for the regular Levenberg-Marquardt method: if a sample set $\mathcal{S}^{(t)}$ remains constant for a number of iterations, the method eventually approaches a stationary point of $f_{\mathcal{S}^{(t)}}$ leading to diminishing reductions S_K. Consequently, Eq. (13) will not hold after a finite number of iterations, and the batch size strictly increases until $K^+ = N$ is reached.

5   Experiments

We choose dense image alignment (with homography model and photometric errors), and essential matrix estimation (with geometric errors) to evaluate the performance our proposed algorithm. Experiments for bundle adjustment can be found in the supplementary. The image pairs used throughout our experiments are obtained from a variety of publicly available datasets, including the ETH3D,[5] EPFL Multi-view stereo[6] and AdelaideMRF[7] dataset [41]. In this section, we focus on presenting representative results that highlight the performance of our approach. More detailed results and studies of parameters are provided in the supplementary material. Two types of problems are tested in our experiments:

– Standard NLLS (Problem (1)): To test this type of problem, we perform dense homography estimation with photometric errors, and essential matrix refinement using sparse key points (outliers are assumed to be rejected by a pre-processing step, e.g. using RANSAC [13]).
– Problems with robustified residuals: We also investigate the performance of our approach on model fitting problems with robust kernels (Problem (2)). The essential matrix estimation on a sparse set of putative correspondences (containing outliers) is performed, where the outliers are directly discarded during the optimization process by applying a robust kernel ψ to the residuals (in contrast to the previous experiments where RANSAC is used to discard outliers). We choose ψ to be the smooth truncated least squares kernel,

$$\psi(r) = \tfrac{\tau^2}{4}\left(1 - \max\{0, 1 - r^2/\tau^2\}^2\right) \tag{22}$$

where τ is the inlier threshold. In this case, the upper bound b on the residual changes that is used in Eq. (13) is $\tfrac{1}{4}\tau^2$.

---

[5] https://www.eth3d.net/datasets.
[6] https://www.epfl.ch/labs/cvlab/data/data-strechamvs/.
[7] https://tinyurl.com/y9u7zmqg.

The standard LM algorithm is used as the baseline to assess the performance of our proposed approach. In addition, we also compared our method against L-BFGS. All algorithms are implemented in C++ and executed on an Ubuntu workstation with an AMD Ryzen 2950X CPU and 64GB RAM. We employ the open-source OpenCV library[8] for pre-processing tasks such as SIFT feature extraction and robust fitting with RANSAC. We set δ to 0.1 and α to 0.9 in all experiments. The initial sample size (K_0) is set to $0.1N$ (N is the number of total measurements). All the experiments use the relaxed version as shown in Eq. (18), where the parameter η is set to 0.5. A comparison between Eq. (13) and its relaxed version is provided in the supplementary material.

5.1 Dense Image Alignment with Photometric Errors

This problem is chosen to demonstrate the efficiency of our proposed method as it often requires optimizing over a very large number of residuals (the number of pixels in the source image). In particular, given two images I_1 and I_2, the task is to estimate the parameters $\theta \in \mathbb{R}^d$ that minimize the photometric error,

$$\min_{\theta} \sum_{\mathbf{x} \in I_1} \|I_1(\mathbf{x}) - I_2(\pi(\mathbf{x}, \theta))\|^2, \tag{23}$$

where $\mathbf{x}$ represents the pixel coordinates, and $\pi(\mathbf{x}, \theta)$ is the transform operation of a pixel $\mathbf{x}$ w.r.t. the parameters θ. In this experiment π is chosen to be the homography transformation, thus $\theta \in \mathbb{R}^8$ (as the last element of the homography matrix can be set to 1). When linearizing the residual we utilize the combined forward and backward compositional approach [42] (which averages the gradient contribution from I_1 and I_2), since this is more stable in practice and therefore a more realistic scenario.

We select six image pairs from the datasets (introduced above) to test our method (results for more image pairs can be found in the supplementary materials). Figure 1 shows the optimization progress for the chosen image pairs, where we plot the evolution of the objectives vs. the run times for our method and conventional LM. We also compare the results against L-BFGS, where it can clearly be observed that L-BFGS performs poorly for this particular problem (note that for image pairs where L-BFGS does not provide reasonable solutions, we remove their results from the plots).

As can be observed from Fig. 1, ProBLM achieves much faster convergence rates compared to LM. Moreover, Fig. 1 also empirically shows that our proposed method always converges to the same solutions as LM, thanks to our efficient progressive batching mechanism. Due to the non-linearity of the underlying problem this is somewhat surprising, since the methods will follow different trajectories in parameter space.

5.2 Essential Matrix Estimation with Squared Residuals

High-resolution image pairs from the *"facade"* sequence extracted from the ETH3D dataset are used in this experiment. For each image, we extract SIFT

---

[8] https://github.com/opencv/opencv.

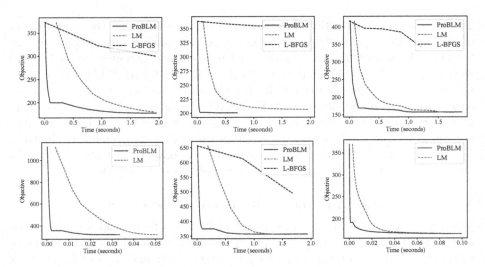

Fig. 1. Plots of objective vs. time for our method in comparison with LM and L-BFGS on dense image alignment. The image pairs used are (from left to right, top to bottom): Head, Hartley Building, Union House, Old Classics Wing, Johnson, and Napier Building.

key points, and use nearest neighbor search to get approximately 5000 putative correspondences per image pair. The key points are normalized using the corresponding intrinsic matrices provided with the dataset. To obtain an outlier-free correspondence set, we run 100 RANSAC iterations on the putative matches to obtain around 2000 inliers per image pair, which are then fed into the nonlinear least squares solvers for refinement. The objective of interest is the total Sampson error induced by all residuals, and we use the parameterisation of [14].

We first evaluate the performance of the algorithms on a single pair of images with different random starting points. Figure 2a shows the objectives versus run time for a single pair of image on 20 runs, where at the beginning of each run, a random essential matrix is generated and used as starting solution for all methods. Similar to the case of dense image alignment shown in Fig. 1, ProBLM demonstrates superior performance throughout all the runs.

The experiment is repeated for 50 different pairs of images. For each pair, we execute 100 different runs and record their progresses within a run time budget of 10 ms. The results are summarized in Fig. 3a, where we use performance profiles [43] to visualize the overall performance. For each image pair, we record the minimum objective f^* obtained across 100 runs, then measure the percentage of runs (denoted by ρ) that achieves the cost of $\leq \tau f^*$ ($\tau \geq 1$) at termination. Figure 3a shows the results. Observe that within a time budget of 10 ms, a large fraction of ProBLM runs achieve the best solutions, while most LM runs take much longer time to converge. This shows that our method is of great interest for real-time applications.

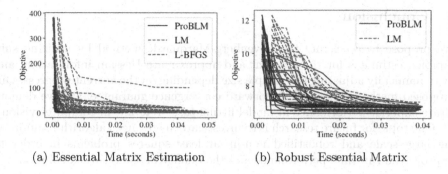

Fig. 2. Objectives vs run-time for 20 runs with random initializations for non-robust (left) and robust essential matrix essential matrix estimation (right).

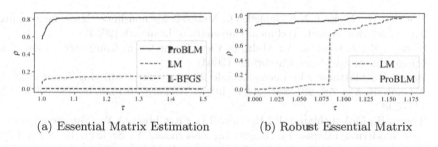

Fig. 3. Performance profiles for (left): essential matrix estimation with run time budget set to 10 ms, and (right): robust essential matrix estimation with run time budget set to 200 ms.

5.3   Robust Essential Matrix Fitting

As introduced earlier, our method is directly applicable to model fitting problems with robust kernels. To demonstrate this, we repeat the essential matrix fitting problem as discussed in the previous section, but we use the set of 5000 putative correspondences as input. To enforce robustness, we apply the smooth truncated least squares kernel shown in Eq. (22). Graduated Non-convexity [44] with 5 graduated levels is employed as the optimization framework. At each level (outer loop), our method is used to replace LM and the problem is optimized until convergence before switching to the next level. We compare this traditional approach where LM is used in the nested loop. Figure 2b and 3b show the evolution and performance profile (with the time budget of 200 ms) for this experiment. Similar to the case of clean data, our proposed method outperforms traditional LM by a large margin. A comparison with RANSAC can be found in the supplementary material, where we demonstrate that by applying ProBLM, one achieves comparable solutions to RANSAC within the same amount of run time, which further strengthens the applicability of our method for a wide range of vision problems.

6 Conclusion

We propose to accelerate the Levenberg-Marquardt method by utilizing subsampled estimates for the gradient and approximate Hessian information, and by dynamically adjusting the sample size depending on the current progress. Our proposed method has a straightforward convergence guarantee, and we demonstrate superior performance in model fitting tasks relevant in computer vision.

One topic for future research is to investigate in advanced algorithms addressing large-scale and robustified non-linear least-squares problems in order to improve the run-time performance and the quality of the returned solution.

References

1. Madsen, K., Nielsen, N., Tingleff, O.: Methods for non-linear least squares problems. Technical report, Technical University of Denmark (2004)
2. Hartley, R., Zisserman, A.: Multiple View Geometry in Computer Vision. Cambridge University Press, Cambridge (2003)
3. Baker, S., Matthews, I.: Lucas-Kanade 20 years on: a unifying framework. Int. J. Comput. Vis. **56**, 221–255 (2004). https://doi.org/10.1023/B:VISI.0000011205.11775.fd
4. Triggs, B., McLauchlan, P.F., Hartley, R.I., Fitzgibbon, A.W.: Bundle adjustment — a modern synthesis. In: Triggs, B., Zisserman, A., Szeliski, R. (eds.) IWVA 1999. LNCS, vol. 1883, pp. 298–372. Springer, Heidelberg (2000). https://doi.org/10.1007/3-540-44480-7_21
5. Nocedal, J., Wright, S.: Numerical Optimization. Springer, Heidelberg (2006). https://doi.org/10.1007/978-0-387-40065-5
6. Levenberg, K.: A method for the solution of certain non-linear problems in least squares. Q. Appl. Math. **2**, 164–168 (1944)
7. Marquardt, D.W.: An algorithm for least-squares estimation of nonlinear parameters. J. Soc. Ind. Appl. Math. **11**, 431–441 (1963)
8. Golub, G.H., Pereyra, V.: The differentiation of pseudo-inverses and nonlinear least squares problems whose variables separate. SIAM J. Numer. Anal. **10**, 413–432 (1973)
9. Okatani, T., Deguchi, K.: On the Wiberg algorithm for matrix factorization in the presence of missing components. Int. J. Comput. Vis. **72**, 329–337 (2007). https://doi.org/10.1007/s11263-006-9785-5
10. Hong, J.H., Zach, C., Fitzgibbon, A.: Revisiting the variable projection method for separable nonlinear least squares problems. In: 2017 IEEE Conference on Computer Vision and Pattern Recognition, pp. 127–135 (2017)
11. Jurie, F., Dhome, M.: Hyperplane approximation for template matching. IEEE Trans. Pattern Anal. Mach. Intell. **24**, 996–1000 (2002)
12. Agarwal, S., Snavely, N., Seitz, S.M., Szeliski, R.: Bundle adjustment in the large. In: Daniilidis, K., Maragos, P., Paragios, N. (eds.) ECCV 2010. LNCS, vol. 6312, pp. 29–42. Springer, Heidelberg (2010). https://doi.org/10.1007/978-3-642-15552-9_3
13. Fischler, M.A., Bolles, R.C.: Random sample consensus: a paradigm for model fitting with applications to image analysis and automated cartography. Commun. ACM **24**, 381–395 (1981)

14. Rosten, E., Reitmayr, G., Drummond, T.: Improved RANSAC performance using simple, iterative minimal-set solvers. Technical report (2010)
15. Davis, T.A., Gilbert, J.R., Larimore, S.I., Ng, E.G.: Algorithm 836: COLAMD, a column approximate minimum degree ordering algorithm. ACM Trans. Math. Softw. (TOMS) **30**, 377–380 (2004)
16. Kalman, R.E.: A new approach to linear filtering and prediction problems. Trans. ASME-J. Basic Eng. **82**, 35–45 (1960)
17. Pearl, J.: Reverend Bayes on inference engines: a distributed hierarchical approach. In: Proceedings of the Second AAAI Conference on Artificial Intelligence, AAAI 1982, pp. 133–136. AAAI Press (1982)
18. Drummond, T., Cipolla, R.: Real-time tracking of highly articulated structures in the presence of noisy measurements. In: Proceedings Eighth IEEE International Conference on Computer Vision, ICCV 2001, vol. 2, pp. 315–320 (2001)
19. Robbins, H., Monro, S.: A stochastic approximation method. Ann. Math. Stat. **22**, 400–407 (1951)
20. Kiefer, J., Wolfowitz, J., et al.: Stochastic estimation of the maximum of a regression function. Ann. Math. Stat. **23**, 462–466 (1952)
21. Wilson, D.R., Martinez, T.R.: The general inefficiency of batch training for gradient descent learning. Neural Netw. **16**, 1429–1451 (2003)
22. Keskar, N.S., Mudigere, D., Nocedal, J., Smelyanskiy, M., Tang, P.T.P.: On large-batch training for deep learning: generalization gap and sharp minima. arXiv preprint arXiv:1609.04836 (2016)
23. Byrd, R.H., Hansen, S.L., Nocedal, J., Singer, Y.: A stochastic quasi-Newton method for large-scale optimization. SIAM J. Optim. **26**, 1008–1031 (2016)
24. Bollapragada, R., Nocedal, J., Mudigere, D., Shi, H.J., Tang, P.T.P.: A progressive batching L-BFGS method for machine learning. In: International Conference on Machine Learning, pp. 620–629 (2018)
25. Zhao, R., Haskell, W.B., Tan, V.Y.: Stochastic L-BFGS: improved convergence rates and practical acceleration strategies. IEEE Trans. Signal Process. **66**, 1155–1169 (2018)
26. Curtis, F.E., Shi, R.: A fully stochastic second-order trust region method. arXiv preprint arXiv:1911.06920 (2019)
27. Nocedal, J.: Updating quasi-Newton matrices with limited storage. Math. Comput. **35**, 773–782 (1980)
28. Liu, D.C., Nocedal, J.: On the limited memory BFGS method for large scale optimization. Math. Program. **45**, 503–528 (1989). https://doi.org/10.1007/BF01589116
29. Bottou, L., Curtis, F.E., Nocedal, J.: Optimization methods for large-scale machine learning. SIAM Rev. **60**, 223–311 (2018)
30. Tran-Dinh, Q., Pham, N.H., Nguyen, L.M.: Stochastic Gauss-Newton algorithms for nonconvex compositional optimization. arXiv preprint arXiv:2002.07290 (2020)
31. Byrd, R.H., Chin, G.M., Nocedal, J., Wu, Y.: Sample size selection in optimization methods for machine learning. Math. Program. **134**, 127–155 (2012). https://doi.org/10.1007/s10107-012-0572-5
32. Bollapragada, R., Byrd, R., Nocedal, J.: Adaptive sampling strategies for stochastic optimization. SIAM J. Optim. **28**, 3312–3343 (2018)
33. Mohr, R., Stein, O.: An adaptive sample size trust-region method for finite-sum minimization. arXiv preprint arXiv:1910.03294 (2019)
34. Agarwal, N., Bullins, B., Hazan, E.: Second-order stochastic optimization for machine learning in linear time. J. Mach. Learn. Res. **18**, 4148–4187 (2017)

35. Pilanci, M., Wainwright, M.J.: Newton sketch: a near linear-time optimization algorithm with linear-quadratic convergence. SIAM J. Optim. **27**, 205–245 (2017)
36. Roosta-Khorasani, F., Mahoney, M.W.: Sub-sampled Newton methods. Math. Program. **174**, 293–326 (2019). https://doi.org/10.1007/s10107-018-1346-5
37. Byrd, R.H., Lu, P., Nocedal, J., Zhu, C.: A limited memory algorithm for bound constrained optimization. SIAM J. Sci. Comput. **16**, 1190–1208 (1995)
38. Holland, P.W., Welsch, R.E.: Robust regression using iteratively reweighted least-squares. Commun. Stat.-Theory Methods **6**, 813–827 (1977)
39. Hoeffding, W.: Probability inequalities for sums of bounded random variables. In: Fisher, N.I., Sen, P.K. (eds.) The Collected Works of Wassily Hoeffding. SSS, pp. 409–426. Springer, New York (1994). https://doi.org/10.1007/978-1-4612-0865-5_26
40. Cohen, A., Zach, C.: The likelihood-ratio test and efficient robust estimation. In: IEEE International Conference on Computer Vision (ICCV) (2015)
41. Wong, H.S., Chin, T.J., Yu, J., Suter, D.: Dynamic and hierarchical multi-structure geometric model fitting. In: 2011 IEEE International Conference on Computer Vision (ICCV), pp. 1044–1051. IEEE (2011)
42. Malis, E.: Improving vision-based control using efficient second-order minimization techniques. In: IEEE International Conference on Robotics and Automation, Proceedings, ICRA 2004, vol. 2, pp. 1843–1848. IEEE (2004)
43. Dolan, E.D., Moré, J.J.: Benchmarking optimization software with performance profiles. Math. Program. **91**, 201–213 (2002). https://doi.org/10.1007/s101070100263
44. Zach, C., Bourmaud, G.: Descending, lifting or smoothing: secrets of robust cost optimization. In: Ferrari, V., Hebert, M., Sminchisescu, C., Weiss, Y. (eds.) ECCV 2018. LNCS, vol. 11216, pp. 558–574. Springer, Cham (2018). https://doi.org/10.1007/978-3-030-01258-8_34

Fast and Differentiable Message Passing on Pairwise Markov Random Fields

Zhiwei Xu[1,2](✉) [iD], Thalaiyasingam Ajanthan[1] [iD], and Richard Hartley[1] [iD]

[1] Australian National University and Australian Centre for Robotic Vision, Canberra, Australia
{zhiwei.xu,thalaiyasingam.ajanthan,richard.hartley}@anu.edu.au
[2] Data61, CSIRO, Canberra, Australia

Abstract. Despite the availability of many Markov Random Field (MRF) optimization algorithms, their widespread usage is currently limited due to imperfect MRF modelling arising from hand-crafted model parameters and the selection of inferior inference algorithm. In addition to differentiability, the two main aspects that enable learning these model parameters are the forward and backward propagation time of the MRF optimization algorithm and its inference capabilities. In this work, we introduce two fast and differentiable message passing algorithms, namely, Iterative Semi-Global Matching Revised (ISGMR) and Parallel Tree-Reweighted Message Passing (TRWP) which are greatly sped up on a GPU by exploiting massive parallelism. Specifically, ISGMR is an iterative and revised version of the standard SGM for general pairwise MRFs with improved optimization effectiveness, and TRWP is a highly parallel version of Sequential TRW (TRWS) for faster optimization. Our experiments on the standard stereo and denoising benchmarks demonstrated that ISGMR and TRWP achieve much lower energies than SGM and Mean-Field (MF), and TRWP is two orders of magnitude faster than TRWS without losing effectiveness in optimization. We further demonstrated the effectiveness of our algorithms on end-to-end learning for semantic segmentation. Notably, our CUDA implementations are at least 7 and 700 times faster than PyTorch GPU implementations for forward and backward propagation respectively, enabling efficient end-to-end learning with message passing.

1 Introduction

Optimization of Markov Random Fields (MRFs) has been a well-studied problem for decades with a significant impact on many computer vision applications such as stereo vision [1], image segmentation [2], texture modeling [3]. The widespread use of these MRF optimization algorithms is currently limited due to imperfect MRF modelling [4] because of hand-crafted model parameters, the usage of inferior inference methods, and non-differentiability for parameter learning. Thus,

Electronic supplementary material The online version of this chapter (https://doi.org/10.1007/978-3-030-69535-4_32) contains supplementary material, which is available to authorized users.

H. Ishikawa et al. (Eds.): ACCV 2020, LNCS 12624, pp. 523–540, 2021.
https://doi.org/10.1007/978-3-030-69535-4_32

better inference capability and computing efficiency are essential to improve its performance on optimization and modelling, such as energy optimization and end-to-end learning.

Even though parameter and structural learning with MRFs has been employed successfully in certain cases, well-known algorithms such as Mean-Field (MF) [5,6] and Semi-Glocal Matching (SGM) [7], are suboptimal in terms of optimization capability. Specifically, the choice of an MRF algorithm for optimization is driven by its inference ability, and for learning capability through efficient forward and backward propagation and parallelization capabilities.

In this work, we consider message passing algorithms due to their generality, high inference ability, and differentiability, and provide efficient CUDA implementations of their forward and backward propagation by exploiting massive parallelism. In particular, we revise the popular SGM method [1] and derive an iterative version noting its relation to traditional message passing algorithms [8]. In addition, we introduce a highly parallelizable version of the state-of-the-art Sequential Tree-Reweighted Message Passing (TRWS) algorithm [9], which is more efficient than TRWS and has similar minimum energies. For both these methods, we derive efficient backpropagation by unrolling their message updates and cost aggregation and discuss massively parallel CUDA implementations which enable their feasibility in end-to-end learning.

Our experiments on the standard stereo and denoising benchmarks demonstrate that our Iterative and Revised SGM method (ISGMR) obtains much lower energies compared to the standard SGM and our Parallel TRW method (TRWP) is two orders of magnitude faster than TRWS with virtually the same minimum energies and that both outperform the popular MF and SGM inferences. Their performance is further evaluated by end-to-end learning for semantic segmentation on PASCAL VOC 2012 dataset.

Furthermore, we empirically evaluate various implementations of the forward and backward propagation of these algorithms and demonstrate that our CUDA implementation is the fastest, with *at least 700 times speed-up* in backpropagation compared to a PyTorch GPU version. Code is available at https://github.com/zwxu064/MPLayers.git.

Contributions of this paper can be summarised as:

- We introduce two message passing algorithms, ISGMR and TRWP, where ISGMR has higher optimization effectiveness than SGM and TRWP is much faster than TRWS. Both of them outperform the popular SGM and MF inferences.
- Our ISGMR and TRWP are massively parallelized on GPU and can support any pairwise potentials. The CUDA implementation of the backpropagation is at least 700 times faster than the PyTorch auto-gradient version on GPU.
- The differentiability of ISGMR and TRWP is presented with gradient derivations, with effectiveness validated by end-to-end learning for semantic segmentation.

2   Related Work

In MRF optimization, estimating the optimal latent variables can be regarded as minimizing a particular energy function with given model parameters. Even if the minimum energy is obtained, high accuracy cannot be guaranteed since the model parameters of these MRFs are usually handcrafted and imperfect. To tackle this problem, learning-based methods were proposed. However, most of these methods rely greatly on finetuning the network architecture or adding learnable parameters to increase the fitting ability with ground truth. This may not be effective and usually requires high GPU memory.

Nevertheless, considering the highly effective MRF optimization algorithms, the field of exploiting their optimization capability with parameter learning to alleviate each other's drawbacks is rarely explored. A few works provide this capability in certain cases, such as CRFasRNN in semantic segmentation [5] and SGMNet in stereo vision [7], with less effective MRF algorithms, that is MF and SGM respectively. Thus, it is important to adopt highly effective and efficient MRF inference algorithms for optimization and end-to-end learning.

MRF Optimization. Determining an effective MRF optimization algorithm needs a thorough study of the possibility of their optimization capability, differentiability, and time efficiency. In the two main categories of MRF optimization algorithms, namely move-making algorithms (known as graph cuts) [10–15] and message passing algorithms [1,9,16–21], the state-of-the-art methods are α-expansion [12] and Sequential Tree-Reweighted Message Passing (TRWS) [9] respectively. The move-making algorithms, however, cannot easily be used for parameter learning as they are not differentiable and are usually limited to certain types of energy functions.

In contrast, message passing algorithms adapt better to any energy functions and can be made differentiable and fast if well designed. Some works in probabilistic graphical models indeed demonstrate the learning ability of TRW algorithms with sum-product and max-product [16,20] message passing. A comprehensive study and comparison of these methods can be found in Middlebury [4] and OpenGM [22]. Although SGM [1] is not in the benchmark, it was proved to have a high running efficiency due to the fast one-dimensional Dynamic Programming (DP) that is independent in each scanline and scanning direction [1].

End-to-End Learning. Sum-product TRW [23–25] and mean-field [5,26,27] have been used for end-to-end learning for semantic segmentation, which presents their highly effective learning ability. Meanwhile, for stereo vision, several MRF/CRF based methods [7,28,29], such as SGM-related, have been proposed. These further indicate the high efficiency of selected MRF optimization algorithms in end-to-end learning.

In our work, we improve optimization effectiveness and time efficiency based on classical SGM and TRWS. In particular, we revise the standard SGM and make it iterative in order to improve its optimization capability. We denote the resulting algorithm as ISGMR. Our other algorithm, TRWP, is a massively parallelizable version of TRWS, which greatly increases running speed without losing the optimization effectiveness.

3 Message Passing Algorithms

We first briefly review the typical form of a pairwise MRF energy function and discuss two highly parallelizable message passing approaches, ISGMR and TRWP. Such a parallelization capability is essential for fast implementation on GPU and enables relatively straightforward integration to existing deep learning models.

3.1 Pairwise MRF Energy Function

Let X_i be a random variable taking label $x_i \in \mathcal{L}$. A pairwise MRF energy function defined over a set of such variables, parametrized by $\Theta = \{\theta_i, \theta_{i,j}\}$, is written as

$$E(\mathbf{x} \mid \Theta) = \sum_{i \in \mathcal{V}} \theta_i(x_i) + \sum_{(i,j) \in \mathcal{E}} \theta_{i,j}(x_i, x_j) , \qquad (1)$$

where θ_i and $\theta_{i,j}$ denote unary potentials and pairwise potentials respectively, $\mathcal{V}$ is the set of vertices (corresponding, for instance, to image pixels or superpixels), and $\mathcal{E}$ is the set of edges in the MRF (usually encoding a 4-connected or 8-connected grid).

3.2 Iterative Semi-Global Matching Revised

We first introduce the standard SGM for stereo vision supporting only a single iteration. With its connection to message passing, we then revise its message update equation and introduce an iterative version. Figure 1 shows a 4-connected SGM on a grid MRF.

3.2.1 Revised Semi-Global Matching

We cast the popular SGM algorithm [1] as an optimization method for a particular MRF and discuss its relation to message passing as noted in [8]. In SGM, pairwise potentials are simplified for all edges $(i, j) \in \mathcal{E}$ as

$$\theta_{i,j}(\lambda, \mu) = \theta_{i,j}(|\lambda - \mu|) = \begin{cases} 0 & \text{if } \lambda = \mu , \\ P_1 & \text{if } |\lambda - \mu| = 1 , \\ P_2 & \text{if } |\lambda - \mu| \geq 2 , \end{cases} \qquad (2)$$

where $0 < P_1 \leq P_2$. The idea of SGM relies on cost aggregation in multiple directions (each direction having multiple one-dimensional scanlines) using Dynamic Programming (DP). The main observation made by [8] is that, in SGM the unary potentials are over-counted $|\mathcal{R}| - 1$ times (where $\mathcal{R}$ denotes the set of directions) compared to the standard message passing and this over-counting

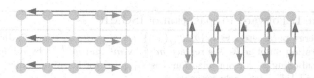

Fig. 1. An example of 4-connected SGM on a grid MRF: left-right, right-left, up-down, down-up. Message passing along all these scanlines can be accomplished in parallel.

corrected SGM is shown to perform slightly better in [30]. Noting this, we use symbol $m_i^r(\lambda)$ to denote the message-vector passed to node i, along a scan-line in the direction r, **from** the previous node, denoted $i-r$. This is a vector indexed by $\lambda \in \mathcal{L}$. Now, the SGM update is *revised* from

$$m_i^r(\lambda) = \min_{\mu \in \mathcal{L}} \left(\theta_i(\lambda) + m_{i-r}^r(\mu) + \theta_{i-r,i}(\mu, \lambda) \right) , \tag{3}$$

which is the form given in [1], to

$$m_i^r(\lambda) = \min_{\mu \in \mathcal{L}} \left(\theta_{i-r}(\mu) + m_{i-r}^r(\mu) + \theta_{i-r,i}(\mu, \lambda) \right) . \tag{4}$$

The $m_i^r(\lambda)$ represents the minimum cost due to possible assignments to all nodes previous to node i along the scanline in direction r, and assigning label λ to node i. It does not include the cost $\theta_i(\lambda)$ associated with node i itself.

Since subtracting a fixed value for all λ from messages preserves minima, the message $m_i^r(\lambda)$ can be reparametrized as

$$m_i^r(\lambda) = m_i^r(\lambda) - \min_{\mu \in \mathcal{L}} m_i^r(\mu) , \tag{5}$$

which does not alter the minimum energy. Since the values of $\theta_i(\lambda)$ are not included in the messages, the final cost at a particular node i at label λ is *revised* from

$$c_i(\lambda) = \sum_{r \in \mathcal{R}} m_i^r(\lambda) \tag{6}$$

to

$$c_i(\lambda) = \theta_i(\lambda) + \sum_{r \in \mathcal{R}} m_i^r(\lambda) , \tag{7}$$

which is the sum of messages over all the directions plus the unary term. The final labelling is then obtained by

$$x_i^* = \operatorname*{argmin}_{\lambda \in \mathcal{L}} c_i(\lambda) , \quad \forall i \in \mathcal{V} . \tag{8}$$

Here, the message update in the revised SGM, *i.e.*, Eq. (4), is performed in parallel for all scanlines for all directions. This massive parallelization makes it suitable for real-time applications [31] and end-to-end learning for stereo vision [7].

Algorithm 1: Forward Propagation of ISGMR

Input: Energy parameters $\Theta = \{\theta_i, \theta_{i,j}(\cdot, \cdot)\}$, set of nodes $\mathcal{V}$, edges $\mathcal{E}$, directions $\mathcal{R}$, iteration number K. We replace $m^{r,k}$ by m^r and $m^{r,k+1}$ by $\hat{m}^r$ for simplicity.

Output: Labelling $\mathbf{x}^*$ for optimization, costs $\{c_i(\lambda)\}$ for learning, indices $\{p^r_{k,i}(\lambda)\}$ and $\{q^r_{k,i}\}$ for backpropagation.

1   $\hat{\mathbf{m}} \leftarrow 0$ and $\mathbf{m} \leftarrow 0$ ▷initialize all messages

2   **for** iteration $k \in \{1, \ldots, K\}$ **do**

3   **forall** directions $r \in \mathcal{R}$ **do**   ▷**parallel**

4   **forall** scanlines t in direction r **do**   ▷**parallel**

5   **for** node i in scanline t **do**   ▷**sequential**

6   **for** label $\lambda \in \mathcal{L}$ **do**

7                  $\Delta(\lambda, \mu) \leftarrow \theta_{i-r}(\mu) + \theta_{i-r,i}(\mu, \lambda) + \hat{m}^r_{i-r}(\mu) + \displaystyle\sum_{d \in \mathcal{R} \setminus \{r, r^-\}} m^d_{i-r}(\mu)$

8                  $p^r_{k,i}(\lambda) \leftarrow \mu^* \leftarrow \mathrm{argmin}_{\mu \in \mathcal{L}} \Delta(\lambda, \mu)$ ▷store index

9                  $\hat{m}^r_i(\lambda) \leftarrow \Delta(\lambda, \mu^*)$ ▷message update (9)

10                 $q^r_{k,i} \leftarrow \lambda^* \leftarrow \mathrm{argmin}_{\lambda \in \mathcal{L}} \hat{m}^r_i(\lambda)$ ▷store index

11                 $\hat{m}^r_i(\lambda) \leftarrow \hat{m}^r_i(\lambda) - \hat{m}^r_i(\lambda^*)$ ▷reparametrization (5)

12      $\mathbf{m} \leftarrow \hat{\mathbf{m}}$ ▷update messages after iteration

13   $c_i(\lambda) \leftarrow \theta_i(\lambda) + \sum_{r \in \mathcal{R}} m^r_i(\lambda), \forall i \in \mathcal{V}, \lambda \in \mathcal{L}$ ▷Eq. (7)

14   $x^*_i \leftarrow \mathrm{argmin}_{\lambda \in \mathcal{L}} c_i(\lambda), \forall i \in \mathcal{V}$ ▷Eq. (8)

3.2.2   Iteration of Revised Semi-Global Matching

In spite of the revision for the over-counting problem, the 3-penalty pairwise potential in Eq. (2) is insufficient to obtain dominant penalties under a large range of disparities in different camera settings. To this end, we consider more general pairwise potentials $\theta_{i,j}(\lambda, \mu)$ and introduce an iterative version of the revised SGM. The message update for the iterative version is

$$m_i^{r,k+1}(\lambda) = \min_{\mu \in \mathcal{L}} \left(\theta_{i-r}(\mu) + \theta_{i-r,i}(\mu, \lambda) + m_{i-r}^{r,k+1}(\mu) + \sum_{d \in \mathcal{R} \setminus \{r, r^-\}} m_{i-r}^{d,k}(\mu) \right), \quad (9)$$

where r^- denotes the opposite direction of r and $m_{i-r}^{r,k+1}(\mu)$ denotes the updated message in kth iteration while $m_{i-r}^{r,k}(\mu)$ is updated in $(k-1)$th iteration. The exclusion of the messages from direction r^- is important to ensure that the update is analogous to the standard message passing and the same energy function is minimized at each iteration. A simple combination of several standard SGMs does not satisfy this rule and performs worse than our iterative version, as reported in Tables 1–2. Usually, $\mathbf{m}^r$ for all $r \in \mathcal{R}$ are initialized to 0, the exclusion of r^- from $\mathcal{R}$ is thus redundant for a single iteration but not multiple iterations. Even so, messages can be reparametrized by Eq. (5).

After multiple iterations, the final cost for node $i \in \mathcal{V}$ is calculated by Eq. (7), and the final labelling is calculated in the same manner as Eq. (8). We denote this iterative and revised SGM as ISGMR, summarized in Algorithm 1.

In sum, the improvement of ISGMR from SGM lies in the exclusion of over-counted unary terms by Eq. (4) to increase the effects of pairwise terms as well

---

Algorithm 2: Forward Propagation of TRWP

Input: Energy parameters $\Theta = \{\theta_i, \theta_{i,j}(\cdot, \cdot)\}$, set of nodes $\mathcal{V}$, edges $\mathcal{E}$, directions $\mathcal{R}$, tree decomposition coefficients $\{\rho_{i,j}\}$, iteration number K.

Output: Labelling $\mathbf{x}^*$ for optimization, costs $\{c_i(\lambda)\}$ for learning, indices $\{p^r_{k,i}(\lambda)\}$ and $\{q^r_{k,i}\}$ for backpropagation.

1 $m \leftarrow 0$ ▷initialize all messages
2 **for** iteration $k \in \{1, \dots, K\}$ **do**
3   **for** direction $r \in \mathcal{R}$ **do**   ▷**sequential**
4   **forall** scanlines t in direction r **do**   ▷**parallel**
5   **for** node i in scanline t **do**   ▷**sequential**
6   **for** label $\lambda \in \mathcal{L}$ **do**
7            $\Delta(\lambda, \mu) \leftarrow \rho_{i-r,i}\big(\theta_{i-r}(\mu) + \sum_{d \in \mathcal{R}} m^d_{i-r}(\mu)\big) - m^{r^-}_{i \leftarrow r}(\mu) + \theta_{i-r,i}(\mu, \lambda)$
8            $p^r_{k,i}(\lambda) \leftarrow \mu^* \leftarrow \text{argmin}_{\mu \in \mathcal{L}} \Delta(\lambda, \mu)$ ▷store index
9            $m^r_i(\lambda) \leftarrow \Delta(\lambda, \mu^*)$ ▷message update (10)
10         $q^r_{k,i} \leftarrow \lambda^* \leftarrow \text{argmin}_{\lambda \in \mathcal{L}} m^r_i(\lambda)$ ▷store index
11         $m^r_i(\lambda) \leftarrow m^r_i(\lambda) - m^r_i(\lambda^*)$ ▷reparametrization (5)
12 $c_i(\lambda) \leftarrow \theta_i(\lambda) + \sum_{r \in \mathcal{R}} m^r_i(\lambda), \forall i \in \mathcal{V}, \lambda \in \mathcal{L}$ ▷Eq. (7)
13 $x^*_i \leftarrow \text{argmin}_{\lambda \in \mathcal{L}} c_i(\lambda), \forall i \in \mathcal{V}$ ▷Eq. (8)

---

as the iterative energy minimization by Eq. (9) to further decrease the energy with updated messages.

3.3 Parallel Tree-Reweighted Message Passing

TRWS [9] is another state-of-the-art message passing algorithm that optimizes the Linear Programming (LP) relaxation of a general pairwise MRF energy given in Eq. (1). The main idea of the family of TRW algorithms [32] is to decompose the underlying graph $\mathcal{G} = (\mathcal{V}, \mathcal{E})$ of the MRF with parameters Θ into a combination of trees where the sum of parameters of all the trees is equal to that of the MRF, i.e., $\sum_{T \in \mathcal{T}} \Theta_T = \Theta$. Then, at each iteration message passing is performed in each of these trees independently, followed by an averaging operation. Even though any combinations of trees would theoretically result in the same final labelling, the best performance is achieved by choosing a monotonic chain decomposition and a sequential message passing update rule, which is TRWS. Interested readers please refer to [9] for more details.

Since we intend to enable fast message passing by exploiting parallelism, our idea is to choose a tree decomposition that can be massively parallelized, denoted as TRWP. In the literature, edge-based or tree-based parallel TRW algorithms have been considered, namely, TRWE and TRWT in the probability space (specifically sum-product message passing) rather than for minimizing the energy [32]. Optimizing in the probability domain involves exponential calculations which are prone to numerical instability, and the sum-product version requires $\mathcal{O}(|\mathcal{R}||\mathcal{L}|)$ times more memory compared to the min-sum message passing in backpropagation. More details are in Appendix E.

Correspondingly, our TRWP directly minimizes the energy in the min-sum message passing fashion similar to TRWS, and thus, its update can be written as

$$m_i^r(\lambda) = \min_{\mu \in \mathcal{L}} \left(\rho_{i-r,i}(\theta_{i-r}(\mu) + \sum_{d \in \mathcal{R}} m_{i-r}^d(\mu)) - m_{i-r}^{r^-}(\mu) + \theta_{i-r,i}(\mu, \lambda) \right) . \quad (10)$$

Here, the coefficient $\rho_{i-r,i} = \gamma_{i-r,i}/\gamma_{i-r}$, where $\gamma_{i-r,i}$ and γ_{i-r} are the number of trees containing the edge $(i - r, i)$ and the node $i - r$ respectively in the considered tree decomposition. For loopy belief propagation, since there is no tree decomposition, $\rho_{i-r,i} = 1$. For a 4-connected graph decomposed into all horizontal and vertical one-dimensional trees, we have $\rho_{i-r,i} = 0.5$ for all edges.

Note that, similar to ISGMR, we use the scanline to denote a tree. The above update can be performed in parallel for all scanlines in a single direction; however, the message updates over a scanline are sequential. The same reparametrization Eq. (5) is applied. While TRWP cannot guarantee the non-decreasing monotonicity of the lower bound of energy, it dramatically improves the forward propagation speed and yields virtually similar minimum energies to those of TRWS. The procedure is in Algorithm 2.

In sum, our TRWP benefits from a high speed-up without losing optimization capability by the massive GPU parallelism over individual trees that are decomposed from the single-chain tree in TRWS. All trees in each direction r are paralleled by Eq. (10).

3.4   Relation Between ISGMR and TRWP

Both ISGMR and TRWP use messages from neighbouring nodes to perform recursive and iterative message updates via dynamic programming. Comparison of Eq. (9) and Eq. (10) indicates the introduction of the coefficients $\{\rho_{i-r,i}\}$. This is due to the tree decomposition, which is analogous to the difference between loopy belief propagation and TRW algorithms. The most important difference, however, is the way message updates are defined. Specifically, within an iteration, ISGMR can be parallelized over all directions since the most updated messages $\hat{m}^r$ are used only for the current scanning direction r and previous messages are used for the other directions (refer Eq. (9)). In contrast, aggregated messages in TRWP are up-to-date *direction-by-direction*, which largely contributes to the improved effectiveness of TRWP over ISGMR.

3.5   Fast Implementation by Tree Parallelization

Independent trees make the parallelization possible. We implemented on CPU and GPU, where for the C++ multi-thread versions (CPU), 8 threads on Open Multi-Processing (OpenMP) [33] are used while for the CUDA versions (GPU), 512 threads per block are used. Each tree is headed by its first node by interpolation. The node indexing details for efficient parallelism are provided in Appendix C. In the next section, we derive efficient backpropagation through each of these algorithms for parameter learning.

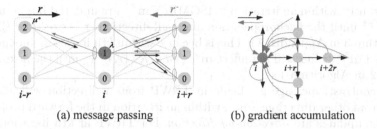

(a) message passing   (b) gradient accumulation

Fig. 2. Forward and backward propagation, a target node is in dark gray, r: forward direction, r^-: backpropagation direction. (a) blue ellipse: min operation as MAP, blue line: an edge having the minimum message. (b) a message gradient at node i accumulated from nodes in r^-. (Color figure online)

4   Differentiability of Message Passing

Effective and differentiable MRF optimization algorithms can greatly improve the performance of end-to-end learning. Typical methods such as CRFasRNN for semantic segmentation [5] by MF and SGMNet for stereo vision [7] by SGM use inferior inferences in the optimization capability compared to ISGMR and TRWP.

In order to embed ISGMR and TRWP into end-to-end learning, differentiability of them is required and essential. Below, we describe the gradient updates for the learnable MRF model parameters, and detailed derivations are given in Appendix D. The backpropagation pseudocodes are in Algorithms 3–4 in Appendix A.

Since ISGMR and TRWP use min-sum message passing, no exponent and logarithm are required. Only indices in message minimization and reparametrization are stored in two unsigned 8-bit integer tensors, denoted as $\{p_{k,i}^r(\lambda)\}$ and $\{q_{k,i}^r\}$ with indices of direction r, iteration k, node i, and label λ. This makes the backpropagation time less than 50% of the forward propagation time. In Fig. 2a, the gradient updates in backpropagation are performed along edges that have the minimum messages in the forward direction. In Fig. 2b, a message gradient at node i is accumulated from all following nodes after i from all backpropagation directions. Below, we denote the gradient of a variable $*$ from loss L as $\nabla * = dL/d*$.

For ISGMR at kth iteration, the gradients of the model parameters in Eq. (9) are

$$
\nabla\theta_i(\lambda) = \nabla c_i(\lambda) + \sum_{v\in\mathcal{L}}\sum_{r\in\mathcal{R}}\sum_{\mu\in\mathcal{L}}\left(\left.\nabla m_{i+2r}^{r,k+1}(\mu)\right|_{v=p_{k,i+2r}^r(\mu)}\right.
$$

$$
\left.+\sum_{d\in\mathcal{R}\backslash\{r,r^-\}}\left.\nabla m_{i+r+d}^{d,k}(\mu)\right|_{v=p_{k,i+r+d}^d(\mu)}\right)\Bigg|_{\lambda=p_{k,i+r}^r(v)}, \tag{11}
$$

$$
\nabla\theta_{i-r,i}(\mu,\lambda) = \left.\nabla m_i^{r,k+1}(\lambda)\right|_{\mu=p_{k,i}^r(\lambda)}. \tag{12}
$$

Importantly, within an iteration in ISGMR, $\nabla \mathbf{m}^{\mathbf{r},k}$ are updated but do not affect $\nabla \mathbf{m}^{\mathbf{r},k+1}$ until the backpropagation along all directions $\mathbf{r}$ is executed (line 18 in Algorithm 3 in Appendix A). This is because within kth iteration, independently updated $\mathbf{m}^{r,k+1}$ in r will not affect $\mathbf{m}^{d,k}, \forall d \in \mathcal{R} \setminus \{r, r^-\}$, until the next iteration (line 12 in Algorithm 1).

In contrast, message gradients in TRWP from a direction will affect messages from other directions since, within an iteration in the forward propagation, message updates are *direction-by-direction*. For TRWP at kth iteration, $\nabla \theta_i(\lambda)$ related to Eq. (10) is

$$
\nabla \theta_i(\lambda) = \nabla c_i(\lambda) + \sum_{v \in \mathcal{L}} \sum_{r \in \mathcal{R}} \sum_{\mu \in \mathcal{L}} \left(-\nabla m_i^{r^-}(\mu) \Big|_{v = p_{k,i}^{r^-}(\mu)} \right.
$$
$$
\left. + \sum_{d \in \mathcal{R}} \rho_{i+r,i+r+d} \nabla m_{i+r+d}^d(\mu) \Big|_{v = p_{k,i+r+d}^d(\mu)} \right) \Bigg|_{\lambda = p_{k,i+r}^r(v)}, \tag{13}
$$

where coefficient $\rho_{i+r,i+r+d}$ is for the edge connecting node $i + r$ and its next one in direction d which is denoted as node $i + r + d$, and the calculation of $\nabla \theta_{i-r,i}(\lambda, \mu)$ is in the same manner as Eq. (12) by replacing $m^{r,k+1}$ with m^r.

The backpropagation of TRWP can be derived similarly to ISGMR. We must know that gradients of the unary potentials and the pairwise potentials are accumulated along the opposite direction of the forward scanning direction. Therefore, an updated message is, in fact, a new variable, and its gradient should not be accumulated by its previous value but set to 0. This is extremely important, especially in ISGMR. It requires the message gradients to be accumulated and assigned in every iteration (lines 17–18 in Algorithm 3 in Appendix A) and be zero-out (lines 4 and 16 in Algorithm 3 and line 14 in Algorithm 4 in Appendix A). Meanwhile, gradient derivations of ISGMR and characteristics are provided in Appendix D.

5   Experiments

Below, we evaluated the optimization capability of message passing algorithms on stereo vision and image denoising with fixed yet qualified data terms from benchmark settings. In addition, differentiability was evaluated by end-to-end learning for 21-class semantic segmentation. The experiments include effectiveness and efficiency studies of the message passing algorithms. Additional experiments are in Appendix F.

We implemented SGM, ISGMR, TRWP in C++ with single and multiple threads, PyTorch, and CUDA from scratch. PyTorch versions are for time comparison and gradient checking. For a fair comparison, we adopted benchmark code of TRWS from [4] with general pairwise functions; MF followed Eq. (4) in [6]. For iterative SGM, unary potentials were reparametrized by Eq. (6). OpenGM [22] can be used for more comparisons in optimization noting TRWS as one of the most effective inference methods.

Our experiments were on 3.6GHz i7-7700 Intel(R) Core(TM) and Tesla P100 SXM2.

5.1 Optimization for Stereo Vision and Image Denoising

The capability of minimizing an energy function determines the significance of selected algorithms. We compared our ISGMR and TRWP with MF, SGM with single and multiple iterations, and TRWS. The evaluated energies are calculated with 4 connections.

Datasets. For stereo vision, we used Tsukuba, Teddy, Venus, Map, and Cones from Middlebury [34,35], 000041_10 and 000119_10 from KITTI2015 [36,37], and delivery_area_11 and facade_1 from ETH3D two-view [38] for different types of stereo views. For image denoising, Penguin and House from Middlebury dataset[1] were used.

MRF Model Parameters. Model parameters include unary and pairwise potentials. In practice, the pairwise potentials consist of a pairwise function and edge weights, as $\theta_{i,j}(\lambda, \mu) = \theta_{i,j} V(\lambda, \mu)$. For the pairwise function $V(\cdot, \cdot)$, one can adopt (truncated) linear, (truncated) quadratic, Cauchy, Huber, etc.., [39]. For the edge weights $\theta_{i,j}$, some methods apply a higher penalty on edge gradients under a given threshold. We set it as a constant for the comparison with SGM. Moreover, we adopted edge weights in [4] and pairwise functions for Tsukuba, Teddy, and Venus, and [11] for Cones and Map; for the others, the pairwise function was linear and edges weights were 10. More evaluations with constant edge weights are given in Appendix F.

Number of Directions Matters. In Fig. 3, ISGMR-8 and TRWP-4 outperform the others in ISGMR-related and TRWP-related methods in most cases. From the experiments, 4 directions are sufficient for TRWP, but for ISGMR energies with 8 directions are lower than those with 4 directions. This is because messages from 4 directions in ISGMR are insufficient to gather local information due to independent message updates in each direction. In contrast, messages from 4 directions in TRWP are highly updated in each direction and affected by those from the other directions. Note that in Eq. (7) messages from all directions are summed equally, this makes the labels by TRWP over-smooth within the connection area, for example, the camera is oversmooth in Fig. 4n. Overall, TRWP-4 and ISGMR-8 are the best.

ISGMR vs SGM. [30] demonstrates the decrease in energy of the overcount corrected SGM compared with the standard SGM. The result shows the improved optimization results achieved by subtracting unary potentials $(|\mathcal{R}|-1)$ times. For experimental completion, we show both the decreased energies and improved disparity maps produced by ISGMR. From Tables 1–2, SGM-related energies are much higher than ISGMR's because of the over-counted unary potentials. Moreover, ISGMR at the 50th iteration has much a lower energy value than the 1st iteration, indicating the importance of iterations, and is also much lower than those for MF and SGM at the 50th iteration.

TRWP vs TRWS. TRWP and TRWS have the same manner of updating messages and could have similar minimum energies. Generally, TRWS has the

---

[1] http://vision.middlebury.edu/MRF/results.

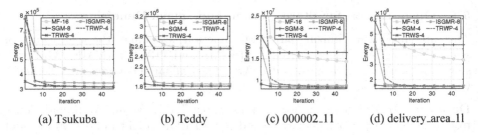

(a) Tsukuba   (b) Teddy   (c) 000002_11   (d) delivery_area_11

Fig. 3. Convergence with the connections having the minimum energy in Table 1.

Table 1. Energy minimization for stereo vision. ISGMR is better than SGM and TRWP obtains similar energies as TRWS. ISGMR and TRWP outperform MF and SGM.

Method	Tsukuba		Teddy		000002_11		delivery_area_11	
	1 iter	50 iter	1 iter	50 iter	1 iter	50 iter	1 iter	50 iter
MF-4	3121704	1620524	3206347	2583784	82523536	44410056	19945352	9013862
SGM-4	873777	644840	2825535	2559016	24343250	18060026	5851489	4267990
TRWS-4	352178	<u>314393</u>	1855625	<u>1807423</u>	9109976	8322635	1628879	1534961
ISGMR-4 (ours)	824694	637996	2626648	1898641	22259606	12659612	5282024	2212106
TRWP-4 (ours)	869363	<u>314037</u>	2234163	<u>1806990</u>	40473776	8385450	9899787	<u>1546795</u>
MF-8	2322139	504815	3244710	2545226	61157072	18416536	16581587	4510834
SGM-8	776706	574758	2868131	2728682	20324684	16406781	5396353	4428411
ISGMR-8 (ours)	684185	<u>340347</u>	2532071	<u>1847833</u>	17489158	8753990	4474404	1571528
TRWP-8 (ours)	496727	<u>348447</u>	1981582	<u>1849287</u>	18424062	8860552	4443931	<u>1587917</u>
MF-16	1979155	404404	3315900	2622047	46614232	14192750	13223338	3229021
SGM-16	710727	587376	2907051	2846133	18893122	16791762	5092094	4611821
ISGMR-16 (ours)	591554	<u>377427</u>	2453592	<u>1956343</u>	15455787	9556611	3689863	1594877
TRWP-16 (ours)	402033	<u>396036</u>	1935791	<u>1976839</u>	11239113	<u>9736704</u>	2261402	<u>1630973</u>

lowest energy; at the 50th iteration, however, TRWP-4 has lower energies, for instance, Tsukuba and Teddy in Table 1 and Penguin and House in Table 2. For TRWP, 50 iterations are sufficient to show its high optimization capability, as shown in Fig. 3. More visualizations of Penguin and House denoising are in Appendix F.

5.2   End-to-End Learning for Semantic Segmentation

Although deep network and multi-scale strategy on CNN make semantic segmentation smooth and continuous on object regions, effective message passing inference on pairwise MRFs is beneficial for fine results with auxiliary edge information. The popular denseCRF [6] demonstrated the effectiveness of using MF inference and the so-called dense connections; our experiments, however, illustrated that with local connections, superior inferences, such as TRWS, ISGMR, and TRWP, have a better convergence ability than MF and SGM to improve the performance.

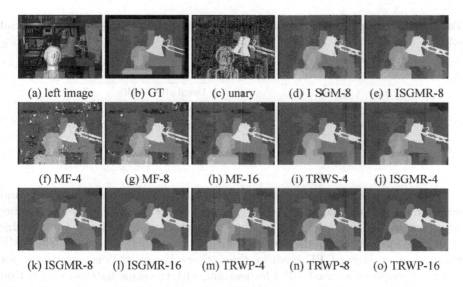

(a) left image   (b) GT   (c) unary   (d) 1 SGM-8   (e) 1 ISGMR-8

(f) MF-4   (g) MF-8   (h) MF-16   (i) TRWS-4   (j) ISGMR-4

(k) ISGMR-8   (l) ISGMR-16   (m) TRWP-4   (n) TRWP-8   (o) TRWP-16

Fig. 4. Disparities of Tsukuba. (d)–(e) are at 1st iteration. (f)–(o) are at 50th iteration. (j) and (l) have the lowest energies in ISGMR-related and TRWP-related methods respectively. TRWP-4 and TRWS-4 have similar disparities for the most parts.

Table 2. Energy minimization for image denoising at 50th iteration with 4, 8, 16 connections (all numbers divided by 10^3). Our ISGMR or TRWP performs best.

Method	Penguin	House
MF-4	46808	50503
SGM-4	31204	66324
TRWS-4	15361	37572
ISGMR-4 (ours)	16514	37603
TRWP-4 (ours)	15358	37552
MF-8	21956	47831
SGM-8	37520	76079
ISGMR-8 (ours)	15899	39975
TRWP-8 (ours)	16130	40209
MF-16	20742	55513
SGM-16	47028	87457
ISGMR-16 (ours)	17035	46997
TRWP-16 (ours)	17516	47825

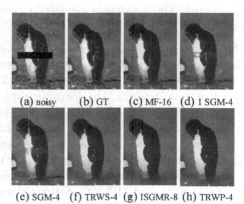

(a) noisy   (b) GT   (c) MF-16   (d) 1 SGM-4

(e) SGM-4   (f) TRWS-4   (g) ISGMR-8   (h) TRWP-4

Fig. 5. Penguin denoising corresponding to the minimum energies marked with gray color in Table 2. ISGMR-8 and TRWP-4 are our proposals.

Table 3. Learning for semantic segmentation with mIoU on PASCAL VOC2012 val set.

(a) term weight for TRWP-4

Method	λ	mIoU (%)
+TRWP-4	1	79.27
+TRWP-4	10	79.53
+TRWP-4	20	79.65
+TRWP-4	30	79.44
+TRWP-4	40	79.60

(b) full comparison

Method	λ	mIoU (%)
DeepLabV3+ [40]	–	78.52
+SGM-8 [1]	5	78.94
+MF-4 [6]	5	77.89
+ISGMR-8 (ours)	5	78.95
+TRWP-4 (ours)	20	79.65

Below, we adopted TRWP-4 and ISGMR-8 as our inference methods and negative logits from DeepLabV3+ [40] as unary terms. Edge weights from Canny edges are in the form of $\theta_{ij} = 1 - |e_i - e_j|$, where e_i is a binary Canny edge value at node i. Potts model was used for pairwise function $V(\lambda, \mu)$. Since MF required much larger GPU memory than others due to its dense gradients, for practical purposes we used MF-4 for learning with the same batch size 12 within our GPU memory capacity.

Datasets. We used PASCAL VOC 2012 [41] and Berkeley benchmark [42], with 1449 samples of the PASCAL VOC 2012 val set for validation and the other 10582 for training. These datasets identify 21 classes with 20 objects and 1 background (Fig. 5).

CNN Learning Parameters. We trained the state-of-the-art DeepLabV3+ (ResNet101 as the backbone) with initial learning rate 0.007, "poly" learning rate decay scheduler, and image size 512×512. Negative logits from DeepLabV3+ served as unary terms, the learning rate was decreased for learning message passing inference with 5 iterations, *i.e.*, 1e−4 for TRWP and SGM and 1e−6 for ISGMR and MF. Note that we experimented with all of these learning rates for involved inferences and selected the best for demonstration, for instance, for MF the accuracy by 1e−6 is much higher than the one by 1e−4.

In Table 3, ISGMR-8 and TRWP-4 outperform the baseline DeepLabV3+ [40], SGM-8 [1], and MF-4 [6]. Semantic segmentation by ISGMR-8 and TRWP-4 are more sharp, accurate, and aligned with the Canny edges and ground-truth (GT) edges, shown in white, than the other inference methods, such as SGM-8 and MF-4 (see Fig. 6).

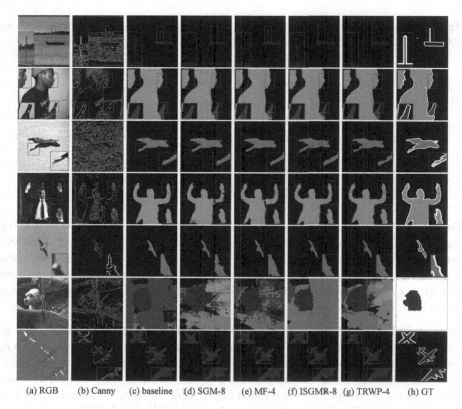

(a) RGB   (b) Canny   (c) baseline   (d) SGM-8   (e) MF-4   (f) ISGMR-8   (g) TRWP-4   (h) GT

Fig. 6. Semantic segmentation on PASCAL VOC2012 val set. Last two rows are failure cases due to poor unary terms and missing edges. ISGMR-8 and TRWP-4 are ours.

Table 4. Forward propagation time with 32 and 96 labels. Our CUDA version is averaged over 1000 trials; others over 100 trials. Our CUDA version is 7–32 times faster than PyTorch GPU version. C++ versions are with a single and 8 threads. Unit: second.

Method	PyTorch CPU		PyTorch GPU		C++ single		C++ multiple		CUDA (ours)		Speed-up PyT/CUDA	
	32	96	32	96	32	96	32	96	32	96	32	96
TRWS-4	–	–	–	–	1.95	13.30	–	–	–	–	–	–
ISGMR-4	1.43	11.70	0.96	1.13	3.23	25.19	0.88	5.28	0.03	0.15	32×	8×
ISGMR-8	3.18	24.78	1.59	1.98	8.25	71.35	2.12	15.90	0.07	0.27	23×	7×
ISGMR-16	7.89	52.76	2.34	4.96	30.76	273.68	7.70	62.72	0.13	0.53	18×	9×
TRWP-4	1.40	11.74	0.87	1.08	1.84	15.41	0.76	4.46	0.03	0.15	29×	7×
TRWP-8	3.19	24.28	1.57	1.98	6.34	57.25	1.88	14.22	0.07	0.27	22×	7×
TRWP-16	7.86	51.85	2.82	5.08	28.93	262.28	7.41	60.45	0.13	0.52	22×	10×

5.3 Speed Improvement

Speed-up by parallelized message passing on a GPU enables a fast inference and end-to-end learning. To be clear, we compared forward and backward propagation times for different implementations using 256×512 size images with 32 and 96 labels.

Table 5. Backpropagation time. PyTorch GPU is averaged on 10 trials and CUDA on 1000 trials. Ours is 716–1081 times faster than PyTorch GPU. Unit: second.

Method	PyTorch GPU		CUDA (ours)		Speed-up PyT/CUDA	
	32	96	32	96	32	96
ISGMR-4	7.38	21.48	0.01	0.03	738×	716×
ISGMR-8	18.88	55.92	0.02	0.07	944×	799×
ISGMR-16	58.23	173.02	0.06	0.18	971×	961×
TRWP-4	7.35	21.45	0.01	0.02	735×	1073×
TRWP-8	18.86	55.94	0.02	0.06	943×	932×
TRWP-16	58.26	172.95	0.06	0.16	971×	1081×

Forward Propagation Time. In Table 4, the forward propagation by CUDA implementation is the fastest. Our CUDA versions of ISGMR-8 and TRWP-4 are at least 24 and 7 times faster than PyTorch GPU versions at 32 and 96 labels respectively. In PyTorch GPU versions, we used tensor-wise tree parallelization to highly speed it up for a fair comparison. Obviously, GPU versions are much faster than CPU versions.

Backpropagation Time. In Table 5, the backpropagation time clearly distinguishes the higher efficiency of CUDA versions than PyTorch GPU versions. On average, the CUDA versions are at least 700 times faster than PyTorch GPU versions, and only a low memory is used to store indices for backpropagation. This makes the backpropagation much faster than the forward propagation and enables its feasibility in deep learning. Analysis of PyTorch GPU version and our CUDA implementation are in Appendix D.4.

6   Conclusion

In this paper, we introduce two fast and differentiable message passing algorithms, namely, ISGMR and TRWP. While ISGMR improved the effectiveness of SGM, TRWP sped up TRWS by two orders of magnitude without loss of solution quality. Besides, our CUDA implementations achieved at least 7 times and 700 times speed-up compared to PyTorch GPU versions in the forward and backward propagation respectively. These enable end-to-end learning with effective and efficient MRF optimization algorithms. Experiments of stereo vision and image denoising as well as end-to-end learning for semantic segmentation validated the effectiveness and efficiency of our proposals.

Acknowledgement. We would like to thank our colleagues Dylan Campbell and Yao Lu for the discussion of CUDA programming. This work is supported by the Australian Centre for Robotic Vision (CE140100016) and Data61, CSIRO, Canberra, Australia.

References

1. Hirschmuller, H.: Stereo processing by semiglobal matching and mutual information. TPAMI **30**, 328–341 (2008)
2. Boykov, Y., Jolly, M.: Interactive graph cuts for optimal boundary and region segmentation of objects in N-D images. In: ICCV (2011)
3. Hassner, M., Sklansky, J.: The use of Markov random fields as models of texture. Comput. Graph. Image Process. **12**(4), 357–370 (1980)
4. Szeliski, R., et al.: A comparative study of energy minimization methods for Markov random fields with smoothness-based priors. TPAMI **30**, 1068–1080 (2008)
5. Zheng, S., et al.: Conditional random fields as recurrent neural networks. In: CVPR (2015)
6. Krähenbühl, P., Koltunz, V.: Efficient inference in fully connected CRFs with Gaussian edge potentials. In: NeurIPS (2011)
7. Seki, A., Pollefeys, M.: SGM-Nets: semi-global matching with neural networks. In: CVPR (2017)
8. Drory, A., Haubold, C., Avidan, S., Hamprecht, F.A.: Semi-global matching: a principled derivation in terms of message passing. In: Proceedings of German Conference on Pattern Recognition (GCPR) (2014)
9. Kolmogorov, V.: Convergent tree-reweighted message passing for energy minimization. TPAMI **28**, 1568–1583 (2006)
10. Ajanthan, T., Hartley, R., Salzmann, M.: Memory efficient max-flow for multi-label submodular MRFs. In: CVPR (2016)
11. Ajanthan, T., Hartley, R., Salzmann, M., Li, H.: Iteratively reweighted graph cut for multi-label MRFs with non-convex priors. In: CVPR (2015)
12. Boykov, Y., Veksler, O., Zabih, R.: Fast approximate energy minimization via graph cuts. TPAMI **23**, 1222–1239 (2001)
13. Carr, P., Hartley, R.: Solving multilabel graph cut problems with multilabel swap. In: DICTA (2009)
14. Hartley, R., Ajanthan, T.: Generalized range moves. arXiv:1811.09171 (2018)
15. Veksler, O.: Multi-label moves for MRFs with truncated convex priors. IJCV **98**, 1–14 (2012). https://doi.org/10.1007/s11263-011-0491-6
16. Jordan, M.: Learning in Graphical Models. MIT Press, Cambridge (1998)
17. Kwon, D., Lee, K.J., Yun, I.D., Lee, S.U.: Solving MRFs with higher-order smoothness priors using hierarchical gradient nodes. In: Kimmel, R., Klette, R., Sugimoto, A. (eds.) ACCV 2010. LNCS, vol. 6492, pp. 121–134. Springer, Heidelberg (2011). https://doi.org/10.1007/978-3-642-19315-6_10
18. Murphy, K., Weiss, Y., Jordan, M.: Loopy belief propagation for approximate inference: an empirical study. In: UAI (1999)
19. Pearl, J.: Probabilistic Reasoning in Intelligent Systems. Morgan Kaufmann, Burlington (1988)
20. Wainwright, M.J., Jordan, M.I.: Graphical models, exponential families, and variational inference. Found. Trends Mach. Learn. **1**, 1–305 (2008)
21. Wang, Z., Zhang, Z., Geng, N.: A message passing algorithm for MRF inference with unknown graphs and its applications. In: Cremers, D., Reid, I., Saito, H., Yang, M.-H. (eds.) ACCV 2014. LNCS, vol. 9006, pp. 288–302. Springer, Cham (2015). https://doi.org/10.1007/978-3-319-16817-3_19
22. Kappes, J., et al.: A comparative study of modern inference techniques for discrete energy minimization problems. In: CVPR (2013)

23. Domke, J.: Learning graphical model parameters with approximate marginal inference. TPAMI **35**, 2454–2467 (2013)
24. Taskar, B., Guestrin, C., Koller, D.: Max-Margin Markov Networks. MIT Press, Cambridge (2003)
25. Tsochantaridis, I., Joachims, T., Hofmann, T., Altun, Y.: Large margin methods for structured and interdependent output variables. JMLR **6**, 1453–1484 (2005)
26. Liu, Z., Li, X., Luo, P., Loy, C.C., Tang, X.: Semantic image segmentation via deep parsing network. In: ICCV (2015)
27. Lin, G., Shen, C., Hengel, A., Reid, I.: Efficient piecewise training of deep structured models for semantic segmentation. In: CVPR (2016)
28. Zhang, F., Prisacariu, V., Yang, R., Torr, P.H.: GA-Net: guided aggregation net for end-to-end stereo matching. In: CVPR (2019)
29. Knobelreiter, P., Reinbacher, C., Shekhovtsov, A., Pock, T.: End-to-end training of hybrid CNN-CRF models for stereo. In: CVPR (2017)
30. Facciolo, G., Franchis, C., Meinhardt, E.: MGM: a significantly more global matching for stereo vision. In: BMVC (2015)
31. Hernandez-Juare, D., Chacon, A., Espinosa, A., Vazquez, D., Moure, J., Lopez, A.M.L.: Embedded real-time stereo estimation via semi-global matching on the GPU. In: International Conference on Computational Sciences (2016)
32. Wainwright, M., Jaakkola, T., Willsky, A.: MAP estimation via agreement on (hyper) trees: message-passing and linear-programming approaches. Trans. Inf. Theory **51**(11), 3697–3717 (2005)
33. Dagum, L., Menon, R.: OpenMP: an industry standard API for shared-memory programming. Comput. Sci. Eng. **5**, 46–55 (1998)
34. Scharstein, D., Szeliski, R.: A taxonomy and evaluation of dense two-frame stereo correspondence algorithms. Int. J. Comput. Vis. **47**, 7–42 (2002). https://doi.org/10.1023/A:1014573219977
35. Scharstein, D., Szeliski, R.: High-accuracy stereo depth maps using structured light. In: CVPR (2003)
36. Menze, M., Heipke, C., Geiger, A.: Object scene flow. ISPRS J. Photogram. Remote Sens. **140**, 60–76 (2018)
37. Menze, M., Heipke, C., Geiger, A.: Joint 3D estimation of vehicles and scene flow. In: ISPRS Workshop on Image Sequence Analysis (2015)
38. Schops, T., et al.: A multi-view stereo benchmark with high-resolution images and multi-camera videos. In: CVPR (2017)
39. Hartley, R., Zisserman, A.: Multiple View Geometry in Computer Vision. Cambridge University Press, Cambridge (2003)
40. Chen, L.-C., Zhu, Y., Papandreou, G., Schroff, F., Adam, H.: Encoder-decoder with Atrous separable convolution for semantic image segmentation. In: Ferrari, V., Hebert, M., Sminchisescu, C., Weiss, Y. (eds.) ECCV 2018. LNCS, vol. 11211, pp. 833–851. Springer, Cham (2018). https://doi.org/10.1007/978-3-030-01234-2_49
41. Everingham, M., Eslami, S., Gool, L., Williams, C., Winn, J., Zisserman, A.: The PASCAL visual object classes challenge a retrospective. Int. J. Comput. Vis. **111**, 98–136 (2015). https://doi.org/10.1007/s11263-014-0733-5
42. Hariharan, B., Arbelaez, P., Bourdev, L., Maji, S., Malik, J.: Semantic contours from inverse detectors. In: ICCV (2011)

A Calibration Method for the Generalized Imaging Model with Uncertain Calibration Target Coordinates

David Uhlig$^{(\boxtimes)}$ (D) and Michael Heizmann (D)

Institute of Industrial Information Technology, Karlsruhe Institute of Technology,
Karlsruhe, Germany
{david.uhlig,michael.heizmann}@kit.edu

Abstract. The developments in optical metrology and computer vision require more and more advanced camera models. Their geometric calibration is of essential importance. Usually, low-dimensional models are used, which however often have insufficient accuracy for the respective applications. A more sophisticated approach uses the generalized camera model. Here, each pixel is described individually by its geometric ray properties. Our efforts in this article strive to improve this model. Hence, we propose a new approach for calibration. Moreover, we show how the immense number of parameters can be efficiently calculated and how the measurement uncertainties of reference features can be effectively utilized. We demonstrate the benefits of our method through an extensive evaluation of different cameras, namely a standard webcam and a microlens-based light field camera.

1 Introduction

Accurate optical measurement methods are becoming increasingly important for high-precision manufacturing. The rising demand can be satisfied by modern imaging systems with advanced optics. The exact geometric calibration of these systems is of essential importance for computer vision and optical metrology. Most systems use perspective projection with a single projection center and are referred to as central cameras. They can often be described by low-dimensional, parametric models with few intrinsic parameters, *e.g.* the well-known pinhole model which even can compensate imperfections of the system, such as lens aberrations, with the help of polynomial correction parameters [1]. In some applications in the field of optical metrology, more complex imaging systems are needed. These can often no longer be described by a central camera model and are in many cases non-parametric and non-central, *e.g.* multi camera systems, catadioptric cameras or light field cameras [2–5]. Here, more sophisticated

Electronic supplementary material The online version of this chapter (https://doi.org/10.1007/978-3-030-69535-4_33) contains supplementary material, which is available to authorized users.

© Springer Nature Switzerland AG 2021
H. Ishikawa et al. (Eds.): ACCV 2020, LNCS 12624, pp. 541–559, 2021.
https://doi.org/10.1007/978-3-030-69535-4_33

models are needed, which always have to be precisely adapted to the specific camera.

The disadvantage of low-dimensional models is that they have poor explanatory power and in modern cameras not every pixel of the many millions can be perfectly described by these models. The more complexity an imaging system has, the more difficult it becomes to model it. The more elaborate the optical elements are, the more challenging it becomes to find a mathematically adequate mapping between the light of the captured scene and the physical sensor plane of the camera. Consequently, in the recent years, the lack of flexibility and precision has led to the development of new camera models, where cameras can be described as generalized imaging systems, which are independent of the specific camera type and allow high-precision calibration.

The generalized camera model was originally introduced in the work of Grossberg and Nayar [6,7]. An arbitrary imaging system is modeled as a nonparametric discrete black box containing photosensitive elements. Each pixel collects light from a bundle of rays that enter the imaging system, referred to as *raxel* which consists of geometrical ray coordinates and radiometric parameters. The set of all *raxels* builds the complete generalized imaging model. The authors perform the calibration by measuring the intersection of camera rays with known reference targets: a monitor that is moved by a linear translation stage with known steps. Sturm and Ramalingam [8,9] and Ramalingam *et al.* [10] excluded the radiometric properties and proposed a calibration of the generalized model where poses may be unknown. A closed form solution can be obtained, if the same pixel sees three points of the reference objects. The downside of their method is that the ray distribution of the camera has to be known in advance. For example, different models apply when the imaging system is non-central or a perspective camera and complicated parametrization steps are necessary. Bothe *et al.* [11] and Miraldo *et al.* [12] achieve pixel wise calibration by bypassing the estimation of the target pose by simply tracking it using an external stereo-camera-system or an IR tracker, respectively. Some work has been done to simplify the calibration by reducing the number of parameters by, *e.g.*, fitting a spline surface onto the set of rays [13,14]. Thus, the camera is evaluated on a subset of control points. However, this only works when the imaging system is smooth, *i.e.* multi camera systems, light field cameras or more complex optical systems are excluded. The work most similar to ours is that of Bergamasco *et al.* [15,16]. They assume unknown poses and calibrate the camera by iteratively calculating the projection of the rays onto a coded calibration monitor, and by minimizing the resulting coding-error on a pixel level. In a second step, they estimate the reference pose using an adapted iterative closest point method [17]. However, they don't use a unified global objective function during the minimization of the calibration error and without proper initialization their method tends to diverge.

Due to these disadvantages, we present in this article a new method to calibrate the generalized imaging model, which improves the work of Bergamasco *et al.* Our goal is to find a flexible calibration procedure that can accurately describe the geometrical properties of an arbitrary imaging system. In the end, however, one does not obtain an "image", but rather a set of rays with corresponding intensities. Still, this does not interfere with most applications in optical metrology, e.g., profilometry, deflectometry or laser triangulation, where only the geometric ray properties are relevant [18–20]. For our method, we assume unknown poses of the calibration target and iteratively solve the subproblems of camera calibration and pose estimation, without the use of an additional translation or rotation stage. By processing every pixel individually and updating each pose one at a time, we can efficiently reduce the computational costs, whereby every camera ray and each observed point contribute to the result. Our main contributions are the following. We present a closed form least squares solution for the ray calibration subproblem. We correctly solve the pose estimation subproblem using a gradient descend optimization on the rotation manifold. And most importantly, we propose to use the measurement uncertainty of the target feature to increase the accuracy of the entire camera calibration. All is achieved by minimizing a single objective function, where convergence can be always achieved. Finally, acceleration techniques are applied to obtain an almost quadratic convergence rate.

In the next sections we outline the basic calibration procedure and its difficulties. We present how to measure reference target features and their corresponding uncertainties. After describing how to include this uncertainty in the optimization procedure, we will explain the individual calibration steps in more detail. Finally, experiments validate the accuracy of the proposed calibration method by analyzing different camera systems.

2 Background

2.1 Plücker-Line

The portion of the light that is sampled by a single pixel has a cone-like shaped expansion due to the effects of the depth-of-field. For simplicity's sake, one models a *raxel* as a ray running through the center of this cone along the direction of light propagation. There are various possibilities for a mathematical description of rays, but in this work the concept of Plücker-coordinates is used [21,22]. In 6D-Plücker-space a Plücker-line $\mathbf{L} \in \mathbb{P}^6$ is defined by its direction $\mathbf{d} \in \mathbb{R}^3$ and its moment $\mathbf{m} \in \mathbb{R}^3$. A line in 3D-space has four degrees of freedom, therefore two constraints apply to the Plücker-line:

$$\mathbb{P}^6 = \left\{ \begin{pmatrix} \mathbf{d} \\ \mathbf{m} \end{pmatrix} \middle| \mathbf{d}, \mathbf{m} \in \mathbb{R}^3, \mathbf{d}^\mathsf{T}\mathbf{m} = 0, \|\mathbf{d}\| = 1 \right\}. \tag{1}$$

The moment can be calculated with $\mathbf{m} = \mathbf{p} \times \mathbf{d}$, where $\mathbf{p} \in \mathbb{R}^3$ is an arbitrary point on the line $\mathbf{L}$. The moment vector stands perpendicular on the line and its norm $\|\mathbf{m}\|$ corresponds to the Euclidean distance of the line to the origin. The Euclidean distance of a line $\mathbf{L}$ to an arbitrary point $\mathbf{x}$ can be found by calculating the distance to the closest point on the line, which results in [23]:

$$d(\mathbf{L}, \mathbf{x}) = \|\mathbf{x} \times \mathbf{d} - \mathbf{m}\|. \tag{2}$$

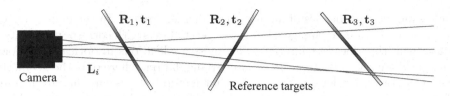

Fig. 1. Generalized calibration: The imaging system is treated as a black box that is independently of the internal optics described by a set of vision rays. Each individual ray observes the intersected reference target point. The ideal calibration results in a minimal distance between rays and points.

2.2   Alternating Minimization

Now, calibrating the camera just means to estimate for every single pixel its ray $\mathbf{L}$, with direction $\mathbf{d}$ and moment $\mathbf{m}$. In conclusion, we are looking for ray parameters that minimize a suitable distance measure between the camera rays and observed reference points, whereby the positions of the references are assumed to be unknown. The calibration can now be formulated in the sense of a least squares problem. Figure 1 illustrates the approach.

$$f(\mathcal{R}, \mathcal{T}, \mathcal{L}) = \sum_{k,i} d\left(\mathbf{p}_{ik}, \mathbf{L}_i\right)^2 . \tag{3}$$

Here, index i represents the individual rays and index k the reference coordinate system. $d(\cdot)$ is a suitable ray-to-point distance measure and $\mathbf{p}_{ik} = \mathbf{R}_k \mathbf{x}_{ik} + \mathbf{t}_k$ are the observed features in 3D-space, where $\mathbf{x}_{ik}$ is a local point on a reference target. $\mathbf{R}_k, \mathbf{t}_k$ are the corresponding transformations to the camera coordinate system. And for the remainder of this article, we define $\mathcal{R} := \{\mathbf{R}_1, \mathbf{R}_2, \dots\}, \mathcal{T} := \{\mathbf{t}_1, \mathbf{t}_2, \dots\}, \mathcal{L} := \{\mathbf{L}_1, \mathbf{L}_2, \dots\}$.

Regardless of the actual used distance measure, it is very difficult to minimize such a problem in a reasonable time and with appropriate use of computational resources. The ray model with six parameters and two constraints has four degrees of freedom per pixel. Even for today's standard cameras, this leads to a huge number of parameters that have to be optimized (*e.g.* a 40-megapixel camera has 240 million parameters). In addition, the reference target pose is in general not known. Thus, at the same time six degrees of freedom per pose have to be estimated. The coupling of poses and rays and the immense number of parameters results in an extremely high dimensional problem that cannot be solved using a single optimization method. The calculation of a gradient or a Hessian and the corresponding function evaluations would be computationally too expensive.

Therefore it is useful to divide the problem into subproblems and then solve them iteratively in the sense of an *Alternating Minimization* (AM) [24]. Accordingly, problem (3) is split into a camera calibration and a reference target pose estimation. The approach of an AM is to fix a parameter set and to solve the resulting problem. This way one has two particular problems to solve in each iteration:

$$\mathbf{L}_i^{(n)} = \underset{\mathbf{L}_i \in \mathbb{P}^6}{\arg\min}\ f\left(\mathcal{R}^{(n-1)}, \mathcal{T}^{(n-1)}, \mathbf{L}_i\right),\tag{4}$$

$$\mathbf{R}_k^{(n)}, \mathbf{t}_k^{(n)} = \underset{(\mathbf{R}_k, \mathbf{t}_k) \in \mathrm{SE}(3)}{\arg\min}\ f\left(\mathbf{R}_k, \mathbf{t}_k, \mathcal{L}^{(n)}\right),\tag{5}$$

where an appropriate initialization $\mathcal{R}^{(0)}, \mathcal{T}^{(0)}$ has to be chosen. The first problem is solved for each pixel i individually by fixing all of the reference target poses and the second one is solved for each single pose k by assuming fixed ray parameters.

2.3 Dense Feature Acquisition

To present the camera calibration as a per pixel problem and to treat each pixel independently from its neighbors, sufficient observations of reference features have to be available for every pixel. However, the widely used checkerboard patterns can provide only sparse features which aren't nearly enough for a generalized camera calibration. Instead, it is a good idea to use active targets, *e.g.* flat monitor displays, and active encoding strategies, to assign each camera ray a 2D point in the local reference target plane. Thus, each ray can observe one feature per pose.

The detection of features in the reference target plane and with it the registration of camera rays $\mathbf{L}_i$ to monitor display points $\mathbf{x}_{ik}$ is found in our approach via a temporal coding of the monitor pixels. Phase shift methods are particularly suitable because they are robust against noise, low-pass filtering by defocusing of the camera and variation of ambient light [25]. They encode a normalized reference coordinate $x \in [0, 1]$, where the encoding is done in horizontal and vertical direction separately, by generating a signal sequence of K sinusoidal patterns shifted by $\varPsi_k = \frac{2\pi k}{K}$ with phase $\varphi(x) = 2\pi f x$:

$$g_k(x) = A + B\cos\left(\varphi(x) + \varPsi_k\right).\tag{6}$$

The camera records the signal sequence $\tilde{g}_k$ with $k = 0 \ldots K - 1$, calculates the phase and decodes the reference coordinate from it $x = \frac{\varphi}{2\pi f}$, with:

$$\varphi = \mathrm{atan2}(-a, b)\ \mathrm{mod}\ 2\pi, \quad a = \sum_{k=0}^{K-1} \tilde{g}_k \sin\left(\varPsi_k\right), \quad b = \sum_{k=0}^{K-1} \tilde{g}_k \cos\left(\varPsi_k\right).\tag{7}$$

For symmetric K step phase shift methods, the uncertainty of the phase measurement σ_φ can be specified as a function of the sensor noise σ_I [26]:

$$\sigma_\varphi = \frac{1}{f}\sqrt{\frac{2}{K}}\frac{\sigma_I}{B},\tag{8}$$

where $\widehat{B} = \frac{2}{K}\sqrt{a^2 + b^2}$ is an estimate of the modulation B of the signal. By using multi frequency phase shift coding methods [27], dense features and their local coordinates can be found for every camera ray in subpixel precision, with respect to monitor pixels. In addition, the uncertainty of this measurement can be quantified and used in the subsequent calibration procedure. The interested reader is advised to refer to the literature for more details [26,28].

3   Generalized Camera Calibration

With the previous results, we can define an objective function that needs to be minimized in order to calibrate the camera and find all ray parameters $\mathbf{d}_i, \mathbf{m}_i$. Simultaneously, we estimate the pose of the calibration targets $\mathbf{R}_k, \mathbf{t}_k$ with respect to the camera. This is done in a weighted least squares sense by minimizing the distance between uncertain target points $\mathbf{x}_{ik}$ with uncertainty σ_{ik} and their corresponding camera rays. To this end, we utilize the phase shift coding strategy to estimate the uncertainties of the reference target points which results in a weighting factor $w_{ik} = \sigma_{ik}^{-2}$. In conclusion, we obtain the objective function:

$$f(\mathcal{R}, \mathcal{T}, \mathcal{L}) = \sum_{i,k} w_{ik} \left\| (\mathbf{R}_k \mathbf{x}_{ik} + \mathbf{t}_k) \times \mathbf{d}_i - \mathbf{m}_i \right\|^2 . \tag{9}$$

As mentioned before, even with today's computing power, it is very difficult (or even impossible) to estimate the enormous number of parameters of this problem simultaneously and in a reasonable time. We therefore divide it into two subproblems, one for camera calibration and another for pose estimation, which are then handled iteratively. This allows to solve the subproblems more easily and to get an optimal result, which further leads to the overall problem converging towards a solution.

3.1   Camera Ray Calibration

One step in the camera calibration procedure is to estimate the ray parameters by assuming known poses of the calibration targets. This greatly reduces the complexity. Instead of calculating every parameter at once, we can calibrate the ray $\mathbf{L}_i = (\mathbf{d}_i^{\mathrm{T}}, \mathbf{m}_i^{\mathrm{T}})^{\mathrm{T}} \in \mathcal{L}$ of each pixel individually (or in parallel). Hence, for every single ray we obtain a new optimization problem which we can write in a more compact form:

$$f(\mathbf{d}_i, \mathbf{m}_i) = \sum_k w_{ik} \left\| \mathbf{p}_{ik} \times \mathbf{d}_i - \mathbf{m}_i \right\|^2$$

$$= \mathbf{d}_i^{\mathrm{T}} \mathbf{A}_{\mathrm{dd},i} \mathbf{d}_i + \mathbf{m}_i^{\mathrm{T}} \mathbf{A}_{\mathrm{md},i} \mathbf{d}_i + a_{\mathrm{mm},i} \left\| \mathbf{m}_i \right\|^2 . \tag{10}$$

Here, $\mathbf{p}_{ik} = \mathbf{R}_k \mathbf{x}_{ik} + \mathbf{t}_k$ represents the target point in camera coordinates and $\mathbf{A}_{\mathrm{dd},i} = \sum_k w_{ik} [\mathbf{p}_{ik}]_\times^{\mathrm{T}} [\mathbf{p}_{ik}]_\times$, $\mathbf{A}_{\mathrm{md},i} = \sum_k 2 w_{ik} [\mathbf{p}_{ik}]_\times^{\mathrm{T}}$, $a_{\mathrm{mm},i} = \sum_k w_{ik}$ are found by summing over the pose index k, reordering and extracting the ray parameters $\mathbf{d}_i$ and $\mathbf{m}_i$. In addition, for better readability, we neglect the index i in the remainder of this section.

It can be easily shown that $\mathbf{A}_{dd}$ is almost always positive definite and invertible. Thus, problem (10) is convex. Considering the characteristics of the Plücker-rays (1), finding the optimal rays results in minimizing a quadratic program with quadratic equality constraints: $\|\mathbf{d}\| = 1$, $\mathbf{d}^T\mathbf{m} = 0$. Although the minimization of such a problem in general requires a difficult nonlinear minimization, we are able to find a global minimum in this specific case, using a few simple steps.

At first, it should be obvious that the solution of the constraint problem is scale ambiguous and that the norm of the ray direction $\|\mathbf{d}\|$ does not influence the actual ray properties [22]. Thus, after having found a solution, we can apply a normalization to the ray $\mathbf{L_n} = \mathbf{L}/\|\mathbf{d}\| = (\mathbf{d}/\|\mathbf{d}\|, \mathbf{m}/\|\mathbf{d}\|)$ to obtain a geometrical meaningful point-to-ray distance (2). To deal with the inequality constraints, we formulate the Lagrangian:

$$g = \mathbf{d}^T\mathbf{A}_{dd}\mathbf{d} + \mathbf{m}^T\mathbf{A}_{md}\mathbf{d} + a_{mm}\|\mathbf{m}\|^2 + \lambda\mathbf{d}^T\mathbf{m} + \mu\left(\mathbf{d}^T\mathbf{d} - 1\right), \quad (11)$$

with the Lagrange multipliers λ, μ. Further, the first order conditions for a minimum are:

$$\frac{\partial g}{\partial \mathbf{d}} = 2\mathbf{A}_{dd}\mathbf{d} + \mathbf{A}_{md}^T\mathbf{m} + \lambda\mathbf{m} + 2\mu\mathbf{d} \overset{!}{=} 0, \quad (12) \qquad \frac{\partial g}{\partial \lambda} = \mathbf{d}^T\mathbf{m} \overset{!}{=} 0, \quad (14)$$

$$\frac{\partial g}{\partial \mathbf{m}} = 2a_{mm}\mathbf{m} + \mathbf{A}_{md}\mathbf{d} + \lambda\mathbf{d} \overset{!}{=} 0, \quad (13) \qquad \frac{\partial g}{\partial \mu} = \|\mathbf{d}\|^2 - 1 \overset{!}{=} 0. \quad (15)$$

Using (13) and (14), this results in a solution for the ray moment $\mathbf{m}$ and λ:

$$\mathbf{m} = -\frac{1}{2a_{mm}}\left(\mathbf{A}_{md} + \lambda\mathbf{I}\right)\mathbf{d}, \quad (16)$$

$$\mathbf{d}^T\mathbf{m} = -\frac{1}{2a_{mm}}\mathbf{d}^T\left(\mathbf{A}_{md} + \lambda\mathbf{I}\right)\mathbf{d} \overset{!}{=} 0, \quad (17)$$

$$\Rightarrow \lambda = \frac{\mathbf{d}^T\mathbf{A}_{md}\mathbf{d}}{\mathbf{d}^T\mathbf{d}} \overset{(15)}{=} \mathbf{d}^T\mathbf{A}_{md}\mathbf{d} = \mathbf{d}^T\left(\sum_k 2w_{ik}[\mathbf{p}_{ik}]_\times^T\right)\mathbf{d}$$

$$= -\mathbf{d}^T\left(\left(\sum_k 2w_{ik}\mathbf{p}_{ik}\right)\times\mathbf{d}\right) = 0, \quad (18)$$

where the last equation holds because $\mathbf{d}$ is orthogonal to $\mathbf{p}\times\mathbf{d}$, $\forall\,\mathbf{p}\in\mathbb{R}^3$. Inserting these results into (12) leads to a simple eigenvalue problem for the solution of the ray direction $\mathbf{d}$ and Lagrange multiplier μ:

$$\left(\mathbf{A}_{dd} - \frac{1}{4a_{mm}}\mathbf{A}_{md}^T\mathbf{A}_{md}\right)\mathbf{d} = \mu\mathbf{d}. \quad (19)$$

These equations still contain the trivial solution $\mathbf{d} = \mathbf{m} = 0$ which however has no geometric meaning for the calibration and is excluded by (15). Apart from that, the solution space of (19) consists of three eigenvalues μ_j with corresponding eigenvectors $\mathbf{d}_j$. After estimating a possible $\mathbf{d}_j$ and corresponding

Lagrange multiplier μ_j, we need to scale the eigenvalue probem to normalize the ray such that $\|\mathbf{d}_j\| = 1$ in order to keep the geometrical meaning of (2) and to obtain an unambiguous scaling. We can get the corresponding ray momentum $\mathbf{m}_j$ through (16). And finally, from these at most three possible stationary points, we select the one with the smallest objective function value (11) to be the optimal solution. In conclusion, we find a closed form solution for the least squares problem of the weighted ray-to-point distance minimization.

3.2 Generalized Pose Estimation

As before, the estimation of the calibration target pose can drastically be simplified by assuming known ray parameters. Therefore we optimize each pose individually. The objective function for each pose k becomes:

$$f(\mathbf{R}_k, \mathbf{t}_k) = \sum_i w_{ik} \left\| (\mathbf{R}_k \mathbf{x}_{ik} + \mathbf{t}_k) \times \mathbf{d}_i - \mathbf{m}_i \right\|^2 . \tag{20}$$

However, solving for a pose $\mathbf{R}_k, \mathbf{t}_k$ is non-trivial because the solution space is restricted to the special Euclidean group SE(3), which combines rotations and translations in three dimensions, $\mathbf{R}_k \in$ SO(3) and $\mathbf{t}_k \in \mathbb{R}^3$, respectively. Directly applying a nonlinear optimization procedure is not advisable, because every function evaluation results in the summation over all rays and is thus computationally very expensive. Therefore, as before, we need to find a more compact form of this quadratic function. Again for the sake of brevity, we omit the index k for the remainder of this section. Further, we use the vectorization operator $\mathbf{r} = \text{vec}(\mathbf{R}) \in \mathbb{R}^9$ that stacks the columns of the 3×3 matrix $\mathbf{R}$. While computing the summation over all ray indices i only once, we obtain independence of the actual number of rays, which simplifies and speeds up later optimization steps:

$$\min f(\mathbf{R}, \mathbf{t}) = \mathbf{r}^{\mathrm{T}} \mathbf{A}_{rr} \mathbf{r} + \mathbf{t}^{\mathrm{T}} \mathbf{A}_{tt} \mathbf{t} + \mathbf{t}^{\mathrm{T}} \mathbf{A}_{tr} \mathbf{r} + \mathbf{b}_r^{\mathrm{T}} \mathbf{r} + \mathbf{b}_t^{\mathrm{T}} \mathbf{t} + h$$
$$\text{s.t.} \ \ \mathbf{r} = \text{vec}(\mathbf{R}), \ (\mathbf{R}, \mathbf{t}) \in \text{SE}(3). \tag{21}$$

While observing the constraint quadratic objective (21), we notice that the main constraint lies in the rotational part and moreover the objective is convex in the translation part. Thus, the problem can further be reduced by decoupling of translation and rotation, which means that $\mathbf{t}$ can be expressed in terms of $\mathbf{R}$. We can find the optimal translation vector with the first order condition for a minimum, using $\frac{\partial f(\mathbf{R}, \mathbf{t})}{\partial \mathbf{t}} \overset{!}{=} 0$. This leads to:

$$\mathbf{t} = -\frac{1}{2} \mathbf{A}_{tt}^{-1} \left(\mathbf{A}_{tr} \mathbf{r} + \mathbf{b}_t \right) . \tag{22}$$

Inserting (22) into (21) results in the decoupling of the rotation and translation subproblem, which then again yields a quadratic optimization problem ($\mathbf{A}, \mathbf{b}, c$ are calculated from $\mathbf{A}_{rr}, \mathbf{A}_{tt}, \mathbf{A}_{tr}, \mathbf{b}_r, \mathbf{b}_t, h$, see supplemental material for more details):

$$f(\mathbf{R}) = \mathbf{r}^{\mathrm{T}} \mathbf{A} \mathbf{r} + \mathbf{b}^{\mathrm{T}} \mathbf{r} + c, \quad \text{s.t.} \ \ \mathbf{r} = \text{vec}(\mathbf{R}), \ \mathbf{R} \in \text{SO}(3). \tag{23}$$

After finding a solution for the rotation matrix we obtain the optimal translation vector with (22), assuming invertibility of $\mathbf{A}_{tt}$. It can be shown that $\mathbf{A}_{tt}$ is positive definite in most cases with the exception of a few exotic camera ray distributions (e.g. parallel rays, telecentric optics), and hence we truly get the minimum of the objective with respect to the translation.

Although minimization of (23) seems simple at first, we have the constraint to find an optimum in SO(3). This is equivalent to a non-convex problem with quadratic and cubic constraints on the rotation parameters. Bergamasco et al. [15] use an iterative closest point algorithm that iteratively calculates the transformation from the observed points to the closest point on the corresponding rays, which however only converges near the optimum. Kanatani [29] suggests a fast method by first calculating an Euclidean solution, with $\mathbf{R} \in \mathbb{R}^{3 \times 3}$, and projecting it onto the SO(3)-manifold using singular value decomposition, which results in a not entirely correct minimization. Schweighofer and Pinz [30] solve the problem using sum-of-squares optimization and constrain the algorithm to SO(3). Ventura et al. [31] and Kneip et al. [32] find a solution computationally very efficient, using Gröbner basis [33]. This however requires further "root polishing" to resolve ambiguities and to achieve good results. Hence, since our main focus is not real-time optimization, but rather highly precise pose estimation, we are obliged to find an accurate minimum to ensure convergence of the AM calibration. In order to find this, we therefore directly use a gradient-based optimization approach on the Riemannian manifold $SO(3) = \{ \mathbf{R} \in \mathbb{R}^{3 \times 3} \,|\, \mathbf{R}^{\mathrm{T}} \mathbf{R} = \mathbf{I}, \det(\mathbf{R}) = 1 \}$, which implicitly considers all constraints. The mapping from any element of the tangent space $\boldsymbol{\eta} \in \mathfrak{so}(3)$ to $\mathbf{R} \in SO(3)$ is called the exponential map $\mathbf{R} = e^{[\boldsymbol{\eta}]_{\times}}$, and the reverse map is called the logarithmic map $[\boldsymbol{\eta}]_{\times} = \log(\mathbf{R})$. Both can be calculated in closed form, using the skew operator [34]:

$$[\boldsymbol{\eta}]_{\times} = \begin{bmatrix} 0 & -\eta_3 & \eta_2 \\ \eta_3 & 0 & -\eta_1 \\ -\eta_2 & \eta_1 & 0 \end{bmatrix}. \tag{24}$$

If a function is to be optimized on the manifold, the corresponding direction of descent must be sought in the local tangent space $f_{\boldsymbol{\eta}}(\mathbf{R}) = f(e^{[\boldsymbol{\eta}]_{\times}} \mathbf{R})$. In order to use conventional optimization methods, a valid representation for both the gradient and the Hessian must be identified. These can be easily found by using directional derivatives of the locally parameterized manifold in the direction of the tangent space [35]:

$$Df_{\boldsymbol{\eta}}(\mathbf{R})[\boldsymbol{\eta}] = \lim_{\varepsilon \to 0} \frac{\partial}{\partial \varepsilon} f_{\boldsymbol{\eta}\varepsilon}(\mathbf{R}) = \boldsymbol{\eta}^{\mathrm{T}} \mathrm{grad}(f), \tag{25}$$

$$D\,\mathrm{grad}(f)[\boldsymbol{\eta}] = \lim_{\varepsilon \to 0} \boldsymbol{\eta}^{\mathrm{T}} \frac{\partial}{\partial \varepsilon} \mathrm{grad}(f) = \boldsymbol{\eta}^{\mathrm{T}} \mathrm{Hess}(f) \boldsymbol{\eta}. \tag{26}$$

Looking back at our original problem (23), this approach leads to the explicit formulas for the Riemannian gradient and Riemannian Hessian (the interested reader is advised to refer to the supplementary material or the literature for further details [35, 36]):

$$\text{grad}(f) = 2\mathbf{H}^{\text{T}} (\mathbf{R} \otimes \mathbf{I}) (\mathbf{A}\mathbf{r} + \mathbf{b}) , \tag{27}$$

$$\text{Hess}(f) = 2\mathbf{H}^{\text{T}} \left((\mathbf{R} \otimes \mathbf{I}) \mathbf{A} (\mathbf{R} \otimes \mathbf{I})^{\text{T}} - \mathbf{I} \otimes \text{mat} (\mathbf{A}\mathbf{r} + \mathbf{b}) \mathbf{R}^{\text{T}} \right) \mathbf{H} . \tag{28}$$

Here, the reshape operator $\text{mat}(\cdot)$ is the inverse of $\text{vec}(\cdot)$. $\otimes$ is the Kronecker product, $\mathbf{e}_1, \mathbf{e}_2, \mathbf{e}_3$ are unit base vectors and $\mathbf{H} = \left[\text{vec}([\mathbf{e}_1]_\times), \text{vec}([\mathbf{e}_2]_\times), \text{vec}([\mathbf{e}_3]_\times) \right] \in \mathbb{R}^{9 \times 3}$.

After the formulas for the gradient and the Hesse matrix have been established, we can build a quadratic model of the local tangent space and are then able to minimize the objective (23) with the help of an appropriate Newton descend algorithm. Apart from important differences, the procedure is quite similar to the classic Euclidean approach. For the current iterate, we calculate $\text{grad}f(\mathbf{R}^{(n)})$ and $\text{Hess}f(\mathbf{R}^{(n)})$. After the search direction $\boldsymbol{\eta}^{(n)}$ has been found by solving the Newton equation, one has to calculate a projection of the tangent space back to the manifold to obtain a valid descend [36]:

$$\text{Hess}f(\mathbf{R}^{(n)}) \, \boldsymbol{\eta}^{(n)} = -\text{grad}f(\mathbf{R}^{(n)}) , \tag{29}$$

$$\mathbf{R}^{(n+1)} = e^{\left(\alpha [\boldsymbol{\eta}^{(n)}]_\times \right)} \mathbf{R}^{(n)} . \tag{30}$$

Finally, a subsequent 1D backtracking line search in SO(3) finds a sufficient step size α and accelerates the convergence. In order to initialize the algorithm an appropriate start is required, where in the context of an AM-camera-calibration, the pose estimate from the previous iteration may be used.

3.3   Convergence, Acceleration and Summary

The camera ray calibration provides the globally optimal solution in every step. Furthermore, the pose estimation converges towards a minimum and provides no inferior result than the previous iteration. Following the researches in the field of AM [24,37], it is easy to show the convergence of the optimization procedure to a stationary point with an $\mathcal{O}(\frac{1}{n})$ convergence rate (see supplementary material). In order to obtain a faster convergence, acceleration techniques may be applied. We modified Nesterov's acceleration scheme to obtain an almost $\mathcal{O}(\frac{1}{n^2})$ convergence rate [38]. During the acceleration step, a weighted rate of the change of the pose parameters is added to the next estimate. When accelerating the rotation, of course, this has to be done on the SO(3)-manifold: The current rotation is reversed by the previous rotation, projected onto the $\mathfrak{so}(3)$ tangent space using the log-map, weighted by an acceleration parameter and finally transformed back into a rotation matrix using the exp-map and multiplied onto the current estimate. Algorithm 1 summarizes the complete AM calibration.

Although we have a strictly convergent algorithm, of course, there does not exist a unique solution. Depending on the starting value, the optimization runs into an arbitrary coordinate system. Therefore, it is advisable to initialize the algorithm with a rough estimate of the reference target poses, which could for example be obtained using standard model-based approaches presented in the

---

Algorithm 1. Alternating minimization

Input: For every pixel i and target pose k: measure monitor coordinates $\mathbf{x}_{ik}$ and weight w_{ik}

Output: Calibrated ray $\mathbf{L}_i$ for each pixel and pose $\mathbf{R}_k, \mathbf{t}_k$ of all reference targets

Initialize: Set poses of reference targets $\mathcal{R}^{(0)}, \mathcal{T}^{(0)}$ (*e.g.* use Ramalingam *et al.* [10])

Set acceleration parameter $\beta_0 = 0$

1: **for** $n = 1, 2, 3, \ldots$ **do**
2:     **for** $i = 1, 2, 3, \ldots$ **do**
3:         Hold pose parameters and optimize rays
4:         $\mathbf{L}_i^{(n+1)} = \arg\min_{\mathbf{L}_i \in \mathbb{P}^6} f\left(\mathcal{R}^{(n)}, \mathcal{T}^{(n)}, \mathbf{L}_i\right)$
5:     **end for**
6:     **for** $k = 1, 2, 3, \ldots$ **do**
7:         Hold ray parameters and optimize poses
8:         $\mathbf{R}_k^*, \mathbf{t}_k^* = \arg\min_{(\mathbf{R}_k, \mathbf{t}_k) \in \mathrm{SE}(3)} f\left(\mathbf{R}_k, \mathbf{t}_k, \mathcal{L}^{(n+1)}\right)$
9:         Accelerate translation and rotation update
10:       $\mathbf{t}_k^{(n+1)} = \mathbf{t}_k^* + \beta_n \left(\mathbf{t}_k^* - \mathbf{t}_k^{(n)}\right)$
11:       $\mathbf{R}_k^{(n+1)} = e^{\beta_n \log\left(\mathbf{R}_k^{\mathrm{T}(n)} \mathbf{R}_k^*\right)} \mathbf{R}_k^*$
12:       with a sequence β_n as defined by Nesterov [38].
13:     **end for**
14: **end for**

---

literature [1,39] or the generalized approach by Ramalingam *et al.* [10]. However, here it is of utmost importance that the camera model is properly chosen. Of course, one can also randomly select starting poses with the downside of an increased optimization time and the risk to converge to a non-optimal local minimum. Nonetheless, the arbitrary coordinate system doesn't change the geometrical properties of the rays and, accordingly, the calibrated camera can be used without loss of accuracy. Even more, the final calibration can be easily transformed to a standardized coordinate system, *e.g.* by defining the origin to be the point that is closest to all rays and by selecting the z-axis to be the mean ray direction.

4 Experiments

For the evaluation, a 27" monitor with a resolution of 2560×1440 and a pixel pitch of $233\,\mu\mathrm{m}$ was used to display the necessary calibration patterns. Two different imaging systems were used to evaluate the proposed method: A standard webcam (Logitech C920 HD Pro Webcam) and a more exotic example, a microlens-based light field camera (Lytro Illum). The latter one has a microlens array placed in front of the sensor, which allows to sample the plenoptic function of a scene [3,40–42]. This ultimately results in a non-central camera with multiple projection centers, which can be used as a 3D-camera and in addition requires a much more complex camera model to be efficiently calibrated. The monitor was captured from 30 different poses, whereby several phase shift patterns have to be recorded at each pose to encode the target features [28]. The distances between monitor and camera were in the range of 5 cm to 2 m. In order to compare the proposed technique to the classic methods, checkerboard patterns were displayed at the same positions. The webcam was calibrated using OpenCV [39] and Zhang's algorithm [1]. The light field camera was calibrated using the state-of-the-art method by Bok *et al.* [43]. Both methods use checker patterns. The proposed generalized calibration procedure was initialized with a rough pose estimation. The webcam was initialized with OpenCV and for the light field camera we used the calibration by Bok *et al.* with a succeeding standard pose estimation. As an alternative, one could also initialize using the generalized relative pose estimation algorithm proposed by Ramalingam *et al.* [10]. In many cases, we observed that it was acceptable to just "guess" the positions of the monitor, *e.g.* see Fig. 2, where the monitor poses at start and after convergence are shown. We eventually terminated the alternating minimization after 100 iterations, due to sufficient convergence. Since each ray is independent from one another, it is possible to process them in parallel, using a GPU. The optimization of 40 million pixels (Lytro Illum) thus only takes a few seconds per iteration (Intel Core i7-6700, Nvidia GTX 1080 Ti, 16 GB RAM). The calibration procedure therefore converges after 10 min, whereas the method by Bok *et al.* uses a highly advanced model which takes more than three hours to calibrate. Our method is even faster when calibrating the two megapixel webcam.

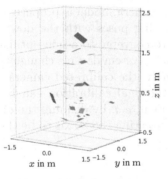
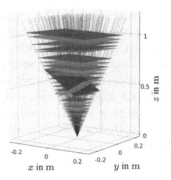

(a) Iteration 0: $d_e \approx 0.6$ m.   (b) Iteration 100: $d_e \approx 80\,\mu$m.

Fig. 2. Convergence of the calibration: Depict are the observed area of the monitor, the calibrated camera rays and the mean Euclidean distances at start and end. Even with an initially very bad pose estimation, the procedure converges towards reasonable results. Note the difference in scale.

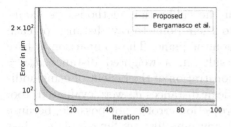

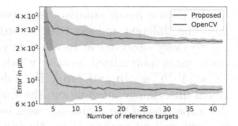

Fig. 3. Convergence and initialization of AM-calibration: The plot shows the mean value and the $\pm\sigma$-range of the convergence.

Fig. 4. Dependency on the number of patterns: The plot shows the mean value and the $\pm\sigma$-range of the error.

Figure 3 shows the convergence of the proposed method as a function of the root mean square error (RMSE) over the number of iterations. The plot shows the calibration of the webcam, which was initialized with the model-based OpenCV pose estimation. To investigate the robustness against bad initialization, the convergence behavior was investigated for 100 trials while random translations in the range ±10 cm and rotations $\pm10°$ were added to each initialization. Therefore, the start of the plot corresponds approximately to the error of the OpenCV calibration. For comparison, the convergence behavior of the generalized calibration method of Bergamasco *et al.* [15] was also investigated, using the same initializations. Figure 3 shows that the proposed method converges significantly faster than their method and that it is less sensitive to a bad initialization, which is shown by the smaller standard deviation in the RMSE.

Theoretical we need two different point observations to fit a ray, then A_{dd} is positive definite. And to fit a pose, we need three non-parallel rays (then A_{tt} is positive definite) that observe different points (then A_{rr} is positive definite). With only two reference targets, we always converge to a perfect fit, which of course is useless. An unambiguous solution however can theoretically be obtained with at least three reference poses [10]. But of course, because we use a least squares based minimization approach and we want to reduce the impact of noise, we need more reference targets. This becomes apparent in Fig. 4. Here, we investigate the calibration error when different numbers of reference targets are used. For this purpose, the camera was calibrated 100 times, where each time a fixed number of target patterns was randomly selected from a total set of 60 poses. The mean error of all calibrations and their $\pm\sigma$ standard deviation are plotted over the number of used patterns. It can be seen that the overall calibration error needs at least a minimum of 15–20 poses to result in a good calibration, whereas more poses increase the overall robustness of the method. Too few patterns, on the other hand, result in a very unreliable calibration. We see similar results for the OpenCV calibration, although the dependency on the number of patterns is not as strong as compared to the proposed method. In summary, the proposed calibration needs more reference poses to correctly estimate the immense number of parameters. However, even with fewer poses, the error of the proposed calibration is several times smaller than the model-based calibration.

To ensure a fair comparison between the calibration methods, we examined the different models with regard to their point-to-ray distance of each ray to every observed feature in every monitor plane. The comparison is here done using normalized values, which results in a weighted distance $d_{\mathbf{w}} = (\sum w_{ik})^{-1} \sum w_{ik} \| \mathbf{p}_{ik} \times \mathbf{d}_i - \mathbf{m}_i \|$. For a demonstration of the benefit of using additional uncertainty information, the Euclidean distances d_e were evaluated, too. A comparison of the commonly used re-projection error is not possible, because in a generalized camera model there isn't anything like an "image plane", just a set of rays. Table 1 summarizes the respective calibration results.

Table 1. Calibration errors: Methods with the suffix "checker" were evaluated only at the sparsely detected checker features. For all others, the error was calculated over all observed phase-shift features. "Proposed (E)" does not use the uncertainty and only minimizes the Euclidean distance.

	Logitech Webcam				Lytro Illum			
	$d_{\mathbf{w}}$ in µm		d_e in µm		$d_{\mathbf{w}}$ in µm		d_e in µm	
	Mean	RMSE	Mean	RMSE	Mean	RMSE	Mean	RMSE
OpenCV [39] (checker)	–	–	267.4	340.0	–	–	–	–
OpenCV	243.1	323.8	343.3	375.3	–	–	–	–
Bok *et al.* [43] (checker)	–	–	–	–	–	–	448.4	851.8
Bok *et al.*	–	–	–	–	375.6	758.8	7165.1	8686.0
Bergamasco *et al.* [15]	88.8	121.0	93.9	130.3	922.1	1696.5	1041.8	1720.5
Proposed (E)	83.3	117.6	86.8	**124.3**	77.1	185.3	163.1	**438.5**
Proposed	**81.6**	**117.0**	**84.6**	125.5	**49.4**	**105.8**	**155.5**	457.4

We can see that the proposed method produces the best results. Even for the webcam, with its relatively simple optics, the generalized approach delivers both a smaller mean error and RMSE, resulting in a more precise geometric calibration with fewer outliers at the same time. In the classic model, these outliers cannot be used because they are too far away from the model description. The generalized model, however, can effectively use each individual pixel as a source of information. This becomes particularly visible for the webcam if only the error regarding the checkerboard features is evaluated. Here, the error is smaller than when all phase shift features are used for every pixel. This demonstrates that the classic calibrations optimize the camera model for only a part of the pixels, by neglecting outliers, while the generalized model optimally calibrates every pixel. Also, our proposed method performs better than the generalized approach by Bergamasco *et al.*, even if we don't take the uncertainties into account and only minimize the Euclidean distance. Furthermore, it can be seen that additional information about the coordinate uncertainty improves the calibration even more. Inaccurate points are weighted less strongly and therefore have a weaker effect on the result. Figure 5a illustrates the results by showing the distribution of all point-to-ray distances.

Similar conclusions can be drawn with the Lytro Illum camera. Due to the more complex optics and the more extensive optimization associated with it, the differences here are much greater and the superiority of the proposed generalized calibration becomes even clearer. Although the model by Bok *et al.* is highly advanced, it is strongly adapted to the few checker features and only produces good results here. But if the model is evaluated using the phase shift features for every pixel, then this leads to high RMSE values caused by many outliers. In this case, we can see particularly well that a low dimensional model-based approach cannot ideally describe every pixel of a camera with complex optics, such as the light field camera. Moreover, the benefit of using uncertainties becomes very well apparent: the quality of pixels in microlens-based light field cameras (and the ability to accurately model the corresponding rays) deteriorates towards the edges of the microlenses [43,44], leading to increased uncertainties. These can however be effectively suppressed by the proposed procedure, leading to much smaller mean errors and RMSE values. The method by Bok *et al.* can calibrate the center of each microlens very well. Here, their calibration error reduces to about 60 μm for the best pixels. But, the more the pixels move away from the center, the worse becomes the error. This reduces the overall calibration quality, as seen in the results. Also, the method by Bok *et al.* returns only 35 million of the total 41 million pixels. The worst pixels, which are between neighboring microlenses, cannot be modeled and are therefore cut off. Thus, they cannot be analyzed in the evaluation made here. However, our proposed model can effectively calibrate the rays of every pixel of the sensor, whereby we not only get good calibration results in the centers of the microlenses, but also at the edges, where it is very difficult to describe the light field camera with a uniform model. While the method by Bergamasco *et al.* delivers good results for the webcam, we weren't able to get a good calibration for the light field camera. Although the calibration of the webcam shows that their approach works, it seems that it does not generalize as well as the proposed method and that it has difficulties with the poor quality of the pixels at the edges of the microlenses. The procedure diverged in our experiments. Only after improving the initialization for a few iterations using our method and by excluding the pixels with highest uncertainty, we were able to obtain a convergent result for their method, which still has a smaller error than the calibration by Bok *et al.*

Figure 5b summarizes these results and shows the distribution of all point-to-ray distances for the Lytro Illum. The method by Bok *et al.* results in a flat distribution with a peak at 60 μm. Also, several peaks systematically appear at higher distances, which are due to the difficulties of modeling a light field camera. The method by Bergamasco *et al.* results in an overall flat distribution with errors at high values (more than 1 mm). Our proposed methods, on the other hand, are much tighter with peaks at far lower values. Moreover, larger errors from minimizing only the Euclidean distance can be shifted to smaller ones by using the generalized calibration with uncertainty-based weighting.

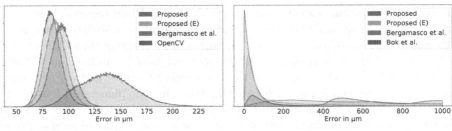

(a) Histogram of errors (Logitech Webcam).   (b) Histogram of errors (Lytro Illum).

Fig. 5. The generalized model creates a much tighter distribution with less outliers as compared to the classical calibrations. Outliers can be suppressed even more with uncertainty information.

5   Summary

We presented a new calibration technique for the generalized imaging model. We proposed to split the calibration into two parts, ray calibration and pose estimation, and to apply an alternating minimization to efficiently optimize the immense number of parameters. Dense calibration features were obtained using phase shifting techniques, where we accounted for the measurement uncertainty that were estimated during the pre-processing. We presented a simple analytical solution to minimize the ray subpoblem. And further, we optimized the pose by decoupling rotation and translation and by using a gradient descent on the rotation manifold. Finally, experimental evaluation verified the advantages of the proposed method over conventional and other generalized approaches and demonstrated the benefit of using additional information about the uncertainty of the calibration target coordinates. We make the source code of our method publicly available and encourage others to use it to their own needs [45].

References

1. Zhang, Z.: A flexible new technique for camera calibration. IEEE Trans. Pattern Anal. Mach. Intell. **22**, 1330–1334 (2000)
2. Hartley, R., Zisserman, A.: Multiple View Geometry in Computer Vision, 2nd edn. Cambridge University Press, Cambridge (2000)
3. Ng, R., Levoy, M., Brédif, M., Duval, G., Horowitz, M., Hanrahan, P.: Light field photography with a hand-held plenoptic camera. Computer Science Technical Report CSTR 2, 1–11 (2005)
4. Pless, R.: Using many cameras as one. In: 2003 IEEE Computer Society Conference on Computer Vision and Pattern Recognition, II-587-93, Los Alamitos, Calif. IEEE Computer Society (2003)
5. Swaminathan, R., Kang, S.B., Szeliski, R., Criminisi, A., Nayar, S.K.: On the motion and appearance of specularities in image sequences. In: Heyden, A., Sparr, G., Nielsen, M., Johansen, P. (eds.) ECCV 2002. LNCS, vol. 2350, pp. 508–523. Springer, Heidelberg (2002). https://doi.org/10.1007/3-540-47969-4_34

6. Grossberg, M.D., Nayar, S.K.: A general imaging model and a method for finding its parameters, pp. 108–115. In: Proceedings/Eighth IEEE International Conference on Computer Vision, Los Alamitos, Calif. IEEE Computer Society (2001)

7. Grossberg, M.D., Nayar, S.K.: The raxel imaging model and ray-based calibration. Int. J. Comput. Vis. **61**, 119–137 (2005)

8. Sturm, P., Ramalingam, S.: A generic concept for camera calibration. In: Pajdla, T., Matas, J. (eds.) ECCV 2004. LNCS, vol. 3022, pp. 1–13. Springer, Heidelberg (2004). https://doi.org/10.1007/978-3-540-24671-8_1

9. Ramalingam, S., Sturm, P.: A unifying model for camera calibration. IEEE Trans. Pattern Anal. Mach. Intell. **39**, 1309–1319 (2017)

10. Ramalingam, S., Sturm, P., Lodha, S.K.: Towards complete generic camera calibration. In: Schmid, C., Tomasi, C., Soatto, S. (eds.) CVPR 2005, Los Alamitos, Calif, pp. 1093–1098. IEEE Computer Society, (2005)

11. Bothe, T., Li, W., Schulte, M., Kopylow, C.V., Bergmann, R.B., Jüptner, W.P.O.: Vision ray calibration for the quantitative geometric description of general imaging and projection optics in metrology. Appl. Optics **49**, 5851–5860 (2010)

12. Miraldo, P., Araujo, H., Queiro, J.: Point-based calibration using a parametric representation of the general imaging model. In: 2011 IEEE International Conference on Computer Vision (ICCV), Piscataway, NJ, pp. 2304–2311. IEEE (2011)

13. Miraldo, P., Araujo, H.: Calibration of smooth camera models. IEEE Trans. Pattern Anal. Mach. Intell. **35**, 2091–2103 (2013)

14. Schops, T., Larsson, V., Pollefeys, M., Sattler, T.: Why having 10,000 parameters in your camera model is better than twelve. In: Proceedings of the IEEE/CVF Conference on Computer Vision and Pattern Recognition (CVPR) (2020)

15. Bergamasco, F., Albarelli, A., Rodola, E., Torsello, A.: Can a fully unconstrained imaging model be applied effectively to central cameras? In: 2013 IEEE Conference on Computer Vision and Pattern Recognition (CVPR), Piscataway, NJ, pp. 1391–1398. IEEE (2013)

16. Bergamasco, F., Albarelli, A., Cosmo, L., Torsello, A., Rodola, E., Cremers, D.: Adopting an unconstrained ray model in light-field cameras for 3D shape reconstruction. In: 2015 IEEE Conference on Computer Vision and Pattern Recognition (CVPR), Piscataway, NJ, pp. 3003–3012. IEEE (2015)

17. Chen, C.S., Chang, W.Y.: On pose recovery for generalized visual sensors. IEEE Trans. Pattern Anal. Mach. Intell. **26**, 848–861 (2004)

18. Balzer, J., Werling, S.: Principles of shape from specular reflection. Measurement **43**, 1305–1317 (2010)

19. Pankaj, D.S., Nidamanuri, R.R., Prasad, P.B.: 3-D imaging techniques and review of products. In: Proceedings of International Conference on Innovations in Computer Science and Engineering (2013)

20. van der Jeught, S., Dirckx, J.J.: Real-time structured light profilometry: a review. Opt. Lasers Eng. **87**, 18–31 (2016)

21. Shevlin, F.: Analysis of orientation problems using plücker lines. In: Proceedings of MD and Los Angeles, CA, pp. 685–689. IEEE Computer Society Press (1984)

22. van der Hodge, W., Pedoe, D.: Methods of Algebraic Geometry. Cambridge University Press, Cambridge (1994)

23. Brox, T., Rosenhahn, B., Gall, J., Cremers, D.: Combined region and motion-based 3D tracking of rigid and articulated objects. IEEE Trans. Pattern Anal. Mach. Intell. **32**, 402–415 (2010)

24. Grippo, L., Sciandrone, M.: On the convergence of the block nonlinear Gauss-Seidel method under convex constraints. Oper. Res. Lett. **26**, 127–136 (2000)

25. Zuo, C., Feng, S., Huang, L., Tao, T., Yin, W., Chen, Q.: Phase shifting algorithms for fringe projection profilometry: a review. Opt. Lasers Eng. **109**, 23–59 (2018)
26. Fischer, M., Petz, M., Tutsch, R.: Model-based noise prediction for fringe projection systems - a tool for the statistical analysis of evaluation algorithms. TM Technisches Messen **84**, 111–122 (2017)
27. Zuo, C., Huang, L., Zhang, M., Chen, Q., Asundi, A.: Temporal phase unwrapping algorithms for fringe projection profilometry: a comparative review. Opt. Lasers Eng. **85**, 84–103 (2016)
28. Salvi, J., Pagès, J., Batlle, J.: Pattern codification strategies in structured light systems. Pattern Recogn. **37**, 827–849 (2004)
29. Kanatani, K.: Analysis of 3-D rotation fitting. IEEE Trans. Pattern Anal. Mach. Intell. **16**, 543–549 (1994)
30. Schweighofer, G., Pinz, A.: Globally optimal O(n) solution to the PnP problem for general camera models. In: BMVC (2008)
31. Ventura, J., Arth, C., Reitmayr, G., Schmalstieg, D.: A minimal solution to the generalized pose-and-scale problem. In: 2014 IEEE Conference on Computer Vision and Pattern Recognition, pp. 422–429. IEEE (2014)
32. Kneip, L., Li, H., Seo, Y.: UPnP: an optimal $O(n)$ solution to the absolute pose problem with universal applicability. In: Fleet, D., Pajdla, T., Schiele, B., Tuytelaars, T. (eds.) ECCV 2014. LNCS, vol. 8689, pp. 127–142. Springer, Cham (2014). https://doi.org/10.1007/978-3-319-10590-1_9
33. Kukelova, Z., Bujnak, M., Pajdla, T.: Automatic generator of minimal problem solvers. In: Forsyth, D., Torr, P., Zisserman, A. (eds.) ECCV 2008. LNCS, vol. 5304, pp. 302–315. Springer, Heidelberg (2008). https://doi.org/10.1007/978-3-540-88690-7_23
34. Ma, Y., Soatto, S., Kosecka, J., Sastry, S.S.: An Invitation to 3-D Vision: From Images to Geometric Models. Springer, New York (2003). https://doi.org/10.1007/978-0-387-21779-6
35. Absil, P.A., Mahony, R., Sepulchre, R.: Optimization algorithms on matrix manifolds. Princeton University Press, Princeton (2009)
36. Boumal, N.: Optimization and estimation on manifolds. Ph.D. thesis, Catholic University of Louvain, Louvain-la-Neuve, Belgium (2014)
37. Niesen, U., Shah, D., Wornell, G.: Adaptive alternating minimization algorithms. In: 2007 IEEE International Symposium on Information Theory, pp. 1641–1645, Piscataway, NJ. IEEE Service Center (2007)
38. Nesterov, Y.E.:A method for solving the convex programming problem with convergencerate O(1/k^2).Dokl. akad. nauk Sssr. 269, pp. 543–547 (1983)
39. Bradski, G.: The openCV library. Dr. Dobb's J. Softw. Tools, **120**, 122–125 (2000)
40. Ihrke, I., Restrepo, J., Mignard-Debise, L.: Principles of light field imaging: briefly revisiting 25 years of research. IEEE Signal Process. Mag. **33**, 59–69 (2016)
41. Zhang, Q., Zhang, C., Ling, J., Wang, Q., Yu, J.:A generic multi-projection-center model and calibration method for light field cameras. IEEE Trans. Pattern Anal. Mach. Intell. (2018)
42. Zhang, Q., Ling, J., Liu, Y., Yu, J.:Ray-space projection model for light field camera. In: CVPR 2019 (2019)
43. Bok, Y., Jeon, H.G., Kweon, I.S.: Geometric calibration of micro-lens-based light field cameras using line features. IEEE Trans. Pattern Anal. Mach. Intell. **39**, 287–300 (2017)

44. Dansereau, D.G., Pizarro, O., Williams, S.B.: Decoding, calibration and rectification for lenselet-based plenoptic cameras. In: 2013 IEEE Conference on Computer Vision and Pattern Recognition, pp. 1027–1034 (2013)
45. Institute of Industrial Information Technology, Karlsruhe Institute of Technology: Public GitLab repositories. GNU GPLv3 License (2020). https://gitlab.com/iiit-public

Graph-Based Heuristic Search for Module Selection Procedure in Neural Module Network

Yuxuan Wu[(⊠)] and Hideki Nakayama

The University of Tokyo, Tokyo, Japan
{wuyuxuan,nakayama}@nlab.ci.i.u-tokyo.ac.jp

Abstract. Neural Module Network (NMN) is a machine learning model for solving the visual question answering tasks. NMN uses programs to encode modules' structures, and its modularized architecture enables it to solve logical problems more reasonably. However, because of the non-differentiable procedure of module selection, NMN is hard to be trained end-to-end. To overcome this problem, existing work either included ground-truth program into training data or applied reinforcement learning to explore the program. However, both of these methods still have weaknesses. In consideration of this, we proposed a new learning framework for NMN. Graph-based Heuristic Search is the algorithm we proposed to discover the optimal program through a heuristic search on the data structure named Program Graph. Our experiments on FigureQA and CLEVR dataset show that our methods can realize the training of NMN without ground-truth programs and achieve superior program exploring efficiency compared to existing reinforcement learning methods. (The code of this work is available at https://github.com/evan-ak/gbhs)

1 Introduction

With the development of machine learning in recent years, more and more tasks have been accomplished such as image classification, object detection, and machine translation. However, there are still many tasks that human beings perform much better than machine learning systems, especially those in need of logical reasoning ability. Neural Module Network (NMN) is a model proposed recently targeted to solve these reasoning tasks [1,2]. It first predicts a program indicating the required modules and their layout, and then constructs a complete network with these modules to accomplish the reasoning. With the ability to break down complicated tasks into basic logical units and to reuse previous knowledge, NMN achieved super-human level performance on challenging visual reasoning tasks like CLEVR [3]. However, because the module selection is a discrete and non-differentiable process, it is not easy to train NMN end-to-end.

Electronic supplementary material The online version of this chapter (https://doi.org/10.1007/978-3-030-69535-4_34) contains supplementary material, which is available to authorized users.

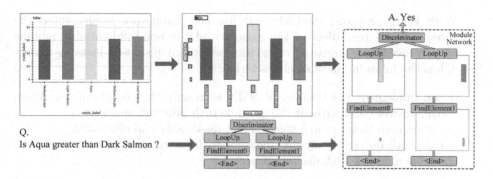

Fig. 1. Our learning framework enables the NMN to solve the visual reasoning problem without ground-truth program annotation.

To deal with this problem, a general solution is to separate the training into two parts: the program predictor and the modules. In this case, the program becomes a necessary intermediate label. The two common solutions to provide this program label are either to include the ground-truth programs into training data or to apply reinforcement learning to explore the optimal candidate program. However, these two solutions still have the following limitations. The dependency on ground-truth program annotation makes NMN's application hard to be extended to datasets without this kind of annotation. This annotation is also highly expensive while being hand-made by humans. Therefore, program annotation cannot always be expected to be available for tasks in real-world environments. In view of this, methods relying on ground-truth program annotation cannot be considered as complete solutions for training NMN. On the other hand, the main problem in the approaches based on reinforcement learning is that with the growth of the length of programs and number of modules, the size of the search space of possible programs becomes so huge that a reasonable program may not be found in an acceptable time.

In consideration of this, we still regard the training of NMN as an open problem. With the motivation to take advantage of NMN on broader tasks and overcome the difficulty in its training in the meanwhile, in this work, we proposed a new learning framework to solve the non-differentiable module selection problem in NMN (Fig. 1).

In this learning framework, we put forward the Graph-based Heuristic Search algorithm to enable the model to find the most appropriate program by itself. Basically, this algorithm is inspired by Monte Carlo Tree Search (MCTS). Similar to MCTS, our algorithm conducts a heuristic search to discover the most appropriate program in the space of possible programs. Besides, inspired by the intrinsic connection between programs, we proposed the data structure named Program Graph to represent the space of possible programs in a way more reasonable than the tree structure used by MCTS. Further, to deal with the cases that the search space is extremely huge, we proposed the Candidate Selection Mechanism to narrow down the search space.

With these proposed methods, our learning framework implemented the training of NMN regardless of the existence of the non-differentiable module selection procedure. Compared to existing work, our proposed learning framework has the following notable characteristics:

- It can implement the training of NMN with only the triplets of {question, image, answer} and without the ground-truth program annotation.
- It can explore larger search spaces more reasonably and efficiently.
- It can work on both trainable modules with neural architectures and non-trainable modules with discrete processing.

2   Related Work

2.1   Visual Reasoning

Generally, Visual Reasoning can be considered as a kind of Visual Question Answering (VQA) [4]. Besides the requirement of understanding information from both images and questions in common VQA problems, Visual Reasoning further asks for the capacity to recognize abstract concepts such as spatial, mathematical, and logical relationships. CLEVR [5] is one of the most famous and widely used datasets for Visual Reasoning. It provides not only the triplets of {question, image, answer} but also the functional programs paired with each question. FigureQA [6] is another Visual Reasoning dataset we focus on in this work. It provides questions in fifteen different templates asked on five different types of figures.

To solve Visual Reasoning problems, a naive approach would be the combination of Convolutional Neural Network (CNN) and Recurrent Neural Network (RNN). Here, CNN and RNN are responsible for extracting information from images and questions, respectively. Then, the extracted information is combined and fed to a decoder to obtain the final answer. However, this methodology of treating Visual Reasoning simply as a classification problem sometimes cannot achieve desirable performance due to the difficulty of learning abstract concepts and relations between objects [3,4,6]. Instead, more recent work applied models based on NMN to solve Visual Reasoning problems [3,7–12].

2.2   Neural Module Network

Neural Module Network (NMN) is a machine learning model proposed in 2016 [1, 2]. Generally, the overall architecture of NMN can be considered as a controller and a set of modules. Given the question and the image, firstly, the controller of NMN takes the question as input and outputs a program indicating the required modules and their layout. Then, the specified modules are concatenated with each other to construct a complete network. Finally, the image is fed to the assembled network and the answer is acquired from the root module. As far as we are concerned, the advantage of NMN can be attributed to the ability to break down complicated questions into basic logical units and the ability to reuse previous knowledge efficiently.

By the architecture of modules, NMN can further be categorized into three subclasses: the feature-based, attention-based, and object-based NMN.

For feature-based NMNs, the modules apply CNNs and their calculations are directly conducted on the feature maps. Feature-based NMNs are the most concise implementation of NMN and were utilized most in early work [3].

For attention-based NMNs, the modules also apply neural networks but their calculations are conducted on the attention maps. Compared to feature-based NMNs, attention-based NMNs retain the original information within images better so they achieved higher reasoning precision and accuracy [1,2,7,9].

For object-based NMNs, they regard the information in an image as a set of discrete representations on objects instead of a continuous feature map. Correspondingly, their modules conduct pre-defined discrete calculations. Compared to feature-based and attention-based NMNs, object-based NMNs achieved the highest precision on reasoning [10,11]. However, their discrete design usually requires more prior knowledge and pre-defined attributes on objects.

2.3 Monte Carlo Methods

Monte Carlo Method is the general name of a group of algorithms that make use of random sampling to get an approximate estimation for a numerical computing [13]. These methods are broadly applied to the tasks that are impossible or too time-consuming to get exact results through deterministic algorithms. Monte Carlo Tree Search (MCTS) is an algorithm that applied the Monte Carlo Method to the decision making in game playing like computer Go [14,15]. Generally, this algorithm arranges the possible state space of games into tree structures, and then applies Monte Carlo estimation to determine the action to take at each round of games. In recent years, there also appeared approaches to establish collaborations between Deep Learning and MCTS. These work, represented by AlphaGo, have beaten top-level human players on Go, which is considered to be one of the most challenging games for computer programs [16,17].

3 Proposed Method

3.1 Overall Architecture

The general architecture of our learning framework is shown as Fig. 2. As stated above, the training of the whole model can be divided into two parts: a. Program Predictor and b. modules. The main difficulty of training comes from the side of Program Predictor because of the lack of expected programs as training labels. To overcome this difficulty, we proposed the algorithm named Graph-based Heuristic Search to enable the model to find the optimal program by itself through a heuristic search on the data structure Program Graph. After this searching process, the most appropriate program that was found is utilized as the program label so that the Program Predictor can be trained in a supervised manner. In other words, this searching process can be considered as a procedure targeted to provide training labels for the Program Predictor.

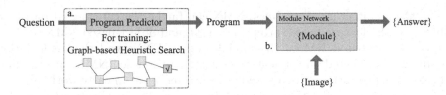

Fig. 2. Our Graph-based Heuristic Search algorithm assists the learning of the Program Predictor.

The abstract of the total training workflow is presented as Algorithm 1. Note that here q denotes the question, p denotes the program, $\{module\}$ denotes the set of modules available in the current task, $\{img\}$ denotes the set of images that the question is asking on, $\{ans\}$ denotes the set of answers paired with images. Details about the *Sample* function are provided in Appendix A.

Algorithm 1. Total Training Workflow

1: **function** TRAIN()
2:     Program_Predictor, $\{module\}$ ← Intialize()
3:     **for** loop in range(Max_loop) **do**
4:         q, $\{img\}$, $\{ans\}$ ← Sample(Dataset)
5:         p ← Graph-based_Heuristic_Search(q, $\{img\}$, $\{ans\}$, $\{module\}$)
6:         Program_Predictor.train(q, p)
7:     **end for**
8: **end function**

3.2   Program Graph

To start with, we first give a precise definition of the program we use. Note that each of the available modules in the model has a unique name, fixed numbers of inputs, and one output. Therefore, a program can be defined as a tree meeting the following rules:

i) Each of the non-leaf nodes stands for a possible module, each of the leaf nodes holds a ⟨END⟩ flag.
ii) The number of children that a node has equal to the number of inputs of the module that the node represents.

For the convenience of representation in prediction, a program can also be transformed into a sequence of modules together with ⟨END⟩ flags via pre-order tree traversal. Considering that the number of inputs of each module is fixed, the tree form can be rebuilt from such sequence uniquely.

Then, as for the Program Graph, Program Graph is the data structure we use to represent the relation between all programs that have been reached throughout the searching process, and it is also the data structure that our algorithm

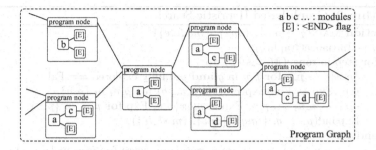

Fig. 3. Illustration of part of a program graph

Graph-based Heuristic Search works on. A Program Graph can be built meeting the following rules:

i) Each graph node represents a unique program that has been reached.
ii) There is an edge between two nodes if and only if the edit distance of their programs is one. Here, insertion, deletion, and substitution are the three basic edit operations whose edit distance is defined as one. Note that the edit distance between programs is judged on their tree form.
iii) Each node in the graph maintains a score. This score is initialized as the output probability of the program of a node according to the Program Predictor when the node is created, and can be updated when the program of a node is executed.

Figure 3 is an illustration of a Program Graph consisting of several program nodes together with their program trees as examples. To distinguish the node in the tree of a program and the node in the Program Graph, the former will be referred to as m_n for "module node" and the latter will be referred to as p_n for "program node" in the following discussion. Details about the initialization of the Program Graph are provided in Appendix B.

3.3 Graph-Based Heuristic Search

Graph-based Heuristic Search is the core algorithm in our proposed learning framework. Its basic workflow is presented as the *Main* function in line 1 of Algorithm 2. After Program Graph g gets initialized, the basic workflow can be described as a recurrent exploration on the Program Graph consisting of the following four steps:

i) Collecting all the program nodes in Program Graph g that have not been fully explored yet as the set of candidate nodes $\{p\_n\}_c$.
ii) Calculating the Expectation for all the candidate nodes.
iii) Selecting the node with the highest Expectation value among all the candidate nodes.
iv) Expanding on the selected node to generate new program nodes and update the Program Graph.
   The details about the calculation of Expectation and expanding strategy are as follows.

Algorithm 2. Graph-based Heuristic Search

1: **function** MAIN(q, $\{img\}$, $\{ans\}$, $\{module\}$)
2:     $g \leftarrow$ InitializeGraph(q)
3:     **for** step in range(Max_step) **do**
4:         $\{p\_n\}_c \leftarrow p\_n$ **for** p_n in g **and** p_n.fully_explored $==$ False
5:         p_n_i.Exp $\leftarrow$ FindExpectation(p_n_i, g) **for** p_n_i in $\{p\_n\}_c$
6:         $p\_n_e \leftarrow p\_n_i$ s.t. p_n_i.Exp $= max\{p\_n_i$.Exp **for** p_n_i in $\{p\_n\}_c\}$
7:         Expand(p_n_e, g, $\{img\}$, $\{ans\}$, $\{module\}$)
8:     **end for**
9:     $p\_n_{best} \leftarrow p\_n_i$ s.t. p_n_i.score $= max\{p\_n_i$.score **for** p_n_i in $\{p\_n_i\}\}$
10:     **return** p_n_{best}.program
11: **end function**

12: **function** EXPAND(p_n_e, g, $\{img\}$, $\{ans\}$, $\{module\}$)
13:     p_n_e.visit_count $\leftarrow p\_n_e$.visit_count $+ 1$
14:     **if** p_n_e.visited $==$ False **then**
15:         p_n_e.score $\leftarrow$ accuracy(p_n_e.program, $\{img\}$, $\{ans\}$, $\{module\}$)
16:         p_n_e.visited $\leftarrow$ True
17:     **end if**
18:     $\{m\_n\}_c \leftarrow m\_n$ **for** m_n in p_n_e.program **and** m_n.expanded $==$ False
19:     $m\_n_m \leftarrow$ Sample($\{m\_n\}_c$)
20:     $\{program\}_{new} \leftarrow$ Mutate(p_n_e.program, m_n_m, $\{module\}$)
21:     **for** $program_i$ in $\{program\}_{new}$ **do**
22:         **if** LegalityCheck($program_i$) $==$ True **then**
23:             g.update($program_i$)
24:         **end if**
25:     **end for**
26:     m_n_m.expanded $\leftarrow$ True
27:     p_n_e.fully_explored $\leftarrow$ True if $\{m\_n\}_c$.remove(m_n_m) $== \varnothing$
28: **end function**

Expectation. Expectation is a measurement defined on each program node to determine which node should be selected for the following expanding step. This Expectation is calculated through the following Eq. 1.

$$
p\_n_i.\text{Exp} = \sum_{d=0}^{D} w_d * max\{p\_n_j.\text{score} \mid p\_n_j \text{ in } g, \ distance(p\_n_i, p\_n_j) \leq d\}
$$
$$
+ \frac{\alpha}{p\_n_i.\text{visit\_count} + 1}
\tag{1}
$$

Intuitively, this equation estimates how desirable a program is to guide the modules to answer a given question reasonably. Here, D, w_d, and α are hyperparameters indicating the max distance in consideration, a sequence of weight coefficients while summing best scores within different distances d, and the scale coefficient to encourage visiting less-explored nodes, respectively.

In this equation, the first term observes the nodes nearby and find the highest score within each different distance d from 0 to D. Then, these scores are weighted by w_d and summed up. Note that the distance here is measured on the Program Graph, which also equals to the edit distance between two programs. The second term in this equation is a balance term negatively correlated to the number of times that a node has been visited and expanded on. This term balances the Expectation levels that unexplored or less-explored nodes get.

Expansion Strategy. Expansion is another essential procedure of our proposed algorithm as shown in line 12 of Algorithm 2. The main purpose of this procedure is to generate new program nodes and update the Program Graph. To realize this, the five main steps are as follows:

i) If the program node p_n_e is visited for the first time, try its program by building the model with specified modules to answer the question. The question answering accuracy is used to update its score. If there are modules with neural architecture, these modules should also be trained here, but the updated parameters are retained only if the new accuracy exceeds the previous one.

ii) Collect the module nodes that have not been expanded on yet within the program, then sample one from them as the module node m_n_m to expand on.

iii) Mutate the program at module m_n_m to generate a set of new programs $\{program\}_{new}$ with three edit operations: insertion, deletion, and substitution.

iv) For each new program judged to be legal, if there is not yet a node representing the same program in the Program Graph g, then create a new program node representing this program and add it to g. The related edge should also be added to g if it does not exist yet.

v) If all of the module nodes have been expanded on, then mark this program node p_n_e as fully explored.

For the Mutation in step iii), the three edit operations are illustrated by Fig. 4. Here, insertion adds a new module node between the node m_n_m and its parent. The new module can be any of the available modules in the model. If the new module has more than one inputs, m_n_m should be set as one of its children, and the rest of the children are set to leaf nodes with $\langle END \rangle$ flag.

Deletion removes the node m_n_m and set its child as the new child of m_n_m's parent. If m_n_m has more than one child, only one of them should be retained and the others are abandoned.

Substitution replaces the module of m_n_m with another module. The new module can be any of the modules that have the same number of inputs as m_n_m.

For insertion and deletion, if there are multiple possible mutations because the related node has more than one child as shown in Fig.4, all of them are retained.

These rules ensure that newly generated programs consequentially have legal structures, but there are still cases that these programs are not legal in the sense of semantics, e.g., the output data type of a module does not match the input data type of its parent. Legality check is conducted to determine whether a program is legal and should be added to the Program Graph, more details about this function are provided in Appendix C.

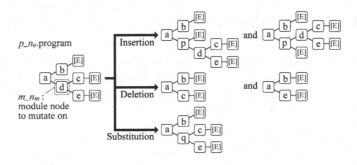

Fig. 4. Example of the mutations generated by the three operations insertion, deletion, and subsitution.

3.4   Candidate Selection Mechanism for Modules

The learning framework presented above is already a complete framework to realize the training of the NMN. However, in practice we found that with the growth of the length of programs and the number of modules, the size of search space explodes exponentially. This brings trouble to the search. To overcome this problem, we further proposed the Candidate Selection Mechanism (CSM), which is an optional component within our learning framework. Generally speaking, if CSM is activated, it selects only a subset of modules from the whole of available modules. Then, only these selected modules are used in the following Graph-based Heuristic Search. The abstract of the training workflow with CSM is presented as Algorithm 3.

Algorithm 3. Training Workflow with Candidate Selection Mechanism

---

1: **function** TRAIN()
2:     Program_Predictor, Necessity_Predictor, {$module$} ← Intialize()
3:     **for** loop in range(Max_loop) **do**
4:         q, {img}, {ans} ← Sample(Dataset)
5:         {$module$}$_{candidate}$ ← Necessity_Predictor(q, {$module$})
6:         p ← Graph-based_Heuristic_Search(q, {img}, {ans}, {$module$}$_{candidate}$)
7:         Necessity_Predictor.train(q, p)
8:         Program_Predictor.train(q, p)
9:     **end for**
10: **end function**

Here, we included another model named Necessity Predictor into the learning framework. This model takes the question as input, and predicts a N_m-dimensions vector as shown in Fig. 5. Here, N_m indicates the total number of modules. Each component of this output is a real number between zero and one indicating the possibility that each module is necessary for solving the given question. N_p and N_r are the two hyperparameters for the candidate modules selection procedure. N_p indicates the number of modules to select according to the predicted possibility value. The N_p modules with the top N_p values of predictions are selected. N_r indicates the number of modules that are selected randomly besides the N_p selected ones. The union of these two selections with $N_p + N_r$ modules becomes the candidate modules for the following search.

For the training of this Necessity Predictor, the optimal program found in the search is transformed into a N_m-dimensions boolean vector indicating whether each module appeared in the program. Then, this boolean vector is set as the training label so that the Necessity Predictor can also be trained in a supervised manner as Program Predictor does.

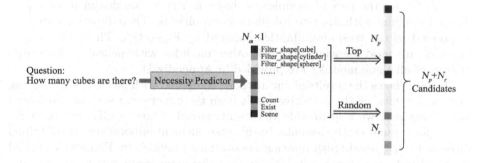

Fig. 5. The process to selecte the $N_p + N_r$ candidate modules

4   Experiments and Results

Our experiments are conducted on the FigureQA and the CLEVR dataset. Their settings and results are presented in the following subsections respectively.

4.1   FigureQA Dataset

The main purpose of the experiment on FigureQA is to certify that our learning framework can realize the training of NMN on a dataset without ground-truth program annotations and outperform the existing methods with models other than NMN.

An overview of how our methods work on this dataset is shown in Fig. 6. Considering that the size of the search space of the programs used in FigureQA is relatively small, the CSM introduced in Sect. 3.4 is not activated.

Table 1. Setting of hyperparameters in our experiment

Max_loop	Max_step	D	w_d	α
100	1000	4	(0.5, 0.25, 0.15, 0.1)	0.05

Generally, the workflow consists of three main parts. Firstly, the technique of object detection [18] together with optical character recognition [19] are applied to transform the raw image into discrete element representations as shown in Fig. 6a. For this part, we applied Faster R-CNN [20,21] with ResNet 101 as the backbone for object detection and Tesseract open source OCR engine [22,23] for text recognition. All the images are resized to 256 by 256 pixels before following calculations.

Secondly, for the part of program prediction as shown in Fig. 6b, we applied our Graph-based Heuristic Search algorithm for the training. The setting of the hyperparameters for this part are shown in Table 1. The type of figure is treated as an additional token appended to the question.

Thirdly, for the part of modules as shown in Fig. 6c, we designed some pre-defined modules with discrete calculations on objects. Their functions are corresponded to the reasoning abilities required by FigureQA. These pre-defined modules are used associatively with other modules with neural architecture. Details of all these modules are provided in Appendix D.

Table 2 shows the results of our methods compared with baseline and existing methods. "Ours" is the primitive result from the experiment settings presented above. Besides, we also provide the result named "Ours + GE" where "GE" stands for ground-truth elements. In this case, element annotations are obtained directly from ground-truth plotting annotations provided by FigureQA instead of the object detection results. We applied this experiment setting to measure the influence of the noise in object detection results.

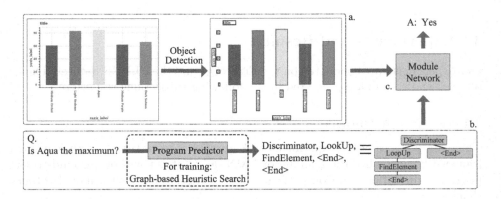

Fig. 6. An example of the inference process on FigureQA

Table 2. Comparison of accuracy with previous methods on the FigureQA dataset.

Method	Accuracy			
	Validation sets		Test sets	
	Set 1	Set 2	Set 1	Set 2
Text only [6]	50.01%		50.01%	
CNN+LSTM [6]	56.16%		56.00%	
Relation Network [6, 24]	72.54%		72.40%	
Human [6]			91.21%	
FigureNet [25]			84.29%	
PTGRN [26]	86.25%		86.23%	
PReFIL [27]	94.84%	93.26%	94.88%	93.16%
Ours	95.74%	95.55%	**95.61%**	**95.28%**
Ours + GE	**96.61%**	**96.52%**		

Through the result, firstly it can be noticed that both our method and our method with GE outperform all the existing methods. In our consideration, the superiority of our method mainly comes from the successful application of NMN. As stated in Sect. 2.2, NMN has shown outstanding capacity in solving logical problems. However, limited by the non-differentiable module selection procedure, the application of NMN can hardly be extended to those tasks without ground-truth program annotations like FigureQA. In our work, the learning framework we proposed can realize the training of NMN without ground-truth programs so that we succeeded to apply NMN on this FigureQA. This observation can also be certified through the comparison between our results and PReFIL.

Compared to PReFIL, considering that we applied the nearly same 40-layer DenseNet to process the image, the main difference we made in our model is the application of modules. The modules besides the final Discriminator ensure that the inputs fed to the Discriminator are related to what the question is asking on more closely.

Here, another interesting fact shown by the result is the difference between accuracies reached on set 1 and set 2 of both validation sets and test sets. Note that in FigureQA, validation set 1 and test set 1 adopted the same color scheme as the training set, while validation set 2 and test set 2 adopted an alternated color scheme. This difference leads to the difficulty of the generalization from the training set to the two set 2. As a result, for PReFIL the accuracy on each set 2 drops more than 1.5% from the corresponding set 1. However, for our method with NMN, this decrease is only less than 0.4%, which shows a better generalization capacity brought by the successful application of NMN.

Also, Appendix E reports the accuracies achieved on test set 2 by different question types and figure types. It is worth mentioning that our work is the first one to exceed human performance on every question type and figure type.

4.2   CLEVR Dataset

The main purpose of the experiment on CLEVR is to certify that our learning framework can achieve superior program exploring efficiency compared to the classic reinforcement learning method.

For this experiment, we created a subset of CLEVR only containing the training data whose questions appeared at least two times in the whole training set. This subset contains 31252 different questions together with their corresponding annotated programs. The reason for applying such a subset is that the size of the whole space of possible programs in CLEVR is approximately up to 10^{40}, which is so huge that no existing method can realize the search in it without any prior knowledge or simplification on programs. Considering that the training of modules is highly time-consuming, we only activated the part of program prediction in our learning framework, which is shown as Fig. 6b. With this setting, the modules specified by the program would not be trained actually. Instead, a boolean value indicating whether the program is correct or not is returned to the model as a substitute for the question answering accuracy. Here, only the programs that are exactly the same as the ground-truth programs paired with given questions are considered as correct.

In this experiment, comparative experiments were made on the cases of both activating and not activating the CSM. The structures of the models used as the Program Predictor and the Necessity Predictor are as follows. For Program Predictor, we applied a 2-layer Bidirectional LSTM with hidden state size of 256 as the encoder, and a 2-layer LSTM with hidden state size of 512 as the decoder. Both the input embedding size of encoder and decoder are 300. The setting of hyperparameters are the same as FigureQA as shown in Table 1 except that Max_loop is not limited. For Necessity Predictor, we applied a 4-layer MLP. The input of the MLP is a boolean vector indicating whether each word in the dictionary appears in the question, the output of the MLP is a 39-dimensional vector for there are 39 modules in CLEVR, the size of all hidden layers is 256. The hyperparameters N_p and N_r are set to 15 and 5 respectively. For the sentence embedding model utilized in the initialization of the Program Graph, we applied the GenSen model with pre-trained weights [28,29].

For the baseline, we applied REINFORCE [30] as most of the existing work [3, 12] did to train the same Program Predictor model.

The searching processes of our method, our method without CSM, and REINFORCE are shown by Fig. 7. Note that in this figure, the horizontal axis indicates the times of search, the vertical axis indicates the number of correct programs found. The experiments on our method and our method without CSM are repeated four times each, and the experiment on REINFORCE is repeated eight times. Also, we show the average results as the thick solid lines in this figure. They indicate the average times of search consumed to find specific numbers of correct programs. Although in this subset of CLEVR, the numbers of correct programs that can be finally found are quite similar for the three methods, their searching processes show great differences. From this result, three main conclusions can be drawn.

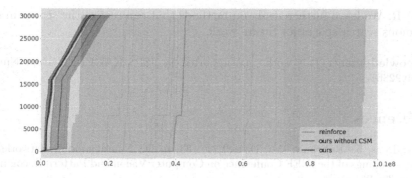

Fig. 7. Relation between the times of search and the number of correct programs found within the searching processes of three methods.

Firstly, in terms of the average case, our method shows a significantly higher efficiency in exploring appropriate programs.

Secondly, the searching process of our method is much more stable while the best case and worst case of REINFORCE differ greatly.

Thirdly, the comparison between the result of our method and our method without CSM certified the effectiveness of the CSM.

5 Conclusion

In this work, to overcome the difficulty of training the NMN because of its non-differentiable module selection procedure, we proposed a new learning framework for the training of NMN. Our main contribution in this framework can be summarized as follows.

Firstly, we proposed the data structure named Program Graph to represent the search space of programs more reasonably.

Secondly and most importantly, we proposed the Graph-based Heuristic Search algorithm to enable the model to find the most appropriate program by itself to get rid of the dependency on the ground-truth programs in training.

Thirdly, we proposed the Candidate Selection Mechanism to improve the performance of the learning framework when the search space is huge.

Through the experiment, the experiment on FigureQA certified that our learning framework can realize the training of NMN on a dataset without ground-truth program annotations and outperform the existing methods with models other than NMN. The experiment on CLEVR certified that our learning framework can achieve superior efficiency in searching programs compared to the classic reinforcement learning method. In view of this evidence, we conclude that our proposed learning framework is a valid and advanced approach to realize the training of NMN.

Nevertheless, our learning framework still shows weakness in dealing with the extremely huge search spaces, e.g., the whole space of possible programs in

CLEVR. We leave further study on methods that can realize the search in such enormous search spaces for future work.

Acknowledgment. This work was supported by JSPS KAKENHI Grant Number JP19K22861.

References

1. Andreas, J., Rohrbach, M., Darrell, T., Klein, D.: Neural module networks. In: Proceedings of the IEEE Conference on Computer Vision and Pattern Recognition, pp. 39–48 (2016)
2. Andreas, J., Rohrbach, M., Darrell, T., Klein, D.: Learning to compose neural networks for question answering. In: Proceedings of the 2016 Conference of the North American Chapter of the Association for Computational Linguistics: Human Language Technologies, pp. 1545–1554 (2016)
3. Johnson, J., et al.: Inferring and executing programs for visual reasoning. In: Proceedings of the IEEE International Conference on Computer Vision, pp. 2989–2998 (2017)
4. Antol, S., et al.: VQA: visual question answering. In: Proceedings of the IEEE International Conference on Computer Vision, pp. 2425–2433 (2015)
5. Johnson, J., Hariharan, B., van der Maaten, L., Fei-Fei, L., Lawrence Zitnick, C., Girshick, R.: Clevr: a diagnostic dataset for compositional language and elementary visual reasoning. In: Proceedings of the IEEE Conference on Computer Vision and Pattern Recognition, pp. 2901–2910 (2017)
6. Kahou, S.E., Michalski, V., Atkinson, A., Kádár, Á., Trischler, A., Bengio, Y.: Figureqa: an annotated figure dataset for visual reasoning. In: International Conference on Learning Representations (2018)
7. Hu, R., Andreas, J., Rohrbach, M., Darrell, T., Saenko, K.: Learning to reason: end-to-end module networks for visual question answering. In: Proceedings of the IEEE International Conference on Computer Vision, pp. 804–813 (2017)
8. Hu, R., Andreas, J., Darrell, T., Saenko, K.: Explainable neural computation via stack neural module networks. In: Ferrari, V., Hebert, M., Sminchisescu, C., Weiss, Y. (eds.) ECCV 2018. LNCS, vol. 11211, pp. 55–71. Springer, Cham (2018). https://doi.org/10.1007/978-3-030-01234-2_4
9. Mascharka, D., Tran, P., Soklaski, R., Majumdar, A.: Transparency by design: closing the gap between performance and interpretability in visual reasoning. In: Proceedings of the IEEE Conference on Computer Vision and Pattern Recognition, pp. 4942–4950 (2018)
10. Shi, J., Zhang, H., Li, J.: Explainable and explicit visual reasoning over scene graphs. In: Proceedings of the IEEE Conference on Computer Vision and Pattern Recognition, pp. 8376–8384 (2019)
11. Yi, K., Wu, J., Gan, C., Torralba, A., Kohli, P., Tenenbaum, J.: Neural-symbolic VQA: disentangling reasoning from vision and language understanding. In: Advances in Neural Information Processing Systems, pp. 1031–1042 (2018)
12. Mao, J., Gan, C., Kohli, P., Tenenbaum, J.B., Wu, J.: The neuro-symbolic concept learner: interpreting scenes, words, and sentences from natural supervision. In: International Conference on Learning Representations (2019)
13. Metropolis, N., Ulam, S.: The Monte Carlo method. J. Am. Stat. Assoc. **44**, 335–341 (1949)

14. Kocsis, L., Szepesvári, C.: Bandit based Monte-Carlo planning. In: Fürnkranz, J., Scheffer, T., Spiliopoulou, M. (eds.) ECML 2006. LNCS (LNAI), vol. 4212, pp. 282–293. Springer, Heidelberg (2006). https://doi.org/10.1007/11871842_29
15. Coulom, R.: Efficient selectivity and backup operators in Monte-Carlo tree search. In: van den Herik, H.J., Ciancarini, P., Donkers, H.H.L.M.J. (eds.) CG 2006. LNCS, vol. 4630, pp. 72–83. Springer, Heidelberg (2007). https://doi.org/10.1007/978-3-540-75538-8_7
16. Silver, D., et al.: Mastering the game of go with deep neural networks and tree search. Nature 529, 484 (2016)
17. Silver, D., et al.: Mastering the game of go without human knowledge. Nature 550, 354 (2017)
18. Girshick, R., Donahue, J., Darrell, T., Malik, J.: Rich feature hierarchies for accurate object detection and semantic segmentation. In: Proceedings of the IEEE Conference on Computer Vision and Pattern Recognition , pp. 580–587 (2014)
19. Singh, S.: Optical character recognition techniques: a survey. J. Emerg. Trends Comput. Inf. Sci. 4, 545–550 (2013)
20. Ren, S., He, K., Girshick, R., Sun, J.: Faster R-CNN: towards real-time object detection with region proposal networks. In: Advances in Neural Information Processing Systems (NIPS) (2015)
21. Yang, J., Lu, J., Batra, D., Parikh, D.: A faster pytorch implementation of faster R-CNN (2017). https://github.com/jwyang/faster-rcnn.pytorch
22. Smith, R.: An overview of the tesseract OCR engine. In: Ninth International Conference on Document Analysis and Recognition (ICDAR 2007), vol. 2, pp. 629–633. IEEE (2007)
23. Smith, R.: Tesseract open source OCR engine (2019). https://github.com/tesseract-ocr/ tesseract
24. Santoro, A., et al.: A simple neural network module for relational reasoning. In: Advances in Neural Information Processing Systems, pp. 4967–4976 (2017)
25. Reddy, R., Ramesh, R., Deshpande, A., Khapra, M.M.: FigureNet: a deep learning model for question-answering on scientific plots. In: 2019 International Joint Conference on Neural Networks (IJCNN), pp. 1–8. IEEE (2019)
26. Cao, Q., Liang, X., Li, B., Lin, L.: Interpretable visual question answering by reasoning on dependency trees. IEEE Trans. Pattern Anal. Mach. Intell. (2019)
27. Kafle, K., Shrestha, R., Price, B., Cohen, S., Kanan, C.: Answering questions about data visualizations using efficient bimodal fusion. arXiv preprint arXiv:1908.01801 (2019)
28. Subramanian, S., Trischler, A., Bengio, Y., Pal, C.J.: Learning general purpose distributed sentence representations via large scale multi-task learning. In: International Conference on Learning Representations (2018)
29. Subramanian, S., Trischler, A., Bengio, Y., Pal, C.J.: Gensen (2018). https://github.com/Maluuba/gensen
30. Williams, R.J.: Simple statistical gradient-following algorithms for connectionist reinforcement learning. Mach. Learn. 8, 229–256 (1992)

Towards Fast and Robust Adversarial Training for Image Classification

Erh-Chung Chen[(✉)] and Che-Rung Lee[(✉)]

National Tsing Hua University, Hsinchu, Taiwan
s107062802@m107.nthu.edu.tw, crlee@cs.nthu.edu.tw

Abstract. The adversarial training, which augments the training data with adversarial examples, is one of the most effective methods to defend adversarial attacks. However, its robustness degrades for complex models, and the producing of strong adversarial examples is a time-consuming task. In this paper, we proposed methods to improve the robustness and efficiency of the adversarial training. First, we utilized a re-constructor to enforce the classifier to learn the important features under perturbations. Second, we employed the enhanced FGSM to generate adversarial examples effectively. It can detect overfitting and stop training earlier without extra cost. Experiments are conducted on MNIST and CIFAR10 to validate the effectiveness of our methods. We also compared our algorithm with the state-of-the-art defense methods. The results show that our algorithm is 4–5 times faster than the previously fastest training method. For CIFAR-10, our method can achieve above 46% robust accuracy, which is better than most of other methods.

1 Introduction

Deep neural networks have demonstrated a strong capability to solve many challenging computer vision tasks, such as classification [1], object detection [2] and image captioning [3]. These successful achievements not only shift the paradigm of AI researches, but also enable many useful applications, such as self-driving car [4] and medical image analysis [5].

However, the current neural network models for image classification are vulnerable to the adversarial attack, which means slight perturbations in the input data can significantly degrade the accuracy of classification, even though those perturbed images are indistinguishable from the original ones by human's eyes. Adversarial attacks can be a potential threat to real applications, such as the cell-phone camera attack [6] and the road sign attack [7]. Hence, designing models that can have better resistance to adversarial attacks is one of the most important tasks to make practical AI applications.

Adversarial attacks have many different forms. For white-box attacks, such as L-BFGS [8], FGSM [9], and CW attack [10], attackers can access complete information about the target networks, including the architecture, model parameters, or even the training data, from which the adversarial examples can be generated.

© Springer Nature Switzerland AG 2021
H. Ishikawa et al. (Eds.): ACCV 2020, LNCS 12624, pp. 576–591, 2021.
https://doi.org/10.1007/978-3-030-69535-4_35

For black-box attacks, attackers have little knowledge about the target models, but they can still fool the target models, even with one pixel modification [11]. Moreover, the adversarial examples are transferable, which means an adversarial example generated by one model can fool different models. As a result, attackers can make use of this property to generate universal adversarial examples [12].

In this paper, we focus on the defense of the white-box attacks with epsilon bound on L_∞ norm since major attacks of this type generate adversarial examples from the gradient of the loss function [9]. Many attempts of defenses try to eliminate the gradient information during the training, however, the paper [13] showed those types of defenses are unworkable. Another strategy is adversarial training, which adds adversarial examples into training data. Despite its safety and efficacy, adversarial training needs strong enough adversarial examples to avoid the over-fitting to the perturbations. Nevertheless, searching powerful adversarial examples is a time consuming task.

Many defense strategies have been proposed, such as gradient regularization [14], TRADES [15] and feature denoising [16]. Fast training methods have been proposed as well [17–19]. Besides, recent works have investigated how robustness can achieve on large scale datasets [16,20,21]. We propose a new training architecture to enhance the robustness of the adversarial training, and design a new method for producing adversarial examples to accelerate the training speed. The proposed training architecture concatenates a re-constructor to the classifier, whose objective is to produce an identical image to the original clean image. The purpose of such architecture is to force the classifier not only to output a correct label for each input image, but also to project adversarial images onto a manifold, on which the inter-class distance can be reduced. With such kind of training model, even a weaker model can learn non-trivial classifiers with good robustness against adversarial attacks.

Our adversarial images generator is called enhanced FGSM (Fast Gradient Sign Method [9]), which can produce strong attacks without computing them from iterative PGD. The signSGD algorithm and its variations have been used for different applications in machine learning, such as distributed learning [22] and the producing of adversarial examples for black-box attacks [23]. FGSM can generate a good initial point for adversarial examples [17], but it suffers the catastrophic overfitting, which can slow down the train process. With the mechanism to check the robust accuracy during training process, we can terminate the training earlier and avoid the catastrophic overfitting.

We evaluated our method using MNIST and CIFAR10 datasets, and compared our methods with the state-of-the-art defense algorithms proposed by [15,18,24]. The experimental results show that our methods are about 5 times and 4 times faster than AdvFree [18] for MNIST and CIFAR10 respectively. In addition, for MNIST, our method can achieve better accuracy under projection gradient decent attacks compares to AdvFree. And for CIFAR10, our method can achieve 46.06% robust accuracy. If the enhanced FGSM is combined with TRADES, the robust accuracy of CIFAR10 can be 48.05%.

Our main contributions are summarized as follows:

- We investigate the importance of inter-class distance.
- We propose a new training architecture with a lightweight attack, which reduces heavy computing cost.
- We show that our model's capacity is much smaller than competitor but have similar or better accuracy.

The rest of this paper is organized as follows. Section 2 introduces the necessary background about the adversarial attacks and defense methods. Section 3 presents our algorithms, and model architecture. Section 4 shows the experimental results and the discussions. Conclusion and future work are given in the last section.

2   Preliminary

This section introduces notations and describes mathematical background of adversarial attacks and defenses.

Given an input image x, whose value is defined in the domain $[0, 1]^{W \times H \times C}$, the classifier outputs one of the indices in a set of labels $\{c_1, c_2, \ldots, c_k\}$. The classification process can be represented as a function,

$$F(x)_i = \text{softmax}(Z^o(x)), \tag{1}$$

where $F(x)_i$ represents the probability of that image x is labeled with class i and $Z^o(x) \in R^k$ is the output of the last layer of the network before the softmax layer,

$$\text{softmax}(z_i) = \frac{e^{z_i}}{\sum_{j=1}^{k} e^{z_j}}, \tag{2}$$

that normalizes the output $Z^o(x)$ to a probability distribution over predicted output classes. The network predicts that x belongs to label t by one of the flowing two functions,

$$\begin{cases} F(x) = \arg \max F(x)_i, \\ H(x) = \arg \max Z^o(x)_i. \end{cases} \tag{3}$$

The training of the classifier can be viewed as a minimization process of the loss function $L(x, y)$ over a given training dataset X, where $x \in X$ and y is the corresponding label for the image x.

2.1   Formulating Adversarial Attack

An adversarial example is an image with indistinguishable perturbation that causes model to make incorrect prediction. An adversarial example is the solution of the following optimization problem:

$$\min ||\delta||_p, \text{ subject to } F(x + \delta) \neq F(x). \tag{4}$$

We can define conditions in Eq. (4) as a constraint set Ω,

$$\Omega = \{x | F(x)_t - \arg\max_{i \neq t} F(x)_i \leq 0\}. \tag{5}$$

In [9], authors first proposed a method, called Fast Gradient Sign Method (FGSM), to generate adversarial examples x^{adv} as follows,

$$x^{\text{adv}} = \mathcal{P}_{[0,1]}(x + \alpha \text{sign}(\nabla L(x, y))) \tag{6}$$

where $L(x, y)$ is the loss function, α is the step size, and $\mathcal{P}_{[0,1]}$ is a projection function to ensure that x^{adv} is a valid image. The major idea is to add perturbations along the direction of $\text{sign}(\nabla L(x, y))$, such that image could be misclassified.

The attack can be a small perturbation on the original image. One way to characterize this property is to constrain the size of perturbation to a small range, say ϵ. To satisfy the ϵ constrain, the Projection Gradient Decent (PGD) algorithm is usually applied to the generate valid perturbations. PGD runs for T iterations. In each iteration i, it follows the Eq. (6):

$$x_{i+1}^{\text{PGD}} = \mathcal{P}_{[0,1]}(x_i^{\text{PGD}} + \alpha \text{sign}(\nabla L(x, y))) \tag{7}$$

and applies projection operator on x_{i+1}^{PGD} such that $\|x_{i+1}^{\text{PGD}} - x\|_\infty < \epsilon$. If a random start is allowed, noise from $-\epsilon$ to ϵ will be added in the beginning or at each step.

For FGSM attack, α in (6) is set to ϵ, so x^{adv} moves to the boundary immediately; for PGD attack, x_{t+1}^{PGD} moves to the boundary by T steps, so α in (7) is ϵ/T which is smaller than ϵ. Therefore, PGD is able to make more powerful adversarial images.

2.2 Linear Approximation and DeepFool

FGSM and PGD discussed in Sect. 2.1 can find feasible solutions of the Eq. (4), but the solutions may not be optimal. The geometric meanings of the optimal δ in Eq. (4) is the smallest step toward to the boundary of the constraint set Ω.

In the paper of DeepFool [25], the authors argued that the optimization problem can be linearized by Taylor expansion, by which a better solution with smaller perturbation than that of FGSM and PGD can be found. In DeepFool, the constraint set Ω is replaced with another equivalent set $\hat{\Omega}$,

$$\hat{\Omega} = \{x | Z^o(x)_t - \arg\max_{i \neq t} Z^o(x)_i \leq 0\}. \tag{8}$$

If $Z^o(x)$ is an affine function, problem (8) has a closed-form solution,

$$\min_{i \neq t} \frac{|Z^o(x)_t - Z^o(x)_i|}{\|\nabla Z^o(x)_t - \nabla Z^o(x)_i\|_q}, \tag{9}$$

where p and q follow Holder's Inequality's constraint $1/p + 1/q = 1$. The detail of the proof can be found in [25].

By linearizing the lost function of a network, we can use the formula in (9) as a solution to (8). The error term depends on how close the initial point is to the decision boundary and the magnitude of the Hessian. Principally, the latter is more important than the former. Nevertheless, the magnitude of the Hessian is difficult to estimate even if function is Lipschitz continuity [26]. A practical strategy is trying to regularize gradient which implicitly reduce the upper bound [14].

2.3 Adversarial Training

The adversarial training, which injects adversarial examples into the training dataset. The state-of-the-art method was proposed by Madry [24], in which they showed that the adversarial training is to solve the following min-max problem:

$$\min_{\theta} \max_{x':D(x',x)<\epsilon} L(x',y;\theta) \tag{10}$$

The maximization problem is to search the strongest adversarial examples; while the minimization problem is to minimize the adversarial loss given by inner attacks. They also argued that adversarial attacks generated by PGD is the strongest first-order attack, which means if a model is robust enough against the PGD attack, it will be defensive against any gradient-based attack. Therefore, PGD attack is a best choice for the inner attack.

To reduce the heavy computation of adversarial training, Adversarial training for Free (AdvFree) [18] calculates mini-batch's one-step adversarial images with step size ϵ immediately during backward phase, re-uses adversarial images in the next forward phase, and repeats such loop m times. Compared with the standard adversarial training, which requires m times forward and backward phases to generate adversarial images, AdvFree needs no extra cost. However, AdvFree is not exactly equal to PGD attack [24], because it chooses ϵ as step size instead of $\frac{\epsilon}{T}$ and moves to the boundary in one step. If ϵ is large, AdvFree cannot compute an accurate adversarial images during iterations. On the other hand, if AdvFree chooses a smaller step size, attacks at each step would not be strong enough, except the last step. As a result, AdvFree takes longer time to converge.

2.4 Gradient Masking

Since most attacks are based on the gradient information of target networks, the gradient masking methods defend the attacks by making the gradient indeterminable. However, the gradient masking methods are vulnerable to other types of attacks other than the gradient based ones [13]. On the other hand, if a model can defend the gradient based attacks without using gradient masking methods, it can resist almost all kinds of attacks, as shown in [13]. Therefore, it is important to ensure that no gradient masking is used explicitly or implicitly in the design of the defending method.

In [13], authors enumerated some rules to judge whether the gradients information of a model is hidden or not. If a model satisfies one or more properties listed below, it may use the gradient masking methods.

1. The random sampling method can find adversarial examples but gradient based attacks cannot.
2. One-step PGD attacks have better performance than iterative PGD attacks.
3. Increasing the distortion bound does not decrease robust accuracy.
4. Unbounded PGD attacks do not reach 100% success.
5. Black-box attacks are better than white-box attacks.

We are going to scrutinize that the above phenomena do not occur on our trained model.

3   Model and Algorithm

This section introduces the training architecture and the adversarial image generator.

3.1   Adversarial Image Generator

Our adversarial image generator is based on the FGSM method, because of its computational advantages over the optimization based algorithms. However, it is well-known that models trained by FGSM attacks can easily overfit to adversarial images, especially for a large ϵ [6,24]. This phenomenon is called catastrophic over-fitting, where the model's robust accuracy drops to 0% suddenly during training phase.

The root cause of the overfitting problem is that the adversarial examples generated by FGSM cannot fully represent the ϵ-ball attacks [24]. There are two major problems of FGSM. First, the direction of FGSM x^{FGSM} is obtained from $\nabla_x L(x)$, along which the loss function $L(x)$ increases most. However, such direction is not the solution to the problem (5), because it does not consider the inter-class relation. Second, the step size of the FGSM is a fixed value, which cannot represent the attacks of smaller sizes.

In this paper, we proposed a fast adversarial image generator, called enhanced FGSM (eFGSM), which modifies FGSM to generate a better solution for problem (5). eFGSM has two steps. First, we will use the direction generated by FGSM as an initial point, because as shown in [17], FGSM still gives an approximate solution to the problem (5).

$$x^{\text{eFGSM}} = \mathcal{P}_{[0,1]}(x + \mathcal{P}_{[-\epsilon,\epsilon]}(\kappa \, \text{sign}(\Gamma))), \tag{11}$$

where κ and Γ are the magnitude and the estimated attack respectively. Second, a more accurate adversarial example x^{adv} is computed with linear approximation Δ and x^{eFGSM},

$$\Delta = \min_{i \neq t} \frac{|Z^o(x^{\text{eFGSM}})_t - Z^o(x^{\text{eFGSM}})_i|}{||\nabla Z^o(x^{\text{eFGSM}})_t - \nabla Z^o(x^{\text{eFGSM}})_i||_1}$$
$$x^{\text{adv}} = \mathcal{P}_{[0,1]}(x^{\text{eFGSM}} + \text{sign}(\nabla Z^o(x^{\text{eFGSM}}))\Delta). \tag{12}$$

This is because the direction of linear approximation can solve the problem (5), as shown in Sect. 2.2.

For each image, eFGSM generates a quick perturbation with the majority vote version of FGSM [22]. Equation (11) is similar to the original FGSM, except two modifications. First, Γ is calculated from the gradient direction obtained in each epoch,

$$\Gamma^{j+1} = 0.95\Gamma^j + \text{sign}(x^{adv} - x). \tag{13}$$

where the Γ^{j+1} at $j+1$th epoch is a weighted accumulated sum of gradients. Compared with the single gradient direction used in FGSM, Γ will stick on the weighted gradient direction of each pixel and hence produce stronger attacks. Second, κ is obtained from the Gaussian distribution with the mean equal to $\text{sign}(\Gamma)\epsilon$,

$$\kappa = \mathcal{N}(\text{sign}(\Gamma)\epsilon, \sigma^2). \tag{14}$$

And the variance σ is a hyperparameter to be decided. By doing so, the generated adversarial examples can better represent the attacks than those generated by FGSM.

The formulation of Γ can be considered as Bagging [27], which produces more accurate decisions than those produced by a single targeted model, even though each attack is weak and noisy. However, we need not generate multiple models for each epoch. Instead, like the idea proposed in [18], we only compute the gradient of the trained model during backward phase, and store the cumulative signs of gradients, so that Γ can be updated in each epoch. The updated Γ can be used to generate the adversarial images in the next epoch. Comparing to AdvFree [18], our method is more flexible and converges faster.

The design of κ is a heuristic strategy. Comparing with Madry's PGD with random start, which selects a random point in ϵ-ball as initial point. Instead, Γ gives us a hint of gradient information. To start from a random point without losing much gradient information and keeping diversity, we suggest that κ is generated by Gaussian distribution with mean equal to $\text{sign}(\Gamma)\epsilon$.

3.2   Inter-class Distance

We argue that network's vulnerabilities come from one-hot encoding. In categorical classification problems, labels are usually encoded as one-hot vectors, and cross entropy loss encourages network to fit one-hot encoding labels. Thus, it forces each class to be mutually orthogonal to each other. The disadvantage of the one-hot encoding is ignoring the relationship among classes. For example, image 0 and image 6 on MNIST have similar stroke, and there are ambiguous images between those two classes. On the contrary, the difference between image 0 and 7 on MNIST is significant.

To solve this issue, the label smoothing technique was proposed [28], which is a regularization technique avoiding classifier predicting a too confident result. In [28], authors suggested that this skill helps networks' pre-softmax layer to get better representation.

Equation (9) suggests inter-class distance should also be taken into consideration in the design of a robust classifier. If $|\Delta|$ is greater than ϵ, no feasible adversarial examples exist for the ϵ-ball attack. In other words, the perturbation reaches the boundary of ϵ-ball or physical constraint($x \in [0,1]$) before reaching decision boundary. To enlarge Δ as much as possible, we can either increase the magnitude of numerator or decrease the magnitude of denominator of Eq. (9). In the L_2 norm attack for an affine classifier, the denominator is

$$\arg\min_{i \neq t} ||W_t - W_i||_2 ||\nabla Z^{o-1}(x)||_2 =$$
$$\arg\min_{i \neq t}(|W_t|^2 + |W_i|^2 - 2|W_t||W_i|)||\nabla Z^{o-1}(x)||_2, \tag{15}$$

where W is the last layer's weights and Z^{o-1} is the output of the second last layer. If two classes are orthogonal, $-2|W_t||W_i|$ will be 0 and Δ will be minimum. Moreover, this result can be extended to L_∞ norm attack as well; for L_1 norm attack, denominator is $|| \cdot ||_\infty$, whose magnitude cannot be reduced efficiently. Thus, defending against L_1 norm attacks is still problematic [29].

Inter-class distance provides another benefits to check the occurrence of catastrophic overfitting. We can roughly estimate the distance between x^{adv} and the decision boundaries during the training phase without extra cost. That means we can quickly check the robust accuracy without the PGD-k attack. An image x is considered as robust if the minimal distance is always greater than ϵ. Catastrophic overfitting can be detected once robust accuracy at this epoch is tremendously decreased. If such case happens, the training procedure should be terminated immediately to avoid the catastrophic overfitting.

3.3 Training Model

In a seminal paper [24], authors had pointed out the characters of the defense models for effective adversarial training. One of them is "weak models may fail to learn non-trivial classifiers". However, as mentioned in Sect. 3.2, no strong evidences suggest that model's capacity is related to robustness. The inter-class distance should be the key point. To show that, we employ the idea of denoising auto-encoder [30] to design the training architecture. A denoising auto-encoder concatenates an encoder with a re-constructor, whose objective is to force the encoder to project the noisy data back onto a lower dimension manifold where the clean data reside. Because on the manifold, the noisy data are more clustered to the clean data, a weak model can still learn non-trivial classifiers.

The proposed architecture is presented in Fig. 1, which consists of two networks: a classifier C and a re-constructor R. The network has three inputs: $\hat{x}$ is an adversarial example, x is the original image, and y is the ground-truth label with label smoothing. When receiving an input image $\hat{x}$, the classifier outputs a label $\hat{y}$, which is a vector showing the probability of each category for the input image. The output $\hat{y}$ is then fed into the re-constructor R, whose goal is to produce an identical image to x. The loss function of the network contains two terms: L_G and L_C, which are reconstruction loss and categorical loss respectively. Loss function is formulated as follows:

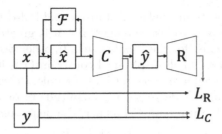

Fig. 1. The network architecture for training. y is ground-label with label smoothing, $\hat{x}$ is adversarial image generated by input image x and $\mathcal{F}$ is adversarial image generator which collecting gradient information from $\hat{x}$. For inference, only the classifier C is used.

$$\min_{\theta} L_R(\hat{x}, x; \theta) + \lambda \cdot L_C(\hat{x}, y; \theta). \tag{16}$$

The goal is to find parameters θ that minimizes the risk of misclassification. The categorical loss L_C, which is also considered as sparse regularization, helps the classifier to output the correct label for the input image $\hat{x}$, even with noises. The reconstruction loss L_R enlarges the misclassified images' penalty. Because the latent code $\hat{y}$ is totally different from y, the re-constructor R is not able to generate the images which belong to the same class. On the other hand, it is allowable to classifier predict wrong class but is adjacent to the ground-truth label. The reason is those classes share similar representations in hidden layers.

To refine the distribution of latent space, the label smoothing technique is applied, which adds small perturbations in the ground-truth labels. Without label smoothing, $\hat{y}$ is almost a one-hot vector. It is because feeding a one-hot vector into re-constructor is equivalent to solving a one-to-many mapping problem, which means one-hot vector represents the images of the same class with arbitrary shapes or textures. This is not what we want.

The network R is used to improve inter-class distance. It is not used in the inference time. The hyper-parameter λ balances the functions of those two terms. We will justify its optimal value in the experiments.

3.4   Models for MNIST and CIFAR10

The specific model designs for MNIST and CIFAR10 are given below. For MNIST, all classifiers use CNN architecture. Our classifier requires smaller filter size and fewer unit of fully connected layer than others, which makes our model smaller and faster. More specifically, the number of parameters in our model is only 0.2 million, while it is 0.76 millions in TRADES and 3.3 millions in Madry's model. The architecture of re-constructor is a simple model with two dense layers and three transpose convolutional layers, whose number of parameters is 0.26 millions.

For CIFAR10, the architecture of the classifier is a variation of the wide residual networks WRN22-5. Comparing to AdvFree, TRADES and Mardy's model, they use WRN34-10 [31] as the classifier model. Our WRN-22-5 model has 6.7 millions parameters, and WRB34-10 model has near 46 millions. Our re-constructor uses the upsamping version of WRN22-3 model, whose number of parameters is 5.1 millions.

4 Experiments

This section presents three sets of experiments. The first set of experiments compare the accuracy under attacks and the training performance of our model with others. The second set of experiments perform ablation study on various factors, including hyperparameter λ in Eq. (16), label smoothing, and the effectiveness of adversarial training and the re-constructor model. The third set of experiments justify that our model does not belong to the gradient masking methods, and therefore can resist most kinds of attacks.

4.1 Performance and Robustness

We evaluated our method on MNIST and CIFAR10 datasets. For both datasets, we followed the instructions in [32] and reported robust accuracy with adaptive PGD (PGD-ADP). For ablation tests, we used the standard PGD with cross-entropy loss (PGD_{CE}) and PGD with CW loss (PGD_{CW}) against the defense models [24]. For MNIST, we set $\epsilon = 0.3/1.0$ on L_∞ norm. Standard attacks iterates 100 steps and the step size is 0.01. For CIFAR10, we set $\epsilon = 8.0/255$ on L_∞ norm. Attacks iterates 20 steps and the step size is 2.0/255. Adaptive attacks iterate 100 steps and search the optimal step size at each step.

We also compared our model with other competitive models. For MNIST, Madry's model uses adversarial training with PGD_{CE}-40 on training set; TRADES sets β to 1; and AdvFree sets m to 15 and step size to 0.01. For CIFAR10, Madry's model uses adversarial training with PGD_{CE}-10 on the training set; TRADES sets β to 6; and AdvFree sets m to 8.

Table 1 summarizes the experimental results. The first column is the total time for training; the second column is the elapsed time of each epoch; the third column is accuracy of natural data, and the forth column is accuracy

Table 1. Comparison of different models.

MNIST	T_{train}[s]	T_{epoch}[s]	acc$_{\text{nat.}}$	acc$_{\text{adv.}}$	CIFAR10	T_{train}[s]	T_{epoch}[s]	acc$_{\text{nat.}}$	acc$_{\text{adv.}}$
Ours	268	6.7	99.01	92.37	Ours	7,095	141.9	88.01	46.06
Madry's	69,993	77.0	97.26	88.45	Madry's	240,177	1351.0	87.25	44.04
TRADES	8,000	80.0	99.48	95.41	TRADES	118,560	1526.0	84.92	52.76
AdvFree	1,430	2.6	99.40	87.62	AdvFree	29,120	183.0	86.07	43.80

under adversarial attacks. As can be seen, our model is the fastest model for both datasets, although our training has a little extra computational cost for re-constructor. The reason is our model is much smaller than others. Also, we have the fastest rate of convergence. For CIFAR10, our model achieves 46.06% robust accuracy, which is similar to Madry's method. For MNIST, TRADES's natural and robust accuracy is slightly higher than our model. MNIST is a good example for large ϵ. If AdvFree's step size is increased, it would fail to converge.

4.2   Ablation Study

Hyperparameter λ. This experiment verifies how the hyperparameter λ in Eq. (16) affects the robust accuracy of our model on MNIST and CIFAR10. Table 2 lists the model accuracy for MNIST and CIFAR10 under different attacks respectively. The result shows the best choice of λ for MNIST is near 0.1, and the best λ for CIFAR10 is 0.05. If a smaller λ is chosen, the categorical loss in Eq. (16) will be neglected, which means the model is like to solve an unsupervised clustering problem.

Label Smoothing. This experiment investigates the influence of the label smoothing for the model accuracy. Table 3 shows the results of the model trained without using the label smoothing technique. Comparing to the results shown in Table 2, one can find that the model's robust accuracy increases significantly with label smoothing technique.

Adversarial Training and Re-constructor. This experiment compares the effectiveness of two techniques used in our method: adversarial training with enhanced FGSM attack and re-constructor model. For each dataset, we tried three different combinations:

- AdvTrain: using adversarial training with enhanced FGSM attack only.
- REC: using re-constructor model only. The input images are unmodified.
- Combined: using both techniques.

The results, which are the model accuracy under different kinds of attacks, are shown in Table 4 for MNIST and CIFAR10 respectively. AdvTrain successfully generates good quality of adversarial images. The robust accuracy for PGD_{CE} is similar to Madrey's model for both dataset, but here is a gap between the robust accuracy for PGD_{CE} and robust accuracy for PGD_{CW}. It implies that AdvTrain may not to defense against arbitrary attacks.

   The goal of re-constructor is to make the classifier converge faster and more robust. Without any adversarial training data, the re-constructor is useless, because it does not help the original classifier to capture more features. Hence, re-constructor model only method fails completely for MNIST. On the other hand, the images in CIFAR10 have a large variation even for the objects in

Table 2. Influence of λ on the model accuracy (%). Left: MNIST. Right CIFAR10.

λ	1.0	0.5	0.1	0.01	0.001	λ	1.0	0.5	0.1	0.05	0.01
Natural	99.22	99.13	99.02	96.72	53.19	Natural	88.00	87.97	87.76	88.01	83.19
PGD-ADP	91.24	91.54	92.37	86.66	26.08	PGD-ADP	36.89	39.82	44.03	46.06	38.51
PGD$_{CE}$-100	96.75	96.49	96.55	92.10	36.08	PGD$_{CE}$-20	59.47	59.73	64.65	65.36	54.02
PGD$_{CW}$-100	96.58	96.47	96.33	91.27	30.50	PGD$_{CW}$-20	54.84	59.20	64.48	65.21	55.17

Table 3. Accuracy (%) of the model trained without using label smoothing technique. Left: MNIST. Right CIFAR10.

λ	1.0	0.5	0.1	0.01	0.001	λ	1.0	0.5	0.1	0.05	0.01
Natural	99.31	99.31	99.17	98.46	70.91	Natural	86.82	86.85	86.18	86.67	84.88
PGD-ADP	87.70	88.33	90.63	89.31	54.58	PGD-ADP	22.63	22.90	26.91	31.43	28.23
PGD$_{CE}$-20	94.60	94.58	95.68	95.15	62.72	PGD$_{CE}$-20	24.85	25.69	35.22	41.39	56.32
PGD$_{CW}$-20	94.79	94.68	95.72	94.81	59.22	PGD$_{CW}$-20	25.49	27.00	39.22	43.61	57.04

Table 4. Accuracy (%) of models trained by different techniques. Left: MNIST. Right: CIFAR10

Techniques	AdvTrain	REC	Combined	Techniques	AdvTrain	REC	Combined
Natural	99.02	98.98	99.01	Natural	87.05	90.05	88.01
PGD-ADP	90.05	0.00	92.37	PGD-ADP	40.21	0.07	46.06
PGD$_{CE}$-100	96.06	0.18	96.27	PGD$_{CE}$-20	62.22	41.20	65.36
PGD$_{CW}$-100	95.24	0.00	96.23	PGD$_{CW}$-20	56.32	43.59	65.21

the same class. Moreover, the image background are not unified. Thus, the reconstructor alone can enhance the ability of classifier to learn better features. The images augmented by sampled noise just enlarge the variation of training data, whose function is not significant.

Early Stopping Estimation. This experiment evaluates the robust accuracy by Eq. (9). For MNIST, we get 14.7% high risk data; for CIFAR10, we get 43.12% high risk data. That means the distance between those data and the decision boundary is less than ϵ. Comparing with Table 4, our method gives a better bound than that of the standard PGD attacks.

TRADES with Enhanced FGSM. The enhanced FGSM can be applied not only to our model, but also others. We combined eFGSM with TRADES, and evaluated its performance. The robust accuracy of such combination for CIFAR10 is 48.05%, which is less than that of TRADES (54.02%), but is slightly better than that of our original method (46.07%). However, its average epoch time is about 250 s, which is much faster than that of TRADES 1526 s). Therefore, for fast training, eFGSM has its value to achieve good descent accuracy with significant acceleration.

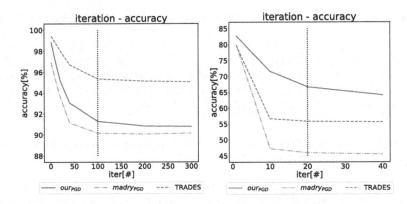

Fig. 2. Robust accuracy decreases when PGD iteration increases. Left: $\epsilon = 0.3/1.0$ on MNIST. Right: $\epsilon = 8/255$ on CIFAR10.

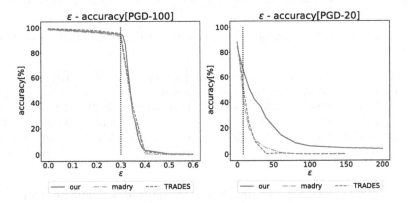

Fig. 3. Robust accuracy decreases when ϵ increases. Left: MNIST. Right CIFAR10.

4.3   Justification of Gradient Masking Issues

This set of experiments checked whether our model shows some properties of gradient masking with three experiments.

- Increase the number of iterations for PGD attack (checking property 2).
- Increase the size of ϵ (checking property 3 and 4).
- Attack the models using other methods (checking property 1 and 5).

The result of the first experiment is shown in Fig. 2. As can be seen, the accuracy converges when the number of iterations of PGD increases, which means the attacks are stronger.

Figure 3 shows the robust accuracy for MNIST and CIFAR10 when the size of ϵ increases. First, the accuracy are decreased monotonically as the size of ϵ grows. Second, when ϵ is large enough, the accuracy drops to 0. For CIFAR10, the degradation of our method is slower than that of others and the curve does not reach to 0% when ϵ is larger than 200.

Table 5. Robust accuracy for black-box PGD$_{CE}$-20 attack on our model

	Conv-4	ResNet-56	Madry's
Accuracy [%]	85.03	83.42	72.0

We want to emphasize that our method seems to perform better result than others but this does not mean that our method is quite robust than others. We selected standard PGD as attacker since we get quite suspicious result in ablation study. This phenomenon is reasonable because the purpose of those sets of experiments is verifying gradient masking issue. Once we strengthen the power of PGD with several times with random restarts, robust accuracy will be zero eventually. From the experimental results, we believe that obfuscating gradient does not occur in our training method.

The last experiment uses the transferability of attacks on CIFAR10 to show that other kinds of attacks are weaker than the PGD based method for our model. We used the attacks generated for other three models: (1) a four layer convolution neural network (Conv-4), (2) Resnet-56 [33], and (3) Madry's adversarial trained model. The accuracy for our model under the attacks transferred from other models are shown in Table 5. As can be seem the values are between the accuracy under PGD attacks (46.06%) and the natural accuracy (88.01%). Attacks generated from Madry's model are stronger than others because our model is similar to Madry's. These experiments confirmed that the gradient masking does not occur in our model.

5   Conclusion

In this paper, we presented two methods to improve the robustness and the performance of adversarial training. The first one is a training architecture, which leverages a re-constructor to make the model learn the classifier on a lower dimension manifold, on which the inter-class distance is shrunken, so the trained model can be more robust and the model size can be reduced. The second method is a fast way to generate the adversarial examples. We enhanced FGSM so that it can generate more representable attacks without solving the optimization problems. Experimental results show that the models generated by our methods for MNIST and CIFAR10 require less parameters and run faster than other training methods.

In the future, we have several research directions to explore. First, we want to try our methods on more complicated models and datasets, such as ImageNet. Second, for the training architecture, how to build a suitable re-constructor to help the training of more robust classifiers requires further investigation. Third, for adversarial example generator, more computationally economic ways still need to research. Last, we would like to extend our methods to other applications, besides image classification, to resist different kinds of adversarial attacks.

References

1. Krizhevsky, A., Sutskever, I., Hinton, G.E.: ImageNet classification with deep convolutional neural networks. Adv. Neural Inf. Process. Syst. **25**, 1097–1105 (2012)
2. Redmon, J., Farhadi, A.: Yolo9000: better, faster, stronger. In: Proceedings of the IEEE Conference on Computer Vision and Pattern Recognition, pp. 7263–7271 (2017)
3. Hossain, M., Sohel, F., Shiratuddin, M.F., Laga, H.: A comprehensive survey of deep learning for image captioning. ACM Comput. Surv. (CSUR) **51**, 118 (2019)
4. Huval, B., et al.: An empirical evaluation of deep learning on highway driving. arXiv preprint arXiv:1504.01716 (2015)
5. Litjens, G., et al.: A survey on deep learning in medical image analysis. Med. Image Anal. **42**, 60–88 (2017)
6. Kurakin, A., Goodfellow, I., Bengio, S.: Adversarial examples in the physical world. arXiv preprint arXiv:1607.02533 (2016)
7. Eykholt, K., et al.: Robust physical-world attacks on deep learning models. arXiv preprint arXiv:1707.08945 (2017)
8. Szegedy, C., et al.: Intriguing properties of neural networks. arXiv preprint arXiv:1312.6199 (2013)
9. Goodfellow, I.J., Shlens, J., Szegedy, C.: Explaining and harnessing adversarial examples. arXiv preprint arXiv:1412.6572 (2014)
10. Carlini, N., Wagner, D.: Towards evaluating the robustness of neural networks. In: 2017 IEEE Symposium on Security and Privacy (SP), pp. 39–57. IEEE (2017)
11. Su, J., Vargas, D.V., Sakurai, K.: One pixel attack for fooling deep neural networks. IEEE Trans. Evol. Comput. **23**, 828–841 (2019)
12. Papernot, N., McDaniel, P., Goodfellow, I., Jha, S., Celik, Z.B., Swami, A.: Practical black-box attacks against machine learning. In: Proceedings of the 2017 ACM on Asia Conference on Computer and Communications Security, pp. 506–519. ACM (2017)
13. Athalye, A., Carlini, N., Wagner, D.: Obfuscated gradients give a false sense of security: circumventing defenses to adversarial examples. arXiv preprint arXiv:1802.00420 (2018)
14. Ross, A.S., Doshi-Velez, F.: Improving the adversarial robustness and interpretability of deep neural networks by regularizing their input gradients. In: Thirty-Second AAAI Conference on Artificial Intelligence (2018)
15. Zhang, H., Yu, Y., Jiao, J., Xing, E.P., Ghaoui, L.E., Jordan, M.I.: Theoretically principled trade-off between robustness and accuracy. arXiv preprint arXiv:1901.08573 (2019)
16. Xie, C., Wu, Y., Maaten, L.V.D., Yuille, A.L., He, K.: Feature denoising for improving adversarial robustness. In: Proceedings of the IEEE Conference on Computer Vision and Pattern Recognition, pp. 501–509 (2019)
17. Wong, E., Rice, L., Kolter, J.Z.: Fast is better than free: revisiting adversarial training. arXiv preprint arXiv:2001.03994 (2020)
18. Shafahi, A., et al.: Adversarial training for free! In: Advances in Neural Information Processing Systems, pp. 3353–3364 (2019)
19. Zhang, D., Zhang, T., Lu, Y., Zhu, Z., Dong, B.: You only propagate once: accelerating adversarial training via maximal principle. In: Advances in Neural Information Processing Systems, pp. 227–238 (2019)
20. Raff, E., Sylvester, J., Forsyth, S., McLean, M.: Barrage of random transforms for adversarially robust defense. In: Proceedings of the IEEE Conference on Computer Vision and Pattern Recognition, pp. 6528–6537 (2019)

21. Kannan, H., Kurakin, A., Goodfellow, I.: Adversarial logit pairing. arXiv preprint arXiv:1803.06373 (2018)
22. Bernstein, J., Zhao, J., Azizzadenesheli, K., Anandkumar, A.: signSGD with majority vote is communication efficient and fault tolerant. arXiv preprint arXiv:1810.05291 (2018)
23. Liu, S., Chen, P.Y., Chen, X., Hong, M.: signSGD via zeroth-order oracle. In: International Conference on Learning Representations (2018)
24. Madry, A., Makelov, A., Schmidt, L., Tsipras, D., Vladu, A.: Towards deep learning models resistant to adversarial attacks. arXiv preprint arXiv:1706.06083 (2017)
25. Moosavi-Dezfooli, S.M., Fawzi, A., Frossard, P.: DeepFool: a simple and accurate method to fool deep neural networks. In: Proceedings of the IEEE Conference on Computer Vision and Pattern Recognition, pp. 2574–2582 (2016)
26. Virmaux, A., Scaman, K.: Lipschitz regularity of deep neural networks: analysis and efficient estimation. In: Advances in Neural Information Processing Systems, pp. 3835–3844 (2018)
27. Opitz, D., Maclin, R.: Popular ensemble methods: an empirical study. J. Artif. Intell. Res. 11, 169–198 (1999)
28. Müller, R., Kornblith, S., Hinton, G.E.: When does label smoothing help? In: Advances in Neural Information Processing Systems, pp. 4694–4703 (2019)
29. Sharma, Y., Chen, P.Y.: Attacking the Madry defense model with l-1-based adversarial examples. arXiv preprint arXiv:1710.10733 (2017)
30. Vincent, P., Larochelle, H., Lajoie, I., Bengio, Y., Manzagol, P.A.: Stacked denoising autoencoders: learning useful representations in a deep network with a local denoising criterion. J. Mach. Learn. Res. 11, 3371–3408 (2010)
31. Zagoruyko, S., Komodakis, N.: Wide residual networks. arXiv preprint arXiv:1605.07146 (2016)
32. Carlini, N., et al.: On evaluating adversarial robustness. arXiv preprint arXiv:1902.06705 (2019)
33. He, K., Zhang, X., Ren, S., Sun, J.: Deep residual learning for image recognition. In: Proceedings of the IEEE Conference on Computer Vision and Pattern Recognition, pp. 770–778 (2016)

Few-Shot Zero-Shot Learning: Knowledge Transfer with Less Supervision

Nanyi Fei[1], Jiechao Guan[1], Zhiwu Lu[2(✉)], and Yizhao Gao[2]

[1] School of Information, Renmin University of China, Beijing, China
[2] Beijing Key Laboratory of Big Data Management and Analysis Methods, Gaoling School of Artificial Intelligence, Renmin University of China, Beijing, China
luzhiwu@ruc.edu.cn

Abstract. Existing zero-shot learning (ZSL) methods assume that there exist sufficient training samples from seen classes, each annotated with semantic descriptors such as attributes, for knowledge transfer to unseen classes without any training samples. However, this assumption is often invalid because collecting sufficient seen class samples can be difficult and attribute annotation is expensive; it thus severely limits the scalability of ZSL. In this paper, we define a new setting termed Few-Shot Zero-Shot Learning (FSZSL), where only a few annotated images are collected from each seen class (i.e., few-shot). This is clearly more challenging yet more realistic than the conventional ZSL setting. To overcome the resultant image-level attribute sparsity, we propose a novel inductive ZSL model termed sparse attribute propagation (SAP) by propagating attribute annotations to more unannotated images using sparse coding. This is followed by learning bidirectional projections between features and attributes for ZSL. An efficient solver is provided for such knowledge transfer with less supervision, together with rigorous theoretic analysis. With our SAP, we show that a ZSL training dataset can also be augmented by the abundant web images returned by image search engine, to further improve the model performance. Extensive experiments show that the proposed model achieves state-of-the-art results.

1 Introduction

Due to the difficulty in collecting sufficient training images for large-scale object recognition [1–4] where deep convolutional neural networks (CNNs) are often employed, zero-shot learning (ZSL) has become topical in computer vision [5–13]. To recognize unseen classes without any training images, existing ZSL models leverage a semantic space as the bridge for knowledge transfer from seen classes to unseen ones, and the semantic attribute space is the most commonly used [14]. Given a set of seen class images, the visual features are first extracted, typically using CNNs pretrained on ImageNet. With the feature representations

Electronic supplementary material The online version of this chapter (https://doi.org/10.1007/978-3-030-69535-4_36) contains supplementary material, which is available to authorized users.

H. Ishikawa et al. (Eds.): ACCV 2020, LNCS 12624, pp. 592–608, 2021.
https://doi.org/10.1007/978-3-030-69535-4_36

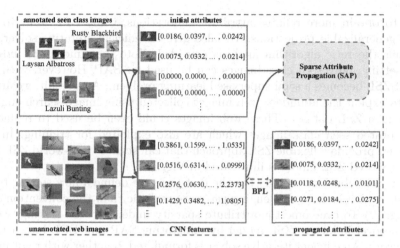

Fig. 1. Schematic illustration of the proposed ZSL model including SAP and BPL. The web images are obtained by Google with the query 'North American Bird'. The few annotated seen class images are augmented with these unannotated external data.

of images and the semantic representations of class names, the next task is to learn a joint embedding space using seen class data. In such a space, both feature and semantic representations are projected to be directly compared. Once the projection functions are learned, they are applied to test images and unseen class names, and the nearest neighbor class name is found for each test image.

Although ZSL can avoid the need of collecting unseen class images for training, it still requires a large number of attribute/label annotations per seen class: hundreds of class-level attribute annotations are often needed, along with hundreds of image-level class label annotations. This severely limits the scalability of ZSL. In this paper, to study how to overcome this limitation associated with existing ZSL models and make ZSL truly scalable, we define a new ZSL setting termed Few-Shot Zero-Shot Learning (FSZSL), where only a few annotated images are collected from each seen class. This is clearly more challenging yet *more realistic* than the conventional ZSL setting. Note that our new FSZSL setting is often encountered in real-world application scenarios such as fine-grained classification and medical image recognition. More specifically, in these scenarios, each image is hard to annotate with a class label even for an expert and thus only a few annotated images per seen class can be obtained; meanwhile, recognizing unseen classes is always needed because the new/rare classes will unavoidably occur when more data is accumulated.

To overcome the resultant image-level attribute sparsity, we propose a novel inductive ZSL model termed sparse attribute propagation (SAP) by propagating attribute annotations to more unannotated images using sparse coding [15,16]. This is followed by learning bidirectional projections between features and attributes for ZSL. We formulate sparse attribute propagation (SAP) and bidirectional projection learning (BPL) within a unified ZSL framework: SAP aims to obtain more reliable attribute annotations, while BPL aims to learn more generalizable projections. We also give an efficient iterative solver, with rigorous theoretic algorithm analysis provided. Note that under the inductive ZSL setting, only seen class images can be used for SAP. However, with SAP, our FSZSL becomes a semi-supervised learning problem. As a result, we are now able to exploit the abundant web images collected using image search engine to augment a ZSL dataset. These web images could even be used to replace the unannotated seen class images which are also exploited for training. In summary, we provide a flexible ZSL approach that can scale to real-world ZSL tasks. Our proposed ZSL model is illustrated in Fig. 1.

Our contributions are: (1) For the first time, we define a new setting termed FSZSL, which is more challenging yet more realistic than the conventional ZSL setting. (2) To overcome the attribute sparsity under our new setting, we propose a novel inductive ZSL model by integrating SAP and BPL into a unified framework. An efficient iterative solver is formulated, together with rigorous theoretic analysis. (3) Our model is highly flexible and can be generalized to other vision problems such as social image annotation (SIA) [17–19] (see the suppl. material). Extensive experiments show that our model achieves state-of-the-art results on both problems (i.e., ZSL and SIA).

2   Related Work

Knowledge Transfer for ZSL. Since both seen and unseen classes can be defined in a same semantic space, it is often leveraged as a bridge for knowledge transfer from seen classes to unseen ones. Existing ZSL methods typically learn a projection between the visual feature space and the semantic space, and can be divided into three groups depending on how the projection function is built: (1) The first group projects both visual and semantic spaces into a latent embedding space [20–23]. (2) Methods in the second group learn projections from the visual space to the semantic one [6,7,24]. (3) The third group projects semantic representations into the visual space [25,26], which can reduce the hubness problem [27]. Moreover, several works [12,28–31] first projects visual representations into the semantic space and then projects them back, which can help reduce the domain shift problem. Note that Semantic AutoEncoder (SAE) and our BPL are closely related. The main difference is that the weight hyperparameter for balancing the two projection directions is removed from our BPL. Moreover, our algorithm is given a theoretic analysis while such an analysis is missing for SAE. Notably, as we have stated our contributions above, BPL is not the focus of this work, and it can be replaced by any other embedding method (see Table 3).

ZSL with Less Human Annotation. A ZSL model typically exploits two types of human annotations for recognizing unseen classes without any training images: (1) the human-annotated class labels of training images from seen classes; (2) the human-defined semantic representations of seen/unseen classes. In the area of ZSL, much attention has been paid to reducing the annotation cost of generating human-defined semantic representations (e.g., the semantic space is formed using online textual documents [7,8], human gaze [10], or visual similes [11,32] instead of attributes), which leads to significantly less annotation cost. Different from these ZSL models, we focus on ZSL with less human annotation by defining a new ZSL setting, i.e., only a few annotated images are collected from each seen class. Although our ZSL model is proposed based on attributes in this paper, it can be easily generalized to other forms of semantic space [7,8,10,11] to further reduce the annotation cost. To our best knowledge, we are the first to define this new setting in the area of ZSL.

Semi-Supervised ZSL. In this paper, attribute propagation is performed from a few annotated seen class images to more unannotated images so that more reliable attribute annotations can be obtained. This can be regarded as a form of semi-supervised ZSL. Note that the test images from unseen classes are not used for training our model, i.e., we take an inductive ZSL setting. However, in the area of ZSL, when semi-supervised learning is applied to ZSL, the unlabelled test images from unseen classes are typically used for training. This results in a transductive ZSL setting: either label propagation [5,6,9,33] or self-training [28,34–38] is employed for semi-supervised learning. Since these transductive ZSL models assume the access to the whole test set, they have limited applications in real-world scenarios. Note that although the test set is not involved in the training process, our model still exploits the unannotated seen class images for attribute propagation. Given that it is not easy to obtain the unannotated seen class images, we choose to perform attribute propagation with unannotated external data from image search engine, which thus provides a feasible/convenient approach to applying our model to real-world ZSL tasks.

ZSL with Web Images. In computer vision, web images have been widely used to promote the performance of existing recognition models as in [39–42]. However, there is less attention on exploiting web images for ZSL. Two exceptions are: the web images are utilized to augment the unseen class data in [43] and discover event composition knowledge for zero-shot event detection in [44]. In this work, although web images are also employed as external data, our model is quite different from [43] in that we do not search web images *directly with unseen class names* since this is against the zero-shot setting.

3 Methodology

3.1 Problem Definition

Let $C_s = \{cs_1, \cdots, cs_p\}$ denote a set of seen classes and $C_u = \{cu_1, \cdots, cu_q\}$ denote a set of unseen classes, where p and q are the numbers of seen and unseen classes, respectively. These two sets of classes are disjoint. Similarly, $\mathbf{Z}_s = [\mathbf{z}_1^{(s)}, \cdots, \mathbf{z}_p^{(s)}] \in \mathbb{R}^{k \times p}$ and $\mathbf{Z}_u = [\mathbf{z}_1^{(u)}, \cdots, \mathbf{z}_q^{(u)}] \in \mathbb{R}^{k \times q}$ denote the corresponding seen and unseen class semantic representations (e.g., k-dimensional attribute vectors). We are given a set of seen class training images $\mathcal{D}_s = \{(\mathbf{x}_i^{(s)}, l_i^{(s)}), \mathbf{y}_i^{(s)} : i = 1, \cdots, r, r + 1, \cdots, N_s\}$, where $\mathbf{x}_i^{(s)} \in \mathbb{R}^{d \times 1}$ is the d-dimensional feature vector of the i-th training image, $l_i^{(s)} \in \{1, \cdots, p\}$ is the label of $\mathbf{x}_i^{(s)}$ according to $\mathcal{C}_s$, $\mathbf{y}_i^{(s)} = \mathbf{z}_{l_i^{(s)}}^{(s)}$ is the semantic representation of $\mathbf{x}_i^{(s)}$ (i.e., only class-level attributes are needed), and N_s is the number of training images. In this paper, only the first r annotated training images $\mathbf{x}_i^{(s)}$ ($1 \leq i \leq r$) have non-zero attribute vectors, i.e., $\mathbf{y}_i^{(s)} = \mathbf{0}$ ($r + 1 \leq i \leq N_s$). Moreover, let $\mathcal{D}_u = \{(\mathbf{x}_i^{(u)}, l_i^{(u)}), \mathbf{y}_i^{(u)} : i = 1, \cdots, N_u\}$ denote a set of unseen class test images, where $\mathbf{x}_i^{(u)} \in \mathbb{R}^{d \times 1}$ is the feature vector of the i-th test image, $l_i^{(u)} \in \{1, \cdots, q\}$ is the unknown label of $\mathbf{x}_i^{(u)}$ according to $\mathcal{C}_u$, $\mathbf{y}_i^{(u)}$ denotes the unknown semantic representation of $\mathbf{x}_i^{(u)}$, and N_u is the number of test images. The goal of FSZSL is to predict the labels of test images by learning a classifier $f : \mathcal{X}_u \to \mathcal{C}_u$, where $\mathcal{X}_u = \{\mathbf{x}_i^{(u)} : i = 1, \cdots, N_u\}$. Under the generalized FSZSL setting (following [45–47]), the test samples can come from both seen and unseen classes, so the classifier becomes $f : \mathcal{X} \to \mathcal{C}_s \cup \mathcal{C}_u$, where $\mathcal{X}$ denotes the set of all test samples.

Note that the above problem definition is consistent with the inductive ZSL setting, where the unannotated seen class training images are given along with the annotated seen class training ones. Their uniform notations make the model formulation more concise. As we have mentioned, the unannotated seen class images can be replaced by the unannotated web images from image search engine (see Fig. 1), resulting in a feasible approach for real-world ZSL tasks. The details of such FSZSL with external data are given at the end of Sect. 3.

3.2   Model Formulation

When learned with only a few annotated images per seen class under our new ZSL setting, the projection function between the feature and semantic spaces is not reliable. Therefore, we choose to propagate such sparse attribute annotations to more unannotated images using sparse coding [15,16]: more attribute annotations enable us to learn a more reliable projection, but the noise caused by attribute propagation should also be suppressed by sparse coding, which is thus called sparse attribute propagation (SAP). Moreover, given all seen class training images (with ground truth/predicted attribute vectors), we integrate the forward and reverse projections for ZSL, since either projection suffers from the projection domain shift [5,25]. By bidirectional projection learning (BPL), a visual feature vector is first projected into a semantic space and then back into visual feature space to reconstruct itself. Such self-reconstruction can improve the generalization ability of the model and help tackle the projection domain shift. Our unified framework including SAP and BPL is given below.

Concretely, with the whole seen class training set $\mathcal{X}_s = \{\mathbf{x}_i^{(s)} : i = 1, \cdots, N_s\}$, we construct first a graph $\mathcal{G} = \{\mathcal{V}, \mathbf{A}\}$ with its vertex set $\mathcal{V} = \mathcal{X}_s$ and affinity matrix $\mathbf{A} = [a_{ij}]_{N_s \times N_s}$, where a_{ij} denotes the similarity between training images $\mathbf{x}_i^{(s)}$ and $\mathbf{x}_j^{(s)}$. The affinity matrix $\mathbf{A}$ can be defined as: $a_{ij} = \exp(-\|\mathbf{x}_i^{(s)} - \mathbf{x}_j^{(s)}\|_2^2 / (2\sigma^2))$, where the parameter σ can be determined empirically ($\sigma = 1$ in this paper). The normalized Laplacian matrix $\mathbf{L}$ is given by

$$\mathbf{L} = \mathbf{I} - \mathbf{D}^{-\frac{1}{2}} \mathbf{A} \mathbf{D}^{-\frac{1}{2}}, \tag{1}$$

where $\mathbf{I}$ is an identity matrix, and $\mathbf{D}$ is a diagonal matrix with its i-th diagonal element being $\sum_j a_{ij}$. We derive a new matrix $\mathbf{B} \in \mathbb{R}^{N_s \times N_s}$ from $\mathbf{L}$: $\mathbf{B} = \Sigma^{\frac{1}{2}}\mathbf{V}^T$, where $\mathbf{V}$ is an orthonormal matrix with each column being an eigenvector of $\mathbf{L}$, and Σ is a diagonal matrix with its diagonal element Σ_{ii} being an eigenvalue of $\mathbf{L}$ (sorted as $0 \leq \Sigma_{11} \leq \cdots \leq \Sigma_{N_s N_s}$). Denoting the eigen-decomposition of $\mathbf{L}$ as $\mathbf{L} = \mathbf{V}\Sigma\mathbf{V}^T$, $\mathbf{L}$ can be represented as: $\mathbf{L} = (\Sigma^{\frac{1}{2}}\mathbf{V}^T)^T\Sigma^{\frac{1}{2}}\mathbf{V}^T = \mathbf{B}^T\mathbf{B}$.

We further collect the feature and attribute vectors of the training set as $\mathbf{X}^{(s)} = [\mathbf{x}_1^{(s)}, \cdots, \mathbf{x}_{N_s}^{(s)}] \in \mathbb{R}^{d \times N_s}$ and $\mathbf{Y}^{(s)} = [\mathbf{y}_1^{(s)}, \cdots, \mathbf{y}_{N_s}^{(s)}] \in \mathbb{R}^{k \times N_s}$. Our ZSL model solves the following optimization problem:

$$\min_{\mathbf{Y},\tilde{\mathbf{Y}},\mathbf{W}} \{\|\mathbf{Y} - \tilde{\mathbf{Y}}\|_F^2 + \lambda_1\|\mathbf{B}\tilde{\mathbf{Y}}^T\|_1 + \lambda_2\|\mathbf{Y} - \mathbf{Y}^{(s)}\|_1$$

$$+ \lambda_3(\|\mathbf{W}\mathbf{X}^{(s)} - \mathbf{Y}\|_F^2 + \|\mathbf{X}^{(s)} - \mathbf{W}^T\mathbf{Y}\|_F^2 + \lambda_4\|\mathbf{W}\|_F^2)\}, \qquad (2)$$

where $\mathbf{W} \in \mathbb{R}^{k \times d}$ is a projection matrix from the visual feature space to the semantic space, $\mathbf{Y} \in \mathbb{R}^{k \times N_s}$ collects the optimal attribute vectors of all seen class training images, $\tilde{\mathbf{Y}} \in \mathbb{R}^{k \times N_s}$ denotes an intermediate matrix that approaches $\mathbf{Y}$, and $\lambda_1, \lambda_2, \lambda_3, \lambda_4$ are free parameters.

The first and third terms of Eq. (2) are the L_2-norm and L_1-norm fitting constraints, respectively. Particularly, the third term enforces the noise sparsity in $\mathbf{Y}$, which is a commonly used constraint for data noise and has been proven to be effective. Also, by adding this term, the reliable entries of $\mathbf{Y}$ (with large values) will remain large, while the unreliable entries (with small values) are forced to be close to zero, leading to noise reduction. Figure 3(b) shows that removing the third term of Eq. (2) leads to significant performance degradation (see 'Single L_1' vs. 'No L_1' in Fig. 3(b)). The second term is a graph smoothness constraint, different from the conventional graph smoothness constraint as a trace norm term. Here, L_1-norm is used to promote the sparsity on the inferred attribute vectors and thus noise reduction (see Fig. 3(b)). Additionally, the last three terms denote the loss function of projection learning for ZSL. The two projection matrices are transpose of each other, similar to those in an auto-encoder [48,49].

Note that introducing both $\mathbf{Y}$ and $\tilde{\mathbf{Y}}$ makes Eq. (2) much easier to solve. If we do not introduce the intermediate attribute matrix $\tilde{\mathbf{Y}}$, the SAP part of Eq. (2) becomes $\lambda_1\|\mathbf{B}\mathbf{Y}^T\|_1 + \lambda_2\|\mathbf{Y} - \mathbf{Y}^{(s)}\|_1$. That is, the objective function would have two L_1-norm terms, and solving an optimization problem with such an objective function is notoriously hard. We thus replace $\mathbf{Y}$ in $\lambda_1\|\mathbf{B}\mathbf{Y}^T\|_1$ with $\tilde{\mathbf{Y}}$ and add a term $\|\mathbf{Y} - \tilde{\mathbf{Y}}\|_F^2$ to ensure that $\tilde{\mathbf{Y}}$ and $\mathbf{Y}$ are close.

3.3 Optimization Algorithm

Let $\mathcal{F}(\mathbf{Y}, \tilde{\mathbf{Y}}, \mathbf{W})$ denote the objective function in Eq. (2). The optimization problem in Eq. (2) can be solved in two alternating steps as follows:

$$\mathbf{SAP}: \mathbf{Y}^*, \tilde{\mathbf{Y}}^* = \arg\min_{\mathbf{Y},\tilde{\mathbf{Y}}} \mathcal{F}(\mathbf{Y}, \tilde{\mathbf{Y}}, \mathbf{W}^*), \qquad (3)$$

$$\mathbf{BPL}: \mathbf{W}^* = \arg\min_{\mathbf{W}} \mathcal{F}(\mathbf{Y}^*, \tilde{\mathbf{Y}}^*, \mathbf{W}), \qquad (4)$$

where $\mathbf{Y}^*$ is initialized with $\mathbf{Y}^{(s)}$, and $\mathbf{W}^*$ is initialized by solving the BPL problem in Eq. (4) with $\mathbf{Y}^* = \tilde{\mathbf{Y}}^* = \mathbf{Y}^{(s)}$.

Sparse Attribute Propagation (SAP). The SAP subproblem in Eq. (3) is solved with the alternating optimization technique as follows: 1) SAP-I: fix $\mathbf{Y} = \mathbf{Y}^*$, and update $\tilde{\mathbf{Y}}$ by $\tilde{\mathbf{Y}}^* = \arg\min_{\tilde{\mathbf{Y}}} \mathcal{F}(\mathbf{Y}^*, \tilde{\mathbf{Y}}, \mathbf{W}^*)$; 2) SAP-II: fix $\tilde{\mathbf{Y}} = \tilde{\mathbf{Y}}^*$, and update $\mathbf{Y}$ by $\mathbf{Y}^* = \arg\min_{\mathbf{Y}} \mathcal{F}(\mathbf{Y}, \tilde{\mathbf{Y}}^*, \mathbf{W}^*)$.

1) SAP-I. Directly solving the SAP-I subproblem is of high computational cost mainly due to the dimension of $\mathbf{B}$ ($N_s \times N_s$). Fortunately, we find a way to dramatically reduce this dimension by using only a small subset of eigenvectors of $\mathbf{L}$. Specifically, we decompose $\tilde{\mathbf{Y}}$ to $\tilde{\mathbf{Y}} = (\mathbf{V}_m \alpha)^T$, where $\alpha = \{\alpha_{ij}\}_{m \times k}$ is an $m \times k$ matrix that collects the reconstruction coefficients and $\mathbf{V}_m$ is an $N_s \times m$ matrix whose columns are the m smallest eigenvectors of $\mathbf{L}$ (i.e., the first m columns of $\mathbf{V}$). The SAP-I subproblem can be reformulated as follows:

$$
\begin{aligned}
\alpha^* &= \arg\min_{\alpha} \|\mathbf{V}_m \alpha - \mathbf{Y}^{*T}\|_F^2 + \lambda_1 \|\mathbf{BV}_m \alpha\|_1 \\
&= \arg\min_{\alpha} \sum_{j=1}^{k} (\|\mathbf{V}_m \alpha_{.j} - \mathbf{Y}_{.j}^{*T}\|_2^2 + \lambda_1 \|\mathbf{BV}_m \alpha_{.j}\|_1),
\end{aligned}
\tag{5}
$$

where $\alpha_{.j}$ and $\mathbf{Y}_{.j}^{*T}$ denote the j-th column of α and $\mathbf{Y}^{*T}$, respectively. The above problem can be decomposed into k independent subproblems:

$$
\begin{aligned}
&\arg\min_{\alpha_{.j}} \|\mathbf{V}_m \alpha_{.j} - \mathbf{Y}_{.j}^{*T}\|_2^2 + \lambda_1 \|\mathbf{BV}_m \alpha_{.j}\|_1 \\
&= \arg\min_{\alpha_{.j}} \|\mathbf{V}_m \alpha_{.j} - \mathbf{Y}_{.j}^{*T}\|_2^2 + \lambda_1 \|\sum_{i=1}^{m} \Sigma^{\frac{1}{2}} \mathbf{V}^T \mathbf{V}_{.i} \alpha_{ij}\|_1 \\
&= \arg\min_{\alpha_{.j}} \|\mathbf{V}_m \alpha_{.j} - \mathbf{Y}_{.j}^{*T}\|_2^2 + \lambda_1 \sum_{i=1}^{m} \Sigma_{ii}^{\frac{1}{2}} |\alpha_{ij}|,
\end{aligned}
\tag{6}
$$

where the orthonormality of $\mathbf{V}$ is used to simplify $\|\mathbf{BV}_m \alpha_{.j}\|_1$. Many off-the-shelf solvers exist for solving L_1-optimization problems like Eq. (6). L1General[1] is employed here, which can solve Eq. (6) at a linear time cost.

To further improve the efficiency, we compute the affinity matrix $\mathbf{A}$ over a k_g-nearest neighbor graph with $k_g \ll N_s$. The time complexity for finding m eigenvectors with the smallest eigenvalues of the sparse matrix $\mathbf{L}$ is $O(m^3 + m^2 N_s + k_g m N_s)$, which scales well to the data.

2) SAP-II. Let $\bar{\mathbf{Y}} = \mathbf{Y} - \mathbf{Y}^{(s)}$. The SAP-II subproblem can be reformulated as

$$
\begin{aligned}
\bar{\mathbf{Y}}^* &= \arg\min_{\bar{\mathbf{Y}}} \{\|\bar{\mathbf{Y}} + \mathbf{Y}^{(s)} - \tilde{\mathbf{Y}}^*\|_F^2 + \lambda_2 \|\bar{\mathbf{Y}}\|_1 \\
&\quad + \lambda_3 (\|\mathbf{W}^* \mathbf{X}^{(s)} - (\bar{\mathbf{Y}} + \mathbf{Y}^{(s)})\|_F^2 + \|\mathbf{X}^{(s)} - \mathbf{W}^{*T}(\bar{\mathbf{Y}} + \mathbf{Y}^{(s)})\|_F^2)\} \\
&= \arg\min_{\bar{\mathbf{Y}}} \{\mathrm{loss}(\bar{\mathbf{Y}}) + \lambda_2 \|\bar{\mathbf{Y}}\|_1\},
\end{aligned}
\tag{7}
$$

---

[1] https://www.cs.ubc.ca/schmidtm/Software/L1General.html.

Algorithm 1. Inductive FSZSL with Joint SAP and BPL

Input: Feature representation of the training set $\mathbf{X}^{(s)}$
   Initial semantic representation $\mathbf{Y}^{(s)}$
   Parameters $k_g, m, \lambda_1, \lambda_2, \lambda_3$
Output: $\mathbf{W}^*$
1: Construct a k_g-NN graph with its affinity matrix $\mathbf{A}$ being defined over $\mathbf{X}^{(s)}$;
2: Find m smallest eigenvectors of the Laplacian matrix $\mathbf{L}$ and store them in $\mathbf{V}_m$;
3: Initialize $\mathbf{W}^*$ by solving Eq. (8) with $\mathbf{Y}^* = \mathbf{Y}^{(s)}$;
4: **for** all iteration $= 1, ..., $ MaxIteration **do**
5: SAP-I: find α^* with Eq. (5) and compute $\tilde{\mathbf{Y}}^*$ as $\tilde{\mathbf{Y}}^* = (\mathbf{V}_m \alpha^*)^T$;
6: SAP-II: find $\bar{\mathbf{Y}}^*$ with Eq. (7) and compute $\mathbf{Y}^*$ as $\mathbf{Y}^* = \bar{\mathbf{Y}}^* + \mathbf{Y}^{(s)}$;
7: BPL: find $\mathbf{W}^*$ by solving Eq. (8);
8: **end for**
9: return $\mathbf{W}^*$.

---

where $\operatorname{loss}(\bar{\mathbf{Y}}) = \|\bar{\mathbf{Y}} + \mathbf{Y}^{(s)} - \tilde{\mathbf{Y}}^*\|_F^2 + \lambda_3(\|\mathbf{W}^*\mathbf{X}^{(s)} - (\bar{\mathbf{Y}} + \mathbf{Y}^{(s)})\|_F^2 + \|\mathbf{X}^{(s)} - \mathbf{W}^{*T}(\bar{\mathbf{Y}} + \mathbf{Y}^{(s)})\|_F^2)$. Since $\operatorname{loss}(\bar{\mathbf{Y}})$ is a quadratic function w.r.t. $\bar{\mathbf{Y}}$, the above L_1-optimization problem can also be solved efficiently with L1General.

Bidirectional Projection Learning (BPL). By setting $\frac{\partial \mathcal{F}(\mathbf{Y}^*, \tilde{\mathbf{Y}}^*, \mathbf{W})}{\partial \mathbf{W}} = 0$, the BPL subproblem in Eq. (4) can be solved using a Sylvester equation:

$$(\mathbf{Y}^*\mathbf{Y}^{*T} + \lambda_4\mathbf{I})\mathbf{W} + \mathbf{W}(\mathbf{X}^{(s)}\mathbf{X}^{(s)T}) = 2\mathbf{Y}^*\mathbf{X}^{(s)T}, \tag{8}$$

which is solved (using Matlab built-in function) with a time complexity of $O((k^2 + d^2 + kd)N_s + k^3 + d^3)$. We empirically set $\lambda_4 = 0.01$.

By joint SAP and BPL for inductive FSZSL, our algorithm is given in Algorithm 1. Once learned, given the optimal projection matrix $\mathbf{W}^*$ found by our algorithm, we predict the label of a test image $\mathbf{x}_i^{(u)}$ as

$$l_i^{(u)} = \arg\min_j \|\mathbf{x}_i^{(u)} - \mathbf{W}^{*T}\mathbf{z}_j^{(u)}\|_2^2. \tag{9}$$

Since each of iteration steps 5–7 in Algorithm 1 has an efficient solver and our algorithm is shown to converge very quickly (≤ 5 iterations) in the experiments, it has a linear time complexity with respect to the data size.

3.4 Algorithm Analysis

We provide a rigorous analysis on the properties and behaviors of Algorithm 1 as follows. Without loss of generality, we first normalize all of $\|\mathbf{x}_i^{(s)}\|_2$, $\|\mathbf{y}_j^{(s)}\|_1$ to 1, and thus have: $\|\mathbf{Y}^{(s)}\|_F \leq \|\mathbf{Y}^{(s)}\|_1 \leq \sqrt{r}$.

Proposition 1. *The solutions* $(\mathbf{Y}^*$ *and* $\mathbf{W}^*)$ *found by Algorithm 1 are bounded.*

Proof. (a) Eq. (7) is equivalent to: $\bar{\mathbf{Y}}^* = \arg\min_{\bar{\mathbf{Y}}} \operatorname{loss}(\bar{\mathbf{Y}})$, s.t. $\|\bar{\mathbf{Y}}\|_1 \leq M(\lambda_2)$, where $M(\lambda_2)$ is a constant depended on λ_2. Since $\mathbf{Y}^* = \bar{\mathbf{Y}}^* + \mathbf{Y}^{(s)}$, we have

$\|\mathbf{Y}^*\|_F \leq \|\bar{\mathbf{Y}}^*\|_F + \|\mathbf{Y}^{(s)}\|_F \leq C_1$, where $C_1 = M(\lambda_2) + \sqrt{r}$.

(b) Given that $\mathbf{Y}^*\mathbf{Y}^{*T} + \lambda_4\mathbf{I}$ and $\mathbf{X}^{(s)}\mathbf{X}^{(s)T}$ in Eq. (8) are non-negative definite, there exist orthogonal matrices $\mathbf{P}$, $\mathbf{Q}$ s.t. $\boldsymbol{\Sigma_1}\mathbf{P}^T\mathbf{WQ} + \mathbf{P}^T\mathbf{WQ}\boldsymbol{\Sigma_2} = 2\mathbf{P}^T\mathbf{Y}^*\mathbf{X}^{(s)T}\mathbf{Q}$, where $\boldsymbol{\Sigma_1} = \mathrm{diag}(\theta_1^1,...\theta_k^1)$ and $\boldsymbol{\Sigma_2} = \mathrm{diag}(\theta_1^2,...\theta_d^2)$ collect the eigenvalues of $\mathbf{Y}^*\mathbf{Y}^{*T} + \lambda_4\mathbf{I}$ and $\mathbf{X}^{(s)}\mathbf{X}^{(s)T}$, respectively. Obviously, $\theta_i^1 \geq \lambda_4$ $(i = 1,...,k), \theta_j^2 \geq 0$ $(j = 1,...,d)$. Let $\tilde{\mathbf{W}} = \mathbf{P}^T\mathbf{WQ}$ and $\tilde{\mathbf{R}} = \mathbf{P}^T\mathbf{Y}^*\mathbf{X}^{(s)T}\mathbf{Q}$. We have $\boldsymbol{\Sigma_1}\tilde{\mathbf{W}} + \tilde{\mathbf{W}}\boldsymbol{\Sigma_2} = 2\tilde{\mathbf{R}}$. Since $\tilde{w}_{ij} = 2\tilde{r}_{ij}/(\theta_i^1 + \theta_j^2)$, $\|\mathbf{W}^*\|_F = \|\tilde{\mathbf{W}}\|_F \leq 2\|\mathbf{Y}^*\mathbf{X}^{(s)T}\|_F/\lambda_4$. Given that $\|\mathbf{Y}^*\|_F \leq C_1$, we further obtain: $\|\mathbf{W}^*\|_F \leq 2\|\mathbf{Y}^*\|_F\|\mathbf{X}^{(s)T}\|_F/\lambda_4 \leq C_2$, where $C_2 = 2C_1\sqrt{N_s}/\lambda_4$. $\square$

Proposition 2. *The optimal projection matrix* $\mathbf{W}^*$ *found by Algorithm 1 is insensitive to the perturbation of* $\mathbf{Y}^*$, *i.e.,* $\|\triangle\mathbf{W}^*\|_F \to 0$, *if* $\|\triangle\mathbf{Y}^*\|_F \to 0$.

Proof. Given $\mathbf{W}^*$ found by Algorithm 1, we have

$$(\mathbf{Y}^*\mathbf{Y}^{*T} + \lambda_4\mathbf{I})\mathbf{W}^* + \mathbf{W}^*(\mathbf{X}^{(s)}\mathbf{X}^{(s)T}) = 2\mathbf{Y}^*\mathbf{X}^{(s)T}. \qquad (10)$$

When a perturbation $\triangle\mathbf{Y}^*$ is added to $\mathbf{Y}^*$, the optimal projection matrix found by Algorithm 1 is $\hat{\mathbf{W}}^*$:

$$\mathbf{H}\hat{\mathbf{W}}^* + \hat{\mathbf{W}}^*(\mathbf{X}^{(s)}\mathbf{X}^{(s)T}) = 2(\mathbf{Y}^* + \triangle\mathbf{Y}^*)\mathbf{X}^{(s)T}, \qquad (11)$$

where $\mathbf{H} = (\mathbf{Y}^* + \triangle\mathbf{Y}^*)(\mathbf{Y}^* + \triangle\mathbf{Y}^*)^T + \lambda_4\mathbf{I}$. Let $\triangle\mathbf{W}^* = \hat{\mathbf{W}}^* - \mathbf{W}^*$. Subtracting Eq. (10) from Eq. (11), we obtain $\mathbf{H}\triangle\mathbf{W}^* + \triangle\mathbf{W}^*(\mathbf{X}^{(s)}\mathbf{X}^{(s)T}) = \mathbf{K}$, where $\mathbf{K} = 2\triangle\mathbf{Y}^*\mathbf{X}^{(s)T} - (\triangle\mathbf{Y}^*\triangle\mathbf{Y}^{*T} + \mathbf{Y}^*\triangle\mathbf{Y}^{*T} + \triangle\mathbf{Y}^*\mathbf{Y}^{*T})\mathbf{W}^*$. According to the proof of Proposition 1, we similarly obtain $\|\triangle\mathbf{W}^*\|_F \leq \|\mathbf{K}\|_F/\lambda_4$. We further have:

$$\|\triangle\mathbf{W}^*\|_F \leq [2\sqrt{N_s}\|\triangle\mathbf{Y}^*\|_F + C_2\|\triangle\mathbf{Y}^*\|_F(\|\triangle\mathbf{Y}^*\|_F + 2\|\mathbf{Y}^*\|_F)]/\lambda_4$$
$$\leq \|\triangle\mathbf{Y}^*\|_F[2\sqrt{N_s} + C_2(\|\triangle\mathbf{Y}^*\|_F + 2C_1)]/\lambda_4, \qquad (12)$$

which means that $\|\triangle\mathbf{W}^*\|_F \to 0$, if $\|\triangle\mathbf{Y}^*\|_F \to 0$. $\square$

Note that Proposition 1 is used in the proof of Proposition 2 as a preliminary proposition. Importantly, from Proposition 2, the optimal projection matrix $\mathbf{W}^*$ used for final recognition is insensitive to the perturbation of $\mathbf{Y}^*$. This thus provides guarantee that Algorithm 1 is robust under our new ZSL setting.

3.5   FSZSL with External Data

Although the test images from unseen classes are not involved in the training process (see Algorithm 1), the proposed algorithm still exploits the unannotated seen class images for SAP. Sometimes, even collecting unannotated seen class images becomes a burden. To address this issue, we thus choose to perform SAP with the unannotated external data from image search engine. By searching relevant images with high-level semantic abstraction (i.e., query) of seen classes, we obtain many free web images to augment the few annotated seen class images at hand. These unannotated web images can be readily exploited for SAP, instead of the unannotated seen class images used in Algorithm 1. When the few annotated seen class images are fused with the unannotated external data, the proposed algorithm can be implemented without any modifications.

Note that the unannotated web images are obtained at a low cost (search key words on a image search engine), and thus unavoidably contain some images that do not belong to the seen classes. For example, given the benchmark seen/unseen class split (i.e., 150/50) of the CUB-200-2011 Birds (CUB) dataset [50], we collect the external data by Google with the query 'North American Bird' (i.e., high-level semantic abstraction of seen classes). With this high-level query, it is very likely that a returned image comes from either seen or unseen classes, and beyond (see Fig. 2). In this paper, we choose to classify the obtained web images using the CNN model proposed in [51], and then discard the images that are classified to unseen classes. Given that [51] has reported a very high accuracy in fine-grained classification, *the effect of possible unseen class images can be suppressed dramatically* during training our SAP model. Therefore, the achieved improvements (if any) are mainly contributed to our SAP model itself.

4   Experiments

4.1   FSZSL on Benchmark Datasets

Datasets and Settings. 1) Datasets. Four widely-used benchmark datasets are selected: (a) Animals with Attributes (AwA) [14] has 30,475 images, 85 attributes, and the seen/unseen class split of 40/10; (b) CUB-200-2011 Birds (CUB) [50] has 11,788 images, 312 attributes, and the seen/unseen split of 150/50; (c) aPascal&Yahoo (aPY) [52] has 15,339 images, 64 attributes, and the class split of 20/12; (d) SUN Attribute (SUN) [53] has 14,340 images, 102 attributes, and the split of 707/10.

2) Semantic and Feature Spaces. First, we establish the semantic space with attributes for the four benchmark datasets, all of which provide the attribute annotations for seen/unseen classes. Second, we extract the ResNet101 [4] features to form the visual feature space as in [54–56].

3) Evaluation Metrics. For the standard FSZSL setting, we compute the multi-way top-1 accuracy as in previous works. For the generalized FSZSL setting (following [45–47]), we compute the harmonic mean of the following two accuracies: acc_u – the top-1 accuracy of classifying the test samples from unseen classes to all seen/unseen classes, and acc_s – the top-1 accuracy of classifying the test samples from seen classes to all seen/unseen classes.

4) Parameter Settings. Our algorithm has five hyperparameters: k_g, m, λ_1, λ_2, λ_3. Given only a few annotated seen class images, it is impossible to select the parameters by cross-validation. Fortunately, our algorithm is shown to be insensitive to these parameters (see the suppl. material). We thus uniformly set $k_g = 300$, $m = 50$, $\lambda_1 = 0.01$, $\lambda_2 = 1e - 4$, and $\lambda_3 = 1e - 6$. Note that λ_1, λ_2 and λ_3 are small but such small values are needed. For λ_1 and λ_3, they need to be small because the associated terms have much larger values than others.

Table 1. Comparative results (%) of standard FSZSL. Average top-1 accuracy is reported (with standard deviation in bracket).

Dataset	K	RPL [27]	ESZSL [24]	SSE [20]	SAE [12]	ZSKL [57]	RN [55]	PQZSL [23]	AREN [58]	Ours
CUB	5	29.4(1.4)	24.1(1.4)	15.6(2.8)	29.7(1.5)	32.2(1.6)	27.5(7.9)	26.5(1.1)	29.9(0.9)	**40.9(1.5)**
	10	34.3(1.0)	27.7(0.8)	16.3(1.4)	35.8(1.9)	37.8(0.8)	28.0(3.2)	31.0(1.5)	30.9(0.9)	**45.8(0.8)**
	15	38.2(0.9)	30.3(0.6)	18.2(0.9)	39.1(0.8)	40.5(0.5)	31.3(6.5)	36.9(0.5)	31.5(0.7)	**47.5(0.8)**
	20	40.0(0.5)	32.9(0.4)	19.2(1.2)	41.0(0.2)	41.5(0.7)	32.6(4.0)	38.7(1.0)	31.9(0.6)	**48.4(0.3)**
	25	41.4(1.0)	34.9(0.6)	21.0(0.6)	43.0(0.4)	42.3(0.3)	35.4(1.8)	40.3(0.3)	32.0(0.3)	**49.3(0.7)**
AwA	5	50.3(2.0)	26.4(4.0)	39.9(3.2)	58.1(5.3)	54.5(2.7)	28.7(3.2)	40.9(2.9)	60.0(1.1)	**71.0(3.1)**
	10	53.6(2.2)	26.8(5.7)	41.4(5.8)	62.6(4.1)	61.0(2.2)	29.7(1.8)	43.3(7.2)	60.8(0.4)	**74.5(1.8)**
	15	53.8(2.3)	34.4(1.8)	42.2(4.4)	63.2(2.0)	62.6(2.4)	31.1(4.0)	51.2(1.8)	61.1(0.8)	**75.7(1.7)**
	20	55.2(1.7)	40.8(1.7)	42.6(4.5)	65.4(1.7)	65.6(1.5)	32.4(5.2)	54.2(1.9)	61.3(0.6)	**76.0(1.4)**
	25	55.7(1.4)	41.5(2.0)	42.9(3.5)	66.6(1.5)	66.7(1.9)	35.2(3.3)	56.5(2.9)	64.2(5.3)	**77.5(0.9)**
aPY	5	21.4(5.7)	19.2(4.4)	13.1(3.0)	25.5(5.2)	33.6(3.4)	8.0(4.3)	24.8(1.7)	34.1(2.5)	**42.5(8.3)**
	10	22.3(3.6)	19.8(4.0)	14.0(3.4)	31.6(6.8)	35.0(6.1)	27.4(4.6)	26.6(5.4)	36.6(2.5)	**44.1(4.8)**
	15	23.0(2.6)	20.8(5.3)	14.1(4.0)	35.5(6.2)	37.1(4.7)	32.2(2.8)	29.1(2.9)	37.3(3.6)	**44.8(5.0)**
	20	24.9(2.8)	20.6(3.4)	15.3(2.3)	39.2(5.4)	38.7(6.5)	32.7(2.8)	30.7(2.2)	37.5(3.3)	**45.7(4.7)**
	25	25.5(2.8)	21.8(2.1)	17.6(2.1)	40.6(5.0)	40.4(4.6)	35.1(2.5)	32.0(2.2)	37.7(2.6)	**47.4(4.7)**
SUN	1	57.2(3.2)	58.0(4.4)	58.1(3.1)	53.4(2.1)	58.9(5.5)	54.2(3.8)	55.0(3.3)	57.3(1.1)	**81.7(1.9)**
	2	62.4(3.3)	62.5(4.7)	60.2(3.3)	64.4(1.5)	67.8(1.6)	58.7(4.8)	57.8(3.0)	59.4(1.7)	**83.0(2.2)**
	3	64.0(4.1)	65.8(5.2)	60.8(3.2)	70.1(3.1)	70.3(2.4)	60.4(4.0)	66.1(2.6)	61.0(1.0)	**83.3(1.4)**
	4	66.5(3.2)	68.9(4.5)	62.1(3.4)	74.5(2.6)	71.4(2.6)	62.1(5.5)	71.5(2.1)	61.0(1.0)	**83.9(1.4)**
	5	69.1(1.9)	70.2(2.1)	62.6(2.2)	76.8(2.0)	73.4(2.2)	64.6(4.4)	75.9(3.3)	61.5(0.3)	**84.3(1.3)**

For λ_2, it controls the strength of noise reduction and it needs to be small since the entries of the associated matrix are mostly small (otherwise most entries are forced to be zeros). However, having such small values does not mean that the corresponding terms can be dropped. Concretely, when the second term of Eq. (2) is removed (i.e., $\lambda_1 = 0$), the performance drops (see SAP-I+BPL vs. BPL in Fig. 3(a)). When the third term of Eq. (2) is removed (i.e., $\lambda_2 = 0$), the performance drops significantly (see SAP-I+SAP-II+BPL vs. SAP-I+BPL in Fig. 3(a)). As for λ_3, it surely cannot be zero since BPL is needed for ZSL.

5) Compared Methods. We select eight representative/state-of-the-art ZSL models as the baselines: RPL [27], ESZSL [24], SSE [20], SAE [12], ZSKL [57], RN [55], PQZSL [23], and AREN [58]. Note that for the comparison in Table 3, some baselines are selected because they can utilize the propagated attributes (with continuous, rather than binary values) as inputs for ZSL.

Results of Standard FSZSL. The comparative results under the standard FSZSL setting are shown in Table 1. Note that all seen class images from each dataset are provided for training, but only K images per seen class are annotated (the others are unannotated). Since there are only 20 images in each class of SUN, we take $K \in \{1, 2, 3, 4, 5\}$. For fair comparison, all eight ZSL alternatives apply the nearest neighbor classifier over a few annotated seen class images to classify each unannotated image to a seen class (thus its pseudo label and the corresponding attribute vector can be obtained)[2]. We have the following

---

[2] Due to the insufficient initial supervision, stronger label propagation models often induce too much noise. In contrast, with only one-step propagation, such nearest

Table 2. Comparative results (%) of generalized FSZSL. Harmonic mean is reported (with standard deviation in bracket).

Dataset	K	RPL [27]	ESZSL [24]	SSE [20]	SAE [12]	ZSKL [57]	RN [55]	PQZSL [23]	AREN [58]	Ours
CUB	5	16.8(1.5)	9.4(0.6)	6.9(1.4)	18.5(1.1)	18.6(0.9)	12.4(2.5)	19.9(1.3)	23.1(2.4)	**27.7(0.5)**
	10	21.3(0.8)	9.9(0.5)	8.7(1.4)	24.9(0.9)	22.2(0.5)	14.3(1.4)	22.5(0.9)	25.9(1.2)	**33.9(0.4)**
	15	23.7(0.3)	10.6(0.9)	9.0(0.6)	28.4(0.6)	24.1(0.3)	15.3(2.6)	24.8(0.7)	26.7(0.6)	**36.1(0.9)**
	20	25.3(0.2)	11.8(0.4)	9.9(0.3)	30.2(0.5)	25.3(0.3)	17.3(1.4)	26.6(0.5)	27.1(0.8)	**37.9(0.7)**
	25	26.1(0.3)	12.7(1.4)	10.5(1.2)	31.8(0.6)	26.0(0.3)	19.9(4.6)	28.1(0.3)	28.1(0.6)	**39.0(0.3)**
AwA	5	40.6(1.6)	27.7(4.1)	19.4(2.4)	33.5(3.9)	45.6(1.7)	36.8(2.4)	37.0(3.1)	37.6(2.0)	**55.1(2.8)**
	10	41.3(1.7)	29.2(4.0)	21.7(2.2)	44.0(2.4)	46.9(1.7)	37.8(4.8)	38.1(2.2)	41.1(2.6)	**59.0(1.7)**
	15	41.4(0.9)	33.2(2.6)	24.2(2.6)	47.8(2.1)	47.4(1.8)	40.3(1.8)	47.3(1.8)	42.4(2.7)	**61.2(1.3)**
	20	41.5(1.6)	37.1(1.5)	28.6(0.6)	50.4(1.4)	48.1(1.5)	41.7(0.6)	50.3(1.1)	42.5(4.3)	**62.7(1.3)**
	25	41.6(1.4)	39.7(2.4)	32.5(0.6)	51.8(0.6)	48.5(1.5)	42.7(3.5)	51.1(1.6)	42.7(1.6)	**63.0(2.0)**

Table 3. Comparative accuracies (%) of FSZSL with external data on the CUB+Web dataset. Note that RPL, ESZSL, SAE, and ZSKL also exploit the propagated attributes obtained by our SAP method for fair comparison.

K	RPL0 [27]	RPL [27]	ESZSL0 [24]	ESZSL [24]	SAE0 [12]	SAE [12]	ZSKL0 [57]	ZSKL [57]	Ours
1	21.5	26.9	10.4	12.8	22.0	27.8	23.0	26.5	**29.1**
2	23.5	29.4	20.6	23.5	24.7	30.6	26.2	30.3	**32.9**
3	26.2	31.4	22.1	27.6	25.1	33.3	28.5	32.7	**36.4**
4	28.9	35.0	23.5	30.8	27.9	35.7	30.5	34.5	**39.1**
5	29.4	37.3	24.1	32.2	29.7	37.6	32.2	35.8	**41.2**

observations: (1) Our model achieves the best results on all four datasets, and the improvements over the second-best range from 6% to 23%. This clearly validates the effectiveness of our model in overcoming the attribute sparsity problem. (2) The performance margin between our model and eight ZSL alternatives generally becomes bigger as fewer annotated seen class images are provided for training. Our explanation is that: other than eight ZSL alternatives, our model exploits more accurately propagated attribute annotations (obtained by SAP) for BPL. (3) Our model significantly outperforms the state-of-the-art deep ZSL models RN [55] and AREN [58], suggesting that deep models tend to suffer from the annotation sparsity and thus may not be suitable for our new setting.

Results of Generalized FSZSL. We take the generalized FSZSL setting by following [45]. K annotated images per seen class are given for model training as in the standard setting. The comparative results are presented in Table 2. Our model is still shown to achieve the best results under this more challenging setting. Importantly, the obtained even bigger margins suggest that both SAP and BPL can promote the generalization ability of our model.

---

neighbor based label propagation (NN-LP) induces much less noise. Experiments in the suppl. material also show that NN-LP is comparable to MixMatch [59] (one of the strongest, but without denoising) under our FSZSL setting. Therefore, it is reasonable to use NN-LP for all compared ZSL models.

Fig. 2. Examples of the top images returned by Google with the query 'North American Bird'. We discard the images containing multiple bird classes (marked with red boxes). (Color figure online)

4.2 FSZSL with External Data

Dataset and Settings. We construct a new dataset called CUB+Web[3] as follows: 1) The training set has 750 annotated images (5 per class) from the 150 seen classes of standard CUB [50], along with 1,205 unannotated web images obtained by Google with the query 'North American Bird'; 2) The test set has 2,946 unannotated images from the 50 unseen classes of CUB. Particularly, we first download top-2,000 web images from Google and discard the images with bird objects from multiple classes (see Fig. 2). Furthermore, we classify the obtained web images using the CNN model proposed in [51], and discard the images that are classified to unseen classes, resulting in 1,205 unannotated web images left. Since [51] has reported a very high accuracy in fine-grained classification, *the effect of possible unseen class images can be suppressed dramatically* during training our SAP model. Additionally, for CUB+Web, the semantic and feature spaces are formed exactly the same as in Section 4.1.

Comparative Results. We compare with eight closely-related ZSL models: 1) RPL0 – the reverse projection learning model [27] trained with only a few annotated seen class images; 2) RPL – the RPL model trained with not only a few annotated seen class images but also the web images with the propagated attributes obtained by our model; 3) ESZSL0 – the ESZSL model [24] trained like RPL0; 4) ESZSL – ESZSL trained like RPL; 5) SAE0 – the SAE model [12] trained like RPL0; 6) SAE – SAE trained like RPL; 7) ZSKL0 – the ZSKL model [57] trained like RPL0; 8) ZSKL – ZSKL trained like RPL.

  Note that four baselines (i.e., SSE, RN, PQZSL, and AREN) require class labels of training samples as inputs. Applying the nearest neighbor classifier like Table 1 makes no sense here, because the external images are not even guaranteed to belong to seen classes (there may be outliers although the unseen class images have been mostly removed). These baselines thus are inapplicable, but others can still benefit from external data (with propagated attributes).

---

[3] https://github.com/anonymous04321/cub-web

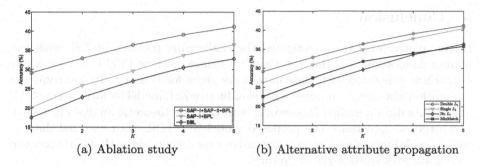

(a) Ablation study   (b) Alternative attribute propagation

Fig. 3. (a) Ablation study results for our full model on the CUB+Web dataset. (b) Comparative results obtained by different attribute propagation models (the same BPL is used for ZSL) on the CUB+Web dataset.

The comparative results in Table 3 (with K annotated images per seen class) show that: (1) The five models (i.e., RPL, ESZSL, SAE, ZSKL and ours) trained using extra web images with propagated attributes lead to significant improvements over those without using extra web images (i.e., RPL0, ESZSL0, SAE0 and ZSKL0), validating the effectiveness of our SAP method. (2) Due to iterative optimization between BPL and SAP, our model still outperforms RPL, ESZSL, SAE, and ZSKL (although they also utilize the web images with propagated attributes obtained by our SAP method).

Further Evaluation. 1) Ablation Study. To evaluate the contribution of each component (SAP-I, SAP-II, or BPL) of our full model, we conduct experiments by adding more components to the BPL model. The ablative results in Fig. 3(a) show that: (1) The SAP-I step by solving Eq. (5) yields better results (see SAP-I+BPL vs. BPL). (2) The SAP-II step by solving Eq. (7) obtains further improvements (see SAP-I+SAP-II+BPL vs. SAP-I+BPL), which become more significant with fewer annotated seen class images (i.e., smaller K).

2) Alternative Attribute Propagation. We compare four alternative attribute propagation models: 1) 'Double L_1': our model formulated in Eq. (2); 2) 'Single L_1': $\|\mathbf{B}\tilde{\mathbf{Y}}^T\|_1$ used in our model is replaced by $\|\mathbf{B}\tilde{\mathbf{Y}}^T\|_F^2$; 3) 'No L_1': $\|\mathbf{Y} - \mathbf{Y}^{(s)}\|_1$ is removed from the second model 'Single L_1'; 4) 'MixMatch' [59]: our SAP is replaced by the state-of-the-art semi-supervised learning (SSL) method to perform attribute propagation. The comparative results are presented in Fig. 3(b). As expected, more L_1-norm regularization terms used for attribute propagation lead to better results, due to the stronger noise reduction ability. Interestingly, under our FSZSL setting where only few labelled seen class samples can be used as initial supervision, MixMatch (one of the strongest, but without denoising) performs even worse than 'Double L_1' and 'Single L_1'. This shows the importance of noise reduction during performing attribute propagation for FSZSL (which is also our main motivation of developing SAP).

5   Conclusion

In this paper, we have investigated the challenging problem of ZSL with less human annotation. For the first time, we define the new FSZSL setting where only a few annotated seen class images are given for training. To overcome the annotation sparsity, we propose a novel inductive ZSL model by formulating SAP and BPL within a unified framework, with rigorous theoretic analysis provided. Moreover, we generalize the proposed model to FSZSL with external data as well as social image annotation. Extensive experiments show that the proposed model achieves state-of-the-art results.

Acknowledgements. This work was supported in part by National Natural Science Foundation of China (61976220 and 61832017), and Beijing Outstanding Young Scientist Program (BJJWZYJH012019100020098).

References

1. Krizhevsky, A., Sutskever, I., Hinton, G.E.: ImageNet classification with deep convolutional neural networks. Adv. Neural Inf. Process. Syst. **25**, 1097–1105 (2012)
2. Simonyan, K., Zisserman, A.: Very deep convolutional networks for large-scale image recognition. arXiv preprint arXiv:1409.1556 (2014)
3. Russakovsky, O., et al.: ImageNet large scale visual recognition challenge. IJCV **115**, 211–252 (2015)
4. He, K., Zhang, X., Ren, S., Sun, J.: Deep residual learning for image recognition. In: CVPR, pp. 770–778 (2016)
5. Fu, Y., Hospedales, T.M., Xiang, T., Gong, S.: Transductive multi-view zero-shot learning. TPAMI **37**, 2332–2345 (2015)
6. Fu, Z., Xiang, T., Kodirov, E., Gong, S.: Zero-shot object recognition by semantic manifold distance. In: CVPR, pp. 2635–2644 (2015)
7. Ba, L.J., Swersky, K., Fidler, S., Salakhutdinov, R.: Predicting deep zero-shot convolutional neural networks using textual descriptions. In: ICCV, pp. 4247–4255 (2015)
8. Qiao, R., Liu, L., Shen, C., van den Hengel, A.: Less is more: zero-shot learning from online textual documents with noise suppression. In: CVPR, pp. 2249–2257 (2016)
9. Ye, M., Guo, Y.: Zero-shot classification with discriminative semantic representation learning. In: CVPR, pp. 7140–7148 (2017)
10. Karessli, N., Akata, Z., Schiele, B., Bulling, A., et al.: Gaze embeddings for zero-shot image classification. In: CVPR, pp. 4525–4534 (2017)
11. Long, Y., Shao, L.: Learning to recognise unseen classes by a few similes. In: ACM-MM, pp. 636–644 (2017)
12. Kodirov, E., Xiang, T., Gong, S.: Semantic autoencoder for zero-shot learning. In: CVPR, pp. 3174–3183 (2017)
13. Wang, W., Pu, Y., Verma, V., et al.: Zero-shot learning via class-conditioned deep generative models. In: AAAI, pp. 4211–4218 (2018)
14. Lampert, C.H., Nickisch, H., Harmeling, S.: Attribute-based classification for zero-shot visual object categorization. TPAMI **36**, 453–465 (2014)
15. Lee, H., Battle, A., Raina, R., Ng, A.: Efficient sparse coding algorithms. In: Advances in Neural Information Processing Systems, pp. 801–808 (2007)

16. Sinha, K., Belkin, M.: Semi-supervised learning using sparse eigenfunction bases. In: Advances in Neural Information Processing Systems, pp. 1687–1695 (2010)
17. Johnson, J., Ballan, L., Fei-Fei, L.: Love thy neighbors: image annotation by exploiting image metadata. In: ICCV, pp. 4624–4632 (2015)
18. Hu, H., Zhou, G.T., Deng, Z., Liao, Z., Mori, G.: Learning structured inference neural networks with label relations. In: CVPR, pp. 2960–2968 (2016)
19. Liu, F., Xiang, T., Hospedales, T.M., Yang, W., Sun, C.: Semantic regularisation for recurrent image annotation. In: CVPR, pp. 4160–4168 (2017)
20. Zhang, Z., Saligrama, V.: Zero-shot learning via semantic similarity embedding. In: ICCV, pp. 4166–4174 (2015)
21. Changpinyo, S., Chao, W., Gong, B., Sha, F.: Synthesized classifiers for zero-shot learning. In: CVPR, pp. 5327–5336 (2016)
22. Liu, G., Guan, J., Zhang, M., Zhang, J., Wang, Z., Lu, Z.: Joint projection and subspace learning for zero-shot recognition. In: ICME, pp. 1228–1233 (2019)
23. Li, J., Lan, X., Liu, Y., Wang, L., Zheng, N.: Compressing unknown images with product quantizer for efficient zero-shot classification. In: CVPR, pp. 5463–5472 (2019)
24. Romera-Paredes, B., Torr, P.H.S.: An embarrassingly simple approach to zero-shot learning. In: ICML, pp. 2152–2161 (2015)
25. Kodirov, E., Xiang, T., Fu, Z., Gong, S.: Unsupervised domain adaptation for zero-shot learning. In: ICCV, pp. 2452–2460 (2015)
26. Zhang, F., Shi, G.: Co-representation network for generalized zero-shot learning. In: ICML, pp. 7434–7443 (2019)
27. Shigeto, Y., Suzuki, I., Hara, K., Shimbo, M., Matsumoto, Y.: Ridge regression, hubness, and zero-shot learning. In: Appice, A., Rodrigues, P.P., Santos Costa, V., Soares, C., Gama, J., Jorge, A. (eds.) ECML PKDD 2015. LNCS (LNAI), vol. 9284, pp. 135–151. Springer, Cham (2015). https://doi.org/10.1007/978-3-319-23528-8_9
28. Zhao, A., Ding, M., Guan, J., Lu, Z., Xiang, T., Wen, J.R.: Domain-invariant projection learning for zero-shot recognition. In: Advances in Neural Information Processing Systems, pp. 1027–1038 (2018)
29. Li, A., Lu, Z., Guan, J., Xiang, T., Wang, L., Wen, J.R.: Transferrable feature and projection learning with class hierarchy for zero-shot learning. IJCV **128**, 1–18 (2020)
30. Huo, Y., Guan, J., Zhang, J., Zhang, M., Wen, J.R., Lu, Z.: Zero-shot learning with few seen class samples. In: ICME, pp. 1336–1341 (2019)
31. Guan, J., Lu, Z., Xiang, T., Li, A., Zhao, A., Wen, J.R.: Zero and few shot learning with semantic feature synthesis and competitive learning. TPAMI, 1–14 (2020)
32. Long, Y., Shao, L.: Describing unseen classes by exemplars: zero-shot learning using grouped simile ensemble. In: WACV, pp. 907–915 (2017)
33. Li, A., Lu, Z., Wang, L., Xiang, T., Wen, J.R.: Zero-shot scene classification for high spatial resolution remote sensing images. IEEE Trans. Geosci. Remote Sens. **55**, 4157–4167 (2017)
34. Li, X., Guo, Y., Schuurmans, D.: Semi-supervised zero-shot classification with label representation learning. In: ICCV, pp. 4211–4219 (2015)
35. Guo, Y., Ding, G., Jin, X., Wang, J.: Transductive zero-shot recognition via shared model space learning. In: AAAI, pp. 3494–3500 (2016)
36. Shojaee, S.M., Baghshah, M.S.: Semi-supervised zero-shot learning by a clustering-based approach. arXiv preprint arXiv:1605.09016 (2016)
37. Wang, Q., Chen, K.: Zero-shot visual recognition via bidirectional latent embedding. IJCV **124**, 356–383 (2017)
38. Yu, Y., et al.: Transductive zero-shot learning with a self-training dictionary approach. arXiv preprint arXiv:1703.08893 (2017)

39. Bergamo, A., Torresani, L.: Exploiting weakly-labeled web images to improve object classification: a domain adaptation approach. Adv. Neural Inf. Process. Syst. **23**, 181–189 (2010)
40. Duan, L., Xu, D., Chang, S.F.: Exploiting web images for event recognition in consumer videos: a multiple source domain adaptation approach. In: CVPR, pp. 1338–1345 (2012)
41. Zhang, H., Liu, S., Zhang, C., Ren, W., Wang, R., Cao, X.: SketchNet: sketch classification with web images. In: CVPR, pp. 1105–1113 (2016)
42. Niu, L., Tang, Q., Veeraraghavan, A., Sabharwal, A.: Learning from noisy web data with category-level supervision. In: CVPR, pp. 7689–7698 (2018)
43. Niu, L., Veeraraghavan, A., Sabharwal, A.: Webly supervised learning meets zero-shot learning: a hybrid approach for fine-grained classification. In: CVPR, pp. 7171–7180 (2018)
44. Gan, C., Sun, C., Nevatia, R.: Deck: discovering event composition knowledge from web images for zero-shot event detection and recounting in videos. In: AAAI, pp. 4032–4038 (2017)
45. Chao, W.-L., Changpinyo, S., Gong, B., Sha, F.: An empirical study and analysis of generalized zero-shot learning for object recognition in the wild. In: Leibe, B., Matas, J., Sebe, N., Welling, M. (eds.) ECCV 2016. LNCS, vol. 9906, pp. 52–68. Springer, Cham (2016). https://doi.org/10.1007/978-3-319-46475-6_4
46. Rahman, S., Khan, S.H., Porikli, F.: A unified approach for conventional zero-shot, generalized zero-shot and few-shot learning. arXiv preprint arXiv:1706.08653 (2017)
47. Xian, Y., Schiele, B., Akata, Z.: Zero-shot learning - the good, the bad and the ugly. In: CVPR, pp. 4582–4591 (2017)
48. Lu, X., Tsao, Y., Matsuda, S., Hori, C.: Speech enhancement based on deep denoising autoencoder. In: Interspeech, pp. 436–440 (2013)
49. Feng, F., Wang, X., Li, R.: Cross-modal retrieval with correspondence autoencoder. In: ACM-MM, pp. 7–16 (2014)
50. Wah, C., Branson, S., Welinder, P., Perona, P., Belongie, S.: The Caltech-UCSD birds-200-2011 dataset. Technical report CNS-TR-2011-001, California Institute of Technology (2011)
51. Yu, C., Zhao, X., Zheng, Q., Zhang, P., You, X.: Hierarchical bilinear pooling for fine-grained visual recognition. In: ECCV, pp. 595–610 (2018)
52. Farhadi, A., Endres, I., Hoiem, D., Forsyth, D.: Describing objects by their attributes. In: CVPR, pp. 1778–1785 (2009)
53. Patterson, G., Xu, C., Su, H., Hays, J.: The sun attribute database: beyond categories for deeper scene understanding. IJCV **108**, 59–81 (2014)
54. Chen, L., Zhang, H., Xiao, J., Liu, W., Chang, S.F.: Zero-shot visual recognition using semantics-preserving adversarial embedding networks. In: CVPR, pp. 1043–1052 (2018)
55. Sung, F., Yang, Y., Zhang, L., Xiang, T., Torr, P.H., Hospedales, T.M.: Learning to compare: relation network for few-shot learning. In: CVPR, pp. 1199–1208 (2018)
56. Xian, Y., Lorenz, T., Schiele, B., Akata, Z.: Feature generating networks for zero-shot learning. In: CVPR, pp. 5542–5551 (2018)
57. Zhang, H., Koniusz, P.: Zero-shot kernel learning. In: CVPR, pp. 7670–7679 (2018)
58. Xie, G.S., et al.: Attentive region embedding network for zero-shot learning. In: CVPR, pp. 9384–9393 (2019)
59. Berthelot, D., Carlini, N., Goodfellow, I.J., Papernot, N., Oliver, A., Raffel, C.: Mixmatch: a holistic approach to semi-supervised learning. In: Advances in Neural Information Processing Systems, pp. 5050–5060 (2019)

Lossless Image Compression Using a Multi-scale Progressive Statistical Model

Honglei Zhang[1]([✉])[iD], Francesco Cricri[1][iD], Hamed R. Tavakoli[1][iD],
Nannan Zou[1,2][iD], Emre Aksu[1][iD], and Miska M. Hannuksela[1][iD]

[1] Nokia Technologies, Tampere, Finland
{honglei.1.zhang,francesco.cricri,hamed.rezazadegan_tavakoli,
nannan.zou,emre.aksu,miska.hannuksela}@nokia.com
[2] Tampere University, Tampere, Finland
http://www.nokia.com

Abstract. Lossless image compression is an important technique for image storage and transmission when information loss is not allowed. With the fast development of deep learning techniques, deep neural networks have been used in this field to achieve a higher compression rate. Methods based on pixel-wise autoregressive statistical models have shown good performance. However, the sequential processing way prevents these methods to be used in practice. Recently, multi-scale autoregressive models have been proposed to address this limitation. Multi-scale approaches can use parallel computing systems efficiently and build practical systems. Nevertheless, these approaches sacrifice compression performance in exchange for speed. In this paper, we propose a multi-scale progressive statistical model that takes advantage of the pixel-wise approach and the multi-scale approach. We developed a flexible mechanism where the processing order of the pixels can be adjusted easily. Our proposed method outperforms the state-of-the-art lossless image compression methods on two large benchmark datasets by a significant margin without degrading the inference speed dramatically.

1 Introduction

A lossless image compression system converts an input image into a bitstream that is smaller in size and the original image can be fully reconstructed. These systems bring several benefits in data storage, manipulating, and transferring where information loss is not allowed. On the other hand, lossy image compression aims at a much higher compression rate by allowing the data to be reconstructed with a certain amount of degradation. PNG [1] and FLIF [2] are image formats that support lossless image compression. Other image compression techniques, such as JPEG 2000 [3], WebP[4], and HEVC [5] support both lossy and lossless image compression.

Electronic supplementary material The online version of this chapter (https://doi.org/10.1007/978-3-030-69535-4_37) contains supplementary material, which is available to authorized users.

© Springer Nature Switzerland AG 2021
H. Ishikawa et al. (Eds.): ACCV 2020, LNCS 12624, pp. 609–622, 2021.
https://doi.org/10.1007/978-3-030-69535-4_37

A typical lossless image compression system contains a probability model and an entropy codec. The probability model is built up from a statistical model that gives an estimation of the statistical characteristics of an input image. The entropy codec encodes/decodes symbols in the input data into/from variable-length prefix-free codes according to the statistics given by the probability model. According to Shannon's source coding theorem [6], the optimal code length of a symbol is $-\log_2 P$, where P is the probability of the symbol to be encoded. Arithmetic coding is an efficient entropy coding algorithm that has been adopted in many image/video coding systems, such as HEVC [5].

Accurate probability estimation is the most critical aspect of a lossless image compression system. Traditional lossless image compression system, such as PNG [1] uses a static statistical model with Huffman coding to encode the difference of the pixels and the predicted value based on its neighboring pixels. AVC [7] and HEVC [5] applies an adaptive model, known as CABAC, to give a better estimation of the probabilities [8]. The CABAC model updates the model parameters during the process of encoding/decoding according to the content of the image. With the fast development of deep learning techniques, deep neural networks have been used to achieve more accurate statistical estimations [9–15]. Unlike traditional image/video coding systems [5,7], which encode residuals between the input symbols and the predicted symbols, deep neural network-based image/video compression systems normally use the estimated value distribution function directly, since deep neural networks are more capable of modeling complicated distribution functions.

An autoregressive statistical model uses pixels that have already been processed as a context to derive the value distribution function of the pixels to be encoded/decoded [16–18]. These models can achieve good compression rates. However, at the inference stage, i.e. encode/decoding stage, the input data are processed sequentially and an expensive deep neural network is involved to process every pixel. Thus, the systems based on these models are only capable of encoding/decoding small images [15]. To address this problem, L3C [15] and SReC [14] adopt a multi-scale approach. Pixels at each scale are processed in a parallel manner, which greatly speeds up the encoding/decoding procedure. However, the compression rate is compromised significantly. In [13], the authors proposed another type of context-based statistical model where an input image is first compressed with a lossy compression method and then used as the context to infer the value distribution function of the pixels in an input image.

Flow-based approach [9,12,19] learns a invertible function that converts an input image into a latent representation with a predefined distribution function. At the decoding stage, the inverse function of the encoding function is applied to reconstruct the input image. These algorithms also process pixels in a parallel manner and have similar computation complexities for encoding and decoding. However, the capacity of these methods is limited by the constrain that the encoding and decoding functions must be mutually invertible. Large neural networks have to be used to improve the performance of the system.

In this paper, we propose a lossless image compression system based on a multi-scale progressive statistical model. The proposed method significantly improves the compression rate without heavily degrading the encoding/decoding speed. Our system incorporates a flexible framework where the compression rate and encoding/decoding speed can be adjusted easily. Using the proposed model, we have improved the state-of-the-art compression rate on the ImageNet64 dataset and the OpenImage dataset by a significant margin.

2   Related Work

2.1   Pixel-Wise Autoregressive Statistical Model

Pixel-wise autoregressive statistical models, such as PixelRNN [17], PixelCNN [16] and PixelCNN++ [18], model the joint distribution of the pixels in an image as the product of the distribution of each pixel conditioned on the previous pixels. Let x be an image, N be the number of pixels, and $x_1, x_2, \cdots, x_N$ be the pixels arranged in a certain order, for example, a raster scan order. The joint distribution of x is defined by

$$p(x) = \prod_{i=1}^{N} p\left(x_i | x_1, x_2, \cdots, x_{i-1}\right), \tag{1}$$

where $p\left(x_i | x_1, x_2, \cdots, x_{i-1}\right)$ is modeled by a deep neural network. During the training and encoding stage, a masked convolutional neural network (CNN) is applied to ensure that the probability estimation of the current pixel only depends on the previous pixels. More importantly, with the masked CNN architecture the system can be trained efficiently as a standard deep CNN. However, at the decoding stage, pixels can only be processed sequentially. This limitation prevents the pixel-wise autoregressive model from being used in practice [15].

2.2   Multi-scale Autoregressive Statistical Model

Multi-scale autoregressive statistical models proposed in L3C [15] and SReC [14] model the joint distribution of x as the product of the conditional distributions in multiple scales. Let M be the number of scales, and $x^{(i)}$ be the representation at scale i. For simplicity, we use $x^{(0)}$ to denote the input image. We have $x^{(i)} = E\left(x^{(i-1)}\right)$, where $E(\cdot)$ is a encoding function that performs a type of downsampling operation to an input representation. Let $C^{(i)} = \left\{x^{(i)}, x^{(i+1)}, \cdots, x^{(M)}\right\}$ be the set of representations from scale i to scale M. The joint distribution of $x^{(0)}, x^{(1)}, \cdots, x^{(M)}$ is defined by

$$p\left(x^{(0)}, x^{(1)}, \cdots, x^{(M)}\right) = \left(\prod_{i=0}^{M-1} p\left(x^{(i)} | C^{(i+1)}\right)\right) p\left(x^{(M)}\right), \tag{2}$$

where $p\left(x^{(M)}\right)$ is the distribution function of the last scale and modeled by the assumption that the elements in $x^{(M)}$ are independent and uniform distributed. The conditional distribution at scale i is parameterized as

$$p\left(x^{(i)}|C^{(i+1)}\right) = p\left(x^{(i)}|y^{(i+1)}\right), \tag{3}$$

where $y^{(i)} = D\left(y^{(i+1)}, x^{(i)}\right)$, and $D(\cdot)$ is a decoder function implemented using a deep neural network. The system is trained to optimize the cross entropy with respect to the estimated probability distribution $p\left(x^{(0)}|y^{(1)}\right)$.

2.3   Flow-Based Statistical Model

Flow-based generative method is another technique that has been recently used for lossless image compression, for example, in LBB [9], Integer Flows [12], and Real-NVP [19]. A flow-based method learns an invertible mapping function from the image space to a latent space where the dependent variable follows a predefined distribution function. Let the mapping function be $z = f(x)$ where z is the dependent variable in the latent space with a predefined distribution function $p_Z(z)$. The distribution function of input x is defined by

$$p(x) = p_Z(f(x)) \left| \det\left(\frac{\partial f(x)}{\partial x}\right) \right|, \tag{4}$$

where $\det(\cdot)$ is the determinant of a matrix. Because of the determinant operation, the Jacobian of $f(x)$ at x must have certain forms, for example, be a diagonal or upper triangular matrix. In Real-NVP [19], Dinh et.al. proposed a invertible function using coupling layers that are defined by

$$z_{1:d} = x_{1:d} \tag{5}$$
$$z_{d+1:N} = x_{d+1:N} \odot \exp\left(s\left(x_{1:d}\right)\right) + t\left(x_{1:d}\right), \tag{6}$$

where N is the dimension of the input variable, $s(\cdot)$ and $t(\cdot)$ are scale and translation functions, and $\odot$ is element-wise product. The coupling layer partition the variables in x into two sets $x_{1:d}$ and $x_{d+1:N}$. $x_{1:d}$ is directly mapped to the corresponding output variables. $x_{d+1:N}$ is mapped to the output variables using scale and translation factors that are derived from $x_{1:d}$.

Next, we will give a detailed description of our proposed statistical model and our lossless image compression system.

3   Multi-scale Progressive Statistical Model

3.1   Statistical Model

Similar to multi-scale approaches [14,15], we downsample an input image into a number of low-resolution representations. Pixels in lower resolution representations are used as a context to estimate the distribution function of the pixels in a higher resolution representation.

In L3C [15], a representation $x^{(i+1)}$ is derived from representation $x^{(i)}$ using an encoder function $E(\cdot)$. This design not only complicates the system but also makes the training less efficient since the system becomes a very deep neural network from the end-to-end point of view. Experiments show that increasing the number of scales does not improve the performance [15]. In SReC [14], the encoder function is defined as an average pooling function. SReC can be trained more efficiently than L3C. However, extra bits must be used to encode round errors. Inspired by the coupling layer in Real-NVP [19], we simply take a subset of pixels in $x^{(i)}$ as $x^{(i+1)}$. With this simplification, the probability distribution function $p\left(x^{(0)}\right)$ can be directly factorized as

$$p\left(x^{(0)}\right) = \left(\prod_{i=0}^{M-1} p\left(x^{(i)}|C^{(i+1)}\right)\right) p\left(x^{(M)}\right) \qquad (7)$$

To further improve the compression rate without dramatically compromizing the encoding/decoding speed, we partition the pixels at each scale into groups, i.e. $x^{(i)} = g_1^{(i)} \cup g_2^{(i)} \cup \cdots \cup g_{B_i}^{(i)}$, where B_i is the number of groups at scale i. The details of the grouping methods will be described in Sect. 3.3. The groups are processed sequentially. Once all pixels in a group are processed, they are added to the context to improve the estimation accuracy of the pixels in the next group. Taking this grouping operation into consideration, we can further factorize Eq. 7 to

$$p\left(x^{(i)}|C^{(i+1)}\right) = \prod_{j=1}^{B_i} p\left(g_j^{(i)}|g_1^{(i)}, g_2^{(i)}, \cdots, g_{j-1}^{(i)}, C^{(i+1)}\right), \qquad (8)$$

where $g_j^{(i)}$ is the pixel group j at scale i, B_i is the number of groups at scale i, and $i = 0, 1, \cdots, M - 1$. Let $G_j^{(i)} = \left\{g_1^{(i)}, g_2^{(i)}, \cdots, g_{j-1}^{(i)}, C^{(i+1)}\right\}$ be the context for group $g_j^{(i)}$. Assuming the pixels in a group are conditional independent, we have the probability distribution function

$$p\left(g_j^{(i)}|G_j^{(i)}\right) = \prod_{k=1}^{N_j^{(i)}} p\left(x_{j,k}^{(i)}|G_j^{(i)}\right), \qquad (9)$$

where $x_{j,k}^{(i)} \in g_j^{(i)}$ is pixel k in group j at scale i, and $N_j^{(i)}$ is the number of pixels in group $g_j^{(i)}$.

Next, we use a mixture of logistic distributions to model $p\left(x_{j,k}^{(i)}|G_j^{(i)}\right)$ in a similar way as defined in PixelCNN++ [18]. The parameters of the mixture model $p\left(x_{j,k}^{(i)}|G_j^{(i)}\right)$ are derived from a function of context $G_j^{(i)}$ using a deep neural network. Note that, in this model, the logistic mean of the distribution function of a subpixel is modeled as a weighted sum of the logistic means of previous subpixels.

Given the statistical model defined by Eqs. 7, 8, and 9, the deep neural network is trained to minimize the cross entropy of the input $x^{(0)}$, i.e.

$$\mathbb{E}_{x^{(0)} \sim q(x)} \left[-\log p \left(x^{(0)} \right) \right], \tag{10}$$

where $q(x)$ is the true distribution of the input image and $\mathbb{E}(\cdot)$ is the expectation of a random variable.

3.2   Lossless Image Compression System

Figure 1 illustrates our lossless image compression system using the proposed multi-scale progressive statistical model. For clarity, the figure only shows a system of two scales.

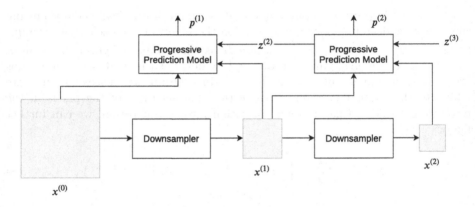

Fig. 1. The lossless image compression system using the proposed multi-scale progressive statistical model. Yellow boxes indicate tensors. (Color figure online)

In this system, an input image $x^{(0)}$ is first downsampled to low-resolution representations $x^{(1)}$ and $x^{(2)}$. As mentioned in Sect. 3.1, we take a subset of pixels in $x^{(i)}$ as $x^{(i+1)}$. If the pixels are selected in a checkerboard pattern, the system is equivalent to using the nearest neighbor downsampling operation as the encoder function $E(\cdot)$ as used in [14,15]. This simplification improves training efficiency and helps us to develop a more flexible architecture to achieve better performance. With this design, we can increase the number of scales without suffering from the gradient vanishing/exploding problem that a very deep neural network system may encounter.

Figure 2 illustrates the progressive prediction model at scale i, which is the core component of our system. An input tensor $x^{(i)}$ is first upsampled to $\hat{x}_1^{(i)}$ to have the same size as tensor $x^{(i-1)}$. For simplicity, we choose the nearest-neighbor upsampling method in our experiments. Next, $\hat{x}_1^{(i)}$ is partitioned into multiple groups as described in Sect. 3.1. For each group of pixels, a deep CNN is used to estimate the parameters for the value distribution functions of the pixels

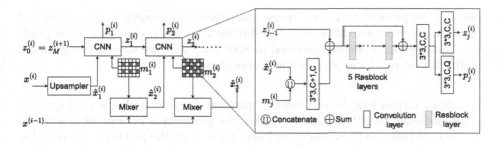

Fig. 2. The architecture of the progressive prediction model in Fig. 1. The notations in convolution blocks are in the format of "kernel_size*kernel_size, input_channels,output_channels". The Resblock layer is the basic Resnet block defined in [20]. No batch normalization is used in the system. C is the network size and Q is the number of parameters for the mixture of logistic distributions model.

in that group. The detailed structure of this deep CNN is illustrated on the right side of Fig. 2. The deep CNN takes three inputs: $\hat{x}_j^{(i)}$ is the tensor that holds a mixture of predicted and true values of pixels in $x^{(i-1)}$; $m_j^{(i)}$ is the binary mask that indicates the true values in $x_j^{(i)}$; $z_{j-1}^{(i)}$ is the context information passed from the previous stage. The initial context $z_0^{(i)}$ is set to be the output context of scale $i + 1$. For the last scale when there is no context information available, we set the context to be zero, i.e. $z_0^M = 0$. The deep CNN outputs parameters $p_j^{(i)}$ for the estimated value distribution functions of the pixels in group j, and the context information $z_j^{(i)}$.

At the training and encoding stage, where the ground truth $x^{(i-1)}$ is available, after the pixels in group j have been processed, the system sets the corresponding values in $\hat{x}_{j+1}^{(i)}$ with the true pixel values using the mixer component, and updates mask $m_{j+1}^{(i)}$ accordingly. Then, $\hat{x}_{j+1}^{(i)}$, $m_{j+1}^{(i)}$ and $z_j^{(i)}$ are passed to the deep CNN to derive $p_{j+1}^{(i)}$ and $z_{j+1}^{(i)}$. The entropy of the pixels in group $j+1$ is calculated using $p_{j+1}^{(i)}$ and $x^{(i)}$ at the training stage. At the encoding stage, the pixels are encoded by the arithmetic encoder according to the estimated value distribution function using parameters $p_{j+1}^{(i)}$. At the decoding stage, the estimated value distribution functions for pixels in group j are used to decode the true values from the bitstream using the arithmetic decoder. $\hat{x}_{j+1}^{(i)}$ and $m_{j+1}^{(i)}$ are updated in the same way as the training and encoding stage. This procedure continues until all $B^{(i)}$ groups are processed.

3.3   Pixel Grouping Methods

Using the binary mask $m_j^{(i)}$, one can easily set the number of groups and the method to group the pixels. The grouping methods determine the order of the pixels to be processed. In an extreme case when $B^{(i)}$ is equal to the number of pixels to be processed at scale i, the statistical model is equivalent to a pixel-wise autoregressive model described in Sect. 2.1. Next, we show some grouping methods that can be applied in the proposed system.

Random Grouping. In this method, pixels to be processed at scale i are randomly assigned to $B^{(i)}$ groups. Note that the grouping is performed in advance and agreed between the encoder and decoder so that the pixels can be decoded correctly at the decoding stage.

Grouping with a Fixed Pattern. With this method, the pixels are grouped by a predetermined fixed pattern. Figure 3 shows two options for the fixed pattern grouping. In (a), an input image is first partitioned into 4×4 blocks and the pixels are grouped according to the index number shown in the figure. Note that this grouping method is similar to the architecture in [14]. Since the value distribution function are estimated using the available pixels in the neighboring area as the context, it is intuitive to process the pixels that have the most available pixels in its neighboring area. In (b), the pixels are assigned to 6 groups in the order of the number of available neighboring pixels.

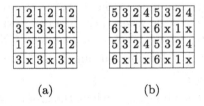

(a)   (b)

Fig. 3. Two grouping methods with fixed patterns. (a) Grouping method (3 groups) by a fixed pattern similar to [14]; (b) Grouping method (6 groups) according to the number of availability pixels in the neighboring area. "x" indicates available pixels before grouping. The number indicates the group to which the pixel belongs. Pixels are processed group by group according to their group index number.

Dynamic Grouping. Instead of using a predefined fixed pattern, one can also group the pixels dynamically according to the content of the image. For example, the grouping can be determined by the expected entropy values of the pixels. As the progressive statistical model outputs the parameters of the value distribution functions, the expected entropy values can be calculated. However, this calculation is quite expensive. We chose to use an upper bound to approximate the expected entropy values. Let random variable X follow a mixture of logistic distributions determined by the number of mixtures K, mixture weights π_k, means μ_k and scales s_k where $k = 1, 2, \cdots, K$. An upper bound of the expected entropy of X can be defined by

$$U(X) = \sum_{k=1}^{K} \pi_k \log \pi_k + \sum_{k=1}^{K} \pi_k (\ln s_k + 2). \tag{11}$$

The derivation of this upper bound can be found in the appendix. Given the approximation of the expected entropy values defined by Eq. 11, the pixels can be processed in an ascending order or descending order. Our experiments have shown that the descending order yields a better compression rate. In practice, this means that the system should process the most difficult pixels first. This counter-intuitive behavior actually helps to improve the overall compression rate since determining the most difficult pixels can make other pixels more predictable. This can be easily understood in the case of determining the borderline of two homogeneous areas.

4 Experiments

4.1 Impact of Grouping Method

We first evaluate the impact of the grouping methods described in Sect. 3.3. In this experiment, we trained the proposed probability model with different grouping methods using the training split of the CIFAR-10 dataset [21]. 3-scale architecture is used. For the dynamic grouping method, we partitioned the pixels into 3 groups at each scale according to the estimated entropy upper bound calculated using Eq. 11. We used the Adam optimization method with a learning rate of 1E-4 and a batch size of 128. Since CIFAR-10 is a dataset of small images (size 32×32), we trained the system until the training converged. Table 1 shows bits-per-pixel (BPP) results on the validation split of the CIFAR-10 dataset.

Table 1. Compression rate in bits-per-pixel on the validation split of the CIFAR-10 dataset using different grouping methods described in Sect. 3.3.

Random grouping	Fixed pattern (a)	Fixed pattern (b)	Dynamic grouping
10.83	10.66	**10.45**	10.60

Table 1 shows that an ordered grouping method performs better than the random grouping method. It also shows that the dynamic grouping method described in Sect. 3.3 has a better compression rate comparing to the fixed pattern (a) in Fig. 3. It should be noted that the two methods have the same number of groups at each scale. According to the results, increasing the number of groups can significantly improve the compression rate as the fixed pattern (b), which contains 6 groups of pixels at each scale, outperforms all other grouping methods (3 groups) with a significant margin. In our experiments, we also noticed that the system with a fixed pattern grouping method converged faster than the dynamic grouping method.

4.2   Impact of the Number of Scales

In this experiment, we evaluated the impact of the number of scales using the CIFAR-10 dataset. We use the fixed pattern (a) as the grouping method. All other system parameters are the same except for the number of scales.

The results in Table 2 show that increasing the number of scales can improve the compression rate. However, the improvement from 4 scales to 5 scales is negligible. Note that the tensor size at scale 4 accounts for less than 0.4% of the input image. Compressing this small amount of data does not bring much benefit to the overall compression rate.

Table 2. Compression rate in bits-per-pixel on the validation split of the CIFAR-10 dataset using different scales.

2 scales	3 scales	4 scales	5 scales
10.95	10.66	10.614	**10.612**

4.3   Compression Performance on the ImageNet64 and the OpenImage Dataset

Next, we compare the proposed method against other state-of-the-art methods on the two main datasets that have been used to benchmark lossless image compression methods. The ImageNet64 dataset [22] contains images from the ImageNet dataset [23] that are downsampled to 64×64 pixels. The training split contains 1.28M images and the validation split contains 50K images. The OpenImage dataset [24] is a dataset with 9M images with annotations for various computer vision tasks. For a fair comparison, we prepared the training and the validation split of the OpenImage dataset in the same way as [13–15]. PNG format of the OpenImage dataset was used to avoid JPEG compression artifacts as suggested in [14].

We define three profiles, as shown in Table 3, for our lossless image compression system and evaluated their performance on the ImageNet64 and the OpenImage dataset. The difference between the "big" and the "normal' profile is the grouping method. Note that fixed pattern (b) has 6 groups at each scale while fixed pattern (a) has 3 groups. The "extra" profile defines a bigger system by increasing the number of scales from 3 to 4, the network size (the number of channels used in convolution layers) from 64 to 128, and the number of mixtures of the mixture of logistic distributions from 5 to 10. Note that the "big" profile does not increase the network size compared to the "normal" profile.

Table 3. The three profiles used to evaluate system performance.

	Normal	Big	Extra
Scales	3	3	4
Grouping method	Fixed pattern (a)	Fixed pattern (b)	Fixed pattern (b)
Network size	64	64	128
Number of mixtures	5	5	10

The system is trained with Adam optimization and learning rate 2×10^{-4} without weight decay. For the ImageNet64 dataset, the batch size is set to 64. For the OpenImage dataset, we use randomly cropped $128x \times 128$ patches from input images as the input. The batch size for the "normal" profile is 64, the "big" profile is 32, and the "extra" profile is 16. The learning rate is dropped by 10 times if a plateau is reached. The ImageNet64 dataset is trained for 40 epochs and the OpenImage dataset is trained for 20 epochs. All experiments had been executed on an NVIDIA DGX-1 system with Tesla V100 GPUs. All training was performed on a single GPU training mode.

The validation split of the OpenImage dataset contains 500 images randomly selected from the original validation set of the OpenImage dataset. The selected images are the same as those used in [13–15]. If an input image is too large to be processed because of the limitation of the GPU memory, we partition the image into patches and the bitstreams of all patches are concatenated to generate the final output file. The size of the patches is 496×496 for the "normal" and the "big" profile, and 256 for the "extra" profile. We note that this tiling operation degrades the compression rate because of the border effects. The reported compression rates of our methods are calculated from the size of the final output file which includes also extra metadata information such as image size and the number of scales.

Table 4 shows the compression results on the validation split of the ImageNet64 and the OpenImage dataset. To be compared with other literature, both bits-per-pixel and bits-per-subpixel (shown in parenthesis) are reported. The parameter column shows the number of parameters for the neural network-based methods.

Table 4. Compression results on the validation split of the ImageNet64 dataset and the OpenImage dataset. The numbers under the datasets columns are bits-per-pixel and bits-per-subpixel (in parenthesis). An empty cell indicates that the field is not relevant and "-" symbol indicates that the value is not reported by the authors.

	Method	Parameters	ImageNet64	OpenImage
Traditional	PNG [14]		17.22 (5.74)	12.09 (4.03)
	WebP [14]		13.92 (4.64)	9.09 (3.03)
	FLIF [14]		13.62 (4.54)	8.61 (2.87)
Flow-based	IDF [12]	84.33M	11.70 (3.90)	8.28 (2.76)
VAE-based	HiLLoC [10]	-	11.70 (3.90)	-
Context-based	RC [13]	-	-	8.37 (2.79)
	L3C [15]	5.01M	13.26 (4.42)	8.97 (2.99)
	SReC [14]	4.20M	12.90 (4.29)	8.10 (2.70)
	Ours (normal)	**1.87M**	11.89 (3.96)	8.14 (2.71)
	Ours (big)	**1.87M**	11.78 (3.93)	7.88 (2.63)
	Ours (extra)	9.93M	**11.33 (3.78)**	**7.48 (2.49)**

The results in Table 4 show that our methods significantly improve the compression rate on the ImageNet64 dataset with a much smaller model. The previous state-of-the-art method achieved 11.70 BPP with a model of 84.33M parameters and the proposed model achieved 11.33 BPP with a model of 9.93M parameters. On the OpenImage validation dataset, the "normal" profile achieves the same level of performance as the previous state-of-the-art methods with a much smaller model. The "big" and "extra" profile of the proposed method improves the state-of-the-art results by a big margin.

4.4   Encoding/Decoding Time

In this experiment, we evaluate the encoding and decoding time of the proposed method versus other lossless image compression methods. Methods that are based on pixel-wise autoregressive models are not included in the investigation since it is well-known that these methods are very slow and only capable of processing small images [14,15,25]. For L3C, SReC, and our methods, we selected an input image of size 256×256 and compressed/decompressed the image using different methods on the same system. Model loading time is not included in the measurement. For the IDF method, we recorded the encoding time using a pretrained CIFAR10 model on the CIFAR10 dataset. The LBB [9] method is a flow-based method that requires auxiliary bits to be sent together with the images to be encoded/decoded. It is included in the comparison since it works similar to pixel-wise statistical models that process pixels sequentially during the inference time. The values of the HiLLoC and the LBB methods are calculated from the numbers reported in [10] and [9] respectively. and We normalize the encoding/decoding time to be seconds per 32x32 pixels since the reported numbers in literature are for different sizes of images. Table 5 shows the encoding and decoding time in seconds. Note that our implementation is not optimized to achieve a fast encoding/decoding speed.

Table 5. Encoding/decoding time in seconds per 32×32 pixels.

	L3C [15]	SReC [14]	Ours (normal)	Ours (big)	Ours (extra)	HiLLoC [10]	IDF [12]	LBB [9]
Encoding	0.0078	0.025	0.031	0.052	0.074	0.159	0.430	64.4
Decoding	0.0070	0.025	0.029	0.049	0.070	-	-	65.9

As shown in Table 5, the proposed method has the same level of speed as SReC [14] with the "normal" profile. The "big" and the "extra" profile show significant compression rate gains without heavily sacrificing the inference speed. The results also show that the proposed methods are also significantly faster than HiLLoC and IDF which also process pixels in groups. Compared to pixel-wise methods like LBB, our proposed methods have a tremendous advantage.

5 Discussions

In this paper, we presented a multi-scale progressive statistical model and a lossless image compression system based on it. The proposed statistical model efficiently balances the accuracy that pixel-wise models achieve and the speed that multi-scale models obtain. Experiments show that the proposed system outperforms the state-of-the-art methods by a significant margin on the two large benchmark datasets. The proposed system achieves superior performance with smaller models compared to other systems. The proposed system has a slightly higher computation complexity compared to other "fast" methods with significant gains in the compression rate. The proposed system incorporates a flexible mechanism where the pixel grouping method can be specified easily. We evaluated the static grouping methods using fixed patterns and a dynamic grouping method based on the upper bound of the estimated entropy. Experiments show that increasing the number of groups at each scale significantly improves the compression rate. The dynamic method shows certain gains compared to the static methods using fixed patterns when the number of groups at each scale is the same. However, the convergence speed at the training stage is much slower. This behavior needs to be further studied and a mechanism that can speed up the training with dynamic grouping methods shall be developed.

References

1. http://libpng.org/pub/png/libpng.html (libpng Home Page)
2. Sneyers, J., Wuille, P.: FLIF: free lossless image format based on MANIAC compression. In: 2016 IEEE International Conference on Image Processing (ICIP), pp. 66–70. IEEE (2016)
3. https://jpeg.org/jpeg2000/: (JPEG - JPEG 2000)
4. https://developers.google.com/speed/webp: (A new image format for the Web|WebP)

5. Sullivan, G.J., Ohm, J.R., Han, W.J., Wiegand, T.: Overview of the high efficiency video coding (HEVC) standard. IEEE Trans. Circuits Syst. Video Technol. **22**, 1649–1668 (2012). IIEEE
6. Shannon, C.E.: A mathematical theory of communication. Bell Syst. Tech. J. **27**, 379–423 (1948). _eprint: https://onlinelibrary.wiley.com/doi/pdf/10.1002/j.1538-7305.1948.tb01338.x
7. Marpe, D., Wiegand, T., Sullivan, G.: The H.264/MPEG4 advanced video coding standard and its applications. IEEE Commun. Mag. **44**, 134–143 (2006). Conference Name: IEEE Communications Magazine
8. Marpe, D., Schwarz, H., Wiegand, T.: Context-based adaptive binary arithmetic coding in the H.264/AVC video compression standard. IEEE Trans. Circuits Syst. Video Technol. **13**, 620–636 (2003). Conference Name: IEEE Transactions on Circuits and Systems for Video Technology
9. Ho, J., Lohn, E., Abbeel, P.: Compression with Flows via Local Bits-Back Coding arXiv:1905.08500 [cs, math, stat] (2020)
10. Townsend, J., Bird, T., Kunze, J., Barber, D.: HiLLoC: lossless image compression with hierarchical latent variable models (2019)
11. Johnston, N., et al.: Improved Lossy Image Compression with Priming and Spatially Adaptive Bit Rates for Recurrent Networks. arXiv:1703.10114 [cs] (2017)
12. Hoogeboom, E., Peters, J.W.T., Berg, R.V.D., Welling, M.: Integer Discrete Flows and Lossless Compression. arXiv:1905.07376 [cs, stat] (2019)
13. Mentzer, F., Van Gool, L., Tschannen, M.: Learning Better Lossless Compression Using Lossy Compression. arXiv:2003.10184 [cs, eess] (2020)
14. Cao, S., Wu, C.Y., Krähenbühl, P.: Lossless Image Compression through Super-Resolution. arXiv:2004.02872 [cs, eess] (2020)
15. Mentzer, F., Agustsson, E., Tschannen, M., Timofte, R., Van Gool, L.: Practical Full Resolution Learned Lossless Image Compression. arXiv:1811.12817 [cs, eess] (2019)
16. Oord, A.v.d., Kalchbrenner, N., Vinyals, O., Espeholt, L., Graves, A., Kavukcuoglu, K.: Conditional Image Generation with PixelCNN Decoders. arXiv:1606.05328 [cs] (2016)
17. Oord, A.V.D., Kalchbrenner, N., Kavukcuoglu, K.: Pixel Recurrent Neural Networks. arXiv:1601.06759 [cs] (2016)
18. Salimans, T., Karpathy, A., Chen, X., Kingma, D.P.: PixelCNN++: Improving the PixelCNN with Discretized Logistic Mixture Likelihood and Other Modifications (2016)
19. Dinh, L., Sohl-Dickstein, J., Bengio, S.: Density estimation using Real NVP. arXiv:1605.08803 [cs, stat] (2017)
20. He, K., Zhang, X., Ren, S., Sun, J.: Deep Residual Learning for Image Recognition. arXiv:1512.03385 [cs] (2015)
21. Krizhevsky, A., Hinton, G.: Learning Multiple Layers of Features from Tiny Images. Princeton, Citeseer (2009)
22. Chrabaszcz, P., Loshchilov, I., Hutter, F.: A Downsampled Variant of ImageNet as an Alternative to the CIFAR datasets. arXiv:1707.08819 [cs] (2017)
23. Deng, J., Dong, W., Socher, R., Li, L.J., Li, K., Fei-Fei, L.: ImageNet: a large-scale hierarchical image database. In: CVPR09 (2009)
24. Kuznetsova, A., et al.: The open images dataset V4. Int. J. Comput. Vis. **128**(7), 1956–1981 (2020). https://doi.org/10.1007/s11263-020-01316-z. ISSN 1573-1405
25. Ramachandran, P., et al.: Fast Generation for Convolutional Autoregressive Models. arXiv:1704.06001 [cs, stat] (2017)

Spatial Class Distribution Shift in Unsupervised Domain Adaptation: Local Alignment Comes to Rescue

Safa Cicek[1]([✉]), Ning Xu[2], Zhaowen Wang[2], Hailin Jin[2], and Stefano Soatto[1]

[1] University of California, Los Angeles, USA
{safacicek,soatto}@ucla.edu
[2] Adobe Research, San Jose, USA
{nxu,zhawang,hljin}@adobe.com

Abstract. We propose a method for semantic segmentation in the unsupervised domain adaptation (UDA) setting. We particularly examine the domain gap between spatial-class distributions and propose to align the local distributions of the segmentation predictions. Despite its simplicity, the proposed method achieves state-of-the-art results in UDA segmentation benchmarks.

1 Introduction

Unsupervised domain adaptation (UDA) consists of modifying a model trained on a labeled dataset, called the "source" so it can function on data from a different "target" domain, for which no annotations are available [1–6]. More in general, we want to train a model to operate on input data from both the source and target domains, despite the absence of annotated data for the latter. For instance, one may have a synthetic dataset, where annotation comes for free, but wish for the resulting model to work well on real data, where the manual annotation is scarce or absent. UDA setting is even more vital for semantic segmentation tasks where annotation and quality control per a single image requires more than $1.5\,\mathrm{h}$ on average [7].

In this work, we focus on the UDA segmentation task where the goal is to estimate the segmentation map $y \in \{0,1\}^{K \times H \times W}$ for a given RGB image where K is the number of classes. For the source samples, we have access to ground-truth labels $y^s \in Y$ which are used to minimize cross-entropy loss[1],

$$L_{ce}(P^s; f) := \mathbb{E}_{(x^s,y^s) \sim P^s} \frac{1}{HW} \sum_{i=1}^{H} \sum_{j=1}^{W} \ell_{CE}(f(x^s)_{ij}; y_{ij}^s) \qquad (1)$$

---

[1] We denote label and prediction corresponding to a pixel coordinates of (i,j) with $y_{ij} \in \{0,1\}^K$ and $f(x)_{ij} \in \mathbb{R}^K$ respectively.

Electronic supplementary material The online version of this chapter (https://doi.org/10.1007/978-3-030-69535-4_38) contains supplementary material, which is available to authorized users.

© Springer Nature Switzerland AG 2021
H. Ishikawa et al. (Eds.): ACCV 2020, LNCS 12624, pp. 623–638, 2021.
https://doi.org/10.1007/978-3-030-69535-4_38

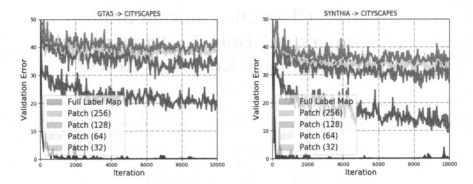

Fig. 1. Spatial-class distribution shift correlates with the receptive field on the segmentation maps. Validation errors for a binary classifier trained to distinguish binary domain labels from segmentation maps are given for GTA5 → Cityscapes (left) and SYNTHIA → Cityscapes (right). If the domain gap between segmentation maps are large, then error decays faster. We repeat this experiment for different receptive fields. When the binary classifier is trained on the entire segmentation maps (blue curve), errors decay quickly, whereas, for smaller patch sizes, learning slows down. For patch sizes smaller than 128, predictions of the classifiers are close to luck (50%). Errors for SYNTHIA are slightly lower due to the larger spatial-class shift between SYNTHIA and Cityscapes. This experiment verifies that even when the spatial class distribution shift is large between the global segmentation maps, local segmentation maps are still almost indistinguishable. (Color figure online)

Fig. 2. Samples from the datasets. Spatial-class distributions vary from source to target domains for the UDA segmentation benchmarks; namely, SYNTHIA → Cityscapes and GTA5 → Cityscapes. SYNTHIA images are generated with random camera views, unlike Cityscapes which only have dashcam views. On the other hand, in GTA5, there are unrealistic scenarios e.g. ego-vehicle driving on the sidewalk. (Color figure online)

where f is the segmentation network and P^s is the distribution of source domain samples and corresponding labels, $\ell_{CE}(f(x)_{ij}; y_{ij}) := -\langle y_{ij}, \log f(x)_{ij} \rangle$ is calculated using the one-hot ground-truth vector $y_{ij} \in \{0,1\}^K$ and class label estimates $f(x)_{ij} \in \mathbb{R}^K$ from the output of a deep neural network with input x. Next, we discuss the proposed methods for leveraging unlabeled target data and our contribution in relation to this vast literature (Sect. 2). In the following section, we describe the proposed method (Sect. 3). Finally, we put it to the test on UDA segmentation benchmarks (Sect. 4).

2   Related Work

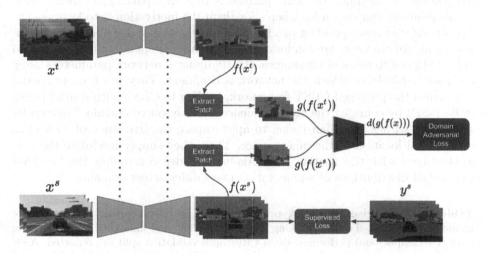

Fig. 3. The network structure of the proposed approach. Our binary domain discriminator (blue) acts on the *random* patches of predictions ($g(f(x))$) and not on the global segmentation maps ($f(x)$). (Color figure online)

In the following, we present some of the previous works on the UDA segmentation tasks excluding the ones focusing on different tasks for the sake of space. AdvEnt [8] is the baseline method. It is observed that in the source-only training, entropy is mostly low for the source predictions and only high at the edges, while the entropy is mostly high on the predictions of the target images. Hence, they proposed to align the "weighted self-information" to minimize the entropy of target predictions while aligning them to source predictions. We improved this work in an orthogonal direction by performing a random-patch alignment. [9,10] proposed heuristics to have class-conditional alignments. [11] follows a curriculum learning approach: where they sequentially learn pseudo-labels for the entire image, superpixels, and finally the dense predictions.

[12] proposed to use a fully convolutional network (PatchGAN) for image translation which is later employed in several UDA works [13]. However, unlike PatchGAN that divides the image into a fixed collection of patches, we randomize the location of patches. Therefore, the distributions we align using the domain discriminator have supports defined by the values of these prediction patches.

While the cardinality of the patch set exponentially increases with the size of the image for the proposed method, PatchGAN always uses a small subset of this set. Hence, the aligned distributions for the proposed method and PatchGAN are significantly different.

Work of [14] looks similar to ours as they partition images into 3 by 3 regions before alignment. But actually, it has the exact opposite motivation and outcome as they only align the corresponding patches while we choose our partitions completely randomly. This saddle difference has great importance. Our motivation for aligning "random" patches is that the spatial-class distribution across domains can vary a lot wheres for them the motivation is to leverage the hypothesis that corresponding patches have similar spatial distributions. But, in reality, as camera views are random in SYNTHIA, corresponding patches should not be aligned to those of Cityscapes. [18,19] updates network parameters using the pseudo-labels for which the network is confident. They incorporate spatial priors into the proposed CBST framework, leading to CBST with spatial priors (CBST-SP) by counting the class frequencies in the source domain, followed by smoothing with a Gaussian kernel to approximate the frequency of each class at a spatial location in the image space. Then, they simply modulate the network output with this spatial prior. Again, this idea contradicts the fact that the spatial distributions of segmentation maps differ across domains.

Table 1. Comparison to SOA on SYNTHIA → Cityscapes. All models are trained on the labeled source training data (SYNTHIA) and unlabeled target training data (Cityscapes) and performances on Cityscapes validation split are reported. A+E [8] refers to the ensemble of two networks: one trained with the adversarial loss and the other is with entropy minimization. In the literature, two different mIoU scores are reported for this task: one is for 16 common classes between two domains (mIoU) and the other is for the 13 classes (mIoU-13) excluding *wall, fence, pole*. Our method outperforms all the previous methods in both metrics.

Method	Road	SW	Build	Wall*	Fence*	Pole*	TL	TS	Veg	Sky	PR	Rider	Car	Bus	Motor	Bike	mIoU	mIoU-13
Source	14.9	11.4	58.7	1.9	0.0	24.1	1.2	6.0	68.8	76.0	54.3	7.1	34.2	15.0	0.8	0.0	23.4	26.8
MCD [15]	84.8	43.6	79.0	3.9	0.2	29.1	7.2	5.5	83.8	83.1	51.0	11.7	79.9	27.2	6.2	0.0	37.3	43.5
Source	55.6	23.8	74.6	-	-	-	6.1	12.1	74.8	79.0	55.3	19.1	39.6	23.3	13.7	25.0	-	38.6
AdaptSegNet [13]	84.3	42.7	77.5	-	-	-	4.7	7.0	77.9	82.5	54.3	21.0	72.3	32.2	18.9	32.3	-	46.7
CLAN [16]	81.3	37.0	80.1	-	-	-	16.1	13.7	78.2	81.5	53.4	21.2	73.0	32.9	22.6	30.7	-	47.8
MinEnt [8]	73.5	29.2	77.1	7.7	0.2	27.0	7.1	11.4	76.7	82.1	57.2	21.3	69.4	29.2	12.9	27.9	38.1	44.2
AdvEnt [8]	87.0	44.1	79.7	9.6	0.6	24.3	4.8	7.2	80.1	83.6	56.4	23.7	72.7	32.6	12.8	33.7	40.8	47.6
A+E [8]	85.6	42.2	79.7	8.7	0.4	25.9	5.4	8.1	80.4	84.1	57.9	23.8	73.3	36.4	14.2	33.0	41.2	48.0
Source	64.3	21.3	73.1	2.4	1.1	31.4	7.0	27.7	63.1	67.6	42.2	19.9	73.1	15.3	10.5	38.9	34.9	40.3
CBST [17]	68.0	29.9	76.3	10.8	1.4	33.9	22.8	29.5	77.6	78.3	60.6	28.3	81.6	23.5	18.8	39.8	42.6	48.9
MRL2 [18]	63.4	27.1	76.4	14.2	1.4	35.2	23.6	29.4	78.5	77.8	61.4	29.5	82.2	22.8	18.9	42.3	42.8	48.7
MRENT [18]	69.6	32.6	75.8	12.2	1.8	35.3	23.3	29.5	77.7	78.9	60.0	28.5	81.5	25.9	19.6	41.8	43.4	49.6
MRKLD [18]	67.7	32.2	73.9	10.7	1.6	37.4	22.2	31.2	80.8	80.5	60.8	29.1	82.8	25.0	19.4	45.3	43.8	50.1
LRENT [18]	65.6	30.3	74.6	13.8	1.5	35.8	23.1	29.1	77.0	77.5	60.1	28.5	82.2	22.6	20.1	41.9	42.7	48.7
Ours	90.6	51.34	81.96	11.77	0.32	29.51	11.72	12.38	82.69	84.7	58.57	24.73	81.94	36.37	17.11	41.75	**44.84**	**51.99**

[20] combined previous works of curriculum [11] and self training [19]. Instead of super-pixels, they use patches of sizes 4 and 8. The key idea is to alternatively update labels and network weights. They apply average pooling on the predictions and pseudo labels and minimize a classification loss between them. Our

approach fundamentally differs from this as we align the predictions on the source and the target images whereas they align the predictions of the pre-trained network (providing pseudo-labels) and the main network both on the target images. Hence, unlike us, their algorithm may not align the local-prediction distributions across domains, which is the main motivation of this work.

The proposed method is orthogonal to most of the methods from this rich and multi-faceted context and can be improved by incorporating some of these ideas.

3   Proposed Method

As can be seen in Fig. 2, spatial-class distribution can greatly differ from source to target domains, due to scene structure, camera view changes, etc. This contradicts with the idea of aligning the segmentation network outputs globally via minimax losses.

Before describing the proposed method, we conducted a motivational experiment to verify and quantify this hypothesis. For this purpose, we train a binary domain classifier on the ground-truth segmentation maps to measure the identifiability of the domain label from segmentation maps. See Fig. 1 where the left panel is for GTA5-Cityscapes and the right one is for SYNTHIA-Cityscapes. When the task is to distinguish the global segmentation maps, classifiers can easily detect the domain (blue curves). As we decrease the receptive field on the segmentation maps, by cropping smaller patch sizes, it is getting harder for the classifier to find the correct domain label. For very small patch sizes, the performance of the classifier is close to chance (50%). Details on the training is given in the Sect. 4.1.

This experiment quantifies and verifies two almost obvious claims: First, the global segmentation maps can have different distributions across domains (i.e. spatial-class distribution shift) hence one should not align the global segmentation predictions at the training time. Second, even if the spatial-class distribution is very large (e.g. SYNTHIA → Cityscapes), the local segmentation maps can have similar distributions across domains. Assuming this as a fact for any cross-domain task -which we only verify for UDA segmentation benchmarks-, one should align random patches of predictions at the training time, for network predictions on different domains to abide by this phenomenon.

3.1   Loss Functions

A natural choice for aligning the cropped prediction distributions for the source and the target domains is to optimize a domain adversarial loss on the extracted patches from the segmentation predictions:

$$L_{adv}(P_x^s, P_x^t; f, d) := \mathbb{E}_{x^s \sim P_x^s, x^t \sim P_x^t} \ell_{CE}\Big(\psi(x^s), [0,1]\Big) + \ell_{CE}\Big(\psi(x^t), [1,0]\Big) \quad (2)$$

where $\psi(x) := d(g(f(x))$, g randomly extracts a patch of size $i < H$ and $j < W$ from the segmentation prediction $f(x)$, and ℓ_{CE} is cross entropy loss. P_x^s, P_x^t

are marginal distributions of the source and the target domains. $d : x \mapsto \mathbb{R}^2$ is binary domain discriminator (see Fig. 3).

As in the previous work of [8], instead of applying domain adversarial loss on the segmentation maps $y \in \{0,1\}^{K \times H \times W}$ directly, we found aligning the "self-information maps", $\overline{y} = h(y) \in \mathbb{R}^{K \times H \times W}$ where $\overline{y}_{kij} = h(y_{kij}) := -y_{kij} \log y_{kij}$ more effective.[2] Hence, the final objective function becomes,

$$L_{advent}(P_x^s, P_x^t; f, d) := \mathbb{E}_{x^s \sim P_x^s, x^t \sim P_x^t} \ell_{CE}\left(\overline{\psi}(x^s), [0,1]\right) + \ell_{CE}\left(\overline{\psi}(x^t), [1,0]\right) \tag{3}$$

where $\overline{\psi}(x) := d(g(h(f(x))))$. Then, the overall optimization problem solved by the segmentation network f is,

$$\min_f \max_d L_{ce}(P^s; f) - \lambda L_{advent}(P_x^s, P_x^t; f, d). \tag{4}$$

Since there is no closed form solution, the objective function is optimized by the segmentation network f and the domain discriminator d in an alternating fashion using SGD.

4   Empirical Evaluation

4.1   Implementation Details

Datasets. To evaluate the performance of the proposed method, we put it to test on the standard UDA segmentation benchmarks: GTA5 $\rightarrow$ Cityscapes and SYNTHIA $\rightarrow$ Cityscapes and compare against SOA and baseline methods.

GTA5 dataset consists of 24966 images with a resolution of 1914×1052 and collected from the video game based on the city of Los Angeles. The resolution of the images in the target set Cityscapes is 2048×1024. The number of target training images is 2975. Methods are tested on the 500 samples of the validation split of Cityscapes. For GTA5 $\rightarrow$ Cityscapes, 19 common classes are used. These are the same classes as the ones used in Cityscapes benchmark [7] where rare classes are excluded from the evaluation.

SYNTHIA [21] is generated by rendering a virtual city created with the Unity development platform. RANDCITYSCAPES subset of SYNTHIA is used as the source training set. This subset consists of 9400 frames of the city taken from a virtual array of cameras moving randomly. We choose the 16 overlapping classes between SYNTHIA and Cityscapes following the earlier works

---

[2] Note that this is not exactly entropy of the predictions as the y_{kij} terms are not summed over the class dimension k. But, the source sample predictions have low entropy as cross-entropy is minimized on them. Adversarial alignment results in aligned $\overline{y}_{kij}$ distributions and thus, results in low entropy for the target predictions as well. As in [8], we found this weighted-scheme more effective because this adversarial loss promotes both the low entropy target predictions and aligned prediction maps across domains.

[9,11,17,19]. Classes that do not exist in this setting, compared to GTA5 setting are *terrain, truck, train.* There is another setting only considering 13 classes excluding the classes *wall, fence* and *pole* [10,13]. Mean scores corresponding to these 13 classes are reported as mIoU-13.

Table 2. Comparison to SOA on GTA5 → Cityscapes. Same as Table 1 except for GTA5 → Cityscapes. Here, the results are reported on 19 common classes (mIoU). The proposed method outperforms 3 of 4 scores that previous SOA [18] reported and it is only 0.12% less than the best method (MRKLD) of [18] which selectively samples for hard classes. The proposed method can be combined with MRKLD, but we choose to report naked results to show the effectiveness of the proposed *random*-patch alignment.

Method	Road	SW	Build	Wall	Fence	Pole	TL	TS	Veg	Terrain	Sky	PR	Rider	Car	Truck	Bus	Train	Motor	Bike	mIoU
Source	42.7	26.3	51.7	5.5	6.8	13.8	23.6	6.9	75.5	11.5	36.8	49.3	0.9	46.7	3.4	5.0	0.0	5.0	1.4	21.7
CyCADA [22]	79.1	33.1	77.9	23.4	17.3	32.1	33.3	31.8	81.5	26.7	69.0	62.8	14.7	74.5	20.9	25.6	6.9	18.8	20.4	39.5
Source	36.4	14.2	67.4	16.4	12.0	20.1	8.7	0.7	69.8	13.3	56.9	37.0	0.4	53.6	10.6	3.2	0.2	0.9	0.0	22.2
MCD [15]	90.3	31.0	78.5	19.7	17.3	28.6	30.9	16.1	83.7	30.0	69.1	58.5	19.6	81.5	23.8	30.0	5.7	25.7	14.3	39.7
Source	75.8	16.8	77.2	12.5	21.0	25.5	30.1	20.1	81.3	24.6	70.3	53.8	26.4	49.9	17.2	25.9	6.5	25.3	36.0	36.6
AdaptSegNet [13]	86.5	36.0	79.9	23.4	23.3	23.9	35.2	14.8	83.4	33.3	75.6	58.5	27.6	73.7	32.5	35.4	3.9	30.1	28.1	42.4
CLAN [16]	87.0	27.1	79.6	27.3	23.3	28.3	35.5	24.2	83.6	27.4	74.2	58.6	28.0	76.2	33.1	36.7	6.7	31.9	31.4	43.2
MinEnt [8]	84.4	18.7	80.6	23.8	23.2	28.4	36.9	23.4	83.2	25.2	79.4	59.0	29.9	78.5	33.7	29.6	1.7	29.9	33.6	42.3
MinEnt + ER [8]	84.2	25.2	77.0	17.0	23.3	24.2	33.3	26.4	80.7	32.1	78.7	57.5	30.0	77.0	37.9	44.3	1.8	31.4	36.9	43.1
AdvEnt [8]	89.9	36.5	81.6	29.2	25.2	28.5	32.3	22.4	83.9	34.0	77.1	57.4	27.9	83.7	29.4	39.1	1.5	28.4	23.3	43.8
A+E [8]	89.4	33.1	81.0	26.6	26.8	27.2	33.5	24.7	83.9	36.7	78.8	58.7	30.5	84.8	38.5	44.5	1.7	31.6	32.4	45.5
Source	-	-	-	-	-	-	-	-	-	-	-	-	-	-	-	-	-	-	-	29.2
FCAN [23]	-	-	-	-	-	-	-	-	-	-	-	-	-	-	-	-	-	-	-	46.6
Source	71.3	19.2	69.1	18.4	10.0	35.7	27.3	6.8	79.6	24.8	72.1	57.6	19.5	55.5	15.5	15.1	11.7	21.1	12.0	33.8
CBST [17]	91.8	53.5	80.5	32.7	21.0	34.0	28.9	20.4	83.9	34.2	80.9	53.1	24.0	82.7	30.3	35.9	16.0	25.9	42.8	45.9
MRL2 [18]	91.9	55.2	80.9	32.1	21.5	36.7	30.0	19.0	84.8	34.9	80.1	56.1	23.8	83.9	28.0	29.4	20.5	24.0	40.3	46.0
MRENT [18]	91.8	53.4	80.6	32.6	20.8	34.3	29.7	21.0	84.0	34.1	80.6	53.9	24.6	82.8	30.8	34.9	16.6	26.4	42.6	46.1
MRKLD [18]	91.0	55.4	80.0	33.7	21.4	37.3	32.9	24.5	85.0	34.1	80.8	57.7	24.6	84.1	27.8	30.1	26.9	26.0	42.3	47.1
LRENT [18]	91.8	53.5	80.5	32.7	21.0	34.0	29.0	20.3	83.9	34.2	80.9	53.1	23.9	82.7	30.2	35.6	16.3	25.9	42.8	45.9
Ours	89.72	32.54	82.19	31.27	25.12	30.11	38.0	24.64	84.68	41.36	76.59	60.25	29.2	86.27	39.05	51.43	1.37	29.07	39.73	46.98

Training Details. We used ResNet101-based DeepLabv2 [24] without CRF post-processing [25] to have a fair comparison with SOA methods [17,18]. We compare our method with the ones reporting in the same setting where they do not exploit more advanced segmentation networks like DeepLabv3+ [26,27], thus we exclude [20,28] from the comparison. This is necessary to make fair comparison possible as DeepLabv3+ includes a decoder replacing bilinear interpolation with atrous convolutions. This results in better recovering of the object boundaries. Intersection Over Union (IoU) has been the standard evaluation metric for semantic segmentation task: $(IoU) = \frac{TP}{TP+FN+FP}$ where TP, FN and FP correspond to true positive, false negative and false positive respectively. Then, mean IoU (mIoU) is calculated by averaging IoU of all the classes. Pixel accuracy, $\frac{TP+TN}{TP+TN+FN+FP}$ also considers TN (pixels correctly identified as not belonging to the class). This is not a good metric if some classes are seen in a few pixels only. A trivial solution would be to never estimate such classes. So, we also do not report on this metric. Batch size is set to be one due to memory constraints. Hence, batch norm parameters are updated with momentum but current batch statistics are not used during training. Image width and height are resized to (760, 1280) for SYNTHIA, (720, 1280) for GTA5 and (512, 1024) for Cityscapes during training. The weight for the adversarial loss (λ) given in

Eq. 3 is set to be 0.001. The number of training iterations is 150000. The learning rate for segmentation network and domain discriminator are 2.5×10^{-4} and 10^{-4} respectively. SGD and Adam are used for optimizing segmentation and discriminator networks respectively.

Table 3. Ablations on SYNTHIA → Cityscapes. We compare the performance of the proposed method to the following baselines. (1) The source-only model is only trained on the labeled source examples minimizing the cross-entropy loss. (2) In AP-CI (Align Predictions of Cropped Images), *RGB images are cropped instead of prediction maps.* (3) AGP-GI (Align Global Predictions of Global Images) refers to minimizing the same adversarial loss (Eq. 3) *on the global segmentation maps.* The proposed method, ALP-GI (Align Local Predictions of Global Images) outperforms all baselines with 15.13%, 31.59% and 4.69% (in mIoU) compared to Source-only, AP-CI (Align Predictions of Cropped Images) and AGP-GI (Align Global Predictions of Global Images) respectively. The last row shows the relative increase compared to the source-only baseline.

Method	Road	SW	Build	Wall*	Fence*	Pole*	TL	TS	Veg.	Sky	PR	Rider	Car	Bus	Motor	Bike	mIoU	mIoU-13
Source-only	57.18	26.41	72.05	6.29	0.15	25.56	8.87	11.12	74.06	80.6	53.69	12.39	49.46	5.25	7.66	20.39	31.95	36.86
AP-CI	33.12	21.75	58.02	0.21	0.0	10.82	0.0	0.37	53.43	42.52	24.12	0.58	24.16	1.22	0.01	1.24	16.97	20.04
AGP-GI	83.42	38.16	77.33	4.34	0.17	25.5	6.2	6.82	77.81	83.97	55.29	18.76	79.13	40.55	15.86	31.62	40.31	47.3
ALP-GI	90.6	51.34	81.96	11.77	0.32	29.51	11.72	12.38	82.69	84.7	58.57	24.73	81.94	36.37	17.11	41.75	44.84	51.99
Relative	33.42	24.93	9.91	5.48	0.17	3.95	2.85	1.26	8.63	4.1	4.88	12.34	32.48	31.12	9.45	21.36	12.89	15.13

Table 4. Ablations on GTA5 → Cityscapes. Same as Table 3 except for GTA5 → Cityscapes. The proposed method, ALP-GI (Align Local Predictions of Global Images) outperforms all baselines with 9.22%, 26.36% and 6.42% (in mIoU) compared to Source-only, AP-CI (Align Predictions of Cropped Images) and AGP-GI (Align Global Predictions of Global Images) respectively. The last row shows the relative increase compared to the source-only baseline.

Method	Road	SW	Build	Wall	Fence	Pole	TL	TS	Veg.	Terrain	Sky	PR	Rider	Car	Truck	Bus	Train	Motor	Bike	mIoU
Source-only	75.46	24.6	65.09	11.91	10.58	28.19	27.45	14.64	79.71	32.04	70.56	52.26	20.1	71.91	28.7	48.5	1.42	16.89	37.36	37.76
AP-CI	44.41	14.72	58.47	12.14	1.0	16.64	1.28	1.67	70.77	12.19	65.4	41.38	0.16	27.9	9.43	13.93	0.0	0.25	0.0	20.62
AGP-GI	86.62	10.48	81.79	27.41	17.29	25.19	29.36	14.85	84.27	34.7	78.16	57.3	28.3	83.65	31.93	35.52	0.15	22.59	21.05	40.56
ALP-GI	89.72	32.54	82.19	31.27	25.12	30.11	38.0	24.64	84.68	41.36	76.59	60.25	29.2	86.27	39.05	51.43	1.37	29.07	39.73	46.98
Relative	14.26	7.94	17.1	19.36	14.54	1.92	10.55	10	4.97	9.32	6.03	7.99	9.1	14.36	10.35	2.93	-0.05	12.18	2.37	9.22

Training Details for the Experiment in Fig. 1. The implementation details for the motivational experiment are as follows. We report validation errors after each 100 training iterations. We randomly choose 500 samples from the source domains for validation and did not use them during training. Cityscapes have already the validation split of size 500 samples. In total, 1000 samples is used to calculate the validation errors. Errors are averaged over three runs. Deviations over different runs are shaded but in some regions, they are too small to be visible. Standard classifier, ResNet18 [29] is used as a binary classifier. Label maps are resized to (512, 1024) before and after cropping, to have the same size segmentation maps for both domains. SGD with momentum 0.9, weight decay 10^{-4}, and fixed learning rate of 10^{-3} is used.

4.2 Quantitative Evaluation

In Tables 1, 2, we compare the proposed method against SOA methods. The proposed method especially shines on SYNTHIA $\rightarrow$ Cityscapes as for this task, spatial-class distribution shift is larger (See Fig. 1, 2).

Our method surpasses all the previous SOA methods in both metrics of SYNTHIA $\rightarrow$ Cityscapes. Previous SOA [18] applies mining on rarely predicted classes and manages to get relatively high scores even in the very challenging classes. For instance, our method could only achieve 1.37% in *train* class of GTA5 setting, while previous SOA [18] could perform 26.9%. Similarly, for *fence* class of SYNTHIA setting, we perform poorly. Domain shift for segmentation maps and RGB images of these classes is too large for achieving robust performance in these classes.

Other methods we compare are as follows. FCAN [23] which proposed to combine the image alignment and translation losses. FCAN does not report class-wise performance and only report on GTA5. [13] applied domain adversarial loss both at the hidden layers and the network outputs. [15] encourages the consistency of different classifiers by having one encoder and two classifiers. Both classifiers are trained on the labeled source samples. The distance between predictions of two classifiers on the same target sample is minimized by the encoder and maximized by classifiers. [16] leverages the consistency between two classifiers in a different way. If two classifiers agree on the prediction, they keep the adversarial loss weight for that prediction small. In both tasks, we outperform all these methods which are orthogonal to ours and it could be combined with them but here we report the naked results to highlight the role of *random*-patch alignment.

The closest apple-to-apple comparison to our method is with [8] AdvEnt which applies the same loss without random cropping on the predictions. The proposed method improves baseline AdvEnt method [8] from 47.6% to 51.99% in SYNTHIA $\rightarrow$ Cityscapes and 43.8% to 46.98% in GTA5 $\rightarrow$ Cityscapes. Moreover, note that A+E reported in [8] is an ensemble of two networks trained with different losses, so it is not directly comparable to our method. Nonetheless, the relative accuracy improvements to their reported numbers are 3.15% for GTA5 and 8.12% for SYNTHIA. More controlled ablations are discussed next.

In Tables 3, 4, we compare the proposed method Align Local Predictions of Global Images (ALP-GI) against the following baselines: (1) Source-only, (2) Align Predictions of Cropped Images (AP-CI) and (3) Align Global Predictions of Global Images (AGP-GI).

Source-only baselines are only trained on the labeled source samples minimizing the cross-entropy loss. Our method improves source-only baselines with

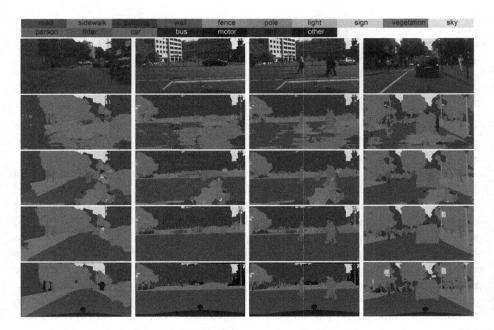

Fig. 4. Qualitative results for SYNTHIA → Cityscapes. Visuals of Cityscapes test set predictions are presented along with the corresponding RGB images. From top to bottom: (1) RGB image, (2) source-only prediction, (3) global alignment prediction, (4) our prediction and (5) ground truth segmentation. The proposed method especially performs well on the more common classes like *road* or *sidewalks* whereas it misses some of the small and rare objects like *traffic signs*.

15.13% and 9.22% for SYNTHIA → Cityscapes and GTA5 → Cityscapes respectively. Since the network and other training details are the same for all the methods, the improvement verifies the effectiveness of the proposed loss in leveraging the unlabeled target samples.

Similarly, the proposed method improves AGP-GI (Align Global Predictions of Global Images) baselines with 4.69% and 6.42% for SYNTHIA → Cityscapes and GTA5 → Cityscapes respectively. The improvement compared to AGP-GI verifies the significance of the *random*-patch alignment. Note that the results reported here for AGP-GI are slightly lower than those reported in [8]. The difference from AdvEnt-only (ours is 47.3, theirs is 47.6) is due to implementation differences. Moreover, they report the best results by ensembling two different networks (A+E) whereas we report a single network's predictions for each method for having a controlled-experimental setting.

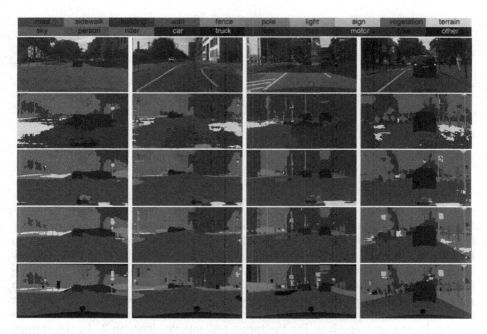

Fig. 5. Qualitative results for GTA5 → Cityscapes. Same as Fig. 4 except for GTA5 → Cityscapes. Again, network can correctly capture objects belonging to classes *road, car* while missing tiny objects (e.g. *traffic light, traffic sign*) or classes with large domain gap (e.g. *fence*).

Another way to align the prediction patches is simply to feed the cropped images to the network. But, the problem with this approach is that the network cannot leverage the scene information (i.e. larger context) when inferring the semantic segmentation map for small crop sizes. That is why in the proposed method, we minimize the cross-entropy loss on the entire images, and for the adversarial loss, *we randomly extract the patches of the predictions and not of the RGB images*. For completeness, we also evaluate this choice and report AP-CI (Align Predictions of Cropped Images) in Tables 3, 4 where we compare the proposed method to simply cropping the RGB images with the same crop sizes. This baseline gives terrible results for the patch size of 256 as such a small receptive field makes it hard for the network to correctly capture the scene. As a result, the performance of this baseline is even lower than the source-only baseline which does not leverage any target sample. The proposed method surpasses this baseline with 31.59% and 26.36% for SYNTHIA → Cityscapes and GTA5 → Cityscapes respectively.

Fig. 6. Entropy of predictions. The entropy of the predictions on the source samples (columns 1, 3) and the target test samples (columns 2, 4) are given. From top to bottom: RGB image, the entropy of the source-only trained model and the entropy of the proposed method. Left two columns are for models trained on SYNTHIA → Cityscapes and right two columns are for GTA5 → Cityscapes. Color transitions from purple to yellow as the value of entropy increases. Entropy values are low on the source images for both the source-only and the proposed models (column 1, 3) except edges due to the cross-entropy loss. For the target test samples (column 2, 4), the entropy of predictions are small for the proposed method thanks to the adversarial loss while source-only models have high uncertainty on the target images.

For SYNTHIA → Cityscapes, our method outperforms the source-only model for all the classes as can be seen in the last row Table 3. But, the improvements are especially significant for the classes *road, sidewalk, car, bus* where accuracies (IoU) increased from 57.18, 26.41, 49.46, 5.25 to 90.6, 51.34, 81.94, 36.37 respectively. These are more common classes and the shapes of these objects do not significantly differ from one domain to other as in *fence* class. Hence, the proposed *random*-patch alignment method can leverage the object shapes learned from the source data. For GTA5 → Cityscapes, the proposed method improves the source-only baseline in all classes except *train*, which is a challenging class for this task as objects belonging to *train* class in GTA5 are far away from the ego-vehicle and they are hardly perceivable. The advantage of the proposed method is most apparent in the classes *building* and *wall* where IoU scores increased from 65.09 and 11.91 to 82.19 and 31.27 respectively.

4.3   Qualitative Evaluation

In Fig. 4 and 5, we present several qualitative results for SYNTHIA → Cityscapes and GTA5 → Cityscapes. In each figure, predictions of the source-only, global alignment, and the proposed methods along with corresponding RGB images and ground-truth segmentation maps are given. Black regions in the ground-truth maps belong to *other* class which are not evaluated at the test time. Thanks to the proposed random-patch alignment regularization, the network

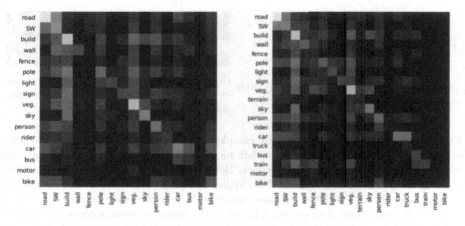

Fig. 7. Confusion matrices. Log-scaled confusion matrices for SYNTHIA →
Cityscapes (left) and GTA5 → Cityscapes (right) are given. Confusion matrices are
calculated by averaging over all the target test set. The value of the matrix at row i
and column j is equal to the number of observations that should be classified as i and
predicted to be j. As the value increases, color changes from purple to yellow. Networks
are confused between *sidewalk* and *road* classes in both tasks. The classes *building* and
vegetation are attracting classes that networks tend to misclassify objects belonging to
other classes as one of two. (Color figure online)

learns the shape of the objects like *car, traffic signs*, and corrects the mistakes
of the global alignment method. Even though the proposed method is quite
successful in capturing the common classes *road, sidewalks* accurately, sometimes
it can miss tiny and rare objects (e.g. belonging to class *fence*). In Fig. 6, we
give the entropy of predictions for the source-only baseline and the proposed
method for both tasks along with the corresponding RGB images. As expected,
entropy values of the predictions on the target test set (column 2, 4) are less for
the proposed method thanks to the adversarial loss. Entropies have high values
mostly on the edges. For source images (column 1, 3), both models have small
uncertainty as both minimize cross-entropy loss on them. In Fig. 7, we give log-
confusion matrices on the target test set predictions of the proposed method
for both tasks. As can be observed, some classes are more likely to be confused
(e.g. sidewalks and road). Furthermore, the false-positive ratio is high for some
classes like building and vegetation (i.e. network is tempted to predict objects
belonging to other classes as one of the two). In Fig. 8a, we plot the performance
on the target test set as a function of patch size. We get the best results when
aligning the prediction crops of size 256 for both tasks. Based on the experiment
in Fig. 1, for this size of segmentation maps, a strong discriminator can have
predictions that are better than luck. However, still, the discriminator cannot
reduce validation error below 20% (green curve) unlike the global alignment case
(blue curve) where the validation error quickly drops to 0%. Moreover, aligning
the predictions with this crop size is sufficient to have aligned predictions for
smaller path sizes. In Fig. 8b, we present an illustrative example of how the

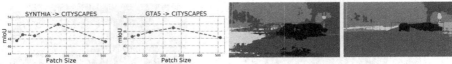

(a) Performance as a function of the patch size.

(b) The proposed method learns the shape of the objects from the labeled source domain.

Fig. 8. (a) mIoU on the target test samples are given for models trained to align different patch size predictions. The left panel is for SYNTHIA → Cityscapes and the right one is for GTA5 → Cityscapes. Both models achieve the best results when aligning the predictions of size 256. For smaller and larger patch sizes, the performance of the model decays. **(b)** Blue regions denoted with the red rectangles are estimated as a *car*. Such a *car* shape does not exist in any of the source segmentation patches, hence unless we perform the proposed adversarial loss, a discriminator can easily tell apart domains only by looking at the segmentation maps. So, this prediction will be corrected with the proposed loss. On the other hand, we do not promote global segmentation map alignment unlike previous works as the global segmentation distributions are not necessarily the same across domains. (Color figure online)

proposed adversarial loss helps to learn the shapes of the objects from the labeled source domain and results in improved predictions compared to the source-only predictions.

5 Conclusion

We proposed a simple yet, effective solution to the spatial-class distribution shift problem and proved its effectiveness by performing at the state-of-the-art in UDA segmentation benchmarks. We further verified its success in the more controlled settings with the ablation studies. The method performs the best for UDA tasks with large spatial-class shifts (e.g. SYNTHIA Cityscapes). The proposed method adds no computational cost to the baseline method and it takes approximately 25 h to train with a single Nvidia Tesla V100. Results on the Berkeley Deep Driving dataset are given in Supp. Mat.

Acknowledgment. Research supported by ONR N00014-19-1-2229.

References

1. Wang, M., Deng, W.: Deep visual domain adaptation: A survey. Neurocomputing (2018)
2. Sun, B., Feng, J., Saenko, K.: Return of frustratingly easy domain adaptation. In: AAAI, vol. 6 (2016)
3. Tzeng, E., Hoffman, J., Saenko, K., Darrell, T.: Adversarial discriminative domain adaptation. In: Computer Vision and Pattern Recognition (CVPR), vol. 1 (2017)

4. Cicek, S., Soatto, S.: Unsupervised domain adaptation via regularized conditional alignment. In: Proceedings of the IEEE International Conference on Computer Vision, pp. 1416–1425 (2019)
5. Cicek, S., Fawzi, A., Soatto, S.: SaaS: speed as a supervisor for semi-supervised learning. In: Ferrari, V., Hebert, M., Sminchisescu, C., Weiss, Y. (eds.) ECCV 2018, Part II. LNCS, vol. 11206, pp. 152–166. Springer, Cham (2018). https://doi.org/10.1007/978-3-030-01216-8_10
6. Cicek, S., Soatto, S.: Input and weight space smoothing for semi-supervised learning. In: Proceedings of the IEEE International Conference on Computer Vision Workshops (2019)
7. Cordts, M., et al.: The cityscapes dataset for semantic urban scene understanding. In: Proceedings of the IEEE Conference on Computer Vision and Pattern Recognition, pp. 3213–3223 (2016)
8. Vu, T.H., Jain, H., Bucher, M., Cord, M., Pérez, P.: Advent: Adversarial entropy minimization for domain adaptation in semantic segmentation. arXiv preprint arXiv:1811.12833 (2018)
9. Hoffman, J., Wang, D., Yu, F., Darrell, T.: Fcns in the wild: Pixel-level adversarial and constraint-based adaptation. arXiv preprint arXiv:1612.02649 (2016)
10. Chen, Y.H., Chen, W.Y., Chen, Y.T., Tsai, B.C., Frank Wang, Y.C., Sun, M.: No more discrimination: Cross city adaptation of road scene segmenters. In: Proceedings of the IEEE International Conference on Computer Vision, pp. 1992–2001 (2017)
11. Zhang, Y., David, P., Gong, B.: Curriculum domain adaptation for semantic segmentation of urban scenes. In: The IEEE International Conference on Computer Vision (ICCV), vol. 2 (2017)
12. Isola, P., Zhu, J.Y., Zhou, T., Efros, A.A.: Image-to-image translation with conditional adversarial networks. In: Proceedings of the IEEE Conference on Computer Vision and Pattern Recognition, pp. 1125–1134 (2017)
13. Tsai, Y.H., Hung, W.C., Schulter, S., Sohn, K., Yang, M.H., Chandraker, M.: Learning to adapt structured output space for semantic segmentation. In: Proceedings of the IEEE Conference on Computer Vision and Pattern Recognition, pp. 7472–7481 (2018)
14. Chen, Y., Li, W., Van Gool, L.: Road: reality oriented adaptation for semantic segmentation of urban scenes. In: Proceedings of the IEEE Conference on Computer Vision and Pattern Recognition, pp. 7892–7901 (2018)
15. Saito, K., Watanabe, K., Ushiku, Y., Harada, T.: Maximum classifier discrepancy for unsupervised domain adaptation. In: Proceedings of the IEEE Conference on Computer Vision and Pattern Recognition, pp. 3723–3732 (2018)
16. Luo, Y., Zheng, L., Guan, T., Yu, J., Yang, Y.: Taking a closer look at domain shift: category-level adversaries for semantics consistent domain adaptation. In: Proceedings of the IEEE Conference on Computer Vision and Pattern Recognition, pp. 2507–2516 (2019)
17. Zou, Y., Yu, Z., Kumar, B., Wang, J.: Domain adaptation for semantic segmentation via class-balanced self-training. arXiv preprint arXiv:1810.07911 (2018)
18. Zou, Y., Yu, Z., Liu, X., Kumar, B., Wang, J.: Confidence regularized self-training. In: Proceedings of the IEEE International Conference on Computer Vision, pp. 5982–5991 (2019)
19. Zou, Y., Yu, Z., Vijaya Kumar, B.V.K., Wang, J.: Unsupervised domain adaptation for semantic segmentation via class-balanced self-training. In: Ferrari, V., Hebert, M., Sminchisescu, C., Weiss, Y. (eds.) ECCV 2018, Part III. LNCS, vol. 11207, pp. 297–313. Springer, Cham (2018). https://doi.org/10.1007/978-3-030-01219-9_18

20. Lian, Q., Lv, F., Duan, L., Gong, B.: Constructing self-motivated pyramid curriculums for cross-domain semantic segmentation: a non-adversarial approach. In: Proceedings of the IEEE International Conference on Computer Vision, pp. 6758–6767 (2019)
21. Ros, G., Sellart, L., Materzynska, J., Vazquez, D., Lopez, A.M.: The synthia dataset: a large collection of synthetic images for semantic segmentation of urban scenes. In: Proceedings of the IEEE Conference on Computer Vision and Pattern Recognition, pp. 3234–3243 (2016)
22. Hoffman, J., et al.: Cycada: Cycle-consistent adversarial domain adaptation. arXiv preprint arXiv:1711.03213 (2017)
23. Zhang, Y., Qiu, Z., Yao, T., Liu, D., Mei, T.: Fully convolutional adaptation networks for semantic segmentation. In: Proceedings of the IEEE Conference on Computer Vision and Pattern Recognition, pp. 6810–6818 (2018)
24. Chen, L.C., Papandreou, G., Kokkinos, I., Murphy, K., Yuille, A.L.: Deeplab: semantic image segmentation with deep convolutional nets, Atrous convolution, and fully connected CRFs. IEEE Trans. Pattern Anal. Mach. Intell. **40**, 834–848 (2017)
25. Krähenbühl, P., Koltun, V.: Parameter learning and convergent inference for dense random fields. In: International Conference on Machine Learning, pp. 513–521 (2013)
26. Chen, L.C., Papandreou, G., Schroff, F., Adam, H.: Rethinking atrous convolution for semantic image segmentation. arXiv preprint arXiv:1706.05587 (2017)
27. Chen, L.-C., Zhu, Y., Papandreou, G., Schroff, F., Adam, H.: Encoder-decoder with Atrous separable convolution for semantic image segmentation. In: Ferrari, V., Hebert, M., Sminchisescu, C., Weiss, Y. (eds.) ECCV 2018, Part VII. LNCS, vol. 11211, pp. 833–851. Springer, Cham (2018). https://doi.org/10.1007/978-3-030-01234-2_49
28. Zhang, Q., Zhang, J., Liu, W., Tao, D.: Category anchor-guided unsupervised domain adaptation for semantic segmentation. In: Advances in Neural Information Processing Systems, pp. 433–443 (2019)
29. He, K., Zhang, X., Ren, S., Sun, J.: Deep residual learning for image recognition. In: Proceedings of the IEEE Conference on Computer Vision and Pattern Recognition, pp. 770–778 (2016)

Robot Vision

Robot Vision

Point Proposal Based Instance Segmentation with Rectangular Masks for Robot Picking Task

Satoshi Ito$^{(\boxtimes)}$ and Susumu Kubota

Corporate Research and Development Center, Toshiba Corporation, Kawasaki, Japan
{satoshi13.ito,susumu.kubota}@toshiba.co.jp

Abstract. In this paper, we focus on instance segmentation of a top-view image for robot picking task. One difficulty in this setting is that objects are located in various orientations and highly overlapped, where a traditional box proposal approach such as Mask R-CNN does not work well because more than one objects often have very similar bounding-boxes. To address this issue, we adopt a recently developed point proposal approach. This approach firstly generates point proposals instead of box proposals, then an instance mask is predicted over an image for each proposal point. This procedure enables us to obtain pixel-precise masks even for objects sharing the same bounding-box. However, mask prediction over an image may produce a few false positive pixels apart from objects and these false positives are problematic for robot picking task. To suppress them, we introduce rectangular masks. A rectangular mask for each proposal point restricts the existence area of the corresponding object within the rectangle. The experimental result on WISDOM dataset shows that our method achieves superior performance to Mask R-CNN with the same backbone model and introduction of rectangular masks gives small improvement of mask AP and large improvement of box AP.

1 Introduction

With the recent increase of e-commerce, automation technologies using robots to reduce logistics costs attract great attention. In order to grasp and move objects, it's important for robots to understand each object's shape and location accurately. The task of segmenting objects in an image is called instance segmentation in computer vision. A lot of instance segmentation methods have been proposed so far and the detection performance has been much improved with recent advances of deep learning techniques. However, most of the methods were evaluated on benchmark datasets consisting of natural scenes such as Microsoft COCO [1] and Cityscapes [2] while instance segmentation of a top-view image is usually required for robot picking task. Therefore, those methods are not necessarily suitable for this task.

In this work, we study instance segmentation of a top-view image for robot picking task. Segmenting objects in a top-view image is difficult because objects

© Springer Nature Switzerland AG 2021
H. Ishikawa et al. (Eds.): ACCV 2020, LNCS 12624, pp. 641–653, 2021.
https://doi.org/10.1007/978-3-030-69535-4_39

can be located in various orientations and highly overlapped. In this situation, since object shape cannot be approximated with an axis-aligned bounding-box, a traditional box proposal approach such as Mask R-CNN [3] does not work well. Furthermore, overlapped objects often have very similar bounding-boxes or even share the same bounding-box, and a box proposal approach cannot distinguish them.

To overcome the above problem, we use recently developed point proposal based methods [4,5]. This approach firstly proposes points in objects instead of bounding-boxes of objects, then predicts a pixel-precise instance mask over an image based on each proposal point. Thus, a point proposal approach can deal with non-axis-aligned objects and objects sharing the same bounding-box. However, since the number of background pixels is much larger than the number of object pixels, it is likely that a predicted mask includes a few false positive pixels. For robot picking task, false positive pixels apart from an object are problematic. Therefore, we introduce rectangular masks to suppress those false positives. For each proposal point, our model generates a rectangular mask to restrict the existence area of the corresponding object within the rectangle.

Experimental results on WISDOM dataset [6] show that our method achieves superior performance to Mask R-CNN. In ablation study, introduction of rectangular masks gives a large improvement of box AP by 7.5 points and a small improvement of mask AP by 0.5 points.

2   Related Work

Two-stage methods with object detector/proposal [3,7,8] became the first main-stream of instance segmentation in deep learning. Mask R-CNN [3] is the most famous method and widely used even today. There are methods [9–11] to improve mask R-CNN performance. This two-stage approach firstly detects RoIs by using Region Proposal Network (RPN) [12] then classifies and segments an object in each RoI. Because this approach assumes that an RoI contains only one object, it cannot deal with objects sharing the same RoI. Recently, single-stage methods [13–16] based on the successful single-stage object detector FCOS [17] have been proposed and achieve comparable performance to mask R-CNN. However, these methods are still based on an object detector, hence they have the same problem as two-stage methods.

Another approach on instance segmentation is based on pixel embeddings [18, 19]. In this approach, the network is trained to output similar embeddings for the pixels of the same objects while dissimilar embeddings for the pixels belonging to different objects. Then, after outputting pixel embeddings, some clustering method is applied to them in order to obtain instance masks. This approach can produce a pixel-precise mask even for objects sharing the same bounding-box. However, this solution is suboptimal since the trained network is not optimized for instance segmentation. As a result, this approach is not competitive to the above mentioned detector based approach in terms of detection performance.

There are a few methods [4,5] based on point proposal. These methods firstly propose points in objects, then predict an instance mask over an image for each proposal point. Neven et al. [4] uses pixel embeddings for instance mask prediction. Therefore, this approach inherits both advantages of detector based approach and pixel embedding approach. Our method is based on this approach, and some techniques are introduced to improve the performance of instance segmentation of a top-view image.

Recently, a single stage method named SOLO [20] has been proposed. SOLO utilizes a uniform grids instead of proposal points. That is, it divides an image into grid cells. Then, for each grid cell, it predicts the mask of the object which the cell belongs to. Therefore, if the cell size is enough small, SOLO has the same advantages as point proposal approach.

3   Method

The overview of our instance segmentation method is shown in Fig. 1. Our model is built on a backbone such as ResNet [23] and FPN [21]. Multi-scale feature maps P2, P3, P4 and P5 are fused to a single scale shared features $\vec{f} \in \mathrm{R}^{H \times W \times 256}$ by the method described in [22] where H and W are height and width of P2, respectively. Then, shared features are input to five branches. Each branch has its own learnable parameters of two convolution layers. A point proposal branch outputs proposal points $\vec{p}$, and instance masks $\vec{M}$ are predicted by using pixel embeddings, scales, and proposal points. At the same time, rectangular masks $\vec{B}$ are generated by using an output of box branch and proposal points. Then, each instance mask is refined by the corresponding rectangular mask in order to suppress false positive pixels. Finally, confidence scores of instances are computed from the refined instance masks and a semantic segmentation score map.

3.1   Point Proposal

A point proposal branch transforms shared features to a heat map $\vec{h} \in \mathrm{R}^{H \times W}$ in which the pixels belonging to objects have larger values than background. Then, the at most K largest local maximum points $\{\vec{p}_k = (u_k, v_k)\}_{k=1}^{K}$ are sampled from the heat map. u_k and v_k represent y and x coordinates, respectively. These points $\{\vec{p}_k\}_{k=1}^{K}$ are used as proposal points. We use $K = 500$ in our experiments.

3.2   Mask Prediction

For each proposal point $\vec{p} = (u, v)$, its corresponding instance mask $\vec{M}_{\vec{p}} \in \{0, 1\}^{H \times W}$ is obtained by thresholding $\vec{m}_{\vec{p}} \in \mathrm{R}^{H \times W}$ whose elements are computed by the following function:

$$m_{\vec{p}}(i, j) = \exp\left(-(\vec{x}(i, j) - \vec{x}_{\vec{p}})^T \vec{\Sigma}_{\vec{p}}^{-1}(\vec{x}(i, j) - \vec{x}_{\vec{p}})\right), \tag{1}$$

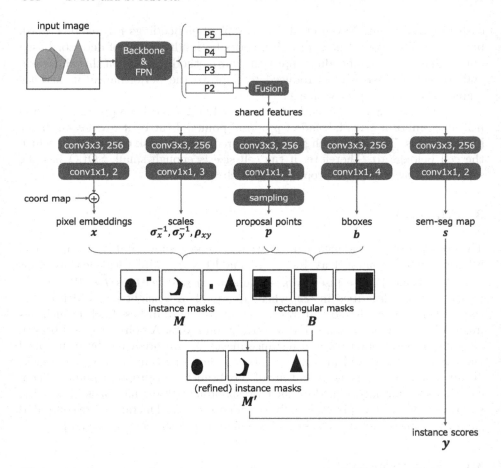

Fig. 1. The overview of our instance segmentation method. There are five branches after shared features, obtained by fusing P2, P3, P4 and P5 of FPN [21]. Fusion process is the same as UPerNet [22]. Instance masks are computed from pixel embeddings, scales, and proposal points, and rectangular masks are computed from bounding-boxes and proposal points, in parallel. Then, instance masks are refined by rectangular masks in order to suppress false positive pixels. Finally, confidence scores for instances are calculated from the refined masks and semantic segmentation map.

where $\vec{x}(i,j) \in \mathrm{R}^2$ is the pixel embedding at the coordinates (i,j) and $\vec{x}_{\vec{p}} = \vec{x}(u,v)$. $\Sigma_{\vec{p}}^{-1} \in \mathrm{R}^{2\times2}$ is a positive definite symmetric matrix at the proposal point $\vec{p}$ and used for distance calculation in the pixel embedding space. $m_{\vec{p}}(i,j)$ represents a probability that a pixel (i,j) belongs to the object which $\vec{p}$ belongs to. In order to make pixel embeddings $\vec{x}$ more discriminative, a coordinate map is added as mentioned in [4,24]. Equation (1) is similar to [4], but our $\vec{\Sigma}_{\vec{p}}^{-1}$ is a full matrix while their method adopts a diagonal one. We believe that a full matrix is more suitable for this task because objects are not axis-aligned. The matrix $\vec{\Sigma}_{\vec{p}}^{-1}$ is represented as:

$$\vec{\Sigma}_{\vec{p}}^{-1} = \frac{1}{1 - \rho_{xy,\vec{p}}^2} \begin{pmatrix} \sigma_{y,\vec{p}}^{-2} & -\rho_{xy,\vec{p}}\sigma_{x,\vec{p}}^{-1}\sigma_{y,\vec{p}}^{-1} \\ -\rho_{xy,\vec{p}}\sigma_{x,\vec{p}}^{-1}\sigma_{y,\vec{p}}^{-1} & \sigma_{x,\vec{p}}^{-2} \end{pmatrix}, \tag{2}$$

where

$$\vec{\Sigma}_{\vec{p}} = \begin{pmatrix} \sigma_{y,\vec{p}}^2 & \rho_{xy,\vec{p}}\sigma_{x,\vec{p}}\sigma_{y,\vec{p}} \\ \rho_{xy,\vec{p}}\sigma_{x,\vec{p}}\sigma_{y,\vec{p}} & \sigma_{x,\vec{p}}^2 \end{pmatrix} \tag{3}$$

$$\sigma_{y,\vec{p}}^{-1} = \sigma_y^{-1}(u,v) \tag{4}$$

$$\sigma_{x,\vec{p}}^{-1} = \sigma_x^{-1}(u,v) \tag{5}$$

$$\rho_{xy,\vec{p}} = \rho_{xy}(u,v). \tag{6}$$

Hence, our scales branch outputs three parameter maps $\vec{\sigma}_x^{-1}, \vec{\sigma}_y^{-1} \in \mathrm{R}_{>0}^{H \times W}$ and $\vec{\rho}_{xy} \in (-1,1)^{H \times W}$ for constructing each $\vec{\Sigma}_{\vec{p}}^{-1}$. The exponential activation function is used for $\vec{\sigma}_x^{-1}$ and $\vec{\sigma}_y^{-1}$, and the tanh activation function is used for $\vec{\rho}_{xy}$.

3.3   False Positive Suppression with Rectangular Masks

As mentioned above, since the majority of pixels are background, a few false positive pixels accidentally occur in background region. We suppress them in the instance mask $\vec{M}_{\vec{p}}$ by using a rectangular mask $\vec{B}_{\vec{p}} \in \{0,1\}^{H \times W}$:

$$\vec{M}_{\vec{p}}' = \vec{M}_{\vec{p}} \circ \vec{B}_{\vec{p}}, \tag{7}$$

where $\circ$ denotes Hadamard product. The rectangular mask $\vec{B}_{\vec{p}}$ is constructed from $\vec{b}_{\vec{p}} = (t_{\vec{p}}, l_{\vec{p}}, b_{\vec{p}}, r_{\vec{p}})^T \in \mathrm{R}_{>0}^4$, an output of our box branch at the proposal point $\vec{p} = (u,v)$, as follows:

$$B_{\vec{p}}(i,j) = \begin{cases} 1 & \text{if } u - \alpha t_{\vec{p}} \le i \le u + \alpha b_{\vec{p}} \wedge v - \alpha l_{\vec{p}} \le j \le v + \alpha r_{\vec{p}} \\ 0 & \text{otherwise} \end{cases}, \tag{8}$$

where α is a constant parameter to expand a predicted rectangle. We use $\alpha = 1.1$ in our experiments. The exponential activation function is applied after the last convolution layer in the box branch so that $\vec{b}_{\vec{p}}$ is positive. Note that this suppression procedure is not used in training phase.

Finally, an average of a semantic segmentation score map $\vec{s}$ over an instance region is used as a confidence score for the instance mask.

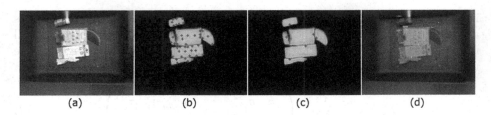

Fig. 2. Visualization of proposal points. (a) input image. (b) proposal points represented as red cross over proposal heat map $\vec{h}$. (c) remaining proposal points after post-processing. (d) instance segmentation result.

3.4 Post-processing

Our model outputs $\{(\vec{M}'_k, y_k)\}_{k=1}^{K}$ where $\vec{M}'_k$ is the (refined) instance mask obtained in Eq. (7) and y_k is the corresponding confidence score. The obtained masks are generally redundant because there can be more than one proposal points in each object region. In order to remove redundant masks, we select the instance masks in descending order of confidence scores so that each instance mask includes only one proposal point. Then, redundant masks are removed from remaining masks based on overlap ratio. Figure 2 shows that an example of proposal points before and after post-processing. We can see that there is only one proposal point in each instance after post-processing.

3.5 Training

For training our model, we compute four losses $L_{\text{prop}}, L_{\text{mask}}, L_{\text{box}}$ and L_{sseg}. Then, these losses are combined by using multitask uncertainty weighting [25] which is one of the adaptive multitask loss balancing techniques. As described later, proposal points are required to compute L_{prop} and L_{mask}. However, the quality of point proposal is poor at an early stage of training. Therefore, we use points randomly sampled from ground-truth instance masks as proposal points during training. In our experiments, we sample 100 points per image. Each loss is briefly described below.

L_{prop} **for Point Proposal.** We train the network so that heat map $\vec{h}$ can be used as a proxy to the quality of the instance mask generated at each proposal point. The quality at (i, j) is approximated with the following equation:

$$q(i,j) = \frac{1}{Z} \min_{k} m_{(i,j)}(u_k, v_k), \tag{9}$$

where (u_k, v_k) is the k-th random proposal point as described above and Z is a normalization parameter to ensure $\max_{i,j} q(i,j) = 1$. By using $q(i,j)$, we define L_{prop} as follows:

$$L_{\text{prop}} = \frac{1}{HW} \left| \vec{h} - \hat{\vec{h}} \right|_{F}^{2}, \tag{10}$$

where $| * |_F$ denotes Frobenius norm and

$$\hat{h}(i,j) = \begin{cases} \beta + (1-\beta)q(i,j) & \text{if } (i,j) \in \text{foreground pixels} \\ 0 & \text{otherwise} \end{cases}.$$ (11)

$\beta \in (0,1)$ is a minimum value for foreground pixels and we set it to 0.7. This value is the same as [5].

L_{mask} **for Mask Prediction.** For L_{mask}, we adopt a simple soft-IoU loss [26] as follows:

$$L_{\text{mask}} = \frac{1}{K} \sum_{k=1}^{K} \left(1 - \frac{\epsilon + \sum_{i,j} m_{\vec{p}_k}(i,j)\hat{M}_{\vec{p}_k}(i,j)}{\epsilon + \sum_{i,j} m_{\vec{p}_k}(i,j) + \hat{M}_{\vec{p}_k}(i,j) - m_{\vec{p}_k}(i,j)\hat{M}_{\vec{p}_k}(i,j)} \right),$$ (12)

where $\epsilon = 1$ is a smoothing constant and $\hat{M}_{\vec{p}_k}$ is the ground-truth instance mask to which the point $\vec{p}_k$ belongs.

L_{box} **for Rectangular Masks.** For L_{box}, we compute box IoU loss [27] at every foreground pixels as below:

$$L_{\text{box}} = \frac{1}{N} \sum_{\vec{p} \in \text{foreground}} \left(1 - \frac{I_{\vec{p}} + \epsilon}{U_{\vec{p}} + \epsilon} \right),$$ (13)

where N is the number of foreground pixels, $\epsilon = 1$ is a smoothing constant,

$$I_{\vec{p}} = \left(\min(t_{\vec{p}}, \hat{t}_{\vec{p}}) + \min(b_{\vec{p}}, \hat{b}_{\vec{p}}) \right) \left(\min(l_{\vec{p}}, \hat{l}_{\vec{p}}) + \min(r_{\vec{p}}, \hat{r}_{\vec{p}}) \right),$$ (14)

$$U_{\vec{p}} = (\hat{t}_{\vec{p}} + \hat{b}_{\vec{p}})(\hat{l}_{\vec{p}} + \hat{r}_{\vec{p}}) + (t_{\vec{p}} + b_{\vec{p}})(l_{\vec{p}} + r_{\vec{p}}) - I_{\vec{p}},$$ (15)

and $\hat{*}$ denotes the corresponding ground-truth, respectively.

L_{sseg} **for Semantic Segmentation.** For the semantic segmentation loss L_{sseg}, we adopt a standard soft-max cross entropy loss with label smoothing [28]. Its smoothing parameter is set to 0.1 in our experiments.

4   Experiments

The performance of our method is evaluated on WISDOM Dataset [6]. This dataset provides 400 color top-view images of $1{,}032 \times 772$. We use the same training/test split as [6]. This split provides 100 training images including 25 objects and 300 test images including different 25 objects. For all experiments, each input image is resized so that the longer side is equal to 512. The detection performance is evaluated three times with different random seeds, and their averaged score is reported.

Here, we consider evaluation metrics. As described above, false positive pixels apart from an object are problematic for robot picking task, hence an evaluation

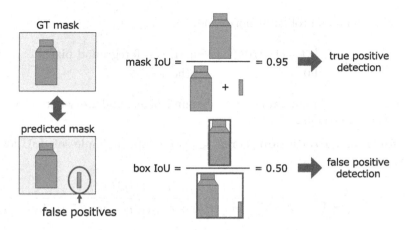

Fig. 3. Comparison of mask IoU and box IoU. A predicted mask including a few false positive pixels apart from an object is judged as true positive detection by mask IoU while judged as false positive detection by box IoU under an IoU threshold in $(0.5, 0.95]$.

metric should be sensitive to them. Box AP, an object detection evaluation metric, is such a metric while mask AP, commonly used as an instance segmentation evaluation metric, is insensitive to a few false positive pixels. Figure 3 shows a typical example. A predicted mask including a few false positives is judged as true positive by mask IoU while judged as false positive by box IoU. On the other hand, box AP is insensitive to mask accuracy while mask AP is sensitive to it. Therefore, we use both evaluation metrics box AP and mask AP in our experiments.

We use ResNet50 model pre-trained on ImageNet [29]. Our model is trained for 10,000 iterations with a batch-size of 4. We use the SGD optimizer with learning rate of 0.02, momentum of 0.9 and weight decay of 0.0005. The learning rate is scheduled using a cosine annealing scheduler [30]. During training, parameters of stem and stage1 in ResNet50 are fixed and the learning rate for the other parameters in ResNet50 is multiplied by 0.1. We apply data augmentation similar to that used to train an SSD model [31]. Data augmentation is implemented by using Albumentations library [32]. We use PyTorch framework [33] for all our experiments.

4.1   Main Results

Table 1 shows comparison of our model with other methods. The evaluation result of Mask R-CNN with ResNet50-FPN is obtained by using maskrcnn-benchmark [34]. Our model achieves mask AP of 52.3% and box AP of 48.1%, which are 12.2 points and 11.4 points higher than those of Mask R-CNN with the same ResNet50-FPN backbone, respectively. As compared with D-SOLO [20],

| Input | GT | Ours | Mask R-CNN | D-SOLO |

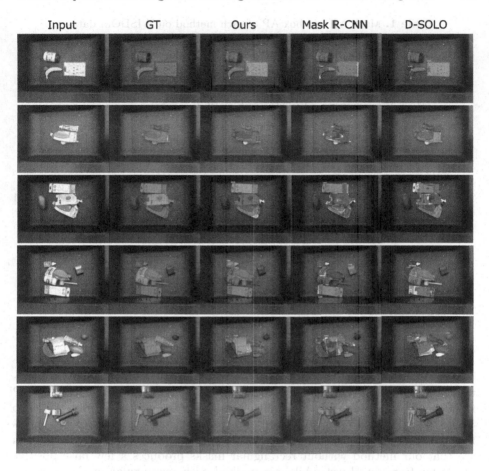

Fig. 4. Visualization results of our method, Mask R-CNN and D-SOLO.

our mask and box APs are 10.3 and 9.0 points higher, respectively. Furthermore, our method is comparable to SD Mask R-CNN[1] [6] which uses depth information.

Table 2 shows mask APs at IoU threshold of 0.5 and 0.75. We can see that mask AP@IoU = 0.75 of our method is much higher than mask R-CNN and D-SOLO. This means that our method can predict object shapes more precisely than those methods. We show some visualization results of each method in Fig. 4. It also shows that our method produces more accurate instance masks than Mask R-CNN and D-SOLO. Moreover, our method generates good instance segmentation results even for highly overlapped objects. Typical failure case is found in the bottom-most row in Fig. 4. All the methods over-segment a hammer-shaped object. This is because there is no object of similar shape in training data.

---

[1] Since their ResNet35 model is not standard, we could not compare the performance with the same backbone. The configuration of ResNet35 can be found in their code.

Table 1. Mask AP and box AP of each method on WISDOM dataset.

Method	Backbone	Input type	Mask AP @all [%]	Box AP @all [%]
SD Mask R-CNN [6]	ResNet35-FPN	Depth	51.6	-
Mask R-CNN [6]	ResNet35-FPN	RGB	38.4	-
Mask R-CNN	ResNet50-FPN	RGB	40.1	36.7
D-SOLO	ResNet50-FPN	RGB	42.0	39.1
Ours	ResNet50-FPN	RGB	52.3	48.1

Table 2. Mask APs [%] of each method with ResNet50-FPN backbone on WISDOM dataset.

Method	AP@all	AP@IoU = 0.5	AP@IoU = 0.75
Mask R-CNN	40.1	76.4	38.0
D-SOLO	42.0	75.1	42.9
Ours	52.3	82.8	55.1

4.2 Ablation Study

The results of ablation experiments are shown in Table 3. Our instance segmentation method with rectangular masks achieves a large improvement of box AP from 40.6% to 48.1% while a small improvement of mask AP from 50.7% to 52.3%. This means that introduction of rectangular masks successfully suppress false positive pixels apart from objects. An example is shown in Fig. 5. We can see that our method without rectangular masks produces a few false positive pixels far from an object while our method with rectangular masks does not produces such a false positive pixels.

By using a full matrix $\vec{\Sigma}$, the performance mask AP is slightly improved from 51.8% to 52.3%. Computational cost is almost unchanged between our model with a full matrix and that with diagonal one. Hence, introducing a full matrix is a good choice for this task.

Table 3. Ablation experiments on WISDOM dataset.

Full $\vec{\Sigma}$	Rectangular masks	Mask AP@all [%]	Box AP@all [%]
		49.2	39.1
✓		50.7	40.6
	✓	51.8	47.4
✓	✓	52.3	48.1

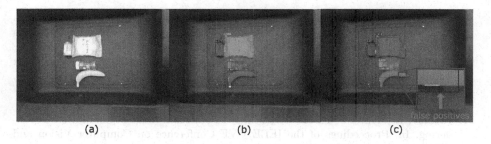

(a)   (b)   (c)

Fig. 5. Instance masks obtained by our method with or without rectangular masks. (a) Input image. (b) Instance masks with rectangular masks. (c) Instance masks without rectangular masks. The instance mask for upper-right object includes a few false positives under the banana-shaped object.

5 Conclusions

In this work, we focus on instance segmentation of a top-view image for robot picking task. We propose a point proposal based instance segmentation method with rectangular masks, which suppress false positive pixels apart from objects. The experimental results on WISDOM dataset show that our method achieves superior performance to Mask R-CNN and D-SOLO with the same backbone model.

References

1. Lin, T.-Y., et al.: Microsoft COCO: common objects in context. In: Fleet, D., Pajdla, T., Schiele, B., Tuytelaars, T. (eds.) ECCV 2014, Part V. LNCS, vol. 8693, pp. 740–755. Springer, Cham (2014). https://doi.org/10.1007/978-3-319-10602-1_48
2. Cordts, M., et al.: The cityscapes dataset for semantic urban scene understanding. In: The IEEE Conference on Computer Vision and Pattern Recognition (CVPR) (2016)
3. He, K., Gkioxari, G., Dollar, P., Girshick, R.: Mask R-CNN. In: The IEEE International Conference on Computer Vision (ICCV) (2017)
4. Neven, D., Brabandere, B.D., Proesmans, M., Gool, L.V.: Instance segmentation by jointly optimizing spatial embeddings and clustering bandwidth. In: The IEEE Conference on Computer Vision and Pattern Recognition (CVPR) (2019)
5. Sofiiuk, K., Barinova, O., Konushin, A.: Adaptis: adaptive instance selection network. In: The IEEE International Conference on Computer Vision (ICCV) (2019)
6. Danielczuk, M., et al..: Segmenting unknown 3D objects from real depth images using mask R-CNN trained on synthetic data. In: The IEEE International Conference on Robotics and Automation (ICRA) (2019)
7. Li, Y., Qi, H., Dai, J., Ji, X., Wei, Y.: Fully convolutional instance-aware semantic segmentation. In: The IEEE Conference on Computer Vision and Pattern Recognition (CVPR) (2017)
8. Viet Pham, S.I., Kozakaya, T.: BiSeg: simultaneous instance segmentation and semantic segmentation with fully convolutional networks. In: The British Machine Vision Conference (BMVC) (2017)

9. Huang, Z., Huang, L., Gong, Y., Huang, C., Wang, X.: Mask scoring R-CNN. In: Proceedings of the IEEE/CVF Conference on Computer Vision and Pattern Recognition (CVPR) (2019)

10. Cheng, T., Wang, X., Huang, L., Liu, W.: Boundary-preserving mask R-CNN. In: Vedaldi, A., Bischof, H., Brox, T., Frahm, J.-M. (eds.) ECCV 2020, Part XIV. LNCS, vol. 12359, pp. 660–676. Springer, Cham (2020). https://doi.org/10.1007/978-3-030-58568-6_39

11. Kirillov, A., Wu, Y., He, K., Girshick, R.: Pointrend: mage segmentation as rendering. In: Proceedings of the IEEE/CVF Conference on Computer Vision and Pattern Recognition (CVPR) (2020)

12. Ren, S., He, K., Girshick, R., Sun, J.: Faster R CNN: towards real-time object detection with region proposal networks. In: Cortes, C., Lawrence, N.D., Lee, D.D., Sugiyama, M., Garnett, R. (eds.) Advances in Neural Information Processing Systems, vol. 28, pp. 91–99. Curran Associates, Inc. (2015)

13. Ying, H., Huang, Z., Liu, S., Shao, T., Zhou, K.: Embedmask: Embedding coupling for one-stage instance segmentation (2019)

14. Wang, Y., Xu, Z., Shen, H., Cheng, B., Yang, L.: Centermask: single shot instance segmentation with point representation. In: IEEE/CVF Conference on Computer Vision and Pattern Recognition (CVPR) (2020)

15. Lee, Y., Park, J.: Centermask: real-time anchor-free instance segmentation. In: IEEE/CVF Conference on Computer Vision and Pattern Recognition (CVPR) (2020)

16. Tian, Z., Shen, C., Chen, H.: Conditional convolutions for instance segmentation. In: Vedaldi, A., Bischof, H., Brox, T., Frahm, J.-M. (eds.) ECCV 2020, Part I. LNCS, vol. 12346, pp. 282–298. Springer, Cham (2020). https://doi.org/10.1007/978-3-030-58452-8_17

17. Tian, Z., Shen, C., Chen, H., He, T.: FCOS: fully convolutional one-stage object detection. In: The IEEE International Conference on Computer Vision (ICCV) (2019)

18. Fathi, A., et al.: Semantic instance segmentation via deep metric learning. CoRR abs/1703.10277 (2017)

19. De Brabandere, B., Neven, D., Van Gool, L.: Semantic instance segmentation for autonomous driving. In: The IEEE Conference on Computer Vision and Pattern Recognition (CVPR) Workshops (2017)

20. Wang, X., Kong, T., Shen, C., Jiang, Y., Li, L.: SOLO: segmenting objects by locations. In: Vedaldi, A., Bischof, H., Brox, T., Frahm, J.-M. (eds.) ECCV 2020, Part XVIII. LNCS, vol. 12363, pp. 649–665. Springer, Cham (2020). https://doi.org/10.1007/978-3-030-58523-5_38

21. Lin, T.Y., Dollar, P., Girshick, R., He, K., Hariharan, B., Belongie, S.: Feature pyramid networks for object detection. In: The IEEE Conference on Computer Vision and Pattern Recognition (CVPR) (2017)

22. Xiao, T., Liu, Y., Zhou, B., Jiang, Y., Sun, J.: Unified perceptual parsing for scene understanding. In: Ferrari, V., Hebert, M., Sminchisescu, C., Weiss, Y. (eds.) ECCV 2018, Part V. LNCS, vol. 11209, pp. 432–448. Springer, Cham (2018). https://doi.org/10.1007/978-3-030-01228-1_26

23. He, K., Zhang, X., Ren, S., Sun, J.: Deep residual learning for image recognition. In: The IEEE Conference on Computer Vision and Pattern Recognition (CVPR) (2016)

24. Novotny, D., Albanie, S., Larlus, D., Vedaldi, A.: Semi-convolutional operators for instance segmentation. In: Ferrari, V., Hebert, M., Sminchisescu, C., Weiss, Y. (eds.) ECCV 2018, Part I. LNCS, vol. 11205, pp. 89–105. Springer, Cham (2018). https://doi.org/10.1007/978-3-030-01246-5_6

25. Kendall, A., Gal, Y., Cipolla, R.: Multi-task learning using uncertainty to weigh losses for scene geometry and semantics. In: The IEEE Conference on Computer Vision and Pattern Recognition (CVPR) (2018)

26. Rahman, M.A., Wang, Y.: Optimizing intersection-over-union in deep neural networks for image segmentation. In: Bebis, G., et al. (eds.) ISVC 2016, Part I. LNCS, vol. 10072, pp. 234–244. Springer, Cham (2016). https://doi.org/10.1007/978-3-319-50835-1_22

27. Rezatofighi, H., Tsoi, N., Gwak, J., Sadeghian, A., Reid, I., Savarese, S.: Generalized intersection over union: a metric and a loss for bounding box regression. In: The IEEE Conference on Computer Vision and Pattern Recognition (CVPR) (2019)

28. Szegedy, C., Vanhoucke, V., Ioffe, S., Shlens, J., Wojna, Z.: Rethinking the inception architecture for computer vision. In: The IEEE Conference on Computer Vision and Pattern Recognition (CVPR) (2016)

29. Russakovsky, O., et al.: ImageNet large scale visual recognition challenge. Int. J. Comput. Vis. 115(3), 211–252 (2015). https://doi.org/10.1007/s11263-015-0816-y

30. Loshchilov, I., Hutter, F.: SGDR: stochastic gradient descent with warm restarts. In: International Conference on Learning Representations (ICLR) 2017 Conference Track (2017)

31. Liu, W., et al.: SSD: single shot MultiBox detector. In: Leibe, B., Matas, J., Sebe, N., Welling, M. (eds.) ECCV 2016, Part I. LNCS, vol. 9905, pp. 21–37. Springer, Cham (2016). https://doi.org/10.1007/978-3-319-46448-0_2

32. Buslaev, A., Iglovikov, V.I., Khvedchenya, E., Parinov, A., Druzhinin, M., Kalinin, A.A.: Albumentations: fast and flexible image augmentations. Information 11, 125 (2020)

33. Paszke, A., et al.: Pytorch: an imperative style, high-performance deep learning library. In: Advances in Neural Information Processing Systems, vol. 32, pp. 8024–8035. Curran Associates, Inc. (2019)

34. Massa, F., Girshick, R.: Mask R-CNN benchmark: Fast, modular reference implementation of Instance Segmentation and Object Detection algorithms in PyTorch (2018). https://github.com/facebookresearch/maskrcnn-benchmark

Multi-task Learning with Future States for Vision-Based Autonomous Driving

Inhan Kim$^{(\boxtimes)}$, Hyemin Lee , Joonyeong Lee , Eunseop Lee ,
and Daijin Kim

Department of Computer Science and Engineering, POSTECH, Pohang-si, Korea
{kiminhan,lhmin,joonyeonglee,eunseop90,dkim}@postech.ac.kr

Abstract. Human drivers consider past and future driving environments to maintain stable control of a vehicle. To adopt a human driver's behavior, we propose a vision-based autonomous driving model, called Future Actions and States Network (FASNet), which uses predicted future actions and generated future states in multi-task learning manner. Future states are generated using an enhanced deep predictive-coding network and motion equations defined by the kinematic vehicle model. The final control values are determined by the weighted average of the predicted actions for a stable decision. With these methods, the proposed FASNet has a high generalization ability in unseen environments. To validate the proposed FASNet, we conducted several experiments, including ablation studies in realistic three-dimensional simulations. FASNet achieves a higher Success Rate (SR) on the recent CARLA benchmarks under several conditions as compared to state-of-the-art models.

Keywords: Vision-based autonomous driving · Controller with future actions · Multi-task learning based autonomous driving

1 Introduction

Traditionally, an autonomous vehicle can drive itself using localization information and motion equations defined by the kinematic vehicle model. With advances in deep learning, the classical rules for manipulating the vehicle can be learned by deep neural networks. Recently, we have witnessed wide and significant progress in autonomous driving, especially in the field of computer vision [1–5]. Furthermore, starting with a Conditional Imitation Learning (CIL) [6], several successive studies [6–11] apply high-level navigational commands (i.e., Follow Lane, Go Straight, Turn Right, and Turn Left) as provided by a navigation system to guide the global optimal path to reach the final destination.

Despite the impressive progress, vision-based autonomous vehicles face unexpected situations that can reduce driving accuracy and stability. For example,

Electronic supplementary material The online version of this chapter (https://doi.org/10.1007/978-3-030-69535-4_40) contains supplementary material, which is available to authorized users.

H. Ishikawa et al. (Eds.): ACCV 2020, LNCS 12624, pp. 654–669, 2021.
https://doi.org/10.1007/978-3-030-69535-4_40

the autonomous vehicle can turn abruptly or stop and never move. Once an abnormal behavior is caused by an incorrectly predicted control value, unsafe situations are likely to occur and it may take a long time to recover to a safe driving situation. In addition, several authors [7,9,11–13] have highlighted limited capability of a model trained with a single task learning manner or single RBG image as an input. To tackle this problem, we focus on the ways to reduce unstable control and increase the generalization ability of the vehicle controller.

First, we observed that human drivers manipulate vehicles safely by anticipating future situations. For example, when human drivers approach an intersection, they anticipate when to slow down and when to turn the steering wheel. This is the main reason why human drivers can usually control a vehicle with stability. However, most autonomous driving research uses only current information for decision making, which can lead to unstable longitudinal or lateral control. Motivated by this observation, we utilize the generated future frame using the concept of Deep Predictive-Coding Network (PredNet) [14] and calculated future localization information using kinematic motion equations [15].

Second, it improves the generalization and regularization abilities of the trained model with Multi-task Learning (MTL). MTL is a good solution for generalization by leveraging domain-specific information contained in training representations of other tasks through a joint optimization strategy [16]. Furthermore, learning with auxiliary tasks in MTL will improve the generalization for the main tasks without introducing any extra computational burden at inference time. Finally, MTL acts as a regularizer, which reduces the risk of overfitting, by introducing an inductive bias. With these benefits, MTL has displayed success in the field of autonomous driving [7,9,12,13].

Our key contributions are summarized as follows: 1) We present a successful vision-based driving architecture based on the weighted average of future actions by preventing the situation wherein a single incorrect control action makes the vehicle's movement unstable; 2) We designed the MTL model, including auxiliary tasks, by generating future representations and future localization information without additional knowledge compared with a baseline model; and 3) We achieve enhanced and stable driving results, especially in unseen environments by applying these concepts to base networks.

2 Related Work

2.1 Deep Learning Based Autonomous Driving

There has been a steady release of various driving models that map camera pixels directly to the longitudinal and lateral controls. End-to-end driving models automatically learn important representations of the necessary processing steps, such as recognizing useful road features. Bojarski et al. [3] demonstrated that a vehicle could potentially be controlled using a deep Convolutional Neural Network (CNN) based solely on a front-facing camera. Following this research, various CNN-based end-to-end networks have been investigated [4,6,7,17–19].

Other researchers are investigating Reinforcement Learning (RL) for controlling vehicles using, which trains a deep neural network based on a policy-based reward [8,20,21]. These systems can be generalized for unseen scenarios, and their performance will be coverage of human driving. In these studies, the main aim is to learn human-controllable policy in a trial-and-error manner without explicit human supervision. However, RL-based approaches are difficult to apply in the real world because the training process is not reliable and fatal accidents may occur.

Recently, many studies have employed MTL to achieve the optimal information exchange between highly correlated tasks [7,9,12,21–23]. Furthermore, based on these approaches, some studies employ auxiliary tasks, such as the result of segmentation network and optical flow as well as raw image [11,13]. One of the reasons for this success is attributed to the inbuilt sharing mechanism, which allows deep neural networks to learn representations shared across different categories. This insight naturally extends to sharing between tasks and leads to further performance improvements.

Many studies have contributed to significant driving performance improvements; however, these studies may predict the unexpected control values that can reduce driving accuracy and stability. While driving, the vehicle can become quite unstable with just one wrong control value, particularly at higher speeds. Thus, we focus on a stable driving model and propose FASNet, which employs a weighted average action based on multiple predicted actions.

2.2   Action Prediction with Generated Representation

Various methods to predict realistic pixel values in future frames have been investigated [24,25]. Most state-of-the-art approaches use generative neural networks to represent the pixel-wise appearance of a given image in a video sequence. The performance of these networks is undoubtedly impressive.

However, future frame prediction is a challenging task due to the complex appearance and motion dynamics. To address this problem, joint learning is the most commonly explored approach to model complex motion fields [26,27]. In [26], the authors attempt to jointly train the network to resolve the prediction problems that derive from complex pixel-level distributions in natural images. In addition, an effective future frame prediction method for complex urban driving scenes utilizing video and optical flow sequences has been proposed [27].

Furthermore, recent research shows that learning correlated tasks simultaneously can enhance the performance of individual tasks [28]. In [29], the authors proposed a MTL approach by jointly predicting steering angles and future frame sequences. In addition, the latent variables of a multi-task generative network can be effectively used to predict vehicle steering angles [14,30]. In this paper, we utilize an enhanced PredNet that has a specialized neural network branches, similar to the conditional branch in [6]. The branches are also selectively trained via high-level commands that indicate where the vehicle will go. With the conditional branches, we can generate more accurate future images and latent variables for angle prediction.

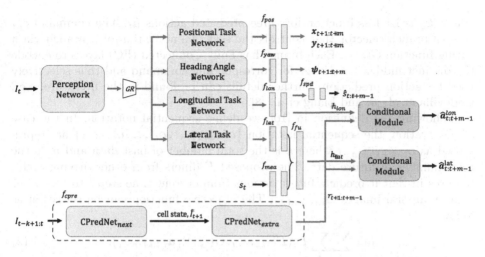

Fig. 1. Overall architecture of the FASNet. A perception network processes an input image to a latent space followed by four task-specific networks: two for localization tasks and two for control tasks. The subnetwork f_{cpre}, which has two submodules CPredNet$_{next}$ and CPredNet$_{extra}$, generates future representations from past sequential images. The future representations and embedded features by FC layers fused and fed into the conditional module, which predicting future longitudinal and lateral control values according to the navigational command.

3   Method

3.1   Task Definition

Conditional Imitation Learning (CIL) [6] for autonomous driving is a form of supervised learning that can learn a driving policy from human driver experts using given N video sequences v_i, $i \in (1, \ldots, N)$ with observations $o_{i,t}$, actions $a_{i,t}$, and high-level navigational commands $c_{i,t}$. Basically, all datasets have at least one command: follow the lane (Follow Lane). Various additional commands are added according to the driving scenarios, such as drive straight (Go Straight), turn left at the next intersection (Turn Left), and turn right at the next intersection (Turn Right). The observations consist of tuples, each of which contains an image ($I_{i,t}$) and measured signals, such as speed ($s_{i,t}$). Here, $a_{i,t}$ actions include steering angle ($a_{i,t}^{str}$), an acceleration value ($a_{i,t}^{acc}$) and braking value ($a_{i,t}^{brk}$) of the human driver to manipulate the vehicle. The dataset is defined $D = \{(o_{i,t}, a_{i,t}, c_{i,t})\}_{i=1}^{N}$.

The expanded strategy of the CIL is that CIL with a ResNet backbone Speed prediction (CILRS) model [7]. The CILRS objective function, which minimizes the parameters θ of the action prediction network (F), is expressed as follows:

$$\min_{\theta} \sum_{i}^{N} \sum_{t}^{T_i} L_a(F(I_{i,t}, s_{i,t}, G(c_{i,t})), a_{i,t}), \tag{1}$$

where L_a is L1 loss function for three predicted actions $\hat{a}_t$. The command $c_{i,t}$ acts as branch selector that controls the selective activation of a branch via a gating function $G(c_{i,t})$. Each branch has Fully Connected (FC) layers to encode the distinct hidden knowledge for corresponding command and thus selectively used for action prediction. Further details can be found in the literature, e.g., Codevilla et al. [6] and Liang et al. [8].

Following the definition in [10], we define sequential notation. In the case of observation, the sequential notation $\{o_{t-k+1}, \ldots, o_t, \ldots, o_{t+m-1}\}$ are represented as $o_{t-k+1:t+m-1}$ where k is the total number of past data and m is the total number of future data. The proposed F differs from other driving architectures in that it predicts future actions from current time step t to $t+m-1$ using temporal images $(I_{i,t-k+1:t})$. The objective function can be rewritten as follows:

$$\min_\theta \sum_i^N \sum_t^{T_i} L_a(F(I_{i,t}, s_{i,t}, G(c_{i,t})), a_{i,t:t+m-1}), \tag{2}$$

where $a_{i,t:t+m-1}$ is the sequential ground truth of actions, T_i is total time at each video sequence, and L_a is also the L1 loss function for predicted sequential actions $\hat{a}_{t:t+m-1}$:

$$L_a = \sum_t^{t+m-1} ||\hat{a}_{i,t}^{str} - a_{i,t}^{str}||^1 + ||\hat{a}_{i,t}^{acc} - a_{i,t}^{acc}||^1 + ||\hat{a}_{i,t}^{brk} - a_{i,t}^{brk}||^1. \tag{3}$$

3.2 Conditional Future Actions and States Prediction Network

We propose a novel architecture to predict future actions $(\hat{a}_{t:t+m-1})$. Note that for simplicity, hereafter, the index of video sequences will be omitted in the definitions. We use a ResNet34 architecture [31] pretrained on the ImageNet as a backbone network for generalized driving on learning reactions to dynamic objects in complex environments [7]. As shown in Fig. 1, the ResNet34 architecture is divided into two groups: 1) Convolution stages from *Conv1* to *Conv4* are utilized for the perception network. The output feature map of the perception network is shared between all related task-specific subnetworks on hard parameter sharing manner. 2) The last convolution stage (*Conv5*) is used for task-specific networks. The feature maps, which are fed into each subnetworks, are trained to represent features that focus more on each task. Specifically, the task-specific network has a FC layer to embed the extracted features.

The positional task and heading angle networks in Fig. 1 estimate the future localization states such as positions of the vehicle in global coordinates $(x_{t+1:t+m}, y_{t+1:t+m})$ and heading angles $(\psi_{t+1:t+m})$. These localization tasks, which are closely related to target control tasks, are considered the auxiliary tasks to improve the generalization of the main tasks. Therefore, the positional task and heading angle networks are utilized only at the training time. The loss function of the localization states is defined as follows:

$$L_l = \sum_t^{t+m-1} ||\hat{x}_{t+1} - x_{t+1}||^2 + ||\hat{y}_{t+1} - y_{t+1}||^2 + ||\hat{\psi}_{t+1} - \psi_{t+1}||^2, \tag{4}$$

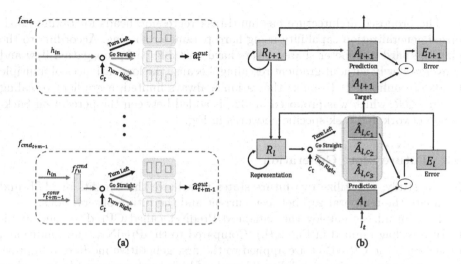

Fig. 2. (a) Architecture of the conditional module. The h_{in} can be the h_{lon} or h_{lat}. Additionally, the $\hat{a}^{out}$ can be the $\hat{a}^{lon}$ or $\hat{a}^{lat}$ as well. (b) Information flow in two level modules in CPredNet. Each module consists of a recurrent representation layer (R_l), an input convolutional layer (A_l), a prediction layer ($\hat{A}_l$), and an error representation unit (E_l). In addition, a gating function choose activation layer in the first level using a command (c_t).

The longitudinal task network considers longitudinal outputs by processing the latent space followed by two prediction branches: one for hidden variables h_{lon} to predict longitudinal actions ($\hat{a}^{acc}_{t:t+m-1}$, $\hat{a}^{brk}_{t:t+m-1}$) and one for speed sequence ($\hat{s}_{t:t+m-1}$) to achieve an effect of regularization [7]. The output, which passes through the lateral task network and f_{lat}, is fuse with the output of f_{mea} by f_{ffu} in Fig. 1.

f_{cpre} comprises two modified PredNets, which we refer to as CPredNets. The CPredNets generate future representations using sequential past images ($I_{t-k+1:t}$) and high-level command (c_t) as inputs. The outputs of f_{cpre} are defined as $r_{t+1:t+m-1}$, where each r_t is the lowest representation layer in the CPredNet, which learned latent variables to generate future frames $\hat{I}_{t+1:t+m-1}$. Note that the model can make optimal actions when there is no temporal gap between o and $\hat{a}$. Therefore, predicting $\hat{a}_{t+1:t+m-1}$ without $o_{t+1:t+m-1}$ may reduce the accuracy. To prevent such loss of accuracy, the representational features $r_{t+1:t+m-1}$ act as the observation of the corresponding time step.

Each conditional module of $f_{cmd_{t+n}}$ has FC layers and a gating function to encode the distinct hidden knowledge for the corresponding command and thus is selectively used for prediction. However, in the case of $n > 0$, there is additional FC layer f^{cmd}_{fu} in Fig. 2(a) to combine inputs. Before fusing these features, we apply some 3×3 convolutional layers to $r_{t+1:t+m-1}$ to extract meaningful information named r^{conv}_{t+n}.

The proposed architecture has multi-task regression heads for taking maximized generalization capability using hard parameter sharing. According to the [32], the hard parameter shared layers have unstable backpropagation flow and converge slowly without gradient rescaling, because the loss variances of multiple heads are unlimited. To make the variance always limited, a gradient rescaling module GR, which was proposed in [32], is added between the perception backbone network and task-specific networks in Fig. 1.

3.3 Future State Generation

In this study, we utilize two future states to achieve the benefits of MTL and eliminate the temporal gap between current and the future observations.

First of all, we employ the enhanced PredNet called CPredNet and architecture is diagrammed in Fig. 2.(b). Compared to the PredNet, the conditional branches in the CPredNet are applied to the first generative module to improve future frame generation capability. The role of high-level command (c_t) is a clear indicator of the directional change and acts as a switch that selects which representation branch is used at any given situation. The CPredNet follows all the PredNet training rules, except for the conditional learning. The further details and full set of update rules can be found in supplementary material.

The second way to generate the future state is to employ motion equations defined by the kinematic vehicle model. In this study, a discrete kinematic bicycle model with the desired point on the center of the front axle is used to describe the vehicle dynamics. According to the kinematic analysis, the vehicle localization information, which the position of the vehicle in global coordinates (x, y) and consists of heading angle (ψ), at that time $t + 1$ are given as follows:

$$x_{t+1} = x_t + s_t cos(\delta_t + \psi_t)\Delta t \tag{5}$$

$$y_{t+1} = y_t + s_t sin(\delta_t + \psi_t)\Delta t \tag{6}$$

$$\psi_{t+1} = \psi_t + \frac{s_t tan(\delta_t)}{l}\Delta t \tag{7}$$

where δ is the wheel steering angle and l is the wheel base.

Because we consider the offset of localization information from current position and heading angle, the first current states x_t, y_t, and ψ_t can be set to zero. And then we can calculate the future coordinates and heading angles recursively. In addition, we set the constant values Δt and l to 0.1 and 3, respectively.

3.4 Kinematic Relation Based Learning

The main goal of kinematic-relation based learning is that leveraging useful representation contained in multiple related task-specific networks to help improve the generalization performance of the control tasks. In order to utilize the effect of this relation to the proposed architecture, we define implicit relation loss functions.

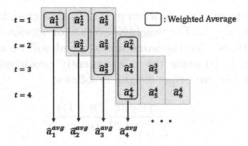

Fig. 3. Illustration of weighted average concept.

The Eqs. (5)–(7) can be expressed with respect to the speed s_t and steering angle δ_t.

$$s_t = \frac{x_{t+1}}{cos(\delta_t)} = \frac{y_{t+1}}{sin(\delta_t)} \tag{8}$$

$$\delta_t = tan^{-1}(\frac{\psi_{t+1}}{s_t}) \tag{9}$$

We can reformulate the Eqs. (5) and (6) to define the formula expressed with respect to the steering angle δ_t, but we use the Eq. (7). Because if we use the Eqs. (5) and (6), an arccosine and arcsine functions are included. Kinematic motion equations are utilized in training process with predicted outputs from the network. In this case, as the domain of the arccosine and arcsine functions are from -1 to $+1$ inclusive, the inputs of both functions should be restricted by clipping or scaling. This human intervention in the learning process can produce unexpected results.

The Eq. (8) and (9) indicate that the current vehicle control value and localization state of $t+1$ can be determined by each other. According to the relation, assuming that the steering angle δ_t and next position x_{t+1}, y_{t+1} are well estimated, we can calculate the accurate speed s_t. In addition, the δ_t is calculated as well as the predicted ψ_{t+1} and s_t using Eq. (9). The output from the each task-specific head has a relation with other outputs. To add the relationship between the prediction heads directly, the explicit relational loss function is defined as follows:

$$L_r = \sum_{t}^{t+m-1} ||\frac{\hat{y}_{t+1}}{sin(\hat{\delta}_t)} - s_t||^2 + ||\frac{\hat{x}_{t+1}}{cos(\hat{\delta}_t)} - s_t||^2 + ||tan^{-1}(\frac{\hat{\psi}_{t+1}}{\hat{s}_t}) - \delta_t||^2, \tag{10}$$

where $\hat{\delta}_t$ can be replaced by $\hat{a}^{str}$. The pair of related regression heads can be jointly optimized with backpropagation to estimate accurate prediction.

3.5   Weighted Average Action

In order to make a stable action value, we utilize a weighted average method. Here, we redefine a predicted action as $\hat{a}_q^p$, where p is a time step index and q is an index of the predicted sequence corresponding to the time step.

In Fig. 3, we show an example when m is 3. In that case, for each time step t, the FASNet predicts $\hat{a}_{t:t+2}^{t}$. The weighted average of actions $(\hat{a}_t^{avg})$ is calculated using predicted actions with the same index q and will be used as the control signal at that time t. To make the most recently predicted value contributes more to the final result, we define weight as follows:

$$w_q^p = \frac{e(log_b(q - p + 1))}{\sum_{i=1}^{min(q,m)} e(log_b(i)))}, \tag{11}$$

where b is greater than 0 and less than 1. The contribution of the predicted actions can be adjusted using b.

4   Experiments

4.1   Implementation in Detail

Before training whole network, we first update the weights of f_{cpre}. During the training stage, CPredNets are trained using the same experimental setting as PredNet [14]. CPredNet$_{next}$ is pretrained using sequences of the previous k frames, and then the weights are fine-tuned for extrapolation. To prevent a decrease in computation speed, the CPredNets comprise three-level generative modules with a channel size of (3, 48, and 96). In addition, the input images are resized to 100×44 by interpolation.

As mentioned previously, the representation layer r_t passes through convolutional layers and then fused by f_{fu}^{cmd}. We use six convolutional layers, and all layers are followed by Batch Normalization (BN) and Rectified Linear Unit (ReLU) activation. The detailed setting of each layer for r_t is shown in Table 1.

The number of hidden units of the f_{pos}, f_{yaw}, f_{lon}, f_{lat}, f_{mea}, f_{spd}, and f_{fu} layers are same as the CILRS network [7]. Additionally, the sizes of the last FC layer of f_{pos} and f_{yaw} are $2 \times m$ and m, respectively. Finally, the size of f_{fu}^{cmd} is 512. In our experiment, sequences of 9 frames are sampled for training, and our model predicts 3 consecutive actions ($k = 6$, $m = 3$). In addition, we set b to 0.4 for the weighted average. Our model is trained using the Adam solver with mini-batches of 200 samples. The learning rate is set to 0.0001 at the beginning and then it decreases by a factor 0.1 at 50 % and 75 % of the total number of training epochs. The total multi-task loss function is defined as:

$$L_t = \lambda_a L_a + \lambda_l L_l + \lambda_c L_c + \lambda_r L_r + \lambda_s L_s, \tag{12}$$

where L_c is the f_{cpre} loss and L_s is a loss for speed prediction branch. We set the λ_a, λ_l, λ_c, λ_r, and λ_s to 0.5, 0.15, 0.15, 0.1 and 0.1, respectively.

4.2   Benchmark and Dataset

The CARLA simulator has a large variety of driving environments, such as traffic lights and dynamic obstacles, including dynamic vehicles and pedestrians. We employ the original CARLA benchmark [33], *NoCrash* benchmark [7], and

Table 1. Network architecture applied to representation layers $r_{t+1:t+m-1}$.

Layer type	Kernel size	Feature maps	Stride
Conv-BN-ReLU	(3, 3)	32	2
Conv-BN-ReLU	(3, 3)	32	1
Conv-BN-ReLU	(3, 3)	64	2
Conv-BN-ReLU	(3, 3)	64	1
Conv-BN-ReLU	(3, 3)	128	2
Conv-BN-ReLU	(3, 3)	128	1

AnyWeather benchmark[19] on CARLA simulator to evaluate the proposed method. For a fair comparison with the other methods, we follow the benchmark polices [7,33]. All benchmarks evaluate the driving performance under four environments "Training Conditions", "New Weather", "New Town", and "New Town & Weather" in terms of Success Rate (SR).

We collect the training data while using the autopilot [34] of the CARLA simulator for approximately 100 h. For augmentation and teaching the model how to recover from a poor position [3], we use three RGB cameras by adjusting the roll values of the left and right cameras by −20 and 20 degrees from the middle camera, respectively. As most of the data are collected from straight driving scenes, we refer to the idea of sampling [10] to solve the data imbalance problem. Additionally, we perform extensive data augmentation by adding Gaussian blur, additive Gaussian noise, additive and multiplicative brightness variation, contrast variation, and saturation variation to prevent overfitting.

4.3 Experimental Result

We compare our FASNet model with the recent state-of-the-art approaches: the Conditional Imitation Learning (CIL) [6] extension with a ResNet backbone and speed prediction model (CILRS) [7], Learning By Cheating (LBC) [11] model, Implicit Affordances based Reinforcement Learning (IARL) [21] model, and Learning Situational Driving (LSD) [19] model. The closest baseline model to ours is the CILRS model. We set the same experimental settings, such as dataset conditions (including image resolution) and perception network. The LBC and IARL models rely on different prior information such as the 3D position of all external dynamic agents or semantic segmentation. Although the LSD uses an RGB image only, it utilizes a deeper backbone network (ResNet50) and a larger image resolution (256×256).

Table 2 reports the quantitative comparison on the original CARLA 0.8.4 benchmark with state-of-the-art networks. This benchmark consists of four driving tasks "Straight", "One Turn", "Navigation", and "Navigation with Dynamic Obstacles" [33]. Compared to the baseline model, the proposed FASNet exhibits significant improvements especially under the "New Town" environment. In addition, we achieved the state-of-the-art driving performance among the models, which use only RGB images for training and evaluation.

Table 2. Comparison with the state-of-the-art networks on the original CARLA 0.8.4 benchmark in terms of Success Rate (SR) in each condition. The results are percentage (%) of SR and higher values are better.

Task	Training conditions					New Weather				
	CILRS[7]	LSD[19]	FASNet	LBC [11]	IARL [21]	CILRS [7]	LSD [19]	FASNet	LBC [11]	IARL [21]
Straight	96	-	100	100	100	96	-	100	100	100
One Turn	92	-	100	100	100	96	-	100	96	100
Navigation	95	-	100	100	100	96	-	99	100	100
Nav. Dynamic	92	-	100	100	100	96	-	98	96	100
Task	New Town					New Town & Weather				
	CILRS [7]	LSD [19]	FASNet	LBC [11]	IARL [21]	CILRS [7]	LSD [19]	FASNet	LBC [11]	IARL [21]
Straight	96	100	100	100	100	96	100	100	100	100
One Turn	84	99	100	100	100	92	100	100	100	100
Navigation	69	99	99	100	100	92	100	100	100	100
Nav. Dynamic	66	98	99	99	98	90	98	100	100	100

Table 3. Comparison with the state-of-the-art networks on the *NoCrash* CARLA benchmarks in terms of success rate in each condition.

Task	Training conditions					New weather				
	CILRS [7]	LSD [19]	FASNet	LBC [11]	IARL [21]	CILRS [7]	LSD [19]	FASNet	LBC [11]	IARL [21]
Empty	97 ± 2	-	96±0	97	100	96 ± 1	-	98 ± 0	87	36
Regular	83 ± 0	-	90 ± 1	93	96	77 ± 1	-	80 ± 1	87	34
Dense	42 ± 2	-	44 ± 2	71	70	47±5	-	38 ± 4	63	26
Task	New Town					New Town & Weather				
	CILRS[7]	LSD[19]	FASNet	LBC[11]	IARL[21]	CILRS[7]	LSD[19]	FASNet	LBC[11]	IARL[21]
Empty	66 ± 2	94 ±1	95 ± 1	100	99	90 ± 2	95±1	92±2	70	24
Regular	49±5	68±2	77±2	94	87	56±2	65±4	66±4	62	34
Dense	23±1	30±4	37±2	51	42	24±8	32±3	32±4	39	18

The *NoCrash* benchmark [7] measures the capability of the controller to react to dynamic objects for three driving tasks: "Empty", "Regular Traffic", and "Dense Traffic". Quantitative comparisons on the *NoCrash* benchmark are reported in Table 3. The LBC and IARL, which utilize additional prior knowledge, are evaluated on the version of CARLA 0.9.6. Compared to the RGB-based models, we achieve state-of-the-art performances in the "New Town" conditions and "Regular" tasks. We established that training with various related tasks could make a more generalized model under unseen environments. Additionally, we observe that the accidents caused by unexpected single control value are alleviated through the weighted average action of future predictions. Moreover, our proposed model significantly improves over the baseline model except for the "Dense Traffic" tasks in the training town. Most of our failure, in the "Dense Traffic" task, is that pedestrians and other vehicles crash into the ego-vehicle. In some cases, the intersection is already blocked by an accident.

The *AnyWeather* benchmark is a new benchmark to quantify the ability of drastically diverse weather conditions. The evaluation condition is a new town under all ten weathers unseen in training. The results are presented in Table 4. It is observable that FASNet achieves state-of-the-art SRs under all tasks. This aspect means that the proposed architecture has higher generalization capability and robustness to unseen environments. We observe that most of our failure cases

Table 4. Experimental results the harsh environments on the *AnyWeather* benchmark in terms of success rate.

Task	New Town & Weather		
	CILRS	LSD	FASNet
Straight	83.2	85.6	**93.2**
One Turn	78.4	81.6	**87.0**
Navigation	76.4	79.6	**82.8**
Nav. Dynamic	75.6	78.4	**81.2**

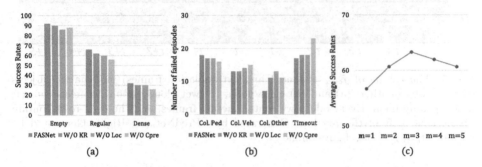

Fig. 4. Results of the ablation studies on the CARLA *NoCrash* benchmark under "New Town & Weather" conditions, which requires the highest generalization. (a) success rates, (b) number of failed episodes, and (c) average success rates of FASNet with different number of future actions.

are under the "MidRainSunset" and "HardRainSunset". As the lane on the road is invisible, predicting stable steering control value is difficult.

During the inference stage, the computation time required by FASNet is approximately 0.04~0.06 ms on a Titan RTX.

4.4   Ablation Studies

To evaluate whether our approaches improve accuracy, we conducted another experiment without the explicit kinematic relational loss (W/O KR), the localization task-specific networks (W/O Loc), and the f_{cpre} network (W/O Cpre) in Fig. 4. In the case of "W/O Cpre", future representations are not used, including future actions. In summary, the absence of any module causes the Success Rate (SR) to decrease, as shown in Fig. 4.(a). As seen in Fig. 4.(b), the number of collisions with others (Col. Other) shows a considerable increase even in the absence of a single component. This indicates that the vehicle has come off the road owing to unexpected behavior with a lack of generalization ability. Further, the high failure rates of "Col. Other" confirm the usefulness of the localization tasks for safe driving. The major cause of failure in the case of "W/O Cpre" is "Timeout". This happens because the vehicle stops and never moves caused by

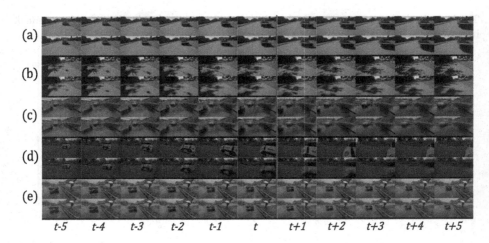

Fig. 5. The results of f_{cpre} (for next and extrapolation frames) in dynamic objects with various weather: (a) and (b) clear noon, (c) wet cloudy noon, (d) clear sunset, and (e) rainy noon. Every odd rows contain actual frames, and the even rows contain predictions. Left of the red line: Generated by CPredNet$_{next}$; Right: Generated by CPredNet$_{extra}$. (Color figure online)

an unexpected longitudinal control value. In addition, few input images prevent a car from operating normally, and this has led to a suspension from driving on the simulator. The weighted average action of future predictions can overcome this problem by degrading an effect of the incorrect prediction. The average SR values of FASNet for different number of future states to use (m) are shown in Fig. 4.(c). Parameter m indicates the number of future states employed. In the case of $m = 1$, the model equals to the "W/O Cpre" case. Our observation can be proven, because when $m > 1$, every average SR value is greater than that when $m = 1$.

4.5   Future State Generation

We make future representations using the CPredNets and localization information using a kinematic vehicle model without additional annotations. To verify that these methods can generate the knowledge successfully, we show the results for both approaches.

Fig. 5 shows the qualitative predictions on the test scenarios on the CARLA simulator. The CPredNets can generate fairly accurate frames under the various environments. The results of various weather and scenarios are represented in Fig. 5: (a) sunny/straight, (b) sunny/go straight with dynamic object, (c) wet cloudy/turn left, and (d) sunset/straight with dynamic object. Sometimes the CPredNets generate blurry objects and backgrounds (i.e., shadow of tree in (c) and yellow vehicle in (d)). However, as can be seen in Fig. 5, primarily activated factors for a making decision [3], such as road, lane, and curb are perfectly generated. This indicates that the generated future frame will not negatively affect

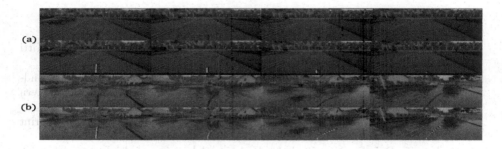

Fig. 6. Each image shows the coordinate changes from current position for 10 time steps: (a) stop scenario, (b) right turn scenario. Every odd row contains the ground truth coordinates and the even row contains the calculated coordinates with vehicle motion equations.

the prediction of the vehicle's action. Additionally, we report the comparison results between the CPredNet and PredNet in supplementary material.

Figure 6 shows the coordinates change from current to future positions qualitatively. Note that we calculate the positions of the vehicle in global coordinates with speed and the steering angle. As observable in Fig. 6, future locations are successfully calculated. Furthermore, the quantitative errors of calculated coordinates and vehicle heading are under 0.04 in terms of the mean square error.

5   Conclusion

In this study, we investigated a stable end-to-end vision-based autonomous driving model by weighted averaging of predicted future actions. We attempted to prevent a situation wherein a single incorrect control action renders the vehicle's movement unstable. To achieve enhanced generalization ability, we designed multi-head networks that are supervised by task-specific objectives including auxiliary localization tasks. During the training, the related tasks are jointly optimized with the shared layers, which serve as the regularizer. Thus, we generated training knowledge without any additional annotations. We have empirically shown that such a strategy can improve the generalization and driving performance of the base model through various experiments.

Acknowledgments. This work was supported by Institute of Information & communications Technology Planning & Evaluation (IITP) grant funded by the Korea government (MSIT) (No. 2014-0-00059, Development of Predictive Visual Intelligence Technology), (No. 2017-0-00897, Development of Object Detection and Recognition for Intelligent Vehicles) and (No. 2018-0-01290, Development of an Open Dataset and Cognitive Processing Technology for the Recognition of Features Derived From Unstructured Human Motions Used in Self-driving Cars).

References

1. Geiger, A., Lenz, P., Stiller, C., Urtasun, R.: Vision meets robotics: the Kitti dataset. Int. J. Robot. Res. **32**, 1231–1237 (2013)
2. Cordts, M., et al.: The cityscapes dataset for semantic urban scene understanding. In: Proceedings of the IEEE Conference on Computer Vision and Pattern Recognition, pp. 3213–3223 (2016)
3. Bojarski, M., et al.: End to end learning for self-driving cars. arXiv preprint arXiv:1604.07316 (2016)
4. Hecker, S., Dai, D., Van Gool, L.: End-to-end learning of driving models with surround-view cameras and route planners. In: Ferrari, V., Hebert, M., Sminchisescu, C., Weiss, Y. (eds.) ECCV 2018, Part VII. LNCS, vol. 11211, pp. 449–468. Springer, Cham (2018). https://doi.org/10.1007/978-3-030-01234-2_27
5. Huang, Z., Zhang, J., Tian, R., Zhang, Y.: End-to-end autonomous driving decision based on deep reinforcement learning. In: 2019 5th International Conference on Control, Automation and Robotics (ICCAR), pp. 658–662. IEEE (2019)
6. Codevilla, F., Miiller, M., López, A., Koltun, V., Dosovitskiy, A.: End-to-end driving via conditional imitation learning. In: 2018 IEEE International Conference on Robotics and Automation (ICRA), pp. 1–9. IEEE (2018)
7. Codevilla, F., Santana, E., López, A.M., Gaidon, A.: Exploring the limitations of behavior cloning for autonomous driving. In: Proceedings of the IEEE International Conference on Computer Vision, pp. 9329–9338 (2019)
8. Liang, X., Wang, T., Yang, L., Xing, E.: CIRL: controllable imitative reinforcement learning for vision-based self-driving. In: Ferrari, V., Hebert, M., Sminchisescu, C., Weiss, Y. (eds.) ECCV 2018, Part VII. LNCS, vol. 11211, pp. 604–620. Springer, Cham (2018). https://doi.org/10.1007/978-3-030-01234-2_36
9. Sauer, A., Savinov, N., Geiger, A.: Conditional affordance learning for driving in urban environments. arXiv preprint arXiv:1806.06498 (2018)
10. Wang, Q., Chen, L., Tian, B., Tian, W., Li, L., Cao, D.: End-to-end autonomous driving: An angle branched network approach. IEEE Trans. Veh. Technol.(2019)
11. Chen, D., Zhou, B., Koltun, V., Krähenbühl, P.: Learning by cheating. arXiv preprint arXiv:1912.12294 (2019)
12. Li, Z., Motoyoshi, T., Sasaki, K., Ogata, T., Sugano, S.: Rethinking self-driving: Multi-task knowledge for better generalization and accident explanation ability. arXiv preprint arXiv:1809.11100 (2018)
13. Chowdhuri, S., Pankaj, T., Zipser, K.: Multinet: Multi-modal multi-task learning for autonomous driving. In: 2019 IEEE Winter Conference on Applications of Computer Vision (WACV), pp. 1496–1504. IEEE (2019)
14. Lotter, W., Kreiman, G., Cox, D.: Deep predictive coding networks for video prediction and unsupervised learning. arXiv preprint arXiv:1605.08104 (2016)
15. Kong, J., Pfeiffer, M., Schildbach, G., Borrelli, F.: Kinematic and dynamic vehicle models for autonomous driving control design. In: 2015 IEEE Intelligent Vehicles Symposium (IV), pp. 1094–1099. IEEE (2015)
16. Zhang, Y., Yang, Q.: A survey on multi-task learning. arXiv preprint arXiv:1707.08114 (2017)
17. Xu, H., Gao, Y., Yu, F., Darrell, T.: End-to-end learning of driving models from large-scale video datasets. In: Proceedings of the IEEE Conference on Computer Vision and Pattern Recognition, pp. 2174–2182 (2017)
18. Chi, L., Mu, Y.: Deep steering: Learning end-to-end driving model from spatial and temporal visual cues. arXiv preprint arXiv:1708.03798 (2017)

19. Ohn-Bar, E., Prakash, A., Behl, A., Chitta, K., Geiger, A.: Learning situational driving. In: Proceedings of the IEEE/CVF Conference on Computer Vision and Pattern Recognition, pp. 11296–11305 (2020)

20. Yu, A., Palefsky-Smith, R., Bedi, R.: Deep reinforcement learning for simulated autonomous vehicle control, pp. 1–7. Course Project Reports, Winter (2016)

21. Toromanoff, M., Wirbel, E., Moutarde, F.: End-to-end model-free reinforcement learning for urban driving using implicit affordances. In: Proceedings of the IEEE/CVF Conference on Computer Vision and Pattern Recognition, pp. 7153–7162 (2020)

22. Tai, L., Yun, P., Chen, Y., Liu, C., Ye, H., Liu, M.: Visual-based autonomous driving deployment from a stochastic and uncertainty-aware perspective. arXiv preprint arXiv:1903.00821 (2019)

23. Yang, Z., Zhang, Y., Yu, J., Cai, J., Luo, J.: End-to-end multi-modal multi-task vehicle control for self-driving cars with visual perceptions. In: 2018 24th International Conference on Pattern Recognition (ICPR), pp. 2289–2294. IEEE (2018)

24. Mathieu, M., Couprie, C., LeCun, Y.: Deep multi-scale video prediction beyond mean square error. arXiv preprint arXiv:1511.05440 (2015)

25. Srivastava, N., Mansimov, E., Salakhudinov, R.: Unsupervised learning of video representations using LSTMs. In: International Conference on Machine Learning, pp. 843–852 (2015)

26. Liang, X., Lee, L., Dai, W., Xing, E.P.: Dual motion GAN for future-flow embedded video prediction. In: Proceedings of the IEEE International Conference on Computer Vision, pp. 1744–1752 (2017)

27. Wei, H., Yin, X., Lin, P.: Novel video prediction for large-scale scene using optical flow. arXiv preprint arXiv:1805.12243 (2018)

28. Ranjan, R., Patel, V.M., Chellappa, R.: Hyperface: a deep multi-task learning framework for face detection, landmark localization, pose estimation, and gender recognition. IEEE Trans. Pattern Anal. Mach. Intell. 41, 121–135 (2017)

29. Du, L., Zhao, Z., Su, F., Wang, L., An, C.: Jointly predicting future sequence and steering angles for dynamic driving scenes. In: ICASSP 2019–2019 IEEE International Conference on Acoustics, Speech and Signal Processing (ICASSP), pp. 4070–4074. IEEE (2019)

30. Jin, X., et al.: Predicting scene parsing and motion dynamics in the future. In: Advances in Neural Information Processing Systems, pp. 6915–6924 (2017)

31. He, K., Zhang, X., Ren, S., Sun, J.: Deep residual learning for image recognition. In: Proceedings of the IEEE Conference on Computer Vision and Pattern Recognition, pp. 770–778. (2016)

32. Song, G., Chai, W.: Collaborative learning for deep neural networks. In: Advances in Neural Information Processing Systems, pp. 1832–1841 (2018)

33. Dosovitskiy, A., Ros, G., Codevilla, F., Lopez, A., Koltun, V.: Carla: An open urban driving simulator. arXiv preprint arXiv:1711.03938 (2017)

34. felipecode: Carla 0.8.4 data collector (2018). https://github.com/carla-simulator/data-collector

MTNAS: Search Multi-task Networks for Autonomous Driving

Hao Liu[1](✉), Dong Li[2], JinZhang Peng[2], Qingjie Zhao[1], Lu Tian[2], and Yi Shan[2]

[1] Beijing Institute of Technology, Beijing, China
{3120181007,zhaoqj}@bit.edu.cn
[2] Xilinx Inc., Beijing, China
{dongl,jinzhang,lutian,yishan}@xilinx.com

Abstract. Multi-task learning (MTL) aims to learn shared representations from multiple tasks simultaneously, which has yielded outstanding performance in widespread applications of computer vision. However, existing multi-task approaches often demand manual design on network architectures, including shared backbone and individual branches. In this work, we propose MTNAS, a practical and principled neural architecture search algorithm for multi-task learning. We focus on searching for the overall optimized network architecture with task-specific branches and task-shared backbone. Specifically, the MTNAS pipeline consists of two searching stages: branch search and backbone search. For branch search, we separately optimize each branch structure for each target task. For backbone search, we first design a pre-searching procedure t1o pre-optimize the backbone structure on ImageNet. We observe that searching on such auxiliary large-scale data can not only help learn low-/mid-level features but also offer good initialization of backbone structure. After backbone pre-searching, we further optimize the backbone structure for learning task-shared knowledge under the overall multi-task guidance. We apply MTNAS to joint learning of object detection and semantic segmentation for autonomous driving. Extensive experimental results demonstrate that our searched multi-task model achieves superior performance for each task and consumes less computation complexity compared to prior hand-crafted MTL baselines. Code and searched models will be released at https://github.com/RalphLiu/MTNAS.

Keywords: Multi-task learning · Neural architecture search · Autonomous driving

1 Introduction

Multi-task learning (MTL) [1] is one of the popular research topics among a broad family of machine learning algorithms, which aims at learning multiple

Electronic supplementary material The online version of this chapter (https://doi.org/10.1007/978-3-030-69535-4_41) contains supplementary material, which is available to authorized users.

H. Ishikawa et al. (Eds.): ACCV 2020, LNCS 12624, pp. 670–687, 2021.
https://doi.org/10.1007/978-3-030-69535-4_41

tasks simultaneously. By learning shared representations across different tasks, MTL can further improve the performance for each task and reduce model complexity for inference. With the remarkable success of deep Convolutional Neural Networks (CNNs), Multi-task networks have shown outstanding performance in widespread applications of computer vision such as joint learning of face detection and landmark prediction [2], object detection and instance segmentation [3], pose estimation and action recognition [4]. MTL also has great significance in practical systems (e.g. autonomous driving) where both high performance and fast inference speed are required, especially on the resource-constrained devices.

However, most of the existing MTL methods directly use hand-crafted network architectures for joint learning of multiple tasks. This might be sub-optimal because: (1) The backbone is typically designed for large-scale image classification tasks (e.g., ImageNet). Thus the backbone architecture is not adaptive for different downstream tasks; (2) The branch often consists of simple architectures (e.g., a few stacked convolution or deconvolution layers), which may not sufficiently transfer the shared representations to each specific task.

Recently, neural architecture search (NAS) has achieved great progress by automatically seeking the optimal network architectures, instead of relying on expert knowledge and tedious trials. Much effort has been made on employing NAS for different tasks such as image classification [6–9], object detection [10–12] and semantic segmentation [13,14]. However, there have been little considerations on NAS for MTL in a unified framework. It is infeasible to simply apply existing NAS methods for jointly learning multi-task networks. First, proxy datasets/tasks are often required for searching architectures [6–9], which are often based on relatively small input and aim at classifying images only. The resulting structure is likely to be sub-optimal for other tasks, especially for those requiring high-resolution inputs. Although recent work [15] has been explored by directly optimizing the target task, it mainly focuses on the single basic classification task. Second, for more challenging tasks beyond classification, existing NAS algorithms only search part of networks, e.g., backbone [11,13], FPN structure [10] and ASPP architecture [14], which would not suffice the requirement of overall optimization for multiple tasks. Third, conventional ImageNet pre-training procedure is usually adopted to learn initialized network weights but can not optimize the network architectures for target downstream tasks.

To alleviate these problems, we propose a multi-task neural architecture search (MTNAS) algorithm in this work. We aim to optimize an *overall* network architecture for MTL with two stages: branch search and backbone search. For branch search, we optimize each branch architecture for each task separately. We observe that searching for *task-specific* branch architectures helps better adapt the feature representations to each target task. For backbone search, our goal is to optimize *task-shared* backbone architecture for better learning general shared representations with different tasks. To this end, we first design a pre-searching procedure to learn the initialized backbone architecture and further optimize it under the overall multi-task guidance. Unlike ImageNet pre-training, our pre-searching procedure can optimize architecture parameters and network weights simultaneously, offering good initialization for subsequent optimization. Our MTNAS pipeline is built on the recent differentiable NAS algorithms [9,16,17] by searching for the optimal computation cells in both of branch and backbone search stages.

We apply the proposed MTNAS approach for joint learning of object detection and semantic segmentation for autonomous driving using both single and mixed datasets. We focus on automatically generating light-weight multi-task networks for fast inference speed and high performance in such practical scenarios. Experimental results consistently demonstrate our MTNAS method performs favorably against the existing single-task/multi-task learning baselines. In particular, on the challenging mixed-set benchmark (i.e., combination of CityScapes, Waymo and BDD100K), our searched multi-task model, with 65% FLOPs only, achieves 3.5% higher mAP on detection and 2.0% higher mIoU on segmentation compared to the hand-crafted MTL counterpart. Besides, compared to the conventional ImageNet pre-training which only updates the network weights, our pre-searching procedure achieves superior performance (e.g., 1.2% gain on segmentation) by simultaneously optimizing network weights and architectures.

The main contributions of this paper are summarized as follows:

- We propose a practical and principled neural architecture search algorithm beyond single-task to multi-task learning. We search for the complete architectures instead of sub-optimal parts of network structure by optimizing task-specific branches and task-shared backbone.
- We develop a simple but effective pre-searching procedure by simultaneously optimizing the network weights and architectures for backbone. Such scheme serves as a better alternative of conventional ImageNet pre-training and provides good initialization of backbone structure for subsequent optimization.
- We apply the proposed MTNAS method to the joint learning of object detection and semantic segmentation in the autonomous driving scenarios. Extensive experimental results demonstrate the superiority of our searched multi-task model over the existing hand-crafted MTL baselines in terms of recognition performance and computation complexity.

2 Related Work

2.1 Multi-task Learning

Multi-task learning is a learning framework where multiple tasks are learned simultaneously [1]. By sharing commonalities across different tasks, MTL has widely shown promising performance for various applications [2–4]. Owing to the shared architectures and weights, multi-task networks can also improve the inference efficiency compared to separate models of each task.

One line of recent research on MTL is balancing different tasks [18,19] or seeking solutions with trade-offs between different tasks [20]. These works either learn fixed optimal weights or learn a set of optimal solutions. Another line of literature on MTL is investigating the optimal strategies of sharing network activations or parameters across different tasks [21–23]. Our approach is orthogonal to these strategies as we focus on searching optimal network architectures by jointly learning multiple tasks in this work.

Recently, some work has attempted to use one single network architecture for MTL by exploiting network redundancies to pack multiple tasks [24], developing multiple internal virtual models with different configurations for different tasks [25] or dynamically selecting the optimal model from a pool of candidates [26]. However, these approaches are often built for different classification tasks (e.g., ImageNet classification, scene classification, and fine-grained classification). Differently, our method can address more challenging tasks beyond classification.

Previous work that is mostly related to our method includes [27,28]. The work of [27] builds a self-organized neural network by dynamically composing different function blocks for each input. The work of [28] explores different evolution ways of routing and shared modules in MTL. Our method differs from these related approaches in three aspects. First, they perform architecture search by reinforcement learning or evolutionary algorithms, while we employ the efficient differentiable NAS to search for the optimal cell structure. Second, only final fully-connected layers are routed in the network by [27], whereas our method aims to optimize the overall multi-task network architecture instead of parts of the network. Third, these methods are only applied to classification tasks. Differently, we bring the best practices to realize a multi-task NAS on more challenging tasks (e.g., object detection and semantic segmentation) simultaneously.

2.2 Neural Architecture Search

In the past years, plentiful efforts have been made into manual design of high-performance networks [5,29–33]. Neural architecture search, as an emerging alternative approach, aims at designing networks automatically, which has attracted recent research interests. Three key components of NAS lie in search space, search algorithm and performance evaluator. (1) For search space, existing work constructs the final network architectures by directly searching for the entire network [6,7,34], searching for the repeatable cell structure [9,35,36] or exploiting hierarchical structure [13,37,38]. (2) For search algorithms, some works exploit reinforcement learning (RL) [7,15,34,39] to train recurrent neural network controllers for generating architectural hyperparameters of networks. Evolutionary algorithms (EA) provide an alternative to searching for neural architectures by evolving them with crossover and mutation [8,11]. However, these RL and EA methods tend to require intensive computation even on small input images. Recent work attempts to reduce the computational cost by weight sharing [6] or gradient-based optimization [9,35,40]. (3) For performance evaluator, existing work has explored mono-objective (i.e., accuracy) or multi-objective (e.g., accuracy, latency, and FLOPs) schemes. In this work, we follow the differentiable NAS [9,16,17] to search for the optimal cell structure for both branches and backbone, and combine multiple rewards from different tasks to guide the search procedures in an alternating way.

Most of existing NAS approaches target on image classification tasks, either requiring proxy datasets/tasks [7,9,12,35] or directly optimizing on target tasks [15]. The most recent NAS papers [41–43] mainly focus on improving the search algorithm for a single task while we aim to realize a multi-task NAS pipeline. Recent methods have investigated NAS for more tasks, e.g., object detection [11,12,44] and semantic segmentation [13]. However, these methods only search parts of networks such as the backbone or other functional units. In contrast, our method extends NAS from single-task to multi-task learning and aims to search for the overall network architecture.

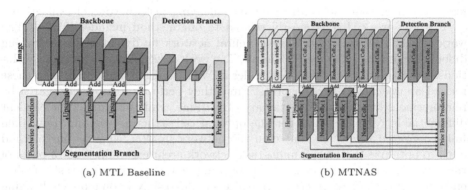

(a) MTL Baseline   (b) MTNAS

Fig. 1. Illustration of our hand-crafted multi-task network baseline and MTNAS architecture which includes backbone, detection branch, and segmentation branch.

3   Proposed Method

3.1   Hand-Crafted Multi-task Network Baseline

We first introduce the hand-crafted multi-task network baseline in this section. As shown in Fig. 1 (a), we build a backbone architecture to learn task-shared representations, followed by task-specific decoders that learn adapted representations for each task.

Backbone acts as a feature extractor to extract different abstract levels of shared representations in a multi-task network, which has a great impact on the performance of consecutive tasks. We use ImageNet pre-trained networks (e.g., ResNet) as our backbone but remove the last fully-connected classification layer associated with the pre-training task. We consider joint learning of object detection and semantic segmentation in this work. For the detection branch, we employ the SSD detection head [45] and aggregate prior box predictions from multiple feature maps of different resolutions. For the segmentation branch, similar to FCN [32], we stack several upsampling layers (each followed by ReLU activation and Batch Normalization) for pixel-wise prediction. We also integrate FPN structure [46] to further improve the quality of representations for both tasks.

3.2   Multi-task Neural Architecture Search

In this section, we first describe our search space design and search algorithm and then introduce the proposed MTNAS pipeline.

Search Space. We follow [9] to search for two types of computation cells (i.e., normal cell and reduction cell) as the building block of network architecture. Each cell is a directed acyclic graph $\mathcal{G} = (\mathcal{V}, \mathcal{E})$ where $\mathcal{V} = \{v_i\}|_{i=0}^{N-1}$ and $\mathcal{E} = \{e(i,j)\}|_{0 \le i < j \le N-1}$. Each node v_i represents a certain feature map in CNNs and each directed edge $e(i,j)$ represents a certain operation $o(i,j) \in \mathcal{O}$ transforming v_i to v_j. In this work, each cell has $|\mathcal{V}| = 7$ nodes (i.e., two input nodes, four intermediate nodes and one output node) and we set $|\mathcal{O}| = 8$ candidate operations [1] as our base search space. The base search space is shared across the entire search process including searching for architectures of backbone and branches.

Search Algorithm. Following [9], we solve the bi-level optimization problem to attain the optimal architecture parameters ϕ:

$$\min_{\phi} \mathcal{L}_{\text{val}}(\omega^*(\phi), \phi) \quad s.t. \quad \omega^*(\phi) = \arg\min_{\omega} \mathcal{L}_{\text{train}}(\omega, \phi) . \tag{1}$$

where $\mathcal{L}_{\text{train}}$ and $\mathcal{L}_{\text{val}}$ mean the training loss and validation loss, respectively. After obtaining the optimized architecture parameters, we can derive the final network architecture by preserving operations with the two largest probabilities. We also apply strategies of partial connection [17] and early stopping [16,47] to reduce the computation overhead during the multi-task search process. Besides, we apply SyncBN [48] to allow calculation of batch statistics across multiple GPU cards for the challenging tasks (e.g., detection and segmentation) which often require high-resolution input.

Multi-task Search Pipeline. We denote a multi-task network as $\mathcal{N}(\phi, \omega)$ where $\phi = \{\phi_0, \phi_1, \ldots, \phi_n\}$ and $\omega = \{\omega_0, \omega_1, \ldots, \omega_n\}$ represent the architecture parameters and network weights, respectively. Specifically, the index 0 indicates backbone and $\{i\}|_1^n$ indicate n branches in the multi-task network. Our goal is to search for the overall multi-task model with optimal architectures and weights:

$$\mathcal{N}(\phi^*, \omega^*)|_{\phi^{(0)}, \omega^{(0)}} . \tag{2}$$

where $\phi^{(0)}$ and $\omega^{(0)}$ mean the initialization of architecture parameters and network weights, respectively. We note that it is hard to directly optimize the overall multi-task architecture ϕ in practice because (1) Different optimization targets of each task may incur conflicts during searching for the task-specific branch

---

[1] *zero, skip-connect, max-pool-3x3, avg-pool3x3, sep-conv-3x3, sep-conv-5x5, dil-conv-3x3, dil-conv5x5.*

architectures; (2) It requires substantial GPU memory consumption since large search space is caused by optimizing different normal and reduction cells for multiple tasks at the same time. Thus, to reduce the search space and ease the optimization of joint search, we propose a two-stage multi-task search process: branch search and backbone search, as illustrated in Fig. 2. Specifically, we first search for the optimal branch architectures for each task separately and then search for the optimal backbone architecture under the overall guidance. For the reason of search order, we explain that our goal is to search for task-specific branches and task-shared backbone. When optimizing the backbone, we need to compute the loss from all the tasks. After obtaining the optimal branch architectures, backbone can benefit from each branch architecture and then learn shared knowledge across all tasks, leading to overall optimization for MTL.

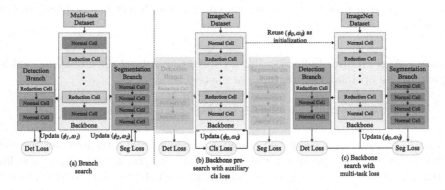

Fig. 2. Proposed multi-task neural architecture search (MTNAS) algorithm pipeline.

S1: Branch Search. The goal of this search stage is to optimize the task-specific branch architectures for each task. Thus, we address each target task separately so that these tasks will not affect each other. In other words, when optimizing i-th branch, only the loss $\mathcal{L}_i$ associated with this task is backpropagated through the network. The architectures and weights of other branches $(\phi_j, \omega_j)|_{j=1, j \neq i}^n$ are frozen. The backbone will be initialized with the same cells as the current branch and will be re-initialized when searching for another branch. After the branch search stage, we can obtain the task-specific branch models:

$$\mathcal{N}(\phi_i^*, \omega_i^*)|_{\phi_i^{(0)}, \omega_i^{(0)}}, \quad i \in \{1, 2, \ldots, n\} . \tag{3}$$

S2: Backbone Search. The goal of this search stage is to optimize task-shared backbone architectures for all tasks of interest. ImageNet pre-training has been widely used for various vision tasks as it can learn from large-scale data and provide a good weight initialization for different downstream tasks. We observe that large-scale data is also important to help optimize the backbone architecture. Thus, we propose a simple but effective pre-searching procedure to search for an initialized backbone architecture under the guidance of auxiliary ImageNet classification task. To this end, we freeze all branches (including architectures and weights) and append a fully-connected classification layer to the backbone. After pre-searching, a well-initialized backbone model is obtained:

$$\mathcal{N}(\phi'_0, \omega'_0)|_{\phi_0^{(0)}, \omega_0^{(0)}} \ . \tag{4}$$

The proposed pre-searching procedure can be viewed as a better alternative of ImageNet pre-training in the context of NAS. The auxiliary large-scale data not only helps learn the low-/mid-level features but also helps learn general cell architectures. Unlike ImageNet pre-training which only updates the network weights, our pre-searching can update both of architecture parameters and network weights, and provide better initialization of backbone structure for subsequent optimization.

With the pre-searched architecture parameters and network weights of the backbone as initialization, we further optimize the backbone structure under the overall multi-task guidance. Specifically, we design an alternating optimization strategy by incorporating iterative supervision from each task. For each iteration, only one loss from a single task will be backpropagated. The benefits of such scheme are two-fold. First, it helps improve training stability for the collaborative optimization of multiple tasks empirically. Second, it is flexible for MTL since it enables the utilization of datasets where only annotations of a single task are available. That is, we do not require complete labeled data of all tasks on a single dataset. In the stage of backbone search, branch architectures remain unchanged. Backbone can benefit from the optimal branches to learn shared knowledge from all tasks. The task-shared backbone will be generated after this backbone search stage:

$$\mathcal{N}(\phi_0^*, \omega_0^*)|_{\phi_0^{(0)}=\phi'_0, \omega_0^{(0)}=\omega'_0} \ . \tag{5}$$

The entire MTNAS algorithm pipeline is also described in Algorithm 1. We show in Fig. 1 (b) an example of the final overall architecture of the searched multi-task network.

Multi-task Finetuning. After obtaining the optimized multi-task network architecture, we further finetune the overall network weights $\hat{\omega}^* \leftarrow \omega^*$ and the overall network architectures $\phi_i^*|_{i=0}^n$ remain unchanged during this process.

4   Experiments

4.1   Datasets and Evaluation Metrics

In this work, we apply the proposed MTNAS method to joint learning of object detection and segmentation for autonomous driving. Our experiments are conducted on four public datasets, including KITTI [49], CityScapes [50],

---

Algorithm 1. MTNAS - Multi-Task Neural Architecture Search

Input:
  Base search space $\mathcal{O}$.
  ImageNet dataset $\mathcal{D}_0$.
  Task-specific datasets $\mathcal{D}_i|_{i=1}^n$ associated with n tasks.
  Hyperparameters of early stopping policy: K, T.
Branch Search:
  for $i = 1 \rightarrow n$ **do**
    Initialize ϕ_i with task-specific search space and initialize ω_i randomly.
    repeat
        Update (ϕ_i, ω_i) according to Eq. 1
    until $\mathcal{N}(\phi_i, \omega_i)$ does not change for K iterations.
  end for
  Output the resulting branches $(\phi_i^*, \omega_i^*)|_{i=1}^n$.
Backbone Search:
  Freeze branches and add an auxiliary ImageNet classification layer.
  Initialize ϕ_0 and ω_0 randomly.
  while number of *skip-connect* operation $\leq T$ **do**
    Update (ϕ_0, ω_0) according to Eq. 1
  end while
  Output the pre-searched backbone (ϕ_0', ω_0').
  Activate branches and remove the ImageNet classification layer.
  Initialize (ϕ_0, ω_0) with (ϕ_0', ω_0') and fix branch architectures $\phi_i|_{i=1}^n$.
  repeat
      Update (ϕ_0, ω_0) according to Eq. 1
  until $\mathcal{N}(\phi_0, \omega_0)$ does not change for K iterations.
  Output the resulting backbone $\mathcal{N}(\phi_0^*, \omega_0^*)$.
Output:
  Derive the final optimal multi-task network architecture $\mathcal{N}(\phi_i^*, \omega_i^*)|_{i=0}^n$.

BDD100K [51] and Waymo [52]. The KITTI dataset contains 7,481 training images and 7,518 test images with three categories of *car, pedestrian* and *cyclist* for object detection. The Cityscapes dataset contains 2,975 training, 500 validation and 1525 test images of 19 categories for semantic segmentation. Waymo and BDD100K are recent large-scale datasets with diverse autonomous driving scenes and are challenging for both detection and segmentation tasks. BDD100K includes annotations for both detection and segmentation while Waymo includes detection annotations only. Note that our method can be flexibly applied to the case that annotations are available for a certain task but not for other tasks. Based on these datasets, we create two sets of benchmarks for evaluating multi-task networks in our experiments.

Single Set. We apply a single small dataset for each task in this version. Specifically, KITTI is used for detection and CityScapes is used for segmentation. This single-set benchmark is used for performance comparisons with existing work on each task.

Mixed Set. We also employ large-scale data to further improve the performance for the practical application. In detail, we combine Waymo and BDD100K by merging their common categories for detection and combine CityScapes and BDD100K for segmentation similarly. This leads to 4 classes for detection and 16 classes for segmentation. We also randomly divide the mixed data into *train*, *validation* and *test* sets. For object detection, we have 120 k, 2 k, 10 k images for *train*, *validation* and *test* sets, respectively. For semantic segmentation, we have 10k, 500, 1500 images for *train*, *validation* and *test* sets, respectively. This mixed-set benchmark is used for our main multi-task results.

For evaluation metrics, we use the standard mean Average Precision (mAP) for detection and mean Intersection over Union (mIoU) for segmentation.

4.2 Implementation Details

MTL Baseline. We take Resnet-18 as the backbone of our hand-crafted multi-task network baseline. For all tasks, we resize images to the same 320×512 resolution as input. We train the multi-task network with a batch size of 32 for 150 k iterations on 2 NVIDIA V100 GPUs. We use SGD for optimization with an initial learning rate of 0.01 (decreased with a linear cosine policy), momentum of 0.9 and weight decay of 3×10^{-5}. As for balancing different branches' losses, we simply set the loss weights of detection and segmentation as 1:1.

MTNAS. We set $K = 10$ and $T = 2$ in Algorithm 1. We use the same batch size of 32 with MTL baseline but different initial learning rate of 0.1 for searching. The maximum iterations of searching for each branch and backbone are set as 5 k and 10 k, respectively. On the single-set benchmark, the branch search, backbone search and multi-task finetuning processes cost 2, 12, 4 GPU days, respectively. All of our experiments are conducted on PyTorch.

4.3 MTL Results on Mixed Set

After obtaining the searched cells for both backbone and branches on the mixed set, we stack a light-weight multi-task network and further finetune its weights. We show the main multi-task results on the mixed-set benchmark in Table 1. We compare the single-task baseline (i.e., SSD for detection and FCN for segmentation) and the multi-task baseline described in Sect. 3.1. We also implement recent MTL methods on our mix-set benchmark including Pareto MTL [20] and TripleNet [53]. Since there are little considerations of NAS methods on MTL, we also implement several related differentiable NAS baselines and extend them to our multi-task setting by searching on a proxy CIFAR10 dataset. Table 1 shows that the proposed MTNAS method achieves the best performance on both tasks and simultaneously consumes the least computation cost compared to the single-task, multi-task and NAS baselines. (1) Our method obtains significant improvement over each single task baseline (e.g., 3.5% mIoU gain for segmentation). By sharing representations in the multi-task network, the computation complexity of the model is largely reduced. We only require around 35% fewer FLOPs than a summation of two separate models (i.e., 9.0 vs. 13.5 + 12.1 = 25.6) but obtain higher performance (i.e., 43.7% vs. 41.5% for detection, 46.2% vs. 42.7% segmentation). (2) Our method outperforms the hand-crafted MTL baseline with 3.5% higher mAP for detection, 2.0% higher mIoU for segmentation and only consumes 65% fewer FLOPs. We also compare MTNAS with other state-of-the-art MTL methods [20,53] using the same network and experimental setting as MTL baseline. The results show that MTNAS outperforms Pareto MTL by 1.9% for detection and 1.3% for segmentation, and outperforms TripleNet by 1.5% for detection and 1.0% for segmentation. (3) We compare our method with those demanding proxy tasks (CIFAR10 classification). The results show the consistent superiority of MTNAS, e.g., 43.7% (Ours) vs. 38.6% (DARTS) for detection.

Table 1. Performance comparisons of multi-task learning on mixed set in terms of detection accuracy (mAP), segmentation accuracy (mIoU) and computation complexity (FLOPs). [†] denotes conventional Imagenet pre-training and [*] denotes the proposed ImageNet pre-searching procedure.

Methods		mAP (%)	mIoU (%)	FLOPs (G)
Manual design[†]	SSD [45]	41.5	-	13.5
	FCN [32]	-	42.7	12.1
	MTL baseline	40.2	44.2	13.7
	Pareto MTL [20]	41.8	44.9	13.7
	TripleNet [53]	42.2	45.2	21.2
Search on proxy tasks	DARTS [9]	36.2	40.1	9.7
	DARTS[†] [9]	38.6	42.6	9.7
	PC-DARTS [17]	34.0	43.0	11.4
	PC-DARTS[†] [17]	36.0	44.5	11.4
	DARTS+ [16]	34.8	44.2	11.4
	DARTS+[†] [16]	37.7	45.0	11.4
Search on target tasks	Random search [54]	38.6	41.5	10.4
	Co-search	41.1	43.0	10.5
	Ours[†], w/o branch search	41.4	45.5	10.9
	Ours[†], w/o backbone search	40.5	44.5	11.8
	Ours[†]	42.1	45.4	**9.0**
	Ours[*]	**43.7**	**46.2**	**9.0**

We show our contributions from the algorithmic components in the last group of Table 1. (1) By discarding either branch or backbone search stage, the performance on both tasks will drop. This validates the necessity of searching for overall architecture in MTL. (2) Compared with the results of the last two rows in Table 1, we demonstrate the effectiveness of our pre-searching procedure. Unlike

ImageNet pre-training that updates network weights only, our pre-searching procedure can optimize both of architecture parameters and network weights and
provide good initialization for the subsequent backbone search process. (3) To
demonstrate the effectiveness of our search method, we follow [54] to implement
the random search baseline and the result is worse than our baseline, and we
tried the co-search scheme (searching backbone and branches at same time) but
get worse results than MTNAS, because we need to reduce the batch size to
fit the memory limit in the co-search manner (only 2 images can be loaded for
training with 32 G memory) and the performance is harmed. We further test the
latency on P100: MTL baseline (8.4 ms), SSD (8.2 ms), FCN (8.1 ms), MTNAS
(6.2 ms). More results on CIFAR10 [55], VOC12 [56] and cross dataset are in
our supplementary material.

We show more detailed ablation studies on backbone search as well as the
searching time in Table 2. In these experiments, we use the searched architecture for two branches. (1) Our method (PS+BS) outperforms that of using the
pre-trained hand-crafted ResNet as backbone (PT) by a large margin, which
validates the superiority of optimizing the backbone structure. (2) Our method
outperforms pre-searching only or searching with the multi-task loss only, which
demonstrates that both auxiliary large-scale data and task-specific data are beneficial for optimizing the backbone architecture. (3) Compared to ImageNet pre-
training, our pre-searching procedure obtains higher performance on both tasks
(43.7% vs. 42.1% for detection, 46.2% vs. 45.4% for segmentation).

Table 2. Ablation studies with respect to backbone search on the mixed-set benchmark. PS: Pre-search backbone on ImageNet. BS: Search backbone with the multi-task
loss. PT: Pre-train backbone on ImageNet.

PS	BS	PT	Time (GPU days)	mAP (%)	mIoU (%)
		✓	14	40.5	44.5
✓			8	40.5	44.3
	✓		12	41.2	44.7
	✓	✓	26	42.1	45.4
✓	✓		20	**43.7**	**46.2**

4.4   Comparisons to State-of-the-Arts on Single Set

We search for another light-weight multi-task network on the single set. Table 3
compares our MTNAS with the state-of-the-art methods on each task. We group
these existing methods by their FLOPs and our searched network achieves competitive performance with other light-weight models on both tasks. For example, compared to RTSeg-MobileNet [57] for segmentation, we achieve 1.9% higher
mIoU and consumes less FLOPs (12.6 G vs. 13.8 G). Compared to SSD-ResNet18

[45] for detection, we achieve 6.1% higher mAP and also consumes less FLOPs (12.6 G vs. 13.5 G).

Table 3. Performance comparisons on single set in terms of per-class AP and mAP on KITTI, mIoU accuracy on CityScapes and FLOPs.

Methods	Car	Pedestrian	Cyclist	mAP (%)	mIoU (%)	FLOPs (G)
PSPNet [58]	-	-	-	-	81.2	412.2
DeepLabv2 [59]	-	-	-	-	63.1	457.8
DeepLabv3+ [60]	-	-	-	-	82.1	496
SegNet [61]	-	-	-	-	57.0	286
SQ [62]	-	-	-	-	59.8	270
DPN [63]	-	-	-	-	59.1	270
SSD-VGG16 [64]	75.9	50.6	50.2	58.9	-	157.4
Faster-RCNN [65]	81.6	65.6	63.4	70.2	-	181
RTSeg-MobileNet [57]	-	-	-	-	61.5	13.8
FCN-ResNet18 [32]	-	-	-	-	51.1	12.1
SSD-ResNet18 [45]	77.4	56.1	54.6	62.7	-	13.5
SqueezeDet [66]	66.1	-	-	-	-	9.7
YOLOv2 [67]	62.8	-	-	-	-	35
MTNAS (Ours)	79.2	65.4	61.8	68.8	63.4	12.6

4.5   MTNAS Architecture and Discussions

Figure 3 shows our searched backbone architectures on the target tasks and those searched by DARTS on the proxy task. Our searched normal cell has a deeper structure which is likely to help improve the representation ability of networks. In terms of reduction cell, DARTS suffers from the collapse problem as it only generates weight-free operations like max-pooling and skip-connection. We observe that these weight-free operations are easier to converge, which incur selection bias during the optimization process. Besides, many pooling operations will cause location information loss and negatively affect the performance of detection and segmentation tasks. In contrast, our MTNAS method leads to more diverse architecture for learning richer information in the reduction cell.

Figure 4 shows our searched branch architectures. By optimizing the branch structure for each task separately, we can learn task-specific cell architectures, e.g., separate convolution for detection and dilated convolution for segmentation, which are crucial for good performance.

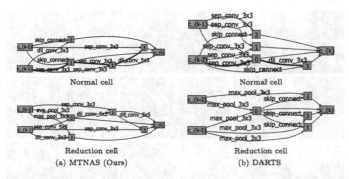

Fig. 3. Searched cell architectures of backbone by our MTNAS algorithm and the original DARTS method.

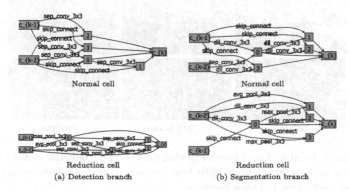

Fig. 4. Searched cell architectures for our detection and segmentation branches by our method.

4.6 Qualitative Evaluations

Figure 5 visualizes some examples of MTL results on the BDD100K dataset. In general, our MTNAS method can achieve more accurate detection and segmentation results compared to the hand-crafted MTL baseline. For example, MTNAS can better detect small objects (e.g., *traffic sign*) in the first row and crowd people in the second row. Besides, MTNAS can better segment the objects with a well-defined shape (e.g., *car*) and amorphous background regions (e.g., *sidewalk* and *sky*) as shown in the last three rows of Fig. 5.

(a) Input   (b) MTL baseline   (c) MTNAS

Fig. 5. Example results of multi-task learning on the BDD100K dataset. Our MTNAS method can achieve more accurate detection and segmentation results compared to the hand-crafted multi-task network baseline.

5   Conclusion

In this paper, we propose a practical and principled neural architecture search algorithm for multi-task learning, named MTNAS. Our method aims to search for the overall optimized network architecture for multi-task learning with two stages. For branch search, we separately optimize the task-specific neural architecture for each branch based on its own optimization objective. For backbone search, we first propose a pre-searching procedure to obtain the initial backbone structure and then refine them under the overall multi-task guidance. We apply the proposed MTNAS pipeline for the challenging autonomous driving scenarios by jointly learning object detection and semantic segmentation. Experimental results demonstrate our searched multi-task model surpasses the hand-crafted single-task and multi-task baselines largely and consumes less computation cost. We believe that our proposed method can provide new insights into neural architecture search on multi-task learning and has broad real-world applications.

References

1. Caruana, R.: Multitask learning. Mac. Learn. **28**, 41–75 (1997). https://doi.org/10.1023/A:1007379606734

2. Zhang, K., Zhang, Z., Li, Z., Qiao, Y.: Joint face detection and alignment using multitask cascaded convolutional networks. SPL **23**, 1499–1503 (2016)
3. He, K., Gkioxari, G., Dollár, P., Girshick, R.: Mask R-CNN. In: ICCV (2017)
4. Luvizon, D.C., Picard, D., Tabia, H.: 2D/3D pose estimation and action recognition using multitask deep learning. In: CVPR (2018)
5. He, K., Zhang, X., Ren, S., Sun, J.: Deep residual learning for image recognition. In: CVPR (2016)
6. Pham, H., Guan, M., Zoph, B., Le, Q., Dean, J.: Efficient neural architecture search via parameters sharing. In: ICML (2018)
7. Zoph, B., Vasudevan, V., Shlens, J., Le, Q.V.: Learning transferable architectures for scalable image recognition. In: CVPR (2018)
8. Real, E., Aggarwal, A., Huang, Y., Le, Q.V.: Regularized evolution for image classifier architecture search. In: AAAI. (2019)
9. Liu, H., Simonyan, K., Yang, Y.: Darts: differentiable architecture search. In: ICLR (2018)
10. Ghiasi, G., Lin, T.Y., Le, Q.V.: NAS-FPN: learning scalable feature pyramid architecture for object detection. In: CVPR (2019)
11. Chen, Y., Yang, T., Zhang, X., Meng, G., Xiao, X., Sun, J.: Detnas: backbone search for object detection. In: NeurIPS (2019)
12. Peng, J., Sun, M., Zhang, Z.X., Tan, T., Yan, J.: Efficient neural architecture transformation search in channel-level for object detection. In: NeurIPS (2019)
13. Liu, C., et al.: Auto-DeepLab: hierarchical neural architecture search for semantic image segmentation. In: CVPR (2019)
14. Chen, L.C., et al.: Searching for efficient multi-scale architectures for dense image prediction. In: NeurIPS (2018)
15. Cai, H., Zhu, L., Han, S.: Proxylessnas: direct neural architecture search on target task and hardware. In: ICLR (2019)
16. Liang, H., et al.: Darts+: Improved differentiable architecture search with early stopping. arXiv preprint arXiv:1909.06035 (2019)
17. Xu, Y., et al.: Pc-darts: partial channel connections for memory-efficient architecture search. In: ICLR (2019)
18. Kendall, A., Gal, Y., Cipolla, R.: Multi-task learning using uncertainty to weigh losses for scene geometry and semantics. In: CVPR (2018)
19. Chen, Z., Badrinarayanan, V., Lee, C.Y., Rabinovich, A.: Gradnorm: gradient normalization for adaptive loss balancing in deep multitask networks. In: ICML (2018)
20. Lin, X., Zhen, H.L., Li, Z., Zhang, Q.F., Kwong, S.: Pareto multi-task learning. In: NeurIPS (2019)
21. Misra, I., Shrivastava, A., Gupta, A., Hebert, M.: Cross-stitch networks for multi-task learning. In: CVPR (2016)
22. He, X., Zhou, Z., Thiele, L.: Multi-task zipping via layer-wise neuron sharing. In: NeurIPS (2018)
23. Meyerson, E., Miikkulainen, R.: Beyond shared hierarchies: deep multitask learning through soft layer ordering. In: ICLR (2018)
24. Mallya, A., Lazebnik, S.: Packnet: dding multiple tasks to a single network by iterative pruning. In: CVPR (2018)
25. Kim, E., Ahn, C., Torr, P.H., Oh, S.: Deep virtual networks for memory efficient inference of multiple tasks. In: CVPR (2019)
26. Ahn, C., Kim, E., Oh, S.: Deep elastic networks with model selection for multi-task learning. In: ICCV (2019)
27. Rosenbaum, C., Klinger, T., Riemer, M.: Routing networks: Adaptive selection of non-linear functions for multi-task learning. In: ICLR (2018)

28. Liang, J., Meyerson, E., Miikkulainen, R.: Evolutionary architecture search for deep multitask networks. In: GECCO (2018)
29. Sandler, M., Howard, A., Zhu, M., Zhmoginov, A., Chen, L.C.: Mobilenetv 2: Inverted residuals and linear bottlenecks. In: CVPR (2018)
30. Yu, F., Koltun, V.: Multi-scale context aggregation by dilated convolutions. In: ICLR (2015)
31. Ma, N., Zhang, X., Zheng, H.-T., Sun, J.: ShuffleNet V2: practical guidelines for efficient CNN architecture design. In: Ferrari, V., Hebert, M., Sminchisescu, C., Weiss, Y. (eds.) ECCV 2018ECCV 2018ECCV 2018, Part XIV. LNCS, vol. 11218, pp. 122–138. Springer, Cham (2018). https://doi.org/10.1007/978-3-030-01264-9_8
32. Long, J., Shelhamer, E., Darrell, T.: Fully convolutional networks for semantic segmentation. In: CVPR (2015)
33. Li, Z., Peng, C., Yu, G., Zhang, X., Deng, Y., Sun, J.: DetNet: design backbone for object detection. In: Ferrari, V., Hebert, M., Sminchisescu, C., Weiss, Y. (eds.) ECCV 2018, Part IX. LNCS, vol. 11213, pp. 339–354. Springer, Cham (2018). https://doi.org/10.1007/978-3-030-01240-3_21
34. Zoph, B., Le, Q.V.: Neural architecture search with reinforcement learning. In: ICLR (2016)
35. Xie, S., Zheng, H., Liu, C., Lin, L.: SNAS: stochastic neural architecture search. In: ICLR (2019)
36. Dong, J.-D., Cheng, A.-C., Juan, D.-C., Wei, W., Sun, M.: DPP-Net: device-aware progressive search for pareto-optimal neural architectures. In: Ferrari, V., Hebert, M., Sminchisescu, C., Weiss, Y. (eds.) ECCV 2018, Part XI. LNCS, vol. 11215, pp. 540–555. Springer, Cham (2018). https://doi.org/10.1007/978-3-030-01252-6_32
37. Liu, H., Simonyan, K., Vinyals, O., Fernando, C., Kavukcuoglu, K.: Hierarchical representations for efficient architecture search. In: ICLR (2018)
38. Tan, M., et al.: Mnasnet: platform-aware neural architecture search for mobile. In: CVPR (2019)
39. He, Y., Lin, J., Liu, Z., Wang, H., Li, L.-J., Han, S.: AMC: AutoML for model compression and acceleration on mobile devices. In: Ferrari, V., Hebert, M., Sminchisescu, C., Weiss, Y. (eds.) ECCV 2018, Part VII. LNCS, vol. 11211, pp. 815–832. Springer, Cham (2018). https://doi.org/10.1007/978-3-030-01234-2_48
40. Wu, B., et al.: Fbnet: hardware-aware efficient convnet design via differentiable neural architecture search. In: CVPR (2019)
41. Yu, J., et al.: BigNAS: scaling up neural architecture search with big single-stage models. In: Vedaldi, A., Bischof, H., Brox, T., Frahm, J.-M. (eds.) ECCV 2020, Part VII. LNCS, vol. 12352, pp. 702–717. Springer, Cham (2020). https://doi.org/10.1007/978-3-030-58571-6_41
42. Cai, H., Gan, C., Wang, T., Zhang, Z., Han, S.: Once-for-all: train one network and specialize it for efficient deployment. In: ICLR (2019)
43. He, C., Ye, H., Shen, L., Zhang, T.: Milenas: efficient neural architecture search via mixed-level reformulation. In: CVPR, pp. 11993–12002 (2020)
44. Guo, J., et al.: Hit-detector: hierarchical trinity architecture search for object detection. In: CVPR, pp. 11405–11414 (2020)
45. Liu, W., et al.: SSD: single shot MultiBox detector. In: Leibe, B., Matas, J., Sebe, N., Welling, M. (eds.) ECCV 2016. LNCS, vol. 9905, pp. 21–37. Springer, Cham (2016). https://doi.org/10.1007/978-3-319-46448-0_2
46. Lin, T.Y., Dollár, P., Girshick, R., He, K., Hariharan, B., Belongie, S.: Feature pyramid networks for object detection. In: CVPR (2017)
47. Chen, X., Xie, L., Wu, J., Tian, Q.: Progressive differentiable architecture search: Bridging the depth gap between search and evaluation. In: ICCV (2019)

48. Peng, C., et al.: Megdet: a large mini-batch object detector. In: CVPR (2018)
49. Geiger, A., Lenz, P., Urtasun, R.: Are we ready for autonomous driving? The Kitti vision benchmark suite. In: CVPR (2012)
50. Cordts, M., et al.: The cityscapes dataset for semantic urban scene understanding. In: CVPR (2016)
51. Yu, F., et al.: Bdd100k: A diverse driving video database with scalable annotation tooling. arXiv preprint arXiv:1805.04687 (2018)
52. Waymo open dataset: An autonomous driving dataset (2019)
53. Cao, J., Pang, Y., Li, X.: Triply supervised decoder networks for joint detection and segmentation. In: CVPR. (2019)
54. Li, L., Talwalkar, A.: Random search and reproducibility for neural architecture search. In: Uncertainty in Artificial Intelligence, PMLR, pp. 367–377 (2020)
55. Krizhevsky, A., et al.: Learning multiple layers of features from tiny images (2009)
56. Hariharan, B., Arbelaez, P., Bourdev, L., Maji, S., Malik, J.: Semantic contours from inverse detectors. In: International Conference on Computer Vision (ICCV) (2011)
57. Siam, M., Gamal, M., Abdel-Razek, M., Yogamani, S., Jagersand, M.: Rtseg: real-time semantic segmentation comparative study. In: ICIP (2018)
58. Zhao, H., Shi, J., Qi, X., Wang, X., Jia, J.: Pyramid scene parsing network. In: CVPR (2017)
59. Chen, L.C., Papandreou, G., Kokkinos, I., Murphy, K., Yuille, A.L.: DeepLab: semantic image segmentation with deep convolutional nets, atrous convolution, and fully connected CRFs. TPAMI 40, 834–848 (2017)
60. Chen, L.-C., Zhu, Y., Papandreou, G., Schroff, F., Adam, H.: Encoder-decoder with atrous separable convolution for semantic image segmentation. In: Ferrari, V., Hebert, M., Sminchisescu, C., Weiss, Y. (eds.) ECCV 2018, Part VII. LNCS, vol. 11211, pp. 833–851. Springer, Cham (2018). https://doi.org/10.1007/978-3-030-01234-2_49
61. Badrinarayanan, V., Kendall, A., Cipolla, R.: Segnet: a deep convolutional encoder-decoder architecture for image segmentation. TPAMI 39, 2481–2495 (2017)
62. Treml, M., et al.: Speeding up semantic segmentation for autonomous driving. In: MLITS, NeurIPS Workshop (2016)
63. Liu, Z., Li, X., Luo, P., Loy, C.C., Tang, X.: Semantic image segmentation via deep parsing network. In: ICCV (2015)
64. Kim, H., Lee, Y., Yim, B., Park, E., Kim, H.: On-road object detection using deep neural network. In: ICCE-Asia (2016)
65. Ren, S., He, K., Girshick, R., Sun, J.: Faster R-CNN: towards real-time object detection with region proposal networks. In: NeurIPS (2015)
66. Wu, B., Iandola, F., Jin, P.H., Keutzer, K.: Squeezedet: uinified, small, low power fully convolutional neural networks for real-time object detection for autonomous driving. In: CVPR (2017)
67. Redmon, J., Farhadi, A.: Yolo9000: better, faster, stronger. In: CVPR (2017)

Compact and Fast Underwater Segmentation Network for Autonomous Underwater Vehicles

Jiangtao Wang[1] , Baihua Li[1(✉)] , Yang Zhou[1] , Emanuele Rocco[2],
and Qinggang Meng[1]

[1] Department of Computer Science, Loughborough University, Loughborough, UK
{J.Wang5,B.Li,Y.Zhou5,Q.Meng}@lboro.ac.uk.com
[2] Witted SRL, Piazza della Manifattura 1, 38068 Rovereto, Italy
emanuele@witted.it

Abstract. Reliable and real-time semantic segmentation is crucial for vision-based navigation tasks undertaken by AUVs (Autonomous Underwater Vehicles). However state-of-art deep learning segmentation networks could not be deployed on embedded devices with limited onboard resources, due to the required high computation capacity and the lack of capability to deal with poor underwater image quality. In this work we present a new deep underwater segmentation network, featured by a compact encoder and a lightweight decoder. We use only one step upsampling block to recover features maps from the encoder to significantly speed up the inference time. Furthermore, we adopt three strategies to improve the network accuracy. Firstly, in parallel with the main decoder path, we introduce a branch path to extract additional low-level features. Secondly, we use position attention module to enhance the high-level semantic information and use channel attention module to introduce extra global context as well as refine the inter-dependencies of each features. Thirdly, we proposed to use two additional auxiliary loss and smooth loss functions to better train the network, such that it will be more robust in segmenting images at varying resolutions and generating smooth boundaries. We validate our network accuracy on two different underwater segmentation datasets, a generalistic and a specialist one, and our model achieves the same level of accuracy of state-of-art networks. We also tested the network speed on different embedded platforms, and we showed it reaches real-time inference speed on both Nvidia Jetson GPU platforms TX2 and Nano, with respectively around 24 and 18 FPS (Frame Per Second). The proposed network inference is up to 27 times faster than other considered networks. Its high accuracy and speed will so pave the way for its deployment and application on AUVs systems.

1 Introduction

In the past years, Autonomous underwater vehicles (AUVs) have been developed to autonomously carry out various missions in the underwater environment,

© Springer Nature Switzerland AG 2021
H. Ishikawa et al. (Eds.): ACCV 2020, LNCS 12624, pp. 688–703, 2021.
https://doi.org/10.1007/978-3-030-69535-4_42

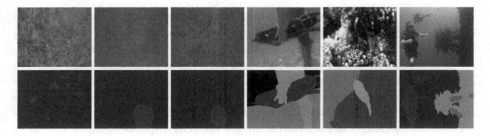

Fig. 1. Examples of underwater semantic segmentation. The first row presents the underwater images and the second row presents their corresponding segmentation ground truth. The first three columns from the left are related to the seagrasses segmentation task [1] while the others comes from SUIM dataset [2] for general underwater segmentation task.

which would be otherwise too expensive and dangerous for the human labor. These range from wreckage search and localization, to marine science, and environmental protection. To be autonomous, those AUVs need similar abilities of UGVs (Unmanned Ground Vehicles) or UAVs (Unmanned Aerial vehicles), for example, free navigation, obstacle avoidance, semantic simultaneous localization and mapping. Scene understanding is the key to support the above tasks and, depending on water conditions, semantic segmentation driven by RGB imagery of the underwater environment could provide it in a cheap, efficient and reliable way. However underwater segmentation cannot be yet widely adopted on AUVs due to that it is still challenging to run segmentation algorithms that are both accurate and, due to computational capability constrains, still achieve real-time inference on the AUVs embedded platforms.

In fact, on one side the underwater environment negatively affects the accuracy of semantic segmentation by continuously modifying the outlook and appearances of the same underwater biological entities or instances. Figure 1 presents six examples of underwater images and their corresponding segmentation ground truth. Those images come with various color shift in the green or blue and different levels of haziness and illumination; those depend on the sea physical parameters, such as depth, salinity or temperature, the presence and activity of biological entities, as plankton or algae, or density of dispersed particles. As in the case of seagrasses at shallow depths, water mass flows given by underwater currents or wave motion keep as well the underwater scenarios in continuous motion. All those unavoidable effects exacerbate the challenge of underwater segmentation.

On the hardware side, the AUVs have only the limited computational capabilities of their GPU embedded platforms, such as Nvidia Jetson TX2 or Nvidia Jetson Nano. On those deep learning-based segmentation methods, which achieve real time state-of-art performance on desktop GPU, do not reach the same inference speed. This speed loss could become a problem for AUVs navigation and control system since it requires vision perceptions - such as object detection and segmentation - to provide scene understanding information fast enough to make real-time decisions for navigation. Given the slow motion of AUVs (2–3 m/s) even during fast surveys, we consider a safe time delay threshold around 100 ms.

To address the above challenges, we present so a lightweight segmentation neural network, which has a reduced number of parameters and FLOPs (floating point operations) and achieves realtime inference speed. We use also multiple segmentation predictions with different resolutions to help our proposed network address the challenges of underwater images taken at disparate seafloor distances with various resolutions. This approach helps also to optimize network training, as well as to improve the segmentation accuracy. We evaluated the proposed network on two datasets, the Seagrass [1] and SUIM [2] datesets, against which we validated its accuracy, and measured its inference speed on two Nvidia embedded platforms.

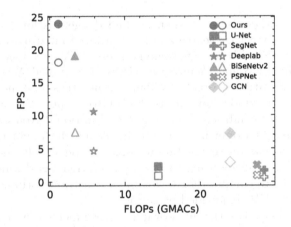

Fig. 2. This figure shows the FLOPs of ours and the other compared segmentation networks (small is better), and their inference speed as frame per second (high is better) on two different platforms. The solid symbols denote the speed test results on Nvidia Jetson TX2, while the hollow symbols relate to the ones on the Nvidia Jetson Nano. It shows that our proposed network is the fastest one with respect to other six networks.

In summary, the main contributions of this work are:

1) we present a new segmentation network which can achieve high accuracy for underwater segmentation. In particular, we employ two additional loss functions, a smooth loss and auxiliary loss, to help train the network reach even higher accuracies. On both the Seagrass [1] and SUIM [2] datasets, our network respectively reaches 89.74 and 51.87 mIoU (mean Intersection Over Union), which are at the state-of-art level.

2) we design such network with a lightweight and well-designed decoder to reduce its total computational demands. Our network has just 1.153M parameters

and 0.278G FLOPs which are respectively at least to 65% and 92% smaller than the ones of the considered alternatives as showed in Fig. 2.

3) we showed then the modest computational needs of the proposed network enable it to overcome the computational limitations of embedded platforms. Such network reaches real-time inference with 24 and 18 FPS respectively on Nvidia Jetson TX2 and Nvidia Jetson Nano GPU platforms; those are respectively at least 9.54× and 19.22× faster than the most accurate network, PSPNet [3].

The proposed network is so optimal for deployment on AUVS embedded platforms for accurate and realtime segmentation inference.

2 Related Work

Underwater Segmentation. Seagrass meadows coverage is a key index to measure for evaluating the health status of the marine ecological environment [4]. To automatically measure it from benthic RGB images, [5,6], and [7] developed patches classification based methods. Those split the whole benthic images into super-pixels and patches at first, then use traditional machine learning methods, such as SVM (Support Vector Machine), to classify each patch and obtain the segmentation. Those authors deployed their segmentation methods on underwater robotics and AUVs where they tested their performances on embedded devices. However, these method cannot achieve the realtime inference, and had weak segmentation accuracies. A few authors, [8,9] and [10], proposed instead end2end deep learning segmentation networks to attain high accuracies on seagrass region detection and segmentation. [11] developed a fast seagrass segmentation network running on GPU Desktop platform and, as well as, compared the existing state-of-art methods against a public seagrass dataset [1]. Instead, for general underwater segmentation on various semantic classes, [2] presented a light-end segmentation network and published its companion generalist underwater segmentation dataset, the SUIM dataset. Our proposed network is an end2end deep learning network optimised for embedded GPU platforms.

Semantic Segmentation Network. Although current state-of-art segmentation networks have been originally proposed for medical image analysis, driverless cars or other surface applications, those successful networks could be applied as well to underwater segmentation tasks. The authors of [2] and [11] already proved that segmentation networks such as U-Net [12], deeplab [13], SegNet [14], PSPNet [3], FCN [15] can achieve excellent segmentation accuracy on different underwater datasets, while [16–19] and [20] proposed a fast inference segmentation networks for real time use on Desktop GPU, which could be potentially deployed on AUVs while still achieve high accuracy.

Light Weight Encoder. Classic Segmentation networks generally consist of two parts, an encoder (or backbone) and a decoder. The encoder is used to downsample the input image to low resolution to generate high-level features, while the decoder is used to restore the resolution of feature maps to achieve pixel-wise segmentation. To compress the segmentation network, it is a common strategy to adopt light weight convolutional networks as encoder, such as MobileNet [21], EfficientNet [22], and ShuffleNet [23]. For example employing MobileNet as backbone in PSPNet [3] or deeplab [13] can significantly reduce the inference FLOPs and accelerate its speed with respect to using ResNet [24] as backbone. In our work, we utilize the mobilenet backbone [21] as encoder to optimize computational demands.

Attention Modules. Attention modules have been wildly used in convolution neural networks. CAM (Channel Attention Modules), such as SENet (Squeeze Excitation Network) [25], CBAM (Convolutional Block Attention Module) [26], and SKNet (Selective Kernal Network) [27] can generate channel-wise weight to demarcate the feature maps across channel. In particular, CAM can enhance the essential and important feature maps to let the network focus on learning those. In our network we applied CAM to differentiate the inter-dependencies of low-level features maps across its channel dimensions, and re-rank relative importance of the features.

General position based attention (PAM) modules instead can generate instead pixel-wise attention maps. Those have abundant high level and global context information, which can significantly help to refine the segmentation prediction. In particular, works such as the PAM of [28] and the non-local block of [29] can generate position attention weights of one pixel to all other pixels. However, even if non-local block and other modules can improve the segmentation accuracy by introducing some global context, they will also increase the network computational demands due to increased network complexity. For a more efficient solution, it is possible to adopt other PAM structures such as GCNet (Global Context Network) [30], CCNet (Criss Cross Network) [31], and ANN (Asymmetric Non-local Neural Network) [32], to improve segmentation accuracy with global context awareness but with contained computational demands. In our network we also employs PAM to generate high level context information at the decoder level.

3   Our Approach

We present a lightweight segmentation network which follows an encoder-decoder architecture. Its overall architecture is shown in Fig. 3. The network encoder can down sample the input images and generate different level feature maps, while the decoder can recover the resolution of the feature maps and make the pixel-wise segmentation prediction. Even if the proposed network can accept input images of any resolution, we experimentally choose the input resolution to be 320×256, as a balance between segmentation accuracy and computational overhead.

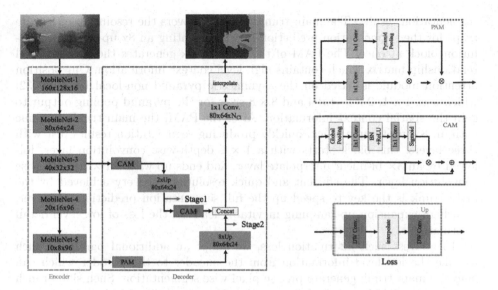

Fig. 3. This figure shows the overall architecture of our proposed segmentation network, which follows an encoder and decoder architecture. It has CAM (Channel Attention Module) to enhance the feature maps via channel-wise. It also has PAM (Position Attention Module) to get the high-level context information associated with pixel-to-pixel relationship. The two stages of segmentation prediction are shown as red arrows in decoder. Numbers under the block name refers to the width, height and channels number of output feature maps. (Color figure online)

3.1 Encoder

We utilize MobileNet V2 [21] as encoder, as the blue box shown in Fig. 3, which is an optimal network for mobile and embedded platforms. This encoder has a low parameter number and FLOPs, allowing fast inference on embedded platforms. In particular, the encoder down-samples the input image for five times (the orange block in the encoder as shown in Fig. 3), reducing the resolution by half after each down sampling step. Those down sampling convolutions generate also different resolution feature maps, from low-level to high-level features. We feed the final feature maps into the decoder. Since the high-level features have, in general, abundant context information, they can help improve the pixel-wise accuracy of the decoder. Additionally, other low-level and low resolution features can provide extra low-level information to the decoder for segmentation result refining.

3.2 Decoder

As shown in Fig. 3 in the red box, the decoder consists of two paths: the one showed as starting with the PAM block, which is main path for the segmentation; a side path, showed as starting with the CAM block, which helps to refine the segmentation results. The main trunk quickly recovers the resolution of feature maps for the segmentation prediction by implementing an 8x up-sample convolution block at once. The PAM of the main trunk generates the pixel-to-pixel relationship matrix which contains high level context information. Our position attention module is based on the asymmetric pyramid non-local block of [32] which uses 1×1, 2×2, 4×4 and 8×8 sizes for the pyramid pooling output to gain the spatial context information. After the PAM, the main trunk continue with an 8× up-sample block, quickly producing segmentation results just with three layers: this block starts with a 1×1 depth-wise convolution layer, followed by an 8× bi-linear interpolate layer, and ends up with a 1×1 depth-wise convolution layer. The efficient and quick resolution recovery achieved by the main trunk is the key to speed up the full segmentation prediction. However, such high expansion up-sampling inevitably leads to the loss of low level detail information.

To address such information loss, we adopt an additional parallel branch to take the low-level information from the encoder to the decoder which can help the main trunk generate precise pixel-wise segmentation. Such side branch starts with a CAM, and the follows with a 2× up-sampling block and ends with another CAM. The detailed structure of such channel attention module is shown within the blue box in Fig. 3. We calculate the channel attention according to global pooling and convolution. This method obtain the inter-dependencies of each feature maps, and also capture the global semantic context. By doing so, the CAM enriches the final inference with both the low-level detail information and the high-level context information. Both main path and branch path generate so the recovered 8× feature maps with respect to the encoder output.

To make the final segmentation prediction, we then concatenate both feature maps together and connect with an additional convolution layer and a 4× bi-linear interpolate layer, which recovers the full resolution segmentation prediction.

As presented, the proposed light decoder structure reduces the computational burden of the inference. This will speed up the segmentation inference on the limited computational capabilities of embedded platforms, while keep the accuracy performances.

3.3 Loss Function

Our total loss function combines three different loss estimates, of which two are based on weighted cross entropy (WCE). We define as the $WCE(y, p)$ of the network prediction p and its corresponding segmentation ground truth y as:

$$WCE(y,p) = \frac{1}{N} \sum_i -\beta^{y_i} \log \left(\frac{\exp(p^{y^i})}{\sum_j \exp(p^j)} \right) \tag{1}$$

where the cross entropy calculation is based on the log softmax of the prediction p, β is the class weight, i is the pixel index and j is the class index. Both p and y should have the same resolution with N pixels.

Cross Entropy Loss. Cross entropy loss l_{ce} is the main loss function used for the segmentation network training and is defined as follows:

$$l_{ce} = WCE(GT, Seg(X)) \tag{2}$$

where GT is the ground truth label towards input X, and $Seg(X)$ is the segmentation prediction generated by the segmentation network.

Smooth Loss. From $Seg(X)$, we calculate the edge smooth loss as [33] to let the network generate the smooth segmentation boundaries. Smooth loos is defined as follows:

$$l_{smooth} = \left| \partial_x \frac{Seg(X)}{Seg(X)} \right| e^{-|\partial_x X|} + \left| \partial_y \frac{Seg(X)}{Seg(X)} \right| e^{-|\partial_y X|} \tag{3}$$

Auxiliary Loss. As indicated in Fig. 3 with red arrows, the up-sampling blocks generate two additional low-resolution segmentation predictions, which we use to calculate two auxiliary losses for the network training. Their loss function is defined as following:

$$l_{aux}^i = WCE(GT, Seg_i(X)) \tag{4}$$

where $Seg_i(X)$ is the i-th stage prediction of segmentation network.

Total Loss. We define so the total loss as weighted sum of the previous losses as Eq. (5):

$$loss = l_{ce} + \sum_i^2 \lambda_{aux}^i l_{aux}^i + \lambda_{Smooth} l_{smooth} \tag{5}$$

where λ_{aux} and λ_{Smooth} are the weights of the respective loss functions.

4   Experiment

In this section, we evaluate our network on two different underwater segmentation datasets: Seagrass [1] and SUIM [2]. The experiments compare our proposed method with six existing state-of-art segmentation approaches. The experiment results validate the advantages of our proposed segmentation network with respect to segmentation accuracies, network parameter numbers, computational demands (FLOPs) and inference speeds.

4.1   Dataset

Seagrass Dataset. The seagrass dataset proposed by [1] involves 12682 images in total, which were taken by underwater cameras at different distances to the sea floor. 6037 of them, taken within the 0 m to 6 m range, have been labeled with ground truth information by human experts. They indicated two possible classes for each pixel: either 1 for seagrass meadows or 0 for the background. The first column of Fig. 4 presents six examples taken from the Seagrass dataset, while the second column presents their ground truth. The first three row of these seagrass examples refers to close range (0 m–2 m) images, while the other three were taken at higher seafloor distances (2 m–6 m). As shown in Fig. 4, with the increase of the distance to seafloor and seagrasses, the imaging conditions such as luminosity, hue and haziness can rapidly change depending on water and weather conditions. This make the seagrass images have varying visual patterns as, for example, different colours, outlines and feature appearances. All this imaging variability increases the challenges of seagrass segmentation.

SUIM Dataset. [2] recently published the SUIM (Segmentation of Underwater Imagery) which is instead a more general underwater semantic segmentation dataset. In this dataset, there are 1630 labelled images in total, which have eight unbalanced classes for pixel-wise annotation: BW (background and waterbody, 31%), HD (human divers, 1.9%), PF (Aquatic plants and sea-grass, 2%), WR (wrecks or ruins, 7.3%), RO (robots, 0.3%), RI (reefs and invertebrates, 35.7%), FV (fish and vertebrates, 7.8%), and SR (seafloor and rocks, 13.9%). The example segmentation images and their annotations are shown in Fig. 5.

4.2 Implementation Details

To increase the data available for the network training, we combined several different image processing methods: we randomly crop a 320×256 patch from the original images (Crop); we rotate the images by a random angle from -20 to $20°$ (Rotation); we horizontally flip the image with 50% probability (Flip). After the data augmentation processing, we normalize each image with pre-calculated mean and variance. In experiments, we used PyTorch 1.5 [34] to implement and train all the networks on a single Nvidia RTX 2080ti GPU, with 100 (500) epochs on Seagrass (SUIM) dataset with Adam optimizer [35]. The batch size is set to 32 during training, momentum is 0.6 and weight decay is 0.001. Initial learning rate is 0.001, and we use linear schedule for the learning rate decay, as $\left(1 - \frac{E_{Current}}{E_{Total}+1}\right) * lr_{initial}$ to update learning rate after each training epoch.

4.3 Segmentation Accuracy Results

Segmentation Metrics. We calculate mIoU (mean Intersection Over Union) and F1 Score ($\mathcal{F}$) to validate the network segmentation accuracy as in [2] and [1]. These two metrics are defined as following equations:

$$mIoU = \frac{1}{Classes} \sum_{class} \frac{|GT \cap Seg(X)|}{|GT \cup Seg(X)|} \tag{6}$$

$$\mathcal{F} = 2 * \frac{1}{Classes} \sum_{class} \frac{|GT \cap Seg(X)|}{|GT| + |Seg(X)|} \tag{7}$$

where *Classes* refers to the total number of segmentation classes.

Table 1. All networks comparison of the segmentation metrics on the Seagrasses dataset

Range	Metrics	Ours	U-Net [12]	SegNet [14]	Deeplab [13]	BiSeNetv2 [36]	PSPNet [3]	GCN [37]
0–2 m	mIoU	88.63	87.73	83.92	88.05	88.34	88.98	87.77
	$\mathcal{F}$	93.93	93.42	91.22	93.61	93.77	94.14	93.45
2–6 m	mIoU	89.31	73.42	82.93	89.33	89.85	88.76	89.39
	$\mathcal{F}$	94.35	84.58	90.60	94.36	94.64	94.04	94.39

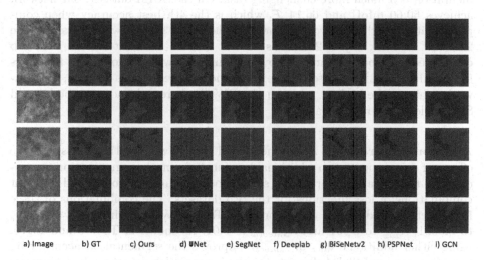

a) Image   b) GT   c) Ours   d) UNet   e) SegNet   f) Deeplab   g) BiSeNetv2   h) PSPNet   i) GCN

Fig. 4. Segmentation qualitative results on the Seagrass dataset. First three rows are taken from 0 m to 2 m distance ranges and last three rows are taken from 2 m to 6 m distance ranges. The red pixels on segmentation present seagrass and yellow pixels present the seabed (background). (Color figure online)

Seagrass Segmentation. To compare the seagrass segmentation accuracy on Seagrass dataset [1], we equally train all the networks with 100 epochs, using the l_{ce} loss only. As shown in Table 1 and Fig. 4, our network achieves the same segmentation accuracy level of the others, in particular 88.63 mIoU and 93.93 $\mathcal{F}$, the second best accuracy over 0–2 m range Seagrass dataset. Over the 2–6 seafloor distance dataset, it achieves instead 89.31 mIoU and 94.35 $\mathcal{F}$, which is the fifth best accuracy on such dataset. The gap between our proposed network and the best accurate network is 0.35 mIoU on 0–2 m range and 0.54 mIoU on 2–6 m range. However, the ablation experiments of the end of this section will show that our networks can also be improved and achieve the 2nd best accuracy on 2–6 m range dataset when trained with the two additional proposed loss functions.

SUIM Segmentation. For a more general evaluation, we also trained the networks on the SUIM dataset [2] with 500 epochs, and compared their segmentation accuracies. For fairness, our network was initially trained with only the l_{ce}. Figure 5 and Table 2 present the segmentation results on such dataset.

In general the estimated segmentation accuracies are smaller than the ones obtained on the Seagrass dataset, which means the generalist underwater segmentation is a much more challenging task. On the SUIM dataset, our network achieves 50.60 mIoU and 66.14 $\mathcal{F}$, which is the 4th best accuracy when compared with all other networks. However, the mIoU gap between ours and the 2nd best network is just 2.08%; as we will show in the next section, this gap can be reduced to less than 0.8% by including the two additional loss functions for training. Yet, on the total 8 segmentation classes of this dataset, our network achieves the highest miou on the BW (background and waterbody) and SR (seafloor and rocks) classes.

Ablation Experiment. As we mentioned earlier, we investigated as well the effects of our proposed two additional loss functions on the segmentation accuracies. We trained all networks with same epoch number but considered different combinations of loss functions for the two datasets. The combinations of these loss functions and results are reported in Table 3. We experimentally set λ_{aux}^1 to 0.0001, λ_{aux}^2 to 0.001 and λ_{Smooth} to 0.01. As shown in Table 3 and Fig. 6, using either additional l_{aux} or l_{smooth} improves the segmentation accuracy on both Seagrass and SUIM dataset. On the seagrass dataset, the mIoU increases from 88.63 up to 88.96 on 0–2 m range images, and from 89.31 to 89.74 on 2–6

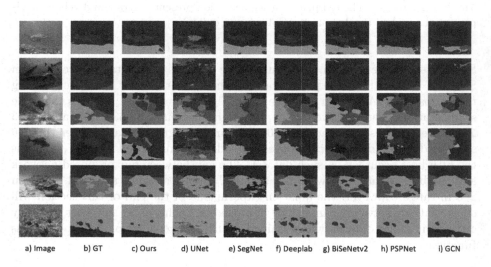

a) Image   b) GT   c) Ours   d) UNet   e) SegNet   f) Deeplab   g) BiSeNetv2   h) PSPNet   i) GCN

Fig. 5. Segmentation qualitative results on the SUIM dataset. The first column shows the test images and the second cloumn shows segmentation ground-truth. The third columns presents the segmentation prediction generated by our proposed network while the other columns refer to the results given by other networks.

Table 2. All networks comparison of the segmentation metrics on the SUIM dataset

	Ours	U-Net [12]	SegNet [14]	Deeplab [13]	BiSeNetv2 [36]	PSPNet [3]	GCN [37]
BW	84.62	79.46	80.63	81.82	83.67	82.51	79.32
HD	52.99	32.24	45.69	50.26	59.29	65.06	38.57
PF	11.46	21.86	17.45	17.06	11.27	28.54	15.09
WR	41.84	33.94	32.24	43.32	39.58	46.55	30.38
RO	49.67	23.66	55.74	63.63	56.54	62.88	54.25
RI	53.70	50.30	47.60	57.15	58.16	55.81	49.94
FV	45.98	38.15	43.93	43.60	56.00	46.75	36.09
SR	60.30	42.16	51.50	55.34	56.93	55.98	52.02
mIoU	50.60	39.85	46.85	51.52	52.68	55.51	44.46
$\mathcal{F}$	66.14	57.10	62.61	68.35	68.58	71.75	61.43

m range images. On SUIM, such improvement is stronger: just using only l_{aux} loss, our network mIoU increases from 50.6 to 51.87. With the accuracy gains given by these two additional loss functions, our networks reaches the 2nd best accuracy on Seagrass dataset and 3nd best accuracy on SUIM dataset.

Table 3. Results from the ablation experiment evaluating the effect of different loss functions on our network mIoU

l_{ce}	l_{aux}	l_{smooth}	Seagrass 0 m–2 m mIoU	Seagrass 2 m–6 m mIoU	SUIM mIoU
✓			88.63	89.31	50.60
✓	✓		88.93	89.40	51.87
✓		✓	88.66	89.54	50.87
✓	✓	✓	88.96	89.74	50.79

4.4 Computational Need and Speed Results

Of all the networks, we measured the FLOPs with respect to a single input image of 320 × 256 resolution, and the total parameter numbers. The FLOPs estimate directly measures the total computational overhead of network inference, which is inversely proportional to inference speed. We timed so also the inference speeds of the networks on the GPUs of two different embedded platforms, an Nvidia Jetson TX2 and Nvidia Jetson Nano. Table 4 presents the measurement results.

We found that our proposed network has less parameters and FLOPs than all other networks. Our network has just 1.153 M parameters and 0.278 G FLOPs which are respectively at least 65% and 92% smaller than the ones of the considered alternatives as showed in Fig. 4. Thanks to this, can execute the segmentation inferences with the highest FPS. By averaging over 100 inferences, our proposed network achieves 23.95 FPS and 18.04 FPS respectively on the TX2 and Nano. As comparison, our network inference is, on average, 1.255 and 2.43 times faster than bisenetv2 (2nd fastest network), and 13.9 and 27.37 times faster than SegNet (the slowest one) respectively on the TX2 and Nano. Furthermore, we observed that with respect to PSPNet, which is the most accurate

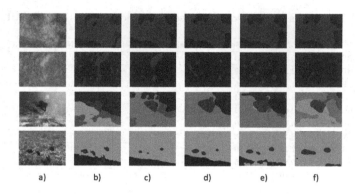

Fig. 6. The results of ablation experiment. Column a) presents test image samples and b) their corresponding ground truth; column c) shows the segmentation results by our network trained with l_{ce} only, d) with l_{ce} and l_{aux} only, and e) with l_{ce} and l_{smooth} only. The last column shows the segmentation results by our network trained with all the three loss functions.

network on the SUIM dataset and on the Seagrasses dataset on the 0–2 m range, our network is 9.5 and 19 times faster on the Nvidia Jetson TX2 and Nano.

On the Nvidia TX2 and, in particular, on the Nano these measurements show that the existing networks, although they achieve high accuracy on underwater segmentation tasks, they are not optimal to be deployed on AUVs for real-time use. Our proposed network instead reaches high accuracies without compromising on inference speed.

Table 4. All network comparison of total parameter number, FLOPs and inference speed achieved on two Nvidia Jetson GPU embedded platforms

		Ours	U-Net [12]	SegNet [14]	Deeplab [13]	BiSeNetv2 [36]	PSPNet [3]	GCN [37]
Params (M)		1.153	14.396	28.442	5.813	3.347	27.501	23.952
FLOPs (GMACs)		0.278	38.793	61.390	8.278	3.830	49.782	7.087
FPS GPU	TX2	23.95	2.297	1.723	10.52	19.07	2.509	7.224
	NANO	18.07	0.89	0.66	4.63	7.42	0.94	2.96

5   Conclusion

In this paper, we present a lightweight underwater segmentation network well suited for deployment on the embedded platforms of AUVs. On two datasets, the generalist SUIM dataset and the specialist Seagrasses dataset, we showed that the new proposed network achieves the same accuracy level of other six state-of-art segmentation networks. We proposed also two additional loss functions to help further our network training and we demonstrated that they let it reach even higher segmentation accuracies. Our network attains 51.87 mIoU

(3rd best) on the generalist dataset SUIM and 89.74 mIoU (2nd best) on 2–6 m range Seagrass dataset. Anyhow, given a light encoder with mobilenet and simple decoder with single step resolution recovery, the proposed network is characterized by a much smaller parameter number and requires much less FLOPs than the other considered segmentation networks. Our network has at least 65% less parameter number and 92% less FLOPs than the ones of the considered alternatives. Contrary to those, it is so much less limited by the computational constrains of the embedded platform and achieves faster inferences. The speed tests shows in fact that the reduced computational requirements of our network allow it to attain much higher FPS than the others segmentation network on different Nvidia embedded platforms; for example it reaches up to 24 FPS on Nvidia Jetson TX2 which is 14 times faster than SegNet. The advantages of such fast inference speed and high segmentation accuracy make so our segmentation network optimal for deployment and real-time use on the embedded platforms of AUVs.

References

1. Reus, G., et al.: Looking for seagrass: Deep learning for visual coverage estimation. In: 2018 OCEANS-MTS/IEEE Kobe Techno-Oceans (OTO), pp. 1–6. IEEE (2018)
2. Islam, M.J., et al.: Semantic segmentation of underwater imagery: Dataset and benchmark. arXiv preprint arXiv:2004.01241 (2020)
3. Zhao, H., Shi, J., Qi, X., Wang, X., Jia, J.: Pyramid scene parsing network. In: Proceedings of the IEEE Conference on Computer Vision and Pattern Recognition, pp. 2881–2890 (2017)
4. Boudouresque, C.F., Bernard, G., Pergent, G., Shili, A., Verlaque, M.: Regression of mediterranean seagrasses caused by natural processes and anthropogenic disturbances and stress: a critical review. Botanica Marina **52**, 395–418 (2009)
5. Gonzalez-Cid, Y., Burguera, A., Bonin-Font, F., Matamoros, A.: Machine learning and deep learning strategies to identify posidonia meadows in underwater images. In: OCEANS 2017-Aberdeen, pp. 1–5. IEEE (2017)
6. Bonin-Font, F., Burguera, A., Lisani, J.L.: Visual discrimination and large area mapping of posidonia oceanica using a lightweight AUV. IEEE Access **5**, 24479–24494 (2017)
7. Bonin-Font, F., Campos, M.M., Codina, G.O.: Towards visual detection, mapping and quantification of posidonia oceanica using a lightweight AUV. IFAC-PapersOnLine **49**, 500–505 (2016)
8. Martin-Abadal, M., Guerrero-Font, E., Bonin-Font, F., Gonzalez-Cid, Y.: Deep semantic segmentation in an AUV for online posidonia oceanica meadows identification. IEEE Access **6**, 60956–60967 (2018)
9. Martin-Abadal, M., Riutort-Ozcariz, I., Oliver-Codina, G., Gonzalez-Cid, Y.: A deep learning solution for posidonia oceanica seafloor habitat multiclass recognition. In: OCEANS 2019 – Marseille, pp. 1–7 (2019)
10. Sengupta, S., Ersbøll, B.K., Stockmarr, A.: Seagrassdetect: a novel method for detection of seagrass from unlabelled under water videos. Ecol. Inform. **57**, 101083 (2020)
11. Weidmann, F., et al.: A closer look at seagrass meadows: Semantic segmentation for visual coverage estimation. In: OCEANS 2019-Marseille, pp. 1–6. IEEE (2019)

12. Ronneberger, O., Fischer, P., Brox, T.: U-Net: convolutional networks for biomedical image segmentation. In: Navab, N., Hornegger, J., Wells, W.M., Frangi, A.F. (eds.) MICCAI 2015, Part III. LNCS, vol. 9351, pp. 234–241. Springer, Cham (2015). https://doi.org/10.1007/978-3-319-24574-4_28

13. Chen, L.-C., Zhu, Y., Papandreou, G., Schroff, F., Adam, H.: Encoder-decoder with Atrous separable convolution for semantic image segmentation. In: Ferrari, V., Hebert, M., Sminchisescu, C., Weiss, Y. (eds.) ECCV 2018, Part VII. LNCS, vol. 11211, pp. 833–851. Springer, Cham (2018). https://doi.org/10.1007/978-3-030-01234-2_49

14. Badrinarayanan, V., Kendall, A., Cipolla, R.: SegNet: a deep convolutional encoder-decoder architecture for image segmentation. IEEE Trans. Pattern Anal. Mach. Intel. **39**, 2481–2495 (2017)

15. Long, J., Shelhamer, E., Darrell, T.: Fully convolutional networks for semantic segmentation. In: Proceedings of the IEEE Conference on Computer Vision and Pattern Recognition, pp. 3431–3440 (2015)

16. Wu, T., Tang, S., Zhang, R., Zhang, Y.: CGNet: A light-weight context guided network for semantic segmentation. arXiv preprint arXiv:1811.08201 (2018)

17. Zhang, X., Chen, Z., Wu, Q.J., Cai, L., Lu, D., Li, X.: Fast semantic segmentation for scene perception. IEEE Trans. Industr. Inf. **15**, 1183–1192 (2018)

18. Poudel, R.P., Liwicki, S., Cipolla, R.: Fast-scnn: Fast semantic segmentation network. arXiv preprint arXiv:1902.04502 (2019)

19. Paszke, A., Chaurasia, A., Kim, S., Culurciello, E.: Enet: A deep neural network architecture for real-time semantic segmentation. arXiv preprint arXiv:1606.02147 (2016)

20. Lo, S.Y., Hang, H.M., Chan, S.W., Lin, J.J.: Efficient dense modules of asymmetric convolution for real-time semantic segmentation. In: Proceedings of the ACM Multimedia Asia. MMAsia 2019, New York, NY, USA. Association for Computing Machinery (2019)

21. Sandler, M., Howard, A., Zhu, M., Zhmoginov, A., Chen, L.C.: Mobilenetv 2: inverted residuals and linear bottlenecks. In: Proceedings of the IEEE Conference on Computer Vision And Pattern Recognition, pp. 4510–4520 (2018)

22. Tan, M., Le, Q.V.: Efficientnet: Rethinking model scaling for convolutional neural networks. arXiv preprint arXiv:1905.11946 (2019)

23. Ma, N., Zhang, X., Zheng, H.-T., Sun, J.: ShuffleNet V2: practical guidelines for efficient CNN architecture design. In: Ferrari, V., Hebert, M., Sminchisescu, C., Weiss, Y. (eds.) ECCV 2018, Part XIV. LNCS, vol. 11218, pp. 122–138. Springer, Cham (2018). https://doi.org/10.1007/978-3-030-01264-9_8

24. He, K., Zhang, X., Ren, S., Sun, J.: Deep residual learning for image recognition. In: Proceedings of the IEEE Conference on Computer Vision and Pattern Recognition, pp. 770–778 (2016)

25. Hu, J., Shen, L., Sun, G.: Squeeze-and-excitation networks. In: Proceedings of the IEEE Conference on Computer Vision and Pattern Recognition, pp. 7132–7141 (2018)

26. Woo, S., Park, J., Lee, J.-Y., Kweon, I.S.: CBAM: convolutional block attention module. In: Ferrari, V., Hebert, M., Sminchisescu, C., Weiss, Y. (eds.) ECCV 2018, Part VII. LNCS, vol. 11211, pp. 3–19. Springer, Cham (2018). https://doi.org/10.1007/978-3-030-01234-2_1

27. Li, X., Wang, W., Hu, X., Yang, J.: Selective kernel networks. In: Proceedings of the IEEE Conference on Computer Vision and Pattern Recognition, pp. 510–519 (2019)

28. Fu, J., Liu, J., Tian, H., Li, Y., Bao, Y., Fang, Z., Lu, H.: Dual attention network for scene segmentation. In: Proceedings of the IEEE Conference on Computer Vision and Pattern Recognition, pp. 3146–3154 (2019)
29. Wang, X., Girshick, R., Gupta, A., He, K.: Non-local neural networks. In: Proceedings of the IEEE Conference on Computer Vision and Pattern Recognition, pp. 7794–7803 (2018)
30. Cao, Y., Xu, J., Lin, S., Wei, F., Hu, H.: GCNet: non-local networks meet squeeze-excitation networks and beyond. In: Proceedings of the IEEE International Conference on Computer Vision Workshops (2019)
31. Huang, Z., Wang, X., Huang, L., Huang, C., Wei, Y., Liu, W.: CCNet: criss-cross attention for semantic segmentation. In: Proceedings of the IEEE International Conference on Computer Vision, pp. 603–612 (2019)
32. Zhu, Z., Xu, M., Bai, S., Huang, T., Bai, X.: Asymmetric non-local neural networks for semantic segmentation. In: Proceedings of the IEEE International Conference on Computer Vision, pp. 593–602 (2019)
33. Heise, P., Klose, S., Jensen, B., Knoll, A.: PM-Huber: patchmatch with huber regularization for stereo matching. In: Proceedings of the IEEE International Conference on Computer Vision, pp. 2360–2367 (2013)
34. Paszke, A., et al.: Pytorch: an imperative style, high-performance deep learning library. In: Advances in Neural Information Processing Systems, pp. 8026–8037 (2019)
35. Kingma, D.P., Ba, J.: Adam: a method for stochastic optimization. In: Bengio, Y., LeCun, Y. (eds.) 3rd International Conference on Learning Representations, ICLR 2015, San Diego, CA, USA, 7–9 May 2015, Conference Track Proceedings (2015)
36. Yu, C., Gao, C., Wang, J., Yu, G., Shen, C., Sang, N.: Bisenet v2: bilateral network with guided aggregation for real-time semantic segmentation. arXiv preprint arXiv:2004.02147 (2020)
37. Peng, C., Zhang, X., Yu, G., Luo, G., Sun, J.: Large kernel matters-improve semantic segmentation by global convolutional network. In: Proceedings of the IEEE Conference on Computer Vision and Pattern Recognition, pp. 4353–4361 (2017)

L2R GAN: LiDAR-to-Radar Translation

Leichen Wang[1,2(✉)], Bastian Goldluecke[2], and Carsten Anklam[1]

[1] Research and Development of Radar Sensor, Daimler AG, Sindelfingen, Germany
{leichen.wang,carsten.anklam}@daimler.com
[2] Department of Computer and Information Science, University Konstanz,
Konstanz, Germany
bastian.goldluecke@uni-konstanz.de

Abstract. The lack of annotated public radar datasets causes difficulties for research in environmental perception from radar observations. In this paper, we propose a novel neural network based framework which we call L2R GAN to generate the radar spectrum of natural scenes from a given LiDAR point cloud.

We adapt ideas from existing image-to-image translation GAN frameworks, which we investigate as a baseline for translating radar spectra image from a given LiDAR bird's eye view (BEV). However, for our application, we identify several shortcomings of existing approaches. As a remedy, we learn radar data generation with an occupancy-grid-mask as a guidance, and further design a set of local region generators and discriminator networks. This allows our L2R GAN to combine the advantages of global image features and local region detail, and not only learn the cross-modal relations between LiDAR and radar in large scale, but also refine details in small scale.

Qualitative and quantitative comparison show that L2R GAN outperforms previous GAN architectures with respect to details by a large margin. A L2R-GAN-based GUI also allows users to define and generate radar data of special emergency scenarios to test corresponding ADAS applications such as Pedestrian Collision Warning (PCW).

1 Introduction

In the past years, environmental perception based on cameras and Light Detection and Ranging (LiDARs) has made significant progress by using deep learning techniques. The basic idea is to design and train a deep neural network by feeding quantities of annotated samples. The training process enables the networks to effectively learn a hierarchical representation of pixels or points using high-level semantic features.

In contrast to LiDARs and camera, Frequency-Modulated Continuous-Wave (FMCW) radar operates at longer ranges and is substantially more robust to adverse weather and lighting conditions. Besides, on account of its compact size and reasonable price, radar is becoming the most reliable and most widely used

Electronic supplementary material The online version of this chapter (https://doi.org/10.1007/978-3-030-69535-4_43) contains supplementary material, which is available to authorized users.

H. Ishikawa et al. (Eds.): ACCV 2020, LNCS 12624, pp. 704–720, 2021.
https://doi.org/10.1007/978-3-030-69535-4_43

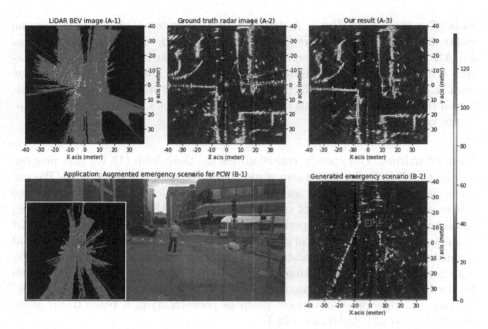

Fig. 1. A: We propose the L2R GAN for synthesizing radar spectrum images from given LiDAR point clouds. A-1: Input LiDAR BEV image with corresponding occupancy grid mask (black is unknown area, gray is free area). A-2: ground truth radar spectrum. A-3: generated radar spectrum of L2R GAN. B: An L2R-GAN-based GUI allows to define and generate the radar data of emergency scenarios to test corresponding ADAS application such as Pedestrian Collision Warning (PCW). B-1: example of an augmented emergency scenario for PCW in a camera and LiDAR BEV image, the pedestrian in red box is inserted 10 m in front of ego car. B-2: corresponding generated radar spectrum. Please zoom in for details.

sensor in Advanced Driver Assistance Systems (ADAS) applications. However, the research on deep learning for analyzing radar signals is still at a very early stage [1–6].

The most important reason for this apparent contradiction is that only a few datasets provide radar data [7]. Inspired by KITTI [8] in the year 2013, most of the 3D object detection datasets include RGB camera images and LiDAR point clouds [9–13]. To the best of our knowledge, only nuScenes [14], Oxford Radar RobotCar [15], and Astyx HiRes2019 Datasets [16] contain radar data. Through careful analysis, we found that the radar data of the nuScenes and Astyx HiRes2019 datasets are sparse radar points instead of raw radar spectra. On the other hand, the Oxford Radar RobotCar supplies radar spectra, but without any object annotation. In short, until now, there has neither been a high-quality public dataset nor a benchmark for radar environmental perception.

Motivated by the above problems, we define automatic LiDAR-to-radar translation as the task of generating radar data from given LiDAR point clouds. It is trained with the broad set of paired LiDAR-radar samples from the Oxford

RobotCar dataset, see Fig. 1. A challenge that needs to be addressed is how the radar and LiDAR data are represented. Image-based representations (such as LiDAR BEV and radar spectrum images) are valid for image-to-image translation GAN frameworks that have a fixed relationship, but fewer details in raw data, *e.g.* intensity, and height of point clouds. Otherwise, point-wise representation bases such as radar pins or point clouds are not well-suited for image-to-image translation GANs.

Contributions. Our specific contributions are three-fold: (1) We first propose a conditional L2R GAN that can translate data from LiDAR to radar. We use an occupancy grid mask for guidance and a set of local region generators to create a more reliable link of objects between LiDAR and radar for refining small-scale regions. (2) In experiments, we demonstrate the effectiveness of our framework for the generation of raw, detailed radar spectra. Both qualitative and quantitative comparison indicate that L2R GAN outperforms previous GANs with respect to details by a large margin. (3) We show that our framework can be used for advanced data augmentation and emergency scene generation by editing the appearance of objects (such as pedestrian) in a real LiDAR scene and feeding to L2R GAN, see Fig. 1.

2   Background and Related Work

In this section, we briefly review recent existing work on data translation with conditional GAN (cGAN) and different representations of LiDAR and radar sensors.

2.1   Cross-Domain Data Translation with Conditional GAN

Cross-Domain data translation, especially image-to-image translation, involves generating a new synthetic version of a given image with a specific modification, such as translating a winter landscape to summer. Generally speaking, image-to-image translation can be divided into supervised and unsupervised translation. Some early works expected to generate an output image close to a ground-truth image by reducing pixel-wise losses, for example, $L1$-loss or MSE in pixel space [17]. From 2016 on, [18] and [19] trained a conditional GAN network on paired data to translate across different image domains (like sketc.hes to photos). In pix2pix [19], the generator is creatively designed as a U-Net architecture [20], while the discriminator classifies each $N \times N$ patch as real or fake instead of the whole image. To synthesize more photo-realistic images given an input map image, pix2pixHD uses a new multi-scale generator and discriminator [21]. In [22], authors demonstrate that conditional GAN models highly benefit from scaling up. In [23] and [24], high-resolution images are scaled using a memory bank composed of a training image segment. Spatially-adaptive normalization to transform semantic information is proposed in [25]. Very recently, LGGAN uses a local class-specific generative network with an attention fusion module to combine the multi-scaled features in the GAN [26].

representation of radar data.PNG

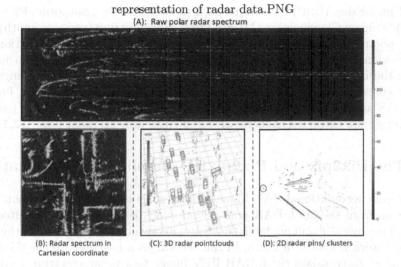

Fig. 2. Different representation of radar data used in the datasets. (a): raw polar radar spectrum, Navtech CTS350-X Millimetre-Wave FMCW radar [15]; (b): the same radar spectrum in Cartesian coordinates; (c): 3D radar point clouds, Astyx 6455 HiRes radar [16]; (d): 2D radar pins/clusters, Continental ARS40X radar [14].

Meanwhile, lots of research aims to train the network in an unsupervised way using unpaired samples from different training sets [27–30]. Furthermore, [31–33] have presented a remarkable technique for training unsupervised image translation models via utilizing a cycle consistency loss. In 2018, to handle translation between multiple-domains without training for each pair of domains, [34] propose StarGAN, which performs this task using only a single model.

2.2 Representations of Radar Data

FMCW radars are widely used for autonomous driving with the ability to measure range (radial distance), velocity (Doppler), azimuth and received power, which is a function of the object's reflectively, size, shape, and orientation relative to the receiver, in some cases also named as radar cross section (RCS). FMCW radars continuously transmit chirp signal and receive echo signal reflected by objects. The radar measurement process is very complicated and the resulting scan is also susceptible to contamination by speckle noise, reflection, and artifacts [35]. According to the increasing levels of data abstraction and handcrafted feature extraction, radar data can be divided into the following representations: raw polar radar spectrum, radar spectrum in Cartesian coordinates, 3D radar point clouds and 2D radar pins, see Fig. 2.

The original radar raw data is in the form of a 2D array, whose row is formed by the target echo returned from each radar pulse. However, as technical secrets, such data is not available to users. Radar manufacturers use digital signal processing (DSP) algorithms such as Fast Fourier Transform (FFT) and Multiple Signal Classification (MUSIC) to obtain spectrum (range-azimuth) data under polar coordinate system [15,36]. Through coordinate transformation into a Cartesian coordinate system, we can further get the BEV spectrum images where the intensity represents the highest power reflection within a range bin. There are several radar researches take radar spectra as input [4,6,37]. Further to ADAS applications, radar data are more heavily processed by DSP (such as clustering) and extracted to sparse 3D radar clusters or 2D radar pins [1,2,14,38].

3   The Pix2pix and Pix2pixHD Baseline Implementations

We propose a conditional GAN framework for generating a high-resolution radar spectrum from the 3D LiDAR point cloud which is based on the architectural ideas of pix2pix [19] and pix2pixHD [21] architectural. An illustration of the overall framework is shown in Fig. 3. In this section, as a baseline, we use the above approaches to translate the LiDAR BEV image to a radar spectrum Cartesian image, which can be formulated as a problem of image-to-image domain translation.

3.1   Architecture of Pix2pix and Pix2pixHD

The pix2pix method is a conditional GAN framework for paired image-to-image translation with an additional $L1$ loss. It consists of a U-Net [20] generator G and a patch-based fully convolutional network discriminator D. The conditional adversarial loss with an input x and ground truth y is formulated as

$$\mathcal{L}_{cGAN}(G, D) = \mathbb{E}_{x,y}[\log D(x, y)] + \mathbb{E}_x[\log(1 - D(G(x)))]. \tag{1}$$

Moreover, training aims to find the saddle point of the objective function

$$\arg \min_G \max_D \mathcal{L}_{cGAN}(G, D) + \lambda \mathcal{L}_{pix}(G), \tag{2}$$

with a pixel-wise reconstruction loss $\mathcal{L}_{pix}$. A typical choice here is the L_1-norm.

The recently proposed pix2pixHD model is based on pix2pix, but has shown better results for high-resolution images synthesis. A multi-scale generator and different discriminators for multiple scales are leveraged to generate high-resolution images with details and realistic textures. The objective function is extended with the matching loss of the multiple layers' features.

We choose the same range (80×80 m) for both LiDAR and radar images. The reason is that the LiDAR point clouds in the far range are very sparse and few measurements are available at distances above 40m. The radar spectrum Cartesian image and BEV LiDAR image have the same representation as an image with a resolution of $N \times N = 400 \times 400$ pixels, where N is the cardinality of the set of bins in the discretized range, and each pixel represents an area of 0.2×0.2 m.

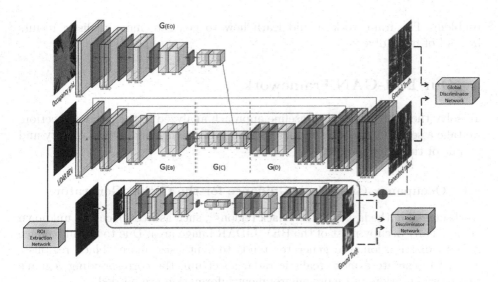

Fig. 3. Overview of L2R GAN network. The L2R GAN consists of four parts: a global generator, a set of local region generators, a ROI extraction network and discriminator network. The local region generator uses a U-Net framework to synthesis radar data in small-scaled ROIs , which is showed in red box. The global generator G_{Global} concatenates the feature maps of occupancy grid mask and LiDAR BEV images. It also consists of four subcomponents: an occupancy grid mask encoder network $G_{(E_O)}$, a BEV image encoder network $G_{(E_B)}$, a concatenation block $G_{(C)}$, and a fusion decoder network $G_{(D)}$. See text below for details. (Color figure online)

3.2 Drawbacks of the Baseline Approaches

It turns out that if we directly apply one of [19] or [21], the generated radar spectrum is quite unsatisfactory, see Fig. 4. After careful analysis, we can identify four main reasons for this. First, due to the difference in sensor characteristics, there is no strict pixel-wise correspondence between the LiDAR BEV and Cartesian radar spectrum image. In particular cases, some objects can only be detected by either LiDAR or radar.

Second, "Black regions", such as free space and unknown regions, usually occupy most of the image area, see the radar spectrum images in Fig. 2. This highly imbalanced data adds to the difficulty, which makes the GAN tend to generate more "black regions" than what would be realistic. In contrast, smaller-scaled regions (vehicles and pedestrians) can not be effectively learned by a global image-level generation, and such regions are much more critical for ADAS.

Third, since pix2pix and pix2pixHD are mainly designed for Semantic-map-guided or edge-map-guided scene generation, whose performance heavily relies on the boundaries of segments. In our case, a LiDAR BEV image alone is not able to provide boundary-like features. Furthermore, neither instance-level semantic label map nor instance maps is available.

Finally, different from a one-to-many mapping problem *e.g.* image synthesis from semantic label maps, LiDAR to radar translation is a one-to-one mapping problem. The framework should learn how to generate more realistic results instead of more diverse.

4   Our L2R-GAN Framework

To solve the problems of the baseline approach analyzed in the previous section, we take a series of measures to increase the performance and overall quality and details of the results.

4.1   Occupancy-Grid-Mask Guidance for the Global Generator

As discussed in the last section, "black regions", such as free space and unknown area, usually occupy most of the BEV LiDAR image area. Due to the imbalance in data distribution, the generator tends to synthesize more "black regions". Thus, to generate a more realistic radar spectrum, the corresponding region's real representation and more environment information are needed.

Inspired by [39] and [40], we assume that an occupancy grid mask of the BEV image allows the generator to better understand environmental information. The mask divides "black regions" into two classes, namely free region and unknown region. Although both regions seem similar in the BEV LiDAR image, there are obviously more radar reflections in unknown space than free space, see Fig. 4. The reason behind this phenomenon is the different working principle, with phenomena such as multipath propagation, refraction, and scattering, which lets radar see part of the objects which are occluded and can not be detected by LiDAR.

To retain the basic structure of the traffic scene, we design an occupancy-grid-mask-guided global generator G_{Global}. The occupancy mask is generated via ray casting through the scene, which is implemented using Bresenham's line rendering algorithm [41]. For details, please see the additional material. The generator G_{Global} follows an architecture in the spirit of U-Net [20] and consists of four components. The occupancy grid mask encoder network $G_{(E_O)}$ learns the features of the occupancy grid mask M. The BEV image encoder network $G_{(E_B)}$ is designed to encode the input BEV image I_{BEV}. A concatenation block $G_{(C)}$ relays the feature maps of $G_{(E_B)}$ and $G_{(E_O)}$ to the backbone framework. Finally, the fusion decoder network $G_{(D)}$ generates a coarse image of resolution 400×400. The complete layout is visualized in Fig. 3.

4.2   Local Region Generator and Discriminator

To produce a truly realistic radar spectrum, a model must be able to synthesize the data of objects which occupy a smaller region, such as vehicles and pedestrians. However, most of the existing cGANs use only a global generator to capture features and texture from a large receptive field. Inspired by the idea of a coarse-to-fine generator to enhance local details [21], we separate the generator into the two sub-components G_{Global} and G_{Local}. However, different from [21], our local generator consists of several independent local region generators, whose input is a small region of interest (ROI) instead of a whole image.

To extract ROIs from LiDAR point clouds effectively, we utilize the feature encoder network from PointPillars [42] as an extraction network. This network is designed to convert a point cloud into a sparse pseudo-image. In our case, the feature encoder network receives the point cloud in a volume of $L \times W \times H = 80 \times 80 \times 5$ m as input and generates a pseudo-image at resolution $w \times h \times c = 400 \times 400 \times 8$ as output, where c is the number of channels of the pseudo-image. We then add a 2D region proposal network (RPN) to detect ROIs in the pseudo-image. The output of whole extraction network consists of serevel ROIs, each has size of $30 \times 30 \times 3$, see Fig. 3. Notably, the Oxford Radar RobotCar dataset has no object annotation. Thus, the extraction network is trained on the nuScenes dataset, whose LiDAR sensor is the same as Oxford Radar RobotCar's.

The local region generator then processes the data on small scale ROIs extracted by the extraction net. The input of each local generation is a segment $L_i \in \mathbb{R}^{30 \times 30 \times 3}$, which is a part of BEV image that contains the segment. To control the training process and results of the local region generators, a global discriminator such as in pix2pix or multi-scale discriminator such as in pix2pixHD is insufficient. Thus, we define corresponding local region discriminators, whose input is a small-scale radar spectrum instead of a large receptive field.

For the global generator, we integrate local generator and discriminator networks which are based on the U-Net architecture, see Fig. 3. In summary, the global generator network aims to learn the large scale features of each scenario to generate globally consistent images, while the local region generator is focusing on small ROIs to enhance and refine the details in the radar spectrum. Finally, we use a fusion structure to combine the outputs of local and global generator to provide more scene details while retaining global structure. In particular, our L2R GAN is therefore capable of effectively producing high-quality radar data of each road user.

4.3   Objective Functions

Different from other conditional GANs, the main purpose of L2R GAN is to generate a unique and as real as possible radar spectrum – no variety, but more fidelity. So the objective of L2R GAN is not only to focus on how to fool the discriminator (GAN loss), but also to reduce the difference to the corresponding ground truth. We have tried several metrics for this pixel-wise loss, such as $L1$, $L2$, and MSE, which we analyze in the next section.

The final objective for the global and local generators and discriminators is an expanded version of Eq. (1),

$$\arg \min_G \max_D \mathcal{L}_{cGAN}(G, D) + \lambda \mathcal{L}_{Lpix}(G) + \mu \mathcal{L}_P(G, D). \tag{3}$$

Here, $\mathcal{L}_P$ is a perceptual loss function known from other cGANs [21], which measures the distribution of high-level features between transformed images and ground-truth images from a discriminator. The parameters λ and μ control the

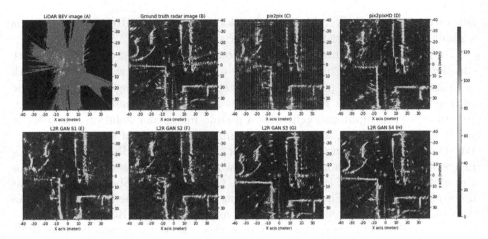

Fig. 4. Comparison on the Oxford robot car dataset [40]. (A) is in put LiDAR BEV image (B) is corresponding ground truth radar image. Our method (H) generates more realistic than pix2pix (B) and pix2pixHD (C). In comparison with other baseline (E), (F), and (G), Our method (H) is closer to ground truth (B). Please zoom in for details.

weight of pixel-wise and perceptual loss, respectively, and are different for the local and global losses. In experiments, it will turn out that the local perceptual loss does not improve results, so $\mu_{\mathrm{local}} = 0$ for optimal results. We first train both generators separately, then jointly fine-tune them, see below for details.

5   Experimental Results

In this section, we describe the set of experiments to evaluate our method and to demonstrate the extension of its capabilities. We then show the effectiveness of our method as a radar translator and conduct a qualitative as well as quantitative comparison against baseline methods. Due to the particularity and uniqueness of the task, we first explain the evaluation methods and metrics in Sect. 5.1. We then validate the structure of L2R GAN with a set of ablation studies to in Sect. 5.2. Finally, we show applications of our method in radar data augmentation from a novel LiDAR point clouds, and performing emergency scene generation in Sect. 6.

5.1   Baseline Comparisons

Implementation Details. We train the entire architecture by optimizing the objectives in Eq. (3). However, in our model, the generators G_{Global} and G_{local} have a considerably different number of parameters. While G_{Global} is trying to learn large scale features, G_{local} aims at refining the details in small scale regions. To mitigate this issue, we employ an adaptive training strategy. In order to adapt the training process at each iteration, if either discriminator's accuracy is higher than 75%, we skip its training. To avoid overfitting, we use dropout layers, which

Table 1. qualitative experiments

	Oxford	nuScenes
Ours >Pix2pix	96.5%	90.5%
Ours >Pix2pix HD	80.5%	85.0%
Ours >GT	24.0%	no GT

Table 2. quantitative experiments

	PSNR(dB)	SSIM
Pix2pix	7.722	0.031
Pix2pix HD	23.383	0.372
Ours	**29.367**	**0.660**

Fig. 5. Table 1 shows the results of blind randomized A/B tests on Amazon MTurk. Each entry is calculated from 200 tests made by at least 5 workers. The results indicate the percentage of comparisons in which the radar spectrum synthesized by our method are considered more realistic than the corresponding synthesized one by Pix2pix or the Pix2pixHD. Opportunity is 50%. To be noticed, for nuScenes dataset, there is no ground truth radar images. Table 2 indicates L2R GAN has less image distortion than pix2pix and pix2pixHD.

are applied to the global generator at training time. We also set different learning rates for the global discriminator, the local discriminator, the global generator, and the local generators, which are 10^{-5}, 0.0025, 10^{-5}, and 0.0025, respectively. We use ADAM with $\beta = 0.5$ for the optimization.

Training, Validation and Test Datasets. We use the recently released Oxford Radar RobotCar Dataset [15], which consists of 280 km of urban driving data under different traffic, weather and lighting conditions. The test vehicle is equipped with 2 LiDAR and 1 radar with the following specifications:

- Navtech CTS350-X Millimetre-Wave FMCW radar, 4 Hz, 400 measurements per rotation, 4.38 cm range resolution, 1.8° beamwidth, 163 m range.
- Velodyne HDL-32E 3D LIDAR, 360° HFoV, 41.3° VFoV, 32 channels, 20 Hz, 100 m range, 2 cm range resolution.

The dataset consists of several approximately 9 km trajectories in the Oxford city map. Similar to the strategy used in prior work, we manually divide the trajectories of the dataset into training, validation, and test set according to a 70:15:15 split. So in following experiments, we use 8500 paired sample as training set, 1200 as validation and test set. Note that the LiDAR scans from each sensor are gathered 20 Hz, whereas radar streams are collected 4 Hz. Due to this temporal difference in synchronization and the dynamic environment, the translation from LiDAR to radar suffers from misalignment. We correct for this misalignment by down-sampling and interpolating the point cloud in the BEV images. In the same fashion, each radar scan is related to the closest LiDAR data in time.

For advanced data augmentation, we also use the nuScenes dataset [14] to validate the generalization ability of L2R GAN. Notably, it has no similar radar ground truth images.

Evaluation Metrics. Evaluating the quality of synthesized radar data is an open problem and more difficult than other synthesized image. In particular, there is no common metric yet to evaluate generated radar data. To highlight

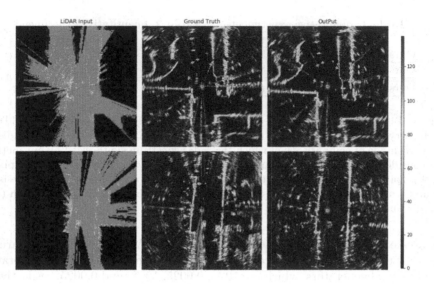

Fig. 6. Example radar results on the Oxford robot car dataset. Please zoom in for details.

the qualities of L2R GAN, we focus attention on how to generate radar data as close as possible to the ground truth. For the quantitative evaluation, we use Peak Signal to Noise Ratio (PSNR, in the range $(0, 100]$) and structural similarity (SSIM, in the range $(0, 1]$) to measure image distortion and derive the similarity between two images [43]. The larger SSIM and PSNR, the less the image distortion.

Meanwhile, as a qualitative experiment, we also investigate a human subjective study. The evaluation metric is based on large batches of blind randomized A/B tests deployed on the Amazon Mechanical Turk platform (Amazon MTurk). To learn the characteristic of a radar spectrum, the workers were asked to first read an introduction to radar signals and browse 100 randomly selected radar spectra from the Oxford radar dataset for 10 min. After this, we assume that the workers have a general understanding of the characteristics and distribution of real radar data. They subsequently will be presented two images at a time, one is ground truth, the other is synthesized from the corresponding LiDAR point clouds. The workers are asked to find the real one in 8 s, as adopted in prior work [21].

Baseline Comparisons. Figure 4 and Fig. 5 report the results of baseline comparisons. Both qualitative and quantitative experiments give evidence that radar images synthesized by our approach are more accurate than the ones synthesized by Pix2pix or the Pix2pix HD. In Table 1, each entry in the table reports the percentage of comparisons in which a radar spectrum image synthesized by our approach was considered more realistic in Amazon MTurk than a corresponding

Method	PSNR(dB)			SSIM		
	min	max	mean	min	max	mean
S1: G_{Global}	23.006	24.206	23.635	0.360	0.406	0.381
S2: S1+G_{Local}	28.430	29.253	28.426	0.576	0.598	0.588
S3: S1+ occupancy grid	23.911	25.079	24.434	0.417	0.473	0.450
S4: S3+G_{Local} (/w $\mathcal{L}_1$)	**29.076**	**29.697**	**29.367**	**0.647**	0.671	0.660
S4 /w $\mathcal{L}_2$	28.261	29.040	28.781	0.643	**0.674**	**0.662**
S4 /w $\mathcal{L}_{MSE}$	29.053	29.423	29.219	0.637	0.665	0.656
S4 /w $\mathcal{L}_1 + \mathcal{L}_{P-local}$	27.601	28.211	27.912	0.543	0.598	0.572
S4 /w $\mathcal{L}_2 + \mathcal{L}_{P-local}$	26.970	27.498	27.201	0.550	0.592	0.570
S4 /w $\mathcal{L}_{MSE} + \mathcal{L}_{P-local}$	27.054	27.431	27.284	0.550	0.601	0.574

Fig. 7. Ablation study to evaluate different components of our framework. The upper half shows the result of different framework structure, while the lower left is analysis of loss functions. The baseline of comparison is S4 (/w $\mathcal{L}_1$), whose loss function is $\mathcal{L}_{cGAN} + \mathcal{L}_1 + \mathcal{L}_{P-Global}$.

one synthesized by Pix2pix or the Pix2pix HD. Figure 6 shows more examples on the Oxford robot car dataset.

5.2 Ablation Analysis

Analysis of the Framework Structure. We evaluate the proposed L2R GAN in four variants S1, S2, S3, S4 as follows: (a) S1 employs only the global generator without occupancy grid mask, (b) S2 combines the global generator without occupancy grid mask and the local region generators to produce the final results, where the local results are produced by using a point pillar based extraction network, (c) S3 uses the proposed occupancy-grid-mask-guided global generator, (d) S4 is our full model. See Fig. 7 for the evaluation result.

Analysis of the Loss Functions. Here, we show how the loss function influences the synthesis performance. For a fair comparison, we retain the same network framework and data setting as S4 and utilize a combination of different losses, see Fig. 7 for results.

Interestingly, the perceptual loss does not improve the quality of local region generators, but tends to make the training process unstable and result in collapse. We speculate that the perceptual loss may not be suitable for a small receptive field, which has few common high-level features. The experiments also show that the $L1$ loss can learn image details more effectively than $L2$ and MSE.

6   Application: Data Augmentation for ADAS

A big problem in ADAS is how to collect data for an emergency scenario to test a corresponding ADAS application. For example, to test Pedestrian Collision

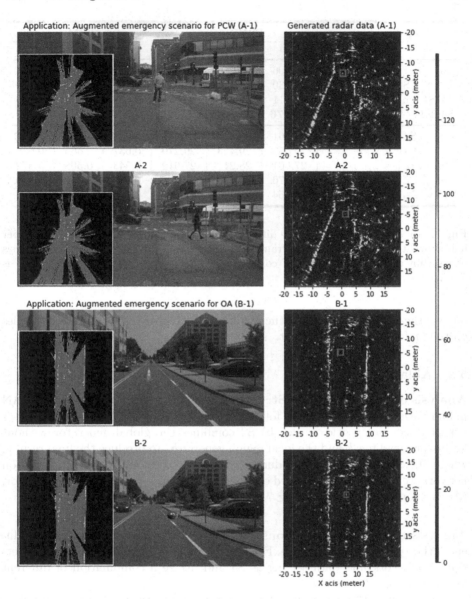

Fig. 8. Example radar data of augmented emergency scenario on the nuScenes dataset. In nuScenes dataset, there is no radar spectrum ground truth. A is augmented emergency scenario for Pedestrian Collision Warning (PCW): A-1 inserts a pedestrian 10 m in front of ego car, A-2 inserts a pedestrian 2 m east and 10 m forward of ego car. B is augmented emergency scenario for Obstacle Avoidance (OA): B-1 inserts a traffic cone 10 m in front of ego car, B-2 inserts a tire 2 m east and 10 m forward of ego car. Here camera images just help the reader understand. Please zoom in for details.

Warning (PCW), on the one hand, a sufficient number of experiments is necessary before the application is released. On the other hand, it is too dangerous to implement such a collision test under real road conditions. For this reason, researchers artificially insert real LiDAR objects into a real LiDAR scene to produce a fake dangerous traffic scenario [44]. The occluded points in the original LiDAR scene can be calculated and removed by mathematical methods, such as applying a cube map [44] or raycasting [39]. However, it is quite difficult to augment radar data in similar way. Due to refraction and scattering, the intersection of radar beams and inserted objects is much more complicated than for LiDAR. In the worst case, the radar wave returning from a target object can get reflected on those surfaces and result in so-called "ghost" targets that do not actually exist.

Given these observations, we propose to generate radar data of a dangerous traffic scenario by manually editing the appearance of individual objects in LiDAR data as above, then feeding the data into our L2R GAN. A GUI allows users to design their own augmented emergency scenario. To implement this idea, we collect several 3D semantically labeled objects from the nuScenes dataset (such as pedestrians, lost cargo and traffic cones) to create an object database for the user to choose from. The user can also manually select which LiDAR scenes to use as background, and where to insert a "dangerous object" of a specific class. For example, the user can add 3D points of a pedestrian 10 m in front of the vehicle into an existing urban scenario to simulate a emergency scenario. Our L2R GAN will then automatically produce a corresponding radar spectrum. This kind of simulation data is urgently required for ADAS development and validation, which can be hardly obtained through test drive. Figure 8 shows four of these augmented scenarios.

7   Conclusion

In summary, we propose a new method for LiDAR-to-radar translation. Based on the pix2pix and pix2pixHD methods, our L2R GAN generates a radar spectrum image through an occupancy-grid-mask-guided global generator, a set of local region generators, a ROI extration network and discriminator networks. Results on synthetic and real radar data show promising qualitative and quantitative results which surpass the previous baseline. A L2R-GAN-based GUI also allows users to define and generate special radar data of emergency scenarios to test corresponding ADAS applications, such as pedestrian collision warning and obstacle avoidance. Our research will serve as a reference for future testing and development of various radar ADAS applications. Future investigations will focus on validating the accuracy of augmented radar data by doing experiments in the field.

Acklowdegment. This work was supported by the DFG Centre of Excellence 2117 'Centre for the Advanced Study of Collective Behaviour' (ID: 422037984).

References

1. Lombacher, J., Hahn, M., Dickmann, J., Wöhler, C.: Potential of radar for static object classification using deep learning methods. In: 2016 IEEE MTT-S International Conference on Microwaves for Intelligent Mobility (ICMIM), pp. 1–4 (2016)
2. Schumann, O., Hahn, M., Dickmann, J., Wöhler, C.: Semantic segmentation on radar point clouds. In: 2018 21st International Conference on Information Fusion (FUSION), pp. 2179–2186 (2018)
3. Dubé, R., Hahn, M., Schütz, M., Dickmann, J., Gingras, D.: Detection of parked vehicles from a radar based occupancy grid. In: IEEE Intelligent Vehicles Symposium (IV), pp. 1415–1420 (2014)
4. Cen, S.H., Newman, P.: Radar-only ego-motion estimation in difficult settings via graph matching. In: 2019 International Conference on Robotics and Automation (ICRA), pp. 298–304 (2019)
5. Bartsch, A., Fitzek, F., Rasshofer, R.: Pedestrian recognition using automotive radar sensors. Adv. Radio Sci. ARS **10**, 45–55 (2012)
6. Dong, X., Wang, P., Zhang, P., Liu, L.: Probabilistic orientated object detection in automotive radar. arXiv preprint arXiv:2004.05310 (2020)
7. Feng, D., et al.: Deep multi-modal object detection and semantic segmentation for autonomous driving: datasets, methods, and challenges. IEEE Trans. Intell. Transp. Syst. (2020)
8. Geiger, A., Lenz, P., Stiller, C., Urtasun, R.: The Kitti vision benchmark suite (2015). http://www.cvlibs.net/datasets/kitti
9. Huang, X., et al.: The apolloscape dataset for autonomous driving. In: Proceedings of the IEEE Conference on Computer Vision and Pattern Recognition Workshops, pp. 954–960 (2018)
10. Sun, P., et al.: Scalability in perception for autonomous driving: Waymo open dataset. In: CVPR, pp. 2446–2454 (2020)
11. Pham, Q.H., et al.: A* 3d dataset: Towards autonomous driving in challenging environments. arXiv preprint arXiv:1909.07541 (2019)
12. Hwang, S., Park, J., Kim, N., Choi, Y., So Kweon, I.: Multispectral pedestrian detection: benchmark dataset and baseline. In: IEEE Conference on Computer Vision and Pattern Recognition (CVPR), pp. 1037–1045 (2015)
13. Jung, H., Oto, Y., Mozos, O.M., Iwashita, Y., Kurazume, R.: Multi-modal panoramic 3D outdoor datasets for place categorization. In: 2016 IEEE/RSJ International Conference on Intelligent Robots and Systems (IROS), pp. 4545–4550 (2016)
14. Caesar, H., et al.: nuscenes: A multimodal dataset for autonomous driving. arXiv preprint arXiv:1903.11027 (2019)
15. Barnes, D., Gadd, M., Murcutt, P., Newman, P., Posner, I.: The oxford radar robotcar dataset: A radar extension to the oxford robotcar dataset. arXiv preprint arXiv:1909.01300 (2019)
16. Meyer, M., Kuschk, G.: Automotive radar dataset for deep learning based 3d object detection. In: 2019 16th European Radar Conference (EuRAD), pp. 129–132 (2019)
17. Dong, C., Loy, C.C., He, K., Tang, X.: Image super-resolution using deep convolutional networks. IEEE Trans. Pattern Anal. Mach. Intell. **38**, 295–307 (2015)
18. Sangkloy, P., Lu, J., Fang, C., Yu, F., Hays, J.: Scribbler: controlling deep image synthesis with sketch and color. In: IEEE Conference on Computer Vision and Pattern Recognition (CVPR), pp. 5400–5409 (2017)

19. Isola, P., Zhu, J.Y., Zhou, T., Efros, A.A.: Image-to-image translation with conditional adversarial networks. In: IEEE Conference on Computer Vision and Pattern Recognition (CVPR), pp. 1125–1134 (2017)
20. Ronneberger, O., Fischer, P., Brox, T.: U-net: convolutional networks for biomedical image segmentation. In: International Conference on Medical Image Computing and Computer-Assisted Intervention, pp. 234–241 (2015)
21. Wang, T.C., Liu, M.Y., Zhu, J.Y., Tao, A., Kautz, J., Catanzaro, B.: High-resolution image synthesis and semantic manipulation with conditional gans. In: IEEE Conference on Computer Vision and Pattern Recognition (CVPR), pp. 8798–8807 (2018)
22. Brock, A., Donahue, J., Simonyan, K.: Large scale gan training for high fidelity natural image synthesis. arXiv preprint arXiv:1809.11096 (2018)
23. Qi, X., Chen, Q., Jia, J., Koltun, V.: Semi-parametric image synthesis. In: IEEE Conference on Computer Vision and Pattern Recognition (CVPR), pp. 8808–8816 (2018)
24. Chen, Q., Koltun, V.: Photographic image synthesis with cascaded refinement networks. In: IEEE International Conference on Computer Vision (ICCV), pp. 1511–1520 (2017)
25. Park, T., Liu, M.Y., Wang, T.C., Zhu, J.Y.: Semantic image synthesis with spatially-adaptive normalization. In: IEEE Conference on Computer Vision and Pattern Recognition (CVPR), pp. 2337–2346 (2019)
26. Tang, H., Xu, D., Yan, Y., Torr, P.H., Sebe, N.: Local class-specific and global image-level generative adversarial networks for semantic-guided scene generation. In: IEEE Conference on Computer Vision and Pattern Recognition (CVPR), pp. 7870–7879 (2020)
27. Liu, M.Y., Breuel, T., Kautz, J.: Unsupervised image-to-image translation networks. In: Advances in Neural Information Processing Systems, pp. 700–708 (2017)
28. Liu, M.Y., Tuzel, O.: Coupled generative adversarial networks. In: Advances in Neural Information Processing Systems, pp. 469–477 (2016)
29. Shrivastava, A., Pfister, T., Tuzel, O., Susskind, J., Wang, W., Webb, R.: Learning from simulated and unsupervised images through adversarial training. In: IEEE Conference on Computer Vision and Pattern Recognition (CVPR), pp. 2107–2116 (2017)
30. Bousmalis, K., Silberman, N., Dohan, D., Erhan, D., Krishnan, D.: Unsupervised pixel-level domain adaptation with generative adversarial networks. In: IEEE Conference on Computer Vision and Pattern Recognition (CVPR), pp. 3722–3731 (2017)
31. Zhu, J.Y., Park, T., Isola, P., Efros, A.A.: Unpaired image-to-image translation using cycle-consistent adversarial networks. In: IEEE International Conference on Computer Vision (ICCV), pp. 2223–2232 (2017)
32. Yi, Z., Zhang, H., Tan, P., Gong, M.: Dualgan: unsupervised dual learning for image-to-image translation. In: IEEE International Conference on Computer Vision (ICCV), pp. 2849–2857 (2017)
33. Kim, T., Cha, M., Kim, H., Lee, J.K., Kim, J.: Learning to discover cross-domain relations with generative adversarial networks. In: Proceedings of the 34th International Conference on Machine Learning, vol. 70, pp. 1857–1865 (2017)
34. Choi, Y., Choi, M., Kim, M., Ha, J.W., Kim, S., Choo, J.: Stargan: unified generative adversarial networks for multi-domain image-to-image translation. In: IEEE Conference on Computer Vision and Pattern Recognition (CVPR), pp. 8789–8797 (2018)

35. de Martini, D., Kaul, P., Gadd, M., Newman, P.: RSS-Net: weakly-supervised multi-class semantic segmentation with FMCW radar. In: IEEE Intelligent Vehicles Symposium (IV) (2020)
36. Lim, J.S., et al.: Digital signal processing. Technical report, Research Laboratory of Electronics (RLE) at the Massachusetts Institute of ... (1988)
37. Patel, K., Rambach, K., Visentin, T., Rusev, D., Pfeiffer, M., Yang, B.: Deep learning-based object classification on automotive radar spectra. In: 2019 IEEE Radar Conference (RadarConf), pp. 1–6 (2019)
38. Wang, L., Chen, T., Anklam, C., Goldluecke, B.: High dimensional frustum point-net for 3D object detection from camera, LiDAR, and radar. In: IEEE Intelligent Vehicles Symposium (IV) (2020)
39. Hu, P., Ziglar, J., Held, D., Ramanan, D.: What you see is what you get: Exploiting visibility for 3D object detection. arXiv preprint arXiv:1912.04986 (2019)
40. Wirges, S., Fischer, T., Stiller, C., Frias, J.B.: Object detection and classification in occupancy grid maps using deep convolutional networks. In: 2018 21st International Conference on Intelligent Transportation Systems (ITSC), pp. 3530–3535 (2018)
41. Bresenham, J.: A linear algorithm for incremental digital display of circular arcs. Commun. ACM **20**, 100–106 (1977)
42. Lang, A.H., Vora, S., Caesar, H., Zhou, L., Yang, J., Beijbom, O.: Pointpillars: fast encoders for object detection from point clouds. In: IEEE Conference on Computer Vision and Pattern Recognition (CVPR), pp. 12697–12705 (2019)
43. Hore, A., Ziou, D.: Image quality metrics: PSNR vs. SSIM. In: 2010 20th International Conference on Pattern Recognition, pp. 2366–2369 (2010)
44. Fang, J., et al.: Augmented LiDAR simulator for autonomous driving. IEEE Robot. Autom. Lett. **5**, 1931–1938 (2020)

V2A - Vision to Action: Learning Robotic Arm Actions Based on Vision and Language

Michal Nazarczuk[✉][iD] and Krystian Mikolajczyk[iD]

Imperial College London, London, UK
{michal.nazarczuk17,k.mikolajczyk}@imperial.ac.uk

Abstract. In this work, we present a new AI task - Vision to Action (V2A) - where an agent (robotic arm) is asked to perform a high-level task with objects (*e.g.* stacking) present in a scene. The agent has to suggest a plan consisting of primitive actions (*e.g.* simple movement, grasping) in order to successfully complete the given task. Queries are formulated in a way that forces the agent to perform visual reasoning over the presented scene before inferring the actions. We propose a novel approach based on multimodal attention for this task and demonstrate its performance on our new V2A dataset. We propose a method for building the V2A dataset by generating task instructions for each scene and designing an engine capable of assessing whether the sequence of primitives leads to a successful task completion.

1 Introduction

Our goal is to develop an intelligent agent capable of perceiving and reasoning about the environment by combining information from different modalities. Visual Question Answering (VQA) [1] is a related task that requires combining language and visual input. Recently, Embodied Question Answering (EQA) [2] was proposed as a new challenging problem incorporating navigation as the necessary step for successful question answering. We propose a new task, Vision to Action (V2A), to bridge the gap between visual reasoning and action planning which requires the agent to perform a multimodal perception. We introduce a dataset generated for this purpose, along with an engine capable of assessing the correctness of predicted sequences of actions.

VQA and EQA tasks involve an agent to provide a specific answer to a given question. For the question: *What is the weight of the big blue box?*, the answer can be *heavy*. Humans typically interact with the object before answering such question. We gain knowledge about the properties of the objects in the world through exploration as well as from the external knowledge. When asked a given question, our answer may be *let me check that in the Internet* or *let me hold it to estimate the weight, or use a scale* for a more accurate answer. In our work, we focus specifically on the latter, planning the exploration using simple, primitive actions. We consider a scenario with objects on a table in the context of

© Springer Nature Switzerland AG 2021
H. Ishikawa et al. (Eds.): ACCV 2020, LNCS 12624, pp. 721–736, 2021.
https://doi.org/10.1007/978-3-030-69535-4_44

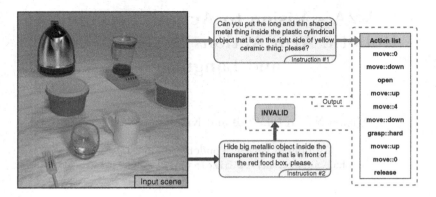

Fig. 1. Vision to Action task. Given the scene and instruction, the task is to predict a sequence of primitive actions leading to a successful completion of the task. In order to enforce multimodal perception, data includes instructions correct linguistically, although some not possible to complete given the scene.

robotic manipulation. Programming a manipulator is a similar task to composing a sequence of primitive actions. In addition, we claim that the tasks of visual reasoning and planning should be done jointly - a plan cannot be made based on the instruction only, but must rely on the current state of the environment.

The main focus of EQA is to include navigation in the task of Visual Question Answering. While its goal is to perform on-line prediction of the best exploration path, our proposed V2A is concerned with manipulation actions. Our main objective is to maximise information gain from the visual and language input such that, in combination with experience gained through exploration, the system is capable of assessing the validity of the given query and preparing a plan which can then be implemented in a real-world or simulated scenario.

V2A considers semantically high-level primitives and high-level description of the scene, which decouple the model from a particular robotics hardware or a simulated environment. Nonetheless, we keep the primitive actions similar to a high-level programming language, with the goal of being able to transfer the sequences into the real settings by wrapping primitives in code functions specific to the equipment. Realistic scenarios often require action planning that cannot be replaced with an online decision making process *e.g.* picking up lighter out of two objects requires planning to measure the weight of both of them. In such a situation, one needs to plan a sequence of action based on the current observation. An overview of the V2A task is presented in Fig. 1. Given the input scene and a textual instruction, the system predicts the sequence of the actions, if the task can be performed given the scene. Otherwise, the system indicates invalidity of the task. To this end, we provide a new dataset for the V2A task along with an engine to assess the completion of a given instruction. Our dataset is inspired by the common robotic setup including a manipulator placed on a table-top equipped with a camera. We also propose an evaluation protocol consisting of different metrics to assess different aspects of model performance. Finally, we propose a novel approach to perform the V2A task. Our approach incorporates a Multimodal Attention Model that is used to simultaneously translate sequences of attribute vectors (corresponding to objects in the scene) and natural language instructions into a sequence of primitive actions that fulfils the given task.

2   Related Work

Our work involves visual and linguistic reasoning, and action planning , intended for robotics applications. It is a new problem and there are no existing methods that are suitable for this task, however the relevant literature include papers from the area of VQA, EQA and action planning that we review below.

Visual Question Answering [1] is the task of providing the precise answer to a given question that is related to a given image. VQA follows two main approaches: projecting images and text onto a common subspace to predict the answer [3–5], or disentangling the scene and question into understandable forms to perform a human-like reasoning to discover the answer. The latter emerged as a new task, called Visual Reasoning, which along with predicting the correct answer, attempts to produce a logical reasoning that resembles a human approach to the problem. Neural Module Networks [6–8] propose to stack network modules to predict the flow of the focus over the image objects, and therefore explain the origin of the final answer. NS-VQA [9] and NS-CL [10] focus on fully disentangling the scene into a human-readable form, such that the reasoning can be performed by executing symbolic programs on the new representation.

Embodied Question Answering [2] adds an additional component to the VQA - navigation in a simulated environment. An agent is asked a simple question and its task is to navigate to the correct location and answer the question after. Current methods [11] split the task into two streams: navigation and question answering. The agent switches between modules to gather clues necessary to answer the query. The task of navigating an agent based on language and visual input was further explored for both simulated and real world scenarios [12–14].

Action planning focuses on producing a plan consisting of simple components based on the given input. A common source of the information about how to perform the action is a linguistic description. Detailed textual instructions on how to perform a task are translated into a series of actions in [15]. Generating plans for a high-level task in the setting of incomplete world knowledge is proposed in [16]. Video action recognition is used in [17] to generate sequences of actions corresponding to the presented task.

Available datasets include examples with multimodal data, but none of them have annotation in form of instruction/image pairs accompanied with ground truth sequences of actions. Furthermore, there are no tools to assess the correctness of predicted actions. The most relevant datasets are Visual Reasoning benchmarks. CLEVR [18] provides a number of simple synthetically generated scenes composed of spheres, cylinders and cubes. CLEVR includes questions, answers and programs to obtain the answer given the scene graph. SHOP-VRB [19] builds upon CLEVR and provides a more realistic scenario of a tabletop with common household items. In addition to CLEVR structure, it provides some simple text descriptions for the objects along with questions grounded in the image and text simultaneously. SHOP-VRB also addresses the problem of reasoning about unseen instances of object classes. On the other end of the spectrum there exist robotics datasets concerning the performance of different tasks in simulated environments. DeepMind Control Suite [20] provides a number of control tasks for different types of robotic agents. ALFRED [21] focuses on language in robotics, as it provides detailed task descriptions along with action sequences grounded in that text that are to be executed in a simulated environment. RoboTurk [22] is mainly focused on imitation learning, as it contains a large base of different tasks paired with crowdsourced demonstrations for each. Surreal [23] provides a reinforcement learning framework for manipulation tasks.

V2A attempts to bridge the gap between the visual reasoning task, robotics action planning and available datasets. It is based on SHOP-VRB annotations, allowing for easy generation of new samples. It provides an engine that works on scene graphs that allows for very quick executions. The queries force the model to perform multimodal perception. Unlike ALFRED [21], that provides detailed descriptions linking high level tasks to sequence primitives, we allow the model to learn visual-action dependencies through exploration. Additionally, V2A remains very challenging from visual reasoning standpoint.

3   Dataset and Engine

V2A involves generating a sequence of actions that, performed on a given scene, would lead to a successful completion of a given instruction or question. Hence, we introduce a new dataset containing natural language instructions along with an engine that allows for testing solutions and validating the result of the performed actions. We build on closely related SHOP-VRB datasets [19] that has recently been introduced for VQA in robotics.

3.1   Engine

The engine operates on a level of abstraction, that allows to decouple the task from real machines or specific simulating environments. It works as a state machine operating on two main abstractions - state of the scene, and state of the robotic arm. The dictionary of the state extends the one in SHOP-VRB scene graphs state by adding properties related to object manipulations (*e.g. is opened, current location*). The manipulator dictionary describes the current state of the manipulator and the gripper (*e.g. gripper closed, current location*).

Our engine performs all operations by calling a sequence of primitive actions on the scene and manipulator states. Primitive actions, presented in Table 1,

Table 1. Primitive actions in the proposed engine. The primitives are composed of action verbs, and parameters if needed. Parameters can include an index, a direction of movement or a property characteristic to the given action. If not specified, the action is performed on the object in focus.

Command	Argument	Functioning
avoid	index	Avoid object *index* during next move.
move	index	Move arm towards object *index*.
move	direction	Move arm in cardinal *direction*.
move	[up/down]	Lift or lower the arm.
grasp	[soft/hard/attach]	Grasp the object next to the arm using given grip.
release	-	Release object from the gripper.
open	-	Open the object next to the arm.
close	-	Close the object next to the arm.
measure	property	Measure *property* of the object next to the arm.
shake	-	Shake the object in the gripper.
rotate	-	Rotate the object in the gripper.
flip	-	Flip the object in the gripper.
button press	-	Press the button on the object next to the arm.
fill	-	Fill the object next to the arm.

require the scene and the manipulator to be in particular states to be possible to execute, and modify these states according to the performed action. Construction of primitives and operation on state dictionaries allow new tasks to be easily added to the engine, simply by specifying the required conditions and changes in the state due to the action performed. As proposed in Table 1, primitive actions take the form of operations related to robotic manipulation. The primitives are on high semantic level in order for the benchmark to avoid limitations from any specific language. It is assumed that any presented action can be wrapped in a software-specific function such that, given the proper parameters, it would result in similar changes in the scene as we describe. The parameters of the scene and the manipulator that are required for the primitive action, reflect the behaviour of a robotic arm. The set of requirements and changes are effectively creating the rules of the environment for the agent. For example, when moving the manipulator towards an object, one has to plan the trajectory such that the arm does not collide with any other object (*avoid::[close neighbors]* has to precede *move::down*). Similarly, when pushing the object by sliding it on the tabletop, the trajectory should avoid the neighbors in the movement direction. On the other hand, when the object is lifted, there is no need to avoid obstacles. Furthermore, when putting an object into a container with a lid, one has to open it to put the object in. Similar rules apply to all primitive actions presented.

The proposed engine is equipped with a functionality of checking whether the agent, given a task, can succeeded in completing it by preforming the sequence of inferred primitive actions. All benchmarking tasks are presented in Table 2.

Table 2. List of benchmark tasks available in V2A. The tasks, together with visual reasoning cues, are the base for the provided instructions. Each task is characterised with a different engine state that allows to assess whether the task can be completed with a given sequence of primitive actions.

# Task	# Task
1 Pick the *OBJ* up	12 Check if there are moving parts inside the *OBJ*
2 Open the *OBJ*	13 Check what is on the other side of the *OBJ*
3 Measure weight of the *OBJ*	14 Pick the *OBJ* up and move it *DIR*
4 Measure stiffness of the *OBJ*	15 Pick the *OBJ1* up and move it over the *OBJ2*
5 Measure roughness of the *OBJ*	16 Push the *OBJ DIR*
6 Measure elasticity of the *OBJ*	17 Push the *OBJ1* towards the *OBJ2*
7 Empty the *OBJ*	18 Stack the *OBJ1* on top of the *OBJ2*
8 Fill the *OBJ* with liquid	19 Put the *OBJ1* in the *OBJ2*
9 Turn the *OBJ* on	20 Hide the *OBJ1* inside the *OBJ2*
10 Boil the liquid inside the *OBJ*	21 Flip the *OBJ1* and shake it over the *OBJ2*
11 Shatter the *OBJ* (drop it)	22 Rotate the *OBJ1* and put it in the *OBJ2*

Due to the construction of the engine, checking the success is simply comparing the state of the manipulator and the state of the scene to the model state. Such an approach also makes the addition of more tasks very simple - by setting requirements on the final states of the scene and the manipulator. For example, when picking up an object, the target action is to simply change the state of the object to *picked up*. When hiding an object in another object, a container, one has to verify whether both are at the correct positions, and the lid of the container has been closed after putting the object in.

The ground truth action sequences for each given task are generated by the engine based on *prototype* sequences provided by human annotators. Prototypes contain a series of primitives always necessary to be performed to complete the given task (*e.g.* picking the object up has to contain *moving towards* and *grasping*). Based on the prototype along with the knowledge of the environment (required states of the primitives) the instructions are provided additional primitives such that the task is ultimately executed with success. We consider this ground truth to be the shortest sequence to achieve the goal for each task.

Due to the possibility of multiple correct solutions the ground truth sequences are intended for measuring only the efficiency of the system, and not for a supervised training of a predictor. Alternatively, such ground truth can be used for initialising a model that is then trained on other data.

3.2   Dataset

We generate a V2A dataset of challenging instructions grounded in visual inputs. We use the same scenes as in [19]. For each scene we provide 9 to 10 visually grounded instructions asking the agent to perform one of the tasks specified in Table 2. Each instruction is equipped with a corresponding task, as well as the objects and parameters concerned by the task. Figure 2 contains sample scenes and corresponding instructions from V2A dataset.

Could you push the medium-sized light metal portable thing behind the light yellow metal portable object on the right side of the table, please?

Pick up and move the metal portable cylindrical thing that is on the left side of the medium-sized blue metal cylindrical thing over the brown portable thing.

There is a medium-sized light object that is both on the right side of the white bowl and left of the portable thermos; could you hide it inside the heavy metallic object, please?

Fig. 2. Example scenes and queries from V2A dataset. Note the complexity of visual reasoning process required to successfully plan the set of primitive actions that fulfils the instruction.

Dataset instructions are generated in a procedural way. We employ 77 different instruction templates. Each template corresponds to one of the aforementioned tasks. Templates are chosen randomly for generating instructions while keeping the distribution of instructions over templates uniform. Each template is used to instantiate valid instructions, such that there exist a sequence of actions resulting in a successfully executed task, as well as invalid instructions, such that no sequence is able to lead to a positive result for a given task (*e.g.* asking to turn on a fork). Invalid instructions require the system to specifically indicate that a query is invalid (not only producing any invalid primitives sequence). Distribution of valid and invalid instructions is also uniform over the templates. While being generated, each new instruction is tested for correctness, and both the task and the concerned objects are returned as the answer. This allows the engine to test any generated sequence for execution correctness given the task, as well as to generate the ground truth sequence of primitives. Furthermore, the instructions provide a challenge for visual perception as they describe objects by their properties and their relations to other objects. Finally, functional programs, similar to those in CLEVR are also provided as a part of the ground truth.

V2A includes 4 splits: *training, validation, test* and *benchmark*. The *benchmark* split is comprised of scenes that contain the same classes as, but different instances of the objects as the other splits. In Table 3, we provide details of the V2A dataset containing the number of samples in each split.

Table 3. Number of instructions in V2A dataset for valid and invalid tasks. Note that some scenes do not contain enough objects to generate 10 distinct questions, hence, some of them contain fewer.

Split	training	validation	test	benchmark
valid	49965	7500	7500	7500
invalid	49911	7487	7494	7492
total	99876	14987	14994	14992

4   Multimodal Attention Model for V2A

We propose a three step approach as a Multimodal Attention Model for the V2A task. Additionally, we analyse the performance of a simple translation model in a blind scenario (without visual input).

Our proposed approach is inspired by NS-VQA [9]. It consists of three main components - scene segmentation, attributes extraction and multi-modal sequence-to-sequence instruction to action translation. The approach is illustrated in Fig. 3.

Scene segmentation is performed using Mask R-CNN [24]. The network predicts the segmentation mask and category of each object.

Attributes extraction is implemented with the use of ResNet-34 [25]. Masked images of objects obtained from the segmentation step are concatenated with the full image and passed through the network to predict their properties and coordinates on the supporting plane. Scene segmentation and attributes extraction are trained with the ground truth provided with the scenes, resulting in a disentangled representation of the visual scene.

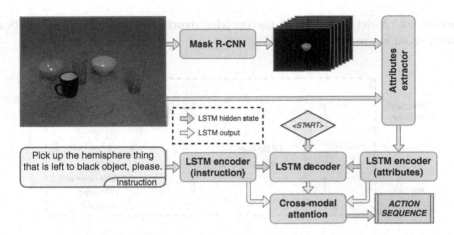

Fig. 3. Proposed Multimodal Attention Model. Input image is segmented with Mask R-CNN and processed by attributes extraction network to provide a disentangled representation of the scene. Both, attributes and a text instruction are parsed by LSTM encoders in order to decode the final instruction sequence using an LSTM decoder with a cross-modal attention layer.

Instruction to action translation is based on the Seq2seq machine translation scheme [26]. Disentangled attributes vectors of the scene corresponding to the input instruction are passed as a sequence to the Bidirectional LSTM [27] encoder. Considering the input as a sequence of objects allows the model to point towards particular items within the scene. Similarly, instruction words are embedded to vector representations and passed through a second Bidirectional LSTM network. Further, hidden states for both representations are concatenated and set as the hidden state of the decoder network, which is a unidirectional LSTM. Both outputs from the image and the instruction LSTMs are projected with linear layers to match the output of the decoder LSTM. An attention mechanism is then applied to the pair of outputs from the image encoder-decoder output and the instruction encoder-decoder. The attention is implemented in a similar manner to that proposed in [28] and adopted in NS-VQA. Given the output decoder vector $\mathbf{q}_t$ for timestep t, and the encoder output $\mathbf{e}_i$ for timesteps i a new context vector for timestep t, $\mathbf{c}_t$ is calculated by a weighted sum of the encoded states according to the attention distribution:

$$\mathbf{c}_t = \sum_i \alpha_{ti}\mathbf{e}_i \qquad \text{where:} \qquad \alpha_{ti} = \frac{\exp(\mathbf{q}_t^\mathsf{T}\mathbf{e}_i)}{\sum_k \exp(\mathbf{q}_t^\mathsf{T}\mathbf{e}_k)} \qquad (1)$$

The context vector is concatenated with the decoder output and projected back to its original size inside the attention layer. New representations for the attributes-focused decoding and the instruction-focused decoding are projected such that, after concatenation, their dimensions match those of the original decoder output. Finally, the obtained multimodal vector is projected onto the output vocabulary space in order to predict the next action token for the final action list. A detailed view of the decoder structure along with the attention mechanism is presented in Fig. 4.

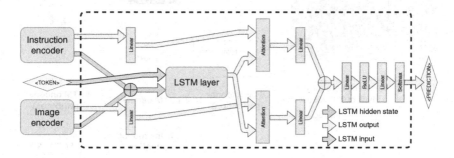

Fig. 4. Detailed view of the decoder and attention layers. Hidden states of both encoders are concatenated and used to initialise the decoder state. Outputs of the encoders are projected to the size of the decoder output in order to use the attention mechanism that produces context-aware outputs. These are further concatenated and used to predict the next token in action sequence.

The training regime for translating instructions to actions is divided into two steps: weakly-supervised and reinforced. The weakly-supervised part of the training uses randomly selected ground truth action lists for the given instructions. Selected actions are uniformly distributed among the instruction templates, while keeping the ratio of valid to invalid templates at a given value. A total number of ground truth annotated instructions for the supervised part of the training does not exceed 3% of the whole training set size.

The reinforced step follows the weakly supervised part. We use REINFORCE [29] to further train the model on the full set of instructions. The reward is generated based on the execution of the generated action list in V2A engine. We allow the setting of different rewards for valid and invalid instructions.

5   Evaluation Protocol

Success rate (SR) is a natural way of evaluating any agent performance in interactive tasks. It is defined as the ratio of successful attempts to all attempts. In our case, it is the ratio of correctly evaluated sequences to all given queries. However, we argue that such simple information is not sufficient to assess the performance of the agent in detail.

Valid success rate (VSR) is therefore a new metric we propose. By considering queries for which there exist a valid answer, we measure how well the model is able to generate successful plans.

Invalid success rate (ISR) is the complement of VSR and allows assessment of to whether the system is not overfitting to seemingly easier queries which do not have a valid answer. Considering the simple scenario of creating model that outputs only invalid tokens, one would obtain SR close to 0.5 (with the V2A valid/invalid ratio of roughly 1:1) but score exactly 0.0 in VSR.

Harmonic success rate (HSR) is our proposal of a metric combining the afore-mentioned scores into one based on the harmonic mean of VSR and ISR (being an analogue of F_1 score for precision and recall):

$$HSR = 2 \frac{VSR \cdot ISR}{VSR + ISR} \tag{2}$$

Efficiency of the sequence (E_{score}) prevents the agent from *gaming* the engine by outputting all the possible moves that do not break the sequence (*e.g.* avoiding all obstacles one by one before every move). Efficiency is calculated as the ratio of the length of the primitives list generated by the model to the ground truth one (the shortest possible). Efficiency is calculated only for valid entries for which the model performed a successful task completion.

Action sequence accuracy (A_{acc}) assesses the accuracy of the focus on the given task by the model. To obtain the score, we calculate the ratio of successful task completions to all actions produced by the model that lead to correct execution according to the engine (with no errors, calculated only for valid instructions).

All suggested metrics, with information whether the goal is to maximise or minimise each score, and bounding values for each are presented in Table 4.

Table 4. Summary of the evaluation metrics with bounding values and indicated maximisation or minimisation goal.

Metric	SR	VSR	ISR	HSR	E_{score}	A_{acc}
better	↑	↑	↑	↑	↓	↑
min	0.0	0.0	0.0	0.0	1.0	0.0
max	1.0	1.0	1.0	1.0	∞	1.0

6 Experiments

We perform experiments on the *test* and *benchmark* splits of V2A dataset. *Test* split consists of new scenes generated with the same instances of objects as *train* and *validation* splits, whereas *benchmark* split challenges the system with scenes generated with the same classes of objects but new instances. We consider *benchmark* split to be an analogue of zero-shot learning capable of evaluating generalisation properties of the system in an unknown setting. We provide results for our two models, both blind and multimodal. Both models follow the training regime of supervised pretraining and reinforced fine-tuning. The amount of data sampled for the supervised part is the same for both models and does not exceed 3% of all *training* split instructions.

6.1   Blind Model

Additionally to our full model, we propose an ablation evaluation with only the language part of the model. The method becomes a standard sequence-to-sequence model trained with the same regime as the full model (weakly-supervised + reinforced). The ablation study is proposed to show the importance of correct visual perception in the V2A task.

Seq2seq blind model is trained only with instruction-action sequence pairs for the supervised part and with instructions and engine rewards for the reinforced part. The supervised part uses negative log-likelihood as the loss function and is trained with Adam [30] with learning rate $1e-3$ as an optimiser. We use *validation* split as an early stopping criterion. For the reinforced part, learning rate is decreased to $1e-5$ and the reward is set to be 0.2 for invalid queries and 5.0 for valid ones.

6.2   Multimodal Attention Model

Multimodal attention model uses an attribute extraction pipeline similar to that in NS-VQA [9] . Firstly, we train Mask R-CNN for 30000 iterations with the supervision of ground truth masks. Thereafter, we train the attributes extractor, a ResNet-34, using *training* split. We apply early stopping based on *validation* split. In order to draw conclusions on the action planning for *test* and *benchmark* splits, we provide the attributes extraction accuracy for V2A scenes in Table 5. We train our multimodal action planner similarly to the blind model. We use the same optimisers and loss functions, and keep rewards the same. Additionally, we train the model with ground truth attribute vectors as well as those inferred from the attributes extraction network in order to assess how the quality of features affects performance.

Table 5. Attributes recognition accuracy for V2A scenes.

Split	Category	Size	Weight	Colour	Material	Mobility	Shape	Overall	Dist err
Test	88.3	88.9	88.9	88.5	88.4	89.2	88.7	88.7	0.062
Bench	43.2	61.2	53.7	50.8	48.8	65.4	38.0	51.4	0.102

6.3   Results

The results for the aforementioned models are presented in Table 6.

Table 6. Results for V2A task. Text LSTM is a blind model without visual input, MAM refers to the full proposed approach, *test* and *benchmark* refer to the splits of the dataset and *GT* and *inferred* correspond to use of attributes from ground truth or extracted via the attributes extraction network, respectively.

Model	SR	VSR	ISR	HSR	E_{score}	A_{acc}
Text LSTM test	32.1	3.1	61.1	5.9	1.09	12.4
Text LSTM benchmark	31.9	2.5	61.4	4.8	1.08	12.6
MAM test GT	44.9	24.9	65.0	36.0	1.04	38.4
MAM test inferred	44.7	23.8	65.0	34.8	1.04	36.3
MAM benchmark GT	42.3	10.7	73.9	18.7	1.02	16.2
MAM benchmark inferred	40.2	6.4	79.9	11.9	1.02	10.2

The blind model performs very poorly overall which is the expected behaviour. One can quickly notice that with no visual input the challenge of *benchmark* split is not presented to the model, hence, the results are very similar for both *test* and *benchmark*. As explained in the evaluation protocol, one can expect balancing valid and invalid recognition to be a complex task. It can be inferred that the blind model has overfitted to be predicting a majority of sequences with invalid tokens as the answer. However, by looking at VSR and HSR scores one may instantly notice that in fact, the blind model was not able to learn the actual planning. Based on E_{score}, we can notice that correctly predicted action plans were not much longer that ground truth ones. A_{acc} is showing that the model was able to produce more programs that were executed by the engine with no errors (which means they can be performed on the given scene), however, only a small fraction of them were focused on the given task.

MAM system preforms significantly better than the blind one. We observed that both models were performing similarly for invalid queries. However, the multimodal attention model generated many more correct sequences for instructions with a valid answer. Increase in VSR drastically improved the harmonic mean HSR, proving it to be a very useful metric to assess the performance of various systems in the V2A task. In case of the multimodal approach, we observe a significant difference between *test* and *benchmark* splits. Seemingly, presenting a new, never-before-seen combination of attributes poses a nontrivial challenge to the system. One can notice that ISR improved for *benchmark* split with respect to *test* split. It may be inferred that the model learned to associate specific attributes as preventing the instruction to be fulfilled and such ones were associated with the valid instructions in *benchmark* split. Furthermore, all models seem not to add too many additional instructions to the ground truth action sequence (E_{score}). This is possibly due to the supervised pretraining step, presenting the system with some shortest model sequences. We can see a clear difference in action sequence accuracy A_{acc} between *test* and *benchmark* splits. This indicates that the model was more precise in performing the task correctly for *test* split, which may be caused by misleading attributes from *benchmark* split. Finally, one may notice a significant impact of the attributes recognition accuracy on the given model. A difference in the performance between models using the ground truth attributes and the attributes extracted by the network correspond to attributes recognition accuracy (Table 5. We observe bigger gap in performance for *benchmark* split, which attributes were extracted with much lower accuracy than for *test* split.

Breakdown of success rates among different task with distinction for valid and invalid queries was also investigated. In Fig. 5 we present the breakdown of success rates, keeping the numbering consistent with Table 2. We observe that the

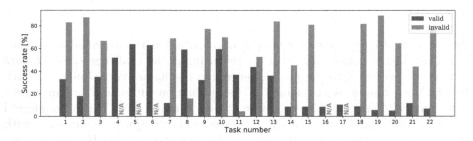

Fig. 5. Breakdown of success rates for the full model (experiment on *test* split). Task numbers refer to Table 2. Note that some tasks can always be performed no matter the scene given (*e.g.* we assume objects cannot always be picked up but can always be pushed), hence some columns are not present for *invalid* part.

distribution of accuracies is not even among the tasks, especially for valid samples. One can notice a significant decrease in performance for tasks 14 to 22. Those tasks correspond to instructions asking to manipulate more than one object within the same sequence. It is then not surprising that the system finds such a task harder than manipulating a single object, as it also follows the human intuition of being a harder task.

7   Conclusions

In this work, we presented a new challenging task for experiments in computer vision and high-level action planning. We believe that V2A bridges the gap between visual and language reasoning and action planning, and in particular, object manipulation with a robotic arm. We show that the task poses a significant challenge for multimodal perception. An agent has to be developed with the understanding of natural language instructions that are grounded in an image - visual input. The grounding forces the planning to be performed in a multimodal space. We believe that V2A defines a task that resembles modalities that are offered to an agent working in a real-world environment.

Along with the task, we provide a dataset containing natural language instructions for an agent, and an engine capable of assessing whether the task has been performed successfully. The engine operates on functional primitives that are actions assigned to be performed by the robotic arm. Primitives operate on a high level of abstraction as we want to decouple the task from any particular hardware or simulation software. Additionally, we believe that such an approach enables further integration with a real system by wrapping primitive actions in a syntax specific to a terminal system.

Our experiments proved V2A to be a challenging, but well-defined task. We observe that challenges that are naturally hard for a human are also hard for the system (manipulating more objects in a sequence is much harder than manipulating one). An experiment with a blind system trying to learn primitive action sequences directly from instructions shows that visual perception is an integral part of the task, and must necessarily be addressed when trying to solve it.

Acknowledgements. This research was supported by UK EPSRC IPALM project EP/S032398/1.

References

1. Agrawal, A., et al.: VQA: visual question answering. In: International Conference on Computer Vision (ICCV) (2015)
2. Das, A., Datta, S., Gkioxari, G., Lee, S., Parikh, D., Batra, D.: Embodied question answering. In: IEEE Conference on Computer Vision and Pattern Recognition (CVPR) (2018)
3. Anderson, P., et al.: Bottom-up and top-down attention for image captioning and visual question answering. In: IEEE Conference on Computer Vision and Pattern Recognition (CVPR) (2018)
4. Kim, J.H., Jun, J., Zhang, B.T.: Bilinear attention networks. In: Advances in Neural Information Processing Systems (2018)
5. Tan, H., Bansal, M.: LXMERT: learning cross-modality encoder representations from transformers. In: Proceedings of the 2019 Conference on Empirical Methods in Natural Language Processing (2019)
6. Andreas, J., Rohrbach, M., Darrell, T., Klein, D.: Neural module networks. In: IEEE Conference on Computer Vision and Pattern Recognition (CVPR) (2016)
7. Hu, R., Andreas, J., Rohrbach, M., Darrell, T., Saenko, K.: Learning to reason: end-to-end module networks for visual question answering. In: IEEE International Conference on Computer Vision (ICCV) (2017)
8. Hu, R., Andreas, J., Darrell, T., Saenko, K.: Explainable neural computation via stack neural module networks. In: Ferrari, V., Hebert, M., Sminchisescu, C., Weiss, Y. (eds.) ECCV 2018, Part VII. LNCS, vol. 11211, pp. 55–71. Springer, Cham (2018). https://doi.org/10.1007/978-3-030-01234-2_4
9. Yi, K., Wu, J., Gan, C., Torralba, A., Pushmeet, K., Tenenbaum, J.B.: Neural-symbolic VQA: disentangling reasoning from vision and language understanding. In: Advances in Neural Information Processing Systems (2018)
10. Mao, J., Gan, C., Deepmind, P.K., Tenenbaum, J.B., Wu, J.: The neuro-symbolic concept learner: interpreting scenes, words, and sentences from natural supervision. In: International Conference on Learning Representations (ICLR) (2019)

11. Yu, L., Chen, X., Gkioxari, G., Bansal, M., Berg, T.L., Batra, D.: Multi-target embodied question answering. In: IEEE Conference on Computer Vision and Pattern Recognition (CVPR) (2019)
12. Roh, J., Paxton, C., Pronobis, A., Farhadi, A., Fox, D.: Conditional driving from natural language instructions. In: Conference on Robot Learning (2019)
13. Wang, X., et al.: Reinforced cross-modal matching and self-supervised imitation learning for vision-language navigation. In: IEEE Conference on Computer Vision and Pattern Recognition (CVPR) (2019)
14. Vasudevan, A.B., Dai, D., Van Gool, L.: Talk2Nav: long-range vision-and-language navigation with dual attention and spatial memory. Int. J. Comput. Vis. **129**, 246–266 (2020). https://doi.org/10.1007/s11263-020-01374-3
15. Feng, W., Zhuo, H.H., Kambhampati, S.: Extracting action sequences from texts based on deep reinforcement learning. In: Proceedings of the Twenty-Seventh International Joint Conference on Artificial Intelligence (IJCAI) (2018)
16. Nyga, D., et al.: Grounding robot plans from natural language instructions with incomplete world knowledge. In: 2nd Conference on Robot Learning (2018)
17. Zhang, H., Lai, P.J., Paul, S., Kothawade, S., Nikolaidis, S.: Learning collaborative action plans from YouTube videos. In: International Symposium on Robotics Research (ISRR) (2019)
18. Johnson, J., Fei-Fei, L., Hariharan, B., Zitnick, C.L., Van Der Maaten, L., Girshick, R.: CLEVR: a diagnostic dataset for compositional language and elementary visual reasoning. In: IEEE Conference on Computer Vision and Pattern Recognition (CVPR) (2017)
19. Nazarczuk, M., Mikolajczyk, K.: SHOP-VRB: a visual reasoning benchmark for object perception. In: International Conference on Robotics and Automation (ICRA) (2020)
20. Tassa, Y., et al.: DeepMind Control Suite. CoRR (2018)
21. Shridhar, M., et al.: ALFRED a benchmark for interpreting grounded instructions for everyday tasks. In: IEEE Conference on Computer Vision and Pattern Recognition (CVPR) (2020)
22. Mandlekar, A., et al.: Scaling robot supervision to hundreds of hours with RoboTurk: robotic manipulation dataset through human reasoning and dexterity. In: International Conference on Intelligent Robots and Systems, (IROS) (2019)
23. Fan, L., et al.: SURREAL: open-source reinforcement learning framework and robot manipulation benchmark. In: Conference on Robot Learning (2018)
24. He, K., Gkioxari, G., Dollár, P., Girshick, R.: Mask R-CNN. In: International Conference on Computer Vision (ICCV) (2017)
25. He, K., Zhang, X., Ren, S., Sun, J.: Deep residual learning for image recognition. In: IEEE Conference on Computer Vision and Pattern Recognition (CVPR) (2016)
26. Sutskever, I., Vinyals, O., Le, Q.V.: Sequence to sequence learning with neural networks. In: Advances in Neural Information Processing Systems (2014)
27. Hochreiter, S., Schmidhuber, J.: Long short-term memory. Neural Comput. **9**, 1735–1780 (1997)
28. Bahdanau, D., Cho, K., Bengio, Y.: Neural machine translation by jointly learning to align and translate. In: International Conference on Learning Representations (ICLR) (2015)
29. Williams, R.J.: Simple statistical gradient-following algorithms for connectionist reinforcement learning. Mach. Learn. **8**, 229–256 (1992)
30. Kingma, D.P., Lei Ba, J.: Adam: a method for stochastic optimization. In: International Conference on Learning Representations (ICLR) (2015)

To Filter Prune, or to Layer Prune, That Is the Question

Sara Elkerdawy[1]([⊠])[iD], Mostafa Elhoushi[2], Abhineet Singh[1], Hong Zhang[1],
and Nilanjan Ray[1]

[1] Department of Computing Science, University of Alberta, Edmonton, Canada
{elkerdaw,asingh1,hzhang,nray1}@ualberta.ca
[2] Toronto Heterogeneous Compilers Lab, Huawei, Canada

Abstract. Recent advances in pruning of neural networks have made it
possible to remove a large number of filters or weights without any per-
ceptible drop in accuracy. The number of parameters and that of FLOPs
are usually the reported metrics to measure the quality of the pruned
models. However, the gain in speed for these pruned models is often
overlooked in the literature due to the complex nature of latency measurements. In this paper, we show the limitation of filter pruning methods
in terms of latency reduction and propose LayerPrune framework. Layer-
Prune presents a set of layer pruning methods based on different criteria
that achieve higher latency reduction than filter pruning methods on
similar accuracy. The advantage of layer pruning over filter pruning in
terms of latency reduction is a result of the fact that the former is not
constrained by the original model's depth and thus allows for a larger
range of latency reduction. For each filter pruning method we examined, we use the same filter importance criterion to calculate a per-layer
importance score in one-shot. We then prune the least important layers
and fine-tune the shallower model which obtains comparable or better
accuracy than its filter-based pruning counterpart. This one-shot process
allows to remove layers from single path networks like VGG before fine-
tuning, unlike in iterative filter pruning, a minimum number of filters per
layer is required to allow for data flow which constraint the search space.
To the best of our knowledge, we are the first to examine the effect
of pruning methods on latency metric instead of FLOPs for multiple
networks, datasets and hardware targets. LayerPrune also outperforms
handcrafted architectures such as Shufflenet, MobileNet, MNASNet and
ResNet18 by 7.3%, 4.6%, 2.8% and 0.5% respectively on similar latency
budget on ImageNet dataset (Code is available at https://github.com/
selkerdawy/filter-vs-layer-pruning).

Keywords: CNN pruning · Layer pruning · Filter pruning · Latency
metric

Electronic supplementary material The online version of this chapter (https://
doi.org/10.1007/978-3-030-69535-4_45) contains supplementary material, which is
available to authorized users.

H. Ishikawa et al. (Eds.): ACCV 2020, LNCS 12624, pp. 737–753, 2021.
https://doi.org/10.1007/978-3-030-69535-4_45

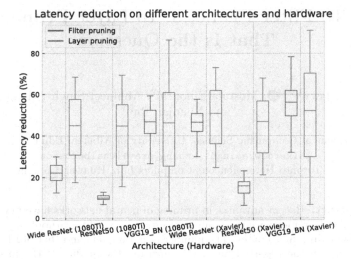

Fig. 1. Example of 100 randomly pruned models per boxplot generated from different architectures. The plot shows layer pruned models have a wider range of attainable latency reduction consistently across architectures and different hardware platforms (1080Ti and Xavier). Latency is estimated using 224 × 224 input image and batch size = 1.

1   Introduction

Convolutional Neural Networks (CNN) have become the state-of-the-art in various computer vision tasks, e.g., image classification [1], object detection [2], depth estimation [3]. These CNN models are designed with deeper [4] and wider [5] convolutional layers with a large number of parameters and convolutional operations. These architectures hinder deployment on low-power devices, e.g., phones, robots, wearable devices as well as real-time critical applications, such as autonomous driving. As a result, computationally efficient models are becoming increasingly important and multiple paradigms have been proposed to minimize the complexity of CNNs.

A straight forward direction is to manually design networks with a small footprint from the start such as [6–10]. This direction does not only require expert knowledge and multiple trials (e.g. up to 1000 neural architectures explored manually [11]), but also does not benefit from available, pre-trained large models. Quantization [12,13] and distillation [14,15] are two other techniques, which utilize the pre-trained models to obtain smaller architectures. Quantization reduces bit-width of parameters and thus decreases memory footprint, but requires specialized hardware instructions to achieve latency reduction. While distillation trains a pre-defined smaller model (student) with guidance from a larger pre-trained model (teacher) [14]. Finally, model pruning aims to automatically remove the least important filters (or weights) to reduce the number of parameters or FLOPs (i.e indirect measures). However, prior work [16–18] showed that neither number of pruned parameters nor FLOPs reduction directly correlate with latency (i.e a direct measure) consumption. Latency reduction, in that case, depends on various aspects, such as the number of filters per layer (signature) and the deployment device. Most GPU programming tools require careful compute kernels[1] tuning for different matrices shapes (e.g., convolution weights) [19,20]. These aspects introduce non-linearity in modeling latency with respect to the number of filters per layer. Recognizing the limitations in terms of latency or energy by simply pruning away filters, recent works [16,17,21] proposed optimizing directly over these direct measures. These methods require per hardware and architecture latency measurements collection to create lookup-tables or latency prediction models which can be time-intensive. In addition, these filter pruned methods are bounded by the model's depth and can only reach a limited goal for latency consumption.

In this work, we show the limitations of filter pruning methods in terms of latency reduction. Figure 1 shows the range of attainable latency reduction on randomly generated models. Each box bar summarizes the latency reduction of 100 random models with filter and layer pruning on different network architectures and hardware platforms. For each filter pruned model i, a pruning ratio $p_{i,j}$ per layer j such that $0 \leq p(i,j) \leq 0.9$ is generated thus models differ in signature/width. For each layer pruned model, M layers out of total L layers (dependent on the network) are randomly selected for retention such that $1 \leq M \leq L$ thus models differ in depth. As to be expected, layer pruning has a higher upper bound in latency reduction compared to filter pruning especially on modern complex architectures with residual blocks. However, we want to highlight quantitatively in the plot the discrepancy of attainable latency reduction using both methods. Filter pruning is not only constrained by the depth of the model but also by the connection dependency in the architecture. An example of such connection dependency is the element-wise sum operation in the residual block between identity connection and residual connection. Filter pruning methods commonly prune in-between convolution layers in a residual to respect the number of channels and spatial dimensions. BAR [22] proposed an atypical residual block that allows mixed-connectivity between blocks to tackle the issue. However, this requires special implementations to leverage the speedup gain. Another limitation in filter pruning is the iterative process and thus is constrained to keep a minimum number of filters per layer during optimization to allow for data passing. LayerPrune performs a one-shot pruning before fine-tuning and thus it allows for layer removal even from single path networks.

Motivated by these points, what remains to ask is how well do layer pruned models perform in terms of accuracy compared to filter pruned methods. Figure 2 shows accuracy and images per second between our LayerPrune, several state-of-the-art pruning methods, and handcrafted architectures. In general, pruning methods tend to find better quality models than handcrafted architectures. It is worth noting that filter pruning methods such as ThiNet [23] and Taylor [24]

---

[1] A compute kernel refers to a function such as convolution operation that runs on a high throughput accelerator such as GPU.

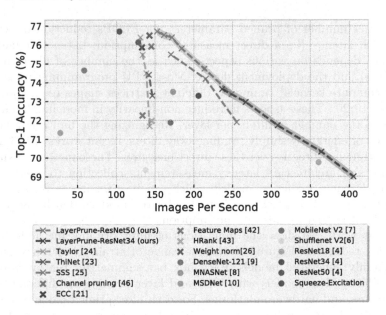

Fig. 2. Evaluation on ImageNet between our LayerPrune framework, handcrafted architectures (dots) and pruning methods on ResNet50 (crosses). Inference time is measured on 1080Ti GPU.

show small speedup gain as more filters are pruned compared to LayerPrune. That shows the limitation of filter pruning methods on latency reduction.

2 Related Work

We divide existing pruning methods into four categories: weight pruning, hardware-agnostic filter pruning, hardware-aware filter pruning and layer pruning.

Weight Pruning. An early major category in pruning is individual weight pruning (unstructured pruning). Weight pruning methods leverage the fact that some weights have minimal effect on the task accuracy and thus can be zeroed-out. In [25], weights with small magnitude are removed and in [26], quantization is further applied to achieve more model compression. Another data-free pruning is [27] where neurons are removed iteratively from fully connected layers. L_0-regularization based method [28] is proposed to encourage network sparsity in training. Finally, in lottery ticket hypothesis [29], the authors propose a method of finding winning tickets which are subnetworks from random initialization that achieve higher accuracy than the dense model. The limitation of the unstructured weight pruning is that dedicated hardware and libraries [30] are needed to achieve speedup from the compression. Given our focus on latency and to keep the evaluation setup simple, we do not consider these methods in our evaluation.

Hardware-Agnostic Filter Pruning. Methods in this category (also known as structured pruning) aim to reduce the footprint of a model by pruning filters without any knowledge of the inference resource consumption. Examples of these are [23,24,31–33], which focus on removing the least important filters and obtaining a slimmer model. Earlier filter-pruning methods [23,33] required layer-wise sensitivity analysis to generate the signature (i.e number of filters per layer) as a prior and remove filters based on a filter criterion. The sensitivity analysis is computationally expensive to conduct and becomes even less feasible for deeper models. Recent methods [24,31,32] learn a global importance measure removing the need for sensitivity analysis. Molchanov et al. [24] propose a Taylor approximation on the network's weights where the filter's gradients and norm are used to approximate its global importance score. Liu et al. [31] and Wen et al. [32] propose sparsity loss for training along with the classification's cross-entropy loss. Filters whose criterion are less than a threshold are removed and the pruned model is finally fine-tuned. Zhao et al. [34] introduce channel saliency that is parameterized as Gaussian distribution and optimized in the training process. After training, channels with small mean and variance are pruned. In general, methods with sparsity loss lack a simple approach to respect a resource consumption target and require hyperparameter tuning to balance different losses.

Hardware-Aware Filter Pruning. To respect a resource consumption budget, recent works [17,21,35,36] have been proposed to take into consideration a resource target within the optimization process. NetAdapt [17] prunes a model to meet a target budget using a heuristic greedy search. A lookup table is built for latency prediction and then multiple candidates are generated at each pruning iteration by pruning a *ratio* of filters from each layer independently. The candidate with the highest accuracy is then selected and the process continues to the next pruning iteration with a progressively increasing *ratio*. On the other hand, AMC [36] and ECC [21] propose an end-to-end constrained pruning. AMC utilizes reinforcement learning to select a model's signature by trial and error. ECC simplifies the latency reduction model as a bilinear per-layer model. The training utilizes the alternating direction method of multipliers (ADMM) algorithm to perform constrained optimization by alternating between network weight optimization and dual variables that control the layer-wise pruning ratio. Although these methods incorporate resource consumption as a constraint in the training process, the range of attainable budgets is limited by the depth of the model. Besides, generating data measurements to model resource consumption per hardware and architecture can be expensive especially on low-end hardware platforms.

Layer Pruning. Unlike filter pruning, little attention is paid to shallow CNNs in the pruning literature. In SSS [37], the authors propose to train a scaling factor for structure selection such as neurons, blocks, and groups. However, shallower models are only possible with architectures with residual connections to allow data flow in the optimization process. Closest to our work for a general (unconstrained by architecture type) layer pruning approach is the work done by

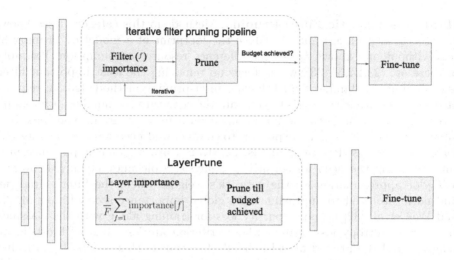

Fig. 3. Main pipeline illustrates the difference between typical iterative filter pruning and proposed LayerPrune framework. Filter pruning (top) produces thinner architecture in an iterative process while LayerPrune (bottom) prunes whole layers in one-shot. In LayerPrune, layer's importance is calculated as the average importance of each filter f in all filters F at that layer.

Chen et al. [38]. In their method, linear classifiers probes are utilized and trained independently per layer for layer-ranking. After the layer-ranking learning stage, they prune the least important layers and fine-tune the shallower model. Although [38] requires rank training, it is without any gain in classification accuracy compared to our one-shot LayerPrune layer ranking as will be shown in the experiments section.

3   Methodology

In this section, we describe in detail LayerPrune for layer pruning using existing filter criteria along with a novel layer-wise accuracy approximation. A typical filter pruning method follows a three-stage pipeline as illustrated in Fig. 3. Filter importance is iteratively re-evaluated after each pruning step based on a pruning meta-parameter such as pruning N filters or pruning those $\leq$ threshold. In LayerPrune, we remove the need for the iterative pruning step and show that using the same filter criterion, we can remove layers in a one-shot to respect a budget. This simplifies the pruning step to a hyper-parameter free process and is computationally efficient. Layer importance is calculated as the average of filter importance in this layer.

3.1 Statistics-Based Criterion

Although existing filter pruning methods are different in algorithms and optimization used, they focus more on finding the optimal per-layer number of filters and share common filter criteria. We divide the methods based on the filter criterion used and propose their layer importance counterpart used in LayerPrune.

Preliminary Notion. Consider a network with L layers, each layer l has weight matrix $W^{(l)} \in \mathbb{R}^{N_l \times F_l \times K_l \times K_l}$ with N_l input channels, F_l number of filters and K_l is the size of the filters at this channel. Evaluated criteria and methods are:

Weight Statistics. [21,25,33] differ in the optimization algorithm but share weight statistics as a filter ranking. Layer pruning for this criteria is calculated as:

$$\text{weights-layer-importance}[l] = \frac{1}{F_l} \sum_{i=1}^{F_l} \left\| W^{(l)}[:, i, :, :] \right\|_2 \tag{1}$$

Taylor Weights. Taylor method [24] is slightly different from previous criterion in that the gradients are included in the ranking as well. Filter f ranking is based on $\sum_s (g_s w_s)^2$ where s iterates over all individual weights in f, g is the gradient, w is the weight value. Similarly, layer ranking can be expressed as:

$$\text{taylor-layer-importance}[l] = \frac{1}{F_l} \sum_{i=1}^{F_l} \left\| G^{(l)}[:, i, :, :] \odot W^{(l)}[:, i, :, :] \right\|_2 \tag{2}$$

where $\odot$ is element-wise product and $G^{(l)} \in \mathbb{R}^{N_l \times F_l \times K_l \times K_l}$ is the gradient of loss with respect to weights $W^{(l)}$.

Feature Map Based Heuristics. [23,39,40] rank filters based on statistics from output of layer. In [23], ranking is based on the effect on the next layer while [39], similar to Taylor weights, utilizes gradients and norm but on feature maps.

Channel Saliency. In this criterion, a scalar is multiplied by the feature maps and optimized within a typical training cycle with task loss and sparsity regularization loss to encourage sparsity. Slimming [31] utilizes Batch Normalization scale γ as the channel saliency. Similarly, we use Batch Normalization scale parameter to calculate layer importance for this criteria, specifically:

$$\text{BN-layer-importance}[l] = \frac{1}{F_l} \sum_{i=1}^{F_l} (\gamma_i^{(l)})^2 \tag{3}$$

Ensemble. We also consider diverse ensemble of layer ranks where the ensemble rank of each layer is the sum of its rank per method, more specifically:

$$\text{ensemble-rank}[l] = \sum_{m \in \{1...M\}} (\text{LayerRank}(m, l)) \tag{4}$$

where l is the layer's index, M is the number of all criteria and LayerRank indicates the order of layer l in the sorted list for criterion m.

3.2 Efficiency-Based Criterion

In addition to existing filter criteria, we present a novel layer importance by layer-wise accuracy approximation. Motivated by the few-shot learning literature [41,42], we use imprinting to approximate the classification accuracy up to each layer. Imprinting is used to approximate a classifier's weight matrix when only a few training samples are available. Although we have adequate training samples, we are inspired by the efficiency of imprinting to approximate the accuracy in one pass without the need for training. We create a classifier proxy for each prunable candidate (e.g. convolution layer or residual blocks), and then the training data is used to imprint the classifier weight matrix for each proxy. Since each layer has a different output feature shape, we apply adaptive average pooling to simplify our method and unify the embedding length so that each layer produces roughly an output of the same size. Specifically, the pooling is done as follows:

$$d_i = \text{round}(\sqrt{\tfrac{N}{n_i}})$$
$$E_i = \text{AdaptiveAvgPool}(O_i, d_i), \tag{5}$$

where N is the embedding length, n_i is layer i's number of filters, O_i is layer i's output feature map, and AdaptiveAvgPool [43] reduces O_i to embedding $E_i \in \mathbb{R}^{d_i \times d_i \times n_i}$. Finally, embeddings per layer are flattened to be used in imprinting. Imprinting calculates the proxy classifier's weights matrix P_i as follows:

$$P_i[:, c] = \frac{1}{N_c} \sum_{j=1}^{D} \mathbb{I}_{[c_j == c]} E_j \tag{6}$$

where c is the class id, c_j is sample's j class id, N_c is the number of samples in class c, D is the total number of samples, and $\mathbb{I}_{[.]}$ denotes the indicator function.

The accuracy at each proxy is then calculated using the imprinted weight matrices. The prediction for each sample j is calculated for each layer i as:

$$\hat{y}_j = \operatorname*{argmax}_{c \in \{1,...,C\}} P_i[:, c]^T E_j, \tag{7}$$

where E_j is calculated as shown in Eq. (5). This is equivalent to finding the nearest class from the imprinted weights in the embedding space. Ranking of each layer is then calculated as the gain in accuracy from previous pruning candidate.

4 Evaluation Results

In this section we present our experimental results comparing state-of-the-art pruning methods and LayerPrune in terms of accuracy and latency reduction on two different hardware platforms. We show latency on high-end GPU

1080Ti and on NVIDIA Jetson Xavier embedded device, which is used in mobile vision systems and contains 512-core Volta GPU. We evaluate the methods on CIFAR10/100 [44] and ImageNet [1] datasets.

4.1 Implementation Details

Latency Calculation. Latency model is averaged over 1000 forward pass after 10 warm up forward passes for lazy GPU initialization. Latency is calculated using batch size 1, unless otherwise stated, due to its practical importance in real-time application as in robotics where we process an online stream of frames. All pruned architectures are implemented and measured using PyTorch [45]. For a fair comparison, we compare latency reduction on similar accuracy retention from baseline and reported by original papers or compare accuracy on similar latency reduction with methods supporting layer or block pruning.

Handling Filter Shapes After Layer Removal. If the pruned layer l with weight $W^{(l)} \in \mathbb{R}^{N_l \times F_l \times K_l \times K_l}$ has $N_l \neq F_l$, we replace layer $(l+1)$'s weight matrix from $W^{(l+1)} \in \mathbb{R}^{F_l \times F_{l+1} \times K_{l+1} \times K_{l+1}}$ to $W^{(l+1)} \in \mathbb{R}^{N_l \times F_{l+1} \times K_{l+1} \times K_{l+1}}$ with random initialization. All other layers are initialized from the pre-trained dense model.

4.2 Results on CIFAR

We evaluate CIFAR-10 and CIFAR-100 on ResNet56 [4] and VGG19-BN [46].

Random Filters vs. Random Layers. Initial hypothesis verification is to generate random filter and layer pruned models, then train them to compare their accuracy and latency reduction. Random models generation follows the same setup as explained in Sect. (1). Each model is trained with SGD optimization for 164 epochs with learning rate 0.1 that decays by 0.1 at epochs 81, 121, and 151. Figure 4 shows the latency-accuracy plot for both random pruning methods. Layer pruned models outperform filter pruned ones in accuracy by 7.09% on average and can achieve up to 60% latency reduction. Also, within the same latency budget, filter pruning shows higher variance in accuracy than layer pruning. This suggests that latency constrained optimization with filter pruning is complex and requires careful per layer pruning ratio selection. On the other hand, layer pruning has small accuracy variation, in general within a budget.

VGG19-BN. Results on CIFAR-100 are presented in Table 1. The table is divided based on the previously mentioned filter criterion categorization in Sect. 3.1. First, we compare with Chen et el. [38] on a similar latency reduction as both [38] and LayerPrune perform layer pruning. Although [38] requires training for layer ranking, LayerPrune outperforms it by 1.11%. We achieve up to 56% latency reduction with 1.52% accuracy increase from baseline. As VGG19-BN is over-parametrized for CIFAR-100, removing layers act as a regularization and

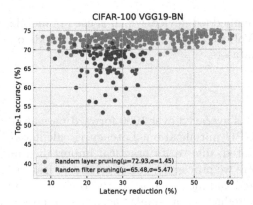

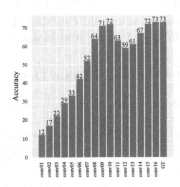

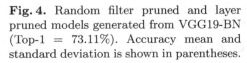

Fig. 4. Random filter pruned and layer pruned models generated from VGG19-BN (Top-1 = 73.11%). Accuracy mean and standard deviation is shown in parentheses.

Fig. 5. Layer-wise accuracy using imprinting on CIFAR-100. Red indicates drop in accuracy. (Color figure online)

can find models with better accuracy than the baseline. Unlike with filter pruning methods, they are bounded by small accuracy variations around the baseline. It is worth mentioning that latency reduction of removing the same number of filters using different filter criteria varies from -0.06% to 40.0%. While layer pruned models, with the same number of pruned layers, regardless of the criterion range from 34.3% to 41%. That suggests that latency reduction using filter pruning is sensitive to environment setup and requires complex optimization to respect a latency budget.

To further explain the accuracy increase by LayerPrune, Fig. 5 shows layer-wise accuracy approximation on baseline VGG19-BN using the imprinting method explained in Sect. (3.2). Each bar represents the approximated classification accuracy up to this layer (rounded for visualization). We see a drop in accuracy followed by an increasing trend from conv10 to conv15. This is likely because the number of features is the same from conv10 to conv12. We start to observe an accuracy increase only at conv13 that follows a max-pooling layer and has twice as many features. That highlights the importance of downsampling and doubling the number of features at this point in the model. So layer pruning does not only improve inference speed but can also discover a better regularized shallow model especially on a small dataset. It is also worth mentioning that both the proxy classifier from the last layer, conv16, and the actual model classifier, GT, have the same accuracy, showing how the proxy classifier is a plausible approximation of the converged classifier.

ResNet56. We also compare on the more complex architecture ResNet56 on CIFAR-10 and CIFAR-100 in Table 2. On a similar latency reduction, LayerPrune outperforms [38] by 0.54% and 1.23% on CIFAR-10 and CIFAR-100

Table 1. Comparison of different pruning methods on VGG19-BN CIFAR-100. The accuracy for baseline model is shown in parentheses. LR, bs stands for latency reduction and batch size respectively. x in LayerPrune$_x$ indicates number of layers removed. −ve LR indicates increase in latency. Shallower indicates whether a method prunes layers. Best is shown in **bold**.

VGG19 (73.11%)						
Method	Shallower?	Top1 Acc. (%)	1080Ti LR (%)		Xavier LR (%)	
			bs = 8	bs = 64	bs = 8	bs = 64
Chen et al. [38]	✓	73.25	56.01	52.86	58.06	49.86
LayerPrune$_8$-Imprint	✓	**74.36**	56.10	53.67	57.79	49.10
Weight norm [25]	✗	73.01	−2.044	−0.873	−4.256	−0.06
ECC [21]	✗	72.71	16.37	36.70	29.17	**36.69**
LayerPrune$_2$	✓	73.60	17.32	14.57	19.512	10.97
LayerPrune$_5$	✓	**74.80**	**39.84**	**37.85**	**41.86**	34.38
Slimming [31]	✗	72.32	16.84	**40.08**	40.55	**39.53**
LayerPrune$_2$	✓	73.60	17.34	13.86	18.85	10.90
LayerPrune$_5$	✓	**74.80**	**39.56**	37.30	**41.40**	34.35
Taylor [24]	✗	72.61	15.87	19.77	−4.89	17.45
LayerPrune$_2$	✓	73.60	17.12	13.54	18.81	10.89
LayerPrune$_5$	✓	**74.80**	**39.36**	**37.12**	**41.34**	**34.44**

respectively. On the other hand, within each filter criterion, LayerPrune outperforms filter pruning and is on par with the baseline in accuracy. In addition, filter pruning can result in latency increase (i.e negative LR) with specific hardware targets and batch sizes [47] as shown with batch size 8. However, LayerPrune consistently shows latency reduction under different environmental setups. We also compare with larger batch size to further encourage filter pruned models to better utilize the resources. Still, we found LayerPrune achieves overall better latency reduction with a large batch size. Latency reduction variance, LR var, between different batch sizes within the same hardware platform is shown as well. Consistent with previous results on VGG, LayerPrune is less sensitive to changes in criterion, batch size, and hardware than filter pruning. We also show results up to 2.5× latency reduction with less than 2% accuracy drop.

4.3 Results on ImageNet

We evaluate the methods on ImageNet dataset for classification. For all experiments in this section, PyTorch pre-trained models are used as a starting point for network pruning. We follow the same setup as in [24] where we prune 100 filters each 30 mini-batches for 10 pruning iterations. The pruned model is then fine-tuned with learning rate $1e^{-3}$ using SGD optimizer and 256 batch size. Results on ResNet50 are presented in Table 3. In general, LayerPrune models improve accuracy over the baseline and their counterpart filter pruning meth-

Table 2. Comparison of different pruning methods on ResNet56 CIFAR-10/100. The accuracy for baseline model is shown in parentheses. LR and bs stands for latency reduction and batch size respectively. subscript x in LayerPrune$_x$ indicates number of blocks removed.

Method	Shallower?	Top1 Acc. (%)	1080Ti LR (%)		Xavier LR (%)	
			bs = 8	bs = 64	bs = 8	bs = 64
CIFAR-10 ResNet56 baseline (93.55%)						
Chen et al. [38]	✓	93.09	**26.60**	**26.31**	26.96	25.66
LayerPrune$_8$-Imprint	✓	**93.63**	26.41	26.32	**27.30**	**29.11**
Taylor weight [24]	✗	93.15	0.31	5.28	−0.11	2.67
LayerPrune$_1$	✓	**93.49**	2.864	**3.80**	5.97	5.82
LayerPrune$_2$	✓	93.35	**6.46**	**8.12**	**9.33**	**11.38**
Weight norm [25]	✗	92.95	−0.90	5.22	1.49	3.87
L1 norm [33]	✗	93.30	−1.09	−0.48	2.31	1.64
LayerPrune$_1$	✓	**93.50**	2.72	3.88	7.08	5.67
LayerPrune$_2$	✓	93.39	**5.84**	**7.94**	**10.63**	**11.45**
Feature maps [39]	✗	92.7	−0.79	6.17	1.09	**8.38**
LayerPrune$_1$	✓	**92.61**	3.29	2.40	7.77	2.76
LayerPrune$_2$	✓	92.28	**6.68**	**5.63**	**11.11**	5.05
Batch Normalization [31]	✗	93.00	0.6	3.85	2.26	1.42
LayerPrune$_1$	✓	**93.49**	2.86	3.88	7.08	5.67
LayerPrune$_2$	✓	93.35	**6.46**	**7.94**	**10.63**	**11.31**
LayerPrune$_{18}$-Imprint	✓	92.49	57.31	55.14	57.57	63.27
CIFAR-100 ResNet56 baseline (71.2%)						
Chen et al. [38]	✓	69.77	**38.30**	34.31	38.53	39.38
LayerPrune$_{11}$-Imprint	✓	**71.00**	**38.68**	35.83	**39.52**	**54.29**
Taylor weight [24]	✗	71.03	2.13	5.23	−1.1	3.75
LayerPrune$_1$	✓	**71.15**	3.07	3.74	3.66	5.50
LayerPrune$_2$	✓	70.82	**6.44**	**7.18**	**7.30**	**11.00**
Weight norm [25]	✗	71.00	2.52	6.46	−0.3	3.86
L1 norm [33]	✗	70.65	−1.04	4.06	0.58	1.34
LayerPrune$_1$	✓	**71.26**	3.10	3.68	4.22	5.47
LayerPrune$_2$	✓	71.01	**6.59**	**7.03**	**8.00**	**10.94**
Feature maps [39]	✗	70.00	1.22	9.49	−1.27	**7.94**
LayerPrune$_1$	✓	**71.10**	2.81	3.24	4.46	5.56
LayerPrune$_2$	✓	70.36	**6.06**	**6.70**	**7.72**	**7.85**
Batch Normalization [31]	✗	70.71	0.37	2.26	−1.02	2.89
LayerPrune$_1$	✓	**71.26**	3.10	3.68	4.22	5.47
LayerPrune$_2$	✓	70.97	**6.36**	**6.78**	**7.59**	**10.94**
LayerPrune$_{18}$-Imprint	✓	68.45	60.69	57.15	61.32	71.65

ods. Although feature maps criterion [39] achieves better accuracy by 0.92% over LayerPrune₁, LayerPrune has higher latency reduction that exceeds by 5.7%.

It is worth mentioning that the latency aware optimization ECC has an upper bound latency reduction of 11.56%, on 1080Ti, with accuracy 16.3%. This stems from the fact that iterative filter pruning is bounded by the network's depth and structure dependency within the network, thus not all layers are considered for pruning such as the gates at residual blocks. Besides, ECC builds a layer-wise bilinear model to approximate the latency of a model given the number of input channels and output filters per layer. This simplifies the non-linear relationship between the number of filters per layer and latency. We show the latency reduction on Xavier for an ECC pruned model optimized for 1080Ti, and this pruned model results in a latency increase on batch size 1 and the lowest latency reduction on batch size 64. This suggests that a hardware-aware filter pruned model for one hardware architecture might perform worse on another hardware than even a hardware-agnostic filter pruning method. It is worth noting that the filter pruning HRank [40] with 2.6x FLOPs reduction shows large accuracy degradation compared to LayerPrune (71.98 vs 74.31). Even with aggressive filter pruning, speed up is noticeable with large batch size but shows small speed gain

Table 3. Comparison of different pruning methods on ResNet50 ImageNet. * manual pre-defined signatures. ** same pruned model optimized for 1080Ti latency consumption model in ECC optimization

ResNet50 baseline (76.14)						
Method	Shallower?	Top1 Acc. (%)	1080Ti LR (%)		Xavier LR (%)	
			bs = 1	bs = 64	bs = 1	bs = 64
Batch Normalization	✗	75.23	2.49	1.61	−2.79	4.13
LayerPrune₁	✓	**76.70**	15.95	4.81	21.38	6.01
LayerPrune₂	✓	76.52	**20.41**	**8.36**	**25.11**	**9.96**
Taylor [24]	✗	76.4	2.73	3.6	-1.97	6.60
LayerPrune₁	✓	**76.48**	15.79	3.01	21.52	4.85
LayerPrune₂	✓	75.61	**21.35**	**6.18**	**27.33**	**8.42**
Feature maps [39]	✗	**75.92**	10.86	3.86	20.25	8.74
Channel pruning* [48]	✗	72.26	3.54	6.13	2.70	7.42
ThiNet* [23]	✗	72.05	10.76	**10.96**	15.52	**17.06**
LayerPrune₁	✓	75.00	16.56	2.54	23.82	4.49
LayerPrune₂	✓	71.90	**22.15**	5.73	**29.66**	8.03
SSS-ResNet41 [37]	✓	75.50	25.58	24.17	31.39	21.76
LayerPrune₃-Imprint	✓	**76.40**	22.63	25.73	30.44	20.38
LayerPrune₄-Imprint	✓	75.82	**30.75**	**27.64**	**33.93**	**25.43**
SSS-ResNet32 [37]	✓	74.20	**41.16**	29.69	**42.05**	29.59
LayerPrune₆-Imprint	✓	**74.74**	40.02	**36.59**	41.22	34.50
HRank-2.6x-FLOPs* [40]	✗	71.98	11.89	36.09	20.63	**40.09**
LayerPrune₇-Imprint	✓	**74.31**	**44.26**	**41.01**	**41.01**	38.39

with small batch size. Within shallower models, LayerPrune outperforms SSS on the same latency budget even when SSS supports block pruning for ResNet50, which shows the effectiveness of accuracy approximation as layer importance.

4.4 Layer Pruning Comparison

In this section, we analyze different criteria for layer pruning under the same latency budget as presented in Table 4. Our imprinting method consistently outperforms other methods, especially on higher latency reduction rates. Imprinting is able to get 30% latency reduction with only 0.36% accuracy loss from baseline. The ensemble method, although has better accuracy than the average accuracy, is still sensitive to individual errors. We further compare layer pruning by imprinting on a similar latency budget with smaller ResNet variants. We outperform ResNet34 by 1.44% (LR = 39%) and ResNet18 by 0.56% (LR = 65%) in accuracy showing the effectiveness of incorporating accuracy in block importance. Detailed numerical evaluation can be found in supplementary.

Table 4. Comparison of different layer pruning methods supported by LayerPrune on ResNet50 ImageNet. Latency reduction is calculated on 1080Ti with batch size 1.

ResNet50 (76.14)				
	1 block (LR $\approx$ 15%)	2 blocks (LR $\approx$ 20%)	3 blocks (LR $\approx$ 25%)	4 blocks (LR $\approx$ 30%)
LayerPrune-Imprint	**76.72**	**76.53**	**76.40**	**75.82**
LayerPrune-Taylor	76.48	75.61	75.34	75.28
LayerPrune-Feature map	75.00	71.9	70.84	69.05
LayerPrune-Weight magnitude	**76.70**	**76.52**	76.12	74.33
LayerPrune-Batch Normalization	**76.70**	76.22	75.84	75.03
LayerPrune-Ensemble	**76.70**	76.11	75.76	75.01

5 Conclusion

We presented LayerPrune framework which includes a set of layer pruning methods. We show the benefits of LayerPrune on latency reduction compared to filter pruning. The key findings of this paper are the following:

- For a filter criterion, training a LayerPrune model based on this criterion achieves the same, if not better, accuracy as the filter pruned model obtained by using the same criterion.
- Filter pruning compresses the number of convolution operations per layer and thus latency reduction depends on hardware architecture, while LayerPrune removes the whole layer. As result, filter pruned models might produce non-optimal matrix shapes for the compute kernels that can lead even to latency increase on some hardware targets and batch sizes.

- Filter pruned models within a latency budget have a larger variance in accuracy than LayerPrune. This stems from the fact that the relation between latency and number of filters is non-linear and optimization constrained by a resource budget requires complex per-layer pruning ratios selection.
- We also showed the importance of incorporating accuracy approximation in layer ranking by imprinting.

Acknowledgment. We thank Compute Canada and WestGrid for their supercomputers to conduct our experiments.

References

1. Krizhevsky, A., Sutskever, I., Hinton, G.E.: Imagenet classification with deep convolutional neural networks. In: Advances in Neural Information Processing Systems, pp. 1097–1105 (2012)
2. Redmon, J., Farhadi, A.: Yolov3: An incremental improvement. arXiv preprint arXiv:1804.02767 (2018)
3. Elkerdawy, S., Zhang, H., Ray, N.: Lightweight monocular depth estimation model by joint end-to-end filter pruning. In: 2019 IEEE International Conference on Image Processing (ICIP), pp. 4290–4294. IEEE (2019)
4. He, K., Zhang, X., Ren, S., Sun, J.: Deep residual learning for image recognition. In: Proceedings of the IEEE CVPR, pp. 770–778 (2016)
5. Wu, Z., Shen, C., Van Den Hengel, A.: Wider or deeper: revisiting the resnet model for visual recognition. Pattern Recognit. **90**, 119–133 (2019)
6. Ma, N., Zhang, X., Zheng, H.-T., Sun, J.: ShuffleNet V2: practical guidelines for efficient CNN architecture design. In: Ferrari, V., Hebert, M., Sminchisescu, C., Weiss, Y. (eds.) ECCV 2018, Part XIV. LNCS, vol. 11218, pp. 122–138. Springer, Cham (2018). https://doi.org/10.1007/978-3-030-01264-9_8
7. Howard, A.G., et al.: Mobilenets: Efficient convolutional neural networks for mobile vision applications. arXiv preprint arXiv:1704.04861 (2017)
8. Wang, R.J., Li, X., Ling, C.X.: Pelee: A real-time object detection system on mobile devices. In: Advances in Neural Information Processing Systems, pp. 1963–1972 (2018)
9. Huang, G., Liu, Z., Van Der Maaten, L., Weinberger, K.Q.: Densely connected convolutional networks. In: Proceedings of the IEEE Conference on Computer Vision and Pattern Recognition, pp. 4700–4708 (2017)
10. Huang, G., Chen, D., Li, T., Wu, F., van der Maaten, L., Weinberger, K.Q.: Multi-scale dense networks for resource efficient image classification. arXiv preprint arXiv:1703.09844 (2017)
11. Kurt Keutzer, E.A.: Abandoning the dark arts: Scientific approaches to efficient deep learning. In: The 5th Workshop on Energy Efficient Machine Learning and Cognitive Computing, Conference on Neural Information Processing Systems (2019)
12. Wang, K., Liu, Z., Lin, Y., Lin, J., Han, S.: HAQ: hardware-aware automated quantization with mixed precision. In: Proceedings of the IEEE CVPR, pp. 8612–8620 (2019)
13. Hubara, I., Courbariaux, M., Soudry, D., El-Yaniv, R., Bengio, Y.: Quantized neural networks: training neural networks with low precision weights and activations. J. Mach. Learn. Res. **18**, 6869–6898 (2017)

14. Yang, C., Xie, L., Su, C., Yuille, A.L.: Snapshot distillation: teacher-student optimization in one generation. In: Proceedings of the IEEE CVPR, pp. 2859–2868 (2019)
15. Jin, X., et al.: Knowledge distillation via route constrained optimization. In: Proceedings of the IEEE ICCV, pp. 1345–1354 (2019)
16. Yang, T.J., Chen, Y.H., Sze, V.: Designing energy-efficient convolutional neural networks using energy-aware pruning. In: Proceedings of the IEEE Conference on Computer Vision and Pattern Recognition, pp. 5687–5695 (2017)
17. Yang, T.-J., et al.: NetAdapt: platform-aware neural network adaptation for mobile applications. In: Ferrari, V., Hebert, M., Sminchisescu, C., Weiss, Y. (eds.) ECCV 2018, Part X. LNCS, vol. 11214, pp. 289–304. Springer, Cham (2018). https://doi.org/10.1007/978-3-030-01249-6_18
18. Bianco, S., Cadene, R., Celona, L., Napoletano, P.: Benchmark analysis of representative deep neural network architectures. IEEE Access 6, 64270–64277 (2018)
19. van Werkhoven, B.: Kernel tuner: a search-optimizing GPU code auto-tuner. Future Gener. Comput. Syst. 90, 347–358 (2019)
20. Nugteren, C., Codreanu, V.: CLTune: a generic auto-tuner for opencl kernels. In: 2015 IEEE 9th International Symposium on Embedded Multicore/Many-core Systems-on-Chip, pp. 195–202. IEEE (2015)
21. Yang, H., Zhu, Y., Liu, J.: Ecc: Platform-independent energy-constrained deep neural network compression via a bilinear regression model. In: Proceedings of the IEEE CVPR, pp. 11206–11215 (2019)
22. Lemaire, C., Achkar, A., Jodoin, P.M.: Structured pruning of neural networks with budget-aware regularization. In: Proceedings of the IEEE Conference on Computer Vision and Pattern Recognition, pp. 9108–9116 (2019)
23. Luo, J.H., Wu, J., Lin, W.: Thinet: A filter level pruning method for deep neural network compression. In: Proceedings of the IEEE ICCV, pp. 5058–5066 (2017)
24. Molchanov, P., Mallya, A., Tyree, S., Frosio, I., Kautz, J.: Importance estimation for neural network pruning. In: Proceedings of the IEEE CVPR, pp. 11264–11272 (2019)
25. Han, S., Pool, J., Tran, J., Dally, W.: Learning both weights and connections for efficient neural network. In: Advances in Neural Information Processing Systems, pp. 1135–1143 (2015)
26. Han, S., Mao, H., Dally, W.: Compressing deep neural networks with pruning, trained quantization and Huffman coding. In: IC LR 2017, (2015)
27. Srinivas, S., Babu, R.V.: Data-free parameter pruning for deep neural networks. arXiv preprint arXiv:1507.06149 (2015)
28. Louizos, C., Welling, M., Kingma, D.P.: Learning sparse neural networks through l_0 regularization. arXiv preprint arXiv:1712.01312 (2017)
29. Frankle, J., Carbin, M.: The lottery ticket hypothesis: Finding sparse, trainable neural networks. arXiv preprint arXiv:1803.03635 (2018)
30. Sharify, S., et al.: Laconic deep learning inference acceleration. In: Proceedings of the 46th International Symposium on Computer Architecture, pp. 304–317 (2019)
31. Liu, Z., Li, J., Shen, Z., Huang, G., Yan, S., Zhang, C.: Learning efficient convolutional networks through network slimming. In: Proceedings of the IEEE ICCV, pp. 2736–2744 (2017)
32. Wen, W., Wu, C., Wang, Y., Chen, Y., Li, H.: Learning structured sparsity in deep neural networks. In: Advances in Neural Information Processing Systems, pp. 2074–2082 (2016)
33. Li, H., Kadav, A., Durdanovic, I., Samet, H., Graf, H.P.: Pruning filters for efficient convnets. In: ICLR (2017)

34. Zhao, C., Ni, B., Zhang, J., Zhao, Q., Zhang, W., Tian, Q.: Variational convolutional neural network pruning. In: Proceedings of the IEEE Conference on Computer Vision and Pattern Recognition, pp. 2780–2789 (2019)
35. Chin, T.W., Zhang, C., Marculescu, D.: Layer-compensated pruning for resource-constrained convolutional neural networks. In: NeurIPS (2018)
36. He, Y., Lin, J., Liu, Z., Wang, H., Li, L.-J., Han, S.: AMC: AutoML for model compression and acceleration on mobile devices. In: Ferrari, V., Hebert, M., Sminchisescu, C., Weiss, Y. (eds.) ECCV 2018, Part VII. LNCS, vol. 11211, pp. 815–832. Springer, Cham (2018). https://doi.org/10.1007/978-3-030-01234-2_48
37. Huang, Z., Wang, N.: Data-driven sparse structure selection for deep neural networks. In: Ferrari, V., Hebert, M., Sminchisescu, C., Weiss, Y. (eds.) ECCV 2018, Part XVI. LNCS, vol. 11220, pp. 317–334. Springer, Cham (2018). https://doi.org/10.1007/978-3-030-01270-0_19
38. Chen, S., Zhao, Q.: Shallowing deep networks: layer-wise pruning based on feature representations. IEEE Trans. Pattern Anal. Mach. Intell. **41**, 3048–3056 (2018)
39. Molchanov, P., Tyree, S., Karras, T., Aila, T., Kautz, J.: Pruning convolutional neural networks for resource efficient transfer learning. arXiv preprint arXiv:1611.06440 3 (2016)
40. Lin, M., et al.: HRank: Filter pruning using high-rank feature map. In: Proceedings of the IEEE/CVF Conference on Computer Vision and Pattern Recognition, pp. 1529–1538 (2020)
41. Qi, H., Brown, M., Lowe, D.G.: Low-shot learning with imprinted weights. In: Proceedings of the IEEE CVPR, pp. 5822–5830 (2018)
42. M. Siam, B.O., Jagersand, M.: AMP: adaptive masked proxies for few-shot segmentation. In: Proceedings of the IEEE ICCV (2019)
43. He, K., Zhang, X., Ren, S., Sun, J.: Spatial pyramid pooling in deep convolutional networks for visual recognition. In: Fleet, D., Pajdla, T., Schiele, B., Tuytelaars, T. (eds.) ECCV 2014, Part III. LNCS, vol. 8691, pp. 346–361. Springer, Cham (2014). https://doi.org/10.1007/978-3-319-10578-9_23
44. Krizhevsky, A., Hinton, G., et al.: Learning multiple layers of features from tiny images (2009)
45. Baydin, A.G., Pearlmutter, B.A., Radul, A.A., Siskind, J.M.: Automatic differentiation in machine learning: a survey. J. Mach. Learn. Res. **18**, 5595–5637 (2017)
46. Simonyan, K., Zisserman, A.: Very deep convolutional networks for large-scale image recognition. In: ICLR (2015)
47. Sze, V., Chen, Y.H., Yang, T.J., Emer, J.S.: Efficient processing of deep neural networks: a tutorial and survey. Proc. IEEE **105**, 2295–2329 (2017)
48. He, Y., Zhang, X., Sun, J.: Channel pruning for accelerating very deep neural networks. In: Proceedings of the IEEE ICCV, pp. 1389–1397 (2017)

Author Index

Printed in the United States
By Bookmasters